THE TEACHER EDUCATOR'S HANDBOOK

THE TEACHER
EDUCATOR'S
HANDBOOK

Building a Knowledge Base for the Preparation of Teachers

Frank B. Murray, Editor

A publication sponsored by the American Association of Colleges for Teacher Education

Foreword by David Imig

Jossey-Bass Publishers
San Francisco

Substantial discounts on bulk quantities of Jossey-Bass books are available to corporations, professional associations, and other organizations. For details and discount information, contact the special sales department at Jossey-Bass Inc., Publishers.

(415) 433–1740; Fax (800) 605–2665.

For sales outside the United States, please contact your local Simon & Schuster International Office.

Manufactured in the United States of America.

Library of Congress Cataloging-in-Publication Data

The teacher eduator's handbook : building a knowledge base for the
   preparation of teachers / [edited by] Frank B. Murray. — 1st ed.
      p.   cm. — (The Jossey-Bass education series)
   Includes bibliographical references and index.
   ISBN 0-7879-0121-0 (alk. paper)
    1. Teacher educators—United States—Handbooks, manuals, etc.
  2. Education—Study and teaching (Higher)—United States—Handbooks,
manuals, etc. 3. Teachers—Training of—United States—Handbooks,
manuals, etc. I. Murray, Frank B. II. Series.
  LB1737.5.U5T43   1996
370.71'0973—dc20   95-22317
  CIP

FIRST EDITION
HB Printing   10 9 8 7 6 5 4 3 2 1

THE JOSSEY-BASS EDUCATION SERIES

CONTENTS

FOREWORD

The Teacher Educator's Handbook builds on the substantial efforts of many con- tributors, in particular the American Association of Colleges for Teacher Ed- ucation's Committee on the Professional Knowledge Base. The committee's first volume, *Knowledge Base for the Beginning Teacher,* proposed to describe "that body of knowledge that people should possess and ultimately be able to apply in order to begin teaching." The rationale for this first volume established as central premises the need to move teacher education from a normative to a "state of the art" en- terprise and the urgency of basing substance and structure of teacher education on professional standards for knowledge rather than on conventional wisdom.

Events in the intervening years have both confirmed the soundness of this ra- tionale and made clear the distance yet to be traveled toward these goals. The publication of *Knowledge Base for the Beginning Teacher* in early 1989 preceded the governors' education summit and the national Goals 2000 agenda that grew from the governors' conference. An unprecedented sequence of federal and state pol- icy initiatives now promotes the "systemic reform" of education from early child- hood through postsecondary education. Related initiatives of the national discipline organizations have produced standards for student and teacher per- formance, with standards-based accountability structures now being created in many locations. Within the sphere of teacher preparation, state policy shifts have begun significantly to alter the structure of licensure and its connection to an evolving system of professional certification, as well as to draw accreditation more firmly into the configuration of educational quality control measures.

During the same period, experience gained from the implementation of ac- creditation standards on the professional knowledge base has pointed toward an emerging research agenda on the conceptual framework for teacher education programs. Responses by approximately five hundred teacher preparation institutions to the knowledge-base standards of the National Council for Accreditation of Teacher Education (NCATE) have raised issues about conceptual coherence within the structure of teacher education across individual program (subject matter) areas; about the connection between faculty capacity and credibility of the knowledge base underlying programs; and about the decision-making process for program design in teacher education units.

The present book is a logical successor to address implications arising from the knowledge base that supports teaching and learning. It looks at important questions basic to the design of teacher preparation within the larger context of current policy structures and standards-based accountability. It focuses primarily on preservice preparation of teachers but in doing so addresses the entirety of each disciplinary or pedagogical area. By asking individual scholars to address their statements to faculty who are not experts in the given specialty area, the volume takes on two challenges often lacking in the academic conversation: the reality of designing programs based on mutual understandings about specialized knowledge and the increasing need for effective communication across ever-expanding areas of expertise and specialization.

Like its predecessor, this publication is not intended as a definitive statement. It is meant to serve as a solid foundation for conversations that need to take place inside and outside the institutions that prepare teachers. The value of this work will reside largely in the quality of the dialogue it stimulates; its creators welcome responses from colleagues in all branches of the teacher education enterprise.

August 1995   David Imig
Washington, D.C.

PREFACE

When teacher educators design collegiate programs for novice teachers, they must make decisions that will have wide-ranging effects, decisions that will trickle down to change not just the lives of the teachers themselves but the students they teach, right down to the individual child in the individual public school. The *knowledge base* for teacher educators—the body of work that encompasses opinions and information—offers a way to approach those crucial decisions. It is this knowledge base that teacher educators rely on when they decide—as many do throughout the country—to establish programs that comprise survey courses in the liberal arts and specialized teaching courses as well as educational foundations, methods, and clinical field work courses.

The knowledge base contains a promising body of scholarly literature, as this volume demonstrates. Within this book, leading scholars address a range of issues, ideas, and research findings in the field of teacher education. They examine specific disciplines, social foundations, and program structures as well as crucial broader concepts such as school reform and diversity. It is hoped that education faculty will use this book as a basic reference handbook when planning course content and curricula and establishing program requirements in the 1,279 institutions in the United States that offer academic degree programs leading to teaching licenses.

The authors pay particular attention to the nonspecialized academic information and knowledge that today's teacher education faculty, as a collective, should know about each discipline and subfield of education. For example, mathematics educators as well as their colleagues in nonmath disciplines will need to make decisions about what kind and what quantity of mathematics instruction to require of prospective elementary school teachers or secondary social studies teachers. What approach to mathematics would best guide the teacher education faculty to a considered and productive set of mathematics requirements for teachers in general?

Part One shows how the context of teacher education has changed radically since the *Nation at Risk* report a decade or so ago. The goals of the major educational reform groups, for example, demand a more ambitious kind of teaching in the public schools, which is difficult to learn and is dependent on an unusual kind of knowledge. Part One closes with a review of the various genres of research that support the choices teacher educators make in the design of the teacher education program.

These choices are also critically dependent on the views teacher educators have about the various disciplines that comprise the school curriculum. Therefore, Part Two presents issues, findings, and questions about approaches to teaching some of the major disciplines; all teacher educators, regardless of specialization, will need to consider these issues and questions as they raise the education requirements for future teachers.

Part Three deals more specifically with the discipline of education itself. Here, too, the authors raise issues and questions and report on findings in order to examine in critical detail the components of the discipline.

In the end, teacher educators must make a number of fairly practical decisions about the structure, format, and design of the course of study for our future teachers. Part Four provides guidance and information for today's teacher educators at the highest level of scholarship.

Finally, the book in Part Five addresses the nature of the teacher education professoriate and considers how today's teacher educators might advance scholarship in the field.

In most cases, because of limited space, the chapters provide only general guidance, illustrated by prototypical accounts, in the hope that readers will pursue the particular and specialized aspects of each topic that are of personal and professional interest.

As the authors worked on their individual chapters, many of them struggled with the temptation to write authoritative reviews of the literature in their fields or definitive statements about what prospective teachers should learn. It was indeed a more challenging task to consider what their own teacher education colleagues need to know for the thoughtful determination of the components of the teacher education program that should be retained, dropped, added, or invented.

The book also constitutes an argument for college- and university-based professional teacher education and can be taken as a suggested outline or proposal for a graduate curriculum for teacher educators.

Of course, literature is sometimes only speculative and suggestive, so this book is best seen as simply the *beginning* of a knowledge base for teacher educators. Perhaps most important, it offers a set of questions that the teacher education faculty must ask of itself.

In *The Education of Henry Adams: An Autobiography,* the author mused that teachers influence an eternity, as, generation after generation, no one can tell where (or if) the influence ends. So, too, may the influence of this book linger on , but more surely it stands as a testimony to the work of prior generations of teachers and scholars, whose contributions are acknowledged throughout the volume.

If we are to develop teachers who have the professional knowledge and skills needed to succeed in today's classroom, this volume can provide an essential resource for strengthening teacher education programs.

The idea for a book about a knowledge base for teacher educators was crafted during the 1991 meetings of the American Association of Colleges for Teacher Education's Committee on the Knowledge Base, whose members are Linda Darling-Hammond, Columbia University Teachers College; William Gardner, University of Minnesota and former chair of the committee; Antoine Garibaldi, Xavier University; Marilyn Guy, Concordia College; Gene Hall, University of Northern Colorado; Frank Murray, University of Delaware, chair of the committee; Virginia Richardson, University of Arizona; and Alan Tom, University of North Carolina at Chapel Hill. This group developed an outline for the volume and solicited proposals for chapters from the institutional representatives of the members of AACTE and from members of other professional associations, most notably Division K of the American Educational Research Association. The committee's request for proposals attracted a large number of excellent chapter outlines, for which the committee expresses appreciation. The committee struggled over several months to select the proposals that fit best with its overall vision of the volume and was very grateful for the support its work received from all participants.

The committee was assisted in its work by an able set of reviewers, teachers, and faculty, who gave the authors detailed comments about their manuscripts. These comments and criticisms were especially valuable to the authors and the committee.

Of the many persons who assisted the committee, Carol Smith, senior director for professional issues, AACTE, and Elaine Stotko, assistant dean of the College of Education at the University of Delaware, merit special mention. Carol was a tireless advocate for the committee within AACTE and provided superb staff work for the committee at each and every stage of development of *The Teacher Educator's Handbook.* She and Elaine guided the substantive discussions with the committee, the publisher, and various authors at several critical points in the volume's progress. Elaine managed the editorial process with such high standards that despite her exacting demands, the authors uniformly and gratefully acknowledged the improvements she made in their chapters. Finally, Cynthia Graddy, program associate for professional issues, contributed significant professional support in the process of soliciting proposals, organizing chapter materials, and corresponding with authors on a wide variety of issues related to production of this volume.

As *The Teacher Educator's Handbook* is launched, the committee and the authors feel not unlike Henry Adams felt in 1871 when, as a novice professor of history at Harvard College, he pondered how to organize and structure his subject, which seemed to him both incoherent and immoral. He knew he would have a hand in whether his students became "priests or atheists, plutocrats or socialists, judges or anarchists. . . . Not that his ignorance troubled him," he wrote in *The Education of Henry Adams,* speaking of himself in the third person. "He knew enough to be ignorant. His course had led him through oceans of ignorance; he had tumbled from one ocean into another till he learned how to swim; but even to him, education was a serious thing. . . . A teacher is expected to teach truth, and may perhaps flatter himself that he does so, if he stops with the alphabet or the multiplication table . . . but morals are quite another truth and philosophy is more complex still."

And so, we would add, is a knowledge base for teacher educators.

August 1995
University of Delaware, Newark

Frank B. Murray

THE EDITOR

Frank B. Murray is H. Rodney Sharp Professor in the Departments of Educational Studies and Psychology at the University of Delaware and served as dean of the College of Education between 1979 and 1995. He received his B.A. degree from St. John's College in Annapolis, Maryland, and his M.A.T. and Ph.D. in education from Johns Hopkins University. He has served in various capacities on the editorial boards of several journals in educational and developmental psychology and is a fellow of the American Psychological Association and the American Psychological Society. Currently, he chairs the National Board of the Holmes Group and was president and cofounder of the Project 30 Alliance, a national consortium of faculty in education and the liberal arts. Since 1994, he has been coeditor of the *Review of Educational Research* for the American Educational Research Association. For his contributions to the fields of child development and teacher education reform, he was awarded an honorary doctorate from Heriot–Watt University in Edinburgh, Scotland, in 1994. Since 1991, he has been appointed by Delaware's governors as a commissioner in the Education Commission of the States.

THE CONTRIBUTORS

Mark Amsler is a professor of English and linguistics at the University of Delaware.

Deborah Anders is an adjunct assistant professor at the University of Arizona.

Richard I. Arends is dean of the School of Education and Professional Studies at Central Connecticut State University.

Kathy Carter is an associate professor in the Department of Teaching and Teacher Education at the University of Arizona.

Gary K. Clabaugh is director of the graduate program in education and coordinator of the arts and sciences graduate programs at La Salle University.

Velma L. Cobb is a senior research associate at the National Center for Restructuring Education, Schools, and Teaching and associate director of the National Commission on Teaching and America's Future at Columbia University Teachers College.

Ardra L. Cole is an assistant professor in the Department of Applied Psychology at the Ontario Institute for Studies in Education.

Larry Copes is chairman of the Department of Mathematics at Augsburg College.

Zoubeida Dagher is an assistant professor in the Department of Educational Development at the University of Delaware.

Beatriz S. D'Ambrosio is an associate professor in the School of Education at Indiana University–Purdue University at Indianapolis.

Linda Darling-Hammond is William F. Russell Professor of Education and co-director of the National Center for Restructuring Education, Schools, and Teaching at Columbia University Teachers College.

Robert Donmoyer is a professor in the Department of Educational Policy and Leadership at Ohio State University.

Joseph P. Ducette is an associate dean and professor of Educational Psychology at Temple University.

Edward R. Ducharme is Ellis and Nellie Levitt Distinguished Professor of Education at Drake University.

Mary Kluender Ducharme is an associate professor of education at Drake University.

Patricia A. Edwards is a professor of language and literacy at Michigan State University.

Linnea C. Ehri is Distinguished Professor in the Program in Educational Psychology at the City University of New York Graduate School.

Sharon Feiman-Nemser is a professor in the Department of Teacher Education at Michigan State University.

Lynn Galbraith is an assistant professor of art at the University of Arizona.

Michael F. Graves is a professor and head of literacy education at the University of Minnesota.

Janice Grow-Maienza is a professor of education at Northeast Missouri State University.

Kenneth R. Howey is a professor of teacher education at Ohio State University.

Mary M. Kennedy is director of the Institute for Research on Teaching and Learning at Michigan State University.

J. Gary Knowles is an assistant professor of education at the University of Michigan.

Marsha Levine is a research professor in the School of Education and Human Development at George Washington University.

Amy Raths McAninch is an assistant professor at St. Mary College.

Stuart A. McAninch is an assistant professor in the School of Education at the University of Missouri.

G. Williamson McDiarmid is co-director of the National Center for Research on Teacher Learning and a professor of teacher education at Michigan State University.

Frank B. Murray is H. Rodney Sharp Professor and dean of the College of Education at the University of Delaware.

Leo W. Pauls is executive director of the Jones Institute for Educational Excellence and assistant dean of the Emporia State University Teachers College.

Andrew C. Porter is director of the Wisconsin Center for Education Research and a professor of educational psychology at the University of Wisconsin, Madison.

Janine T. Remillard is an assistant professor in the Department of Educational Studies at the University of Utah.

Virginia Richardson is a professor in the College of Education at the University of Arizona.

Edward G. Rozycki is an assistant professor at the Center for Education at Widener University.

Terry Salinger is the director of research for the International Reading Association.

Trevor E. Sewell is a professor and dean of the Department of Psychological Studies in Education at Temple University.

Joan Poliner Shapiro is an associate professor of educational leadership and policy studies at Temple University.

Barbara Senkowski Stengel is an associate professor at the Stayer Education Center, Millersville University.

Elaine M. Stotko is assistant dean of the College of Education at the University of Delaware.

Alan R. Tom is a professor of education at the University of North Carolina, Chapel Hill.

Joanna P. Williams is a professor of psychology and education at Columbia University Teachers College.

Suzanne M. Wilson is an associate professor at the National Center for Research on Teacher Learning, Michigan State University.

Nancy Winitzky is an assistant professor in the Department of Educational Studies at the University of Utah.

Lauren S. Jones Young is an associate professor of teacher education and educational administration at Michigan State University.

Nancy L. Zimpher is a professor and dean of the College of Education at Ohio State University.

THE TEACHER EDUCATOR'S HANDBOOK

PART ONE

THE NEED FOR A
KNOWLEDGE BASE

CHAPTER ONE

BEYOND NATURAL TEACHING: THE CASE FOR PROFESSIONAL EDUCATION

FRANK B. MURRAY

There is a resurgence of the popular but contested view that the nation's need for new teachers can be provided by well-meaning liberal arts graduates who are willing to sacrifice temporarily the career benefits of their prestigious degrees to work in the schools. This view takes comfort in the analogy that the needs of higher education have been traditionally met, although perhaps not as well as had been hoped, by those who were trained to research their subjects and are willing to accept positions as college instructors.

This popular argument against professional teacher education has merit, less now than in the past, and relies heavily on the fact that teaching is a naturally occurring human behavior that precedes formal schooling and formal teacher education by several centuries and is a longstanding feature of the ancient repertoire of human behaviors. The question implicitly raised by this book is whether university- and college-based teacher education offers anything that can take novices much beyond the natural teaching skills possessed by all. Furthermore, even if formal teacher education improves teaching, can the nation's needs for schooling still be met less expensively yet adequately by natural teaching techniques and styles?

J. M. Stephens (1967) catalogued the features of naturally occurring teaching in his theory of spontaneous schooling. His argument was that schooling, a feature of all anthropological groups, is dependent on a set of natural human tendencies that some persons have to greater degrees than others. Those who have these tendencies in generous proportions will be teachers, whether they intend to be or not. Teaching and learning will take place naturally and not with any particular motive to benefit the pupil. They will occur merely because the tendencies, which meet the teacher's needs, lead incidentally and inevitably to learning in those persons in the teacher's company. Teaching, in other words, is spontaneous and nondeliberate and occurs whenever a person with these tendencies is with any other person.

These tendencies, which sustain natural teaching and schooling, Stephens thought to be the following:

1. The tendency to collect and manipulate things, classify them, dwell on and play with simple and basic ideas, create systems for grouping things that have no immediate payoff, and so forth
2. The tendency to talk about what one knows, on the view that an unshared experience is painful and burdensome and must be eased through telling
3. The tendency to correct others' mistakes, not with any view to making them better persons, but because an error—whether in a book or spoken on television—must be corrected even when the correction cannot possibly affect or benefit the author, publisher, or actor
4. The tendency to supply the word for which someone is groping, not to help the person, but to satisfy one's own need to provide the answer
5. The tendency to "point the moral," to show others how things are related, to show that x leads to y as in "I told you that would happen"

The theory of spontaneous schooling was meant to account for two pervasive findings: the universality of schooling and the fact that most educational research overwhelmingly finds insignificant differences between educational treatments. It accounts for universality by arguing that wherever there are people, these five spontaneous tendencies exist, and the person who possesses those tendencies will be a natural teacher, whether in a school or not. Stephens's theory explained the pervasive no-difference findings in educational research as the natural outcome of the fact that the tendencies were operating in both the treatment and control groups (for example, in large and small classes, in TV and conventional instruction, in mixed and segregated ability groups, in classrooms with textbook A and B). The tendencies, by themselves, caused powerful learning effects that overwhelmed any effects that could be attributed to the researcher's treatment. These effects were explained adequately by the prevailing Skinnerian/Thorndike learning theories because the spontaneous tendencies forged the defining stimulus-response learning link. They caused the stimulus to be presented, they permitted the opportunity to respond to it, and they rewarded and shaped a response to the stimulus.

The theory, like other sociobiological theories, provides a convenient base for arguing that knowledge of subject matter in the company of these tendencies will outfit a person as a teacher, especially in situations where the teacher and the pupil are a lot like each other, as they are in families and other anthropological groups.

This theory and the view of teaching that is based on it, however, have a number of problematic consequences for modern schooling. Reliance on the theory can be expected to lead to serious pedagogical mistakes for both weak and superior students. The theory promotes an outdated mode of instruction that is not supported by modern views of cognition and cognitive development and provides insufficient guidance for the solution of difficult and novel problems in schooling.

When the teacher and the pupil are not alike and when the teacher has, as a result, lower expectations for the "different" pupil, the natural tendencies lead to very unfortunate consequences (Brophy and Good, 1986). When the teacher and the pupil have dissimilar backgrounds, we can expect that the natural teaching mechanisms that support familial instruction will not operate to benefit the student.

American teachers are a relatively homogenous set of lower-middle-class suburban white women, while the American pupil is increasingly variable with regard to every demographic feature (Choy and others, 1993; Howe, 1990). Thus, the teacher, even if she were to rely exclusively on the spontaneous tendencies, must somehow come to terms with a maturing literature on sexism, racism, bilingualism, and cultural and class diversity.

Even if the teacher has acquired such information about the diverse groups in the classroom, there are a predictable number of pedagogical mistakes novices, and regrettably some licensed teachers, make unless they also have had the opportunity to practice some counterintuitive and learned teaching techniques. For example, it is very likely that well-meaning and well-read teachers with good college grades will still make certain pedagogical mistakes with the pupils for whom they have low expectations, regardless of how they came to have these expectations. They will treat these pupils not as individuals but as a group, seat them farther away and outside the zone of frequent teacher-pupil interaction, look at them less, ask them low-level questions, call on them less often, give them less time to respond, give them fewer hints when they are called upon, and give them less praise and more blame than other pupils. They will do all this out of a mistaken sense of kindness that is seemingly oblivious to the pedagogical harm their undisciplined actions will cause their pupils (Hawley and Rosenholtz, 1984; Murray, 1986).

These untrained and kind teachers, believing the pupil does not know very much, will not want to embarrass the pupil by calling on him or her often, will ask *appropriately* easy questions when they do, will give fewer hints and allow less time when the pupil fails to respond, as it would be unkind to prolong the embarrassment, and so on. Professional teachers, like all professionals and in contrast to *spontaneous* teachers, must control many of their kinder instincts and implement an equitable and disciplined professional approach to bring about high levels of achievement from those pupils for whom they would otherwise have low expectations (Oakes, 1985). These professional actions are frequently counterintuitive and therefore require practice.

A further limitation of the natural teaching regime, apart from the harm caused to weaker pupils, is that it does not take the superior pupil much beyond the kind of information that can be told and demonstrated and conforms to the stimulus-response and imitative forms of learning. While declarative knowledge is important, the forms of knowledge that are constructed by the pupil, not merely transmitted to the pupil, are increasingly seen as key to the student's performance at the advanced levels of the disciplines (Murray, 1992; Ogle, Alsalam, and Rogers, 1991). A pupil can be told and shown that the shortest distance between two points is a straight line, for example, but the knowledge that it *must be* a straight line and not some other kind of line cannot be merely given to the pupil. The notion of necessity has its origins elsewhere; showing and telling have not been found, except in very unusual circumstances, to be effective means of "teaching" necessity (Beilin, 1971; Murray, 1978, 1990; Smith, 1993). It is one thing to know that a statement is true but quite another to know that it *must* be true. The origins of necessity and other pivotal concepts seem to lie in *dialectical* instruction and the student's intellectual action. It is a less direct and more subtle form of instruction than that supported by the natural teaching tendencies.

Along with the natural teaching techniques, there often comes a naive and serviceable theory of the human mind (Baldwin, 1980; Heider, 1958). In this naive or commonsense theory, the pupil's school achievement is tied to four commonplace factors: ability, effort, task difficulty, and luck. With these four factors, the natural teacher can completely explain the pupil's success or failure. The problem with this naive theory, apart from the circularity in the four factors, is that more sophisticated theories have been developed, which show that ability, to take only one example, is not fixed or stable and that it varies from moment to moment interactively with many other mental factors, not just the few in the naive theory (Baldwin, 1980; Murray, 1991).

Naive theories yield such maxims as "practice makes perfect" when it is clear that practice only makes tired and it is *reinforced* practice that makes perfect. Moreover, these naive theories give contradictory maxims, such as "he who hesitates is lost" and its converse, "fools rush in where angels fear to tread." Naive theories, for example, see forgetting as the inevitable decay of stored knowledge, when the educated view is that forgetting is an active thinking process of interference and reorganization (Rose, 1993).

These naive views of how the mind works coupled with equally naive views about the nature of subject matters as received, fixed, and unchanging truth further limit the benefits that can be expected from nonprofessional teaching. The teacher's evaluation of the pupil's correct and incorrect responses provides a telling and targeted arena for distinguishing naive and professional teachers. A pupil's reasoning may look illogical to a naive teacher, while the educated teacher will see that the pupil's reasoning is intact but the pupil has operated on different premises from those of a given problem. The naive teacher will be distressed when a pupil who had pluralized the word *mouse* correctly suddenly pluralizes it as *mouses,* while the professional teacher will see the new plural not as an unfortunate regression but as a positive sign of cognitive advancement, in which the pupil is exhibiting a newly developed appreciation of a linguistic rule and is merely overgeneralizing in this instance. Other decrements in performance may also indicate educational progress; for example, a child's ability to identify the color of the ink in which the name of a color is printed is affected by whether the two colors are the same or not. Readers find it easier to identify the red color of the ink in the printed word *red,* for example, than the red ink in the printed word *blue,* but performance is equally high in both situations if the child cannot read (the Stroup effect). Along similar lines, some six-year-old pupils not only maintain incorrectly that the longer row of two rows of five beans has more beans, but also maintain that the longer row *must* have more beans and would always have more beans. These errors occur even after the pupil has just counted the equal number of beans in each row. It happens that the there-*must*-be-more-beans error, which seems the more serious error, is actually indicative of more developed reasoning than the there-are-more-beans error. Naturally, it is very difficult for the naive or spontaneous teacher to accept any error or poor performance as a marker of progress, yet the failure to see some errors as markers of progress is another serious pedagogical mistake that stems from the naive theory of teaching and learning (Bruner, 1961).

The fact that many liberal arts graduates have succeeded in meeting the expectations of the faculty in their fields of study should also not be taken as evidence that, having studied the fundamental ideas of their field, they are ready to take up work as teachers, because many of these graduates, despite their high grades, have not mastered many of the fundamental ideas of their disciplines (McDiarmid, 1992; Tyson, 1994). Large numbers of undergraduate science and engineering majors, for example, are simply unable to write an equation to represent the fact that there are six times as many cows in the field as farmers. Their errors are systematic: they write the equation as *6 cows = 1 farmer,* rather than correctly as *1 cow = 6 farmers.* Their mistake reveals a shallow grasp of the logic of the algebraic equation, the core idea in high school mathematics, and presumably would be revealed once they attempted to solve the equation.

While mistakes in the subject matter are a problem under any view of teacher employment, there are some who hold that some level of professional knowledge should be acquired but that a sufficient level can be reached easily and in a short period. However, such a view, while it represents a small advance in professional education for teachers, has its own problems. For example, on a simple reading of Skinner, prospective teachers will believe that positive reinforcement (or reward) is an effective and preferred way to increase the likelihood of desirable pupil behavior. Without an awareness of the important exceptions and qualifications in which rewards actually weaken a response (the *overjustification phenomenon*), teachers will make mistakes by implementing procedures that run counter to their intentions (see, for example, Cameron and Pierce, 1994).

Similarly, upon a quick reading, the prospective teacher could get the idea that student grades should be normally distributed or that reliability is a property of a test rather than a property of those who took the test. These professional lessons cannot be easily abridged or rushed because many educational innovations are counterintuitive and subtly tied to hidden factors.

For example, it makes a difference whether addition problems, like $8 + 5 = ?$, are presented horizontally or vertically. While a seven-year-old child, to take another example, may understand that the amount of clay in a ball would be unaffected if the ball were flattened, she would more than likely believe incorrectly that the pancake would weigh more and take up less space than the ball. Furthermore, it is now acknowledged that many research findings are inherently provisional and must be qualified by the cohort or generation of subjects who participated in the study, as different results are obtained from different cohorts on such basic questions as whether intellectual performance decreases after a certain age. Thus, having studied the research literature at one time is not a guarantee that the results can be applied at a later time.

Fortunately, it is possible to perform many routine tasks, even teaching tasks, without the benefit of great theoretical sophistication, but errors of judgment multiply when events in the classroom are not routine and when past practice is an insufficient guide. Even though there are significant gaps in it, over the past twenty-five years, a body of literature has developed that supports the way some teachers approach certain educational practices and allows the teacher to evaluate the merits of some educational innovations, techniques, and policies. For example, this literature provides sound advice about whether a teacher should adopt *ita* (the initial teaching alphabet), which regularizes spelling by having forty-four *letters,* one for each of the phonemes of English. The argument is that *ita* facilitates early reading by reducing the discrepancies between English orthography and pronunciation. The teacher who had studied Osgood's transfer surface (Osgood, 1962), unlike the thousands of teachers in the United States and Britain who adopted the innovation in the 1970s or in the 1860s (when the innovation was called *phonotaby*), would know the innovation's likely benefits to reading and harm to spelling.

Similarly, there is a substantial literature on the controversial question of whether failing pupils should repeat a grade or be *socially* promoted to the next grade, or whether a gifted pupil should skip a grade, enter school early, or be grouped separately from less gifted pupils. How can the *natural* teacher decide whether or not pupils should use calculators in their arithmetic lessons and homework? How can naive teachers avoid making mistakes in answering these questions unless they study the relevant research and scholarly literature?

For teaching to become the genuine profession it aspires to be, it must overcome formidable obstacles: the lack of an encompassing, systematic, and authoritative body of scholarly knowledge about teaching as well as about the education of teachers. However, despite the many weaknesses in the naive approach to teaching, a strong case for professional education is difficult to make due to the failure of educational scholarship to coalesce around any powerful and generative theory of schooling and teaching. Although it is unfortunately a negative example, one test of the tentative and embryonic nature of educational scholarship is that there is still no consensus among educational scholars and practitioners about what would constitute educational malpractice (Collis, 1990).

Although there are some teacher activities that are expressly illegal, there is regrettably no accepted view, except in a few extreme instances (like no longer forcing left-handers to switch hands to write), about what educational practices should not be employed in classrooms. Even antithetical practices, like "whole word" and "phonic" reading methods, have reasonable levels of current scholarly support. Without a sure sense of what constitutes educational malpractice, teaching and teacher education are behind other professions that have fairly well-articulated codes of good practice, which by extension define malpractice as the failure to follow good practice. The formulation of issues in a knowledge base for teacher educators, one objective of this volume, is a step in defining a knowledge base and a precondition of an accepted standard for good practice (Berliner, 1988).

Surprisingly, the field of teacher education is also held back by the fact that teacher education programs are not clearly connected to the educational needs of children and adolescents. These needs of course should be the driving principle in the design of teacher education programs, but the influence of other factors is more clearly seen (Gardner, 1991). The overriding question, whose answer legitimizes any requirement in the program, is, can the requirement be connected, on some credible line of reasoning, to the teacher's response to the student's true educational need? The more distant the connection, the less convincing the requirement is to the students and the public. The more distant the connection to the child's needs, the less university-based teacher education is actually warranted, because naive or spontaneous teaching would be adequate in this regard, as it primarily serves the needs of the teacher and only indirectly and sporadically the needs of the pupil.

Educational scholarship, unfortunately, is not currently organized around the needs of children and adolescents but rather around the academic disciplines and the separate clinical methods. Were educational scholarship organized around children's needs and teachers' responses to them, prospective teachers would be guided by the view that the curriculum must be shaped so that it really solves a problem that the student has. The teacher's art is in organizing the activities of the classroom so that the student's work solves a genuine problem that the student brings to the classroom—by reducing a conflict or a discrepancy in the pupil's thinking or by some other means that enables the pupil's thinking to move past an obstacle. As it is now, students' problems are not brought in by the students themselves, but are imposed by the school and are largely artificial—namely, students must avoid school failure by taking actions that meet the teacher's expectations, whatever they are and no matter how unrelated they are to anything the students directly care about. To connect the curriculum to real student problems is an exceptionally demanding task for the teacher, which is another reason why teachers need specialized knowledge and skill.

The study of pedagogy is probably not warranted at the university level if the teacher is held only to the standard of presenting material truthfully and clearly, to giving students an opportunity to practice, and to testing the students' grasp of the material. The modern teacher's obligation, however, is at a much higher level. It is not enough to have the students simply learn the material; they must understand the material (Gardner, 1991).

Understanding, it would appear, cannot be produced by the naive teacher's art alone, by didactic telling, or by showing and coaching, although the pupil may learn and remember what the teacher said and may imitate what the teacher did. It seems to be dependent upon the student's active investigation and experimentation, guided by *dialectic*—the teacher's skillful questioning and conversation. These are aimed at the student's misconceptions and provoke the student to resolve discrepancy, thereby forging a coherent understanding of the events at hand. Unlike *solutions* that are merely learned, the dialectical outcomes are personal and extraordinarily resistant to forgetting.

Pupils will not understand their lessons if the teacher's role is merely to deliver information, however important information is in high-level thinking. While dialectic requires the pupil to do something overtly—to speak, respond, and question—there are other features of teaching for understanding that require the pupil to assist the teacher, because nothing will be understood if the pupil is not active.

Modern views of intelligence and cognition, for example, are clear that knowing is negotiated, distributed, situated, constructed, developmental, and affective, all features that entail action and alter traditional schooling based on the naive view of teaching and subject matter.

The teacher does not in fact have the power, regardless of how well the school is managed, to transfer knowledge to the pupil, and this means that the pupil's intellectual cooperation is a precondition of his inventing what he knows and understands. The teacher must begin the lessons with what the pupil brings to the classroom; they must negotiate what is important and privileged and to what aspects of the pupil's prior understanding the lesson will be linked and assimilated.

Because the range of things to be known and understood exceeds the cognitive capacities of our minds, knowing must be distributed across technological devices, books, lists, and, increasingly, other people with whom we must cooperate and interact. The amount of mental space available for active processing is severely limited (perhaps to as few as seven simultaneous events), and consequently, complex thought is critically dependent upon other devices for assisting the mind in its handling of the multiple factors embedded in complex problems.

In particular, the use of computer technology in the classroom not only shifts instruction from the teacher to the student, but shifts the student's activity from learning to understanding (Sheingold, 1991). The Geometric Supposer is a computer program that encourages students to "do geometry," for example. Its use irrevocably changes the predetermined sequential nature of the school curriculum, the authority for knowledge, and generally forces instruction into a modern format (for example, Scardamalia and Bereiter, 1991).

In the past several years, the cognitive science literature unequivocally demonstrates that understanding is also dependent upon, and critically shaped by, the situation and state in which it takes place. It proves very difficult to document aspects of thought that transcend particular circumstances and generalize as widely as traditional school pedagogy and curricula assume.

Several lines of theory suggest that what we understand is best seen as an invention or construction, provisionally and personally erected to permit sense to be made of a particular set of physical, social, and historical factors. The mind is increasingly seen as a "top down," expectancy-driven and meaning-seeking system.

These mental constructions also seem to be qualitatively different from each other over time and are based upon different mechanisms and logic. It is not simply that the older pupil has more information than the younger one, which of course she does, but rather that the older pupil reasons in a new and novel manner that is not available to the younger pupil. Similarly, and more importantly perhaps, the manner of the younger pupil's and adolescent's reasoning is not available to the adult teacher, especially the *spontaneous teacher,* who would have no reason to suspect that there would be these documented qualitative changes in the student's thinking over the school years.

The pupil's understanding, in other words, cannot be reduced or decomposed into the intellectual possessions of his younger self. His new understanding emerges from his prior understanding, the way moisture emerges from the combination of two gasses, oxygen and hydrogen. The later constructions cannot be predicted from any features of the child's prior understanding, just as water could not be predicted from any feature of a gas.

Cognition and intellectual functioning are increasingly seen as integrated with the other features of the mind. The systematic and ancient links between knowing, emotion, and motivation must be respected in pedagogy, as knowing is surely in the primary service of pervasive and powerful noncognitive factors.

Finally, the teaching profession is held back, ironically, by the very fact that it looks like a profession. Teaching has all the attributes of the other professions: accreditation of academic degrees, professional associations, standardized tests, licenses and credentials, advanced degrees, and so forth. Since the end of the second world war, teachers have been required to have college degrees (in some cases, graduate degrees), pass standardized examinations, meet state license standards, fulfill the school districts' requirements for tenure, complete annual inservice update courses, and show other evidence of professional growth. The irony is that none of these requirements of teachers, all demanding in their appearance, has credibility within or outside the profession, as each is routinely waived when there are shortages of qualified persons for the public schools. In the case of the private schools, the states typically neither set nor require any standards at all, which only reinforces the lack of standing of the current standards.

None of these standards, collectively or separately, provides the public any assurance that the teacher is competent. There are not many high school graduates, for example, who are unable to meet the standards for teaching that are set by the colleges and universities, the respective states, the testing agencies, and the school districts.

Few feel the nation is at risk over these lax professional standards because the naive or spontaneous theory of schooling is implicitly held by large numbers of policy makers and the public. Yet many feel the nation is still at risk educationally and it is largely due to the fact that graduates do not seem to understand very much of what they have learned. This book proposes a remedy: it points to a program of university- and college-based teacher education that demands a much higher standard for the teacher's work—to have all students understand the curriculum.

References

Baldwin, A. (1980). *Theories of child development*. (2nd ed.). New York: Wiley.

Beilin, H. (1971). "The training and acquisition of logical operations." In M. F. Rosskopf, L. P. Steffe, and S. Taback (eds.), *Piagetian cognitive-development research and mathematical education*. Washington, D.C.: National Council of Teachers of Mathematics.

Berliner, D. C. (1988). "Implications of studies of expertise in pedagogy for teacher education and evaluation." *New Directions for Teacher Assessment: Proceedings of the 1988 ETS Invitational Conference*. Princeton, N.J.: Educational Testing Service.

Brophy, J. E., and Good, T. L. (1986). "Teacher behavior and student achievement." In M. C. Wittrock (ed.), *Handbook of research on teaching*. (3rd ed.). New York: Macmillan.

Bruner, J. (1961). *The process of education*. Cambridge, Mass.: Harvard University Press.

Cameron, J., and Pierce, W. (1994). "Reinforcement, reward, and intrinsic motivation: A meta-analysis." *Review of Educational Research, 64*, 363–423.

Choy, S. P., and others (1993). *America's teachers: Profile of a profession*. Washington, D.C.: National Center for Education Statistics.

Collis, J. (1990). *Educational malpractice*. Charlottesville, Va.: Michie Co.

Gardner, H. (1991). *The unschooled mind: How children think and how schools should teach*. New York: Basic Books.

Hawley, W. D., and Rosenholtz, S. J. (1984). "Good schools: What research says about improving student achievement." *Peabody Journal of Education, 61*(4), 1–178.

Heider, F. (1958). *The psychology of interpersonal relations*. New York: Wiley.

Howe, H. (1990). "Thinking about the forgotten half." *Teachers College Record, 92*, 293–305.

McDiarmid, G. W. (1992). *The arts and sciences as preparation for teaching*. (Issue Paper 92-3). East Lansing, Mich.: National Center for Research on Teacher Learning.

Murray, F. B. (1978). "Teaching strategies and conservation training." In A. M. Lesgold, J. W. Pellegrino, S. Fokkema, and R. Glaser (eds.), *Cognitive psychology and instruction*. New York: Plenum.

Murray, F. B. (1986). "Teacher education." *Change*, Sept.-Oct., pp. 18–21.

Murray, F. B. (1990). "The conversion of truth into necessity." In W. Overton (ed.), *Reasoning, necessity and logic: Developmental perspectives*. Hillsdale, N.J.: Erlbaum.

Murray, F. B. (1991). "Questions a satisfying developmental theory would answer: The scope of a complete explanation of developmental phenomena." In H. Reese (ed.), *Advances in child development and behavior*, Vol. 23. San Diego, Calif.: Academic Press.

Murray, F. B. (1992). "Restructuring and constructivism: The development of American educational reform." In H. Beilin and P. Pufall (eds.), *Piaget's theory: Prospects and possibilities*. Hillsdale, N.J.: Erlbaum.

Oakes, J. (1985). *Keeping track: How schools structure inequality.* New Haven, Conn.: Yale University Press.

Ogle, L., Alsalam, N., and Rogers, G. (1991). *The condition of education, 1991.* Washington, D.C.: National Center for Educational Statistics.

Osgood, R. (1962). *Method and theory in experimental psychology.* New York: Oxford University Press.

Rose, S. (1993). *The making of memory.* New York: Anchor Books.

Scardamalia, M., and Bereiter, C. (1991). "Higher levels of agency for children in knowledge building: A challenge for the design of new knowledge media." *Journal of the Learning Sciences, 1,* 37–68.

Sheingold, K. (1991). "Restructuring for learning with technology: The potential for synergy." *Phi Delta Kappan, 73,* 17–27.

Smith, L. (1993). *Necessary knowledge: Piagetian perspectives on constructivism.* Hillsdale, N.J.: Erlbaum.

Stephens, J. M. (1967). *The process of schooling: A psychological examination.* Austin, Texas: Holt, Rinehart & Winston.

Tyson, H. (1994). *Who will teach the children? Progress and resistance in teacher education.* San Francisco: Jossey-Bass.

CHAPTER TWO

THE CHANGING CONTEXT
OF TEACHER EDUCATION

LINDA DARLING-HAMMOND AND VELMA L. COBB

This is a time of great challenge and growing possibility for teacher preparation. As the nation continues the work begun more than a decade ago to redesign its schools for the twenty-first century, the importance of teacher development becomes increasingly clear. Major changes in the nature and contexts of schooling are linked to changes in the nature and contexts of teacher education—changes that are transforming its goals, processes, clientele, governance, and outcomes. This chapter describes how the context for teacher education is evolving and examines the implications of these changes for the development of a profession of teaching that can ensure well-prepared teachers for every child.

A Changing Society and a Changing Occupation of Teaching

In 1983, the report of the National Commission on Excellence in Education, *A Nation at Risk,* brought to the forefront a score of concerns regarding the nation's educational system. This report and a barrage of others that followed focused on perceptions of declining student achievement in an era requiring greater levels of educational success for all students. The educational reform imperative was pursued in the next several years through greater state control of educational processes and mandates for higher educational standards.

The work for this chapter was supported in part by a grant from the Office of the Under Secretary, U.S. Department of Education. The views presented here are those of the authors and do not necessarily represent the views of the Department.

A "second wave" of educational reform followed, with reports from the National Governors' Association (1986), the Carnegie Forum on Education and the Economy (1986), the Holmes Group (1986), and others. These reports affirmed the need to improve education by emphasizing the need to professionalize teaching (Darling-Hammond and Berry, 1988). Reforms aimed at building the capacity of teachers differed from past educational change efforts that mandated new programs (courses, tests, curricula, and management systems) by acknowledging the importance of teachers' knowledge and the nature of the school environments in which they work. The recruitment, preparation, licensure, and renewal of a competent teaching force are now widely recognized as among the central policy issues facing the United States in its educational reform efforts.

In the wake of these reports, efforts to restructure America's schools for the demands of a knowledge-based economy are redefining the mission of schooling and the job of teaching. Because the great masses of students now need to be educated for thinking work rather than low-skilled factory tasks, and educational success is a necessity rather than a luxury for a chosen few, schools are being asked to restructure themselves to ensure higher levels of success for all. Rather than merely "offering education," schools are now expected to ensure that all students learn and perform at high levels. Rather than merely "covering the curriculum," teachers are expected to find ways to support and connect with the needs of all learners (Darling-Hammond, 1990a). Furthermore, they are expected to prepare all students for thinking work: framing problems; finding, integrating, and synthesizing information; creating new solutions; learning on their own; and working cooperatively.

The new mission for education clearly requires substantially more knowledge and radically different skills for teachers, as well as changes in the ways in which schools operate. The kind of teaching required to meet these demands for more thoughtful learning cannot be produced through teacher-proof materials or regulated curriculum. In order to create bridges between common, challenging curriculum goals and individual learners' experiences and needs, teachers must understand cognition and the many different pathways to learning. They must understand child development and pedagogy as well as the structures of subject areas and a variety of alternatives for assessing learning. And they must have a base of knowledge for making decisions traditionally reserved for others in the educational hierarchy (Darling-Hammond, 1990a; Shulman, 1987).

There is another challenge as well that requires a more knowledgeable and highly skilled teaching force: the social setting for teaching is more demanding than ever. Teachers are currently striving to address the needs of a growing number of low-income children (one out of four American children now lives in poverty), the largest wave of immigrants since the turn of the last century, and children who often encounter greater stresses and fewer supports in their communities and families. Furthermore, educators are striving to attain more ambitious goals at a time when schools are more inclusive than they have ever been. More students stay in school longer, and more students with special needs—many of them unserved several decades ago—are now served in more mainstreamed settings.

If all children are to be effectively taught, teachers must be prepared to address the substantial diversity in experiences that children bring with them to school: the wide range of languages, cultures, learning styles and challenges, talents, and intelligences that require in turn an equally rich and varied repertoire of teaching strategies. In addition, teaching for universal learning demands a highly developed ability to discover what children know and can do, how they think and how they learn, and how to match learning and performance opportunities to the needs of individual children. This mission for teaching defies the single, formulaic approach to delivering lessons and testing results that has characterized the goals of much regulation of teaching, many staff development programs, and a number of teacher testing and evaluation instruments.

While these school reforms occur, major changes are taking place in teacher preparation programs across the country; approaches to accreditation, licensing, and induction are being reconsidered; and a new National Board for Professional Teaching Standards is beginning to offer recognition to highly accomplished teachers. These changes are evidence of a deepening commitment to professionalism in teaching as a means to improve education. There is increasing recognition that the capacities teachers need in order to succeed at the twenty-first-century agenda for education can only be widely acquired throughout the teaching force by major reforms in teacher preparation and major restructuring of the systems by which states and school districts license, hire, induct, support, and provide for the continual learning of teachers (Wise and Darling-Hammond, 1987).

While these challenges and changes are being tackled, teaching is faced with the perennial problem it has experienced for centuries: disparities in salaries and working conditions have recreated teacher shortages in central cities and poor rural areas. And, for a variety of reasons, the responses of many governments continues to be to lower or eliminate standards for entry rather than to create incentives that will attract an adequate supply of teachers. As a consequence, this era is developing an even more sharply bimodal teaching force than ever before. While some children are gaining access to teachers who are more qualified and better prepared than in years past, a growing number of poor children and children of color are being taught by teachers who are sorely unprepared for the task they face (Darling-Hammond, 1990b, 1994b). This creates heightened inequality in opportunities to learn and in the outcomes of schooling, with all of the implied social dangers, at the very time we most need to prepare all students more effectively for the greater challenges they face.

If the new forms of schooling that are emerging in this school reform era are to succeed, teaching as an occupation must recruit and retain able and well-prepared individuals for *all* classrooms, not just the most affluent. These entrants must be equipped with the knowledge, skills, and dispositions that will enable them to succeed with all students, and their workplaces must offer them the supports to do so along with the tangible and intangible incentives that will allow them to develop a lifelong career in the profession.

The 1980s launched the most sustained and far-reaching set of efforts to "reform" American elementary and secondary education since the formation of the common school nearly a century earlier. Spurred by massive changes in the nation's economy and social fabric, these initiatives have involved unlikely—indeed previously unthinkable—alliances between chief executive officers of major U.S. corporations, the heads of teachers' unions, state governors, and educators. Reform efforts are addressing every aspect of schooling: curriculum, instruction, assessment, school organization, governance, management, and policy.

Professional standard-setting initiatives undertaken by national professional associations, as well as by state and local education agencies, are rethinking the goals of education. The National Council of Teachers of Mathematics, the National Science Teachers Association, the National Council of Teachers of English, and many other professional groups are working alongside and sometimes in concert with federal and state government agencies to redefine standards for teaching and for student learning. These are linked in turn to the creation of curriculum frameworks and new forms of performance-based testing in many states and to exhortations for more constructivist approaches to teaching. Nearly all states are now engaged in curriculum and assessment reforms aimed at encouraging higher-order thinking and performance abilities. The recent enactment of the "Goals 2000" legislation at the federal level creates an additional stimulus for this work as it provides funds for states to engage these curriculum and assessment reforms linked to voluntary national standards.

The implications for teacher education are many. Teachers will need to be prepared to teach in the ways these new standards demand, with deeper understandings of their disciplines, of interdisciplinary connections, and of inquiry-based learning. They will need skills for creating learning experiences that enable students to construct their own knowledge in powerful ways. In addition, teachers will need to understand and use a variety of more authentic and performance-based means for assessing students' knowledge and understanding as well as for evaluating students' approaches to learning and their prior experiences and conceptions. These kinds of assessments will require keen observation conducted in the context of a highly developed understanding of how children learn, develop, and demonstrate their knowledge. They will rely on teachers' capacities to invent their own means for looking carefully and deeply at student learning processes and products as well as to use—and teach for—much more sophisticated performance assessments developed by others.

School organizations are also changing. Like current restructuring initiatives in business, efforts to restructure schools are seeking to flatten and reduce hierarchies, push decision making closer to the school and classroom, and reshape roles for teachers so that they can be more fully accountable for students. These initiatives also have implications for teacher preparation. Teachers and other educators will need to know a great deal about learning and instruction, about research and theory as well as classroom practice, and about areas of curriculum and assessment development previously reserved for "specialists" at the top of the educational hierarchy or "outside experts."

In addition to the increasingly widespread use of school-based management approaches, there are many proposals to restructure schools, to break up what is viewed as a gridlock in public bureaucracies that manage schooling, to introduce market mechanisms and other new approaches ranging from public school choice to charters, vouchers, and private management of public schools. In some communities, substantial reform energy is going into the creation of new schools, and in many schools and districts, policy makers are introducing results-based strategies for regulating education. All of these initiatives are aimed at opening up schools to greater client input and participation in decision making, and they focus on the results of schooling rather than the continued regulation of schooling processes. Not all of these approaches will have equally beneficial outcomes for educational quality and equality. However, their emergence from a deep well of public frustration with the regulation of public schools must be acknowledged.

However the tussle over these various strategies for stimulating school reform turns out, the strategies do have some common implications for teaching and teacher education. They all require deeper knowledge and greater responsibility for teachers. And to the extent that radical changes in governance and regulation are pursued, the reliance on increased professional accountability increases. Professional accountability starts from the presumption that the basis for quality teaching is knowledgeable and committed teachers. If regulatory accountability mechanisms that define teaching procedures and practices are swept aside, it is more important than ever that educators can be trusted to have the knowledge upon which to base responsible decisions. As Shulman (1983) states, "The teacher remains the key. The literature on effective schools is meaningless, debates over educational policy are moot, if the primary agents of instruction are incapable of performing their functions well. No microcomputer will replace them, no television system will clone and distribute them, no scripted lessons will direct and control them, no voucher system will bypass them" (p. 504).

Efforts to strengthen professional accountability assume that, since decisions about different clients' needs are too complex and individualistic to be prescribed from afar, practitioners must be educated so that they will be able to make those decisions appropriately. Professional accountability aims to ensure competence through rigorous preparation, certification, selection and evaluation of practitioners, as well as continuous peer review. It requires that educators make decisions on the basis of the best available professional knowledge; it also requires that they pledge their first commitment to the welfare of the client. Thus, rather than encouraging teaching that is procedure-oriented and rule-based, professional accountability seeks to create practices that are *client-oriented* and *knowledge-based.*

In addition, professional accountability requires that members of the profession take collective responsibility for defining, transmitting, and enforcing standards of professional practice so that clients are well served.

These conditions for a profession, though central to much of the work of teacher education, have not been universally present in teaching. However, this too is beginning to change.

Standard Setting in Teaching

Over the years, the occupation of teaching has had difficulty defining standards and enforcing a common knowledge base. This is partly because, in contrast to other professions that have developed throughout the twentieth century, teaching has been governed through lay political channels and government bureaucracies—state legislatures, school boards, and departments of education—rather than through professional bodies charged with articulating and enforcing knowledge-based standards. A related problem has been the political inefficacy of professional standard-setting initiatives, which have traditionally been largely ignored by politicians engaged in regulating teaching.

The Problems of Political Governance

Policy makers have typically adopted a view of teaching as relatively simple, straightforward work conducted by semi-skilled workers and controlled by prescriptions for practice. This view is reinforced by the "apprenticeship of experience" adults lived through during their years as students in schools. When some of these adults are later charged with making decisions about the regulation of teaching, they often view questions of required knowledge and skill through the lens of a former pupil rather than the lens of a trained practitioner.

In addition, legislatures and state agencies have a conflict of interest in enforcing rigorous standards for entry to teaching, since they must ensure a warm body in every classroom—and prefer to do so without boosting wages—even while they are charged with defining the minimum preparation needed to teach (Darling-Hammond, 1989). Teacher salaries have continually lagged behind the salaries of other professions requiring similar educational qualifications. Consequently, "despite brief periods of surplus, there has always been a shortage of willing and qualified teachers" (Sedlak and Schlossman, 1986, p. vii). Thus, there has been a constant tension between raising standards of practice and keeping pace with the need for teachers.

> The states . . . [have] found themselves with a set of internally conflicting demands: Improve quality, but guarantee a body in every public classroom. Periodic severe shortages of teachers are much more obvious and compelling than the need for higher quality. . . . Temporary and emergency certificates ease the

shortage in times of undersupply; while in times of oversupply, a glut of teachers removes any rising interest in providing incentives for the improvement of quality. The call for higher salaries is muted when many of those teaching have done little to be temporarily certified, just as it is muted when there are dozens of applicants for each vacancy [Goodlad, 1990, pp. 94–95].

Apple (1987) suggests that "we have built whatever excellence we have in schools on the backs of the low-paid labor of a largely women's work force" (p. 73). In a society that continues to measure status according to compensation, teaching as a meagerly paid, predominantly female occupation has had low prestige. Until the 1960s, teaching was viewed as an "in and out" career (Lortie, 1975), with women continually entering and leaving the profession for child-rearing purposes, and many men and women staying only a short time before leaving for other pursuits. For these reasons and many others—including the differentials in resources committed to schools of education compared to other university departments and the public's ambivalence about education generally—investments in building, codifying, and transmitting a knowledge base for teaching have historically been small (Darling-Hammond, 1990a; Ebmeier, Twombly, and Teeter, 1991; Sedlak and Schlossman, 1986).

And while teaching requires a great deal of discretion and flexibility if it is to be effective, the structure of teaching jobs in bureaucratized schools presses for routine implementation of standardized procedures. This contradiction frequently places teachers in the unprofessional position of having to treat diverse students uniformly, even when the standardized practice required for bureaucratic accountability would be viewed as malpractice if evaluated by the standards of professional accountability.

Whereas professions assume responsibility for defining, transmitting, and enforcing standards of practice, historically teachers have had little or no control over most of the mechanisms that determine professional standards. Instead, in most states, authority for determining the nature of teacher preparation, the types and content of tests used for licensure, and the regulations that govern practice has resided in governmental bodies (legislatures and school boards) and in administrative agencies (state departments of education and central offices). These authority relations ultimately tend to produce bureaucratic rather than professional controls over the content and structure of the work—that is, controls aimed at standardizing procedures rather than at building knowledge that can be applied differentially depending on the needs of a given child.

Finally, there is not yet a highly developed professional accountability structure in teaching. Whereas professional standards boards establish standards for education and entry in professions like medicine, nursing, architecture, accounting, and law, until quite recently such boards have been absent in teaching. Instead, hundreds of individual state mandates have historically controlled what is taught as well as the standards—and loopholes—that are used to grant a teaching license. Educators have not yet been able to establish the kinds of peer review and other accountability mechanisms that will guarantee that only those who can meet acceptable standards of practice will be admitted, graduated, licensed, hired, and retained in the profession. It is this kind of self-regulation that ultimately will justify and legitimize the role of teaching in the ranks of the professions.

Because regulation of entry to practice has not been rigorous, regulation of practice itself has been intrusive. Rules governing curriculum and testing, course requirements, procedures for tracking and promoting students, for organizing instruction and schooling, and for specific educational programs are promulgated by legislatures, state agencies, and lay boards of education at the state and local levels (Wise, 1979).

This micromanagement of teachers' work can be predicted by the laissez-faire approach to admitting individuals to teaching. Forty-six states grant emergency licenses to untrained entrants. In 1985–86, more than thirty thousand emergency licenses were granted in just the few states that kept track of these numbers (Darling-Hammond, 1989). In addition, more than thirty states have authorized "alternative" routes to certification, some of which require only a few weeks of training prior to assumption of full responsibility as a teacher (Darling-Hammond, 1992). Shortages in specific subject areas and in locations like central cities are a major reason for the adoption of such loopholes to regular preparation and licensing requirements. Since the public has had no airtight guarantee about what teachers can be expected to know and be able to do, the perceived need to regulate practice against the prospect of incompetence creates a highly regulated occupation that has sometimes discouraged highly talented candidates from entering and remaining (Darling-Hammond, 1984).

Despite this rather gloomy analysis of the status of teaching, important progress has been made in each of these areas in recent years, and developments on the horizon hold great promise. The ultimate outcome of current initiatives to professionalize teaching will depend in large measure on the extent to which teachers are able to articulate and justify a more professional conception of teaching work than has been common until now, and the extent to which they are willing to accept responsibility for more professional accountability structures to support this view.

Below we examine the current status of supply and demand for teachers; current characteristics of the teaching occupation that influence who enters and stays in teaching, as well as what they can do while they are in the profession; and the characteristics of individuals now entering teacher preparation and teaching. We then discuss the evolution of preparation programs and standards for teaching, as these are being influenced by changes in conceptions of teaching and increased professional governance of the teaching occupation.

Supply and Demand

The teaching force is growing and changing in a number of important respects. Teacher demand has been increasing since the mid 1980s as a function of increasing birth rates and immigration, declining pupil/teacher ratios, and increasing turnover of teachers, primarily due to retirement. The total number of full-time equivalent teachers in public and private schools increased from 2.5 million in 1980 to 2.8 million in 1991 and is projected to reach 3.3 million by the year 2002 (Gerald and Hussar, 1991). Between 1995 and 2005, the demand for newly hired teachers is expected to reach 2.5 million or about 250,000 annually, with a similar rate of demand in the decade following (Darling-Hammond, 1990b; National Center for Education Statistics, 1991).

Recurring shortages of teachers have characterized the United States labor market for most of the twentieth century, with the exception of a brief period of declining student enrollments during the late 1970s and early 1980s (Sedlak and Schlossman, 1986). Currently, increases in demand and recent declines in supply have re-created shortages in a number of areas and teaching fields. In the 1980s, teacher shortages appeared in areas such as bilingual education, special education, physics, chemistry, mathematics, and computer science. Recently, areas such as biology, general science, industrial arts, foreign languages, and positions such as school psychologist, elementary guidance counselor, and librarian have joined the list (Akin, 1989; Darling-Hammond, 1990b). Shortages are most severe in central cities and in growing regions of the country, such as the South and West. The Northwestern and Great Lakes states have had the fewest shortages, in part because of declining student enrollments in many school districts throughout much of the decade (Association for School, College, and University Staffing, 1984).

In addition to enrollments, other factors that influence the demand for teachers are community wealth and goals for education. The types of teachers sought by different communities also vary. Education in many suburban communities has traditionally stressed an academic college preparatory curriculum that requires more mathematics, science, art, and humanities teachers. In urban areas, which have stressed more vocational education and serve a wide variety of special populations of students, bilingual, vocational, and special education teachers are more in demand. Current reforms, however, are heightening demand for academic teachers in all communities, especially in mathematics and science, where course-taking expectations are increasing (Darling-Hammond, 1990c).

While demand is increasing, the supply of newly prepared teachers is also beginning to increase once again, after a dramatic decline from the early 1970s through the mid 1980s. Between 1972 and 1987, the number of bachelor's degrees conferred in education plummeted by well over 50 percent, from 194,229 to 87,083 (American Council on Education, 1989; National Council on Educational Statistics, 1989). The declines were most pronounced for candidates of color, dropping by over 40 percent for Hispanic and Native American candidates between 1975 and 1987, and by two-thirds for African-American candidates (American Council on Education, 1989; National Council on Educational Statistics, 1989). By 1987, only 8,019 candidates of color received bachelor's degrees in education, representing 9 percent of all education degrees, a substantial drop from the 13 percent of a much larger number of degrees that had been awarded to people of color ten years earlier (American Council on Education, 1989).

The decrease in education degrees earned by women between 1975 and 1985 (from 30 percent to 13 percent of all female college students) was matched by an increase in degrees in business (from 5 percent to 20 percent) and other professional fields, such as the sciences, along with preprofessional programs for fields such as law and medicine at the undergraduate level (Darling-Hammond, 1990a, 1990c). Many of the same factors influenced enrollments of students of color: greater enrollment in fields like business and preprofessional fields drew students away from majors in education. As with women generally, these shifts were most pronounced for African-American and Hispanic women.

Since the late 1980s, however, the total number of bachelor's degrees in education has increased, reaching 111,000 in 1990–91 (Snyder and Hoffman, 1993). This represents about three-fourths of all newly prepared teachers each year. The remainder receive degrees in their disciplines with a minor or certificate in education or receive master's degrees. In 1991, about 9 percent of entering teachers had earned a master's degree, nearly double the proportion since 1980 (Choy and others, 1993a; Gray and others, 1993). In addition to some state policies that now require master's degrees for teachers before they can receive a full regular certificate, this increase is also due to the many midcareer entrants who already have bachelor's degrees and are attracted by master's level teacher preparation programs (Darling-Hammond, Hudson, and Kirby, 1989).

At current rates of increase, we might optimistically expect that the total number of new teachers who are fully prepared could grow to about 150,000 annually over the next five years. Beyond that, a wide range of policy choices yet unmade will determine future trends. Recall that this compares to an estimated demand of nearly 250,000 annually. Obviously, teaching vacancies are being and will continue to be filled from other sources, including the reserve pool of teachers (which has recently supplied about a third of newly hired teachers each year) and a number of individuals who are not prepared to teach.

In 1991, the total number of "newly qualified teachers" (who had prepared to teach, were certified, or had taught within a year of their graduation) was 140,000; of these, 121,000 were eligible or certified for teaching, while 19,000 taught without credentials (Gray and others, 1993). Not surprisingly, those who were hired without certification were concentrated in shortage fields. A third or more of all new teachers assigned to teach mathematics, science, social studies, physical education, and special education were neither certified nor eligible for certification in those fields (Gray and others, 1993).

As compared to other newly qualified teachers, those who taught without certification were younger, and they exhibited lower levels of academic achievement; most uncertified entrants (57 percent) had grade point averages (GPAs) *below* 3.25 (and 20 percent had GPAs below 2.25). In contrast, most of those prepared for teaching (51 percent) had GPAs *above* 3.25.

Shortages of qualified candidates are generally location- and field-specific. Overall, 15 percent of all schools and 23 percent of central city schools reported in 1991 that they had vacancies they could not fill with a qualified teacher. Schools with higher enrollments of people of color, whether in central cities, urban fringe, or rural areas, had the most difficulty filling vacancies (Choy and others, 1993b). English as a Second Language and bilingual positions were the most difficult to fill; 37 percent of schools reported they could not find qualified applicants for their vacant positions. Other fields where large numbers of schools reported that qualified applicants were difficult or impossible to find included foreign languages (27 percent of schools), special education (26 percent), and physical sciences (20 percent) (Choy and others, 1993b). As a consequence of these conditions, inner-city high school students in schools having high enrollments of people of color, for example, have only a 50 percent chance of being taught by a certified mathematics or science teacher (Oakes, 1990).

Ironically, while shortages lead to the hiring of unqualified entrants, a great many newly qualified teachers do not immediately enter the profession after they complete their preparation. Of those who prepare to teach, only about 60 to 70 percent actually enter teaching the year after their graduation, and the proportion is even lower for teacher candidates of color (Choy and others, 1993a; Darling-Hammond, 1990b; Haggstrom, Darling-Hammond, and Grissmer, 1988). In 1985, about 74 percent of those newly qualified to teach applied for teaching jobs, and just under 50 percent ended up teaching full time. Only 38 percent of the newly qualified candidates of color entered teaching full time. Continuing the trend, only 76 percent of newly qualified teachers in 1990 applied for teaching jobs and only 58 percent were employed as teachers in 1991 (Choy and others, 1993a; Gray and others, 1993).

Those who prepare to teach but never enter the field do so for a number of reasons. Many have trouble finding employment in areas where they live and want to work. Although most jobs for new teachers are in less affluent central cities, most teacher education students want to teach in well-heeled suburban schools that tend to have lower turnover and that hire experienced teachers rather than new teachers. Some have prepared to teach in fields where there is an oversupply of teachers rather than in fields where there are shortages. Others have prepared to teach in fields like mathematics or science but find the alternative jobs in business and industry more appealing. Still others take time off to do something else (graduate school, travel, or homemaking) after graduating. Some of these individuals enter teaching later. Some education students prepare to teach as a kind of insurance, while pursuing other possible career opportunities. Finally, some teachers decide not to enter the profession when they encounter difficulties in negotiating the shoals of large districts' hiring procedures or when they experience unprofessional hiring practices (Wise, Darling-Hammond, and Berry, 1987).

Reasons for the general undersupply of teachers include the following: salaries lower than those earned by similarly educated professionals, a flat career structure, few opportunities for advancement, and relatively poor working conditions (Darling-Hammond, 1990c). These problems are more severe in low-wealth districts, where shortages are also more severe.

While schools of education can do little to counteract these structural forces in teaching, they can attend to the need to prepare as many of their students as possible for employment in those districts and fields where most jobs will be available; for teaching a diverse population of learners in central city and poor rural districts; for teaching in fields like mathematics and science where demand will remain substantial; and for knowledge in fields like bilingual education and special education, which most beginning teachers will need to use to some extent, even if they are not specialists in these areas. Preparing students well for the schools and kinds of teaching they will likely enter may also help stem the high levels of attrition experienced by beginning teachers, especially those who find themselves unprepared for the demands of their jobs.

Maintaining an adequate supply of well-prepared recruits is even harder during times of substantial new hiring. With heightened demand and greater hiring of new teachers, annual attrition rates can be expected to increase, since new teachers leave at much greater rates than midcareer teachers (Grissmer and Kirby, 1987; Haggstrom, Darling-Hammond, and Grissmer, 1988). In teaching, as in other professions, attrition follows a U-shaped curve, with high attrition in the early years, very low attrition during midcareer (fifteen to twenty years), and an increasing attrition rate during retirement eligibility. Highest attrition rates are among beginning teachers with three or fewer years of experience, particularly those who do not receive mentoring or support during their first years of teaching. Typically, 30 to 50 percent of beginning teachers leave teaching within their first five years (Darling-Hammond, 1990b; Grissmer and Kirby, 1987). Teachers in shortage fields, such as the physical sciences, also tend to leave more quickly and at higher rates (Murnane and Olsen, 1988; Murnane, Singer, and Willett, 1989).

Some states have addressed shortages by increasing salaries and providing scholarships for prospective teachers. However, rather than ensuring competitive salaries and recruitment incentives in shortage areas, most states have tended to reduce standards for entry by establishing alternative routes to certification, expanding the use of substandard and/or temporary credentials, and/or lowering cutoff scores on tests required for licensure (Cobb, 1993; Coley and Goertz, 1990; Darling-Hammond, 1988). In 1990–91, 15 percent of all newly hired teachers did not have any license[1] to teach; another 12 percent held substandard licenses (temporary, provisional, or emergency).

At the local level, teacher shortages can be addressed by assigning teachers to teach outside of their field of licensure, raising class sizes, or canceling courses (Haggstrom, Darling-Hammond, and Grissmer, 1988). Overall, about 16 percent of all teachers teach some classes outside their field of preparation and licensure, and 9 percent spend most of their time teaching in an area outside of their field of preparation. At the secondary level, as many as 11 percent teach outside their area of licensure and 17 percent have less than a college minor in the field they most frequently teach (National Education Association, 1981, 1987).

The prevalence of unlicensed teachers and out-of-field teaching should pose real concerns for every member of the profession and for those who care about the education of all children. Although the issue is hotly debated, the great preponderance of evidence from many dozens of studies demonstrates that fully certified teachers are more effective with students than teachers whose background lacks one or more of the elements required for licensure—that is, subject matter preparation, knowledge about teaching and learning, and a period of guided clinical experiences (see Darling-Hammond, 1992, for a review). Until serious and sustained progress is made toward ensuring qualified teachers in all classrooms, neither the goals of school reform nor the promises of a learner-centered teaching profession can be achieved.

Characteristics of Teaching Employment

The shape of the teaching work force depends not only on the qualities and qualifications of individuals who enter, but also on how occupational and workplace factors affect teachers' decisions to enter, stay in, or leave the profession (Haggstrom, Darling-Hammond, and Grissmer, 1988; McLaughlin and Talbert, 1993; Rosenholtz, 1989). For talented candidates to decide to teach and to remain in teaching, they must perceive opportunities for professional growth, advancement, and financial rewards and experience conditions that enable them to do their jobs well.

The conditions under which teachers work vary substantially across the nearly sixteen thousand local education agencies (LEAs) that hire teachers and are beginning to change in important ways. In general, though, they still reflect a conception of teaching as consisting primarily of instructing large groups of students for most of the day and implementing a curriculum developed for them by others (Darling-Hammond, 1990a).

United States elementary teachers worked an average of forty-four hours per week and secondary teachers spent an average of fifty hours per week on all duties in 1991. The average elementary class size has consistently decreased over the past three decades from twenty-nine in 1961 to twenty-four in 1991. Secondary class size has fluctuated, dropping to twenty-three in 1981 but increasing again to twenty-six in 1991. In both the public and private sectors, classes in the central cities are larger than those in other community types (National Center for Education Statistics, 1993). Teachers in the United States teach 180 days and work an average of 5 nonteaching days per year, a policy that has not changed over the past three decades (National Education Association, 1992).

Despite a shorter school year, no other nation requires teachers to teach more hours per week than the United States. Japanese and most European teachers have substantial time for preparation, curriculum development, and one-on-one work with students, parents, or colleagues, generally teaching large groups of students only about fifteen to twenty hours out of a forty- to fifty-hour work week (Darling-Hammond, 1990a). By contrast, most elementary teachers in the United States have three or fewer hours for preparation per week, while secondary teachers generally have five preparation periods per week. At these levels, 10 and 5 percent, respectively, reported having no preparation periods (National Education Association, 1992).

In most schools, teachers are not expected to meet jointly with other teachers, to develop curriculum or assessments, to observe or discuss each other's classes, nor is time generally provided for these kinds of activities. Not surprisingly, in 1987–88, fewer than 10 percent of public school teachers said they were highly satisfied with the extent and quality of opportunities to collaborate with colleagues (Choy and others, 1993a).

A recent survey of teachers regarding the extent and effects of recent school reform illustrates how professional working conditions affect teachers' attitudes about their work as well as their practices. Those who reported that site-based management (SBM) had been introduced in their schools (about 50 percent of the total) were also much more likely to report that a whole series of other curriculum and organizational reforms had also had an impact on their schools. For example, 72 percent of teachers in SBM schools said that cooperative learning had had a major impact on their school, as compared to only 35 percent of those teachers in non-SBM schools. Also more prevalent in SBM schools were mixed ability group classrooms, tougher graduation standards, authentic assessment practices, emphasis on in-depth understanding rather than superficial content coverage, accelerated learning approaches, connections between classroom practices and home experiences and cultures of students, and teacher involvement in decisions over how school funds are spent.

These kinds of changes in governance seem to be associated with other changes that provide teachers with the teaching circumstances they need to feel effective. Teachers in schools that had been impacted by reform were much more likely to report that their schools had become much better in the previous three years at providing structured time for teachers to work with each other on professional matters, enabling them to observe each other in the classroom and provide feedback about their teaching, allowing teachers to work in teams, giving teachers more time to plan instruction, and being willing to counsel students in home visits.

These changes appear to affect teachers' views of their work. Teachers in reform-impacted schools felt they had more opportunity to adapt their instruction to the needs of their students and to invent more effective methods rather than being constrained by district routines or standardized curricula. They were more optimistic about principal-teacher relationships, about working conditions for teachers, about the educational performance of students, about the professional status of teachers, and about their own job satisfaction. They were much more likely to report themselves very satisfied with their careers as teachers (61 percent as compared to 44 percent) and to see teachers as the agents of reform rather than as the targets of reform (LH Research, 1993).

The relationships between school reform and teachers' working conditions, teaching practices, and satisfaction with teaching are reflected in growing school restructuring initiatives of the two major teachers' unions, the National Education Association (NEA), which represented 66 percent of the teaching force in 1991, and the American Federation of Teachers (AFT), which represented 12 percent of teachers (National Education Association, 1992). Although unions continue to function primarily as the guardians of a collective bargaining system governing economic advancement and procedural due-process issues for employees, they have increasingly become involved in setting standards for teachers, working on school reform, and initiating new educational programs (Kerchner and Koppich, 1993). In a number of districts, unions have been at the forefront of introducing new roles for teachers—such as the consulting teacher programs in Rochester, New York, and Toledo and Cincinnati, Ohio—and stimulating school restructuring initiatives, as in Dade County, Florida, and Wells, Maine. Some of these new initiatives have also begun to influence the ways in which teachers are compensated for taking on new and different responsibilities.

Compensation

The average public school teacher with more than fifteen years of experience and a master's degree earned a salary of $34,934 in 1992 (National Center for Education Statistics, 1993). Private school salaries are lower. Beginning teachers earned $23,054 on average. This was just slightly higher in real dollar terms than salaries in 1972, before the decline in purchasing power that occurred during the 1970s and 1980s. In general, teachers earn 20 to 30 percent less than professionals in other occupations requiring similar educational preparation (Darling-Hammond and Berry, 1988). Though some of the differential in compensation can be accounted for by the fact that most other professionals work more than 185 days per year, a substantial gap remains after this is taken into account (Darling-Hammond, 1990b).

Salaries are not governed by market conditions, but by state and local governmental budgetary actions (Sykes, 1989). These depend in turn on local wealth, tax rates, and willingness to spend on education. Salary levels vary greatly among LEAs within states and among the states themselves. For example, average salaries in 1990–91 ranged from $20,354 in South Dakota to $43,326 in Connecticut (Choy and others, 1993b). Even within a single labor market, there is often a marked difference in teachers' salaries based on the wealth and spending choices of various districts. Typically, teachers in affluent suburban districts earn more than those in central cities or more rural communities within the same area. These variations influence the teacher labor market, contributing to surpluses of qualified teachers in some locations and shortages in others.

These differences also affect teacher retention, especially early in a teacher's career. Better paid elementary and secondary school teachers throughout the 1970s tended to stay in teaching longer than those with lower salaries, especially during their first year of teaching (Murnane and others, 1991). The influence of salary on early career retention appears to continue more recently: in 1987–88, highly paid first-year teachers were more likely to say they planned to stay in teaching than those who were paid less (Sclan, 1993).

For most of the past fifty years, salary scales within districts have been fixed and uniform. The amount a teacher earns is based on his or her years of experience and level of education. In order to boost salaries, during the 1980s many states created statewide minimum salaries. Thirty states presently have mandated minimum compensation levels for teachers statewide, and nineteen states have statewide salary schedules beyond the minimum, usually with a one-step increase in salary for each year of experience. In other states, salary schedules are developed at the local district level, also featuring annual "steps" for experience and additional pay for additional education beyond the bachelor's degree.

The fight for uniform salary schedules was taken up by unions when women were routinely paid at lower rates than men, elementary teachers were paid less than secondary teachers, and black teachers were paid at lower rates than whites. Though there have been major equity benefits of the move to a single salary schedule, there are also some drawbacks to the way in which schedules have been developed. Typically, schedules are flat and guarantee smaller salary increases with increasing years of experience. Thus, there is typically not a wide range between the salaries of beginning teachers and those of the most experienced ones in any given district. This does not provide much incentive for long-term commitments to teaching or for taking on a variety of roles.

Differentiated Compensation and Roles

During the 1980s, twenty-nine states introduced some kind of career ladder, merit pay, or incentive pay system for teachers. These systems may be local or statewide. Such ladders were intended to raise salary levels based on performance and make teaching more attractive to talented teachers. However, most merit pay schemes have already been discontinued due to administration and evaluation problems. A few career ladders continue to exist. Programs designating teachers as "master" or "mentor" teachers with special responsibilities continue in larger numbers, although they exist only in a minority of districts. These programs allow teachers to engage in work such as curriculum development or assistance to new teachers, work traditionally reserved for administrators (Darling-Hammond, 1990a; Darling-Hammond and Berry, 1988).

The proportions of teachers actually receiving incentive pay of any kind was small in 1990–91: about 2 percent on average for each of several forms of incentive pay, such as individual merit pay, a schoolwide bonus, or additional pay for teaching in a shortage field or high-priority location. More noticeable numbers received payment for serving as master or mentor teachers (9 percent) or for participating in a career ladder program (23 percent).

These initiatives attempt not only to differentiate pay but also to alter the "flat" career structure of teaching. In the work environment, there has been little differentiation between beginning and veteran teachers in salary and responsibilities, and little variety at any career point in teachers' work roles. Because there are few rewards for longevity in teaching, a seniority system has emerged that often permits veterans to opt for "easier" assignments.

Novice teachers, having the least experience, are usually assigned the least desirable tasks within a school and the most educationally needy children and are disproportionately hired in the least economically advantaged schools. Veteran teachers in large districts frequently transfer to more desirable schools at their earliest opportunity (Darling-Hammond and Berry, 1988; Darling-Hammond and Goodwin, 1993).

These conditions are also beginning to change. Some models are emerging that demonstrate how incentive structures in teaching may be reshaped to encourage the provision of highly qualified teachers to less advantaged students and to enable expert veterans to provide support for new entrants.

In Charlotte-Mecklenburg, North Carolina, and in Rochester, New York, for example, "lead" teachers who have been recognized for their demonstrated expertise can be called upon, as part of their privilege and their obligation, to teach children and to create new programs in the schools that currently need transforming. In such experiments, and in policy changes they incorporate, lies one part of the hope for equalizing opportunities to learn. In a growing number of districts, mentor teachers are taking on the responsibility for supporting and helping to prepare new teachers as well. The responsibility for helping prepare and induct new members of the profession is increasingly being recognized by school districts and is increasingly being assumed in concert with schools of education.

Induction into Teaching

A growing number of first-year teachers are participating in programs that formally socialize them into teaching: by 1991, 48 percent of all teachers with fewer than three years of experience and 54 percent of public school teachers had experienced some kind of induction program during their first year. The number of teachers who participated in formal induction programs almost doubled during the decade 1981–1991 and more than tripled since the early 1970s (Choy and others, 1993b). Depending on the nature of the programs—including the extent to which they focus on support as well as evaluation, and the extent to which they help teachers address real problems of practice—these induction initiatives may make a substantial difference in teacher recruitment and retention.

Previous research on teacher induction programs shows that there are major differences in the strategies adopted by states during the 1980s. While places like California and Connecticut funded mentor programs that enabled expert veteran teachers to work in a sustained fashion with beginners, many of the first wave induction programs focused more on evaluation than mentoring. They required new teachers to pass an observational evaluation prior to receiving a continuing license. Though these were called induction programs, most did not fund the work of mentors, and the mandated evaluation strategies typically looked for the demonstration of predetermined generic behaviors rather than for the development of contextually appropriate good practice (Darling-Hammond with Sclan, 1992; MacMillan and Pendlebury, 1985; Peterson and Comeaux, 1989; Wise and Darling-Hammond, 1987).

Since then, more states and districts have sought to create programs that support new teachers in the development of guided, collegial practice and inquiry likely to promote higher levels of efficacy and effectiveness (Darling-Hammond with Sclan, 1992; Little, 1987; Rosenholtz, 1985). Some mentoring programs have already been shown to improve beginning teachers' effectiveness and decrease their typically high attrition (Smylie, 1994). Further research will be needed to ascertain what kinds of induction programs most new teachers are experiencing and how they are affecting teachers' effectiveness and commitment to stay in teaching.

Teachers of all experience levels agree on the importance of supervised induction. When asked what would have helped them in their first years of teaching, 47 percent felt that a skilled, experienced teacher assigned to provide advice and assistance would have benefited them, and 39 percent felt that more practical training, such as a year's internship before having their own classroom, would have been most helpful (Metropolitan Life, 1991). Among the many changes evolving in teacher education programs and policies is a growing commitment to extend clinical preparation through more extensive student teaching and internships. Many of these models create a more seamless bridge between university-based and school-based preparation through school-university partnerships explicitly focused on beginning teacher induction. These and other trends in teacher education programs are described below.

Teacher Education Programs

Teacher education in the United States takes place in a wide range of higher education institutions. Among the 1,978 four-year colleges and universities in the nation, approximately 1,279 have schools, colleges, or departments of education (SCDEs) engaged in teacher education (National Council for Accreditation of Teacher Education, 1993; Sykes, 1985). These include large public institutions, private independent and religious-affiliated liberal arts colleges, and private universities. The greatest number of SCDEs are in the central region of the country, with the fewest located in the western region.

The majority (approximately 65 percent) of higher education institutions having teacher education programs are private, but these produce only 25 percent of the new teachers. About one-third of all teacher-preparing institutions, most in large public universities, actually produce 75 percent of all teachers. Many of these colleges began as state normal schools for teachers, and they continue to emphasize the preparation of teachers in their current broader role as liberal arts colleges. Some prepare as many as a thousand teachers annually. Overall, teacher candidates comprise about 10 percent of total college and university enrollments and about 13 percent of undergraduate enrollments (American Association of Colleges for Teacher Education, 1987).

While national estimates of teacher education expenditures are not available, the relative claim on higher education dollars made by teacher education is clearly small relative to other fields. In comparison to other university departments and programs, teacher education programs bring in substantially more resources than they expend for services to their students (Sykes, 1985). One recent analysis of expenditures at six research universities found that schools of education are generally the lowest-funded unit within the university and have lost ground over the past decade (Ebmeier, Twombly, and Teeter, 1990). On one common state index for allocating funds based on the relative cost of training in professional fields, education ranks lowest with an index of 1.04, in comparison to engineering at 2.07 and nursing at 2.74 (Sykes, 1985). Support for teacher candidates in the way of state or federal tuition support or stipends is limited.

Teacher Education Students

In contrast to some other countries' policies, there is no established number of annual teacher education entrants determined or subsidized by the government. Program size has tended to increase or decrease with the number of interested candidates who can meet the minimum entry requirements and pay the tuition. "Traditionally, the number of participants in a teacher preparation program is driven by the size of the applicant pool" (Miller and Silvernail, 1994, p. 37). Additionally, preservice programs often provide an excellent source of revenue for the institution as a whole; therefore, some institutions are reluctant to limit enrollment. Frequently, the number of applicants admitted to a program is based on economic considerations rather than quality standards, such as faculty/student ratios or the number of qualified field placements. There are substantial fluctuations in the number of individuals preparing to teach from year to year.

During the 1980s, there was a widespread belief and some evidence that the "quality" of new entrants to teaching was declining. For example, during the lowest recruitment point in the early 1980s, education was one of the fields least selected by those students scoring highest on aptitude and achievement tests (Lanier and Little, 1986; Southern Regional Education Board, 1985; Vance and Schlechty, 1982). This was particularly true for women and college students of color (Astin, 1993; Darling-Hammond, 1984). In addition, those who defected from teaching at each point after choosing an education major (that is, failing to enter teaching and failing to remain) were disproportionately comprised of high test scorers (Vance and Schlechty, 1982; Murnane and others, 1991).

This confluence of circumstances was due to a combination of low demand for teachers, unfavorable salaries and working conditions, and the opening up of more widespread career opportunities for women and for college students of color. Many of these factors have begun to change, however, as demand and interest have increased alongside salary improvements and school reforms. Recent indicators suggest that discouraging trends in the composition of the future teaching force have substantially changed since the 1980s.

Applications have increased generally, particularly from higher achieving college entrants. In addition, to ensure adequate preparation, many teacher education institutions began to require higher GPAs and test scores for admission (Darling-Hammond and Berry, 1988; Howey and Zimpher, 1993). Consequently, the academic qualifications of prospective teachers are now stronger than they were a decade ago and stronger than those of the average college graduate. For example, the GPAs of newly qualified teachers in 1990 were noticeably higher than those of other bachelor's degree recipients, with 50 percent of newly qualified teachers earning an average of 3.25 or better as compared to 40 percent of all graduates (Gray and others, 1993).

While the academic ability of prospective teachers has increased, there are other recruitment needs. Compared to current teachers, the gender and racial/ethnic profile of prospective teachers enrolled in the subset of teacher education programs surveyed by the Research About Teacher Education (RATE) project in 1991 was even less representative of men and people of color. Men represented only 19 percent of these teacher education students, and they were academically the least well prepared of teacher candidates (American Association of Colleges for Teacher Education, 1992; Brookhart and Loadman, 1993). The percentage of people of color enrolled in undergraduate teacher education programs (8 percent) was substantially lower than the proportion enrolled in higher education overall and the proportion in the current teaching force (Goodlad, 1990; Howey and Zimpher, 1993).

Both recruitment and retention of candidates of color are problematic during and after teacher education. In a study conducted by the American Association of Colleges for Teacher Education (1992), African-American teacher education students who had enrolled in the fall of 1985 and 1986 had a higher attrition rate than white or Hispanic teacher education students. At the same time, African-Americans who were newly qualified to teach in 1985 were the most likely group to have received certification but not entered teaching (Darling-Hammond,

1990b). While over 14,000 African-American 1984 degree recipients were eligible or certified to teach, only 8,500 of them were actually teaching a year later. For Hispanics, of 4,100 certified recent graduates, only 2,700 were employed in teaching (National Center for Education Statistics, 1983, 1985). These data demonstrate that the decline in the number of teachers of color is due not only to failure to enter or complete teacher education but also to other factors that dissuade candidates from entering and staying in teaching.

There are many reasons to be concerned about the growing shortages of teachers of color. The importance of teachers of color as role models for majority students and students of color alike is one reason for concern. In addition, teachers of color often bring a special level of understanding to the experiences of students of color and a perspective on school policy and practice that is critical for all schools and districts to include. Finally, with the exception of teachers of color, most prospective teachers do not prefer to teach in inner-city schools, even though that is where a disproportionate number of new jobs are (Howey and Zimpher, 1993). This also presents a challenge with implications for the content and processes of teacher preparation, which need to better ensure all teachers' preparation for urban school teaching. To address the shortages of teachers of color, higher education institutions, in conjunction with states and districts, will need to develop strategies to attract and keep candidates in teacher education programs and support their entry into the profession (Dilworth, 1990).

A related concern is that financial assistance is not available in any substantial amount for teacher education students. Although teacher education students generate money from several sources (loans, grants, employment, etc.), the predominant source of financial income through the 1980s came from family resources, not unlike other undergraduate students (Howey and Zimpher, 1993). Most preservice teacher education students report that they enroll in programs close to where they are living at the time, mainly for the sake of convenience and due to a belief that staying in the area will increase chances for getting a job when they complete their programs (American Association of Colleges for Teacher Education, 1992; Goodlad, 1990; Howey and Zimpher, 1993). Goodlad (1990) found that over 70 percent of the preservice students in his study commuted to school, and the large majority held part-time or full-time jobs.

Policy Guidance

Teacher preparation programs are governed by decisions made within their institutions (at the institutional level as well as within the SCDE), by state requirements for program approval, and—for the 40 percent of programs that are professionally accredited—by the standards of the national accrediting agency, the National Council for Accreditation of Teacher Education (NCATE). NCATE accredits just over 500, or about 40 percent, of the 1,279 higher education institutions operating teacher education programs (National Council for Accreditation of Teacher Education, 1993). However, NCATE-accredited programs produce over 70 percent of the nation's teachers.

In contrast to teaching, where accreditation is voluntary, most other professions require graduation from an accredited professional program as a prerequisite for licensure. In those cases where this is not required, candidates graduating from nonaccredited programs may experience some differentiation in when they can sit for licensing examinations, status, compensation, and/or restrictions in the authorization to practice. Universal accreditation of teacher education programs is now the policy in three states, and a growing number of others are providing incentives for accreditation by participating in state partnerships with NCATE. Currently, about twenty-seven states have partnership agreements with NCATE. These agreements enable institutions to receive accreditation *and* meet state program approval standards by addressing NCATE standards.

Programs are also indirectly guided by their state's licensing requirements for teachers, as these often describe the kinds of courses candidates must complete in order to receive a license. Program approval guidelines and licensing requirements vary from state to state. Generally, these are set by the state department of education. Recently, however, twelve states have established professional standards boards for teaching like those that exist in other professions. In these states, the teachers, other educators, and public members who sit on the standards board have assumed responsibility for setting standards for teacher education program approval and licensing.

In state program approval, states approve teacher education programs based on the programs' abilities to prepare candidates to meet state requirements for teacher licensure. Until recently, most states licensed teachers by requiring them to complete an approved program of teacher education. Upon successful completion of the state-approved program, a recommendation for licensure was submitted to the state. The approval process typically assesses the learning experiences offered rather than what candidates have learned and can do. State program approval is typically coordinated by the state's department of education, under the auspices of a state board of education or a professional teaching standards board. All teacher education programs leading to licensure must be approved by the state.

Unhappiness with the results of this approach led to the enactment of tests for teacher licensing in most states during the 1980s, providing an additional check on the process. Now states are looking at a variety of new approaches to licensing and program approval, including performance-based approaches that would rely more heavily on assessments of teacher knowledge and skill conducted during and after teacher education and induction. These are described more fully below.

State legislatures and state boards of education also sometimes exert authority over schools of education, much more so than any schools or departments within universities. Because of the special state interest in education, legislatures have sometimes been active in mandating admissions and graduation requirements for schools of education, testing requirements, and even specific course requirements. At least twenty-two states now require some form of testing for entry into teacher education, and fifteen states have set minimum grade point averages for entry. Fifteen states require both testing and minimum GPAs (Coley and Goertz, 1990). At their own initiative or due to state mandate, at least 70 percent of teacher education programs now have minimum grade requirements that must be met before a student is admitted. Half also require that students pass a proficiency test before completing the program, a number that has doubled since 1980 (Holmstrom, 1985).

The Preservice Teacher Preparation Curriculum

The large scope of policy activity regarding teacher education during the 1980s and early 1990s has led to greater diversity in program structures. Increased requirements for licensing in some states have led to the growth of five-year programs, while master's degree programs and other postgraduate certification programs for those already holding a bachelor's degree have also expanded in size and number. A variety of approaches are represented in alternate route programs, ranging from short summer programs operated exclusively by school districts to two-year master's programs that combine university-based preparation and an intensive internship.

For most candidates, however, professional preparation still takes place in a four-year program leading to the baccalaureate degree. The typical program has three principal components. First, most coursework during the four years is in the liberal arts, with a major emphasis for secondary teachers on a single content area in which the candidate will be licensed, such as history, mathematics, or biology. Most elementary teachers have traditionally majored in elementary education, but increasingly they attain a major in one of the liberal arts disciplines or a field like psychology or human development.

Second, the remaining coursework is taken in the study of education as a field of inquiry, including teaching methods. Typically, these courses include an introduction to education, educational psychology, general or specific methods courses, and, at least for elementary teacher candidates, child development. What was once a standard requirement for all teacher education students, a course in educational history and philosophy, is now taken by very few (Goodlad, 1990). Education courses typically constitute only about one-fifth of the total program for secondary education majors (26 credit hours on average out of a total of 135), while candidates in elementary education usually complete more education courses (an average of 50 credit hours in pedagogy and other educational courses out of a total of 125).

Finally, there are a variety of field experiences for candidates. Generally, candidates in most elementary and secondary teacher education programs (about 86 percent) are required to go through some kind of observational and tutorial field experiences prior to student teaching (American Association of Colleges for

Teacher Education, 1987). Often during the initial phases of the program, students spend one or two days per week observing or tutoring in schools. In over two-thirds of the teacher education programs, field experiences are also required in one or more methods courses later in the program's sequence. Such experiences allow candidates to apply what they are learning through classroom observations and work with students before entering an intensive student teaching experience (American Association of Colleges for Teacher Education, 1987).

Building on these field experiences, all candidates are involved in practice teaching (also called student teaching), which takes place near the completion of a preparation program and occurs in elementary and secondary schools under the supervision of a cooperating teacher. Typically, student teaching occupies 350 hours during one full fifteen-week semester of the higher education institution, which is slightly less than a full school semester in an elementary or secondary school, due to differences in academic calendars. Increasingly, however, student teaching is based on the school semester rather than a college or university semester (American Association of Colleges for Teacher Education, 1987).

Sometimes, student teaching engages students in two different placements, so that they can experience varied classrooms. Some colleges require as much as a full school year of student teaching, although this is not the norm. Typically, candidates in student teaching experiences are supervised by faculty from the SCDEs as well as by their "cooperating teacher" in the school in which they are placed. College supervisors are usually doctoral students, teacher education faculty, or other SCDE staff. College supervisors average six or seven visits to a student teacher per semester (American Association of Colleges for Teacher Education, 1987). Given the limited amount of time that the college supervisor spends with the student during the student teaching experience, the cooperating teacher is very influential in the student's practical or clinical experience.

Several studies have observed that there are often "loose linkages" between the three components of teacher preparation programs—liberal arts education, professional study, and practical experiences—reducing the connections made among subject matter content, educational theory, and practical application (Goodlad, 1990; Schwartz, 1988; Zeichner, 1986). The fact that colleges have traditionally exerted little influence on the nature or quality of the practicum or student teaching placements is one example of this fragmentation. Principals often choose cooperating teachers "based on administrative convenience rather than educational value" or based on those who volunteer (Darling-Hammond and Goodwin, 1993, p. 33). Cooperating teachers often receive little or no training for their roles and frequently have very little contact with the preparation program directly. Such lack of connections may reinforce teachers' conceptions that content and theory have little utility in the "real world" of the classroom.

To encourage greater continuity between theory and practice, a number of institutions have begun to create professional development schools in close collaboration with nearby school districts. These are partnerships between schools of education and local schools in which the school becomes a site for the clinical preparation of groups of prospective teachers. The Professional Development School (PDS) models state-of-the-art practice, involves school- and university-based faculty in developing a program of learning for beginning teachers, and frequently also provides a site for developing collegial research on teaching (Darling-Hammond, 1994a). Based on surveys of teacher preparation institutions, by 1994 more than two hundred professional development schools had been started across the country (Darling-Hammond, 1994a).

In general, faculty (70 percent) and students (69.7 percent) view their preservice program as having been good or outstanding in preparing candidates for teaching (American Association of Colleges for Teacher Education, 1988). The majority of the remaining faculty and students assessed their programs as adequate. The area of greatest discomfort concerns preparation for diverse learners. When asked whether teacher education graduates were prepared to teach in culturally diverse settings or to teach academically "at-risk" students, many faculty (29.7 percent) and students (28.6 percent) indicated that graduates were "less than adequately" prepared (American Association of Colleges for Teacher Education, 1988). While a similar percentage of each group reported that they were very prepared or adequately prepared, this is clearly an area where changes in the conditions of schooling and the expectations of teachers are demanding greater changes of schools of education as well.

Differences Among Teacher Preparation Programs

Because no universal standards for either licensing or accreditation are enforced, the range in teacher preparation programs is wide. Most of the reform efforts impacting teacher preparation in the past decade focus on structural differences. These structural differences include adding a fifth year, increasing (or, in a few states, limiting) the number of credit hours in professional education, increasing the amount of field-based experience, or creating alternate routes to teaching (Feiman-Nemser, 1990).

A fifth-year program involves completing teacher preparation in a five-year extended bachelor's program or a fifth-year master's degree program following undergraduate school. Some argue that a fifth-year program provides greater flexibility for the integration of theory and practice because the extended time allows greater opportunity for an in-depth supervised internship connected to coursework. Though many of the reform reports of the past decade have advocated this change in teacher preparation, four-year baccalaureate programs are still the norm (Wong and Osgathorpe, 1993).

Preparation programs also differ due to different conceptual orientations and different levels of quality. In some, students learn a great deal about learning and child development; in others, they do not. In some, a subject-specific view of pedagogy is emphasized; in others, generic approaches to pedagogy are taught. In some, teachers learn a great deal about curriculum development and student assessment; in others, they do not. These differences are attributable to several different causes. State regulations governing licensing and program approval are one source of variation. For example, when legislative edicts in New Jersey, Texas, and Virginia reduced the amount of professional education coursework undergraduates could take to no more than eighteen credits, most programs had to eliminate or greatly reduce coursework in learning and child development and focus on generic rather than subject-specific approaches to pedagogy.

On the other hand, a number of states, such as New York, Connecticut, and Arizona, require at least a master's degree on top of a strong subject matter degree for full professional certification; these requirements generally incorporate thirty-six to forty credits of professional education coursework and a lengthy supervised practicum or internship in addition to subject matter preparation. Thus, the meaning of a teaching license, in terms of knowledge and skills represented, varies tremendously from state to state (Darling-Hammond, 1992).

Similarly, although teachers are increasingly expected to major in a discipline while also preparing to teach, this too varies according to state licensing requirements. By 1991, for example, an average of 63 percent of mathematics teachers had majored in their field. However, this ranged from 25 percent in Alaska to 87 percent in Maryland. The proportion of science teachers who had majored in their field increased from 64 percent in 1988 to 70 percent in 1991 but ranged from 41 percent in New Mexico to 85 percent in Connecticut (Blank and Gruebel, 1993).

Because professional accreditation is not universal, a great many programs operate without the core set of standards that guide those that are accredited. Additional sources of variation in program content include the conceptions of teaching and teacher knowledge underlying state program approval guidelines and assessments of beginning teachers (Darling-Hammond with Sclan, 1992), the recent proliferation of state-approved "alternate routes" to certification, and the view of teaching adopted by individual institutions.

Alternative Teacher Education Programs

During the 1980s, more than half of the states (thirty-nine as of 1991) implemented alternate routes to licensure. Most of these alternate routes were aimed at recruiting candidates with bachelor's degrees in other fields. These programs range from one- or two-year master's degree programs, structured to enable entry for midcareer changers or others who already hold a bachelor's degree, to short summer courses prior to hiring.

Most states' alternate routes aimed at recruiting nontraditional entrants into teaching are actually graduate-level, university-based programs structured to ensure that those who have already received other degrees do not have to repeat their undergraduate coursework (Feistritzer, 1990). A few states, however, have authorized programs offered by school districts or the state itself; these require little formal preparation and rely instead on on-the-job supervision, which unfortunately does not always materialize (Darling-Hammond, 1992).

Unlike traditional entrants of teacher education programs, candidates in these shorter-term routes take little education coursework and no student teaching prior to entering; they assume full-time teaching responsibilities following a brief orientation seminar, usually six to eight weeks. Some states' alternate route programs are restricted to areas of teacher shortages or to specific geographic areas; others are not (Choy and others, 1993a). However, most of the short-term non-university-based programs target inner-city school districts with serious shortages (Darling-Hammond, 1992).

The requirements for alternate route certification vary widely. Some states' alternate route requirements are more stringent than the requirements for regular certification in other states. For example, the amount of professional education beyond a liberal arts degree required of alternate route candidates can vary from only nine credit hours in Virginia to the forty-five credit hours required for a full master's degree or its equivalent in Alabama or Maryland (Cornett, 1992; Feistritzer, 1990). Even among programs that require alternate route candidates to complete all regular certification requirements, there is a stark difference between the rigorous twelve-month preparation program required *prior to* entry in Maryland (Maryland State Department of Education, 1990) and the Tennessee requirement that allows candidates to enter without professional preparation while earning credits toward certification at the leisurely rate of six hours every five years (Cornett, 1992). At that rate, a teacher could spend twenty-five years in the classroom before meeting the certification requirements still on the books in most states.

At the same time, some states have much lower expectations for all candidates' academic attainment and preparation than others. Thus, alternate route candidates in "high standards" states such as Maryland or Connecticut, for example, are subjected to higher selection standards and receive a substantially more rigorous professional preparation than either "regular" or "alternative" certification candidates in "low standards" states such as New Jersey or Texas (Darling-Hammond, 1992).

Keeping all of these ambiguities in mind, one estimate places the number of recruits entering teaching through alternate routes at about twenty thousand between 1985 and 1990 (Feistritzer and Cherster, 1991, cited in Choy and others, 1993a). Although this constitutes well under 5 percent of new hires during those years, the number is reportedly growing.

In a RAND Corporation study of nontraditional recruits into teaching, two types of alternate route programs were compared: one category included graduate-level preservice preparation targeted to the needs of midcareer entrants, including carefully focused coursework, an intensive supervised internship or student teaching experience, and usually resulting in a master's degree. The other category included short-term programs, usually only a few weeks, which placed recruits directly into jobs as full-fledged teachers. Recruits in the more extended university-based programs were much more satisfied with the amount and quality of preparation they received, reported fewer difficulties when they entered classroom teaching, and were more likely to say they planned to stay in the profession (Darling-Hammond, Hudson, and Kirby, 1989).

These differences between the outcomes of extended university-based programs and short-term routes appear repeatedly in the literature. A number of reviews of research have summarized the results of recent studies, along with studies conducted during the shortage era of the 1960s and early 1970s, when many teachers entered through temporary and alternate routes. All of them conclude that fully prepared and certified teachers are generally more highly rated and more successful with students than teachers without full preparation (Ashton and Crocker, 1986, 1987; Evertson, Hawley, and Zlotnik, 1985; Greenberg, 1983; Haberman, 1984; Olsen, 1985). As Evertson and colleagues conclude in their research review, "The available research suggests that among students who become teachers, those enrolled in formal preservice preparation programs are more likely to be effective than those who do not have such training" (p. 8).

The importance of full preparation also shows up strongly in a number of specific fields that have been studied. For example, a review of research on science education, incorporating the results of more than sixty-five studies, found consistently positive relationships between student achievement in science and the teacher's background in both education courses and science courses (Davis, 1964; Druva and Anderson, 1983; Taylor, 1957). These effects are particularly noticeable when achievement is measured on higher-order tasks such as students' abilities to apply and interpret scientific concepts (Perkes, 1968). The same influence of preparation on teacher performance has been found for mathematics teachers (Begle, 1979); elementary school teachers (Hice, 1970; McNeil, 1974; LuPone, 1961); teachers of gifted students, again particularly with respect to the development of students' higher-order thinking skills (Hansen, 1988); and early childhood teachers (Roupp, Travers, Glantz, and Coelen, 1979).

Other studies demonstrate that the typical problems of beginning teachers are lessened for those who have had adequate preparation prior to entry (Adams, Hutchinson, and Martray, 1980; Glassberg, 1980; Taylor and Dale, 1971). Studies of teachers admitted through quick-entry alternate routes frequently note that the candidates have difficulty with curriculum development, pedagogical content knowledge, attending to students' differing learning styles and levels, classroom management, and student motivation (Feiman-Nemser and Parker, 1990; Grossman, 1989; Lenk, 1989; Mitchell, 1987). In comparison to beginners who have completed a teacher education program, novices who enter without full preparation show more ignorance about student needs and differences and about the basics of teaching, are less sensitive to students, less able to plan and redirect instruction to meet students' needs (and less aware of the need to do so), and less skilled in implementing instruction (Bents and Bents, 1990; Bledsoe, Cox, and

Burnham, 1967; Copley, 1974; Darling-Hammond, 1992, 1994b; Grossman, 1988; Rottenberg and Berliner, 1990). They are less able to anticipate students' knowledge and potential difficulties and less likely to see it as their job to do so, often blaming the students if their teaching is not successful.

These findings are reflected in a study of the performance of alternate route candidates in Dallas (Gomez and Grobe, 1990). Though these candidates were rated about as well on average as traditional education candidates on several aspects of teaching, they were rated lower on such factors as their knowledge of instructional techniques and instructional models. The performance of alternate route candidates was also much more uneven than that of trained teachers, with a much greater proportion of them—from two to sixteen times as many—likely to be rated "poor" on each of the teaching factors evaluated.[2] The effects of this unevenness showed up most strongly on their students' achievement in language arts, where the achievement gains of students of alternate route teachers were significantly lower than students of traditionally trained teachers. Two recent studies of alternate route recruits to teaching found that their strongest recommendation was for a heavier dose of subject-specific teaching methods, including pedagogical guidance combined with more information about child and adolescent motivation, development, and cognition (Coley and Thorpe, 1985; Darling-Hammond, Hudson, and Kirby, 1989).

Perhaps it is not surprising that alternate route teachers from short-term programs often experience less job satisfaction than fully certified beginning teachers (Lutz and Hutton, 1989; Sciacca, 1987) or that they report less satisfaction with their preparation and less commitment to remaining in teaching than other recruits (Darling-Hammond, Hudson, and Kirby, 1989; see also, regarding attrition, Lutz and Hutton, 1989; Roth, 1986). Problems resulting from inadequate preparation headed the list of complaints of the 20 percent of Los Angeles alternate route candidates who quit before they completed their programs in 1984 and 1985, as well as many of those who remained but voiced dissatisfaction (Wright, McKibbon, and Walton, 1987).

Interestingly, a state evaluation of the Los Angeles program compared several different kinds of teaching recruits, including one group of alternate route entrants who decided to enroll in regular university teacher education programs rather than the short alternate route summer program, while still receiving state-funded mentor support. This group far outscored any of the other recruits on every criterion of classroom effectiveness, suggesting the cumulative power of adding adequate preservice preparation to intensive on-the-job supervision (Wright, McKibbon, and Walton, 1987).

The importance of guidance in learning to teach is confirmed by studies showing that induction support for entering teachers improves the quality of their teaching (Huling-Austin and Murphy, 1987). Beginning teachers who receive such support move more quickly from concerns about discipline and basic classroom management to concerns about instruction and student progress (Odell, 1986).

Virtually all studies of alternate routes to teacher education note the vital importance of high-quality, intensive supervision and related clinical learning opportunities to candidates' success and the problems that occur when such support is absent (Adelman, 1986; Darling-Hammond, Hudson, and Kirby, 1989; Wright, McKibbon, and Walton, 1987).

While studies of short-term alternative certification programs find they rarely provide the intensive supervision they promise (Darling-Hammond, 1992), reviews of the availability and quality of preparation and supervision offered by university-based alternate route programs have been more consistently positive (Coley and Thorpe, 1985; Darling-Hammond, Hudson, and Kirby, 1989; Smith, 1990; Sundstrom and Berry, 1989). Many studies have found that, over time, alternate certification programs have added coursework requirements as gaps in teachers' preparation have been identified, and states and districts have increasingly turned to universities to provide coursework and supervision (Carey, Mittman, and Darling-Hammond, 1988; Cornett, 1992; Hudson and others, 1988).

In light of these findings, policies and programs providing alternate routes to teacher certification may be evaluated in terms of the extent to which they incorporate opportunities to acquire the fundamental elements of teaching knowledge: disciplinary knowledge, knowledge about teaching and learning, and guided clinical practice. This kind of evaluation is critical to a determination of whether states and programs are acting responsibly on behalf of the students their candidates will eventually teach.

Rethinking Teacher Education Programs

All of the forces described in this chapter have influenced changes in teacher education courses, processes, and structures. Over the past decade, many schools of education have made great strides in incorporating new understandings of teaching and learning in their curriculum for prospective teachers. More attention to learning theory, cognition, and learning strategies has accompanied a deepening appreciation for content pedagogy and constructivist teaching strategies. In addition, teacher preparation and teacher induction programs are increasingly introducing strategies that help teachers develop a reflective and problem-solving orientation. This is done by engaging prospective teachers and interns in teacher research, in school-based inquiry, and in learning about students' experiences so that they are building an empirical understanding of learners and a capacity to analyze and reflect on their practice.

These efforts to develop teachers as managers of their own inquiry stands in contrast to earlier assumptions about teacher induction and about teaching generally—that beginning teachers needed to focus only on the most rudimentary tasks of teaching with basic precepts and cookbook rules to guide them and that teachers in general should be the recipients of knowledge rather than the generators of knowledge and understandings about students. The function of teacher preparation is increasingly seen as empowering teachers to own, use, and develop knowledge about teaching and learning as sophisticated and powerful as the demands of their work require.

In addition to preparation that is rigorous and relevant to today's educational needs, teacher education programs are increasingly seeking to offer prospective teachers opportunities to work with effective guidance in diverse settings and underserved areas. Traditionally, many teacher education students have had little or no experience working in low-income urban or rural schools where they are most likely to find jobs later as well as little prior experience working with students with greatly diverse learning needs. In 1991, while the great majority of newly qualified teachers (84 percent) felt adequately prepared to teach all of the subjects they were teaching, a much smaller number felt adequately prepared to teach the full range of diverse learners in their classrooms. Of those who taught limited-English-proficient students, only 57 percent felt adequately prepared to do so, and of those who taught students requiring special education, only 60 percent felt adequately prepared (Gray and others, 1993).

An important part of the current redesign of teacher preparation includes efforts to extend the concept of mentoring in more systematic ways within restructured school settings, especially in urban areas. A growing number of education schools are working with school systems to create institutions like professional development schools and internship sites that will allow new teachers to be inducted into schools as they must *become*, not only schools as they *are*. Too often there is a disjunction between the conceptions of good practice beginning teachers learn in their preparation programs and those they encounter when they begin teaching. Typically, beginning teachers are placed in the most difficult schools, those with the highest rates of teacher turnover, the greatest numbers of inexperienced staff, and the least capacity to support teacher growth and development. These are also often schools where the kinds of learner-centered practices that current reforms are seeking to develop are either not well developed or not well supported. Thus, it is difficult for beginning teachers to develop ways of really connecting what they know to what students know when there are so few supports in the school environment for learning to practice in this more challenging way.

The conditions for thoughtful, adaptive teaching must be well supported by expert, experienced staff in order to be emulated by and instilled in beginning teachers. Because the development of learner-centered practice is enormously difficult, untutored novices often fail at their early attempts. The application of knowledge about learning, teaching, curriculum-building, development, motivation, and behavior to the individual needs of diverse students is a daunting task requiring skillful observation, diagnosis, and integration of many different concepts and abilities. Unless this occurs with the support of an able mentor, the effort can quickly become overwhelming. This is one of the reasons that knowledge acquired in preservice courses is often not put to use—and that beginning teachers' practices often become less sensitive to students' needs rather than more so over the course of their initial year in teaching.

Beginning teachers must develop the ability to apply knowledge appropriately in different contexts while handling the dozens of cognitive, psychological, moral, and interpersonal demands that simultaneously require attention in a classroom. Learning to manage the different personalities and needs of twenty-five or thirty children while prioritizing and juggling often conflicting goals does not happen quickly, automatically, or easily. These are skills that have to be developed. Clinical experiences must enable teachers to learn firsthand about the variability in students' cognitive development and approaches to learning while they are supported with guided instruction and opportunities for reflection on their teaching and its effects on learners. These educative complements to classroom work should assist novices in acquiring wider repertoires of teaching strategies and help them relate problems of teaching practice to research on teaching and human development. Having these kinds of opportunities available should encourage beginners to teach reflectively, to evaluate what they are doing, to assess whether it is working and why, to understand how to make better decisions, and to juggle the many concerns of teaching.

A growing number of teacher educators have argued that professional development schools may be the best hope for addressing beginning teachers' needs. Like teaching hospitals in the medical profession, they may be structured to provide an environment in which new teachers are gradually introduced to the responsibilities of teaching and are given assistance from experienced colleagues as well as their university-based teachers. In such environments, beginning teachers receive ongoing evaluation and feedback from other teachers about their teaching as well as more formal learning opportunities that enable them to link theory and practice. During a formalized internship or induction year, beginning teachers have opportunities for professional development that encourage collaboration and provide the support that is associated with stronger beginning teacher commitment and efficacy.

In many reform models, such as those offered by the Holmes Group (1986, 1990), the Carnegie Forum on Education and the Economy (1986), the RAND Corporation (Wise and Darling-Hammond, 1987), and the National Board for Professional Teaching Standards, all prospective teachers would undertake their student teaching and a more intensive internship in professional development schools. The hope is that there they would encounter state-of-the-art practice and a range of diverse experiences under intensive supervision so that they learn to teach diverse learners effectively, rather than merely to cope, or even to leave the profession, as so many do. Ideally, professional development schools will also provide serious venues for developing the knowledge base for teaching by becoming places in which practice-based and practice-sensitive research can be carried out collaboratively by teachers, teacher educators, and researchers. By creating settings that merge theoretical and practical learning, PDSs may help transmit a common set of expectations that link preparation and practice.

Probably the most important recognition of these various teacher education reforms is that prospective teachers must be taught in the same ways in which they will be expected to teach. Like their students must do, teachers also construct their own understandings by doing: collaborating, inquiring into problems, trying and testing ideas, evaluating and reflecting on the outcomes of their work. As teacher educators, beginning teachers, and experienced teachers work together on real problems of practice in learner-centered settings, they develop a collective knowledge base, along with ownership and participation in a developing a common set of understandings about practice. This development promotes deep understanding that cannot be obtained in coursework alone, although the foundation may be laid in coursework that provides a broader, theoretical frame for developing and interpreting practice.

Professional Standard Setting

The emphasis on professionalism in teaching urged by the 1980s reform reports is one that follows the path of many other professions in the United States over the past hundred years, starting with medicine, and continuing through law, architecture, engineering, nursing, and many other occupations. Professions can be characterized by a specialized knowledge base, a commitment to client welfare, and the definition and transmission of professional standards (Darling-Hammond, 1990a). Occupations that have sought to become professions have increased their requirements for education, created standards of knowledge and ethical behavior that govern entry and practice, and created means for enforcing these standards.

By these tenets, teaching in the United States is only a quasi-profession. It is the only licensed occupation that allows individuals to enter the profession without preparation and without meeting common standards. In most states, standards (requirements for teacher education, licensing, and testing) are not developed or enforced by the profession. Except in the small number of states with professional standards boards for teaching, standards are set by legislatures, lay boards, and commercial testing companies. While professional teaching associations have worked to define a common knowledge base, state policies are not based on a universal commitment to ensuring that all practicing teachers have mastered that knowledge base. The issues of how better to define, transmit, and enforce professional teaching standards are among those a variety of governmental and professional agencies are currently tackling.

In recent years, several major reports calling for the professionalization of teaching have noted that teachers must take hold of professional standard setting if teaching is to make good on the promise of competence that professions make to the public (Carnegie Forum, 1986; Holmes Group, 1986). Teacher education leaders recognize that teachers and teacher educators "must take greater control over their own destiny. A powerful place where this can be done is in standards-setting. . . . Professionals must define high standards, set rigorous expectations, and then hold peers to these standards and expectations" (Imig, 1991, p. 14).

Accreditation, licensing, and advanced certification are the three major quality control mechanisms for any profession. In the field of teaching, these three mechanisms have historically been weak, in large part because of the lay governance structure described earlier. Meanwhile, "the generally minimal state-prescribed criteria remain subject to local and state political influences, economic conditions within the state, and historical conditions which make change difficult" (Dennison, 1992, p. A40).

As noted earlier, professional accreditation is not required in teaching, and licensing standards are frequently waived to ensure that classrooms are covered. Professional certification has until recently been nonexistent. Licensing is distinguished from certification in that licensing is a state function that seeks to ensure that practitioners allowed to practice in the state meet minimum standards of competence—in other words, that they are "safe" to practice. Certification is a professional function that generally indicates higher standards of accomplishment as determined by a national professional body, such as the National Board of Medical Examiners or the National Architectural Registration Board.

The historic lack of rigorous standard setting in teaching is changing, however (Wise and Leibbrand, 1993). In addition to the establishment of autonomous professional standards boards for teaching in twelve states, efforts are currently underway to develop and implement more meaningful standards for teaching. These efforts are being led by the new National Board for Professional Teaching Standards, established in 1987 as the first professional body in teaching to set standards for the advanced certification of highly accomplished teachers; the Interstate New Teacher Assessment and Support Consortium (INTASC), a consortium of twenty-eight states working together with teachers and teacher educators on "National Board–compatible" licensing standards and assessments that are performance-based; and NCATE, which has been strengthening standards for teacher education programs, recently heightening its expectations for the use of a defined knowledge base in the design of teacher education programs and incorporating the performance standards developed by INTASC. These initiatives are also stimulating efforts to develop more sophisticated and authentic assessments of teaching that will enable teachers to demonstrate skills and knowledge in real teaching contexts.

The National Board's voluntary national certification standards and accompanying assessments define what expert, experienced teachers need to know and be able to do and what highly accomplished teaching looks like. As districts and states begin to recognize certification as a meaningful indicator of expertise for salary and appointment purposes, as well as for designing evaluation programs, the standards are likely to have increasing practical effect and reach. The INTASC standards translate the National Board standards into analogous standards for what beginning teachers should be prepared to know and be able to do in order to develop over time into Board-certifiable highly accomplished teachers.

These initiatives have in common a view of teaching as complex, grounded in decisions that are contingent on students' needs and instructional goals, and reciprocal—that is, continually shaped and reshaped by students' responses to learning experiences. This view contrasts with that of the recent "technicist" era of teacher training and evaluation, in which teaching was seen as the implementation of set routines and formulas for behavior, which were standardized and disconnected from the diverse needs and responses of students. The new standards and assessments also take into explicit account the multicultural, multilingual nature of a student body that also harbors multiple intelligences and approaches to learning. In so doing, these efforts seek to encourage teacher education that will address teachers' needs for deeper and more varied understandings of learners and learning so that they can be more effective in their work.

Other important professional and policy efforts support these efforts to identify a common core of understandings that characterizes what all teachers need to know and be able to do to address the individual needs of all children. A number of professional associations have initiatives that focus on defining the common core of knowledge for teachers. The American Association of Colleges for Teacher Education has undertaken ongoing efforts to articulate the essential knowledge base for beginning teachers. The Association of Teacher Educators produces the *Handbook of Research on Teacher Education,* which translates much of the essential knowledge base for teachers into foundations for teacher education programs. The Holmes Group is working to define a common core of ideas and experiences for teacher education. All of these groups have recently articulated a view of teaching knowledge, skills, and dispositions that emphasizes the following:

- Teachers' moral and professional commitment to students and their learning, grounded in an understanding of learners, a commitment to equity, and a pledge to continually seek strategies that will produce success for each learner
- Teachers' understanding of subjects in ways that allow them to make core concepts and modes of inquiry accessible to diverse learners as they construct their own understandings
- Teachers' understanding of learners and learning in ways that allow them to identify different strengths, intelligences, and approaches to learning, as well as to facilitate development of the whole child
- Teachers' active involvement in assessing and supporting student learning by evaluating student thinking and performance and adapting teaching to students' prior knowledge, interests, motivations, and learning
- Teachers' capacities to reflect on their teaching and its consequences for learners, to revise their strategies as needed, and to collaborate with others in creating conditions that support school improvement as well as individual student success

It should be noted, however, that despite this rhetorical consensus among professional associations, there is much less commonality in actual practice. This is because government policy tools still often conflict with these conceptions of teaching, while substantial unevenness in program quality results from unequal funding and lack of commonly applied program standards. Transforming what entering teachers know and can do will require policy moves on several fronts that support the efforts of the profession to define and transmit new standards.

Reforms of Teacher Licensing and Assessment

During the 1980s, most states adopted changes in specific teacher licensing requirements that affected the content of teacher education in one way or another. The most notable changes by a number of states include increases in required hours of college credit in a subject area for secondary teachers, evaluation of classroom performance for beginning teachers in their first year of practice, and continuing education requirements for relicensure. While most states increased the amount of coursework teachers would need to undertake to learn about teaching, a few, such as New Jersey, Texas, and Virginia, actually limited the amount of professional education coursework undergraduates could take. As a consequence, prospective teachers in these states take few if any courses in child development or pedagogy before they are licensed.

Most states added requirements for teacher testing prior to licensure. Of the forty-seven states requiring such tests, twenty-six test for basic skills competency; seventeen test for general knowledge; twenty-seven test for professional knowledge; and twenty-three states test for subject area content knowledge (Coley and Goertz, 1990). In contrast to licensing tests in most other professions, which are developed and administered by members of the profession, tests for teachers have been developed by commercial vendors or state agencies. About half of these states use all or parts of tests put out by commercial vendors—for example, the National Teacher Examinations (NTE) developed and administered by the Educational Testing Service. The other half use tests developed and administered by the state itself.

Many critics have charged that first generation tests of teachers' general and professional knowledge tap very little of what might be called a knowledge base for teaching (Darling-Hammond, 1986; MacMillan and Pendlebury, 1985; Shulman, 1987). Haertel (1991) summarizes the many concerns expressed by researchers and members of the profession: "The teacher tests now in common use have been strenuously and justifiably criticized for their content, their format, and their impacts, as well as the virtual absence of criterion-related validity evidence supporting their use. . . . These tests have been criticized for treating pedagogy as generic rather than subject-matter specific, for showing poor criterion-related validity or failing to address criterion-related validity altogether, for failing to measure many critical teaching skills, and for their adverse impact on minority representation in the teaching profession" (pp. 3–4).

Consequently, efforts are underway in many states to develop new approaches to assessing teachers. In response to concerns that the previous generation of teacher tests, based largely on multiple choice responses to brief, simplified questions, failed to measure teaching knowledge and skill, test developers have also been redesigning their assessments. For example, the Educational Testing Service has recently replaced the NTE with a new testing series called Praxis, which aims for some more performance-based assessments of teaching knowledge. Although multiple-choice questions still predominate, more items in the paper and pencil component require essay responses by teachers, and a classroom observational instrument has been added. Similar changes are occurring in other teacher assessments.

The National Board for Professional Teaching Standards has gone many steps further in its new examinations for the advanced certification of highly accomplished veteran teachers. For NBPTS certification, the assessment is entirely performance-based, using an extensive portfolio assessment completed over several months of classroom work augmented by complex performance tasks completed in an assessment center. Teachers demonstrate their practices through videotapes and other evidence of their teaching, accompanied by discussions of their goals and intentions as well as samples of student work over time. They evaluate textbooks and teaching materials, analyze teaching events, assess student learning and needs, and defend teaching decisions based on their knowledge of curriculum, students, and pedagogy.

The states and professional associations involved in the INTASC consortium are creating licensing standards and assessments for beginning teachers that are compatible with those developed by NBPTS. These include portfolio assessments and other performance-based assessments of teaching, tied to the new standards. Together, the INTASC and NBPTS standards establish a continuum of what teachers need to know and be able to do from entry into teaching through the development of highly accomplished practice. More than a dozen states have already adapted or adopted these standards for their state licensure requirements, and many others are considering doing so.

An important attribute of all of the standards described above is that they are performance-based; that is, they describe what teachers should know, be like, and be able to do rather than listing courses that teachers should take in order to be awarded a license. This shift toward performance-based standard setting is in line with the approach being taken to standard setting for students as well as the approach taken to licensing in other professions. This approach, which is already underway in several states, should clarify the criteria for assessment and licensing, placing more emphasis on the abilities teachers develop than on the titles of classes they take. Ultimately, performance-based licensing standards should enable states to permit greater innovation and diversity in how teacher education programs operate by assessing their outcomes rather than merely regulating their inputs or procedures.

A performance-based licensing system would thus include several key components:

- The adoption of clear standards for performance that are thoroughly evaluated through *performance-based assessments for licensing.* These assessments must be good representations of the actual tasks, knowledge, and skills needed for teaching.

- The *replacement of course-counting strategies* for licensing and program approval with two kinds of standards: (1) licensing based on successful completion of performance-based assessments and completion of an approved/accredited program and (2) program review and accountability based on a demonstration that the school's program provides learning opportunities that lead to the successful attainment of the knowledge, skills, and dispositions needed to teach.

Implied in a performance-based licensing and accreditation system is the expectation that more rigorous and meaningful assessments for licensing will be created and used for all candidates (that is, no one will be licensed without having accomplished all of the necessary demonstrations of readiness to practice). Also implied in such a system is the expectation that rigorous program accountability will rely on evidence that programs both offer learning opportunities responsive to the standards and do so successfully enough that their graduates can meet the standards.

Balancing Standards and Supply

A legitimate question can be raised as to whether improving standards will exacerbate teacher shortages. Interestingly, the reverse has historically been true. Throughout the twentieth century, teacher shortages have been an impetus for upgrading salaries and standards within the profession. Shortages following World War I and World War II, and again in the 1960s, propelled substantial real increases in teacher salaries accompanied by increases in the educational requirements for teaching. As Sedlak and Schlossman (1986) note, "Contrary to what many modern-day educators tend to assume, teacher shortages have been commonplace throughout the twentieth century. Nonetheless, it has proved possible, time and again, to raise certification standards during periods of protracted shortage. Not only has the raising of standards not exacerbated teacher shortages, it may even—at least where accompanied by significant increases in teachers' salaries—have helped to alleviate them (and, at the same time, enhanced popular respect for teaching as a profession)" (p. 39).

Their research demonstrated that teacher shortages generally followed periods of real income decline for teachers and that in most instances the shortages produced both salary gains and heightened standards for teaching.

The dilemma, however, is that while teacher shortages create a political climate within which standards and salaries may be raised, they also create conditions that work against the continuation of these initiatives. The effect of having standards, however high, with large loopholes available to satisfy demand pressures, is that salaries will always remain somewhat depressed. In the past, although teacher salaries have always increased in times of short supply, they have never reached comparability with those of other professions requiring similar training, and they have tended to slip again when the supply crisis was "solved." If no substantial improvement occurs in the attractions to teaching, it will be difficult to improve overall teacher quality, since the pool of potential candidates who can meet the standards will not be sufficiently enlarged. In circular fashion, the failure to attract sufficient numbers of well-qualified teachers will lessen teachers' claims for professional responsibility and autonomy and will increase the press for regulation of teaching, thus further decreasing the attractions to teaching for professionally oriented candidates.

Because education is a public service not only offered to all children by state governments but required of them by law, classrooms cannot be left unstaffed when shortages of qualified teachers occur. However, for the same reasons, the state has the obligation of not only staffing classrooms, but doing so in a manner that does no harm to students. This argues against allowing exceptions to meaningful licensing standards. The problem is that states' current standards for licensure are not accepted as meaningful—that is, related to desired knowledge and skill—by the profession, the public, or even state policy makers themselves (who, as we have seen, are quick to sidestep the very standards they themselves have created). Screens to the profession must be legitimized if they are to be respected and observed; solutions to shortages must be found that protect clients as well as the profession itself.

In considering the supply and standards dilemma, it is important to remember three things. First, there is not an absolute shortage of teachers but a shortage in particular fields and locations. In fact, twice as many teachers are prepared as actually enter teaching each year. The most pressing need is to equalize resources and create incentives that will fill vacancies in places that are not now sufficiently attractive to these nonentrants. Second, with nearly half of all beginning teachers leaving within a few years of entry, strategies that keep teachers in the profession will greatly reduce the demand for new teachers over time.

Finally, the most important concern regarding standards is that they represent meaningful kinds of knowledge and skills for candidates to acquire and for schools of education to address. The goal in standard setting is not to increase the failure rates of candidates seeking to enter but to provide clarity, incentives, and supports to ensure more adequately prepared candidates when they do enter. The goal of more educationally meaningful standard setting is critical to providing teachers with the knowledge and skills they will need to succeed in today's classrooms and to continue as committed members of the profession.

Ultimately, improving the means by which teachers are prepared, inducted, and selected into teaching can provide the impetus for deeper structural changes in the recruitment and responsibilities of teachers. As has occurred in other professions, as teachers receive more rigorous and relevant preparation, their voice, effectiveness, and responsibilities within schools should increase, and the public (including potential recruits) should increasingly recognize teaching as a challenging, vital career requiring expertise and talent.

As schools of education take a leadership role in standard setting for the profession, they can ultimately contribute to both the attractions of teaching as a profession and the capability of their own students to make a positive difference in the lives of children. These challenges and possibilities frame the current context of teacher education and create new opportunities for teacher education to strengthen its role as the foundation for a learner-centered profession of teaching.

Notes

1. The term *certification* is generally used by states to describe their system for ensuring minimal qualifications of candidates allowed to practice. However, *licensing* is the more accurate term, analogous to this function performed by states for other occupations. Licensure indicates that a candidate has governmentally sanctioned legal authority to practice. Certification is the recognition by the profession of a higher level of competence and attainment. Professional certification is just beginning to become available to United States teachers, through the auspices of a National Board for Professional Teaching Standards.

2. The proportions of alternate route candidates rated "poor" ranged from 8 percent on reading instruction to 17 percent on classroom management.

References

Adams, R. D., Hutchinson, S., and Martray, C. (1980). "A developmental study of teachers' concerns across time." Paper presented at the annual meeting of the American Educational Research Association, Boston.

Adelman, N. E. (1986). *An exploratory study of teacher alternative certification and retraining programs.* Washington, D.C.: Policy Study Associates.

Akin, J. N. (1989). *Teacher supply and demand in the United States: 1989 report.* (ASCUS Research Report). Addison, Ill: Association for School, College, and University Staffing.

American Association of Colleges for Teacher Education (1987). *Teaching teachers: Facts and figures (RATE I).* Washington, D.C.: American Association of Colleges for Teacher Education.

American Association of Colleges for Teacher Education (1988). *Teaching teachers: Facts and figures (RATE II).* Washington, D.C.: American Association of Colleges for Teacher Education.

American Association of Colleges for Teacher Education (1992). *Academic achievement of white, black, and Hispanic students in teacher education programs.* Washington, D.C.: American Association of Colleges for Teacher Education.

American Council on Education (1989). *Eighth annual status report on minorities in higher education.* Washington, D.C.: American Council on Education.

Apple, M. W. (1987). "The de-skilling of teaching." In F. S. Bolin and J. M. Falk (eds.), *Teacher renewal.* New York: Teachers College Press.

Ashton, P., and Crocker, L. (1986). "Does teacher certification make a difference?" *Florida Journal of Teacher Education, 3,* 73–83.

Ashton, P., and Crocker, L. (1987). "Systemic study of planned variations: The essential focus of teacher education reform." *Journal of Teacher Education, 38*(3), 2–8.

Association for School, College, and University Staffing (1984). *Teacher supply/demand.* Madison, Wis.: Association for School, College, and University Staffing.

Astin, A. W. (1993). *What matters in college? Four critical years revisited.* San Francisco: Jossey-Bass.

Begle, E. G. (1979). *Critical variables in mathematics education.* Washington, D.C.: Mathematical Association of American and National Council of Teachers of Mathematics.

Bents, M., and Bents, R. (1990). "Perceptions of good teaching among novice, advanced beginner and expert teachers." Paper presented at the annual meeting of the American Educational Research Association, Boston.

Blank, R. K., and Gruebel, D. (1993). *State indicators of science and mathematics education, 1993.* Washington, D.C.: Council of Chief State School Officers.

Bledsoe, J. C., Cox, J. V., and Burnham, R. (1967). *Comparison between selected characteristics and performance of provisionally and professionally certified beginning teachers in Georgia.* Washington, D.C.: U.S. Department of Health, Education, and Welfare.

Brookhart, S. M., and Loadman, W. E. (1993). "Critical minority: Males entering elementary teacher education programs." Paper presented at the annual meeting of the American Educational Research Association, Atlanta.

Carnegie Forum on Education and the Economy (1986). *A nation prepared: Teachers for the 21st century.* New York: Carnegie Foundation.

Carey, N., Mittman, B., and Darling-Hammond, L. (1988). *Recruiting mathematics and science teachers through nontraditional programs.* Santa Monica, Calif.: RAND.

Choy, S. P., and others (1993a). *America's teachers: Profile of a profession.* Washington, D.C.: National Center for Education Statistics, U.S. Department of Education.

Choy, S. P., and others (1993b). *Schools and staffing in the United States: A statistical profile, 1990–91.* Washington, D.C.: National Center for Education Statistics, U.S. Department of Education.

Cobb, V. L. (1993). "Accreditation in teacher education." *Dissertation Abstracts International, 54*(12A). (University Microfilms no. 9414422).

Coley, R. J., and Goertz, M. E. (1990). *Educational standards in the 50 states, 1990.* Princeton, N.J.: Educational Testing Service.

Coley, R. J., and Thorpe, M. E. (1985). *Responding to the crisis in math and science teaching: Four initiatives.* Princeton, N.J.: Educational Testing Service.

Copley, P. O. (1974). *A study of the effect of professional education courses on beginning teachers.* Springfield: Southwest Missouri State University Press. (ED 098 147)

Cornett, L. M. (1992). "Alternative certification: State policies in the SREB states." *Peabody Journal of Education, 67*(3): 55–83.

Darling-Hammond, L. (1984). *Beyond the commission reports: The coming crisis in teaching.* Santa Monica, Calif.: RAND. (R-3177-RC).

Darling-Hammond, L. (1986). "A proposal for evaluation in the teaching profession." *Elementary School Journal, 86*(4), 1–21.

Darling-Hammond, L. (1988). "Teacher quality and educational equality." *College Board Review, 148,* Summer, 16–23, 39–41.

Darling-Hammond, L. (1989). "Teacher supply, demand and standards." *Education Policy, 3*(1), 1–17.

Darling-Hammond, L. (1990a). "Teacher professionalism: Why and how." In A. Lieberman (ed.), *Schools as collaborative cultures; Creating the future now.* Washington, D.C.: Falmer Press.

Darling-Hammond, L. (1990b). "Teacher supply, demand and quality: A mandate for the National Board." Paper prepared for the National Board of Professional Teaching Standards.

Darling-Hammond, L. (1990c). "Teachers and teaching: Signs of a changing profession." In W. R. Houston (ed.), *Handbook of research on teacher education.* New York: Macmillan.

Darling-Hammond, L. (1992). "Teaching and knowledge: Policy issues posed by alternate certification for teachers." *Peabody Journal of Education, 67*(3), 123–154.

Darling-Hammond, L. (1994a). "Developing professional development schools: Early lessons, challenge, and promise." In L. Darling-Hammond (ed.), *Professional development schools: Schools for developing a profession.* New York: Teachers College Press.

Darling-Hammond, L. (1994b). "Who will speak for the children? How Teach for America hurts urban schools and students." *Phi Delta Kappan, 76*(1), 21–34.

Darling-Hammond, L., and Berry, B. (1988). *The evolution of teacher policy.* Santa Monica, Calif.: RAND.

Darling-Hammond, L., and Goodwin, A. L. (1993). "Progress toward professionalism in teaching." In G. Cawelti (ed.), *Challenges and achievements of American education.* Alexandria, Va.: Association for Supervision and Curriculum Development.

Darling-Hammond, L., Hudson, L., and Kirby, S. N. (1989). *Redesigning teacher education: Opening the door for new recruits to science and mathematics teaching.* Santa Monica, Calif.: RAND.

Darling-Hammond, L., with Sclan, E. (1992). "Policy and supervision." In C. D. Glickman (ed.), *Supervision in transition.* Alexandria, Va.: Association for Supervision and Curriculum Development.

Davis, C. R. (1964). "Selected teaching-learning factors contributing to achievement in chemistry and physics." University of North Carolina (unpublished doctoral dissertation).

Dennison, G. (1992). "National standards in teacher preparation: A commitment to quality." *Chronicle of Higher Education,* A40.

Dilworth, M. E. (1990). *Reading between the lines: Teachers and their racial/ethnic cultures.* Washington, D.C.: ERIC Clearinghouse on Teacher Education and American Association of Colleges for Teacher Education.

Druva, C. A., and Anderson, R. D. (1983). "Science teacher characteristics by teacher behavior and by student outcome: A meta-analysis of research." *Journal of Research in Science Teaching, 20*(5), 467–479.

Ebmeier, H., Twombly, S., and Teeter, D. (1991). "The comparability and adequacy of financial support for schools of education." *Journal of Teacher Education, 42*(3), 226–235.

Evertson, C. M., Hawley, W. D., and Zlotnik, M. (1985). "Making a difference in educational quality through teacher education." *Journal of Teacher Education, 36*(3), 2–12.

Feiman-Nemser, S. (1990). "Teacher preparation: Structural and conceptual alternatives." In W. R. Houston (ed.), *Handbook of research on teacher education.* New York: Macmillan.

Feiman-Nemser, S., and Parker, M. B. (1990). *Making subject matter part of the conversation or helping beginning teachers learn to teach.* East Lansing, Mich.: National Center for Research on Teacher Education.

Feistritzer, C. E. (1990). *Alternative teacher certification: A state-by-state analysis.* Washington, D.C.: National Center for Education Information.

Gerald, D. E., and Hussar, W. J. (1991). *Projections of education statistics to 2002.* Washington, D.C.: National Center for Education Statistics, U.S. Department of Education.

Glassberg, S. (1980). "A view of the beginning teacher from a developmental perspective." Paper presented at the annual meeting of the American Educational Research Association, Boston.

Gomez, D. L., and Grobe, R. P. (1990). "Three years of alternative certification in Dallas: Where are we?" Paper presented at the annual meeting of the American Educational Research Association, Boston.

Goodlad, J. I. (1990). *Teachers for our nation's schools.* San Francisco: Jossey-Bass.

Gray, L., and others (1993). *New teachers in the job market: 1991 update.* Washington, D.C.: Office of Educational Research and Improvement, U.S. Department of Education.

Greenberg, J. D. (1983). "The case for teacher education: Open and shut." *Journal of Teacher Education, 34*(4), 2–5.

Grissmer, D., and Kirby, S. N. (1987). *Understanding teacher attrition: The uphill climb to staff the nation's schools.* Santa Monica, Calif.: RAND.

Grossman, P. L. (1988). "A study in contrast: Sources of pedagogical content knowledge for secondary English." Stanford University (unpublished doctoral dissertation).

Grossman, P. L. (1989). "Learning to teach without teacher education." *Teachers College Record, 91*(2), 191–208.

Haberman, M. (1984). "An evaluation of the rationale for required teacher education: Beginning teachers with or without teacher preparation." Paper prepared for the National Commission on Excellence in Teacher Education, University of Wisconsin.

Haertel, E. H. (1991). "Should the National Assessment of Educational Progress be used to compare the states?" *Educational Researcher, 20*(3), 17.

Haggstrom, G., Darling-Hammond, L., and Grissmer, D. (1988). *Assessing teacher supply and demand.* Santa Monica, Calif.: RAND.

Hansen, J. B. (1988). "The relationship of skills and classroom climate of trained and untrained teachers of gifted students." Purdue University (unpublished doctoral dissertation).

Hice, J.E.L. (1970). "The relationship between teacher characteristics and first-grade achievement." *Dissertation Abstracts International, 25*(1), 190.

Holmes Group (1986). *Tomorrow's teachers: A report of the Holmes Group.* East Lansing, Mich.: Holmes Group.

Holmes Group (1990). *Tomorrow's schools: A report of the Holmes Group.* East Lansing, Mich.: Holmes Group.

Holmstrom, E. I. (1985). *Recent changes in teacher education programs.* Washington, D.C.: American Council on Education.

Howey, K. R., and Zimpher, N. L. (1993). "Patterns in prospective teachers: Guides for designing preservice programs." Ohio State University (unpublished manuscript).

Hudson, L., and others (1988). *Recruiting mathematics and science teachers through nontraditional programs: Case studies.* Santa Monica, Calif.: RAND.

Huling-Austin, L., and Murphy, S. C. (1987). "Assessing the impact of teacher induction programs: Implications for program development." Paper presented at the annual meeting of the American Educational Research Association, Washington, D.C.

Imig, D. G. (1991). *The professionalization of teaching: Relying on a professional knowledge base.* St. Louis, Mo.: American Association of Colleges for Teacher Education.

Kerchner, C. T., and Koppich, J. E. (1993). *A union of professionals: Labor relations and educational reform.* New York: Teachers College Press.

Lanier, J. E., and Little, J. W. (1986). *Research on teacher education.* (Occasional Paper no. 8). Washington, D.C.: National Institute on Education.

Lenk, H. A. (1989). "A case study: The induction of two alternative route social studies teachers." Teachers College (unpublished doctoral dissertation).

LH Research (1993). *A survey of the perspective of elementary and secondary school teachers on reform.* Prepared for the Ford Foundation. New York: LH Research.

Little, J. W. (1987). "Teachers as colleagues." In V. Richardson-Koehler (ed.), *Educator's handbook: A research perspective.* White Plains, N.Y.: Longman.

Lortie, D. C. (1975). *Schoolteacher: A sociological study.* Chicago: University of Chicago Press.

LuPone, L. J. (1961). "A comparison of provisionally certified and permanently certified elementary school teachers in selected school districts in New York State." *Journal of Educational Research, 55,* 53–63.

Lutz, F. W., and Hutton, J. B. (1989). "Alternative teacher certification: Its policy implications for classroom and personnel practice." *Educational Evaluation and Policy Analysis, 11*(3), 237–254.

MacMillan, J. B., and Pendlebury, S. (1985). "The Florida performance measurement system: A consideration." *Teachers College Record, 87,* 69–78.

McLaughlin, M. W., and Talbert, J. E. (1993). *Contexts that matter for teaching and learning.* Stanford, Calif.: Stanford University Press.

McNeil, J. D. (1974). "Who gets better results with young children—experienced teachers or novices? " *Elementary School Journal, 74,* 447–451.

Maryland State Department of Education (1990). *Maryland's alternative programs for teacher preparation.* Baltimore: Maryland State Department of Education.

Metropolitan Life (1991). *The first year: New teachers' expectations and ideals.* New York: Metropolitan Life Insurance Co.

Miller, L., and Silvernail, D. L. (1994). "Wells Junior High School: Evolution of a professional development school." In L. Darling-Hammond (ed.), *Professional development schools: Schools for developing a profession.* New York: Teachers College Press.

Mitchell, N. (1987). *Interim evaluation report of the alternative certification program.* Dallas, Texas: DISD Department of Planning, Evaluation, and Testing. (REA 87–027–2).

Murnane, R. J., and Olsen, R. J. (1988). "Factors affecting length of stay in teaching." Paper presented at the annual meeting of the American Education Research Association, New Orleans.

Murnane, R. J., Singer, J. D., and Willett, J. B. (1989). "The influences of salaries and 'opportunities costs' on teachers' career choices: Evidence from North Carolina." *Harvard Educational Review, 59*(3), 325–346.

Murnane, R. J., and others (1991). *Who will teach? Politics that matter.* Cambridge, Mass.: Harvard University Press.

National Center for Education Statistics (1983). *Condition of education, 1983.* Washington, D.C.: U.S. Department of Education.

National Center for Education Statistics (1985). *Recent college graduate survey.* Washington, D.C.: U.S. Department of Education.

National Center for Education Statistics (1991). *The condition of education, 1991,* Vol. 1: *Elementary and secondary education.* Washington, D.C.: U.S. Department of Education.

National Center for Education Statistics (1993). *The condition of education, 1993.* Washington, D.C.: U.S. Department of Education.

National Commission on Excellence in Education (1983). *A nation at risk.* Washington, D.C.: National Commission on Excellence in Education.

National Council for Accreditation of Teacher Education (1993). *State/NCATE Partnership Program packet: A state-by-state analysis.* Washington, D.C.: National Council for Accreditation of Teacher Education.

National Education Association (1981). *Status of the American public school teacher, 1980–1981.* Washington, D.C.: National Education Association.

National Education Association (1987). *Status of the American public school teacher, 1985–1986.* Washington, D.C.: National Education Association.

National Education Association (1992). *Status of the American public school teacher, 1990–1991.* Washington, D.C.: National Education Association.

National Governors' Association (1986). *Time for results: The governors' 1991 report on education.* Washington, D.C.: National Governors' Association.

Oakes, J. (1990). *Multiplying inequalities: The unequal distribution of mathematics and science opportunities.* Santa Monica, Calif.: RAND.

Odell, S. (1986). "Induction support of new teachers: A functional approach." *Journal of Teacher Education, 37,* 26–30.

Olsen, D. G. (1985). "The quality of prospective teachers: Education vs. noneducation graduates." *Journal of Teacher Education, 36*(5), 56–59.

Perkes, V. A. (1968). "Junior high school science teacher preparation, teaching behavior, and student achievement." *Journal of Research in Science and Teaching, 6*(4), 121–126.

Peterson, P. L., and Comeaux, M. A. (1989). "Evaluating the systems: Teachers' perspectives on teacher evaluation." Paper presented at the annual meeting of the American Educational Research Association, San Francisco.

Rosenholtz, S. J. (1985). "Effective schools: Interpreting the evidence." *American Journal of Education, 93,* 352–388.

Rosenholtz, S. J. (1989). *Teacher's workplace: The social organization of schools.* White Plains, N.Y.: Longman.

Roth, R. A. (1986). "Alternate and alternative certification: Purposes, assumptions, implications." *Action in Teacher Education, 8*(2), 1–6.

Rottenberg, C. J., and Berliner, D. C. (1990). "Expert and novice teachers' conceptions of common classroom activities." Paper presented at the annual meeting of the American Educational Research Association, Boston.

Roupp, R., Travers, J., Glantz, F., and Coelen, C. (1979). *Children at the center: Summary findings and their implications.* Cambridge, Mass.: ABT Associates.

Schwartz, H. (1988). "Unapplied curriculum knowledge." In L. N. Tanner (ed.), *Critical issues in curriculum.* (87th yearbook of the National Society for the Study of Education). Chicago: University of Chicago Press.

Sciacca, J. R. (1987). "A comparison of levels of job satisfaction between university-certified first-year teachers and alternatively certified first-year teachers." East Texas State University (unpublished doctoral dissertation).

Sclan, E. (1993). "The effect of perceived workplace conditions on beginning teachers' work commitment, career choice commitment, and planned retention." *Dissertation Abstracts International, 54*(08A). (University Microfilms no. 9400594).

Sedlak, M. W., and Schlossman, S. (1986). *Who will teach? Historical perspectives on the changing appeal of teaching as a profession.* Santa Monica, Calif.: RAND.

Shulman, L. S. (1983). "Autonomy and obligation: The remote control of teaching." In L. S. Shulman and G. Sykes (eds.), *Handbook of teaching and policy.* White Plains, N.Y.: Longman.

Shulman, L. S. (1987). "Knowledge and teaching: Foundations of the new reform." *Harvard Educational Review, 57,* 1–22.

Smith, J. M. (1990). "A comparative study of the state regulations for and the operation of the New Jersey provisional teacher certification program." Paper presented at the annual meeting of the American Educational Research Association, Boston.

Smylie, M. A. (1994). "Redesigning teacher's work: Connections to the classroom." In L. Darling-Hammond (ed.), *Review of research in education,* Vol. 20. Washington, D.C.: American Educational Research Association.

Snyder, T. D., and Hoffman, C. M. (1993). *Digest of education statistics, 1993.* Washington, D.C.: National Center for Education Statistics, U.S. Department of Education.

Southern Regional Education Board (1985). *Access to quality undergraduate education.* Atlanta: Southern Regional Education Board.

Sundstrom, K., and Berry, B. (1989). "Assessing the initial impact of the South Carolina critical needs certification program." Report to the State Board of Education.

Sykes, G. (1985). "Teacher education in the United States." In B. R. Clark (ed.), *The school and the university.* Los Angeles: University of California Press.

Sykes, G. (1989). "Examining the contradictions of licensure." *Education Week, 8*(27), 32.

Taylor, J. K., and Dale, R. (1971). *A survey of teachers in the first year of service.* Bristol, England: Institute of Education, University of Bristol.

Taylor, T. W. (1957). "A study to determine the relationships between growth in interest and achievement of high school students and science teacher attitudes, preparation, and experience." North Texas State College (unpublished doctoral dissertation).

Vance, V. S., and Schlechty, P. C. (1982). "The distribution of academic ability in the teaching force: Policy implications." *Phi Delta Kappan, 64*(1), 22–27.

Wise, A. E. (1979). *Legislated learning.* Berkeley: University of California Press.

Wise, A. E., and Darling-Hammond, L. (1987). *Licensing teachers: Design for a profession.* Santa Monica, Calif.: RAND.

Wise, A. E., Darling-Hammond, L., and Berry, B. (1987). *Effective teacher selection: From recruitment to retention.* Santa Monica, Calif.: RAND. (R-3462-NIE/CSTP).

Wise, A. E., and Leibbrand, A. (1993). "Accreditation and the creation of a profession of teaching." *Phi Delta Kappan, 75*(2), 133–173.

Wong, M. J., and Osgathorpe, R. T. (1993). "The continuing domination of the four-year teacher education program: A national survey." *Journal of Teacher Education, 44*(1), 64–70.

Wright, D. P., McKibbon, M., and Walton, P. (1987). *The effectiveness of the teacher trainee program: An alternate route into teaching in California.* Sacramento: California Commission on Teaching Credentialing.

Zeichner, K. M. (1986). "Social and ethical dimensions of reform in teacher education." In J. V. Hoffman and S. A. Edwards (eds.), *Reality and reform in clinical teacher education.* New York: Random House.

Annotated Bibliography

Darling-Hammond, L. (1990). "Teachers and teaching: Signs of a changing profession." In W. R. Houston (ed.), *Handbook of research on teacher education.* New York: Macmillan. Against the backdrop of efforts to reform the teaching profession, this chapter explores the current and potential status of teaching and teachers in light of political, social, and economic trends. Darling-Hammond outlines occupational features of teaching including low financial compensation, a flat career structure with few opportunities for advancement, and relatively poor working conditions when compared with other professional lines of work. Defining professionalism as the extent to which members of an occupation share a common body of knowledge and use shared standards of practice in exercising that knowledge on behalf of clients, the author then traces the historical recurrences of attempts to professionalize teaching throughout the past 150 years. After concluding that "in each of its iterations, progressivism gave way to standardizing influences," Darling-Hammond argues that if teaching is to become a true profession, bureaucratic accountability systems will need to be replaced with rigorous, professionally determined standards for education, internship, and licensure of teachers. Such a system would guarantee that all members of the profession are competent to exercise good judgment, in exchange for professional control over the structure and content of their work, monitored through peer review of practice.

Darling-Hammond paints a thorough, statistically based portrait of the teaching force and analyzes supply and demand trends in light of current educational policy structures. She concludes by discussing critical issues related to teacher shortages, teacher preparation, and induction of new teachers, arguing that investment in better recruitment and preparation of teachers would allay some of the present hindrances to the professionalization of teaching.

Darling-Hammond, L., Wise, A. E., and Klein, S. (1995). *A license to teach: Building a profession for 21st century schools.* Boulder, Colo.: Westview Press. There is a growing realization that the intense national quest to improve education for students requires attention to the knowledge and skills of teachers as well as attention to the capacities of teachers to teach a more demanding curriculum to the increasingly diverse groups of learners who are present—and who must become successful— in American schools. In this volume, Darling-Hammond, Wise, and Klein reconceptualize and propose a more effective and meaningful licensing system for teachers; their concept is based on their work with the Minnesota Board of Teaching and modeled after the licensing systems of other professions.

In a chapter that further fleshes out Shulman's sketch (1987) of the knowledge base for teaching, the authors meticulously lay out what teachers need to know and be able to do, then call for, and describe in detail, a teacher licensing plan that would provide for prospective teachers to complete a carefully designed and supervised internship program. The internship program would operate under state guidelines in local school districts and would occur after teacher candidates had completed liberal arts and professional education courses and undergone assessments of their basic skills and professional teaching knowledge. Successful completion of the internship would then be a prerequisite for taking a final state examination of teaching skills based on performance assessments of contextualized, complex teaching tasks.

Feiman-Nemser, S. (1990). "Teacher preparation: Structural and conceptual alternatives." In W. R. Houston (ed.), *Handbook of research on teacher education*. New York: Macmillan.

This chapter focuses on different ways of conceiving and carrying out teacher preparation. After examining standard notions of teacher preparation and offering frameworks for looking at distinctive approaches and alternatives, Feiman-Nemser discusses the state of the art concerning programs of initial teacher preparation and indicates where conceptual, empirical, and practical work are needed.

Feiman-Nemser begins with a brief overview of historic traditions that have influenced ways of thinking about teacher education and learning to teach: the normal-school tradition, the liberal arts tradition, and the university-based professional graduate school tradition. She then discusses what is known about different institutional arrangements and program structures, including undergraduate programs, extended (five-year) programs, graduate-level programs, and alternative certification programs.

Feiman-Nemser goes on to examine various conceptual orientations that have shaped the professional sequence, which she identifies as academic, practical, technological, personal, and critical/social orientation. A conceptual orientation refers to ideas about the goals of teacher preparation and the means for achieving them, and, unlike the structural alternatives discussed earlier, conceptual orientations are not tied to particular forms of teacher preparation. The chapter closes with an introduction to promising research-in-progress designed to illuminate different ideas about, and approaches to, preparing teachers.

Gideonse, H. D. (1993). "The governance of teacher education and systemic reform." *Educational Policy, 7*(4), 395–426.

Gideonse argues that systemic reform for teacher education will come only through actions taken to enhance the professionalism of teaching as it is performed, and that it is performed in highly idiosyncratic sites with changing particularities, by use of means and toward ends that are themselves warmly contested. In this article, he examines the governance of teacher education in pursuit of systemic reform in light of (1) what is known about instances of change in schooling, (2) state-of-the-art understandings about the nature of human learning and the roles of teachers in facilitating learning, (3) alternative modes of governing teacher education, and (4) serious impediments to systemic reform in the teacher education arena.

Gideonse takes the position that systemic reform of teacher education must be driven by a national system of accreditation for teacher education. He makes two recommendations in this article: (1) a comprehensive professional development effort for all teacher educators on standards development activities and (2) the outright rejection of inadequate routes to licensure and/or employment in teaching.

Murnane, R. J., and others (1991). *Who will teach? Policies that matter.* Cambridge, Mass.: Harvard University Press.

In light of the fact that in the 1990s, America's public schools will hire more than two million new teachers due to the demographics of an aging, retiring teaching force and the "baby boomlet" entering schools, the authors of this volume explore the issues related to the current increased demand for new teachers.

The questions addressed include whether dollars make a difference in relation to teacher salary scales affecting career decisions. The authors examine how fiscal resources affect school district hiring practices, showing that adequate funding levels can facilitate creative solutions to the challenges districts face in hiring skilled teachers. They also conclude that salaries make a difference in how long teachers stay in the classroom.

The problem of recruiting and retaining skilled math and science teachers is discussed, as is the academic quality of teaching recruits. Differences in career paths of teachers according to grade levels and subject specialties are mapped out.

The authors also investigate the declining percentage of minority, and specifically African-American, teachers and the growing disparity between the ethnic composition of public school student bodies and that of the teaching force. Included in this discussion are the issues of licensing requirements and working conditions.

The authors conclude that the career decisions of prospective teachers, current teachers, and former teachers are influenced by the opportunities they face in teaching and in other fields. They use their evidence to compare the effectiveness of alternative strategies for staffing our schools with racially diverse faculties of skilled teachers and to argue for the strategies they find most promising, which include the reform of licensing laws, a carefully structured set of salary increases, and improvements in working conditions.

Sedlak, M. W., and Schlossman, S. (1986). *Who will teach? Historical perspectives on the changing appeal of teaching as a profession.* Santa Monica, Calif.: RAND.

This report examines, from a historical perspective, the desirability of teaching as a career. Focusing particularly on the profession's economic reward structure and social composition, the study attempts to provide a chronological, conceptual, and empirical framework to guide future case-study research. Sedlak and Schlossman report several findings emerging from this study that are relevant to the current reform movement in public education:

1. Reform movements in education (as in many other fields) are notorious for their tendencies toward presentism—for painting the past in the darkest possible light in order to stress the urgent need for rapid and major transformation of the status quo.

2. Contrary to what many modern-day educators tend to assume, teacher shortages have been commonplace throughout the twentieth century.

3. No single subject is more central to the history of the teaching profession than the changing role of women in American society; in unsettling the traditional assumptions linking women to teaching, the women's movement appears to have opened up new prospects for the professionalization of teaching that might never otherwise have developed.

Shulman, L. S. (1987). "Knowledge and teaching: Foundations of the new reform." *Harvard Educational Review, 57*(1), 1–22.

This article follows closely on the spate of national commission reports issued in 1986, which called for the professionalization of teaching. In it, Shulman presents an argument, informed by philosophy, psychology, and studies of novice and experienced teachers, regarding the content, character, and sources for a knowledge base of teaching on which the professionalization of teaching can be built. The questions that focus his argument are these: What are the sources of the knowledge base for teaching? In what terms can these sources be conceptualized? What are the implications for teaching policy and educational reform?

After elucidating general categories of the knowledge base for teaching—content knowledge, general pedagogical knowledge, curriculum knowledge, pedagogical content knowledge, knowledge of learners, knowledge of educational contexts, and knowledge of educational ends—Shulman cites four major sources for the teaching knowledge base: (1) scholarship in content disciplines; (2) the materials and settings of the institutionalized educational process; (3) research on schooling, social organization, human learning, teaching, and development; and (4) the wisdom of practice itself. Calling on educational practitioners, scholars, and policy makers to rethink how teachers are prepared and evaluated, Shulman discusses a conception of teaching, based on both philosophical and empirical foundations, which views teaching as comprehension and reasoning, as transformation and reflection.

CHAPTER THREE

PERSPECTIVES ON LEARNING TO TEACH

SHARON FEIMAN-NEMSER AND JANINE REMILLARD

This chapter provides teacher educators with perspectives on learning to teach that have implications for the structure, content, and pedagogy of teacher education. For some time, teacher educators have looked to research on teaching for guidance in designing programs for teachers. But knowing what good teachers do, how they think, or what they know is not the same as knowing how teachers learn to think and act in particular ways and what contributes to their learning. Researchers, policy makers, and teacher educators are beginning to recognize that understanding more about teachers as learners, what they need to know and how they learn their craft, can help in clarifying the role of formal teacher education in learning to teach.

The phrase *learning to teach* rolls easily off the tongue, giving the impression that this is a straightforward, easily understood process. In fact, we do not have well-developed theories of learning to teach and the phrase itself covers many conceptual complexities. What does learning teaching entail? How is teacher learning similar to and different from other learning? What sort of teaching is being learned? What sort of teaching do we hope teachers will learn? As these questions imply, learning to teach raises both descriptive and normative issues that must be addressed in any serious effort to build a model of learning to teach.

The work for this chapter was sponsored in part by the National Center for Research on Teacher Learning, College of Education, Michigan State University. The National Center for Research on Teacher Learning is funded primarily by the Office of Educational Research and Improvement, U.S. Department of Education. The views expressed in this chapter do not necessarily represent those of the Office or the Department.

Of course, commonsense theories abound. "Anyone can teach." "If you know your subject, you can teach it." "Teachers are born not made." "Everything you need to know about teaching can be learned on the job." Widely held in our society, these assertions find little support in the field or the research literature, nor do they accord a significant role to teacher education.

Despite the absence of dependable theories, teacher education programs and policies reflect different ideas about learning to teach. For instance, the traditional structure of preservice programs—foundations courses followed by methods courses followed by student teaching—implies that learning to teach is a matter of first acquiring formal knowledge and then applying it in the field. Policies that limit professional education requirements for undergraduates and increase academic requirements endorse the view that academic study offers the most important preparation for teaching. And policies that mandate the assessment of beginning teachers without providing them with assistance rest on an implicit assumption that learning to teach is not a lengthy or serious undertaking since it can be completed in a short time. Like the commonsense theories mentioned above, these ideas also lack compelling empirical support.

A major purpose in writing this chapter is to persuade teacher educators that attending to issues subsumed by the phrase *learning to teach* can enhance the design and conduct of university- and school-based teacher education. In order to unpack the phrase *learning to teach,* we have to ask questions about *who* is doing the learning, *what* they are learning, *how* the learning proceeds, and *when/where* the learning takes place. By exploring questions about teachers as learners, about teaching as a practice to be learned, about teacher learning as a complex social-psychological process that occurs over time in different contexts, we can begin to understand some of the theoretical, practical, and normative issues covered by the phrase *learning to teach.*

We organize this chapter around different though related aspects of learning to teach, pulling each forward one at a time to discuss salient issues and to present illustrative findings. The first section presents a temporal perspective on learning to teach. The second section looks at preservice and beginning teachers as learners. The third section examines different ways that people have conceptualized the content of learning to teach, while the fourth section discusses learning processes and opportunities. By presenting ideas about the when, where, who, what, and how of learning to teach, we hope to raise teacher educators' consciousness about a neglected part of the conceptual and practical foundations of their work.

Times and Places in Learning to Teach

Learning to teach is not synonymous with teacher education. Teacher educators intervene in a process that begins long before teachers take their first education course and that continues afterward on the job; nor can teachers' formal learning about teaching be confined to professional studies, since teachers learn about their subjects and the teaching and learning of those subjects in other academic contexts, including elementary and secondary school, as well as on the job. These basic facts about the times and places of learning to teach have important implications for teacher education. In this section, we outline the chronology of learning to teach, locating formal teacher education in a broad temporal framework and identifying important issues concerning the curriculum of teacher education that derive from this perspective.

The Chronology of Learning to Teach

It is hard to say exactly when learning to teach begins. From an early age, we are surrounded by teaching, most notably by parents and teachers. These early experiences with authority figures help shape teachers' pedagogical tendencies (Nemser, 1983; Stephens, 1969; Wright and Tuska, 1968).

The influence of schooling is especially strong. Future teachers spend thousands of hours in elementary and secondary school watching what teachers do and developing images about and dispositions toward teaching, learning, and subject matter. This long, informal "apprenticeship of observation" (Lortie, 1975) distinguishes learning to teach from other kinds of professional learning, posing unique challenges for teacher educators.

Formal preparation for teaching occurs in universities and schools. Teachers are supposed to lay an intellectual and practical foundation for teaching in education courses and field experiences. Many teachers say that their preservice program did not prepare them for teaching, and a variety of research using both surveys and case methods documents the limited impact of teacher education on prospective teachers' perspectives and beliefs (for example, National Center for Research on Teacher Education, 1991; Tabachnick, Popkewitz, and Zeichner, 1979–80). At the same time, we have some evidence that powerful and innovative teacher preparation can affect the way teachers think about teaching and learning, students, and subject matter (see, for example, Ball, 1990; Cochran-Smith, 1991; Florio and Lensmire, 1990; Feiman-Nemser and Featherstone, 1992).

Preparation for teaching also includes academic study in liberal arts courses, where intellectual dispositions are shaped and subject matter knowledge is acquired. Research on what prospective teachers actually learn in liberal arts courses raises questions about whether academic study automatically provides teachers with the kind of subject matter knowledge they need in order to foster meaningful and integrated understandings in their students (McDiarmid, 1990). Still, university study of academic subjects does influence the way teachers think about knowledge and approach the teaching of academic content (Grossman, 1990; Wilson, Shulman, and Richert, 1987; Wilson and Wineburg, 1988).

No matter how much teachers learn during preservice preparation, learning teaching inevitably occurs on the job. First-year teachers essentially have two jobs: they have to teach and they have to learn to teach (Wildman, Niles, Magliaro, and McLaughlin, 1989). The spread of induction programs suggests that policy makers recognize what teachers know and research confirms—that the first year of teaching is an intense and potentially formative phase in learning to teach (Lortie, 1975; Nemser, 1983).

No one learns to teach in a year. Efforts to describe the stages teachers go through in learning to teach generally posit an initial stage of survival and discovery, a second stage of experimentation and consolidation, and a third stage of mastery and stabilization (see, for example, Berliner, 1986; Field, 1979; Fuller and Bown, 1975; Watts, 1980). These stages are loosely tied to amounts of experience with stabilization occurring around the time of tenure.

Self-knowledge appears to be a major fruit of early teaching (Kagan, 1992). In what Featherstone (1993) calls "the journey in, the journey out," novices begin to craft a professional identity through their struggles with and explorations of students and subject matter. Over time, teachers develop instructional routines and classroom procedures and learn what to expect from pupils. Experience generally yields greater confidence, flexibility, and a sense of professional autonomy. After five to seven years, most teachers feel they know how to teach. Whether we choose to call these teachers "masters" or "experts" depends on how we define mastery and expertise (Carter and others, 1987; Leinhardt, 1988; Livingston and Borko, 1989).

Research on teachers' professional lives reveals that learning and change do not necessarily stop once teachers consolidate a teaching style. Still, it becomes more difficult to describe a common trajectory (Huberman, 1989). Personal dispositions, educational opportunities, and social and political movements provide incentives for continued learning, but whether learning is incremental or dramatic seems to vary with the individual teacher, the school, and the sociopolitical context.

Lessons for Teacher Educators

This temporal portrait of learning to teach sets the stage for thinking about what teacher education should be like at different times and in different places. It also foreshadows our discussion about who teachers are as learners, what they need to learn, and how that learning can be fostered. For example, knowing that biography plays a powerful role in learning to teach does not tell us what teacher candidates have come to believe about teaching or how we should work with those beliefs during teacher preparation. It does, however, focus our attention on the content of teacher candidates' beliefs and how that content helps or hinders professional learning. Similarly, the fact that the first year of teaching is mostly a time of learning does not tell us what novices need to learn. It should, however, push us to conceptualize the content of learning to teach and to sort out what can best be taught and learned at the university prior to teaching, what can best be learned through guided practice in someone else's classroom, what should be learned through structured induction support, and what depends on learning from teaching over time.

Teacher Candidates as Learners

All good teachers, including teacher educators, draw on knowledge about their students in deciding what and how to teach. Fortunately, there is a growing literature on who teacher education students are and what they bring to teacher education in the way of entering knowledge, beliefs, and dispositions. In this section, we sample three areas of scholarship that shed light on teacher candidates as learners: demographic surveys, studies of women's ways of knowing, and research on the content of teacher candidates' beliefs. We also consider the obligation of teacher educators to learn about their own students' backgrounds and entering beliefs and the ways they make sense of their professional studies and teaching experience.

Who Prospective Teachers Are

Demographic profiles of teachers and teacher education students suggest remarkable similarity and stability. The data also reveal several characteristics that distinguish teacher education students as a group from their higher education colleagues. Because of limitations in the research (for example, too little attention to subpopulations such as elementary versus secondary candidates and too much reliance on samples from single institutions), we should regard the generalizations with caution (Brookhart and Freeman, 1992). Still, the patterns help us think about who teacher education students are in relation to what they need to become professional teachers.

Teacher education students are not likely to upset the demographic stability of the current teaching population. The typical American teacher is a Caucasian female, married with two children. She teaches in a suburban elementary school. She is not politically active (Feistritzer, 1986). The typical teacher candidate is female; 75 percent of prospective secondary teachers and 93 percent of those intending to teach elementary, compared to 54 percent of all students in higher education, are women. Ninety-three percent are Caucasian, 10 percent more than all higher education students. Over half of these students grew up in small, rural towns or suburbs. Few are from large, urban areas. Most attend college full time. The average age is twenty-five and a third of those intending to teach elementary school are already married (Book and Freeman, 1986; Brookhart and Freeman, 1992).

Teacher education students have been characterized as "culturally insular" with "limited career horizons." Most selected their university because of its proximity to home and few wish to travel or work more than a hundred miles from their hometown. A majority prefer to teach middle-class children of average ability in traditional settings. In one national survey, 57 percent said they wanted to teach in suburban areas, while only 15 percent expressed interest in teaching in urban settings (Zimpher, 1989).

Although generalized, this portrait of prospective teachers highlights domains of experience that could be informative to teacher educators. Three areas seem especially salient: (1) prospective teachers' experiences as women; (2) prospective teachers' limited exposure to people who are socially, ethnically, and culturally different from themselves; and (3) prospective teachers' experiences as students.

Orientations to Learning

Research on feminist epistemology and on women's perceptions of the work of teaching sheds light on the ways in which women perceive themselves as learners and teachers (Belenky, Clinchy, Goldberger, and Tarule, 1986; Biklen, 1983; Gilligan, 1982; Laird, 1988). Given the preponderance of women in teaching and teacher education, this research can help us think about how preservice students may approach teacher preparation and teaching.

Many students who choose to become teachers are hard working and serious. They have grown up in a school system that rewards passivity and obedience rather than self-directed learning. They have learned to see teachers and texts as authoritative sources of knowledge. Seldom have they been encouraged to build their own knowledge or value their own ideas and questions. Disenfranchised as learners, they have achieved success by figuring out what the teacher wants and by doing it (Belenky, Clinchy, Goldberger, and Tarule, 1986).

For many women, success in formal education is strongly linked to a sense of self. While men are more apt to blame poor school performance on bad luck or circumstances beyond their control, women tend to interpret bad grades and teacher reproofs as indicators of their own inadequacies (Belenky, Clinchy, Goldberger, and Tarule, 1986; Holland and Eisenhart, 1990; McDade, 1988). Large numbers of women describe their college classes as stifling and disempowering, reminding them of their mental shortcomings. These orientations toward schooling and higher education are likely to influence how preservice teachers think about themselves as learners and how they approach learning to teach.

Teacher candidates' orientations toward learning to teach are also influenced by their views of teaching as work. Many preservice teachers, particularly those who are women, choose teaching because of its nurturing and caring attributes. In a survey of over four hundred elementary teacher candidates, Book, Byers, and Freeman (1983) found that many viewed teaching as "an extended form of parenting" learned through experience and dependent on natural instincts and intuitions. Because respondents emphasized the nurturing aspects of the teacher's role over responsibilities for intellectual development, they assumed that teacher education had little to teach them.

By telling us about a significant proportion of our students, research on women's ways of knowing highlights a central challenge for teacher educators—helping intending teachers develop intellectual confidence. Unless teacher candidates experience their own intellectual powers, they may not value this quality in their pupils.

Experience with Diversity

In order to build bridges between students and subject matter, teachers need to know how their students think about what they are learning. Attending to the thinking of others means trying to see the world through the others' eyes. Like most people, teachers often assume that students who share their language and culture experience it as they do (Jackson, 1986). Like the teacher candidates interviewed by Holt-Reynolds (1992), they ask, "What works for me?" in deciding what will work for their students. One of the central tasks of teacher education is to help teacher candidates overcome this "presumption of shared identity" in order to learn to attend to the thinking and actions of others (Jackson, 1986).

When we consider the ethnic and cultural diversity of American school children and the homogeneity and cultural insularity of those intending to teach, this task becomes increasingly more complex. The "narrow framework of experience" (Paine, 1989) that teacher candidates often bring to teacher education has provided limited contact with people who are ethnically or culturally different from themselves and few opportunities in their formal schooling to consider that others may learn, understand, or experience things differently. Drawing on their own experience, they develop assumptions about the learning and thinking of others that fit with their own. Even more problematic is the tendency to interpret differences in approaches or orientations to learning or schooling as indicators of limited cognitive ability or lack of motivation. Wary of racial stereotypes, teacher candidates resist cultural or ethnic explanations for student performance (Paine, 1989).

Teacher educators must help prospective teachers learn to look beyond their own experience and actively seek to know students, their thinking, and their culture. Teachers and teacher candidates can also benefit from gaining perspective on their own cultural roots and the beliefs they have developed as a consequence (Cazden and Mehan, 1989).

Prospective Teachers' Beliefs

The beliefs and commitments held by teachers-to-be significantly influence what they learn in teacher education (Bird and Anderson, 1992; Borko, Livingston, McCaleb, and Mauro, 1988; Calderhead, 1991). Having spent more than thirteen years in classrooms learning about teaching through an "apprenticeship of observation" (Lortie, 1975), prospective teachers have beliefs about what teachers do and say, how children learn, and what should be taught (Ball, 1988; Feiman-Nemser and Featherstone, 1992; Weinstein, 1988). Recent research on the content of these beliefs can alert teacher educators to images and ideas their students may hold while providing a map of relevant categories of beliefs to explore (Nespor, 1987).

Beliefs About Teaching and Learning. Like much of our society, prospective teachers believe that teaching is a process of passing knowledge from teacher to student and that learning involves absorbing or memorizing information and practicing skills (Ball and McDiarmid, 1987; Calderhead and Robson, 1991; Cohen, 1988; Cuban, 1984). Students wait like empty vessels to be filled and teachers do the filling. Teachers tell students what they need to know and students listen and learn (that is, memorize) what they have been told. When prospective teachers imagine themselves teaching, they often picture themselves standing before a group of students presenting, talking, explaining, showing, "going over" the material to be learned (Ball, 1988).

This perspective places sole authority for knowing on the teacher, making her the source and provider of information. It is reflected in a common concern of teacher candidates—that they might not be able to answer students' questions. Deeply rooted, these views of teaching and learning are not likely to change unless alternative experiences challenge their validity (Duckworth, 1987; McDiarmid, 1992; see also the discussion on conceptual change and learning to teach in the last section of this chapter).

Beliefs About Subject Matter. The views of teaching and learning sketched above relate to and are supported by beliefs about subject matter. Most often, the subject matter is seen as a fixed collection of facts, concepts, and skills that must be "learned" before they can be applied (Ball, 1988; Florio and Lensmire, 1990; Grossman, 1990; Leinhardt and Smith, 1985). For example, mathematics is often viewed and treated as a set of discrete rules best learned through repeated practice. Based on their own experiences as students, prospective teachers think of "doing math" as a matter of completing a page of forty problems. While reading and writing may be viewed as more creative, expressive, and pleasurable, many preservice teachers also regard these subjects as highly prescriptive and rule-based (Hollingsworth, 1989). They consider approaches to instruction that are not rigidly sequenced or structured—or that encourage student collaboration—to be unsettling (Florio and Lensmire, 1990). Given these views of knowledge, it is not surprising that many prospective teachers believe they already know most of what they need to teach (McDiarmid, 1992).

Beliefs About Students. Prospective teachers also have preconceptions about their future students that are rooted in their experiences in and outside school and their commitments to the altruistic, nurturing ideals of teaching (Brookhart and Free-man, 1992; Weinstein, 1988). Often these beliefs are contradictory. On the one hand, prospective teachers believe that they should treat all students fairly. This generally means treating them all the same. However, they also believe that every child is unique and deserves an education suited to his or her special needs (Mc-Diarmid, 1991; Paine, 1989). The tension between treating students as individu-als and treating all students alike may cause prospective teachers to disregard or overlook student diversity that is race or class related and that reflects social in-equities.

Limited experience and exposure to stereotypes embraced in mainstream so-ciety shape preservice teachers' perceptions of diverse groups. In one study, re-searchers found that many preservice teachers are willing to accept ethnic or cultural stereotypes about groups of students to explain certain behaviors or to adjust their expectations for students (Paine, 1989; McDiarmid, 1992). Some believe that certain ethnic groups are more "concrete-oriented" or respond more readily to particular instructional styles (McDiarmid, 1992). Others confound low achievement with lower class. Such views hardly represent dependable bases for pedagogical decisions.

Learning About the Learners of Teacher Education

We have sampled three areas of scholarship that shed light on who teacher can-didates are as learners and what they bring to teacher preparation. The research sensitizes us to possible beliefs and orientations that intending teachers might hold and helps us think about what we can build on and what needs to be challenged. It underscores the need for teacher educators to investigate their own students' backgrounds and beliefs. Finally, it highlights an opportunity for teacher educa-tors to add to the knowledge base of teacher education by extending and refining our understanding of teacher education students as learners.

The Content of Learning to Teach

We cannot talk about learning to teach without considering the content of that learning. In learning to teach, what do teachers need to learn? Answers to this question bear on decisions about the curriculum and pedagogy of teacher edu-cation. They also reflect ideas and assumptions about what teaching is like and what forms of knowledge and expertise guide teachers' practice.

Most often the question of what teachers need to learn is framed in terms of professional knowledge and skills. We ask, "What do teachers need to know and be able to do in order to teach?" Whereas lack of knowledge and skill may limit what teachers can do, having them does not guarantee their wise use. Recently, some researchers and teacher educators have begun to use the term *dispositions* to signal additional qualities, sensibilities, attitudes, and commitments required for teaching. Dispositions are tendencies or inclinations to act in particular ways. Tied to occasions, they unite ability with desire (Schwab, 1976).

Thinking of the content of learning to teach in terms of knowledge, skills, and dispositions provides a rough analytic starting point. The larger challenge is specifying what these categories consist of and how their contents interact in teaching. This is generally referred to as defining a knowledge base for teaching, though the term *knowledge base* often connotes a narrower undertaking (Tom and Valli, 1990). Even though the knowledge base rhetoric far outstrips the reality, some progress has been made. This progress reflects shifting paradigms in research on teaching from a focus on what teachers do to a focus on how they think and then on what they know and how they organize and use their knowledge (see Shulman, 1986, for a review).

We organize this discussion around three contemporary efforts to frame the content of learning to teach. The first, *Knowledge Base for the Beginning Teacher* (Reynolds, 1989), outlines various domains of professional knowledge that beginning teachers need to know about in order to do their work. The second, formulated by Anne Reynolds at the Educational Testing Service (Reynolds, 1992), identifies core teaching tasks on the assumption that if novices can perform these tasks, they possess the requisite knowledge and skills required for beginning teaching. The third, based on work of the National Board for Professional Teaching Standards (1990), offers a set of standards that integrate knowledge, skills, and dispositions required for excellence in teaching. While they illustrate the state of the art, these examples also reveal the limits of our knowledge about what teachers need to learn and the challenges that face teacher educators in trying to figure out what to teach.

Domains of Professional Knowledge

Commissioned by the American Association of Colleges of Teacher Education, *Knowledge Base for the Beginning Teacher* (KBBT) (Reynolds, 1989) purports to offer a book-length statement of what every beginning teacher should know. The preface spells out the assumptions guiding the project: (1) we know enough to codify a knowledge base for teaching, (2) the knowledge base is inevitably incomplete and changing, (3) it takes various forms and comes from diverse sources, and (4) it can be structured in different ways.

The project organizers identified domains with which, in their judgment, every beginning teacher should be familiar. Then they invited experts associated with each domain to write a chapter outlining "confirmed knowledge" appropriate for "professionally responsible beginning teachers." The table of contents reveals topics that are part of the emerging work on professional knowledge for teaching (Shulman, 1987; Grossman, 1990): classroom organization and management, learners and learning, classroom instruction, the developmental needs of pupils, subject matter knowledge for teaching, subject specific pedagogy, knowledge about reading and writing, students with special needs, the social organization of classes and schools, the school district, ethical dimensions of teaching, to name about half of the chapter titles.

KBBT reflects the range and richness of professional knowledge that bears on teachers' work, but it leaves open the question of what it means to know and use such knowledge in teaching. To explore this issue, we briefly examine the treatment of four domains of knowledge directly related to the central task of teaching, which is to connect students with worthwhile subject matter. This allows us to highlight the special status of subject matter knowledge and its interaction with other domains and to acknowledge the role and limits of propositional knowledge as a guide to practice.

Traditionally not part of the teacher education curriculum, subject matter knowledge is a central component of the content of learning to teach. Whatever else teachers need to know, they need to know their subjects. Current educational reforms have prompted renewed interest in teachers' subject matter knowledge because they call for a kind of teaching that promotes powerful and flexible knowledge and understanding in students (see, for example, Brophy, 1989; Cohen, 1989). Still, the question of what teachers need to know about their subjects to realize this goal has been difficult to answer (Kennedy, 1991).

Grossman, Wilson, and Shulman (1989) provide a very general answer by specifying three kinds of subject matter knowledge for teaching: content knowledge, which includes knowledge of facts, concepts, and procedures within a discipline; substantive knowledge, or knowledge of explanatory frameworks in a field; and syntactic knowledge, or knowledge of the ways in which new knowledge is brought into a field. A growing body of case studies of subject matter teaching reveals how the presence or absence of this kind of knowledge affects the learning opportunities that prospective and practicing teachers provide for their students. (For one review of this work, see Ball and McDiarmid, 1990). These portraits make a compelling case for why teachers need deeper and more flexible subject matter knowledge than they generally have a chance to learn. Combined with mounting evidence that even prospective teachers who major in the subjects they teach often cannot explain fundamental concepts in their discipline (National Center for Research on Teacher Education, 1991), the research underscores the importance of addressing this often neglected domain of knowledge for teaching.

McDiarmid, Ball, and Anderson (1989) extend the argument about subject matter knowledge in their treatment of subject-specific pedagogy (also called pedagogical content knowledge). They concentrate on the role of instructional representations, which include all the different ways that teachers convey messages to pupils about the substance and nature of a subject—activities, questions, problems, explanations—as well as the way answers are sought and validated. They argue that prospective teachers need to develop a repertoire of representations for the subjects they teach and standards for judging the validity and appropriateness of different representations. This will enable teachers to design and adapt learning activities that foster ideas and patterns of thinking parallel to knowledge and ways of thinking in the academic disciplines.

In two related chapters, Anderson (1989a, 1989b) outlines compatible perspectives on learners, learning, and classroom instruction. Arguing that beginning teachers need to develop coherent personal theories to guide their perceptions and decisions, she presents a small set of core ideas about learners and learning, which she translates into a perspective on classroom instruction. Rooted in constructivist theory and research, these concepts about knowledge, metacognition, and motivation, on the one hand, and academic tasks, scaffolding, and learning environments on the other, provide the intellectual foundation for a personal theory of learning and teaching. Besides learning what these concepts mean, Anderson argues, prospective teachers must learn how the concepts relate to each other and how they come together in particular teaching episodes.

Framing a professional knowledge base around discrete domains helps us appreciate the range of knowledge and values that bear on teaching. At the same time, it misrepresents the interactive character of teachers' knowledge and side-steps the issue of knowledge use. Teachers do not draw on knowledge one domain at a time; rather, they weave together different kinds of knowledge as they reason about what to do and take action in particular situations (McDiarmid, Ball, and Anderson, 1989). For instance, in planning an instructional activity, a teacher may consider what concepts she wants students to learn (content), how those topics fit with previous and future topics (curriculum), how appropriate the activity is for her particular group of students (learners), what might be difficult for them (learning), how she will find out what students do and do not understand. Researchers are just beginning to study the processes by which teachers meld different kinds of knowledge in teaching and to consider how best to represent the results.

General propositional knowledge can never be a complete guide to practice. For one thing, teaching depends on judgment and reasoning, which must also be learned. Moreover, much of what teachers need to know to respond to immediate classroom situations must be discovered by them over time in their particular context (Richardson, 1994). If expertise in teaching consists of knowledge and commitments tied to actions, then we must consider not only what teachers know (or need to learn) but how they transform their knowledge into professional activity (Kennedy, 1987).

Tasks of Teaching

A second approach to framing the content of learning to teach begins with the question, "What should teachers be able to do?" and then reasons backward to the knowledge and skills required for performing these tasks. This is the tack taken by the Educational Testing Service in its recent efforts to design new performance assessments for beginning teachers.

To lay the intellectual foundation for this initiative, Reynolds (1992) prepared a synthesis of research reviews on effective teaching and learning to teach. She acknowledges serious problems with the literature: (1) the research does not reflect teachers' perspective, (2) empirical evidence linking teacher actions and student learning is limited and does not generalize across settings, (3) the differences between effective experienced teachers and effective beginning teachers is not well understood, and (4) what we know about teaching from the research literature may not fit our vision of good teaching. Still, she uses it to frame a set of teaching tasks that beginning teachers should be able to perform. These tasks, she argues, fit any teaching situation regardless of the teacher's philosophy, subject matter, or students. Having an adequate knowledge base means being able to do the following:

1. Plan lessons that enable students to relate new learning to prior understanding and experience
2. Develop rapport and personal interactions with students
3. Establish and maintain rules and routines that are fair and appropriate to students
4. Arrange the physical and social conditions of the classroom in ways that are conducive to learning and that fit the academic task
5. Represent and present subject matter in ways that enable students to relate new learning to prior understanding and that help students develop metacognitive strategies
6. Assess student learning using a variety of measurement tools and adapt instruction according to the results
7. Reflect on their own actions and students' responses in order to improve their teaching [Reynolds, 1992, p. 26]

The idea of framing a knowledge base around tasks of teaching has a certain face validity. Teaching is a practical art and the tasks of teaching cover familiar territory. Additional support for this approach comes from research on teachers' classroom knowledge, which also uses the construct of "tasks" to describe the way individual teachers acquire and organize their knowledge of classroom events. According to the researchers, teachers organize their knowledge around particular tasks of teaching such as teaching lessons or maintaining order (Doyle, 1986; Leinhardt and Greeno, 1986). While these tasks are common to all classrooms, the meaning individual teachers bring to them is a function of their unique knowledge and experience. Furthermore, as teachers act to accomplish tasks of teaching, their understanding of what a given task involves and what it means to accomplish it changes. From this perspective, teachers learn to teach as they make sense of and take on the tasks of teaching (Carter, 1990).

Reynolds does not actually work out the connections between the ability to perform the tasks and the knowledge, skills, and dispositions required to do so; rather, she identifies broad requirements such as knowledge of pedagogy appropriate to the content being taught and the disposition to find out about one's students and school and the skills to do so. But it is also the case that we simply do not know enough about how teachers think through and pull off these tasks in particular contexts or upon what combination of general and "local" knowledge they depend.

Any performance model rests on ideas about the nature of teaching and the role of the teacher. Reynolds' tasks of teaching framework gives the impression that teaching is relatively straightforward work. Teachers plan lessons, arrange classroom conditions, and present content so that students will learn. Teachers note the results of their actions and make appropriate adjustments. Teaching seems like a form of technical problem solving in which teachers apply familiar means to accomplish predetermined ends (Schön, 1983).

A different picture emerges from studies that describe what teaching is like for teachers. Jackson (1968) portrays classrooms as complex, unpredictable, and multidimensional settings. Research on teachers' "practical" or "classroom knowledge" (Carter and Doyle, 1987; Doyle, 1990; Elbaz, 1983) further reveals the complexities and uncertainties of interactive teaching and the need for considerable thinking in action (Schön, 1987). For example, in a study of her own practice, Lampert (1985) argues that teachers do not solve problems; rather, they navigate among competing goals as they make moment-to-moment decisions about what to do in particular instructional situations.

Both portraits capture important aspects of teaching with implications for defining the content of learning to teach. Besides learning to handle the routine and the predictable, teachers must develop the capacity to think on their feet and to respond in appropriate ways to an ever-changing situation. Just as uncertainty challenges teachers, so preparing teachers for uncertainty challenges teacher educators (Floden and Buchmann, 1993).

While teaching performance depends on knowledge and skills, it cannot be defined independently of purposes, commitments, and values. Except for the reference to "fairness" in relation to classroom rules and routines, the tasks of teaching framework avoids moral language. But teaching is a moral practice as well as a technical activity, and this has implications for thinking about the content of learning to teach. Besides acquiring requisite knowledge and skills, teachers must also develop values, commitments, and images of good teaching.

Professional Standards

Values and commitments figure prominently in the standards framework generated by National Board for Professional Teaching Standards (NBPTS), which was founded in 1987 in response to a major recommendation in a Carnegie-commissioned report on education and the economy (Carnegie, 1986). Governed by a sixty-three-member board dominated by classroom teachers, this independent, nonprofit organization is devoted to creating a voluntary national certification system for experienced elementary and secondary teachers.

As a first step in defining professional standards, the board adopted a policy statement entitled "What Teachers Should Know and Be Able to Do" (National Board for Professional Teaching Standards, 1990). The statement sets out five core propositions that reflect what the board values in teaching and serve as a foundation for its work.

1. Teachers are committed to students and their learning.
2. Teachers know the subjects they teach and how to teach those subjects to students.
3. Teachers are responsible for managing and monitoring student learning.
4. Teachers think systematically about their practice and learn from experience.
5. Teachers are members of learning communities.

The policy statement underscores the value and limits of formal knowledge in teaching. In relation to the first proposition, for example, we are told that highly accomplished teachers base their practice on prevailing theories of cognition and intelligence as well as on "observation and knowledge of their students' interests, abilities, skills, knowledge, family circumstances and peer relationships." We are also told that "teaching ultimately requires judgement, improvisation, and conversation about ends and means" (p. 13).

The propositions reflect teachers' responsibilities both inside and outside the classroom. For example, teachers orchestrate learning in group settings, assess student progress on a regular basis, and use multiple methods to meet their goals (proposition 3). They strengthen their teaching by seeking advice, studying educational research, reflecting on their own classroom experience (proposition 4). They work collaboratively with parents and other professionals (proposition 5).

Professional values and commitments lie at the heart of the standards. The first proposition articulates the ethical foundation of teachers' practice: the conviction that all students can learn and the commitment to making knowledge accessible to all. References to other commitments appear throughout the document: respect for disciplinary thinking, a commitment to lifelong professional development, reverence for the craft of teaching. The document invokes teachers who exemplify the personal and intellectual virtues they seek to cultivate in their students—curiosity and love of learning, tolerance and open-mindedness, fairness and justice, respect for human diversity and dignity, and the ability to question received wisdom (p. 25).

The policy statement projects a vision of good teaching and an image of what it means to be a professional teacher. Good teaching emphasizes conceptual understanding, problem solving, multiple perspectives. Professional teachers make decisions based on personal experience and the best knowledge available. Excellence in teaching depends on human qualities, expert knowledge and skill, and professional commitment.

These propositions and their elaboration serve as a philosophical basis for more focused standards in thirty different areas defined by disciplines (for example, mathematics, English/language arts, science) and developmental levels (for example, early childhood, middle childhood, early adolescence). Compatible standards for beginning teachers have been developed by the Interstate New Teacher Assessment and Support Consortium (INTASC), a program of the Council of Chief State School Officers (1993). Both sets of professional standards reflect a vision of good teaching that is a necessary prerequisite to figuring out what teachers need to learn.

Lessons for Teacher Educators

These three examples represent "state of the art" efforts to frame a knowledge base for teaching. Associated with different purposes—teacher education, teacher assessment, teacher licensure, and teacher certification—they draw mainly on research and scholarship and, in the case of the NBPTS, on the "wisdom of practice." Overlap among the three examples suggests consensus about broad domains of knowledge and values and agreement about core tasks of teaching. Differences in focus and format highlight the absence of a shared structure to frame a knowledge base and a way to represent expertise in teaching.

What lessons can teacher educators derive from this brief discussion of these efforts to frame the content of learning to teach? First, there is a lot to learn, more than teachers could possibly master in the limited time allotted to teacher preparation. Some of this content falls outside the traditional boundaries of the teacher education curriculum; much of it has not been codified. Second, what teachers need to learn not only includes knowledge, skills, and dispositions, but also ways of knowing, thinking, caring, and acting. Third, since much of what teachers need to know can only be learned in situ, an important part of learning to teach involves learning to learn in context. Fourth, defining the content of learning to teach depends on clarifying a vision of good teaching.

On the one hand, we seem to know quite a lot about what teachers need to learn. On the other hand, we still have mostly general statements and fragmented research. This means that teacher educators have to figure out for themselves what to teach in light of who their students are and what the time frame is. Getting clear about the kind of teaching they want teachers to learn will not only help teacher educators make decisions about what to teach, it will also ensure that this "content" adds up to a coherent vision of teaching.

Until now, we have separated the "what" from the "how" of learning to teach in order to focus on the question of what teachers need to learn. Ultimately, content and processes of learning to teach must be brought together, since how teachers learn shapes what they learn and is often part of what they need to know. Unfortunately, we know even less about the processes of learning to teach than we do about the content.

Processes and Opportunities in Learning to Teach

As we turn to the "how" of learning to teach, we gather together the threads of our argument in order to relate them to a consideration of learning processes and opportunities. The following general points bear on this discussion: (1) different times and places are more or less suited to the learning of different aspects of teaching; (2) what gets learned at one time influences teachers' readiness for and openness to subsequent learning; (3) the constellation of disposition and beliefs, knowledge, and understandings that teachers bring to a given learning opportunity affects what they learn from it; (4) the content of learning to teach takes different forms that, in turn, call for different kinds of learning opportunities; and (5) how teachers learn affects what they learn.

When we talk about the "how" of learning to teach, we mean both cognitive processes and learning opportunities. Cognitive processes loosely refer to what goes on in teachers' heads. Learning opportunities include both the contexts of learning (programs, settings, interventions, and so on) and the social interactions within these contexts that promote learning. To understand how teachers learn to teach, we need to attend to teacher cognitions and to the conditions and opportunities that facilitate their learning (Cobb, 1994).

By and large, research on how teachers learn has tended to focus on (1) how their beliefs, perceptions, attitudes, orientations, understandings, knowledge, and skills change over time or (2) on descriptions of the contexts of learning. Connecting the changes to the learning opportunities is at the heart of research on teacher learning. Scholars and researchers are just beginning to define this messy and ill-structured domain through their programs of research (Carter, 1990; Kagan, 1992; Kennedy, 1993).

Promising lines of work include studies of (1) efforts to transform prospective teachers' beliefs; (2) how teachers gain subject matter knowledge and pedagogical content knowledge; (3) teachers' practical knowledge and how it develops; (4) how teachers learn ambitious forms of teaching on their own and in the company of other teachers; and (5) how teachers' knowledge, skills, and dispositions change as they participate in different teacher education programs. Because they focus on how teachers learn particular aspects or versions of teaching under specific conditions, these studies represent an important advance over previous research, which tended to treat learning to teach as a global and undifferentiated process.

Conventional teacher education reflects a view of learning to teach as a two-step process of knowledge acquisition and application or transfer. Lay theories assume that learning to teach occurs through trial and error over time. Neither view captures the prevailing position that learning occurs through an interaction between the learner and the learning opportunity. If we want to understand how and why teachers learn what they do from a given learning opportunity, we have to investigate both what the experience was like and what sense teachers made of it. If we want to design an appropriate learning opportunity, we have to clarify what we want teachers to learn, what kind of intellectual work that will entail, where teachers are in relation to the desired outcome, and what kinds of resources and activities are likely to help teachers move in the desired direction.

No single theory or model of learning can adequately account for all aspects of learning to teach; rather, we need perspectives that fit with what is being learned and that take into account who is doing the learning and when or where the learning is taking place. In this section, we briefly examine a cluster of theoretical ideas from cognitive psychology, anthropology, and sociology that seem especially relevant in thinking about how some of the important constituents of teaching are or should be learned. These ideas also help explain why teacher education has not been a powerful force in teacher learning. We use cases to link this discussion with what has come before.

Conceptual Change and Learning to Teach

We have already described the kinds of beliefs about teaching, learning, subject matter, and diversity that many teacher candidates bring to teacher preparation. While teacher educators often intend to change those beliefs, prospective teachers frequently leave teacher preparation with their beliefs intact. When such beliefs limit the range of ideas and actions that teachers consider, this consequence is problematic.

Feiman-Nemser and Buchmann (1986) report a case of mislearning during teacher preparation that illustrates the problem. The researchers describe how Janice, an elementary education major, fits ideas she encounters in her courses into a framework of beliefs based on what she saw and heard growing up, leaving her with beliefs that work against equal educational opportunities. Asked to describe an article that stood out to her, Janice selected Anyon's critique (1981) of the unequal distribution of school knowledge by social class and school location, which she misinterpreted as simply a description of the way things are. She connected this to something she read in math methods on motivation—that poor children are more present-oriented and require immediate reinforcement. Asked whether she had any experiences with children from backgrounds different from her own, Janice talked at length about Mexican migrant workers on the family farm whose children were not interested in going to school. Adding a final piece to the picture, she recalled a discussion in her curriculum class about "why teach poetry to lower class, low achievers" that made her think that "maybe certain things should be stressed in certain schools, depending on where they're located" (p. 247).

While current beliefs and conceptions can serve as barriers to change, they also provide frameworks for interpreting and assessing new and potentially conflicting information. That is the paradoxical role of prior beliefs. Like all learners, teachers can only learn by drawing on their own beliefs and prior experiences, but their beliefs may not help them learn new views of teaching and learning advocated by teacher educators (Anderson and Bird, 1994). Recognizing the challenge of transforming prospective teachers' beliefs and committed to promoting new visions of teaching and learning, some teacher educators have turned to conceptual change models for insights about the conditions under which people are more likely to change their minds.

Conceptual change theory (Posner, Strike, Hewson, and Hertzog, 1982; Strike and Posner, 1985) suggests that changing teachers' beliefs depends on their recognizing discrepancies between their own views and those underlying new visions of teaching and learning. Research on human judgment suggests that change is more likely to occur if alternatives are vivid, concrete, and detailed enough to provide a plausible alternative (Nesbitt and Ross, 1980).

From these theoretical perspectives and from the work of teacher educators interested in transforming teacher candidates' beliefs (see, for example, Bird, Anderson, Sullivan, and Swidler, 1993; Feiman-Nemser and Featherstone, 1992; Florio and Lensmire, 1990; Holt-Reynolds, 1992; Wilcox, Schram, Lappan, and Lanier, 1992), several conditions seem necessary to induce conceptual change. First, teachers need an opportunity to consider why new practices and their associated values and beliefs are better than more conventional approaches. Second, they must see examples of these practices, preferably under realistic conditions. Third, it helps if teachers can experience such practices firsthand as learners. If we also want teachers to incorporate these ideas and practices into their own teaching, we need to provide ongoing support and guidance (Kennedy, 1991). All these requirements find additional justification in theories of situated cognition.

Situated Cognition and Learning to Teach

Teacher educators generally assume that knowledge and skills exist independently of the contexts in which they are acquired. The notion that teachers can first learn concepts and skills and then apply them in real-world teaching situations reflects this assumption. Cognitive psychologists (for example, Brown, Collins, and Duguid, 1989; Lave, 1988; Resnick, 1989) challenge this notion by claiming that all knowledge is situated in and grows out of the contexts of its use. Besides providing a compelling explanation for why teachers use so little of what they are taught, the theory of situated cognition directs teacher educators to embed teacher learning in "authentic" activity (Brown, Collins, and Duguid, 1989).

From studies of learning in and out of school, it appears that people build up knowledge by solving real problems using available clues, tools, and social supports (Resnick, 1987). Traditional apprenticeships provide one model of this kind of learning. In an apprenticeship, a beginner develops flexible skills and conditional knowledge by working on genuine tasks in the company of a master. In pioneering studies of tailoring apprenticeships, for example, Lave and Wenger

(1991) describe the situated and sequenced process by which apprentices learn to produce garments. From observing masters, apprentices develop an image of how an entire garment is produced while they work on specific components (such as a sleeve) and practice specific skills, such as cutting, pressing, using the sewing machine. In this type of apprenticeship, knowing cannot be separated from doing.

Cognitive Apprenticeship. The term "cognitive apprenticeship" has been applied to classroom-based instructional models that incorporate key features of an apprenticeship (Brown, Collins, and Duguid, 1989; Collins, Brown, and Newman, 1989). These features include authentic activity, social interaction, collaborative learning, and a teacher/coach who makes his or her knowledge and thinking visible to the learner(s). Adding "cognitive" is intended to convey the idea that the same conditions or opportunities that support the development of physical skills can also support the development of cognitive skills.

An obvious application of cognitive apprenticeship to learning to teach is student teaching, internships, and other mentored learning situations where the teacher's learning is "situated" in the context of practice. Ideally, the novice would learn how to think and act like a teacher by observing and engaging in the activities of teaching alongside a more experienced practitioner. The mentor would model ways of thinking and acting, coach the novice in her attempts to carry out particular tasks, and gradually withdraw support as the novice learns to perform on her own. This calls for classroom teachers to take on the role of school-based teacher educator, which requires special preparation and coaching.

Assisted Performance. Vygotsky's theory (1978) of assisted performance in the zone of proximal development (ZPD) accounts for how learning occurs through social interaction with a more capable other. The ZPD is the distance between what an individual can do independently and what he or she can do with assistance. Assistance from and cooperative activity with a teacher, expert, or more capable peer enables the learner to perform at levels beyond his or her level of independent performance. Knowledge and skills that initially exist in the interaction between the novice and the more capable other eventually get internalized by the learner. Vygotsky's work is primarily concerned with children. Some contemporary proponents (for example, Tharp and Gallimore, 1988), claiming that identical processes operate in the learning adult, are beginning to explore the application of these ideas to teacher education. We should not let the terms *situated learning, cognitive apprenticeship,* and *assisted performance* mislead us into thinking that these theories only apply to teacher learning in school settings. They pertain to education courses, which are often criticized for being "too theoretical" and "not very practical," as well as to teachers' academic preparation. In these university classrooms, teachers often encounter concepts and ideas disconnected from any meaningful contexts, or they work alone without the benefits of collaboration or modeling.

Advocates of case-based teacher education see the use of cases as one way to situate teacher learning in problems of practice. (See Sykes and Bird, 1992, for a review of different uses of cases in teacher education.) Through the analysis of cases, teachers can learn concepts in ways that reveal their use and practice the kind of reasoning and problem solving that "real" teaching entails.

The learning theories and instructional models that we have reviewed constitute a valuable resource for teacher educators interested in promoting and understanding teacher learning. Besides suggesting important features of powerful interventions, these theoretical perspectives give us lenses to use in explaining the learning that does (or does not) occur. To illustrate what this could look like, we describe a unique teacher education intervention designed to help an experienced, successful, elementary teacher learn to teach mathematics in new ways (Heaton and Lampert, 1993). This intervention honors the contextualized quality of knowing and learning in teaching. It also shows how the kind of teaching to be learned shapes the content of the learning.

A Case of Learning to Teach for Understanding

As a doctoral student, Heaton read about the kind of mathematics teaching and learning advocated by reformers. Unsure how, as a prospective teacher educator, she would be able to help novices learn to teach in ways that she herself had never taught, Heaton decided to try to learn a new kind of mathematics teaching. She arranged to teach fourth-grade mathematics next door to Lampert, a scholar and teacher educator, who was teaching math in the fifth grade and using her classroom as a setting for prospective and practicing teachers and teacher educators to study a new kind of teaching practice (Lampert, 1992).

Once a week, Lampert observed Heaton's teaching and wrote notes about specific teaching problems that occurred. Heaton also observed Lampert's teaching and they met regularly to talk about their practice. Sometimes they looked at samples of children's work or designed problems to use with their students. They also worked math problems and discussed connections between the elementary mathematics curriculum and the discipline of mathematics.

Lampert based her approach to helping Heaton on ideas about what teachers need to know and how that knowledge is learned. The approach consisted primarily of classroom observation and discussion of situated problems of practice and alternative solutions. Lampert justifies this approach by drawing a parallel between teaching for understanding and teaching *teaching* for understanding. In both cases, deciding whether a solution or a practice is appropriate depends on having a contextualized understanding of the problem or circumstance. By observing and reflecting on Heaton's lessons, Lampert modeled ways of thinking about teaching and learning. Through this process, she hoped to help Heaton develop what Shulman calls "strategic knowledge"—the knowledge that "comes into play as the teacher confronts particular situations or problems, whether theoretical, practical, or moral, where principles collide and no simple solution is possible" (Heaton and Lampert, 1993, p. 58).

The kind of teaching Heaton wanted to learn requires the teacher to manage the exchange of mathematical ideas in the context of managing complex social interactions. This not only depends on having different kinds of knowledge about subject matter, students, curriculum, social interactions, teaching, and so on. It also requires holding that knowledge flexibly, "not in the form of a script, but in the form of a web of multiply connected ideas for things to try. . . . It is not a matter of learning the rules and then following them; it is a matter of casing out the situation you are in on a moment by moment basis, watching how students react to your response, constructing a new response in a cyclical improvisation" (Heaton and Lampert, 1993, p. 58).

This description recalls our earlier discussion about the interactive nature of teachers' knowledge and reinforces the intersection of the "what" and the "how" in learning to teach. In trying to conceptualize what teaching mathematics for understanding entails, Lampert is describing what we usually treat as tacit knowledge. Her formulation illustrates some of the problems with framing a knowledge base around discrete domains of knowledge or generic tasks of teaching. Teacher education rarely helps teachers develop the kind of contextualized and coordinated knowledge that Lampert works on with Heaton. This may help explain why teacher candidates have difficulty constructing new kinds of pedagogy even when they have come to believe that it is both possible and desirable and when they have acquired new subject matter understandings (Wilcox, Schram, Lappan, and Lanier, 1992).

Describing her own learning, Heaton reports that she was faced with struggles "everywhere I turned" (Heaton and Lampert 1993, p. 60). "The difficulties began with planning . . . trying to follow a script yet teach in ways that opened up the discourse to students' ideas. They also encompassed how to get students to talk and then, when they did, what to do with their ideas. Deciding which ideas to pursue, which to drop, and which to suspend for the moment was hard" (p. 61). Heaton also struggled with mathematical concepts and with fundamental questions about what it means to know and do mathematics (see also Heaton, 1994).

In many ways, Heaton represents our best foot forward in terms of candidates for teacher development. She had been a successful student of mathematics through college calculus. When she began working with Lampert, she was already a competent teacher who had done the kind of teaching in social studies that she wanted to learn in mathematics. So it is instructive for teacher educators to note that Heaton still needed to learn new mathematical and pedagogical knowledge in order to teach in a way that was responsive to students' thinking and to the mathematical ideas under discussion.

Heaton's story raises many question about what and how we teach teachers at the preservice and induction levels as well as during inservice. If preservice teacher education provided a stronger foundation in subject matter and pedagogy, what kinds of learning needs would novices present? Could those needs be addressed by creating cognitive apprenticeships with experienced teachers who are also trying to change their practice? Do experienced teachers have more to unlearn than novices when they try to embrace new forms of teaching and learning?

We note that the Lampert-Heaton case says relatively little about how teachers learn to teach mathematics to diverse students. Researchers are just beginning to frame and study the question of how teachers learn to teach demanding content to all students, a question that is central to the current reform agenda. Still, we believe that this story and other stories of learning to teach for understanding bear careful reading and rereading by teacher educators not only for images and insights about what new pedagogies can look like, but also for ideas about how to help teachers learn to teach in these ways and to think deeply about their practice.

Clearly, there is a lot that we do not know about the content and processes of learning to teach. Teacher educators are in a good position to enlarge our understanding by inventing and studying new ways to situate teacher learning in practice. The story that Heaton and Lampert tell is a model both for what such learning opportunities might look like and for how we can tell about them.

References

Anderson, L. M. (1989a). "Classroom instruction." In M. C. Reynolds (ed.), *Knowledge base for the beginning teacher.* Elmsford, N.Y.: Pergamon Press.

Anderson, L. M. (1989b). "Learners and learning." In M. C. Reynolds (ed.), *Knowledge base for the beginning teacher.* Elmsford, N.Y.: Pergamon Press.

Anyon, J. (1981). "Social class and school knowledge." *Curriculum Inquiry, 11,* 3–41.

Ball, D. L. (1988). "Knowledge and reasoning in mathematical pedagogy: Examining what prospective teachers bring to teacher education." Michigan State University (unpublished doctoral dissertation).

Ball, D. L. (1990). "Breaking with experience in learning to teach mathematics: The role of a preservice methods course." *For the Learning of Mathematics, 10*(2), 10–16.

Ball, D. L., and McDiarmid, G. W. (1987). "Understanding how teachers' knowledge changes." *National Center for Research Teacher Education Colloquy, 1*(1), 9–13.

Ball, D. L., and McDiarmid, G. W. (1990). "The subject-matter preparation of teachers." In W. R. Houston (ed.), *Handbook of research on teacher education.* New York: Macmillan.

Belenky, M. F., Clinchy, B. M., Goldberger, N. R., and Tarule, J. M. (1986). *Women's ways of knowing: The development of self, voice, and mind.* New York: Basic Books.

Berliner, D. C. (1986). "In pursuit of the expert pedagogue." *Educational Researcher, 15*(7), 5–13.

Biklen, S. K. (1983). *Teaching as an occupation for women: A case study of an elementary school.* Syracuse, N.Y.: Education Designs Group.

Bird, T., and Anderson, L. M. (1992). *How three prospective teachers construed three cases of teaching.* (Research Report 94–3). East Lansing, Mich.: National Center for Research on Teacher Learning.

Bird, T., Anderson, L. M., Sullivan, B. A., and Swidler, S. A. (1993). "Pedagogical balancing acts: Problems in influencing prospective teachers' beliefs." *Teaching and Teacher Education, 9*(3), 253–267.

Book, C. L., Byers, J., and Freeman, D. J. (1983). "Student expectations and teacher education traditions with which we can and cannot live." *Journal of Teacher Education, 34*(1), 9–13.

Book, C. L., and Freeman, D. J. (1986). "Differences in entry characteristics of elementary and secondary teacher candidates." *Journal of Teacher Education, 37*(2), 47–54.

Borko, H., Livingston, C., McCaleb, J., and Mauro, L. (1988). "Student teachers' planning and post-lesson reflections: Patterns and implications for teacher preparation." In J. Calderhead (ed.), *Teachers' professional learning.* Washington, D.C.: Falmer Press.

Brookhart, S. M., and Freeman, D. J. (1992). "Characteristics of entering teacher candidates." *Review of Educational Research, 62*(1), 37–60.

Brophy, J. E. (1989). *Advances in research on teaching.* Greenwich, Conn.: JAI Press.

Brown, J. S., Collins, A., and Duguid, P. (1989). "Situated cognition and the culture of learning." *Educational Researcher, 18*(1), 32–43.

Calderhead, J. (1991). "The nature and growth of knowledge in student teaching." *Teaching and Teacher Education, 7*(5/6), 531–535.

Calderhead, J., and Robson, M. (1991). "Images of teaching: Student teachers' early conceptions of classroom practice." *Teaching and Teacher Education, 7*, 1–8.

Carnegie Forum on Education and the Economy (1986). *A nation prepared: Teachers for the 21st century.* New York: Carnegie Foundation.

Carter, K. (1990). "Teachers' knowledge and learning to teach." In W. R. Houston (ed.), *Handbook of research on teacher education.* New York: Macmillan.

Carter, K., and Doyle, W. (1987). "Teachers' knowledge structures and comprehension processes." In J. Calderhead (ed.), *Exploring teachers' thinking.* London: Cassell Educational.

Carter, K., and others (1987). "Processing and using information about students: A study of expert, novice and postulant teachers." *Teaching and Teacher Education, 3*, 145–157.

Cazden, C. B., and Mehan, H. (1989). "Principles from sociology and anthropology: Context, code, classroom, and culture." In M. C. Reynolds (ed.), *Knowledge base for the beginning teacher.* Elmsford, N.Y.: Pergamon Press.

Cobb, P. (1994). "Where is the mind? Constructivist and sociocultural perspectives on mathematical development." *Educational Researcher, 23*(7), 13–20.

Cochran-Smith, M. (1991). "Learning to teach against the grain." *Harvard Educational Review, 61*(3), 279–310.

Cohen, D. K. (1988). "Teaching practice: *Plus ça change . . .*" In P. W. Jackson (ed.), *Contributing to educational change: Perspectives on research and practice.* Berkeley, Calif.: McCutchan.

Cohen, D. K. (1989). "Practice and policy: Notes on the history of instruction." In D. Warren (ed.), *American teachers: Histories of a profession at work.* New York: Macmillan.

Collins, A., Brown, J. S., and Newman, S. E. (1989). "Cognitive apprenticeship: Teaching the craft of reading, writing and mathematics." In L. B. Resnick (ed.), *Knowing, learning and instruction: Essays in honor of Robert Glaser.* Hillsdale, N.J.: Erlbaum.

Cuban, L. (1984). *How teachers taught: Constancy and change in American classrooms, 1890–1980.* White Plains, N.Y.: Longman.

Doyle, W. (1986). "Classroom organization and management." In M. C. Wittrock (ed.), *Handbook of research on teaching.* (3rd ed.). New York: Macmillan.

Doyle, W. (1990). Classroom knowledge as a foundation for teaching. *Teachers College Record, 91*, 247–260.

Duckworth, E. (1987). *The having of wonderful ideas.* New York: Teachers College Press.

Elbaz, F. (1983). *Teacher thinking: A study of practical knowledge.* London: Croom Helm.

Featherstone, H. (1993). "Learning from the first years of classroom teaching: The journey in, the journey out." *Teachers College Press, 95*(1), 93–112.

Feiman-Nemser, S., and Buchmann, M. (1986). "The first year of teacher preparation: Transition to pedagogical thinking?" *Journal of Curriculum Studies, 18*(3), 239–256.

Feiman-Nemser, S., and Featherstone, H. (1992). *Exploring teaching: Reinventing an introductory course.* New York: Teachers College Press.

Feistritzer, C. E. (1986). *Teacher crisis: Myth or reality?* Washington, D.C.: National Center for Education Information.

Field, K. (1979). *Teacher development: A study of the stages in the development of teachers.* Brookline, Mass.: Brookline Teacher Center.

Floden, R. E., and Buchmann, M. (1993). "Between routines and anarchy: Preparing teachers for uncertainty." In M. Buchmann and R. E. Floden (eds.), *Detachment and concern: Conversations in the philosophy of teaching and teacher education.* New York: Teachers College Press.

Florio, S., and Lensmire, T. J. (1990). "Transforming prospective teachers' ideas about writing instruction." *Journal of Curriculum Studies, 22,* 277–289.

Fuller, F., and Bown, O. H. (1975). "On becoming a teacher." In K. Ryan (ed.), *Teacher education.* (74th yearbook of the National Society for the Study of Education). Chicago: University of Chicago Press.

Gilligan, C. (1982). *In a different voice: Psychological theory and women's development.* Cambridge, Mass.: Harvard University Press.

Grossman, P. L. (1990). *The making of a teacher.* New York: Teachers College Press.

Grossman, P. L., Wilson, S. M., and Shulman, L. S. (1989). "Teachers of substance: Subject matter knowledge for teaching." In M. C. Reynolds (ed.), *Knowledge base for the beginning teacher.* Elmsford, N.Y.: Pergamon Press.

Heaton, R. (1994). "Creating and studying a practice of teaching elementary mathematics for understanding." Michigan State University (unpublished doctoral dissertation).

Heaton, R., and Lampert, M. (1993). "Learning to hear voices: Inventing a new pedagogy of teacher education." In D. K. Cohen, M. W. McLaughlin, and J. E. Talbert (eds.), *Teaching for understanding: Challenges for policy and practice.* San Francisco: Jossey-Bass.

Holland, D. C., and Eisenhart, M. A. (1990). *Educated in romance: Woman, achievement and college culture.* Chicago: University of Chicago Press.

Hollingsworth, S. (1989). "Prior beliefs and cognitive change in learning to teach." *American Educational Research Journal, 26*(2), 160–189.

Holt-Reynolds, D. (1992). "Personal history-based beliefs as relevant prior knowledge in course work." *American Educational Research Journal, 29,* 325–349.

Huberman, M. (1989). The professional life cycle of teachers. *Teachers College Record, 91,* 31–57.

Interstate New Teacher Assessment and Support Consortium (1993). *Model standards for beginning teacher licensing and development: A resource for state dialogue.* Washington, D.C.: Council of Chief State School Officers.

Jackson, P. W. (1968). *Life in classrooms.* Austin, Texas: Holt, Rinehart & Winston.

Jackson, P. W. (1986). "On knowing how to teach." In *The practice of teaching.* New York: Teachers College Press.

Kagan, D. M. (1992). "Professional growth among preservice and beginning teachers." *Review of Educational Research, 62*(2), 129–169.

Kennedy, M. M. (1987). "Inexact sciences: Professional development and the education of expertise." In E. Z. Rothkopf (ed.), *Review of research in education,* Vol. 14. Washington, D.C.: American Educational Research Association.

Kennedy, M. M. (1991). *Teaching academic subjects to diverse learners.* New York: Teachers College Press.

Kennedy, M. M. (1993). *An agenda for research on teacher learning.* East Lansing, Mich.: National Center for Research on Teacher Learning.

Laird, S. (1988). "Reforming 'women's true profession': A case of 'feminist pedagogy' in teacher education. *Harvard Education Review, 58*(4), 449–463.

Lampert, M. (1985). "How do teachers manage to teach?" *Harvard Educational Review, 55*(2), 178–194.

Lampert, M. (1992). "Practices and problems in teaching authentic mathematics in school." In F. K. Oser, A. Dick, and J. L. Patry (eds.), *Effective and responsible teaching: The new synthesis.* San Francisco: Jossey-Bass.

Lave, J. (1988). *Cognition in practice.* Cambridge: Cambridge University Press.

Lave, J., and Wenger, E. (1991). *Situated learning: Legitimate peripheral participation.* Cambridge: Cambridge University Press.

Leinhardt, G. (1988). "Situated knowledge and expertise in teaching." In J. Calderhead (ed.), *Teachers' professional learning.* Washington, D.C.: Falmer Press.

Leinhardt, G., and Greeno, J. (1986). "The cognitive skill of teaching." *Journal of Educational Psychology, 78,* 75–95.

Leinhardt, G., and Smith, D. (1985). "Expertise in mathematics instruction: Subject matter knowledge." *Journal of Educational Psychology, 77,* 247–271.

Livingston, C., and Borko, H. (1989). "Expert/novice differences in teaching: A cognitive analysis and implications for teacher education." *Journal of Teacher Education, 40*(4), 36–42.

Lortie, D. C. (1975). *Schoolteacher: A sociological study.* Chicago: University of Chicago Press.

McDade, L. A. (1988). "Knowing the 'right stuff': Attrition, gender and scientific literacy." *Anthropology and Education Quarterly, 19,* 93–114.

McDiarmid, G. W. (1990). "Liberal arts: Will more result in better subject matter understanding?" *Theory into Practice, 29*(1), 21–29.

McDiarmid, G. W. (1991). "What do prospective teachers need to know about culturally different children?" In M. M. Kennedy (ed.), *Teaching academic subjects to diverse learners.* New York: Teachers College Press.

McDiarmid, G. W. (1992). "Tilting at webs of belief: Field experiences as a means of breaking with experience." In S. Feiman-Nemser and H. Featherstone (eds.), *Exploring teaching: Reinventing an introductory course.* New York: Teachers College Press.

McDiarmid, G. W., Ball, D. L., and Anderson, C. R. (1989). "Why staying one chapter ahead doesn't really work: Subject-specific pedagogy." In M. C. Reynolds (ed.), *Knowledge base for the beginning teacher.* Elmsford, N.Y.: Pergamon Press.

National Board for Professional Teaching Standards (1990). *Toward high and rigorous standards for the teaching profession: Initial policies and perspectives of the National Board for Professional Teaching Standards.* (2nd ed.). Washington, D.C.: National Board for Professional Teaching Standards.

National Center for Research on Teacher Education (1991). *Teacher education and learning to teach: Final report.* East Lansing, Mich.: National Center for Research on Teacher Education.

Nemser, S. (1983). "Learning to teach." In L. S. Shulman and G. Sykes (eds.), *Handbook of teaching and policy.* White Plains, N.Y.: Longman.

Nesbitt, R. E., and Ross, L. (1980). *Human inference: Strategies and shortcomings of social judgement.* Englewood Cliffs, N.J.: Prentice Hall.

Nespor, J. (1987). "The role of beliefs in the practice of teaching." *Journal of Curriculum Studies, 19*(4), 317–328.

Paine, L. (1989). *Orientation toward diversity: What do prospective teachers bring?* (Research Report no. 89–9). East Lansing, Mich.: National Center for Research on Teacher Education.

Posner, G. J., Strike, K. A., Hewson, P., and Hertzog, W. (1982). "Accommodation of a scientific conception: Toward a theory of conceptual change." *Science Education, 66,* 211–227.

Resnick, L. B. (1987). "Learning in school and out." *Educational Researcher, 16*(9), 13–20.

Resnick, L. B. (1989). Introduction. In L. B. Resnick (ed.), *Knowing, learning and instruction.* Hillsdale, N.J.: Erlbaum.

Reynolds, A. (1992). "What is competent beginning teaching? A review of the literature." *Review of Educational Research, 62*(1), 1–35.

Reynolds, M. C. (ed.) (1989). *Knowledge base for the beginning teacher.* Elmsford, N.Y.: Pergamon Press.

Richardson, V. (1994). "Conducting research on practice." *Educational Researcher, 23*(5), 5–10.

Schön, D. A. (1983). *The reflective practitioner.* New York: Basic Books.

Schön, D. A. (1987). *Educating the reflective practitioner.* San Francisco: Jossey-Bass.

Schwab, J. J. (1976). "Education and the state: Learning community." In *Great Ideas Today.* Chicago: Encyclopaedia Britannica.

Shulman, L. S. (1986). "Paradigms and research programs in the study of teaching: A contemporary perspective." In M. C. Wittrock (ed.), *Handbook of research on teaching.* (3rd ed.). New York: Macmillan.

Shulman, L. S. (1987). "Knowledge and teaching: Foundations of the new reform." *Harvard Educational Review, 57*(1), 1–22.

Stephens, J. M. (1969). "Research in the preparation of teachers: Background factors that must be considered." In J. Herbert and D. P. Ausubel (eds.), *Psychology in teacher preparation.* Toronto: Ontario Institute for Studies in Education. (Monograph Series no. 5).

Strike, K. A., and Posner, G. J. (1985). "A conceptual change view of learning and understanding." In L.H.T. West and A. L. Pines (eds.), *Cognitive structure and conceptual change.* San Diego, Calif.: Academic Press.

Sykes, G., and Bird, T. (1992). "Teacher education and the case idea." *Review of Research in Education, 18,* 457–521.

Tabachnick, B. R., Popkewitz, T. S., and Zeichner, K. M. (1979–1980). "Teacher education and the professional perspectives of student teachers." *Interchange, 10*(4), 12–29.

Tharp, R., and Gallimore, R. (1988). *Rousing minds to life.* Cambridge: Cambridge University Press.

Tom, A. R., and Valli, L. (1990). "Professional knowledge for teachers." In W. R. Houston (ed.), *Handbook of research on teacher education.* New York: Macmillan.

Vygotsky, L. (1978). *Mind and society.* Cambridge, Mass.: Harvard University Press.

Watts, H. (1980). *Starting out, moving on, running ahead, or how the teachers' center can attend to stages in teachers' development.* (Teachers' Centers Exchange Occasional Paper no. 8). San Francisco: Far West Laboratory for Educational Research and Development.

Weinstein, C. S. (1988). "Preservice teachers' expectations about the first year of teaching." *Teaching and Teacher Education, 4*(1), 31–41.

Wilcox, S. K., Schram, P., Lappan, G., and Lanier, P. (1992). "The role of a learning community in changing preservice teachers' knowledge and beliefs in teacher education." *For the Learning of Mathematics, 2,* 31–39.

Wildman, M. T., Niles, J. A., Magliaro, S. G., and McLaughlin, R. A. (1989). "Teaching and learning to teach: The two roles of beginning teachers." *Elementary School Journal, 89*(4), 471–494.

Wilson, S. M., Shulman, L. S., and Richert, A. E. (1987). " '150 different ways' of knowing: Representations of knowledge in teaching." In J. Calderhead (ed.), *Exploring teachers' thinking.* London: Cassell Educational.

Wilson, S. M., and Wineburg, S. S. (1988). "Peering at history from different lenses: The role of disciplinary perspectives in the teaching of American history." *Teachers College Record, 89,* 525–539.

Wright, B., and Tuska, S. (1968). "From dream to life in the psychology of becoming a teacher." *School Review, 76,* 253–293.

Zimpher, N. L. (1989). "The RATE project: A profile of teacher education students." *Journal of Teacher Education, 40*(6), 27–30.

Annotated Bibliography

Feiman-Nemser, S., and Featherstone, H. (1992). *Exploring teaching: Reinventing an introductory course.* New York: Teachers College Press.
    Written by teacher educators, this book provides examples of learning opportunities designed to transform prospective teachers' entering beliefs about teaching, learning, subject matter, and schooling. Besides providing insights into how teacher educators are thinking about their own teaching, the book offers concrete examples of university-based learning opportunities that embody many of the features of cognitive apprenticeship and conceptual change teaching.

Grossman, P. L. (1990). *The making of a teacher: Teacher knowledge and teacher education.* New York: Teachers College Press.
    This book focuses on how secondary teachers acquire and develop subject matter knowledge and pedagogical content knowledge. It is organized around cases of six prospective English teachers, three with professional preparation and three without. While all six teachers have a strong background in English, those with professional preparation were able to reconceptualize their subject for purposes of teaching it. The cases show that what teachers learn from experience about teaching English to adolescents depends on the knowledge and beliefs they bring to that experience. One chapter describes the content and pedagogy of a curriculum and instruction course designed to help prospective teachers learn to teach English in responsive ways.

Heaton, R., and Lampert, M. (1993). "Learning to hear voices: Inventing a new pedagogy of teacher education." In D. K. Cohen, M. W. McLaughlin, and J. E. Talbert (eds.), *Teaching for understanding: Challenges for policy and practice.* San Francisco: Jossey-Bass.
    This chapter describes a unique teacher educational intervention designed to help a successful, experienced elementary teacher learn to teach mathematics in new ways. Written by the learning teacher and her mentor, it gives teacher educators an image of a practice-centered pedagogy that is all too rare in teacher education whether at the preservice, induction, or inservice levels. While some aspects of this intervention are unique, teacher educators can still get insights about what learning to teach for understanding entails and how teachers can be helped to develop this kind of practice. In terms of our discussion of learning to teach, this reading integrates a consideration of "what" and "how."

Kennedy, M. M. (1987). "Inexact sciences: Professional development and the education of expertise." In E. Z. Rothkopf (ed.), *Review of research in education,* Vol. 14. Washington, D.C.: American Educational Research Association.
    Kennedy identifies four ways that professions have defined the expertise critical to professional performance. These include the application of general principles, technical skill, critical analysis, and deliberative action. Kennedy argues that teaching involves deliberative action, the ability to connect knowledge to action. If we define the "what" of learning to teach as deliberative action, then we need to provide the kinds of professional learning opportunities that will help teachers develop this ability.

Reynolds, M. C. (ed.) (1989). *Knowledge base for the beginning teacher.* Elmsford, N.Y.: Pergamon Press.
    Despite the problems of framing a knowledge base for teaching around discrete domains of knowledge, this book still provides a good overview of important categories of knowledge that bear on teaching. It can help teacher educators think about what is

important for beginning teachers to know about subject matter, students, classroom culture, evaluation, learning, and so on. The handbook does not say much about how teachers can be helped to learn this.

Tharp, R., and Gallimore, R. (1988). *Rousing minds to life.* Cambridge: Cambridge University Press.
This book talks about how Vygotsky's ideas can be applied to classroom teaching and learning and to teacher education and teacher learning. The authors present a unified educational theory rooted in cognitive and cultural psychology, which they illustrate with examples of teaching, classroom, and school organization from the Kamehameha Elementary Program (KEEP). Of special interest is the discussion of teacher learning through assisted performance in chapters ten and eleven that provides a detailed case and a theoretical framework for the "how" of learning to teach.

CHAPTER FOUR

THE CONCEPT OF A KNOWLEDGE BASE

ROBERT DONMOYER

The publication of this book can be seen as both a relatively routine and a somewhat audacious act—routine because since the beginning of this century scholars have attempted to articulate knowledge that could provide the basis for professional rather than political control of education; audacious because, to put the matter simply, knowledge today is not what it used to be.

Today a growing number of scholars argue that no knowledge is objective and that all knowledge is inevitably political. This cadre includes philosophers and historians of science such as Kuhn (1962), Feyerabend (1970), and Toulmin (1983, 1972); sociologists of knowledge (Berger and Luckmann, 1967; Young, 1971; Gusfield, 1976); critical theorists (Williams, 1963; Habermas, 1984–1987, 1978); feminist scholars (Harding, 1991, 1986; Haraway, 1989, 1988; Hesse, 1980); postmodern social critics (Foucault, 1972; Lyotard, 1988); avant-garde anthropologists (Marcus and Clifford 1986; Tyler, 1987); African-American scholars (Stanfield, 1985; Gordon, Miller, and Rollock, 1990); and a host of education scholars influenced by a variety of scholarly traditions (Apple, 1979, 1982; Donmoyer, 1983, 1985, 1990c; Eisner, 1988, 1990; Giroux, 1981; Gitlin, Siegel, and Boru, 1988; Lather, 1986, 1991; Guba and Lincoln, 1989; Scheurich and Imber, 1991; Wexler, 1982). This argument appears to undermine the traditional rationale for professional control of educational decision making and suggests those who put together a book purporting to articulate a knowledge base about anything in the social realm are either incredibly naïve or engaged in a clandestine political act.

Furthermore, it is not simply academics who have become skeptical about the possibility of generating objective knowledge and the desirability of professional control of education. Skepticism about these matters can be found in popular culture as well. Recently, I sat in theaters on both coasts and heard audiences respond with knowing laughter when Lily Tomlin, as Trudy the Bag Lady, referred to reality as "nothin' but a collective hunch" and "a primitive method of crowd control that got out of hand" (Wagner, 1987, p. 18).

A similar sort of skepticism about professionalism is evident in many recent school reform proposals. School reforms recently implemented in Chicago, for instance, were expressly designed to minimize professional control and to reinstitute the sort of local, layperson control of education that reformers during the first part of this century tried to eliminate. In short, in Chicago and elsewhere, yesterday's heroes (educational professionals) are increasingly seen as villains, and yesterday's solution (professional control) is now often seen as the problem.

The purpose of this chapter therefore is to briefly review the argument linking knowledge and politics—the argument that seemingly undermines the case for professional control—and then to consider four possible responses to it. Any one of these responses, if deemed adequate, could reestablish, at least in some form, the professional/political distinction accepted as self-evident throughout most of this century. An adequate response should also help legitimate current efforts to establish a knowledge base in the areas of teaching and teacher education as well as the general notion of professionalism in education.

Before proceeding with this agenda, however, I will place the current efforts to articulate a knowledge base in the areas of teaching and teacher education in a historical context and show how the various efforts represented in this book are both different from and similar to earlier efforts to articulate a knowledge base in the field of education.

A Historical Perspective

The attempts in this book to articulate a knowledge base for teacher education differ in significant ways from earlier attempts; nevertheless, there are sufficient similarities to earlier efforts to make the book's general purpose problematic for scholars who have talked about an inevitable linkage between knowledge and politics.

Early-Twentieth-Century Thinking

In 1910, E. L. Thorndike authored the lead article in the inaugural issue of the *Journal of Educational Psychology*. He wrote:

> A complete science of psychology would tell every fact about everyone's intellect and character and behavior, would tell the cause of every change in human nature, would tell the result which every educational force—every act of every person that changed any other or the agent himself—would have. It would aid

us to use human beings for the world's welfare with the same surety of the result that we now have when we use falling bodies or chemical elements. In proportion as we get such a science we shall become masters of our own souls as we are now masters of heat and light. Progress toward such a science is being made [p. 6].

Thorndike was hardly a voice crying in the wilderness during the first part of this century. A belief in the power of scientific research was virtually an article of faith of the progressive movement. Another well-known progressive, economist George Counts (1926), declared, "If in the history of the development of educational technique the present period is to be marked off from the periods which have gone before, the reason will be found in the fact that it has recognized the importance of scientific method and has sought to use that method in the solution of educational problems" (pp. 87–88).

Counts wrote this in an article contained in the *Twenty-Sixth-Yearbook of the National Society for the Study of Education,* which dealt with curriculum making; contributors were a virtual who's who of progressive educators concerned with questions of curriculum and teaching. In reviewing the *Twenty-Sixth Yearbook* years later, Walker (1975) observed that its contributors not only "affirmed the value of scientific method in curriculum making" but that they did so "with greater unanimity than they could muster in favor of any other explicit commitment" (p. 10). At another point, Walker observed, "Science's competitors as grounds of appeal for justification of curricular practice—judgment of experienced persons, tradition, popular preference, educational ideals or philosophies—were either rejected outright by such pejorative labeling as 'subjective opinion,' 'blind traditionalism,' or 'vested interests,' or subordinated to science" (p. 12).

Given the emerging curriculum field's faith in science, it is not surprising that Franklin Bobbitt began his classic 1924 text, *How to Make a Curriculum,* by likening the work of curriculum development to work in the applied science of engineering. Social engineering imagery also dominated thinking within the field of educational administration (Callahan, 1964). Early figures in this field were particularly impressed with the notion of scientific management that had been employed by business to make factories more productive. Elwood P. Cubberly, the father of the field of educational administration, explicitly likened schools to factories and explicitly endorsed the notions of scientific management: "Our schools are, in a sense, factories in which the raw products (children) are to be shaped and fashioned into products to meet the various demands of life. The specifications for manufacturing come from the demands for the twentieth-century civilization, and it is the business of the school to build its pupils according to the specialized machinery, continuous measurement of production to see if it is according to specifications, the elimination of waste in manufacture, and a large variety in the output" (Cubberly, 1909, p. 338).

Early educational reformers' enthusiasm for science and for applied scientific fields such as engineering must be seen, in part at least, as a response to a very real and very obvious problem: political control of education. The evils of political control were particularly obvious in urban areas where brutal ward politics and corrupt political machines were commonplace. Tyack (1974), for instance, documents the sort of behavior that might make even a Tammany Hall politician blush: teachers buying their positions from political bosses; politically powerful textbook publishers engineering the hiring of particular school superintendents who were then expected to purchase the publishers' wares; unscrupulous textbook salesmen using prostitutes to entice school board members into illicit liaisons that could later be used as blackmail. Given such a context, it is not surprising that reformers such as Bobbitt and Cubberly sought to substitute professional for political control of education and that scholars such as Thorndike were intent on creating a knowledge base that would make professional control defensible.[1]

Successes, Failures, and Successful Failures

Reformers generally succeeded in maximizing professional control and minimizing political influence. Ultimate control of course remained in the hands of publicly elected school boards. Over time, however, members of these boards began to be elected at large rather than by local wards. One result was the election of board members who tended to be less interested in the day-to-day running of schools. Board members elected at large also tended to share the values of university-trained educational professionals (including the valuing of professionals) and consequently were inclined to turn responsibility for educational decision making over to them (Tyack, 1974). All of this occurred, ironically, even though scholars failed to provide the sort of knowledge base that Thorndike had promised and that was presupposed by those who argued for professional control.

The search for such a knowledge base went on, however. As late as the 1970s, federal policy makers funded elaborate planned variation studies, which policy analysts assured them would tell which policies and programs were most effective (Rivlin, 1971). Within education, Project Follow Through (Abt Associates, 1977; Haney and Villaume, 1977) is the best-known example of a planned variation study. The goal of this program was to determine the relative effectiveness of different early childhood education models in educating disadvantaged (the adjective of choice of the time) students.

The continuing dominance of Thorndike's thinking is also quite obvious in Thorndike's highly influential field of educational psychology throughout the first three-quarters of this century. Until the mid 1970s, for instance, research on teaching relied almost exclusively on a process-product paradigm oriented toward identifying teacher behaviors that correlated with and presumably caused greater amounts of student learning (Good, Biddle, and Brophy, 1975).

Now what is interesting about Thorndike's work, and later work such as process-product studies of teaching, is the influence it has had *in the absence of any very definitive results.* It was Thorndike's *notion* of a knowledge base, for example, not the actual existence of one, which was instrumental in promoting the cause of professional control.

Similarly, process-product studies of teaching provided precious little insight that was not already available through common sense; even the statistically significant findings that were produced were only true at the aggregate level and could in no way be applied to particular individuals or particular groups of students or teachers (see Donmoyer and Kos, 1993). Still, the a priori assumptions and images that guided work within the Thorndike tradition were quite influential in terms of how we conceptualized the role of research in education and even how we conceptualized teaching and teacher education. The role of research was to discover and validate formulas for practice, and practice itself was often thought of in terms of systems, techniques, routines, and standard operating procedures. Indeed, an array of past educational reforms such as teacher-proof curricula and competency-based teacher education were at least partially legitimated by the social engineering imagery that served as the a priori grounding of the Thorndike research tradition, even though that research tradition netted very little in the way of definitive results.

Rethinking Fundamental Assumptions

By the 1970s, the absence of results had begun to be a cause for concern. The traditional defense, which asserted that educational research was a young science that simply needed time to provide the sort of definitive findings promised by Thorndike, became less than convincing to many. A team of top-ranking scholars commissioned by the Ford Foundation to review Project Follow Through evaluation data took note of the probabilistic nature of those data. They pointed out, for instance, that the approaches to early childhood education that aggregate data suggested were most effective were *not* effective in all places, and approaches that aggregate data certified as relatively ineffective were in certain settings among the most effective of all the strategies studied. The team concluded that this aspect of the results "should be honored widely and serve as a basis of educational policy. Local schools do seem to make a difference. The peculiarities of individual teachers, schools, neighborhoods, and homes influence pupils' achievement far more than whatever is captured by labels such as basic skills or affective education" (House, Glass, McLean, and Walker, 1978, p. 462).

Even Thorndike's field of education psychology began to undergo some rather dramatic changes. By the mid 1970s, for instance, a new line of research on teaching had emerged, one that focused on the complex process of teacher thinking rather than discrete teaching behaviors (for example, Clark and Yinger, 1977; Shulman and Lanier, 1977). In 1978, even Gage, a die-hard supporter of process-product models of research on teaching, was forced to acknowledge that such research could at best only provide a general knowledge base for teaching and that teacher artistry would always be required to adjust and shape that knowledge base to the needs of particular students and particular situations.

Today, process-product studies are difficult to find within the contemporary research literature on teaching. That literature is now dominated by studies of teacher thinking, a subject that is normally investigated with methods more associated with the largely descriptive discipline of anthropology or descriptively oriented work in cognitive psychology than with Thorndike's social engineering-oriented version of educational psychology.

The Case of Cronbach

The shifts in perspective outlined above probably can be seen most clearly by tracing the career of the eminent educational psychologist Lee Cronbach. By the 1950s, Cronbach had already established himself as a skilled player of Thorndike's research game. In 1957, however, Cronbach told the American Psychological Association that the complexity of human phenomena required a minor alteration in the traditional game plan. Rather than searching for laws that were universal and context-free, Cronbach argued, researchers should attempt to identify cause-and-effect relationships between certain educational treatments on the one hand and certain types of individuals (in Cronbach's terms, individuals with certain "aptitudes") on the other. In colloquial terms, he made the case for researchers attending to learning styles.

In the mid 1970s, however, after nearly twenty years of searching for "aptitude x treatment interactions" and nearly twenty years of frustration brought on by "inconsistent findings coming from roughly similar inquiries," Cronbach (1975) told the American Psychological Association, "Once we attend to interactions, we enter a hall of mirrors that extends to infinity. However far we carry our analysis—to third order or fifth order or any other—untested interactions of still higher order can be envisioned" (p. 119).

Compounding the problem of complexity is the problem of culture. Cronbach cited Bronfenbrenner's historical look at child-rearing practices of middle- and lower-class parents to demonstrate the significance of this variable: class differences documented in the 1950s were often just the reverse of practices that had been observed in the 1930s. Cronbach concluded, "The trouble, as I see it, is that we cannot store up generalizations and constructs for ultimate assembly into a network. It is as if we needed a gross of dry cells to power an engine and could only make one a month. The energy would leak out of the first cells before we had half the battery completed. So it is with the potency of our generalizations" (p. 123).

In his 1975 article, Cronbach emphasized that the social world was no less lawful than the physical world. The problem was that social laws were too complex and the social world too changeable to identify them. By the early 1980s, however, Cronbach had rejected even the notion of social laws. He began suggesting that the entire cause-and-effect way of thinking that undergirds the social engineering view of professionalism and traditional view of research is an inappropriate way to characterize social phenomena. By 1982, in fact, Cronbach had arrived at a position similar to that of symbolic interactionists (Blumer, 1969) and ethnomethodologists (Garfinkel, 1967): human action is constructed, not caused; those who expect research to produce the sort of definitive cause-and-effect generalizations that he and Thorndike had promised in earlier days are simply, in Cronbach's words, "waiting for Godot."

An Emerging Consensus

Not everyone in the field of teacher education in particular or education more generally has embraced a position as radical as Cronbach's. Today, however, there is a general distrust of systems and standard operating procedures as solutions to educational problems. There is also a growing recognition of the importance of teachers and the need for teachers to have both the skill and the flexibility to respond appropriately to the idiosyncracies of particular students and particular classrooms (Donmoyer and Kos, 1993).

Implicit within this need-for-flexibility argument is also an altered view of how knowledge contributes to professional expertise: today, knowledge is more likely to be seen as a heuristic to guide practice rather than as a source of formulas that dictate what professionals are to do (Donmoyer and Kos, 1993). In the popular vernacular, knowledge must be used in a context of teacher empowerment, not as the basis for organizing educational factories.

This book for the most part reflects this new awareness. (The very fact that it is addressed to teacher educators rather than school administrators or those who educate school administrators is one indication of this fact.) Thus, this book also represents a bit of a departure from earlier attempts to articulate a knowledge base in education.

There are some important similarities, however. Those who have put together this book share with earlier reformers a belief in professionals and a belief that knowledge is a primary source (possibly even *the* primary source) of professional expertise. The professionals in question differ, of course. Teachers are now front and center, whereas in the past they played a supporting role to school administrators. Knowledge, too, plays a significantly different role in grounding professionalism; it is now seen as contributing to the clinical ability of teachers rather than as a source of systems and standard operating procedures. Still, the fundamental faith in expertise and scientific knowledge as a source of that expertise has not been abandoned. It is this very faith of course that is problematic for those who see an inevitable link between knowledge and politics.

The next section briefly summarizes the argument linking knowledge and politics, and the subsequent section outlines and critiques four possible responses to it—attempts to salvage the notion of professionalism in light of the contemporary critique of knowledge.

Knowledge as Politics

As noted at the outset of this chapter, various scholarly traditions have developed theories linking knowledge and politics. The argument that will be presented here has certainly been informed by this theoretical work but will be presented in relatively simple, straightforward terms. Wherever possible, concrete examples from the field of education, rather than references to abstract theory, will be used to make key points.[2]

A Different Conception of Politics

Those who argue that knowledge is inevitably political are not talking about the sort of conscious, self-interested Machiavellian activity that so troubled educational reforms during the first part of this century. Those who see an inevitable linkage between knowledge and politics view politics as something that is much more subtle and much more indirect, a politics of perceptions and procedures, of standard operating ways of thinking and doing things. This sort of politics is deeply embedded in culture and the culturally sanctioned categories and conduct that members of a culture take to be natural and inevitable.

One can begin to grasp how this subtle, indirect politics operates by attending to a phenomenon that is now recognized by a wide array of disciplines and fields of study, though different disciplines and fields often talk about the phenomenon in somewhat different ways. Philosophers talk of paradigms or conceptual frameworks; psychologists, of cognitive structures or schemata; anthropologists, of cultural constructs; literary critics, of interpretive frameworks. None of these terms is a precise synonym for any other, of course. Each, however, refers to the fact that we do not have direct access to empirical reality, that the mind is not a blank slate, that what we know, even in rigorous research, is in part a product of the a priori assumptions we make and the categories and language we employ.

Psychologist Ulric Neisser (1976) demonstrated long ago that even the most rudimentary acts of perception are influenced by a priori assumptions, but the impact of these assumptions is most visible when we examine the effect of language on thought and action. The significance of language for a field like education can be demonstrated by considering how Piagetian and Skinnerian psychologists would approach evaluating a kindergarten program. If the focus of the evaluation were on outcomes, for instance, Piagetians would undoubtedly want to examine variables related to the central Piagetian concept of conservation.[3] Because there is no equivalent concept in Skinner's learning theory, behaviorists would undoubtedly choose very different outcome variables to study.

Even if Skinnerians attempted to focus on the phenomena of conservation, it is unlikely that their theoretical translation of this concept would be acceptable to Piagetians. Indeed, Piagetians and Skinnerians see the processes of teaching and learning in fundamentally different ways. For Skinnerians, learning occurs because someone has carefully structured a curriculum built around incrementally sequenced behaviors to be mastered and reinforced. For Piagetians, learning is itself a process of structuring that must be engaged in by learners themselves. Teaching cannot be turned into a mechanical process of reinforcement choreographed in advance by a curriculum developer. Indeed, in Piagetian thought there is no analog for the Skinnerian concept of reinforcement. The best a teacher can do, from a Piagetian perspective, is create a rich environment with which students can interact, allow students the freedom to interact, and then fashion instruction improvisationally to respond—frequently in the form of questions—to what students do and say.

It is important to note that the problems of language and meaning just alluded to can arise even when we eschew the use of formal theory. The term *learning,* for instance, will mean different things to fundamentalist parents who want the schools to go back to basics and to artists who want schools to promote productive idiosyncracy. Before an evaluator can determine whether program A produces more learning than program B, the evaluator must define learning. The definition selected—whether it comes from formal or folk theory—will influence the evaluator's findings at least as much as the empirical reality being studied.

The situation is further complicated by the fact that evaluators' traditional cause-and-effect way of thinking is inconsistent with certain value orientations within education. Freire (1970), Buber (1965), peace educators such as Galtung (1974), curriculum theorists such as Jardine and Clandinin (1987) and a humanist reading of Dewey (see Kliebard, 1975), for example, suggest that teachers should not manipulate students in a classroom the way scientists manipulate variables in a laboratory; rather than attempting to control students, teachers should engage in dialogue with students, and rather than transmitting predetermined objectives to students, teachers should work with students to jointly construct the curriculum for the class.

These prescriptive theories about what education ought to be are compatible with ethnomethodologists' and symbolic interactionists' descriptive theories of what human action is. Blumer (1969), the father of symbolic interactionism, for example, argued that human beings act toward things on the basis of the meanings that things have for them and that meanings are generated by social interaction; he also argued that meanings are not static but must constantly be constructed and reconstructed by actors during social interaction. Thus, even if meanings and reasons are allowed to substitute for causes in a cause-and-effect explanatory framework—if we treat them, in other words, as independent or possibly as intervening variables—Blumer would not be satisfied. According to Blumer, the cause-and-effect explanatory framework itself sends an inaccurate message regardless of its substantive content.

Whether or not one accepts Blumer's conception of human action, this conception does provide an alternative to a cause-and-effect conception of how the social world operates, and as such it reminds us that the cause-and-effect conception of the social world is just that, a conception. In short, Blumer and like-minded scholars have reinforced an idea put forth by Kant long ago: it is impossible to talk about the nature of reality with any sense of certainty because we can never know reality independent of the cognitive structures that influence our perceptions of it.

The bottom line is that no knowledge is objective; all knowledge, whether we are talking about the folk knowledge of ordinary people or the formal knowledge generated by research, is subjective; it reflects the conceptions and metaphors of the knower. These conceptions and metaphors are not so much determined by the data; rather, they help determine what the data mean and in some instances (for example, in the cases of Piagetian and Skinnerian psychology) even what the data are.[4] In short, the conclusions generated by a study and the recommendations coming out of it will have as much (and often more) to do with a priori assumptions and metaphors employed by the researcher as with the "empirical" phenomena that the researcher studied.

Perceptions, Procedures, and Politics

But what does all of this have to do with politics, a notion that, in commonsense parlance at least, implies a process for allocating scarce resources, for legitimating certain values rather than others, and ultimately for determining who wins and who loses? The answer to this question is suggested by two examples.

Several years ago, elementary school teacher Mark Carter's school district hired some high-priced consultants to develop a teacher evaluation instrument. The consultants developed an instrument based on the findings of teacher effectiveness research. Unfortunately for Mark, his conceptions of teaching and learning differed substantially from the conception held by researchers who design teacher effectiveness studies. Whereas teacher effectiveness studies presumed teaching to be something reasonably equivalent to direct instruction, Mark thought of teaching in the more Piagetian manner described above. Also, the notion of learning operationalized in the dependent variables of most teacher effectiveness studies differed radically from Mark's view of learning, which incorporated attitudinal and affective factors and even in the cognitive realm emphasized conceptual understanding and application rather than the mastery of discrete skills.

Not surprisingly, when it was time to evaluate Mark with the district's newly developed instrument, there was a problem. The evaluator kept coming to his classroom and then leaving without administering the instrument. Finally, Mark realized what was wrong: the evaluator was waiting for Mark to "teach," which the evaluation instrument assumed meant standing in front of the class and engaging in direct instruction. Fortunately, this particular story has a happy ending. Mark was a tenured teacher with an admirable track record; hence, he survived his evaluation ordeal. Undoubtedly, however, other teachers with less experience, confidence, and credibility would not have fared so well.

Teachers who follow the "rules" of teacher effectiveness research, of course, could easily find themselves in the same predicament as Mark if a different body of empirical research were used to generate a teacher evaluation instrument. A district could, for instance, base its evaluation instrument on the literature about language acquisition and literacy development (see, for example, DeFord and Harste, 1984), the literature that grounds the whole language movement. If this were the case, teachers like Mark would be the winners and those who taught primarily through direct instruction would be judged inadequate.

In the second example demonstrating the political implications of the analysis presented above, the potential losers are not teachers of a certain philosophical persuasion but rather a group of students who in the past were labeled "disadvantaged." Critics correctly charge that this label often led to a process of "blaming the victim." When the label was uncritically accepted—as it was for a considerable period of time by a large number of educators, including educational researchers who often provided the data to legitimate the use of the label—there was also uncritical acceptance of the "fact" that the disproportionately high failure rate for minority students resulted from inadequacies in the children, their families, and their cultures rather than from inadequacies within the mainstream culture and its schools.

In time, of course, the notion of "culturally different" began to replace the idea of "culturally disadvantaged." This new perspective, however, did not emerge from empirical data; rather, a shift in perspective was a prerequisite for both seeing data differently and seeking different data.

Three Implications

These two examples suggest three things. First, they demonstrate quite clearly that the subtle, indirect process being talked about by those who describe an inevitable link between knowledge and politics does indeed produce winners and losers and therefore is quite compatible with our commonsense notion of politics.

Second, they demonstrate that the sort of politics being talked about by those who see knowledge as inevitably political is indeed quite different from the Machiavellian politics that led earlier reformers to turn to professionals as a way of "taking the schools out of politics." A Machiavellian view assumes that individuals see the world in the same way but have different, often mutually exclusive, interests, which they attempt to maximize through the use of power. The sort of politics being talked about here is a politics of perceptions—a "fascism in our heads," as postmodern scholar Michael Foucault might call it. It is also a politics that plays itself out in our language and in the routines and standard operating procedures of organizational life.

Each of these realms of human experience—our thoughts, words, and "normal" activities—helps legitimate and in turn is legitimated by the others. Together they can create the illusion of reality. They can make humanly constructed artifacts seem natural and inevitable and blind us to alternative ways of thinking, talking, and acting. Hence, although perceptions and procedures can certainly be consciously manipulated to serve Machiavellian purposes (consider, for example, television commercials in most political campaigns), no Machiavellian intent is required for perceptual/procedural politics to allocate resources, legitimate values, and determine winners and losers. This characteristic makes this version of politics more subtle, more difficult to recognize, and therefore potentially more insidious than the sort of Machiavellian politics practiced during the first part of this century.

One final and, given the purposes of this book, crucial implication can be drawn from the two examples presented above: empirical research cannot free us from the spell of perceptual and procedural politics. Indeed, in the two examples presented here, empirical research was at least partially the source of the spell. Therefore, a professionalism grounded in a knowledge of empirical research is not an alternative to political control of education but only a different kind of political control.[5]

Four Responses to the Knowledge-as-Politics Critique

The critique just presented appears to put us on the horns of a dilemma: either we can do what people in places like Chicago are trying to do, that is, reestablish non-professional control of education and in the process open the door to the sort of Machiavellian politics practiced in the past, or we can attempt to perpetuate the illusion that research and evaluation provide an objective basis for making educational decisions and justify professional control of education on the basis of that illusion. The above critique also suggests a related, more immediate problem: given the critique presented above, it would appear that those who put together a book that attempts to articulate a knowledge base for teacher education—or for any other sort of professional activity in the social realm, for that matter—must be either consciously or unconsciously engaged in the process of perpetuating an illusion.

Is there another possibility, a way out of this dilemma? Four responses to the analysis presented in the previous section are implicitly and occasionally explicitly present in the literature. Three are less than adequate; one may have the potential to salvage the political/professional distinction and the notion of professional knowledge, but it will require that we rethink fundamental assumptions about what constitutes professionalism in education and about how educational professionals should be educated.

The Traditional Response

As noted in the historical discussion, educational researchers' traditional response to what has just been said would emphasize the relative immaturity of educational research and the belief that in time empirical solutions will be found to the sort of problems suggested in the examples above. This position was recently resurrected by Murray (1989) in his lead-off chapter for an earlier work sponsored by the American Association of Colleges for Teacher Education (AACTE), *Knowledge Base for the Beginning Teacher.*

Murray is a developmental psychologist with a distinguished publication record in his field. His impressive body of work is not the subject of discussion; rather, the focus here is exclusively on Murray's chapter in the first AACTE *Knowledge Base* book, a chapter that represents a departure from his usual line of scholarship. This chapter is a very visible, quite recent, and well-argued presentation of the traditional point of view.

For instance, Murray (1989) specifically indicates that "the discipline of education still is in its earliest period of development" and cautions "the student of teaching . . . to adopt a skeptical view toward the claims of educational theorists and researchers" (p. 11). He leaves little doubt, however, about what could and should happen in time. "In the end," he writes, "the choice between one model or another of educational change lies in which gives the more truthful account of the changes in question" (p. 7). Elsewhere, he says, "In considering the truth of educational practices as they may be derived from a theory, we must be concerned with the status of three factors: (a) the correctness of the theory, (b) the correctness of the educational practices, and (c) the correctness of the deduction by which the first might generate the second" (pp. 7–8).

To his credit, Murray does acknowledge the existence of value differences within the field of education, but he quickly downplays their significance:

> The clearest educational recommendations from the operant theory for education are programmed instruction, computer-assisted instruction (which is the technological extension of the first), contingency-managed classrooms, and token economies. An often-cited educational recommendation from Piagetian theory (other than the structure of the discipline curriculum innovations) is discovery learning. The premise of discovery learning is that the information pupils discover for themselves will be learned easier and remembered longer than information acquired in some other way. When one teaches by the discovery method, however, one teaches in much the same way as by the operant method. In both cases, the environment (the classroom) is arranged in a way that ensures that some responses by pupils are more likely to occur than others. . . . The differences between these theories may not be great when considering them for educational practice. In a very real sense, the rat in the Skinner box discovers the solution to its thirst just as the laboratory scientist is programmed by his or her laboratory, and so on [p. 9].

Ultimately, Murray's attempt to minimize the significance of paradigmatic differences is less than convincing. Consider, for instance, Murray's claim that, educationally speaking, the difference between Piagetian and behaviorist educational orientations is not great since both orientations are concerned with arranging the environment to promote learning. At some abstract level, of course, Murray's claim is correct; at the level of action, however, the claim obscures far more than it reveals. A teacher trained exclusively in a Piagetian-oriented teacher education program would not be well equipped to work in an operant-oriented school, and vice versa. Furthermore, the outcomes each orientation values are sufficiently different from the outcomes valued by the other to make it highly unlikely that anything resembling a critical experiment could be devised to determine which is the better way of structuring the learning environment. The failed attempts to find a common empirical basis for assessing the relative worth of whole language and traditional approaches to language instruction are instructive in this regard. (See, for example, the Edelsky, 1990/McKenna, Robinson, and Miller, 1990, *Educational Researcher* debate.)

In short, Murray's claim that operant and Piagetian teaching are essentially alike because both kinds of teaching are concerned with structuring the classroom environment to maximize learning is more than a little reminiscent of the claim that Adolf Hitler and Pope John XXIII are the same because both were skilled politicians who presided over complex bureaucracies. This comparison also is not wrong; it obscures so much more than it reveals, however, that the comparison seems pointless.

Equally problematic is the traditional view's cavalier treatment of the notion of truth and its equally cavalier assumption that scientific procedures allow us to discover truth. Murray, for instance, in his restatement of the traditional view, simply ignores the critiques of sociologists of knowledge, critical theorists, feminist scholars, and postmodern social critics (he does cite three philosophers of science, but his citations are from 1952, 1964, and 1965) and asserts that scientific research is the source of truth. Such an assertion is difficult to defend, however, given the fact that long ago even the relatively conservative philosopher of science, Karl Popper, declared, "We cannot identify science with truth, for we think that both Newton's and Einstein's theories belong to science, but they cannot both be true, and may well both be false" (Popper, in Magee, 1973, p. 78).

Murray's talk of true educational practices seems especially problematic. Even if we assume that what Murray is talking about is the truth of propositions about practice, using truth as the criteria to assess the worth of a practice seems a bit odd. Normally, we talk of educational practices being effective or ineffective, good or bad, better or worse, or adequate or inadequate, not true or false. This is not merely a meaningless semantic distinction. Our traditional ways of talking have implicit within them an acknowledgment of the importance of values and the need for value-laden criteria in decision making about educational practice. By contrast, talk of truth and falsity further obscures the role of values in research.

Murray makes a valiant attempt to salvage the traditional response. Ultimately, however, his argument—and the traditional response in general—is undermined by an unwillingness to take seriously the very real value differences that often are at the heart of paradigm disputes within the social sciences.

The Eclecticism Response

There is a second response that does clearly acknowledge the value differences embedded within empirical research, although this response is more implicit in teacher educators' actions than explicitly discussed in the literature. The approach is often evident in course syllabi, particularly syllabi for survey or introductory courses, which are built around explicating different paradigms or models. The response also can be seen in books such as Joyce and Weil's *Models of Teaching* (1992), which offers a smorgasbord of instructional strategies, Wolfgang and Glickman's *Solving Discipline Problems* (1986), which presents a similar sort of eclectic array of strategies related to discipline and management, and Dembo's *Applying Educational Psychology in the Classroom* (1988), a text that describes the tenets of three different schools of psychology and explicates the differing views of teaching and learning implicit in each.

The eclecticism response has an obvious advantage over the traditional response in that it clearly acknowledges the values differences implicit in different schools of empirical research. Ultimately, however, it is also a less than adequate response to those who challenge the idea of professionalism: although the eclectic response does a good job of exposing teachers and prospective teacher educators to alternative possibilities, it says little or nothing about how to choose among these alternatives. Simply articulating an array of alternative paradigms and perspectives does nothing to legitimate the notion of professionalism; indeed, Broudy (1981) has argued that the presence of conflicting educational paradigms is the source of professional educators' credibility problem. It is not surprising, therefore, that the National Council for Accreditation of Teacher Education (NCATE), the national accrediting organization for teacher education programs, does not consider eclecticism an adequate response to its standard that a teacher education program be based on a clearly defined knowledge base.

The Coherence/Consistency Response

NCATE itself has at least implicitly endorsed a third possible response to the knowledge-as-politics critique, one which centers around the principles of coherence and consistency. The organization allows a program it reviews to choose its knowledge base. To be sure, NCATE does require that the knowledge base selected be "based on essential knowledge, established and current research findings, and sound professional practice" (National Council for Accreditation of Teacher Education, 1992, p. 47), but since there are established and current research findings and respected professional practice to justify everything from informal, whole language teaching to highly structured, direct instruction, this requirement allows for quite different, even antithetical knowledge bases to be employed. Indeed, the focus of most NCATE evaluations with respect to the knowledge base standard is not on the adequacy of the knowledge base employed; rather, the central question in most instances is whether the articulated knowledge base has been implemented throughout the program. A program is normally judged, in other words, not primarily on the adequacy of the foundation on which it is built but rather on the consistency with which that foundation has been implemented. In short, coherence is the operative criterion in making accreditation decisions with respect to NCATE's knowledge base standard.

The difficulty with the coherence response can be seen by looking at another chapter in the first AACTE knowledge base book, in which Carolyn Evertson (1989) presents a coherent framework for approaching classroom management and discipline. Evertson emphasizes that her framework is research based and her discussion of this matter reflects the research-as-heuristic notion that the above historical analysis indicates is typical of more sophisticated contemporary views. Evertson writes, "The knowledge base, while critical as a foundation, does not provide a set of simple prescriptions, independent behaviors, or even strategies, but rather provides evidence of important constructs that must be examined to establish a workable management system" (p. 59). Nowhere, however, does Evertson acknowledge the values implicit in the research that gave rise to her framework and constructs—the heuristics she presents—and hence the values implicit in the heuristics themselves. This is typical of the coherence response. Coherence is, in fact, possible only if we ignore value differences and include in our knowledge base the research that shares our values and a priori conceptions of learning and teaching.

This is certainly what Evertson has done. In contrast to Wolfgang and Glickman's eclectic discussion of discipline and classroom management (1986), Evertson's framework rests on literature with similar a priori assumptions about what learning is and how it should be promoted in schools. The learning outcomes in the literature Evertson employed, for instance, tend to be in the cognitive rather than the social or affective domains, and even within the cognitive domain, dependent variables tend to be skewed in the direction of bits of information and isolated skills, which can be transmitted to students in a fairly direct manner. It is not surprising therefore that the image of the ideal teacher implicit in the framework Evertson has drawn from this work emphasizes tight teacher control. With respect to the category "Planning Before School Begins," for example, Evertson declares without qualification, "Areas in need of advance planning include the organization of physical environment and the establishment of expectations, rules, and procedures for behavior and academic work among others" (p. 60).

Others operating from a different knowledge base rooted in different values and different conceptions of teaching and learning might come to a somewhat different conclusion about what planning should and should not be done in advance. One middle-school teacher, for instance, purposely does not arrange the physical environment of her classroom before the school year begins. By most criteria, this teacher would be judged excellent. Almost every year, several of her students win prestigious state and national writing competitions. She herself has been named teacher of the year by the state-level professional association in her field and received one of ten cash awards for excellence given to teachers in all fields, K–12, by one of the state's businesses. The school's psychologist and principal, as well as parents and fellow teachers, attest to this teacher's ability to work miracles with difficult students. And students themselves, even six or seven years after they have had her as a teacher, frequently remember her as the kindest teacher they have ever had as well as the teacher from whom they learned the most and who best prepared them for college.

According to the teacher, her success is not unrelated to her decision not to arrange the classroom before the start of the school year; she wants her students to be involved in decision making about how *their* space should be organized. The strategy is one of many she uses to create a sense of student ownership of classroom life and in the process to build a classroom culture conducive to learning as she defines the term.

This teacher shares a concern articulated by sociolinguist Susan Florio-Ruane in another chapter of *Knowledge Base for the Beginning Teacher* titled "Social Organization of Classes and Schools." Florio-Ruane writes:

> Significant here for beginning teachers is the realization that a social context awaits in the classrooms where they will comfortably (or uncomfortably) assume social and intellectual authority over children. But, as Waller's work asserts, there is an essential mismatch between such a social arrangement and teachers' work: the education of children. Learners who are subordinates cannot participate in many of the activities and forms of discourse that would lead to genuine education. Thus, beginning teachers need to learn to mitigate aspects of their authority not only because they like children and want to be liked in return, but because they want to teach well [p. 166].

The concerns articulated in the Florio-Ruane chapter—for example, the concern that "learners who are subordinates cannot participate in many of the activities and forms of discourse that would lead to genuine education" and the concern that teachers "learn to mitigate aspects of their authority"—are nowhere in evidence in the chapter by Evertson. This is not surprising since Evertson is not a sociolinguist; her framework is based on a very different knowledge base from the one used by Florio-Ruane, a knowledge base generated out of fundamentally different conceptions of learning and teaching. This does not mean that Evertson's framework is useless, of course. (Indeed, many teachers will attest to the utility of Evertson's work.) It does mean, however, that Evertson's research-based position (and the research-based position of Florio-Ruane, for that matter) contains a value bias. This same sort of value bias is built into any program emerging out of the coherence response.

The problem here should be obvious. The tale of Mark Carter recounted above demonstrates the difficulties created when a research literature's value biases get codified into formal policies or organizational structures such as a district's evaluation system, but there are also problems for individual teachers independent of the formal policy structure. Consider, for example, a beginning teacher deciding how to handle classroom management and discipline. We would certainly want the teacher to know about the methods articulated in Evertson's framework, but we would also want the teacher to know about the educational ends Evertson's framework tacitly embraces, and we would want our beginning teacher to be aware of the quite different concerns sociolinguists like Florio-Ruane have expressed and have some way of dealing with contradictions inherent in these different research traditions.

To the extent that we take the coherence response seriously and design teacher education programs around the principle of consistency, however, our programs will not only not prepare teachers to choose among or thoughtfully combine rival paradigms and purposes (also a failing of the eclectic approach) but teachers we educate will not even be made aware of the existence of different paradigms and the differing purposes and values they serve.

The Practical Reasoning Response

The image of the novice teacher thinking intelligently about how to approach discipline and classroom management suggests a fourth and final way we might ground professionalism at a time when all knowledge is seen as inevitably political. This response takes its cue from the field of law, which Gardner (1989), in his preface for AACTE's first knowledge base book, notes is not so much grounded in a knowledge base as in a process of reasoning. Those who educate lawyers certainly want to pass on a knowledge of legal principles and the cases in which these principles are contextualized, but this goal is secondary in importance to the development of skill in legal reasoning.

The focus in educational programs would not be on legal reasoning, of course, but it could be on practical reasoning. The idea of practical reasoning is as old as Aristotle's conception of politics[6] and as contemporary as Dewey's (1916, 1929) and Schön's (1983) conceptions of reflective practice. An array of scholars within the field of education have discussed the relevance of this notion for educational decision making (for example, see Fenstermacher, 1986; Zumwalt, 1982; Schwab, 1969; Donmoyer, 1983, 1985, 1990b, 1991; Reid 1978; Rentel, 1993; Walker, 1990; Cherryholmes, 1988; Beyer, 1990).

Schwab (1969) defines practical reasoning as a "complex and arduous" process. He writes,

> It treats both ends and means and must treat them as mutually determining one another. It must try to identify, with respect to both, what facts may be

relevant. It must try to ascertain the relevant facts in the concrete case. It must try to identify the desiderata in the case. It must generate alternative solutions. It must make every effort to trace the branching pathways of consequences which flow from each alternative and affect desiderata. It must then weigh alternatives and choose, not the right alternative, for there is no such thing, but the best one [pp. 318–319].

One of the reviewers of an earlier draft of this chapter, after reading Schwab's definition, wrote: "Would not a chemist looking for a more efficient reaction chain be doing exactly this?" The answer is no. The difference can be seen by focusing on the word *efficient*. For a chemist, what the term *efficiency* means generally is not problematic. The chemist's problem therefore is basically a technical one; it can be resolved with empirical evidence alone.

For an educator engaged in practical reasoning, the meaning of efficiency or even whether efficiency, however it is defined, should be the main criterion for assessing an educational practice's worth, is potentially problematic. Efficiency will undoubtedly mean one thing to Carolyn Evertson and something quite different to Susan Florio-Ruane, because the outcomes they would have teachers strive for differ.

Thus, our beginning teacher, using practical reasoning to decide whether to follow Evertson's advice and be an unabashedly authoritative teacher or to respond to Florio-Ruane's concern and attempt to mitigate the authority that is inevitably part of the teacher role, must confront value questions, questions of ends, as well as technical questions about means. Indeed, our hypothetical teacher will treat questions of ends and means as inextricably linked.

Our hypothetical teacher can illustrate two additional characteristics of practical reasoning that differentiate it from the work of the chemist or anyone else searching for theoretical knowledge. First, the focus of practical reasoning is on the particular rather than the general. The hypothetical teacher described above, for instance, might conclude that the view of learning that undergirds Florio-Ruane's thinking is generally better than Evertson's view but might still conclude that Evertson's management framework is more helpful during the first year of teaching when a paramount concern is teacher survival.

The second characteristic is related to the first: in a public policy field like education,[7] in which we must constantly balance conflicting purposes, our choices are sometimes not between good and bad or even good and less good options but between equally desirable alternatives. In this situation, practical reasoning may involve balancing alternative orientations and ways of doing things rather than choosing among them. Consider, for example, the beginning teacher employing Evertson's management framework because he or she has decided that survival concerns should be the primary criteria on which decisions are made during the first year of teaching. This same teacher might also try to find other opportunities to mitigate against the authoritative teacher role the framework tends to promote, particularly as the year progresses and the teacher feels more secure in his or her new role.

What would it mean to take the practical reasoning response seriously within a teacher education context? How would a teacher education program built around practical reasoning differ from programs built around the three other responses outlined above? To answer these questions, I will focus on what a language arts methods course might look like in each of the four contexts.

The traditional response, of course, provides no short-term solution to the problem of designing a language arts methods course and, if the analysis presented here is on target, no long-term solution either. The eclectic and coherence responses, by contrast, do provide relatively clear-cut guidelines.

At one institution, for instance, program planners generally opt for coherence as an organizing principle, although the ideas and practices around which different programs cohere vary greatly. Special education students learn to teach reading and language arts in a manner that would make B. F. Skinner proud: the ideas they are exposed to, the methods they practice, and the teaching methods they see modeled all reflect a behaviorist view. General elementary education majors are also exposed to a highly consistent program; here, however, the focus is almost exclusively on informal, whole language versions of teaching and learning, even for students with special needs. In each case, programmatic coherence is purchased at a rather high price: students are kept in the dark about the ideas and methods that are at the center of the other program.

By contrast, the eclectic response would make students aware of differing positions. Such awareness, in fact, is the primary goal of the eclectic approach. Students enrolled in a language arts methods course built around eclecticism undoubtedly would learn about whole language and behaviorist approaches and probably several other approaches to language arts teaching and learning as well. They might even learn about the advantages and disadvantages of the various approaches they study. What they would not have an opportunity to learn about, and certainly would not have an opportunity to practice, is a method for choosing among or appropriately balancing the differing approaches.

Such a method would be front and center in the practical reasoning response. To be sure, at first glance this response may look very much like the eclectic approach. We would certainly want students in a practical reasoning-based language arts methods course, for instance, to become aware of ideas and skills associated with a wide range of knowledge bases, even when their recommendations for practice conflict. But in a course built around practical reasoning, acquiring such knowledge would not be an end in itself; rather, the various knowledge bases students would learn about would serve as heuristics as students think, talk, and write about (1) what actions could be taken in *specific* language learning contexts, (2) what the likely consequences of each of the different courses of action would be, (3) what the relative worth of each of the likely consequences is, and (4) ultimately what should be done.

Operationally, the practical reasoning response would mean building language arts methods courses around problem-based rather than subject-centered learning (Stepien, Gallagher, and Workman, 1993; Bridges, 1992). Undoubtedly case material—either in text form or in the sort of technologically advanced forms being developed by Ball, Lampert, and Rosenberg (1993) in the mathematics education field—would be used to simulate real-world problems and to stimulate practical reasoning in the preservice methods classroom. A range of other strategies and techniques—everything from sociodramas (Donmoyer, 1990a) to the one-way-mirror critique sessions used in Reading Recovery training (Rentel, 1993)—might also be used to give future and practicing teachers an opportunity to practice practical reasoning.

To summarize, the focus of the practical reasoning response is reasoning about ends as well as means, with the full realization that questions of ends and means cannot be ordered in a neat and tidy linear fashion. An eclectic collection of visions of educational practice and the eclectic research literature that supports these visions would be used to inform this reasoning process both about the likely consequences of particular courses of action and the different sorts of educational ends that might be pursued.

Conclusion

The practical reasoning response appears to provide a way to salvage the notion of professionalism in postpositivist times because it does not ground professionalism in any particular knowledge base that will inevitably serve some interests at the expense of others. Instead, as in the profession of law, the claim to expertise here is rooted in an ability to reason in a particular way. In this case, the form of reasoning employed focuses on ends as well as means, and in fact sees questions about what ends we should value and what means we should pursue as inevitably interconnected.

The practical reasoning response seems especially defensible if we conceptualize practical reasoning, in part, at least, as a public process; that is, if we assume that professionals have an obligation to make their reasoning public and to listen and take seriously the public's response.[8] This notion is certainly consistent with much of the recent rhetoric on site-based management and shared decision making. The shared decision making teams that have been established in many schools in response to this rhetoric, in fact, can be seen as forums in which practical reasoning can occur.

We should not be naïve about the implementation difficulties associated with the practical reasoning response, of course. Empirical work reported by Zeichner and Liston (1987) and Ross (1989), for instance, suggests that developing beginning teachers' practical reasoning ability will require much more than a single course, and my own empirical work suggests that practical reasoning can be difficult and psychologically painful even for experienced teachers (Donmoyer, 1983, 1990b, 1991). The stakes are particularly high when we ask teachers to use practical reasoning in a public context, for example, on-site-based management teams composed of parents and community members. In such contexts, teachers who are unprepared or insecure may tend to hide behind outmoded notions of professionalism to shield themselves from public scrutiny and criticism.

Unfortunately, a discussion of implementation issues is beyond the scope of this chapter. The purpose here is much more modest: to provide a philosophical rationale for professionalism in light of the knowledge-as-politics critique. A second related but more parochial purpose is to provide a frame through which informed, contemporary readers might view this book's other chapters. That frame suggests the need to do two things: first, to read critically, to be as concerned with the a priori conceptions and values that helped shape researchers' empirical findings as with the empirical findings themselves, and second, to be cautious in translating the contents of this book into action. Just as teachers must employ practical reasoning to balance rival perspectives and fit them to particular contexts, the teachers of teachers must do the same.

Notes

1. Certain progressives—George Counts, the economist quoted earlier, for example— sometimes used the term *political* less pejoratively. Counts and his fellow social reconstructionists, for example, would probably have acknowledged that their attempt to use schools to transform society was, in some sense, a political agenda. Since, in their minds, they were doing what was right and those who opposed them were acting out of self-interest, social reconstructionists applauded the efforts of other progressives who were trying to wrest control of education away from politicians and turn it over to professionals whose expertise, social reconstructionists assumed, would naturally lead them to support and try to enact the social reconstructionists' agenda.

2. This bid for accessibility and relevance has its price, of course. Among other things, it obscures differences among the different scholarly traditions that argue for the political nature of knowledge. These differences are subtle but not insignificant. In addition, certain postmodern scholars caution against the "tyranny of lucidity," that is, the conclusion that an author's argument must be true because it seems so obvious. To avoid this problem, postmodern scholars often utilize a discourse style that is intentionally opaque. Some postmodern scholars also argue that commonsense assumptions can only be challenged if uncommon modes of discourse are employed.

3. Piaget talked about the conservation of number, for instance, a concept that most preschoolers have not yet acquired. If one takes seven blocks and seven balls, lays out the blocks in a row and the balls in another row right beside the blocks, and then asks whether there are more blocks, more balls, or the same amount of blocks and balls, most preschoolers will give the latter answer. If one then spreads the row of blocks out so that the row of blocks is longer even though no more blocks have been added, most preschoolers will say that there are more blocks. Piagetians would say that the preschool child has not yet developed the notion of conservation of number; the child does not know that seven is seven no matter how the seven objects are arranged.

4. I do not want to overstate this point. There is a two-way street here: the data we gather can certainly alter our understanding of the metaphors and the a priori conceptions we employ. My point is simply that there is no such thing as immaculate perception and that no amount of methodological sophistication can alter the fact that all data are inevitably "tainted" by the subjectivity of the knower.

5. For a more detailed discussion of differing conceptions politics, see Donmoyer, 1990a.

6. Aristotle's conception of politics is radically different from the Machiavellian conception and the perceptual and procedural view described above. For a more detailed discussion of this point, see Donmoyer, 1990a.

7. I am using the term *public policy field* broadly here. I assume that the classrooms are important policy-making arenas and that teachers are significant policy makers. For a more thorough discussion of this view and a rationale for its appropriateness, see Schwille, Porter, and Gant, 1980.

8. I should acknowledge that not all postpositivist scholars would agree with this point. Certain feminist scholars, for example, argue that practical reasoning has a gender bias built into it because the sort of public discourse around which this approach would be built does not reflect women's natural or preferred way of operating in the world (Belenky, Clinchy, Goldberger, and Tarule, 1986). Scheurich and Imber (1991) suggest that a public practical reasoning process may have an inevitable social class bias built in as well. In addition, postmodern scholars challenge the very notions of communication and understanding that ground a practical reasoning approach. According to them, the world will always consist of a cacophony of voices talking past each other. In such a world, the idea that discourse and deliberation can lead to consensus about a course of action to be pursued is considered at best romantic and at worst dangerous. Feminists' objections might be accommodated by broadening the definition of reasoning beyond an Aristotelian one and by instituting the sort of group process procedures that Scheurich and Imber allude to in their article. The postmodern critique cannot be so easily accommodated, but it can be challenged on instrumental grounds: even if the postmodern critique is essentially correct, should we not at least attempt to reach some degree of understanding and resolve disputes on that basis before resorting to brute politics?

References

ABT Associates (1977). *Education as experimentation: A planned variation model.* Boston: ABT Associates.

Apple, M. W. (1979). *Ideology and curriculum.* New York: Routledge & Kegan Paul.

Apple, M. W. (1982). *Education and power.* New York: Routledge & Kegan Paul.

Ball, D. L., Lampert, M., and Rosenberg, M. (1993). "Using multimedia technology to support a new pedagogy of teacher education." Presentation at the Annual Meeting of the American Educational Research Association, Atlanta.

Belenky, M., Clinchy, B., Goldberger, N., and Tarule, J. (1986). *Women's ways of knowing: The development of self, voice and mind.* New York: Basic Books.

Berger, P., and Luckmann, T. (1967). *The social construction of reality.* New York: Anchor Books.

Beyer, L. E. (1990). "Curriculum deliberation: Value choices and political possibilities." In J. Sears and D. Marshall (eds.), *Teaching and thinking about curriculum.* New York: Teachers College Press.

Blumer, H. (1969). *Symbolic interactionism: Perspective and method.* Englewood Cliffs, N.J.: Prentice Hall.

Bobbitt, J. F. (1924). *How to make a curriculum.* Boston: Houghton Mifflin.

Bridges, E. (1992). *Problem-based learning for administrators.* Eugene, Oreg.: ERIC Clearinghouse on Educational Management.

Broudy, H. S. (1981). *Truth and credibility: The citizen's dilemma.* White Plains, N.Y.: Longman.

Buber, M. (1965). "Education." In *Between man and man* (R. Smith, trans.). New York: Macmillan.

Callahan, R. E. (1964). *The cult of efficiency: A study of the social forces that have shaped the administration of public schools.* Chicago: University of Chicago Press.

Cherryholmes, C. (1988). *Power and criticism: Poststructural investigation in education.* New York: Teachers College Press.

Clark, C. M., and Yinger, R. (1977). "Research on teacher thinking." *Curriculum Inquiry, 7,* 279–309.

Counts, G. S. (1926). "Current practices in curriculum-making in public high schools." In G. Whipple (ed.), *26th yearbook of the National Society for the Study of Education.* Bloomington, Ill.: Public School Publishing Co.

Cronbach, L. (1957). "The two disciplines of scientific psychology." *American Psychologist, 12,* 671–684.

Cronbach, L. (1975). "Beyond the two disciplines of scientific psychology." *American Psychologist, 30,* 116–127.

Cronbach, L. (1982). "Prudent aspirations of social inquiry." In W. Kruskal (ed.), *The social sciences: Their nature and lines.* Chicago: University of Chicago Press.

Cubberly, E. P. (1909). *Changing conceptions of education.* Boston: Houghton Mifflin.

DeFord, D., and Harste, J. C. (1984). "Child language research and curriculum." In J. Britton (ed.), *English teaching: An international exchange.* Portsmouth, N.H.: Heinemann Educational Books.

Dembo, M. (1988). *Applying educational psychology in the classroom.* White Plains, N.Y.: Longman.

Dewey, J. (1916). *Democracy and education.* New York: Macmillan.

Dewey, J. (1929). *The sources of a science of education.* New York: Liverwright.

Donmoyer, R. (1983). *Evaluation as deliberation: Issues, assumptions and findings from an exploratory study.* Washington, D.C.: National Institute of Education.

Donmoyer, R. (1985). "The rescue from relativism." *Educational Researcher, 14,* 13–20.

Donmoyer, R. (1990a). "Curriculum, community and culture: Reflections and pedagogical possibilities." In J. Sears and D. Marshall (eds.), *Teaching and thinking about curriculum: Critical inquiries.* New York: Teachers College Press.

Donmoyer, R. (1990b). "Curriculum evaluation and the negotiation of meaning." *Language Arts, 67,* 274–286.

Donmoyer, R. (1990c). "Generalizability and the single case study." In E. W. Eisner and A. Peshin (eds.), *Qualitative research in education.* New York: Teachers College Press.

Donmoyer, R. (1991). "Postpositivist evaluation: Give me a for instance." *Educational Administration Quarterly, 27*(3), 265–296.

Donmoyer, R., and Kos, R. (1993). "At-risk students: Insights from/about research." In R. Donnmoyer and R. Kos, *At-risk students: Portraits, policies, programs, and practices.* Albany: State University of New York Press.

Edelsky, C. (1990). "Whose agenda is this anyway? A response to McKenna, Robinson, and Miller." *Educational Researcher, 19*(8), 7–11.

Eisner, E. W. (1988). "The primacy of experience and the politics of method." *Educational Researcher, 7*(5), 15–20.

Eisner, E. W. (1990). "Objectivity." Paper presented at the annual meeting of the American Educational Research Association, Boston.

Evertson, D. (1989). "Classroom organization and management." In M. C. Reynolds (ed.), *Knowledge base for the beginning teacher.* Elmsford, N.Y.: Pergamon Press.

Fenstermacher, G. D. (1986). "Philosophy of research on teaching: Three aspects." In M. C. Wittrock (ed.), *Handbook of research on teaching.* (3rd ed.). New York: Macmillan.

Feyerabend, P. (1970). "Against method: Outline of an anarchistic theory of knowledge." In M. Rodner and S. Winokur (eds.), *Analyses of theories and methods of physics and psychology.* Minneapolis: University of Minnesota Press.

Florio-Ruane, S. (1989). "Social organization of classes and school." In M. C. Reynolds (ed.), *Knowledge base for the beginning teacher.* Elmsford, N.Y.: Pergamon Press.

Foucault, M. (1972). *The archaeology of knowledge* (A. M. Sheridan Smith, trans.). New York: Pantheon Books.

Freire, P. (1970). *Pedagogy of the oppressed.* New York: Seabury Press.

Gage, N. L. (1978). The scientific basis of the art of teaching. New York: Teachers College Press.

Galtung, J. (1974). "On peace education." In C. Wolf (ed.), *Handbook on peace education.* Frankfurt, Germany, and Oslo, Norway: International Peace Research Association.

Gardner, W. E. (1989). Preface. In M. C. Reynolds (ed.), *Knowledge base for the beginning teacher.* Elmsford, N.Y.: Pergamon Press.

Garfinkel, H. (1967). *Studies in ethnomethodology.* Englewood Cliffs, N.J.: Prentice Hall.

Giroux, H. A. (1981). *Ideology, culture and the process of schooling.* Philadelphia: Temple University Press.

Gitlin, A., Siegel, M., and Boru, K. (1988). "The politics of method: From leftist ethnography to evaluative research." *International Journal of Qualitative Studies in Education, 2*(3), 235–253.

Good, T. L., Biddle, B., and Brophy, J. E. (1975). *Teachers make a difference.* Austin, Texas: Holt, Rinehart & Winston.

Gordon, E. W., Miller, F., and Rollock, D. (1990). "Coping with communicentric bias in knowledge production in the social sciences." *Educational Researcher, 19*(3), 14–19.

Guba, E. G., and Lincoln, Y. (1989). *Fourth generation evaluation.* Newbury Park, Calif.: Sage.

Gusfield, J. (1976). "The literary rhetoric of science." *American Sociologist, 41,* 11–33.

Habermas, J. (1978). *Knowledge and human interests* (J. Shapiro, trans.). Portsmouth, N.H.: Heinemann Educational Books.

Habermas, J. (1984–1987). *The theory of communicative action,* Vols. 1–2 (T. McCarthy, trans.). Boston: Beacon Press.

Haney, W., and Villaume, J. (1977). *"The follow through planned variation experiment."* Washington, D.C.: Department of Health, Education, and Welfare (Education Division), Office of Education, Office of Planning, Budgeting, and Evaluation. (OEC-O-74–0394)

Haraway, D. (1988). "Situated knowledges: The science question in feminism and the privilege of partial perspective." *Feminist Studies, 14*(3), 575–599.

Haraway, D. (1989). *Primate visions: Gender, race, and nature in the world of modern science.* New York: Routledge & Kegan Paul.

Harding, S. (1986). *The science question in feminism.* Ithaca, N.Y.: Cornell University Press.

Harding, S. (1991). *Whose science? Whose knowledge?* Ithaca, N.Y.: Cornell University Press.

Hesse, M. (1980). *Revolutions and reconstructions in the philosophy of science.* Brighton, England: Harvester Press.

House, E., Glass, G., McLean, D., and Walker, P. (1978). "No simple answer: Critique of the follow-through evaluation." *Educational Leadership, 35,* 462–464.

Jardine, D., and Clandinin, D. J. (1987). "Does it rain on Vancouver Island? Teaching as storytelling." *Curriculum Inquiry, 17,* 471–481.

Joyce, B. R., and Weil, M. (1992). *Models of teaching.* Needham Heights, Mass.: Allyn & Bacon.

Kliebard, H. M. (1975). "Reappraisal: The Tyler rationale." In W. Pinar (ed.), *Curriculum theorizing: The reconceptualists.* Berkeley, Calif.: McCutchan.

Kuhn, T. (1962). *The structure of scientific revolutions.* Chicago: University of Chicago Press.

Lather, P. (1986). "Research as praxis." *Harvard Educational Review, 56*(3), 257–277.

Lather, P. (1991). *Getting smart: Feminist research and pedagogy with/in the postmodern.* New York: Routledge & Kegan Paul.

Lyotard, J. (1988). *The differend: Phrases in dispute.* Minneapolis: University of Minnesota Press.

McKenna, M., Robinson, R. E., and Miller, J. "Whole language: A research agenda for the nineties." *Educational Researcher, 19*(8), 3–6.

Magee, B. (1973). *Karl Popper.* New York: Viking Penguin.

Marcus, G., and Clifford, J. (1986). *Writing culture: The poetics and politics of ethnography.* Berkeley: University of California Press.

Murray, F. B. (1989). "Explanation in education." In M. C. Reynolds, (ed.), *Knowledge base for the beginning teacher.* Elmsford, N.Y.: Pergamon Press.

National Council for Accreditation of Teacher Education (1992). *Standards, procedures, and policies for the accreditation of professional education units.* Washington, D.C.: National Council for Accreditation of Teacher Education.

Neisser, U. (1976). *Cognition and reality: Principles and implications of cognitive psychology.* New York: Freeman.

Reid, W. (1978). *Thinking about the curriculum.* New York: Routledge & Kegan Paul.

Rentel, V. M. (1993). "Preparing clinical faculty members: Research on teachers' reasoning." In K. R. Howey and N. L. Zimpher (eds.), *The professional development of teacher educators.* Norwood, N.J.: Ablex.

Rivlin, A. (1971). *Systematic thinking in social action.* Washington, D.C.: Brookings Institution.

Ross, D. D. (1989). "First steps in developing a reflective approach." *Journal of Teacher Education, 40*(2), 22–30.

Scheurich, J., and Imber, M. (1991). "Educational reforms can reproduce societal inequities: A case study." *Educational Administration Quarterly, 27,* 297–320.

Schön, D. A. (1983). *The reflective practitioner.* New York: Basic Books.

Schwab, J. J. (1969). "The practical: A language for curriculum." *School Review, 76,* 1–23.

Schwille, J. R., Porter, A. C., and Gant, M. (1980). "Content decision making and the politics of education." *Educational Administration Quarterly, 16*(2), 21–40.

Shulman, L. S., and Lanier, J. E. (1977). "The Institute for Research in Teaching: An overview." *Journal of Teacher Education, 28*(4) 44–49.

Stanfield, J. H. (1985). "The ethnocentric bias of social science knowledge production." *Review of Research in Education, 12,* 387–415.

Stepien, W., Gallagher, S., and Workman, D. (1993). "Problem based learning for traditional and interdisciplinary classrooms." Center for Problem Based Learning, Illinois Math and Science Academy (unpublished manuscript).

Thorndike, E. L. (1910). "The contribution of psychology to education." *Journal of Educational Psychology, 1,* 5–12.

Toulmin, S. (1972). *Human understanding.* Princeton, N.J.: Princeton University Press.

Toulmin, S. (1983). "The construal of reality: Criticism in modern and postmodern science." In W.J.T. Mitchel (ed.), *The politics of interpretation.* Chicago: University of Chicago Press.

Tyack, D. B. (1974). *The one best system.* Cambridge, Mass.: Harvard University Press.

Tyler, S. (1987). *The unspeakable: Discourse, dialogue, and rhetoric in the postmodern world.* Madison: University of Wisconsin Press.

Wagner, J. (1987). *The search for signs of intelligent life in the universe.* New York: HarperCollins.

Walker, D. C. (1975). "Straining to lift ourselves: A critique of the foundations of the curriculum field." *Curriculum Theory Network, 5,* 3–25.

Walker, D. C. (1990). *Fundamentals of curriculum.* San Diego, Calif.: Harcourt.

Wexler, P. (1982). "Ideology and education: From critique to class action." *Interchange, 13*(1), 53–78.

Williams, R. (1963). *Culture and society, 1790–1950.* Harmondsworth, England: Penguin.

Wolfgang, C., and Glickman, C. D. (1986). *Solving discipline problems.* Needham Heights, Mass.: Allyn & Bacon.

Young, M. (ed.) (1971). *Knowledge and control: New directions for the sociology of education.* New York: Macmillan.

Zeichner, K. M., and Liston, D. P. (1987). "Teaching student teachers to reflect." *Harvard Educational Review, 57*(1), 23–48.

Zumwalt, K. K. (1982). "Research on teaching: Policy implementation for teacher education." In A. Lieberman and M. W. McLaughlin (eds.), *Policy making in education.* (81st yearbook of the National Society for the Study of Education). Chicago: National Society for the Study of Education.

Annotated Bibliography

Anderson, L. (1989). "Learners and learning." In M. C. Reynolds (ed.), *Knowledge base for the beginning teacher.* Elmsford, N.Y.: Pergamon Press.

This chapter is normally read for its substantive content: Anderson describes two quite different paradigms of learning and argues for the superiority of one over the other. The chapter is included in this annotated bibliography, however, because of the way Anderson makes her case. She does not claim that one paradigm is superior because it has more or better empirical evidence supporting it; rather, her argument is a pragmatic and ultimately an ethical one. She models, in short, in a rudimentary way, the process of practical reasoning discussed in this article. To be sure, teachers who must make decisions about what to do in their particular classrooms and teacher educators engaged in making decisions about a specific program need to take contextual factors into account to a greater extent than Anderson does in making her relatively abstract case; the basic "line" of argument would be quite similar, however.

Belsey, C. (1992). *Critical practice.* New York: Routledge & Kegan Paul.

This is a concise and quite readable account of some of the key ideas frequently associated with the terms *postmodernism* or *poststructuralism.* The focus is on the fields of literary criticism and linguistics, but implications for the field of education can easily be seen.

Donmoyer, R. (1991). "Postpositivist evaluation: Give me a for instance." *Educational Administration Quarterly, 27,* 265–296.

The article describes an approach to program evaluation built around the idea of practical reasoning. The approach was designed to simultaneously evaluate a school program and contribute to the professional development of teachers and administrators involved with the program. The article also presents data describing what happened when the evaluation approach was tried out in practice. These data suggest some of the factors that are problematic for teachers asked to engage in practical reasoning in a public forum.

Gusfield, J. (1976). "The literary rhetoric of science." *American Sociologist, 41,* 11–33.

This article presents one of the clearest demonstrations of how the language employed in a research article rather than the data reported can influence the article's conclusions and recommendations. This article could be read as a public policy variant of Kuhn's treatise on the importance of paradigms on thought in the physical sciences.

Kuhn, T. (1962). *The structure of scientific revolutions.* Chicago: University of Chicago Press.
This classic text in the philosophy of science popularized the notion of paradigms and, in the process, challenged the academic community's faith in empiricism. Kuhn's discussion of the role and function of paradigms is limited to a physical science context. Others, however, quickly applied Kuhn's ideas to the social sciences in general and education in particular.

Ross, D. D. (1989). "First steps in developing a reflective approach." *Journal of Teacher Education, 40,* 22–30.
Ross describes an introductory course in an elementary teacher education program at the University of Florida designed to engage students in reflection. Outcome data generated from that class are also presented. The definition of reflection Ross and her colleagues used is reasonably consistent with the notion of practical reasoning employed in this paper. The data presented suggest that a single course is just a first step in developing reflection or practical reasoning ability in preservice teachers.

Schwab, J. J. (1969). "The practical: A language for curriculum." *School Review, 76,* 1–23.
This article represents an early attempt to resurrect the Aristotelian notion of deliberation or practical reasoning and apply it to the field of education. Schwab's focus is on the making of curriculum but his analysis can easily be applied to teacher decision making and especially to curriculum development in the field of teacher education.

Toulmin, S. (1972). *Human understanding.* Princeton, N.J.: Princeton University Press.
Toulmin, S. (1983). "The construal of reality: Criticism in modern and postmodern science." In. W.J.T. Mitchel (ed.), *The politics of interpretation.* Chicago: University of Chicago Press.
In *Human Understanding,* Toulmin covers much of the same ground covered by Kuhn, but he moves the discussion beyond a physical science context. The distinction Toulmin draws between academic disciplines and public policy fields should be particularly helpful for academics in the field of education. It should help educational academics better understand how their work and the problems they confront might differ from the activities of sociologists, anthropologists, political scientists, linguists, and researchers in the field of psychology. In the 1983 paper, Toulmin emphasizes the importance of value issues and questions of justice in scientific discourse.

Zeichner, K. M., and Liston, D. P. (1987). "Teaching student teachers to reflect." *Harvard Educational Review, 57,* 23–48.
The authors describe an elementary teacher education program at the University of Wisconsin, Madison, that is built around the notion of reflection. Since the developers of the program assume that teachers must address value-oriented criteria in the reflection process (a basic assumption of the program's developers is that teachers are "moral craftpersons"), their view of reflection seems consistent with the idea of practical reasoning discussed in this paper. Outcome data about the program presented by the authors suggest that students have difficulty implementing the moral craftperson component of the teacher role even though they appear to understand and accept the idea.

CHAPTER FIVE

RESEARCH GENRES IN TEACHER EDUCATION

MARY M. KENNEDY

Almost since its inception, teacher education has suffered from doubts about its contribution to teaching. Outside observers have asked, usually skeptically, whether teacher education makes a difference, and teacher educators themselves have wondered what they have been able to accomplish and how they could accomplish more. Presumably, research could help both teacher educators and teacher education policy makers to better understand whether and how teacher education makes a difference.

I began this chapter with the idea of summarizing the available empirical evidence on the effects of teacher education. I wanted a review that would differ from Koehler's review (1985), which summarized a variety of research efforts associated with teacher education, and from Katz and Raths' typology (1985) of research areas in the field. Rather than reviewing what was known about any particular aspect of teacher education, I wanted to see what was known about the benefits (or lack of benefits) of teacher education *as a whole*. This proved difficult. The studies that address the question "Does teacher education make a difference?" do so in such diverse ways that it is virtually impossible to summarize their findings.

One problem is that the boundaries between what is teacher education and

An earlier version of this paper was presented at the annual meeting of the Association of Teacher Educators, February 1991. Preparation of the paper was supported by the National Center for Research on Teacher Learning under a grant from the U.S. Department of Education, Office of Research. However, the views expressed here are the author's, and no official endorsement should be inferred.

what is not are unclear. Some researchers attend to preservice teacher education, while others attend to inservice. Within preservice, some researchers focus on experiences in schools as part of teacher education, some focus on courses in the liberal arts as teacher education, and some focus on those courses that occur within education departments as teacher education. I decided not to address preservice arts and sciences courses, inservice education, or even student teaching. Though each of these is important to teaching, the biggest and most controversial part of teacher education is the set of courses known as the professional component of the undergraduate curriculum. Preservice teacher education is a huge enterprise, producing a hundred thousand new teachers each year and occurring in a wide variety of institutions of higher education. Thus, even with this delimitation, I found that different authors attend to different aspects of teacher education: some to the number of courses people took, some to the content, some to the type of institution offering the program, and so forth. In fact, Galluzzo and Craig (1990) argued that even faculty within a program can differ in what they think the central features of their program are.

Not only is the enterprise itself difficult to get a handle on, but the outcomes of teacher education are similarly diffuse. As a field, we suffer from enduring disagreements about what counts as a valid outcome and about how to measure those outcomes that do count. Some people want evidence of teacher thinking, others of teacher skills. Some think you assess thinking through paper-and-pencil tests, others that you need to see it in the context of practice, and so forth.

A variety of approaches have been devised over time to try to get a better handle on preservice teacher education. But because of the complexity of the enterprise, and because of the ambiguity about its intended outcomes, no study can accommodate all aspects of teacher education and all outcomes. Every researcher necessarily limits his or her attention. Every researcher makes difficult decisions about which aspects of teacher education will be studied, about which outcomes will be examined, and about how the study will be designed to determine the relationship between teacher education and its outcomes.

On reviewing these various studies, I realized that they can be grouped into a few broad categories. The available research on preservice teacher education tends to fall into five distinct categories, or *genres*. I call them genres because each represents a coherent and internally consistent way of thinking about whether teacher education makes a difference. The differences among these genres is most apparent in the delimiting decisions they make. They differ, for instance, in the *aspects of teacher education* that they choose to examine. Some focus on completed programs, some on particular components within preservice programs, and others on the volume, or number of courses taken, in teacher education. They also differ in *what counts as an outcome*. Some examine skills, some examine teacher knowledge or beliefs, and still others look for evidence of gains in pupil achievement. They even differ in the *kinds of arguments* they make about whether or how teacher education makes a difference.

These groups can also be called genres in that each has been used on numerous occasions by numerous researchers and because researchers within each genre tend to build on other work within their genre more than on work in other genres. Most of them represent communities of scholars who share a set of norms and values and who share a particular view of, and interest in, teacher education. In addition, they rarely attend to the research done by scholars in other genres.

My aim in this chapter is to examine these genres with an eye toward the kind of knowledge each gives us. My hope is that, through such a review, teacher educators and researchers can learn more about how research can contribute to our knowledge and understanding of teacher education and perhaps how we can improve on these genres in the future. As I review each genre, I ask three questions: (1) What aspects of teacher education does it look at, and are those aspects relevant to the needs of teacher educators who want to use research to improve their programs? (2) What outcomes does it look at, and are these outcomes sufficient? (3) What is the argument about the relationship between these programs and outcomes, and is the argument credible?

Searches for Contributions to Student Learning

The first genre is done by researchers who are interested in influencing policies, not policies in teacher education necessarily, but policies in the K–12 school system. Researchers working within this genre are engaged in a relatively open-ended search for contributions to pupil learning, and one of the possible contributions is teacher education. Also, they are especially interested in contributions that policy makers can control. For instance, if they found that library size did not make a difference, but that class size did, they would advise local school boards to spend their money reducing class size rather than building up their libraries. Their audiences are state and local policy makers, not teacher educators per se. Yet because they examine all the factors that might be relevant to student achievement, they often wind up doing research on whether teacher education makes a difference.

Many of these studies were stimulated by, and are based on, the Equality of Educational Opportunity Study (Coleman and others, 1966), and many actually used the EEOS data. One of the earliest of these studies that included teacher education was conducted by Eric Hanushek (1971, 1972). He began by asking whether teachers differed in their ability to increase student achievement after taking into account the child's initial achievement and various aspects of the child's background. Hanushek found that teachers did make a difference. That is, the teacher a child happened to have could significantly influence the child's achievement for the school year. Seeing that this was the case, Hanushek then tried to see which particular teacher characteristics seemed to account for these differences. Among the variables Hanushek examined were college major, number of hours of graduate coursework, and length of time since the teachers' most recent educational experience. Hanushek found that neither college major nor the number of graduate credits teachers had taken were significantly related to student achievement. Variables that were related, on the other hand, included the teachers' general verbal ability and the recency of their last educational experience. These two variables do not necessarily reflect teacher education courses per se, although verbal ability may reflect the effect of college education in general. The recency of the teachers' educational experiences may reflect either the nature of the experiences or the teachers' interest in continued professional learning.

Another important study that focused on teacher education was done by Murnane and Phillips (1981). Like Hanushek, these researchers began by testing to see whether teachers made a difference, found that they did, and then tried to see what aspects of teachers seemed to account for these differences. But instead of generating a single equation that included all possible contributions to student achievement, they developed two separate equations, one of which included measures of teacher *behaviors* (for example, circulating around the room to correct seatwork, using demonstrations, or making students repeat poor work) and the second of which included measures of teacher *characteristics* (for example, years of experience, possession of a master's degree, and the prestige of the college attended). Their data indicated that teacher behaviors were better predictors of student achievement than were teacher characteristics. Moreover, of those characteristics that Murnane and Phillips examined, neither of their education-related variables—possession of a master's degree or prestige of college attended—appeared to be relevant to student achievement.

Another early study by Begle and Geeslin (1972) looked more closely at the pattern of courses that teachers took. They focused specifically on mathematics teachers and examined some twenty different features of their teachers' educations, including whether the teachers majored or minored in mathematics and the number of course credits teachers took in mathematics. Like the others, they also found that these measures of teachers' undergraduate course taking were not clearly associated with student gains in achievement in mathematics.

If these studies were all we had available on the question of whether teacher education made a difference, we would probably conclude that it did not. In a recent review of literature in this genre, Hanushek (1989) summarized 113 studies that included some aspect of teacher education. Only 13 of these 113 education-related variables were statistically significant; of these, 8 indicated that the teachers' education was positively related to student achievement and 5 indicated that it was negatively related to student achievement. Unfortunately, Hanushek's summary did not indicate *which aspects* of the teachers' educations were measured in these studies. That is, some studies may have measured whether or not the teacher majored in an academic subject, others may have measured the number of credits taken beyond the bachelor's degree, while still others may have measured the recency of the education experience. Thus, the meaning of this finding is less clear than it might have been. Now let me address my three questions about this genre of research.

Aspects of Teacher Education Examined

The aspects of teacher education that these researchers examine are often called policy parameters: broad parameters of teacher education that can be manipulated by policy makers. That is, these researchers do not ask about the details of any particular teacher education program because details cannot be regulated through policy. On the other hand, of course, policy parameters tend to be less relevant to teacher educators because they give few hints of *why* these parameters do or do not make a difference. They may not be of much real use to those who want to improve teacher education, for two reasons.

First, virtually every teacher in these studies *already holds a bachelor's degree* and is already certified to teach. The percentage of teachers lacking a bachelor's degree was only 7 percent in 1966 and has since fallen to less than 1 percent (National Center for Education Statistics, 1989). Presumably, then, all of these teachers have attained the minimum educational background required for teaching. The variations among these teachers that are measured, therefore, are not variations in the core of teacher education but instead are peripheral variations. That the population of teachers involved in these studies is so homogeneous in its educational attainment can produce a problem that statisticians call "restricted range." If there is little variation on a particular measure, such as education level, it will be difficult to show a relationship between that variable and any other. A wider range is needed in order to see such relationships. Studies done in other countries, for instance, where teachers' education may range from secondary to college degrees, show that the amount of a teacher's education does make a difference (Murnane, 1985).

A second reason these studies might lack utility, even for policy makers, has to do with variations in educational backgrounds that are *not* measured. Since the United States does not have a centralized curriculum, and since many states give teacher educators considerable leeway in their program designs, teacher education programs can look remarkably different from one institution to the next. A recent report from the Council of Chief State School Officers (1988) indicated that the number of credits of professional education required for elementary teacher candidates ranged from eighteen to ninety across the states. Not only do the number of credits taken within the professional curriculum differ, but their content and character differ as well. These differences reflect different ideas about what teachers need to know and about how teachers learn. It is reasonable to suppose that such differences are relevant to the outcomes of teacher education, but they are not differences that can easily be measured. By failing to measure the substantive differences among programs, researchers in this genre may miss the very aspect of teacher education that is most likely to make a difference. Moreover, because there is so much variation in the content and character of teacher education programs, measures of the *amount* of teacher education do not necessarily measure a unitary thing. Some teachers may have received extensive education in a mediocre program while others received modest education in a very good program. It should not be surprising, therefore, that measures of amount generally do not correlate highly with measures of student achievement gains. When a scale does not measure a unitary thing, it is hard to show a relationship between it and other things.

A recent study by Ferguson and Womack (1993) corrects this problem in two ways. First, instead of simply tallying up courses, they document the actual courses students took during their undergraduate preparation and correlated the presence or absence of each course with teaching performance during student teaching. Second, instead of using presence or absence of a major in a subject as their indicator of subject matter knowledge, they use both grade point average within the subject and score on the subject matter portion of the National Teacher Examinations (NTE). With these alterations in method, the researchers found substantial relationships between the teacher education courses that teacher candidates took and the quality of the teaching they demonstrated.

Outcomes

Researchers practicing within this genre take student achievement—or better still, gains in student achievement—as their primary outcome. Early studies tended to use achievement at a single point in time as the outcome, but by the late 1970s it became clear that only gains in achievement made sense as an outcome. Still, the reliance on student achievement is a limitation in that these tests measure some but not all of the important goals of education. And a good teacher education program will try to prepare teachers to teach many things other than the basic skills that are measured on standardized achievement tests. In fact, whether such tests even measure the most important outcomes of schooling is a highly debatable issue, as the contemporary debate over authentic assessments suggests. Gains in student achievement, then, constitute a very narrow outcome for estimating the contributions of teacher education to teaching. Perhaps when and if alternative strategies for assessing students are found, the associations between these and teachers' backgrounds may change.

Credibility of the Argument

The logic of these studies goes something like this: if teachers who have taken more credits in teacher education foster greater gains in student achievement than teachers with fewer credits (after taking into account differences in students' entering achievement, family background, and so forth), then teacher education has made a difference. Because such differences have not often been observed, some researchers within this genre have argued against policies that require teachers to take certain numbers of credits, for instance, or that pay teachers more if they have master's degrees. It is a relatively simple argument, but it depends on quite a complex statistical approach called "multiple regression." Multiple regression is designed not to estimate the effects of any one variable by itself but instead to weigh individual contributions *relative to* the contribution of other factors that might influence student learning.

This statistical technique creates a mathematical model of the set of influences and then estimates the relative importance of each. The success of the study depends on how accurately the researcher's *model* of the phenomenon matches the *real phenomenon*. Suppose, for instance, that the researcher develops a model like this: "achievement gain is a function of earlier achievement, family support, amount of education the teacher has had, and recency of the teacher's education." But suppose further that the real phenomenon is that achievement gain is a function of earlier achievement, family support, quality of the teacher's education, teacher's desire to improve, and school climate.

The point of the statistical analysis, of course, is to find out how this complex of influences actually relates to the outcome of interest. But the analysis depends on devising a model that adequately matches the real phenomenon. In this example, the real phenomenon differs from the model in several ways. For one thing, the model measures the recency of the teacher's last educational experience, and this is not relevant in the real phenomenon. Instead, in the real phenomenon, the variable that matters is the teacher's *desire to improve*. It is reasonable to suppose that these two variables are related; that is, when teachers have a high desire to improve, they are likely to voluntarily continue their education and so will have had more recent educational experiences than other teachers. The researcher's erroneous model may lead to the conclusion that the courses themselves, rather than the teacher's disposition to improve her practice, were responsible for these gains in student achievement. This would be a case of a false positive, a conclusion that something makes a difference when it really does not.

Another difference between the model and the real phenomenon is that the model measures the *quantity* of teacher education whereas in the real phenomenon it is the *quality* of the teacher's education program that is most important. Again, the model errs by measuring the wrong variable. However, in this case, there may be no relationship between quantity and quality. So if the researcher finds that quantity of teacher education is unrelated to student achievement, he (and his audience of policy makers) may erroneously conclude that teacher education *in general* is unrelated to student achievement when in fact it is. This would be an instance of a false negative—concluding that something does not make a difference when it really does.

Yet another difference between the model and the real phenomenon is that the real phenomenon includes a variable that is entirely missing from the model: school climate. This mismatch also can create a problem of interpretation. There is ample evidence now that school climate is an important contributor to student achievement (Good and Brophy, 1986), and it may also be an important contributor to the teacher's ability to teach well. Since the model does not include school climate, variation in this factor adds "noise" to the equation and makes it harder to see the relationship between all other variables and the outcome. It is possible that teachers' educational backgrounds make a difference *within each school climate*, but these effects are not apparent when a wide range of school climates are involved in the study—or it is possible that teacher education only makes a difference within reasonably positive school climates and that it cannot help teachers teach better when they are working in especially difficult schools.

This research genre, then, is limited in all three of the areas we examined. The aspects of teacher education that it measures often include such things as completed degrees, quantities of coursework, or courses taken after the bachelor's degree, rather than quality or content of these courses. Its outcome, student achievement test scores, represents only a narrow slice of the outcomes educators may want to see. Finally, to the extent that its arguments about the relationship between teacher education and student achievement are based on misspecified models, it lacks credibility.

Researchers working within this genre have learned a great deal about how best to do this research. They have learned, for instance, that they need to use gains in pupil achievement, rather than achievement at one point in time, as their outcome measure. They have learned that they need to examine school resources and pupil outcomes at the level of the individual pupil rather than using school or district averages and to try to measure the resources that individual children actually receive rather than summing up all the resources that exist (Murnane, 1981). And they have learned some of the ways in which their models might not work (see, for instance, Fortune, 1993). These insights provide at least the potential for models to become increasingly sophisticated over time. Yet despite these conceptual advances, many researchers (see, for example, Strauss and Sawyer, 1986; Ferguson, 1990; Dolan and Schmidt, 1987) continue to use techniques that have been rejected by others (such as analyzing district averages) because these data are available and because the researchers still hope to provide policy makers with knowledge about things policy makers can manipulate.

Comparing the Haves and the Have-Nots

The second research genre, too, tends to be geared toward policy makers. Like the first genre, this one focuses on teachers who have completed their education and are already teaching and then looks backward to see their education. But instead of measuring a wide range of variables, researchers working within this genre focus specifically on teaching practice as the outcome of interest and teacher education as the predictor of interest. These researchers actively seek teachers who come from different educational backgrounds. Usually, they work within a particular school district or geographic region, find all the teachers who are teaching with provisional or emergency credentials, and compare them with teachers in the same region who are fully certified. Once two groups of teachers have been identified, the researchers observe the classroom practices of both groups, searching for differences. One advantage of these studies over those in the first genre is that, because these begin with a search for noncertified teachers, they often have a larger proportion of such teachers in their sample than do open search studies. But these studies can be done only during periods when school districts are experiencing serious personnel shortages so that they need to hire a lot of provisionally certified teachers. Several were done in the early 1960s, comparing certified and noncertified teachers (for example, Beery, 1960; Hall, 1964; Gerlach, 1964; Gray, 1962; Bledsoe, Cox, and Burnham, 1967), and a new crop are now being done comparing regularly certified and alternatively certified teachers (for instance, Cornett, 1984; Brown, Edington, Spencer, and Tinafero, 1989; Peck, 1989).

One early study in this genre, which has often been cited as evidence against the value of teacher education, was conducted by Popham (1971). Popham's intent was to develop a strong measure of teaching skill, but he went about it by devising teaching assignments and then asking both certified teachers and college students to do these teaching assignments. Each assignment entailed nine hours of teaching and students were randomly assigned to teachers. Teachers were not told how to teach the content but instead were given the instructional objectives and some materials. This study differed from many in the genre by using student achievement as the outcome rather than teaching practices per se. Popham found no significant differences between teachers and college students and attributed this lack of difference to the way teachers were prepared.

A more typical example of the genre is LuPone's comparison (1961) of elementary teachers in New York. This study used a "high-inference" observation system—that is, one that asked observers to make their own judgments about whether, for instance, the teacher is maintaining order, or is friendly or aloof with pupils. LuPone compensated for differences in observer judgment by using multiple observers in each classroom. In addition, he grouped his teachers according to whether they had one, two, or three years of experience, so that differences in credentials would not be confused with differences in experience. LuPone found that fully certified teachers surpassed provisionally certified teachers, across all levels of experience, on five of his eight observation scales. The scales on which teacher education made a difference included preparation and management, treatment of subject matter, pupil-teacher relations, evaluation, and use of instructional materials and methods. On another scale, LuPone found no difference between first-year teachers but did find differences between teachers in the other experience categories. The two scales on which no differences were found were parent-teacher relations and human relations, both skills that are demonstrated outside the classroom.

Dewalt and Ball's 1987 study, by way of contrast, used a "low-inference" observation system: observers simply checked whether they saw a particular behavior or not but made no judgments as to whether that behavior indicated orderliness or friendliness or any other general teaching concept. The teaching behaviors were drawn from research literature on effective teaching strategies. When the researchers observed the teachers, they specifically asked their teachers to demonstrate these competencies. Thus, their observations do not reflect what teachers might normally do in their classrooms but instead reflect the teachers' ability to do these specific things on demand. One group of teachers had taken no teacher education courses, the other had had at least twelve credit hours in teacher education but had not done student teaching. So the comparison really asks whether taking at least twelve credits in teacher education makes a difference. The two groups were found to differ on several variables, but the comparisons did not always favor the same group. Behaviors that were more often demonstrated by teachers who had taken teacher education courses were those having to do with creating a nonpunitive classroom climate and accommodating individual differences. Those that favored teachers who had taken no courses in teaching had to do with holding students accountable for their work and asking a wide range of questions about the material. These researchers also found, incidentally, a wider range of practices among the nonprepared teachers than among the prepared teachers.

Several recent studies have extended this genre to include comparisons of teachers who participated in alternative routes with regularly certified teachers. For instance, Brown, Edington, Spencer, and Tinafero (1989) compared emergency-permit teachers with both fully certified teachers and interns who were participating in an alternative route program. They pooled their data across grade levels and found no differences among the three groups on four of the five scales they used. Emergency-permit teachers were significantly higher on the fifth scale, called "growth and responsiveness," a scale that could reflect a higher degree of on-the-job learning among these teachers who have received no advance preparation for their work.

The studies in this genre are remarkably diverse in the outcomes they measure and in the way they select groups for contrast. Not surprisingly, given this diversity, their findings are mixed as well. Most reviewers of this genre (for example, Haberman, 1985; Evertson, Hawley, and Zlotnik, 1985) perceive the overall pattern of differences as indicating that teacher education does make a difference, though they also point out that such studies, like the open search studies, do not take account of the content or character of teacher education programs. Now let us consider our three questions.

Aspects of Teacher Education Examined

Whereas the open search researchers are likely to tally up courses or degrees *beyond* the bachelor's degree or to determine whether teachers majored in education or not, researchers in this genre usually define teacher education as whatever set of courses is required for initial certification. The aspect of teacher education that is of interest to them is the completed program relative to the incomplete program. Since presumably these programs are designed to make a difference to teaching practice, questions about the merits of the completed program are of interest. Comparisons among different types of programs—for instance, alternative routes versus traditional programs—are also of interest, particularly in the current policy climate, where numerous efforts are under way to devise alternatives to the traditional preservice program.

Many of these researchers also document the number of undergraduate, as opposed to graduate, education courses taken by teachers in the noncertified group. An important finding from this research is that very few provisionally certified or emergency-certified teachers have had absolutely no exposure to teacher education. Instead, they have taken a few courses but not enough to become certified. So the comparisons are actually between teachers who have taken everything that is required to become fully certified and teachers who have taken some portion of the requirements. Again, this difference is relevant, since both policy makers and teacher educators expect the completed undergraduate program to make a difference.

Still, these researchers continue to treat the undergraduate program as a black box. They do not document which courses were taken, or from which institution. Since programs are so various, it is possible that differences in conclusions reflect differences in local teacher education programs from which samples of teachers are drawn. Rarely do these researchers document the nature of the programs whose impact they are presumably studying. A nice exception to this general rule is Arch's comparison (1989) of teachers prepared through a traditional undergraduate program versus a M.A.T. program. While Arch found only slight differences between graduates of the two programs in supervisors' ratings of teaching competence, she was able to interpret these similarities and differences in light of the specific characteristics of the two programs. Without such an in-depth examination, findings from comparison studies can indicate only the potential impact of teacher education; they can provide no clues about what aspects of teacher education make a difference or why some do and others do not.

Outcomes

Although a few comparison studies use tests of knowledge, such as the NTE or a state-required test (for example, Cornett, 1984), most depend on observations of teachers for their outcomes. But even within the observation studies, there is still a great deal of room for variability in what counts as evidence of good teaching. These studies have relied on a variety of different observation systems and a variety of different outcomes, depending on what is fashionable and on what observation instruments are available at the time. One could argue, of course, that even though the criteria used in comparison studies may change over time, each criterion is likely to reflect views of good teaching that would also have guided teacher education programs at the time the studies were done. If this is true, it is not unreasonable to expect certified teachers to perform better than noncertified teachers in most of these studies. But to the extent that observation instruments lack reliability or validity, and to the extent that they focus on too narrow a range of teaching behaviors, they may fail to discover differences that actually exist.

Credibility of the Argument

Studies in this genre actually represent a two-sided argument. On one side, if we find greater skill among provisionally certified teachers, we might argue that teacher education *hinders* teaching and that teachers are better off taking more liberal arts courses than they are taking teacher education courses. On the other side, if we find greater skill among certified teachers, we might argue that teacher education *facilitates* teaching and should continue to be required.

But there is a serious limitation to both sides of this argument, for all of these studies examine practice *after* teachers begin teaching. Like the open search studies, they may confuse teachers' motivation to improve with their inclination to enroll in a teacher education program. They cannot determine what these teachers were like when they were still in college, making decisions to enter or not to enter a teacher education program, or making decisions to take a few courses but not to complete the program. If people with different patterns of capabilities choose different educational paths in the first place, the differences we observe when they are teaching could reflect nothing more than differences that were there years earlier. Thus, a major problem with these studies is that we cannot be sure that the observed differences reflect the actual programs or courses teachers took.

In fact, even a finding of *no difference* does not avoid this dilemma, for it is possible that different kinds of people enroll in different programs and that the programs washed out the initial differences. An interesting study by Skipper and Quantz (1987) illustrates this point. They followed a group of arts and sciences students and a group of teacher education students from freshman year through senior year. They found that substantial differences existed between the two groups as freshmen, but that these differences had disappeared by the time they were seniors. No difference at the end of a program, then, means no evidence that teacher education has hindered teaching, no evidence that teacher education has contributed to teaching, and no evidence that different kinds of people enrolled in different programs to start with.

Beery's study (1960) also illustrates the problem of interpretation. Beery found that certified teachers were more different from teachers who had taken *some* courses in teacher education than they were from teachers who had taken *no* teacher education courses. Why would such a pattern exist? One strong hypothesis is that the teachers who formed these different groups differed in important ways that may have led them to take the particular configuration of courses they did, so that the differences Beery observed had more to do with what kinds of people chose these curricular paths than with the courses they actually took.

Grossman's case studies (1990) of six novice teachers is an improvement over many comparison studies in two important ways. First, Grossman interviewed her teachers in addition to observing them and asked them where they got their ideas for teaching. Many referred to specific teacher educators. Second, Grossman visited the teacher education program attended by her sample of certified teachers so that she could test the idea that this program in fact provided content that was consistent with the ideas her novice teachers held. Finally, one of the certified teachers in Grossman's study had actually tried teaching earlier and, based on this experience, returned to college to obtain a teaching credential. This teacher's recollections of the first teaching experience provided yet another source of evidence to justify the inference that credentialed teachers taught differently because of what they had been taught in their teacher education program.

Overall, then, comparisons of the haves and the have-nots focus on a more relevant aspect of teacher education—completed programs or alternatives to completed programs—than have open search studies, and their outcomes are more relevant as well. But comparison studies suffer a logic problem that is very similar to that of open searches in that neither genre enables researchers to separate the impact of the courses or programs teachers took from their reasons for taking those courses or programs in the first place. Because this genre requires naturally occurring populations of teachers who have received different types of preparation, it is not a widely used genre. Moreover, those who do such studies are often capitalizing on a situation and are unaware of others who have used the genre in the past. For this reason, researchers often do not learn from the mistakes of others. Even recent studies make mistakes in design that researchers long ago identified—drawing a sample of alternatively certified teachers from the school's most inexperienced teachers and drawing a sample of fully certified teachers from its more experienced teachers, for instance, or failing to match teachers on the grade level they teach. Because researchers in this genre are often unaware that they are following in a research tradition, they do not benefit from that tradition and the genre has failed to become more sophisticated over time.

Ask the Teacher

The third genre also focuses on teachers who have completed their educational programs but assumes that teachers themselves might be the best judges of the contributions of teacher education to their teaching. Teacher educators often try to determine whether particular aspects of teacher education made a difference by surveying their own graduates and asking them if their educational program made a difference to their practice. This strategy is popular in part because it is

relatively inexpensive and simple to do, and in part because the National Council for Accreditation of Teacher Education (NCATE) accreditation requirements
have continually stressed the need for such program evaluations. Adams and Craig
(1983) surveyed teacher education programs in 1980 and found that 74 percent
claimed to be conducting some sort of follow-up of their graduates.

Ask-the-teacher studies generally use two strategies to estimate the contributions of teacher education. One is to ask teachers to assess their own knowledge
and skills—that is, to assess their own ability to teach. The other is to ask them
to assess the contributions to their teaching of their preservice program or of particular courses within that program.

Pigge's survey (1978) is a good example of the genre. Pigge developed a list
of twenty-six competencies taken from the Bowling Green curriculum on which
the respondents were to rate themselves. On Pigge's five-point scale, most self-
assessments were quite high. The lowest average self-assessment was close to the
midpoint of the scale. Few teachers, then, viewed themselves as seriously lacking
in any of these teaching competencies. Pigge also asked teachers to estimate
how important these various competencies were to their work and to indicate
where they learned these competencies. Generally speaking, teachers thought that
those competencies *most* necessary to their work were learned on the job, whereas
those considered *least* necessary were acquired in their teacher education programs.

Henry (1986) provides a more recent example. He surveyed the 1983 and
1984 graduates from Indiana State, asking them to rate themselves on a three-
point scale: strong, adequate, and needs improvement. These were beginning
teachers, who presumably should not have been embarrassed to say that they
needed improvement on some aspects of teaching. Of the forty-five dimensions
Henry asked about, only five were areas in which 15 percent or more teachers felt
they needed improvement. On nine of these forty-five items, no one claimed to
need improvement. Henry also asked his beginning teachers to indicate their preference for different forms of assistance that might be helpful in their beginning
years of teaching. The most often selected options were other teachers or a
newsletter. The option least often selected was "University supervision similar
to that received during student teaching." Like Pigge's teachers, then, these beginning teachers felt they were doing quite well as teachers and felt that they
learned more from their experience and their colleagues than they did from formal teacher education.

In addition to asking teachers to rate themselves and their programs, a prominent part of many institutionally based studies is a list of the specific courses or
program components required by the program and a request that teachers rate
the quality or relative value of particular aspects of their programs. Many of these
studies are only available through the Educational Resources Information Center
(ERIC) system (for example, Reed, 1975; Drummond, 1976; Warren, Dilts,
Thompson, and Blaustein, 1982; Benz, 1984; Schmelter, n.d.). If student teaching is included in the list, it invariably is the highest rated part of preservice teacher

education, usually followed by one or more methods courses. If subject matter preparation is included in the list, it receives a higher rating than do professional courses. If something called "foundations" is included, or a course with a title like *School and Society*, it receives the lowest rating.

In an interesting study by Clark, Smith, Newburg, and Cosk (1985), teachers were observed in their classrooms and then asked where they got the ideas for what they did. The most frequently cited source for a teaching idea was that the teacher generated it himself or herself. Second most prominent was the cooperating teacher with whom the teacher had undergone student teaching. Teacher education faculty were given credit for only 17 percent of the practices teachers were asked about.

Though most ask-the-teacher studies are conducted by teacher education institutions and include only graduates of those institutions, a few studies survey a broader population of teachers. For instance, the National Education Association (NEA) recently surveyed its members and asked them to evaluate the contributions of fourteen different sources of knowledge about teaching, one of which was preservice teacher education (Smylie, 1989). The preservice teacher education program was ranked thirteen of fourteen. The highest-rated sources of knowledge were direct experience, consultation with other teachers, and independent study and observations of other teachers, all of which are entirely in the control of the individual teacher. The only item rated less positively than undergraduate teacher education was school district-provided inservice programs. Another study, quite different in design, is Ryan and others' (1979) series of case studies of beginning teachers. While their sample had a variety of views about their teacher education, a theme running through many of their interviews was that one can only learn to teach through experience in teaching.

Studies conducted by asking the teacher are probably the most numerous of all studies aimed at learning whether teacher education makes a difference. However, many of these studies are not published in journals and are difficult to find. The scattered sample I reviewed, however, gave the distinct impression that teachers do not attribute much value to their teacher education courses. But before drawing a firm conclusion from these studies, let us consider our three questions.

Aspects of Teacher Education Examined

Because these studies are usually conducted by the institutions providing teacher education, because these institutions presumably know what their programs offer, and because these studies often ask teachers about particular program components, in addition to asking them about the program as a whole, these studies can be far more informative to the teacher educators than either of the first two research genres. But their benefit is highly localized. That is, most of these studies examine teacher education as it exists in one particular institution. They ask their graduates to assess the math methods course, the student teaching component, the placement service, and so on. The aspects of teacher education that are examined, then, are of less interest to the field as a whole than they are to the institutions that generate them. In fact, the more useful a survey becomes to its institution, the less useful it will likely become to others, for local utility depends on forming questions that are highly specific to the local situation. Furthermore, to the extent that ask-the-teacher studies depend on unique question formats and response options, it is close to impossible to compare findings from one study to the next or to aggregate the findings and identify patterns regarding different features of preservice teacher education.

Outcomes

Almost universally, ask-the-teacher studies use teachers' judgments of their own knowledge or skill as the primary indicator of program impact. Most of them provide the teachers with a list of knowledge or skill areas or a list of program courses and ask the teachers to rate themselves or their alma mater on a five-point scale. Reliance on teacher judgment is a substantial limitation in these studies, for several reasons. First, we do not know what *criteria* teachers use when they make these assessments. Are the teachers' criteria the same as an independent observer's criteria might be? In fact, even when teachers are asked simply to describe their practice, without evaluating its adequacy, their descriptions often differ considerably from those of an independent observer. Teachers' self-reports are more likely to agree with those of an independent observer when the reporting form focuses on specific situations (for instance, first-period social studies or the teaching of a particular body of content) rather than on teaching in general and when the same set of questions is asked more than once, so that teachers learn to attend to those practices that interest the researchers (Koziol and Burns, 1986). These conditions are never met in follow-up surveys, though Browne and Hoover (1990) move in that direction by asking their teachers to indicate how frequently they use a selection of teaching strategies that their faculty recommended. Few strategies were regularly used, and the authors concluded that situational factors prevented teachers from using these desirable teaching strategies.

Teacher self-assessments may also be influenced by emotional responses to their teaching situations. Gaede (1978), for instance, found that teachers' assessment of their own knowledge increased as they moved through their teacher education programs but decreased substantially during their first year of teaching. Certainly these teachers did not suddenly know less once they entered their own classrooms, but just as certainly, they *felt* they knew less once they encountered the demands of real teaching.

Similarly, when a teacher claims a program has contributed to her knowledge or skill, or has *not* contributed to her knowledge or skill, we do not know how accurate these judgments are. It is highly likely that teachers do not recall what they knew or were able to do five years earlier. Strang, Badt, and Kauffman (1987) provide some evidence that teachers do not accurately recall their prior capability. They measured teachers' skills both before and after a program treatment, and they also asked teachers afterward to estimate the degree to which they had changed during the program. The researchers' independent assessment of teacher change showed their proficiency moving from 52 percent to 87 percent. However, the *teachers'* assessments of their own change indicated movement from 81 percent to 85 percent. Teachers, then, may not be good judges of whether they have learned from a program or not.

If these data are construed as indicators of teacher's *felt problems,* on the other hand, rather than as valid assessments of what teachers have learned, the data may have some value to the field. Veenman (1984) recently reviewed over eighty-three follow-up surveys in the United States and other countries. He found that classroom discipline was most mentioned in seventy-seven studies as a major problem and was nominated in the bulk of the studies he reviewed. The second most often cited problem was motivating students, mentioned in forty-eight studies, and third most often mentioned was dealing with individual differences, this problem cited in forty-three of the studies. From findings such as these, we can distinguish those areas in which teachers feel relatively more capable from those in which they feel relatively less capable, the latter tending to be those areas having to do with their moment-to-moment interactions with students. Thus, though it is not possible to draw many inferences about teacher education programs, it is possible to learn what teachers think they can do well and what they think they cannot do well.

Credibility of the Argument

The logic of ask-the-teacher studies goes something like this: if teachers who choose to respond to the survey claim that they are competent in certain areas or if they claim that they have (or have not) learned something valuable from their teacher education programs, we can assume that they are correct and that their estimates of the contributions of teacher education are also correct. Since there is no direct measure of teachers' knowledge or skill, the burden of the argument falls entirely on the teachers' judgments.

Moreover, these studies almost never include comparison groups and never include data on what teachers were like prior to program participation, so it is not possible to attribute findings to the program unless we take the teachers' word for it. No independent corroborating evidence is available. An interesting effort designed to at least partially correct for this problem is under way at Ohio State University (Loadman and Gustafson, 1990), where a group of institutions have agreed to use a common survey instrument for their follow-up studies. Once a sufficient number of institutions have conducted surveys with this instrument, it may be possible to draw some simple contrasts among respondents from different institutions or different types of institutions.

Finally, none of the studies takes into account the teaching context. Some teaching situations are far more challenging than others, some provide less assistance to new teachers than others, and some provide considerably different expectations of teachers than their programs may have been striving for. To the extent that any of these contextual differences might influence teacher judgments, the findings are even more difficult to interpret.

Thus, to make any sense of these data, we have to assume that (1) teachers use the same criteria to judge themselves and their programs as teacher educators, policy makers, or educational researchers would use; (2) teachers' assessments of their own knowledge and skills, and of their prior knowledge and skills, are accurate; and (3) the context in which teachers are teaching has no bearing on their assessments of themselves or their teacher education programs. And even after making these assumptions, we do not know what to make of the ratings that we see, for we have no common metric against which to define them.

Overall, then, ask-the-teacher studies have only limited utility. Although the aspect of teacher education that they examine is the core of teacher education, the undergraduate program that leads to a credential, each study is limited to a particular institution and cannot offer much guidance to either policy makers or teacher educators at other institutions. Even more important, though, the credibility of the argument hinges almost entirely on the validity and reliability of teachers' judgments of their own teaching ability. Problems with these judgments limit the credibility of the entire genre.

Experiments in Teacher Education

The fourth way to find out whether teacher education makes a difference is to experimentally test the effects of different approaches to teacher education. This genre of research has been especially popular among teacher educators who are interested in microteaching, but experiments have also been used to study the effects of hypermedia (Goldman and Barron, 1990), video demonstrations (Winitzky and Arends, 1991), direct instruction (Klesius, Searls, and Zielonka, 1990), and a variety of other teacher education strategies. Generally, researchers working within this genre contrast two or more approaches to teacher education in an effort to discern the relative merits of each.

Experiments avoid several of the limitations of the first three genres. They always contrast two or more clearly defined program variations rather than leaving teacher education as an undefined event; they often assess teachers' knowledge or skill *prior to* their participation in the program as well as after it so that they can be more sure that whatever differences are eventually observed are due to program differences rather than preexisting differences; and they usually assess the outcome of interest directly rather than asking teachers to judge their own performance. In addition, they often randomly assign teacher candidates to program variations to ensure that groups receiving different variations do not differ in their prior knowledge or motivations before participating. The combination of these features gives experimental researchers a tremendous advantage over those using open searches, those comparing have and have-nots, and those asking the teacher. Experimental researchers can ascertain how teachers differed both before and after program participation and they know what the program actually did.

Copeland's study (1975) of the relationship between microteaching and student teaching is a good example of such an experiment. In this study, Copeland first sorted students into two groups, one of which received microteaching training in the skill of "asking probing questions." He then observed a number of cooperating teachers and divided them into two groups, depending on the extent to which they tended to ask probing questions in their own teaching. Finally, he gave half of each group of cooperating teachers training in the supervision of student teachers. That is, he created four groups of cooperating teachers, split both by whether or not they tended to ask probing questions on their own and by whether or not they were trained in the supervision of student teachers. He then assigned his two groups of student teachers across the four groups of cooperating teachers and looked at the combined effects of microteaching training with different kinds of cooperating teachers. Copeland found that microteaching alone did not increase the likelihood that students would ask probing questions during student teaching but neither did either of the other two treatments, whether alone or together. However, the combination of all three forms of assistance did make a difference.

A more recent example of experiments is a series of studies reported at the Annual Meeting of the American Educational Research Association by Winitzky and Arends (1989). These researchers first contrasted the effects of visiting exemplary classrooms with observing videotapes and found both to be equally effective in helping teachers use cooperative grouping in their own microteaching. In a second study, they contrasted two methods of developing novices' intellectual schemata regarding cooperative grouping, and in the third, they contrasted learning in the exemplary classrooms with learning via microteaching and found them to be equally effective. Like many such studies, these did not follow the students into their own student teaching experiences to see the extent to which they carried their new skills into their own teaching practice.

Most of the experimental literature in teacher education defines the outcome of teacher education as observable skills—questioning skills or presentational skills, for instance, rather than, say, knowledge or attitudes or beliefs. Also, most of it contrasts a few basic forms of teacher education: microteaching versus modeling versus seminars versus combinations of these approaches, for example. Despite the similarities in style, the studies are diverse and those who try to summarize them often see different patterns. For instance, Gage (1977, 1985) relied on this literature to conclude that the field was indeed moving toward developing a true scientific basis for teaching while Cornfield's conclusion (1991) was that microteaching is effective with inservice teachers but that there is little reliable evidence of its effectiveness with preservice teachers. Tisher and Klinzing (1992) found more positive evidence in favor of microteaching than in favor of any of the other approaches (simulations, modeling, and so forth) and Cruickshank and Metcalf (1990) managed to draw a series of recommendations from this literature for how to organize a training program; yet Copeland (1982) argued that there was little evidence that teacher candidates used their new skills once they were in their own classrooms.

Now let us consider my three questions.

Aspects of Teacher Education Examined

More than any of the other studies, these studies tend to focus on the actual practice of teacher education. Researchers who conduct experiments are not interested in the amount of additional courses teachers take, as open search researchers are, or in whole certification programs, as researchers who compare arts and sciences graduates with teacher education graduates are, nor are they interested in teachers' retrospective judgments, as ask-the-teacher survey researchers. They are interested in particular segments of teacher education and in rather fine-grained variations in strategies used within these segments of teacher education. Studies in this genre seem to be especially relevant to those who want to improve teacher education.

On the other hand, many of these studies suffer because they are *too* short in duration. They may contrast relatively small program units: three hours of approach A versus three hours of approach B or even three weeks of A versus three weeks of B. They do this of course in part because smaller units are easier to manage for research purposes. But it is not clear that evidence of effectiveness within such small units can be used to make larger-scale changes in the structure of teacher education programs, nor is it necessarily realistic to expect such brief programs to have lasting effects on teacher candidates.

Outcomes

With respect to outcomes, most of these researchers evaluate teacher candidates' abilities to perform the specific skills for which they have been trained. They look, for instance, at candidates' questioning skills or at their skill in responding to student disruptions. The outcomes assessed are by definition directly relevant to teacher education, since they are selected specifically to reflect the program goals. But they do tend to be behavioristic. Researchers rarely examine, for instance, teachers' affective response to the skill. Yet if teachers learn to implement a skill on demand, but also learn to dislike the skill because of some other aspect of the experimental condition, we would not expect them to demonstrate the skill when they are under no pressure to do so—nor do researchers often examine the extent to which teacher candidates understand the point of using this skill or why it is valuable in teaching. One important exception to this rule is Gliessman (1987; Gliessman and Pugh, 1987), whose work emphasizes the importance of teachers' conceptual rationale for the skills they are learning, especially when those skills are complex.

Another general problem with the outcomes of these experiments is that they often are limited to immediate impact: they examine teacher behavior immediately after the teachers complete the various program approaches. Rarely do these researchers follow teachers to see whether the changes initially observed will be sustained several months later. Those who do follow teachers longer generally follow them only into student teaching and so they still do not know whether their short-term effects will be demonstrated once the teachers are teaching in their own classrooms. In fact, several studies suggest that the learned skills are not practiced by teachers when they enter their own classrooms, and it is their eventual classroom practice, after all, that we ultimately want to influence.

Credibility of the Argument

The logic of these studies is persuasive: if teachers participating in one program approach improve their skill more than other teachers do, then this approach has a greater impact. Because researchers have assessed their candidates' skills both before and after the candidates participated in these approaches, and because candidates were randomly assigned to the approaches, these researchers can be more sure than other researchers that the outcomes they observe do not reflect preexisting differences among groups.

Overall, then, these studies are more relevant to teacher educators in the aspects of teacher education they examine, more relevant in the outcomes they assess, and more powerful in their ability to draw unambiguous findings regarding the relative merits of one program approach over another. They could be strengthened a great deal by following teacher candidates over a longer period of time and by extending the outcomes beyond discrete behaviors.

Watch Teacher Candidates Change

The fifth way to find out whether or how teacher education makes a difference is to follow teacher candidates as they proceed through their college education, gathering data on them at several points along the way, to see whether and how their ideas about teaching change over time. Researchers working within this genre want to learn what students are like when they enter their programs, how they change over time in response to their programs, and what they are like when they finish. Like experiments, these studies offer us the advantage of being able to document *change* so that, if differences exist at the end of the study, we can interpret these differences relative to differences that may have existed at the outset. And like experiments, change studies sometimes enable us to look inside the black box, to see the details of the programs in which students participate and to see the interaction between the program and the students. Unlike experiments, though, these studies rarely allow us to compare students who participated in different kinds of programs. While we learn more about how they change as they encounter particular aspects of their programs, we cannot say with any confidence how they might have changed if they had participated in some other kind of program.

Change studies have been especially popular among researchers who are interested in the student teaching component of teacher education (Hodges, 1982; Silvernail and Costello, 1983; Tabachnick and Zeichner, 1984; Goodman, 1986). The student teaching component is a more definable and therefore manageable piece of the teacher education puzzle. In the typical research design, researchers contrast before and after data on student teachers' beliefs or knowledge or skills. One advantage of these studies is that, since student teaching experiences are the least well controlled aspect of teacher education, it is possible to capitalize on the variation in student teaching experiences to learn more about what features make the most difference to the outcomes (for example, McIntyre and Killian, 1986, 1987). But this variation is also a disadvantage precisely because student teaching is the least controlled aspect of teacher education. Moreover, while these studies are valuable, and have increased our understanding of the student teaching component of teacher education, they leave untouched the centerpiece of the enterprise—the large, diffuse, complicated web of courses and other events that we call preservice teacher education.

One of the earliest and best examples of an effort to move this genre into the university program is Feiman-Nemser and Buchmann's study (1989) of teacher candidates participating in two different teacher education programs. They followed six students participating in two preservice teacher education programs, interviewing them on several occasions about their understanding of what they were learning and about their views of teaching. They also observed the teacher education courses these students took. Through their descriptions of these students, they were able to demonstrate gradual shifts in views and to demonstrate ways in which the messages provided in these programs were sometimes misinterpreted by the candidates. The study demonstrates the importance of the teachers' entering assumptions and the ways in which they combine their own childhood experiences with the lessons they are being taught to form their ideas about teaching and learning.

Another good illustration of this genre is Hollingsworth's study (1989) of M.A.T. candidates. She followed candidates both through their university courses and their teaching internships. Through her investigation, she was able to show not only the role that prior beliefs played in these teachers' learning but also how their university learning connected to their practical experience. She found that candidates' prior beliefs influenced their receptivity to the program and that they went through several distinct phases in their practice as they tried to accommodate what they had learned in the program with their classroom experiences. Change studies range from cases of individuals (for example, Valli and Agnostinelli, 1992) to large-scale quantitative studies. Galluzzo (1984) provided an example of a quantitative study of change when he gave a sample of candidates the NTE each year of their college program. Interestingly, he found that candidates did not change on the general studies portion of the NTE but did change significantly on their professional knowledge. Quantitative studies are particularly popular for assessing the impact of the entire college experience, and Pascarella and Terenzini (1991) provide a remarkably thorough summary of this literature.

And now to my three questions.

Aspects of Teacher Education Examined

The aspect of teacher education that change researchers tend to focus on is the patterns of courses that students take. Qualitative researchers are especially interested in courses *as they are perceived by the candidates themselves.* A program brochure may claim, for instance, that Education 201 introduces students to findings from research on teaching. But the researcher who is documenting change in teacher candidates wants to know what Education 201 actually does. In addition, he or she wants to know what Education 201 looks like to student A, to student B, to student C, and so forth. Instead of allowing official program rhetoric to define the courses students take, they may actually attend courses with their sample students or ask students to describe what the faculty are telling them and what they make of that. Moreover, they are interested in how the impact of these courses accumulates over time to create particular changes in the candidate's knowledge or understanding of the practice of teaching. In this sense, the aspects of teacher education that they examine are more relevant than those of experiments, for change studies tend to examine entire programs. To the extent that students receive messages that are different from the messages faculty intended, these findings can help both individual faculty members and groups of faculty to revise their programs.

Outcomes

With respect to outcomes, these researchers tend to be more interested in teachers' knowledge, beliefs, and attitudes than in their teaching skills, in part because they cannot really examine skills until teachers begin teaching and in part because these are the domains they expect to see changing as candidates participate in university courses. Often, however, these studies are limited by their failure to follow candidates into practice, to learn whether the changes observed during a program extend into the teachers' classroom practices. An exception to this general trend is the Teacher Education and Learning to Teach (TELT) study conducted by the National Center for Research on Teacher Education (1991; Kennedy, 1991), in which several hundred teachers, participating in ten teacher education programs, were followed through their programs and into their first year of teaching.

Credibility of the Argument

Many change studies are based on the assumption that teacher candidates enter their college programs with a set of initial beliefs that will influence their responses to the courses they take. As candidates participate in teacher education courses, they respond by incorporating some new ideas but also by altering the messages they receive to make them more consistent with what they already believed. The influence of teacher education, or of college more generally, therefore, is not unidirectional. Instead, there is an interaction between students and their programs. Researchers who watch teachers change want to learn how students who enter with different patterns of beliefs are influenced in different ways. They often gather extensive family and education background data on their students and use these background data to interpret the changes they later observe.

Studies of change share with open searches a tendency to document a wide range of variables, most of which are defined in advance. Just as the success of open searches depends on the model used to generate the data, the success of change studies depends heavily on the theory of learning and development that guides data collection. That is, since researchers are following students over time, since numerous possible changes can occur, and since these changes can be influenced by numerous possible student background characteristics as well as by numerous possible program characteristics, the quality of this research depends on the quality of theory that guides data collection.

Among the five research genres reviewed here, this is the only one that assumes that the outcome of teacher education depends not only on what the program teaches but also on the candidates' initial attitudes and beliefs. Rather than limiting their investigation to whether candidates learned the particular knowledge or skills transmitted by a program, researchers in this genre are interested in the ways in which candidates' own beliefs interact with program messages to create a unique set of new ideas about teaching and learning. The range of attitudes and beliefs examined, together with the interactive nature of these studies, gives them an advantage over experiments, in that experiments are often limited to a much smaller question having to do with whether candidates learn a very specific outcome, regardless of what else they may have learned along the way.

One difficulty that some such studies encounter is a confusion between change due to student development and change due to program impact. The fact that students are changing and developing over time does not necessarily mean that these changes are a result of a program impact. Many college students are still in a highly formative stage in their lives and may be changing in several ways that have little to do with the particular courses or curricula they encounter as students. Thus, the credibility of change studies depends either on comparison groups, which permit changes to be contrasted across program types, or on background data and program data, which enable changes to be interpreted in light of these context variables. The Teacher Education and Learning to Teach study, for instance, included data on teachers participating in ten programs, data on their attitudes and beliefs prior to as well as after program participation, and data on the programs themselves. Feiman-Nemser and Buchmann (1989) provide a smaller-scale example of the same principles in their study of six teacher candidates in that these candidates were participating in two different programs and the researchers collected data on the programs as well as on the students. In both cases, researchers increased the credibility of their argument by showing specific relationships between the students' initial ideas, the ideas that were presented in the courses, and the students' final ideas.

Another difficulty that can arise in change studies derives from the number of observations made on students. Students are often interviewed, or respond to questionnaires, on numerous occasions, and it is highly likely that over time they learn not only what will be asked but also how to respond. Thus, there is a chance that the researchers themselves are at least partly responsible for the changes they describe.

Overall, then, these studies focus on relevant aspects of teacher education (undergraduate programs and components within those programs) and on relevant outcomes—changes in knowledge and beliefs about teaching. The logic is also sound, provided that attention is given to sorting out natural maturation from program effects. While the findings are rich and informative, and provide many insights into how college students interpret and respond to their undergraduate programs, they also are rather complex, leaving us with so many patterns of change that it may be difficult to gauge the pervasiveness of any particular pattern of change. And they often do not tell us whether the observed changes are sustained in practice.

Conclusions

All five of these research genres are intended to document whether or how teacher education makes a difference. But even though they are designed to examine the same *general* question, they address it in quite different ways. Here are the questions they actually ask:

1. Do teachers who have majored in education or taken extra teacher education credits beyond the baccalaureate degree raise their pupils' achievement scores more than teachers who have not?

2. Do certified teachers teach differently on a set of prespecified observable dimensions than uncertified teachers?
3. Do teacher education graduates think they have the necessary knowledge and skills to teach and do they think their teacher education courses gave them any particular knowledge or skills?
4. Does one type of program format do better than another in helping teacher candidates perform a specific skill?
5. How do the attitudes, knowledge, or beliefs of college students change while they are participating in teacher education programs?

Researchers necessarily limit their investigations in many ways. They must decide which aspects of teacher education to study, which outcomes to measure, and which form of argument they will use. While a study cannot be done without making these limiting decisions, each decision also limits the ultimate value of the study.

Choosing the Aspect of Teacher Education to Examine

In reviewing these genres, it seems clear that some aspects of teacher education are more fruitful to examine than others. For instance, the first two genres I reviewed—the open searches and the comparisons of liberal arts graduates and teacher education graduates—treat teacher education as a black box. Because they study teachers who have already completed their programs, they rarely know about the content and character of the teacher education programs themselves. So they treat teacher education as if all programs were the same, as if the enterprise of teacher education were a homogeneous, fixed entity. This is a serious limitation for both policy makers and teacher educators, for we can learn nothing about the relative merits of different approaches to teacher education or about how teacher education programs actually influence teacher candidates.

The remaining three genres enable us to examine the contents of teacher education programs, but they do so in differing ways. When a survey asks teachers to rate particular courses, we may still not know which section of the course each teacher took, or which faculty member taught the course, or at what point in the teachers' curriculum sequence the course was taken. In contrast, many experiments and change studies are able to describe in detail the actual program components or courses that students take.

Choosing the Outcomes

It also seems clear from this review that there are numerous relevant outcomes that could be examined and that nearly every genre examines only a narrow range of outcomes. Open searches limit their attention to student achievement test scores, as if these were the only outcomes teachers tried to influence, and experiments tend to focus on one or two specific skills. Ask-the-teacher studies limit their attention to teachers' judgments of their own capabilities, and we can never be sure what criteria teachers are using to judge their own knowledge and skills. Comparison studies and change studies both rely on broader ranges of outcomes, the former by observing real teaching in all of its complexity, and the latter by allowing teachers to express their ideas about a variety of topics. Still, rarely do either of these genres often incorporate the outcomes of any of the others.

Teachers may benefit from teacher education in many qualitatively different ways: they may acquire knowledge, alter their beliefs, gain skills, or develop new attitudes and dispositions, and all of these outcomes may be important to teaching practice. Moreover, in any given segment of teacher education, regardless of its primary intent, teachers may be influenced in more than one way. Even when the program is concentrating on skills, teachers will acquire some new knowledge and may change their beliefs or dispositions, particularly regarding the specific skills being taught. Any study that addresses only one of these outcomes is therefore automatically too narrow in its focus. Conversely, studies that focus on attitudes and beliefs do so on the assumption that these are important to practice, but rarely follow students into practice to test that assumption.

Enhancing the Credibility of the Argument

Three of the genres described here suffer in credibility because they examined teachers only *after* the teachers had completed their education, not before. In these genre—open searches, comparison studies, and ask-the-teacher studies—we have difficulty drawing inferences about whether or how teacher education has made a difference because we do not know how the various teachers in the study differed from one another *before* their college educations and why different teachers chose the particular programs or courses that they did. The effects of program participation are confounded with the effects of self-selection into the programs.

The sad fact is that poorly designed studies are not merely *non*informative. Often, they are *mis*informative: by failing to consider what teacher candidates already knew prior to participating in teacher education, for instance, researchers may draw conclusions that either over- or underestimate the value of teacher education. They may mislead policy makers to erroneously add or remove requirements from their programs or mislead teacher educators to over- or underuse particular program features.

The experiments and the studies of teacher change are least susceptible to this error and offer the most potentially credible arguments about whether and how teacher education has made a difference. These two genres provide two important advantages over the others: both allow us to see what teacher candidates were like before they participated in their programs and both allow us to observe firsthand the relationship between program character and content, on one hand, and outcomes on the other. Change studies have the additional advantage that they can be used to evaluate whole programs rather than only discrete parts of programs. They offer numerous advantages over, for instance, follow-up surveys as means of evaluating local programs where comparison groups are rarely available. In fact, to encourage teacher educators to adopt change studies for their program evaluations, the National Center for Research on Teacher Learning has recently released for general use all the data collection instruments used in the TELT study, along with an analysis of what can be learned about teacher candidates by using these instruments (Kennedy, McDiarmid, and Ball, 1993).

Notice, too, that these two genres, experiments and change studies, rest on quite different assumptions about *how* teacher education is likely to make its difference. Experiments focus on program format—videos versus microteaching, for instance—while change studies focus on program content. Experiments focus on predefined skills whereas change studies look for altered beliefs. Experiments tend to assume that program influences are unidirectional, whereas change studies tend to assume that programs interact with candidates' entering ideas to produce new ideas about teaching. So these two strategies are based on substantially different assumptions, both about what teachers need to learn and about the relationship between programs and teacher candidates. Yet they share research design features that are important to those who want to learn more about whether or how teacher education makes a difference, for both enable us to learn the details of how candidates respond and change as they participate in particular aspects of teacher education.

What I have tried to show in this chapter is that the way a researcher poses his or her research question constrains what can be learned from the study. Such constraining decisions are necessary, for the enterprise of teacher education is too large, complicated, and amorphous to succumb to an all-encompassing study. The challenge facing researchers in teacher education is to maximize the potential of their studies by assuring that the aspects of teacher education they study are meaningful and relevant to teacher educators who want to use research to improve their programs, that the outcomes they examine are valid and sufficient, and that the evidence they gather will enable them to develop credible arguments about whether and how teacher education has made a difference.

References

Adams, R. D., and Craig, J. R. (1983). "A status report of teacher education program evaluation." *Journal of Teacher Education, 34*(2), 33–36.

Arch, E. C. (1989). "Comparison of student attainment of teaching competencies in traditional preservice and fifth-year Master of Arts in Teaching programs." Presented at the annual meeting of the American Educational Research Association, San Francisco.

Beery, J. R. (1960). *Professional preparation and effectiveness of beginning teachers.* Coral Gables, Fla.: Graphic Arts Press.

Begle, E. G., and Geeslin, W. (1972). *Teacher effectiveness in mathematics instruction.* (National

Longitudinal Study of Mathematical Abilities Reports no. 28). Washington, D.C.: Mathematical Association of America and National Council of Teachers of Mathematics.

Benz, C. R. (1984). *The practical value of what first-year teachers have been taught in college: Implications for teacher competency exams.* Akron, Ohio: University of Akron Press. (ED 249 268).

Bledsoe, J. C., Cox, J. V., and Burnham, R. (1967). *Comparison between selected characteristics and performance of provisionally and professionally certified beginning teachers in Georgia.* Washington, D.C.: U.S. Department of Health, Education, and Welfare. (ED 015 553).

Brown, D., Edington, E., Spencer, D. A., and Tinafero, J. (1989). "A comparison of alternative certification, traditionally trained, and emergency permit teachers." *Teacher Education and Practice, 5*(2), 21–23.

Browne, D., and Hoover, J. H. (1990). "The degree to which student teachers report using instructional strategies valued by university faculty." *Action in Teacher Education, 12*(1), 20–24.

Clark, D. C., Smith, R. B., Newburg, J. J., and Cosk, V. A. (1985). "Perceived origins of teaching behavior." *Journal of Teacher Education, 36*(6), 49–53.

Coleman, J. S., and others (1966). *Equality of educational opportunity.* Washington, D.C.: U.S. Department of Health, Education, and Welfare.

Copeland, W. D. (1975). "The relationship between micro-teaching and student teacher classroom performance." *Journal of Educational Research, 68,* 289–293.

Copeland, W. D. (1982). "Laboratory experiences in teacher education." In *Encyclopedia of Educational Research,* Vol. 2. (5th ed.). New York: Free Press.

Cornett, L. M. (1984). *A comparison of teacher certification test scores and performance evaluations of graduates in teacher education and liberal arts and sciences in three southern states.* Atlanta: Southern Regional Education Board.

Cornfield, I. R. (1991). "Microteaching skill generalization and transfer: Training preservice teachers in introductory lesson skills." *Teaching and Teacher Education, 7*(1), 25–56.

Council of Chief State School Officers (1988). *State education indicators, 1988.* Washington, D.C.: Council of Chief State School Officers.

Cruickshank, D. R., and Metcalf, K. K. (1990). "Training within teacher preparation." In W. R. Houston (ed.), *Handbook of research on teacher education.* New York: Macmillan.

Dewalt, M., and Ball, O. W. (1987). "Some effects of training on the competence of beginning teachers." *Journal of Educational Research, 80*(6), 343–347.

Dolan, R. C., and Schmidt, R. M. (1987). "Assessing the impact of expenditure on achievement: Some methodological and policy considerations." *Economics of Education Review, 6*(3), 285–299.

Drummond, R. J. (1976). *Follow-up of 1970–76 College of Education graduates.* Orono: University of Maine Press. (ED 141 306).

Evertson, C. M., Hawley, W. D., and Zlotnik, M. (1985). "Making a difference in educational quality through teacher education." *Journal of Teacher Education, 36*(3), 2–12.

Feiman-Nemser, S., and Buchmann, M. (1989). "Describing teacher education: A framework and illustrative findings from a longitudinal study of six students." *Elementary School Journal, 89,* 365–377.

Ferguson, P., and Womack, S. T. (1993). "The impact of subject matter and education coursework on teaching performance." *Journal of Teacher Education, 44*(1), 55–63.

Ferguson, R. (1990). *Racial patterns in how school and teacher quality affect achievement and earnings.* Cambridge, Mass.: Kennedy School of Government (photocopied).

Fortune, J. C. (1993). "Why production function analysis is irrelevant in policy deliberations concerning educational funding equity." *Education Policy Analysis Archives, 1*(11).

Gaede, O. F. (1978). "Reality shock: A problem among first-year teachers." *Clearinghouse, 51*(9), 405–409.

Gage, N. L. (1977). *The scientific basis of the art of teaching.* New York: Teachers College Press.

Gage, N. L. (1985). *Hard gains in the soft sciences: The case of pedagogy.* Bloomington, Ind.: Phi Delta Kappa.

Galluzzo, G. (1984). "An evaluation of a teacher education program." Paper presented at the annual meeting of the American Educational Research Association, New Orleans.

Galluzzo, G., and Craig, J. R. (1990). "Evaluation of preservice teacher education programs." In W. R. Houston (ed.), *Handbook of research on teacher education.* New York: Macmillan.

Gerlach, D. E. (1964). "An analysis of administrators' evaluations of selected professionally and provisionally certified secondary school teachers." Doctoral dissertation, Florida State University. (University Microfilm no. 65–5580).

Gliessman, D. H. (1987). "Changing complex teaching skills." *Journal of Education for Teaching, 13*(3), 267–275.

Gliessman, D. H., and Pugh, R. C. (1987). "Conceptual instruction and intervention as methods of acquiring teaching skills." In H. Tellema and S.A.M. Veenman (eds.), Developments in training methods for teacher education. *International Journal of Education, 11,* 555–563.

Goldman, E., and Barron, L. (1990). "Using hypermedia to improve the preparation of elementary teachers." *Journal of Teacher Education, 41*(3), 21–31.

Good, T. L., and Brophy, J. E. (1986). School effects. In M. C. Wittrock (ed.), *Handbook of research on teaching.* (3rd ed.). New York: Macmillan.

Goodman, J. (1986). "What students learn from early field experiences: A case study and critical analysis." *Journal of Teacher Education, 36*(6), 42–48.

Gray, H. B. (1962). "A study of the outcomes of preservice education associated with three levels of teacher certification." Doctoral dissertation, Florida State University. (University Microfilm no. 63–1814).

Grossman, P. L. (1990). *The making of a teacher: Teacher knowledge and teacher education.* New York: Teachers College Press.

Haberman, M. (1985). "Does teacher education make a difference? A review of comparisons of liberal arts and teacher education majors." *Journal of Thought, 20*(2), 25–34.

Hall, H. O. (1964). "Professional preparation and teacher effectiveness." *Journal of Teacher Education, 15*(1), 72–76.

Hanushek, E. A. (1971). "Teacher characteristics and gains in student achievement: Estimation using micro data." *American Economic Review, 61*(2), 280–288.

Hanushek, E. A. (1972). *Education and race: An analysis of the educational production process.* Lexington, Mass.: Heath.

Hanushek, E. A. (1989). "The impact of differential expenditures on school performance." *Educational Researcher, 18*(3), 45–51, 62.

Henry, M. K. (1986). "Strengths and needs of first-year teachers." *Teacher Educator, 22*(2), 10–18.

Hodges, C. (1982). "Implementing methods: If you can't blame the cooperating teacher, who can you blame?" *Journal of Teacher Education, 33*(6), 25–29.

Hollingsworth, S. (1989). "Prior beliefs and cognitive change in learning to teach." *American Educational Research Journal, 26*(2), 160–189.

Katz, L. G., and Raths, J. D. (1985). "A framework for research on teacher education programs." *Journal of Teacher Education, 36*(10), 9–15.

Kennedy, M. M. (1991). "Some surprising findings on how teachers learn to teach." *Educational Leadership, 49*(11), 14–17.

Kennedy, M. M., McDiarmid, G. W., and Ball, D. L. (1993). *A study package for examining and tracking changes in teachers' knowledge.* East Lansing, Mich.: National Center for Research on Teacher Learning.

Klesius, J. P., Searls, E. F., and Zielonka, P. (1990). "A comparison of two methods of direct instruction of preservice teachers." *Journal of Teacher Education, 41*(4), 34–43.

Koehler, V. (1985). "Research on preservice teacher education." *Journal of Teacher Education, 36*(1), 23–30.

Koziol, S. M., Jr., and Burns, P. (1986). "Teachers' accuracy in self-reporting about instructional practices using a focused self-report inventory." *Journal of Educational Research, 79*(4), 205–209.

Loadman, W. E., and Gustafson, G. L. (1990). *National database for teacher education program follow-up.* Columbus: College of Education, Ohio State University.

LuPone, L. J. (1961). "A comparison of provisionally certified and permanently certified elementary teachers in selected school districts in New York State." *Journal of Educational Research, 55*(2), 53–63.

McIntyre, D. J., and Killian, J. E. (1986). "Students' interactions with pupils and cooperating teachers in early field experiences." *Teacher Educator, 22*(2), 2–9.

McIntyre, D. J., and Killian, J. E. (1987). "The influence of supervisory training for cooperating teachers on preservice teacher development during early field experiences." *Journal of Educational Research, 80*(5), 277–282.

Murnane, R. J. (1981). "Interpreting the evidence on school effectiveness." *Teachers College Record, 83*(1), 19–35.

Murnane, R. J. (1985). "Do effective teachers have common characteristics? Interpreting the quantitative evidence." Paper presented to the National Research Council Conference on Teacher Quality in Science and Mathematics, Washington, D.C.

Murnane, R. J., and Phillips, B. R. (1981). "What do effective teachers of inner-city children have in common?" *Social Science Research, 10,* 83–100.

National Center for Education Statistics (1989). *Digest of education statistics, 1989.* Washington, D.C.: National Center for Education Statistics.

National Center for Research on Teacher Education (1991). *Initial findings from the Teacher Education and Learning to Teach (TELT) study.* East Lansing, Mich.: National Center for Research on Teacher Education.

Pascarella, E. T., and Terenzini, P. T. (1991). *How college affects students: Findings and insights from twenty years of research.* San Francisco: Jossey-Bass.

Peck, H. I. (1989). "The effect of certification status on the performance of mathematics teachers: A pilot study." Paper presented at the annual meeting of the American Educational Research Association, San Francisco.

Pigge, F. L. (1978). "Teacher competencies: Need, proficiency, and where proficiency was developed." *Journal of Teacher Education, 29*(4), 70–76.

Popham, W. J. (1971). "Performance tests of teaching proficiency: Rationale, development, and validation." *American Educational Research Journal, 8*(1), 105–117.

Reed, H. B. (1975). *Evaluation of alternative approaches to teacher preparation.* Amherst: University of Massachusetts Press. (ED 147 335).

Ryan, K., and others (1979). "'My teacher education program? Well, . . .': First-year teachers reflect and react." *Peabody Journal of Education, 56,* 267–271.

Schmelter, R. C. (n.d.). A follow-up study of mathematics education majors from the University of Wisconsin, Oshkosh, 1985. Oshkosh: University of Wisconsin. (ED 265 034).

Silvernail, D. L., and Costello, M. H. (1983). "The impact of student teaching and internship programs on preservice teachers' pupil control perspectives, anxiety levels, and teaching concerns." *Journal of Teacher Education, 36*(4), 32–36.

Skipper, C. E., and Quantz, R. (1987). "Changes in educational attitudes of education and arts and sciences students during four years of college." *Journal of Teacher Education, 38*(3), 39–44.

Smylie, M. A. (1989). "Teachers' views of the effectiveness of sources of learning to teach." *Elementary School Journal, 89*(5), 543–558.

Strang, H. R., Badt, K. S., and Kauffman, J. M. (1987). "Microcomputer-based simulations for training fundamental teaching skills." *Journal of Teacher Education, 38*(1), 20–26.

Strauss, R. P., and Sawyer, E. A. (1986). "Some new evidence on teacher and student competencies." *Economics of Education Review, 5*(1), 41–48.

Tabachnick, B. R., and Zeichner, K. M. (1984). "The impact of student teaching experience on the development of teacher perspectives." *Journal of Teacher Education, 35*(6), 28–36.

Tisher, R. P., and Klinzing, H. G. (1992). "Procedures to develop classroom teaching skills: Modeling, cases, simulations and microteaching." *South Pacific Journal of Teacher Education, 20*(1), 35–47.

Valli, L., and Agnostinelli, A. (1992). "Teaching with and without formal preparation." Paper presented at the annual meeting of the American Educational Research Association, San Francisco.

Veenman, S.A.M. (1984). "Perceived problems of beginning teachers." *Review of Educational Research, 54,* 143–178.

Warren, R. D., Dilts, H. E., Thompson, A. D., and Blaustein, M. H. (1982). *Follow-up study of first-year Iowa State graduates: General frequency report.* Ames: Iowa State University Press. (ED 270 436).

Winitzky, N. E., and Arends, R. I. (1991). "Translating research into practice: The effects of various forms of training and clinical experiences on preservice students' knowledge, skills, and reflectiveness." *Journal of Teacher Education, 42*(1), 52–65.

Annotated Bibliography

Copeland, W. D. (1982). "Laboratory experiences in teacher education." In *Encyclopedia of educational research,* Vol. 2. (5th ed.). New York: Free Press.
This article is a good review of experimental literature. It illustrates the aspects of teacher education programs that these researchers focus on and it summarizes findings as well. He reviews research on microteaching, protocols, and simulations.

Evertson, C. M., Hawley, W. D., and Zlotnik, M. (1985). "Making a difference in educational quality through teacher education." *Journal of Teacher Education, 36*(3), 2–12.
This is a good review of a variety of research approaches to teacher education. It is aimed more at making sense of the findings than at analyzing the merits of different designs, but the authors do point out that many studies fail to take into account program content and goals.

Feiman-Nemser, S., and Buchmann, M. (1989). "Describing teacher education: A framework and illustrative findings from a longitudinal study of six students." *Elementary School Journal, 89,* 365–377.
The "watch teachers change" genre is still relatively new in teacher education and no good reviews of this literature currently exist. This study, and the one below, offer good examples of what can be learned from such studies.

Haberman, M. (1985). "Does teacher education make a difference? A review of comparisons of liberal arts and teacher education majors." *Journal of Thought, 20*(2), 25–34.
This paper reviews a set of recent studies comparing liberal arts graduates with teacher education graduates. In addition to reviewing the findings, Haberman also

discusses some of the issues that are not addressed in these studies but that should be if we are to improve their value.

Hanushek, E. A. (1989). "The impact of differential expenditures on school performance." *Educational Researcher, 18*(3), 45–51, 62.
This paper reviews findings from open search studies and discusses some of the methodological issues but concentrates mainly on the findings and their implications for educational policy. It offers a good example of how findings from these studies are interpreted for policy.

Hollingsworth, S. (1989). "Prior beliefs and cognitive change in learning to teach." *American Educational Research Journal, 26*(2), 160–189.
The "watch teachers change" approach is still relatively new in teacher education and no good reviews of this literature currently exist. This study, and the one above, offer good examples of what can be learned from such studies.

Katz, L. G., and others (1981). "Follow-up studies: Are they worth the trouble?" *Journal of Teacher Education, 32*(2), 18–24.
This paper reviews a sample of twenty-six ask-the-teacher studies, all of which are follow-up surveys of program graduates. The authors summarize some of the methodological problems in these studies, including response rates, problems of validity and reliability of the survey instruments, and credibility of the conclusions that are drawn from the studies.

Veenman, S.A.M. (1984). "Perceived problems of beginning teachers." *Review of Educational Research, 54,* 143–178.
This literature review focuses more on the perceived needs of beginning teachers than on the impact of teacher education per se. It has the advantage, however, of being international in its scope.

PART TWO

SUBJECT MATTER KNOWLEDGE

CHAPTER SIX

PATHWAY FROM THE LIBERAL ARTS CURRICULUM TO LESSONS IN THE SCHOOLS

FRANK B. MURRAY AND ANDREW PORTER

Teacher educators are confronted by five broad questions about the liberal arts component of their teacher education programs. The issues and problems raised within each of these questions constitute a rough map of a complex pathway by which subject matter travels back and forth, so to speak, between the prospective teacher in the university and the student in the school. The questions cannot be avoided and they are often answered by omission but answered nevertheless, as each teacher education faculty, one way or another, takes an implicit or explicit stand on each question.

Question 1. Subject matter understanding. How should teachers acquire a knowledge of the discipline(s) they are licensed to teach? The traditional college major would seem to be the right answer to this question, but it is not the complete answer as it can be shown to be insufficient, and sometimes misleading, preparation (McDiarmid, 1990).

Question 2. General and liberal knowledge. How do teacher education graduates become well-informed persons? Beyond being well informed, however, how do prospective teachers come to have the habits of mind that have always been claimed for a liberal education? These habits are essential if teachers are to become more than technicians.

Question 3. Pedagogical content knowledge. How do teacher education students learn how to convert their knowledge of the subject matter into lessons for a wide range of pupils? This is the weakest link in teacher education programs and the area that requires the most intense cooperation between faculties in education and in the arts and sciences.

Question 4. Multicultural, international, and other human perspectives. For all persons, but especially for prospective teachers, the college curriculum must be accurate with respect to the best of recent scholarship on matters of race, gender, ethnicity, and cultural perspective. Making the curriculum accurate in this way is difficult in view of the fact that scholarship is often incomplete and merely suggestive and most higher education faculty were educated in a period when there was very little sensitivity to, or awareness of, alternative perspectives in each curricular domain. How will teachers acquire the dispositions to act on their new knowledge in the sensitive and accepting manner that leads to high levels of achievement for all their pupils?

Question 5. The teacher's decisions about the content to be taught. However the teacher education and arts and science faculties answer the four questions above about what students in teacher education programs will study, there are other issues that need to be considered and addressed in the teacher education program. These center on the guidance that can be provided to prospective teachers about such matters as the following:

1. How much time should the teacher allocate to a subject?
2. What topics are to be taught within the time allocated?
3. Which students will study what topics?
4. When and in what order will the topics be taught?
5. What standards of achievement should the teacher set?

Question 1: How Should Teachers Learn the Subjects They Will Teach?

Everyone agrees that teachers must know the subject matters they hope to teach their pupils (Buchmann, 1984). The academic major, however, is not by itself an adequate preparation in the subject matter the student will teach (Kennedy, 1991). By and large, since the traditional academic major is geared toward graduate study or entry-level employment, it does not induce in students the kind of basic subject matter understanding necessary to be an effective teacher.

Apart from the purposes of major, there are problems with the scope of a major's contents for some teaching assignments such as elementary school teaching. The prospective elementary teacher, for example, needs to be well grounded in mathematics, literature, writing, history, geography, the natural and social sciences, the fine arts, language, and much more. Similar problems are found at the secondary level in social studies or general science teaching, which are informed by several distinct university subjects or majors, each of which is a full university course of study in its own right.

We do know that reasonably well-educated college and university graduates find themselves in difficulty in their attempts to answer coherently, and with integrity, the questions that young children are likely to put to them (Ball, 1991). Ball (1990) reported, for example, that mathematics majors were no more successful than were nonmajors in thinking of real-world events that corresponded to the arithmetical problem "divide the fraction $1^3/_4$ by the fraction $1/2$." Apart from the mistake of providing examples of dividing by 2 instead of $1/2$, the student who had majored in mathematics did not have the kind of mathematical understanding that would support the teaching of this and other elementary topics.

If the traditional academic major provides inadequate preparation for school teaching, what would constitute adequate subject matter preparation? Murray (1991) suggested six approaches to the academic major for elementary teachers, each of which illustrates how complicated it would be for teacher educators to provide for the prospective teacher's mastery of the elementary subject matter.

Interdisciplinary Major

This option, while clearly appropriate for elementary education majors, also applies to some secondary education majors (for example, social studies or general science). In the case of the elementary school teacher, the option would consist of reformed minors in the areas of the school curriculum: mathematics, foreign language, history and social science, English, natural science, and fine arts. Apart from the fact that each minor would need to be responsive to the unique requirements of the elementary school teacher, the interdisciplinary minor option is fairly conservative and administratively feasible. It is an honest approach insofar as each major area of the elementary school curriculum is addressed, but it would suffer from the same weaknesses that are found in the traditional major if the minor were not reformed along the lines that follow.

Philosophy and Structure of the Subject Matter Major

This option might be a major in philosophy with an emphasis on the philosophy or basic structure of the appropriate subject matters (for example, the philosophy of science, mathematics, language, and so forth), in which essential and fundamental aspects of the subject matter are covered.

Text Approach or "Great Books" Major

This approach entails a close reading of seminal texts in each area (the "great books") coupled with an examination of school textbooks for the assumptions they make about the discipline in question. The logic of this approach, like the philosophy of the disciplines approach, is that the core structure of the discipline is addressed directly but in the introductory manner in which it was first presented historically. This approach also has the advantage of providing some guidance about whether some subject matter conceptions are more sophisticated, elegant, or powerful than other conceptions. Does quantum mechanics, for example, provide a "better" way of thinking about light than wave, particle, or phlogiston theories of light? How will the teacher determine which subject matter concepts are more advanced (above the standard, and so on)—those that came later historically, those espoused by older students, those that have greater "meaning" for the student? In the field of descriptive statistics, for example, how would the teacher determine which way of thinking about central tendency and variation is "above standard" or superior? Which mental representation of central tendency and variation is more sophisticated, one based upon physical models of equilibrium, or upon computer graphics representations of data points, or upon calculation formulas, or one seen as the solution to certain questions in the behavioral sciences, or as derivations of algebraic equations, or as part of a system of expressions in calculus or some other branch of mathematics? Whatever the answer, the study of subject matter in the teacher education program needs to yield guidance on these kinds of questions—questions that the teacher also cannot avoid in the evaluation of student performance.

The Cognitive Psychology Major

In this option, the student would simply major in cognitive psychology and specialize in the workings of the mind. The subject matter content would be picked up through the consideration of how the mind operates mathematically, aesthetically, and so forth. Like the philosophy of the disciplines or text approaches, this approach would provide a structure for the reformed minors in each subject area. Each area would be approached from the perspective of how we think about and know the content in question. The approach fits well with the current trend in cognitive psychology that stresses the domain specificity of our thinking, but it suffers like those above from the lack of fit with the current organization of the higher education faculty and curriculum.

Genetic Epistemology as a Major

This option has a distinct advantage in that it addresses another dimension of standards-based reform by providing a way of determining whether the pupil's performance is "developmentally" or "cognitively" above, at, or below an academic standard. It entails the study of the developmental psychological literature of the concepts that make up the curriculum.

In this approach, the teacher education student learns the relevant developmental constraints upon the pupil's acquisition of the curriculum and also learns, as an unavoidable part of the discussion, the nature of the subject matter itself. The story of how the young child develops the notion of number, for example, is valuable in its own right, but it also reveals salient portions of number theory, the arithmetical algorithms, and other aspects of mathematics. Similarly, the account of the child's moral development reveals the principal issues in moral philosophy and political theory.

It would not be possible to study the development of the child's concept of weight without studying the same notion as it appears in Newtonian mechanics and other branches of physics. The young child, for example, can be shown to operate with the following "equation" for weight (Murray and Johnson, 1970, 1975):

Weight $= f$ (the object's mass, size, shape, texture, temperature, hardness, continuity, label, but not the object's horizontal or vertical position in space)

The elementary school teacher needs to be aware of the young child's view of weight because it is based on a consistent "child logic" that conceals many misconceptions about weight. These misconceptions obviously have implications for pedagogy and curriculum design (Murray and Markessini, 1982). Adolescents and many adults operate with the following simpler and to some degree more sophisticated "equation":

$$\text{WEIGHT} = f \text{ (the object's mass)}$$

In other words, the only way adults can think of to change an object's weight is to alter its mass, that is, add something or take something away from the object. The young child can imagine many other ways for altering weight, all unfortunately incorrect.

The educated person operates with another, presumably more advanced, expression:

$$\text{Weight} = f \frac{\text{(mass of the object x mass of the planet)}}{\text{(square of the distance between their centers)}}$$

In addition, the educated person may be able to convert the expression into a still more advanced form as a genuine equation via a value, g, for the gravitational constant, which permits algebraic manipulation of the terms in the expression. At this point, other more "advanced" factors may be introduced into the expression to treat certain buoyant forces or variations in the earth's g, and so forth. This series of expressions, or one similar to it, provides at the moment the only guidance the field has in the determination of criteria for standards for this aspect of the science curriculum.

There is a similar developmental progression for the child's understanding of the beam balance, in which the young child's understanding of "weighing" is controlled solely by the effects of adding or subtracting weight from a beam balance pan without regard to the influence of any other factor (Siegler, 1981). Later, the distance of the balance pan from the fulcrum is gradually factored into the child's scheme for the operation of the balance, and after several more developmental steps, we see the product moment law in place in the adolescent's thinking.

All concepts and relations in the curriculum can be profitably approached from this perspective. The approach also has face validity in teacher education because it contains the kinds of information that prospective teachers accept as clearly relevant for their future work, particularly the evaluation of whether the pupil's understanding meets a content standard.

The prospective teacher's study of genetic epistemology, however, is more than a device by which students in teacher education might learn their academic disciplines. It goes to the core of the kind of knowledge the teacher needs, namely generative ways of organizing information and knowledge. It entails the search for structures, alternate ways of representing the subject matter, analogies and metaphors, that could take *each* pupil well beyond what can be held together temporally and spatially through rote memorization.

The Pedagogical Content Knowledge Minor

This approach presupposes a "genetic epistemological approach" and addresses the fact that teachers go beyond these developmental considerations as they inevitably transform what they know into a teachable subject. They give the subject a new structure and meaning, one that is appropriate to their students' level of understanding. These structures can be studied and codified, although the literature in this aspect of education is regrettably scarce. Since the reformulation of the discipline is inevitable in teaching, one might as well address it directly and examine it in the context of learning the academic disciplines.

Question 2: What Are the Uses of a Liberal Arts Education in Teacher Education?

Almost every educational reform report has made the unchallenged claim that teachers need to be well schooled in the liberal arts. Rarely have reasons been advanced for this claim, as it has almost a self-evident quality to it. When reasons have been advanced, they have been in support of a somewhat different proposition, namely that teachers ought to be well grounded in the subjects they teach to their pupils. Sometimes the claim for the liberal arts has been made on the grounds that teachers ought to be well-educated persons, and well-educated persons are only those who have been schooled in the liberal arts. Even here, there is confusion, because being well informed is not the same thing as being liberally educated. General and liberal education are about different things, the one being about having good and dependable information and the other about knowing what the point of something is and what is worth doing (Blits, 1985).

Liberal arts education is about knowledge and information that the teacher does not teach directly and may not ever teach, yet it is about knowledge that is presumed to influence teaching and other human endeavors in several important ways. The historical claims for the study of the liberal arts are the following:

1. They are worth knowing for their own sake; they are ends in themselves, activities that make human life complete.
2. They are appropriate for the free person—free of utilitarian concerns, free from the need of labor; in other words, they are studies that are appropriate for leisure.
3. They promote the full realization of what it means to be human and intelligent and support the selection of wise and good ends for the community and oneself.
4. They set the student free from the bondage of convention, from unanalyzed custom and opinion, from the tyranny of dogma and assertion—free to search out and construct truth.
5. They make a difference when they are heard; they have an effect of persuading others to take up virtuous and just courses of action, and they yield good citizens who can lead the society wisely and to good ends.
6. They show the student how, by the power of human reason, to search for and construct truths not heretofore known and truths that are inevitably provisional because all the thinkers have not, and could not have, completed their work.
7. They enable the student to tell the truth eloquently about the most durable and best of what has been learned.
8. Most important, the liberal arts should lead to the invention and understanding of good ends and to a clear conception of the good and proper outcomes of teaching.

Though the actual content of the liberal course of study may be somewhat arbitrary, its outcome is not: it must take the prospective teacher beyond technique and algorithms. It is not widely appreciated in this regard that the so-called foundation courses in teacher education are also properly a part of the liberal arts component. Rarely do these courses have direct relevance for the classroom and they are, as a result, often criticized by teacher education students and teachers in the field. It is a misguided criticism, however, because these courses offer explanations of schooling, not prescriptions or remedies for schooling. Their function in the teacher education program is the same as the claims made for the function of the liberal arts, and therefore they should be held to the standard we set for the liberal arts component.

Question 3: How Are Academic Disciplines Transformed into School Lessons?

All teachers know that the subject matter they teach is different from the subject matter they learned from their own teachers. The teacher inevitably transforms the subject matter into something else: a teachable subject that has its own structure and logic that will help the student make sense of the subject matter. The knowledge that supports this conversion of the storehouse of knowledge into the school curriculum, into something that has meaning for the pupil, is what we meant earlier by the expression *pedagogical content knowledge.*

Pedagogical content knowledge (Shulman, 1986, 1987) rests upon the structures of genetic epistemology and confers some appropriate level of understanding and is ultimately about those structures that actually advance our understanding (see Murray and Fallon, 1989).

As an example, the young elementary school child will be taught one of the algorithms for subtraction. There are several options for taking 67 from 95, for example. The two numbers in the problem can be regrouped and represented as (60 + 7) taken from (80 + 15), by a strategy known as "decomposition," or the numbers in the problem may be represented as (70 + 7) taken from (90 + 15), by a strategy known as "equal additions"; or more elaborate and equally correct algorithms can be taught in which the correct answer, 28, is reached by making different combinations of calculations that are also sound and academically sensible. On what basis should the teacher choose an algorithm for the lesson since mathematically there is no basis for selecting one algorithm over another, except perhaps elegance or parsimony? Kamii (1989), for example, found that young children will invent yet other strategies that are a more natural outgrowth of the young child's understanding of numbers than are the usual school-taught algorithms of decomposition or equal additions.

This knowledge—of what is a telling example, a good analogy, algorithm or heuristic, a provocative question, a compelling theme—is a proper object of study of educators and could yield a deep and generative understanding of the disciplines. To have multiple ways of representing a subject matter, to have more than one example or metaphor, to have more than one mode of explanation requires a high order and demanding form of subject matter understanding.

Educational critics often say that, owing to the low quality of teaching, school pupils and university students are driven to memorize by rote large portions of the curriculum, with the point of education being little more than to return this rotely memorized and undigested material to the teacher on an examination. However, the human mind cannot memorize very much material by rote, in fact probably not much more than half a dozen unrelated items at a time. Even the marginal pupil who confronts the massive amounts of material in the school and university curriculum finds a way to impose some structure, some organizational scheme, on the material. The question is never whether or not there was some structure, theory, scheme, and so forth but only whether the structure was good or poor, above, below, or at standard. Whatever the teacher actually did in the lesson, the pupils will find some way to make sense of it, to code it, to assimilate it into what they already know, often with an outcome the teacher may never have intended. The nearly universal error of the pupil's mistaking Martin Luther King for Martin Luther in the world history class is just one of a thousand examples, many quite humorous, of the pupil's often desperate attempt to make sense of what is presented by the teacher.

In the end, the discussion of pedagogical content knowledge becomes a discussion of the appropriate ways of organizing information and knowledge. It is the search for structures, ways of representing the subject matter, analogies and metaphors, that will take *each* pupil well beyond what can be held together temporally and spatially through rote memorization. At the lowest pedagogical content knowledge level, there are mnemonic structures that can carry the student past the half-dozen rotely memorized items, but these structures accomplish very little other than improving retention and defending the memorized items against the rapid forgetting that is the hallmark of most rotely learned material. The mnemonic device *roygbiv* can provide the student with the order of the spectral colors. Like all mnemonic devices, however, it fails to provide understanding, giving no clue about how or why the spectral phenomenon takes place, why the order of colors is reversed in the second rainbow of a double set, and so on. Knowing the order of the colors can be very helpful and may be essential information for the solution to many higher order problems, but education requires more than this. Pedagogical content knowledge is fundamentally about those structures that confer some appropriate level of understanding, and it is ultimately about those structures that actually advance our understanding.

Discussions of pedagogical content knowledge are at the heart of the teacher educator's work and cannot be avoided. *Hamlet* will undoubtedly be taught at some point, but how should it be represented, what is it about—the use of language to talk about language, the pathology of indecision, the unconscious mind of the adolescent, or the recreation of a historical event? The discussion of pedagogical content knowledge needs to acknowledge that some structures are scaffolds, and as scaffolds they are provisional and designed solely to advance the pupil to another place. Thus, it may be appropriate to introduce the *1812 Overture,* and by implication all classical music, as the recreation of an event, as program music, in which the two national anthems battle each other in the overture as the armies did on the battlefield. This representation, or structure, which is hopelessly inadequate for any later understanding of musical composition, may provide a beginning scaffold that will engage the pupil. At the same time, other provisional structures, such as comparing gravitational force to magnetic force or pulmonary circulation to a hot air return heating system, may inhibit the subsequent understanding of topics in physics or physiology.

Question 4: How Can the Teacher Education Curriculum Be Made More Accurate?

Tomorrow's teachers will face classrooms of pupils that will be markedly more diverse and varied than today's classrooms. Tomorrow's teachers and tomorrow's pupils will be very different from each other.

The issue of cultural diversity is not a peripheral matter or merely a desirable add-on in teacher education. The issue is at the heart of the reform of the courses of study in both education and the arts and sciences because the honesty and accuracy of the curriculum is at stake. The charge that higher education is parochial and insensitive to international and global matters, as well as to matters of significance to the nation's many minority groups, is fundamentally a charge that the curriculum is wrong, the very thing it cannot be! To give one example, the discipline of psychology turns out to be very different from what is presented in the standard introductory textbook when it is qualified by the contributions of African-American psychologists (see Guthrie, 1976, for examples).

The point is that the study of minority issues or the study of global or international issues will fail as they have in the past if they are not anchored, passionately and with conviction, in the core values of the academy. Attempts to secure a place for these matters in federal law and regulation, in arguments about compensation for past injustice, in assertions about fairness and decency, in appeals to the specter of failure in the international markets, or in the realization that minorities can exert political power over the allocation of public dollars may produce short-term gains. They will fail ultimately to win a place for cultural diversity in higher education, however, because the effort can be deflected so easily by its critics when it is based on these short-term considerations and arguments. Moreover, the diversity in the educational history of the various American minority groups is too complex and inconsistent for such an approach.

The stories of the various European immigrant minority groups, Native American groups, black Americans (for example, African, Jamaican, Haitian, Melanesian, and others), Hispanic groups (Mexican, Cuban, Puerto Rican, Dominican, Spanish, and more) are each unique and different within themselves in various historical periods and within and between geographical regions.

The one sure anchor for international education and the study of cultural diversity is the core value of the academy, namely the pursuit of truth. At each stage of cognitive development, an individual's cognitive growth is enhanced by the confrontation of divergent views, by the clash of paradigms, perspectives, and theories. The history of the great universities is largely the story of an ever widening inclusion, however slow, of different groups and views, based in part on inclusion as a value in its own right. More important, the core values of the academy are enhanced by the inclusion of more groups, both among the students and the faculty, in the quest for a more coherent account of things. Intellectual evolution, like biological evolution, is enhanced by a base of variability, a base of multiple perspectives and interests, which contains many different kinds of candidates for success.

The prospective teacher, however, needs more than a firm grasp of subject matter that is shaped by important modern and postmodern scholarship and by the political tension among Western traditionalists, multiculturalists, and Afrocentrists (Banks, 1993). There can never be, for all practical purposes, a close match between the deep knowledge of various cultures and language groups and the actual variation a teacher can expect to find in any classroom of a large urban school system, several of which have speakers from more than a hundred different language groups. Consequently, the teacher cannot be expected to actually know that, for example, an Eskimo child might resist summarizing a story because of a cultural prohibition against speaking for another, or that some Native American students might subvert the school's policy on cheating because their culture requires cooperation among peers. Rather, the prospective teacher has little option but to acquire the attitudes and skills of the teacher of English as a Second Language (ESL). ESL teachers teach English to classrooms of students, none of whom know English and all of whom speak a language the ESL teacher either does not or in any case need not speak. Teachers' attitudes, dispositions, and skills need not be restricted to language teaching but carry equal force in the teaching of other subject matters to students with diverse backgrounds.

Question 5: How Does the Teacher Decide What Subject Matter to Teach?

However the teacher education and arts and science faculties answer the four questions above about what teacher education students will study in the college or university, there remains another set of questions that needs to be considered and addressed in the teacher education program.

Regardless of a teacher's subject matter knowledge, many decisions must be made about exactly what to teach, first in creating a syllabus but most importantly in actually delivering instruction. Teachers, as professional educators, are responsible for deciding how their classroom will be organized and what pedagogical strategies will be employed. No one doubts a teacher's responsibility for deciding if cooperative groups are to be used, if class discussion is to be emphasized, when and under what circumstances student behavior is to be rewarded. Few limits are placed on how teachers are to teach, essentially only limits set by standards of safety and fairness to students. But what about content? Putting aside for the moment the how of teaching, who should have a say in deciding what is to be taught? What is the teacher's role in making content decisions?

Regardless of who should have a say in specifying what should be taught, the teacher is the one who ultimately decides what content is covered in the classroom. A teacher may or may not choose the textbook used, but the teacher invariably decides how to use the book: what chapters will be covered and which will be skipped, what will be emphasized and what will be downplayed, and how fast to go (Freeman and Porter, 1989). Teachers also decide whether or not to emphasize in instruction the content that is emphasized on tests given for purposes of external accountability. In practice, teachers may teach pretty much what they taught last year. Beginning teachers may teach what they remember having been taught when they were students. Teachers may teach only that which they think their students are capable of learning; these expectations about students may or may not be accurate. Teachers may teach only that which they think students are willing to work to learn (Sedlak, Wheeler, Pullin, and Cusick, 1986). Alternatively, teachers may resist student demands for less work, clinging instead to standards that they have inferred from others or their own sense of what is right. Teachers may believe that the subject they are teaching has a hierarchical structure so that, for example, in mathematics, problem solving cannot be taught until computational skills are mastered; or teachers may be persuaded by cognitive science research that shows that students are capable of understanding complex problem solving long before they have mastered computational skills and that in fact their mastery of computation is often enhanced by integrating instruction on computation with instruction on problem solving (Romberg and Carpenter, 1986).

While teachers must ultimately decide what to teach, in doing so they face a near infinite number of possible sources of advice on how to make those decisions. Sorting through the possibilities, they may take into account their own knowledge, believing that it is not possible for them to teach something effectively that they do not really understand themselves.

What Is Content?

Distinguishing between content and pedagogy is not easy. At a crude level, the distinction works quite well. Content is the "what" of instruction. If instruction is 100 percent effective, then content is what students would know and know how to do. In contrast, pedagogy is the "how" of instruction. But when one pushes hard on the distinction between content and pedagogy, the distinction begins to blur. A page of story problems in a mathematics textbook may seem like problem solving content, and it may be. But what if all fifteen story problems on the page have the same form, and what if each requires a solution of multiplying one single-digit number times another single-digit number? At some point, as the student works through the problems, the task changes from one of problem solving to one of drill- and-practice on single-digit multiplication.

Nevertheless, at a conceptual level, distinguishing between content and pedagogy is often useful. In deciding upon the content of instruction, teachers must make a number of decisions that collectively define a student's opportunity to learn (Porter and others, 1988).

Teachers must decide *how much time* to allocate to a content area. In elementary school, decisions about time include decisions regarding how long a lesson should be, whether a subject should be taught every day of the week, and whether or not time must be made up when a lesson is missed due to a convocation or field trip. In high school, many decisions about time are made by the structure of the school day. An instructional period may be fifty minutes or two hours; a subject may be scheduled to meet five days a week or three days a week. To some extent, at the high school level, decisions about time are delegated to students. For example, students must decide which courses to take, although they are frequently advised into one track or another.

A teacher must decide upon *what topics to cover* within the allocated time. In a course on U.S. history, what events will be covered and what are students are to know about those events? Will students be expected to draw inferences from what they know?

A teacher must decide *whether all students will be taught the same content* or whether different students will receive different content according to the teacher's perceptions of students' interests and/or abilities. Again, in elementary school, decisions about which students study what content are largely under the teacher's direct control, with the exception of pullout programs for compensatory and special education. Teachers may form instructional groups with differentiated content, they may individualize instruction, or they may use whole group instruction. At the high school level, a great deal of differentiation is beyond the teacher's direct control—for example, what track a student is placed in and what electives a student decides to take. Still, there is room within a particular course for a teacher to differentiate among students in assignments given.

Finally, teachers must decide *what standards to hold* for student accomplishment. Obviously, the more stringent the standards, the more likely the pace of instruction will be slowed and the breadth of content covered narrowed. Lundgren (1972) discovered that teachers use a "steering group"—a small group of students that the teacher monitors most closely for their understanding—to make pacing decisions. According to Lundgren, in classrooms in Western cultures, the typical teacher's steering group consists of two or three students at approximately the 20th percentile on achievement/aptitude for that class.

A student's opportunity to learn is defined by decisions about how much time to allocate, what topics to cover, which students study which topics, and to what standards of achievement. Student opportunity to learn is not only an output of schooling in its own right; it is also the single most powerful school-controlled determinant of student achievement (Sebring, 1987; Schmidt, 1983a, 1983b). Clearly, opportunity to learn is a necessary yet insufficient ingredient for student achievement. In addition, instruction must be pedagogically sound, and students must be ready and motivated.

Because decisions about the content of instruction are decisions that are typically made without much deliberation, teachers lack a language for describing content. Research on teachers' content decision making in elementary school mathematics created a language defined by a three-dimensional taxonomy: (1) general intent (for example, conceptual understanding, skills, applications), (2) the nature of material presented to students (fractions, decimals, and so on), and (3) the operation the student must perform (for example, estimate, multiply) (Kuhs and others, 1979). The three dimensions are crossed so that a topic is defined as the intersection (for example, story problems involving addition of whole numbers, basic subtraction facts, understanding the concept of place value). More general topics are described by the marginals of each of the three dimensions (for example, the emphasis given to conceptual understanding). More recently, this work has been extended to create languages for describing the content of high school mathematics and science (Porter and others, 1993). Again, the languages are represented by taxonomies, one for math and one for science. The first two dimensions describe what usually comes to mind first when thinking of content. In mathematics, distinctions are made among such general areas as arithmetic, measurement, geometry, trigonometry, and within each general area, finer distinctions such as for statistics, distinguishing among distributional shapes, central tendency variability, correlation or regression sampling, and point estimates of parameters. General content areas for science include biology of the cell, human biology, chemistry, physics, and the like. Each of these general areas is further broken down by the second dimension of the taxonomy. The third and fourth dimensions of the taxonomies are common to both mathematics and science. Modes of instruction distinguish between exposition, pictorial models, concrete models, equations/formulas, graphical, laboratory work, and field work. The types of knowledge or skills that students are expected to acquire are broken down into memorize facts/definitions/equations; understand concepts; collect data; order, compare, estimate, and approximate; perform procedures; solve routine problems; replicate experiments/replicate proofs; interpret data and recognize patterns; recognize, formulate, and solve novel problems/design experiments; build and revise theories/develop proofs. Again, topics are defined by the intersection of the four dimensions; more general distinctions can be made with the marginals of the taxonomy.

What Is the Intended Curriculum?

While teachers ultimately decide what is taught in their classrooms, they receive a great deal of advice, both formally and informally, as to what those decisions should be. These sources of advice, especially the formal ones emanating from the formal school hierarchy, can be thought of as the intended curriculum.

Curriculum Frameworks. The most direct formal advice that teachers receive regarding what to teach comes from curriculum frameworks, curriculum guides, or lists of instructional goals and objectives. Most states have something like a curriculum framework, which can be more or less detailed and which can be required or only advisory (Archbald, 1994). The best-known examples of state curriculum frameworks come from California and New York. In California, in the mid 1980s, curriculum frameworks were used as the lead policy instrument for attempting to bring about a massive curriculum reform, placing greater emphasis upon conceptual understanding, problem solving, and reasoning, in an attempt to bring those desired student outcomes into better balance with the traditional emphasis upon facts and skills. New York, with its Regents diplomas, has the oldest and most established set of curriculum frameworks, though they are limited to high school courses supporting a Regents diploma.

In addition to state curriculum frameworks, most large school districts have their own curriculum guides, sometimes quite specific and sometimes but not always in alignment with the state frameworks. Regardless of whether the state frameworks and district curriculum guides are required or advisory, and regardless of how detailed they are, they stop short of prescribing exactly each topic that must/should be taught. State and district curriculum frameworks and guides vary dramatically in the degrees of discretion they leave to teachers.

Tests. There is a well-known saying that what is taught is what is tested. Like most sayings, there is some degree of truth. Historically, externally mandated tests of student achievement have attempted to reflect what is taught. In fact, where tests are used with high stakes attached for students, such as high school graduation tests, the law requires that students be provided a reasonable opportunity to learn that which is tested (*Debra P.* v. *Turlington, 1981*). Coming into alignment with a test is not much of a challenge to schools and teachers when the test is a minimum competency/basic skills–oriented test. But tests could significantly influence what is taught if (1) what is on the test were to differ significantly from normative instructional practice and (2) the results of the test were to be used for purposes of accountability.

Textbooks. Just as there is the saying that what is taught is what is tested, there also is the saying that teachers teach what is in the textbook. Obviously, the only way these two sayings can both be true is if tests and textbooks are in alignment with each other. When careful content analyses have been done of tests and textbooks to determine their overlap, considerable alignment has been found—but so have important areas of uniqueness. For example, in a study that compared four commonly used textbooks and five commonly used tests in fourth-grade mathematics, of the textbook topics covered, the percent covered on the test ranged from a low of 14 percent to a high of 30 percent. Obviously, not everything in the textbook is tested. Of the topics tested, the percentage covered in a book ranged from a low of 52 percent to a high of 87 percent. For one test and textbook combination, only half of what was tested was covered in the textbook, and only 20 percent of what was covered in the textbook was tested (Freeman and others, 1983).

Textbooks can be an important influence on teacher content decision making, in part because of the authority of the textbook and in part because the textbook is an instructional resource that makes teaching more manageable. But rarely do teachers cover everything in a textbook. For example, in a study of elementary mathematics, the most ardent textbook follower failed to use 40 percent of the lessons in her textbook. Other teachers skipped lessons and whole chapters and spent as much as 12 percent of their time teaching content that was not even considered in the textbook. Not only do textbooks not necessarily dictate the topics that are taught but they provide little or no guidance for three of the other content decisions teachers must make: how much time to devote to instruction, whether or not to present different content to different groups of students, and what standards of achievement should be held to which students (Freeman and Porter, 1989).

Advice from Individuals. In addition to curriculum frameworks, tests, and textbooks, all of which may be mandated by the formal school hierarchy, teachers receive advice directly from parents; other teachers, especially those teaching more advanced courses; and the principal. In a policy-capturing study asking elementary school teachers about what influenced their mathematics content decisions, parents, teachers, and the principal were all seen as legitimate sources of advice (Floden and others, 1981). In another study, however, teachers in schools serving affluent neighborhoods were more likely to see parents as a legitimate source of advice as to what should be taught than were teachers in schools serving high concentrations of students from poor families (Irwin and others, 1986).

What Gives Weight to Potential Influences of Teacher Content Decisions?

In deciding what to teach, the teacher stands between a host of potential influences, on the one hand, and the students in the classroom, on the other hand. In their role as content decision makers, teachers can be viewed more as political brokers than as implementers (Schwille and others, 1983). Because the content advice teachers receive comes from so many different sources and in so many different forms, sometimes with one source of advice conflicting with the next, a great deal of teacher autonomy is created. In attempting to determine what is best and most appropriate for their students, teachers must weigh their own predilections against the various sources of advice that they receive. As political brokers, teachers straddle the fence between professional autonomy and bureaucratic subordination.

Several attributes of potential external influences on teachers' content decision making can be identified that help to explain the degree of likely influence. *Prescriptiveness* is an attribute describing the extent to which a potential influence is explicit and specific in stating what content is desired. For example, a mandated textbook is more prescriptive if the textbook is accompanied by a requirement that the book be taught page-by-page from beginning to end than if the book is simply required but with no explanation as to how the book is to be used. *Consistency* describes the extent to which an influence is aligned with other influences in the designated content. If an external test covers content that is not in a mandated textbook, the two policies are inconsistent. Potential influences on teacher content decision making can vary in their degree of *authority* (Spady and Mitchell, 1979). Authority can be established through law (that is, being the official policy of the school hierarchy), through input from experts (in other words, having curriculum experts involved in the development of a curriculum framework), through consistency with social norms (calling for that which is already commonplace), or through being promoted by charismatic leaders (such as having a state superintendent promote a state curriculum framework). The *power* of a potential influence can be strengthened through rewards and sanctions (for example, externally mandated tests can be used for decisions about high school graduation).

Together, the four attributes of prescriptiveness, consistency, authority, and power are useful in predicting the strength of a particular content policy or the likelihood that content advice from an individual will be taken. In addition, the likelihood of influence upon teachers' content decisions is a function of the nature of the request. If teachers are asked to make substantial and difficult changes, the influence is less likely than if the requested change is modest.

The amount of content advice or requirements that teachers receive has varied over the years. Within a given time period, the amount of content advice has varied substantially from state to state and district to district. In the late 1950s and early 1960s, there was a curriculum reform to upgrade content for the academically elite. High school mathematics (this was the time of "new math") and science curricula in particular were made more demanding. In the late 1960s and 1970s, the basic skills reform took over. The pendulum swung from upgrading content for the academically elite to guaranteeing basic skills for the academically less able. In the mid 1980s, the most demanding aspects of the two earlier curriculum reforms were combined into a reform that has been labeled hard content for all students (Porter, Archbald, and Tyree, 1991). To some extent, the 1985 mathematics curriculum framework in California foreshadowed this late 1980s reform. The most visible document of the reform is the NCTM's *Curriculum and Evaluation Standards for School Mathematics* (National Council of Teachers of Mathematics, 1989). Since then, similar curriculum standards have been or are being written for virtually every academic subject.

Also, the thinking about curriculum control has shifted considerably over time. Minimum competency testing was the lead policy instrument of the basic skills reform. Test results were typically reported school by school; student grade-to-grade promotion and graduation were often determined on the basis of test performance. In the early 1980s, this curriculum control strategy came under attack. An attempt was made to replace curriculum control with teacher empowerment. Advocates of the empowerment strategy believe that you cannot legislate excellence in education. Rather, the best approach to better teaching is to have qualified and committed teachers with decision-making power. At the heart of the empowerment strategy is the concept of professional control over technical decision making. Empowerment, it is argued, makes better use of teacher expertise and garners greater teacher commitment. School restructuring, especially site-based decision making, has been the lead policy instrument.

The empowerment strategy did not go long without significant challenge. With the curriculum reform of hard content for all students came the idea of systemic reform. The argument for systemic reform is that if there is to be a massive shift in the enacted curriculum away from a heavy emphasis upon facts and skills and toward a better balance with conceptual understanding and application, then leadership will be needed. The decentralized approach of teacher empowerment seems unlikely, at least by itself, to move practice in a new and predetermined direction (for example, the NCTM's *Curriculum Standards*). In essence, systemic reform replaces the often piecemeal and fragmented policy initiatives of curriculum control with policies that are internally consistent and aligned to the goal of hard content for all students. The lead policy instrument of systemic reform is a curriculum framework. Tests and instructional materials are to be aligned to that framework. Significant staff development is to be provided so that teachers have the knowledge and skills necessary to implement the reform (Smith and O'Day, 1990).

At the time of this writing, neither the teacher empowerment strategy nor the systemic reform strategy has been implemented in pure form. Most of the districts with site-based decision making are in states with curriculum control policies left over from the basic skills era. As for systemic reform, probably the best example is California, where the curriculum frameworks are in place and testing is coming into alignment with the frameworks. Instructional materials are lagging badly behind, however, and there is nothing anywhere near the magnitude of staff development needed.

If systemic reform becomes a serious strategy, the degree of teacher discretion in content decision making will be greatly reduced. However, until that happens, teachers will continue to be confronted with the difficult task of deciding upon the enacted curriculum.

Why Is Teacher Content Decision Making an Important Concern?

As has been said, teacher content decisions determine a student's opportunity to learn. Opportunity to learn, in turn, is the single most powerful school-controlled determinant of student achievement. When teachers decide what to teach, for how much time, to which students and to what standards, they are placing important parameters around what their students will learn.

Teachers differ one from another in important ways in the content decisions that they make. In addition, teachers as a group make content decisions that stand in sharp contrast to recommendations from professional societies.

Too Many Facts and Skills

In two studies of Michigan elementary school teachers, three-fourths of mathematics instructional time was spent teaching skills: how to add, subtract, multiply, and divide. One teacher spent over 90 percent of instructional time on computational skills, leaving only 6 percent for the development of conceptual understanding and 1 percent for the study of problem solving. In contrast, another teacher devoted only 40 percent of instructional time to skill development, leaving much more time for emphasizing conceptual understanding and applications. While developing computational skills with decimals and fractions was a priority for fifth-grade instruction, two-thirds of the fifth-grade teachers gave less than one hour of instruction on problem solving involving fractions. Fifty percent of the teachers gave less than one hour of instruction to problem solving involving decimals (Porter, 1989).

Studies show that in high school mathematics, instruction emphasizes computational procedures, while in science, emphasis is upon memorizing facts. Only 4 percent of instructional time was given to collecting and interpreting data. Only 2 percent of instructional time was devoted to students working with novel problems. In mathematics, no instructional time was allocated to students learning to develop proofs, not even in geometry. In science, essentially no time was allocated to students designing experiments or building and revising theories (Porter, Smithson, and Osthoff, 1994).

Teaching for Exposure

In the two studies of elementary school mathematics instruction (Porter, 1989), not only was the emphasis upon skill development as opposed to conceptual understanding and application but a very large percentage of topics taught received only brief coverage. For the typical elementary school teacher of mathematics, a full 70 percent of the topics taught at one time or another during a school year received less than thirty minutes of instructional time. Less than 10 percent of the topics taught received the equivalent of two hours or more of instruction. Not surprisingly, the topics emphasized were all skill development topics, while the topics taught for exposure with no real intention for student mastery were the topics concerning conceptual understanding and application.

In the curriculum reform of hard content for all students, breadth of coverage is to be replaced by depth of coverage. If students are to have deep conceptual understanding that allows them to use their knowledge to solve novel problems and to reason, then students will need to study less content in greater depth and detail (Newmann and Wehlage, 1993). This call for depth rather than breadth stands in direct contrast to typical instructional practice. Further, in a policy-capturing study of teacher content decision making, teachers were found to be influenced by a variety of policies and individuals when adding new content to the content that they had been already teaching. However, when the attempted influence was to cause to teachers to discontinue teaching content that they had been teaching, they were resistant (Floden and others, 1981). In an interview study of teachers of elementary school mathematics, after having described all of the mathematics content taught over the course of a full school year, teachers were asked if there were more time, what topics they might add. The responses were several and interesting. Teachers were then asked if there were less time, what topics would they delete. The question left teachers stymied. At least in elementary school mathematics, then, teachers' content decisions are more easily influenced by calls for additional content than they are influenced by calls for greater focus and depth.

What Is the Teacher's Role in Content Decision Making?

As an individual, the teacher has the responsibility for delivering the enacted curriculum, the content and pedagogical strategies that make up instruction as it occurs. In making decisions about pedagogical strategies, teachers draw upon their professional knowledge, what they have learned from their teacher education program, from inservice professional development experiences, from colleagues, and from their own trial-and-error experiences. Content decision making should be just as purposeful. But unlike pedagogical strategies, the content of instruction is in large part a political matter. State and school district boards of education are elected, and those boards are charged with the responsibility of setting policy, including policy concerning the intended curriculum. As public employees, public school teachers have a responsibility to be knowledgeable about the content policies of their school district and state.

State and district policies concerning the intended curriculum are, however, not so prescriptive that they dictate exactly what must be taught, for how long, to whom, and to what standards of achievement, nor are these policies always consistent one with another. Thus, individual teachers are forced into the role of political broker, making sense of the requirements from their state and district, along with the advice and wishes of colleagues, parents, and students, as they decide what is in the best interest of their students and within their own technical capability to deliver.

Policies and advice that have authority actually change the beliefs of a teacher so that, once persuaded, the teacher attempts to deliver the intended content as much because of a belief that the content is appropriate as because the content was advised or required. Policies that gain their weight through power (rewards and sanctions) may have influence on teachers' content behaviors, even without persuading the teacher that what is being taught is most appropriate. Obviously, content decisions influenced by authoritative policies and advice are likely to continue long after the policy or advice has disappeared, while content decisions influenced by power policies are more fragile.

A teacher's role in content decision making, however, extends beyond what the teachers do as individuals in their own classes. Each teacher is, or at least should be, a member of one or more professional groups. These professional groups—for example, the National Commission on Social Studies in the Schools—deliberate on questions of what should be taught and from time to time issue statements—such as the commission's *Charting a Course: Social Studies for the Twenty-First Century* (Curriculum Task Force, 1989). Teachers as professionals have the responsibility to participate in these content deliberations; as members of a collective, teachers become involved in attempts to influence the content decisions that they will ultimately make.

Individual teachers also have a responsibility to become active in the policy formulation and policy critique of their school, their district, and their state. Increasingly, representatives from the teacher corps are involved in the formal content policy-making apparatus of the state, district, and school; for example, they are invariably included on boards that develop curriculum frameworks and that select textbooks and other instructional materials. Increasingly, teachers are becoming involved in test development and policies about test use. Surprisingly, teachers have less involvement in designing and delivering staff development, and for that matter staff development often has little to say about the actual content of instruction. This may change as the curriculum reform of the late 1980s gains steam.

Also surprisingly, given the importance of content decision making in determining student achievement, content decision making receives relatively little explicit attention in preservice teacher education programs. For example, prospective math teachers take math courses where they learn math and math methods courses where they learn pedagogical strategies. But in neither of these two types of courses is much, if any, attention given to how a teacher should think through questions about how much time to allocate to a subject, what topics to cover, for which students, and to what standards of achievement. There is no part of the preservice teacher education curriculum that can be counted upon to help prospective teachers understand that content decision making is problematic, that it is important, and that teachers have responsibilities in making content decisions not only for their own instruction but in participating in deliberations about what should be taught by their colleagues. Content decisions are too important a part of being a teacher to receive so little attention in teacher education. This should be corrected.

References

Archbald, D. A. (1994). "Reflections on the design and purposes of state curriculum guides: A comparison of mathematics and social studies guides from four states." In R. F. Elmore and S. H. Fuhrman (eds.), *The governance of curriculum.* (1994 yearbook of the Association for Supervision and Curriculum Development). Alexandria, Va.: Association for Supervision and Curriculum Development.

Ball, D. L. (1990). "The mathematical understandings that preservice teachers bring to teacher education." *Elementary School Journal, 90,* 449–466.

Ball, D. L. (1991). "Teaching mathematics for understanding: What do teachers need to know about subject matter?" In M. M. Kennedy (ed.), *Teaching academic subjects to diverse learners.* New York: Teachers College Press.

Banks, J. A. (1993). "The canon debate, knowledge construction, and multicultural education." *Educational Researcher, 22*(5), 4–14.

Blits, J. (1985). "The search for ends: Liberal education and the modern university." In J. Blits (ed.), *The American university.* Buffalo, N.Y.: Prometheus Books.

Buchmann, M. (1984). "The priority of knowledge and understanding in teaching." In J. D. Raths and L. Katz (eds.), *Advances in teacher education,* Vol. 1. Norwood, N.J.: Ablex.

Curriculum Task Force (1989). *Charting a course: Social studies for the 21st century.* Washington, D.C.: National Commission on Social Studies in the Schools.

Debra P. v. Turlington, 474 F. Supp. 244 (M.D. Fla. 1979); affirmed in part 644 F. 2d 397 (5th Cir. 1981).

Floden, R. E., and others (1981). "Responses to curriculum pressures: A policy capturing study of teacher decisions about content." *Journal of Educational Psychology, 73,* 129–141.

Freeman, D. T., and others (1983). "Do textbooks and tests define a national curriculum in elementary school mathematics?" *Elementary School Journal, 83,* 501–513.

Freeman, D. T., and Porter, A. C. (1989). "Do textbooks dictate the content of mathematics instruction in elementary schools?" *American Educational Research Journal, 26*(3), 403–421.

Guthrie, R. (1976). *Even the rat was white: A historical view of psychology.* New York: Harper-Collins.

Irwin, S., and others (1986). "The effects of school socioeconomic status on student opportunities to learn mathematics." Paper presented at the annual meeting of the American Educational Research Association, San Francisco.

Kamii, C. (1989). *Young children continue to reinvent arithmetic: 2nd grade.* New York: Teachers College Press.

Kennedy, M. M. (ed.) (1991). *Teaching academic subjects to diverse learners.* New York: Teachers College Press.

Kuhs, T. M., and others (1979). *A taxonomy for classifying elementary school mathematics content.* (Research Series no. 4). East Lansing: Institute for Research on Teaching, Michigan State University.

Lundgren, U. P. (1972). *Frame factors and the teaching process.* Stockholm: Almqvist & Wiksell.

McDiarmid, G. W. (1990). "The liberal arts: Will more result in better subject matter understanding?" *Theory into Practice, 29*(1), 21–29.

Murray, F. B. (1991). "Alternative conceptions of academic knowledge for prospective elementary teachers." In M. C. Pugach and H. L. Barnes (eds.), *Changing the practice of teacher education: The role of the knowledge base.* Washington, D.C.: American University Press.

Murray, F. B., and Fallon, D. (1989). *The reform of teacher education for the 21st century: Project 30 year one report.* Newark: University of Delaware Press.

Murray, F. B., and Johnson, P. (1970). "A note on using curriculum models in analyzing the child's concept of weight." *Journal of Research in Science Teaching, 7,* 377–381.

Murray, F. B., and Johnson, P. (1975). "Relevant and some irrelevant factors in the child's concept of weight." *Journal of Educational Psychology, 67,* 705–711.

Murray, F. B., and Markessini, J. (1982). "A semantic basis of nonconservation of weight." *Psychological Record, 32,* 375–379.

National Council of Teachers of Mathematics (1989). *Curriculum and evaluation standards for school mathematics.* Reston, Va.: National Council of Teachers of Mathematics.

Newmann, F. M., and Wehlage, G. G. (1993). "Five standards of authentic instruction." *Educational Leadership, 50*(7), 8–12.

Porter, A. C. (1989). "A curriculum out of balance: The case of elementary school mathematics." *Educational Researcher, 18*(5), 9–15.

Porter, A. C., Archbald, D. A., and Tyree, A. K., Jr. (1991). "Reforming the curriculum: Will empowerment policies replace control?" In S. H. Fuhrman and B. Malen (eds.), *The politics of curriculum and testing.* (1990 yearbook of the Politics of Education Associations). London: Taylor & Francis.

Porter, A. C., Smithson, J., and Osthoff, E. (1994). "Standard setting as a strategy for upgrading high school mathematics and science." In R. F. Elmore and S. H. Fuhrman (eds.), *The governance of curriculum.* (1994 yearbook of the Association for Supervision and Curriculum Development). Alexandria, Va.: Association for Supervision and Curriculum Development.

Porter, A. C., and others (1988). "Content determinants in elementary school mathematics." In D. A. Grouws and T. J. Cooney (eds.), *Perspectives on research on effective mathematics teaching.* Hillsdale, N.J.: Erlbaum.

Porter, A. C., and others (1993). "Reform up close: A classroom analysis." Final Report to the National Science Foundation. (Grant no. SPA-8953446).

Romberg, T. A., and Carpenter, T. P. (1986). "Research on teaching and learning mathematics: The discipline of scientific inquiry." In M. C. Wittrock (ed.), *Handbook of research on teaching.* (3rd ed.). New York: Macmillan.

Schmidt, W. H. (1983a). "High school course-taking: A study of variation." *Journal of Curriculum Studies, 15*(2), 167–182.

Schmidt, W. H. (1983b). "High school course-taking: Its relationship to achievement." *Journal of Curriculum Studies, 15*(3), 311–332.

Schwille, J. R., and others (1983). "Teachers as policy brokers in the content of elementary school mathematics." In L. S. Shulman and G. Sykes (eds.), *Handbook on teaching and policy.* White Plains, N.Y.: Longman.

Sebring, A. P. (1987). "Consequences of differential amounts of high school coursework: Will the new graduation requirements help?" *Educational Evaluation and Policy Analysis, 9*(3), 257–273.

Sedlak, M. W., Wheeler, C. W., Pullin, D. C., and Cusick, P. A. (1986). *Selling students short: Classroom bargains and academic reform in the American high school.* New York: Teachers College Press.

Shulman, L. S. (1986). "Those who understand: Knowledge growth in teaching." *Educational Researcher, 15*(2), 4–14.

Shulman, L. S. (1987). "Knowledge and teaching: Foundations of the new reform." *Harvard Educational Review, 57*(1), 1–22.

Siegler, R. (1981). *Developmental sequences within and between concepts.* Monographs of the Society for Research in Child Development, *46*(189).

Smith, M. S., and O'Day, J. (1990). "Systemic school reform." In S. H. Fuhrman and B. Malen (eds.), *The politics of curriculum and testing.* (1990 yearbook of the Politics of Education Association). London: Taylor & Francis.

Spady, W. G., and Mitchell, D. E. (1979). "Authority and the management of classroom activities." In D. L. Duke (ed.), *Classroom management.* (78th yearbook of the National Society for the Study of Education). Chicago: University of Chicago Press.

Annotated Bibliography

Dill, D. D., and others (1990). *What teachers need to know: The knowledge, skills, and values essential to good teaching.* San Francisco: Jossey-Bass.

> A group of scholars in education and the other academic disciplines attempt to answer the question, What are the knowledge, skills, and values essential for the preparation of middle-school and secondary school teachers? This very readable and accessible book, all chapters of which are based upon talks at a Chapel Hill conference, provides a

grounded treatment of pedagogical content knowledge within a humanistic tradition. The book gives special weight to the arts and science perspective of teacher education.

Kimball, B. A. (1986). *Orators and philosophers: A history of the idea of liberal education.* New York: Teachers College Press.

Orators and Philosophers superbly documents how complex and confused the history of the liberal arts is. The historical record will not unequivocally support any single claim about the nature and function of a liberal arts education, either now or at some earlier golden period. With such a shaky and uncertain foundation, it is hard to know how teacher educators could respond to the universal call to base the education of teachers on a firm education in the liberal arts. *Orators and Philosophers* finds two distinct forms of liberal arts education: the *orator* tradition, in which the orator speaks the truth about the best and most noble of what is known so that his or her pupils will act virtuously and govern themselves wisely, and the *philosopher* tradition, in which the pupil's honest and unending pursuit of truth is the outcome of a liberal education. Implicit in the orator tradition is a commitment to a canon of the best of what is known and thought. No such commitment is required in the philosopher tradition other than the mastery of the modes of inquiry, some of which are naturally a part of the orator's canon. To which tradition should teacher education be anchored? Kimball makes a case for the reestablishment of the orator tradition, which he claims has been displaced by the philosopher tradition, in liberal education.

Tyson, H. (1994). *Who will teach the children? Progress and resistance in teacher education.* San Francisco: Jossey-Bass.

A journalist's critical view of the arts and science component of America's teacher education programs is presented in her report of five schools of education and one state system that have been active in the school reform movements. The study reports good and bad news about how teacher education students learn the subject matters they plan to teach.

CHAPTER SEVEN

A KNOWLEDGE BASE IN THE FINE ARTS

LYNN GALBRAITH

My task is to present a case for what all prospective teachers should ideally learn about the fine arts and why. In presenting this case, I would like to describe briefly the way in which important integrative elements in learning can be identified with the fine arts. For my purposes, I employ *fine arts* as an umbrella term to encompass the disciplines of the performing and visual arts, specifically the areas of dance, music, theater, and visual arts. I make the following broadly based claims for the teaching of the fine arts:

1. The fine arts are central to society and culture (Margolis, 1978). As a collective body of knowledge, they represent some of the most powerful and impression-forming achievements, images, and experiences of humanity (Weitz, 1950).

2. Intrinsic to the knowledge base within the fine arts is a distinct body of ideas, images, concepts, metaphors, and principles (Smith, 1987) that are generated as individuals create or respond to works of art. The study of the expressive and appreciative significance of works of art is grounded in the general notions of aesthetic education (Broudy, 1972; Eisner, 1963): our encounters with works of art help shape our expressive, perceptual, and imaginative capacities (Dewey, 1934; Goodman, 1968; Greene, 1981). Enhancing these capacities is essential to general education (Broudy, 1990): thus, all prospective teachers should be introduced to aspects of aesthetic education through the fine arts. Specific coursework should include (a) the creation and expression of ideas through the study of different art media, (b) an understanding of means of aesthetic and critical inquiry, and (c) an awareness of the historical and cultural significance of works of art.

3.   An understanding of aesthetic learning within the fine arts knowledge base can provide all teachers with thoughtful and relevant curricula and pedagogy that will enrich, translate, and give life to not only the arts but to other school subjects within their classrooms.

In presenting my case, I will provide specific examples drawn from my particular area of expertise, the visual arts, to illustrate the way in which knowledge of some aspects of the fine arts live up to these claims. I want to be quite clear that my emphasis on the visual arts is not intended to diminish the other fine arts forms of dance, theater, and music. I acknowledge that content knowledge within the four separate fine arts disciplines varies, and each warrants specialized instruction. The fine arts disciplines are broad, and my examples serve as illustrations that attest to the viability of all or any of its disciplines. We must help prospective teachers gain, in their encounters with the fine arts, not only knowledge about its various disciplines but a willingness and propensity to hear the meaning in a piece of music or to delight in the movement of a dance (Sibley, 1965). Also, importantly, we must assist them in considering how they might pass on this enjoyment to their pupils.

In the last part of this chapter, I go on to suggest that an understanding of the fine arts, particularly in terms of aesthetic education, is critical not just for the specialist subjects of the fine arts but also for the school curriculum as a whole. I then raise a number of issues that must be addressed if the fine arts are to become a substantial component of any teacher education program.

Claims for the Teaching of the Fine Arts

Claim 1: The fine arts knowledge base is essential to society and culture.

As revealed from the first brush strokes on the walls of the caves at Lascaux in the Gironde in southern France, the fine arts have long been an important part of human aesthetic development and achievement (Berleant, 1991). From the archaeological record, we can trace the emergence of the fine arts to a position of prominence, prototypically for Western society, with the classical Greek culture. The aesthetic treatises of Plato and Aristotle provide some of our earliest detailed interpretations of how the fine arts were valued within that society. These philosophers were amongst the first to identify and discuss questions relating to how art works are created, their intrinsic meaning and beauty, and their cultural and moral implications (Beardsley, 1966). These fundamental aesthetic questions remain directly relevant to the present day.

It was not until the Italian Renaissance, however, that the fine arts assumed the high profile within Western society that they still carry today. During this period, the fine arts became an integral component of the humanistic and classical education advanced by Renaissance thought (Kristeller, 1961). This integration was specifically shaped by the achievements of painters, sculptors, musicians, and architects, who created works of art that could simultaneously elicit artistic pleasure, beauty, empathy, and contemplation and act as avenues of patronage (Baxandall, 1972). This attention to aesthetics (Wilds and Lottich, 1962) and the wishes of patrons easily separated these finer art works from the lowly crafts, practices, and artifacts that were products of artisans, monks, and guildsmen of the early medieval era (Martindale, 1972). During the Renaissance, art works were admired not just for their usefulness and function in society but as objects unto themselves as well as ideal representations of Renaissance thought and values. This departure from earlier thinking paved the way over the following centuries for our modern concepts of the fine arts (Efland, 1990) and the elevated status of the artist within society.

However, as this century comes to a close, developments in the form of new artistic media, materials, techniques, and technologies, as well as attention to racial, ethnic, and cultural concerns have accelerated us toward a new era in the definition of the fine arts. Drawing a clear line among the traditional fine arts areas has become increasingly more difficult. Firstly, advances in telecommunications, computer-generated imagery and software, electronically synthesized sounds, and mixed and multimedia productions have redefined the accepted ways with which we view and thereby interact with the world. Secondly, changes in demographics and cultural, ethnic, and gender perspectives have offered serious challenges to the concepts, canons, and values of the fine arts within what is generally considered "Western" society (Piper, 1984). Finally, technological and multicultural and multiethnic concerns have been joined by new interpretations of the fine arts spurred by hermeneutic inquiry (Heidegger, 1964) and postmodern perspectives (Foucault, 1972) that demand that the relationships among artists, their works and texts, and their audiences be continually reassessed and revisited. Now more than ever, the immediacy of the fine arts, from painting to visual imagery displayed via the Internet, both reflects the cultural and technological changes occurring in society and provides a vehicle through which these changes can permeate society at large.

Claim 2: Intrinsic to the knowledge base within the fine arts is a distinct body of ideas, images, concepts, metaphors, and principles, which are generated as individuals create or respond to works of art.

Works of art have the capacity to intensify and enlarge the scope of human experience and understanding (Langer, 1957) by allowing for the expression of human feelings and messages through their various media. How individuals create, give meaning to, and value works of art are therefore fundamental elements of aesthetic education and consequently an obvious and important component of the fine arts knowledge base. Inquiry into the aesthetic dimensions of the fine arts allows for the organization of the feelings, experiences, and ideas of each individual (Beardsley, 1981; Gulbenkian Foundation, 1982; Reid, 1973). This inquiry also shapes our emotions, perception, and imagination (Broudy, 1987; Osborne, 1970).

Aesthetic learning and sensitivities are encountered, for example, by performing a piece of music, or by articulating art historical knowledge, or by exploring basic human sensibilities, or by provoking the viewer's imagination about all art objects, contemporary, premodern, or a product of another culture (Csikszentmihalyi and Robinson, 1990). Works of art are "created expressly for their aesthetic purposes, and to intrigue and delight us" (Clark, Day, and Greer, 1987, p. 139). Dialogue continually changes with every rehearsal and performance (Aspin, 1991).

If aesthetic education can be viewed as the essential glue that binds together, and thereby gives form to, the different elements within the fine arts disciplines, what understanding with the fine arts—derived from aspects of aesthetic education—is essential learning for all prospective teachers? Coursework in three major areas of the fine arts knowledge base seems integral to the aesthetic learning of prospective teachers: (1) the creation and expression of ideas through the study of different art media, (2) an understanding of means of aesthetic and critical inquiry, and (3) an awareness of the historical and cultural significance of art works.

It is perhaps helpful to visualize the content within these three areas through use of the case study format, since this avoids repetition and both enlivens and lends verisimilitude to the problems that teacher educators are trying to solve. As I suggested earlier, I will touch on specific examples in the visual arts. We will follow a student, "Jane," who has entered a teacher education program. Her required coursework includes the following:

1. *The creation and expression of ideas through the study of different art media.* Humans have the capacity to create or re-create (as in the performances of dance, music, and theater) works of art that communicate and represent information, expressions, and meanings. Using the role of the *artist, dancer, musician, actor,* and so forth as models, all prospective teachers should have the opportunity to enact or reenact the art-making experience in terms of the actual creation or performance of art works. Dewey (1934) noted, "Art denotes a process of doing or making. This is as true of fine as of technological art. Art involves molding of clay, chipping of marble, laying on of pigments, construction of buildings, playing instruments, enacting roles on stage, going through the rhythmic movements in the dance. Every art does something with some physical material, the body or something outside the body, with or without the use of intervening tools, and with a view to production of something visible, audible, or tangible" (p. 47).

Jane, our prospective teacher, is expected to take on the role of the artist in a required visual arts studio course housed within the College of Fine Arts. Titled "The Foundations of the Visual Arts," the course helps college-level students thoroughly explore and manipulate selected artistic materials, concepts, and techniques. Although Jane has limited experiences in the visual arts and certainly does not have a particular penchant for drawing and painting, she will be expected to be involved in the art-making experience during this semester's course. She will investigate and try to solve firsthand a number of pictorial, symbolic, and practical problems. She will learn that artists have their own vocabulary—form, rhythm, texture, space, balance, surface, words that retain their own meaning within the visual arts yet act as metaphors elsewhere.

Jane's instructor will stress the similarities and differences between various artistic media—painting, sculpture, papermaking, printmaking—so that she will learn to appreciate why a sketch is different from a finished drawing, why an artist's plate is different from a finished print, and why working artists strive to develop portfolios. Jane will be asked to make aesthetic and critical judgments about her work from its initiation to its completion.

Jane should ideally come to realize that the creation of art forms provides direct experience with artistic materials and techniques, which in turn will help foster her own imagination and perceptual skills (Spratt, 1987). As Jane undertakes this creative process, there is no doubt that she will experience the aspects of pleasure and frustration, time and hard work, and problem solving intrinsic to making a work of art. She will learn about the techniques involved in art making, and she will also develop an understanding about the commitment and disciplined inquiry required for such an activity. It is most likely that Jane will learn about herself and her own individual and cognitive capabilities as an artist. A quote from Dewey (1934) illustrates the task of the artist (in this case a painter) this way: "The painter must consciously undergo the effect of his every brush stroke or he will not be aware of what he is doing and where his work is going. Moreover, he has to see each particular connection of doing and undergoing in relation to the whole that he decides to produce. To apprehend such relations is to think, and is one of the most exacting modes of thought" (p. 45).

2. *An understanding of means of aesthetic and critical inquiry.* One of the most important ways in which we can make sense of the world we inhabit is to employ the skills of appreciation and critical analysis that are central to an understanding of the fine arts in our aesthetic responses to objects in our everyday environment. Berleant (1991) and Dewey (1934) have described the need for human beings to actively develop interpretative skills to enable them to understand, enjoy, and appreciate the fine arts from the consumer's standpoint. This therefore comprises another important element of the fine arts knowledge base.

Let us return to Jane and her experiences within the visual arts for an example relevant to this area. Jane is halfway through a college-level visual arts course entitled "Appreciating the Visual Arts." This course examines issues in creating, appreciating, and criticizing works of art. Her instructor challenges her to reflect upon and thereby define the nature of art by introducing her to a variety of visual forms and to a group of alternative aesthetic viewpoints (Dickie, 1971; Goodman, 1978; Osborne, 1970). She is encouraged to investigate traditional aesthetic issues—for example, concepts of beauty (Santayana, 1955), formalism (Pepper, 1949), expressionism (Hospers, 1982), and emotionalism (Collingwood, 1938) and to compare them with aesthetic issues that have emerged from the study of poststructuralism (Foucault, 1972), sociology (Becker, 1982), psychology (Arnheim, 1967; Gardner, 1973; Gombrich, 1969), anthropology (Maquet, 1986), and the feminist viewpoint (Ecker, 1985; Garber, 1992).

Jane learns that in aesthetic education the visual metaphor is important: images precede language. Broudy (1987) has argued that the fine arts develop the imagination, resulting in a store of images upon which the individual can draw to view the world (Clark, Day, and Greer, 1987). Jane takes heed of Arnheim's notions (1967) that humans must develop their ability to observe and to think about what they see. Further, she is mindful of Sibley's assertion (1965) that individuals should not just obtain mere knowledge of the fine arts but instead actually experience aesthetic enjoyment, appreciation, and judgment themselves. They must see, hear, and feel the communicative spirit intrinsic to the powerful images inherent within the fine arts (Spratt, 1987).

In this class, Jane develops her notion of what it means to have an aesthetic experience. She learns to understand how artists experiment and take risks and how aesthetic experiences may differ qualitatively between and across cultures (Maquet, 1986). Ultimately she struggles with the question, what is art? Fortunately, her instructor provides her with ways in which to observe, talk about, and analyze specific works of art and means with which to make valid aesthetic and critical judgments. She accomplishes this by visiting local museums and galleries, in which she is asked to identify her preferences (verbally and in written form) among specific pieces of sculpture or painting and to try to develop an understanding of what underlies her preferences. As one of the benefits provided by this course, Jane comes to realize that humans are responsible for making informed aesthetic judgments during their lifetimes and these judgments carry over to other aspects of their lives. Also, at the more personal level, Jane recognizes that she is beginning to appreciate, respond to, and enjoy the visual arts. Csikszentmihalyi and Robinson (1990) put it this way: "The aesthetic experience develops sensitivity to the being of other persons, to the excellence of form, to the style of distant historical periods, to the essence of unfamiliar civilizations. In so doing, it changes and expands the being of the viewer" (p. 183).

3. *An awareness of the historical and cultural significance of art works.* All prospective teachers must have some sense of how the fine arts have evolved over the centuries and within different cultures, past and present. Moreover, they must have some knowledge of how the fine arts are viewed in our postmodern world (Heidegger, 1964) in that our ability to respond to art forms is affected by their cultural context (Lanier, 1991).

Let us consider this next example, again from the visual arts. It is a new semester, and Jane is participating in an art history course, "Contemporary and Cultural Images in the Visual Arts." This course compares and contrasts past and contemporary imagery and ethnic and racial traditions within and across societies. One of the major goals of this course is to provide the students with a greater global awareness within the context of the fine arts and education in general.

The instructor asks Jane to speculate about visual form in terms of anthropological, cultural, historical, political, and social perspectives (Arnheim, 1967; McPhee and Degge, 1977), as well as to examine the impact of present day technology both on the visual arts and on culture in general. Jane learns that as the structure of the world constantly changes through the passage of time, so does the knowledge base of the fine arts in that it evolves in terms of its purposes, concepts, and methods. She also learns that the historical, geographical, and sociological contexts of a work of art are important in that they document and provide insights into these changes (Blandy and Congdon, 1987; Heidegger, 1964; Lanier, 1991). Jane begins to realize that it is almost impossible to understand the role of the fine arts within a specific society without knowledge of the history of that society.

During this course, Jane becomes cognizant that works of art are couched within certain world views or contexts, which in turn provoke specific aesthetic responses (Berger, 1972). She learns that works of art such as Picasso's painting *Guernica*, a Maori carving, a Martha Graham dance, and a play by Samuel Beckett all provide cues that enable her to develop an aesthetic response in terms of the art works, their meaning, and the pleasure that they can instill in her as the viewer. However, it is also the contextual nature of these art works, provided by historical and cultural features, that open up more possibilities for appreciation. Jane acknowledges that the deepest appreciation of the painting *Guernica*, for example, can only be experienced through development of an understanding of the Spanish Civil War. Similarly, a Maori sculpture can only be appreciated with reference to the many layers of meaning inherent within Maori culture and experiences (Chalmers, 1974).

Claim 3: An understanding of aesthetic learning within the fine arts knowledge base can provide all teachers with thoughtful and relevant curricula and pedagogy that will enrich, translate, and give life within their classrooms both to the arts and to other school subjects.

Schools have a number of different purposes and these purposes often differ from those of academicians within the framework of higher education. As part of her training within the fine arts, Jane will need to learn to teach those things that matter most to pupils in ways that are meaningful to them. This is particularly true for classes that comprise a diverse range of students from varying racial, cultural, and ethnic backgrounds.

Keeping the above points in mind, Jane will need to consider carefully the ways in which principles, concepts, metaphors, images, and means of thinking, knowing, and inquiry, gained from her personal encounters with the fine arts knowledge base, can be used to inform, enrich, and embody her own teaching and curriculum (Jackson, 1991). An earlier suggestion was that experiences within aesthetic education (in terms of creating, performing, and responding to works of art) can serve as a glue to tie together the various fine arts disciplines. This can now be extended more broadly; thus, elements from aesthetic education can also serve to improve the quality of the entire curriculum within schools, not just the fine arts disciplines: "We should have schools that seek to enlarge the students' sense of aesthetics by engaging them in creating and thinking about beauty. But we should also value aesthetic education because of the role that emotions and sense play in thinking, and because thinking aesthetically is as demanding and important to students' lives as thinking scientifically, quantitatively, or historically" (Lazerson, McLaughlin, McPherson, and Bailey, 1985, p.74).

Jane's preparation needs must be grounded in an understanding of actual classroom practices within the fine arts in schools (Boardman, 1990; Davis, 1990; Galbraith, 1990; Koehler, 1979) and their relationship to the school curriculum as a whole. This preparation must take place within courses that stress the connections between aesthetic education (Madeja, 1977) and teaching within schools. At the present time, however, most prospective teachers take some variant of a *methods* course grounded in one of the specific arts areas: dance, music, theater, or the visual arts. It is rare in teacher education programs for prospective teachers to take separate arts education courses in each of the four distinct fine arts disciplines or for them to take a methods course that combines one or more of the disciplines. The following course description exemplifies how the required fine arts coursework can be connected to educational practice.

In this course, "The Aesthetic Dimensions of Teaching," Jane will be asked to identify important aesthetic concepts and ideas suitable for classroom use. She will learn, for example, that in many classrooms, teachers often ask pupils to illustrate written work in other subjects, such as social studies or language arts, in order to make the unit of study more acceptable to pupils (Rico, 1993). Jane acknowledges that these traditional practices have some worth, but she learns that pupils should be encouraged to create or to respond to drawings or plays on their own merits (National Art Education Association, 1986). Her previously acquired grounding in aesthetic and critical knowledge and skills will help her pupils develop informed and sensitive responses as they discuss the aesthetic merits of their own work and that of their peers and so move beyond the critique clichés of pupils' work ("nice job," "super," the omnipresent smiley face). Jane will also learn that the fine arts provide a store of images from which she can draw to enhance her teaching (Broudy, 1987). Teachers often ask pupils to "imagine," or "listen for," propensities that encourage pupils to engage in different ways of learning.

Jane will examine works of art within the fine arts that originate from different ethnic perspectives and viewpoints (Chanda, 1992). It is possible, using Banks's model (1989), that she will seek to modify her own curricular orientations and goals to reflect more intercultural understanding. Jane will encounter aesthetic, critical, and historical activities within the fine arts that discuss and interpret art works from alternative aesthetic and cultural positions and from social, political, and postmodern perspectives, including those that are controversial in nature.

Arnheim (1993) has indicated that teaching is greatly enhanced by the use of visual materials. For visual learning, it seems self-evident that teachers use visible examples (charts, diagrams, bulletin boards) and do not solely rely on verbal explanations within classrooms. Being able to distinguish among quality visuals as well as being able to recognize their appropriate use in the classroom will be a critical element in Jane's education. Moreover, Arnheim's notions are even more apt as prospective teachers consider the impact of technology on the activity of teaching and pupil learning. Multimedia technology (laser discs, videotapes, synthesized sounds, and CD-ROMs) is very much a part of the fine arts in terms of its visual and auditory components and capacities. All prospective teachers will not only need to be versed in how to run this multimedia technology and software but they will need to be aware of how this technology can be fused successfully (and ethically) within classrooms.

Jane will also learn that it is from within the fine arts that many forms of alternative assessment are derived. Eisner (1991) has written extensively on how aesthetic and critical concepts can be employed in the evaluation of teaching. Portfolio assessment (Gardner, 1989) comes directly from within the fine arts. Jane's encounters with the fine arts will allow her to experience firsthand the uses of portfolios and their contribution to her own personal aesthetic development and that of her pupils.

By being informed in aspects of the fine arts knowledge base, Jane can begin to dissolve the boundaries among in-school subjects. As a prospective teacher, she will be able to work with all teachers and help them integrate the fine arts (Hanna, 1992) and specifically aesthetic education throughout her school.

Issues for Teacher Education Decision Making in the Fine Arts

There is no doubt that the fine arts are neglected within elementary and secondary schooling. (See, for example, Eisner, 1992; Greene, 1981; Reimer, 1991.) Given their contributions to a well-rounded education, the following issues related to this lack of support for the fine arts in schools must be addressed by teacher educators.

First, teacher education candidates and teacher educators frequently have only a rudimentary background, if any, in the various fine arts disciplines. The state of neglect is often exacerbated within the context of discussions about teacher education coursework, since the fine arts can be stereotyped either as anti-intellectual or nonessential. If we examine any cross-section of educators at any level, we find little formal training in the fine arts. Thus, commitment for the fine arts knowledge base is mandatory.

Second, and more troubling, we also find that teacher educators and teacher candidates cling to preconceptions about the fine arts, developed when they were school pupils themselves (Galbraith, 1991). These typically are based on a poor self-image concerning a lack of ability in the production of fine arts and a lack of awareness in the area of arts appreciation and aesthetics. Paradoxically, although these negative self-images and inadequate background can often be linked to poor teaching and teacher preparation in the fine arts, they do not translate to increased support for curricular reform.

Third, support for the fine arts has also been eroded indirectly as a consequence of social and political pressures to teach basic skills within the sciences, mathematics, and language arts (Engel, 1980). These pressures leave little instructional time or curricular resources for the fine arts. Yet the intellectual strengths intrinsic to the fine arts, such as creativity in performance and development of the aesthetic sense (to name just two), are important skills required in many disciplines (Hanna, 1992; Lazerson, McLaughlin, McPherson, and Bailey, 1986; Smith, 1989).

Fourth, teacher educators may argue that perspective teachers need little exposure to the fine arts, if any, if they are to teach in schools with fine arts specialists. This is a false argument. Many elementary classroom teachers are now held accountable for teaching the fine arts (Efland, 1976), and in reality there are few dance and theater specialists in schools (Martin and Ross, 1988). Thus, the work of fine arts specialists can be greatly augmented by collaboration with nonspecialists and with specialists in other areas. Therefore, some basic grounding in the fine arts becomes essential for all teachers (Martin, 1986).

Taken together, these problems explain to a large degree the overall lack of importance of the fine arts within schools and also serve to legitimize the inequities in assignment of institutional resources to this area. If this is to change, it seems clear that teacher educators nationally must take the lead in demonstrating commitment to promoting education within, and allocating resources to, the fine arts. The following reasons are particularly relevant:

1. As previously stressed, the fine arts are essential to a general education that includes aesthetic education. We must help prospective teachers and pupils find reasons to care about the fine arts, their history, their role in society and culture, their means of expression and communication, and their pedagogical methods. The fine arts make a difference in our lives, and schools should be in the business of helping make that difference and educating the future generation in aspects of the fine arts knowledge base and its subject-specific and interdisciplinary relationships within the overall school curriculum.

2. The fine arts provide us with visual imagery, sounds, dance forms, and so forth, that are representative of intercultural and international view points (Mason, 1988). Teachers (at all levels of schooling) are being asked to redesign school curricula so as adequately to instruct students who represent an enormous diversity in language, culture, and family background (Fenstermacher, 1990). The fine arts are key to representing some of the most powerful forms of expression, performance, and aesthetic attitudes and beliefs inherent within our diverse society and cultural groups, especially as we move toward the twenty-first century. The impact of the media, television, gang graffiti, clothing, and other forms of expression and communication all contribute to the lives of today's youth. Recognition of how music, visual imagery, computer technology, dance forms, and so forth play an important part in the lives of today's youth and the communities in which they live is an essential component in teacher preparation.

3.   Prospective teachers must also take coursework that they believe will improve their classroom practice (May, 1989). Coursework that orchestrates and models alternative ways of knowing and learning, uses alternative assessment methods, values creative activity and performance, underscores historical investigation and the appreciation of the arts, and promotes aesthetic development and critical inquiry is essential in improving our schools.

Conclusions

The worlds of the stage, the concert hall, and the museums and galleries are substantial (Becker, 1982; Dickie, 1971). The talents of the creators and performers within these worlds have far-reaching effects. The opportunities offered for critics, arts historians, aestheticians, audience members, and participants to appreciate, consume, and engage in these art worlds are unlimited (Berleant, 1991). Furthermore, these art worlds reflect the changing racial, ethnic, cultural, and technological fabric of our society.

In this brief essay, I have chosen examples from the visual arts to make my case for including parts of this immense fine arts knowledge base in the preservice education of teachers. I reiterate my earlier recommendation that teacher education candidates will need to acquire knowledge in the other fine arts disciplines of dance, music, and theater. I also acknowledge that I may have perhaps skirted a major concern: whether teacher education candidates should explore one or more of the fine arts disciplines in depth or possess a more broadly based education across the fine arts. Both sides of the coin are viable options; it will be the task of teacher educators to examine their own campuses to seek out coursework that allows prospective teachers, within the fine arts, to be actively engaged in (1) art making or performance activities, (2) aesthetic and critical inquiry, and (3) developing an understanding of the historical and cultural dimensions of the fine arts. Arguably, these three strands of learning can be achieved either through the study of one or more of the specific disciplines or within more interdisciplinary fine arts coursework.

I have proposed that experiences within aesthetic education can function as the essential glue that holds the various fine arts disciplines together and that elements derived from aesthetic education can benefit the entire fabric of the school curriculum. Further, I have maintained that prospective teachers must take additional coursework that enables them to visualize the connecting threads and questions that link the various fine arts disciplines and the practices of education within our diverse schools.

I now wish to add that attention to aesthetic education and experiences can also help guide a teacher education curriculum (Beyer, 1986). As teacher educators actively search for and institute course work on their campuses, this coursework must be taught by instructors who model ways of thinking that will augment the aesthetic education of teacher education candidates. There is no doubt that some college courses are inadequate models for future teachers (large entry-level classes in which rote memorization of slides serves as learning about the fine arts!). Prospective teachers must be steered toward faculty who are passionately engaged in the fine arts and responsive to how its subject matter can inform, enrich, question, and change, rather than merely mimic, existing classroom practices in schools. The inclusion of the fine arts knowledge base within a teacher education program provides teacher education candidates, at the very least, with an active engagement with the aesthetic dimensions of teaching and learning. Moreover, this knowledge base provides teacher educators with a rich educational canvas that is a vital component in any teacher education program today.

References

Arnheim, R. (1967). *Art and visual thinking.* Berkeley: University of California Press.

Arnheim, R. (1993). "Learning by looking and thinking." *Educational Horizons, 75*(2), 94–98.

Aspin, D. (1991). "Justifying music education." In R. A. Smith and A. Simpson (eds.), *Aesthetics and arts education.* Urbana: University of Illinois Press.

Banks, J. A. (1989). *Multicultural education: Issues and perspectives.* Needham Heights, Mass.: Allyn & Bacon.

Baxandall, M. (1972). *Painting and experience in fifteenth century Italy.* Oxford: Oxford University Press.

Beardsley, M. C. (1966). *Aesthetics from classical Greece to the present: A short history.* New York: Macmillan.

Beardsley, M. C. (1981). *Aesthetics: Problems in the philosophy of criticism.* Indianapolis: Hackett.

Becker, H. S. (1982). *Art worlds.* Berkeley: University of California Press.

Berger, J. (1972). *Ways of seeing.* Harmondsworth, England: Penguin.

Berleant, A. (1991). *Art and engagement.* Philadelphia: Temple University Press.

Beyer, L. E. (1986). "Critical theory and the art of teaching." *Journal of Curriculum and Supervision, 1*(3), 221–232.

Blandy, D., and Congdon, K. (1987). *Art in a democracy.* New York: Teachers College Press.

Boardman, E. (1990). "Music teacher education." In W. R. Houston (ed.), *Handbook of research on teacher education.* New York: Macmillan.

Broudy, H. S. (1972) *Enlightened cherishing: An essay on aesthetic education.* Urbana: University of Illinois Press.

Broudy, H. S. (1987). *The role of imagery in learning.* (Occasional Paper no. 1). Los Angeles: Getty Center for Education in the Arts.

Broudy, H. S. (1990). "Cultural literacy and general education." *Journal of Aesthetic Education, 24*(1), 7–16.

Chalmers, G. (1974). "A cultural foundation for education in the arts." *Art Education, 27*(1), 21–25.

Chanda, J. (1992). "Multicultural education and the visual arts." *Arts Education Policy Review, 94*(1), 12–16.

Clark, G., Day, M., and Greer, D. W. (1987). "Discipline-based art education: Becoming students of art." In R. A. Smith (ed.), *Discipline-based art education: Origins, meaning and development.* Urbana: University of Illinois Press.

Collingwood, R. G. (1938). *The principles of art.* Oxford: Clarendon Press.

Csikszentmihalyi, M., and Robinson, R. E. (1990). *The art of seeing.* Malibu, Calif.: Getty Museum/Getty Center for Education in the Arts.

Davis, D. J. (1990). "Teacher education for the visual arts." In W. R. Houston (ed.), *Handbook of research on teacher education.* New York: Macmillan.

Dewey, J. (1934). *Art as experience.* New York: Capricorn Books.

Dickie, G. (1971). *Aesthetics: An introduction.* New York: Bobbs-Merrill.

Ecker, G. (1985). *Feminist aesthetics.* Boston: Beacon Press.

Efland, A. D. (1976). "The school art style: A functional analysis." *Studies in Art Education, 17*(2), 37–44.

Efland, A. D. (1990). *A history of art education.* New York: Teachers College Press.

Eisner, E. W. (1963). "Knowledge, knowing and the visual arts." *Harvard Educational Review, 33*(2), 208–218.

Eisner, E. W. (1985). *The educational imagination.* (2nd ed.). New York: Macmillan.

Eisner, E. W. (1991). *The enlightened eye: Qualitative inquiry and the enhancement of educational practice.* New York: Macmillan.

Eisner, E. W. (1992). "The misunderstood role of the arts in human development." *Phi Delta Kappan, 73*(8), 591–595.

Engel, M. (1980). "Getting serious about arts education." *Principal,* Sept., pp. 6–10.

Fenstermacher, G. D. (1990). "Some moral considerations on teaching as a profession." In J. I. Goodlad, R. Soder, and K. A. Sirotnik (eds.), *The moral dimensions of teaching.* San Francisco: Jossey-Bass.

Foucault, M. (1972). *The archeology of knowledge.* New York: Colophon Books.

Galbraith, L. (1990). "Examining issues from general teacher education: Implications for preservice art education methods courses." *Visual Arts Research, 16*(2), 51–58.

Galbraith, L. (1991). "Analyzing an art methods course: Implications for preparing primary art student teachers." *Journal of Art and Design Education, 10*(3), 329–342.

Garber, E. (1992). "Feminism, aesthetics and art education." *Studies in Art Education, 33*(4), 210–225.

Gardner, H. (1973). *The arts and human development.* New York: Wiley.

Gardner, H. (1989). "Zero-based arts education: An introduction to ARTS PROPEL." *Studies in Art Education, 30*(2), 71–83.

Gombrich, E. (1969). *Art and illusion: A case study of pictorial representation.* Princeton, N.J.: Princeton University Press.

Goodman, N. (1968). *The languages of art.* New York: Bobbs-Merrill.

Goodman, N. (1978). *Ways of worldmaking.* Indianapolis: Hackett.

Greene, M. (1981). "Aesthetic literacy in general education." In J. Soltis (ed.), *Philosophy and education.* (80th yearbook of the National Society for the Study of Education, pt. 1). Chicago: University of Chicago Press.

Gulbenkian Foundation (1982). *The arts in schools.* London: Oyez Press.

Hanna, L. J. (1992). "Connections: Arts, academics and productive citizens." *Phi Delta Kappan, 73*(8), 601–606.

Heidegger, M. (1964). "The origin of a work of art" (A. Hofstadter, trans.). In A. Hofstadter and R. Kuhns (eds.), *Philosophies of art and beauty.* New York: Modern Library.

Hospers, J. (1982). *Understanding the arts.* Englewood Cliffs, N.J.: Prentice Hall.

Jackson, P. W. (1991). "On learning to see what is not there." *Keynote addresses, 1991 NAEA annual convention.* Reston, Va.: National Art Education Association.

Koehler, V. (1979). "Research on teaching: Implications for research on the teaching of the arts." In G. L. Knieter and J. A. Stallings (eds.), *The teaching process and arts and aesthetics.* St. Louis, Mo.: Central Midwestern Regional Education Laboratory.

Kristeller, P. O. (1961). *Renaissance thought: The classic, scholastic and humanistic strains.* New York: HarperCollins.

Langer, S. (1957). *Problems of art.* New York: Scribner.

Lanier, V. (1991). *The world of art education according to Lanier.* Reston, Va.: National Art Education Association.

Lazerson, M., McLaughlin, J. B., McPherson, B., and Bailey, S. K. (1985). *An education of value.* Cambridge: Cambridge University Press.

McPhee, J., and Degge, R. M. (1977). *Art, culture, and environment: A catalyst.* Belmont, Calif.: Wadsworth.

Madeja, S. (1977). *Arts and aesthetics: An agenda for the future.* St. Louis, Mo.: Central Midwestern Regional Educational Laboratory.

Maquet, J. (1986). *The aesthetic experience.* New Haven, Conn.: Yale University Press.

Margolis, J. (1978). *Philosophy looks at the arts.* Philadelphia: Temple University Press.

Martin, K. (1986). "On teaching teachers to teach." Paper presented at the National Symposium on Teaching in the Arts, Baton Rouge, La.

Martin, K., and Ross, G. (1988). "Developing professionals for arts education." In J. B. McLaughlin (ed.), *Toward a new era in arts education.* New York: American Council for the Arts.

Martindale, A. (1972). *The rise of the artist in the Middle Ages and early Renaissance.* London: Thames & Hudson.

Mason, R. M. (1988). *Art education and multiculturalism.* London: Croom Helm.

May, W. T. (1989). "Teachers, teaching, and the workplace: Omissions in curriculum reform." *Studies in Art Education, 30*(3), 142–156.

National Art Education Association (1986). *Quality art education.* Reston, Va: National Art Education Association.

Osborne, H. (1970). *The art of appreciation.* New York: Oxford University Press.

Pepper, S. C. (1949). *The basis of criticism in the arts.* Cambridge, Mass.: Harvard University Press.

Piper, D. (1984). *Looking at art.* New York: Random House.

Reid, L. A. (1973). "Aesthetics and aesthetic education." In D. Field and J. Newick (eds.), *The study of education and art.* New York: Routledge & Kegan Paul.

Reimer, B. (1991). "Essential and nonessential characteristics of aesthetic education." *Journal of Aesthetic Education, 25*(3), 193–214.

Rico, G. L. (1993). "Toward an expanded conception of knowing: Qualitative thought in recreations." *Educational Horizons, 71*(2), 99–108.

Santayana, G. (1955). *The sense of beauty.* New York: Dover.

Sibley, R. (1965). "Aesthetic and nonaesthetic." *Philosophical Review, 74*(2), 135–159.

Smith, R. A. (1987). "The changing image of art education: Theoretical antecedents of discipline-based art education." In R. A. Smith (ed.), *Discipline-based art education: Origins, meaning and development.* Urbana: University of Illinois Press.

Smith, R. A. (1989). *A sense of art: A study in aesthetic education.* New York: Routledge & Kegan Paul.

Spratt, F. (1987). "Art production in discipline-based art education." In R. A. Smith (ed.), *Discipline-based art education: Origins, meaning and development.* Urbana: University of Illinois Press.

Weitz, M. (1950). *Philosophy of the arts.* Cambridge, Mass.: Harvard University Press.

Wilds, E., and Lottich, K. (1962). *The foundations of modern education.* Austin, Texas: Holt, Rinehart & Winston.

Annotated Bibliography

As the reference list suggests, there are many books related to education within the fine arts. The following are two publications that may be of use to teacher educators:

McLaughlin, J. B. (1988). *Toward a new era in arts education.* New York: American Council for the Arts.

This book comprises the proceedings of the Interlochen Symposium that examined the arts, the teaching of the arts, and learning the arts in order to develop a common conceptual base through the examination of critical issues in arts education. The symposium recommended thirty-two specific proposals for improving arts education in the United States. Six papers from the symposium are presented. Topics discussed include teacher preparation, curriculum development, and advocacy for the arts.

Smith, R. A., and Simpson, A. (1991). *Aesthetics and arts education.* Urbana: University of Illinois Press.

This book comprises a series of thirty-two essays written by a distinguished set of international writers involved with aesthetic education in the arts. It is a resource that sets forth some of the fundamental goals of arts education in general and issues within aesthetics as a field of study.

CHAPTER EIGHT

CHANGING THE SUBJECT: TEACHER EDUCATION AND LANGUAGE ARTS

MARK AMSLER AND ELAINE M. STOTKO

Recent work in literary and cultural theory and in linguistics has posed new challenges and opened new possibilities to teachers of reading and language arts. A critical inquiry into the curriculum includes questions about the relation between textbooks and real-world language, about the cultural and linguistic differences among students in today's classrooms, and about what to do tomorrow in language arts. New theories and approaches to literacy, drawn from sociolinguistics, text theory, and critical pedagogy, also present challenges and possibilities to teachers of teachers in education programs. How effective are methods and content area courses for developing teachers' abilities to "read" their classrooms and motivate students to use literate discourse in productive and powerful ways? Also, as teachers of teachers, can we effect changes in teaching and critical understanding in the schools by considering more reflectively our own positions in the college classroom as critics, language "experts," and readers?

Typically, language arts is defined as instruction in speaking, listening, reading, writing, and critical thinking. This definition is workable but problematic. So defined, language arts as a skill can inform the teaching and understanding of all other subjects in the curriculum. But often, this definition of language arts is used narrowly to mean instruction in "correct" spoken and written standard English, with little attention to how the subject of "English" defines both a set of activities and a subject for critical study. Language arts need not be just a service to the rest of the curriculum, a place where proper reading and writing are taught. Literacy education is not just about process or form or socially appropriate usage, though it includes all these practical skills.

Above all, literacy education is about using and understanding discourse. By discourse, we mean language use appropriate to different social contexts and communicative goals. In addition to being able to decode and inscribe, being literate means understanding how different discourses are used in and out of school and other settings, what different discourses signify, and how to think reflectively about these discourses. Being literate means being able to identify oneself as a member of a socially empowered group and to imagine the possibilities that this entails.

Therefore, language arts as a school subject connects with the question of what kinds of knowledge and what beliefs are promoted or fostered in the curriculum. Thinking of language arts as discursive activities reshapes the "subject" in the curriculum and also redescribes how we think of ourselves as subjects. That is, rather than individuals who use language merely as an instrument of our own thought, we are discursive subjects positioned within social discourses and at the same time agents who find ways to use language to construct meaning, or personal knowledge, around ourselves through psychosocial processes of identification, resistance, and habits of community.

A teacher occupies a specific and socially constructed position in the classroom. Whether we choose to accept the role or not, as language arts, literacy, or literature teachers we represent or express specific attitudes about language and discourse. How often have we heard, "Oh, you teach English? I'd better watch my language." But as teachers of English and linguistics, we often find ourselves living out a double role within the same activity. When we teach grammar in the classroom, for example, our own attitudes toward English (the version we speak and write as well as the versions we do not) have a direct bearing on the grammar lesson. We cannot presume that the variety of English we teach is transmitted in an unmediated way through the variety we use. Whether we consider ourselves "traditional," "radical," or "nurturing" teachers, our beliefs about language and learning shape the subject of language in the classroom.

As teachers of fourth graders or prospective high school teachers, our teaching practices are constituted as a series of social and epistemological dialogues between the institutionally shaped subject, English, and the specific interests and goals of teachers and students. Of all the knowledges and experiences we have, which ones do we think are appropriate for school and for the world that school stands before? Which ones are appropriate for our students to learn? Rather than assuming that we teachers are the only ones who set the context for learning, we also need to think carefully about the context within which learning—both our students' and our own—is already taking place. The teacher is immediately responsible for the classroom context, but who shares in the knowledge presumed to be classroom knowledge? How is the authority of the teacher constructed in the classroom situation and in cultural discourse? How is English as a social practice made into a subject for study, and how does it construct our subjectivity?

Language Arts: Variation and Power

The question of authority and knowledge surfaces very insistently when our roles of teacher and parent intersect. The subject is homework. During her first eight years of school, Elaine's daughter discovered that her mother was not a very reliable help for her English assignments from school, even though she is both a linguist and an English teacher. Elaine in turn feels distanced from many of the language arts and English grammar exercises her daughter brings home. Last year in eighth grade, for example, she spent several frustrating weeks trying to understand the teacher's and textbook's distinction between *me* as an indirect object ("Bake me a cake") and *me* as the object of a preposition ("Bake a cake for me"). Speakers of English can agree that these two sentences are generally synonymous and that, from the perspective of case grammar and "sentence roles," the word *me* in each instance functions as a receiver or indirect object (the one who receives the cake). However, the textbook included more than ten pages of exercises designed to get students to distinguish between the term *indirect object* and the term *object of a preposition.*

The only purpose of the textbook exercises seemed to be to make sure the students could identify each surface structure by its "proper" name; that is, the students were learning a particular way of talking about language, a grammatical metalanguage, and how to apply it appropriately according to the definitions and examples in the textbook. Mother and daughter spent hours struggling over these exercises. While Elaine's daughter was able to see that the sentences were synonymous, neither could see why it was so important to learn two sets of labels for what appeared to be essentially the same grammatical structure, nor did there seem to be any classroom discussion that acknowledged that there are different ways in which sentence structures can be described.

Why should there be such a distinction between a functional understanding of English grammar and the formal classroom presentation of grammatical categories? Why should students who are native speakers spend so much time learning labels for structures they already know and can use (for example, the plural ending *-s*)? How do the structures of language arts discourse shape students' and teachers' and ultimately teachers of teachers' attitudes about "correct" language, language "deficits," "good" and "bad" usage, and appropriate language study? How does school knowledge about language differ from what children already know about and do with language? Does learning a specific grammatical metalanguage (object of a preposition, indirect object) really help students communicate more effectively? Whose usage is privileged in the curriculum or the classroom? How do we imagine or shape a community in the classroom when we "do" language arts?

The "subject" of language arts affects how we as speaking "subjects" think about and use language for expression and communication. Historically, language arts instruction has had more effect on how students think about English, language variation, and the role of language in social order than it has on their specific linguistic usage. Following the work of Bakhtin (1981, 1986) and Vygotsky (1986) on language acquisition and speech genres, we can say that beneath the school exercises in pluralization, syntactic description, and appreciating "great literature," language arts is about understanding the uses of language in particular contexts.

Recently, Mark was teaching a general introduction to English linguistics for college undergraduates. The class was trying to determine the degree to which English word order is fixed and the range of acceptable variations there might be when using indexical words, such as pronouns and spatial/temporal adverbs *(here, there, now, then)*. Mark asked students to consider the sentence "Look at that rock there." How movable is the adverb *there*? One student in the class said that the word *there* could be used properly only in the final slot in the sentence. "Look at that there rock," she said, was incorrect and a sign of poor education. An important pedagogical moment was emerging in the classroom, but we were not certain yet in which direction the class would go. Then, another student in the back of the room raised her hand and said, "But that's the way I really talk. Where I come from, everybody says, 'Look at that there rock.' " The moment had arrived in the classroom dialogue.

Finding ways to talk about (we are not saying "handle" or "manage") these dialectal differences and the attitudes they carry with them is an example of what a critical language arts pedagogy is all about. After the two students spoke, the class was surprised to find itself in a conflict over grammaticality and acceptability. We focused on two questions: (1) how are syntactic patterns, which are systematic, related to dialectal differences, and (2) how do dialectal differences enable some speakers to stigmatize certain constructions, such as "that there rock," as "inferior"? We analyzed the underlying syntactic forms of the two sentences, using our knowledge of English phrase structures, recent linguistic descriptions of syntactic dependency and case grammar, and theories of sentence roles. The discussion of the first question went more smoothly than the discussion of the second. As long as the students could maintain what they regarded as an "objective" distance, they could discuss the sentences. But when we turned to our beliefs about correctness, standard and nonstandard usage, and what most language arts textbooks prescribe, the discussion became bumpy. The class worked hesitantly, describing some of the differences between what someone *could* say and what was acceptable or proper for someone to say.[1] Nonetheless, the mostly suburban, white, middle-class students did risk entering a difficult but important discussion about how linguistic identities are shaped in discursive positions and about how some of their conceptions of "hick" speech or "redneck" speech depended not on grammatical but on social criteria.

The nonstandard construction "that there rock" does not appear in any language arts or grammar handbook as an acceptable construction. Yet the group was presented with an unequivocal statement that the construction was acceptable to more than one person in the class. For the teacher, the study of syntax (or pronunciation or spelling or morphology) cannot be isolated from community norms of usage and correctness. Not all unacceptable forms are grammatically incorrect. The students had to acknowledge that there was not a single, univocal linguistic norm in the community or at least that there was more than one linguistic community represented in the classroom. Our discussion did not produce a unified community understanding in which "that there rock" came to be thought of as interchangeable with "that rock there." That was not the goal of our discussion. Rather, we talked about how our ideas of "standard English" or "linguistic community" are informed by specific linguistic features and more broadly based social attitudes (for example, as several students said, "that there rock" is a sign of poor education).[2] Mark tried (not always successfully) to keep the discussion inclusive and nonconfrontational, because it is important for students, especially prospective teachers, to find ways to talk together about deep-seated language attitudes and also to see how as teachers they are implicated in the construction of distinctions between standard and nonstandard English. The discussion was productive to the extent the class became more aware of how different linguistic and social communities exist within the idealized description of "standard" English. By considering the relation between grammatical structures and pedagogical gestures such as repeating "correctly" a student's speech, they also opened up a critical discussion of the degree to which language arts instruction is implicated in the construction of our notions about what counts as "standard."

When teaching about reading, writing, and literature, we need to adopt a more functional discourse and consider grammar instruction from the perspective of the linguistic distinction between a "prescriptive" and "descriptive" account of language. Attitudes about language use and correctness presented in school are mostly characterized by a prescriptive approach to language, in which only one type of English (typically the teacher's or the textbook's) is acceptable. By adopting this view, schools separate the language of the teacher (or the language the teacher claims to profess) from the languages of the students and further divide students of different social, economic, or ethnic backgrounds from mainstream schooling. This approach also positions the teacher, right or wrong, as the sole arbiter of appropriate usage, the "grammar God," at least in the language arts classroom. Those students who are able to harness a "standard" English dialect for school purposes are at a clear advantage within the system (although at times they may find themselves at a disadvantage within their peer group), and membership within the dominant culture has a direct bearing on perceptions of one's intelligence, group identity, and self-worth.

Coupled with a more critical linguistic pedagogy, the descriptive approach encourages teachers to investigate the normal variations that naturally occur in language and to reflect more on their own language, their attitudes toward correctness, and their attitudes toward students whose language use differs in some way from their own. Such inquiries are not objective studies in the sense that the teacher is simply discovering the features already there. There is no purely descriptive understanding of language, only positions within which we come to understand language practices. Nor are we prescribing the "correct" descriptive approach. Rather, the tools of descriptive linguistics can be used to understand and to help students grasp the ways linguistic structures (of pronunciation, morphology, syntax, or vocabulary) are organized according to discourse rules, community identities, and cultural values. The empirical approach of descriptive linguistics, in other words, paying close attention to what speakers and writers actually do with language, can help students perceive the complex ways in which linguistic communities are organized and understand the importance of standard English as cultural capital.

A more self-reflective language arts curriculum can foreground the fact that not all linguistic differences are the same. Among mainstream speakers, for example, some dialectal differences are tolerated or acceptable while others are not. Kaplan (1989) notes that different kinds of language variation evoke different responses from the listener. Regional vocabulary differences (she says "hoagie," he says "torpedo," I say "submarine sandwich" or "sub") are often thought to be interesting or amusing but are seldom judged to be either correct or incorrect. Pronunciation differences may cause more complex reactions. Some are not noticed, others are quaint or exotic, while still others are considered substandard. But what counts as standard depends on the community the speaker is perceived to be part of. If a teacher in the United States were to have, say, a British English or Caribbean English speaker in the classroom, it is doubtful that a dialect feature such as "postvocalic *r* drop" would be labeled as incorrect, though there may be some stigma attached to Caribbean English speakers' reducing initial consonant clusters (as when *stomach* is pronounced "tomach"). But when a student from Boston or Atlanta relocated in a West Coast or midwestern classroom speaks with *r* drop, the feature may be considered humorous or cute. Moreover, both New England and southern American English display *r* drop, but speakers in each region tend to think of speakers in the other region as "deviant." All English speakers delete some word-final morphemes when speaking rapidly. But when a Black English Vernacular (BEV) speaker deletes a plural marker at the end of a word, his or her speech is sometimes labeled deficient, even though such a deletion is a rule-governed process in that dialect.[3] When a student belongs to a minority or nonprestigious group, nonstandard features of his or her speech are often perceived to be deficient rather than different.

Reproducing the power of language arts instruction as a cultural symbol, dominant and nondominant language speakers alike often regard grammatical (as opposed to pronunciation) differences as incorrect. Also, dominant language speakers, such as the student in Mark's class with her mainstream dialect (affirmed by school discourse) and her belief that "that there rock" is incorrect, often make judgments about other speakers' *abilities* to use language effectively or about their general intelligence.

All of us as teachers, whether we are working in elementary, high school, or college classrooms, can open the "subject" of language arts to include the structures of language variation. We can also work to include language variation more explicitly as well as implicitly in the curriculum. This is particularly important as the numbers of minority children and children of limited English proficiency in the classroom increase. We are not suggesting teachers give up teaching standard English. Ideally, all students should be able to participate in "official literate culture" in the ways they want and need to. All students should be able to use all the cultural capital that standard English affords them. But we also have an intellectual responsibility to demystify standard English and to set mainstream literate discourse and usage in the context of a broader understanding of language variation, including acceptable and unacceptable differences.

For example, teacher educators can guide their students through a critical examination of how textbooks exclude typical and natural language variation while presuming that a certain dialect of English is correct. Think of the basal reader lessons that contrast pairs of words such as *pin* and *pen* for spelling or phonics practice without taking into account that for a large portion of the United States, the two words are pronounced identically (/PIN/). Similarly, consider a typical lesson on homonyms. Would the teacher accept *caught* and *cot* as homonyms (/kat/), as they are for more than half the English speakers in the United States? When we did homonym projects in the fifth grade in the mid 1950s, there was no discussion of pronunciation differences and dialect patterns. Would there be any place in today's classroom for discussing whether the students' lists of homonyms are based on similar or different pronunciation patterns? Each teacher's dialect and attitudes toward correctness color the classroom discussion. If we are not comfortable with language variation or diversity, how can our students be?

The view of language as an ideal object fostered in schools contributes to other contradictions in the curriculum. For example, students' understanding of school language is often confused by its decontextualized presentation. Teenagers already know a lot about the language they speak with friends: what is "correct," what is "incorrect," which expressions will mark them as a member of the group or as a "geek" or as an outsider, and so forth. Teens have a great deal of context to draw from in forming these judgments, and language arts teachers need to take that context seriously and to reflect on and theorize about how kids know what it means to talk "cool."

Unfortunately, most presentations of school language focus more on autonomous form and ignore context and the social construction of meaning and identity through various discourses. Take, for instance, a standard textbook presentation of relative clause structures. All students (and most writers) have trouble deciding whether a particular relative clause is "essential" or "nonessential," or in students' terms, whether they need to put commas around the clause or not. Why is this so difficult to decide? Textbooks tell students to determine whether the information in the clause is needed or "extra" information. However, these texts miss the point that the overriding factor in whether something is considered to be "essential" or "just additional information" has to do with what the speaker/writer intends. That is, the punctuation must be determined by discourse context or prior information. It cannot be determined simply by looking at a textbook sentence out of context. Yet most language arts textbooks present lists of such decontextualized sentences for practice as if a sentence were some fixed object that could be understood apart from its larger context.

The problems that result from considering language in decontextualized ways in language arts have been recognized and discussed in the research on second-language acquisition for a number of years (see, for example, Di Pietro, 1987). This research shows that second-language learners do better when language practice is situated within realistic and socially appropriate language contexts. Yet we often miss this point in our language arts curriculum for native speakers, with the result that students often come to believe that what they are doing in their language arts or English classes has no relevance in their real world.

Therefore, it is important that language arts and literature teachers both investigate the ways in which standard English empowers certain people and recognize their role in reproducing the cultural capital that standard English carries. In other words, classroom discussions and exercises must be informed by a view of discourse as sociolinguistic variation, community identifications, and forms of cultural power.

Hirsch (1987) has made what looks like a similar claim: that schooling should give everyone, especially "disadvantaged" children, access to the most important and culturally valuable information and forms of cultural knowledge. But Hirsch's program, now being piloted in some American elementary schools, presupposes that socially effective schooling depends on a common curriculum of shared information that everyone masters. Hirsch rightly focuses on literacy as cultural capital, but in his program there is no room for different discourse communities or knowledges or for discussing various forms of understanding or for negotiating knowledges between teachers and students or between different social groups. Hirsch believes that only by "piling up specific, communally shared information can [disadvantaged and middle-class] children learn to participate in complex cooperative activities with other members of their community" (p. xv). When knowledge is organized as a single body, such a view of schooling as Hirsch's gives rise to a monologic rather than a dialogic curriculum (see Bakhtin, 1981).

In theory, whole language approaches address the problem of decontextualized language arts instruction; however, actual classroom practice may or may not achieve this pedagogical goal. Whole language curricula try to involve students in activities that use oral and written language to accomplish literate tasks of communication, persuasion, organizing information, and so on within larger communicative contexts (that is, reasons for knowing and wanting to know something). Rather than being treated as discrete entities, the subject matters are interrelated according to what the students might want to know and what the teacher thinks is relevant. In an elementary school classroom, for instance, the students might decide to learn about chickens using fiction, folklore, and factual material. The students observe a real chicken's behavior, write up their findings, compare information, categorize the information they produce, and discuss the relations between what they observe and what they read about chickens in encyclopedias, picture books, and folktales.[4] Whole language approaches nicely link areas of knowledge and discourse through cognitive and curricular webbing.

However, though whole language activities are student-centered, English is still too often represented as a univocal object looked at in a formal, decontextualized way or regarded only as the instrument of expression, or else language usages are left unexamined and unquestioned in the classroom. Even programs that emphasize whole language curricula could expand their view of the integrated and critical curriculum to include more analysis and discussion of the structure of language, varieties of English, and the different social functions of language use, including formal and informal contexts. In the context of topics about the environment, animal and human life on earth, relationships, or history, students might be asked to compare objective or scientific discourse with fictional discourse, analyze and compare literal and figurative language, and discuss the ways language represents cultural knowledge or stereotypes. To work in these flexible and interdisciplinary ways, which some whole language approaches presume, prospective language arts teachers will need to develop a broad and critical understanding of English as socially situated and multivoiced.

One consequence of taking a more contextualized approach to language arts would be to rethink the way in which students' oral and written "errors" are understood and responded to. Not all student writing needs to be "corrected" according to standard English. Some writing lessons could focus on why certain language forms (first person or third person, contractions, colloquialisms, idioms particular to written English) are appropriate for some contexts but not others. So often, school discourse is said to require standard English because it is "correct" or "more rational." In fact, "standard" English is enforced in schools because it is part of what identifies the school as a legitimate community, what connects school with the larger official community, what marks the relation between schooling and the profit interests of the workplace. By explicitly analyzing the features of standard written English as a code, students can develop a context for thinking about how other communities within the school community, such as their peer groups, are also identified by particular linguistic styles. The language arts classroom, then, can provide students and teachers with ways to conceptualize and theorize the various discourse situations in which they and others participate.

When language differences are not automatically stigmatized as deficits or as indicating the knowledge that students lack, a language arts curriculum can be constituted as a group of activities that students participate in rather than as content to be "poured into" students to make up for what they lack. Furthermore, while some students may need speech therapy to compensate for difficulties with articulation (for example, sibilants such as /s/ or /z/), many purported deficit speakers are unfairly viewed as less intelligent and needing remediation.

Teachers should recognize that from an early age students understand a lot about language use. Teachers and administrators can capitalize on this knowledge and competence when planning or augmenting the school curriculum. Students know, for example, that you do not usually address the school principal in the same manner as your friends or write a letter to your mother in the same way you write a note to a friend in class. Yet so many language arts activities serve to homogenize distinctions that students can already make. The same teacher who refuses to allow the use of contractions in a formal paper might also mark them as incorrect in letter writing. At the same time, students might be confused about why they should not use contractions in their compositions or how formal written English differs from spoken English. Students who ask whether they are "permitted" to use contractions or *I* in a composition are not participating fully in a literate discourse. They are surveying what to them probably seems more like an unknown territory. Also, when middle and high schools divide language and literature into separate classes, students believe that grammar and grammatical analysis are subjects to be learned only for school, to pass the tests. It should be no surprise that many students wonder what all of this language practice is actually about and how it connects to their communicative goals and the language they use every day.

School life is permeated by all sorts of writing by students, teachers, and administrators—official and unofficial, formal and informal, personal and public, some turned in to the teacher, some concealed from the teacher. But when teachers neglect to discuss with students the broader purposes of different kinds of writing, "school" writing becomes something that people are asked to do only in composition classes.

For example, one high school student we know has determined that the most effective way to write a paper for his English teacher, who believes in the importance of revision and requires students to produce revisions of their work, is to write the final version first and then back up and write a series of progressively worse rough drafts, ending (or beginning) with a smudged pencil copy. So far this year, this strategy has earned him good grades in English. But his strategy for turning out drafts reveals his lack of understanding of what revision actually is, how revisions give writers a chance to try out ideas, how readers' feedback can be another way of thinking about the topic for oneself, and how discussing revisions is a way of negotiating between the writer's own point of view and the larger discourse community within which the writing makes sense. Evidently, the high school English teacher assumes that the students already understand and are comfortable with the provisional nature of written drafts and revisions and that they use revisions to extend their thinking about a question or topic. But for the student, revisions are just so many hurdles to get over. In addition, the way teachers themselves treat the writing process and revision can give students the idea that brainstorming, collaborative writing, and revision are simply ways for the teacher to point out "errors" or, worse, to have other students point out the errors under the guise of helping each other.

If Elaine's daughter's struggle with indirect objects can be used as an example, it would seem that the design of exercises throughout the early grades and in particular the middle-school grades focuses on a prescriptive rule-based approach to language and teaching students to apply a particular grammatical metalanguage. But students get little or contradictory guidance about why their teachers think English grammar is important.

Exercises in the early grades try to "teach" children language structures they already know without much direct instruction—how to form plurals or the past tense, for example. Of course, standard English presumes that students must learn to *spell* or *mark* or *punctuate* these forms appropriately. But language arts textbooks and basal readers also give teachers the impression that children need to be taught the grammatical structures themselves, when in fact children are already *using* many of these structures productively in their oral discourse. The fact that some students speaking a nonstandard variety of English might not always form past tenses or plurals with the appropriate standard English markers clearly shows how the typical language arts curriculum privileges traditional middle-class speakers in the United States and rewards them for succeeding at what they already know how to do. At the same time, the curriculum also stigmatizes other speakers who are using their dialects correctly and appropriately but not with the same school success. Teachers need to help students make the bridge to literacy by relying more on students' oral proficiency and knowledge of English grammar, particularly in the case of "nonstandard" speakers.

It is unfortunate that some hostility has developed between English and language arts teachers and contemporary linguists when in fact a good number of linguistic approaches to language incorporate and extend the insights of traditional grammar. Exercises in the later grades tend to focus on learning the "right names" (metalanguage) for parts of speech or certain grammatical constructions. Students are typically expected to learn how to group words into grammatical categories (noun, verb, adjective, adverb, and so forth), but they are not usually encouraged to discover underlying relations and tensions between word classes (for instance, *red* as noun and adjective) or to understand where the standard word class definitions break down or become fuzzy. Grammar lessons (bordering on lessons in the scientific method) might include activities in which students find ways to group and categorize different words and structures beyond the traditional textbook definitions of the parts of speech. Such discussions could conveniently connect language arts subject matter with the procedures for scientific observation and classification. For example, the traditional definition of a noun as a "person, place, or thing" is workable, but only in a limited context. What kind of "thing" is a baseball game, a thunderstorm, or hunger? The traditional definition of a verb as an "action, event, or state" word seems more applicable to these examples. Is school or Congress a "place" in the narrow sense? And what is a story?

An object? An event? An experience? That teachers and students might not have all the answers to such questions does not make them any the less important for a reflective language arts curriculum.

When a student is directed to identify or underline the nouns, verbs, and adjectives in the following sentences, how well do the traditional definitions fit?

1. We spilled punch at the *dance*.
2. The garbage *smells*.
3. It *rained*. Big drops of *rain* fell.
4. Hundreds of people watched the car *race*.

In sentences 1 and 4, *dance* and *race* refer to activities. *Smells* in sentence 2 appears to modify *garbage* and has an intransitive quality. In sentence 3, whether *rain* is a noun or a verb depends on its grammatical marking rather than its semantic meaning. Students using the textbooks' decontextualized word class definitions will have problems choosing the "correct" answer to complete the exercise. On the other hand, students might get the correct answer not because the traditional school definitions are helpful but because they are able to identify nouns, subjects, and verbs by using other syntactic clues (such as the articles *a* or *the* or the past tense marker *-ed*). Grammar exercises, we believe, should include more explicit instruction and discussion of the relations between traditional word classes and grammatical functions.

An English or language arts curriculum has a number of important goals. Perhaps most important is to help students move outside the classroom as strong, critical readers and writers, as individuals who reflect on how they and others construct meaning in various discourses, and as speakers and writers who use appropriate discourses to organize, understand, and improve their worlds. A critically thoughtful curriculum presumes language to be both content and form—the object of discursive analysis and discourse itself. Different teacher education programs will have—indeed, need to have—different curriculum designs that respond to the expertise of the faculty and the makeup of the student population. But both elementary and secondary education programs can include more specific work on language structure and variation. Teacher educators can help prospective teachers develop their understanding of language as a system more variable than the prescriptive rules would have us believe. We also should work to show that such variability need not be tied, as it is in traditional grammatical judgments, to judgments about deviance, deficiency, and cognitive disadvantages. This work may be in individual courses or part of a general foundations sequence, but in either case, it should probably not be left to traditional methods classes.

Prospective teachers also need to be empowered to read textbooks and curriculum materials critically in terms of socially situated meanings. They should be encouraged to explore systematically the relations between skills and content and the functions of linguistic identities in constructing social power. At a minimum, prospective K–12 teachers need to work specifically to understand the structures and functions of both standard and nonstandard English, the latter not as deficiencies but as legitimate discourses. Finally, and perhaps most important, prospective teachers, the majority of whom are women, should be encouraged and challenged to think critically about their own positions in schooling, about the ways in which schooling has silenced women's and minority discourses, and about inventive ways to empower those often silenced discourses.

Literary Studies

Not only have sociolinguistics and critical approaches to language variation and differences offered stimulating ways to rethink conventional language arts curricula, but in literary interpretation and critical reading, discourse studies and new approaches to reading and textuality have also posed important challenges for the language arts curriculum, both at the middle and high school levels and in the elementary grades. Teacher education programs and departments of English and comparative literature, though not always allies, have many subjects and interests in common. In our university, English secondary education majors take most of their courses in British, American, and world literature. The "subject" of the English education major is virtually indistinguishable from the "subject" of the English major. Moreover, elementary education majors specializing in language arts and English are encouraged to take a number of courses in literature, folklore, and critical theory.

The history of literary studies in Britain and America during the twentieth century can be mapped as a movement from (1) a *belles lettres* criticism given to the appreciation of writers' life and times to (2) New Criticism and close reading that focuses rigorously on the poetic text itself and on how linguistic and poetic connections in the text, chiefly metaphor, produce a verbal object constituted by poetic, as opposed to ordinary, language to (3) attention to the ways in which textual meaning and significance are constructed by readers and the ways in which cultural and literary contexts determine and amplify the reading and writing of texts.

The consequences of this historical movement for the practice and theory of literary studies have been profound and far-reaching. Today, English departments in American and British universities and colleges teach not only the traditional canon of English writers (Chaucer, Shakespeare, Pope, Wordsworth, Dickens, and Yeats, or Franklin, Twain, Hawthorne, Melville, Dickinson, James, and Eliot) but also and increasingly writers from other English traditions: Caribbean, African, Indian, Native American, Hispanic, Irish, Scots, Canadian, Australian. English curricula also include more women writers, African-American writers, and Chinese- and Japanese-American writers. Many English departments include critical theory, feminist theory, cultural theory, semiotics, film studies, and linguistic approaches to literature as part of their curricula and as part of what they want English majors to know about when they graduate.

Granted, courses in minority or postcolonial literatures or in new critical and theoretical approaches to literary studies have sometimes been controversial. Shifts in critical paradigms and the canon have not come without anxiety and some difficulty. Still, many English departments offer versions of this new subject called literary studies. Finally, English departments today teach a wide variety of writing courses designed for both majors and nonmajors, including expository and analytic writing, poetry and fiction writing, business and technical writing, and journalism.

Rather than conceiving of poems or stories as containers of meaning, we might think of how we produce and read "texts" as we construct, negotiate, and resist meanings. In his essay "On Reading," Roland Barthes (1986) describes reading as "a plural field of scattered practices, of irreducible effects" (p. 33). Locating and determining the text's (or the writer's) intended meaning is only one of several kinds of close reading, and the intended meaning of a text is not something that is strictly controlled by a writer. Rather, readers comprehend texts in relation to "discourses," those larger, more complex cultural and linguistic practices that shape and limit but also empower readers' "textual competences."

Feminist literary theory in particular has galvanized contemporary literary studies by investigating how, instead of a monolithic or universal reader, there are different "reading positions" and different "implied readers." The lessons of feminist theory and criticism are felt not just in women's literature courses but throughout literary studies. Kate Chopin's book *The Awakening* and Charlotte Perkins Gilman's story "The Yellow Wallpaper" dramatize the difference gender and socialization make in narrative point of view and challenge the assumption that men and women necessarily read alike or identify with characters and situations in the same ways. Several of our colleagues in the English department have described class discussions that explored why some of the boys think the female narrator in Gilman's story is overreacting and why many of the girls think she is justifiably distressed at her treatment. If readers bring parts of themselves and their cultures to the texts they read, the gender of reading and the construction of textual understanding are important for understanding particular readers' literary competence. Likewise, African-American readers, working-class readers, rural readers, or newly literate adult readers do not automatically begin in the same reading position as white middle-class readers. Indeed, as psychoanalytic theory and gender theory in literary studies suggest, the stable notion of a white middle-class reader, male or female, is itself problematic.

In literary studies today, textual meaning has been contextualized in ways that relate texts with one another and that emphasize the production as well as the reception of meanings in the activity of reading. Although not every English major reads Ludwig Wittgenstein, Wittgenstein's concept of "language games" will be familiar to many. In the *Philosophical Investigations*, Wittgenstein (1963) argues that *language game* "is meant to bring into prominence the fact that the *speaking* of language is part of an activity, or of a form of life. . . . For a *large* class of cases—though not for all—in which we employ the word 'meaning' it can be defined thus: the meaning of a word is its use in the language" (paras. 23, 43).

The meaning of a text is structured by the interpretive strategies and assumptions we bring to the activity of reading. An empowering literacy encourages the reader to ask, "What can I do with a text? What risks am I taking as I read?" Yet many students are taught that their role as readers is to determine the "correct" authorial meaning of a text, a single meaning usually controlled by the teacher or textbook writers.

Besides the attention to the question of the reader's position, contemporary literary studies are also informed by a renewal of historical criticism of texts (sometimes referred to as "new historicism" or "cultural materialism"). Traditional literary studies have described history as what is "outside the text," background for a proper understanding of the text. In this view, history is not the proper subject of literary study but ancillary to it.

However, it is just this distinction between what is properly inside and outside the text, between insiders and outsiders, between a primary and a secondary object of reading that is being reexamined in contemporary literary studies and in the humanities in general. Anthropologists now discuss and theorize about the intersubjectivity of observation and about the problematic position of the "participant observer."

A reconceptualized literary history now includes not only the social and political events and cultural ideas surrounding the initial publication of a text but also the history of the reception of a text: for example, how Jane Austen's reputation as an ironic narrator came about and the cultural discourses within which a text might be situated and so understood when we read it. Shakespeare's *Midsummer Night's Dream* can be read alongside the various images of Queen Elizabeth in the 1590s (the Cult of Elizabeth) or as reflecting on the sometimes anxious relations among artists and their patrons and their fictions. *The Tempest* can be juxtaposed with Elizabethan accounts of exploration to investigate the relations between discovery, knowledge, and imperialism in the Renaissance. *As You Like It* and *Macbeth,* more typically taught in high school English courses, can be read in the context of social and political debates over power and authority in the standardization of language and law or the role of demonology and witchcraft in social order or the representations of women, debates that pertain to both the Renaissance and the contemporary world. Reader-oriented and historical criticisms emphasize how poems and the world can be read as texts.

One goal of many recent critical practices in literary studies is to disturb the boundary between what has traditionally been called "literary" and what is "nonliterary" in order to change the subject of inquiry to "reading texts." At the same time, prospective teachers need to imagine, and experience for themselves, how the classroom is both a context for reading and a place to explore reading contexts.

Barthes identified reading positions and contexts along a continuum from "work" to "text":

> The work closes on a signified. There are two modes of signification which can be attributed to this signified: either it is claimed to be evident and the work is then the object of a literal science, of philology, or else it is considered to be secret, ultimate, something to be sought out, and the work then falls under the scope of a hermeneutics, of an interpretation (Marxist, psychoanalytic, thematic, etc.). . . . The Text, on the contrary, practises the infinite deferment of the signified, is dilatory. . . . The logic regulating the Text is not comprehensive (define "what the work means") but metonymic; the activity of associations, contiguities, carryings-over coincides with a liberation of symbolic energy (lacking it, man would die); the work—in the best of cases—is *moderately* symbolic (its symbolic runs out, comes to a halt); the Text is *radically* symbolic . . . [Barthes, 1989, p. 1007].

Following Barthes's schematic polemic, many current forms of literary study depend on the notion that a text is fissured, not entirely consistent with itself, or that there are different positions from which to read a text. From this perspective, the aims of literary study are to understand not only textual intentions but also the implications of different reading positions, to begin to unpack the particular discourses woven together in the text, and to respond critically to the interpretations, associations, and responses that constitute the act of reading. Reading signifies not just getting the writer's or the text's meaning but also coming to understand oneself as an interpreter and to reflect critically and productively on the activity of reading a text—in a sense, to know where we are when we read and to imagine where else we or someone else might be when reading the text.

Many critics have written or spoken eloquently about the profound changes this reconceptualization of literary study has had on their teaching and scholarly practices. For example, in an essay in the *Chronicle of Higher Education* (1992b), Gerald Graff describes his own revaluation of his teaching and reading:

> Recent literary theory teaches us that what we don't see enables and limits what we do see. My reading of *Heart of Darkness* as a universal parable of reason and unreason allowed me to see certain things in the novel that I still think are important. But it also depended on my not seeing certain things or not treating them as worth thinking about. . . . Today I teach *Heart of Darkness* very differently. One critical work that caused me to change was an essay by the Nigerian novelist Chinua Achebe, "An Image of Africa: Racism in Conrad's *Heart of Darkness*." . . . When I assign *Heart of Darkness* to undergraduates now, I also assign the Achebe essay. I don't, however, simply teach his interpretation as correct; I ask my students to weigh it against competing interpretations. . . . In short, I now teach *Heart of Darkness* as part of a critical debate about how to

read it, which in turn is part of a larger theoretical debate about how politics and power affect the way we read literature. With such an approach I think I am following the dominant trend in contemporary theory, which is not to reduce literary works to transparent expressions of ideology. That is the impression that has been given by critics [to theoretical and cultural approaches to literature], whose hostility to current theory exceeds their willingness to read it [p. A48].

Graff's experience, if not his particular teaching strategy, is reproduced in numerous, though not all, college and university departments of English. Graff's story underscores how even if courses in British, American, and world literatures are regularly offered as they have been, they are not necessarily taught as before, nor is the scholarship and criticism that nourishes them informed by the same sort of readings. If a teacher education program is located in a liberal arts majors program rather than cordoned off in a school of education, English students will necessarily be immersed in more critical and interdisciplinary questions of reading response and textual criticism. Students graduating as teachers might have struggled through their reading of Shakespeare's plays in terms of the Cult of Elizabeth or the relation between discovery and imperialism or the construction of gender in cross-dressing. They may have explored Wordsworth's poetry and theories of language and imagination in the context of Wittgenstein's notion of language games or asked how Conrad's *Heart of Darkness* is complicit with yet resists the Eurocentric construction of a racial Other or asked how Charlotte Gilman's narrator in "The Yellow Wallpaper" challenges some of our underlying assumptions about the gender of the "unreliable narrator" or considered how pedagogical gestures and course syllabus are important parts of teaching the text.

These are the sorts of readings and textual juxtapositions that make Mark's aunt in Cambridge, Massachusetts, cringe at what has happened in (or, as she says, "to") the humanities and literary study during the past twenty-five years. These critical questions and readings have much to contribute to language arts teaching if teachers are empowered to imagine and structure a curriculum. Teacher educators can gain much from thinking about these multidisciplinary approaches to literacy and reading and the kinds of teaching and classroom knowledge they imply.

In this two-decade-old paradigm, criticism and theorizing our experiences with textuality, language, reading, and interpretation are conceived to be fundamentally dialogic. Literary language is characterized as a particular kind of discourse. Reading means reading in terms of a frame or context, "reading as . . . " Interpretation is more likely to be thought of as contingent, multiple, and mobile rather than as fixed and singularly authoritative. These ways of thinking about our reading, our relation to the tradition of literature and criticism, and the social roles of literacy suggest two important relations between contemporary literary study and the teaching of language arts and teaching language arts teachers: the multidisciplinary character of literary study and the role of imagination in the practice of reading, writing, and thinking.

Teaching the New Literacy

Language arts teachers are engaged in a multifaceted enterprise: teaching the arts and strategies of spoken and written discourse and critical thinking. This enterprise takes place in a classroom whose racial, ethnic, linguistic, and social contexts are becoming increasingly diverse (see Trueba, 1989) and where the lack of student motivation and interest in the language arts and English curricula is seen not just in "nontraditional" students and the "disadvantaged," though it is rampant there, but in so-called privileged students as well.

To some extent, the institutional structures of schooling have changed to meet these changed circumstances and expectations. Some districts and schools no longer organize their curricula around standardized tests and big-publisher language arts textbook series. Tracking and ability grouping are under scrutiny or are being phased out in some school districts. Class schedules in some schools have been organized more flexibly, with larger blocks of time within which teachers can develop interdisciplinary, open-ended lessons and integrated units. Special kinds of instruction have been devised to help students who do not learn in the ways prescribed by the general curriculum and classroom practices.

But the fact is that these structural changes in the scene of schooling are just beginning to take hold in the United States. Most school districts still use some form of tracking and ability grouping. Schools are regularly evaluated and ranked according to how their students perform on the California Test of Basic Skills and other standardized tests. Classes with thirty to forty students each are organized around recitation and discrete-point question-and-answer sessions. Students read literature and other texts and are tested on their comprehension with worksheets, fact-oriented questions, and problems that can be solved by finding the answer in the book and copying it down. There is not much critical or reflective thinking going on in these classroom practices, nor is there much critical reading or writing.

Language arts teachers-to-be can be guided to find ways to bridge the discourses of literary study and reflective thinking on teaching about language. More important, they need to be able to develop the questions and the "subject" knowledge that can empower them to bridge and reflect critically on language, texts, and responses with their students in their classrooms. They will not do this by merely pursuing a course of literary study, nor will they formulate these questions and contexts simply by taking language arts methods courses. Preparing language arts teachers is the responsibility of subject area teachers as well as methods teachers.

To go further, the very distinction between subject area and methods courses is precisely the sort of bifurcation that contemporary critical theory and critical literacy seeks to break down. As teachers of prospective teachers, those of us in literature programs and certification programs need to provide our students with sustained and guided experiences of reading, responding, theorizing about, and reflecting on powerful language varieties and complex texts (written, oral, and visual) and on the means by which we are shaped or connected or distanced through discursive forms (including popular culture, literature, presidential speeches, advertising, and legal debates).

If reading means "reading as" and if reading is one of several ways we use language in discourse, then language arts teaches what James Moffett more than twenty years ago called "the universe of discourse." Teaching the New Literacy (see Willinsky, 1990) involves rethinking and reimagining not only the relations among authors, texts, and readers but also the relations among teachers, students, parents, and communities and among writing, reading, and thinking critically.

A persistent myth of literacy is that literacy is the acquisition and use of the skills necessary for correct oral and written expression. But as Freire, Hirsch, Graff, Vygotsky, and Trueba have helped us recognize, literacy is much more. Literacy is the formation of cultural power and social identity through the use of knowledge and discourses that are approved but also potentially transformative and transforming.

Language arts teachers need not only be knowledgeable about but also, in Heath's sense (see Heath, 1983), be ethnographers—know how to observe and ask questions—about how children acquire and learn linguistic and literate abilities, about a variety of language uses and dialects, about a variety of texts (literary and nonliterary, canonical and noncanonical, elite and popular), about the relations between theorizing about reading and reading closely, and about the different forms of self-representation and expression in speech and writing.

Notes

1. For example, we might differ on our views of whether "I seen him in town" can be used or not, depending on our dialects. However, the sentence "Baseball the player by the hit was" would not be acceptable because it is ungrammatical, in the sense that it violates the rules of English word order.

2. Movies and television provide students with stereotypes of "hillbilly" and other nonstandard Englishes in that such speech is used only to characterize formally uneducated people (even if the characters themselves have a certain kind of folk wisdom or are represented as authentic regional types). The point is, how can schools rethink the notion of standard English?

3. Black English Vernacular has been studied extensively. See, for example, Labov (1969), Smitherman (1977), and Wolfram (1991).

4. See Dalrymple (1991) for a description of such a study in an elementary classroom.

References

Bakhtin, M. (1981). *The dialogic imagination: Four essays* (M. Holquist, ed.; C. Emerson and M. Holquist, trans.). Austin: University of Texas Press.

Bakhtin, M. (1986). *Speech genres and other late essays* (C. Emerson and M. Holquist., eds.; V. W. McGee, trans.). Austin: University of Texas Press.

Barthes, R. (1986). "On reading." In *The rustle of language* (R. Howard, trans.). New York: Hill & Wang.

Barthes, R. (1989). "From work to text." In D. Richter (ed.), *The critical tradition*. New York: St. Martin's Press.

Dalrymple, K. S. (1991). "The chicken study: Third graders prepare for independent study of animals." In Y. M. Goodman, W. J. Hood, and K. S. Goodman (eds.), *Organizing for whole language*. Portsmouth, N.H.: Heinemann Educational Books.

Di Pietro, R. J. (1987). *Strategic interaction: Learning languages through scenarios*. Cambridge: Cambridge University Press.

Graff, G. (1992a). *Beyond the culture wars: How teaching the conflicts can revitalize American education*. New York: Norton.

Graff, G. (1992b). "What has literary theory wrought?" *Chronicle of Higher Education*, Feb. 12, p. A48.

Heath, S. B. (1983). *Ways with words: Language, life and work in communities and classrooms*. Cambridge: Cambridge University Press.

Hirsch, E. D., Jr. (1987). *Cultural literacy: What every American needs to know*. Boston: Houghton Mifflin.

Kaplan, J. (1989). *English grammar: Principles and facts*. Englewood Cliffs, N.J.: Prentice Hall.

Labov, W. (1969). "The logic of nonstandard English." In J. Alatis (ed.), *Linguistics and the teaching of standard English to speakers of other languages or dialects*. Washington, D.C.: Georgetown University Press. (Monograph Series on Language and Linguistics 22).

Scholes, R. (1988). "Three views of education: Nostalgia, history, and voodoo." *College English, 50*, 323–332.

Smitherman, G. (1977). *Talkin and testifyin: The language of Black America*. Boston: Houghton Mifflin.

Trueba, H. T. (1989). *Raising silent voices: Educating the linguistic minorities for the 21st century*. Boston: Newbury House.

Vygotsky, L. (1986). *Thought and language* (A. Kozulin, ed. and trans.). Cambridge, Mass.: MIT Press.

Willinsky, J. (1990). *The new literacy*. New York: Routledge & Kegan Paul.

Wittgenstein, L. (1963). *Philosophical investigations*. Oxford: Blackwell.

Wolfram, W. (1991). *Dialects and American English*. Englewood Cliffs, N.J.: Prentice Hall.

Annotated Bibliography

American tongues (1987). VHS documentary produced and directed by L. Alvarez and A. Kolker, in consultation with W. Wolfram. New York: Center for New American Media.

Using interviews and narrative, this lively and wide-ranging video presents regional, social, and ethnic differences in American speech, together with the attitudes people have about these differences. The video includes material on the uses of standard and nonstandard English dialects. It is intended for a general audience and is appropriate for elementary through college students.

Bakhtin, M. (1981). *The dialogic imagination: Four essays* (M. Holquist, ed.; C. Emerson and M. Holquist, trans.). Austin: University of Texas Press.

Bakhtin, M. (1986). *Speech genres and other late essays* (C. Emerson and M. Holquist, eds.; V. W. McGee, trans.). Austin: University of Texas Press.
Bakhtin's work has had a marked but controversial influence on contemporary literary, cultural, education, and linguistic theorizing. These two collections include Bakhtin's important essays on "dialogism" and on the relation between heteroglossia and "speech genres," which are embedded in "life genres."

Christian, D. (1979). *Language arts and dialect differences*. Arlington, Va.: Center for Applied Linguistics.
This pamphlet provides an overview of the major issues educators face regarding the teaching of standard English to speakers of nonstandard English dialects and directs readers to more detailed work on topics such as writing assessment, dialect differences versus speech pathology, and teaching about dialects in language arts.

Di Pietro, R. J. (1987). *Strategic interaction: Learning languages through scenarios*. Cambridge: Cambridge University Press.
Di Pietro stresses the importance of situating second and foreign language classroom activities within a context of meaningful social activity through the use of scenarios, a role-playing technique that replicates real-life situations by allowing students to be themselves while requiring that they use the new language to resolve problems and accomplish tasks. Di Pietro's book makes for productive reading for language arts teachers interested in learning more about the role of context, shared knowledge, and meaningful activity in successful language learning.

Fish, S. (1980). *Is there a text in this class? The authority of interpretive communities*. Cambridge, Mass.: Harvard University Press.
Fish's work—always brilliant, witty, cranky, and controversial—has been at the center of the past two decades of change in the teaching of literature and critical theory in colleges and universities. This collection of essays engages with methods of literary interpretation, speech act theory, linguistic semantics, and the relations between readers' responses to texts and the communities of interpretive assumptions that render those responses meaningful. Fish's work provides a rigorous and critical introduction to reader response criticism and an intellectually challenging alternative to Louise Rosenblatt's theory of reading as transactional analysis.

Gee, J. P. (1990). *Social linguistics and literacies: Ideology in discourses*. Washington, D.C.: Falmer Press.
Arguing that people inhabit different discourses as ways of living, Gee examines home-school relationships as a way into the "failure" problem among minority students. Gee speaks to both linguists and educators, claiming that "literacy is always multiple, always tied to social practices that include much more than reading and writing, and is inherently ideological." Gee stresses the sociocultural importance of apprenticeship into various discourses.

Gee, J. P. (1993). *An introduction to human language: Fundamental concepts in linguistics*. Englewood Cliffs, N.J.: Prentice Hall.
This up-to-date and very readable general text surveys all of the major areas of contemporary linguistic research, including grammar, language acquisition, and language

history. Gee's textbook provides an interesting combination of formal linguistic analyses with socially oriented discourse analyses.

Graff, G. (1987). *Professing literature: An institutional history.* Chicago: University of Chicago Press. Graff's critical narrative documents the shift in American education, primarily colleges, from the study of Latin and Greek to the study of modern languages, especially English, as the basis for a language and literature curriculum. Contrary to some nostalgic dreams, the literature curriculum of 1875 was as conflicted as today's curriculum, with sharp disputes about methods of critical reading, the canon, and the goals for reading. As a pedagogical change, Graff proposes that college and university teachers of literature "teach the conflicts" that shape literary studies as a subject matter and a discourse. Graff's more recent book, *Beyond the Culture Wars: How Teaching the Conflicts Can Revitalize American Education* (1992a), takes up similar questions in the context of literary and literacy debates over the past two decades.

Heath, S. B. (1983). *Ways with words: Language, life and work in communities and classrooms.* Cambridge: Cambridge University Press. Heath chronicles the language development of children from two southeastern U.S. communities: a white working-class community whose lives have revolved around the textile mill industry for four generations and a black working-class community recently moved into the life of the mills after generations of farming. Heath uses a participatory ethnographic approach to analyze school, home, and community environments and the acquisition of language practices for classrooms and jobs. She finds clear differences in language development between the two working-class communities, as well as between these communities and the racially mixed middle-class mainstream in power in the town. Heath shows how these language differences are related to educational tracking and assessment, the uses of oral and written discourses, and the language abilities each group values.

Hirsch, E. D., Jr. (1987). *Cultural literacy: What every American needs to know.* Boston: Houghton Mifflin. This *New York Times* best-seller argues that to improve education in America we should teach all students a curriculum organized around a consensual list of information. Hirsch criticizes Deweyan education theory and practice and the "shopping mall curriculum," which, he claims, have fostered a "skills over content" curriculum in the schools and left three generations of America's students without a common academic culture. For one of many critiques of Hirsch's argument, see Scholes (1988), in which he refers to Hirsch's program as "voodoo."

Kutz, E., and Roskelly, H. (1991). *An unquiet pedagogy: Transforming practice in the English classroom.* Portsmouth, N.H.: Boynton Cook. Drawing on the "critical pedagogy" of Freire and on Vygotsky's social theories of learning and language, Kutz and Roskelly provide a clear and "reader-friendly" account of how theorizing about language, literacy, and meaning can be embedded in classroom practices and language arts curricula. Adapting Heath's methods for classroom ethnography, their book includes many accounts by preservice teachers of their experiences, plans, and critiques of classroom practices.

Pratt, M. L., and Traugott, E. (1979). *Linguistics for students of literature.* Englewood Cliffs, N.J.: Prentice Hall. This is a very clear and full survey of linguistics and social approaches to language. Pratt and Traugott present linguistic concepts and analyses from the viewpoint of case grammar and use illustrations and exercises drawn from British and American literature. They include discussions of the uses of linguistics for literary criticism in the classroom.

Scholes, R. (1985). *Textual power: Literary theory and the teaching of English.* New Haven, Conn.: Yale University Press.

In this work, which received an award from the National Council of Teachers of English, Scholes mediates between traditional theories of authorial intention that validate our readings of texts and theories of reading that deny or defer the idea that meaning is in the text itself and that celebrate "free play" and "readers' roles" as the only determiners of textual meaning. In his semiotic approach, Scholes seeks to connect in important ways how readers make meaning with how texts shape our readings. In effect, Scholes tries to amalgamate New Critical close textual reading with the social and political modes of critical reading associated with poststructuralism and some forms of deconstruction.

Wolfram, W. (1991). *Dialects and American English.* Englewood Cliffs, N.J.: Prentice Hall.

This highly readable survey of dialects and sociolinguistic variation in the United States covers regional, ethnic, social, and gender differences. Wolfram also presents proposals for investigating dialects and dialect differences, for teaching standard English, for rethinking school achievement texts, and for incorporating dialect study into the language arts curriculum. Wolfram's conclusions should be compared to those in Smitherman (1977) and Labov (1969).

CHAPTER NINE

READING CURRICULUM AND INSTRUCTION

MICHAEL F. GRAVES, LEO W. PAULS, AND TERRY SALINGER

This chapter is about the first *R*, reading, and about the contents of teacher education programs designed to prepare preservice teachers to assist students as they learn to read and as they become accomplished readers. The intent is to offer an overview of the reading curriculum for teacher educators who work in areas other than reading.

We make several assumptions. The first is that students preparing to be either elementary or secondary teachers are required to take a minimum number of courses in reading methodology or similar content. The International Reading Association (1992), the major professional organization in reading education, recommends a minimum of two three-credit courses in reading for prospective elementary teachers and one three-credit course for prospective secondary teachers. In this chapter, we discuss preparation of elementary teachers first, followed by modifications for prospective secondary teachers. The curriculum we describe could be delivered within those guidelines.

Second, considerable overlap is assumed between the curriculum required of individuals preparing to teach at the elementary level and that of those who plan to teach secondary students. It is important to note that at both the elementary and secondary levels teachers must do much more than teach students mechanical aspects of gaining meaning from print. Students must also learn to use reading as a tool for other learning, for thinking, and for enjoying and contributing to

This chapter was written with collaboration from Jack Cassidy, Daniel Hittleman, and Karen Lunsford.

the world in which they live. The curriculum should create students who value reading and who voluntarily choose to read.

A final assumption is that teacher thought is based in two kinds of knowledge (Roehler and others, 1987). To be effective, teachers must possess specific content or declarative knowledge about reading processes. For example, they must recognize the importance of background knowledge in comprehending what is read. They must also possess knowledge of specific pedagogical strategies for helping students achieve in reading. To carry the example forward, teachers need to know a range of appropriate strategies to motivate students to draw upon their background knowledge as they read. Teachers' actions, both in planning instruction and in responding to students spontaneously during instruction, are influenced by both these knowledge bases, and strong teachers demonstrate ability to access their knowledge bases readily in order to respond to students with information and with appropriate teaching strategies. These knowledge bases contribute to teachers' theoretical stance—that is, the perspective they hold on how children learn to read and write and how their literacy abilities grow over time. Application of this information in actual classrooms enriches teachers' knowledge base further, increasing their competence and ultimately resulting in what has been called "craft knowledge" (Leinhardt, 1990).

Theoretical Models of Reading

Much day-to-day reading instruction is directly motivated by theoretical perspectives or models developed within the past thirty years. These models seek to explain the cognitive processes used while reading and the many variables that influence reading. Ruddell, Ruddell, and Singer (1994) provide detailed descriptions of many important theories about reading; Anderson, Hiebert, Scott, and Wilkinson (1985) describe the educational implications of many significant theories; and Graves and Graves (1994) summarize theories that are relevant for beginning teachers.

It is less important that teachers remember specific names of individual models than that they recognize that models are attempts to explain how individuals learn to read and how competent readers orchestrate strategies and skills in order to make sense of print. Study of the more widely accepted theoretical models can cause prospective teachers to reflect upon their own reading behaviors and to begin to understand cognitive, social, linguistic, attitudinal, and foundational processes that influence reading growth. This understanding helps them conceptualize the complexity of what students at all levels must accomplish as they learn to read and write.

Teachers' stances toward reading should be grounded in a comprehensive, interactive, social-constructivist model of the reading process rather than in any specific instructional approach (International Reading Association, 1992). Teachers need to understand that, according to current researchers, individuals actively seek meaning as they attempt to read. Meaning does not reside solely in a text but is instead constructed as readers bring their background knowledge and experiences to their reading task. Thus, although it is certainly not the case that every interpretation of a text is a valid one, different readers may interpret texts in different, equally accurate ways. This theory of reading is generally termed the *constructivist model* or theory.

Prospective teachers also need to know about "schema theory," which maintains that readers search for connections between their existing schemata—what they already know—and the new information and ideas they encounter in the texts they read (Anderson and Pearson, 1984). Readers engage in an iterative process of moving between existing knowledge and text to construct their own meaning, which will undoubtedly be similar but rarely identical to what the author had in mind.

Finally, prospective teachers need to be familiar with "interactive models" of reading that seek to explain the reading processes used by skilled readers. These models contend that readers use information from many knowledge sources to arrive at meaning and that the information moves iteratively between the reader's background knowledge and the text itself. Information in the text includes letter-sound correspondences, word meanings, sentence structure, graphic features such as illustrations or charts, and the content itself. Readers' background knowledge is their schemata about the topics of text. Good readers learn to rely on both text and background knowledge as they seek meaning, and they balance their reliance on the two as demanded by particular texts.

In addition to shaping their stance toward reading, understanding of theoretical models helps prospective teachers identify the assumptions upon which instructional methodologies are based.

Approaches to Reading Instruction

Prospective teachers need to be familiar with the two approaches to reading instruction that they are most likely to encounter when they begin to teach: traditional "basal readers" and the newer "whole language approach." Many schools still use some form of basal readers (Durkin, 1990; Pearson, Roehler, Dole, and Duffy, 1992), but whole language methodology and its underlying tenets about children's learning have gained increasing acceptance in recent years. It is safe to generalize that adaptations of these two approaches are common in elementary classrooms, and variations are used in middle and secondary schools as well.

The mainstay of traditional basal reader programs is a series of graded readers or anthologies accompanied by worksheets, tests, supplementary materials, and manuals that tell teachers in specific terms how the collected materials should be used (Smith, [1965] 1986). All materials are carefully developed to conform to a predetermined "scope and sequence" that reflects the order in which children are supposed to acquire specific reading skills. Vocabulary and sentence structure are controlled, especially for books used in lower grades.

The underlying assumption of most basal series is that acquisition of reading ability consists of learning many discrete skills. Children in a class are often divided into three reading groups according to placement within the basal series, and instruction is offered according to a prescribed, teacher-dominated routine referred to as a "directed reading lesson." Lessons are sequenced to include preparatory discussion and vocabulary instruction, silent reading of the selection, follow-up questions about the selection, and skills instruction and practice. Most of the texts are short and have been written to support the sequenced skills instruction; stories in basal series are often criticized as simplistic and unchallenging, especially when compared to the richness of children's literature.

Recently, some publishers have been marketing "literature-based" reading series that feature longer selections, often complete pieces of or excerpts from children's literature. While similar to traditional basals, the teachers' manuals are less prescriptive, and teachers are encouraged to vary students' interactions with texts more than in the directed reading lesson (Durkin, 1990). For example, students may write about what they read in response logs, dramatize a selection, or prepare a story to present in a "readers' theater" format.

The whole language approach represents a different perspective about literacy teaching and learning. It emphasizes interactions among teachers, students, and texts as key factors in reading acquisition and takes advantage of the social nature of learning. Learning to read is not perceived as the learning of discrete skills but as a more holistic and developmental process that is similar to the acquisition of oral language skills. Goodman (1985) provides a short introduction to the approach, while Weaver (1990) and Edelsky, Altwerger, and Flores (1991) offer more detail.

Whole language allows teachers and students more autonomy and more choice. Individual selections of children's literature, rather than anthologies, comprise the "basal" material of instruction, and students often select what they will read. These features place tremendous responsibility on teachers and administrators to supply ample libraries of diverse, relevant, and appropriate books. There are no teachers' manuals, and students to a great extent keep track of their own reading. The overall goal is for students to learn a repertoire of strategies they can use flexibly to make sense from and with text. Reading and writing are viewed as mutually reinforcing processes that are learned together.

Taking advantage of the social nature of learning, teachers meet with small groups of students for discussion of books read in common. They frequently work on collaborative projects, learning from and with each other. They provide instruction as determined by students' needs, either in individual conferences or small group sessions, monitor students' progress as part of daily routines, and provide assistance and instruction as needed to support students' emerging sense of competence. Students read and write independently and in small groups brought together because of shared interests, desire to read specific pieces of literature, or other purposes.

Environments to Encourage Children to Become Readers

One responsibility faced by beginning teachers is that of creating what has been called a "literate classroom environment" (Holdaway, 1979). Literate classrooms are filled with books and other print material chosen to reflect the many functional, informational, and recreational uses for reading. For example, when early childhood teachers post signs, lists of words, and class-generated stories rather than commercial decorations, students see the many purposes of print and can actually use classroom "environmental print" to increase a store of words they can recognize and spell on their own. Literate classrooms provide comfortable places where students can read and ample storage space for books. Students are given time to read, talk, write, and think about what they have read; they experience the pleasures of reading for its own sake and the satisfaction of learning from reading.

In all classroom settings, teachers need to demonstrate respect for the diversity that exists in their classes and to provide learning environments that encourage all children to achieve to their maximum abilities. Teachers can demonstrate respect by providing students with opportunities to read and discuss books that accurately present many different cultures, ethnic groups, and lifestyles (Cullinan, 1992, 1993). Teacher sensitivity toward racism, sexism, and ageism in children's books ensures that students' literature experiences are positive.

Teachers also need to know how students' backgrounds can influence their reading. For example, students may appear to be failing to comprehend or miscomprehending something they have read when in fact they lack prerequisite background knowledge or possess conflicting knowledge. In a similar vein, teachers must recognize that children from different backgrounds may respond to instruction in different ways and that it is necessary to vary modes of presentation and accept different modes of response from students. For example, Au and Jordan (1981) found that young native Hawaiian children did poorly in lessons consisting of silent reading and teacher questioning but benefited when reading instruction was offered in a more interactive manner similar to the "talk-story" pattern of interchange they heard in their homes.

Perhaps the most crucial point to be considered in planning classroom environments is the importance of success and the costs of failure. Many times, students who do not do well in school attribute their failure in reading to factors beyond their control—the books they must read are "too hard" or the teacher "doesn't like" them. A pattern of behavior called "passive failure" can develop (Johnston and Winograd, 1985). Because students think that they have no control over their learning, they essentially stop trying to achieve in school. Their initial weaknesses magnify, their sense of failure intensifies, and attempts to address deficits are unsuccessful. If students experiencing these feelings are to have any chance of succeeding in school, teachers must show them that they can play active roles in their own learning and can succeed at reading and writing.

Specific aspects of reading instruction, to be discussed next, include instruction for children's beginning or emergent literacy, strategies for word identification and vocabulary growth, aspects of reading comprehension, and the reading-writing connection.

Emergent Literacy

Until recently, most early childhood reading instruction was based on the premise that children knew little or nothing about reading or writing prior to school entry. Research conducted worldwide has changed this view, and today virtually all reading educators recognize that young children observe print in their environments, hypothesize about reading and writing, and form initial, tentative concepts about print use and production long before they enter school (Ferreiro and Teberosky, 1982; Harste, Woodward, and Burke, 1984; Teal and Sulzby, 1985). Literacy abilities emerge over time as children gain experience with print use and production, both in and out of school. When young children "read" a McDonald's sign, pretend to read a newspaper, or scribble-write a letter to a friend, these are examples of the behaviors that contribute to these initial conceptualizations. This aspect of literacy learning is referred to as "emergent literacy."

Early reading curricula have been influenced by research on emergent literacy. Children are encouraged to experiment with reading and writing behaviors, to browse through books and use illustrations to make up stories before they can actually read, and to express their ideas in writing by using "invented spelling" strategies with which they approximate traditional orthography (Dyson and Freedman, 1991). Instruction, offered in small, flexible groups, provides lessons on the many skills and strategies that students must master; it is balanced with experiences with authentic children's literature rather than with the carefully structured materials of basal reader "readiness" programs. Teachers frequently model and explain reading and writing behaviors. For example, instruction often is centered on a chart-stand display of a "big book" version of a piece of literature. Students can easily see the enlarged print and white space and observe as the teacher reads, runs her hand left to right under each word, swings her hand down and back at the end of each line, and pauses at each mark of punctuation. This mode of instruction seeks to make a complex cognitive process as visible as possible for young learners (Clay, 1979). Additionally, teachers emphasize functional as well as recreational and instructional purposes of reading and writing.

Detailed information about emergent literacy can be found in Goodman (1990), Morrow (1993), and Strickland and Morrow (1989).

Building and Enriching Students' Vocabularies

Students usually enter school with the ability to recognize and read a few words, such as product or store names, labels of parts of the preschool room, and so forth. These form the base of their reading vocabulary, which will grow by three thousand to four thousand words per year to reach approximately twenty thousand words by sixth grade (Nagy and Herman, 1987; White, Graves and Slater, 1990). This figure represents words that students can both recognize and understand. Because there is a strong relationship between the number of words students know and their overall comprehension abilities, teachers need to know ways to assist students in building and enriching their reading vocabularies. Traditional basal reader approaches recommended the direct teaching of individual words in preparation for reading lessons. The disadvantage here is that students may not encounter words presented in this manner again soon enough for them to learn the words thoroughly. Other approaches prepare students to learn words on their own by presenting strategies needed to attend to context and word parts and to use reference sources such as dictionaries or thesauri. Still other approaches address concept development as well as vocabulary growth and have particular value in content area work. Anderson and Nagy (1993), Beck, McKeown, and Omanson (1987), Graves (1992), Heimlich and Pittelman (1986), and Nagy (1988) all describe parts of such a curriculum.

Instruction in Word Identification Strategies

Although there is wide variation in recommendations about how students should be taught to identify unfamiliar words, few educators deny that students often encounter words they do not immediately recognize and that they need to be able to apply strategies to make sense of these words.

The most useful word identification strategies include "phonic analysis"—using letter-sound correspondences to decode unfamiliar words and blending sounds to form words—and "structural analysis"—attending to root words, prefixes, and suffixes to arrive at meaning and pronunciation. Explicit instruction in how to use phonic and structural analysis offered early in students' school experiences and practiced in extensive reading of material at an appropriate level of difficulty should give students a repertoire of strategic behaviors—"attack plans"—that they can use to assist themselves as they read. As students become proficient readers, they learn to recognize words automatically, instantly, and without conscious attention. The term for this kind of behavior is *automaticity*.

Information about word identification strategies can be found in Adams (1990), Durkin (1993), Graves, Watts, and Graves (1994), Salinger (1993), and Stahl (1992). Adams (1990), Beck and Juel (1992), and Adams and others (1991) offer overviews of various perspectives on word identification instruction.

Fostering Students' Reading Comprehension

The goal of all reading instruction should be to enhance students' ability to read with comprehension. Just as they need strategies for word identification, students need to master comprehension strategies, "conscious and flexible plans that [they] apply and adapt to a variety of texts" (Pearson, Roehler, Dole, and Duffy, 1992, p. 169). These strategies are processes that enable readers to understand and remember what they read.

Two methods are commonly used to instruct students in the range of comprehension strategies they need to know. The first approach involves direct instruction of target strategies, such as procedures for creating summaries or asking oneself checkup questions. The other embeds instruction within students' actual reading activities so that students learn to apply specific strategies when they encounter text that invites their use. Whichever approach is used, it is essential that these strategies are taught and learned. For this to happen, prospective teachers need to know what the strategies are and why they are important. The following are generally agreed to be the most important strategies:

- Assessing and making use of prior knowledge about the topics encountered in print
- Asking and answering questions
- Differentiating between important and unimportant aspects of text
- Making inferences
- Summarizing
- Interpreting graphic information
- Creating images about the reading material

Strong readers also monitor what they read by constantly questioning themselves to be sure that they are understanding. This behavior is one aspect of "metacognition," the reader's consciousness about his or her understanding of text along with the ability to use appropriate strategies to "fix" misunderstandings when comprehension processes break down (Garner, 1992).

Teaching reading comprehension strategies are most successful when reading lessons are organized into three distinct parts: prereading, during reading, and postreading. Prereading experiences consist of activities such as prompting students to activate background knowledge related to the text they will read, building needed background knowledge, previewing the section, or making predictions about the text based on its title and illustrations. During-reading experiences might include reading parts of the selection aloud, following study guides, or answering questions to check on comprehension. Postreading activities normally involve summarizing and clarifying parts of text but can also consist of projects such as art, drama, or writing. During the postreading phase, teachers might also reteach sections of text that students have found difficult, thereby offering direct and relevant instruction on comprehension strategies. Prospective teachers need to be able to use these and a variety of other approaches to promote comprehension, and they need to become sensitive to the sorts of activities that will work best with different kinds of texts.

Information about means of fostering reading comprehension is provided in Graves and Graves (1994), Salinger (1993), and Wood, Lapp, and Flood (1992).

Reading-Writing Connection

Informed by recent research, many reading educators stress that reading and writing are mutually reinforcing cognitive processes that ought not to be separated instructionally. They cite how young children move back and forth between experimentation with the two modes of expression, how writing can reinforce content area learning, how reading good writing can influence students' own writing competence, and other examples of the close links that exist between the two processes (Irwin and Doyle, 1992; Langer, 1986).

The instructional implications of this strand of research are obvious: students should be encouraged to write about their reading, to use various modes of writing as vehicles for learning, and to consider the audience of readers as they themselves compose written works. The extent to which students are asked to respond to reading in an "open-ended," written format is a clear sign of the impact of this research on instruction.

Assessment Issues

In addition to understanding basic principles of standardized testing, prospective teachers need to learn a variety of informal means for assessing students' progress in reading. For example, skillful observations of students as they read, answer questions, and talk about their reading can provide insight into how students are actually employing strategies to decode unfamiliar words and make sense of text. By listening to students' oral reading, teachers can infer the kinds of cues (letter-sound correspondence, context, and so forth) students are using as they read. Analysis of patterns of oral deviations from text can provide immediately useful diagnostic information that teachers can use instructionally.

As a rejection of the one-right-answer model of multiple-choice questions and an affirmation of the idea that individuals construct meaning from text, teachers are increasingly asking students to respond to open-ended short-answer or essay questions on tests of reading comprehension (see Mullis, Campbell, and Farstrup, 1993, for a discussion of this kind of question used in large-scale assessment). Other informal, classroom-based assessment methods, such as portfolios of students' work collected over time, give teachers data about students' progress as readers and literacy users in general (Glazer and Brown, 1993). At the same time, since reading is a complex process and since different groups and individuals make use of assessment for different purposes, prospective teachers need to be knowledgeable about a variety of forms of assessment: standardized tests, teacher-made tests, portfolios, and others (Farr, 1992).

A Reading Curriculum for Prospective Secondary Teachers

Most teachers at the secondary level are content specialists; they do not teach reading as a process but rather expect their students to come to them already knowing how to read with comprehension. Unfortunately, this expectation is often not realized (Foertsch, 1992; Mullis, Campbell, and Farstrup, 1993). In many states, prospective secondary teachers must take at least one reading course, often one designated "Reading in the Content Areas." In these courses, prospective teachers learn about reading strategies that students must employ as they read literature, social studies, mathematics, science, and other subjects; and they learn how they can help students whose skills are not adequately developed for the reading tasks presented in content area work.

Secondary teachers must deal with many of the same issues as those who teach in the elementary school, but the emphasis given to many of the topics will differ markedly. For example, it is important that prospective secondary teachers understand the theoretical foundations of reading acquisition, but the extent of their familiarity with theory need not be so deep and extensive as that of elementary school teachers. It is more important that secondary teachers recognize that a dominant theory undergirding much educational practice is the concept that learners actively construct meaning through an interaction of new and previously learned ideas and information. Understanding this perspective should shape the ways in which teachers in all content areas plan and deliver instruction.

Prospective secondary teachers also need to be familiar with what Pearson, Roehler, Dole, and Duffy (1992) call an "emerging expertise" model of reading development. According to this model, students are initially taught skills and strategies in the lower grades and then as they progress through the grades learn to use these strategies in increasingly sophisticated ways through encounters with more challenging texts. Teachers in content areas assist students by providing conceptual and contextual support to foster more sophisticated learning. Conceptual support is usually context-specific, while contextual support is often procedural information about how one goes about reading and learning in a given content area. For example, teachers may need to acclimate students to the format in which information is presented in a content area. Primary source materials such as newspapers in social studies or lab reports in science present different challenges from those students have encountered in more traditional reference and textbooks.

Secondary teachers also need to be familiar with instructional approaches that foster reading comprehension. The model of a three-part reading lesson can be productively modified for any content area. Thus, secondary teachers can assess background knowledge, make students ready for learning, guide their learning, and follow up on learning, just as elementary teachers offer pre-, during-, and postreading instruction. Additional information that secondary teachers need to know at a general level concerns the different approaches to reading instruction and principles for establishing a literate and effective classroom environment. The kind of reading instruction students receive prior to high school often determines how much they have used writing in conjunction with reading, how accustomed they are to working independently, and how critically they are inclined to think about what they read. By recognizing that students will differ along these dimensions, secondary teachers can better plan their own instruction to help students become readers, writers, and thinkers, as well as independent workers in all content areas.

Information about the developmental nature of learning and about the various aspects of learning to read, such as acquiring word identification strategies, is also important to secondary teachers. This information can assist teachers who work with disabled readers or with students who are learning to be literate in English as a second language.

Finally, prospective secondary teachers in all content areas need to know about vocabulary growth and comprehension. Understanding and using the technical vocabulary of each content area are important parts of students' learning, as is mastering strategies for figuring out the specialized meanings of words that may be familiar from other contexts. Teachers ought not to assume that all secondary students have learned these strategies and need to plan instruction to facilitate this learning. Using study guides, semantic webbing for vocabulary and concept growth, learning logs and response journals, discussions, and thoughtful questioning strategies are but a few of the ways in which secondary teachers can make their instruction more effective and enhance their students' comprehension. The classic text on the topic, Herber (1970), and more recent texts by Vacca and Vacca (1993), Ryder and Graves (1994), and Heimlich and Pittelman (1986) offer many useful suggestions for content area teachers.

Conclusion

Because there is so much to know in order to teach reading successfully, it is important that teacher education programs in reading be as thoroughly planned and as efficient as possible. Reading courses can be most effective in offering prospective teachers a balanced view of both theory and methodology to prepare them to help students acquire reading abilities when the content that teachers acquire from reading courses is integrated with the content of other courses in teacher education programs.

References

Adams, M. J. (1990). *Beginning to read: Thinking and learning about print—a summary* (prepared by S. A. Stahl, J. Osborn, and F. Lehr). Newark, Del.: International Reading Association.

Adams, M. J., and others (1991). "Beginning to read: A critique by literacy professionals and a response by Marilyn Jager Adams." *Reading Teacher, 44*, 370–395.

Allington, R. L. (1983). "The reading instruction provided readers of differing abilities." *Elementary School Journal, 83*, 548–559.

Anderson, R. C., Hiebert, E. H., Scott, J. A., and Wilkinson, I.A.G. (1985). *Becoming a nation of readers: The report of the Commission on Reading.* Washington, D.C.: National Institute of Education.

Anderson, R. C., and Nagy, W. E. (1993). *The vocabulary conundrum.* (Technical Report no. 570). Urbana: Center for the Study of Reading, University of Illinois.

Anderson, R. C., and Pearson, P. D. (1984). "A schema-theoretic view of basic process in reading." In P. D. Pearson (ed.), *Handbook of reading research.* White Plains, N.Y.: Longman.

Au, K. H., and Jordan, C. (1981). "Teaching reading to Hawaiian children: Finding a culturally appropriate solution." In H. T. Trueba, J. P. Guthrie, and K. H. Au (eds.), *Culture and the bilingual classroom.* Boston: Newbury House.

Beck, I. L., and Juel, C. (1992). "The role of decoding in learning to read." In S. J. Samuels and A. E. Farstrup (eds.), *What research has to say about reading instruction.* (2nd ed.). Newark, Del.: International Reading Association.

Beck, I. L., McKeown, M. G., and Omanson, R. C. (1987). "The effects and uses of diverse vocabulary instructional techniques." In M. G. McKeown and M. E. Curtis (eds.), *The nature of vocabulary acquisition.* Hillsdale, N.J.: Erlbaum.

Clay, M. (1979). *Teaching: The patterning of complex behavior.* Portsmouth, N.H.: Heinemann Educational Books.

Cullinan, B. E. (ed.) (1992). *Invitation to read: More children's literature in the reading program.* Newark, Del.: International Reading Association.

Cullinan, B. E. (ed.) (1993). *Fact and fiction: Literature across the curriculum.* Newark, Del.: International Reading Association.

Durkin, D. (1990). *Comprehension instruction in current basal reading series.* (Technical Report no. 521). Urbana: Center for the Study of Reading, University of Illinois.

Durkin, D. (1993). *Teaching them to read.* (6th ed.). Needham Heights, Mass.: Allyn & Bacon.

Dyson, A. H., and Freedman, S. W. (1991). "Writing." In J. Flood, J. M. Jensen, D. Lapp, and J. R. Squire (eds.), *Handbook of research on teaching the English language arts.* New York: Macmillan.

Edelsky, C., Altwerger, B., and Flores, B. (1991). *Whole language: What's the difference?* Portsmouth, N.H.: Heinemann Educational Books.

Farr, R. (1992). "Putting it all together: Solving the reading assessment puzzle." *Reading Teacher, 46*, 26–37.

Ferreiro, E., and Teberosky, A. (1982). *Literacy before schooling.* Portsmouth, N.H.: Heinemann Educational Books.

Foertsch, M. A. (1992). *Reading in and out of school.* Princeton, N.J.: Educational Testing Service.

Garner, R. (1992). "Metacognition and self-monitoring strategies." In S. J. Samuels, and A. E. Farstrup (eds.), *What research has to say about reading instruction.* (2nd ed.). Newark, Del.: International Reading Association.

Glazer, S. M., and Brown, C. S. (1993). *Portfolios and beyond: Collaborative assessment in reading and writing.* Norwood, Mass.: Christopher-Gordon.

Goodman, K. S. (1985). *What's whole in whole language?* Richmond Hill, Ontario: Scholastic.

Goodman, Y. M. (ed.) (1990). *How children construct literacy: Piagetian perspectives.* Newark, Del.: International Reading Association.

Graves, M. F. (1992). "The elementary vocabulary curriculum: What should it be?" In M. J. Dreher and W. H. Slater (eds.), *Elementary school literacy: Critical issues.* Norwood, Mass.: Christopher-Gordon.

Graves, M. F., and Graves, B. B. (1994). *Scaffolding reading experiences: Designs for student success.* Norwood, Mass.: Christopher-Gordon.

Graves, M. F., Watts, S. M., and Graves, B. B. (1994). *Essentials of classroom teaching: Elementary reading methods.* Needham Heights, Mass.: Allyn & Bacon.

Harste, J. C., Woodward, V. A., and Burke, C. L. (1984). *Language stories and literacy lessons.* Portsmouth, N.H.: Heinemann Educational Books.

Heimlich, J. E., and Pittelman, S. D. (1986). *Semantic mapping: Classroom applications.* Newark, Del.: International Reading Association.

Herber, H. L. (1970). *Teaching reading in content areas.* Englewood Cliffs, N.J.: Prentice Hall.

Holdaway, D. (1979). *The foundations of literacy.* Portsmouth, N.H.: Heinemann Educational Books.

International Reading Association (1992). *Standards for reading professionals.* Newark, Del.: International Reading Association.

Irwin, J. W., and Doyle, M. A. (eds.) (1992). *Reading/writing connections: Learning from research.* Newark, Del.: International Reading Association.

Johnston, P. H., and Winograd, P. N. (1985). "Passive failure in reading." *Journal of Reading Behavior, 17,* 279–301.

Langer, J. A. (1986). *Children reading and writing: Structures and strategies.* Norwood, N.J.: Ablex.

Leinhardt, G. (1990). "Capturing craft knowledge in teaching." *Educational Researcher, 19*(2), 18–25.

Morrow, L. M. (1993). *Literacy development in the early years.* (2nd ed.). Needham Heights, Mass.: Allyn & Bacon.

Mullis, I.V.S., Campbell, J., and Farstrup, A. E. (1993). *National Assessment of Educational Progress 1992 reading report card for the nation and the states.* Washington, D.C.: Office of Educational Research and Improvement.

Nagy, W. E. (1988). *Teaching vocabulary to improve reading comprehension.* Newark, Del.: International Reading Association.

Nagy, W. E., and Herman, P. A. (1987). "Depth and breadth of vocabulary knowledge: Implications for acquisition and instruction." In M. G. McKeown and M. E. Curtis (eds.), *The nature of vocabulary acquisition.* Hillsdale, N.J.: Erlbaum.

Pearson, P. D., Roehler, L. R., Dole, J. A., and Duffy, G. G. (1992). "Developing expertise in reading comprehension." In S. J. Samuels and A. E. Farstrup (eds.), *What research has to say about reading instruction.* (2nd ed.). Newark, Del.: International Reading Association.

Roehler, L. B., and others (1987). "Exploring preservice teachers' knowledge structures." Paper presented at the American Educational Research Association Meeting, Washington, D.C.

Ruddell, R. B., Ruddell, M. R., and Singer, H. (eds.) (1994). *Theoretical models and processes of reading.* (4th ed.). Newark, Del.: International Reading Association.

Ryder, R. J., and Graves, M. F. (1994). *Reading and learning in content areas.* Columbus, Ohio: Merrill.

Salinger, T. (1993). *Models of literacy instruction.* Columbus, Ohio: Merrill.

Smith, N. B. (1986). *The history of reading instruction.* Newark, Del.: International Reading Association. (Originally published 1965).

Stahl, S. A. (1992). "Saying the 'p' word: Nine guidelines for exemplary phonics instruction." *Reading Teacher, 45,* 618–625.

Strickland, D. S., and Morrow, L. M. (eds.) (1989). *Emerging literacy: Young children learn to read and write.* Newark, Del.: International Reading Association.

Teal, W. E., and Sulzby, E. (eds.) (1986). *Emergent literacy: Writing and writing.* Norwood, N.J.: Ablex.

Vacca, R. T., and Vacca, J. L. (1993). *Content area reading.* (4th ed.). New York: HarperCollins.

Weaver, C. (1990). *Understanding whole language.* Portsmouth, N.H.: Heinemann Educational Books.

White, T. G., Graves, M. F., and Slater, W. H. (1990). "Growth of reading vocabulary in diverse elementary schools: Decoding and word meaning." *Journal of Educational Psychology, 82*(2), 281–290.

Wood, K. D., Lapp, D., and Flood, J. (1992). *Guiding readers through text: A review of study guides.* Newark, Del.: International Reading Association.

Annotated Bibliography

Adams, M. J., and others (1991). "Beginning to read: A critique by literacy professionals and a response by Marilyn Jager Adams." *Reading Teacher, 44,* 370–395.

This is both a series of responses to *Beginning to Read*—a book that examines issues in beginning reading instruction, most specifically, phonics instruction—and a series of discussions for and against phonics instruction and related issues. It serves as an interesting introduction to the debates on phonics instruction and the more general matter of traditional versus whole language instruction.

Anderson, R. C., Hiebert, E. H., Scott, J. A., and Wilkinson, I.A.G. (1985). *Becoming a nation of readers: The report of the Commission on Reading.* Washington, D.C.: National Institute of Education.

This is a concise and very readable summary of much that we know about reading and reading instruction. If one were to read only one book on reading instruction, this would be an excellent choice.

Farr, R. (1992). "Putting it all together: Solving the reading assessment puzzle." *Reading Teacher, 46,* 26–37.

This essay considers the assessment needs of students, teachers, administrators, and the public and proposes a multifaceted approach that meets the needs of various audiences. Farr presents a very balanced position on the strengths and weaknesses of alternate and, all too often, competing forms of assessment.

Graves, M. F., Watts, S. M., and Graves, B. B. (1994). *Essentials of classroom teaching: Elementary reading methods.* Needham Heights, Mass: Allyn & Bacon.

This concise elementary methods text describes the essential knowledge, skills, strategies, and attitudes necessary to effectively teach reading to elementary students. If one were searching for a book that expanded on the content of this chapter, this would be an excellent choice.

Pearson, P. D., Roehler, L. R., Dole, J. A., and Duffy, G. G. (1992). "Developing expertise in reading comprehension." In S. J. Samuels and A. E. Farstrup (eds.), *What research has to say about reading instruction.* (2nd ed.). Newark, Del.: International Reading Association.

This well-constructed essay presents a contemporary view of reading comprehension strategies. It also contrasts contemporary notions of strategy instruction and reading instruction more generally with older notions and thereby provides some history of approaches to reading instruction.

CHAPTER TEN

LEARNING TO READ AND
LEARNING TO TEACH READING

LINNEA C. EHRI AND JOANNA P. WILLIAMS

How should we prepare teacher education students for the task of teaching reading to pupils in grades K through 12? Several factors ought to be considered. Pupils who are learning to read follow a predictable course of development, so developmental issues need to be understood. Development does not occur in a vacuum but requires an instructional context; therefore, being familiar with methods of teaching reading is essential. The appropriateness of methods depends upon which reading processes are being taught at which points in development, so multiple methods rather than a single method must become part of a teacher's repertoire. Moreover, the suitability of methods depends upon how much knowledge and experience the teacher has had in teaching reading. More prescriptive methods will benefit novices but may be too rigid for veteran teachers who have learned to operate flexibly with multiple procedures and activities tailored to the needs of individual students.

The processes involved in reading and learning to read are language-based processes, and teachers need to understand how language is structured, particularly orthographic and phonological aspects of language, so that they can help students learn how the alphabetic system represents speech. Although it is important for teacher education students to acquire background knowledge about many aspects of teaching and learning to read, they also need to receive very specific practical information and experience and to be shown how they as novice teachers can operate in the classroom to teach reading effectively to their students. Learning to teach reading is itself a developmental process that begins in a teacher education program but continues as teachers gain experience teaching reading. What needs to develop in the minds of teachers is a practice-based understanding of how pupils learn to read, how instruction enables their development as readers, and how to assess whether teaching is producing learning in students. Very likely, the way that teacher education programs are structured will determine whether or not such an understanding takes root and grows. These are the topics bearing on a teacher education program in reading that will be explored in this chapter.

Teachers face the need to make many decisions every day. They can take time to deliberate about some problems, but others may require immediate resolution. A good teacher is a good problem solver and decision maker, and it is paramount that teachers be trained to make competent, informed decisions. This means that their education cannot be geared merely to acquiring the current wisdom of the field with respect to principles, theory, and practice. Rather, it must also include an understanding of the way that reliable, verifiable knowledge is derived. This involves becoming familiar with the nature of critical thinking, scientific inquiry, and research evidence, which in turn enables teachers to better interpret and evaluate new ideas and thereby foster their own growth as professionals. Teacher education programs should be designed to help teachers grow professionally in this respect.

Reading Processes and Their Development

To appreciate what reading teachers need to understand about reading processes and their course of acquisition, we have provided a brief sketch of this domain of knowledge. Left out of the sketch, to be addressed in the next section, is instruction, the component that drives development. (For more extensive discussion, see Adams, 1990; Barr, Kamil, Mosenthal, and Pearson, 1991; Gough, Ehri, and Treiman, 1992; Ehri, 1991; Feitelson, 1988.)

When skilled readers read and understand text, many cognitive and linguistic processes operate concurrently and automatically in synchrony. The interactive model presented in Figure 10.1 depicts some of these processes. The center box represents a central processor that receives information from the eyes and interprets it. The boxes around the center depict the various information sources that are stored in the reader's memory and that operate together to enable recognition and interpretation of text.

Knowledge of language enables readers to recognize sentences and their meanings. A specific type of knowledge that is particularly helpful is the understanding of how text is structured: its organization, use of signaling words, and other conventions, especially those that define and differentiate text genres such as narrative and expository text. Knowledge of the world, including both encyclopedic and experiential knowledge, supplies readers with the background for understanding ideas and filling in parts that are left implicit (and assumed known) rather than stated explicitly in the text. Metacognitive knowledge enables readers to monitor their own comprehension to ascertain whether the information makes

FIGURE 10.1. INTERACTIVE MODEL: SOURCES OF KNOWLEDGE USED TO READ TEXT.

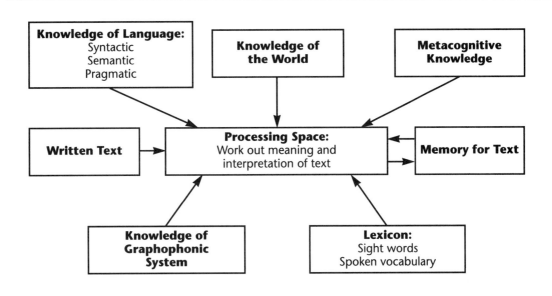

Source: Adapted from Rumelhart, 1977.

sense and meets specific purposes. Metacognitive knowledge about corrective strategies, such as rereading and self-questioning, enables readers to remediate comprehension failures (Baker and Brown, 1984). Knowledge of the alphabetic-phonemic (letter-sound) system involves knowing how the spelling system represents speech, including how to transform graphemes into phonemes, the smallest units of sound (Venezky, 1970). This knowledge may be used to decode unfamiliar words as well as to confirm the identity of words read by sight and by guessing from context (Perfetti, 1985). Lexical knowledge refers to the reader's dictionary of words held in memory, including words known by sight (Ehri, 1991). Accessing sight words in lexical memory is the principal way that readers recognize words in text. All of these knowledge sources support and contribute to text comprehension. Of course, memory is very important for linking the meaning of a text to previously read text as well as for integrating it with information from the other knowledge sources.

The course of development of reading processes and knowledge sources specified in Figure 10.1 has been portrayed by Chall (1983) as a series of stages, which we have modified slightly: Stage 0 is emergent reading; Stage 1 is initial reading and decoding; Stage 2 is fluency and consolidation; Stage 3 is reading to learn. Stage 0 occurs during the preschool years when students may be introduced to reading by listening to storybooks read by parents, by learning to name alphabet letters, by seeing labels and signs marking objects and places in their environment. Children's knowledge of spoken language and knowledge of the world begins to develop during Stage 0. Because written language is different from spoken language in several ways, including structure and information density, children may find it a challenge at first to understand text when it is read to them. They develop familiarity with the patterns of written language as a result of listening to adults read storybooks (Mason, 1980; Sulzby, 1985).

Students move into Stage 1 when formal reading instruction begins, typically during kindergarten or first grade. As they learn how the alphabet represents speech, they become able to read print on their own. Building a sight vocabulary is essential for advancing the beginner's ability to read text. Contrary to traditional views that sight word learning involves visual memorization of word shapes, research has shown that the process of storing sight words in memory involves using grapheme-phoneme knowledge to remember how the letters in spellings of specific words symbolize sounds in their pronunciations (Ehri, 1991). Another important accomplishment is learning how to read unfamiliar words. Children acquire several strategies for doing this: decoding, in which letters are sounded out and blended into recognizable pronunciations; analogizing, in which known sight words are used to read unknown words sharing the same letters; contextual guessing, in which meanings and sentence structure of the prior text are used to anticipate words (Ehri, 1991).

When students master the basics of decoding, usually in second grade, they move into Stage 2. Their word recognition speeds up and becomes automatic, the various processes that operate concurrently in text reading become consolidated and more interactive, and text reading becomes noticeably more fluent. According to Chall (1983), the best way for students to improve fluency is through practice in reading easy text. Stage 3 occurs once students have mastered the mechanics of reading and are able to use reading to acquire new knowledge. It begins around fourth grade, when students are expected to learn history, science, social studies, and other subjects by reading textbooks.

It should be noted that the labels given to these stages identify reading processes that are undergoing major developmental changes and that must be mastered for learners to be able to function adequately at the next stage. The labels do not indicate that learners practice only those processes and no others during this period. For example, during the initial reading and decoding stage, text reading is essential for beginners to acquire a sight vocabulary of function words such as *from, what,* and *the* (Ehri and Roberts, 1979; Ehri and Wilce, 1980).

Students may have difficulty learning to read for a variety of reasons linked to the various stages and knowledge sources in Figure 10.1 (Ehri, 1986; Rack, Snowling, and Olson, 1992; Stanovich, 1980, 1986; Vellutino, 1979). Inadequate knowledge of language will impair reading. Readers who have impoverished experiences or poor memories for information about the world may lack the vocabulary and background knowledge to interpret some kinds of texts. Readers with poor knowledge of the alphabetic-phonemic system or with limited sight vocabularies will have trouble processing words in text. Poor readers typically reveal severe deficiencies in the acquisition of alphabetic-phonemic and lexical skills at Stage 1. Readers may acquire decoding skill but still lack speed and fluency in their reading, which is a deficiency at Stage 2. Later, in Stage 3, poor readers may not be alert to lapses in their comprehension as they read, or, if they are aware, they may not be competent at using appropriate strategies to recover. Teachers need to understand how normal reading skill develops as well as what can go wrong during acquisition so that they can identify those students who are at risk for reading failure and take steps to address their learning problems.

Teaching students to read, at least in the United States, is complicated by the fact that at any one grade, students display large individual differences in reading skill. Even in kindergarten, a classroom will typically include readers as well as nonreaders, children who know many letters as well as those who know only a few. As students progress through the grades, differences among them grow even larger (Juel, 1988; Stanovich, 1986). This means that at any grade teachers must be prepared to teach students who are at various stages of reading development. Even with adequate instruction, some students will have difficulty learning to read and will progress more slowly than their age mates. Teachers who understand how normal reading develops, how to effect progress through instruction, and how to assess strengths and weaknesses in reading skills will be equipped to deal with large individual differences that include severely disabled readers. This is because the best remedy for any reading disability is proper instruction (Chall, 1978).

In sum, having knowledge about reading processes and their acquisition enables teachers to understand what they are doing, why, and where they are headed with their instruction. When they observe students' reading behaviors, they have a cognitive scheme for interpreting these behaviors, what these behaviors indicate about the students' capabilities, and what might be done to promote further growth. When teachers come upon new methods for teaching reading, they have a basis for making informed judgments about the likely effectiveness of these methods. If a method does not work as expected, they have a basis for speculating about why and for checking their hunches. In short, knowledge about reading processes makes teachers informed consumers of instructional materials, sensitive observers of reading behavior in students, and skilled managers of instruction.

Instructional Methods

When educators speak about methods of teaching reading, they may have in mind a variety of types of instruction ranging from very general "philosophies" to very specific instructional procedures. In the United States, beliefs about how to teach reading vary a good deal, with old ideas regularly returning and then fading away again, as in swings of a pendulum (Chall, 1967). Ideas constituting the core of newly advanced methods are usually variants of methods prominent in the past (for example, the ABC method, the whole word method, the phonics method, and currently the whole language method).

The course of the pendulum's swing is predictable. Reading educators are persuaded to embrace one instructional approach. It gains in popularity. Publishers respond to the demand by abandoning the old and constructing new materials and manuals. Teachers adopt the new procedures. Initial enthusiasm gradually turns to disillusionment as the method does not result in the expected success. A new approach comes to the fore. This occurs over and over again primarily because the methods have failed to teach reading in a comprehensive balanced way; they have failed to provide instruction that addresses all of the processes that learners need to acquire to become skillful readers.

Novice teachers of reading need to study instructional methods, materials, and procedures from a historical perspective to become aware of the great variety of approaches that are possible and that might prove effective under some circumstances for some purposes (for instance, language experience, individualized reading, basal reading programs, initial teaching alphabet, skill-based programs, analytic phonics, synthetic phonics, linguistic programs, computerized instruction). With this perspective, teachers are in a much better position to recognize and even combat future swings of the pendulum.

Methods are not an end but rather a means that teachers use to improve students' reading. In any text on reading instruction, methods are discussed in terms of their intended impact on aspects of reading that students must acquire, such as reading readiness, word identification, vocabulary, reading comprehension. Not only must student teachers learn about various methods but they must also understand the specific reading processes targeted by the methods; moreover, they must learn how to evaluate whether the methods have their intended effect on students' learning. Published research findings as well as teachers' own observations, past experience, and reasoning provide important bases for this evaluation.

In addition, there are instructional design criteria that should prove helpful to teachers, not only for evaluating others' methods but also for designing their own instructional activities (E. Gagné, 1985; R. Gagné, 1985). For example, teachers need to recognize when exposure to information is insufficient for enabling students to learn and remember it, when students need to practice the information and to receive corrective feedback as well, when metacognitive strategies contribute, when teacher modeling makes a difference, when student discussion enhances learning, when a task must be subdivided into simpler parts to be learned, when prerequisites are necessary, when metalanguage contributes to learning and when it merely confuses learners (for example, talk of short and long vowels, digraphs, silent *e* rule, two-vowel walking/talking rule) (Adams, 1990).

Being able to state rules or to talk about print is not the same as being able to use this knowledge in reading (Beck, 1981).

Once student teachers actually begin to teach reading, they will have access to a richer source of information about the adequacy of particular methods than descriptions in college texts can provide. They must learn how to be astute observers and to detect signs in pupils' behaviors indicating whether they are making progress. By administering informal assessments to individual students periodically, teachers can check on just those aspects of their reading that are problematic.

Many assessment techniques are available. For example, running records of students' oral reading of unfamiliar texts can be used to evaluate students' fluency and to identify the cues that they use to read unfamiliar words (Clay, 1979, 1991). Noting students' accuracy and speed in reading a list of isolated words that they have encountered frequently in their texts can be used to see whether the words are known by sight. Noting students' accuracy in reading a list of pseudowords can be used to check on their decoding skill. Asking questions that demand inferential thinking and evaluating students' discussion and interpretation of texts will allow an assessment of their overall comprehension. Teachers can assess whether these skills are in place by asking students to write or say the sounds of letters and to use their letter knowledge to spell the sounds they hear in words. Unless teachers have ways to assess the capabilities that students need in order to learn to read, they cannot judge whether they are teaching effectively and whether their students are making progress.

Structures in Language That Are Important for Learning to Read

Reading is a language-based process (Brady and Shankweiler, 1991). Beginning readers must adapt their knowledge of spoken language in order to understand what is being represented in print and how print works. The greatest learning difficulties occur during Stage 1 when students must become analytic about language structures that they have heretofore ignored. Students must learn to segment words into phonemes and match these up to graphemes in the spellings of words. Phonemic segmentation is made difficult by the fact that there are no boundary markers in speech signaling where one phoneme ends and the next begins. Rather, phonemes are folded into each other and pronounced as a blend. Various studies show that beginning readers have a very difficult time segmenting words into phonemes (Liberman and Shankweiler, 1979). Disabled readers also have trouble with this. Phonemic segmentation is hard even for adults who have not learned how to read an orthography that represents phonemes with letters (Morais, Cary, Alegria, and Bertelson, 1979; Read, Yun-Fei, Hong-Yin, and Bao-Qing, 1986).

Another difficult task for beginners is that of learning the entire set of twenty-six letters in their various forms and learning which phonemes are represented by the letters. English consists of about forty-six phonemes, and some of these are spelled in more than one way. Not only phonemes but also names must be associated with letter shapes. For pupils who enter school not knowing any letters, the task of learning all these correspondences is monumental. According to research (Adams, 1990), they cannot make much progress in learning to read print until they acquire knowledge of letters. Indeed, letter knowledge along with phonemic segmentation are the two best predictors of how well kindergartners will learn to read during the first two years in school (Share, Jorm, Maclean, and Matthews, 1984).

To teach beginning reading effectively, teachers would benefit enormously from a course on the structure of written language and how it relates to spoken language. This includes knowledge of phonetics, knowledge about the regularities of the spelling system not only at the level of letters as they represent phonemes (Read, 1971; Venezky, 1970) but also at the level of spelling patterns that recur in words (Treiman, Goswami, and Bruck, 1990) and patterns having to do with the origins of words, including differences among Latin, Anglo-Saxon, and Greek roots (Balmuth, 1982; Henry, 1989). Such a course would provide insights not only into spelling patterns but also into the semantics of words, equipping teachers for vocabulary instruction (McKeown and Curtis, 1987).

Teaching Reading as Thinking

The definition of reading has recently undergone a dramatic modification. Currently reading is viewed as a process that involves constructing meaning from text (Anderson, Hiebert, Scott, and Wilkinson, 1985). This definition emphasizes the integration of information from a variety of sources, including not only the text itself but also the extant knowledge of the reader and the context of the particular reading situation. It is not unlike other types of thinking or comprehension except that it is of course text driven.

Preservice teachers in reading need to complete a course focused on the implications of this conceptualization of the reading process. Specifically, they need to study the ways in which students read strategically as they construct meaning and the ways in which teachers can foster the acquisition of such strategies. Before reading a text, readers can benefit from reviewing headings, skimming the text to activate prior knowledge, and formulating questions. During reading, they can benefit from monitoring their understanding and modifying their strategies when appropriate. After reading, readers can benefit from reflecting on what they have read, attempting to summarize and evaluate the text, or integrating the information they have gleaned from the text with other knowledge (Palincsar, Ogle, Jones, and Carr, 1988).

Teachers should develop competence in those teaching activities that have been identified as particularly effective in fostering comprehension (Pearson and

Fielding, 1991). It is useful to focus on the macrostructural relations in a text—for example, the story grammar components in narrative text (Stein and Glenn, 1979) and the components of various types of expository text such as comparison/contrast and argument (Meyer, 1979). It is also important to emphasize ways in which readers can link textual information to their background knowledge (for example, by introducing relevant prereading discussion). Training in identifying the important information in a text and in producing good summaries is helpful (Brown and Day, 1983; Williams, Taylor, and deCani, 1984). Instructional attention to developing specific metacognitive strategies, sometimes discussed under the rubric of study skills, is particularly effective. Comprehension monitoring training—helping students to develop awareness of when they understand and when they do not—is followed by teaching strategies that help students regulate comprehension (such as slowing down their rate of reading) and repair comprehension failures (such as rereading, reviewing) (Garner, 1987). Students should also be taught to recognize when and where specific metacognitive strategies will be of use (Paris, 1986) and be given many opportunities to write, which has been shown to help them make progress (Bereiter and Scardamalia, 1987). This type of strategy instruction is most effective when teachers are skilled in questioning and leading discussions so that students are actively involved and are truly constructing meaning on their own (Roehler and Duffy, 1991). A teacher's skill in such instruction comes only with considerable experience and specific training (Pressley, Symons, Snyder, and Cariglia-Bull, 1989).

In their reading course, student teachers should learn to determine when this instructional approach is sufficient and when it is not. The approach was developed originally not for beginning reading instruction but primarily for students in Stage 3 (Chall, 1983), when the main goal is to acquire the ability to read for information (and for pleasure). Certainly students who are in the early stages of learning to read can also profit from training in strategic reading and thinking. However, not all aspects of beginning reading instruction can be carried out successfully using only this approach. Instruction that is focused on text processing and comprehension may be sufficient to improve the reading ability of readers at advanced stages, but it is not sufficient to ensure that beginning readers acquire the "mechanics" of word reading and decoding. Other types of instructional activities are required to provide for the acquisition of letter-sound knowledge and word reading (Williams, 1991).

Learning to Teach Reading

It is important to view learning how to teach reading as a process that develops over time. The ability to teach changes in predictable ways as the novice teacher gains experience. From this perspective, the purpose of a preservice teacher education program is to provide teachers with background knowledge about the structure of written language, the nature of reading processes and reading disabilities, alternative methods of teaching reading, and how to assess students' reading capabilities. An additional purpose is to provide teachers with specific methods of teaching reading that will help them to begin the learning/development process. These methods should provide an initial scaffold that is sufficiently prescriptive to allow teachers to begin operating effectively in the classroom. The scaffold should also be sufficiently explanatory to enable teachers to incorporate their experiences into their knowledge base and thus improve their understanding of how to teach reading effectively.

The methods initially taught to beginning teachers probably need to be highly prescriptive. Having instruction available in the form of scripts might sometimes prove helpful to implement some teaching techniques. At the very least, instructional methods and materials should be accompanied by text that explains what the methods are intended to accomplish with learners. They should also be accompanied by directions about how to assess whether the methods are having their intended effect on learners.

As teachers gain experience teaching reading and observing how the skills of learners develop under their guidance, their understanding grows. Three ingredients are central for facilitating growth:

1. Teachers must possess theoretical knowledge about reading processes and their course of development in learners, and they must apply this knowledge in handling their instruction and in observing the progress of their students.
2. Teachers must accumulate a repertoire of instructional materials and activities that they have tested and found useful to promote reading processes in their students.
3. Teachers must have ways of regularly observing and assessing the progress that readers make as well as the adequacy of their own instructional methods.

Recommended Course Requirements

Teacher educator programs should include the following courses to enable their students to begin the process of becoming competent teachers of reading:

- *Psychology of reading processes and acquisition;* the cognitive/linguistic processes involved in reading and learning to read; the course of development of reading processes and the role of instruction in promoting development; ways to assess competence in reading processes; methods of scientific inquiry to derive knowledge from evidence
- *Structure of written and spoken language;* how this relates to methods of teaching reading and to processes involved in reading and spelling acquisition in learners

- *Methods of teaching reading*, including a history of reading instruction; relationship to reading processes
- *Practica in the teaching of reading* in which student teachers learn to implement a prescriptive approach that is carefully scaffolded by their faculty supervisor

In this last approach, teachers should be assisted in integrating these instructional experiences with their background knowledge (about reading processes, learning, and development, about instructional methods, and about assessment) in order to begin the process of constructing their own practice-based understanding about how to teach reading effectively. Two practica courses are recommended, one focusing on emergent reading and the early period when the "mechanics" of reading are acquired and mastered, the other focusing on the later period when skills in comprehension and learning from text become central.

References

Adams, M. J. (1990). *Beginning to read: Thinking and learning about print.* Cambridge, Mass: MIT Press.

Anderson, R. C., Hiebert, E. H., Scott, J. A., and Wilkinson, I.A.G. (1985). *Becoming a nation of readers: The report of the Commission on Reading.* Washington, D.C.: National Institute of Education.

Baker, L., and Brown, A. L. (1984). "Cognitive monitoring in reading." In J. Flood (ed.), *Understanding reading comprehension.* Newark, Del.: International Reading Association.

Balmuth, M. (1982). *The roots of phonics.* New York: Teachers College Press.

Barr, R., Kamil, M. L., Mosenthal, P., and Pearson, P. D. (eds.) (1991). *Handbook of reading research,* Vol. 2. White Plains, N.Y.: Longman.

Beck, I. L. (1981). "Reading problems and instructional practices." In G. Mackinnon and T. G. Waller (eds.), *Reading research: Advances in theory and practice,* Vol. 2. San Diego, Calif.: Academic Press.

Bereiter, C., and Scardamalia, M. (1987). *The psychology of written composition.* Hillsdale, N.J.: Erlbaum.

Brady, S., and Shankweiler, D. (eds.) (1991). *Phonological processes in literacy: A tribute to Isabelle Y. Liberman.* Hillsdale, N.J.: Erlbaum.

Brown, A. L., and Day, J. D. (1983). "Macrorules for summarizing texts: The development of expertise." *Journal of Verbal Learning and Verbal Behavior, 22,* 1–14.

Chall, J. S. (1967). *Learning to read: The great debate.* New York: McGraw-Hill.

Chall, J. S. (1978). "A decade of research on reading and learning disabilities." In S. J. Samuels (ed.), *What research has to say about reading instruction.* Newark, Del.: International Reading Association.

Chall, J. S. (1983). *Stages of reading development.* New York: McGraw-Hill.

Clay, M. (1979). *The early detection of reading difficulties.* Portsmouth, N.H.: Heinemann Educational Books.

Clay, M. (1991). *Becoming literate: The construction of inner control.* Portsmouth, N.H.: Heinemann Educational Books.

Ehri, L. C. (1986). "Sources of difficulty in learning to spell and read." In M. L. Wolraich and D. Routh (eds.), *Advances in developmental and behavioral pediatrics.* Greenwich, Conn.: JAI Press.

Ehri, L. C. (1991). "Development of the ability to read words." In R. Barr, M. L. Kamil, P. Mosenthal, and P. D. Pearson (eds.), *Handbook of reading research*, Vol. 2. White Plains, N.Y.: Longman.

Ehri, L. C., and Roberts, K. T. (1979). "Do beginners learn printed words better in contexts or in isolation?" *Child Development, 50,* 675–685.

Ehri, L. C., and Wilce, L. S. (1980). "Do beginners learn to read function words better in sentences or in lists?" *Reading Research Quarterly, 15,* 451–476.

Feitelson, D. (1988). *Facts and fads in beginning reading: A cross-language perspective.* Norwood, N.J.: Ablex.

Gagné, E. (1985). *The cognitive psychology of school learning.* New York: Little, Brown.

Gagné, R. (1985). *The conditions of learning and a theory of instruction.* (4th ed). Austin, Texas: Holt, Rinehart & Winston.

Garner, R. (1987). *Metacognition and reading comprehension.* Norwood, N.J.: Ablex.

Gough, P. B., Ehri, L. C., and Treiman, R. (eds.) (1992). *Reading acquisition.* Hillsdale, N.J.: Erlbaum.

Henry, M. K. (1989). "Children's word structure knowledge: Implications for decoding and spelling instruction." *Reading and Writing, 2,* 135–152.

Juel, C. (1988). "Learning to read and write: A longitudinal study of 54 children from first through fourth grades." *Journal of Educational Psychology, 80,* 437–447.

Liberman, I. Y., and Shankweiler, D. (1979). "Speech, the alphabet, and teaching to read." In L. B. Resnick and P. Weaver (eds.), *Theory and practice of early reading*, Vol. 2. Hillsdale, N.J.: Erlbaum.

McKeown, M. G., and Curtis, M. E. (1987). *The nature of vocabulary acquisition.* Hillsdale, N.J.: Erlbaum.

Mason, J. (1980). "When *do* children begin to read? An exploration of four-year-old children's letter and word reading competencies." *Reading Research Quarterly, 15,* 203–227.

Meyer, B.J.F. (1979). "Organizational patterns in prose and their use in reading." In M. L. Kamil and A. J. Moe (eds.), *Reading research: Studies and applications.* Clemson, S.C.: National Reading Conference.

Morais, J., Cary, L., Alegria, J., and Bertelson, P. (1979). "Does awareness of speech as a sequence of phones arise spontaneously?" *Cognition, 7,* 323–331.

Palincsar, A. S., Ogle, D. S., Jones, B. F., and Carr, E. G. (1988). *Strategies for teaching reading as thinking (teleconference resource guide).* Elmhurst, Ill.: North Central Regional Educational Laboratory.

Paris, S. G. (1986). "Teaching children to guide their reading and learning." In T. E. Raphael (ed.), *The contexts of school-based literacy.* New York: Random House.

Pearson, P. D., and Fielding, L. (1991). "Comprehension instruction." In R. Barr, M. L. Kamil, P. Mosenthal, and P. D. Pearson (eds.), *Handbook of reading research*, Vol. 2. White Plains, N.Y.: Longman.

Perfetti, C. (1985). *Reading ability.* New York: Oxford University Press.

Pressley, M., Symons, S., Snyder, B. L., and Cariglia-Bull, T. (1989). "Strategy instruction research comes of age." *Learning Disability Quarterly, 12,* 16–31.

Rack, J., Snowling, M., and Olson, R. (1992). "The nonword reading deficit in developmental dyslexia: A review." *Reading Research Quarterly, 27,* 28–53.

Read, C. (1971). "Preschool children's knowledge of English phonology." *Harvard Educational Review, 41,* 1–34.

Read, C., Yun-Fei, Z., Hong-Yin, N., and Bao-Qing, D. (1986). "The ability to manipulate speech sounds depends on knowing alphabetic writing." In P. Bertelson (ed.), *The onset of literacy: Cognitive processes in reading acquisition.* Cambridge, Mass.: MIT Press.

Roehler, L. R., and Duffy, G. G. (1991). "Teachers' instructional actions." In R. Barr, M. L. Kamil, P. Mosenthal, and P. D. Pearson (eds.), *Handbook of reading research*, Vol. 2. White Plains, N.Y.: Longman.

Rumelhart, D. (1977). "Toward an interactive model of reading." In S. Dornic (ed.), *Attention and performance VI.* Hillsdale, N.J.: Erlbaum.

Share, D., Jorm, A., Maclean, R., and Matthews, R. (1984). "Sources of individual differences in reading acquisition." *Journal of Educational Psychology, 76,* 1309–1324.

Stanovich, K. E. (1980). "Toward an interactive-compensatory model of individual differences in the development of reading fluency." *Reading Research Quarterly, 16,* 32–71.

Stanovich, K. E. (1986). "Matthew effects in reading: Some consequences of individual differences in the acquisition of literacy." *Reading Research Quarterly, 21,* 360–406.

Stein, N. L., and Glenn, C. (1979). "An analysis of story comprehension in elementary school children." In R. O. Freedle (ed.), *New directions in discourse processing,* Vol. 2: *Advances in discourse processes.* Norwood, N.J.: Ablex.

Sulzby, E. (1985). "Children's emergent reading of favorite storybooks: A developmental study." *Reading Research Quarterly, 20,* 458–481.

Treiman, R., Goswami, U., and Bruck, M. (1990). "Not all nonwords are alike: Implications for reading development and theory." *Memory and Cognition, 18,* 559–567.

Vellutino, F. R. (1979). *Dyslexia: Theory and research.* Cambridge, Mass.: MIT Press.

Venezky, R. (1970). *The structure of English orthography.* The Hague, Netherlands: Mouton.

Williams, J. P. (1991). "The meaning of a phonics base for reading instruction." In W. Ellis (ed.), *All language and the creation of literacy.* Baltimore: Orton Dyslexic Society.

Williams, J. P., Taylor, M. B., and deCani, J. S. (1984). "Constructing macrostructure for expository text." *Journal of Educational Psychology, 76,* 1065–1075.

Annotated Bibliography

Adams, M. J. (1990). *Beginning to read: Thinking and learning about print.* Cambridge, Mass.: MIT Press.

Many issues involving the development of reading processes and methods of instruction are addressed in this book. Theory and research findings are brought to bear on the issues. The debate regarding how reading should be taught to beginners, phonics versus teaching-for-meaning, is considered. Research findings are reviewed in order to shed light on the important processes involved in learning to read. Processes such as the following are considered: word recognition, orthographic and phonological processing, processes occurring during text reading, the contribution of phonics rules to acquisition, the link between writing and learning to read, precursors of reading acquisition.

Barr, R., Kamil, M. L., Mosenthal, P., and Pearson, P. D. (eds.) (1991). *Handbook of reading research,* Vol. 2. White Plains, N.Y.: Longman.

This book devotes over a thousand pages to a consideration of many aspects of research on reading and literacy. Preservice teachers and teacher educators will find a wealth of information in the thirty-four chapters. Particularly relevant to the concerns we have discussed are Chapter 15 on development of the ability to read words, Chapter 20 on perspectives on reading disability research, Chapter 27 on beginning reading, Chapter 29 on comprehension instruction, and Chapter 30 on teachers' instructional actions.

Ruddell, R. B., Ruddell, M. R., and Singer, H. (eds.) (1994). *Theoretical models and processes of reading.* (4th ed.). Newark, Del.: International Reading Association.

This lengthy edited volume consists of fifty-one chapters addressing issues, theory, and research on literacy. Of the many topics covered are historical changes in reading;

processes of reading and literacy including language processes, social context and culture, literacy development, comprehension, reader response, and metacognition; models of reading and literacy processes; and new paradigms.

Stahl, S. A., Osborn, J., and Lehr, F. (1990). *"Beginning to Read" by Marilyn Jager Adams: A summary*. Urbana: Center for the Study of Reading, University of Illinois.

This book was written to create a shorter version of the book by Adams, a version less detailed and technical but one that preserves information about beginning reading of particular use to teachers, school administrators, and parents.

CHAPTER ELEVEN

HISTORY, PHILOSOPHY, AND SOCIOLOGY OF SCIENCE AND MATHEMATICS

ZOUBEIDA DAGHER AND BEATRIZ D'AMBROSIO

One of my science teachers explained a principle to us, but he first told us, "I do not know why it is that way, I cannot explain it to you but believe me." Was it wise to follow with our eyes closed, without asking questions on the nature or reasons for the existence of this principle? Yet nobody dared challenge him and everybody believed him. . . . Nobody knew why. . . . He made use of his authority, his superiority, to prove the validity of what he was saying.

LAROCHELLE AND DESAUTELS, 1992, P. 164

Traditionally, school science and mathematics have been taught as a series of procedures and rules. A recent study by the National Assessment of Education Programs found that "60 percent of the 8th graders and 46 percent of the 12th graders said they read a textbook in class 'several times a week or more,' and nearly all 8th graders attend classes where teachers place heavy emphasis on knowing science facts, rather than understanding concepts" (Rothman, 1992, p. 15). Teaching science and mathematics merely as facts or vocabulary words is further compounded by the relative isolation of the content from a real-world context, leaving the learner with a distorted understanding of the nature of science and mathematics.

To many individuals, mathematical activity is limited to identifying the appropriate procedure that will solve a contrived school problem. Similarly, scientific activities in schools tend to focus on verification of taught principles rather than on the exploration of relevant issues or applications, rendering scientific knowledge dysfunctional in providing students with meaningful explanatory frameworks. The theories and laws confirmed in experiments fail to apply to life outside school.

The perception of the first-year college student cited above perhaps exemplifies the experience of many at the precollege and college levels. Science concepts are portrayed in schools as facts, a solid account of how the world works. Students are seldom asked to participate in negotiating evidence or reflect on the nature of the concepts they are studying, how and why they were constructed. Carter (1989) points out that "for many science teachers, knowledge of the nature of science arises mainly through internalizing implicit messages from science texts and courses in light of preexisting cultural mythology about scientific activity" (p. 42). Whereas students preparing to be scientists get the opportunity to have their initial ideas of science challenged through subsequent research, Carter points out that this challenge seldom happens for science teachers, whose preparation seldom engages them in scientific research.

Teachers need to study more than the traditional content of mathematics and science. They need to study about mathematics and science by reviewing relevant episodes related to the history, philosophy, and sociology of science. Duschl (1990) claims that an incomplete picture of science is taught by providing learners with the *what*, with scientific knowledge of propositions and processes that justifies what we know, and neglecting to engage students with the *how*, how we have come to believe what we believe and why we employ certain techniques rather than others. Thus, "science instruction is taken out of context and presented without the critical background material necessary for an understanding of the meanings or transitions of science," indirectly denying students the opportunity to see science as "an activity in which change is a normal and rational part of the growth of knowledge" (Duschl, 1990, p. 41). Teachers' emphasis on the facts of science has been attributed by Gallagher to their "lack of education in the areas of the history, philosophy, or sociology of science" (cited in Lederman, 1992, p. 350). The majority of views of the nature of science examined in a study of thirty-four elementary science methods' textbooks (Abell, 1989) were found to be inadequate in presenting the tentative and revisionary nature of science. Gallagher's study suggests that teaching experience seems to make no difference in terms of helping teachers to articulate some basic understanding of science as a way of knowing. Based on this research, two needs for preservice science education were identified: to expose teachers to the nature of science and to provide them with experience in integrating the nature of science in their teaching (Lederman, 1992).

Teaching teachers about how science and mathematics connect to other areas of human culture is as important as teachers' learning of scientific and mathematical concepts. If school mathematics and science are to be understood as human endeavors that have evolved from humanity's efforts to understand and explain its world as experienced, then the teaching of these disciplines would be expected to match or relay the contextual nature of that knowledge. If teachers are expected to meet the challenges of the new reform efforts (for example, the American Association for the Advancement of Science, 1989; the National Council of Teachers of Mathematics, 1989), then their preparation should include knowledge of the nature of science and mathematics, which is considered a major component of scientific and mathematical literacy.

In the following sections, we will discuss the changing perceptions of the nature of school science and mathematics as a consequence of the impact of perceptions of the philosophers of those disciplines. Then we will revisit some connections to educational theories and extend the discussion to include examples and implications for teaching and learning. The three areas (nature of disciplines, teaching, and learning) would merge in teacher preparation in order to provide a postpositivist view of mathematics and science. Such a view would explore rather than ignore or deplore the social and political values that have shaped the development of mathematical and scientific knowledge.

On the Nature of Scientific and Mathematical Knowledge

In his well-known book *The Structure of Scientific Revolutions,* Kuhn (1970) appealed to historical case studies to reexamine the notions of objectivity and the role of logic in justifying scientific claims. His representation of scientists as operating within paradigms that define and prescribe the procedures, questions, and paths undertaken destroyed the commonly and naïvely held stereotype of science as objective and neutral. Lakatos's account (1978) of scientific activity as revolving around research programs (in which scientific knowledge, including mathematical knowledge, is considered fallible, corrigible, and open to revision), provided an alternative to the normal/revolutionary science proposed by Kuhn. Feyerabend (1988) pushed the case to an extreme by highlighting the irrationality of science. The outcome of all these efforts was evident in the way philosophers addressed the nature of knowledge: it was no longer satisfactory to focus on the logical aspects of knowledge production apart from its sociological grounds. The role of values in determining what is to be observed and how, and the sociopolitical forces that determine what knowledge is valid or not, could not be ignored by being brushed off as external to the activity. The external-internal dichotomy does not allow us to escape a reassessment of the notions of science and mathematics as objective, certain, true.

Sociological forces shaping scientific knowledge have been described by several scholars (Knorr-Cetina, 1981; Latour, 1987; Latour and Woolgar, 1979). Parallel to these views and equally forceful have been the voices of feminists (Harding, 1991), who have focused on how the social construction of knowledge is highly influenced by the dominance of certain groups, namely middle-class Western white males, who have long defined what counts as science and what does not. The extreme emphasis on rationality and the Cartesian dichotomies it brings along with it in the teaching and practice of science have been the very reason for excluding many females from pursuing science. This exclusion in turn has influenced the types of questions that are asked and answered as well as the types of methods and procedures that are used. For example, scientific hypotheses attempting to explain Down's syndrome have for a long time focused mainly on two factors:

the rate of coital frequency before conception and oocyte aging in females. The research of Martin-De Leon and Boice (1982) provided further evidence based on animal studies that sperm aging could be a third factor (see also Martin-De Leon and Boice, 1985 and Martin-De Leon and Williams, 1987). This is an instance in which the contribution of female scientists helped modify the direction of questions formerly asked in this field. In education, controversies surrounding IQ research and cultural bias inherent in IQ and other educational standardized testing highlight the values embedded in research activities as well as the far-reaching implications of these values when the findings are used to make crucial decisions about individuals or to stereotype groups.

On the Nature of Learning Mathematics and Science in Schools

Alongside the developments in the philosophy of science and mathematics, parallel developments have occurred in relation to the view of the learner and the process of learning. These developments reflect a shift from a view of the learner as a passive recipient of knowledge *(tabula rasa)* to the learner as an active constructor of knowledge. Connectionism, as represented by E. L. Thorndike, lost its prevalence and support among educators as John Dewey's thoughts on the active learner were more appealing to the social movement for progressive education. In spite of the increasing renewal of the notion of the active learner, current mathematics and science instruction reflects the emphasis on drill and practice of procedures and the recall and accumulation of facts, modes of instruction prevalent since the last century. Currently, mathematics and science educators are engaged in designing curriculum reform initiatives that focus on learning as a constructive as opposed to a transmitted process.

Piaget's idea of constructivism is considered by Kamii (1984) to be one of his most important contributions, along with his notions of autonomy. In Kamii's interpretation (1984) of Piaget, "a child acquires knowledge . . . by constructing it from within, not by internalizing it directly from the environment. . . . children construct knowledge by creating and coordinating relationships" (p. 412). Essential in this conception of knowledge growth in individuals is the active construction of new knowledge on the part of students. The appeal of constructivist philosophies to science and mathematics educators arises from the mounting evidence from a multitude of studies (more than two thousand) on children's alternative frameworks (see Pfundt and Duit, 1994) and studies from other disciplines. These studies show that children's construction of new knowledge is greatly influenced by their prior conceptions in much the same way as scientists' inquiry is shaped by their theoretical frameworks. Various versions of constructivism have emerged in education in the past decade ranging from radical (von Glasersfeld, 1990) to social (Ernest, 1992). It is beyond the scope of this chapter to compare and contrast the many different views of constructivism apparent today. Instead, we focus the reader's attention to the implications of the constructivist views for mathematics and science curricula.

In a very substantial way, an understanding of the nature of science could help teachers see analogically how the larger scale of the construction of knowledge relates in some respects to children's constructions. Piaget's general research program in search for the epistemic subject was an attempt to discern whether ontogeny recapitulates phylogeny (individual development of knowledge recapitulates historical development of thought) (Piaget and Garcia, 1989). One of the major conclusions from this book, according to Chapman (1988, p. 328), is that "scientific progress, like psychogenesis, is a process of constructive evolution." Although Piaget's project failed to account for development beyond one historical stage, it remains pertinent for teachers to realize that not only at the level of logic but also at the level of content many parallels exist between some ideas that children hold about the natural or physical world and some ideas that were held by scientists throughout history. Children's notions of a flat earth, of heat and temperature, and of light traveling from the eye to the object are a few examples. Similarly, in mathematics, children's difficulties with non-unit fractions, irrational numbers, and limits have parallels in the evolution of mathematical thought. It is important that teachers be aware of the historical parallels to children's intuitive ideas because it will temper the tendency to judge those ideas as right or wrong. It will also help teachers to focus on students' reasoning as the teachers engage them in negotiating meaning through thoughtful discussions and relevant activities.

We have pointed out earlier how scientific and mathematics literacy demands not only an understanding of the specific concepts but also of the context in which that knowledge was produced and applied, as well as an awareness of the potential of that knowledge and its limitations. The historical record here could be very helpful, not necessarily for making that knowledge available for students as is but rather for using that knowledge to make appropriate curricular and instructional decisions.

This conception of mathematics and science as socially constructed bodies of knowledge that have their roots in practice has been translated in educational imperatives by Ernest (1992), Cobb, Wood, and Yackel (1990), Confrey (1990), Kamii and De Clark (1985), Kamii and Joseph (1989), and others. In the following sections, we make observations that have implications for how an understanding of the social construction of mathematics and science can affect the teaching of those disciplines.

First

Knowledge of science and math is culturally based. Within the cultural milieu, the notion of community that determines what is accepted as legitimate knowledge cannot be ignored. Kuhn's reference (1970) to normal and revolutionary science—and prevailing paradigms, demonstrated by historical examples—provides a way of understanding how scientific knowledge is legitimized within the scientific community. A study of the issues surrounding historical issues, as in the cases of Galileo and Darwin, can provide teachers with an appreciation of the dynamics between science and society (see McGinnis and Oliver, 1992). This understanding can help them gain critical insights into some of the current controversies (such as creation-evolution) by examining the underlying assumptions inherent in the arguments. Other instances of how the knowledge of cases could enhance science teaching have been proposed (see Duschl, 1990; Matthews, 1988).

The study of the histories of the disciplines illustrates how different forms of knowledge evolved in different cultural settings in response to needs and problems faced by people in a given place and time. For example, the Babylonians are mostly known for the development of a sophisticated numeration system, while the Egyptians are credited with the evolution of geometry. As Kline (1953) points out, the mathematics of these people did not restrict itself to resolving problems in commerce and agriculture but was closely tied to their religious beliefs and reflected in their art and architecture as well. The accomplishments of the Chinese in the areas of printing, gunpowder, and magnetism preceded the discovery of these activities in Europe by five hundred to a thousand years (see Krugly-Smolska, 1992). Their contributions extended to areas of astronomy, optics, acoustics, biology, and medicine. The contributions of Hindu and Islamic scientists, when examined in their historical context, reveal the intricate connections among science, technology, and society. Beyond an examination of the historical accounts of these and other cultures, the study of the cultural basis of science, technology, and mathematics is further pursued and demonstrated in the current research studies on "ethnoscience," "ethnomathematics," and corresponding research programs (see D'Ambrosio, 1985, 1991; Pompeu, 1992; Ascher, 1991; Frank, 1990). These issues do not rest here.

In D'Ambrosio's account of the pedagogical implications of work with ethnomathematics (1985), he suggests the need to recognize and incorporate ethnomathematics into the curriculum in order to make different cultural forms compatible. This view of mathematical pedagogy, which includes a strong cultural component, is put into practice in the works of Gerdes (1991). In his work, the mathematics practiced in Mozambique society is at the heart of the instructional program in teacher education. The mathematics of cultural practices (such as basket making) are analyzed and studied by future teachers, enhancing their awareness of the intuitive mathematics existent in their culture and legitimizing and valuing the people's ways of knowing.

Second

Rationality and objectivity are attributed to science with the assumption that theory choice is made on strictly rational grounds. Given the aforementioned summary on the sociological and historical philosophies, we reaffirm Kuhn's and Feyerabend's stance that "the search for necessary and sufficient conditions or rules of theory-choice is a project doomed to failure. . . . that any statement of rules, procedures, and methods fails to capture the wit, imagination, and judgement required for the invention, testing, and evaluation or justification of scientific hypotheses and theories" (Bernstein, 1983, p. 63).

One of the outward expressions of the rationality and objectivity of science is exemplified in the so-called scientific method, often discussed in introductions to many science textbooks. The myth embodied in the method is destructive because it locks a dynamic process into a particular order and assumes strict dichotomies between observation and theory, between the knower and the known. Most of the definitions of the scientific method and the scientific processes that were discussed in the 1960s and 1970s (and sometimes we find them recurring in the 1990s) are based, according to De Boer (1991, p. 198), "on conceptions of science that had their origins in inductivist and empiricist philosophies that had developed in the seventeenth century." When discussed in textbooks, no reference is usually given to the values underlying and guiding the observation or interpretation or to the nonlinear nature of the steps involved. Creativity, imagination, and intuition are ignored (Cross, 1990). The notion of science as a collective and socially negotiated activity is deemphasized. The textbooks' depiction of the scientific method as the way scientists arrive at their knowledge ignores historical, sociological, and psychological elements of scientific activity. Emphasis on the scientific method may be responsible for creating the perception that by following its steps one is sure to arrive at "certain and secure scientific knowledge" (Oldroyd, 1986, p. 365). Such a perception might be responsible for creating the kind of distorted conceptions in students' understanding of the nature of scientific knowledge as revealed by this college student's comments: "I believed I knew everything about the production of scientific knowledge but, as the course goes on, the less I think that I know something, the more I discover things of which I had never even doubted the existence. The notion that I have questioned is that of objectivity. In my first journal, I saw objectivity as the absence of subjectivity and the way I described it, only computers could reach an acceptable level, since it was related to the elimination of all feelings and emotions" (Larochelle and Desautels, 1992, pp. 162–163).

A significant change in students' perceptions resulted from a philosophy course in which the instructors created a research context to conduct "epistemological questioning that aimed at developing the reflexive and argumentative competencies of the students" (p. 160). This change is expressed by the same student's words: "Now, I relate the concept of objectivity to the capacity of maintaining good communication with other researchers and to constantly put into question our own points of view and research methods" (p. 163).

The lack of adequate attention to the humanistic dimension in science textbooks and instruction leads by omission to an inevitable trust in science as objective, neutral, and certain. The dangers of such attitudes become evident when politicians selectively use that knowledge in debates in order to resolve questions with broad societal ramifications. Advocates of certain points of view select specific pieces of evidence and present it as facts or as theories, depending on the choice that strengthens their case; they ignore disagreements (creation-versus-evolution controversies) among experts and, under the banner of scientific objectivity, disregard the assumptions beneath the kinds of questions that were asked, the methods of research, and the limitations in the conclusions (Harding, 1991; Martin, 1991; Suzuki, 1989).

When driven to an extreme, science as the apex of rationality gets extended to other facets of human experience under the assumption that science is the solution to all problems—which leads to a form of scientism. The formation of scientistic attitudes is undesirable because it ignores the limits of science and dilutes the importance of existing environmental, medical, and even social problems. Furthermore, it results in rejecting other ways of knowing on the basis that they are irrational and inferior. These attitudes are damaging because they define legitimate knowledge by the standards of scientific knowledge viewed narrowly as objective, rational, and infallible.

Third

Scientific knowledge is in a continuous state of flux as is evident both in the history of science and in the personal intellectual history of students. As individuals within a cultural group negotiate explanations of phenomena, those ideas evolve and change. Once true explanations, they get replaced by more functional explanations. Hence, truths are only truths within a certain time and are based on the understandings of the group of individuals attempting to understand or explain a phenomenon. Thus, the role of philosophy of the disciplines is important in helping prospective teachers appreciate the power and the limits of mathematics and science. In this regard, we find that Hersh's perception of the role of mathematical philosophy provides "an account of mathematical knowledge as . . . fallible, corrigible, tentative and evolving, as is every other kind of human knowledge" (1986, p. 21).

The focus on Euclidean geometry in precollege mathematics is an example of how the view of mathematics as an objective, rational, and infallible discipline can limit students' understanding of geometry. Definitions, assuming work exclusively on the plane, make it very difficult for students to conceive of geometrical entities on different surfaces. As an illustration, consider the concept of straight lines, which takes on different meanings if the assumption of working on a plane surface is modified. A much more general understanding of straight lines is needed to interpret that concept on spherical surfaces, hyperbolic surfaces, or even in a "taxicab" space. The act of questioning the assumptions of Euclidean geometry is essential to developing an understanding of its limitations and in encouraging students to explore geometrical entities in different spaces. This practice would help students understand mathematics as a discipline in a constant state of flux and growth.

Fourth

The experimental nature of science and mathematics must be emphasized. Within the context of experimentation in science, Lakatos (1978) reminds us that "mature science is not a trial-and-error procedure, consisting of isolated hypotheses, plus their confirmations or refutations. The great achievements, the great 'theories' are not isolated hypotheses or discoveries of facts, but research programmes, and not of trial-and-error, nor of 'naïve guessing'" (p. 212). He stresses that the seemingly "crucial experiment" is not after all "objectively crucial." An understanding of the nature of experimentation in science is important for teachers of science in order to temper an otherwise unequivocal belief in the power of experiments in settling scientific disputes over competing explanations.

Although there is wider acceptance of the experimental nature of science than of mathematics, there has been growing attention to understanding the nature of mathematics as based on observations and practice. Lakatos (1978) traces the history of this interpretation of the nature of mathematics to the mid 1900s. In this sense, he describes mathematics as quasi-empirical and depicts the development of a quasi-empirical theory in the following way: "It starts with problems followed by daring solutions, then by severe tests, refutations. The vehicle of progress is bold speculations, criticism, controversy between rival theories, problemshifts" (pp. 29–30). This stands in contrast to an a priorist (that is, analytic, known through mental introspection) view of theories, in which Euclidean theory, for instance, is taken to exemplify the outcome of a "search for self-evident axioms" and a methodology that is "puritanical, antispeculative" (Lakatos, 1978, p. 29). According to Polya (1954):

> Mathematics is regarded as a demonstrative science. Yet this is only one of its aspects. Finished mathematics presented in a finished form appears as purely demonstrative, consisting of proofs only. Yet mathematics in the making resembles any other human knowledge in the making. You have to guess a mathematical theorem before you prove it; you have to guess the idea of the proof before you carry through the details. You have to combine observations and follow analogies; you have to try and try again. The result of the mathematician's creative work is demonstrative reasoning, a proof; but the proof is discovered by plausible reasoning, by guessing [p. vi].

Hence, creative mathematical activity can have its origins in observations of the real world, in looking for patterns, and in trying to understand and solve problems. These problems may have their seeds in practical, real-world phenomena or in mathematics itself. Often, the paradoxes generated by formalized mathematical ideas spur the creativity of mathematicians.

The study of the origin of ideas and the struggles of humanity to overcome obstacles in the evolution of the field enhances our understanding of mathematical activity. Ideally, the historical accounts should aid us in this task of understanding. Unfortunately, much of the mainstream history of mathematics and science reported to date focuses on the successes in the evolution of scientific and mathematical thought and emphasizes the study of finished products. Such historical accounts lead one to ignore the humanistic nature of scientific thought and the real process of evolution of ideas. In using the history of mathematics and science to understand the nature of the discipline, it is essential to uncover studies that emphasize the struggles and paradoxes faced by scientists throughout the course of history. In this regard, such accounts need to bring out in the open the contributions and struggles of scientists whose gender or ethnic background affected the type of recognition they received for their work.

As an example of the benefit of studying history to understand the nature of the discipline, let us focus on the evolution of the concept of proof. If we analyze the evolution of the concept of proof as Arcavi (1991) proposes, then "one may grasp the social context of proof by looking at it as a communication device for members of a certain mathematical community at a certain period of time" (p. 11). In this sense, an argument that today may seem inappropriate due to its lack of rigor might have been accepted centuries ago. Controversies over the legitimacy of proofs that rely on the use of computers are still prevalent today. Philosophers argue about whether a theorem can be proven by examining all the cases and whether such a proof can be considered an acceptable mathematical proof. This is particularly relevant as teachers try to help students build a convincing argument in support of a mathematical conjecture. According to Ernest (1992), "Mathematics rests on spoken (and thought and read) natural language, and mathematical symbolism is a refinement and extension of written natural language. Mathematical concepts refine and abstract natural language concepts" (p. 94). Thus, mathematical language used with rigor in mathematical proofs is a refinement of the arguments presented through natural language.

The four implications discussed above capture significant elements of scientific activity. The understanding of this essence is critical for acquiring scientific and mathematical literacy. In the quest for promoting literacy in teachers and their future students, intervention in teacher education programs is necessary. Here, we wish to reiterate Lederman's cautionary remark (1992) that we need to be careful "not to attempt to impose a particular view of science on teachers and students as if it was more informed or unchanging. Rather ways to communicate both the changing nature of science, as well as its various forms, must be included along with any attempt to change teachers' or students' conceptions of scientific knowledge" (p. 352). In the interest of promoting literacy in teachers and their future students, we outline in the following section an intervention strategy to face that challenge.

Model of Implementation

We believe that when teachers understand the nature of science and mathematics, this can lead to more effective teaching of mathematics and science at all levels. We remind the reader, however, that teachers' translation of their understanding into desirable instructional strategies and potentially fruitful learning outcomes is far from straightforward. Case study research on teachers' beliefs reveals, for example, an instance where constraints prevented one teacher from using strategies that were congruent with his beliefs (Brickhouse, 1990). As we propose this model for implementation, we are conscious that "the influence of teachers' conceptions on classroom practice is mediated by a complex set of factors (such as curriculum constraints, administrative policies, teachers' attitudes about students and learning, etc.)" (Lederman, 1992, p. 353). Attention to these constraints is crucial if the knowledge that teachers develop in their teacher education programs is to become functional and effective.

This discussion pertains to the preparation of both elementary and secondary teachers. We encourage the reader to imagine parallel changes that would occur at the elementary and secondary schools with respect to the mathematics and science curriculum. These changes would reflect the ways in which teachers have learned science and mathematics.

The goal of improving teachers' understanding of science and mathematics will necessitate a systemic change in teacher education programs. Such a change involves a reconceptualization of how math and science are taught at the university level, from emphasis on concepts and theories to an understanding of these concepts in the context of their historical construction and their present societal repercussions. The content courses would have to be redesigned with the social studies of science and mathematics in mind. They would have to be experience based with room for conjecture, hypothesis making, and systematic testing of student-generated hypotheses. An element of metacognitive reflection on the thinking process and the implications of the findings is necessary in the context of the classroom and the larger societal context. Questions about whether the constructed claims to knowledge are reasonable and an exploration of the societal implications of that knowledge allow students to recognize the interconnections between science and mathematics and life as they know it (their daily experience). In such classes, students would be asked to develop their own questions and engage in some form of open-ended inquiry.

Along with the change in the content courses comes a change in how methods courses are designed. Ideally, a methods component would be linked to each of the content courses and would provide the forum in which the pedagogical potential of the science and mathematics content is discussed. In considering those possibilities, students would be asked to evaluate the developmental and cultural appropriateness of the various concepts to the various grade levels. They would review studies related to children's preconceptions regarding the given topic. They would review and research historical episodes in connection to that topic taken from various cultures so that the students come to understand and honor the different ways of knowing. This approach would increase students' self-esteem and self-confidence as learners of science and mathematics since their way of thinking is considered plausible and acceptable in the classroom community of learners. We contend that this focus will allow for the development of a multicultural perspective on the learning of mathematics and science in a way that truly integrates multicultural experiences into the learning process.

The clinical experiences integrated with the methods component would require preservice teachers to assume a role of teacher-researcher. As teacher-researchers, they would undertake projects in which they themselves become explorers of ways in which they can build instruction around their students' pre-existing concepts in math and science. During clinical experiences, preservice teachers would experience continuous evaluation of students' learning. Thus, preservice teachers would be aligning the assessment procedure with students' understanding, an approach that focuses on the growth of students' knowledge as opposed to their attainment of expert knowledge. The use of reflective strategies would also assist prospective teachers in attending to "those specific instructional behaviors, activities, and decisions implemented within the context of a lesson," found by Lederman (1992, p. 351) to be most important in influencing students' beliefs about the nature of science.

Setting up this ideal model, we expect readers to find within their institutional settings ways of restructuring their programs in order to permit experiences that are conducive to a better understanding of science and mathematics in the service of instruction. In addition to the suggestions for implementation outlined above, we believe that a course that explores meaningful and relevant challenges to students could be very helpful in restructuring future teachers' ideas (Carter, 1989; Larochelle and Desautels, 1992). We maintain, however, that concerted efforts in the core courses are necessary to counter the effects of twelve years of schooling.

We believe that a powerful understanding of science and math concepts could be attained in a systematic fashion through the inclusion of a special course and the restructuring of content and methods courses. Such programmatic changes will enable future teachers to experience firsthand, and perhaps for the first time, what it means to understand science and mathematics in context and will therefore enable them to develop strong working models of how to teach these disciplines effectively and meaningfully.

References

Abell, S. (1989). "The nature of science as portrayed to preservice elementary teachers via methods textbooks." In D. E. Herget (ed.), *The history and philosophy of science in science teaching: Proceedings of the first international conference.* Tallahassee: Florida State University Press.

American Association for the Advancement of Science (1989). *Science for all Americans: A Project 2061 report on literacy goals in science, mathematics, and technology.* Washington, D.C.: American Association for the Advancement of Science.

Arcavi, A. (1991). "The benefits of using history." *For the Learning of Mathematics, 11*(2), 11.

Ascher, M. (1991). *Ethnomathematics: A multicultural view of mathematical ideas.* Pacific Grove, Calif.: Brooks/Cole.

Bernstein, R. (1983). *Beyond objectivism and realism.* Philadelphia: University of Pennsylvania Press.

Brickhouse, N. (1990). "Teachers' beliefs about the nature of science and their relationship to classroom practice." *Journal of Teacher Education, 41,* 53–62.

Carter, C. (1989). "Scientific knowledge, school science, and socialization into science: Issues in teacher education." In D. E. Herget (ed.), *The history and philosophy of science in science teaching: Proceedings of the first international conference.* Tallahassee: Florida State University Press.

Chapman, M. (1988). *Constructive evolution.* Cambridge: Cambridge University Press.

Cobb, P., Wood, T., and Yackel, E. (1990). "Classrooms as learning environments for teaching and research." In R. B. Davis, C. A. Maher, and N. Noddings (eds.), *Constructivist views on the teaching and learning of mathematics.* Reston, Va.: National Council of Teachers of Mathematics.

Confrey, J. (1990). "What constructivism implies for teaching." In R. B. Davis, C. A. Maher, and N. Noddings (eds.), *Constructivist views on the teaching and learning of mathematics.* Reston, Va.: National Council of Teachers of Mathematics.

Cross, B. (1990). "A passion within reason." *Science and Children, 27,* 16–21.

D'Ambrosio, U. (1985). *Socio-cultural bases for mathematics education.* Campinas, Brazil: University of Campinas.

D'Ambrosio, U. (1991). *On ethnoscience.* Campinas, Brazil: Interdisciplinary Center for the Improvement of Science Education.

De Boer, G. (1991). *A history of ideas in science education.* New York: Teachers College Press.

Duschl, R. (1990). *Restructuring science education.* New York: Teachers College Press.

Ernest, P. (1992). "The nature of mathematics: Towards a social constructivist account." *Science and Education, 1,* 89–100.

Feyerabend, P. (1988). *Against method.* London: Verso.

Frank, R. (1990). *The Basque plenary system and modern mathematics: An essay in ethnomathematics.* Iowa City: University of Iowa Press.

Gerdes, P. (1991). *Etnomatematica: Cultura, matematica e educacão* [Ethnomathematics: Culture, mathematics, and education]. Maputo, Mozambique: Instituto Superior Pedagogico.

Harding, S. (1991). *Whose science? Whose knowledge? Thinking from women's lives.* Ithaca, N.Y.: Cornell University Press.

Hersh, R. (1986). "Some proposals for reviving the philosophy of mathematics." In T. Tymoczko (ed.), *New directions in the philosophy of mathematics.* Boston: Birkhauser.

Kamii, C. (1984). "Autonomy: The aim of education envisioned by Piaget." *Phi Delta Kappan, 65,* 410–415.

Kamii, C., and De Clark, G. (1985). *Young children reinvent arithmetic: Implications of Piaget's theory.* New York: Teachers College Press.

Kamii, C., and Joseph, L. L. (1989). *Young children continue to reinvent arithmetic—2nd grade: Implications of Piaget's theory.* New York: Teachers College Press.

Kline, M. (1953). *Mathematics in Western culture.* New York: Oxford University Press.

Knorr-Cetina, K. (1981). *The manufacture of knowledge: An essay on the constructivist and contextual nature of science.* Elmsford, N.Y.: Pergamon Press.

Krugly-Smolska, E. (1992). "A cross-cultural comparison of conceptions of science." In S. Hills (ed.), *The history and philosophy of science in science education,* Vol. 1. Kingston, Ontario: Queen's University Press.

Kuhn, T. (1970). *The structure of scientific revolutions.* Chicago: University of Chicago Press.

Lakatos, I. (1978). *Mathematics, science and epistemology.* Cambridge: Cambridge University Press.

Larochelle, M., and Desautels, J. (1992). "The epistemological turn in science education: The return of the actor." In R. Duit, F. Goldberg, and H. Neidderer (eds.), *Research in physics learning: Theoretical issues and empirical studies.* Kiel, Germany: Institute for Science Education.

Latour, B. (1987). *Science in action: How to follow scientists and engineers through society.* Cambridge, Mass.: Harvard University Press.

Latour, B., and Woolgar, S. (1979). *Laboratory life: The social construction of scientific facts.* Newbury Park, Calif.: Sage.

Lederman, N. G. (1992). "Students' and teachers' conceptions of the nature of science: A review of the research." *Journal of Research in Science Teaching, 29,* 331–359.

McGinnis, J. R., and Oliver, J. S. (1992). "An examination of the interplay between science and religion using two prominent cases from the history of science: Galileo Galilei and Charles Darwin." In S. Hills (ed.), *The history and philosophy of science in science education,* Vol. 2. Kingston, Ontario: Queen's University Press.

Martin, J. (1991). "What should science education do about gender bias in science?" In M. R. Matthews (ed.), *History, philosophy and science teaching.* Toronto: Ontario Institute for Studies in Education.

Martin-De Leon, P. A., and Boice, M. L. (1982). "Sperm aging in the male and cytogenetic anomalies: An animal model." *Human Genetics, 62,* 70–77.

Martin-De Leon, P., and Boice, M. L. (1985). "Sperm aging in the male after sexual rest: Contribution to chromosome anomalies." *Gamete Research, 12,* 151–163.

Martin-De Leon, P., and Williams, M. B. (1987). "Sexual behavior and Down syndrome: The biological mechanism." *American Journal of Medical Genetics, 27,* 693–700.

Matthews, M. R. (1988). "A role for history and philosophy in science teaching." *Educational Theory and Philosophy, 20,* 69–81.

National Council of Teachers of Mathematics (1989). *Curriculum and evaluation standards for school mathematics.* Reston, Va.: National Council of Teachers of Mathematics.

Oldroyd, D. (1986). *The arch of knowledge.* London: Methuen.

Pfundt, A., and Duit, R. (1994). *Students' alternative frameworks and science education.* Kiel, Germany: Institute of Science Education.

Piaget, J., and Garcia, R. L. (1989). *Psychogenesis and the history of science.* New York: Columbia University Press.

Polya, G. (1954). *Induction and analogy in mathematics.* Princeton, N.J.: Princeton University Press.

Pompeu, G. (1992). "Bringing ethnomathematics into school curriculum: An investigation of teachers' attitudes and pupils' learning." Cambridge University (unpublished doctoral dissertation).

Rothman, R. (1992). "Science reform goals elusive: NAEP find results, survey paint 'sad' classroom picture." *Education Week,* Apr. 1, pp. 1, 15.

Suzuki, D. (1989). *Inventing the future.* Toronto, Ontario: Stoddart.

von Glasersfeld, E. (1990). "An exposition of constructivism: Why some like it radical." In R. B. Davis, C. A. Maher, and N. Noddings (eds.), *Constructivist views on the teaching and learning of mathematics.* Reston, Va.: National Council of Teachers of Mathematics.

Annotated Bibliography

Duschl, R., and Hamilton, R. (eds.) (1992). *Philosophy of science, cognitive psychology, and educational theory and practice.* Albany: State University of New York Press.
This edited volume is interdisciplinary in nature. It presents various ideas from philosophy of science and cognitive psychology that relate to science education. Written by philosophers, psychologists, and educational researchers, the discussions present multidisciplinary views on learning and provide a number of frameworks that would enhance the reader's ability to reflect on science teaching practices and current reform efforts.

Ernest, P. (1991). *The philosophy of mathematics education.* Washington, D.C.: Falmer Press.
One of the main goals of this book is to relate the philosophy of mathematics to educational issues. Ernest challenges the absolutist view of mathematics and describes a pedagogy that values the social construction of mathematics. In this book, the reader will find theoretical elements supporting changes in mathematics instruction in the direction of educating critical thinkers of mathematics. The view of mathematics as a human and social endeavor is portrayed throughout the book and underlies the pedagogical practices proposed.

Joseph, G. G. (1991). *The crest of the peacock: Non-European roots of mathematics.* New York: Viking Penguin.
George Joseph approaches the history of mathematics in a way that highlights the mathematical endeavors of non-European communities. This approach reinforces the view of mathematics as evolving from a rich tapestry of cultural initiatives for the solution of real problems. Readers will find in this resource a novel approach to the study of the history of mathematics and teachers will find examples that will enhance a multicultural approach to the study of mathematics.

Lemke, J. (1990). *Talking science.* Norwood, N.J.: Ablex.
This book poignantly reveals how the nature of science and scientific activity are portrayed and reinforced through interaction patterns between teacher and students. Using a social semiotics approach to analyzing classroom discourse, the author presents actual classroom excerpts to disclose the written and unwritten rules of classroom behavior by showing teachers' and students' strategies of control. Lemke focuses on the thematic patterns and curriculum content, the ideology of evidence and authority, and the many hidden (and not so hidden) lessons that are taught about the nature of scientific knowledge. The author succeeds in communicating very sophisticated ideas in a simple and clear language and presents concrete recommendations that are of importance to science teachers and teacher educators.

Matthews, M. R. (ed.) (1991). *History, philosophy, and science teaching.* Toronto: Ontario Institute for Studies in Education.
The chapters in this edited volume are written by a diverse group of scholars: science educators, philosophers, and scientists. The book's five parts include (1) an introduction to history and philosophy in science teaching; (2) rationality, ethics, and science education; (3) history of science and the psychology of learning; (4) science and

ideology; and (5) history and philosophy in the classroom. The various chapters give the reader a good introduction to issues pertaining to the connections of history and philosophy of science to educational practice.

Restivo, S., Van Bendegem, J. P., and Fischer, R. (eds.) (1993). *Math worlds: Philosophical and social studies of mathematics and mathematics education.* New York: State University of New York Press.

This collection of edited papers serves to raise many important issues about the philosophy and sociology of mathematics and mathematics education. The interesting combination of papers brings forth a wide range of topics from typical philosophical discussions on the nature of mathematics discussions to issues of gender and politics in mathematics and mathematics education. Several authors address implications for mathematics education of the philosophy and sociology of mathematics.

CHAPTER TWELVE

TEACHING WHAT MATHEMATICIANS DO

LARRY COPES

In one of those wistful just-before-sleep moments a couple of years ago, my third-grade daughter, Lynn, was telling me that the final round of the class checkers tournament would take place the next day.

"How many students started the tournament?" I asked.

After listing the students who had been absent that day, she said, "Twenty-four."

"How many games will there be altogether?"

"Well, the first day there were twelve games. The next day there were six. Then there were three. Then there was this thing called a bye, so there was only one game. And tomorrow the winner of that game plays the other person. Let's see: 12 + 6 + 3 + 1 + 1. That's 23."

"Hmm. I wonder if it's a coincidence that 23 is one less than 24."

"I dunno. Probably."

"Some people would say that each of the twenty-four people except the tournament winner has to lose one game, so there will be twenty-three games for people to lose."

"Cool!"

"Yeah. I think so, too. The way you figured out the number of games was arithmetic. The other is *real* math."

"Cool," she repeated, but then I realized that she had started crying quietly.

"What's the matter?"

"What if I never get a teacher who will teach *real* math and all we ever do is boring multiplication tables?"

To think about teaching mathematics, we ought to start with first principles and work up. Several questions arise:

- What is "real math"?
- Why should we teach this mathematics to children?
- How might we teach this mathematics to children?
- Can it be done?
- How might we teach teachers to teach this way?

Real Mathematics

What is this "real mathematics"? Real mathematics is what mathematicians do. Most people's course experience might indicate that mathematicians sit around all day multiplying three-digit numbers by hand, solving complicated algebraic equations, and figuring out the age of their nephews whose ages ten years ago were half their own. But that's *not* what mathematicians do. Real mathematicians don't necessarily do arithmetic or algebra any better than other mortals. As Halmos (1968) says, "You can no more expect a mathematician to be able to add a column of figures rapidly and correctly than you can expect a painter to draw a straight line or a surgeon to carve a turkey—popular legend attributes such skills to these professions, but popular legend is wrong" (p. 376).

So what *do* mathematicians do? They investigate mathematics. And in their investigations, they engage in three basic activities: posing problems, solving problems, and critiquing their work.

Posing Problems

Mathematical investigations focus on problems. But before anything else can be done with a problem, it has to be posed. Where do problems come from?

Let's see if we can find some patterns in a few examples:

- During a recent concert intermission, I wondered how many women's rest rooms were needed for every men's rest room.
- While walking down a sidewalk the other day, I began to wonder why my foot fell on an expansion crack every fifth step.
- How old will I be when my age is twice Lynn's age?

In all three of these examples, as in the case of the checkers tournament, the problem grew out of a common event. But that doesn't mean that the problem is practical. The problem of the women's rest rooms might be a fairly practical problem for an architect, but the question about sidewalk cracks is more whimsical (unless I do indeed break my mother's back). The question about ages is not practical at all, as far as I can see.

Other impractical mathematical problems arise out of games. Chess has spawned many investigations, as has the game of constructing geometric objects using only a compass and straightedge. Another mathematical game is to prove or disprove all conjectures using deductive reasoning. It's the insistence on this kind of proof that distinguishes mathematics from other fields of endeavor.

Sometimes mathematicians will go to some trouble to pose a problem. For example, suppose you are walking through an apple orchard. You might ask how far you can see. (That question could be very practical if you were searching for a lost child.) Or you might be more imaginative. Suppose the orchard were infinite, with the trees neatly aligned in infinitely many rows and columns. But then the trees all shrink until they are infinitely thin (with the rows and columns staying the same distance apart). You cut down one of the trees and stand on a stump (presumably making yourself infinitely thin to do so). Now how far can you see? Can you see out of the orchard?

My students are quick to point out that you can see out if you just look straight up. So we change the problem to eliminate that possibility. Then they claim that if the orchard is infinite, there is no "out." So we rephrase the problem as "seeing infinitely far." But then can you lean over and look between rows? Would parallax interfere with sight? Is the orchard on a sphere and hence curving? And so on. We keep refining the problem until we've represented the orchard by equally spaced points on a plane. You are represented by one of those "tree points." Lines of sight are represented by straight lines that pass through the "tree point" representing you. The question then becomes whether or not any such lines will miss all other "tree points." Now we have posed an interesting mathematical problem.

Solving Problems

Once mathematicians have posed a problem, their goal is to solve it. They do this through a cycle of making and testing conjectures.

For example, let's try to solve the orchard problem. You might conjecture immediately that there is no way that a line through the "tree point" that represents you can miss all other "tree points," since there are infinitely many "tree points." Or you might conjecture the opposite, that since those "tree points" are just points with no length or breadth, a line would be more likely to miss them than hit them.

Making the conjecture, even with an intuitive defense, would not be sufficient for solving the problem, however. You'd have to test your conjecture. Unlike much conjecture testing in science, you wouldn't perform an actual experiment. You wouldn't try to grow an infinite orchard of infinitely thin trees. You wouldn't even lay out many dots on a sheet of paper and try drawing various lines. Rather, you'd play the deductive proof game. To prove the conjecture that every line will hit a tree, you'd have to produce a way of determining which tree will be hit by any given line. To prove the conjecture that at least one line won't hit any trees, you need to describe such a line.

After years of doing math homework, we might think that a mathematician—a "math whiz"—will just sit down and "do" the problem. Rarely are real mathematics problems that easy. For example, suppose you try to prove the conjecture that all lines in the infinite orchard hit trees, but you are unsuccessful. Not only do you not prove the conjecture, you gain some ideas about what some lines that miss all the trees might look like. So you might try to test the opposite conjecture. You might fail here too if you see how those candidates will indeed hit trees, and thus you'll get some new ideas about how to prove the first conjecture true. You may cycle back and forth several times. Some mathematicians have spent their careers alternating between trying to prove a conjecture and trying to disprove it.

Many emotions accompany these attempts to solve problems. The longer a problem remains unsolved, the more unhappy the mathematician might be—and the more delighted the mathematician is when the problem is actually solved. It's this "high" that attracts many mathematicians to the field.

Critiquing Work

Mathematicians don't stop when they solve a problem. They sit back and critique their work.

As students, we were told to "check our calculations," and indeed mathematicians examine their arguments for logical flaws. They also ask about the reasonableness of the solution. (Is it reasonable that I was thirty-five when Lynn was born?) But more importantly, mathematicians critique the *method* they used to solve the problem.

Mathematicians might ask, for example, if there is a *better* method for finding this solution. A mathematician who solved the checkers tournament problem by adding up the numbers might be dissatisfied and search for a better approach. After finding the "real math" method, the mathematician might claim that it's a better approach than the arithmetic method for several reasons:

- It is *more efficient,* since it's easier to subtract 1 than to add up a lot of numbers.
- It demonstrates *more insight* into the nature of the situation of single-elimination tournaments.
- It is *more elegant,* more likely to evoke a comment like "cool!"
- Coming up with the method required *more creative* thought.
- The method *generalizes more easily* to other situations; if we add just one more player, the real math method tells us there will be just one more game, while the arithmetic approach becomes more difficult, since more "byes" have to be considered.

Note that when doing this kind of critique, mathematicians have shifted their focus from the problem's solution to methods for finding the solution. And often there's more than one method. Mathematicians might compare and contrast several approaches to solving the same problem.

Another way mathematicians critique their work is by generating new problems. Now we're back to the step we described first in the cycle: problem posing. What if the checkers tournament were organized differently, say as a double-elimination tournament? Then how many games would be played? How might we organize the tournament to rank the entire class? How many games would be needed then? Questions arising from solutions to problems are the basis of future mathematical research. Since one solution can often spawn many questions, more mathematical research is taking place today than at any previous time.

Finally, mathematicians critique a piece of work by trying to evaluate its significance. Work is considered significant if it produces a new method that generalizes to many other problems. An investigation is significant if it spawns many interesting questions. A *very* significant approach might bring together two branches of mathematics, the way calculus uses techniques for solving motion problems to solve area and volume problems. The *most* significant work might change the way people think about nonmathematical things, such as how Newton's mathematical axiomatization of physics helped lead to the eighteenth-century Enlightenment in Europe (see Kline, 1953).

But Why?

I claim that the mathematics we should be teaching in our schools is the mathematics that mathematicians do: mathematical investigations, complete with problem posing, problem solving, and critiquing. A gamut of emotions, a variety of approaches, elegance, and significance. Even impracticality.

But *why* should we teach real mathematics to children? A critically thinking reader named, say, Chris, has already scribbled in the margin, "But what about beating the Japanese?" Had the margin been larger, Chris might have added, "More Americans need to know more math so that we can produce better engineers. And puzzles and elegance don't count in engineering. Even significance is irrelevant. Engineers must be able to get solutions that are numbers, the right numbers, and get them efficiently. If you want to call that 'arithmetic' instead of 'math,' then what we need is more and better teaching of arithmetic."

I think critical thinking is laudable, until I'm the target of it. Then I'm tempted to respond, "Well, I just said all that stuff earlier to give you something to think critically about."

Chris's marginal ravings can be addressed more directly, though.

First, I think they undervalue the job of an engineer. The modern engineer does not sit at a desk and do numerical calculations by hand. The modern engineer designs and builds and tinkers. Calculators and computers do the numerical manipulations. The engineer thinks, using mathematical concepts.

Moreover, strangely enough, technological progress grows out of the most useless-appearing mathematics. For example, mathematicians do geometry in such generality that the results apply in any number of dimensions, including five dimensions and ten dimensions and a thousand dimensions. Practical? Not apparently. But some theoretical physicists (Crease and Mann, 1986) think that the basic building blocks of the universe are ten-dimensional objects called "strings." And computer designers often find multidimensional mathematical models useful. Sure, the mathematical research often precedes the applications by decades, even centuries. But we learn from the very practical-minded Roman Empire that a culture that discourages creative mathematics eventually runs out of tools for creative engineers (see Kline, 1953).

There's another reason for teaching mathematical investigations rather than arithmetic: we might attract more people into mathematics. Right now, the only professional mathematicians are people who have done well at and enjoyed fourteen or more years of calculation-based courses and then have successfully survived a transition to the uncertainties and different thinking modes of real mathematics. The standard curricula do not emphasize elegance and multiple methods and creativity and connections. And yet research such as that of Belenky, Clinchy, Goldberger, and Tarule (1986) shows that many people, especially many women, learn best through connections and relationships. Research described by Buerk (1985) indicates that some bright students avoid mathematics because it feels cold and unrelated, but they are attracted to mathematics when they experience open-ended mathematical investigations. And people are attracted to beauty, to elegance, to creativity.

"But," Chris adds, "even if people should be taught mathematical investigations, don't they need the basics to do it? And shouldn't the basics come first? After all, you have to learn to walk before you can run."

I don't know about your experience, Chris, but my daughter Lynn was not seen walking until she was about five years old. She went right from crawling to running and couldn't be stopped. Other children skip the crawling.

"What I mean," Chris says, "is not that kids need basic manipulative skills so much as basic concepts."

Apparently, Chris is attuned to concept-based curriculum, a very important trend in mathematics education (see, for example, Cobb and others, 1991; Cobb, Wood, Yackel, and McNeal, 1992; Hiebert and Wearne, 1992, 1993; and Ball, 1993). So let's consider a very basic mathematical concept, that of a variable. If we ask a variety of mathematicians and mathematics teachers what a variable is, we'll get answers like these:

- A variable varies.
- It's a quantity that varies.
- It's a letter.
- It's a letter that represents a set of numbers.

- It's a letter that represents a number in a given set of numbers.
- It's a function from a set of sets to the union of those sets.

It seems clear that the people questioned have different concepts of variable, concepts they have created for themselves. That's not only acceptable; it's necessary. People must construct their own concepts. I cannot teach you the concept of something the way I might be able to teach you how to do something. This understanding is the basis of the constructivist philosophy of knowledge (see Piaget, 1970).

Rather than trying to teach either basic skills or basic concepts, then, we need to provide opportunities and encouragement for our students to construct skills and concepts for themselves. Teaching mathematical investigations can provide those opportunities. Moreover, students will gain skills and concepts through the investigations. Cobb and others (1991) indicate that students in a conceptually focused course can learn manipulative skills well enough to outperform their counterparts in a skill-based course. Similarly, students in an investigation-based course may learn both skills and concepts better than they would in courses in which the mathematical "material" is taught as if it were "out there" rather than to be reconstructed by the students.

So How?

Since we *should* engage students in mathematical investigations, how *can* we?

A natural place to turn in trying to answer this question is the recently published standards of the National Council of Teachers of Mathematics (1991). These standards have compiled the latest thinking of many mathematics educators and are being used as a basis for innovative experiments around the country. The standards emphasize several of the characteristics I have described of doing real math: problem solving, communication, reasoning, and interrelationships among mathematical ideas. The advice most relevant to the question of how to teach mathematical investigation is in Standards 1, 2, and 3, which can be summarized as follows:

1.   The teacher of mathematics should pose tasks that engage students' intellect; develop students' mathematical understandings and skills; stimulate students to make connections and develop a coherent framework for mathematical ideas; call for problem formulation, problem solving, and mathematical reasoning; promote communication about mathematics; represent mathematics as an ongoing human activity (p. 25).

2.   The teacher of mathematics should orchestrate discourse by posing questions and tasks that elicit, engage, and challenge each student's thinking; listening carefully to students' ideas; asking students to clarify and justify their ideas orally

and in writing; deciding what to pursue in depth from among the ideas that students bring up during a discussion; and deciding when to provide information, when to clarify an issue, when to model, when to lead, and when to let a student struggle with a difficulty (p. 35).

3.   The teacher of mathematics should promote classroom discourse in which students listen to, respond to, and question the teacher and one another; use a variety of tools to reason, make connections, solve problems, and communicate; initiate problems and questions; make conjectures and present solutions; explore examples and counterexamples to investigate a conjecture; try to convince themselves and one another of the validity of particular representations, solutions, conjectures, and answers; rely on mathematical evidence and argument to determine validity (p. 45).

The real math teacher, then, should "pose questions and tasks" and "orchestrate discourse."

Here is an example of such teaching that I observed recently:

"Once upon a time," the teacher said, "there was a monk. He lived at the bottom of a not-so-high mountain in Tibet. He had a strange custom. The last day of each month he left his hut at the bottom of the mountain precisely at sunrise. He walked up a particular path to the top of the mountain, timing his trip to arrive precisely at sunset. He meditated all night. Precisely at sunrise the next day, the first day of the new month, he left the top of the mountain and walked down the same path, arriving at the bottom of the mountain precisely at sunset.

"The question is: Is there necessarily a point on the path at which he arrives at the same time of day each of two days, going up and going back down?"

"Sure," said Alpha, "the midpoint."

"The midpoint of what?" the teacher asked.

"The midpoint of the path. Well, the midpoint of the time, too. He's at the midpoint of the path at noon, or whenever the midpoint of the day is."

"But the midpoint of the day changes," added Beta. "It's not the same each day, because the sun sets and rises at different times."

Alpha came back: "Well, not much. Anyway, we should 'mathematize' the problem and assume the sunrise and sunset are the same."

"Even then," said Gamma, "he wouldn't necessarily be at the same point on the path at the same time of day each day. He goes through the midpoint only if his speed is constant."

"Oh, come on. He goes through the midpoint no matter what. He just might not go through it at the midpoint of the trip each day if his pace isn't steady."

Beta: "Let's mathematize the problem and say that he goes at a steady pace. Then it's easy."

"Are we all agreed that if he goes at a constant speed then he'll go through the midpoint at the same time of day each day?" the teacher asked.

"Yes," said Delta, "if we also assume that sunrise and sunset are at the same time each day."

"But that's boring." Epsilon spoke up. "What if we don't make those assumptions?"

"Then he certainly is not at the same place at the same time on those two days," responded Beta.

"Well, he might be," said Delta. "Just because we don't make the assumptions doesn't mean that they can't be true. We just can't say that he's necessarily at the same point at the same time each day."

"Can you describe a case in which he's not?" the teacher interjected.

"Sure," said Alpha, and stood up to write on the board. "He's here at six in the morning—let's say that's sunrise—and he's here at six in the evening, sunset. He runs up the mountain between six and seven in the morning, and then he sits just one inch from the top all day and steps over at six in the evening. The next day he runs down the mountain between six and seven, and he waits near the hut until just before sunset."

"But he might cross the same point at six-thirty on those two days," said Epsilon.

"Well, if he did, he *could* have come down just a little faster and then not crossed at the same point."

"Not at that particular point, maybe," said Gamma, "but at some other point perhaps."

"I have an idea." Delta went up to the board. "Suppose we draw a graph like this. Here he is at the bottom of the mountain, and here's the top, and here are the times. There's no time that he's at the same place on the path."

"That's because you've graphed time all along the *x*-axis. We want the same *time of day*, not the same time." That was Beta.

"Look!" Alpha was almost jumping in her seat. "Just change your graph so that the line coming down is over the same times as the line going up. They have to cross. They're at the same point then."

"Yeah, but it's not the same time, is it?" asked Delta.

"Sure it is. The same time of day, that is."

And so on. Eventually the class (and indeed more than Gamma of them actually contributed) came to a solution that everyone found satisfactory.

Stories

I find it helpful to summarize these suggestions for teaching mathematical investigations with a sociological metaphor. Mathematicians form a community, a subculture, with its own ways of thinking and living. We wish to give students an accurate feeling for this subculture and make them feel welcome in that community. To do so, we should ask how one describes a culture to its visitors and newcomers. One of the best ways of describing a culture is by sharing stories of that culture.

What are the stories of the mathematics culture? Your first thought when putting the words *stories* and *mathematics* together might be of those infamous "story problems" that have been part of the mathematical culture for at least fifteen hundred years. But they are just a small part of the classical problems of mathematics with which every mathematician is familiar. There are other kinds of stories, too. There are stories that are actually solutions to problems. There are stories about the lives of mathematicians. There are stories about connections between mathematics and culture.

Most important are stories that describe investigations. Such stories can be exciting, since a mathematical investigation involves all of the elements of a good adventure: mystery, drama, foreshadowing, missed opportunities, tension, release, catharsis—and beauty. An investigation story usually weaves together many threads and sows the seeds of new stories. It probably contains some element of unreality and thus allows a degree of escape.

Because they have all of these components, investigation stories are very difficult to *tell*. But they can be *acted out*, by the students themselves, while conducted by teachers, as in the case of the monk problem.

We can act out stories about even the simplest of problems. Let's consider an arithmetic problem such as

$$64$$
$$-\underline{28}$$

For years we've tried to teach students the right way to solve that kind of problem. We tell them to borrow a 1 from 6, subtract 8 from 14 to get 6, then subtract 2 from 5 to get 3. The result is 36.

But do we also tell students about Kye's method, as reported by Davis (1970)? Subtract 8 from 4 to get -4. Subtract 20 from 60 to get 40. Then add 40 to -4 to get 36.

No, I'm not advocating that we teach Kye's method *instead* of the other one. Rather, we can start an *investigation* by showing students both methods and asking them to look for others and consider which one is best. In the process of learning about mathematical investigations, they will learn some subtraction skills, and they will construct deep concepts of subtraction for themselves.

Another mathematical investigation might grow out of multiplication. We're accustomed to asking students to engage in exercises such as multiplying 15 by 4. A good mathematical investigation often starts with a "backward question." What numbers can be multiplied together to get 60? You might take 30 times 2 or 20 times 3 or 15 times 4 or 5 times 4 times 3—and so on. Try factoring a lot of numbers and see if you can find a pattern in how many factors numbers have.

Alternatively, perhaps we can start out with one way of factoring 60, say 30 times 2, and break it down further into 6 times 5 times 2. The 6 can be thought of as 3 times 2, so 60 is 3 times 2 times 5 times 2: $60 = 3 \times 2 \times 5 \times 2$. But you could have started off with 60 as 10 times 6. Break down the 10 as 5 times 2, and break down the 6 as 3 times 2. Now 60 is written as 5 times 2 times 3 times 2: $60 = 5 \times 2 \times 3 \times 2$. The two ways of writing 60 are different, and yet they have a lot in common. They contain the same numbers, 2, 3, and 5, for example, and the 2 occurs twice in each list. So we might begin a real mathematical investigation. If we start out with 60 as 15 times 4, will we get a similar representation? Why? What makes the different representations the same and how are they different? Will this work for any number? Investigations along these lines can lead to insights into the nature of multiplication as well as practicing the skills.

Speaking of multiplication, suppose that students are asked to investigate table of numbers shown in Table 12.1, looking for patterns. In this multiplication table, young students might find some patterns that seem pretty obvious in retrospect: in any row, to get from one number to the one next to it on the right, you add the same thing. The number in row 7 and column 6 is the same as the number in row 6 and column 7, and this is true for all rows and columns. And so on. More advanced students might note that if we do a "knight's tour," as on a chessboard, starting at 1, going down 2 rows and over 1 column to the right, and so on, we get the numbers 1, 6, 15, 28, and 45, which are all sums of whole numbers (6 is the sum of the first three whole numbers, 15 the sum of the first five, 28 the sum of the first seven, and 45 the sum of the first nine). Why is this the case? What would happen if we extended the table further? Again, the investigation might not only make students very familiar with the results of multiplying numbers but might also give them opportunities to construct a deeper concept of multiplication while getting an idea of what mathematicians really do.

Oh, my. Here's Chris again: "But this is ridiculous! It flies in the face of civilized society! One purpose of stories—originally oral, now written or on videotape—is to pass on the wisdom of the society to its newest members, to save them

TABLE 12.1. A MULTIPLICATION TABLE.

	1	2	3	4	5	6	7	8	9	10
1	1	2	3	4	5	6	7	8	9	10
2	2	4	6	8	10	12	14	16	18	20
3	3	6	9	12	15	18	21	24	27	30
4	4	8	12	16	20	24	28	32	36	40
5	5	10	15	20	25	30	35	40	45	50
6	6	12	18	24	30	36	42	48	54	60
7	7	14	21	28	35	42	49	56	63	70
8	8	16	24	32	40	48	56	64	72	80
9	9	18	27	36	45	54	63	72	81	90
10	10	20	30	40	50	60	70	80	90	100

from having to 'reinvent the wheel.' Modern education has refined that process beyond that of any previous society. We cannot expect positive growth and development if students are using all their time discussing irrelevant things such as monks on mountains or the different ways of factoring 60! You're just talking about the 'discovery method,' which wasted our time twenty years ago."

Indeed, modern schools have refined the process to the point that students need not reinvent anything at all. We have found ways of telling them all kinds of stuff, and to make it their own, we give them worksheets. Daughter Lynn just brought home a folder of one week's work: thirty worksheets, including a folder of twenty-one on Mexico, one on spelling, one on health, one on Pegasus, and a Venn diagram on Pilgrims and Native Americans. I know those numbers don't add up, because I didn't mention the five worksheets on "mathematics." They dealt with an imaginary supermarket trip: "Three bunches of carrots cost _____ . How much does one bunch cost?" She says that she had to look at some picture of a grocery aisle and read a sign about carrots to fill in the blank. And then she had to divide. Skill development. Practical stuff.

But do we want our children to be machines? I would rather they be inventors and let computers do the mechanical work. If we want to teach Lynn the skill of inventing, however, we have to show her how to do it and give her lots of practice. And her initial inventions may not be all that new; she may be reinventing wheels and other old ideas—just as she was not the first to figure out how much one bunch of carrots cost. Is reinvention bad?

As for the discovery method, I'm talking about something quite different. Teachers used the discovery method to help students learn the mathematical results of others. Programs focusing on discovery don't capture the idea of mathematical research, in which any conjecture is fine as long as it can be defended logically. These programs rarely tolerate the elements of true open-ended investigation: problem posing and critiquing work as well as problem solving. We should engage students in creating stories of mathematical investigations so that they will learn the skills and feelings of investigating and will see that mathematics is not just the results of others.

Can It Be Done?

Can we successfully teach mathematical investigations to children? Is anybody actually doing it?

Collectively, we don't have much experience with teaching mathematical investigations. Nevertheless, the best teachers have been teaching investigation occasionally for years. They want to encourage this kind of teaching.

Some descriptions of mathematical investigations are beginning to appear. For example, Fellows (1992) describes work in which second graders investigated a problem in graph theory. The students' investigations were modeled after the kind of exploration they were accustomed to doing in language arts. Casey (1990, p. 1) writes, "As language teachers we welcome young learners into the community of literate people so that they can find the same joy and satisfaction that we have known as readers and writers. It is natural, then, to ask, how does one participate in a community of mathematicians, and what joys and satisfactions result from doing so?"

I can cite our own AUGMENT program at Augsburg College as an example of helping college students come to know what it means to participate in a community of mathematicians. Replacing the standard calculus/linear algebra sequence for mathematics and science majors (including prospective secondary teachers), the AUGMENT program emphasizes mathematical investigations. The text tells stories of investigations. In class, students participate in investigations, either in small groups or as a whole class. For example, the discussion of the monk problem reported above took place in an AUGMENT class. Students are asked to investigate as part of their homework and exams.[1]

Preparing Teachers

How might we teach teachers to teach mathematical investigations?

Several goals for mathematics teachers follow from what I've been saying:

- Teachers should know what mathematicians do, what mathematical investigations are. They should know that investigations are *not* limited to symbol pushing or even problem solving but also include posing problems and critiquing solutions.
- Teachers should know why their students should learn to investigate mathematically: not because the results are useful or practical, which often they aren't, but because abstract, impractical mathematical results are needed in advance of scientific and then technological progress—and because encounters with elegance and creativity and beauty enrich lives and make people say "cool!"
- Teachers should know ways that they can teach mathematical investigations. When the emphasis is on discovering processes rather than reading answers from Tablets in the Sky, teachers need not be able to read those tablets themselves. They need not know all of the answers to engage students in investigating.

How can we get these messages across to prospective teachers? Telling them, even through this book, will probably not be much more effective than telling answers to mathematics students. All of them need to do some reinventing of their own. Just as stories of mathematical investigations can help teach students about the processes of mathematics, stories about teaching mathematical investigations can help teachers. Stories about classroom investigations, such as the one about the monk problem and the glimpse of the orchard problem, can help.

Stories about individual learning might also lend insight. Casey[2] writes about how her third-grade daughter did some mathematical investigating:

I grab two coffee cups and a jar off the dish drainer. "OK, here we have yellow, white and clear. Lined up like that, in that order, that's one way. How many different orders can you put them in?" "Well, you would have . . . ," she begins. She starts out confidently: "yellow, white, clear, yellow, clear, white." Then like this: "White yellow clear, white . . . " Trails off, loses herself. I can see from the way she began moving the objects that she had a scheme in mind, but she is now bogged down. It is also past her bedtime and I was stern with her about getting her stuff cleaned up out of the living room fast, now, and not playing with that cat because it's bedtime. I can't be keeping her up now just because it's something I want her to do, some experiment I want to perform on her. She wants to go get a piece of paper. "Here, I'll count for you," I say. "Try again." She counts up all six, switching the objects confidently.

"OK," I say, pulling off another cup. (There are certain advantages to not having a dishwasher). "How many for four?" "Oh, man that's hard," she laughs. "What color are we gonna call this cup?" Clearly a good question, it's beige-ish yellow-ish with a flower or two. "Brown," I say. "OK, you've got brown, clear, white, yellow . . . ," she begins. Then, "Whoa, this is hard."

"OK, I'm gonna give you a hint. How many arrangements are there with the brown one first?" And I pull the brown one about two inches away from the others. "Oh," she laughs, "three [*sic*] are six!" Of course I hope she will go on and put one of the other cups first and announce that for each of the different colors first there will be six, based on what she has figured out. (*I* know this because I had just figured it out myself the other day. *Again*, haunted by the fat demeaning woman who had first tried to make it clear to me. I remember all those possibilities swimming. Still don't know where two-to-the-*n* exactly fits in to the scheme of things, what with this and *p*-choose-two. Oh well. When I did get it, it was apparent to me that any kid that can count to 24 can figure out that formula.)

Just as it was clear that there would be six possibilities when there was a brown one in front, it was equally clear to her that there were six possibilities when the clear one was in front. She manipulated them and moved them quickly, tossing out numbers, thinking ahead, skipping steps, and finally bringing herself down into a mire of confusion. "Yikes! Yuck!" She shook her head. "This is too hard." And she went at it again, more slowly, still skipping steps, still trying to generalize. She said "five" lots of times, and "four" too, and finally "twenty" quite a few times, and then she asked, "are there 20?"

"Well," I said, "it's complicated, and you get the idea that there's a lot of figuring to do, and you are really close to figuring out, not just how many for 4, but if you took a look at how many for 3 and how you figured that out, and how many for 4 . . . " "There would be a pattern!" she announced. "Yes, and then it gets so interesting, so many patterns, that we just don't have time to talk about it before you go to bed. But it's something to think about. This is the kind of thing that you could do if you stayed home with me. By the way, did you do any multiplying?" "No," she says. "How did you get 20?" (She very well could have added up something or counted something to there; it was a legitimate question.) "Doyyyyy!" she laughed.

We can ask our teachers and prospective teachers to explore these stories about teaching/learning experiences. How did this kind of teaching encourage investigation? In these stories of mathematical investigations, what did the teachers have in common?

Conclusion

Someone once said that one should never end a class period by "wrapping things up," because such closure would deprive students of a reason to think about the questions themselves. So rather than summarizing, I'll cite a student who, after a year of AUGMENT courses, gave her definition of mathematics: "Mathematics is the quest for the interesting." Her words reveal an understanding of mathematical investigation that is very rare for students in traditional mathematics courses. Words like these testify to the possibility that such an understanding need not be so rare.

Notes

1. L. Copes, *The quest for the interesting: Report to the fund for the improvement of postsecondary education on the AUGMENT Project.* 1993. (Available from Augsburg College, Minneapolis, MN 55454.)
2. N. Casey, "Two stories." Unpublished manuscript. 1993. (Available from Institute for Studies in Educational Mathematics, 10429 Barnes Way, South St. Paul, MN 55454.)

References

Ball, D. L. (1993). "With an eye on the mathematical horizon: Dilemmas of teaching elementary school mathematics." *Elementary School Journal, 93*(4), 373–397.

Belenky, M. F., Clinchy, B. M., Goldberger, N. R., and Tarule, J. M. (1986). *Women's ways of knowing.* New York: Basic Books.

Buerk, D. (1985). "The voices of women making meaning in mathematics." *Journal of Education, 167*(3), 59–70.

Casey, N. (1990). "Language acquisition and mathematics learning." In C. Swenson (ed.), *Connections.* Seattle: Washington State Mathematics Council.

Cobb, P., and others (1991). "Assessment of a problem-centered second-grade mathematics project." *Journal for Research in Mathematics Education, 22*(1), 3–29.

Cobb, P., Wood, T., Yackel, E., and McNeal, B. (1992). "Characteristics of classroom mathematics traditions: An interactional analysis." *American Educational Research Journal, 29*(3), 573–604.

Crease, R. P., and Mann, C. C. (1986). "The gospel of string." *Atlantic, 257*(4), 24–29.

Davis, R. B. (1970). "Report from the states." *Mathematics Teaching, 50,* 6–12.

Fellows, M. (1992). "Computer science in the elementary school." In N. D. Fisher, H. B. Keynes, and P. D. Wagreich (eds.), *Mathematicians and education reform.* Providence, R.I.: American Mathematical Society.

Halmos, P. R. (1968). "Mathematics as a creative art." *American Scientist, 56*(4), 375–389.

Hiebert, J., and Wearne, D. (1992). "Links between teaching and learning place value with understanding in first grade." *Journal for Research in Mathematics Education, 23*(2), 98–122.

Hiebert, J., and Wearne, D. (1993). "Instructional tasks, classroom discourse, and students' learning in second-grade arithmetic." *American Educational Research Journal, 30*(2), 393–425.

Kline, M. (1953). *Mathematics in Western culture.* New York: Oxford University Press.

National Council of Teachers of Mathematics (1991). *Professional standards for teaching mathematics.* Reston, Va.: National Council of Teachers of Mathematics.

Piaget, J. (1970). *Genetic epistemology.* New York: Columbia University Press.

Annotated Bibliography

Brown, S. I., and Walter, M. I. (1983). *The art of problem posing.* Philadelphia: Franklin Institute Press.
This book explores several problem-posing strategies and how they might be taught, with many examples.

Copes, L. (1982). "The Perry development scheme: A metaphor for learning and teaching mathematics." *For the Learning of Mathematics, 3*(1), 38–44.
Copes describes how students' conception of mathematics can interfere with their learning real math.

Newman, J. R. (ed.) (1956). *The world of mathematics.* New York: Simon & Schuster.
This classic collection of essays and excerpts in four volumes has long been an excellent source of insight into various aspects and branches of mathematics.

Rising, G. R., Brown, S. I., and Meyerson, L. N. (1977). "The teacher-centered mathematics classroom." *Organizing for Mathematics Instruction.* (39th yearbook of the National Council of Teachers of Mathematics). Reston, Va.: National Council of Teachers of Mathematics.
This chapter contains many classroom vignettes and analyses of experiences in real mathematics.

CHAPTER THIRTEEN

SCIENCE AND CREATIONISM: A CASE STUDY IN BIOLOGY

NATIONAL ACADEMY OF SCIENCES

State legislatures are considering, and some have passed, bills that would require the introduction of biblical creationism in science classes wherever evidence for the origin of the planet, of life and its diverse forms, or of mankind is presented. Local school boards have passed ordinances intended to restrict the teaching of biological concepts of evolution or to require what is called "balanced treatment" of creationism and evolution. Publishers of science textbooks are under pressure to deemphasize accepted scientific theories of evolution while adding course material on "creation science."

The teachings of creationism as advocated by and exemplified in the writings of the leading proponents of "creation science" include the following judgments: (1) the earth and universe are relatively young, perhaps only 6,000 to 10,000 years old; (2) the present physical form of the earth can be explained by "catastrophism," including a worldwide flood; and (3) all living things (including humans) were created miraculously, essentially in the forms we now find them. These teachings may be recognized as having been derived from the accounts of origins in the first two chapters of Genesis in the Bible.

Generations of able and often devout scientists before us have sought evidence for these teachings without success. Foremost among these was Charles Darwin, a member in good standing of the Church of England and an officer of his parish church at Down, in Kent, for many years. His search more than a century ago gave us instead a hypothesis for the origin of species by means of natural selection. Others have given us hypotheses about the origin and history of the earth and the universe itself. These hypotheses have been tested and validated by many different lines of inquiry. With modifications to include new findings, they have become the central organizing theories that make the universe as a whole intelligible, lend coherence to all of science, and provide fruitful direction to modern research. The hypothesis of special creation has, over nearly two centuries, been repeatedly and sympathetically considered and rejected on evidential grounds by qualified observers and experimentalists. In the forms given in the first two chapters of Genesis, it is now an invalidated hypothesis. To reintroduce it into the public schools at this time as an element of science teaching would be akin to requiring the teaching of Ptolemaic astronomy or pre-Columbian geography.

Confronted by this challenge to the integrity and effectiveness of our national education system and to the hard-won evidence-based foundations of science, the National Academy of Sciences cannot remain silent. To do so would be a dereliction of our responsibility to academic and intellectual freedom and to the fundamental principles of scientific thought. As a historic representative of the scientific profession and designated advisor to the federal government in matters of science, the Academy states unequivocally that the tenets of "creation science" are not supported by scientific evidence, that creationism has no place in a *science* curriculum at any level, that its proposed teaching would be impossible in any constructive sense for well-informed and conscientious science teachers, and that its teaching would be contrary to the nation's need for a scientifically literate citizenry and for a large, well-informed pool of scientific and technical personnel.

The Central Scientific Issues

Five central scientific issues are critical to consideration of the treatment in school curricula of the origin and evolution of the universe and of life on earth:

- The nature of science
- Scientific evidence on the origin of the universe and the earth
- The consistent and validated scientific evidence for biological evolution: specifically, evidence for change over vast realms of time and for relation by common descent, evidence from molecular biology for degree of relationship, and evidence showing mechanisms of evolution
- Human evolution
- The origin of life

Discussions and conclusions concerning each of these issues make up the balance of this chapter and present the basis for the Academy's position that the teaching of creationism is not an appropriate activity in our public schools.

The Nature of Science

It is important to clarify the nature of science and to explain why creationism cannot be regarded as a scientific pursuit. The claim that equity demands balanced treatment of the two in the same classroom reflects misunderstanding of what science is and how it is conducted. Scientific investigators seek to understand natural phenomena by direct observation and experimentation. Scientific interpretations of facts are always provisional and must be testable. Statements made by any authority, revelation, or appeal to the supernatural are not germane to this process in the absence of supporting evidence. In creationism, however, both authority and revelation take precedence over evidence. The conclusions of creationism do not change, nor can they be validated when subjected to test by the methods of science. Thus, there are profound differences between the religious belief in special creation and the scientific explanations embodied in evolutionary theory. Neither benefits from the confusion that results when the two are presented as equivalent approaches in the same classroom.

In broadest terms, scientists seek a systematic organization of knowledge about the universe and its parts. This knowledge is based on explanatory principles whose verifiable consequences can be tested by independent observers. Science encompasses a large body of evidence collected by repeated observations and experiments. Although its goal is to approach true explanations as closely as possible, its investigators claim no final or permanent explanatory truths. Science changes. It evolves. Verifiable facts always take precedence. The beautifully symmetrical and once inspiring hypothesis of an earth-centered universe, apparently supported by the "common sense" observation that the sun and stars orbit the earth, fell before an accumulation of new evidence. Today's theory of an expanding universe of 10 trillion stars, with all its puzzles and uncertainties, is far more consistent with the evidence now available.

Scientists operate within a system designed for continuous testing, where corrections and new findings are announced in refereed scientific publications. The task of systematizing and extending the understanding of the universe is advanced by eliminating disproved ideas and by formulating new tests of others until one emerges as the most probable explanation for any given observed phenomenon. This is called the scientific method.

An idea that has not yet been sufficiently tested is called a hypothesis. Different hypotheses are sometimes advanced to explain the same factual evidence. Rigor in the testing of hypotheses is the heart of science. If no verifiable tests can be formulated, the idea is called an ad hoc hypothesis, one that is not fruitful; such hypotheses fail to stimulate research and are unlikely to advance scientific knowledge.

A fruitful hypothesis may develop into a theory after substantial observational or experimental support has accumulated. When a hypothesis has survived repeated opportunities for disproof and when competing hypotheses have been eliminated as a result of failure to produce the predicted consequences, that hypothesis may become the accepted theory explaining the original facts.

Scientific theories are also predictive. They allow us to anticipate yet unknown phenomena and thus to focus research on more narrowly defined areas. If the results of testing agree with the predictions from a theory, the theory is provisionally corroborated. If not, it is proved false and must be either abandoned or modified to account for the inconsistency.

Scientific theories therefore are accepted only provisionally. It is always possible that a theory that has withstood previous testing may eventually be disproved. But as theories survive more tests, they are regarded with higher levels of confidence. A theory that has withstood as many severe tests as, for example, that of biological evolution by means of natural selection is held with a very high degree of confidence.

In science, then, facts are determined by observation or measurement of natural or experimental phenomena. A hypothesis is a proposed explanation of those facts. A theory is a hypothesis that has gained wide acceptance because it has survived rigorous investigation of its predictions.

Higher levels of generalization are formulated into scientific laws. A law identifies a class of regularities in nature from which there has been no known deviation after many observations or trials. It is usually expressed mathematically. The laws of Newtonian and relativistic motion and those of thermodynamics are examples. Scientific laws tell us the ways but not the whys of nature. They are used in launching and manipulating space probes, investigating the far reaches of the universe, mapping deep-sea topography from the surface, or probing the earth's internal structure. We must heed them in formulating new hypotheses and theories.

By the standards described above, special creation is neither a successful theory nor a testable hypothesis for the origin of the universe, the earth, or of life thereon. Creationism reverses the scientific process. It accepts as authoritative a conclusion seen as unalterable and then seeks to support that conclusion by whatever means possible.

In contrast, science accommodates, indeed welcomes, new discoveries: its theories change and its activities broaden as new facts come to light or new potentials are recognized. Examples of events changing scientific thought are legion. Here, for example, we mention four that are both recent and germane to the subject of this chapter.

1.   The study of the origin of life as a product of chemical evolution became possible only with advances, mostly since World War II, in our understanding of early atmospheres, with the development of geochronological dating and other research methods, and with the discovery of a long sequence of mainly microbial Precambrian fossils.

2.   Evidence for deciphering the earliest stages in the evolution of the solar system arrived on earth in a meteorite that fell in Sonora, Mexico, in 1969.

3. The fortuitous discovery in 1965 of a universal background radiation at a temperature of approximately -270 degrees Celsius (3 degrees Celsius above absolute zero) brought the first concrete evidence about the nature of the earliest universe.

4. Discoveries during the past three decades of hominoid remains in East Africa, Pakistan, and elsewhere have combined with advances in molecular biology to initiate a new subscience—paleoanthropology. This field of inquiry is providing an ever-growing inventory of evidence both for a close evolutionary connection between modern humans *(Homo sapiens)* and their australopithecine ancestors and for a clear genetic affinity between human beings and the chimpanzee.

Prior acceptance of the fixed ad hoc hypotheses of creationism—ideas that are certified as untestable by their most ardent advocates—would have blocked these and other important advances that have led to the great scientific achievements of recent years. When we accept explanations not derived from or tested by the scientific method, we cannot achieve true scientific understanding, nor can we even pursue it effectively.

Scientific Evidence on the Origin of the Universe and the Earth

The processes by which new galaxies, stars, and our own planetary system are formed are sometimes referred to as the "evolution" of the universe, the stars, and the solar system. The word *evolution* in this context has a very different meaning than it does when applied to the evolution of organisms. In both instances there is an unfolding, but the processes involved are entirely different. The relevant sciences involved are also different—the biological sciences in the evolution of organisms and the physical sciences in the evolution of the universe and its constituent domains.

The evidence is overwhelming that the universe has evolved over a period of at least several billion years. Among the most striking indications of this process are the receding velocities of distant galaxies. This general expansion of the universe was first noted in the late 1920s and early 1930s by the American astronomer Edwin Hubble from his studies of the changing wavelengths of light from distant stars and galaxies (Hubble, 1929; Hubble and Humason, 1931). Astronomers today, extrapolating backward, estimate that the expansion probably began some 10 to 20 billion years ago. This concept of expansion from a more dense early state was dramatically confirmed in 1965, when faint radio static left over from the early universe was discovered by radio astronomers at the Bell Laboratories (Penzias and Wilson, 1965). The intensity of this static was just what would be expected to result from the expansion of the universe. Confirming earlier predictions, the discovery strongly reinforced the scientific theory that the universe evolved from an initially dense state at a starting temperature of approximately 100 billion degrees Celsius (Weinberg, 1977).

The invariant spontaneous decay of the radioactive isotopes of some elements, resulting in the formation of inert daughter isotopes of other elements, provides further evidence that the universe is billions of years old. Analyses of the relative abundances of radioactive isotopes and their inert decay products in the earth, meteorites, and moon rocks all lead to the conclusion that these bodies are about 4.5 billion years old. This finding agrees with calculations of the age of the sun based on the theory of stellar evolution and is consistent with estimates of the time that would be required for the origin of life and the evolution of organisms.

Another measure of age comes from the relative abundance of uranium isotopes. The relative rarity of the isotope uranium-235, whose half-life is roughly 0.7 billion years, tells us that the earth's uranium is approximately 7 billion years old. We do not know how long after the beginning of the universe it took to form the uranium found on earth, but its presence and relative abundance require that the age of the universe be at least 7 billion years. Although our picture of the origin and evolution of the universe, the stars, and the earth is tentative, our reservations should not be confused with uncertainty about their great age.

Astrophysicists also have developed plausible hypotheses concerning the formation of galaxies, individual stars, and planetary systems. The sun and planets in our solar system are believed to have been formed by condensations from an interstellar cloud of dust and gas like those now visible in parts of our galaxy. New evidence from the geochemical study of isotopes in the Allende meteorite implies that the condensation resulting in our solar system was initiated by a nearby exploding star (or supernova) about 4.5 billion years ago. Many details are uncertain, but there is general agreement on the broader aspects of this process.

The evolution of stars is understood more quantitatively. Comparisons of computer simulations of stellar evolution with the observed distribution of the temperature and luminosities of stars in large clusters indicate that the clusters are typically 10 billion years old.

A major reason for the creationists' opposition to the geological record and evolution is their belief that earth is relatively young, perhaps only a few thousand years old. In rejecting evidence for the great age of the universe, creationists are in conflict with data from astronomy, astrophysics, nuclear physics, geology, geochemistry, and geophysics. The creationists' conclusion that the earth is only a few thousand years old was originally based on the timing of events in the Old Testament, including the counting of recorded generations (Renckens, 1964). Recent attempts to support this conclusion include arguments that the present magnetic field of the earth is the decaying remnant of a magnetic field that was created with it and that if the earth were more than 10,000 years old the initial strength of the field would have been impossibly large. This is one creationist tenet that can be and has been scientifically tested but that has not withstood scrutiny. Current scientific data support the theory that the earth's magnetic field is a product of the motions of its fluid core. The field varies and shifts, but between shifts it is maintained and is constantly renewed by dynamo effects within the core.

Scientists knew that the earth was old before they knew how old. Today more than a dozen independent radiometric methods are used to measure ages in years, based on different decay systems with different decay constants and on the ratios of the decay products of different uranium isotopes. When the age of a given rock is found to be the same when measured by a variety of different isotopic systems, scientists accept that age with a high level of confidence. There is very low probability that different isotopic systems with different constants would produce the same results by chance. Suffice it to say here that the cumulative geochronological evidence indicates the ages of the earth and solar system to be about 4.5 billion years old.

The Scientific Standing of Biological Evolution

Contrary to popular opinion, neither the term nor the idea of biological evolution began with Charles Darwin and his foremost work, *On the Origin of Species by Means of Natural Selection* (1859). The *Oxford English Dictionary* (1933) tells us that the word *evolution*, to unfold or open out, was derived from the Latin, *evolvere*, which applied to the "unrolling of a book." It first appeared in the English language in 1647 in a nonbiological connection. It became widely used in English in its primary Latin meaning for all sorts of progressions from simpler beginnings. Evolution was first used as a biological term in 1670 to describe the changes observed in the maturation of insects. However, it was not until the 1873 edition of *The Origin of Species* that Darwin first applied the term. Before that he used the expression *descent with modification,* which is still as good a brief definition of biological evolution as any. In later editions of the book, Darwin paid tribute to the earlier views of Jean Baptiste de Lamarck (1802, 1809) and others about the subject we now call biological evolution or simply evolution.

Although it was Darwin, above all others, who first marshaled the convincing critical evidence for biological evolution, earlier alert scholars recognized that the succession of living forms on the earth had changed systematically with the passage of geological time. The first recorded test of the predictive powers of the hypothesis was met in the 1830s. The paleontologist William Lonsdale recognized that fossils from geographically isolated rocks now classified as Devonian were intermediate in their degree of development between Silurian forms in deeper strata and Carboniferous ones above—a sequence that has since been independently confirmed thousands of times (Geikie, 1897; Tasch, 1950).

As applied to biology, a distinction is to be drawn between the questions (1) *whether* and (2) *how* biological evolution happened. The first refers to the finding, now supported by an overwhelming body of evidence, that descent with modification occurred during more than 2.7 billion years of earth's history. The second refers to the theory explaining how those changes developed along the observed lineages. The mechanisms are still undergoing investigation; the currently favored theory is an extensively modified version of Darwinian natural selection.

With that proviso we will now consider three aspects of biological evolution in more detail: relation by common descent, molecular biology as it explains the degree of relationship, and the mechanism of evolution.

Relation by Common Descent. Evidence for relation by common descent has been provided by paleontology, comparative anatomy, biogeography, embryology, biochemistry, molecular genetics, and other biological disciplines. The idea first emerged from observations of systematic changes in the succession of fossil remains found in a sequence of layered rocks. Such layers are now known to have a cumulative thickness of many scores of kilometers and to represent at least 2.7 billion years of geological time. The first observation that the final sequence changes systematically upward in an undeformed succession of stratified rocks (and thus with time) was announced in 1799 by a practical engineer named William Smith (Geikie, 1897). His findings were confirmed and extended by a number of paleontologists and geologists who used the fossils not as proof of evolution but as a basis for working out the original sequences of structurally disturbed rock strata.

The general sequence of fossils had thus already been recognized when Darwin perceived that the observed progression of biological forms strongly implied common descent. The farther back into the past one looked, the less the fossils resembled recent forms, the more the various lineages merged, and the broader the implications of a common ancestry appeared.

In Darwin's time, however, paleontology was still a rudimentary science, and large parts of the geological succession of stratified rocks were unknown or inadequately studied. Darwin therefore worried about the rarity of truly intermediate forms. Creationists have then and now seized on this as a weakness in evolutionary theory. Indeed, although gaps in the paleontological record remain even now, many have been filled by the researches of paleontologists since Darwin's time. Hundreds of thousands of fossil organisms found in well-dated rock sequences represent a succession of forms through time and manifest many evolutionary transitions. Microbial life of the simplest type (i.e., procaryotes, which are cells whose nuclear matter is not bounded by a nuclear membrane) was already in existence 2.7 billion years ago and perhaps even earlier. The oldest evidence suggesting the existence of more complex organisms (i.e., eucaryotic cells with a true nucleus) has been discovered in fossils that had been hermetically sealed in flinty rocks approximately 1.4 billion years old. More advanced forms like true algae, fungi, higher plants, and animals have been found only in still younger geological strata. Table 13.1 presents the order in which progressively complex forms of life appeared.

The sequence of observed forms and the fact that all except the first are constructed from the same basic cellular type strongly imply that all these major categories of life (including plants, true algae, and fungi) have a common ancestry in the first eucaryotic cell. Moreover, there have been so many discoveries of

TABLE 13.1. APPROXIMATE TIME SINCE FIRST
KNOWN APPEARANCE OF VARIOUS LIFE FORMS.

Life Form	Time Since First Known Appearance (Millions of years)
Microbial (procaryotic cells)	2,700
Complex (eucaryotic cells)	1,400
First multicellular animals	670
Shell-bearing animals	540
Vertebrates (simple fishes)	490
Amphibians	350
Reptiles	310
Mammals	200
Nonhuman primates	60
Earliest apes	25
Australopithecine ancestors	5
Homo sapiens (human)	0.05 (50,000 years)

intermediate forms between fish and amphibians, between amphibians and reptiles, between reptiles and mammals, and even along the primate line of descent, that it is often difficult to identify categorically the line to which a particular genus or species belongs. Indeed, nearly all fossils can be regarded as intermediates in some sense—as life forms that come between related forms that preceded them and those that followed.

The fossil record thus provides compelling evidence of systematic change through time—of descent with modification. From this consistent body of evidence it can be predicted that no reversals will be found in future paleontological studies. That is, amphibians will not appear before fishes nor mammals before reptiles, and no complex life will occur in the geological record before the oldest eucaryotic cells. That prediction has been upheld by the evidence that has accumulated thus far: no reversals have been found.

Creationists have sometimes cited an investigation of human footprints said to be associated with those of dinosaurs. These footprints were reported to have been found in a roughly 90-million-year-old layer of rock near Glen Rose, Texas. It was subsequently discovered by a young creationist himself that some of the human-looking footprints had been carved by pranksters and that the reportedly convincing ones were no longer present (Morris, 1980). There is no evidence that humans lived at the time of the dinosaurs. In fact, there is much that is opposed to that conclusion.

Although creationists claim that the entire geological record, with its orderly succession of fossils, is the product of a single universal flood that lasted a little longer than a year and covered the highest mountains to a depth of some 7 meters a few thousand years ago, there is clear evidence in the form of intertidal and terrestrial deposits that at no recorded time in the past has the entire planet been under water. Moreover, a universal flood of sufficient magnitude to deposit the existing strata, which together are many scores of kilometers thick, would require a volume of water far greater than has ever existed on and in the earth, at least since the formation of the first known solid crust about 4 billion years ago. The belief that all this sediment with its fossils was deposited in an orderly sequence in a year's time defies all geological observations and physical principles concerning sedimentation rates and possible quantities of suspended solid matter. We do not doubt that there were periods of unusually high rainfall or that extensive flooding of inhabited areas has occurred, but there is no scientific support for the hypothesis of a universal, mountain-topping flood.

Inferences about common descent derived from paleontology have been reinforced by comparative anatomy. The skeletons of humans, dogs, whales, and bats are strikingly similar, despite the different ways of life led by these animals and the diversity of environments in which they have flourished. The correspondence, bone by bone, can be observed in every part of the body, including the limbs. Yet a person writes, a dog runs, a whale swims, and a bat flies—with structures built of the same bones.

Scientists call such structures homologous and have concurred that they are best explained by common descent. Comparative anatomists investigate such homologies, not only in bone structure but also in other parts of the body as well, working out relationships from degrees of similarity. Their conclusions provide important inferences about the details of evolutionary history that can be tested by comparisons with the sequence of ancestral forms in the paleontological record.

The mammalian ear and jaw offer another instance in which paleontology and comparative anatomy combine to show common ancestry through transitional stages. The lower jaws of mammals contain only one bone, whereas those of reptiles have several. The other bones in the reptile jaw are homologous with bones now found in the mammalian ear. What function could these bones have had during intermediate stages? Paleontologists have now discovered two intermediate forms of mammal-like reptiles *(Therapsida)* with a double jaw joint— one composed of the bones that persist in mammalian jaws, the other consisting of bones that eventually became the hammer and anvil of the mammalian ear. Similar examples are numerous. Some specific findings relating to human beings are described later in this chapter.

Biogeography also has contributed evidence for common descent. The diversity of life is stupendous. Approximately 250,000 species of living plants, 100,000 species of fungi, and perhaps 1.5 million additional species of animals and microorganisms have been described and named, each occupying its own peculiar ecological setting or niche, and the census is far from complete. Some species, such as human beings and our companion the dog, can live under a wide range of environmental conditions. Others are amazingly specialized. One species of the fungus *Laboulbenia* grows exclusively on the rear portion of the covering wings of a single species of beetle *(Aphaenops cronei)* found only in some caves of southern France. The larvae of the fly *Drosophila carcinophila* can develop only in specialized grooves beneath the flaps of the third pair of oral appendages of the land crab *Gecarcinus ruricola*, which is found only on certain Caribbean islands.

How can we make intelligible the colossal diversity of living beings and the existence of such extraordinary, seemingly whimsical creatures as *Laboulbenia*, *Drosophila carcinophila*, and others? Why are island groups like the Galapagos so often inhabited by forms similar to those on the nearest mainland but belonging to different species? Why is the indigenous life so different on different continents? Creationists contend that the curious facts of biogeography result from the occurrence of a special creationary event. A scientific hypothesis proposes that biological diversity results from an evolutionary process whereby the descendants of local or migrant predecessors became adapted to their diverse environments. A testable corollary of that hypothesis is that present forms and local fossils should show homologous attributes indicating how one is derived from the other. Also, there should be evidence that forms without an established local ancestry had migrated into the locality. Wherever such tests have been carried out, these conditions have been confirmed.

A good example is provided by the mammalian populations of North and South America, where strikingly different endemic forms evolved in isolation until the emergence of the Isthmus of Panama approximately 3 million years ago. Thereafter, the armadillo, porcupine, and opossum—mammals of South American origin—were able to migrate to North America along with many other species of plants and animals, while the placental mountain lion and other North American species made their way across the isthmus to the south.

The evidence that Darwin found for the influence of geographical distribution on the evolution of organisms has become stronger with advancing knowledge. For example, approximately 2,000 species of flies belonging to the genus *Drosophila* are now found throughout the world. About one-quarter of them live only in Hawaii. More than a thousand species of snails and other land mollusks are also found in Hawaii. The only natural explanation for the occurrence of such great diversity among closely similar forms is that the differences resulted from adaptive colonization of isolated environments by animals with a common ancestry. The Hawaiian islands are far from and were never attached to any mainland or other islands, and they have had few colonizers. Organisms that reached these islands found many unoccupied and relatively isolated ecological niches where they could then undergo separate evolutionary diversifications.

The vagaries of biogeography cannot be attributed to environmental peculiarities alone. The Hawaiian islands are no better than other Pacific islands for the survival of *Drosophila*, nor are they less hospitable than other parts of the world for many organisms not indigenous to them. For example, pigs and goats have multiplied in Hawaii after their introduction by humans. Thus, organisms are also absent from places well suited to their occupancy where potential ancestors were lacking.

Embryology, the study of biological development from the time of conception, is another source of independent evidence for common descent. Barnacles, for instance, are sedentary crustaceans with little apparent similarity to such other crustaceans as lobsters, shrimps, or copepoda. Yet barnacles pass through a free-swimming larval stage, in which they look unmistakably like other crustacean larvae. The similarity of larval stages supports the conclusion that all crustaceans have homologous parts and a common ancestry. Similarly, human and other mammalian embryos pass through a stage during which they have unmistakable but useless grooves similar to gill slits found in fishes—evidence that they and the other vertebrates shared remote ancestors that respired with the aid of gills.

Finally, the substantiation of common descent that emerges from all the foregoing lines of evidence is being validated and reinforced by the discoveries of modern biochemistry and molecular biology, as discussed in the following section.

Molecular Biology and the Degree of Relationship. Very recent studies in molecular biology have independently confirmed the judgments of paleontologists and classical biologists about relationships among lineages and the order in which species appeared within lineages. They have also provided detailed information about the mechanisms of biological evolution.

DNA (deoxyribonucleic acid), the hereditary material within all cells, and the proteins encoded by genes in the DNA both offer extensive information about the ancestry of organisms. Analysis of such information has made it possible to reconstruct evolutionary events that were previously unknown and to confirm and date events already surmised but not precisely dated. The precision whereby evolutionary events can be thus reconstructed is one reason why the evidence from molecular biology is so compelling.

In unveiling the universality of the chemical basis of heredity, molecular biology has profoundly affirmed common ancestry. In all organisms—bacteria, plants, and animals, including humans—the hereditary information is encoded in DNA, which is in all instances made up of the same four subunits called nucleotides. The genetic code by which the information contained in the nuclear DNA is used to form proteins is essentially the same in all organisms. Proteins in all organisms are invariably composed of the same 20 amino acids, all having a "left-handed" configuration, although there are amino acids in nature with both "right-" and "left-handed" configurations. The metabolic pathways through which the most diversified organisms produce energy and manufacture cell components are also essentially the same.

This unity reveals the genetic continuity of living organisms, thereby giving independent confirmation of descent from a common ancestry. There is no other way consistent with the laws of nature and probability to account for such uniformity. The genetic code may serve as an example. In general, each of the 64 possible sequences of three of the four nucleotides in the nuclear DNA has the same meaning in all organisms. The significance of this can be seen by comparing the genetic code to human languages. Many different languages have evolved, each using certain combinations of symbols and sounds to convey a specific meaning. If similar combinations of symbols and sounds are used to express the same meaning in different languages, we infer that the languages involved had a common source. The genetic code is a universal language, implying a single source.

Consider a comparison between two books of similar length. Let us say that closer examination reveals that the two books are identical page by page and word by word, except that an occasional word, say one in a hundred, is different. It is highly improbable that the two books were written independently: either one book was copied from the other or both were copied from a third source. Now, if each nucleotide in human DNA is represented by one letter, the complete sequence of nucleotides would require over a million pages. When the pages in the human genetic book are compared with those of diverse organisms, correspondence in the sequence of letters gives unmistakable evidence of common origin. Occasional changes provide information about particular species, just as all copies of a specific edition of a book can be identified by common changes.

Thus molecular biology validates the already impressive evidence that all living organisms, from bacteria to humans, are ultimately descended from common ancestors (Dobzhansky, Ayala, Stebbins, and Valentine, 1977). Since evolutionists of earlier times knew nothing about molecular biology, discoveries resulting from studies in this relatively new field of science provide independent and unanticipated reinforcement of their theories.

But the evidence for evolution from molecular biology goes further. The *degree* of similarity in the sequence of nucleotides in DNA (or of amino acids in proteins) can now be precisely quantified. For example, the protein cytochrome-*c* in humans and chimpanzees consists of the same 104 amino acids in exactly the same order, whereas that of rhesus monkeys differs from them by one amino acid, that of horses by 11 amino acids, and that of tuna by 21 amino acids. The extent of deviation corresponds to the time interval since fish, mammals, and human ancestors appeared in the geological record, i.e., the degree of divergence reflects the time that has passed since the respective lineages had a common ancestry. Thus, inferences from paleontology, comparative anatomy, and other disciplines as to the evolutionary history of organisms can be tested by examining the sequences of nucleotides in the DNA or the sequences of amino acids in protein. The potential power of such tests is overwhelming. Each of the thousands of genes and proteins provides an independent test of evolutionary history.

Only a few of the countless possible tests have been performed, of course. But of the many hundreds that have been conducted, none has provided evidence contrary to the concept of evolution. Instead, molecular biology confirms the idea of common descent in every aspect.

Evolution pervades all biological phenomena. To ignore that it occurred or to classify it as a form of dogma is to deprive the student of the most fundamental organizational concept in the biological sciences. No other biological concept has been more extensively tested and more thoroughly corroborated than the evolutionary history of organisms. The *mechanisms* by which evolution occurred, however, are not agreed upon in detail. They remain an area for continuing research, discussion, and discovery.

Mechanisms of Evolution. Students of evolutionary biology seek not only to reconstruct the evolutionary history of organisms but also to discover the specific mechanisms that account for evolutionary change. Research on this subject is currently so lively that we can include in this brief chapter only some well-tested and widely agreed upon generalities.

Darwin proposed that evolution could be explained by hereditary variation followed by natural selection. His original hypothesis has undergone extensive modification and expansion, but the central concepts stand firm. Mendelian genetics and molecular biology were unknown to Darwin, but studies in these fields have explained the occurrence of hereditary variations essential to Darwin's ideas. Genetic variations result from changes in DNA structure, whether by mutation, recombination, or some other yet incompletely understood mechanism. Such changes in DNA can now be physically observed and numerically quantified in many favorable circumstances (Ayala and Valentine, 1979).

There is still much to be learned from new experiments and observations. Meanwhile, biologists and paleontologists are debating the relative importance of the various mechanisms in order to devise questions that will produce the most meaningful inquiries into the methods and rates of evolution.

One point concerning mechanisms deserves emphasis. Mutations and other variations arise by chance. They do not necessarily equip the organism with better means for surviving in its environment. But if a gene variant improves adaptation (for example, by allowing an organism to make use of an available nutrient or to escape predators more effectively), the organisms carrying that gene are more likely to survive and reproduce than those without it. Thus, much as Darwin proposed, natural selection is the process that gives direction to evolution and makes it more than the product of chance. Natural selection accounts for the apparent design of organisms as well as their imperfections. Adaptations, whether expressed as simple metabolic reactions or as a complicated organ like the human eye, are considered by the overwhelming majority of biologists to be the result of natural selection. For this reason, the theory of natural selection is called upon to explain the observable evidence for biological evolution.

Human Evolution

Studies in evolutionary biology have led to the conclusion that mankind arose from ancestral primates. This association was hotly debated among scientists in Darwin's day, before molecular biology and the discovery of the now abundant connecting links. Today, however, there is no significant scientific doubt about the close evolutionary relationships among all primates or between apes and humans (Andrews and Cronin, 1982; Simons, 1980, 1981). The "missing links" that troubled Darwin and his followers are no longer missing. Today, not one but many such connecting links, intermediate between various branches of the primate family tree, have been found as fossils. These linking fossils are intermediate in form and occur in geological deposits of intermediate age. They thus document the time and rate at which primate and human evolution occurred.

The possibility of error in determining ages has been reduced by new methods based on measurements of reversals in the earth's magnetic field in ancient rocks. Furthermore, fossils continue to be found with great frequency. The combination of information from stratigraphy, fossils, and dating techniques and findings from studies in molecular biology has enabled scientists to develop the following scheme of human evolution:

The human line separated from that of the apes approximately 5 million years ago. About 4 million years ago, our ancestors were already bipedal but had brains no larger than those of the contemporary apes. Within 2 million years after that, these small-brained bipeds were making stone tools. In the next half million years, the brain doubled in size and the stone tools became much more complex. Change was very slow until people anatomically similar to ourselves had evolved. Then in a few thousand years, humans reached Australia, the Arctic, and the New World. Tools were improved, and boats, bows, and sleds were invented. This revolution was accompanied by the development of agriculture and shortly thereafter, from an evolutionary point of view, the complex social and industrial world we know today.

From the time of our earliest ancestors onward, there were successive and regular increases in average brain volume and body size, coupled in later stages with a progressive reduction in the thickness of the brain case, the protrusion of brow ridges, and the size of the cheek teeth. These changes occurred through a succession of well-documented intermediate forms or species. Finally, approximately 50,000 years ago, Homo sapiens—the oldest human being of morphologically modern character—appeared. This appearance of fully developed modern man close to 50,000 years ago is of course inconsistent with the creationist view that the earth is perhaps only 10,000 years old or less.

These conclusions from comparative anatomy, stratigraphy, dating techniques, and paleoanthropology are backed up by findings from studies in molecular biology. A 99 percent similarity is found between the DNA of human beings and the DNA of chimpanzees. Such studies link humans, the chimpanzee, and the gorilla in the same biological family.

The Origin of Life

Scientific research on the origin of life is in an exploratory phase, and all its conclusions are tentative. We know that the organisms that lived on the earth

2 billion or more years ago were simple microbial forms. There is even some evidence that life might already have existed when the first known solid crust formed on earth, almost 4 billion years ago. The geological record indicates that liquid water, other chemicals, and a suitable atmosphere for prebiotic chemical activity were present on earth more than 3.8 billion years ago. Earliest life was unicellular or noncellular, existed in the absence of oxygen, and may have been incapable of producing its own nutrients from solar or chemical energy. Experimental results and astronomical observations are consistent with the idea that the steps required to link and set into operation the essential components of a living cell could have occurred under conditions prevailing on the primitive earth. They could not occur now because of the destructive effects of today's abundant molecular oxygen, not only on simple unprotected living systems but also on the intermediate products that might have generated the component molecules of such systems.

Experiments conducted under plausible primitive-earth conditions have resulted in the production of amino acids, large protein-like molecules made from long chains of amino acids, the nucleotide components of DNA, and DNA-like chains of these nucleotides. Many biologically interesting molecules have also been detected by astronomers using radio-telescopes. We can, therefore, explain how the early oxygen-free earth provided a hospitable site for the accumulation of molecules suitable for the construction of living systems. Such molecules could have been formed as a result of chemical reactions on the earth's surface, or they could have arrived in carbonaceous meteorites. Perhaps both sources are responsible for their presence.

Once the starting materials such as amino acids and nucleotides have been formed, larger molecules can then be made experimentally by removing water through a process called dehydration condensation. Amino acids join to form proteins, and nucleotides join to form nucleic acids. Even DNA molecules have been synthesized from purified components taken from the laboratory shelf.

For those who are studying aspects of the origin of life, the question no longer seems to be whether life could have originated by chemical processes involving nonbiological components but rather what pathway might have been followed. The data accumulated thus far imply selective processes. Prebiological chemical evolution is seen as a trial-and-error process leading to the success of one or more systems built from the many possible chemical components. The system that evolved with the capability of self-replication and mutation led to what we now define as a living system.

Will we ever be able to identify the path of chemical evolution that succeeded in initiating life as we know it? This question may be unanswerable. Even if a living cell were to be made in the laboratory, that event would not prove that nature followed the same pathway billions of years ago. Still, the history of science shows that seemingly intractable problems may become amenable to solution as a result of advances in theory or instrumentation or the fortuitous discovery of new facts.

Conclusion

Scientists, like many others, are awestruck at the order and complexity of nature. Religion provides one way for human beings to be comfortable with these marvels. However, the goal of science is to seek natural explanations for phenomena—and the origins of life, the earth, and the universe are, to scientists, such phenomena—within the framework of natural laws and principles and the operational rule of testability.

It is, therefore, our unequivocal conclusion that creationism, with its accounts of the origin of life by supernatural means, is not science. It subordinates evidence to statements based on authority and revelation. Its documentation is almost entirely limited to the special publications of its advocates. And its central hypothesis is not subject to change in light of new data or demonstration of error. Moreover, when the evidence for creationism has been subjected to the tests of the scientific method, it has been found invalid.

No body of beliefs that has its origin in doctrinal material rather than scientific observation should be admissible as science in any science course. Incorporating the teaching of such doctrines into a science curriculum stifles the development of critical thinking patterns in the developing mind and seriously compromises the best interests of public education. This could eventually hamper the advancement of science and technology as students take their places as leaders of future generations.

References

Andrews, P., and Cronin, J. E. (1982). "The relationships of *Sivapithecus* and *Ramapithecus* and the evolution of the orangutan." *Nature, 297,* 541–546.

Ayala, F. J., and Valentine, J. W. (1979). *Evolving: The theory and processes of organic evolution.* Redwood City, Calif.: Benjamin-Cummings.

Darwin, C. (1859). *On the origin of species by means of natural selection, or the preservation of favored races in the struggle for life.* (1st ed.). London, England: Murray. (Facsimile of the first edition published by Harvard University Press, Cambridge, Mass., 1964.)

Dobzhansky, T., Ayala, F. J., Stebbins, G. L., and Valentine, J. W. (1977). *Evolution.* New York: Freeman.

Geikie, A. (1897). *The founders of geology.* New York: Macmillan.

Hubble, E. P. (1929). "A relation between distance and radial velocity among extra-galactic nebulae." *Proceedings of the National Academy of Sciences, 15,* 168–173.

Hubble, E. P., and Humason, M. L. (1931). "The velocity-distance relation among extra-galactic nebulae." *Astrophysics Journal, 74,* 43–80.

Lamarck, J. B., de (1802). *Recherches sur l'organisation des corps vivants et particulièrement sur son origine, sur la cause de son développement et des progrès de sa composition. Précédé du discours d'ouverture du cours de zoölogie donné dans le Musée d'Histoire Naturelle, l'an X de la République* [Research on the organization of living beings, particularly on its origin, the reason for its development, and the evolution of its structure. Preceded by a discourse on the opening up of the zoology course given at the Museum of Natural History, Year 10 of the Republic]. Paris: de Lamarck.

Lamarck, J. B., de (1809). *Philosophie zoölogique, ou exposition des considérations relative à l'histoire naturelle des animaux* [Zoological philosophy, or exposition of reflections on the natural history of the animals]. Paris: Dentu. (Reprinted in 1960 by Lubrecht and Cramer, Monticello, N.Y.)

Morris, J. D. (1980). *Tracking those incredible dinosaurs and the people who knew them.* San Diego, Calif.: CLP Publishers.

Oxford English Dictionary (1933). Oxford: Clarendon Press.

Penzias, A. A., and Wilson, R. W. (1965). "A measurement of excess antenna temperature at 4080 Mc/s." *Astrophysics Journal, 142*(1), 419–421.

Renckens, H. (1964). *Israel's concept of the beginning: The theory of Genesis 1–3* (C. Napier, trans.). New York: Herder & Herder.

Simons, E. L. (1980). "Man's immediate forerunners." *Proceedings of the Royal Society of London, Series B, 292,* 21–42.

Simons, E. L. (1981). "Origins of genus *Homo* from *Australopithecus* and from *Ramapithecus* or from an unknown form." In *Les processus de l'hominisation* [The course of human development]. (Colloques Internationaux du Centre National de la Recherche Scientifique [International Symposiums of the National Center for Scientific Research], no. 599). Paris: Editions du Centre National de la Recherche Scientifique.

Tasch, P. (1950). "Darwin and the forgotten Mr. Lonsdale." *Geology Magazine, 87,* 292–296.

Weinberg, S. (1977). *The first three minutes: A modern view of the origin of the universe.* New York: Basic Books.

CHAPTER FOURTEEN

SOMETHING OLD, SOMETHING NEW: WHAT DO SOCIAL STUDIES TEACHERS NEED TO KNOW?

SUZANNE M. WILSON AND G. WILLIAMSON MCDIARMID

In some ways, the charge for this chapter is a simple one: address the question, What do teacher educators have to know in order to teach social studies? But where to look? There's no empirical basis for answering the question. Researchers haven't gone out, found themselves some good social studies educators, and examined how they work. Surveys haven't been conducted about the content and pedagogy of social studies teacher education. Maybe that's what we should have done.

But we didn't. Maybe we're lazy or didn't have the time. Maybe our excuse is that the field is in transition. Calls for reform come from many corners: the Project 30 Alliance and the Holmes Group call for the integration of pedagogical content knowledge into teacher education even as researchers struggle to delineate the concept (Holmes Group, 1986; Project 30 Alliance, 1991). The National Board for Professional Teaching Standards is developing standards for teacher professional knowledge across all grade levels. Meanwhile, state curricular frameworks (see, for example, California State Department of Education, 1987; Kentucky Department of Education, 1993), as well as statements from the National Council of the Social Studies (NCSS) (Curriculum Task Force, 1989) and the National Standards Project are calling for the reorganization and enrichment of the K–12 curriculum.[1]

In the midst of this cacophonous call for change, studying the status quo in an attempt to answer our question seems insufficient. Social studies teacher educators need to know a lot: how to teach prospective and practicing teachers about social studies content and pedagogy, how teachers learn, what teachers need to know in order to teach well, and what the latest calls are for the reform of curriculum, pedagogy, and assessment. They also need to know how to face the unknown, helping new teachers invent new pedagogies. Perhaps most important, teacher educators need to know how to reinvent themselves, for as we ask teachers to re-create their curriculum—to teach in innovative ways, to assess with alternative means, to convey a different content—teacher educators must re-create their content, assessment, and pedagogy as well. Thus, some of what we need to know is old, some very new.[2]

So the charge for the chapter becomes more complicated: What do teacher educators need to know in order to change their own teaching and help others learn to teach in new ways? Alternatively, we might ask, How can teacher educators act responsibly and responsively in the face of multiple calls to reform? Although we have done research on teaching, we have yet to research the knowledge base of teacher education. Yet as practicing teacher educators, we have struggled with these questions. In this chapter, we propose to examine our practice, using those reflections to examine the questions we have raised.

Tales from the Field

While some researchers have investigated what teachers ought to know, no one to our knowledge has considered the question of what teacher educators ought to know.[3] Considering the question feels like walking into a hall of mirrors. We've done some thinking about what history and social studies *teachers* need to know; so have others. What are the implications, then, for what *teacher educators* need to know? Do they too need to know about subject matter, context, pedagogy, learners? Do they need to know anything else? For example, do they need to know things about how teachers learn? How about adults? Is there, in fact, a pedagogical content knowledge of social studies teacher educators?

Another set of issues relates to the fact that social studies teacher educators do not act in isolation, for they are members of communities of teacher educators who participate in programs of teacher education. So we might also ask other questions: What kinds of things do social studies teacher educators have to know to plan programs of teacher education? What do they have to know about teacher education and learning generally? In what ways might they coordinate the work that they do with other teacher educators or liberal arts faculty?

We can't begin to address all of these questions here, in part because the research hasn't been done. Yet we've thought about these issues as teacher educators: we've read a lot as we prepare to teach teachers, we've tried a number of things, and we've reflected on our experiences. We propose, then, to anchor our chapter in descriptions of two courses that we have designed. In the first story (told by Bill McDiarmid), we lay out the research and scholarship that informs our work. In the second story (told by Suzanne Wilson), we weave in our students' insights into their own experiences learning to teach. We do not offer these descriptions as answers to the question "What should social studies teacher educators do?" for we do not believe that there is one right way to prepare social studies teachers. Rather, we use these concrete instances to generate a set of hypotheses for what teacher educators, ourselves included, might need to know. We conclude with a call for a collective investigation of these hypotheses, a documentation and critical examination of the understandings necessary to teach teachers well.

Reinventing a Preservice Methods Course

During the 1993–94 academic year, I (G.W.D.) collaborated with a colleague in teacher education and another in history in creating a senior-level course to introduce prospective secondary teachers to the teaching of history and social studies (McDiarmid, Thornburg, and Vinten-Johansen, forthcoming).[4] We developed the course as part of a newly created five-year teacher education program at Michigan State University. Prior to the senior-level course, the prospective teachers took three teacher education courses. The first focused on the learning of diverse students, the second on schools as social organizations, and the third on teaching as it is influenced by social, political, and philosophical forces. The teaching and learning of subject matter knowledge is the focus of the senior-level course. Elementary and secondary teachers attend separate sections and subsequently serve a yearlong internship.

In designing this course, we made several assumptions about the preservice teachers' prior experiences. First, we assumed that they rarely have the opportunity to delve deeply into any subject or to develop a connected understanding of the subject matter (Cuban, 1991; McDiarmid, 1994). They tend to take a collection of largely introductory courses in the various social sciences and history and a set of courses in their major. Providing prospective teachers opportunities to understand historical events, ideas, and methods in depth and to experience connected knowledge seems critical. Without experiencing such learning and knowing themselves, future teachers are unlikely to do the same for their own students.

Second, we assumed that most will teach history and government and relatively few will teach social sciences such as economics, sociology, anthropology, or political science. This is not to say that prospective teachers should ignore these subjects. Rather, they need to understand how they can draw on the perspectives of various social science disciplines. Therefore, they need to study historical problems that lend themselves to such examination.

Third, we assumed that prospective history and social studies teachers have, as high school and university students, experienced few modes of teaching (Cuban, 1991; Goodlad, 1984; Lortie, 1975; McDiarmid, 1992; McNeil, 1986). Usually, these modes are variations on the theme of the lecture. Occasionally, students will have been involved in debates or simulations, particularly at the elementary level (Stodolsky, 1988). If we are to help prospective teachers expand their ideas of teaching, we assumed that they need to experience the full range of pedagogical alternatives.

We also assumed that prospective history and social studies teachers have experienced few views of what history is (Evans, 1988, 1989, 1990; Wilson and Wineburg, 1988). For most, history is information about the past, typically limited to political events and actors. If they are to develop competing views of the nature of history—history as a debate, as a sociohistorical construct, as a mirror that reflects contemporary preoccupations—they must encounter such views. We also assumed they would equate learning history with remembering information.

Yet if we are to help them develop other ideas about learning—that learning may involve reading critically, questioning evidence, considering context—they need learning opportunities that involve more than cramming or memorization. They need to assess competing accounts, examine artifacts and primary sources, develop and support written arguments.

In addition to these assumptions about our students, we made another set of assumptions about reform-oriented history teaching and its demands on teachers. We assumed that teachers need to know about key historical events and actors. Such knowledge informs their purposes and curricular decisions. While necessary, this knowledge is not sufficient. Teachers also need to understand how knowledge is created, challenged, revised, and tested. Such understanding is vital if teachers are to help their students see that knowledge is a human construct. A related assumption is that as future teachers, our students need to understand the degree to which their perspectives and ideas have been shaped by their own histories. This is particularly pertinent to their understanding of their views of others who are different from themselves—ethnically, socially, racially, and culturally.

We further assumed that teachers need to be able to hear their students. That is, they need both to take their students' ideas seriously and to be able to place those ideas in the field. For instance, many students operate on the assumption that history is cyclical, that what has happened in the past will happen in the future. Knowing that this idea is largely discredited in the historical community and knowing that students may regard one war or revolution as pretty much like all the others helps teachers raise issues that question that belief. This is related to another assumption: teachers need to know how students make sense of historical accounts. This includes the considerable body of research that has been done on how students of different ages make sense of historical accounts and documents.[5]

Teachers also need to know about pedagogical and curricular traditions in history and the social studies (for example, Cuban, 1991; Dow, 1991; Jenness, 1990; Parker, forthcoming; Ravitch, 1985; Shaver, Davis, and Helburn, 1980; Thornton, 1992). Information about current and past attempts to revise the social studies curriculum and pedagogy constitutes a reservoir of ideas and cautionary tales on which prospective teachers can draw. Teachers need to know ways of engaging students in learning history and the social studies other than conventional approaches.[6] Although reading textbooks might help some students learn about the past, such conventional approaches are unlikely to help many students develop the inquiring capacities called for by reformers. Students need to take textbook accounts apart, as it were, to understand how they were made and therefore what has been left out, obscured, or misrepresented.

Finally, we assumed that teachers need to know how to help students read critically and craft arguments in writing that draw on varied sources of evidence. This requires both knowledge and skill in the teaching of reading and writing as well as knowledge about what is unique in historical reading and writing (see Wineburg, 1991a, 1991b).

Based on these assumptions, our course contained the following components:

1. In-depth examinations of four critical events in U.S. history that included writing analytical essays about each event
2. Analysis of "cases" of teaching history and the social studies
3. Analysis of key documents in the movement to reform history and social studies teaching
4. Writing case studies of students in secondary history and social studies classes
5. Development of a curriculum
6. Observation of, participation in, and writing about secondary history and social studies classrooms

Examinations of critical historical events. The topics we chose were the frontier, the Constitution and the development of a democratic polity, Reconstruction, and the modern civil rights movement. Each met the following criteria: they (1) offered numerous connections with both antecedent and subsequent events, (2) posed genuine problems, (3) involved a broad spectrum of cultures and people, not merely those prominent in the conventional political accounts of the past, and (4) were clearly interconnected thematically. They also constituted a chronological sequence. (For more details on our rationale for these events, see McDiarmid, Thornburg, and Vinten-Johansen, forthcoming.)

Case analysis. Lee and Judy Shulman, among others, have enumerated the value of cases in teacher education (Shulman, 1992; Shulman, 1986, 1987). Recently, a number of case studies of history and social studies teachers have become available. Wilson (forthcoming) relates the unfolding, in her third-grade classroom, of a unit on choosing a site for the Michigan capital. Brophy (1990) portrays an exemplary fifth-grade teacher teaching a unit on the English colonies. Hasbach and her colleagues (Hasbach, Roth, Hoekwater, and Rosaen, 1993) describe their attempt to involve fifth graders in "powerful" social studies. Wineburg and Wilson (1988) present two contrasting cases of high school history teachers. Wineburg (1993) presents the dilemma created by high school students who reach a moral conclusion about the Vietnam War. Holt (1990) describes high school and college students responding to primary documents from the Reconstruction era. McDiarmid (forthcoming) describes an undergraduate historiography seminar. Wilson and Wineburg (1993) present another pair of contrasting cases in which the teachers hold different beliefs about subject matter and students. Beyond presenting diverse instructional approaches, these cases provide context for thinking, writing, and talking about the considerations of learners, context, and curriculum.

Reform document analyses. Recently, a number of documents have appeared urging reform of the historical/social studies curriculum and, to a lesser degree, reform of the teaching of these subjects (see, for example, California State Department of Education, 1987; Gagnon and the Bradley Commission on History in Schools, 1989; Curriculum Task Force, 1989). More documents continue to emerge as states move toward the adoption of frameworks and standards. That prospective teachers should be familiar with these documents seems self-evident. But these documents also offer potent opportunities to learn more about teaching, learning, and educational policy. Just as students interrogate textbooks, they also interrogated these reform documents: Who wrote it? Why? Who is the audience? What views of the role of schools are evident? What views of knowledge and knowing? What views of teaching and learning? What about learners, particularly historically underserved students?

In addition to current reform documents, students also examined a past attempt at reform, Man: A Course of Study (MACOS) (Dow, 1991), with the intent of understanding the ideas behind such a curriculum. MACOS was a curriculum based both on Piagetian ideas and on the conviction that social science methods are as critical for students to learn as propositions are. The MACOS case is also instructive because its failure to flourish may have less to do with the underlying ideas than with its champions' political missteps.

Case writing. During the first semester, the prospective teachers observed and interviewed two high school students. We asked them to select students who differed from them in such areas as ethnicity, social class, or school achievement. We wanted the prospective teachers to see the school subjects through students' eyes, particularly students different from themselves. This is part of a larger goal: to have students develop into teachers who know how to consider their students' perspectives when making pedagogical decisions. Learning things about one's learners is a significant task of teaching. Current research is beginning to document the ways that children understand and interpret historical and social science concepts.[7]

Curriculum development. In addition, we asked the prospective teachers to develop a teachable "unit" around a topic of their choosing. The emphasis of the project was on the process of inquiry in which they engaged to prepare the unit. We wanted the future teachers to understand the relationship between their own subject matter understanding and their capacity to help others learn. We also wanted them to consider how they might go about finding out what their students know—both during the unit and at the end—and the uncertainty inherent in such processes.

Observations in the field. In addition to four hours in class on campus each week, the prospective teachers spent a minimum of four hours weekly in the field. Besides keeping observational logs, they had specific assignments to focus their attention. Although we encouraged the collaborating teachers to include the prospective teachers in classroom activities, we did not require this. We did not conceive of this as an opportunity for the prospective teachers to learn to teach by observation or to practice pedagogical moves. Rather, we structured the experience as another avenue to examine the subject matter, the curriculum, and teaching and learning.

This brief description of the course does it an injustice, for the components were then woven together through class discussions and activities. However, we hope to have provided an overview of our strategies for helping prospective teachers simultaneously learn about history, teaching, learning, learners, curriculum, and schools. We offer this description tentatively, for we have taught the class only once and now have many ideas about how to refine its components and structure. We now turn to another course—one designed for practicing social studies teachers—in a very different context.

Reading, Doing, and Living History

The work I (S.M.W.) describe took place during July 1992. For four weeks, I was assigned to teach a social studies methods course for experienced elementary, middle, and secondary school teachers from international schools. The course was offered in the southeast corner of France, just outside Provence, not too far from Nice.

I hadn't taught a social studies methods course for quite some time, not since I had done a substantial amount of research on the role of subject matter knowledge and pedagogical content knowledge in teaching and teachers' decisions. I had also read much of the same literature my coauthor cited in his description. Taking that work to heart, I wanted to experiment with ways to provide teachers with opportunities to learn simultaneously about subject matter, teaching, and learning history. I hoped that this enterprise might help me clarify some of my ideas about subject matter knowledge and pedagogical content knowledge in social studies.

I chose history as the focus of the course, for it is the area within social studies in which I feel most confident. As I thought through this course, I carried with me the same kinds of assumptions and beliefs that Bill McDiarmid and his colleagues had about teachers and their experiences. I assumed, for example, that it helps teacher educators teach if they themselves know the subject matter. I made other assumptions as well. I assumed that in methods courses, *pedagogy* is the content. That is, the substantive focus of the course was on how to teach (and learn) social studies. For me, this means that my students might learn both from what I do as their teacher and from the ideas that we examine. I assumed that teachers are being asked to teach in ways that they themselves have not experienced and that this works as an impediment in their capacity to teach in such a way.[8] These two assumptions caused me to think about how to weave together my own teaching and the students' learning as strands of the content of the course.

I made other assumptions as well. I assumed that my students might learn history both through the doing of history (posing questions, collecting evidence, interpreting artifacts) and through the reading of history. I assumed that history is multidimensional and interpretive. I assumed that history is significant in part because it provides context for understanding our political, social, economic, and intellectual surroundings. As I began to think through what the course might entail, my mind was awhirl with different assumptions and commitments (see Figure 14.1).

I decided to structure the course around three interwoven tasks. The first task involved doing a local history. By choosing their own topics and exploring them on their own, students would, I hoped, gain insights into history from the inside out. What serendipitous events, accidents of fate, affect the shape of the history one writes? What kinds of assumptions about human action and behavior do historians make as they put together the pieces of their respective puzzles? How does it feel to infer what happened from the incomplete traces left of the past? How are inquiries limited by what we know, who we are, what resources we have available? As students struggled to write histories about local towns or sites, they encountered each of these questions. They also saw directly how their histories were shaped by their assumptions, interests, concerns, capacities.

A second task consisted of reading histories. Because I was interested in helping students see that there are multiple interpretations of the past and because we were in France in July, I structured this task like a book club (I was also hoping that the fact that we were going to be together on Bastille Day might be advantageous). Students paired off; each pair read a different account of the French Revolution, meeting weekly to discuss the different interpretations. These discussions allowed us to explore other questions related to history: Why do these accounts differ? How do the interests of these historians affect what they choose to see in the past? Why does Schama's account differ from the "official" Oxford account? What do feminist historians see that economic historians do not? How are we as readers persuaded or not by the arguments set forth by these historians?

A third task involved reading educational research and tying it to our own experiences as teachers and learners. I gathered together research reports about history teaching and learning that were related to the kinds of experiences that I was crafting for students in the other tasks. So, for example, we read Wineburg's analysis (1991b) of how differently students and historians read texts. We then tried to examine our own reading in light of that analysis, as well as our observations concerning how elementary and secondary school students read. Similarly, we read McDiarmid's forthcoming account of a university historiography seminar and examined the issues he raises in light of our own attempts to write and read histories. I described the course as shown in Exhibit 14.1.

FIGURE 14.1. SUZANNE'S WORRIES AND COMMITMENTS.

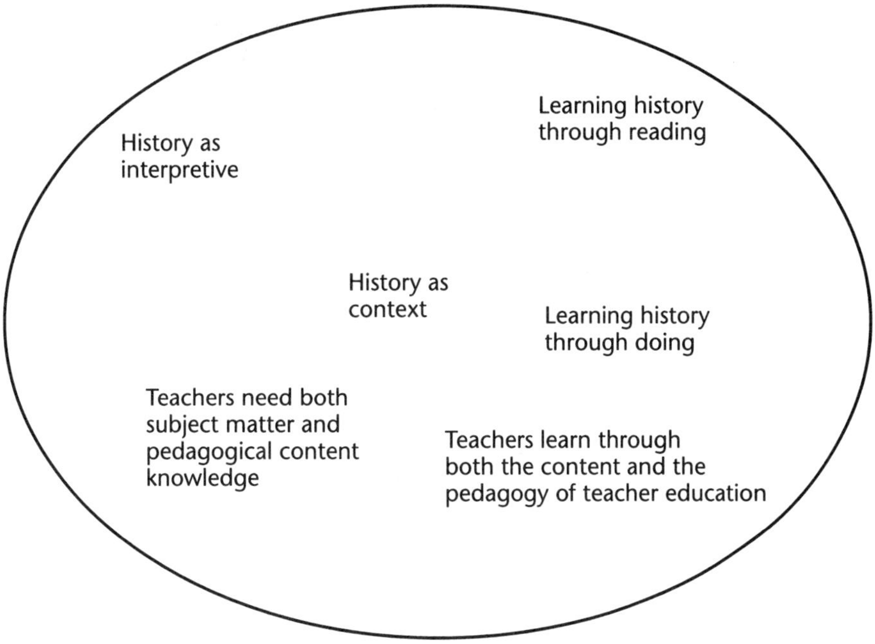

History as
interpretive

Learning history
through reading

History as
context

Learning history
through doing

Teachers need both
subject matter and
pedagogical content
knowledge

Teachers learn through
both the content and the
pedagogy of teacher education

By designing the course as I did, I hoped that teachers might find ways to learn simultaneously about how students learn history, what history is, and how to teach history. I hypothesized that there were multiple sites for such learning, including watching me teach, reflecting on their own experiences as learners, and educational scholarship. Given my previous experience as a teacher educator, I knew that my students would learn as much from what I (and we) did as they would from what we read, and I wanted to take advantage of that.

I neither want to claim that the class was a smashing success nor that I did all this perfectly, but I learned a lot about the promise of such courses designed to weave together questions about subject matter, teaching, and learning. Rather than delineate all of the lessons I learned, I'll focus on a few.

Even teachers who feel they know the subject matter well can learn a lot about content. Several students were initially bothered that the course focused on the French Revolution. As one student observed in the course evaluation, "I wish the subject had not been the French Revolution. Almost all European historians study it. But . . . ," he then noted, "I was surprised at how much I learned. Most of all, I learned that no subject in history is 'done.'" According to his self-report, much of what he learned involved the development of a "more complete picture" through the readings and discussions of the book club. Consider one of Andy's journal entries:

EXHIBIT 14.1. FIRST PAGE OF SUZANNE'S SYLLABUS.

Recent thinking in research on teaching, learning, and teacher learning suggests that content and pedagogy are intimately connected. That is, the ways in which one teaches fundamentally shapes what students learn. In this class, we will explore this connection in several ways. First, we will examine a set of cases of teaching, and consider what students are learning about history and social studies in those cases. Second, we will become learners of history through two different sets of activities: by reading histories and by writing a local history. We will then use those experiences as learners to think about both what it means to know history, and what kinds of teaching best enhance the development of historical understanding.

There are, then, several strands that run throughout the course, and our work will be designed to explore those themes.

Strand 1: What does it mean to understand history? While the social studies include many different disciplines—only one of which is history—we will use history as a strategic example in our discussions of knowledge and knowing, learning and teaching. As we consider this theme, we will pursue questions like: What is the role of fact is history? Of interpretation? Is there truth in history? What uses or applications are to be made of history? How is history related to the lives of ordinary people? What role does history serve? What does it take to do history?

Strand 2: What does it mean to learn history? As teachers, we are constantly making assumptions about what and how students learn. Questions that we might want to consider in the course of pursuing this question include: What aspects of history require require different types of learning? Are there aspects of history as a subject matter that make it a particularly complicated thing to teach? Are there predictable naïve conceptions that students hold that either facilitate or impede their learning of history? What can we learn about learning history from observing our own experiences as learners?

An important subset of questions here involves considering what it takes to read history. History, like every discipline, has characteristic modes of argument, explanation, and rhetoric. What kinds of skills do readers need in order to critically read and consume histories?

Strand 3: What does it take to teach history for deep and complex understandings? A major portion of the intellectual work of teaching involves considering what you want students to learn, how it is that students learn, what materials you have available to you. Drawing on all of this knowledge and more, teachers then decide how best to teach something. In this part of our work, we will consider questions like: Are there any implications for the myriad ways in which one can understand history for an equally wide array of ways in which one might learn about history? What can we learn about teaching history from our own experiences as learners? Are there some ways of teaching history that facilitate the development of particular kinds of historical knowing?

Course Organization. The three strands are difficult to disentangle, for they are interwoven and interconnected. Rather than address these questions in some linear fashion, one at a time, we will approach them by engaging in a set of interrelated tasks that are designed to shed light on each of the three strands in various ways.

1. We will read and discuss a small set of histories about the French Revolution.
2. In three small groups, we will each write a small local history.
3. We will read a series of cases about history teaching.

One of the many outlooks on the teaching of history gained from the book club discussions was that of teaching/learning by comparison. Once the first book had been "reviewed," I noticed that each group constantly made points by referring to the other texts. This building up of a more complete picture I found very helpful. Perhaps in dealing with very young students we do not do enough of this. "Now what does Harold have to say? Is that different from Jones's picture?" [These] are the kinds of comparative references I realize I should do more of. . . . I was grateful that each book club group recounted what they as readers got from the text, not just what the author wrote. I learned more from looking at other people's views on history than simply thinking about my own. Les trusted "events," Jeffrey wanted more follow-up on eyewitness accounts, Keith and Pat sympathized with Socialist movements, and so on. My eyes were opened!

Teachers can learn things about teaching, learning, and subject matter simultaneously. Andy's comment was typical of teachers' musings in journals. Sometimes they would start writing about the subject matter, then move into an observation about themselves as learners or about implications for teaching, and then go back to the subject matter. At other times, they would start with observations about learning, move to discussions about the nature of history, and then go back to implications for teaching. Teaching, learning, history, and epistemology were all interwoven strands in our thinking and discussions. As one teacher observed, "I couldn't really separate myself as a learner or a teacher, so throughout all our activities and readings, I constantly thought of applications in my own teaching." In the past, we have separated subject matter from discussions of teaching and learning, perhaps because it is cleaner that way. Yet it might make more sense to keep them integrated but take care to look at their interrelationships. Consider Pat, a woman who not only knew a lot about the French Revolution but also knew French:

I came into this class not expecting to learn any history but rather to learn *about* history. I've done both and in doing so have learned about myself as a learner. Of course, I always thought I knew how I learned, but I now know something new about my acquisition of knowledge. I learned about the "power" that one feels coming to a subject one knows something about. It is always more comfortable to find oneself in the position of expert. Here I felt doubly empowered as I could also speak the language. However, what got to interest me most was how empowerment works in the individual. At first I wanted to be terribly pedantic and tell everyone what I knew about the French Revolution—been there, done that, so to speak! My pedestal started to shake, however, when I began learning new things, when I got into the realms of not knowing. Our discussion group has been very useful for that. I've had to negotiate. I learned other perspectives. Of course, I was aware that historians write from different perspectives, but I had never thought about what those viewpoints might be and how they can really begin to color your view.

Reading history and doing history contributed equally to teachers' ideas about history teaching and learning. Historians learn in two ways: they read and they write. Learning to "do history," then, means both learning something about how one reads histories and how one constructs them. During the book club discussions, we spoke often of how we were reading, and I used Wineburg's work (1991a, 1991b) to help students think about how they interacted with texts. It was new for students to consider their posture as readers. As Keith explained:

> At the outset of this course, I had never really thought of myself as a reader of history. "Blindly" reading texts on historical events has always been interesting to me, but I feel that I followed the idea and perspective of the writer in a literal sense. I saw history through the eyes of the writer and believed the factual information with no contestation. This way of reading, of course, might have been the result of the way that I was taught. I have learned in this course to approach history in a different way. Although I still read very much as an enthusiastic believer, I now understand some things about the understanding of history and its consequent learning. . . . The historian has his reasons for claiming the truth in certain events, but the reader may not see them as such. Does the reader believe the author and what he states as facts?
>
> What the reader believes depends on many factors which can influence his reaction to the text. One factor that matters is human behavior. Any event in history is dictated by human behavior and the readers' ideas of how and why humans behave as they do. We can never take facts as truisms, nor can we predict human actions.
>
> This discussion of reading has occurred to me as I reread your comments in my journal about Schama. You asked if I was prepared to accept his word as fact. This is not as easy as it once was!
>
> This argument can, of course, be transferred to teaching. Who is to contest what I taught the other day about Tourette? Are my facts correct? Did the Duke have the boy whipped? Did the village move to avoid the plague? Did the man commit suicide? This approach to reading history is novel to me, but its impact has been very deep. Facts are interesting but not always true from everyone's point of view.

Teachers' own experiences as learners can shed much light on their thinking as educators. As Keith's comments demonstrate, examining their own learning served as a powerful source of insight for my students in recognizing their own assumptions. Sometimes these insights were small, details to store for future work, like Andy's remark:

> During our exploratory trip to the French village, I learned a lot about the process of research in connection with trust. I asked a local shop-owner the

meaning of a sign. To my surprise, she didn't know! I asked two others and they gave me two different answers. I put myself in the shoes of my students. (1) Which do I believe? (trust) (2) Which is correct? (if any) (3) Is there something "truthful" in both answers?

It occurred to me that I had chosen to ask three people. Students might have only asked one. It began to occur to me that I need to teach my students the *nature* of the *job* of research.

Other insights revealed teachers who were struggling with their fundamental assumptions about teaching. Pat, for example, mused about her use of small groups and her "flexibility":

I learned to negotiate in the local history study. I use quite a few cooperative learning techniques in my own teaching, and here I have had experience from the other end. I know this does not have to do with history, but I feel it is nevertheless relevant because it has something to do with relinquishing deeply ingrained learning styles. I do not like "group learning." I am much happier doing my own research, probably because of the way I was taught—with an "expert" and isolated learner lapping up the information. I do not want to be bothered with dealing with the social dynamics of a group in addition to acquiring knowledge. I wonder what hidden agenda I have had with my own students when I personally like to learn alone but force them to do a lot of group work. I ended up liking our group work in this class, though, and that fact might change my subconscious messages. It is difficult to give up preconceptions of what you think you know, should know, and how you acquire that knowledge.

From a teaching point of view, this leads me to believe that I am determined to make several adjustments. I thought I was pretty flexible in my teaching approach. I provided as many texts as possible—textbooks, trade books, magazine articles, filmstrips, videos—but I had very precise aims: my own interpretation of specific historical evidence. This leads me to the thought that providing diverse data is all very well and good, but you must be prepared to go with the students' interpretations of the data to build a communal picture. I was, in fact, the opposite of flexible.

As you can see, the teachers' thinking about their assumptions about teaching, history, learning, role, and responsibility were tangled up in their experiences and reflections. It is difficult to sort out what they were learning and whether those were appropriate lessons. Perhaps that is why we tend, as teacher educators, to keep things clean and neat: teach methods or foundations or subject matter—apart. Don't mix them up. It's too much of a tangle. But teaching is a web of subject matter, learning, and teaching, a dynamic of Hawkins's "I, Thou, and It"

([1967] 1974). Perhaps one of the most important things that the students in this class came to understand was the existence of that dynamic and the importance of examining one's actions and assumptions from multiple perspectives.

What Might Social Studies Teacher Educators Need to Know?

So what do these stories suggest about what teacher educators need to know? The simple answer is that they need to know a lot. They need to know everything that social studies teachers need to know and more. If teachers need to know the subject matter and how kids learn about the subject matter, teacher educators need to know those things and also how to help teachers learn those things. They need to know what teachers find relevant, interesting, exciting, motivating. They need to know about teachers' beliefs. They need to know how adults learn and how to help adults learn to teach. They need to know about current changes in the curriculum and pedagogy of the field. These courses, both designed to teach social studies "methods," are quite different, yet as we look across the experiences, we see some patterns in terms of the kinds of understandings that informed our work as teacher educators.

Although we can't begin to delineate everything we would like to know as teacher educators, here we propose a small set of hypotheses and invite readers to explore these hypotheses in their own teaching.

Teacher educators need to know about the history–social studies curriculum and instruction in the schools. Perhaps this is the most obvious of our claims. If teacher educators are to assist prospective and practicing teachers as they learn how to teach social studies, they ought to know something about what teachers are required to teach. But even this claim is not as simple as it appears. Teachers need to know about the curricular traditions, but they also need to know how to examine those traditions critically. They need to know how to analyze and face the challenges presented by the calls for changes in those traditions. Currently, this means that they ought to know about the recent recommendations of the National Council of the Social Studies, the History/Social Studies National Standards Project, state-level frameworks and standards, and the standards drafted by the National Board for Professional Teaching Standards.

By suggesting that teacher educators "know" about these curricula, we mean that they understand their content, their histories, the arguments that both shape and characterize the existence of multiple curricular traditions. We assume that by knowing about the discourse surrounding the social studies curricula, teacher educators will adopt a critical stance that will help them help teachers develop the skills they need to select curricula sensibly.

To judge the value of past and present curricula and reforms, teacher educators need to know something about the disciplines from which those school subjects derive. So we arrive at our second hypothesis:

Teacher educators need to understand the "big" ideas in history and the social studies. Both of us needed to know things about history to design and teach these classes. Suzanne needed to know about the French Revolution; Bill and his colleagues needed to know about the frontier, the Constitution, Reconstruction, and the civil rights movement. However, we neither had to be experts about those topics nor know more than our students. In both courses, the classes were designed to enable students and teachers together to explore the ideas, to learn about them, to delve into them in some depth. Furthermore, given the breadth of disciplines covered by the social studies, it would be impossible to know every field. So if teacher educators need to know something about the subject matters but cannot be experts, how much is enough?

We can't answer that question because each time we learn something new about the subject matter, it only serves to enhance our understandings of how to teach. It seems in many ways that it's OK not to know everything—but one never knows enough. As is the case with all fields of inquiry, the "big" ideas change over time. Sometimes interpretations change, sometimes paradigms shift. Frederick Turner's frontier thesis has been challenged repeatedly since the time we learned about it as high school seniors and undergraduates. Teachers need to keep abreast of such changes, for their responsibility is not to teach the history and social sciences they learned as undergraduates; rather, they are charged with helping students learn about those fields of study in a contemporary sense. If we did not stay abreast of new ideas, we might teach students error-filled information.

But how does one learn these things? What does one read? Both of us have been studying history for a long time. Other teacher educators might select other disciplines in which to ground themselves. After majoring in those fields, we've continued to pursue them. We read histories and book reviews. We have friends who are political scientists and economists. Bill teaches with a practicing historian. To be fully emerged in the literature of the related disciplines and in education would be impossible for either of us. So we do the best we can. We teach and consult with people more expert than we are. We read what Gordon Wood has to say in the *New York Review of Books* or what developments are reported in the *Economist*, the *Atlantic*, the *New Yorker*, the *New Republic*. We scan the local bookstores' shelves for new texts in economics, anthropology, sociology. We get recommendations from colleagues in liberal arts departments about what to read next.

To design these courses, however, we needed to know more than just the latest developments in history and the social sciences. We needed to know things about the nature of historical knowledge: how it is created, tested, critiqued, revised. This leads us to a third hypothesis:

Teacher educators need to understand the nature of knowledge in history and the social sciences. Just as recent research has suggested that teachers need to know about the syntactic as well as the substantive aspects of knowledge (Schwab, 1964; Wilson and Wineburg, 1988), so teacher educators need to know these same things about subject matter. Had Bill not known how historians select, interpret, and use documents, or had Suzanne not known the principles historians use to accumulate and sort through the traces left of the past, we would not have been able to design these courses, nor would we have been able to respond to the problems that students encountered. Moreover, it was our understandings of the ways in which historical knowledge is limited, shaped, and bound that enabled us to explore historical ideas—the French Revolution, the frontier, and so on—without expert knowledge of those ideas. For example, one need not be an expert in French history to know that an Oxford historian will tell a different story than a feminist or a labor historian. Knowing that the disciplinary perspective of an author influences the nature of the history that historian might tell helped us ask questions about interpretation, truth, and fact.

We keep abreast of the epistemological debates in the related fields in ways similar to keeping abreast of the changing ideas: we read, talk to friends, and keep an eye out for books written by philosophers, historians, economists, and others about doing the work of history. For example, we read McCloskey's work on rhetoric in economics (1985) and Schama's antics in history (1991). We comb used bookstores for copies of Collingwood ([1946] 1956) as well as other biographies and autobiographies by historians who write about the doing of history.

Knowing about the subject matters and the curricula that they introduce to their students is but half the story. Teacher educators also need to know about their pupils and how they learn. This leads us to a pair of hypotheses:

Teacher educators need to understand things about their learners, prospective and practicing teachers—their beliefs, experiences, prior knowledge, assumptions, concerns, and interests. Teacher educators need to know how teachers learn—specifically how teachers learn about teaching social studies.

Our descriptions of these classes are chock full of assumptions about what teachers know, the kinds of experiences and beliefs they bring to our classes, and how they learn new things best. Some of these assumptions are about history and social studies. Others are about teachers' beliefs about teaching or learning. For instance, Bill and his colleagues assumed that prospective teachers would bring particular beliefs about the nature of historical knowledge. They also assumed that the prospective teachers would have little experience with reformed images of teaching. Suzanne assumed that teachers might learn to teach in new ways by experiencing alternative teaching themselves. From inside such experiences, they might draw conclusions about how they should tinker with or transform their own practices. Suzanne also assumed that practicing teachers would have little patience for educational scholarship unless it was placed in a context in which its relevance was obvious.

These assumptions seem sensible enough: after all, we developed them through our experiences teaching other kinds of teacher education courses and through our research on teaching (for example, McDiarmid, 1994, forthcoming; Wilson, 1990, 1991, forthcoming; Wilson, Shulman, and Richert, 1987; Wilson and Wineburg, 1988). But we call them assumptions, not knowledge, because they are limited. Research in the area is sketchy, and much remains to be learned.[9] Similarly, although research on teacher learning is growing, this field of scholarship is relatively new.

But knowing things about learners, curriculum and content, and teacher learning is still not sufficient. Teacher educators must then put these ideas together in ways that create educative opportunities for teachers. And so we make one last claim:

Teacher educators need to have their own pedagogical content knowledge. They need to know how to teach their subject matter—social studies methods—well.

In our courses, we were constantly searching for means to help teachers encounter ideas about history and social sciences, about teaching and learning. In a way, one might describe these stories as cases of the development of our pedagogical content knowledge. Through teaching these courses, we have begun to develop a sense of the most compelling representations, of the lessons and experiences that "work," of the ways in which students' experiences and beliefs interact with particular materials and experiences. We believe that in teaching our own content—the pedagogical methods of social studies—well, we model for prospective and practicing teachers what it means to teach well and we also establish credibility. After all, if we want to be effective as teacher educators, mustn't we display the capacity to teach skillfully and thoughtfully? Moreover, by placing teachers in the role of learners, we can help them develop insights into learning as well as teaching. By focusing their attention on their own learning and our teaching, we help them analyze the connections between the two.

In conclusion, then, we believe that some of what social studies teacher educators need to know is subject-specific: the history of social studies teaching and learning in schools, the big ideas in history and the social sciences, the epistemological debates that underlie the development and critique of knowledge in those fields, the beliefs and preconceptions that learners bring to learning those subjects. Other things concern more generic issues: teachers' beliefs about teaching and learning, theories of teacher learning, models and modes of teacher education. Some of these things are well documented, familiar, known; others are less so, yet to be explored. Just like the teachers we are helping to prepare, we too must be prepared to constantly question our assumptions, examine and reflect on promising new practices, and search out new information about the touchstones of our work: teachers, learning, social studies, and teaching. Perhaps most important, teacher educators need to know how to synthesize across these literatures, pulling from adult learning theory and the philosophy of history, from theories of child development and an array of instructional strategies. A list of "things to know" fails to capture this integrative, more dynamic aspect of knowing yet being able to build a house of social studies methods out of the building blocks of history and teaching and learning is one of the most important things teacher educators need to be able to do.

Conclusion

The question this chapter was meant to explore—What do social studies teacher educators need to know?—is not easily answered. Our explorations of the question have been humbling: there is a lot to know, and our time for teaching is finite. In deciding what and how to teach, we have argued that perhaps paramount is creating opportunities for teachers to consider simultaneously the content and nature of the subject matter and the school curriculum, the understandings and interests of the learners, and the teacher's role and pedagogical options. Critical for teachers of any subject matter, these considerations take on particular hues specific to teaching history and the social studies.

Moreover, although teachers have traditionally been viewed as knowers, teacher educators must also view teachers as inquirers: into history and the social sciences and curricula in these subjects; into learners, their ideas, experiences, and understandings; and into teaching, its methods and possibilities. To be practitioners capable of responding to changing circumstances, teachers must come to understand the interrelations of these considerations. Given our changing understanding of what counts as knowledge in history and the social studies and given particular groups of students, how and what should we teach? To address this question, history and social studies teachers need to have experience in pulling together the information and ideas that would help them answer it, as well as the conviction that they should and can. We cannot teach these issues separately and then assume that teachers know how to integrate them in their practice.

This further implies that we, as social studies educators, are also willing to define ourselves as inquirers, prepared to create genuine opportunities to learn in our courses around ideas, topics, activities, texts, and problems in which we too are learners. This is risky behavior; customarily, we are defined by what we know rather than by our willingness to learn. Defining ourselves as inquirers goes against the grain of the institutions in which most of us work. At the same time, we are unlikely to convince teachers that they should be inquirers if we are not willing to engage in genuine inquiry alongside our students.

The debates about history and the social studies are not likely to go away. Rather than viewing this with dismay, we take this as a sign of health. The issues of what we should teach and how we should teach it are kept alive as views of knowledge, knowing, learning, learners, and teaching change. Given the bubbling cauldron of assertions and counterassertions about these issues, the question is, What is the best preparation for prospective and practicing teachers? We respond, Rather than try to convince prospective teachers that there is one "right way" to think about and teach social studies, help them develop their critical inquiry capacities around key issues and ideas in the field. Engage them in the debates about curricula and teaching. Provide them with the opportunities and resources needed for sustained inquiry. Then get out of the way. Meanwhile, we must document and reflect on our own practices; we must contribute to the field of social studies teacher education through writing and arguing about its content, pedagogy, purposes, and promise by developing and analyzing our own practices and the lessons those practices might teach about what we need to know.

Notes

1. For an annotated bibliography of curricular guides and frameworks, we recommend Patrick (1992).
2. Another strategy we might have chosen for this chapter would be to review social studies education. However, we are not experts in such matters and find the reviews and histories of scholars like Dougan (1985), Jenness (1990), Lybarger (1991), Parker (forthcoming), Ravitch (1985), and Thornton (1992) as much more comprehensive, thoughtful, and informed than anything we could write.
3. There is a growing body of literature in which teacher educators reflect on their practice, however, from which one might infer things about what teacher educators need to know. Consider, for example, Duckworth (1987), Feiman-Nemser and Featherstone (1992), Shulman (1992), and Wilson (1990).
4. Although we coauthored the entire chapter, the narrators change here. During the description of the courses, "we" refers to McDiarmid and his collaborators, Laura Thornburg and Peter Vinten-Johansen. Wilson describes her teaching in the first person singular.
5. For examples, see Beck and McKeown, 1988; Beck, McKeown, and Gromoll, 1989; Beck, McKeown, Sinatra, and Loxterman, 1991; Booth, 1978, 1980, 1984; Carretero and Voss, 1994; Downey and Levstik, 1991; McKeown and Beck, 1990; Thornton and Vukelich, 1988; Wineburg, 1991a, 1991b; and Wineburg and Fournier, 1994.
6. For examples, see Clegg, 1991; Dow, 1991; Downey and Levstik, 1991; Drake, 1986; Ehman and Glenn, 1991; Holt, 1990; Jenness, 1990; Jorgensen, 1993; McDiarmid, forthcoming; Parker, 1990; Parker, McDaniel, and Valencia, 1991; Thornton, 1992; Wilson, forthcoming; and Wineburg and Wilson, 1990.
7. See Alleman and Rosaen, 1991; Ashby and Lee, 1987; Berti, 1992; Brophy, Van Sledright, and Bredin, 1992; Carretero, Jacott, Limón, Lopez-Manjón, and León, 1994; Epstein, 1994; Leinhardt, 1994; Levstik, 1986, 1992; Mackey, 1991; Seixas, 1993; Shemilt, 1987; Stodolsky, Salk, and Glaessner, 1991; Thornton and Vukelich, 1988; Torney-Purta, 1994; Wineburg, 1991a, 1991b; and Wyner and Farquhar, 1991.
8. Notice that there is a parallelism here, for reform of teacher education asks us as teacher educators to teach in ways we have never taught before.
9. We are heartened by the fact that history and social studies appear to be becoming a focus of educational scholarship and inquiry. For example, see the special issue of *Educational Psychologist, 29*(2), edited by S. S. Wineburg (1994), titled "The Teaching and Learning of History." As Seixas (1993) points out, there is a much richer and longer tradition of research on history learning in Great Britain.

References

Alleman, J. E., and Rosaen, C. L. (1991). "The cognitive, social-emotional, and moral development characteristics of students: Basis for elementary and middle school social studies." In J. P. Shaver (ed.), *Handbook of research on social studies teaching and learning.* New York: Macmillan.

Ashby, R., and Lee, P. (1987). "Children's concepts of empathy and understanding in history." In C. Portal (ed.), *The history curriculum for teachers.* London: Falmer Press.

Beck, I. L., and McKeown, M. G. (1988). "Toward meaningful accounts in history texts for young learners." *Educational Researcher, 17*(6), 31–39.

Beck, I. L., McKeown, M. G., and Gromoll, E. W. (1989). "Learning from social studies texts." *Cognition and Instruction, 6,* 99–158.

Beck, I. L., McKeown, M. G., Sinatra, G. M., and Loxterman, J. A. (1991). "Revising social studies text from a text-processing perspective: Evidence of improved comprehensibility." *Reading Research Quarterly, 26*(3), 251–276.

Berti, A. E. (1992). "Comprehension of the concept of state in the context of historical events and current affairs in children from 8 to 14 years." Paper presented at the Seminar on Cognitive and Instructional Processes in the Social Sciences and History, Madrid.

Booth, M. (1978). "Children's inductive historical thought." *Teaching History, 21,* 3–8.

Booth, M. (1980). "A modern world history course and the thinking of adolescent pupils." *Educational Review, 32*(3), 245–257.

Booth, M. (1984). "Skills, concepts, and attitudes: The development of adolescent children's historical thinking." *History and Theory, 22,* 101–117.

Brophy, J. E. (1990). *Mary Lake: A case of fifth-grade social studies (American history) teaching.* East Lansing: Center for the Learning and Teaching of Elementary Subjects, Michigan State University.

Brophy, J. E., Van Sledright, B. A., and Bredin, N. (1992). "Fifth graders' ideas about history expressed before and after their introduction to the subject." *Theory and Research in Social Education, 20,* 440–489.

California State Department of Education (1987). *History–social studies framework for California public schools—kindergarten through grade twelve.* Sacramento, Calif.: California State Department of Education.

Carretero, M., Jacott, L., Limón, M., Lopez-Manjón, A., and León, J. A. (1994). "Historical knowledge: Cognitive and instructional implications." In M. Carretero and J. F. Voss (eds.), *Cognitive and instructional processes in history and the social sciences.* Hillsdale, N.J.: Erlbaum.

Carretero, M., and Voss, J. F. (eds.) (1994). *Cognitive and instructional processes in social sciences and history.* Hillsdale, N.J.: Erlbaum.

Clegg, A. A., Jr. (1991). "Games and simulations in social studies education." In J. S. Shaver (ed.), *Handbook of research on social studies teaching and learning.* New York: Macmillan.

Collingwood, R. G. (1956). *The idea of history.* New York: Oxford University Press. (Originally published in 1946.)

Cuban, L. (1991). "History of teaching in the social studies." In J. P. Shaver (ed.), *Handbook of research on social studies teaching and learning.* New York: Macmillan.

Curriculum Task Force. (1989). *Charting a course: Social studies for the 21st century.* Washington, D.C.: National Commission on Social Studies in the Schools.

Dougan, A. M. (1985). "The search for a definition of the social studies: A historical overview." *Indiana Journal of Social Education, 3,* 13–35.

Dow, P. (1991). *Schoolhouse politics: Lessons from the Sputnik era.* Cambridge, Mass.: Harvard University Press.

Downey, M. T., and Levstik, L. S. (1991). "Teaching and learning history." In J. S. Shaver (ed.), *Handbook of research on social studies teaching and learning.* New York: Macmillan.

Drake, F. D. (1986). "Using primary sources and historians' interpretations in the classroom." *Teaching History, 11,* 50–61.

Duckworth, E. (1987). *"The having of wonderful ideas" and other essays on teaching and learning.* New York: Teachers College Press.

Ehman, L. H., and Glenn, A. D. (1991). "Interactive technology in social studies." In J. S. Shaver (ed.), *Handbook of research on social studies teaching and learning.* New York: Macmillan.

Epstein, T. L. (1994). "Sometimes a shining moment: High school students' representations of history through the arts." *Social Education, 22,* 136–141.

Evans, R. W. (1988). "Lessons from history: Teacher and student conceptions of the meaning of history." *Theory and Research in Social Education, 16,* 203–225.

Evans, R. W. (1989). "Teacher conceptions of history." *Theory and Research in Social Education, 17,* 210–240.

Evans, R. W. (1990). "Teacher conceptions of history revisited: Ideology, curriculum, and student belief." *Theory and Research in Social Education, 18,* 101–138.

Feiman-Nemser, S., and Featherstone, H. (eds.) (1992). *Exploring teaching: Reinventing an introductory course.* New York: Teachers College Press.

Gagnon, P., and the Bradley Commission on History in Schools (eds.) (1989). *Historical literacy: The case for history in American education.* New York: Macmillan.

Goodlad, J. I. (1984). *A place called school.* New York: McGraw-Hill.

Hasbach, C., Roth, K. J., Hoekwater, E., and Rosaen, C. L. (1993). *Powerful social studies concepts that count.* East Lansing: Center for the Learning and Teaching of Elementary Subjects, Michigan State University.

Hawkins, D. (1974). "I, thou, and it." In *The informed vision: Essays on learning and human nature.* New York: Agathon. (Originally published in 1967.)

Holmes Group (1986). *Tomorrow's teachers: A report of the Holmes Group.* East Lansing, Mich.: Holmes Group.

Holt, T. (1990). *Thinking historically.* New York: College Entrance Examination Board.

Jenness, D. (1990). *Making sense of the social studies.* New York: Macmillan.

Jorgensen, K. L. (1993). *History workshop: Reconstructing the past with elementary students.* Portsmouth, N.H.: Heinemann Educational Books.

Kentucky Department of Education (1993). *Transformations: Kentucky's curriculum framework.* Lexington: Kentucky Department of Education.

Leinhardt, G., Stainton, C., Virji, S. M., and Odoroff, E. (1994). "Learning to reason in history: Mindlessness to mindfulness." In M. Carretero and J. F. Voss (eds.), *Cognitive and instructional processes in history and the social sciences.* Hillsdale, N.J.: Erlbaum.

Levstik, L. S. (1986). "The relationship between historical response and narrative in a sixth grade classroom." *Theory and Research in Social Education, 14,* 1–19.

Levstik, L. S. (1992). "Narrative and students' historical thinking." Paper presented at the annual meeting of the American Educational Research Association, San Francisco.

Lortie, D. C. (1975). *Schoolteacher: A sociological study.* Chicago: University of Chicago Press.

Lybarger, M. B. (1991). "The historiography of social studies: Retrospect, circumspect, and prospect." In J. P. Shaver (ed.), *Handbook of research on social studies teaching and learning.* New York: Macmillan.

McCloskey, D. N. (1985). *The rhetoric of economics.* Madison: University of Wisconsin Press.

McDiarmid, G. W. (1992). *The arts and sciences as preparation for teaching.* (Issue paper no. 92–3). East Lansing: National Center for Research on Teacher Education, Michigan State University.

McDiarmid, G. W. (1994). "Understanding history for teaching: A study of the historical understanding of prospective teachers." In M. Carretero and J. F. Voss (eds.), *Cognitive and instructional processes in social sciences and history.* Hillsdale, N.J.: Erlbaum.

McDiarmid, G. W. (forthcoming). "Challenging prospective teachers' understandings of history: An examination of a historiography seminar." In R. Glaser and L. Schauble (eds.), *The contributions of instructional innovation to understanding learning.* Hillsdale, N.J.: Erlbaum.

McDiarmid, G. W., Thornburg, L., and Vinten-Johansen, P. (forthcoming). *Reinventing a secondary social studies methods course.*

McKeown, M. G., and Beck, I. L. (1990). "The assessment and characterization of young learners' knowledge of a topic in history." *American Educational Research Journal, 27,* 688–726.

Mackey, J. A. (1991). "Adolescents' social, cognitive, and moral development and secondary school social studies." In J. P. Shaver (ed.), *Handbook of research on social studies teaching and learning.* New York: Macmillan.

McNeil, L. M. (1986). *Contradictions of control: School structure and school knowledge.* New York: Routledge & Kegan Paul.

Parker, W. C. (1990). "Achieving thinking and decision-making objectives in social studies." In J. P. Shaver (ed.), *Handbook of research on social studies teaching and learning.* New York: Macmillan.

Parker, W. C. (forthcoming). "Social studies." In D. Perkins and R. Swartz (eds.), *Teaching thinking in the content areas.*

Parker, W. C., McDaniel, J. E., and Valencia, S. W. (1991). "Helping students think about public issues: Instruction versus prompting." *Social Education, 55*(1), 41–44, 67.

Patrick, J. J. (1992). "Recommended curriculum guides." In *Social studies curriculum resource handbook.* Millwood, N.Y.: Kraus.

Project 30 Alliance (1991). *Year two report: Institutional accomplishments* Newark: University of Delaware Press.

Ravitch, D. (1985). *The schools we deserve: Reflections on the educational crises of our times.* New York: Basic Books.

Schama, S. (1991). *Dead certainties: (Unwarranted speculations).* New York: Knopf.

Schwab, J. J. (1964). "The structures of the disciplines: Meanings and significances." In G. W. Ford and L. Pugno (eds.), *The structure of knowledge and the curriculum.* Skokie, Ill.: Rand McNally.

Seixas, P. (1993). "Historical understanding among adolescents in a multicultural setting." *Curriculum Inquiry, 23,* 301–327.

Shaver, J. P., Davis, O. L., Jr., and Helburn, S. W. (1980). "An interpretative report on the status of precollege social studies education based on three NSF-funded studies." In *What are the needs in precollege science, mathematics, and social science education? Views from the field.* Washington, D.C.: U.S. Government Printing Office.

Shemilt, D. (1987). "Adolescent ideas about evidence and methodology in history." In C. Portal (ed.), *The history curriculum for teachers.* London: Falmer Press.

Shulman, J. H. (ed.) (1992). *Case methods in teacher education.* New York: Teachers College Press.

Shulman, L. S. (1986). "Those who understand: Knowledge growth in teaching." *Educational Researcher, 15*(5), 4–14.

Shulman, L. S. (1987). "Knowledge and teaching: Foundations of the new reform." *Harvard Educational Review, 57,* 1–23.

Stodolsky, S. S. (1988). *The subject matters: Classroom activity in math and social studies.* Chicago: University of Chicago Press.

Stodolsky, S. S., Salk, S., and Glaessner, B. (1991). "Student views about learning math and social studies." *American Educational Research Journal, 28*(1), 89–116.

Thornton, S. J. (1992). "Trends and issues in social studies curriculum." In *Social studies curriculum resource handbook.* Millwood, N.Y.: Kraus.

Thornton, S. J., and Vukelich, R. (1988). "Effects of children's understanding of time concepts on historical understanding." *Theory and Research in Social Education, 16,* 69–82.

Torney-Purta, J. (1994). "Dimensions of adolescents' reasoning about political and historical issues: Ontological switches and developmental processes, and situated learning." In M. Carretero and J. F. Voss (eds.), *Cognitive and instructional processes in social sciences and history.* Hillsdale, N.J.: Erlbaum.

Wilson, S. M. (1990). "The secret garden of teacher education." *Phi Delta Kappan, 72(3),* 204–209.

Wilson, S. M. (forthcoming). "Mastodons, maps, and Michigan: Exploring uncharted territory while teaching elementary school social studies." *Elementary School Journal.*

Wilson, S. M., Shulman, L. S., and Richert, A. E. (1987). "'150 different ways' of knowing: Representations of knowledge in teaching." In J. Calderhead (ed.), *Exploring teachers' thinking.* London: Cassell Educational.

Wilson, S. M., and Wineburg, S. S. (1988). "Peering at history from different lenses: The role of disciplinary perspectives in the teaching of American history." *Teachers College Record, 89,* 525–539.

Wilson, S. W., and Wineburg, S. S. (1993). "Wrinkles in time: Using performance assessments to understand the knowledge of history teachers." *American Educational Research Journal, 30,* 729–769.

Wineburg, S. S. (1991a). "Historical problem solving: A study of the cognitive processes used in the evaluation of documentary and pictorial evidence." *Journal of Educational Psychology, 83,* 73–87.

Wineburg, S. S. (1991b). "On the reading of historical texts: Notes on the breach between school and academy." *American Educational Research Journal, 28(3),* 495–520.

Wineburg, S. S. (1993). *Mr. Stinson's Vietnam: Moral ambiguity in the history classroom.* Fairbanks: Center for Cross-Cultural Studies, University of Alaska.

Wineburg, S. S. (ed.) (1994). "The teaching and learning of history." *Educational Psychologist, 29(2).*

Wineburg, S. S., and Fournier, J. (1994). "Contextualized thinking in history." In M. Carretero and J. F. Voss (eds.), *Cognitive and instructional processes in social sciences and history.* Hillsdale, N.J.: Erlbaum.

Wineburg, S. S., and Wilson, S. M. (1988). "Models of wisdom in the teaching of history." *Phi Delta Kappan, 70,* 50–58.

Wyner, N. B., and Farquhar, E. (1991). "Cognitive, emotional, and social development: Early childhood social studies." In J. P. Shaver (ed.), *Handbook of research on social studies teaching and learning.* New York: Macmillan.

Annotated Bibliography

Each work cited in this chapter has strengths and weaknesses. Here we nominate candidates in several specific categories.

The nature of historical knowledge:

Appleby, J., Hunt, L., and Jacob, M. (1994). *Telling the truth about history.* New York: Norton. Three accomplished female historians examine the nature of what we call "history." They trace the process through which historians and philosophers have come to question key ideas such as "facts" and "truth." In particular, they examine the roles that the history of science and the development of social history have played in the reconsideration of historical knowledge. Their purpose is to rectify what they see as excesses in the postmodern critiques of knowledge. They argue that just because a single, unitary "truth" about the past is no longer a widely accepted goal for historians, they need not abandon the search for "truths" that are more tentative and always qualified.

The history of the social studies:

Jenness, D. (1990). *Making sense of the social studies.* New York: Macmillan.

> This is a comprehensive survey of the social studies—their entry and development as school subjects, their curricular organization, their evolution over time. The author examines each of the disciplines that make up social studies in turn, relating the history of each in schools. In addition, he synthesizes years of research on the teaching and learning of the social studies.

Reform documents:

California State Department of Education (1987). *History–social studies framework for California public schools—kindergarten through grade twelve.* Sacramento: California State Department of Education.

> Many states and professional organizations are currently drafting and publishing standards and frameworks. This is the one we have found most helpful.

What happens to reforms:

Dow, P. (1991). *Schoolhouse politics: Lessons from the Sputnik era.* Cambridge, Mass.: Harvard University Press.

> Dow's examination of the intellectual and political development of the social studies curriculum, Man: A Course of Study (MACOS), is animated by his intimate knowledge of the major actors. Dow was a teacher who became involved in the process of developing and testing the curriculum. MACOS is noteworthy in part because it represented an attempt by a preeminent cognitive psychologist, Jerome Bruner, to instantiate the ideas of Piaget in a curriculum. Dow both explicates the assumptions and ideas that underlay the curriculum and relates the political missteps that led to its demise despite its popularity with teachers and students.

Thinking in history:

Gagnon, P. (1988). "Why study history? *Atlantic Monthly,* Nov.

> Gagnon, who headed up the Bradley Commission on History in the Schools, argues that the study of history is most important because it teaches students judgment. This capacity to judge is, Gagnon contends, the most critical capacity of citizens in a democracy. Using several historical contexts, he demonstrates how genuinely understanding the past involves judgment.

Holt, T. (1990). *Thinking historically.* New York: College Entrance Examination Board.

> A historian at the University of Chicago, Holt illustrates the capacity of both high school and college students to make sense of primary documents. Specifically, Holt reports on how students understood a letter written by freed slaves protesting legislation that dispossessed them of land granted them by General Sherman. As students examine this document, they confront their own assumptions about the capacities of newly freed slaves. Holt also documents how history as it is commonly taught alienates many students and argues that the use of primary documents is an example of how teachers can help students connect, personally and emotionally, with the past.

Teaching history:

Wilson, S. M. (forthcoming). "Mastodons, maps, and Michigan: Exploring uncharted territory while teaching elementary school social studies." *Elementary School Journal.*

> Wilson recounts three teaching and learning incidents in a third-grade classroom and examines the ways in which subject matter knowledge and pedagogical content knowledge affect her capacity to teach effectively.

Wineburg, S. S., and Wilson, S. M. (1991). "Subject matter knowledge in history teaching."
      In J. E. Brophy (ed.), *Advances in research on teaching: Teachers' knowledge of subject matter as it
      relates to their practice*, Vol. 2. Greenwich, Conn.: JAI Press.
      A growing body of work closely examines the myriad ways that accomplished teachers
      can create learning opportunities for their students. In this piece, Wineburg and Wil-
      son contrast two experienced teachers and examine how their knowledge of the sub-
      ject matter and of pedagogy enable them to create educative opportunities for high
      school students.

PART THREE

THE DISCIPLINE
OF EDUCATION

CHAPTER FIFTEEN

DIVERSITY IN EDUCATION: PROBLEMS AND POSSIBILITIES

JOSEPH P. DUCETTE, TREVOR E. SEWELL, AND JOAN POLINER SHAPIRO

All humans are like all other humans, like some other humans, and like no other human.

This paraphrased and often cited aphorism captures a central dilemma in educational practice: to what extent can teachers accommodate the vast range of student diversity that is found in any classroom? This diversity encompasses such educationally relevant dimensions and categories as gender, social class, ethnicity, intelligence, race, religion, disability, and learning style. In combination, these characteristics produce students so distinct and so unique that truly differentiated teaching designed to meet each student's idiosyncratic needs and interests, or to respond to each pupil's specific learning strengths, is difficult if not impossible. As the aphorism says, every student is like no other student.

Yet in every classroom there are distinct groups of students who are more similar than dissimilar and whose similarities facilitate instruction: some students learn better with visual material while others learn better through auditory input; in some situations, girls perform differently than boys; there are some curricular materials that African-American students find more interesting than white students. Viewed from this perspective, every student is like some other students. To carry this analysis to its conclusion, there are certainly some situations where all students in the class respond similarly enough so that each student is like all other students.

How should teachers approach this diversity? How complex and differentiated can instruction be without losing coherence? What aspects of diversity make a difference in a specific situation and which ones are relatively unimportant? As we will attempt to demonstrate throughout this chapter, questions like these, while having a long history in educational practice, have traditionally been considered less important than questions that focus on general issues about the curriculum or about learning. In the present environment, where diversity of all types is becoming more recognized, and where more and more groups are demanding that their specific aspect of diversity must be explicitly acknowledged, these types of questions can no longer be ignored or placed in a secondary position in the educational literature.

The issue of course is neither simple nor easy. From the classroom teacher's perspective, the demands emanating from those who represent different categories of diversity are often perceived as insurmountable problems. Davidson and Phelan (1993) expressed this when they wrote, "For these teachers, conceptions of diversity are found in their description of the inability of students to fit in and act as they 'should,' and in their pejorative comments about students' parents, home lives, neighborhoods, and cultural backgrounds. Many of these teachers believe that a good number of their students are not capable of succeeding and, as a consequence, abdicate any responsibility for helping them do so" (p. 4).

On the other hand, the classroom teacher might choose to deemphasize the problems associated with diversity and instead see what social reconstructionists such as Aronowitz and Giroux (1985) and Freire (1970) consider as possibilities. Davidson and Phelan (1993) describe this perspective in the following way: "For some teachers, diverse student populations provide a catalyst for further training, the development of relevant curricula, and an opportunity to expand their teacher repertories. Many of these teachers express genuine concern for individual students' needs and make special efforts to understand and respond to the unique features of the cultural backgrounds from which their students come. . . . In fact, some become advocates for a curriculum that will empower, rather than impoverish, the chances of *all* youth to succeed" (p. 4).

In this review, we will present both the problems and the possibilities of diversity in education. While we will not dwell on the problems, we will acknowledge that they exist and that they can make teaching into a difficult and perplexing occupation. Our guess is that if given the choice most teachers would choose to teach students who are homogeneous and similar to themselves. We hope that this chapter can demonstrate some of the possibilities for a teacher's own development as well as that of her or his students when diversity is not only accepted but valued.

A Definition of Diversity

For the purposes of this chapter, we define diversity as encompassing the domain of human characteristics that affect an individual's capacity to learn from, respond to, or interact in a school environment. These characteristics can be overt or covert, recognized by the individual or not recognized, and biologically or environmentally or socially determined. Some of the characteristics are meaningful only as they describe an individual; others are more meaningful as they describe a group.

In a single chapter, we cannot encompass the entire range of student diversity, even superficially; thus, it is necessary to exclude many appropriate topics. We have not included, for example, hearing and vision impairments, language differences, and physical disabilities, although such topics could be legitimately covered here since they also impact on school performance. Our hope is that the variables we do cover can serve as effective models for understanding and appreciating other forms of difference.

Types of Diversity

To avoid a laundry list approach to the chapter, we have devised a structure through which the various aspects of diversity can be presented. While there are undoubtedly many alternate ways to do this, we chose one that seemed most inclusive and that made the fewest theoretical assumptions: we have divided the various aspects of diversity into two broad groups, "differences in degree" and "differences in kind," recognizing that any way of characterizing the various kinds of diversity will probably produce problems for some readers. To avoid some of these definitional problems, we are making the following distinction:

One group of individual difference variables is conceptualized as continua or dimensions. Intelligence and learning styles are two clear examples. For these variables, all people are seen as falling along a continuum and in most cases it is possible to assign a number to each individual representing the strength (or amount of presence) of that characteristic for that person. In general, many of these variables are derived from psychology and the issue of operational definition is almost always central. That is, most of these constructs are assessed through some form of standardized (often paper-and-pencil) test.

Conversely, there are other constructs for which the concept of a continuum is largely meaningless. Race, gender, and ethnicity are three examples. To a great extent, these variables are more often the focus of disciplines involving the study of groups, such as sociology and anthropology, and the issue of operational definition is often irrelevant. These "differences in kind," while sharing the underlying theme of tapping an aspect of diversity, are quite different in the way they are discussed in the educational literature.

One way of capturing the differences between these two types of diversity is to recognize that many of the variables that we have included under the rubric of "differences in degree" are viewed as having relatively direct effects on achievement. Thus, a student's intelligence, or learning style, or learning disability, is conceptualized differently from variables such as race or gender. For these latter characteristics, it is assumed that their effects are indirect. That is, girls may not achieve at the same rate as boys in science because the typical science textbook is written in such a way that girls' interests or learning styles are inadequately addressed (see the section on gender later in this chapter). To use a traditional distinction from research methodology, "differences in degree" are often treated as independent variables, while "differences in kind" are often moderator variables.

We realize that this scheme has problems, and we recognize that not all aspects of diversity fit neatly into one or the other of these groups. Moreover, some writers view variables such as gender and ethnic group as also being matters of degree (see, for example, Mead, Dobzhensky, and Light, 1968). Nevertheless, we felt that this structure was a solution to the difficult issue of finding commonalities among variables that in fact are derived from different theoretical bases and that ask very different questions and pose very different solutions to educational problems.

We view the distinction we are making to be similar to the distinction Reynolds made in the previous volume published by the American Association for Colleges of Teacher Education, *A Knowledge Base for the Beginning Teacher* (1989). In the chapter titled "Students with Special Needs," Reynolds distinguishes between individual differences conceptualized as categories versus those conceptualized as variables. He cites as an example of categories such groups as "retarded" or "disturbed" while "chronological age" and "IQ" are examples of variables. While Reynolds intended his discussion to be relevant only to special education, and while he was largely critical of the categorical labeling of children, the essential classification he has made seems to us to be useful in our presentation.

Aspects of Diversity Viewed as Differences in Degree

In this section of the chapter, we will present a selected group of variables that we have termed "differences in degree." In many ways, these variables are similar in definition to what Corno and Snow (1986) have called "aptitudes." In their presentation, individual differences that affect instruction are sorted into three groups: intellectual abilities, viewed as cognitive skills and competencies that enable an individual to learn; personality characteristics, seen as enduring affective or motivational dispositions; and cognitive styles, perceived as propensities for processing information in certain ways. Since space will not permit even a cursory discussion of all the variables that could be presented using this framework, we have decided to focus only on intelligence, learning styles, learning disability, and giftedness. Although this decision excludes many interesting variables, we believe that almost all of the central issues can be considered through an investigation of these four.

As Corno and Snow point out, the three categories they define are not mutually exclusive, nor is it always possible to uniquely classify any specific aspect of diversity into one or another of these groups. Moreover, different authors use different terms to describe essentially identical phenomenon, so the field is at times confusing. Nevertheless, the Corno and Snow distinctions provide at least in a rough way a workable structure for a large number of individual difference variables.

Multiple Intelligences

This construct was chosen as the starting point since the literature in this area demonstrates one of the most notable shifts in educational thinking in recent years: the movement from a unitary and simpler concept of ability to a multivariate and more complex concept. While neither entirely original nor entirely new, the concept of intelligence associated with multiple intelligences, with its emphasis on the pluralistic notion of intelligence and on an individual's ability to develop valuable products in one or more cultural settings, is particularly relevant to the chapter's focus on issues of diversity in general, and ethnicity, social class, and gender in particular.

A complete understanding of multiple intelligences would entail a lengthy presentation of several critical issues, including (1) an historical and theoretical discussion of the development of intelligence tests, (2) a presentation of the literature that has argued for the biological bases of intelligence coupled with the often opposing literature that argues that intellectual competencies can be trained, and (3) the implications for the assessment of intelligence in children from different social classes or from ethnically diverse backgrounds. Obviously, the limited space available to each of the constructs in this chapter precludes an in-depth presentation on any of these topics. We will, however, place the discussion in a historical context.

Theories of Intelligence

First conceived by the French psychologist Alfred Binet, the original intelligence test was commissioned by the French government as a selection device to choose students for appropriate levels of instruction within schools. As such, the 1905 Binet test was designed to determine a child's level of intellectual competence as a basis for effective teaching and remediation. It was when Binet's test was brought to the United States, however, that the concept of intelligence as we presently know it began to take shape. From its very inception in American society, the atheoretical, practical instrument of Binet was transformed and expanded into a tool with far-reaching implications for American education. Legitimized by the expanding science of psychology, the Binet test and the theoretical structure that was devised to validate its use became the basis for a political philosophy marked by a distinction between different racial, ethnic, and cultural groups (Terman, 1916).

This shift in purpose, from helping children with learning difficulties to identifying and labeling children as uneducable (Schiff and Lewontin, 1986), corresponded to the development of theories of intelligence that served as the theoretical justification for the multifaceted uses of intelligence tests. Among the most influential early scientific contributions to the theoretical underpinning of testing instruments were the "general intelligence" theory of Spearman (1927) and the equally influential "primary mental abilities" theory of Thurstone (1938). Framing the Spearman and Thurstone theories in the context of a geographic model depicted as a "map of the mind," Sternberg (1988) points to the emphasis on general intelligence as a major region of the mind in Spearman's model. In contrast, Thurstone discounted the notion of a single major region of the mind and instead identified seven major regions. According to Thurstone, the abilities associated with these regions were verbal comprehension, verbal fluency, inductive reasoning, spatial visualization, perceptual speed, number, and memory.

General Intelligence Versus Several Intelligences

It is in the context of this debate between a unitary concept of intelligence and the idea of several intelligences that Howard Gardner placed his theory of multiple intelligences (MI) (1983). At the core of MI theory is the fundamental belief in the existence of different intellectual strengths and competencies. If, as Gardner and his associates argue (Gardner, 1983; Gardner and Hatch, 1989; Walters and Gardner, 1986), these intellectual competencies can be identified in the manifestation of valued activities in a given cultural setting, MI theory stands in sharp contrast to the notion of general intelligence or a single unitary ability. To understand this conceptual difference, one must not only examine what constitutes intelligence from different theoretical perspectives but more importantly how the conception of intelligence evolves.

Gardner arrived at seven intellectual competencies by investigating the criteria or "signs" of intelligence from a variety of sources. These included studies of normal development; information from neuropsychology, particularly the cognitive functioning of brain-damaged individuals; studies of exceptional individuals and the existence of idiot savants and prodigies; empirical findings from psychometric studies, and support from cross-cultural research. The inclusion of expert end-state performance in adults among the criteria for the definition of intelligence is an important distinguishing characteristic of MI theory, particularly relevant to the issue of fairness in the assessment of culturally diverse populations.

The seven intelligences outlined in Gardner's *Frames of the Mind* (1983) are as follows:

1. *Linguistic Intelligence:* Verbal ability has been a core component of intelligence from its earliest conception and measurement. It also emerges from the various sources providing the criteria for intelligence as a defensible component. Language skills demonstrated by poets and other writers assure an ability to deal with verbal symbols and the various functions of language.

2. *Logical-Mathematical Intelligence:* This form of intelligence is exemplified by

the ability to manipulate mathematical and scientific symbols. The emphasis on the ability to use logical and numerical skills to handle a long chain of reasoning is also fundamental to traditional conceptions of intelligence.

3. *Musical Intelligence:* Biological underpinning has been invoked to suggest that musical expressiveness passes the criterion to be identified as a particular intelligence. Moreover, musical skills yield highly valued cultural products, thus meeting a criterion for consideration. The accomplishments of musical prodigies either through natural talent or by education are remarkable demonstrations of intellectual competence.

4. *Spatial Intelligence:* The expert performances of navigators and architects are reflective of spatial abilities. This form of intelligence is the visual-spatial ability to manipulate or mentally rotate an object to transform it from its original structure.

5. *Interpersonal Intelligence:* The ability to understand the behavior of humans in complex social environments is often indicative of the intellectual competence observed in salespeople and therapists.

6. *Bodily Kinesthetic Intelligence:* This is the ability demonstrated by athletes and dancers; it indicates the skill with which one is able to control bodily movements.

7. *Intrapersonal Intelligence:* Self-awareness and self-knowledge are the salient features of intrapersonal intelligence. It is, however, the ability to capitalize on the understanding of one's self-knowledge to guide one's own behavior that constitutes competence.

If, as Gardner argues, these seven intelligences are fundamentally independent of each other, the notion of a single global measure of intelligence as reflected in the traditional IQ score is of questionable merit. To the proponents of MI theory, the standardized IQ measure, based on weak psychometric support and questionable theories about human functioning, is inadequate to assess the range of human abilities. Furthermore, many culturally meaningful activities such as composing and dancing require different intelligences that cannot be adequately assessed by IQ tests. A central point in Gardner's formulations is the fundamental shift from conventional tests, in which verbal and mathematical abilities are core components of a single measure of intelligence. Gardner argues that only by combining abilities can cultural roles be executed competently.

Issues and Controversies in Multiple Intelligences

Several continuing issues in this field have received attention from researchers and practitioners but are not yet fully resolved. Let us examine some of these issues.

Assessment of Intelligence: IQ Tests Versus Non-IQ Measures.
The psychometric, theoretical, and empirical rationale for the validity and practical utility of the IQ test is firmly entrenched in American psychology and education. Its development

and theoretical justification have been acknowledged by several of the most gifted psychologists as one of the most fundamental accomplishments in psychology. It is therefore quite paradoxical that the theory of multiple intelligences, despite its radical departure from the conception of intelligence underlying IQ tests, has been receiving such favorable attention.

This paradox is cogently presented by Sternberg (1992). If market considerations drive the testing industry as Sternberg implies, it is remarkable that Gardner's conceptualizations are taken seriously when such key school-related demands as accountability, prediction, diagnosis, and placement are apparently not factored into MI's theoretical formulations. Sternberg (1992) has generated a list of what an imaginative test developer might perceive to be the needs of school-based consumers of intelligence tests. Among them are the ability to predict achievement; high correlations with other, similar tests; ease of administration and interpretation; objectivity of scoring and perceived fairness. Given the consistency between the perceived consumer needs and the purposes for which the IQ tests claim validity, the preeminent role of the IQ test seems clearly established.

However, if the quality of educational programming becomes the conceptual basis for testing, then there will inevitably be a conflict between the scientific "purity" of the classic psychometric tradition and the real-life needs of practitioners (Sewell, 1979, 1987). Gardner and his colleagues, instead of following the historical context of testing, have radically shifted the paradigm for the assessment of intelligence. Two central characteristics of their model are worth noting: (1) the model relies heavily on resources from curriculum activities over an extended time period to assess problem-solving skills and to evaluate the ability to fashion products of value, and (2) authentic assessment practices, such as portfolio reviews, are extensively used to measure competence.

Culturally Biased Testing Versus Intelligence-Fair Testing. A fundamental principle underlying the assessment process is the requirement that tests should be selected that are not racially or culturally discriminatory. Nevertheless, the literature on IQ testing is replete with inferences of cultural bias (Mensh and Mensh, 1991; Schiff and Lewontin, 1986), litigations based on charges of discriminatory practices (Elliott, 1986), and systematic documentation of adverse social and economical consequences (Gould, 1981; Karmin, 1974). Since American education must be concerned with the education of an increasingly diverse student population, the challenge of either modifying traditional assessment practices or exploring alternative strategies becomes critical. Presumably, based on the existence of seven relatively independent intelligences, the proponents of the theory of multiple intelligences will point to its potential to assess a wider and more diverse range of human ability. Furthermore, expanding the purpose of testing from the primary historical function of predicting achievement to the use of assessment to identify competencies that are important in everyday life has substantially increased the potential for "intelligence-fair" assessment. If the basic tenet of autonomous intelligences is correct, and if valid assessment procedures emerge to identify these intellectual competencies without resorting to the narrow focus on mathematical and linguistic skills, the potential to assess children from diverse cultures to meet the range of their human potential seems promising.

Implications of MI Theory for Education

Much of the highly acclaimed contribution of psychology to education relates to the uses of intelligence tests in schools. However, despite the impressive scientific and technical qualities associated with the psychometric tradition in testing, evidence has been accumulating for some time to indicate that the IQ test is not an unbiased index of learning ability or relevant real-world competencies. This serious concern is further exacerbated when attention turns to individuals from low socioeconomic and minority backgrounds. The theory of multiple intelligences has challenged the psychometric paradigm and proposed the existence of intellectual competencies that have been grossly neglected by schools. By suggesting a contextual approach to assessment (Kornhaber, Krechevsky, and Gardner, 1990), MI theory has provided fresh thinking to support the focus on competencies applicable to practical, external world experiences.

It is perhaps the sensitivity of MI theory to abilities reflected in neglected areas of schooling such as musical ability, interpersonal and intrapersonal social intelligence, and bodily kinesthetic skills that will provide the impetus for schools to nurture culturally meaningful activities. In the context of this chapter on diversity, MI theory provides a defensible rationale and offers a realistic possibility that schools will be better able to recognize talents in individuals whose cultural experiences make them different from the white, middle-class student on whom so much educational practice has been based.

Learning Styles

The extensive literature on learning styles is based on the assumption that students enter a learning situation with a variety of skills, preferences, and capacities that affect their learning, and that a learning environment that utilizes an individual learner's strengths and is adapted to his or her preferences should facilitate learning for that student. Another student, with different strengths and different preferences, will do better in a different environment. Thus, a student who learns more easily with material presented visually, who prefers working in a small group, and who responds better to bright lighting (to use three examples) would do well academically in an environment modified to contain these three elements.

Learning style theorists claim that explicit attention to learning styles will improve the educational process in four major domains: curriculum design, instructional methods, assessment methods, and student guidance (Curry, 1990). For example, a classroom that is structured so that needs of visual learners as well as auditory learners are met (to use a common example) should be one where student achievement is maximized. While there is little disagreement about the general idea that individual differences should be accommodated in the classroom, there is considerable disagreement about many of the specific details in this area. The primary question that remains unresolved is just how much difference it makes if learning styles are taken into account when organizing a learning environment for instruction.

We have chosen to use the term *learning style* rather than the term *cognitive style* (as Corno and Snow have done) since the focus of the chapter is on instruction and since learning style seems to be the more preferred concept in the educational literature. As Keefe and Ferrell (1990) point out, the two concepts are often confused and the distinctions between them blurred. Cognitive style has been used for a longer period of time (Allport, 1924) and these constructs at least in theory are prerequisites to learning styles. A construct such as "field independence/dependence," for example, defined in the work of Witkin and his associates (1974) as the tendency to approach a situation in an analytic versus a global (or sequential versus holistic) way, is hypothesized to affect a wide variety of behaviors, among which are behaviors in learning environments. Theoretically, therefore, the cognitive style of field independence is both broader and more basic than a learning style such as "auditory processing." Many of the other cognitive style variables (for example, tolerance for ambiguity and locus of control) are assumed to act in essentially the same manner.

Reporting on the results of the National Association of Secondary School Principals' task force on learning styles, Keefe and Languis (1983) present a relatively encompassing and theoretically neutral definition. According to these authors, learning styles are the "composite of characteristic cognitive, affective, and physiological factors that serve as relatively stable indicators of how a learner perceives, interacts with, and responds to the learning environment. It is demonstrated in that pattern of behavior and performance by which an individual approaches educational experiences. Its basis lies in the structure of neural organization and personality which both molds and is molded by human development and the learning experience of home, school, and society" (p. 59).

The main elements of this definition—the cognitive, affective, and physiological aspects of learning styles and their derivation from both innate (that is, genetic) and learned (cultural) sources—allow the authors to straddle most of the thornier issues in this area. In fact, considerable controversy exists about the exact nature of learning styles and about their cause. Of the three comprehensive models of learning style that exist (Dunn, Dunn, and Price, 1975, 1979, 1981, 1985; Hill, 1971; Keefe and Monk, 1986), all assume to some extent that there are significant physiological underpinnings to learning styles, with the Dunns having set forth a fairly elaborate theory linking learning styles to right and left cerebral dominance (Dunn, Beaudry, and Klavas, 1989). On the other hand, writers who are more concerned about cultural influences on learning styles either downplay or deny their physiological basis (see, for example, Shade, 1989, and Hernandez, 1989).

How Many Learning Styles?

While there is some agreement about the essential categories of learning styles (almost all writers, for example, include at least one style similar to the analytic/global distinction made in field independence research), there is little agreement about the exact number of learning style variables or what specific learning styles exist. The work of Dunn, Dunn, and Price (1975), for example, yields twenty-one styles classified into five broad groupings: environmental factors, emotional factors, sociological preferences, physiological needs, and cognitive-psychological inclinations. Table 15.1, again taken from the work of the National Association of Secondary School Principals task force (1983), presents a fairly representative list of learning styles.

It is evident from the table that a wide range of variables are included that cover almost all aspects of the learner/environment interaction. It is also evident that the table includes styles that differ widely in generalizability and importance, a characteristic that almost all of the learning style theories share.

Issues and Controversies

As we have mentioned, the basic idea that individuals differ and that instruction should be modified to take these individual differences into account is not controversial as a general premise. The specifics of how this is accomplished, however, have produced several continuing controversies in this area. Curry (1990) lists three general problems that she perceives in this area: confusion in definitions, weakness in the assessment instruments, and inconclusive results from research involving the matching of learner characteristics and learning environments. Since we have already reviewed some of the issues regarding the definition of learning style, we will briefly comment on the other two issues and will then review the topic of cultural and racial differences in learning style.

The Assessment Instruments. There are several widely used learning style batteries; tests based on the work of the Dunns (Carbo, 1981; Dunn, Dunn, and Price, 1975, 1979, 1981, 1985; Keefe, Languis, Letteri, and Dunn, 1986) are the most common. In general, all of the existing batteries assess a variety of learning styles and produce a profile of an individual learner's strengths and weaknesses (or strong and weak preferences depending on the focus of the learning style theory). Evidence for the reliability of these scales varies from strong to marginal (internal consistency measures, for example, range from .3 to .9 using Cronbach's Alpha; test-retest reliabilities where available range from .2 to .7 over periods of time ranging from two weeks to more than two months).

TABLE 15.1. LEARNING STYLES.

A. Perceptual Styles
    1. Visual—initial reaction to information is visual
    2. Auditory—initial reaction to information is auditory
    3. Emotive—initial reaction to information is emotive

B. Cognitive Styles
    4. Analytic—identifies critical elements of a problem
    5. Spatial—identifies shapes and objects in mental space
    6. Discrimination—visualizes important elements of task
    7. Categorization—uses reasonable criteria for classifying information
    8. Sequential processing—processes information sequentially
    9. Simultaneous processing—processes information visuospatially
    10. Memory—retains information
    11. Verbal—spatial preferences; choice of verbal or nonverbal
    12. Persistence—willingness to finish work
    13. Verbal risk—willingness to express opinions
    14. Manipulative—desire for "hands on" activities
    15. Study time preference (early morning)
    16. Study time preference (late morning)
    17. Study time preference (afternoon)
    18. Study time preference (evening)
    19. Grouping preference—desire to learn in a whole class versus dyadic groupings
    20. Posture preference—desire for formal versus informal study
    21. Mobility preference—desire for taking breaks while studying
    22. Sound preference—desire to study in silence versus study with background sound
    23. Lighting preference—desire for bright or lower lighting
    24. Temperature preference—desire for cool versus warm environments

Source: National Association of Secondary School Principals Learning Styles Task Force (1983), p. 1.

The evidence for validity is a more complex issue, due largely to the fact that the field has not reached consensus about what should and should not be correlated with learning styles. Given this situation, it is difficult if not impossible to make firm statements about the construct validity of any of the batteries. At best, what can be done at this time is to review the evidence by the authors of the scales and judge from these presentations how adequate the scales seem to be. (See Dunn, Beaudry, and Klavas, 1989; and Keefe and Ferrell, 1990, for reviews of research on two of the scales.)

The Matching of Learners and Learning Environments. The critical test of learning style theory is to show that students perform best in learning environments that are matched to their learning style. An ideal research design would create a variety of learning environments structured around major learning styles and would then assign students to these environments so that their learning style matches or does not match the environment. While there is a considerable body of research of this type, a fair generalization of this research is that the evidence is contradictory. As reviewed by Curry (1990), there are about as many studies that show a positive matching effect (see, for example, Douglas, 1979; Tannenbaum, 1982; Steele, 1986) as there are studies that show no effect (Cholakis, 1986; De Gregoris, 1986; Stiles, 1985). Moreover, some studies show that students who are mismatched do better than those who are matched appropriately (Kirby, 1988; Knight, 1990).

Perhaps the most telling criticism of the matching assumption comes from the work of Cohen, Hyman, Ashcroft, and Loveless (1989). In a detailed analysis of the learning style research, these authors found that almost all of the studies demonstrating a positive effect for learning style matching occurred where the instruction was precisely defined, the outcomes were clearly detailed, and both instructors and students knew how the instruction and assessment were aligned. In other words, the treatment produced a positive effect on achievement not because the instruction and the learning style were matched but rather because the research forced the teachers to be clear and coherent in their instruction.

Are There Cultural or Racial Differences in Learning Style? Finally, we wish to review the topic of cultural or racial differences in learning style. While many articles and books in this area have focused on African-Americans, some more recent research has included Latino and Asian students. In general, researchers in this area have attempted to demonstrate that certain cultural or racial groups demonstrate a consistent pattern of learning styles that differs from the pattern demonstrated by other groups. Both Hale-Benson (1982) and Carbo, Dunn, and Dunn (1986), for example, have discussed the "black learning style" and have characterized it as being "global, holistic, simultaneous and field-dependent" (Dunn, Gemake, Jalali, and Zenhausern, 1990). The issue of an African-American learning style has also been raised by Shade (1982, 1986), who argues that the African-American student's culturally induced focus on people and social interactions rather than products or individual achievement may be one of the causes of lower levels of achievement in school. In a more recent and data-based article, Dunn, Gemake, Jalali, and Zenhausern (1990) compared the learning styles of African-American, Chinese-American, Greek-American, and Mexican-American children. These authors found statistically significant differences among the groups, although in some cases the groups were more similar than dissimilar on certain learning style variables.

As is true in many areas of learning style research and theory, the issue of consistent differences between racial or cultural groups is confusing and unclear. It is often the case that the theoretical writing is much stronger than the data base supporting it. Moreover, in any discussion of racial or cultural differences, the effects of social class and/or ethnicity must be taken into account. As we will discuss later in the chapter, the overlapping effects of race, ethnicity, and social class are complex. Since most of the research that has attempted to find racial differences in learning style has not adequately accounted for these overlapping and interactive effects, the existence of racial or cultural differences important enough to be considered in planning instruction must remain an open question.

Implications for Education

It is quite clear that teacher educators should understand the rationale underlying the call for environments that are sensitive and appropriate for individual learners. If nothing else, instruction at all levels should use varied formats and modalities and should in general match instruction to a student's strengths and preferences. To the extent that learning style theorists have furthered this general idea in education, they have had a positive effect. In general, however, the specific claims of these theorists, and particularly the amount of advocacy for their positions, seem unwarranted or at least exaggerated. Currently, learning style theory represents more of a promise than a reality for educational practice. What is clear, however, is that people learn differently and that some learners have strengths in areas that are unique to them and that make them different from other learners (visual learners versus auditory learners; analytic problem solvers versus global problem solvers, and so on). It is a truism to assert that this general idea needs to be taken into account by educators, and the proponents of learning styles have fostered this general notion better than any other group.

Learning Disability and Giftedness

It is estimated that approximately one out of every six children in a typical classroom can be classified as "exceptional" as this term is used in the educational literature (U.S. Department of Education, 1990). Table 15.2 presents a listing of characteristics commonly defined as exceptional and gives the approximate incidence in the U.S. population.

As Gage and Berliner (1991) point out, within the U.S. school population of approximately 45 million students, estimates would indicate that about 6.5 million children would be considered exceptional. Clearly, this form of diversity is one that all teachers will encounter, especially in light of the mandate through Public Law 94–142 to place all students in the least restrictive environment. Since the topic of exceptionality is extremely broad and complex, we will focus in this chapter on only those issues that we feel are central to our main topic. Specifically, we will discuss learning disability and giftedness, not only because these are the two most prevalent aspects of exceptionalities but also because most of the critical issues in this area can be discussed in reference to these topics. (See Reynolds, 1989, for a comprehensive discussion of the major topics in this area.)

TABLE 15.2. INCIDENCE OF EXCEPTIONALITY IN THE U.S. SCHOOL POPULATION.

TYPE OF EXCEPTIONALITY	INCIDENCE IN POPULATION (percent)
Learning disabled	5.0%
Gifted and talented	4.2%
Speech impaired	2.5%
Mentally retarded	1.4%
Emotionally disturbed	1.0%
Hard of hearing and deaf	.14%
Orthopedically impaired	.12%
Other health impaired	.12%
Multihandicapped	.07%
Visually handicapped	.06%

Learning Disability

All students, even the brightest ones, have difficulty learning some material some of the time. When a student who usually does well in school is having trouble, the source for this difficulty is usually sought in such short-term, controllable causes as a temporary illness, lack of interest in the specific topic, or overcommitment in other areas. However, some students consistently have trouble learning yet have no obvious reason for this difficulty. If such a problem persists for a period of time, the student could eventually be classified as learning disabled. As is true of many areas of diversity, there is little disagreement about the general premise that learning disabilities exist. The problem as usual is in the specifics.

Definition. One of the major controversies in the area of learning disabilities concerns the correct definition of this condition. In his recent article, Hammill (1990) reviews eleven different definitions of learning disability, citing the similarities and dissimilarities among them. His preferred definition is the following:

> Learning disabilities is a general term that refers to a heterogeneous group of disorders manifested by significant difficulties in the acquisition and use of listening, speaking, reading, writing, reasoning, or mathematical abilities. These disorders are intrinsic to the individual, presumed to be due to central nervous system dysfunction, and may occur across the life span. Problems in self-regulatory behaviors, social perception, and social interaction may exist with learning disabilities but do not by themselves constitute a learning disability. Although learning disabilities may occur concomitantly with other handicapping conditions (for example, sensory impairment, mental retardation, serious emotional disturbance) or with extrinsic influences (such as cultural differences, insufficient or inappropriate instruction) they are not the results of

those conditions or influences [National Joint Committee on Learning Disabilities, 1988, p. 1].

As Hammill mentions, the one commonality that all definitions share is the notion that a learning-disabled student is an underachiever. In general, this underachievement is defined as either a discrepancy between different achievement domains (for instance, math versus reading) or between a measure of ability, such as an IQ score, and achievement. Moreover, most of the definitions of learning disability exclude a variety of factors (economic and cultural differences, low motivation, poor instruction) as contributing to or causing the condition. Finally, there is a growing consensus that the problem is somehow related to central nervous system functioning, although how and why this occurs is both unclear and controversial.

The second major topic in learning disability concerns the correct instructional approaches teachers should use to help these students achieve their maximum potential. There is a growing literature on this subject focusing on both classroom practices as well as on training in areas such as increasing problem solving abilities, decreasing impulsivity, and improving peer relationships (see Lerner, 1981, for an early review of this area). Gage and Berliner (1991) present a series of actions teachers can use to help deal with the learning disabled in the classroom: a careful observation of the student in various contexts, a comparison of the student with other students to ascertain how atypical the target student's behavior is, a series of steps to determine if the student should be referred for possible special education classification, and some suggestions for developing and implementing an individualized educational plan for the student. The general assumption in most of this literature is that the learning disabled student will be a part of the regular classroom and that it is the responsibility of the teacher to adapt his or her instruction to this form of diversity.

Issues and Controversies. The learning disabled are the fastest growing group of exceptional children in U.S. schools. This rate of increase is evidenced by the following statistics: in 1970, the number of children classified as learning disabled was approximately 150,000; by 1990, the number had increased to 2 million (Yesseldyke and Algozzine, 1983). It is also interesting that a majority of students who are classified as learning disabled are males. Lerner (1981), for example, estimates that there are four to six times as many males as females classified as learning disabled. Since there is no reason to assume that the actual incidence of this condition has increased to the extent noted above, the growing use of the term "learning disabled" is striking testimony to the political and social forces that affect the classification and treatment of exceptional children. Special education (to use the more inclusive term) has always been an arena open to competing political forces as society struggles with both the definition and treatment of children who are viewed as deviant. In an earlier time, a far greater percentage of children were classified as mentally defective, based on either poor school performance, low IQ scores, or both. With the increasing attacks on the traditional IQ test, and the growing awareness that a disproportionate number of minority and low socioeconomic status (SES) children were classified as mentally defective, this label has become increasingly unacceptable. The great advantage to the concept of learning disability is that the construct, by definition, excludes many of the factors (such as cultural differences) that are known to produce those characteristics that have been previously labeled as mental retardation. It should be emphasized that the school-related manifestations of the condition, such as low achievement or lack of attention in class, have not changed. Rather, what has altered is the cause that is believed to produce these behaviors. Furthermore, by placing the etiology in the domain of central nervous system dysfunction, even though the specific action and location are largely unknown, the locus of responsibility for academic failure is shifted away from agents such as parents, teachers, and the school and toward an uncontrollable and unavoidable genetic cause.

All of these factors combine to indicate why learning disability is the classification of choice for the 1990s and why the topic is central to a discussion of diversity in education. By reclassifying a significant number of students who are not achieving at acceptable levels as "learning disabled," a category has been created by which these students can be conveniently grouped and treated as a homogeneous subset of students within a classroom. More important, since writers in this field have carefully excluded such factors as cultural differences or poor academic preparation, charges of racial or ethnic bias, or of poor teaching, cannot be made. Unlike the mentally retarded, the learning disabled are not intellectually deficient, nor do they necessarily have low IQs, nor are they incapable of learning. To push this argument to its logical conclusion, the existence of the construct "learning disability" creates for education a politically correct category in which to put many of its failures, without the necessity of assigning blame to anyone for these failures.

It is not our intent to discredit the general concept of learning disability since underachievement should be a concern of any teacher. Concerns can be raised, however, about the seemingly inevitable tendency to "medicalize" constructs such as learning disability and to transform them into something more closely resembling an illness. For example, there is a clear relationship between learning disability and the diagnostic classification "attention deficit hyperactivity disorder" (ADHD) (Robins, 1992; Rutter, 1989). While this topic is too complex to be covered here, it is interesting to note the movement that seems to be occurring from the general construct of learning disability to the specific, medical syndrome of ADHD. Since ADHD is often treated by medication (Ritalin, generically known as methylphenidate) (Balthazor, Wagner, and Pelham, 1991), the trend to remediate the problem of underachievement through medical means becomes more evident. Some of this movement is undoubtedly warranted, and some of the medical recommendations being made about a growing number of children are correct. The question that education must face is whether this trend has gone too far and whether the medical profession is the proper location for remediating an increasing number of educational problems.

Implications for Education. Our intent in this section is to point out that achievement, like any other student characteristic, is an aspect of diversity. Not all students achieve at the same level or at the same rate, and most students have areas of strength and weakness. The goal of instruction is to adapt to and include this diversity no matter what its cause or its manifestations. The danger with a category such as learning disability is that the label can easily stigmatize (see Cushner, McClelland, and Safford, 1992, for a discussion) and that it becomes too easy to avoid responsibility for adequate instruction. Moreover, the assumed purpose for labeling students as learning disabled is to develop a series of differential treatments for them that will facilitate their achievement. In our opinion, in many cases these treatments are all too often short-lived, uncoordinated, and ineffectual. Nevertheless, there are undoubtedly students for whom the label of learning disabled or ADHD is appropriate. Some of these students can benefit from medication. The problem for education therefore is to assure that students receive the type of special services they need (which all too often means that the student must be classified) without the negative consequences so often contingent on this classification. Clearly, with the recent trend in this direction, most teachers will have students in their classroom who have been classified as learning disabled and/or ADHD and who may be on medication. At the very least, teachers need to be aware of the issues involved in this classification and need to have at their disposal a variety of techniques to deal with these students' special needs.

Gifted and Talented

While it may seem unusual to discuss gifted students in the same section as the learning disabled, in fact many of the underlying issues are similar. As in our previous discussion, two of the major concerns are how the construct should be defined and how this form of diversity should be handled within the regular classroom. As before, both issues are controversial.

Definition. While most general definitions of giftedness are fairly similar, considerable variability exists when the construct is made specific. Gage and Berliner (1991) provide a fairly representative general definition; they say the category usually includes "those demonstrating high performance in one or more of the following areas: general intellectual ability, specific academic aptitude, creative or productive thinking, leadership, or the visual and performing arts" (p. 216).

A similar definition is reported by Cramer (1991), who summarized the responses of twenty-nine experts in the field of gifted education: "Giftedness is the potential for exceptional development of specific abilities as well as the demonstration of performance at the upper end of the talent continuum; it is not limited by age, gender, race, socioeconomic status, or ethnicity" (p. 88).

Finally, Renzulli (1986), one of the leaders in this field, offers what he terms a "three-ring" definition of giftedness: above-average ability, task commitment, and creativity. (For a review of various definitions and the way they are used in school districts throughout the country, see Hunsaker, 1991.)

While all three of the above definitions provide a general framework by which giftedness can be considered, there are obvious problems in their lack of specificity: How high is "high performance"? What is "exceptional development"? At what point do we decide that a student is at the "upper end" of the talent continuum? Questions such as these may not be troubling when the discussion is at a theoretical level; they become critical, however, when the decision must be made about the classification and placement of a specific student.

Issues and Controversies. The controversy over definition touches almost all aspects of programming for gifted and talented students. One basic question, for example, is whether this type of diversity should include only giftedness (which almost always means high aptitude, often defined as high IQ), or talented (which usually means some form of artistic or creative ability, however defined), or both. Where definitions focus on giftedness, a common process for classification is to impose some cutoff score based on an assessment of ability through a standardized test. Assume, for example, that a school district intends to employ an IQ test as the measure of ability and that the criterion for possible admission into the gifted program is an ability level no less than two standard deviations above the mean. If the IQ test used has a mean of 100 and a standard deviation of 15, this means that giftedness would be defined as having an IQ of 130 or more. One would assumed that this would make the rule for classification clear. In practice, however, several complexities arise. For one thing, the standard error of measurement for most tests of this type is at least three points. A student who obtains a score of 129 would therefore have a reasonable case to argue that he or she should be eligible for the gifted program. In addition, the average IQ in any specific district may be more or less than 100, thereby producing a variable cutoff score across districts. Finally, different IQ tests have different means and standard deviations, and different versions of the same test can vary in these characteristics. What seems clear and easy to implement becomes in practice complex and controversial. Moreover, all of the complexity that arises in defining "giftedness" pales in comparison to the problem of defining "talented," a construct whose definition has almost no consensus and whose operationalization is at best in its infancy.

The second major issue in this area concerns the type of program that would be implemented for gifted and talented students after these students have been classified. Getzels and Dillon (1973) list thirty types of programs currently in existence across the country, ranging from separate schools, separate classes within a regular school, pull-out programs several times a week, Saturday classes, and so on. As one might expect, given our previous discussions, there is no real consensus about which type of program is best. There is some agreement among leaders in the field that special programs for gifted and talented students should not be integrated into the regular classroom and that instruction should not simply be more of the same thing that is presented to the regular students. As Renzulli and Reis (1991) point out, the reform movement in education has to some extent had the effect of decreasing attention to gifted programs since many of these reform movements have focused on improving the academic performance of lower achieving students. Given the increasing budgetary restraints in many school districts, gifted programs have often been eliminated in favor of programs focusing on the development of basic skills.

Implications for Education. The inclusion of a section on gifted and talented students is an important part of a chapter on diversity, since this aspect of diversity represents one of the richest resources in any classroom. In many important ways, however, the area has produced a series of controversies that render some of the possible gains from gifted education difficult to attain. One of these issues touches on the discussion earlier in this chapter concerning racial and/or social class bias in IQ tests. If one of the central components in the definition of giftedness is IQ, and if the traditional IQ test is known to be biased against minority groups, it would necessarily follow that minority students would be underrepresented in gifted programs. This is especially critical if a strict IQ definition of giftedness (such as the 130 and above criterion previously mentioned) is used as the sole component for classification and placement. If, for example, the average IQ of African-American students is lower than the average IQ of white students, then a smaller percentage of African-Americans will be classified as gifted as compared to whites. If it can be shown, or if it is believed, that this difference is related to cultural factors inherent in the test, then the decision to place students in the gifted program will be racially biased.

In response to this problem, many school districts have attempted to implement programs for identifying gifted and talented students by the use of multiple criteria. These criteria include, in addition to an IQ measure, such variables as achievement, nominations (parent, teacher, peer, or self), and various ways of assessing creativity. While, in theory, such programs should avoid the problems in the use of the IQ as the sole criterion, in practice this does not always happen. As Reis (1989) points out, "If the youngster has extremely high scores or recommendations on all or many of the other criteria, the multiple criteria are often ignored in favor of a single indicator, an individually administered IQ test" (p. 403). The essential point to be made in this regard is that the use of an IQ measure, even in conjunction with other criteria, will exclude children of limited English proficiency, low-income, and minority backgrounds. While this is a radical departure from current practice, it follows that without a commitment to abandon the use of intelligence tests in the identification process, the problem of identifying minority children as gifted or talented will remain.

Adams (1990) not only presents data demonstrating the underrepresentation of minority children in gifted programs but also goes further in examining the core definition that our society has created for giftedness. As she points out, we have defined giftedness from the perspective of the white, middle-class culture. It should be expected therefore that minority students will not be recognized as gifted when such a definition is applied.

In perhaps one of the most thought-provoking articles in this area, Hoge (1988) reviews the major problems with the concept of giftedness. In addition to the problem with definition that we have already mentioned, he lists three other concerns: (1) there is almost always a discrepancy between the official or conceptual definition of the construct and the operational definition created by the measuring instruments, (2) there is seldom any relationship between the definition of giftedness and the nature of the programming for the students classified, and (3) there is a wide gap between the expectations that society has come to place on giftedness and the operational and conceptual definition of the construct presented by the test makers. While he perceives some positive recent developments in this area, he cautions that at present the construct of giftedness has enough serious problems to question its use in education.

We share the basic idea of Renzulli and Reis (1991) in their discussion of a movement from "being gifted" to "the development of gifted behaviors" and have reproduced part of their argument below:

> Many people have been led to believe that certain individuals have been endowed with a golden chromosome that makes him or her "a gifted person." The further use of terms such as "the truly gifted," "the highly gifted," "the moderately gifted," and "the borderline gifted" only serve to confound the issue because they invariably harken back to a conception of giftedness that equates the concept with test scores. This issue has led us to advocate a fundamental change in the ways the concept of giftedness should be viewed. . . . We believe that labeling students as "gifted" is counterproductive to the education efforts aimed at providing supplementary educational experiences for certain students. We believe that our field should shift its emphasis from a traditional concept of "being gifted" to a concern about the development of gifted behaviors in those youngsters who have the highest potential for benefiting from special educational services" [p. 34].

The implication we draw from Renzulli and Reis's statement is that any static, test-driven definition of giftedness that serves primarily to label and sort one group of students for special placement is unacceptable. Just as there are several intelligences, so are there many ways to be gifted and many different pedagogical implications that can be derived from the varying strengths that students bring to school.

Giftedness, like learning disability, presents a source of diversity in the classroom. Both of these concepts demonstrate the possibilities and the problems that we introduced in the beginning of this chapter: should we treat students like no other human being, like some other human beings, or like all other human beings? Put another way, when is it advantageous for a teacher to conceptualize his or her classroom as consisting of a homogeneous group of "students," when is it preferable to think of the class as composed of recognizable subgroups of students (such as the gifted or the learning disabled) who can be taught in a more or less similar fashion, and when is it better to think of the classroom as containing a group of students each of whom is unique? This is not an issue of choosing a correct or an incorrect position, since each of these ways of conceptualizing diversity is defendable and each is necessary at different times and under different circumstances. While we have no easy answer to these complex questions, we have tried throughout this section to caution against the overreliance on simple schemes for labeling and classifying students. In our opinion, these schemes often obfuscate more than they clarify and are seldom based on sound research that demonstrates that they produce higher levels of achievement or a more manageable classroom.

Aspects of Diversity Viewed as Differences in Kind of Cultural Diversity

In keeping with the distinction made earlier, we have called the topics included in this section of the chapter "differences in kind." Many readers may be more comfortable with the term *cultural diversity*, which is used in the literature in approximately the same way that we are using *differences in kind*. As before, the literature is often inconsistent in the way terms are used and the meaning that is given to concepts. Culture itself is a term laden with meaning. For our purposes, we have chosen to define culture according to Bullivant (1989), who favors discussing it as "a social group's design for surviving in and adapting to its environment" (p. 27). If this definition is applied in an educational setting, then according to Bullivant it is necessary to teach about the "many social groups and their different designs for living in our pluralist society" (p. 27).

Bullivant stresses the importance of studying culture not only by turning to its customs, heritage, history, and aesthetic aspect but especially by dealing with how it has survived. In so doing, issues of power, marginality, and alienation can be directly addressed. The hope is that a feeling of empowerment and the possibility of using one's own agency can be fostered no matter what culture or cultures one belongs to.

Consistent with the definition presented earlier (Bullivant, 1989, p. 4), we have decided to discuss a wide variety of categories in this section: gender, social class, sexual differences, ethnicity, and race. In an attempt to be more inclusive, we have also tried to move beyond the single-group studies approach. Sleeter and Grant (1988) see this approach as "characterized by attention to a single group, for example, women, Asians, Blacks, Hispanics, Native Americans, or the working class" (p. 105). The word *attention* in Sleeter and Grant's definition is pivotal as it indicates that emphasis is placed on the major category for the group. For example, in the area of women's studies, while factors such as race and social class are deemed important, the foundation of this interdisciplinary area is solidly grounded in feminist scholarship, feminist theory, and feminist methodology.

However, it is important to realize that within the single-group areas of women's studies, African-American studies, and ethnic studies, the goal of many writers and academicians is not only to raise the consciousness of others to the literature and history of a single group by teaching its scholarship within a separate department or program, it is also ultimately to transform the traditional curriculum. Transformation means that the mainstream curriculum is decentered to enable the scholarship and methodology of the single groups to be integrated into a new, inclusive curriculum.

The concept of transformation can be seen in phase or stage theory that indicates the steps needed to sensitize students and faculty to the importance of moving the study of a particular group (for example, women) from the margins into the mainstream curriculum (McIntosh, 1984; Schuster and Van Dyne, 1985; Tetreault, 1989). It can also be found in the Afrocentric vision of Asante (1987) and in the levels of ethnic content integration described by Banks and Banks (1989). In all these areas, there is an effort to bring the "new scholarship," the writings and methodologies of previously neglected groups, emanating from the single study areas, into the mainstream curriculum of the schools.

In attempting to pull together salient single-group and other pertinent studies that encompass two or three aspects of cultural diversity, it immediately becomes evident that a number of these differences tend to overlap. The intersection of race and social class issues, for example, can make for different kinds of diversity from those in which gender and social class issues combine. The complexities of overlapping differences continue to create problems in the literature on cultural diversity.

One of the reasons for this complexity has to do with what McCarthy and Apple (1988) have called the "nonsynchronous position" of groups in regard to categories such as gender, race, and ethnicity. Nonsynchrony refers to the situation that occurs when various forms of discrimination act in an asymmetrical fashion on different members of the same group. This position, developed by Hicks (1981), held that "individuals or groups in their relation to their economic and political systems do not share similar consciousness or similar needs at the same point in time" (p. 25). This phenomenon has often meant that areas of difference, such as social class, race, and/or gender, sometimes conflict in educational settings (Parker and Shapiro, 1993).

It is important that those who prepare future educators realize the complexities in this area of cultural diversity. We believe it is especially salient because the

1990s represents a time when there is "a striking discontinuity between teacher and student diversity" (Grant and Secada, 1991). There is also a striking discontinuity between school administrator and student diversity. In both of these cases, demographic information clearly shows that although the student population is becoming increasingly more diverse, the teaching force is remaining predominantly white, female, and upwardly mobile lower class (Apple, 1986; De Lyon and Widdowson Migniuolo, 1989; Grant and Secada, 1991; Sleeter, 1992). Furthermore, despite the student population's diverse composition, school administrators continue to be predominantly white, male, and middle class, although there are a growing number of white, female, middle-class educators preparing for school administrative posts (Jones and Montenegro, 1990). While it is clearly important to recruit teachers and administrators from diverse backgrounds, it is equally important to be cognizant of the homogeneity of the current and future population of professional educators and to be aware that there are striking discontinuities between these educators and the students they teach.

It follows from these striking discontinuities that a major task of educational programming is to provide the predominantly white, female, upwardly mobile, lower-class teachers and the white, male, middle-class school administrators with knowledge of diverse groups in order to develop in them an understanding of differences. In most cases, we also hope that with understanding will come a sense of appreciation of and empathy for those differences. Furthermore, along with this understanding, appreciation, and empathy toward differences, we also believe that it is exceedingly important to provide student teachers and administrative interns with a strong sense of self. We concur with Sleeter and Grant (1988), who have said that "people must first understand themselves before they can hope to understand others" (p. 126). If we do not succeed in this endeavor, we will not have prepared our current educational students properly for the majority of U.S. classrooms and schools in the twenty-first century (American Association of University Women, 1992; Grant and Secada, 1991; Sleeter and Grant, 1988).

Gender

A discussion of gender and the large and growing literature on its relation to education would seem to be a logical starting point for this section of the chapter for several reasons. First, as we mentioned previously, despite the gains in the women's movement over the past twenty years in the United States, the traditional patterns of women as teachers and men as managers of schools persist (Strober and Tyack, 1980). Currently, nearly 69 percent of teachers in the United States are women (85 percent elementary, 53 percent middle/junior high school, and 44 percent secondary) (National Center for Education Statistics, 1989) and approximately 75 percent of school administrators are men (88 percent secondary principals and 66 percent elementary principals) (Jones and Montenegro, 1990). Since almost all female and male children in this society spend a majority of their formative years in institutions in which women teach and men manage, consequently creating environments that are highly structured according to gender, it is obviously important to understand the effects this environment has on students' learning from a cognitive and an affective perspective.

Another reason for beginning this section with a discussion of gender is that this construct represents perhaps better than most the dramatic shift in emphasis that has occurred during the past twenty to thirty years. Traditionally, the topic of differences between girls and boys was listed in textbooks under the heading of "sex differences" and the discussion always included, indeed focused upon, such biological variables as differences in rate of development and possible genetic variations in certain achievement domains (for example, mathematics, science, and verbal skills). It is interesting that the most recent metanalysis of this literature, involving thousands of studies and millions of subjects (Hyde, 1993), concludes that at present there are no appreciable differences between men and women in verbal ability and only a modest difference in math skills. Moreover, a recent review of gender differences in science (Kahle, Parker, Rennie, and Riley, 1993) concludes that almost all of the differences between boys and girls in science achievement result from the misperception by teachers that science is an inherently masculine discipline, involving inherently masculine skills such as analyzing and hypothesizing, and that girls are therefore permitted less access to science-related materials and curriculum. In large part, then, much of the current literature, while not ignoring sex differences, instead focuses on gender differences and the way gender roles and expectations are constructed by our society. The remaining topics in this section of the chapter will maintain this focus on gender rather than on sex as the integrating theme.

Definition. To avoid confusion, we offer Anderson's definition of sex and gender (1988): "Sex refers to the genetic and physical identity of the person and is meant to signify the fact that one is either male or female. One's biological sex usually establishes a pattern of gendered expectations." Anderson, when describing gender, says that it "refers to the socially learned behaviors and expectations that are associated with the two sexes. Thus, whereas 'maleness' and 'femaleness' are biological facts, masculinity and femininity are culturally constructed attributes" (p. 75). She goes on to say that gender is a broad concept encompassing "complex political, economic, psychological, and social relations between men and women in society" (p. 76). As we said above, a significant change has occurred in recent years in which educational effects once viewed as primarily sex-based are now often considered gender-related. To a great degree, the distinctions between sex and gender have been brought about through the interdisciplinary area of women's studies, which has provided considerable scholarship by and about women that has paved the way for discussing these categories within the school as well as within society. Men's studies too is emerging as an important area of research, but it has had only a short period in which to develop. Of all the "differences in kind" that we will discuss in this chapter, the discussion and debate over gender and sex reflect most of the critical points being raised for the other categories included in this section.

Curriculum and Pedagogical Issues and Controversies. As we have already mentioned, there is a long history of research and theorizing on sex differences (see, for example, Maccoby and Jacklin, 1974; Hyde, 1993) in which the different abilities and achievement levels of girls and boys were reviewed, discussed, and explained. We do not intend to review this literature here, since it has been discussed in great detail elsewhere. Our focus instead will be on the more recent reconceptualization of this research from the perspective of gender.

As many writers have noted, the educational environment of schools has not historically been gender neutral, leading to biases of all kinds, even in the 1990s. In fact, Sadker and Sadker (1982) have noted as many as six forms of sex biases within the curriculum today: *linguistic bias,* in which the use of generic *he* and terms such as *caveman, forefathers,* and *mankind* remain; *sex role stereotyping,* in which girls and boys are described in traditional ways: boys as hunters and warriors, girls as princesses and mothers; *invisibility in books and curriculum material,* which simply omits the history and writings of women; *imbalance through the use of only the male perspective,* in which at best the trivial and mundane matters facing girls and women are merely mentioned; *unreality in perpetuating myths,* in which there is a desire to idealize institutions that hardly exist in reality, such as the nuclear family; and *fragmentation of women's contributions,* in which women's works are featured in a box or block in texts rather than being properly integrated into the main body of the subject matter (Sadker, Sadker, and Long, 1989, pp. 107–108).

In the area of instructional practice or pedagogy, in a major report, the American Association of University Women (AAUW) (1991) has indicated that although it is almost two decades since Congress prohibited sex discrimination in education through the passage of Title IX, teachers continue to "have lower expectations for girls than for boys" (p. 1). In fact, in the AAUW report, a clear statement is made concerning often unintentional but very real problems: "Whether one looks at preschool classrooms or university lecture halls, at female teachers or male teachers, research spanning twenty years consistently reveals that males receive more teacher attention than do females. In preschool classrooms boys receive more instructional time, more hugs, and more teacher attention. The pattern persists through elementary school and high school" (p. 68).

In many writings based on classroom research (including Brown and Hoffman, 1991; Culley and Portuges, 1985; Delamont, 1983; Hall and Sandler, 1982; Klein, 1985; Schniedewind and Maher, 1987; Spender, 1982; Stanworth, 1983), what has been found is a recurrent pattern of white boys receiving more attention than white girls. The research shows that boys speak out more than girls without raising their hands; they are provided with teacher comments of praise, acceptance, remediation, and criticism much more often than girls. In fact, the pattern is so prevalent that Dale Spender (1982) has labeled the syndrome "make trouble, get results."

While the area of teacher-student classroom interaction research has not focused strongly on patterns of overlapping categories, such as race, ethnicity, and social class, in relation to gender, a few recent studies have begun to address this issue. In the AAUW (1992) report, for example, evidence is presented that there is a difference in the kinds of interactions associated with white and black children and their teachers (p. 70). What we know thus far is that stereotypes apparently do exist. African-American boys tend to be perceived less favorably by their teachers and are seen as less able than other students (Rosser, 1989). They also tend to have fewer verbal interactions with their teachers yet are the recipients of four to ten times the amount of qualified praise ("That's good, but . . .") as other students (Harris and Carlton, 1990). With black girls, the interactions are extremely complex. "Black girls have less interaction with teachers than white girls, but they attempt to initiate interaction much more often than white girls or than boys of either race" (American Association of University Women, 1992, p. 70). It is hypothesized that teachers may unconsciously rebuff black girls who speak out. Frequently, these children turn to peers for interactions, often becoming the class enforcers or go-betweens for other students (National Science Foundation, 1990). In an even more recent study, Flanagan (1993) reviews the overlap of gender and social class and concludes, "Girls from lower SES families are at a distinct risk of being ignored as long as discussions of class exploitation do not include issues of gender segregation and vice versa, whether these discussions are about school, work, family, or their intersections" (p. 373). Despite these recent studies, however, much more research needs to be carried out dealing not only with the category of gender in the classroom but with the overlapping areas of race, ethnicity, and social class. Despite the limitations, the research clearly shows that girls of all colors are not receiving the kinds of time, attention, and care that they deserve in our nation's classrooms.

Issues Regarding Female Teachers and Administrators. Not only do problems exist for girls in the classroom, they persist for women teachers and administrators. As we have indicated previously, despite the large number of female teachers, the majority of administrators at all levels are men. In the 1990s, the traditional patterns remain intact.

Apple (1986) and others have written extensively about the relatively powerless position of female teachers and how they have been devalued. Apple has written of the belief throughout many eras that teachers might not be professional enough to design a curriculum of their own. This lack of faith in female teachers' abilities has led to what he and others have called the teacher-proof curriculum and the de-skilling of teachers.

In the 1980s and 1990s, despite the rhetoric emphasizing the professionalization of teaching, there seem to be few attempts to raise teachers' self-awareness, which can lead to empowerment. Despite the importance of the topic, few opportunities are provided in teacher preparation programs and inservice training for teachers to learn about gender. In fact, in Sleeter's study (1992) of thirty white teachers who participated in a multicultural education staff development project, the author found many of these experienced teachers were lacking in knowledge of themselves as well as others. In addition, the teachers tended to be conservative, particularly on the issues of race and ethnicity. By the end of her investigation, Sleeter wondered if her sample of teachers understood gender discrimination issues within society at all.

Not only within the classroom but administratively, the problems continue for women. While there are many female teachers, there are still few female principals and superintendents. The lack of females in leadership posts is not a positive influence on girls. We know how important appropriate role modeling is for the young. Furthermore, the problem is not that there are no qualified educators in the pipeline (Pavan, 1985; National Policy Board for Educational Administration, 1989) to take on these roles. It is well documented that highly intelligent and experienced female educators are seldom selected for leadership positions (Marshall, 1985; Ortiz and Marshall, 1988; Pavan, 1985; Shakeshaft, 1987; Shapiro, 1987).

Some of the literature blames women themselves for this apparent career stagnation. Internal or psychological barriers are often cited. Blame is frequently attributed to deficiencies of credentials, degrees, and classroom experience (Shakeshaft, 1987; Shapiro, 1987). Other reasons are more psychologically oriented and include low levels of confidence and autonomy, lack of aspirations and motivation, numerous family and home responsibilities, and the effects of sex role stereotyping and female socialization (Abbey and Melby, 1986; Marshall, 1985; Tetreault and Schmuck, 1985). Although there may be some psychological and internal obstacles that hinder their mobility, there is evidence that formidable, well-defined external factors inhibit development of female school administrators. These factors include the low level of encouragement for women to enter administrative posts, a limited number of role models, lack of networks, and discriminatory practices in hiring and promoting women (Shakeshaft, 1987; Shapiro, 1987).

Issues Regarding Male Teachers and Administrators. Men who teach and administer schools also have their share of problems. Just as women's roles have been socially constructed by society, so have men's. Currently, men are asking themselves questions about their own position in society and are attempting to make sense of changing morals and behavior.

A new literature, dealing with men and masculinity, has appeared recently. Clatterbaugh (1990) presents six perspectives that he believes have begun to dominate this area of research: (1) the *conservative perspective*, which defends the age-old position of men as providers and protectors (Gilder, 1973, 1986; Winner, 1983); (2) the *profeminist perspective*, which charges men to leave behind masculinity that oppresses both women and men (Doyle, 1989; Kimmel, 1987; Pleck, 1981); (3) the *men's rights perspective*, which looks at the discrimination that men face through role expectations (Diamond, 1983; Goldberg, 1987); (4) the *spiritual perspective*, which focuses on men returning to their rites of passages and attempts to offer self-exploration through faith (Bly, 1981; Rowan, 1987); (5) the *socialist perspective*, which turns to the works of Marx and the socialist agenda to empower men to overturn the capitalistic structure of society (Robinson, 1983; Zaretsky, 1976); and (6) the *group-specific perspective*, which looks at masculinity overlapping with other categories such as race, ethnicity, and sexual orientation (Fernback, 1981; Gibbs, 1988; Munoz, 1989).

Implications for Educating Educators. Despite our increasing knowledge of gender issues, our awareness of sex discrimination cases, and the need for gender-fair education (Sadker and Sadker, 1982), little has changed in the preparation of the student teacher (American Association of University Women, 1991) and the school administrator (Parker and Shapiro, 1993; Sadker, Sadker, and Klein, 1991). In fact, there continue to be few curricular reforms, pedagogical changes, staff development modifications, recruitment initiatives, career restructuring programs, and empowerment improvements targeted for girls and women in education in general. There are even fewer reforms available on the study by and about boys' and men's roles related to the field of education.

In the area of the curriculum, the selection of textbooks and other reading matter that takes into account gender balancing can help to combat sexism. Not only should the curriculum of students and their texts deal with gender issues but the texts in teacher education need to be reviewed for gender imbalances. It should be noted that in a 1981 analysis of teacher education texts (American Association of University Women, 1991), a third of them did not even mention the topic of sexism.

In addition, in the area of curriculum development, researchers are already documenting curriculum integration projects that move much of the new scholarship on girls and women into the mainstream (Aiken and others, 1987; Arch, Kirschner, and Tetreault, 1983; Fritsche, 1984; Schmitz and Williams, 1983; Schuster and Van Dyne, 1985; Spanier, Bloom, and Boroviak, 1986). However, only a few of these projects are aimed specifically at the preparation of new and experienced teachers (Shapiro, Parssinen, and Brown, 1992; Styles, 1988).

Administratively, if there is an opportunity to assist in the selection of a new principal or superintendent, there should be an awareness of the need for female role models for girls (Fauth, 1984; Marshall, 1985; Shakeshaft, 1987; Shapiro, 1987). Whenever possible, women need to be encouraged to assume leadership positions as coaches, team leaders, and so forth. In particular, math and science and other traditionally male areas should be taught by female teachers. On the other hand, it could be of value if male teachers taught nontraditional subjects as well as assumed more caretaking functions within schools.

Above all, gender-fair education can make a difference and can help to change attitudes and break down biases. But gender-fair education will not occur until teachers and school administrators are prepared in this area. A focus on female and male theories and issues in teacher training, administrative training, and in-service training programs can help develop self-awareness. Preparation in the category of gender will also enable women teachers and male school administrators, who make up the majority of educators today, to begin to understand their students' and other constituencies' needs. Such training may have a positive effect on the development of both male and female educators and may ultimately lead to a much more empathetic and understanding society.

Social Class

Since social class has been defined in a variety of ways, we have decided that the goals of this chapter are best served by using a broad-based and somewhat less focused definition rather than one which is clearly operationalized but narrow. We agree with Trent (1988), Parker and Shapiro (1993), and others who have noted a distinction between socioeconomic status and social class in discussions of educational issues. The former term has been associated with stratification and has been typically measured by characteristics such as family background, prestige of occupation, and economic status. The latter term has been defined as a large category of people who are of a similar socioeconomic status but who also share commonalities in terms of lifestyles, attitudes, and cultural identification. For our purposes, then, the term *social class* is preferable to *socioeconomic status* because it better captures the issues related to educational practice.

In the United States, it is noteworthy that social class is frequently ignored as an important category in the discussion of cultural diversity, perhaps because of the myth that the term *middle-class* is all-inclusive and relates to most citizens. Rose (1974) believes that the majority of Americans do not want to be part of the lower social class and few think they are wealthy enough to be considered upper class. Hence, most claim that they are somewhere in the middle. Nevertheless, according to Reich (1992), there is a growing segregation of Americans by income, lifestyles, and values. In fact, he writes, "There is only one thing Americans increasingly have in common with their neighbors, and their commonality lies at the heart of the new American 'community.' It is their income levels. You can bet without much risk that you earn about the same amount as the folks down the street. Your educational backgrounds are similar, you pay roughly the same amount in taxes, and you indulge the same consumer impulses. The best definition of 'community' is now the zip code used by direct-mail marketers to target likely customers" (p. 277).

Despite the perception of "middle-classness" held by many Americans, the reality is that this social class group is decreasing and that there are more poor people and more rich people than ever before in this country (Reich, 1992). Things are so polarized that at least one-fourth of all preschool children in the United States now live in poverty (Hodgkinson, 1992).

Whether we wish to admit it or not, social class issues loom large in regard to schooling. Biemiller (1993), in reviewing the data on SES effects on academic achievement, argues that many of the differences noted in the research are in fact attributable to school practices such as grouping. Moreover, inequalities in school support have reached epidemic portions. Great disparities are seen in the amount of money spent per student and the amount paid to teachers when comparing urban and suburban school districts. In an era in which social class issues need to become explicit, educators must obtain an appreciation of the complexity of these issues to better understand their own institution and its place in the community.

Issues and Controversies. A number of issues immediately arise when social class is investigated in the context of schooling, one of which is the tension between equity and excellence. A central element of American consciousness is the belief in equity that is captured by the metaphor of the "melting pot." This metaphor holds that American society is structured in such a way that most immigrants are able to come to the United States, be educated as Americans in American schools, and ultimately succeed. This concept is played out in the focus on public schools as centers to bring together students from diverse social classes. Although we have given lip service to this metaphor, the current reality of the public schools is far different. In fact, where one lives has very much dictated the neighborhood school's composition. Despite the inequities, many still hope that schools will be the salvation of our society (Sarason, 1985) and believe that education is the best weapon for fighting poverty and crime (Hodgkinson, 1992).

Along with a belief in equity through schooling, there is also a belief in excellence in education. Excellence in schooling is often mentioned in eras of "perceived scarcity" when there are dwindling resources and when it becomes important to determine who in fact should receive the most rigorous and most extensive education (Oakes, 1990). The idea of meritocracy is frequently used to rationalize this concept so that the system and the rules appear to be just. Americans want to believe that the contest is a fair one and that all have an opportunity to achieve despite social class. In reality, however, excellence (as it is usually defined and operationalized in these debates) often proves to be the opponent of equity (Oakes, 1990), and students from working-class backgrounds tend frequently to be major victims of the battle. This tension between equity and excellence cannot help but form a backdrop to any discussion of social class and schooling in the United States.

An abiding faith in excellence in education to the detriment of equity is reflected in the perspective of the functionalists. These writers view schools as the major mechanism enabling the best and the brightest to be chosen for future occupational and leadership positions in society. Writers such as Blau and Duncan (1967) contend that schools are the major means by which students are socialized into their future roles in society and they have provided rationales for the creation of American leaders through schooling.

The structuralists' position is similar to that of the functionalists. Bowles and Gintis (1976), for example, demonstrate how social class membership affects a person's place in society and theorize that schools reproduce society's social classes within their classrooms. Writers such as Apple (1982), Ferguson (1984), Shapiro (1990), and many others have offered a model of the economic reproduction of society within schools. To these writers, the schools mirror the greater society, preparing students to fill differentiated roles as workers in society. Gordon (1982) argues that "the normal function of schooling is to produce labor-power according to the demands of capital by making differentiated school knowledge available to advantaged and disadvantaged groups. This in turn reproduces hierarchy, exclusion, and inequality between social class and ethnic groups" (p. 90).

By advantaged, Gordon was referring to those whose backgrounds are economically privileged, who come to school with a significant head start, which is then reinforced through school knowledge that prepares them for the tests that will offer them access to financially rewarding careers. By disadvantaged, he was speaking of the children from poverty who have not had the economic supports at home and who then come to school only to find their options limited by the courses they are prepared to enroll in, the tests they are ready to take, and the role models they meet.

Other scholars have turned to a cultural reproductive rather than an economic reproductive argument to explain the replication of social classes within schools. Bourdieu (1977), Bernstein (1982), Wexler (1982), and others argue that the cultural and linguistic learning disseminated by the school reflects the same values and beliefs found in the dominant society.

Social class issues in the schools have also been raised by writers discussing resistance theory. Willis (1977), Anyon (1987), MacLeod (1987), and others have written about what happens when people from one class, usually the lower class, try to subvert the dominant values in the school and society. Those who resist the values of the dominant culture tend often to be the brighter students who feel that the dominant system does not understand them or reward them (Fine, 1989, 1991). A number of the students in the schools studied by Fine felt that completing school would not enable them to move up to the middle class. In fact, they believed that school was merely encouraging them to continue on in their lower-class existence; in effect, they were being prepared to know their place in society. To avoid the schooling-class-reproduction repetition in many schools, patterns of resistance tended to emerge.

One pattern that has usually led to the reproduction of social classes within the school has been tracking. Unfortunately, although tracking is frequently discussed in teacher education, it is seldom viewed from a social class or from a critical perspective (that is, through other than the dominant culture's lens). The work of cultural and economic reproduction occurs through the concept of tracking when certain students are allowed only certain knowledge because they are in a lower track. Oakes (1990) has looked critically at the concept of tracking and sees it as a way to keep children in their place. Oakes contends that the procedure used to identify, label, regroup, and instruct children tends to lead to a control of knowledge that makes it hard for lower-track children to ever catch up with children placed in a higher track.

The study of tracking leads to a discussion of what has been termed the *hidden curriculum*. Frequently operating through friendship networks or through social class cliques, this curriculum, which is not taught formally, prepares students by providing information for testing, for career opportunities, and for further education. Anyon (1987), Apple (1982), Giroux (1983), McLaren (1989), Purpel (1989), and many others discovered the hidden curriculum that has quietly operated in schools and has frequently tended to be advantageous for white middle-class students and disadvantageous for lower-class children of all colors.

Wexler's approach (1982) was slightly different from those who studied the hidden curriculum. He moved beyond the reproduction of society's social and economic order within schools, looking away from passive acceptance of these realities toward a more interventionist approach. This interventionist approach means that educators need to understand what they do to replicate the system of social class within their institutions and then they need to do something to change the status quo. Welch (1985) also moved in the direction of involvement in changing schools. She asked community leaders to hear the voices of working-class students and respond to their needs through the creation of what she has called "communities of resistance and solidarity."

Social class has also been studied through ethnographies and case studies of schooling (Lubeck, 1985; McNeil, 1986; MacLeod, 1987; Perry, 1988; Weis, 1990). These studies take into account the context of schools and demonstrate how social class emerges as a salient category. Many of the concepts previously discussed—economic reproduction, cultural reproduction, resistance theory, tracking, and the hidden curriculum—are also found in these case studies. They create a powerful illustration of forms of social control that keep the social classes in their place within the school.

Implications for Education. If educators are exposed to the concept that knowledge is reproduced through social and economic means, they have thus already begun a critique of schooling. In addition, if they have dealt critically with the concept of the control of knowledge through tracking, then social class issues have been infused into the curriculum to a degree. Further, in those programs that deal with the hidden curriculum, the stage is set for a review of the writings of others who think and write of oppressed people in relation to education. For example, the work of such educators as Anyon (1987), Freire (1970), Giroux (1983), McLaren (1989), Purpel (1989), Shapiro (1990), and many others may be incorporated into the curriculum to show how social class affects education.

Beyond a critique of schooling and the way social class affects educational outcomes, educators need to be aware of changing demographics and the development of the underclass in American society. From the 1990 U.S. census, we know that the number of poor children is increasing and that at least one-half of the disabled people in our society are not able to obtain employment. Further, if we turn to Philadelphia as an example of one city's problems with an increasing underclass, data tell us that at least twenty-five hundred children live with one or both parents in homeless shelters each year (Philadelphia Citizens for Children and Youth, 1989). Data also indicate that thirteen thousand children who entered public schools in 1990 came from a home with no father present (Yancey, Goldstein, and Webb, 1987). Data also reveal that eighteen thousand or 17 percent of preschool children are at risk because of high levels of lead in their home and in the local environment (Philadelphia Citizens for Children and Youth, 1989). Philadelphia's statistics are not much different from other large cities', and according to Sewell (1990), the situation is worsening. Sewell, Ducette, and Shapiro (1991) expressed their concerns about the environment for underclass and even lower-class children in the following commentary:

> The social reality into which many children from culturally diverse backgrounds are born must be understood as a significant factor. . . . It is a world in which their lives are battered by poverty, social isolation and often racial and ethnic inequities. It is an environment where crime, drug addiction, pollution and abuse are daily realities. There are urban and rural communities where children attend school physically and psychologically unprepared to learn. There are social conditions in which the nutritional status and health care needs of the children adversely affect academic achievement. It is a grim world far removed from the environment of America's privileged middle and upper class youth. It is a world in which taking and doing well on a standardized test is often irrelevant and sometimes impossible. It is a world in which children attend school from environmental conditions which make learning an insignificant objective compared with the issues of personal survival" [pp. 6–7].

In his book *Savage Inequalities,* Kozol (1991) has also warned us of the damages wrought in not acknowledging and doing something about the inequitable environments from which an increasing number of our students come. An educator needs to be aware of the communities of poverty and fear, to read widely in the area of social class, particularly focusing on the problems of the under and lower classes. Clearly, there is a need for the voices of the powerless and oppressed to be recognized and heard.

One way to give educators a feeling of what others are experiencing is to turn to the case studies of schooling that are emerging and that take into account the context of diverse communities. There are a number of insightful case studies that effectively deal with social class. Case studies can simulate for future teachers what they might face within schools when they must deal with students whose backgrounds are different from their own. Analysis of cases may also help to break down myths associated with social class. In addition, the cases may offer some options for ameliorating within the schools some of the grave injustices that have been inflicted by society. For example, in a case study by Lareau (1987), the researcher carried out an investigation of family-school relationships in white working-class and middle-class communities. She discovered in her study that the teachers and principals had a certain expectation regarding the appropriate role of parents in the schooling process. Through interviews with parents, Lareau found that working-class parents wanted their children to do well but tended to leave the education of the child up to the teacher. Middle-class parents on the other hand saw themselves as partners with teachers in their child's education. In the first case, the working-class parents tended to be ill at ease in the school. Many of them had not received a high school diploma. In the second case, the middle-class parents were generally at ease with the teachers. Most were professionals in their own right and had known successes throughout their education. The different backgrounds between working-class and middle-class parents made for different behavior in parents' compliance to school requests. Lareau interpreted her study using the cultural capital model (Bourdieu, 1984). She suggested that the school take into account the difference in cultural backgrounds before assuming that the working-class parents do not want their children to succeed. More studies in the ethnographic tradition are needed to begin to understand some of the misconceptions parents have of schools and schools have of parents, particularly when the category of social class is considered.

Social class should be treated as an important area for inclusion as part of the basic content for all new teachers. It is a category little understood and is often compounded with other factors (race, gender, ethnicity). In this section, to avoid the nonsynchronous situation of compounding categories, we have tried to focus primarily on social class. Social class alone, as a category, is difficult to deal with and is far from simple.

It is hoped that readings in this area will offer educators ways to understand students' problems that are derived primarily from social class issues. Understanding alone, however, will not suffice. Armed with knowledge and empathy, educators can help others surmount social class barriers to attain further education. Education can lead to empowerment and an awareness of options that can enable lower-class students to move beyond a "language of critique" to a life full of "possibilities" (Giroux, 1992).

Sexual Differences

By sexual differences, we are referring to broad categories of sexuality that encompass homosexuality, bisexuality, and heterosexuality. In particular, we will focus on those groups who do not fit the standard societal norm that tends to advocate heterosexuality, primarily for the traditional goal of procreation. For these groups, composed of gays, lesbians, and bisexuals, it has been a difficult struggle to be appreciated as acceptable and normal human beings in American society. In fact, it was not until the early 1970s that the American Psychiatric Association reversed its classification of homosexuals as people with mental disorders (American Psychiatric Association, 1980). It was also not until the same era that universities and corporations adopted sexual orientation nondiscrimination clauses and many states decriminalized consensual, private same-sex activity. Also, this was the time that less stereotypical depictions of gays and lesbians began to appear in the media (Nordin, 1989; Russo, 1981).

Although the definition of homosexuals was modified by the American Psychiatric Association, it did not mean that society accepted sexual differences. In the 1980s, for example, there were major legal setbacks: barring lesbians and gays from military service (*Ben Shalom* v. *Marsh*, 1988), forbidding educators from disclosing their sexual identity (*Rowland* v. *Mad River Local School District*, 1985), retaining the sodomy statutes in numerous states, and retaining housing, schooling, and work discrimination on the basis of sexual orientation (Sears, 1993). Despite the continuing legal barriers, numerous grass-roots organizations sprang up. In higher education, lesbian and gay organizations were recognized; lesbian and gay studies programs were developed; lesbian and gay caucuses appeared in a number of national organizations (including the American Sociological Association, American Language Association, American Anthropological Association, American Educational Research Association). Even religious groups formed their own support groups, such as Roman Catholic's Dignity, Episcopal's Integrity (Adam, 1987; Melton, 1989; Nordin, 1989). In addition, awareness of the high incidence of AIDS cases among members of the gay community led to the formation of political and emotional support groups of all kinds including, Gay Men's Health Crisis, ACT-UP!, and the AIDS Memorial Quilt. These groups created a sense of identity and of concern for those of different sexual orientations.

Issues and Controversies. The schools were slower than higher education to recognize the area of sexual differences. However, by the late 1980s, with the awareness of AIDS, the growth of other communicable diseases, and the help of Surgeon General C. Everett Koop, sex education courses were introduced in greater number in the nation's schools (Haffner, 1990; Sears, 1991).

Within sex education, there has been some emphasis on the study of homosexuality (Sears, 1993). There has also been a first step in the recognition of sexual diversity by a public school system in the development of the Harvey Milk School in New York City (Rofes, 1989), a school for homosexuals and their special needs. Further, gay-affirmative counseling in public high schools has been introduced with Project 10 in Los Angeles (Sears, 1989).

The need to study and understand sexual differences has been made more urgent by the release of demographic data that indicate that sexual minority youth are at high risk. The U.S. Department of Health and Human Services has indicated that one in three lesbian and gay youths attempts suicide; one in four has a serious substance abuse problem. Furthermore, not only do lesbian and gay youths hurt themselves, but they are also subject to stigmatization and verbal and physical assaults by peers. Violence also haunts them not only in the schoolyard but also in their homes, where they are frequently abused for their sexual orientation by family members (*New York Times,* 1992).

In fact, the situation has reached such proportions that the Association for Supervision and Curriculum Development (ASCD), a large organization of educators, passed a resolution in 1990 that encouraged its members to "develop policies, curriculum materials, and teaching strategies that do not discriminate on the basis of sexual orientation." They also urged the schools to provide staff development training and materials to help teachers work more effectively with this "at-risk student population."

The resolution by the ASCD was the first time that a national educational organization made the category of sexual minority visible. It recognized that this particular group has special problems that should be the concern of educators. Like other high-risk groups, these youngsters tend to have "drug/alcohol problems, discipline problems, eating disorders, and youthful suicides; these students often report a history reflecting more fundamental problems such as school curriculum irrelevant to their sexual and personal needs, family problems, and lack of self-esteem and personal security" (Sears, 1993, p. 112).

Implications for Education. Despite the growing awareness of the need for study of sexual differences in schools, the progress in this area has been slow. Textbooks, other than in the field of sex education, tend to ignore the area of sexual orientation. Even in sex education, many of the books are usually superficial. Discussions of this topic continue to be within the hidden curriculum of schools and often are dealt with in unpleasant discussions in the hallways and locker rooms (Sears, 1993). Unless addressed in a formal classroom setting, the prejudices, misinformation, distrust, and guilt will continue. Unless addressed in a sensitive and informed way, the attacks on gay youths will continue.

For the preparation of student teachers and for inservice teacher training, gay and lesbian studies can provide useful and important reading materials. Books such as *Lesbian/Women* and *The Gay Mystique* can be invaluable resources not only for sex education classes but for literature, history, and other courses in schools. Case studies also make for excellent teaching devices. Eric Rofes's book *I Thought People like That Killed Themselves,* the true story of a homosexual high school sophomore in Pennsylvania who committed suicide, could serve as an excellent starting point for a discussion of sexual diversity in the classroom. Comparing and contrasting such a book with Sylvia Plath's novel *The Bell Jar,* for example, could make for fascinating and important discussions within a language arts class.

Educators need to be aware that there are many ways to introduce this material into the classroom. Just the presentation of these topics from time to time could make an important difference to a youth who feels isolated, angry, depressed, and silenced. Two works by Rich, "Compulsory Heterosexuality and Lesbian Existence" (1979) and *On Lies, Secrets, and Silences* (1983), can help break the isolation and open the dialogue on sexual diversity within the classroom.

History classes can also serve as places to open the discussion on sexual differences. Smith-Rosenberg's classic (1983) article "The Female World of Love and Ritual: Relations Between Women in Nineteenth-Century America" can be used to generate an interesting debate on sexual politics and the social construction of gender over time. The readings in the area of sexual differences can break down the taboos and enable those who are different from the norm in their sexual orientation to feel engaged and involved.

While not discussing sexual differences personally, teacher educators can explore with their students the subjects of heterosexuality, homosexuality, and bisexuality. In so doing, teachers can help to break down the myths and prejudices surrounding sexual differences. By breaking down those myths and prejudices, high-risk students will no doubt be helped. What is more, heterosexuals will feel less threatened by those who have different sexual orientations.

Ethnicity and Race

For the purposes of our chapter, we intend to use the umbrella term *ethnicity* to encompass race. We have chosen to define ethnicity using an "expanded definition" that is recommended by Banks (1991), who focuses on ethnic groups. Banks borrowed this expanded approach from Rose (1974), who wrote, "Groups whose members share a unique social and cultural heritage passed on from one generation to the next are known as ethnic groups" (p. 13). Rose expanded this definition further by saying, "Above all else, members of such groups feel a consciousness of kind and 'interdependence of fate' with those who share the customs of the ethnic tradition" (p. 13).

In his discussion, Banks (1991) included white groups such as Italian-Americans or Jewish-Americans as well as ethnic groups of color. However, for the groups of color, Banks categorized them under the heading of ethnic minority groups. Often these groups tend to have "unique physical and cultural characteristics" that enable them to be easily classified by appearance" (p. 14). Although these groups are currently called "minorities," the present demographic trends indicate that they will soon constitute the majority in many U.S. cities. Hence, Banks prefers to call individuals within these groups "people of color" and not refer to them as minorities. In this chapter, we have followed Banks's and many other scholars' preference, and we will speak of them frequently in this way.

Ethnicity seemed to us to form the perfect umbrella for this section because race is such a hard concept to categorize. As Banks (1991) wrote, "Physical anthropologists attempt to divide the human species into subgroups on the basis of biological traits and characteristics. They use the concept of race to differentiate between the various human subgroups. However, anthropologists have had considerable difficulty in trying to structure valid racial categories because of the wide variety of traits and characteristics that human groups share, the extensive mixture among groups, and because the racial categories they have formulated have been largely arbitrary. Consequently, the schemes they have developed for classifying human races vary greatly in number and in characteristics" (p. 73).

In fact, the classification of the human race is so difficult and in many ways arbitrary that Montagu (1974) has called it "man's most dangerous myth" (p. 9). However, when pressured, Montagu did classify humankind into four major groups: Negroid or Black, the Archaic White or Australoid, the Caucasoid or White, and the Mongoloid (p. 9). There are many other kinds of classifications. The U.S. Office of Personnel Management, for example, muddies the waters further by combining race with national origin and by using such categories as American Indian or Alaskan Native; Asian or Pacific Islander; Black, not of Hispanic Origin; Hispanic; and White, not of Hispanic Origin (Banks, 1991).

In many ways, it is not so much the definition of race that is important as it is the social manifestation of this construct that has had a profound effect and helps to create distances among human groups. Racism, derived from the way one group views another, has had powerful effects on society as a whole. According to Banks (1991, pp. 74–75), "Racism is a belief that human groups can be validly grouped on the basis of their biological traits and that these identifiable groups inherit certain mental, personality, and cultural characteristics that determine their behavior."

Racism as a concept has enabled such institutions as slavery to flourish and has allowed murder of certain religious groups, such as during the Holocaust, to be justified. According to Gay (1973), racism allows attitudes to be modified into actions. As van den Berghe (1978, p. 75) sees it, "Racism was congruent with prevailing forms of capitalist exploitation, notably with slavery in the New World and incipient colonial expansion in Africa. There is no question that the desire to rationalize exploitation of non-European peoples fostered the elaboration of a complex ideology of paternalism and racism."

Issues and Controversies. Despite the years of focus on effective teaching, there is still a great deal that we do not know in regard to teaching students of color. According to Murrell (1991):

> There are no well-established criteria for what effective teaching looks like for minority children, nor is there clearly specified practical knowledge about teaching in urban contexts with poor minority students. Indeed, the professional knowledge associated with designing effective pedagogy with diverse populations is more apt to be viewed with awe. The popular educational literature imbues a Marva Collins or a Jaime Escalante with a special sort of

pedagogical magic. They possess knowledge not immediately available to other classroom teachers until they are first demystified, decoded, and spelled out by educational researchers. As a result, we are frequently led up the short road of "teacher effectiveness" by developing decontextualized laundry lists of what expert teachers do, rather than taking the long road of clearly understanding how expert teachers acquire the contextual knowledge they possess [p. 205].

Despite the lack of work on teacher effectiveness with regard to the needs of students of color, there is a body of work that advocates the importance of recruiting teachers of color for the future. Garibaldi (1986), Ladson-Billings (1991), Parker and Hood (1991), and others have raised our consciousness that while African-Americans and Spanish-speaking children make up the majority of students in many large urban school districts, the number of black and minority teachers continues to decline. In fact, by the year 2000, the number of African-American teachers will be a mere 5 percent (Garibaldi, 1986), considerably less than the number of African-Americans (12 percent) in the total population. The demographic imbalance that exists between students of color and teachers of color is one that should be taken seriously.

It is important to recruit people of color into teaching (Garibaldi, 1986; Ladson-Billings, 1991). The recruitment issue is important not only for demographic reasons but for educational purposes, for role modeling, and for mentoring of students of color. Studies of exemplary teaching have demonstrated that having high expectations of students of color can make a difference in helping them to achieve success; additionally, these high expectations can be especially meaningful to the students when they come from someone of the same ethnic background (Foster, 1991; Ladson-Billings, 1991; Murrell, 1991).

One of the current realities in education is that the access to a wider variety of careers for minorities has decreased the number who enter teaching. In this environment, incentives of all kinds are necessary to recruit bright young people from different backgrounds into teaching. Additional thought and effort are needed to retain them in the field (Foster, 1991; Garibaldi, 1986; Ladson-Billings, 1991).

Perspectives of Students of Color on Schooling. To add to the body of literature that focuses on the classroom teacher, recent studies are beginning to document the student's perspective. Some of these investigations deal with broad-based samples of students from different ethnic groups, while others tend to be more context focused and smaller in scope.

Turning to one of the larger studies, Steinberg, Dornbusch, and Brown (1992) surveyed fifteen thousand high school students from nine different high schools in cities throughout the United States. They considered the variables of parenting practices, family values, and youngsters' beliefs about the linkages between academic school success and their future career rewards. The researchers were concerned about ethnic differences in adolescent achievement and were very aware that many studies indicated that African-Americans "generally earn lower grades, drop out more often, and attain less education than do whites" (Mickelson, 1990, p. 44). They were also aware that Hispanic adolescents did not perform as well as whites in school while Asian-American students performed better than whites, African-Americans, and Hispanics.

The researchers found no simple answers. They discovered that adolescents whose parents are "warm, firm, and democratic achieve more in school than their peers" (p. 728) but that parenting style was only part of the picture. Another important factor was the peer group. The differences in the intersection of peer group and parenting seemed to create some very real distinctions among the four ethnic groups studied. In the final analysis, the authors felt that they had a long way to go to explain the phenomenon of ethnic achievement. They advocated the need for more ethnographic studies and for "the ecological approach, with its focus on the multiple contexts in which youngsters live" (p. 729).

Ethnographic Studies of Schools from the Ethnic Perspective. Several recently published ethnographic studies investigated the phenomenon of ethnic achievement from the students' perspective as well as from the perspective of effective teaching. These investigations have begun to document the ways in which schooling and the culture of people of color affect each other. Culture includes not just parenting and the peer group, it also takes into account ethnic rituals, customs, and people's beliefs. This research frequently indicates that the student's culture is often in conflict with the culture in the school. While these ethnographic studies focus on ethnicity, they also include the intersection of ethnicity with social class and gender. They tend to provide rich descriptions of the context of schooling.

For example, some very interesting studies make comparisons between white ethnic groups and African-American groups. In MacLeod's ethnographic study (1987) of the "brothers" and the "hallway hangers," he describes two sets of young working-class males in an urban environment in the Northeast. The brothers are a group of African-American males who for the most part accept the middle-class value that school leads to success. The hallway hangers are predominantly white and believe that schooling will not lead to success in their later lives. Despite their high hopes, the brothers were generally doing only average work academically and were primarily in the vocational track. Although desirous of meeting the school's definition of success, they were not up to the white middle-class standards and faced constant failure. On the other hand, the white working-class group, the hallway hangers, tended to maintain their self-esteem since they did not rely on the school's definition of success. Instead, they looked to wealthy people in the neighborhood, who were often not well educated, to serve as their role models.

The school, according to MacLeod, was doing its job neither for the African-American brothers nor for the white hallway hangers. Different kinds of interventions were needed for the separate ethnic groups. In the case of the former, skill development and other types of compensatory education were needed; in the latter instance, appropriate role models might make a difference. In MacLeod's study, understanding the attitudes and backgrounds of diverse students within the context of the school was essential to determine how to educate each group in the most appropriate ways.

In *Sandbox Society*, Lubeck (1985) compares a white middle-class preschool with an African-American lower-class preschool. Lubeck describes in great detail how teachers worked with the youngsters on the two sites. One such description focuses on the language that enabled teachers to communicate with their students within the classroom. For example, at Harmony, the white, middle-class preschool children were requested to carry out tasks through what Lubeck called "indirect directives." A teacher would ask, "Would you like to sit in that seat over there?" "Would you like to put the salt in the bowl?" "Adam, can you put the oil in?" (p. 119).

On the other hand, at Irving Head Start, the African-American lower-class preschool, teachers tended to give explicit directions: "This is a game: when we go to the restrooms we have to be quiet. If we're not, it will upset other people. The other part of the game is that, if you don't, you're going to get punished for it. You have to have respect for people" (p. 74).

In her discussion, Lubeck indicated that teachers at Harmony Preschool educated white, middle-class youngsters for a society that was made up predominantly of nuclear, individualistic families. At the Irving Head Start School, however, what emerged was a pattern of instruction that prepared the lower-class youngsters for a community of extended families and of shared values. What is especially positive about this study is that a value judgment was not made to indicate what was the best approach to communication or teaching for the young children in the study (Parker and Shapiro, 1993). Lubeck exhibited high regard for difference and indicated the importance of accepting, understanding, and respecting diverse ways of communication and varied ways of teaching appropriate to the population being taught.

In Fine's ethnography (1989) of predominantly working-class Puerto Rican and African-American students, one of her major findings was that school administrators were concerned with controlling knowledge and often censored rather than facilitated the sharing of students' experiences and ideas. Fine describes a process that she calls "silencing," which seemed to occur throughout the school. Although paying lip service to the concept of equal opportunity, in reality, the school administration never really addressed the problems that students faced daily. For example, racism was considered a taboo topic by administrators and teachers; it was thought that a discussion of the topic would demoralize the students. Dropping out of school could not be discussed in class; it was believed that such a discussion might encourage students to do so (p. 136). The silencing often also tended toward fostering behavior alien to the students' cultures. For instance, the African-American and Hispanic students were rewarded for being quiet, obedient, and hard working. When they displayed more assertive behaviors, some of which were more in keeping with their own cultures at home, they were chastised and told that they would end up on welfare (p. 162). Acceptable cultural standards were those of the white middle class and not of the cultures from which the majority of the students came. Studies by Au and Jordan (1980), Heath (1982), and Michaels (1981) are just some of those that have indicated the lack of fit between the culture of schooling and the cultures of diverse ethnic groups.

What is clear from many of these studies is that frequently the students of color who manage to succeed in school have had to sacrifice their own culture to do so. They have turned to what Fordham (1988) has described as a pattern of "racelessness." Fordham believes that many high-achieving African-American students have been forced to cling to an imposed and largely false American dream, thereby achieving the individualistic reward of being a winner within the system. In the process, they have had to forfeit much of their own identity and sense of belonging within the African-American community. Fordham (1988), in a thoughtful article, raises some questions for African-American parents that might be worth consideration by other ethnic minority groups as well. She asks, (1) are we willing to have our children defined as successful even though they display very little commitment to the black community, or (2) are we more committed to the integrity of the existing cultural system in the black community and therefore willing to sublimate our individual goals for the collective advancement of our people? (p. 81).

Fordham, with the help of Le Vine and White (1986), raises another equally important question but this time directed at school administrators and not parents: are you willing to modify existing school curricula to incorporate a more group-centered ethos, thereby enabling black students to "seek self-realization through personal effort in service to the group?" (p. 81).

Implications for Education. Teacher educators need to be aware of the work currently being carried out to transform the curriculum in the area of ethnicity/race. Asante (1991–1992) stated this well when he wrote, "The teacher who teaches American literature and does not refer to the African-American writer is doing a disservice to students of all cultural backgrounds. Equally so, the teacher who teaches music and does not mention one composition by an African-American is de-centering the African-American child and miseducating the rest of the children" (p. 30).

Sleeter and Grant (1988) also recommend what they call the "single-group approach" to change, such as ethnic differences, as a good starting point to making modifications in the curriculum. By this, they mean that Asante's view or Gomez's parallel focus on Hispanic culture could make a difference to students in a classroom who had previously felt invisible. By including the accomplishments of people of color, students from different ethnic groups cannot help but feel a certain pride when their culture's works, ethics, customs, and practices are valued.

The hope would be that their achievement in school would rise because at long last what they learned in school would be connected to and extended beyond what they learned at home.

Murrell (1995) feels that the connections between the culture of the home and the culture of the school have been missing in educational discourse and in the knowledge base of education for far too long. He speaks of the need for teaching and research to be more specifically focused on "experiential knowledge in a social context, particularly as it relates to problematics of race, class, gender, and culture" (p. 206). By this he means the need for a focus more on "connected knowing" (Belenky, Clinchy, Goldberger, and Tarule, 1986) through field-based hands-on projects and, when this is not possible, through simulated experiences. Connected knowing, or knowledge related to experience, is preferred by many educators to the continued focus on abstract or "separate knowing" that is often too remote for the learner to understand and is too removed from the students' own culture at home.

Toward Possibilities Rather than Problems Regarding Diversity

Throughout this chapter, we have presented brief reviews of selected aspects of diversity. Our consistent message has been that teachers and administrators must be able not only to surmount the perceived problems related to diversity in education but also to seek the possibilities associated with pluralism in our nation's schools. Our sense of the current state of education is that we are a long way from attaining these goals. We share Sleeter and Grant's idea (1988) that it is necessary to rethink many of the basic assumptions about teacher preparation and restructure our current programs if we are to prepare teachers for a diverse society. This social constructionist approach is also advocated by Capper (1993) for transforming the preparation programs for administrators in schools and colleges of education.

Brameld (1956) introduced the social reconstructionist approach as a "utopian philosophy." However, over time, this utopian vision has been made more concrete and possible through the writings of scholars such as Aronowitz and Giroux (1985). This movement has also been called conscientization (Freire, 1970); emancipatory pedagogy (Gordon, 1985; Lather, 1991); critical teaching (Shor, 1980); and socialist feminism (Jaggar, 1983; Harraway, 1985). In other contexts, it has been referred to as multicultural education (Suzuki, 1984) or antiracist teaching (Carby, 1982).

This antiracist, multicultural, or social reconstructionist approach turns to the work of critical theorists (such as Anyon, 1987; Apple, 1986), cognitive development theorists (Dewey, 1938; Piaget, 1952), and cultural theorists (Kanter, 1977; Suzuki, 1984). According to Sleeter and Grant (1988), this approach has asked that democratic ideals be practiced in the schools. They wrote, "Practicing democracy also means learning to articulate one's interests, openly debate issues with one's peers, organize and work collectively with others, acquire power, exercise power, and so forth" (p. 187). Further, for oppressed ethnic groups, it also has meant that they "must also develop a sense of political efficacy, and be given practice in social action strategies which teaches them how to get power without violence and further exclusion. . . . Opportunities for social action, in which students have experience in obtaining and exercising power, should be emphasized within a curriculum that is designed to help liberate excluded ethnic groups" (p. 149).

Social reconstructionism has also been used as a way to empower groups such as students who were previously held in check. The goal is to teach students to reflectively organize themselves for action (Freire, 1970) and not passively obey; they would learn about ways to organize an election campaign or means to guide decisions through committee procedures.

Not only does social reconstructionism turn to group action but there is also an emphasis on self-analysis for action. Sleeter and Grant (1988) have advocated the use of one's own autobiography as a way to help others. Through analysis of one's own life and analysis of how one has made decisions over time, Sleeter and Grant and many others believe that much can be learned. Rather than silencing students and teachers (Fine, 1989), there needs to be a discussion of crucial decisions made in people's lives that include the difficult topics of having a baby, dropping out of school, or taking drugs (Aronowitz and Giroux, 1985). Such discussions empower young people and indicate the importance of life choices and options.

The development of social action skills is yet another means for carrying out the social reconstructionist approach to education. This approach emphasizes the ability to use skills that underlie democratic action and to focus these skills on issues related to social inequality. Action research projects can be useful in this pursuit, and they might have the effect of awakening the consciousness of those who carry out the project as well as of those who are the subjects of the research (Anyon, 1987; Banks and Banks, 1989). Development of these skills can lead to an awakening of political interest and can indicate to different groups that a collective effort may lead to change within society.

The preceding suggestions, based on the social reconstructionist approach, can make for a revised knowledge base and curriculum for teacher education. Such suggestions can empower teachers and can in turn lead to the empowerment of their students. By developing these social action skills in students, the voices of many different groups will be heard and respected, and the culture of the community and the school will be more in harmony with each other.

While each of the areas we have reviewed in this chapter has its own set of issues and controversies, there are certain themes and certain questions that seem to recur. Among the ones we think to be central are the following:

1. *The recognition of diversity requires that "education as usual" will no longer work.* There is almost universal agreement that all aspects of diversity require change

in the usual way of instructing students. Almost all writers on diversity agree that education should move away from a focus on changing the students toward a focus on changing the environment. A central difference, however, seems to be how broad this change should be. This question of change can be posed as follows: should we change the teaching methods and the curriculum, or should we transform the schools and the society, or should we do both? In general, writers in the areas we have termed "differences in degree" (for example, learning styles and learning disabilities) tend to focus on more limited change, emphasizing modifications that should occur in the teaching methods and the curriculum. Many of the writers in the areas of "differences in kind" (for example, gender, race, and ethnicity) focus more typically on transforming the schools or society. Almost without exception, however, the writers in both areas agree that fundamental change is mandatory for education to improve.

2. *A diverse curriculum will not solve all of education's problems.* An acceptance of diversity as a basis for educational practices has many positive effects. It should be recognized, however, that it is impossible to be only partially inclusive. If the curriculum is modified to include issues of gender (for example), it is inevitable that demands will be made to include issues of race or class. The inclusion in the curriculum of material representing one ethnic group will ultimately produce requests to include others. Issues of inclusion raise such questions as how differentiated can a curriculum be before it loses coherence? How much individualization can a teacher be expected to handle when attempting to teach thirty or more young people in a classroom?

3. *A totally affective approach for the inclusion of diversity will not suffice.* In large part, education for diversity is the one area of teaching and curriculum where self-knowledge and self-awareness, within the affective domain, are making their most pronounced headway. As many have pointed out, and as we have reiterated in this chapter, an excellent starting point for students who wish to understand and value diversity is to start with themselves: Who am I? Where have I come from? What factors have influenced me to make me the sort of person I am? What critical incidences related to diversity, encompassing such categories as race, gender, or social class, have helped to shape me as a human being? What is my ethnic identity? If I don't have an ethnic identity, why not? As we have pointed out in this chapter, these questions are important for anyone, but they are especially crucial for those members of society who have traditionally considered themselves raceless, genderless, and classless (chiefly the white, middle-class male). As many have pointed out, from this self-knowledge can come an awareness of "otherness," a sensitivity for the sources of other people's personal identities and an empathy for the issues and problems others must deal with in their everyday life.

A review of programs and courses in this area demonstrates the importance of questions such as these and how pervasive group work has become as the prevailing pedagogic technique. We agree with this emphasis, but we offer a caution: self-awareness is an excellent place to begin to understand diversity, but it is a bad place to end. All too often, we fear, an emphasis on diversity leads only to a reiterating, in group format, of personal biases and personal histories. While this may be acceptable in other formats (therapy, for example), it is the central mission of universities in general, and thereby of teacher education programs in particular, to further the cognitive development of their students and to enhance their knowledge base. There is a large and growing literature in the area of diversity. Any program or course whose purpose is to further the understanding of diversity is a failure if this knowledge base is deemphasized or worse yet is missing.

At the beginning of this chapter, we cited the aphorism, "All humans are like all other humans, like some other humans, and like no other human." We would like to conclude this chapter with a more contemporary concept and refer to Stainback and Stainback's definition (1990) of an "inclusive school." According to these writers, an inclusive school is a place where everyone belongs, is accepted, supports, and is supported by peers and other members of the school community in the course of having individual educational needs met.

Although Stainback and Stainback were focusing on the narrow issue of including special needs students in a regular classroom, the description they provide of an inclusive school is easily generalizable to encompass all aspects of diversity. An inclusive school is where the study of diversity inevitably leads. Unfortunately, significant changes need to occur in the preparation of teachers, in the curriculum, in the schools, and in society before this result is achieved.

We live in a society that is becoming increasingly diverse, in which groups no longer will remain silent about the legitimacy of their heritage as an integral part of the curriculum, and in which the needs of individual students can no longer be submerged by uniform teaching practices. In such a society, there can be little question that the only kind of school we can have is an inclusive school; that the only kind of teacher we can certify is one who has self-knowledge and has respect for diversity; and that the only kind of curriculum we can develop is one that recognizes the needs of all students as well as their different cultures. Yet inclusive schools are rare, teachers tend to be homogeneous, and the curriculum is increasingly being driven by standardized tests that focus on uniformity justified on the basis of national educational goals. The gap between our needs and our resources is widening, and we are left, as we so often seem to be in the complex arena of teacher education, with more questions than solutions.

In the face of this paradoxical situation, what can teacher educators do? Although we do not have simple answers for these complex questions, we do have some ideas on how educators can personally begin to value and understand differences:

1. Start by writing an autobiographical account of yourself as an educator and as a person.

2. Analyze the "differences in degree" (for example, learning styles, learning disabilities, exceptionalities) and "differences in kind" (gender, social class, sexual difference, race and ethnicity) that you describe in your story.
3. Begin to read widely in the areas of difference, especially seeking out initially the new scholarship that is most closely related to your own background.
4. Speak to others about what you have learned and try to raise your own consciousness about your differences and how they are perceived in society.
5. Study and teach the literature in other areas of difference, especially those that relate to populations you are working with or may be working with in the future.
6. Be curious about people from other cultures rather than afraid of their differences, and reach out to them not only by reading about their lives but by visiting and assisting them within their own community.

Along with our list of what teachers can do for themselves to value and understand diversity, we would like to include a list of what teachers can do for their students to enable them to appreciate diversity and empower them to deal with intolerance and inequalities. This list comes from the writings of Gollnick and Chinn (1994), who believe, and we concur with them, that teachers should do all of the following:

1. Place the student at the center of the teaching and learning process
2. Promote human rights and respect for cultural differences
3. Believe that all students can learn
4. Acknowledge and build on the life histories and experiences of students' microcultural memberships
5. Critically analyze oppression and power relationships to understand racism, sexism, classism, and discrimination against the disabled, young, and aged
6. Critique society in the interest of social justice and equality
7. Participate in collective social action to ensure a democratic society

The above lists can serve as guidelines to help educators move toward more inclusive schools and toward a language of possibilities rather than problems regarding diversity. As educators, we can choose to focus on the problems represented by diversity, or we can decide to make diversity a central, positive theme in our teaching and learning. It is hoped that this positive approach toward diversity will make the difference for all students, regardless of their race, ethnicity, gender, social class, exceptionality, or any other aspect of difference that might affect their ability to learn and achieve in school.

References

Abbey, A., and Melby, C. (1986). "The effects of nonverbal cues on gender differences in perceptions of sexual intent." *Sex Roles, 15*(5–6), 283–298.

Adam, B. (1987). *The rise of a gay liberation movement.* Boston: Twayne.

Adams, K. (1990). "Examining black underrepresentation in gifted programs." Paper presented at the annual meeting of the National Association for Gifted Education, New Orleans, La.

Aiken, S. H., and others (1987). "Trying transformations: Curriculum integration and the problem of resistance." *SIGNS: Journal of Women in Culture and Society, 12,* 255–275.

Allport, F. H. (1924). *Social psychology.* Boston: Houghton Mifflin.

American Association of University Women (1991). *Stalled agenda: Gender equity and the training of educators.* Washington, D.C.: Educational Foundation and National Education Association.

American Association of University Women (1992). *How schools shortchange girls: A study of major findings on girls and education.* Washington, D.C.: Educational Foundation and National Education Association.

American Psychiatric Association (1980). *Diagnostic and statistical manual of mental disorders.* (3rd ed.). Washington, D.C.: American Psychiatric Association.

Anderson, M. L. (1988). *Thinking about women: Sociological perspectives on sex and gender.* New York: Macmillan.

Anyon, J. (1987). "Social class and school knowledge." *Curriculum Inquiry, 11,* 3–42.

Apple, M. W. (ed.) (1982). *Cultural and economic reproduction in education: Essays on class, ideology and the state.* New York: Routledge & Kegan Paul.

Apple, M. W. (1986). *Teachers and texts: A political economy of class and gender relations in education.* New York: Routledge & Kegan Paul.

Arch, E. C., Kirschner, S. E., and Tetreault, M.K.T. (1983). "Measuring the impact of faculty development in women's studies." Paper presented at the annual conference of the National Women's Studies Association, Humboldt Co., Calif.

Aronowitz, S., and Giroux, H. A. (1985). *Education under siege.* Westport, Conn.: Bergin & Garvey.

Asante, M. K. (1987). *The Afrocentric idea.* Philadelphia: Temple University Press.

Asante, M. K. (1991–1992). "Afrocentric curriculum." *Educational Leadership, 49*(4), 28–31.

Association for Supervision and Curriculum Development (1990). *Resolutions 1990.* Alexandria, Va.: Association for Supervision and Curriculum Development.

Au, K. H., and Jordan, C. (1980). "Teaching reading to Hawaiian children: Finding a culturally appropriate solution." In H. T. Trueba, J. P. Guthrie, and K. H. Au (eds.), *Culture in the bilingual classroom.* Boston: Newbury House.

Balthazor, M. J., Wagner, R. K., and Pelham, W. E. (1991). "The specificity of the effects of stimulant medication on classroom learning-related measures of cognitive processing for attention deficit disorder children." *Journal of Abnormal Child Psychology, 19*(1), 35–52.

Banks, J. A. (1991). *Teaching strategies for ethnic studies.* Needham Heights, Mass.: Allyn & Bacon.

Banks, J. A., and Banks, C. A. (eds.) (1989). *Multicultural education: Issues and perspectives.* Needham Heights, Mass.: Allyn & Bacon.

Belenky, M. F., Clinchy, B. M., Goldberger, N. R., and Tarule, J. M. (1986). *Women's ways of knowing: The development of self, voice, and mind.* New York: Basic Books.

Ben Shalom v. *Marsh,* 690 F. Supp. 774, 777 (E.D. Wis. 1988), 1988.

Bernstein, B. (1982). "Codes, modalities and the process of cultural reproduction: A model." In M. W. Apple (ed.), *Cultural and economic reproduction in education.* New York: Routledge & Kegan Paul.

Biemiller, A. (1993). "Lake Wobegon revisited: On diversity and education." *Educational Researcher, 22*(9), 7–12.

Blau, P. M., and Duncan, O. D. (1967). *The American occupational structure.* New York: Wiley.

Bly, R. (1981). *The man in the black coat turns.* New York: Doubleday.

Bourdieu, P. (1977). "Cultural reproduction and social reproduction." In J. Karabel and A. H. Halsey (eds.), *Power and ideology in education.* New York: Oxford University Press.

Bourdieu, P. (1984). *Distinction: A social critique of the judgment of taste* (R. Nice, trans.). Cambridge, Mass.: Harvard University Press.

Bowles, S., and Gintis, H. (1976). *Schooling in capitalist America.* New York: Basic Books.

Brameld, T.B.H. (1956). *Toward a reconstructed philosophy of education.* Austin, Texas: Holt, Rinehart & Winston.

Brown, L., and Hoffman, N. (eds.) (1991). "Women, girls and the culture of education." *Women's Studies Quarterly* (special issue), *19*(1–2), 1–178.

Bullivant, B. M. (1989). "Culture: Its nature and meaning for educators." In J. A. Banks and C. A. Banks (eds.), *Multicultural education: Issues and perspectives.* Needham Heights, Mass.: Allyn & Bacon.

Capper, C. A. (ed.) (1993). *Educational administration in a pluralistic society.* Albany: State University of New York Press.

Carbo, M. (1981). "Grades 3–12: An adaptation of the Learning Style Inventory." In *Reading Style Inventory.* Englewood Cliffs, N.J.: Prentice Hall.

Carbo, M., Dunn, R., and Dunn, K. (1986). *Teaching students to read through their individual learning styles.* Englewood Cliffs, N.J.: Prentice Hall.

Carby, H. (1982). "Schooling in Babylon." In Center for Contemporary Cultural Studies, *The empire strikes back: Race and racism in '70s Britain.* Wolfeboro, N.H.: Longwood.

Cholakis, M. M. (1986). "An experimental investigation of the relationship between and among sociological preferences, vocabulary instruction and achievement, and the attitudes of New York urban seventh and eighth grade underachievers." *Dissertation Abstracts International, 47,* 11:4046A.

Clatterbaugh, K. (1990). *Contemporary perspectives on masculinity: Men, women, and politics in modern society.* Boulder, Colo.: Westview Press.

Cohen, S. A., Hyman, J. S., Ashcroft, L., and Loveless, D. (1989). "Mastery learning versus learning styles versus metacognitives: What do we tell the practitioner?" Paper presented at the annual meeting of the American Educational Research Association, San Francisco.

Corno, L., and Snow, R. E. (1986). "Adapting teaching to individual differences among learners." In M. C. Wittrock (ed.), *Handbook of research on teaching.* (3rd ed.). New York: Macmillan.

Cramer, R. H. (1991). "The education of gifted children in the United States." *Gifted Child Quarterly, 35*(2), 84–91.

Culley, M., and Portuges, C. (eds.) (1985). *Gendered subjects: The dynamics of feminist teaching.* New York: Routledge & Kegan Paul.

Curry, L. (1990). "Critique of the research on learning styles." *Educational Leadership, 48*(2), 50–56.

Cushner, M., McClelland, A., and Safford, P. (1992). *Human diversity in education: An integrative approach.* New York: McGraw-Hill.

Davidson, A. L., and Phelan, P. (1993). "Cultural diversity and its implications for schooling: A continuing American dialogue." In P. Phelan and A. L. Davidson (eds.), *Renegotiating cultural diversity in American schools.* New York: Teachers College Press.

De Gregoris, C. N. (1986). "Reading comprehension and the interaction of individual; sound preferences and varied auditory distractions." *Dissertation Abstracts International, 47,* 09:3380A.

Delamont, S. (1983). "The conservative school? Sex roles at home, at work, and at school." In S. Walker and L. Barton (eds.), *Gender, class and education.* London: Falmer Press.

De Lyon, H., and Widdowson Migniuolo, F. (eds.) (1989). *Women teachers: Issues and experiences.* Philadelphia: Open University Press.

Dewey, J. (1938). *Experience and education.* New York: Macmillan.

Diamond, J. (1983). *Inside out: Becoming my own man.* San Rafael, Calif.: Fifth Wave.

Douglas, C. B. (1979). "Making biology easier to understand." *American Biology Teacher, 41*(5), 277–281, 298–299.

Doyle, J. (1989). *The male experience.* (2nd ed.). Dubuque, Iowa: Brown.

Dunn, R., Beaudry, J. S., and Klavas, A. (1989). "Survey of research on learning styles." *Educational Leadership, 48*(2), 50–58.

Dunn, R., Dunn K., and Price, G. E. (1975, 1979, 1981, 1985). *Learning style inventory.* Lawrence, Kans.: Price Systems.

Dunn, R., Gemake, J., Jalali, F., and Zenhausern, R. (1990). "Cross-cultural differences in learning styles of elementary-age students from four ethnic backgrounds." *Journal of Multicultural Counseling and Development, 18,* 68–93.

Elliott, R. (1986). *Litigating intelligence: IQ tests, special education and social science in the courtroom.* Dover, Del.: Auburn House.

Fauth, G. C. (1984). "Women in educational administration: A research profile." *Educational Forum, 49,* 65–79.

Ferguson, K. E. (1984). *The feminist case against bureaucracy.* Philadelphia: Temple University Press.

Fernback, D. (1981). *The spiral path.* Boston: Alyson.

Fine, M. (1989). "Silencing and nurturing voice in an improbable context: Urban adolescents in public school." In H. A. Giroux and P. McLaren (eds.), *Critical pedagogy, the state and cultural struggle.* Albany: State University of New York Press.

Fine, M. (1991). *Framing dropouts: Notes on the politics of urban high schools.* Albany: State University of New York Press.

Flanagan, C. (1993). "Gender and social class: Intersecting issues in women's achievement." *Educational Psychologist, 28*(4), 357–378.

Fordham, S. (1988). "Racelessness as a factor in black students' school success: Pragmatic strategy or pyrrhic victory." *Harvard Educational Review, 58,* 54–84.

Foster, M. (1991). " 'Just got to find a way': Case studies of the lives and practice of exemplary black high school teachers." In M. Foster (ed.), *Into schools and schooling.* New York: AMS Press.

Freire, P. (1970). *Pedagogy of the oppressed.* New York: Continuum Press.

Fritsche, J.A.M. (1984). *Toward excellence and equity: The scholarship of women as a catalyst for change in the university.* Orono: University of Maine Press.

Gage, N. L., and Berliner, D. C. (1991). *Educational psychology.* (5th ed.). Boston: Houghton Mifflin.

Gardner, H. (1983). *Frames of mind.* New York: Basic Books.

Gardner, H., and Hatch, T. (1989). "Multiple intelligences go to school: Educational implications of the theory of multiple intelligences." *Educational Researcher, 18*(8), 4–10.

Garibaldi, A. M. (1986). "Sustaining black educational progress: Challenges for the 1990s." *Journal of Negro Education, 55*(3), 386–396.

Gay, G. (1973). "Racism in America: Imperatives for teaching ethnic studies." In J. A. Banks (ed.), *Teaching ethnic studies: Concepts and strategies.* Washington, D.C.: National Council for Social Studies.

Getzels, J. W., and Dillon, J. T. (1973). "The nature of giftedness and the education of the gifted child." In R.M.W. Travers (ed.), *Second handbook of research on teaching.* Skokie, Ill.: Rand McNally.

Gibbs, J. T. (1988). *Young, black and male in America: An endangered species.* Dover, Del.: Auburn House.

Gilder, G. (1973). *Sexual suicide.* New York: Bantam Books.

Gilder, G. (1986). *Men and marriage.* New York: Viking Penguin.

Giroux, H. A. (1983). "Theories of reproduction and resistance in the new sociology of education: A critical analysis." *Harvard Educational Review, 53,* 257–293.

Giroux, H. A. (1992). "Educational leadership and the crisis of democratic government." *Educational Researcher, 20*(4), 4–11.

Goldberg, H. (1987). *The inner male: Overcoming roadblocks to intimacy.* New York: NAL/Dutton.

Gollnick, D. M., and Chinn, P. C. (1994). *Multicultural education in a pluralistic society.* Columbus, Ohio: Merrill.

Gordon, B. M. (1982). "Toward a theory of knowledge acquisition for black children." *Journal of Education, 164,* 90–108.

Gordon, B. M. (1985). "Toward emancipation in citizenship education: The case of African-American cultural knowledge." *Theory and Research in Social Education, 12,* 1–23.

Gould, S. (1981). *The mismeasure of man.* New York: Norton.

Grant, C. A., and Secada, W. G. (1991). "Preparing teachers for diversity." In W. R. Houston (ed.), *Handbook of research on teacher education.* New York: Macmillan.

Haffner, D. (1990). *Sex education 2000: A call to action.* New York: Sex Information and Education Council of the United States.

Hale-Benson, J. E. (1982). *Black children: Their roots, culture, and learning style.* Baltimore: Johns Hopkins University Press.

Hall, R. M., and Sandler, B. (1982). *The classroom climate: A chilly one for women? Project on the status and education of women.* Washington, D.C.: Association of American Colleges.

Hammill, D. D. (1990). "On defining learning disabilities: An emerging consensus." *Journal of Learning Disabilities, 23*(2), 74–84.

Harraway, D. (1985). "A manifesto for cyborgs: Science, technology and socialist feminism in the 1980s." *Socialist Review, 80,* 65–107.

Harris, A., and Carlton, S. (1990). "Patterns of gender differences on mathematics items on the Scholastic Aptitude Test." Paper presented at the annual meeting of the American Educational Research Association, Boston.

Heath, S. B. (1982). "What no bedtime story means: Narrative skills at home and school." *Language in Society, 11*(1), 49–76.

Hernandez, H. (1989). *Multicultural education: A teacher's guide to content and process.* Columbus, Ohio: Merrill.

Hicks, E. (1981). "Cultural Marxism: Nonsychrony and feminist practice." In L. Sargent (ed.), *Women and revolution.* Boston: South End Press.

Hill, J. (1971). *Personalized education programs utilizing cognitive style mapping.* Bloomfield Hills, Mich.: Oakland Community College.

Hodgkinson, H. L. (1992). *A demographic look at tomorrow.* Washington, D.C.: Institute for Educational Leadership.

Hoge, R. D. (1988). "Issues in the definition and measurement of the giftedness construct." *Educational Researcher, 17*(7), 12–16.

Hunsaker, S. (1991). "Instrument use in the identification of gifted and talented children." Paper presented at the meeting of the Jacob K. Javitz Gifted and Talented Education Program Grant Recipients, Washington, D.C.

Hyde, J. S. (1993). "Gender differences." Talk presented at the American Psychological Association, Toronto, Ontario.

Jaggar, A. (1983). *Feminist politics and human nature.* Lanham, Md.: Rowman & Littlefield.

Jones, E. H., and Montenegro, X. P. (1990). *Women and minorities in school administration: Facts and figures, 1989–1990.* Washington, D.C.: Office of Minority Affairs, American Association of School Administrators.

Kahle, J. B., Parker, L. H., Rennie, L. J., and Riley, D. (1993). "Gender differences in science education: Building a model." *Educational Psychologist, 28*(4), 379–404.

Kanter, R. M. (1977). *Men and women of the corporation.* New York: Basic Books.

Karmin, L. (1974). *The science and politics of IQ.* Hillsdale, N.J.: Erlbaum.

Keefe, J. W., and Ferrell, B. G. (1990). "Developing a defensible learning style paradigm." *Educational Leadership, 48*(2), 57–61.

Keefe, J. W., and Languis, M. L. (1983). "Operational definitions." Paper presented to the National Association of Secondary School Principals Learning Styles Task Force, Reston, Va.

Keefe, J. W., Languis M. L., Letteri, C., and Dunn, R. (1986). *Learning style profile.* Reston, Va.: National Association of Secondary School Principals.

Keefe, J. W., and Monk, J. S. (1986). *Learning style profile examiner's manual.* Reston, Va.: National Association of Secondary School Principals.

Kimmel, M. S. (ed.) (1987). *Changing men: New directions in research on men and masculinity.* Newbury Park, Calif.: Sage.

Kirby, J. R. (1988). "Style, strategy, and skill in reading." In R. R. Schmeck (ed.), *Learning strategies and learning styles.* New York: Plenum Press.

Klein, S. (ed.) (1985). *Handbook for achieving sex equity through education.* Baltimore: Johns Hopkins University Press.

Knight, C. B. (1990). "Effects of learning style accommodation on achievement of second graders." Paper presented at the meeting of the Mid-South Educational Research Association, New Orleans, La.

Kornhaber, M., Krechevsky, M., and Gardner, H. (1990). "Engaging intelligence." *Educational Psychologist, 25*(3–4), 177–199.

Kozol, J. (1991). *Savage inequalities: Children in America's schools.* New York: Crown.

Ladson-Billings, G. (1991). "Returning to the source: Implications for educating teachers of black students." In M. Foster (ed.), *Into schools and schooling.* New York: AMS Press.

Lareau, A. (1987). "Social class differences in family-school relationships: The importance of cultural capital." *Sociology of Education, 60*(2), 73–85.

Lather, P. (1991). *Getting smart: Feminist research and pedagogy with/in the postmodern.* New York: Routledge & Kegan Paul.

Lerner, J. (1981). *Learning disabilities: Theories, diagnosis, and teaching strategies.* Boston: Houghton Mifflin.

Le Vine, R., and White, M. (1986). *Human conditions: The cultural basis of educational development.* New York: Routledge & Kegan Paul.

Lubeck, S. (1985). *Sandbox society: Early education in black and white America—a comparative ethnography.* Washington, D.C.: Falmer Press.

McCarthy, C., and Apple, M. W. (1988). "Race, class and gender in American educational research: Toward a nonsynchronous parallelist position." In L. Weiss (ed.), *Class, race and gender in American education.* Albany: State University of New York Press.

Maccoby, E. E., and Jacklin, C. N. (1974). *The psychology of sex differences.* Stanford, Calif.: Stanford University Press.

McIntosh, P. (1984). *Interactive phases of curricular revision: A feminist perspective.* Wellesley, Mass.: Center for Research on Women, Wellesley College.

McLaren, P. (1989). *Life in schools.* White Plains, N.Y.: Longman.

MacLeod, J. (1987). *Ain't no makin' it: Leveled aspirations in a low-income neighborhood.* Boulder, Colo.: Westview Press.

McNeil, L. M. (1986). *Contradictions of control: School structure and school knowledge.* New York: Routledge & Kegan Paul.

Marshall, C. (1985). "From culturally defined to self-defined career stages of women administrators." *Journal of Educational Thought, 19*(2), 134–147.

Mead, M., Dobzhensky, T. G., and Light, D. B. (eds.) (1968). *Science and the concept of race.* New York: Columbia University Press.

Melton, G. (1989). "Public policy and private prejudice: Psychology and law on gay rights." *American Psychologist, 44*(6), 933–940.

Mensh, E., and Mensh, H. (1991). *The IQ mythology.* Carbondale: Southern Illinois University Press.

Michaels, S. (1981). "'Sharing time': Children's narrative styles and differential access to literacy." *Language in Society, 10,* 423–442.

Mickelson, R. (1990). "The attitude-achievement paradox among black adolescents." *Sociology of Education, 63,* 44–61.

Montagu, A. (1974). *Man's most dangerous myth: The fallacy of race.* New York: Oxford University Press.

Munoz, C., Jr. (1989). *Youth, identity and power.* London: Verso.

Murrell, P. C. (1995). "What is missing in the preparation of minority teachers?" In M. Foster (ed.), *Into schools and schooling.* New York: AMS Press.

National Association of Secondary School Principals Learning Styles Task Force (1983). "National task force defines learning style operationally and conceptually." *Learning Styles Network Newsletter, 4*(2), 1.

National Center for Educational Statistics (1989). *Selected characteristics of public school teachers, spring 1961 to spring 1986.* Washington, D.C.: National Center for Educational Statistics.

National Joint Committee on Learning Disabilities (1988). Letter to member organizations.

National Policy Board for Educational Administration (1989). *Improving the preparation of school administrators.* Charlottesville: University of Virginia Press.

National Science Foundation (1990). *Women and minorities in science and engineering.* Washington, D.C.: National Science Foundation.

New York Times (1992). June 14, p. 44.

Nordin, V. (1989). "*GRC* v. *Georgetown:* Autonomy and nondiscrimination." *Thought and Action, 5*(2), 32–47.

Oakes, J. (1990). *Multiplying inequities: The effects of race, social class, and tracking on opportunities to learn mathematics and science.* Santa Monica, Calif.: RAND.

Ortiz, F. I., and Marshall, C. (1988). "Women in educational administration." In N. J. Byran (ed.), *Handbook of research on educational administration.* White Plains, N.Y.: Longman.

Parker, L., and Hood, S. (1991). "Perceptions of minority teacher education students at two Holmes Group institutions: Diversity, equity, and social justice." Paper presented at the annual meeting of the American Educational Research Association, Chicago.

Parker, L., and Shapiro, J. P. (1993). "The context of educational administration and social class." In C. A. Capper (ed.), *Educational administration in a pluralistic society.* Albany: State University of New York Press.

Pavan, B. N. (1985). "Certified but not hired: Women administrators in Pennsylvania." Paper presented at the Research on Women in Education Conference, Boston. (ED 263 689)

Perry, I. (1988). "A black student's reflection on public and private schools." *Harvard Educational Review, 58,* 332–336.

Philadelphia Citizens for Children and Youth (1989). *The health status of Philadelphia's children.* Philadelphia: Philadelphia Citizens for Children and Youth.

Piaget, J. (1952). *The language and thought of the child.* New York: Routledge & Kegan Paul.

Pleck, J. H. (1981). *The myth of masculinity.* Cambridge, Mass.: MIT Press.

Purpel, D. E. (1989). *The moral and spiritual crisis in education: A curriculum for justice and compassion in education.* Westport, Conn.: Bergin & Garvey.

Reich, R. B. (1992). *The work of nations.* New York: Vintage Books.

Reis, S. M. (1989). "Reflections on policy affecting the education of gifted and talented students: Past and future perspectives." *American Psychologist, 44*(2), 399–408.

Renzulli, J. S. (1986). "The three-ring conception of giftedness: A developmental model for creative productivity." In R. J. Sternberg and J. E. Davidson (eds.), *Conceptions of giftedness.* Cambridge: Cambridge University Press.

Renzulli, J. S., and Reis, S. M. (1991). "The reform movement and the quiet crisis in gifted education." *Gifted Child Quarterly, 35*(1), 26–35.

Reynolds, M. C. (1989). "Students with special needs." In M. C. Reynolds (ed.), *A knowledge base for the beginning teacher.* Elmsford, N.Y.: Pergamon Press.

Rich, A. (1979). *On lies, secrets, and silence: Selected prose, 1966–1978.* New York: Norton.

Rich, A. (1983). "Compulsory heterosexuality and lesbian existence." In E. Abel and E. K. Abel (eds.), *The SIGNS reader: Women, gender and scholarship.* Chicago: University of Chicago Press.

Robins, P. M. (1992). "A comparison of behavioral and attentional functioning in children diagnosed as hyperactive or learning-disabled." *Journal of Abnormal of Child Psychology, 20*(1), 65–82.

Robinson, C. J. (1983). *Black Marxism: The making of the black radical tradition.* London: Zed Press.

Rofes, E. (1989). "Opening up the classroom closet: Responding to the educational needs of gay and lesbian youth." *Harvard Educational Review, 59*(4), 444–453.

Rose, P. I. (1974). *They and we: Racial and ethnic relations in the United States.* New York: Random House.

Rosser, P. (1989). *The SAT gender gap.* Washington, D.C.: Center for Women's Policy Studies.

Rowan, J. (1987). *The horned god.* New York: Routledge & Kegan Paul.

Rowland v. *Mad River Local School District, Montgomery County,* 730 F. 2d 444 (1985); 445–446 (6th Cir., 1984); cert. denied, 470 U.S. 1009, 105 S. Ct. 1373, 84 L. ed. 2d. 393 [23 ed. Law Rep. 26].

Russo, V. (1981). *The celluloid closet: Homosexuality in the movies.* New York: HarperCollins.

Rutter, M. (1989). "Attention deficit disorder/hyperkinetic syndrome: Conceptual and research issues regarding diagnosis and classification." In T. Sagvolden and T. Archer (eds.), *Attention deficit disorder: Clinical and basic research.* Hillsdale, N.J.: Erlbaum.

Sadker, M. P., and Sadker, D. M. (1982). *Sex equity handbook for schools.* White Plains, N.Y.: Longman.

Sadker, M. P., Sadker, D. M., and Klein, S. (1991). "The issue of gender in elementary and secondary education." In G. E. Grant (ed.), *Review of Research in Education, 17,* 269–334.

Sarason, S. B. (1985). *Schooling in America: Scapegoat and salvation.* New York: Free Press.

Schiff, M., and Lewontin, R. (1986). *Education and class: The irrelevance of IQ genetic studies.* Oxford: Oxford University Press.

Schmitz, B., and Williams, A. S. (1983). *Sourcebook for integrating the study of women into the curriculum.* Bozeman, Mont.: Northwest Women's Studies Association.

Schniedewind, N., and Maher, F. (eds.) (1987). "Feminist pedagogy." *Women's Studies Quarterly, 15*(3–4), 6–14.

Schuster, M. R., and Van Dyne, S. R. (eds.) (1985). *Women's place in the academy: Transforming the liberal arts curriculum.* Lanham, Md.: Rowman & Littlefield.

Sears, J. (1989). "The impact of gender and race on growing up lesbian and gay in the South." *National Women's Studies Association Journal, 1*(3), 422–457.

Sears, J. (1991). *Growing up gay in the South: Race, gender, and journeys of the spirit.* New York: Haworth Press.

Sears, J. (1993). "Responding to the sexual diversity of faculty and students: Sexual praxis and the critical reflective administrator." In C. A. Capper (ed.), *Educational administration in a pluralistic society.* Albany: State University of New York Press.

Sewell, T. E. (1979). "Intelligence and learning tasks as predictors of scholastic achievement in black and white first grade children." *Journal of School Psychology, 17,* 325–332.

Sewell, T. E. (1987). "Dynamic assessment as a nondiscriminatory procedure." In C. Lidz (ed.), *Dynamic assessment*. New York: Guilford Press.

Sewell, T. E. (1990). "Testing African American children: Have ideological beliefs masked the educational benefits?" *State of Black Philadelphia, 9*, 29–36.

Sewell, T. E., Ducette, J. P., and Shapiro, J. P. (1991). "Cultural diversity and educational assessment." Paper presented at the American Psychological Association Annual Conference, San Francisco.

Shade, B. J. (1982). "African-American cognitive style: A variable in school success?" *Review of Educational Research, 52*(2), 219–244.

Shade, B. J. (1986). "Is there an Afro-American cognitive style?" *Journal of Black Psychology, 13*, 13–16.

Shade, B. J. (1989). *Culture and learning style within the Afro-American community*. New York: Stone.

Shakeshaft, C. (1987). *Women in educational administration*. Newbury Park, Calif.: Sage.

Shapiro, J. P. (1987). "Women in education: At risk or prepared?" *Educational Forum, 51*, 167–183.

Shapiro, J. P., Parssinen, C., and Brown, S. (1992). "Teacher-scholars: An action research study of a collaborative feminist scholarship colloquium between schools and universities." *Teaching and Teacher Education, 8*(1), 91–104.

Shapiro, S. (1990). *Between capitalism and democracy: Educational policy and the crisis of the welfare state*. Westport, Conn.: Bergin & Garvey.

Shor, I. (1980). *Critical teaching and everyday life*. Boston: South End Press.

Sleeter, C. E. (1992). "Resisting racial awareness: How teachers understand the social order from their racial, gender, and social class locations." *Educational Foundations, 6*(2), 7–32.

Sleeter, C. E., and Grant, C. A. (1988). *Making choices for multicultural education: Five approaches to race, class, and gender*. New York: Macmillan.

Smith-Rosenberg, C. C. (1983). "The female world of love and ritual: Relations between women in nineteenth-century America." In E. Abel and E. K. Abel (eds.), *The SIGNS reader: Women, gender and scholarship*. Chicago: University of Chicago Press.

Spanier, B., Bloom, A., and Boroviak, D. (1986). *Women's studies in the United States: A report to the Ford Foundation*. New York: Ford Foundation.

Spearman, C. (1927). *The abilities of man*. New York: Macmillan.

Spender, D. (1982). *Invisible women: The schooling scandal*. London: Writers & Readers.

Stainback, W., and Stainback, S. (1990). "Inclusive schooling." In W. Stainback and S. Stainback (eds.), *Support networks for inclusive schooling*. Baltimore: Brookes.

Stanworth, M. (1983). *Gender and schooling: A study of sexual division in the classroom*. London: Hutchinson.

Steele, G. E. (1986). "An investigation of the relationship between students' interests and the curricular practices of an alternative high school through the perspective of Jung's theory of psychological types." *Dissertation Abstracts International, 47*, 3616A.

Steinberg, L., Dornbusch, S. M., and Brown, B. B. (June 1992). "Ethnic differences in adolescent achievement: An ecological perspective." *American Psychologist, 46*(6), 723–729.

Sternberg, R. J. (1988). "Mental self-government: A theory of intellectual styles and their development." *Human Development, 31*, 197–224.

Sternberg, R. J. (1992). "Ability tests, measurement, and markets." *Journal of Educational Psychology, 84*(2), 134–140.

Stiles, R. H. (1985). "Learning style preferences for design and their relationship to standardized test results." *Dissertation Abstracts International, 43*, 01:68A.

Strober, M. H., and Tyack, D. (Spring 1980). "Why do women teach and men manage? A report on research on schools." *SIGNS: Journal of Women and Culture in Society, 5*, 497.

Styles, E. J. (1988). *SEED project newsletter*. Wellesley, Mass.: Wellesley College Center for Research on Women.

Suzuki, B. H. (1984). "Curriculum transformation for multicultural education." *Education and Urban Society, 16,* 294–322.

Tannenbaum, R. (1982). "An investigation of the relationships between selected instructional techniques and identified field dependent and field independent cognitive styles as evidenced among high school students enrolled in studies of nutrition." *Dissertation Abstracts International, 43,* 01:68A.

Terman, L. M. (1916). *The measurements of intelligence.* Boston: Houghton Mifflin.

Tetreault, M.K.T. (1989). "Integrating content about women and gender into the curriculum." In J. A. Banks and C. A. Banks (eds.), *Multicultural education: Issues and perspectives.* Needham Heights, Mass.: Allyn & Bacon.

Tetreault, M.K.T., and Schmuck, P. (1985). "Equity, educational reform, and gender." *Issues in Education, 3*(1), 45–67.

Thurstone, L. (1938). *Primary mental abilities.* Chicago: University of Chicago Press.

Trent, W. T. (1988). "Class, culture, and schooling: Reframing the questions." A presentation to the faculty of the University of Illinois at the Wingspread Conference Center, Racine, Wis.

U.S. Department of Education (1990). *Current population reports.* Washington, D.C.: U.S. Government Printing Office.

van den Berghe, P. L. (ed.) (1978). *Race and racism: A comparative perspective.* New York: Wiley.

Walters, J., and Gardner, H. (1986). "The theory of multiple intelligences: Some issues and answers." In R. J. Sternberg and R. K. Wagner (eds.), *Practical intelligence.* Cambridge: Cambridge University Press.

Weis, L. (1990). *Working class without work: High school students in a de-industrializing economy.* New York: Routledge & Kegan Paul.

Welch, S. D. (1985). *Communities of resistance and solidarity: A feminist theology of liberation.* Maryknoll, N.Y.: Orbis Books.

Wexler, P. (1982). "Structure, text, and subject: A critical sociology of school knowledge." In M. W. Apple (ed.), *Cultural and economic reproduction in education.* New York: Routledge & Kegan Paul.

Willis, P. (1977). *Learning to labor.* Westmead, England: Saxon House.

Winner, F. D. (1983). *Genetic basis of society.* Dunedin, Fla.: Shakespeare.

Witkin, H. A., and others (1974). *Psychological differentiation: Studies of development.* Hillsdale, N.J.: Erlbaum.

Yancey, L., Goldstein, I., and Webb, D. (1987). *The ecology of health and educational outcomes: An analysis of Philadelphia public elementary schools.* Philadelphia: Institute of Public Policy, Temple University.

Yesseldyke, J. E., and Algozzine, B. (1983). "LD or not LD: That's not the question." *Journal of Learning Disabilities, 16*(1), 29–31.

Zaretsky, E. (1976). *Capitalism, the family, and personal life.* New York: HarperCollins.

Annotated Bibliography

Banks, J. A. (ed.) (1991). (5th ed.). *Teaching strategies for ethnic studies.* Needham Heights, Mass.: Allyn & Bacon.

This book offers diverse perspectives related to pedagogical approaches that deal with ethnic differences. Because its focus is ethnicity, the book is able to offer complex discussions of this one characteristic of diversity. It attempts to cover the major ethnic groups in American society by relating their history, their current place in society, and the pedagogical implications that arise from an understanding of each group's culture.

Banks, J. A., and Banks, C.A. (eds.) (1989, 1993). *Multicultural educations: Issues and perspectives.* Needham Heights, Mass.: Allyn & Bacon.
Turning to experts in multiculturalism, the editors have developed a book that deals not only with the context of diversity but with paradigms and interpretations of difference. The book explores a number of very interesting models on different characteristics of diversity.

Cushner, K., McClelland, A., and Safford, P. (1992). *Human diversity in education: An integrative approach.* New York: McGraw-Hill.
This book explores human differences that affect physical, social, and psychological issues. It is very comprehensive and crosses boundaries dealing not only with individual differences but also with cultural differences. The authors provide an interesting series of exercises relating to each topic introduced, which may be of value to instructors teaching undergraduate or beginning-level graduate courses in multiculturalism.

Hare-Mustin, R. T., and Marecek, J. (eds.) (1990). *Making a difference: Psychology and the construction of gender.* New Haven, Conn.: Yale University Press.
Although focused primarily on the discipline of psychology, the editors have invited authors to develop chapters that can cross boundaries in the area of the construction of gender. The authors of the various chapters move across paradigms with ease and deal with both theory and practice.

Sleeter, C. E., and Grant, C. A. (1988). *Making choices for multicultural education: Five approaches to race, class, and gender.* New York: Macmillan.
Basing their ideas on a review of more than two hundred articles and sixty books, the authors have developed a useful framework for understanding diversity issues. They create five approaches for dealing with race, class, and gender that ultimately lead to a social reconstructionist view of multiculturalism.

CHAPTER SIXTEEN

THE SOCIAL FOUNDATIONS OF EDUCATION: RETROSPECT AND PROSPECT

STUART A. MCANINCH AND AMY RATHS MCANINCH

The "social foundations of education" traditionally refers to the history, philosophy, and sociology of education and, according to the Council of Learned Societies in Education (CLSE) standards (1986), is committed to the "interpretive, normative, and critical" study of education (p. 4). The social foundations as a field is further distinguished from other areas of educational studies in that it embraces a view of education and schooling as a political and ideological process that requires liberal and multidisciplinary inquiry. For example, the problem of what constitutes democratic education (in theory and in practice) has been a central concern for faculty in the social foundations. This issue, as well as related ones, requires the critical analysis of social institutions, conditions, and ideals that is characteristic of scholarship in the social foundations at its best.

In recent years, however, some evidence has emerged to suggest that this conception of the social foundations is not readily attained. A recent survey of best-selling undergraduate social foundations texts found that the content was decidedly uncritical and superficial (Tozer and McAninch, 1987). This conclusion is especially disturbing in light of Shea, Sola, and Jones's survey report (1987) that approximately 48 percent of full-time faculty who teach social foundations courses do not hold a doctoral degree in the field; for adjunct faculty, the percentage is much higher. Furthermore, far from sharing a consensus regarding the goals and purposes of the social foundations such as the one cited above from the CLSE standards, there is some evidence that the social foundations as a field can be currently characterized by retreat from these standards as an ideal and considerable ambivalence over their mission.

Mergers of social foundations departments with educational administration, curriculum and instruction, or departments of elementary and secondary education, loss of faculty positions, and the incidence of nonfoundations faculty teaching "our" courses are all held to be contributing factors to the recent survey finding among members of the American Educational Studies Association (AESA) that the primary purpose of this national professional organization should be to defend foundations programs and courses (Shea, Sola, and Jones, 1987). Moreover, a draft statement of new academic standards for the field recently circulated among AESA members centered on the problem of articulating a justification for the existence of the social foundations altogether (Tozer, 1993). Thus, while this chapter is prepared primarily for faculty outside the field, the ideas reviewed here may also contribute to the internal debate currently taking place among social foundations scholars.

The purpose of this chapter is to provide an overview of the history of the social foundations as a field, to discuss the roles played by the foundations in teacher education, and finally to describe promising lines of research currently being pursued by social foundations scholars.

The Social Foundations in Historical Context

Our characterization of the social foundations as a field in retreat can be more fully clarified through an examination of its historical development. One seminal study that is frequently cited in historical accounts of the social foundations of education is Rugg's book *The Teacher of Teachers* (1952). Rugg, a member of the Teachers College faculty at Columbia University from 1920 to 1951, wrote this history of teacher education as social reconstructionism was waning (significantly, it was published the year John Dewey died). Social reconstructionism is the philosophy that schools should play a key role in reconstructing social institutions and values along democratic lines. Deeply moved by the Great Depression, social reconstructionists believed that the widespread poverty and misery of the 1930s was caused in large part by economic and political beliefs and practices inconsistent with democratic values.

Rugg divided teacher education and the social foundations curriculum into two historical periods, which he called the "first draft," and which spanned approximately 1890 to 1920, and the "second draft," which covered another thirty-year period, from 1920 to 1950. The first draft, Rugg explained, reflected the "conforming way" in American thought, the dominant opinion, which "essentially buttressed the status quo in the culture" (1952, p. 37). Teacher educators embraced a "practical slant" and advanced a conforming, apolitical role for teachers that gave emphasis to adjustment to the new industrial order (Tozer and McAninch, 1986). In the foundations, teacher candidates studied the history, philosophy, or sociology of education divided along disciplinary lines and, according to Tozer and McAninch (1986), the curriculum as reflected in the foundations textbooks of the time was decidedly uncritical; teachers were not expected to be social critics or agents of social change. As Borman (1990) writes, "The textbooks of the times mirrored the accepted norms in teacher education, which emphasized maintenance of the status quo and acceptance of the conservative social and political order" (p. 399).

The second draft signified a rejection of this conformist role for teachers and teacher educators. According to Rugg (1952), the "creative path" in teacher education emerged largely from Teachers College at Columbia, which was the center of social reconstructionist thought during this period. The social foundations' emphasis on social criticism as expressed in the CLSE standards can be traced back to the early shapers of the modern foundations curriculum at Columbia, among them some of the leading social reconstructionists of the 1920s and 1930s. At Teachers College, Rugg's colleagues included John Dewey, William Heard Kilpatrick, George Counts, Kenneth D. Benne, and R. Freeman Butt. These men formed the Teachers College Discussion Group, which met regularly beginning in 1928 to discuss social trends and recent developments in the sciences and arts (Tozer and McAninch, 1986). They sought an integrated approach to the foundations, one that would unite the disciplines in the study of social problems and educational policy and practice.

The Teachers College Social Foundations Texts

One result of this group's work was a two-volume textbook (Rugg, 1941), for use in a graduate foundations sequence at Teachers College, which codified a profound conceptualization of the aims and purposes of both the psychological and social foundations of education. Because these volumes present a particularly compelling and influential view of the social foundations curriculum, a close examination of them is warranted. As Tozer and McAninch (1986) wrote, "The origins of social foundations instruction at Teachers College Columbia appear to be the origins of the field itself" (p. 8).

The introduction to the first volume, written by the foundations faculty, advances the key idea of "education as statesmanship." Teachers in the public schools, according to the authors, are not simply responsible for schooling but are literally statesmen, charged with the responsibility of advancing democratic values and providing educational leadership for society as a whole. The significance of this role stems in part from the growing importance of education as an institution and its potential to effect democratic social change. Thus, the authors conceived of the teacher's role as necessarily political and learned: "organized education, since it constitutes a deliberate effort on the part of society to preserve its possessions and shape its future, is one of the highest and most responsible forms of statesmanship. The American educator working in the public schools is a servant of the American state. As distinguished from the educational job holder, [the educator] is under obligation to foster the most complete development of the capacities of the citizens, upon whose powers the democratic state depends for its existence, its security, and the fulfillment of its ideals" (Rugg, 1941, p. xii).

When the authors refer to the "democratic state," they make it clear that they do not mean that the teacher is a civil servant. Instead, they argue that the true constituency of the educational statesman is the citizenry acting collectively. This distinction parallels Dewey's assertion (1916) that democracy as an ideal does not denote a form of government but rather a quality of social life.

In order to assume this role, educators need much knowledge: they need to "make the fullest use of the empirical findings of social inquiry and thought" and "in the light of the dominant and emergent ethical and aesthetic values of the age and on the basis of the potentialities of the natural endowment, the technological resources, the cultural heritage, the great social trends of the time, and the general conditions of life, he must define problems, make choices, and decide upon courses of action" (Rugg, 1941, p. xii). Thus, for the Teachers College foundations faculty, the justification for the study of the social (and psychological) foundations of education rested on the idea that educators would play a leadership role that required an informed and critical voice. This conception stands in sharp contrast to the current rhetoric surrounding the goals and mission of the foundations today, which are frequently linked to the idea of promoting reflection on and in practice (see Schön, 1983). For the Teachers College Division of Foundations faculty, merely promoting reflection was not enough: educators needed to be critical students of social conditions in order to promote democratic social change.

The introduction to the second volume, written by Rugg, explicitly sets out the perspective from which the editors are working. These pages succinctly summarize social reconstructionist themes: faith in the common man, in democracy and social progress, and in reason and inquiry. This outline of the faculty's point of view is stunning for its commitment to substantive values. One wonders if a social foundations faculty, or any faculty, could ever approach consensus today on a statement equally direct in its espousal of a distinct value position.

The content of the two-volume text consists of short selections of primary source material organized around ideas. In some ways, these texts resemble legal casebooks, in which primary sources (legal cases) are organized by areas of legal theory. The selections under each topic in the Teachers College text offer diverse points of view on the idea under study and like law school texts afford students the opportunity to ferret out principles and arguments from the primary materials. For example, in the first volume, under "The Characteristics of Culture," selections from the works of William F. Ogburn, William Graham Sumner, Ruth Benedict, Alfred North Whitehead, and I. B. Berkson are included. The texts are remarkable for the breadth and depth of intellectual ideas covered in the two-semester sequence.

The Teachers College Legacy to the Foundations

Tozer and McAninch (1986) identify four components of the social foundations curriculum as conceived by the Teachers College foundations faculty: a rigorous study of society, an integrated rather than disciplinary organization, a critical treatment of content, and "an explicitly articulated point of view which gives organization and integration to materials studied" (p. 10).

While the work of the Teachers College faculty spread to other universities, such as the University of Illinois and Ohio State, the creative path in teacher education never became the majority view. What persisted during the height of social reconstructionism and continues to dominate in teacher education is the trade school tradition Rugg called the conforming way. In *The Teacher of Teachers*, Rugg (1952) writes with considerable pathos of the persistence of conservatism and the waning of social reconstructionism: "As I write the men of The Creative Path are scattered and my book has been written to hearten, to help coalesce them, to let them know how right they always have been—and still are. But the dominant word of the Teacher of Teachers from 1900 to this day has been that of The Conforming Way" (p. 38).

The continuing tension between the social reconstructionist legacy in the social foundations of education and the conforming way in teacher education is a theme of the next section.

The Social Foundations and Teacher Education

The role of the social foundations in teacher education is tenuous and shaky—not without good reason. The foundations' mission as explicated by the CLSE standards is not supported by the culture of teaching or teacher education and never has been. As noted above, the roots of the modern social foundations curriculum in social reconstructionism and in liberal learning place it at odds with how teacher education has been historically conceived: as instructional preparation in the narrow, strictly technical sense (see Warren, 1985). In addition, the broader social role that Rugg and his colleagues envisioned for teachers as statesmen, and its requisite grounding in knowledge of society and culture, is one that the vast majority of teachers has not aspired to fill. For example, in 1936, at the height of social reconstructionism, the historian Howard K. Beale published a detailed study of teachers and their attitudes toward academic freedom: *Are American Teachers Free?* Relying on questionnaires, correspondence, and interviews, Beale concluded that "one must not assume that all teachers are unhappy for want of freedom. The vast majority share the views and prejudices and ideals of the community out of which they have sprung and in the midst of which they teach. The vast majority of teachers have never done enough thinking to work out an explicit social philosophy. . . . The majority of teachers do not know what a controversial subject is. All too many have no desire to learn" (pp. 13–14).

Thus, as early as the mid 1930s, there were indications that teachers did not aspire to the "statesman" role. Lortie's study (1975) indicates that teachers enter the profession primarily for the psychic rewards they can accrue from direct work with children. The "subjective warrant" (p. 39) teachers frequently cite for entering the profession is their special gift for working with children—not their desire to change the social order.

This selection bias into the occupation is further complicated by what Lortie (1975) called "the apprenticeship of observation" (p. 61). Unlike other professional candidates, many students of teaching enter their studies with the view that they already know how to teach: they have seen teachers do it for the previous twelve years. Lanier and Little (1986) cite evidence that a widely held view among teacher candidates is that teaching is learned through experience and that it is closely related to parenting. Convincing teacher candidates that teacher educators have something to teach them is difficult enough; for social foundations faculty, those apparently furthest removed from classroom experience, it is frequently impossible.

If Waller (1932), Lortie (1975), and other scholars are correct, the occupation of teaching deepens a conservative outlook that accepts the status quo as a given and seeks to discover what works within the confines of existing arrangements (see Lanier and Little, 1986, for a review). That the culture of teaching deepens a crudely pragmatic and narrow stance signifies an important facet of teacher education: most teacher educators are individuals who themselves were teachers and were socialized into the culture of teaching. To the extent that teacher educators embrace the conforming way, they are at odds with the purposes of those social foundations educators who manifest fidelity to the standards of the field.

But if the social foundations field is fighting an uphill battle vis-à-vis teacher education, it has not only the culture of teaching and teacher education to blame but also the social foundations faculty. First, social foundations educators have been generally reluctant to study the impact of their courses. Teacher educators (and others) justifiably want to know what difference the social foundations coursework makes in the performance of a teacher. Can two teacher candidates, one with foundations coursework and one without, be distinguished? Social foundations faculty have not done the research to be able to answer this question. Borman (1990) notes:

> It is not clear that full knowledge of the foundations perspectives enhances the
> effectiveness of classroom teachers. . . . foundations coursework in teacher edu-
> cation does not easily link up with improved efficiency and achievement in the
> classroom setting on the part of students instructed by those who have had
> such coursework. Most foundations scholars reject an experimentalist orienta-
> tion to the question of whether or not a background in educational foundations
> promotes more effective classroom instruction. . . . These, it is argued, are the
> wrong outcomes to be evaluated in the first place [p. 400].

Instead, Borman suggests that social foundations educators are interested in "whether teachers versed in the foundations are indeed sharper and more knowledgeable in their critique of educational issues, policies, and institutions" (p. 400) and if this in turn translates into some more socially aware orientation in their own students. She concedes, "The impact of coursework in educational foundations on attitudes, beliefs, and behaviors might be, as foundations scholars assert, virtually impossible to measure" (p. 400). Social foundations educators' general unwillingness to attempt to operationalize at least some of their outcomes signifies that the field is operating largely on faith that our courses make a difference.

But rather than relying on faith in the impact of our courses, it seems desirable to seek answers to this outcomes issue. It would be a major contribution to the field to begin to examine the impact (or lack thereof) of social foundations coursework in teacher education. For example, we could seek answers to the following types of questions: Does foundations coursework make a difference with respect to activism in teacher unions, attendance at school board meetings, the frequency with which social issues find their way into the classroom, the disposition to advocate for policies of inclusion, the tendency to read theoretical or critical works on education after graduation, or the tendency to write letters to the editor about educational issues in the community? Social foundations educators' reluctance or resistance to engage in a research program that looks at these or related outcomes leaves the field persistently vulnerable to attack from those unsympathetic to educational theory, both inside and outside the university, and does not serve the teacher candidates we are trying to empower through theoretical coursework.

There is a another way in which social foundations educators have not furthered their own cause with respect to teacher education and it is related to the tension between social foundations educators and teacher educators noted above. Lanier and Little (1986) note that professors who teach social foundations courses tend not to identify themselves as teacher educators. They write, "Identifying primarily with their discipline, the professors teaching foundations courses to prospective teachers (e.g., the psychology, sociology, history, or philosophy of education) tend to deny their teacher education role" (p. 529). To the extent that foundations faculty see themselves as, for example, philosophers who do work in educational theory, they weaken not only the foundations' role in teacher education but also teacher education itself.

Of course, the dilemma is that there is an "inverse relationship between professional prestige and the intensity of involvement with the formal education of teachers" (Lanier and Little, 1986, p. 530). The more directly social foundations faculty engage in teacher education, the lower their professional status. What is considered prestigious is to be associated with a discipline and to do theoretical work as far removed from teacher education as possible. Whereas Broudy (1981) once noted the "Janus-like" (p. 15) nature of philosophy of education as a field, looking at once to its parent discipline and to education, it should be noted that the inducements in higher education are generally to the liberal arts and sciences side and are not associated with teacher preparation. Thus, some social foundations educators may well claim that the weaker their role in teacher education, the better.

Yet it is unclear that social foundations educators have to choose between professorial prestige and contributing in important ways to teacher education. For example, the series of papers written by the philosophers Margaret Buchmann and Robert Floden with their colleagues at Michigan State University (Buchmann and Schwille, 1983; Feiman-Nemser and Buchmann, 1985; Floden, Buchmann, and Schwille, 1987) is a model of the kind of scholarship that contributes both to philosophy and to teacher education. These works examine the efficacy of experience as a teacher, with direct implications for the design of field work and other practica.

Social foundations educators have recently suggested several means of strengthening the role of the social foundations in teacher education. Borman (1990) calls for a closer relationship between foundations faculty and teachers, citing the efforts of George Wood at Ohio University as an exemplar. Tozer (1993), writing on behalf of AESA's Committee on Academic Standards and Accreditation, seeks a more explicitly vocational role for the foundations and thereby appears to renounce the broader, social rationale for foundations study advanced by the Teachers College faculty. Thus, one interpretation of this new draft document is that it signifies a turning back toward the conforming way in the social foundations and is a further sign of retreat in the field.

Developments in Social Foundations Research

Our preceding discussion of the foundations should not be construed as suggesting that there is a lack of vital lines of scholarship and inquiry being pursued by social foundations educators. In our view, the proliferation of social histories of education and ethnographic studies of schools are both positive developments that have facilitated continuing critical dialogue.

Social Histories of Education

In recent years, the field of historical foundations of education has been particularly energized by the influence of social history. Gaining momentum during the 1960s and 1970s, social historians emphasized the need to study history at the microhistorical as well as the macrohistorical level. In other words, they argued that analyzing history is not simply a matter of describing how dominant institutions have developed over time or what it is that political, economic, and cultural leaders have said, written, and done. Rather, social historians working in such areas as labor history, women's history, history of immigration, and African-American history sought to document the centrality to social development of events, dialogues, and patterns of belief and behavior within workplaces, homes, grass-roots organizations, and other community contexts. Without such efforts to understand ideas and actions at the community level, they maintained, the development of political, economic, and cultural institutions could not be accurately understood, since institutional change has inevitably been shaped in important respects by non-elite social groups traditionally not studied by historians.

During the past two decades, research and writing in the history of education have been increasingly informed by methodologies, modes of inquiry, and a knowledge base derived from social history. While intellectual histories such as Kliebard's *Struggle for the American Curriculum, 1893–1958* (1986) and institutional histories such as Tyack and Hansot's *Managers of Virtue: Public School Leadership in America, 1820–1980* (1982) have continued to be written and have contributed to the field, historical accounts of classroom practice, community involvement in schooling, and the educational experiences of various social groups have become more prevalent. Traditionally, educational historians relied most heavily on institutional records, writings of prominent educational figures, and university archival collections. Those influenced by social history have increasingly turned to oral histories, classroom artifacts, diaries and letters of teachers and students, newspapers, newsletters published by community political, labor, ethnic, or religious groups, and statistical analyses aimed at identifying patterns of educational behavior on the part of various demographic groups.

Several examples illustrate the significance of this new emphasis on social history. Reese's *Power and the Promise of School Reform: Grass-Roots Movements During the Progressive Era* (1986) does not deny that networking and alliance building among those whom Tyack (1974) has called "administrative progressives"—elite school board members, school administrators, and university faculty members—did enhance the power of business and educational leaders. Yet based on study of four cities, he also argues that the efforts by elites to consolidate control of urban schooling were intensely contested by complex and often fragile "grass-roots progressive" coalitions that drew on trade union, radical political, Social Gospel, and middle-class women's movements in communities for members, organizational support, and agendas.

In the same vein, the thirteen monographs and theoretical essays in *The Teacher's Voice: A Social History of Teaching in Twentieth Century America,* edited by Altenbaugh (1992), stress the formative impact that decisions and actions on the part of members of non-elite social groups have had on the development of schools. Articles explore the evolution of cultures of teaching and the nature of teachers' work. Major themes include the impact of feminization of teaching on its status and culture; the impacts of social class, race, gender, and religion on the social and educational ideas and behaviors of teachers; variations in how teachers perceived and reacted to school administration and community pressures and expectations; and debates among teachers on teacher unionism and on the nature of their occupation and work.

Cuban's *How Teachers Taught* (1984) is an ambitious attempt to describe patterns of classroom practice in twentieth-century American schools. He addresses constancy and change in teacher practices over time as well as teachers' reactions to efforts to reform curricula and instruction. The primary value of Cuban's study for teacher educators is that it provides grist for reflection and discussion on the persistence of teacher-centered instructional methods despite recurrent progressive critiques and reform efforts—an issue that could not have been addressed from more traditional research perspectives. In *Governing the Young: Teacher Behavior in Popular Primary Schools in the Nineteenth-Century United States,* Finkelstein (1989) combines her analysis of classroom practice in nineteenth-century elementary schools with primary source readings representing a variety of communities and schools. Unlike Cuban, she addresses directly the perspectives of students as well as teachers.

While more traditional institutional and intellectual approaches to the historical foundations allow teacher educators to focus on some issues related to the historical development of the structures of schooling and curriculum theory, social histories of education promote an understanding of the often complex reactions of administrators, teachers, students, or community groups to changes in schools and curriculum theories. Moreover, recent works such as those by Anderson (1988), Markowitz (1993), Rury (1991), and Zilversmit (1993) enable teacher educators to address the impact of schooling on a variety of social groups and to explore from a historical perspective concrete relationships between school and community as well as the broader relationship between schooling and democracy in practice. Consequently, the influence of social history has enhanced the ability of social foundations faculty to critically address vitally important topics in their courses, ranging from historical differences in educational outcomes for students from dissimilar social-class backgrounds to patterns of resistance and accommodation among teachers to bureaucratization of schooling.

Ethnographic Studies of Schools

Ethnography is a form of qualitative research stressing sustained participant observation and extensive formal and informal interviews. Ethnographic research methods were originally systematized during the first half of the twentieth century by social anthropologists such as Bronislaw Malinowski and were first applied to the study of education following World War II. Ethnographers, like social historians, seek to study institutions and cultures by focusing on the interactions that occur within and among social groups and the kinds of meaning-perspectives that individuals within those groups construct in the course of interaction. Ethnographic study, according to Erickson (1986), is governed by two key questions: "What is happening here, specifically? What do these happenings mean to the people engaged in them?" (p. 124).

Ethnographic studies in education have proliferated during the past decade as a means to better understand the day-to-day functioning of schools and classrooms, to augment quantitative research and analyses of schooling that focus on larger structural issues, and to gain better perspective on the impact of race, gender, and social class on educational outcomes, beliefs, and experiences. Often, as in the case of Fine's study of the high dropout rate in a comprehensive high school in New York City (1991), researchers employing ethnographic methodologies have been especially concerned with documenting and exploring in detail the concrete institutional and cultural factors perpetuating unequal educational outcomes in American schools. Fine writes, "I know now that looking deeply at life inside and around this one public high school has given me a close and textured understanding of the nuanced production of education inequities" (p. xi). As in the case of social histories, ethnographic studies have not made more traditional research approaches obsolete but they have opened fertile lines of inquiry previously not possible and have stimulated a critical rethinking of how schools as institutions function.

Michelle Fine's *Framing Dropouts: Notes on the Politics of an Urban Public High School* (1991) is a case in point. Drawing on direct observations, transcribed class discussions and comments at school meetings, stories written by students, and interviews with students, dropouts, parents, faculty members, and administrators, Fine investigates why only 20 percent of the ninth-grade cohort in the school she studied went on to graduate. She describes her growing disenchantment, during the year she spent at the school, with the common stereotypes of dropouts as "depressed, helpless, hopeless, and ever without options" (p. 4). She seeks to identify the complex interweaving of institutional factors and patterns of behavior that contributed to the coercion of students into silence on issues associated with inequity and the pushing of many out of the school and into almost certain poverty through discharges and other less formal means. She attempts to build complexity into her analysis by mapping out patterns of student and parent resistance and acquiescence and by differentiating between those attitudes, beliefs, and actions on the parts of educators that promoted silencing and those that nurtured students' voices and the formation of community in the classroom. Moreover, she notes the often debilitating impact of a rigid bureaucratic structure on educators as well as students and parents. What emerges is a portrait of a school that is dysfunctional in an educative sense but functional in terms of reproduction of social class structure, "an institution that routinely and traditionally has reproduced social injustice, despite even the best intentions of its educators" (Fine, 1991, p. xi).

While other ethnographic studies also tend to focus explicitly on the social reproductive nature of American schools (Grant and Sleeter, 1986, for instance), not all critical ethnographies do so. Metz (1986) examines three middle schools in an urban school system during their first several years as magnet schools. She carefully explores the community and district contexts in which the schools operated, the evolving cultures of teaching within the schools, and the lives of students in three distinctive school environments. While acknowledging social class and race as important categories and the unevenness of educational outcomes, and while exploring what she perceives to be fundamental contradictions in traditional

conceptions of equality of educational opportunity, Metz does not view normative judgment to be part of her role as an ethnographer. Nevertheless, the subject
matter she explores and the concepts she utilizes clearly place this work in the critical tradition in the social foundations.

Conclusion

The social foundations of education have a proud history in the work of Dewey,
Rugg, Counts, and others. Their insistence on a critical perspective on the relationship of school to society is a continuing commitment in the field, although, as
Tozer and McAninch (1987) remind us, it is a commitment not always attained.
While the social foundations field suffers from ambivalence over its relationship
to teacher education and has lost considerable power within schools of education,
the lines of research currently pursued in social history and in ethnography are
two signs of vigor. Whether or not social foundations educators will continue to
maintain a defensive posture or will be able to forge a true consensus around substantive and worthwhile values remains to be seen.

References

Altenbaugh, R. J. (ed.). *The teacher's voice.* Washington, D.C.: Falmer Press.

Anderson, J. D. (1988). *The education of Blacks in the South, 1860–1935.* Chapel Hill: University
of North Carolina Press.

Beale, H. K. (1936). *Are American teachers free?* New York: Scribner.

Borman, K. M. (1990). "Foundations of education in teacher education." In W. R. Houston
(ed.), *Handbook of research on teacher education.* New York: Macmillan.

Broudy, H. S. (1981). "Between the yearbooks." In *Philosophy and education.* (Yearbook of the
80th National Society for the Study of Education, pt. 1). Chicago: University of
Chicago Press.

Buchmann, M., and Schwille, J. R. (1983). "Education: The overcoming of experience."
American Journal of Education, 92, 30–51.

Council of Learned Societies in Education (1986). *Standards for academic and professional instruction in foundations of education, educational studies, and educational policy studies.* Ann Arbor,
Mich.: Praken.

Cuban, L. (1984). *How teachers taught: Constancy and change in American classrooms, 1890–1980.*
White Plains, N.Y.: Longman.

Dewey, J. (1916). *Democracy and education.* New York: Macmillan.

Erickson, F. (1986). "Qualitative methods in research on teaching." In M. C. Wittrock (ed.),
Handbook of research on teaching. (3rd ed.). New York: Macmillan.

Feiman-Nemser, S., and Buchmann, M. (1985). "Pitfalls of experience in teacher preparation." *Teachers College Record, 87,* 53–65.

Fine, M. (1991). *Framing dropouts: Notes on the politics of an urban public high school.* Albany: State
University of New York Press.

Finkelstein, B. (1989). *Governing the young: Teacher behavior in popular primary schools in the nineteenth-
century United States.* Washington, D.C.: Falmer Press.

Floden, R. E., Buchmann, M., and Schwille, J. R. (1987). "Breaking with everyday experience." *Teachers College Record, 88,* 485–517.

Grant, C. A., and Sleeter, C. E. (1986). *After the school bell rings.* Washington, D.C.: Falmer Press.

Kliebard, H. M. (1986). *The struggle for the American curriculum, 1893–1958.* New York: Routledge & Kegan Paul.

Lanier, J. E., and Little, J. W. (1986). "Research on teacher education." In M. C. Wittrock (ed.), *Handbook of research on teaching.* (3rd ed.). New York: Macmillan.

Lortie, D. C. (1975) *Schoolteacher: A sociological study.* Chicago: University of Chicago Press.

Markowitz, R. J. (1993). *My daughter, the teacher.* New Brunswick, N.J.: Rutgers University Press.

Metz, M. H. (1986). *Different by design: The context and character of three magnet schools.* New York: Routledge & Kegan Paul.

Reese, W. J. (1986). *Power and the promise of school reform: Grass-roots movements during the Progressive Era.* New York: Routledge & Kegan Paul.

Rugg, H. (ed.) (1941). *Readings in the foundations of education,* Vols. 1 and 2. New York: Teachers College Press.

Rugg, H. (1952). *The teacher of teachers: Frontiers of theory and practice in teacher education.* New York: HarperCollins.

Rury, J. L. (1991). *Education and women's work: Female schooling and the division of labor in urban American, 1870–1930.* Albany: State University of New York Press.

Schön, D. (1983). *The reflective practitioner: How professionals think in action.* New York: Basic Books.

Shea, C. M., Sola, P. A., and Jones, A. H. (1987). "Examining the crisis in the social foundations of education." *Educational Foundations, 1,* 47–57.

Tozer, S. (1993). "Toward a new consensus among social foundations educators: Draft position paper of the American Educational Studies Association Committee on Academic Standards and Accreditation." *Educational Foundations, 7,* 5–22.

Tozer, S., and McAninch, S. A. (1986). "Social foundation of education in historical perspective." *Educational Foundations, 1,* 8–9.

Tozer, S., and McAninch, S. A. (1987). "Four texts in social foundations of education in historical perspective." *Educational Studies, 18,* 13–33.

Tyack, D. B. (1974). *The one best system: A history of American urban education.* Cambridge, Mass.: Harvard University Press.

Tyack, D. B., and Hansot, E. (1982). *Managers of virtue: Public school leadership in America, 1820–1980.* New York: Basic Books.

Waller, W. (1932). *The sociology of teaching.* New York: Wiley.

Warren, D. (1985). "Learning from experience: History and teacher education." *Educational Researcher, 14,* 5–12.

Zilversmit, A. (1993). *Changing schools: Progressive education theory and practice, 1930–1960.* Chicago: University of Chicago Press.

Annotated Bibliography

Anderson, W. A., and others (1951). *The theoretical foundations of education.* Urbana: Bureau of Research and Service, College of Education, University of Illinois.

This influential report by faculty members at the University of Illinois sought to further clarify the nature of the social foundations of education and to explore issues related to teaching foundations courses at the undergraduate level. Written by professors who had done their graduate work at Teachers College, Columbia University, or Ohio

State University, this document represented an extension into the post–World War II era of the work of Teachers College foundations faculty and close collaborators like Boyd Bode at Ohio State.

Counts, G. S. (1934). *The social foundations of education: Report of the Commission on the Social Studies*, pt. 9. New York: Scribner.
This is a classic articulation of the social foundations of education by one of the most prominent social reconstructionists.
Contemporary scholarship in the social foundations of education is disseminated through the following journals: *Educational Studies*, which publishes book reviews of new books in the field; *Educational Theory*, which focuses on philosophical studies of education; and *Educational Foundations*, a quarterly journal of research in the social foundations of education.

CHAPTER SEVENTEEN

FOUNDATIONS OF EDUCATION AND THE DEVALUATION OF TEACHER PREPARATION

GARY K. CLABAUGH AND EDWARD G. ROZYCKI

Why should Foundations of Education be a part of the knowledge base for teacher preparation? The initial reason is because this field of study emphasizes the cultural context of teaching and schooling, which helps teachers and those that prepare them to understand better and respond more effectively to assertions that the knowledge base itself is largely irrelevant.

In popular culture, many observers maintain that would-be teachers should be given subject matter preparation and a crash course in classroom survival skills and then learn to teach by doing. Public figures such as New Jersey's former chief executive Thomas H. Kean and presidential hopeful H. Ross Perot gained national reputations as "educational reformers" in part by trivializing the importance of formal teacher preparation (Clabaugh and Feden, 1984). In fact, as chair of a Texas school reform commission, Perot gained national press coverage by denouncing teacher education as a "Chinese firedrill" and asserting, "Of the sixty-five education colleges in Texas, maybe ten are worth anything" (wire service report, June 1985).

Confirming that his real quarrel was with the value of the teacher preparation knowledge base itself rather than particular education courses or programs, Perot even convinced the Texas legislature to restrict required teacher preparation coursework to no more than eighteen credit hours *including* student teaching. However, to treat foot disorders in Texas, one must have studied graduate-level biomedical and clinical podiatry for four years and, as of 1995, served a year's residency. That is the equivalent of 240 credits, or more than thirteen times the study it now takes to become a Texas teacher.

Even *A Nation at Risk*, the famous broadside that led off the most recent school reform movement, lamented that a "survey of 1,350 institutions training teachers indicated that 41 percent of the time of elementary school teacher candidates is spent in education courses, which reduces the amount of time available of subject matter courses" (National Commission on Excellence in Education, 1983, p. 22). Imagine a legal schooling reform commission fretting that 41 percent of a law student's time is being taken up with courses in the law. This comparison reveals the low value the commissioners placed on the teacher preparation and the knowledge base that supports it.

All of these fulminations stand in stark contrast to the finding of researchers. Take, for example, Goodlad (1984), who found that while practicing teachers feel well prepared in subject areas, they feel less well prepared in pedagogy. Why, then, is teacher preparation and the knowledge base that sustains it routinely denounced? A partial answer is that many people who have schooling experience presume that having played the role of student, they are possessed of the knowledge needed to produce or direct the play. However, Foundations scholars reveal other factors at work. Scholarship in the history of education, for example, points to our American tradition of promoting schooling as social panacea (see Perkinson, 1990). This tradition involves extreme simplification of issues and a naïve view of causation that requires a simplistic view of what it takes to be a competent teacher.

It is easy to bring this panacea mind-set to the surface. Just follow the approach of Foundations scholars and ask of any particular schooling practice what its costs and benefits are, and for whom. If these questions are raised at all in public forums across the nation, they provoke solemn invocations of communal enterprise, nationhood, and humanity—but the original questions commonly remain unaddressed. Similarly, ask what a school reform slogan such as "Every school a good school" means—good for whom and good for what? There is so little consensus on these matters that reform enthusiasms have oscillated wildly for over a century.

These and similar unanswered questions debunk the tradition of schooling as social panacea. More important, from our knowledge-base perspective, they also discredit the notion that competent teaching is simply a matter of charisma, strength of character, and high expectations. However, encouraged to believe that schooling can magically undo the consequences of social injustice and a host of neglected national concerns, the public is still reassured by assorted public figures, newspaper editors, and other opinion leaders that successful teaching is essentially a matter of purity of heart, subject matter knowledge, and persistent hopefulness. Given the exponential growth of the teaching knowledge base, such a belief is plainly false.

Foundations scholars also point out that character, not technical knowledge, has long been thought to be the primary factor in teaching success or failure. Moreover, "practical coursework" has always been preferred to "speculation"—at least when it comes to training teachers of the "industrial classes" (Beyer, Feinberg,

Pagano, and Whitson, 1989). These and related historic attitudes still influence present-day devaluations of the teacher preparation knowledge base.

Foundations scholarship also reveals that gender and social class inequalities profoundly affect both the teacher work force and the ideas and ideologies of teacher preparation (Beyer, Feinberg, Pagano, and Whitson, 1989). With respect to gender, teaching came to be dominated by large numbers of women who were exploited as cheap labor. Their historically ascribed second-class status rubbed off on the occupation. Furthermore, the time-honored notion that women have a "natural" gift and instinct for nurturance suggested that thorough "theoretical" preparation in teaching was unnecessary, perhaps even perverse (Beyer, Feinberg, Pagano, and Whitson, 1989). With respect to social class, teachers trained for the "common schools" have never served the power elite. The most privileged and powerful Americans have traditionally sent their children to private boarding schools and the universities they feed into. This elite schooling has turned out a disproportionate number of our business, professional, and governmental leaders (Clabaugh and Rozycki, 1990b)—the very same people who often set preparation standards for those who would teach in the very "common schools" that the regulators themselves avoid.

Since elite schooling has traditionally developed a style and state of mind that legitimates unequal relationships while validating the authority of those with power (see Baltzell, 1964), it is predictable that many of its influential graduates dismiss the value of thorough and thoughtful preparation in pedagogy for those who would teach "the masses." Here it is sufficient to industrialize the schooling process and to "teacher-proof" the curriculum through standardization and regulation.

Space prohibits full discussion of it here, but Foundations scholarship also points out that to fully understand the current hostility toward professional teacher preparation and the knowledge base that supports it, one also needs to examine the institutional contexts in which teacher education was created and now takes place. As Schneider (1987) stresses, our present concern with defining and legitimizing teacher preparation has been innate in teacher preparation since its partial takeover by essentially hostile research universities nearly 100 years ago. Thus, part of the difficulty of establishing the full legitimacy of a professional teacher preparation knowledge base lies in the institutional context in which teacher education is now imbedded.

Historical insights are not all that Foundations scholars can contribute to our understanding of past and present devaluations of the teacher preparation knowledge base. These scholars also offer unique distinctions and analytic techniques that can help us understand and counteract these efforts. At a very basic level, for instance, they point out the fundamental difference between necessity and sufficiency. Those who would virtually abandon teacher education have leapt to the conclusion that subject matter knowledge is both necessary *and* sufficient for teaching competence. Subject matter knowledge is certainly necessary but hardly sufficient. To be truly capable, teachers must also understand the ways students learn or fail to learn; the ways they grow and develop mentally, socially, morally, and physically; and the ways they can be motivated. They must also be able to use intelligently a variety of student assessments, integrate the curriculum across subjects, and adapt the rate and type of instruction for the individual learning styles of students. Moreover, and here is where a study of Foundations of Education is critically important, if they are to help govern schools, engage in site-based management, employ strategic planning, and be in command of policy-making perspectives and skills, teachers must be able to do all of the following:

- Analyze the meaning, intent, and effects of educational institutions
- Develop their own value positions regarding education on the basis of critical study
- Understand the decisions and events that have shaped educational thought and practice (Council of Learned Societies in Education, 1986)

Psychological studies of expert performance indicate that it is precisely these kinds of metacognitive skills that differentiate novice from expert (Brown, Bransford, Ferrara, and Campione, 1983; see also Bransford, Stein, Arbitman-Smith, and Vye, 1985) and it is here that Foundations of Education makes a particularly strong contribution to the teacher education knowledge base.

For another example of the unique distinctions and analytic techniques provided by Foundations scholars, consider the relevance of the distinction between absolute and positional benefits developed by Hirsch (1976) and Green (1980). Absolute benefits are those that retain their value no matter how many people enjoy them—for example, self-esteem, joy in reading, or a passion for history. In other words, even if everyone enjoyed these things, their value would be undiminished. Positional benefits, on the other hand, lose value as more people get them. They are, in effect, commodities, articles of commerce, subject to the law of supply and demand.

Now back to the matter of trivializing teacher preparation. Teaching certificates are positional benefits. They would be nearly worthless if they could be had for the asking. Devaluing the teacher preparation knowledge base and minimizing course requirements in education takes on new meaning in this context. By making teaching certificates easy to come by, school "reformers" effectively debase these certificates' positional value. This, in turn, lowers teachers' salaries and the costs of public schooling. So when some governor or presidential hopeful scornfully dismisses the value of the teaching knowledge base by demanding the trivialization of the preparation process, he or she might have Machiavellian intentions.

We see, then, that the insights of Foundations of Education scholarship illumine and suggest methods for countering efforts to cheapen teacher preparation. This, in itself, is a reason for including Foundations in the teacher preparation knowledge base. If teachers cannot understand the factors influencing their own professional preparation, they will never grasp, much less value or fulfill, the possibilities of their profession.

Foundations of Education and the Role of the Teacher

The role of Foundations of Education in the teaching knowledge base ultimately depends on what type of teacher we envision. Foundations of Education specializes in analyzing and assessing schooling's direction, manner, and routines while developing the critical and interpretive skills necessary for understanding schooling in broad perspective. Clearly, such a critical survey of educational thought and practice is unnecessary if educators are merely to be semiskilled operatives in schools that resemble factories. Some influential business executives who would have our schools serve constricted corporate purposes, for example, may have little enthusiasm for teachers who have carefully thought-out value positions and a reflective commitment to the democratic process. Similarly, public officials narrowly concerned with using schooling to promote national competitiveness may not be eager for educators who think in a disciplined manner about fostering and sustaining a free and self-governing citizenry.

Considerations of the type examined in Foundations of Education have always been important to those who hold power, but they are important *to teachers* only if teachers are interested in *professional* practice that involves not only excellence in teaching methods but competence in making broader reflective and interpretive judgments about personal and social interests (Brown, Bransford, Ferrara, and Campione, 1983). However, even experienced teachers sometimes do not see the need for this. Beset with day-to-day problems and impatient with "purely theoretical" issues, they are eager to make classroom decisions without full regard for the broader social and moral matters that Foundational Studies addresses. Sadly, this means that they also ignore the ethical constraints and moral values that separate mere technicians from professionals. (In ancient Rome, an ordinary citizen without the ability to be an active competent social participant at a comprehensive ethical level was considered an *idiota*–a term that does not require translation.

We have just pointed out that Foundations of Education-type issues involve broad-scale values and interests that are central to the professionalization of teaching. Foundations issues also underlie the most pedestrian classroom routines even if, in practice, unthinking practitioners ignore them. Consider these questions that are routinely investigated as part of the Foundations curriculum:

1. What counts as evidence that a student has (or has not) learned something?
2. What counts as evidence that a student can (or cannot) learn something?
3. What assumptions support a particular teaching or testing method and what circumstances might invalidate our judgments about those methods?

Such questions cannot be adequately answered without the sort of inquiry that is a traditional concern of Foundations of Education.

Clearly, then, the problems of teaching cannot properly be confined to the didactics of instruction and the techniques of classroom management. Even if we unwisely confine ourselves to day-to-day classroom issues, important moral issues still arise, and scholarship in the Foundations of Education can help students address with precision the ethical implications of day-to-day matters. Consider this small list of questions and ask, "What is the honorable and principled thing to do?"

1. Should a talkative student be silenced for the sake of the class?
2. Should students be grouped so their individual sense of accomplishment is enhanced, or should they be grouped for the benefit of the least adept among them?
3. When should student infractions of "the rules" be overlooked and why?
4. Should grading be based strictly on achievement or should effort be factored in?
5. Should a teacher ever depart from administrative policies, and if so, when ?
6. When and with what vigor should a teacher intervene when students annoy, insult, or injure one another?
7. Where these may be incompatible, should classroom discipline aim at behavioral change or equality of treatment?

Foundations Studies cannot answer these questions for practitioners, but it can provide a frame of reference for more careful consideration and informed judgment. Foundations scholars such as Tozer (1993) conceptualize this as "constructing meaning" out of otherwise chaotic experience. It is hard to imagine how such questions can better be answered in an untrained and nonreflective state of mind.

General issues such as justice, social inequality, concentrations of power, class differences, race and ethnic relations, or family and community disorganization invariably affect teaching because, as Foundations scholars repeatedly point out, teaching is essentially and inescapably a social and moral enterprise. Teacher preparation that includes these dimensions, therefore, is hardly a frill, and teachers who do not consider these dimensions are incompetent.

Broudy (1985) observes, "Foundational courses are not an intellectual luxury. . . . Put into their appropriate contexts many educational problems cease to be matters of technique" (p. 37).

Developing Critical Understanding

Scholars in the Foundations tradition have long crafted telling interpretations and evaluations of schooling's purposes and practices. The seminal contributions of

John Dewey, William Torrey Harris, William James, or more recently, R. Freeman Butt, Lawrence Cremin, and B. Othanel Smith, demonstrate the discipline's centrally significant contributions to a *critical* understanding of schooling and teaching (Finkelstein, 1982). Dewey, for instance, is widely regarded as America's most influential educator and was the father of the progressive school movement, an idea more frequently abused than understood. His observations on schooling still play an important and controversial role in American life (Bernstein, 1967).

The type of critical understanding epitomized by the work of Dewey is more important now than ever. In *Teachers for the Nation's Schools,* Goodlad (1991) observes that teacher education is at a critical juncture "where a craft either continues to take its cues almost exclusively from practitioners of the craft or opens itself up to the research and theory of those who inquire into it" (p. 30). Goodlad then introduces four dimensions of teaching, the mastery of which requires uniting practice with research and theory:

1. Facilitating enculturation
2. Providing access to knowledge
3. Building an effective teacher-student connection
4. Practicing good stewardship

In each of these dimensions of teaching, Foundations of Education has a contribution to make, as schematized in Table 17.1.

Note that this table links Foundations of Education to the teaching knowledge base. It also points to Foundations' importance as a tool for use by the education professoriate as well as by teachers. Teacher educators, no less than the teachers they train, need to carefully consider the interpretive, normative, and critical dimensions of *their* own practice.

Abandoning the Essence of Foundational Studies

Sadly, some teacher educators discourage the proper utilization of the Foundations knowledge base in teacher preparation. They do this by fostering or tolerating "foundations" courses that totally ignore critical, moral, and ethical concerns. Often taught by people untrained in Foundations of Education (Shea, Sola, and Jones, 1987), these "Introduction to Education" courses are little more than thoughtless or dishonest celebrations of teaching.

This abandonment of the essence of Foundational Studies is reflected in a number of banal textbooks that claim to be in the Foundations tradition. Such texts represent the very antithesis of what it is that the study of Foundations offers to the teaching knowledge base. Analyzing four commonly used texts, Tozer and McAninch (1987, pp. 8–9) focus on typical deficiencies:

TABLE 17.1. CONTRIBUTIONS OF FOUNDATIONS OF EDUCATION.

DIMENSIONS OF TEACHING (AFTER GOODLAD)	FOUNDATIONS' CONTRIBUTIONS
Facilitating Enculturation: Teachers must possess a deep understanding of both the governance structures and processes of political democracy and the requisites of humane citizenship.	Theories and critiques of schooling's purposes. Explorations of conceptions of truth, justice, rights, and so forth as they are applied in educational practice.
Providing Access to Knowledge: Teachers must have a knowledge of subject qua subject and how to teach it as well as a knowledge of what is to count as knowing relative to particular subjects, contexts, and learner characteristics.	Inquiry into the nature of teaching and schooling (see Goodlad, 1991). Inculcating "Canons of Assessment" (see Kerr, 1986) to support pedagogical and administrative judgment. Developing critical intellectual skills (see Goodlad, 1991) applicable to educational practice.
Building an Effective Teacher-Student Connection: Teachers must acquire an epistemology of teaching that goes far beyond the mechanics of teaching to include sensitivity to human potentials and awareness of what enculturation involves.	Examination of the generic-specific learning and teaching controversy (see Phillips and Soltis, 1985). Understanding how one's value commitments affect one's behavior as an educator. Investigation into nature of skills, understandings, and sensitivity.
Practicing Good Stewardship: Teachers must learn the skills necessary for the ongoing renewal of the schools in which they will spend their careers.	Understanding the conflicts and contexts of schooling (see Goodlad, 1991). Acquiring the skills necessary to expand one's action beyond the classroom.

- An exclusively celebrationist approach
- Failure to stimulate critical inquiry
- Unexamined surface realities
- Failure to provide competing accounts or explanations of school or social realities
- Lists of facts, events, and ideas that are not placed in the context of social institutions' processes and ideas
- Topics unrelated from one chapter to another
- Visuals often unintegrated with the text
- Failure to ground improved student judgment in objective, empirical, and disciplined methods of analysis.
- Authoritative declarations that lack supporting evidence or argument

Such texts do not develop in the student a true appreciation of the nature of Foundational Studies; rather, they discourage it.

Approaches to the Foundations of Education

The earliest U.S. efforts to formally prepare teachers emphasized subject matter knowledge and the liberal arts. Knowledge about teaching was confined to a very few courses in pedagogy focusing on instructional methodology. The underlying foundations of teaching and learning were totally neglected (Tozer, Anderson, and Armbruster, 1990). As a typical example, the first catalogue of the State Normal School at Indiana, Pennsylvania, published in 1875, lists such required courses as Higher Arithmetic, Orthography, Writing and Drawing, Physiology, Bookkeeping, Botany, and Chemistry but only *two* courses in pedagogy: School Economy and the Art of Teaching, and Methods of Instruction. However, by 1890, the course of study had expanded to include theoretical training in Applied Psychology and History of Education. The addition of these more theoretical or abstract single academic discipline courses—typically appearing in teacher preparation across the country—marked the beginning of the Foundations tradition.

By the 1920s, single-discipline Foundations of Education coursework, most often history or philosophy of education, was well established, particularly at universities that had been reluctantly drawn into teacher preparation. What is more important, a new cross-disciplinary approach known as Social Foundations of Education was also evolving. Tozer, Anderson, and Armbruster (1990) describe this development emphasizing the role of Teachers College, Columbia University:

> Benefiting from the study and teaching of such scholars as E. L. Thorndike and W. H. Kilpatrick in psychology and philosophy of education, respectively, Teachers College at Columbia University led the nation in developing a theory-based curriculum in teacher education, with teacher candidates expected to take coursework in such foundational disciplines as history, philosophy, sociology, anthropology, and psychology of education. In the 1920s and 1930s, the Foundations Division of Teachers College condensed these several areas of study into two categories: the psychological foundations, which examined the nature of the human mind and learning processes; and the social foundations, which combined the other foundational areas into a cross-disciplinary approach examining the social institutions and processes and ideals underlying educational policy and practice.

In creating this separation, the Foundations Division of Teachers College achieved two significant outcomes. First, they identified mind and culture as the twin foundations on which all teaching and learning processes are built; and second, they created a model for the *professional* preparation of teachers that has been adopted to one degree or another by certification agencies in every state in the nation. We underscore "professional" because the Teachers College faculty deliberately sought to reject what they saw as the technical training model of the normal school in favor of preparing practitioners who were as theoretically informed as practitioners in other professions. [p. 293]

Single-Discipline Approaches

Before examining this interdisciplinary Social Foundations approach, we will briefly examine the earlier-developed single-discipline approaches. Remember, it is a tradition of putting into schooling-related service the insights and paradigms offered by particular academic specializations. The perspectives offered by anthropology, history, philosophy, sociology, and the law, for example, have all been used to provide a broader basis for professional judgment. Unfortunately, as Seymour Sarason observes, the utility of these single-discipline approaches has been limited by the defensively condescending attitude of many subject area academics toward teacher preparation. Academicians with no long-term, disciplined interest in schooling (and often only a rudimentary understanding of teaching) have promoted, rather than remedied, primitive thinking about school-related issues. Gardner (1991) argues that even highly schooled people, unless they take pains to apply the disciplinary knowledge and practices they have acquired, deal with the world from a perspective that is decidedly "primitive." (For instance, Barr and Dreeben, 1983, have soundly criticized the primitive production model of the school. Ignoring such criticisms, however, this model is naïvely resurrected by subject area academics Chubb and Moe, 1990; see also Hogan, 1992.) For these and related reasons, Sarason (1971) notes, most academics who concentrate solely on the traditional concerns of their disciplines merit little consideration when education is seriously discussed.

Despite these limitations, however, three single-discipline modes of inquiry have emerged as central to Foundational Studies, largely, but not exclusively, because of the work of scholars trained in these traditions who have actually studied education: the history of education, the sociology of education, and the philosophy of education. We will briefly examine the role in the knowledge base of each of these traditions.

History of Education

Public discourse on schooling in the United States often resembles the ramblings of an amnesiac. Even college-educated enthusiasts of school reform, for example, have little sense of where we have been or what has already been tried. Moreover, they fail to recognize that educational practices, such as those used in teacher preparation, reflect broader social realities.

Consider the primitive understanding that equates education with schooling. This conflation of two distinct, though related, concepts is a profound confusion that is fostered by historical ignorance. For nearly four million years (well over 99 percent of the human experience), human beings were deliberately taught a whole host of things (education), yet there were *no* schools whatsoever. Significantly, when that formal institutionalized approach to education known as schooling finally did evolve some six thousand years ago in the temples of ancient Sumer, it served only a small social elite who were determined to maintain social control and reinforce their own status (Clabaugh and Rozycki, 1990b). Had Sumer been the only time or place this concern with maintaining control and reinforcing status through schooling played itself out, we might ignore it as an aberration. However, time after time in place after place, these concerns emerge as central to the schooling process. Yes, it is true that ancient China occasionally used schooling for social renewal purposes. (Civil service–type examinations requiring detailed knowledge of Confucianism were used to place middle-class aspirants into upper-class positions.) Nevertheless, a major historical concern of schooling throughout most of human history has been to establish social controls and serve the special interests of a social elite.

Such historical realities should recast our understanding of schooling and even temper our sometimes mindless enthusiasm for schools as instruments of social renewal. In fact, the school curriculum, teacher professionalism, school funding and governance, and, as we noted previously, teacher preparation, all look different when viewed in historical context.

Concerning the knowledge base for teacher preparation, it is not easy to convince novice teachers that educational facts remain mute, isolated, and disconnected until a study of history reveals their pattern. Like most Americans, teacher education candidates find it difficult to look to history for ways to understand and solve problems. Author William Least Heat Moon (1991) astutely observes, "The American Disease is forgetfulness . . . [and] a person or people who cannot recollect their past have little point beyond mere animal existence: it is memory that makes things matter" (p. 266). Foundations scholarship in the history of education supplies that memory in the teacher preparation knowledge base.

Philosophy of Education

Philosophy is often seen as developmentally primary in the teaching knowledge base. Even educators at the earliest stages of training are expected to be ready to explain their "philosophy of education" and show how it is behind nearly every on-the-job decision they make. This is to confuse philosophy with premature rationalizations of personal preference.

Scholarship in the field reveals that philosophy in any form comes late in an educator's development because one must first learn something to have it to analyze. In short, philosophy derives from, even though it illuminates, activity.

In the minds of some, philosophy of education need be no more than a compendium of nostrums. So it is that philosophy is presented as a typology of systems of thought, for example, essentialism, pragmatism, and the like, that are asserted—rarely argued—to have some bearing on the educational enterprise (see Rozycki, 1982). But philosophy as systems of thought is only one of three sometimes conflicting basic aspects to philosophy of education that Passmore (1967) identifies as *wisdoms, ideology,* and *criticism.*

Conceptions of schooling that denigrate the teacher's role to that of a minor functionary would restrict philosophy narrowly to mere wisdoms or ideology. This conception is far less threatening than to conceive of it as a discipline that develops critical capacity—yet that is exactly what it can be.

In teacher preparation, philosophy as wisdoms or ideology tends to hold dominance over the more academic tradition of criticism. However, it is as critical thought in the Socratic tradition that philosophy has made its most significant contribution to Foundations of Education and to the teacher preparation knowledge base. It is in this role that philosophy bridges the gap between the school and a wide variety of traditions of authority (Passmore, 1967).

Philosophers of education working in this critical tradition have developed an entire literature of distinctions and analytical techniques that have great utility in developing value positions regarding teaching, in encouraging policy-making outlooks and expertise, and in searching for resolutions to educational problems and issues. Here is one example. Israel Scheffler, professor of education and philosophy at Harvard University, observes that we cannot make much sense of educational thought and arguments unless we understand that they are entangled in issues relating to language. Taking as an example the use of definitions, Scheffler (1968) identifies four types commonly used in education: descriptive, programmatic, technical, and stipulative.

Descriptive definitions reflect prior usage and clarify terms as they are ordinarily and most clearly applied. Dictionary definitions are descriptive, associating a term with a general account of its prior use. The multiple meanings commonly listed for the same term in dictionaries demonstrate that prior usage often reflects some ambiguity of meaning. For instance, *educate* is defined in *Webster's New World Dictionary* (1968) as "to bring up, rear, or train; or to give knowledge or training to; train or develop by formal schooling or study; teach; instruct" (p. 461). There is, then, both a rearing sense *and* a formal schooling sense of the term. Descriptive definitions are the yardstick by which other types of definitions are measured.

Programmatic definitions are little constrained by prior usage. They are instead used to express serious moral choices, to legislate, and to short-circuit debate. For example, when a suburban Philadelphia school district recently conducted in-service training on "multiculturalism" for middle-school teachers, they invited an outside expert in African-American studies. She told the assembled teachers, "The problem with Eurocentricity is that it has set up hegemony (dominance) or hierarchy. Afrocentricity is to see all cultures as equal" (Finarelli, 1993, p. 15). These definitions violate descriptive usage. *Webster's Encyclopedic Unabridged Dictio-*

nary of the English Language defines *Afro* as "pertaining to black traditions, culture, etc." and *centric* as "pertaining to or situated at the center; central." So *Afrocentric* descriptively means "placing black traditions and culture at the center of things," just as *Eurocentric* means placing European traditions and culture in a similar position. Why, then, would *Eurocentricity* necessarily involve "setting up dominance" and *Afrocentricity* entail "seeing all cultures as equal," as the consultant asserts? There is no logical reason. Indeed, placing black traditions at the center of things makes it more difficult to see all cultures as equal. Accept the consultant's definitions, however, and Eurocentrism is categorized as bad and Afrocentrism as good without either evidence or discussion. That is why the definitions are programmatic.

A handy, though not infallible, method of identifying programmatic definitions is the presence of adjectives such as *true* or *real* in the definition. Consider Pope Pius XI's definition of education: "There can be no true education which is not wholly directed to man's last end, . . . no ideally perfect education which is not Christian education" ([1929] 1981, pp. 353, 372). Accept this definition, telegraphed to the discerning by the adjective *true,* and we embrace the conservative Roman Catholic program of action that underlies it. When we do that, even Albert Einstein becomes uneducated if his schooling was not wholly directed to personal spiritual salvation in the Catholic tradition.

Technical definitions are precise in meaning and call for special knowledge and the use of particular theoretical criteria in their evaluation. For example, when learning theorists speak of "declarative knowledge" versus "procedural knowledge" or when they discuss "long-term" and "short-term" memory, they are using technical language rooted in scientific theory. These terms cannot be understood in abstraction from this body of knowledge. Further, they need not conform to familiar usage or enlighten lay persons. The sole consideration is their theoretical adequacy.

Technical definitions are sometimes scoffed at as mere jargon, but their use in a learned profession is a practical necessity because it is the way experts share common yet complex understandings in an economic manner. In other words, technical definitions serve as a professional shorthand without which communications would be laborious and imprecise.

A limitation of such definitions is that their accurate use is generally restricted to the discipline in which they were developed. Attempts at popularization fail to convey the richness of meaning that is a feature of expert knowledge. *Dyslexia,* for instance, is a technical term referring to a number of specific difficulties in reading and spelling. However, popular usage of the term has continued without any knowledge of these particular difficulties. Thus, *dyslexia* has come to have a very shallow and misleading popular meaning.

Scheffler (1968) points out that sometimes people outside a system of knowledge misuse technical definitions by attempting to extend their meaning beyond the specific context in which they were developed. The hope is that their association with a respected technical field will lend an air of authority to the new usage. Thus, there is a need to be careful of technical definitions that are transplanted outside the borders of the garden where they germinated. These definitions are usually programmatic.

Stipulative definitions establish principles for interpreting terms within certain limited contexts. For example, we would be offering a stipulative definition if we said, "For the purposes of this discussion, let's understand 'learning' to have taken place only when a permanent change is observed in the learner's behavior." Notice there is no claim to necessary agreement with familiar or normal usage. (In that broader context, it is quite possible to imagine that learning has occurred even without any observable change.) We are looking, instead, for a consistent and pragmatic agreement of limited duration. A stipulative definition's sole purpose is facilitating meaningful discussion.

Stipulative definitions sometimes become permanent in the minds of their advocates. When that happens, the definition is no longer stipulative, but programmatic.

A critical approach to the philosophy of education offers literally hundreds of similar distinctions and analytic approaches that are indispensable to thinking with precision about schools and teaching (see Clabaugh and Rozycki, 1990a). Despite the power of philosophical traditions to illuminate critical issues in schooling and teaching, however, American academic philosophers, on the whole, tend not to be interested in education. They are presently preoccupied with the possibility that philosophy as they have practiced it has lost its point. Some prominent philosophers have even given up the notion that philosophy provides one with a special vantage point from which to examine other disciplines disinterestedly (see Baynes, Bohman, and McCarthy, 1987). Happily, many philosophers of education do not take the "end of philosophy" worries of their liberal arts colleagues all that seriously. They understand philosophy's critical tools to be still viable. The contexts of concern in which philosophy of education is carried out enable them in practice to forgo the search for ultimates.

In addition, many philosophers of education believe it is time to cut the umbilical cord to purely academic philosophy altogether. Giarelli (1991) comments:

> Philosophy, in this view, is rooted neither in some privileged access to reality nor in some neutral procedure, but rather in an analysis of those practices by which human communities maintain, extend and renew their continued existence. In short, philosophy is rooted in an analysis of educational practices. . . . education is not dependent upon philosophy for a justification and explanation of its theories, methods and practices. Rather, the future of philosophy depends upon its ability to become an educative element in the life of the community. In this view, it is not the philosopher as midwife delivering a grounding to education, but rather practice, which delivers to philosophy a point and purpose for its existence and identity [p. 36].

Sociology of Education

The sociological tradition has also resulted in major contributions to Foundations of Education. Consider, for example, James Coleman's milestone research on equality of educational opportunity. At the time Coleman was selected to conduct this study, it was assumed that the nation's social inequalities were a by-product of vast differences in school quality. Coleman was employed by the Congress of the United States to determine how great these differences were and to show how the difference in the quality of schools retarded the progress of the poor and minorities. Coleman (1966) expected few surprises but discovered otherwise: "One implication stands out above all: That schools bring little influence to bear on a child's achievement that is independent of his background and general social context; and that this very lack of an independent effect means that the inequalities imposed on children by their home, neighborhood, and peer environment are carried along to become the inequalities with which they confront adult life at the end of school" (p. 325).

Sociologist Christopher Jencks's famed 1972 study, *Inequality*, further developed this important theme. As a conclusion to the massive national survey he directed, Jencks (1972) observed that "children seem to be far more influenced by what happens at home than what happens at school. They also may be more influenced by what happens on the streets and by what they see on television. Everything else—the school budget, its policies, the characteristics of the teachers—is either secondary or completely irrelevant" (pp. 255–256).

These observations are not regarded as dogma in Foundational Studies but as important considerations in the continuing dialogue on the nature of the school *in society*. In fact, they highlight the relevance of sociology in studying the school in society, something that Foundations scholars have advocated since the inception of the discipline.

Experienced teachers know that the world their pupils live in is extremely important to what happens, or fails to happen, at school. Experience has taught and retaught them that nonschool factors too often make *all* the difference in school success or failure, yet they know they can do little about their students' life away from school. These teachers still have to deal with things as they are in the classroom. Nonetheless, if they are to practice professionally, they must not only recognize this sometimes sad reality but master systematic knowledge of how nonschool factors figure in school achievement. Sociology of education provides this knowledge.

Foundations scholars operating within the tradition of sociology have made numerous other contributions to our understanding of schooling. For instance, they have developed the distinction between the manifest functions of schools that are intended and stated openly (literacy, for example) and latent functions (such as child care or legitimating status), which are done inadvertently or which we do not care to recognize (see Collins, 1979). These and similar insights are a product of the sociological tradition focused on schooling.

The Cross-Disciplinary Social Foundations Approach

As previously noted, the interdisciplinary Social Foundations approach to the study of education first coalesced in the 1920s (Tozer and McAninch, 1986). Its unique attribute is that it was specifically designed to provide school practitioners with an integrated *cross-disciplinary* approach to understanding the cultural phenomena that underlie educational ideas and practices (Tozer, 1993). Alterations in values and beliefs, the changing family, the graying of America, changes in the nation's ethnic and racial balance, the transformation of the U.S. economy, the distribution of wealth in America, are all crucial considerations in understanding American schooling as well as the practice of teaching, and Social Foundations' multidisciplinary perspective addresses all of these issues. It should also be noted that a primary concern of Social Foundations of Education since its inception has been its focus on democracy as the chief value commitment of the culture of the United States and what that implies for schooling (Tozer, 1993).

Significantly, Social Foundations scholars often question assumptions that otherwise remain unexamined. For instance, they ask, "Is society best understood as a collective reality that somehow transcends its individual members? If so, should we understand schooling largely in terms of its promotion of harmony, stability, and maintenance of the social order? If, on the other hand, society is better described as an arena in which various groups seek antagonistic goals and special interest groups try to maintain power, are schools best understood as reinforcers of fundamental inequalities? Are the privileged using schooling to preserve their advantage by imposing their values and understandings on those they exploit?" These sorts of considerations, while difficult and controversial, are essential for thoughtful schooling practice.

We have already noted that education is necessarily a moral enterprise and that schools are an important instrument of that endeavor. Schooling willy-nilly inculcates values, and by placing schools in broad social context, the Social Foundations tradition raises the critically important question of *whose* values are being instilled. This is a particularly significant consideration in our profoundly pluralistic society. The breakup of the Soviet monolith and the ongoing struggle in what once was Yugoslavia illustrate how the many pluralisms of a diverse union can degenerate into bloody confusion if such value conflicts remain unexamined and unreconciled.

One can only wonder, viewing America's vast social disparities and growing violence, whether our own pluralistic society can hold. Perhaps we could improve the odds—but not by preparing uninsightful teachers who function as uncritical, even mindless supporters of the status quo. This is not only a moral abdication, it makes no practical long-term sense in a society in which the nature of the status quo is constantly contested. Better that we have thoughtful educators trained to critically appraise the role of the school in a rapidly changing America. Training in the Social Foundations tradition can very effectively aid such critical thinking.

Three Major Perspectives

Using the variety of approaches outlined above, the field of Foundational Studies offers three major common perspectives. The Council of Learned Societies in Education (1986) summarizes these perspectives as follows:

1. The *interpretive perspective,* using theories and resources developed within the humanities and the social and behavioral sciences, assists students in examining and explaining education within different contexts. Foundational Studies promote analyses of the meaning, intent and effects of educational institutions, including schools. A major task of Foundational Studies is to provide the resources, incentive, and skills students require in performing the interpretive functions.

2. The *normative perspective* assists students in examining and explaining education in light of value orientations. Foundational Studies promote understanding of normative and ethical behavior in educational development and recognition of the inevitable presence of normative influences in educational thought and practice—they encourage students to develop their own value position regarding education on the basis of critical study and their own reflections.

3. The *critical perspective* assists students in examining and explaining education in light of its origins, major influences, and consequences. Foundational Studies promote critical understanding of educational thought and practice, and of the decisions and events which have shaped them, in their various contexts. Finally, Foundational Studies encourage the development of policy making perspectives and skills in searching for resolutions to educational problems and issues.

Clearly, these perspectives are useful only if becoming an educator is thought to involve something more than mastering pedagogical technology.

Foundations of Education's Limitations

Some factors limit Foundations of Education's effectiveness as a part of the knowledge base for teacher education. A primary limitation concerns practitioner consensus. Although there is agreement about the scope of Foundational Studies at the level of Council of Learned Societies in Education, Nash and Agne (1982) observe that there still is a widespread lack of consensus among individual practitioners concerning how the specialty should be approached. Whether Foundational Studies is primarily an academic discipline or a utilitarian professional one is at the heart of this disagreement. In this connection, Tozer, Anderson, and Armbruster (1990) surveyed articles relating to this difference of opinion that were published in the *Teachers College Record*, and they found, "Many of the articles explicitly criticize contemporary practices in Foundations of Education for their persistently inadequate integration of Foundational theory and knowledge into teacher education programs. While the research into mind and culture is voluminous and persuasive, teacher education programs, they charge, have failed to present that knowledge in ways that provide teachers with the benefits of that research. Nearly every article in this volume responds to that perceived inadequacy by arguing for attention to the practical contexts of teaching as a guide to integration of research knowledge and theory into the teacher education curriculum" (p. 296).

This dispute need not be fundamental. Admittedly, there is some tension between knowledge pursued for its own sake and knowledge pursued as a basis for action. There is little reason to cast this issue in either/or terms. There are a multitude of connections between "theoretical" studies and practical experience. Indeed, it is often a matter of intelligent practice to recognize "theory" as information that guides decision making.

Another related limitation on Foundations of Education's contribution to the knowledge base concerns a tendency of some Foundations professors to substitute advocacy for analysis. They use their courses to promote factional views and mount partisan appeals for social action. Teacher education candidates can thus find themselves captive to an ideologue whose chief pedagogical approach is to exhort them to his or her particular outlook on schooling and teaching. Such partisan approaches may even involve the exclusive use of *one* of the previously mentioned interpretive, normative, and critical perspectives characteristic of Foundational Studies. However, students are not presented with *competing* accounts of reality. They also are not encouraged to develop their *own* position regarding schooling on the basis of critical study as required by the standards of the Council of Learned Societies in Education. Such an approach is contrary to the Foundations of Education tradition.

Social Foundations does have a tradition of social criticism and, within limited contexts, even social advocacy; and this tradition has become a legitimate and well-considered part of the teaching knowledge base. It is highly relevant, for example, for Foundations scholars to point out potential problems in demanding that U.S. students be first internationally in mathematics and science achievement, while the United States remains last among industrial nations in providing for the physical and mental health of its children. Still, special pleading and propagandistic exhortations that go beyond such observations have little to do with scholarship and even less to contribute to the knowledge base for teacher education.

Teacher Education Programming as the Practice of Philosophy of Education

Foster MacMurray (1975) writes, "As a practical discipline, philosophy of education is an attempt to find the most rationally defensible reasons for doing education one way rather than some other. What makes this kind of educational philosophy different from *(academic)* philosophy is that decisions must be reached as preparation for subsequent action, and the actions that follow upon decisions are intended to have consequences—to make a difference—in human lives" (p. 236).

At the start of this chapter, we noted the utility of Foundations of Education in understanding and defending against the devaluation of teacher education. In this final section, we will deal with how one might use Foundations of Education to select topics and courses for a program in teacher preparation. We offer some criteria and a method for evaluating proposed topics for teacher preparation courses. These criteria suggest a way to prioritize what is to be treated or neglected and to provide rationales for the defense of the choices.

Four criteria are offered by which to judge courses: durability, centrality, consensus, and practicality.

1. *Durability: Is the subject matter ephemeral? Will the content and procedures taught in this course become easily obsolete?* Recall the enthusiasm that preceded the surprisingly quick decline of a variety of heatedly debated course topics, such as interaction analysis, behavioral objectives, time on task, computer literacy, the Paedeia proposal, open classrooms. Such topics as the relation of testing to social stratification, the nature of learning, or the systemic consequences of school structure have proved to be much more enduring.

2. *Centrality: Are the content and procedures taught in this course central to a variety of school and/or disciplinary concerns?* Shall we commit resources to a course whose scope is severely limited? For example, would a course in medieval educational thought take precedence over one on classroom management? It might require strenuous argument to do so.

3. *Consensus: To what extent would the methodology and content of this course be acceptable to a wide variety of scholars in the field?* Does this course require commitment to some exclusive philosophical or ideological precepts? Instructors who confuse college teaching with political action impress students in direct proportion to the

TABLE 17.2. TOPICS FOR ANALYSIS.

	Durability	Centrality	Consensus	Practicality
Learning Theory				
Human Growth and Development				
School Law				
Classroom Management				
Educational Research				
Tests and Measurements				
Educational Psychology				
Philosophy of Education				
History of Education				
Teaching of Reading				
Human Exceptionalities				

naïveté of which they themselves should be disabused by a good teacher preparation program.

4. *Practicality: To what extent do the methods and contents of this course bear on actual schooling practices, not only of classroom teachers, but of educational decision makers in the wide variety of roles they play, as administrators, board members, and so forth?* There is plenty of room for discussion of theory and broad topics, provided one acknowledges the breadth of action expected of a professionally prepared teacher.

One method of using these criteria could be to evaluate each dimension, durability, centrality, consensus, and orientation to schooling practice, from low through moderate to high. The combined rankings constitute a profile that may be further modified by quantifying the individual rankings, low, moderate, high (for example, 1, 3, 5, respectively) and then weighting each dimension with a multiplier according to the traditions and needs of the user's institution. For some situations, this quantification may be useful for quick decisions, although ambiguities and obscurities may result if it is pressed beyond its reasonable limits.

Courses will vary in each of these dimensions depending upon what place in the program they occupy. One might expect, for example, that durability is inversely related to topicality. Thus, topicality may be more tolerable late in the program than early on. Similarly, centrality should be more important in lower level courses. Consensus on content and method is clearly more crucial for core courses than for electives or for orientation to schooling practice. A low scoring course proposal might nonetheless warrant inclusion in a program depending upon to whom it was to be offered or because of considerations of, say, school tradition.

By way of example, we present in Table 17.2 a profiling chart of some current topics or issues that might be analyzed in a program of teacher preparation. We could use a scale of 1 (low) to 5 (high). You are invited to profile the topics in terms of your own perspectives. The very development of such a profile is an exercise in the practice of Foundational thinking.

Conclusion

This chapter illustrates the various ways Foundational Studies forms an essential part of the knowledge base *if* we are serious about the *professional* preparation of teachers. Foundations of Education is centrally important in understanding and combating the devaluation of teacher education by providing special dimensions for critical appraisal. It also helps prospective teachers make better sense of their practice as educational decision makers and promotes the development of expert-level procedural and normative judgments about educational aims and practices. Foundational Studies can also assist the education professoriate in refining and upgrading teacher preparation by providing metacognitive structures for organizing professional development. Foundations of Education thus has an essential role in the knowledge base for teacher education.

References

Baltzell, D. (1964). *The Protestant establishment.* New York: Random House.

Barr, R., and Dreeben, R. (1983). *How schools work.* Chicago: University of Chicago Press.

Baynes, K., Bohman, J., and McCarthy, T. (eds.) (1987). *After philosophy, end or transformation?* Cambridge, Mass.: MIT Press.

Bernstein, R. (1967). *John Dewey.* New York: Washington Square Press.

Beyer, L. E., Feinberg, W. F., Pagano, J. A., and Whitson, A. J. (1989). *Preparing teachers as professionals: The role of educational studies and other liberal disciplines.* New York: Teachers College Press.

Bransford, J. D., Stein, B. S., Arbitman-Smith, R., and Vye, N. J. (1985). "Improved thinking and learning skills: An analysis of three approaches." In J. W. Segal, S. F. Chipman, and R. Glazier (eds.), *Thinking and learning skills,* Vol. 1: *Relating instruction to research.* Hillsdale, N.J.: Erlbaum.

Broudy, H. S. (1985). "Variations in search of a theme." *Journal of Educational Thought, 19*(1), 37.

Brown, A. L., Bransford, J. D., Ferrara, R. A., and Campione, J. C. (1983). "Learning, remembering, and understanding." In P. H. Mussen (ed.), *Handbook of child psychology.* (3rd ed.). New York: Wiley.

Chubb, J., and Moe, T. (1990). *Politics, markets and American schools.* Washington, D.C.: Brookings Institution.

Clabaugh, G. K., and Feden, P. D. (1984). "Commentary: Chiefs can't cast the first stone at the teacher-training system." *Education Week,* Mar. 7, p. 20.

Clabaugh, G. K., and Rozycki, E. G. (1990a). *Instructor's manual for "Understanding schools."* New York: HarperCollins.

Clabaugh, G. K., and Rozycki, E. G. (1990b). *Understanding schools: The foundations of education.* New York: HarperCollins.

Coleman, J. S. (1966). *Equality of educational opportunity.* Washington, D.C.: U.S. Government Printing Office.

Collins, R. (1979). *The credential society.* San Diego, Calif.: Academic Press.

Council of Learned Societies in Education (1986). *Standards for academic and professional instruction in foundations of education, educational studies, and educational policy studies.* Ann Arbor, Mich.: Praken.

Finarelli, L. (1993). "Enfield Middle School faculty gets lesson in multiculturalism." *Springfield Sun,* May 20, p. 15.

Finkelstein, B. (1982). "Technician, mandarins, and witnesses: Searching for professional understanding." *Journal of Teacher Education, 33*(3), 25–27.

Gardner, H. (1991). *The unschooled mind.* New York: Basic Books.

Giarelli, J. M. (1991). "Philosophy, education, and the public practice." In D. P. Ericson (ed.), *Philosophy of education, 1990: Proceedings of the 46th annual meeting of the Philosophy of Education Society.* Normal, Ill.: Philosophy of Education Society.

Goodlad, J. I. (1984). *A place called school: Prospects for the future.* New York: McGraw-Hill.

Goodlad, J. I. (1991). *Teachers for our nation's schools.* San Francisco: Jossey-Bass.

Green, T. (1980). *Predicting the behavior of the educational system.* Syracuse, N.Y.: Syracuse University Press.

Hirsch, F. (1976). *Social limits to growth.* Cambridge, Mass.: Harvard University Press.

Hogan, D. (1992). "School organization and students' achievement: A review essay." *Educational Theory, 42*(1), 83–105.

Jencks, C. (1972). *A reassessment of the effect of family and schooling in America.* New York: HarperCollins.

Least Heat Moon, W. (1991). *Prairyerth.* Boston: Houghton Mifflin.

MacMurray, F. (1975). "Concepts of mind and intelligence in educational theory." *Educational Theory, 25(*3), 236.

Nash, R. J., and Agne, R. (1982). "Beyond marginality: A new role for foundations of education." *Journal of Teacher Education, 33*(3), 2–7.

National Commission on Excellence in Education (1983). *A nation at risk: The imperative for educational reform.* Washington, D.C.: U.S. Government Printing Office.

Passmore, J. (1967). "Philosophy." In P. Edwards (ed.), *The Encyclopedia of Philosophy,* Vol. 6 . New York: Macmillan.

Perkinson, H. J. (1990). *The imperfect panacea: American faith in education, 1865–1990.* (3rd ed.). New York: McGraw-Hill.

Pius XI (1981). "*Divini illius magistri* [Christian education of youth]." In *Papal encyclicals,* Vol. 3. Wilmington, N.C.: McGrath. (Originally published in 1929.)

Rozycki, E. G. (1982). "Review of 'Teaching with Charisma' by Lloyd Duck." *Educational Studies, 13*(1), 70–73.

Sarason, S. B. (1971). *The culture of the school and the problem of change.* Needham Heights, Mass.: Allyn & Bacon.

Scheffler, I. (1968). *The language of education.* Springfield, Ill.: Thomas.

Schneider, B. (1987). "Tracing the provenance of teacher education." In T. S. Popkewitz (ed.), *Critical studies in teacher education: Its folklore, theory and practice.* Washington, D.C.: Falmer Press.

Shea, C. M., Sola, P. A., and Jones, A. H. (1987). "Examining the crises in social foundations of education." *Educational Foundations, 1*(2), 47–57.

Tozer, S. (1993). "Toward a new consensus among social foundations educators: Draft position paper of the American Education Studies Committee on Academic Standards and Accreditation." *Educational Foundations, 7,* 5–22.

Tozer, S., Anderson, T., and Armbruster, B. (1990). "Psychological and social foundations in teacher education: A thematic introduction." *Teachers College Record, 91*(3), 293.

Tozer, S., and McAninch, S. A. (1986). "Social foundations of education in historical perspective." *Educational Foundations, 1,* 8–9.

Tozer, S., and McAninch, S. (1987). "Four texts in the social foundations of education in historical perspective." *Educational Studies, 18,* 13–33.

Webster's Encyclopedic Unabridged Dictionary of the English Language (1989). New York: Dilithium Press.

Webster's New World Dictionary of the American Language (1968). New York: World.

Annotated Bibliography

Beyer, L. E., Feinberg, W. F., Pagano, J. A., and Whitson, A. J. (1989). *Preparing teachers as professionals: The role of educational studies and other liberal disciplines.* New York: Teachers College Press.

Representing a strong liberal arts orientation within Foundations of Education, this book emphatically rejects the customary division between professional and general education. Arguing the need to emphasize wisdom in the determining of ends as well as the means to attain them, the authors examine the nature of educational studies as a liberal, rather than a technical enterprise. Placing the study of education within the broader context of social reproduction, the authors maintain that considerations of technical competence should not be the central element of professionalism.

Broudy, H. S. (1972). *The real world of the public schools.* Orlando, Fla.: Harcourt.

This is a classic of down-to-earth thinking about public education informed with the perspectives and skills of a well-known Foundations scholar. After twenty years, it remains a refreshing contrast to much ideological cant or wishful thinking about schooling.

Clabaugh, G. K., and Rozycki, E. G. (1990). *Understanding schools: The foundations of education.* New York: HarperCollins.

This comprehensive textbook in Foundations of Education is intended to reflect the nature of Foundations as a field and was guided in its writing by the standards of the Council of Learned Societies in Education. It provides numerous analytic techniques for appraising topics of contemporary interest; places education-related facts and events in the context of history, social processes, institutions, and ideas; furnishes competing explanations for school realities; incorporates unifying themes and imagistic analysis; and is accompanied by an instructor's manual that includes numerous learning activities.

Goodlad, J. I., Soder, R., and Sirotnik, K. A. (eds.) (1990). *The moral dimensions of teaching.* San Francisco: Jossey-Bass.

A cross-disciplinary collaboration on important topics, such as the moral responsibility of the public schools, the school as a moral learning community, accountability, teaching as an occupation, professional morals, and so forth, this volume demonstrates how critical focus on very general questions yields insight into the problems of practice.

Soltis, J. F. (ed.) (1985). *Teaching about education series.* New York: Teachers College Press.

This series includes the following texts:

Feinberg, W. F., and Soltis, J. F., *School and society.*
Fenstermacher, G. D., and Soltis, J. F., *Approaches to teaching.*
Phillips, D. C., and Soltis, J. F., *Perspectives on learning.*

Strike, K. A., and Soltis, J. F., *The ethics of teaching*.
Walker, D. C., and Soltis, J. F., *Curriculum and aims*.
This series of books, already well received in the field of Foundations of Education, has
    an added attraction in that its several short volumes may be well employed as supple-
    mental reading in a variety of courses normally found outside the field. Case studies,
    disputes, and dialogues are included to stimulate thinking about important practical
    issues.

CHAPTER EIGHTEEN

EDUCATIONAL PSYCHOLOGY AND THE TEACHER'S REASONING

FRANK B. MURRAY

More than a century ago, in 1892, William James gave a series of lectures to some teachers in Cambridge, Massachusetts, about the implications of his new psychology for teachers, thereby launching educational psychology as a field of study for teachers. His lectures, given thereafter to many audiences of teachers, were published in 1899 under the title *Talks to Teachers*. In the very first lecture, he made a point about what teachers can expect to gain from their study of psychology that still guides the field a hundred years later:

> You make a great, a very great mistake, if you think that psychology, being the science of the mind's laws, is something from which you can deduce definite programmes and schemes and methods of instruction for immediate school-room use. Psychology is a science, and teaching is an art; and sciences never generate arts directly out of themselves. An intermediary inventive mind must make the application, by using its originality.

> A science only lays down the lines within which the rules of the art must fall, laws which the follower of the art must not transgress; but what particular thing he shall positively do within those lines is left exclusively to his own genius [James, 1958, pp. 23–24].

This chapter draws on arguments advanced in other writings by the author (Murray, 1989, 1991, 1992).

The use of psychology in the schools, in James's view, was primarily to sharpen the teacher's thinking and insight about schooling. Its use was actually more proscriptive than prescriptive, a somewhat negative approach because psychology's rules were clearer about what should *not* be done pedagogically than they were about what should be done. While the research literature, on learning, memory, and forgetting, for example, might lead the teacher to avoid requiring the pupil to memorize by rote extensive lists of discrete items, and while it would suggest that learning would be eased if the items were organized into some pattern or structure, it is decidedly less clear from psychology exactly what that structure or pattern should be or how the teacher should create one in the case where such mastery is required. Psychology might tell us, for example, that the beginning and ending items of an unstructured list are remembered better than the middle items (the *serial position effect*), but it would not tell the teacher how that fact could be used to the teacher's advantage in the lesson.[1]

General pedagogical maxims that conform to psychological theory and findings are, even as James acknowledged in 1892, readily available. A teacher might have them uppermost in mind in all teaching situations, but the maxims and principles, no matter how uncontested in psychology, prove themselves of limited value to the teacher on several grounds. First, they tend to be too imprecise to provide the teacher with much functional guidance. A sound rule for all teaching, for example, fully supported in contemporary psychology, is, make the object of instruction the solution to a genuine problem that the student has; thus, pupils will learn and not forget what they are taught. This rule's value is severely limited, however, without some further guidance about how to discover the pupil's genuine problem and how to create the opportunity for the pupil to invent or discover a solution to his or her problem that also meets the standard of the teacher's objectives for the lesson.

In addition to the problem of the functional vagueness in psychological maxims, there are logical difficulties in deriving sound practices from psychological theories because both sound and unsound practices can be derived validly from false theoretical propositions. The truth of theoretical propositions, on the other hand, is always in doubt because it is possible to derive sound practices from both true and false theoretical propositions (Murray, 1989). Thus, we cannot establish the truth of a theoretical proposition by demonstrating that an educational practice works even when the practice can be derived unambiguously from a proposition in the theory. Of course, a theoretical proposition can be disproved, or found to be false, when a properly deduced practice proves to be unsound and that constitutes, incidentally, the principal means by which the discipline of educational psychology advances.

Many sound educational practices, like discovery learning, can be derived validly from propositions in Piagetian theory, for example, and from propositions in other theories, such as Skinner's or Vygotsky's, which, in other respects, are clearly incompatible with certain Genevan propositions about the development of intelligence (Forman and Cazden, 1985; Ginsburg, 1981). Montessori school practices are, to take another example, compatible with Piaget's theory (Elkind, 1976; Gardner, 1966) even though the theories of Montessori and of Piaget are quite different; progressive education made as much sense as an outgrowth of Dewey's account of thinking as it did as an implication of Piaget's view of intelligence (Cremin, 1961; Seltzer, 1977). As James (1958) noted, "And so everywhere teaching must agree with the psychology, but need not necessarily be the only kind of teaching that would so agree; for many diverse methods of teaching may equally well agree with psychological laws" (p. 24).

Educational Practices

Owing to the vagueness in the propositions of many psychological theories, we can expect that different, sometimes contradictory, educational practices can claim to have been derived from the same theoretical principles. J. McVicker Hunt (1961) argued, in this connection, that Piaget's theory implied that a match between the pupil's stage of cognitive development and the demands of the curriculum was needed for proper schooling. Hans Alebi (cited in Flavell, 1963), on the other hand, took Piaget's theory to mean that the pupil, regardless of grade level, needs to have curriculum material presented in a way that recapitulates the entire set of prior stages (see also Granott, 1991, for a discussion of the relationship between micro and macro development). For Hunt, the teacher of adolescents can presume that the student's formal operational competence can be addressed directly in the lesson. For Alebi, the teacher of adolescents needs to begin the lesson with some sensorimotor representation, followed by a figural representation of the lesson's content, and so forth until the lesson can be approached in the way that the teacher who accepts Hunt's perspective had already assumed in the first place.

Over and above these problems of vagueness and logical difficulty in deriving educational practices from psychological theories, there are recently discovered problems with the generality of psychological findings and the laws and principles supported by them. Behavioral scientists typically find more evidence to support the claim that school achievement and performance are dependent upon particular features of contexts and situations in which they occur than to support the claim that performance is dependent upon factors that transcend the context in which the performance occurs. The evidence for the domain specificity, and cohort specificity, of human performance is more convincing than any evidence we have for generalized ability, apart from that captured in a few of the long-standing psychometric measures of ability and personality.

Of course, the problem of the utility of psychological maxims for teaching can be approached from another direction, other than "psychology's talks *to* teachers": it can be approached the other way around, so to speak, as "teachers' talks to, or with, psychology." It can be taken, and often is taken, as the psychological knowledge or maxims teachers implicitly use, might have used, or could have used, to guide their teaching. This line of thinking requires that the competence-performance distinction be respected. What teachers are able to do and what they actually do are often quite different; moreover, even if they have a competence that would be sufficient to accomplish a task, they may accomplish the task in a way that bypasses the competence altogether by drawing upon other abilities and talents.

For example, virtually all adults, and most preschoolers, can give the plural of the following nonsense nouns: *wug, wot,* and *gutch;* in fact, they could give the past tense if these same words were presented as verbs (as in "Today A is wugging B, but yesterday B wugged A," and so on.) Although almost no one knows the linguistic rule for the assignment of the plural (/s/, /z/, /ez/) or past tense (/t/, /d/, /ed/) allomorphs, everyone acts as if they knew the rule for the differential assignment of the allomorphs even though it is obvious that they do not. They have to be basing their flawless plural and past tense performance on some factors of language competence other than their formal knowledge of linguistics even though their formal knowledge of linguistics would be sufficient for them to pluralize nouns and form the past tense of verbs.

Thus, to establish that teachers could have, might have, or even should have, based their teaching performance on some knowledge of educational psychology, or some body of research literature, is no evidence that they in fact did or would. Consequently, any effort to enhance the teacher's knowledge of the educational psychology, or the research literature on effective teaching practices, could prove to be irrelevant; expert teachers, like fluent speakers, can very well base their performance on some area of competence other than the knowledge of the academic discipline that might have, or could have, supported their expert performance (Peterson, 1946). It is essential, particularly in view of the limited time available in the teacher education curriculum, that teacher educators seek to base the instruction in educational psychology upon the psychological knowledge teachers could actually use in their teaching.

Teachers' Reasoning

Unfortunately, very little is known about how teachers actually think about their teaching, other than that teachers employ a kind of naïve psychology in their explanations (Kuhn, 1991). Teachers' reasoning about their pupils' behavior, in fact, proves to be surprisingly indistinguishable from the layperson's explanations. Kuhn (1991) found, for example, when she asked teachers, "What causes children to fail in school?" that teachers' reasoning "shows no superiority over reasoning regarding the other topics . . . performance for the school topic is in fact somewhat inferior to their performance for the other topics" (p. 249). Their reasoning, like about half the subjects in the study, tends to be absolutist—that is, they believe it is possible with sufficient study to know with certainty the causes of a phenomenon, often through a personal commitment to a theory or assertion.

We would expect to find, were teachers asked their reasons for doing what they do, that some scale of sophistication in their reasoning and justification would be found as it has been found in their reasoning about moral dilemmas. It is at least plausible that experts would have better reasons and explanations for what they and pupils do than novices have.

Of course, it would be easy enough to ask teachers to give their reasons and explanations for how and why things happen as they do in the classroom and school. There is hardly any point to it, however, unless there is a way to determine what would constitute a correct, sophisticated, professional, or good reason and explanation. The Kohlberg-Gilligan scales of moral development, despite their widely documented limitations, provide an instructive and prototypical case for the enhancement of professional knowledge about teaching insofar as there are no a priori correct answers to, or conclusions about, any of the moral dilemma problems posed in the assessment (for example, there is no definitive way to conclude that Heinz should steal the otherwise unavailable drug that would save his wife's life or that he should not steal it). There is a way, however, to determine that some responses are more sophisticated or mature than others. The scale is scored solely in terms of the developmental order of the supporting reasons for the decision to steal or not to steal, for example (Harding, 1985).

Unfortunately, there is no equivalent scale of pedagogical development, although the ingredients for one are potentially available. Ammon and Hutcheson (1989) and Black (1989) have speculated about a five-level sequence of teacher conceptions about behavior, development, learning, and teaching, and Kuhn (1991) has proposed an empirically derived scale for skills of teacher's argument and reasoning about evidence. Any number of generic teaching dilemmas or cases could be posed in a way that would reveal the structure of the teacher's reasoning about teaching and schooling. It is the structure that matters—not the specific content or information but rather its form and adequacy.

Education Terms: Assumptions and Problems

While the core of this *new* educational psychology awaits the discovery of the developing amalgam of knowledge, disposition, and skill that professional teachers actually possess, teacher education, in the meantime, could focus on the jargon that permeates the field and masquerades as an explanation for events in the classroom. Educational scholarship, on the whole, operates with a very large number of psychological and other terms that have very low levels of explanatory power—in fact, most constructs are tautologous with the phenomenon they are set up to explain. Nevertheless, genuine distinctions in levels of power and meaning in the educational jargon can be found. These distinctions also provide a potential means for evaluating and scaling the sophistication of the teacher's knowledge.

At the outset, consider these examples of common professional words and expressions we have to describe the psychological differences among pupils in the classroom: *achievers, conservers, field-independent, impulsive, learning deficient, gifted, levelers, analytic, extroverted, ready, subitizers, postconventional reasoners, illiterate, decoders, divergent thinkers, egocentric, anal retentive, at grade level, right-brained, dyslexic, conservative focusers, at risk,* and so on. How can any of these descriptions or labels be of any real use as teachers attempt to understand their pupils and explain what happens in various instructional episodes? Moreover, how can the teacher tell which of these words, and any of the other hundreds of terms encountered in the literature, are useful, and which give nothing more than a label and the illusion that something is understood when it is only named? By what criteria could the teacher tell which of these terms for describing a pupil is worth knowing and which should be discarded? These criteria are critical, of course, but as professional knowledge evolves, a provision for other neologisms must be made. This is especially true for terms invented by teachers if teacher education is to get at the heart of the knowledge teachers actually use to guide their interactions with their clients and colleagues. The criteria must be driven by the uses to which the teacher puts the jargon or neologism and not whether the terms have a privileged place in an academic discipline.

Quite apart from the terms that allegedly capture the psychological differences among children are the terms that describe and differentiate the various kinds of mental activities that are implicated in the children's attempts to master the school curriculum. Consider just one aspect of the mind that is claimed to be at work in the schools: the various kinds of learning. Gagné (1970), for example, argues for the existence of eight types of learning that governed the order in which items in the curriculum should be attempted by the pupil. Claims are made for other distinct kinds of learning as well: incidental, cooperative, perceptual, mastery, verbal and nonverbal, conceptual change, discrimination, motor, discovery, rote, social; signal, active versus passive, place, mathemagenic, structural, trial and error; learning sets, overlearning, learning to learn, oddity learning, and so on. Similar distinctions are claimed for various kinds of teaching: for example, team, reciprocal, Lancastrian, adaptive, maieutic; also direct instruction, tutoring, and subject-matter specific techniques like whole word, phonics, language experience, schema training, metacomprehension training, mapping, SQ3R, QAR training, or ETR method in reading instruction.

At the very least, the teacher education curriculum should make the meaning of these terms clear at the operational level by clarifying the means the teacher would use to produce or measure the phenomenon for which the term is a label. Discovery learning, for example, is what we find when a certain teaching procedure is followed or when the pupil responds in a specified way to certain questions and instructions. Of course, the operations used to measure or produce the concept being defined do not constitute the entire meaning of the concept. The point is that all technical terms should be defined—minimally—by the operations or methods used to measure or produce the concept in question before the terms are accepted as legitimate in teacher's professional knowledge of school events. Thus, it should be perfectly clear, at this primitive stage of professional knowledge, what the teacher means by such terms as *mathematical aptitude, creativity, reciprocal teaching, gifted,* and so on, because the teacher would know how to measure or produce gift-edness, reciprocal teaching, creativity, or mathematical aptitude to explain some aspect of a pupil's performance.

Additional levels of sophistication might be added to the operational definitions of these scholarly terms, as illustrated in the following two examples. In the first, the teacher might explain what could be done to prevent or eliminate a pupil's error or some other inappropriate activity. In the second example, the teacher could explain how much time a pupil might need to learn an element in the curriculum. In the first example, the teacher might draw upon the notion of extinction and in the second example, the teacher might appeal to the pupil's cognitive level and introduce the notion of conservation (in the Piagetian sense) for this purpose. With respect to these two terms, *extinction* and *conservation,* teacher education could seek the following levels of sophistication and distinctions:

Level 1: Definitions state only what the teacher does. Words at this level represent only the procedure the teacher follows in the context that is named by the word. For example, the term *extinction* means only "the teacher's withholding of reward or reinforcement from the pupil." The term *conservation* at the first level refers only to a diagnostic task in which one of two identical objects is transformed by the teacher in some way, and the pupil is asked if the objects have changed in some other way. After one of two clay balls is flattened, for example, a pupil is asked by the teacher whether the flattened ball and the round ball weigh the same.

Level 2: Definitions state only what a pupil does in response to what the teacher did in Level 1. Level 2 definitions are essentially a label for a phenomenon. They also constitute an operational definition. *Extinction* at Level 2 refers to "the decrease in performance when reward is withdrawn," and *conservation* now refers to the fact that children above the age of seven or so will say the transformed object has not changed in weight. Younger children will maintain that the two objects are not equal in weight, or whatever attribute is being assessed *(nonconservation).*

Level 3: The definition states that the phenomenon labeled at Level 2 is caused without stating what the case is. The shift from Level 2 to Level 3 is subtle but significant, because at this point extra meaning is added to the meaning of the term, even though such meaning may be only an affirmation of the assumption that there are no uncaused events in the universe.

Extinction now refers to something that causes school performance to decrease when reward is eliminated; extinction, rather than being merely the label for an event, is now thought of as a process, mechanism, or entity that causes the event. Similarly, *conservation* now refers to the pupil's ability or competence rather than to the task and the pupil's response to it. Thus, we see teachers speaking of conservation ability, or of the pupil who has conservation, or who is a conserver.

Level 3 meaning is speculative and seductive because it gives the unsuspecting teacher the idea that more is known than really is. For example, we may say the reason pupils do poorly in school is because they are educationally handicapped or learning disabled. The evidence for such a handicap or disability, however, may be merely our observation that pupils do poorly in school, in which case we have only learned that pupils do poorly in school because we see them do poorly in school. In other words, we have learned nothing and have not advanced our understanding at all by inventing the terms *educational handicap* or *learning disability*. Regrettably, many terms in educational theories are, as in this case, entirely unsatisfactory because they are tautological and synonymous with the event they purport to explain.

Level 4: The teacher attempts to specify the kind of cause that was assumed at Level 3. Level 4 concepts and terms refer to a proposed mechanism or structure or entity. It is essential that whatever is postulated at this level be adequate to be the cause of more than one lower-level concept or event; otherwise, we are left with the kind of nonsensical and tautological hypothetical constructs encountered in the handicap example. The more phenomena claimed to be caused by the Level 4 concept and the more unrelated they appear to each other, the better the Level 4 concept is likely to be in advancing our understanding.

Neither extinction nor conservation makes it to the fourth level of meaning. Rather, each is hypothesized by theorists to be caused by another term that has sufficient surplus meaning to carry it to this level. Conservation is hypothesized by Jean Piaget to be caused by a Level 4 concept, "concrete operations," which are also alleged to cause and to explain several seemingly unrelated phenomena described by other lower-level concepts such as seriation, transitivity, class inclusion, egocentrism, centration, and horizontality.

Level 5: Few concepts in psychology or education exist at this level, and when they exist, they are used to integrate and summarize sets of Level 4 concepts. In a mathematical sense, a concept at Level 5 is the sum of a term's conceptual meanings at the other levels. Consider the term *reaction potential* (sEr) from Hull's theory of learning. This Level 5 concept describes what the pupil will do (or what his or her potential for reaction is) as a complex mathematical function of a number of lower-level concepts like learning, motivation, fatigue, incentive, and laziness (or a learned tendency not to respond). A Level 5 concept exists for conservation and concrete operations, but it has the form of an entire logical model and structure—the lattice and the Klein four group.

The teacher, in response to the problem of explaining how much time a pupil might need to learn a concept in the curriculum, could go in very different directions by way of accounting for how much time a pupil might need. The problem could be approached through a different analysis and a similar series of levels that lead to a different Level 5 construct, mastery learning, as it is described in Carroll's model of school learning (1989).

Mastery learning (ML), or the degree of pupil learning, is defined by the equation $ML = f(T_s / T_n)$, the components of which can be specified at one of the lower levels of meaning. Time needed for learning (T_n), for example, is a function of pupil ability plus (or minus) the teacher's effectiveness. Time spent on learning (T_s) is seen as a function of either the pupil's perseverance or the time allocated by the teacher for learning the lesson, whichever is less.

Pupil ability, in turn, is taken solely as the personal time the pupil needs to learn something. Teacher effectiveness is taken as the time the pupil saves (or loses, in some unfortunate cases) in learning the task because of the teacher's efforts. Pupil perseverance is simply the time the pupil actually works on the task, and allocated time is nothing more than the time the teacher allocates for the pupil's learning. Each term has a common metric with others, time, so that an unknown or an unspecified term can be found algebraically if the times of the others are determined.

To be sure, many teachers would not think of their work as represented well by the integrated terms of the Carroll model, but nevertheless this representation of the school learning describes a fairly sophisticated and rich possibility for the teacher's thinking because it suggests other factors, besides allocated time, that the teacher could alter.

As a general rule, most concepts in education make sense only at the first two levels of meaning. The few concepts whose meaning carries them to the higher levels have roles in the well-established theories that would assist teachers in the formation of explanations of classroom events.

Educational Explanations

The complete account of an educational phenomenon entails much more, of course. We could expect the teacher to search for answers to a number of additional questions about a phenomenon: what kind of phenomenon is it, how did it get that way, how does it work, how can it work better, and what is the point of it? Educational psychology centers on the question, How does it work? In other words, what mechanisms make schooling work? However, at least three other aspects of any educational event—whether at the pupil or school system level—need to be specified before it can be said that the event is completely intelligible, understood, or explained. The complete account treats the following:

1. The *substance* out of which the event is made: the stuff of behavior in the case of the pupil, that is, which areas of the brain, which muscles, glands, and so

on, are implicated in the event. In the case of a classroom, school, or system, the various tangible components need to be specified.

2.   The *antecedent conditions* that are necessary and sufficient for the event: those that elicit, trigger, and maintain the event. These are the causes of the event, in the usual sense of the term *cause*. In the case of pupil's understanding, it is often thought to be something a teacher does, but other factors are also implicated in this case.

3.   The *form* or *structure* of the event or that which makes the event an instance of one phenomenon rather than another. If a child finally comes to say, "2 + 2 always equals 4 and never any other number," is this a change in language, logic, learning, teaching effectiveness, personality, memory, some combination of these, or what? What is the change a change *of*, and how do we know? If a school begins to group pupils according to their standardized test scores, what kind of change has occurred in the school? In other words, the issue is, what kind of phenomenon are we talking about?

4.   The *purpose* or point of the event, what it leads to, how it fits in with everything else, and how other events in the pupil's life make the event intelligible and vice versa. Does the event mean anything? What is the point, significance, or meaning of the event?

Thus, in the better or fuller explanation of some aspect of the pupil's academic growth, the teacher would be sensitive to the issues of what the behavior is made of, what caused it, what its structure or form is, and what it means (in other words, what is its function and role in the final scheme of things?). Of course, many issues in education are really debates about whether the explanation for a phenomenon (like gender differences in mathematics achievement) is to be found solely in the antecedent conditions for it or in the form or structure of it as well. The debate is not about a research outcome but about what the outcome means. For example, in one view the pupil who argues that Churchill was right to firebomb Dresden gives exactly the opposite answer from the pupil who argues Churchill's act was wrong. Yet in the other view, the two arguments, while contradictory on the surface, may be structurally identical and signify that the two pupils have achieved precisely the same level of moral and logical development. On a larger scale, some see the function of the schools as the liberating transmission of the culture from one generation to the next, while others see the very same events as the imposition of a class structure that represses individual freedom and reduces opportunities.

The attempt to explain educational change totally in terms of antecedent events, the necessary and sufficient conditions, carries with it a determinism that many think precludes the possibility of spontaneous events, of emergent events, of discontinuities, of new stages in the pupil's grasp of a subject matter. After all, spontaneity can exist only when events cannot be reduced to, or linked strictly and solely to, those events that come before them. Thus, it could be said that theories that allow for educational changes that are inherently unpredictable from their antecedents introduce a more sophisticated or advanced view.

If all there is to know about an earlier educational period is known, it still may not allow the teacher to predict the nature of the pupil's subsequent educational accomplishments. The point here is that so much depends upon the teacher's own view of the issue and the way in which he or she thinks about whether the pupil's behavior is determined or open-ended and whether the object of instruction is the pupil's recitation of the correct response or whether the object is the underlying structure of the pupil's correct response, and so forth.

It is best not to have the teacher make too much of the technical aspects of these differences, but it must be borne in mind that every teacher's choice of topic to teach, of behavior to be measured and tested, of kinds of evaluation to use, of instructional groups, of curricular sequences, and so on is critically shaped by some belief in one or another theoretical view of educational development. Basically, teachers attempt only what they believe is possible. The judgment that an aspect of education is impossible, or impossibly difficult, flows from a structure of teacher reasoning that is at the core of professional knowledge and cannot be avoided in the teacher education curriculum and thinking of teacher educators.

Were teacher education ever successful in banishing all jargon that had no explanatory value, teachers, of course, would still construct explanations of their pupils' behavior and accomplishments. Often, as Kuhn (1991) demonstrated, these amateur theories or explanations are unduly restrictive and lead to inappropriate educational decisions, especially regarding unwarranted limitations about what the pupil might attempt and accomplish. Consequently, because teachers, like all reflective people, will invent theories and explanations, teacher educators need some criteria for evaluating the available theories of educational development and learning that will be included in the teacher education curriculum. There simply are differences in the power and adequacy of various educational and psychological theories that must be acknowledged and respected.

Criteria for a Good Theory

What must we have from a good theory? What questions must it answer about the phenomena it attempts to explain? What problems must it resolve or eliminate? All educational phenomena have more or less the same basic form: there is some change, or difference, in student or teacher behavior that is found over a relatively long period of time (weeks, months, years) in the case of development, or in a relatively short time (seconds, minutes, hours, and days) in the case of learning. What must a good psychological theory tell us about these changes and differences?

Contemporary scholarship points to ten categories of information that a good theory must address:

1.   *The form or pattern.* We need to have a way to identify, name, or define the phenomenon, a way to distinguish it from other phenomena. This inevitably means that we must have a way to measure it and perhaps produce it. The act of naming or defining carries the risk that more may be thought to be known and understood than really is, but it is an essential part of any theory, particularly at the beginning, to delineate and name the phenomenon in this way. Thus, to repeat an earlier example, we call the child's response to the changing shape of the clay ball "conservation" and thereby mark it off from other phenomena and begin the act of knowing and making sense of it.

More than the name of the phenomenon, we ask the good theory to tell us the underlying structure, pattern, and organization of the stimuli and responses that make up the phenomenon. What criteria must be met before a pattern of behavior can legitimately claim the label "conservation"?

The bedrock objective facts of psychology, the scientific building blocks of stimulus and response, for example, can only be determined in reference to some other set of propositions that tell us such basic things as how many stimuli and responses there are in a situation.

In the case of Piagetian conservation, after an experimenter spreads five marbles over a wider area, the child observes and asserts, "There as many marbles as before." Is the child's response one response, two responses (one for the subject and one for the predicate of the statement), six responses (one for each word), five responses (one for each marble), or some other number? Apart from the number of responses, what kind of response is it? Is it primarily a perceptual response, a linguistic response, a logical response, a cognitive developmental response, a learned response, an imitative response, and so forth? Similarly, how would we know how many stimuli were responded to by the child in this instance without recourse to some larger view of what the child was thinking about when confronted with this problem?

2.   *Efficient cause.* We ask the good theory to tell us the causes of the phenomenon, the necessary and sufficient conditions for it—the eliciting conditions. This is not to say that the specifications of the necessary and sufficient conditions constitute the whole account or explanation, but only that they are a part of the story, so to speak, and without their specification, a theory would not be satisfying. Thus, we want to know under what conditions the child will assert that there are as many marbles as there were before, and under what conditions the child will claim there are more or fewer marbles as a result of the teacher's actions.

3.   *Mechanisms.* The good theory will tell us what mental mechanisms produce the phenomenon. How do these mechanisms function and how, over the time span during which the change takes place, do they actually produce the change? In the conservation of number example, what role do the mechanisms of learning, social interaction, imitation, cognitive dissonance, mediation, maturation, perception, and so forth play in the child's exhibition of the phenome-

non of conservation? How do they lead the nonconserving child to give conservation responses?

Are there new mechanisms that simply must be invented (or discovered) to account for the phenomenon, or will more parsimonious mechanisms, mechanisms that are merely conditioned links between stimuli and responses, suffice to account for the events researchers document?

4.   *The educational end point.* We assume, for example, that the changes we label as educational are unidirectional, that they lead to a final stage, that there is an educational goal, and we ask that the good theory have a way to specify what the end state is. The earlier steps or stages in a sequence of behaviors, in a curricular progression, are made more intelligible by our knowledge of the end point toward which they are progressing. This is true even though the later periods cannot in any way be the efficient cause of the earlier events because of the unidirectional character of time. Later events cannot cause earlier events, but they can help us make sense of the earlier events by showing what the earlier events lead to. The child's error in the nonconservation response, for example, that the number of marbles changed as they were spread out, would make more sense if we had a way to see what role these "errors," which are primitively consistent with each other, played in the child's subsequent error-free and mature evaluation of the same problem. The very placing of a phenomenon in a developmental or educational sequence and process confers a high degree of intelligibility on it by virtue of securing a place for it in a high-level pattern. Conservation, for example, makes more sense when we can see it as an instance of the child's newly acquired notion of logical necessity and not merely as an episodic peculiarity of the young child's thought (Murray, 1990).

The illumination of the end point of the educational or developmental chain often demonstrates the inadequacy of the nondevelopmental mechanisms to account fully for the phenomenon because usually none has a way to capture the direction of the changes. While the mechanisms mentioned above are adequate in most instances to account for the nonconserving child's eventual acquisition of conservation, they are in a sense too primitive and powerful because they also require that, often as not, the conserving child acquire nonconservation. They account for all changes symmetrically, without regard to a particular direction. Despite the fact that Brownian motion would permit it, the dispersal of dye in water, owing to the higher-order principle of increased entropy, never reconfigures itself into a concentrated drop of dye. Similarly, the conserving child simply does not become a nonconserving one even though the conserver's acquisition of nonconservation is permitted by all the known nondevelopmental mechanisms. Thus, some higher-order mechanism or principle must account for the large-scale movement of cognitive structure in a single direction—preoperativity to operativity in the case of Piagetian theory, for example. We expect a good theory to illuminate the nature of this higher-order guiding mechanism. In fact, the good theory is largely about this higher-order principle because it makes sense of the directional movement in the student's thought. The nature of this principle, or higher-order mechanism, is an area of research and theorizing that continues to remain stubbornly in doubt and contested in contemporary work in psychology.

It must be conceded that the specification of the educational end point of an open-ended system, like education, is nonbinding with respect to any particular outcome. In the same way, the principles of biological evolution are adequate to account for a chain of species development, but they are not of sufficient power to predict the final outcome of species development. Similarly, we would not expect the good theory of educational development, for example, to specify the content of thought but only its general form and power.

The specification of the end point entails, by implication, the specification of the other end of the scale, namely the point of departure. It is helpful to know why the earlier periods fail to hold the developing mind at some point or stage for a longer time even without knowing the character of the next stage or period. Because of the open-ended character of education and the potential for inherently unpredictable outcomes of mental functioning and accomplishment, it may be inevitable that theorists will always understand more of where the mind has been, so to speak, than where it is going.

Moreover, the good theory may provide a way to think about better educational outcomes. Given that many educational outcomes are possible, and that just as many evolutionary solutions are possible for species development, the good theory could be asked to account for, identify, explain, and clarify the better of the available outcomes, outcomes that maximize what it means to be human. We ask that the good theory critically examine the educational outcomes that appear to be necessary and unalterable to determine whether they are really just one of a range of possible educational outcomes.

5. *The meaning of the phenomenon.* Unlike other natural phenomena, behavioral phenomena have the attribute of intentionality insofar as it makes sense to raise the question of what the child, for example, meant or intended by an action. We expect the good theory to address the questions of what the actor intended or meant and what the behavioral phenomenon signifies or means because its identity as a phenomenon resides in its meaning.

Apart from what the child may have meant or intended in her claim that the number of marbles was the same, the question of the meaning or significance of the phenomenon is a micro version of the question of the end point of education. It is an inquiry into the purpose and significance of some aspect of mental life. In this sense, the meaning of the behavioral change may be quite different from what the child meant by what she said or what she intended just as the meaning of a work of art may be, in the end, quite different from what the artist intended.

Just as there is no single interpretation of a text, apart from a framework of interpretation, one would not expect that there could be a single meaning of a behavioral phenomenon that is unrelated to a theory or an interpretative framework that could give meaning to the event. While many different theories, interpretations, translations, and so forth may be compatible with the same facts or texts, progress is made in educational psychology because it can be shown that some theories and interpretations are incompatible with the texts and must be discarded because they simply will not work as interpretations and translations. They lead to inconsistencies and incoherence in the relationships between the facts or text and the interpretation and also among the components of the interpretation itself.

6. *Reductionist mechanisms.* Owing only to the universal commitment to the principle of the unity of science, we would expect that the mental mechanisms that heretofore had a place within the good theory would become tied to physical events and processes within the body. In a similar way, the constructs, gene and vitamin, initially proposed as unseen and wholly hypothetical constructs, eventually came to be seen as physical entities.

This is not to say that the truth of a good psychology theory lies in its physical verification, because the findings of psychological research are true on their own terms. They simply happen that way. The point here is only that the good theory must have the potential for coherence with the other sciences, particularly the biological sciences.

The link between the onset of conservation, for example, and a marked increase in brain lateralization, brain surface, the completion of myelination, increases in EEG alpha activity, and increases in working memory, is undoubtedly part of the complete scientific account of the conservation phenomenon.

7. *Deductive formalism.* Virtually every scientific researcher knows that the way the science is actually conducted is not adequately captured by school accounts of the scientific method. While the logic of discovery and the logic of justification are different, we do expect that the good theory will at some point have a form such that items to be explained are explained by virtue of their being implications of general principles of a theory. The fact that the Pythagorean relation was known by ancient land surveyors and was established independently of the formal system in which it finally came to have a place as a theorem does not take away from the point that a greater degree of understanding is conferred by virtue of the fact that it can be deduced from forty-seven prior propositions in Euclid's system.

The appeal for a deductive formalism in the good theory does not mean that theory building needs to proceed by that route but only that there be a version of the theory that can be expressed in the fashion of the hypothetical-deductive sciences—again in conformity with the unity of science principle.

8. *Cohort specification.* The life span research community has documented that generational effects compromise the generality of many findings, like the shape of the growth of intelligence function, for example (Baltes, Reese, and Nesselroade, 1977). Thus, the good theory would not consider cohort membership to be merely a noisy source of experimental error to be methodologically corrected but rather it would be seen as an integral part of the phenomenon under consideration. Of

course, one would expect that cohort, or time of the subject's birth, is merely a proxy variable for some yet to be discovered factors that operated during a particular historical period, and that these factors would alter significantly the scientific findings that are reported in research paradigms that were not sensitive to generational factors. The good theory would have addressed these. For example, to continue with the nonconservation/conservation literature, it remains to be explained why the very same experimental procedures that failed to train nonconservers to conserve in the 1960s succeeded to a much greater degree in the 1970s (Beilin, 1971, 1977; Murray, 1978, 1982; Strauss, 1972).

9. *Cultural and social determinants.* The identification of factors and mechanisms that operate uniquely in particular historical periods, and not in other periods, has led researchers to consider a much wider range of contextual and interactive factors. Such factors, in earlier research paradigms, would have simply been controlled experimentally or statistically because they were viewed either as uninteresting noise, however potent, or as factors whose investigation had to be postponed until more powerful research techniques became available. The pervasive character of these context-specific factors, however, demonstrated in virtually every area of developmental psychology, has meant that they can no longer be postponed or ignored (Rogoff and Lave, 1984).

At the moment, we are hard pressed to understand why the conservation problems, for example, are more difficult when they are about length rather than number, continuous rather than discontinuous materials, or why the weight of a clay ball would be seen by the young child to change in different amounts when the ball was made colder rather than warmer, rougher rather than smoother, longer rather than wider, in familiar rather than unfamiliar shapes, and so on (Murray and Johnson, 1970, 1975; Murray and Markessini, 1982). We are equally hard pressed to see how and why some groups of children, for example, Native Americans in the Southwest, are not "fooled" as much by these problems about the clay ball's weight as other children appear to be, or why Bedouin children are not "fooled" as much as others about conservation of liquid amount (see Murray, 1981). In virtually every domain of psychology, substantial effects can be attributed to factors that appear to be features of a particular context, social or cultural group, geographic location, historical time period, and so forth. Obviously, the successful theory will find a way to make sense of this—at the moment—bewildering array of context-specific influential factors.

10. *The theorist.* The interdependence of fact and theory or text and interpretation leads to an examination of the theorist as a person and thinker. The interpretive framework that allows events to be "facts" in a science is shaped presumably by personal features of the theorist that heretofore were considered irrelevant when science was viewed exclusively as objective and self-correcting. At the moment, we can only speculate how Piaget's account of moral development would differ had it been formulated outside Protestant Geneva, or how Skin-

ner's account of learning would differ had it not been formulated by an American, and so forth. However, as theories are invariably written and otherwise promulgated, their meaning is also subject to all the hermeneutic issues implicated in the attempt to specify the meaning and significance of an educational change in mental functioning in the first place.

Conclusion

In summary, a good theory of human learning and development in schools is a complete theory, a theory that addresses the ten points cited above and attends to the levels of meaning of the hypothetical terms it introduces.

Teacher educators today would do well to remember the fact found by James (1958) during his years of lecturing to teachers and confirmed repeatedly by generations of educational psychologists since that time, "that what my hearers seem least to relish is analytical technicality, and what they most care for is concrete practical application. So I have gradually weeded out the former, and left the latter unreduced; and now that I have written out the lectures, they contain a minimum of what is deemed 'scientific' in psychology, and are practical and popular in the extreme" (p. 18).

Yet it was equally clear to James in 1899 that teacher educators had to realize that "such a complete knowledge of the pupil, at once intuitive and analytic, is surely the knowledge at which every teacher ought to aim" (p. 26). His objective, when all was said and done, was to go to the heart of the teacher's thinking and have teachers "conceive, and, if possible, reproduce sympathetically in their imagination, the mental life of their pupil as the sort of active unity which he himself feels it to be" (p. 18). And if this sympathetic recreation can be bolstered with a personal theory, which is unencumbered by unproductive jargon, and which falls within the lines of theories that meet the criteria set out above, so much the better for teachers and their pupils.

Note

1. The teacher, for example, might use the serial position effect to uncover whether the pupil were learning spelling words or anything by rote, where the errors would pile up in the middle of the words or text, or whether the pupil had a more structured approach to spelling and learning text.

References

Ammon, P., and Hutcheson, B. P. (1989). "Promoting the development of teachers' pedagogical conceptions." *Genetic Epistemologist, 17*(4), 23–29.

Baltes, P., Reese, H., and Nesselroade, J. (1977). *Life-span developmental psychology: Introduction to research methods.* Pacific Grove, Calif.: Brooks/Cole.

Beilin, H. (1971). "The training and acquisition of logical operations." In M. F. Rosskopf, L. P. Steffe, and S. Taback (eds.), *Piagetian cognitive-development research and mathematical education.* Washington, D.C.: National Council of Teachers of Mathematics.

Beilin, H. (1977). "Inducing conservation through training." In G. Steiner (ed.), *Psychology of the 20th century,* Vol. 7: *Piaget and beyond.* Bern, Switzerland: Kinder.

Black, A. (1989). Developmental teacher education. *Genetic Epistemologist, 17*(4), 5–14.

Carroll, J. (1989). "The Carroll model: A 25-year retrospective and prospective view." *Educational Researcher, 18,* 26–31.

Cremin, L. A. (1961). *The transformation of the school.* New York: Vintage Books.

Elkind, D. (1976). *Child development and education: A Piagetian perspective.* New York: Oxford University Press.

Flavell, J. (1963). *The developmental psychology of Jean Piaget.* New York: Van Nostrand.

Forman, E., and Cazden, C. B. (1985). "Exploring Vygotskian perspectives in education: The cognitive value of peer interaction." In J. V. Wertsch (ed.), *Culture, communication, and cognition: Vygotskian perspectives.* San Diego, Calif.: Academic Press.

Gagné, R. (1970). *The conditions of learning.* (2nd ed.). Austin, Texas: Holt, Rinehart & Winston.

Gardner, R. (1966). "A psychologist looks at Montessori." *Elementary School Journal, 67*(2), 72–83.

Ginsburg, H. (1981). "Piaget and education: The contributions and limits of genetic epistemology." In I. Sigel, D. Brodzinsky, and R. Golinkoff (eds.), *New directions in Piagetian theory and practice.* Hillsdale, N.J.: Erlbaum.

Granott, N. (1991). "From macro to micro and back: On the analysis of microdevelopment." Paper presented at the 21st Annual Symposium of the Jean Piaget Society.

Harding, C. (ed.) (1985). *Moral dilemmas: Philosophical and psychology issues in the development of moral reasoning.* Chicago: Precedent.

Hunt, J. M. (1961). *Intelligence and experience.* New York: Ronald Press.

James, W. (1958). *Talks to teachers on psychology and to students on some of life's ideals.* New York: Norton.

Kuhn, D. (1991). *The skills of argument.* New York: Cambridge University Press.

Murray, F. B. (1978). "Teaching strategies and conservation training." In A. M. Lesgold, J. W. Pellegrino, S. Fokkema, and R. Glaser (eds.), *Cognitive psychology and instruction.* New York: Plenum.

Murray, F. B. (1981). "The conservation paradigm: Conservation of conservation research." In I. Sigel, D. Brodzinsky, and R. Golinkoff (eds.), *New directions in Piagetian theory and practice.* Hillsdale, N.J.: Erlbaum.

Murray, F. B. (1982). "The pedagogical adequacy of children's conservation explanations." *Journal of Educational Psychology, 74,* 656–659.

Murray, F. B. (1989). "Explanations in education." In M. C. Reynolds (ed.), *Knowledge base for the beginning teacher.* Elmsford, N.Y.: Pergamon Press.

Murray, F. B. (1990). "The conversion of truth into necessity." In W. Overton (ed.), *Reasoning, necessity and logic: Developmental perspectives.* Hillsdale, N.J.: Erlbaum.

Murray, F. B. (1991). "Questions a satisfying developmental theory would answer: The scope of a complete explanation of developmental phenomena." In H. Reese (ed.), *Advances in child development and behavior,* Vol. 23. San Diego, Calif.: Academic Press.

Murray, F. B. (1992). "Restructuring and constructivism: The development of American educational reform." In H. Beilin and P. Pufall (eds.), *Piaget's theory: Prospects and possibilities.* Hillsdale, N.J.: Erlbaum.

Murray, F. B., and Johnson, P. (1970). "A note on using curriculum models in analyzing the child's concept of weight." *Journal of Research in Science Teaching, 7,* 377–381.

Murray, F. B., and Johnson, P. (1975). "Relevant and some irrelevant factors in the child's concept of weight." *Journal of Educational Psychology, 67,* 705–711.

Murray, F. B., and Markessini, J. (1982). "A semantic basis of nonconservation of weight." *Psychological Record, 32,* 375–379.

Peterson, H. (ed.) (1946). *Great teachers portrayed by those who studied under them.* New York: Vintage Books.

Rogoff, B., and Lave, J. (eds.) (1984). *Everyday cognition: Its development in social context.* Cambridge, Mass.: Harvard University Press.

Seltzer, E. (1977). "A comparison between John Dewey's theory of inquiry and Jean Piaget's genetic analysis." *Journal of Genetic Psychology, 130,* 323.

Strauss, S. (1972). "Inducing cognitive development and learning: A review of short-term training experiments I: The organismic-developmental approach." *Cognition, 1,* 329–357.

Annotated Bibliography

Farnham-Diggory, S. (1990). *Schooling: The developing child.* Cambridge, Mass.: Harvard University Press.
This lucid book explains two strands of psychological thinking about schooling (Dewey and Thorndike) in the context of modern cognitive psychology. On this base, the book builds the implications for schooling, with particular attention to cultural transmission, technology, basic skills, and school reform.

Gardner, H. (1991). *The unschooled mind: How children think and how schools should teach.* New York: Basic Books.
Gardner addresses the question of what it would take for students actually to understand the lessons they are taught. The author synthesizes a vast scholarly literature about cognitive science and human development as he proposes visionary and practical solutions to the problems of contemporary schooling. The book provides a road map to the theories and literature of modern educational psychology.

James, W. (1958). *Talks to teachers on psychology and to students on some of life's ideals.* New York: Norton.
This beautifully crafted series of lectures gave birth to the field of educational psychology and sets forth the constraints and benefits of psychological knowledge for teaching. Though the findings presented are dated—even outdated—the general argument is as relevant and as persuasive today as it was when teachers first heard these lectures a century ago.

Stephens, J. M. (1967). *The process of schooling: A psychological examination.* Austin, Texas: Holt, Rinehart & Winston.
This book advances one of the few theories of schooling from a psychological and evolutionary perspective. It provides a framework for evaluating most of the educational psychological research that examines the effects of various educational interventions on pupil and student learning.

CHAPTER NINETEEN

PARENTS, FAMILIES, AND COMMUNITIES: OPPORTUNITIES FOR PRESERVICE TEACHER EDUCATION

LAUREN S. JONES YOUNG AND PATRICIA A. EDWARDS

If we dream of the best for our children—at their schools, in their jobs, and throughout their lives—we must help them to aim higher. What was adequate in the past is no longer good enough. . . . And the place to begin is with our expectations for America's educational system.

NATIONAL EDUCATION GOALS PANEL, 1991, P. IX

More is being asked of this nation's schools—the institution, its teachers, and our children. Our eroding global competitiveness, disengagement from democratic processes, parents' worries about their children's futures, and concerns that youth will be ill prepared to succeed in jobs that require complex and collaborative decisions are among the deluge of criticisms being levied at U.S. schools. Accompanying these critiques is an expanding pluralism among the nation's school children, a population notable for its cultural, ethnic, racial, linguistic, and social class diversity. At a time when greater demands are being made of schools, educators now worry about sponsoring more intellectually ambitious learning among children who are members of groups historically excluded from economic, educational, and social advantage. Taken together, these forces powerfully challenge America's commitment to a socially just, democratic society.

Responses to the charge for better-prepared citizens are many and varied: calls for greater school accountability, school choice, higher standards both for pupils and their teachers, rethinking the curricula students should learn. Visions of powerful learning—critical thinking, constructing knowledge, problem solving, advancing understanding—inform other discussions. Critiques of this sort condemn authoritarian school practices based on teaching as telling, learning as a passive process of accumulation, and knowledge as an objective set of facts, laws, and procedures (Cohen, 1988). These critiques reject the narrow scope of teacher responsibility for student learning embedded in a teaching-as-telling orientation: "The teachers' responsibility basically ends when they have told students what they must remember to know and do" (Holmes Group, 1986, pp. 27–28).

Teaching for understanding, as cognitive psychologists sometimes call this vision of powerful learning, takes a different view: knowledge is contested, constructed, and reformulated (Bereiter and Scardamalia, 1987; Goodlad, 1984; Palincsar and Brown, 1984; Shulman, 1987). Students actively participate in conversation, interpretation, and criticism, and what children need to learn rests not on some fixed body of information but on their abilities to "use various and competing ways of understanding the universe" (Haberman, 1991, p. 293).

From the National Center for Research on Teacher Learning (for example, Kennedy, 1991) to the National Council of Teachers of Mathematics (1991), researchers and practitioners are calling for a different view of learning for students and their teachers. For these reformers, it is this kind of teaching and learning—more often accessible in elite, private institutions—that must become available to all the nation's children in public schools.

One feature of good teaching is being able to do it for all the students a teacher will encounter (Carnegie Task Force, 1986; Goodlad, 1990; Holmes Group, 1990; Smith, 1969). Yet while reformers demand a higher-quality education, the typical form of teaching accepted as basic in many inner-city classrooms, for example, constitutes what Haberman (1991) calls a "pedagogy of poverty"—a pedagogy derived both from skewed images of what is good teaching and learning and from limited expectations of children's abilities (see Knapp and Shields, 1990; Means and Knapp, 1991). Extending learning to all children of the sort demanded by reformers rests not just on revisions in how we think about teaching and learning but also on teachers' views of learners and what they can do. From that vantage point, the scope of teacher preparation programs must be extended to examine the dispositions, beliefs, and knowledge about learners and learning that teachers bring to these contexts (Comer, 1990; Dilworth, 1990; Feiman-Nemser and Buchmann, 1986; Paine, 1989).

Delivery of a world-class education does not rest on educators' shoulders alone. The educational and future prospects of America's youth are framed by the context of their lives and by their relative station in the larger society (Apple, 1982; Jencks and others, 1972; Kirst and McLaughlin, 1990). In taking such a view, children are understood to be members of multiple and overlapping contexts. That is, children's learning is not solely dependent on cognition but interacts with the broad ecology of children's lives, a network of familial, cultural, social, economic, political, psychological, and physical factors (Bronfenbrenner, 1979; Bronfenbrenner and Weiss, 1983; Comer, 1980; Heath and McLaughlin, 1987; Nelson-Barber and Mitchell, 1992). One cannot assume that every child will arrive at school rested, well-fed, drug-free, stress-free, healthy, and "ready to learn." Developing a world-class education to meet the democratic, technical, and economic demands of the next century, then, is dependent on wide social and economic changes in society as well as on the collaborative efforts of a broad-based consortium (National Education Goals Panel, 1991; Schorr, 1988).

In this chapter, we consider preservice teachers' knowledge and dispositions that extend ambitious learning for everybody's children. Our particular focus is on everybody's children and the contexts in which they live. We intentionally take a broad view that includes parents, families, and communities in order to argue that teacher preparation programs cannot ignore radical transformations in the social contexts surrounding schools and schoolchildren and the circumstances of children's lives. In this chapter, we respond to three questions: (1) What should be included in teacher education programs about parents, families, and communities? (2) How should teacher educators help teachers facilitate in schools a greater involvement of the adults and institutions that significantly influence children's lives and learning? (3) Given the multiracial and multicultural nature of the school-age population and our ideal of a socially just, democratic society, how will preservice programs prepare future teachers to foster antiracist, multicultural practices?

These three questions emerge from a particular framework. Throughout this discussion, we presume that children are not schooled in isolation but develop as members of multiple and overlapping communities. To consider the questions in their full scope, this chapter begins with a broad account of the contexts in which schoolchildren live. We describe what we consider are critical issues emerging from that context, particularly those about families, communities, and preservice teachers in the last decade of the twentieth century. The second major section is a review of prominent themes in the parent-involvement literature: ways in which schools and parents come together to support children's learning. In the final section, we make proposals for extending the conversation on what beginning teachers should know to include themes about family, community, and social context.

The Social Circumstances of Schoolchildren

Since World War II, the structure, resources, and pluralism of U.S. families with school-age children have undergone stark transitions, changes that are not only altering the ability of both schools and families to carry out traditional responsibilities but also challenging conventional visions of the school's role in society (Comer, 1988).

Family Structure

Families today bear little resemblance to those of the 1950s: two natural parents with mama working at home and daddy in the formal labor force. In sharp contrast, family responsibilities are being shared more broadly, a response due in part to difficult economic and social necessities. Today, most mothers of children under the age of eighteen work outside the home; more than half of new mothers go back to work before their children are a year old (Children's Defense Fund, 1991). While outside work was common among poor mothers in the past, now they are joined in the current labor force by middle- and upper-income mothers. Family structure, expectations of marriage, and marital stability have also shifted radically. About 30 to 35 percent of children today do not live with both biological parents; another 10 percent live in families that include a stepparent (Kirst and McLaughlin, 1990). Hodgkinson (1985, p. 3) provides a profile of 100 children born in the country in 1985:

- 12 will be born out of wedlock.
- 40 will be born to parents who divorce before the child is 18.
- 5 will be born to parents who separate.
- 2 will be born to a parent who will die before the child reaches 18.
- 41 will reach age 18 "normally."

It is becoming much more common for children to be raised by a single parent. The increase in divorce and the rise in births to single mothers account for these greater numbers. Estimates suggest that about one-half of all children will live in a single-parent family for some period before their eighteenth birthday (Kirst and McLaughlin, 1990). While these changing family structures cross racial, ethnic, and socioeconomic lines, the proportions of children living in single-parent families vary substantially by race and ethnic group. Roughly 19 percent of white children, 31 percent of Latino children, and 55 percent of African-American children lived in these family settings in 1989 (U.S. Bureau of the Census, 1990). Children are also being raised in other varieties of family structure: in reconstituted and blended families, in gay and lesbian families, and in the homes of foster parents, grandparents, and other relatives. In fact, only 7 percent of U.S. families are comprised of the two-parent family of a working father and homemaker mother common just four decades ago (Hodgkinson, 1985).

Children's Pluralism

Threaded through changes in family structure is the multiracial and multilingual pluralism of the school population, an expanding mosaic of races, ethnicities, religions, languages, and cultural traditions and values. In the largest metropolitan areas today, for example, more than half of the public school students are children of color (American Council on Education, 1988). These data underscore the growing number of children of color nationally, relative to the population of white children. Children of color, for example, represented 30 percent of the fall 1986 enrollment in U.S. public elementary and secondary schools

(National Center for Education Statistics, 1989). That national proportion of African-American, Latino, Asian-American/Pacific Islander, and American Indian/Alaskan Native children is projected to grow in the coming decades (Natriello, McDill, and Pallas, 1990). Despite the learning opportunities for inclusion presented by this pluralism, insidious structural factors within schools continue to exacerbate societal inequities: prejudicial attitudes and expectations; biases in texts, curricula, discipline, and assessments; discriminatory placements in tracked classrooms and ability groups; low per pupil expenditures; and dilapidated conditions of the physical structure (Comer, 1988; Kozol, 1991; Nieto, 1992; Ogbu, 1990).

These demographic shifts also force us to reexamine our implicit assumptions of schools as white mainstream institutions (Perry and Fraser, 1993). From this reexamination, other inequities become more visible, particularly those arising when children deviate from culturally based "norms" (Auerbach, 1989). Differences in cultural styles of language use and interactional patterns, for example, can lead teachers to misread students' aptitudes, intent, and abilities and to make misattributions of student deficiency (Delpit, 1992; Heath, 1983, 1988). It is relatively difficult for children of color, particularly children with fewer socioeconomic advantages, to overcome teachers' assumptions that their failure to thrive intellectually is due to some deficit in them rather than to a deficit in teaching, in curricular perspectives, or in what students have opportunities to learn. Variabilities in the academic performances of students from particular backgrounds often can be explained by the social and political features of their school environments (Cummins, 1987; Heath, 1988; Ogbu, 1987). Such phenomena reinforce Young and Melnick's proposition (1988) that children at risk of school failure are in some serious way unserved, underserved, or inappropriately served by schools.

Children's Poverty

The circumstances of many children's lives are growing worse. This is not true for some children; many African-American, Latino, Asian-American, Native American, and white children will grow up without knowing impoverishment, neglect, abuse, addiction, homelessness, or hunger. But data on others are not so encouraging. Focusing on poverty as one example, we know that the number of poor children (under age eighteen) in the United States grew by more than 20 percent since 1970 to its current rate of one of every five children (Children's Defense Fund, 1991). Of approximately forty-five million schoolchildren in 1989, about nine million lived in poverty (National Center for Education Statistics, 1991). Most alarming is the rise in poverty among children under the age of six, who have the highest poverty rate for any other age group in our society. Disaggregated by race and ethnicity, these data show that poverty is not evenly experienced across family structures and racial and ethnic groups. In 1984, more than four times as many single women with children than two-parent families lived in poverty, largely the result of lower hourly wages for single mothers and stingy child-support payments, if any support was received (Kirst and McLaughlin, 1990). In 1987, while 42 percent of the five million poor children under six years old were white, children of color were much more likely to be poor. Among children under six in that year, 48 percent of African-American children (1.6 million), 42 percent of young Latino children (1.0 million), 29 percent of young children from other groups of color (0.3 million), and 13 percent of white children (2.1 million) were poor (National Center for Children in Poverty, 1990, pp. 19–20). While no array of statistics can portray the needs and aspirations of real children or the varied ways families manage their limited resources, these data highlight the magnitude of poverty among the next generation of schoolchildren.

Many school communities have experienced significant economic and social change over the past thirty years, particularly in urban areas. Structural changes in the urban economy—for example, the decline in manufacturing jobs—have brought fewer "good-paying" jobs to high school dropouts and graduates as well as high rates of unemployment. Reduced wages, chronic joblessness, and intensified poverty focus attention on families' struggles to raise their children and on the broader structural forces pressing against them. These ills of society are not amenable to correction by schools alone; they underscore the need for broader social and economic change.

In the core inner cities, concentrations of poverty are the result of the mass exodus of African-American middle- and working-class families, who had previously provided important supports to inner-city community and educational institutions (Wilson, 1987). The departure of these families leaves very different communities from those of earlier times, when teachers and parents shared a community, church, and expectations of children; when interactions between teachers and parents outside of school were common (Comer, 1980; Gordon and Breivogel, 1976). Teachers now have fewer opportunities for informal conversations with parents outside of school. Typically, teachers no longer live in the communities of their students and must seek out knowledge about community norms of child rearing and about expectations of schooling. Alliances between home and school, once natural parts of communities, must now be purposefully developed if they are to exist at all.

Children's Future Teachers

The consequences of our multiclass and multi-need school population are not lost on teachers who grapple daily with the out-of-school circumstances of their students, poor and rich alike: physical and emotional abuse of children, substance abuse, latch-key children, the diminished roles of church, school, home, and the authority figures represented in these primary institutions (Houston and Houston, 1992). In a synthesis of fifty-five U.S. studies of beginning teachers, perceived or experienced difficulties in relations with parents ranked among the top (Veenman,

1984). Veteran teachers express far-reaching concerns about the social and physical well-being of their students. The Carnegie Foundation (1990, pp. 115–127),
in a national survey of more than twenty thousand elementary and secondary
teachers, reports that the problems teachers encounter in their classrooms on a
regular basis focus on the welfare of their students. More than half of the teachers surveyed, for example, reported that the following factors are problems in their
school:

- Abused or neglected children
- Poor health among students
- Undernourished children
- More than 20 percent with serious family problems that significantly hindered
  their learning in school
- Lack of parental support
- Parents of children in their school inadequately performing their roles as parents

What was once taken for granted by school people—a familiarity with families and ways that children experience childhood—grows more foreign. Lists such
as the one above highlight the overflow of out-of-school issues into classrooms.
They also presume "failures" on the part of parents to provide schools with children that teachers can teach. Such perspectives will not help children nor foster
positive home-school relations. Educators must learn to see and seek the strengths
within and among families and communities and to build upon these strengths as
a means for fostering children's academic and social development. Greater support for children will depend on different conceptual frameworks for thinking
about partnerships between home and school, frameworks that recognize the contributions that parents do and can make to the academic and social successes of
their children.

The great majority of the 2.5 million teachers in tomorrow's schools will have
come to their decision to teach having had lengthy exposure to unexamined cultural assumptions about individuals, differences, and their place in schooling (Gerald, Horn, Snyder, and Sonnenberg, 1989). More than 90 percent of future
teachers will be white and monolingual, from primarily suburban and small-town
experiences; most will attend a college less than one hundred miles from home
(Zimpher and Ashburn, 1992). Cazden and Mehan (1989) present this profile of
a beginning teacher in the 1990s: "[She will be] female, in the early to mid-
twenties, Anglo, and from a lower-middle-income to middle-income family. It is
important to realize that these will be the characteristics of beginning teachers,
because they will not match those of their pupils" (p. 47).

Most teacher candidates will have grown up with little knowledge about or
genuine contact with others of different racial, religious, or social-class backgrounds (Dilworth, 1990; Goodlad, 1990). The goal of helping every teacher
develop the knowledge, skills, and dispositions necessary to teach a diverse student

population becomes problematic for those who expect to teach children very much like themselves, with little experience with pluralism, with limited understanding of social inequities in schooling, and with expectations that not all children can experience deep learning (McDiarmid and Price, 1990; Paine, 1989; Zimpher and Ashburn, 1992). It is highly likely that this disparity, already common in large numbers of classrooms, will occur more frequently as the size and scale of cross-cultural encounters grow in the coming decades.

Prospective teachers bring much with them to their teacher education programs, including ideas about teaching and learning, about schooling and learners. These ideas—elaborations of home and community values and perspectives—reinforce the need for teacher educators to help novices understand the limitations and parochialism of their personal experience (Buchmann and Schwille, 1983; Feiman-Nemser and Buchmann, 1986; Zimpher and Ashburn, 1992). Paine's analysis (1989) of the orientations prospective teachers bring to understandings of student diversity supports these earlier studies: how teacher education students think about their own teaching and pupils is largely influenced by prior experience. These findings show that prospective teachers' views of student differences are often discussed in the ideal, with few notions of how to apply these abstractions to classroom life. Responses about diversity and social inequality highlight students' lack of knowledge about people different from themselves—by attributions of racial and cultural stereotypes and by attributions of dysfunctionality and deficiency when children's ways of being deviate from a monocultural mainstream. Socially constructed causes of differences and any pedagogical implications of student diversity are largely ignored. Preservice teachers in Paine's sample tended to see differences among students as decontextualized, making it difficult for them to translate abstract notions of fairness and equality to their own teaching. Consequently, they suggest teaching methods that treat diversity as a problem, not as a phenomenon.

While the incongruence between preservice teachers' cultural insularity and children's pluralism is becoming more well known, relatively little attention in professional education programs is focused on preparing teachers for pluralistic classrooms (Grant and Secada, 1990; Liston and Zeichner, 1991; Sleeter, 1985). The marginal treatment of such issues in teacher education programs reinforces a significantly monocultural approach to the preparation of teachers (Goodlad, 1990; McDiarmid, 1990). Some argue that teacher education students should acquire these dispositions, attitudes, and knowledge in their liberal arts courses, but Melnick, Gomez, and Price (1990) report that they receive very little, if anything, there. Some students are offered special "multicultural education" courses developed around presentations about particular racial and ethnic groups. Evidence of deepened student understanding, however, is not encouraging. What is typically offered not only fails to alter beliefs that culturally and economically different students cannot learn but often strengthens those beliefs, as McDiarmid and Price (1990) summarize:

Despite the best intentions of teacher educators, a large proportion [of teachers] appear to be graduating . . . believing that prejudging pupils on the basis of their membership in a particular ethnic group is both valid and a legitimate basis for making instructional decisions. How do we account for such a perverse result? One possibility is that the information prospective teachers encounter about culturally different pupils and the way they encounter such information may reinforce rather than overturn their beliefs. That is, multicultural textbooks, monographs, and lectures on various ethnic groups, in which generalizations about groups is the currency of scholarly discourse, may communicate that generalizations about individuals based on their ethnic group membership are legitimate [p. 5].

Grant (1989) brings a similar reservation to delegating information about culturally diverse learners to one or two selected courses in the teacher education curriculum: "It is not the major point to give teachers a cultural recipe for working with students of color, but to get them to realize that in order to work successfully with any students, especially students whose race and socioeconomic status are different than their own, they will need to raise many questions, starting with questions about themselves. Recipes for teaching students of color can become a means of transmitting racist discourse and practice" (p. 69). This research highlights the difficulty of overcoming years of experience and underscores the need to pay attention both to what teacher candidates should learn in order to extend their world views as well as how they learn it. Involving parents in schools is another strategy recommended to mediate the cultural insularity of teachers and children's pluralism.

Parent Involvement

Building partnerships with parents is widely hailed in education reform efforts as a critical factor in students' school success (Epstein, 1984; Marjoribanks, 1979). Over the past ten or fifteen years, several national education reports—*A Nation at Risk* (National Commission on Excellence in Education, 1983), *A Nation Prepared* (Carnegie Task Force, 1986), and *An Imperiled Generation* (Carnegie Foundation, 1989), for example—have highlighted the centrality of "parent involvement" for bolstering children's academic and social status. There is nothing particularly novel in this view; this nation historically has depended on parents and other community institutions to carry out certain responsibilities to facilitate a school mission of student development (Epstein, 1987; Lightfoot, 1978). This hope is not entirely ill formed. Accumulated evidence supports the importance of parent involvement in fostering children's academic achievement (Bempechat, 1990; Purkey and Smith, 1983; Walberg, 1984). In programs with a strong component of parent involvement, students consistently are better achievers than those in comparable programs with lesser parent involvement (Nieto, 1992). Further, dramatic changes in children's academic progress occur when educators change what Cummins (1986) calls exclusionary patterns of school-community interaction to those of collaboration.

With such strong evidence, why are parent-school collaborations not more extensive? Obstacles exist within both groups. Among parents, differing views on school mission and on their own roles as educators limit participation in school activities (Stallworth and Williams, 1982). While some parents want to be actively involved in the school, others believe that the responsibility for educating children rests solely with the teacher (Nieto, 1992). Still others see themselves in educative roles limited to helping their children at home while remaining distant from schools (Kochan and Mullins, 1992; Siu, 1992).

Others report what many parents feel: an exclusion from routine exchanges with schools reflective of parents' social class, race, ethnicity, and level of education (Comer, 1986; Epstein, 1987; Heath and McLaughlin, 1987; Lightfoot, 1978; McLaughlin and Shields, 1987). Despite extended civil rights over the past two decades, the increased "distrust between school people—largely middle-income, often nonminority, and well-educated—and parents in poor and minority communities" has worked against the two groups coming together (Comer, 1986, p. 444). Lareau (1989) connects variance in parent participation in schools to social-class membership, noting the strong influence of social class on the density of connections between parents and schools, regardless of parents' aspirations for their children. Inequalities in parents' resources and dispositions—for example, education, occupational status, income—critically affect levels of parent involvement (Lareau, 1989).

Other factors inhibit parent-school collaborations. Some parents may be too absorbed or overwhelmed by conditions of living to spend more time with their children, at least in the ways that schools expect. Some parents, especially those from linguistically and culturally diverse communities and from working-class neighborhoods, have a hard time with forms of parent involvement expected by schools, particularly if parents receive little specific assistance from teachers to enable them to comply with expectations, if parents cannot read the communications sent home by the school, or if parents' own school histories are marked by alienation, anger, and difficulty. Even when parents are invited to school, often there is no structure for effectively involving them (Comer, 1986; Epstein, 1988). Meetings scheduled during working hours, few communications to parents from school, contacting parents only when there is a problem, and limited opportunities for meaningful roles in the life of schools further limit the involvement of parents.

While teachers embrace the concept of parent involvement, what they expect from that involvement remains largely ambiguous and narrowly defined. Conceptions of parent roles have ranged from helping children with homework, volunteering in school, and participating in parent-teacher associations to shared governance in school policies (Ascher, 1987; Berger, 1987). In practice, however, what schools want of parents is support of classroom and school activities—assisting children with schoolwork, participating in parent-teacher conferences, and attending school performances. The cooperation solicited often is limited to extending the teacher's role in the home or in the classroom, an orientation underscored by Heath and McLaughlin (1987): "In contrast to the politically based, formalized parent participation models of the preceding era (1965–1980), which failed to elicit widespread or long-term parent involvement, today's strategies stress parents as extensions of the schools' business—supporters of homework, monitors of activities, and reinforcers of school values. Policy makers hope that cooperative efforts between parents and school will help increase in-home support for educational goals and activities" (p. 577). With a few notable exceptions, such as the Chicago school reform and Comer's work in New Haven, parent voices often are silenced in much official and informal school policy. Few efforts are made to extend parents' voice, power, and authority in school policy decisions (Lightfoot, 1978).

Parents from all socioeconomic backgrounds are far more interested in their children's education than many teachers and administrators believe (Kochan and Mullins, 1992; National Commission on Children, 1991). While teachers' expectations of parent involvement have remained largely static (Lindner, 1987), most parents today, regardless of cultural or social-class background, find it difficult to participate with schools in ways that were the norm forty years ago. These changes are not pathologies; they are adult responses to economic and social pressures. What matters are the meanings teachers give to these changes. For example, the incongruence between family life and teacher expectations can fuel teachers' damaging and untrue judgments that parents are uncaring, incompetent, or apathetic (Lareau, 1989; Nieto, 1992; Pang, 1988; Veenman, 1984). As Hale-Benson (1982) and McAdoo (1981) remind us, teacher judgments get translated into perceptions of deficiencies of both families and their children, linking the poor intellectual development of poor children and children of color with inadequacies in their families. Such opinions are not only erroneous but also obscure the need for teachers to rethink partnerships with parents.

By focusing on what are perceived as family deficiencies, teachers who have neither the training nor insight to see beyond surface behaviors will not understand why children and parents act as they do. One teacher's personal account of her changed perceptions and practice is both unusual and telling. Jimmy was a first grader who was not attending school consistently.

> The school counselor and I decided we should make a home visit. At 9:30 one morning, we drove to Jimmy's home in an all-Black neighborhood. . . . When we knocked on the door, Jimmy answered and reluctantly invited us in. Jimmy's mother had been asleep. Still in bed, she graciously invited us into her bedroom. We sat on the end of the bed and discussed our concerns. She was also worried about Jimmy's education. This morning she was tired from working

late and needed Jimmy to stay home and watch her two-year-old. As a single parent, it was difficult for her to maintain her financial stability and care for her two young children. The home visit gave us new insights, and we developed a partnership with Jimmy's mother, sending messages throughout the year. His mother closely monitored his homework assignments, making sure they were completed. Jimmy did well, despite his absences from school. I began to understand how societal pressures were intertwined with the mission of schools. Educators must be sensitive to these variables and refrain from quick decisions. I had adopted the stereotype that Blacks living in ghetto areas did not care about schooling. The stereotypes I had acquired about Black Americans contributed to my ineffectiveness as a teacher. I chose the indulgent belief that the problem was in the student and I had done all I could do [Pang, 1988, p. 377].

What Jimmy's teacher learned from this encounter in terms of altering her own dispositions and practice and what future teachers could learn in their pre-service programs is supported by the work of Taylor and Dorsey-Gaines (1988): "If we are to teach, we must first examine our own assumptions about families and children and we must be alert to the negative images in the literature. . . . Instead of responding to 'pathologies,' we must recognize that what we see may actually be healthy adaptations to an uncertain and stressful world. As teachers, researchers, and policymakers, we need to think about the children themselves and try to imagine the contextual worlds of their day-to-day lives" (p. 203).

Families encourage student achievement in a variety of ways, including but not limited to involvement in schools. Studies of Chinese-American families, especially those of recent immigrants, for example, call into question a definition of parent involvement based solely on participation in school-based activities. Siu (1992) offers this critique of this narrow view of parental involvement for Asian-American parents: "This definition has led to a stereotype that Asian-American parents are inactive and unconcerned. Can a parent care deeply about the child's education, do a lot to encourage and monitor the child's progress, and yet not be present at the school as volunteer, policy-maker, or participant in special presentations and other meetings? The answer seems to be 'Yes' " (pp. 32–33). Like Siu, Nieto's case studies of successful students (1992) show that very few parents, especially parents of color and poor parents, are involved in schools in any but the most superficial ways: few volunteer in school, go to meetings, or even visit the school on a consistent basis. Yet parents were very much involved in supporting their children's academic achievement at home.

Family structure, race, ethnicity, and income tell us little about children's abilities, parents' hopes for their children, or the quality of time families invest with children. Clark's ethnography (1983) of poor, urban African-American families shows that a family's main contribution to children's success in school revolves around parents' dispositions and relationships with children at home. Families where children were achieving academically could not be identified merely by ascriptions of race, class, household structure, or knowing the employment and educational status of the parents. The overall quality of the family's lifestyle, beliefs, and activities, not family structure or social status, influenced children's attitudes, behaviors, and performances in classrooms. Qualities and behaviors nurtured in the home—for example, beliefs about the value of education, setting behavioral standards, monitoring activities—contributed to children's school progress.

Extending What Beginning Teachers Should Know

Throughout this discussion, we have argued that knowledge about parents, families, and communities, their demography, culture, and roles, have a place in the broad set of understandings that comprise teacher education programs. We have tried to build a case for considering contextual influences on children's in-school learning and learning opportunities; for reframing prospective teachers' assumptions about learners and their dispositions toward children, families, and family life; and for extending conceptions of home, school, and community partnerships. These are powerful reasons for schools, families, communities, and teacher preparation programs to grow closer. Without understanding the bigger picture influencing learning in schools, preservice teachers will perpetuate expectations of children and families that diminish students' life chances.

Transformations in society—in the social and economic contexts and in visions of ambitious learning—cannot be accommodated by unchanging content and pedagogy (Griffin, 1989). Knowledge about the worlds that children inhabit, the social contexts influencing schools, how context mediates teaching and learning, and how alliances with families and community organizations promote children's growth and development highlight the complexities involved in linking children's and teachers' experience. These are glaring gaps in what most teacher candidates have opportunities to learn (Comer, 1980; Houston and Houston, 1992; Williams, 1992). Such understandings, particularly the connections to children's learning and learning opportunities, inform what essential understandings might be incorporated in the knowledge frameworks for teacher preparation programs.

Contextual Influences on Children's Learning and Learning Opportunities

We propose that preservice teachers begin their first year of teaching with the disposition to find out about their students, their school, their community, armed with the inquiry skills that will enable them to do so. Griffin (1989) reminds us that a "central understanding of effective teachers is that they have well-developed conceptions of who learners are" (p. 280) in their developmental, cultural, and social senses. That process of inquiry should be founded on current realities of family, community, and context and how these conditions touch the lives of children in and out of school. Epstein (1988) warns, "Unless we examine both family and school structures and practices, we will continue to receive contradictory and often false messages about the capabilities of unconventional, minority, and hard to reach families" (p. 58).

Teachers need to become students of their students: their cultures, languages and linguistic understandings, learning styles, and social conditions (Holmes Group, 1990). The goal is not to replace one set of stereotypes with another but to help teacher candidates know and value children as members of multiple and overlapping contexts that may look very different from those that preservice teachers experienced. Our students will also need to become students of themselves: to assess how their own erroneous and limited understandings of children have harmful consequences for children's learning. Preservice teachers should have opportunities, as Comer (1989) recommends, "to learn the ways in which their behavior can either facilitate or interfere with the development of children" (p. 360). These understandings are developed from "the desire and ability of teachers to learn about the special circumstances of their own students and their communities and the ability to take this kind of knowledge into account in their teaching" (Zeichner, 1993, p. 6).

Understanding children means interacting with a wide range of individuals and institutions (Pugach and Leake, 1991; Schorr, 1988). Griffin (1989) describes how an informed perspective on contextual influences bears on teacher, students, and their work together: "Although it is sometimes comforting to blame changing conditions of teaching on some vague perception that society in general and individual communities in particular are no longer as they once were, teachers and administrators . . . [should] spend the time and energy to explore the deeper and more comprehensive knowledge of the multiple contexts that influence their work. Instead of merely noting that students in school appear to be unresponsive and reluctant learners, they will engage in serious investigation of the students' background characteristics, their home environments, their out-of-school activities, and their expectations of schooling" (p. 279).

Our students will need to develop understandings of how their responses to contextual factors influence children's learning and learning opportunities. When preservice teachers develop the dispositions and skills to inquire about children and to respect children's experiences, when they can connect social foundational knowledge to real classroom practice, and when they can extend their views on children and learning, they will be able to better see, analyze, and respond more appropriately to the possibilities of teaching and learning.

Teaching about subject matter and pedagogy cannot remain separate from teaching about learners and context. Powerful teaching derives from the connections across the domains. Knowing about children and the ways they develop informs discussions about subject matter and pedagogy. In this light, Barnes (1991) notes that understandings beginning teachers need "are not merely the sum of content from the different domains related to teaching" (p. 3). Several studies being conducted at the National Center for Research on Teacher Learning at Michigan State University are attempting to illuminate these relationships. Similarly, a three-nation study of teaching in multicultural, multilingual school settings concludes that subject matter and pedagogy cannot be understood independently of community factors and teachers' dispositions (Beckum and others, 1991). Their findings highlight the need to include several subjects in addition to content and pedagogy, particularly considerations of community and teachers' attitudes and dispositions.

To illuminate this view, we might ask how we would help preservice teachers think through these examples of classroom situations: "What if life experiences have left the student without the confidence to take the risks involved in learning? What if academic learning is not the style of the social network of a child's parents, even though they want their child to succeed in school? Could it be that the 'bad' behavior a child displays is sometimes the result of social and psychological development that is different from or out of sequence with that expected in the classroom?" (Comer, 1986, p. 444). Students differ, as do individuals, as do members of socioeconomic and cultural groups, and these differences should inform instructional and curricular decisions.

By the same token, teacher educators can help preservice teachers to understand the important role of parents and guardians in the education of their children, and educators can strengthen the family-school relationship by encouraging and nurturing parent involvement (Henderson, Marburger, and Ooms, 1986). In addition to adopting a belief about the importance of parent involvement as a principle of good teaching practice, novice teachers can learn various ways of developing their roles as partners with parents in children's education.

Schools alone cannot solve all problems arising from social context, but neither can they ignore them. Mainstream assumptions about schools, families, and communities will not sponsor the kinds of school-community relationships considered so important to children's well-being. In spite of the research on the benefits of parent involvement, few structures are available to teachers to involve parents more broadly (Epstein, 1988). Further, practice based on traditional definitions of parent involvement will fall short for a wide band of this nation's children. Interventions intended to empower parents alone are too narrowly conceived. As it is traditionally defined and practiced, for example, "parent involvement is not powerful enough to have a significant impact on the policies and practices of urban schools" (Davies, 1991, p. 376). Blurring boundaries across home, school, and community question conceptions of parent involvement as one-to-one relationships between parent and teacher, although such relationships can be critical for individual children. Across all social classes, transformations in children's families, contexts, and circumstances press for reconsidering single-issue, "one style fits all" parent-involvement interventions (Epstein, 1988; Lindner, 1987). The scope of these changes challenges us to explore with our students broader definitions of "parent involvement" and more expansive views of teacher, family, and community roles and responsibility.

Davies (1991) and others propose a redefinition of parent involvement developed around the strengths of families and their multicultural communities. This new definition replaces a focus on "parent" with one that includes family and community agencies and institutions that serve children. The rationale is based on three assumptions about children and their families and communities: (1) every child can learn and achieve school success; (2) children's social, emotional, physical, and academic development are linked; and (3) development of the whole child is a shared and overlapping responsibility of the school, family, and other community agencies and institutions. This new definition goes beyond having family members come to school to fulfill schools' agendas but also includes activities and services that arise from and occur in homes and neighborhood settings.

To enact this new definition, schools must become fundamentally different institutions (Kirst and McLaughlin, 1990). Viewing a child as a member of a community social system uncovers the complex interrelationships of children and their environments. Schools become arbiters of services previously provided or arranged for by families: meals, immunizations, shelter, a safe haven. Family-school relations come to mean more than an extension of school into family. This shift in emphasis, from child as student to child as community member, suggests bold departures from traditional relationships of parents and teachers. This view, emerging in school districts across the nation, not only stretches the parameters of past practices around parent involvement but redefines the purpose: not just higher academic achievement but the well-being of children in its fullest sense (Edwards and Young, 1992). Responses are organized around the "functional requirements of healthy, curious, productive, and motivated" children and their families (Heath and McLaughlin, 1987, p. 579). From that vantage point, schools are thought of in new ways: from "deliverers" of educational services, schools become "brokers," tapping community strengths and coordinating the social and resource networks for children and their families from a wide range of local public and private institutions (Heath and McLaughlin, 1987; Hill, Wise, and Shapiro, 1989). A promising example, New Beginnings, is a collaboration among public agencies and schools in San Diego, California, that delivers an integrated package of social and health services to families and school children (Payzant, 1992).

Toward Antiracist, Multicultural Perspectives

Many children, particularly poor children and children of color, are not succeeding in schools in either intellectual or social ways. Prospective teachers will need to understand how the changing demography of learners and visions of powerful learning inform their own standards and expectations of students and families. To help preserve students develop antiracist, multicultural practices, developing understandings about subject matter, pedagogy, learner, and context must be coupled with attention to novices' affective and dispositional qualities. That is, as teacher educators, we will need to develop committed pluralists who have been prepared to work in a wide range of school settings.

The ambitious kind of teaching and learning we hope for will take place in a sustained way for large numbers of students when teachers create classroom environments thoughtfully organized to encourage student voice, participation, conversation, and relationships—where teachers take responsibility for helping each child take part to his or her fullest (Holmes Group, 1990). In these kinds of classrooms, teachers nurture, challenge, guide, and support, providing a stable, safe learning community where every child is a respected and thriving participant. These teachers bridge the worlds of the student with that of the school, building on children's everyday experiences to link new concepts to prior knowledge (Irvine, 1992).

We also see the positive potential in drawing upon the ideas, languages, and perspectives represented by a world view of peoples and ideas. If we are to create the kinds of educational institutions that honor a multiracial, multiethnic, democratic vision of schooling, teachers must take larger roles in "allowing the lives, histories, and cultures of the historically oppressed to critically influence the reconceptualization of knowledge that is represented in the curriculum and the classroom" (Perry and Fraser, 1993, p. 19). That is, we must also negotiate the inclusion in texts and curricular materials of primary stories told by and about members of our pluralistic society. Whether in their liberal arts courses or in teacher education classes, preservice students should graduate with some understandings of the contributions to humankind made by peoples of various cultures. That background will better enable them to "appreciate the potential of those who sit before them" and "to link their students' histories and worlds to the subject matter they present in the classroom" (Delpit, 1992, p. 248).

How Should Teacher Candidates Acquire These Understandings and Dispositions?

How these understandings and dispositions are organized, presented, and developed may be as important as the content itself (Barnes, 1991). We believe there are multiple ways of developing the understandings and dispositions we describe as important. No one model will suffice for the diversity of sociopolitical and cultural contexts found across our communities. Rather than prescribing particular readings, activities, and experiences for a teacher education program, we present several themes to consider about learners, subject matter, pedagogy, and context.

Our university classrooms will need to extend beyond the walls of the college campus, to provide carefully crafted opportunities for students to acquire firsthand experience as participants in community gatherings and in school sites that reinforce and complement our intentions (Griffin, 1989). They will need experience in schools where cultural pluralism is valued and where talk about racial, ethnic, and social-class diversity is a central theme in faculty discussions (Holmes Group, 1990). They should be provided opportunities to reflect with others about meanings they attributed to their experience. Our students will need experiences with a variety of ways of knowing children, in out-of-school places as well as within schools. It is one thing to learn book knowledge about children and families; it is quite another to use ideas in action and to modify one's behavior based on responses to those actions (Nelson-Barber and Mitchell, 1992).

Another avenue is to provide students opportunities to read about, see, and experience models of effective pedagogy for multilingual, multiethnic, multiracial and multi-need children. They should have opportunities to analyze examples from the many successful cases of educating poor children and children of color. In those discussions, the efforts that contribute to children's achievement can be closely examined: to unfold, for example, what it really means to have high standards and expectations for every child. As teacher educators, we will need to refocus our own reliance on labeling those who fall outside a mainstream-determined norm as "disadvantaged," "at risk," "learning disabled," and to break our habit of seeking explanations for student failure outside the classroom or in negative attributions to children. We will need to model the behaviors and dispositions we encourage. We should foster the propensity to ask, "What are the appropriate strategies I can use to further develop my students?" Along with our students, we will need to develop the disposition to search for appropriate matches among the child, pedagogy, and task and to continue exploring when those matches do not fit.

Implications for preservice programs related to the incongruence between children's pluralism and teachers' homogeneity are suggested by Pugach and Leake (1991):

> Our concern is that there are many aspects of the recent research on learning and learners that have profound implications of how teachers approach their work with a diverse group of students. However, if those implications are not explicitly drawn, teacher educators and their students may fail to connect the meaning of that knowledge to the nature of the students they teach. If knowledge is presented in the abstract, in the absence of these linkages, the danger exists that beginning teachers will fail to see its relevance to their own teaching of students whose culture and race differs from their own, particularly when novice teachers may not yet have explored their own feelings regarding working in multiracial, multiethnic schools or classrooms [pp. 29–30].

The goal of developing students' world views will not be accomplished by one course or other brief curricular insertions on particular racial and ethnic groups. Zeichner (1993) reports that it may be "more important to have attitudes and skills for teaching students from all social, cultural, and linguistic backgrounds regardless of the groups from which they come, than it is to study about the characteristics of particular ethnic groups" (p. 6). Delpit (1992) extends this view: "If we are to successfully educate all of our children, we must work to remove the blinders built of stereotypes, monocultural instructional methodologies, ignorance, social distance, biased research, and racism" (p. 248).

Enabling prospective teachers to "remove the blinders," to connect positively to other cultures, to other social classes, to other family structures, and to other races and ethnicities means extending their world views. Such knowledge must become unifying concepts threaded throughout a program, with the continual interplay of theory and practice, in campus laboratories and in field experiences. What are needed are learning experiences that constructively build on preservice students' prior experience and that enable students to push beyond stereotypes and false assumptions about what children and families are willing and able to do. While teacher education efforts have helped students explore their own cultural identities as they examine their dispositions toward different ethnocultural and socioeconomic groups (see, for example, Beyer, 1991; Gomez and Tabachnick, 1991; Hollins, 1990; Ladson-Billings, 1991), greater knowledge alone may be insufficient: "It is difficult for people to see beyond their own cultural walls until they encounter situations where their cultural references no longer serve them. Knowledge of different world views and meanings grows from personal exchanges with those who hold other perspectives. These truths argue for a clinical experience that serves a diverse array of youth and that involves parents and other adults from the children's communities. They also underscore the importance of recruiting and involving school and university faculty of color" (Holmes Group, 1990, p. 40).

Recruiting faculty and students of color and involving parents and community members can also be invaluable resources. We propose that teacher education programs themselves include the diverse voices of adults and children—faculty, teachers, parents, students, and community members—in university classrooms to broaden our students' understandings of learners and families. Furthermore, the inclusion of these perspectives models cultural pluralism and other aspects of diversity that we expect preservice students to value. Finally, the inclusion of diverse voices would diminish the powerful negative messages to our students about authority and power, about participation and inclusion implicit in the prevailing monochrome of university and school faculty.

Conclusion

This nation's classrooms are a key force in the ongoing struggle to build an inclusive society of all children and their families (Perry and Fraser, 1993). Teachers play a vital role in creating those classroom environments (Holmes Group, 1990, 1986). Teacher educators concerned about the learning and social development of citizens for the twenty-first century must also be concerned about the power of social, economic, and political dynamics shaping education futures and about developing a teaching force committed to pluralism and inclusion. What is currently at stake is not just the narrow view of academic achievement as school mission or the purpose of home-school interactions but an expanded purpose of children's positive development. Fulfilling the promise of children's powerful learning for participation in a multiracial, multiethnic democracy provides teacher educators an opportunity to reconsider what is important for beginning teachers to know and how we can help them learn what is important to know. It is also an important reminder about our shared responsibility with other education and community institutions to create conditions in schools and classrooms in which everyone is at home.

References

American Council on Education (1988). *One-third of a nation: A report of the Commission on Minority Participation in Education and American Life.* Washington, D.C.: American Council on Education.

Apple, M. W. (1982). *Education and power.* New York: Routledge & Kegan Paul.

Ascher, C. (1987). *Improving the school-home connection for poor and minority urban students.* New York: Teachers College Institute for Urban and Minority Education.

Auerbach, E. R. (1989). "Toward a social-contextual approach to family literacy." *Harvard Educational Review, 59*(2), 165–182.

Barnes, H. L. (1991). "Reconceptualizing the knowledge base for teacher education." In M. C. Pugach, H. L. Barnes, and L. C. Beckum (eds.), *Changing the practice of teacher education: The role of the knowledge base.* Washington, D.C.: American Association of Colleges for Teacher Education.

Beckum, L. C., and others (1991). "Identifying a knowledge base for teaching multicultural, multilingual students: An international study." In M. C. Pugach, H. L. Barnes, and L. C. Beckum (eds.), *Changing the practice of teacher education: The role of the knowledge base.* Washington, D.C.: American Association of Colleges for Teacher Education.

Bempechat, J. (1990). *The role of parent involvement in children's academic achievement: A review of the literature.* New York: ERIC Clearinghouse on Urban Education.

Bereiter, C., and Scardamalia, M. (1987). "An attainable version of high literacy: Approaches to teaching higher-order skills in reading and writing." *Curriculum Inquiry, 17*(1), 9–30.

Berger, E. H. (1987). *Parents as partners in education: The school and home working together.* (2nd ed.). Columbus, Ohio: Merrill.

Beyer, L. E. (1991). "Teacher education, reflective inquiry and moral action." In B. R. Tabachnick and K. M. Zeichner (eds.), *Issues and practices in inquiry-oriented teacher education.* Washington, D.C.: Falmer Press.

Bronfenbrenner, U. (1979). *The ecology of human development: Experiments by nature and design.* Cambridge, Mass.: Harvard University Press.

Bronfenbrenner, U., and Weiss, H. (1983). *Beyond policies without people: An ecological perspective on child and family policy.* New York: Cambridge University Press.

Buchmann, M., and Schwille, J. R. (1983). "Education: The overcoming of experience." *American Journal of Education, 92*, 30–51.

Carnegie Foundation for the Advancement of Teaching (1989). *An imperiled generation: Saving urban schools.* Princeton, N.J.: Princeton University Press.

Carnegie Foundation for the Advancement of Teaching (1990). *The condition of teaching: A state-by-state analysis.* Princeton, N.J.: Princeton University Press.

Carnegie Task Force on Teaching as a Profession (1986). *A nation prepared: Teachers for the 21st century.* Washington, D.C.: Carnegie Forum on Education and the Economy.

Cazden, C. B., and Mehan, H. (1989). "Principles from sociology and anthropology: Context, code, classroom, and culture." In M. C. Reynolds (ed.), *Knowledge base for the beginning teacher.* Elmsford, N.Y.: Pergamon Press.

Children's Defense Fund (1991). *The state of America's children, 1991.* Washington, D.C.: Children's Defense Fund.

Clark, R. M. (1983). *Family life and school achievement: Why poor black children succeed or fail.* Chicago: University of Chicago Press.

Cohen, D. K. (1988). "Teaching practice: *Plus ça change . . .*" In P. W. Jackson (ed.), *Contributing to educational change: Perspectives on research and practice.* Berkeley, Calif.: McCutchan.

Comer, J. P. (1980). *School power: Implications of an intervention project.* New York: Free Press.

Comer, J. P. (1986). "Parent participation in the schools." *Phi Delta Kappan, 67*(6), 442–446.

Comer, J. P. (1988). "Educating poor minority children." *Scientific American, 259*(5), 42–48.

Comer, J. P. (1989). "Racism and the education of young children." *Teachers College Record, 90*(3), 352–361.

Comer, J. P. (1990). "Home, school, and academic learning." In J. I. Goodlad and P. Keating (eds.), *Access to knowledge: An agenda for our nation's schools.* New York: College Entrance Examination Board.

Cummins, J. (1986). "Empowering minority students: A framework for intervention." *Harvard Educational Review, 56*(1), 18–36.

Cummins, J. (1987). *Empowering minority students.* Sacramento, Calif.: California Association for Bilingual Education.

Davies, D. (1991). "Schools reaching out: Family, school, and community partnerships for student success." *Phi Delta Kappan, 72*(5), 376–382.

Delpit, L. (1992). "Education in a multicultural society: Our future's greatest challenge." *Journal of Negro Education, 61*(3), 237–249.

Dilworth, M. E. (1990). *Reading between the lines: Teachers and their racial/ethnic cultures.* Washington, D.C.: ERIC Clearinghouse on Teacher Education and American Association of Colleges for Teacher Education.

Edwards, P. A., and Young, L.S.J. (1992). "Beyond parents: Family, community, and school involvement." *Phi Delta Kappan, 74*(1), 72–80.

Epstein, J. L. (1984). "Effects of teacher practices and parent involvement on student achievement." Paper presented at the annual meeting of the American Educational Research Association, New Orleans, La.

Epstein, J. L. (1987). "Parent involvement: State education agencies show the way." *Community Educational Journal, 14*(4), 4–10.

Epstein, J. L. (1988). "How do we improve programs for parent involvement?" *Educational Horizons, 66*(2), 58–59.

Feiman-Nemser, S., and Buchmann, M. (1986). "The first year of teacher preparation: Transition to pedagogical thinking." *Journal of Curriculum Studies, 18*(3), 239–256.

Gerald, D. E., Horn, P. J., Snyder, T. D., and Sonnenberg, W. C. (1989). *State projections to 1993 for public elementary and secondary enrollment, graduates and teachers.* Washington, D.C.: National Center for Education Studies.

Gomez, M. L., and Tabachnick, B. R. (1991). "Preparing preservice teachers to teach diverse learners." Paper presented at the annual meeting of the American Educational Research Association, Chicago.

Goodlad, J. I. (1984). *A place called school: Prospects for the future.* New York: McGraw-Hill.

Goodlad, J. I. (1990). *Teachers for our nation's schools.* San Francisco: Jossey-Bass.

Gordon, I. J., and Breivogel, W. F. (1976). *Building effective home-school relationships.* Needham Heights, Mass.: Allyn & Bacon.

Grant, C. A. (1989). "Culture and teaching: What do teachers need to know?" In National Center for Research on Teacher Education, *Competing visions of teacher knowledge: Proceedings from an NCRTE seminar for education policymakers.* East Lansing, Mich.: National Center for Research on Teacher Education.

Grant, C. A., and Secada, W. G. (1990). "Preparing teachers for diversity." In W. R. Houston (ed.), *Handbook of research on teacher education.* New York: Macmillan.

Griffin, G. A. (1989). "Coda: The knowledge-driven school." In M. C. Reynolds (ed.), *Knowledge base for the beginning teacher.* Elmsford, N.Y.: Pergamon Press.

Haberman, M. (1991). "The pedagogy of poverty versus good teaching." *Phi Delta Kappan, 73*(4), 290–294.

Hale-Benson, J. E. (1982). *Black children: Their roots, culture, and learning styles.* Provo, Utah: Brigham Young University Press.

Heath, S. B. (1983). *Ways with words.* New York: Cambridge University Press.

Heath, S. B. (1988). *What no bedtime story means: Narrative skills at home and at school.* Yarmouth, Mass.: Intercultural Press.

Heath, S. B., and McLaughlin, M. W. (1987). "A child resource policy: Moving beyond dependence on school and family." *Phi Delta Kappan, 58*(8), 576–580.

Henderson, A. T., Marburger, C. L., and Ooms, T. (1986). *Beyond the bake sale: An educator's guide to working with parents.* Columbia, Md.: National Committee for Citizens in Education.

Hill, P. T., Wise, A. E., and Shapiro, L. (1989). *Educational progress: Cities mobilize to improve their schools.* Santa Monica, Calif.: RAND.

Hodgkinson, H. S. (1985). *All one system: Demographics of education, kindergarten through graduate school.* Washington, D.C.: Institute for Educational Leadership.

Hollins, E. (1990). "Debunking the myth of a monolithic white American culture, or moving toward cultural inclusion." *American Behavioral Scientist, 34*(2), 201–209.

Holmes Group (1986). *Tomorrow's teachers: A report of the Holmes Group.* East Lansing, Mich.: Holmes Group.

Holmes Group (1990). *Tomorrow's schools: Principles for the design of professional development schools.* East Lansing, Mich.: Holmes Group.

Houston, W. R., and Houston, E. (1992). "Needed: A new knowledge base in teacher education." In L. Kaplan (ed.), *Education and the family.* Needham Heights, Mass.: Allyn & Bacon.

Irvine, J. J. (1992). "Making teacher education culturally responsive." In M. E. Dilworth (ed.), *Diversity in teacher education: New expectations.* San Francisco: Jossey-Bass.

Jencks, C., and others (1972). *Inequality: A reassessment of the effect of family and schooling in America.* New York: HarperCollins.

Kennedy, M. M. (ed.) (1991). *Teaching academic subjects to diverse learners.* New York: Teachers College Press.

Kirst, M. W., and McLaughlin, M. W. (1990). "Rethinking policy for children: Implications for educational administration." In L. L. Cunningham and B. Mitchell (eds.), *Educational leadership and changing contexts in families, communities, and schools.* Chicago: National Society for the Study of Education.

Knapp, M. S., and Shields, P. M. (1990). "Reconceiving academic instruction for the children of poverty." *Phi Delta Kappan, 71*(10), 753–758.

Kochan, F., and Mullins, B. K. (1992). "Teacher education: Linking universities, schools, and families for the twenty-first century." In L. Kaplan (ed.), *Education and the family.* Needham Heights, Mass.: Allyn & Bacon.

Kozol, J. (1991). *Savage inequalities: Children in America's schools.* New York: Crown.

Ladson-Billings, G. (1991). "When difference means disaster: Reflections on a teacher education strategy for countering student resistance to diversity." Paper presented at the annual meeting of the American Educational Research Association, Chicago.

Lareau, A. (1989). *Home advantage: Social class and parental intervention in elementary education.* London: Falmer Press.

Lightfoot, S. L. (1978). *Worlds apart: Relationships between families and schools.* New York: Basic Books.

Lindner, B. (1987). *Family diversity and school policy.* Denver: Education Commission of the States.

Liston, D. P., and Zeichner, K. M. (1991). *Teacher education and the social conditions of schooling.* New York: Routledge & Kegan Paul.

McAdoo, H. P. (1981). *Black families.* Newbury Park, Calif.: Sage.

McDiarmid, G. W. (1990). *What to do about differences? A study of multicultural education for teacher trainees in the Los Angeles Unified School District.* East Lansing, Mich.: National Center for Research on Teacher Learning.

McDiarmid, G. W., and Price, J. (1990). *Prospective teachers' views of diverse learners: A study of the participants in the ABCD project.* East Lansing, Mich.: National Center for Research on Teacher Learning.

McLaughlin, M. W., and Shields, P. M. (1987). "Involving low-income parents in the schools: A role for policy?" *Phi Delta Kappan, 69*(2), 156–160.

Marjoribanks, K. (1979). *Families and their learning environments: An empirical analysis.* New York: Routledge & Kegan Paul.

Means, B., and Knapp, M. S. (1991). "Cognitive approaches to teaching advanced skills to educationally disadvantaged students." *Phi Delta Kappan, 73*(4), 282–289.

Melnick, S. L., Gomez, M. L., and Price, J. (1990). "Getting from here to there: Liberal arts' candidates perspectives on student diversity." Paper presented at the annual meeting of the American Educational Research Association, Boston.

National Center for Children in Poverty (1990). *Five million children: A statistical profile of our poorest young citizens.* New York: School of Public Health, Columbia University.

National Center for Education Statistics (1989). *Digest of education statistics, 1989.* Washington, D.C.: U.S. Department of Education.

National Center for Education Statistics (1991). *Digest of education statistics, 1991.* Washington, D.C.: U.S. Department of Education.

National Commission on Children (1991). *Speaking of kids: A national survey of children and parents.* Washington, D.C.: National Commission on Children.

National Commission on Excellence in Education (1983). *A nation at risk: The imperative for educational reform.* Washington, D.C.: National Commission on Excellence in Education.

National Council of Teachers of Mathematics (1991). *Professional standards for teaching mathematics.* Reston, Va: National Council of Teachers of Mathematics.

National Education Goals Panel (1991). *The national education goals report: Building a nation of learners.* Washington, D.C.: U.S. Government Printing Office.

Natriello, G., McDill, E. L., and Pallas, A. M. (1990). *Schooling disadvantaged children: Racing against catastrophe.* New York: Teachers College Press.

Nelson-Barber, S. S., and Mitchell, J. (1992). "Restructuring for diversity: Five regional portraits." In M. E. Dilworth (ed.), *Diversity in teacher education: New expectations.* San Francisco: Jossey-Bass.

Nieto, S. (1992). *Affirming diversity: The sociopolitical context of multicultural education.* White Plains, N.Y.: Longman.

Ogbu, J. U. (1987). "Variability in minority student performance: A problem in search of an explanation." *Anthropology and Education Quarterly, 18*(4), 312–334.

Ogbu, J. U. (1990). "Overcoming racial barriers to equal access." In J. I. Goodlad and P. Keating (eds.), *Access to knowledge: An agenda for our nation's schools.* New York: College Entrance Examination Board.

Paine, L. (1989). *Orientation toward diversity: What do prospective teachers bring?* (Research

Report no. 89–9). East Lansing, Mich.: National Center for Research on Teacher Education.

Palincsar, A. S., and Brown, A. L. (1984). "Reciprocal teaching of comprehension-fostering and comprehension-monitoring activities." *Cognition and Instruction, 1,* 117–175.

Pang, V. O. (1988). "Ethnic prejudice: Still alive and hurtful." *Harvard Educational Review, 58*(3), 375–379.

Payzant, T. W. (1992). "New beginnings in San Diego: Developing a strategy for interagency collaboration." *Phi Delta Kappan, 74*(2), 139–146.

Perry, T., and Fraser, J. W. (1993). *Freedom's plow: Teaching in the multicultural classroom.* New York: Routledge & Kegan Paul.

Pugach, M. C., and Leake, B. H. (1991). "The KBBT and the preparation of teachers for contemporary American society: An unmatched set?" In M. C. Pugach, H. L. Barnes, and L. C. Beckum (eds.), *Changing the practice of teacher education: The role of the knowledge base.* Washington, D.C.: American Association of Colleges for Teacher Education.

Purkey, S. C., and Smith, M. S. (1983). "Effective schools: A review." *Elementary School Journal, 83*(4), 427–452.

Schorr, L. (1988). *Within our reach: Breaking the cycle of disadvantage.* New York: Doubleday.

Shulman, L. S. (1987). "Knowledge and teaching: Foundations of the new reform." *Harvard Educational Review, 57*(1), 1–22.

Siu, S. F. (1992). *Toward an understanding of Chinese-American educational achievement: A literature review.* (Report no. 2). Boston: Center on Families, Communities, Schools, and Children's Learning.

Sleeter, C. E. (1985). "A need for research on preservice teacher education for mainstreaming and multicultural teacher education." *Journal of Educational Equity and Leadership, 5*(3), 205–215.

Smith, B. O. (1969). *Teachers for the real world.* Washington, D.C.: American Association of Colleges for Teacher Education.

Stallworth, J. T., and Williams, D. L., Jr. (1982). *Executive summary of the final report: A survey of parents regarding parent involvement in schools.* Austin, Texas: Southwest Educational Development Laboratory.

Taylor, D., and Dorsey-Gaines, C. (1988). *Growing up literate: Learning from inner-city families.* Portsmouth, N.H.: Heinemann Educational Books.

U.S. Bureau of the Census (1990). *Marital status and living arrangements, March 1989* (Current Population Reports, Series P-20, no. 445). Washington, D.C.: U.S. Government Printing Office.

Veenman, S.A.M. (1984). "Perceived problems of beginning teachers." *Review of Educational Research, 54*(2), 143–178.

Walberg, H. (1984). "Families as partners in educational productivity." *Phi Delta Kappan, 65*(6), 397–400.

Williams, D. L., Jr. (1992). "Parental involvement teacher preparation: Challenges to teacher education." In L. Kaplan (ed.), *Education and the family.* Needham Heights, Mass.: Allyn & Bacon.

Wilson, W. J. (1987). *The truly disadvantaged: The inner city, the underclass, and public policy.* Chicago: University of Chicago Press.

Young, L.S.J., and Melnick, S. L. (1988). "Forsaken lives, abandoned dreams: What will compel us to act?" *Harvard Educational Review, 58*(3), 380–394.

Zeichner, K. M. (1993). *Educating teachers for diversity.* East Lansing, Mich.: National Center for Research on Teacher Learning.

Zimpher, N. L., and Ashburn, E. A. (1992). "Countering parochialism in teacher candidates." In M. E. Dilworth (ed.), *Diversity in teacher education: New expectations.* San Francisco: Jossey-Bass.

Annotated Bibliography

Henderson, A. T., Marburger, C. L., and Ooms, T. (1986). *Beyond the bake sale: An educator's guide to working with parents.* Columbia, Md.: National Committee for Citizens in Education.
Beyond the Bake Sale provides clear and concise descriptions of ways educators can involve parents in what happens to their children in school. This book is a great starting place for thinking about various forms of parent involvement and the contributions such involvement makes to children's learning. Suggestions about effective ways to build partnerships between schools and families are included throughout the book.

Kaplan, L. (ed.) (1992). *Education and the family.* Needham Heights, Mass.: Allyn & Bacon. This volume is written by members of the Association of Teacher Educators (ATE) Family Ties Commission. This final report is a comprehensive response to the commission's charge: to study what constitutes appropriate relationships between home and school and to make recommendations to ATE regarding teacher educators' roles in preparing beginning teachers to initiate and carry out strategies for strengthening home-school relationships.

Lareau, A. (1989). *Home advantage: Social class and parental intervention in elementary education.* London: Falmer Press.
This book illuminates the relationship between family background and parent involvement in schooling in very telling and powerful ways. Focusing on a working-class and an upper-middle-class community, it helps us to understand the dramatic differences in family-school relationships in these two communities and highlights the influence of social class on opportunities that are afforded children in schools and other social institutions.

Phi Delta Kappan (1991). *72*(5).
The January 1991 issue of *Phi Delta Kappan* includes a special section on parent involvement, with Joyce Epstein as guest editor. This is an excellent resource for gaining a broad sense of the major themes, contributors, dilemmas, and references on parent involvement.

Schorr, L. (1988). *Within our reach: Breaking the cycle of disadvantage.* New York: Doubleday.
There is growing consensus about the need for comprehensive, integrated services for children who are vulnerable to a number of social and health conditions. Schorr describes several intensive health, family support, and education programs that have shown success in breaking the cycle of disadvantage. One chapter in particular, "Schools, Balance Wheel of the Social Machinery," highlights what schools can do as one of several social institutions in the broader community.

PART FOUR

PROGRAM STRUCTURES AND DESIGN

CHAPTER TWENTY

PATTERNS IN PROSPECTIVE TEACHERS: GUIDES FOR DESIGNING PRESERVICE PROGRAMS

KENNETH R. HOWEY AND NANCY L. ZIMPHER

There are understandably several ways in which a chapter discussing prospective teachers could be organized. Given the purposes of this volume, we chose to focus primarily on what we are learning about novice teachers that might inform teacher educators in improving the quality of preservice teacher education. In whatever context and at whatever level, good teachers use student data to plan their instructional activities. Thus, throughout we examine teacher education student data in terms of their implications for helping these beginners learn to teach. An overview of common sociodemographic characteristics of preservice teachers in and of itself has implications not only for teacher education programming but for recruitment strategies. Data from other studies, however, appeared more helpful in terms of their implications for redesigning programs of teacher preparation.

In this regard, the chapter begins with an overview of general characteristics of prospective teachers followed by a brief discussion of implications for teacher recruitment and what might be done programmatically to enable understandings and appreciations of multiple cultures. Section two examines various constructs and dimensions of teacher development and what these suggest for learning to teach. Screening prospective teachers in the early stages of their teacher preparation and monitoring their progress in a more rigorous manner than at present is also examined. Section three reviews studies of teacher beliefs and suggests what might have to be done to alter certain beliefs over time. In section four, the socialization and acculturation of preservice teachers is succinctly addressed, followed again by a short narrative on how positive socialization in particular might be enhanced by teacher educators during professional preparation. Section five very briefly examines the expanding expert-novice literature and what it suggests for how more expert, clinical, supervising, or consulting teachers might be helpful to novice or preservice teachers. We conclude with a discussion of what further data are needed on prospective teachers and how certain data might be captured in portfolios guided by a conceptual framework derived from several of the lines of inquiry reviewed here.

General Student Characteristics

We should underscore at the outset that this chapter is not an analysis of the quality of prospective teachers, however defined. The quality of preservice teachers and more specifically, the effectiveness of their teaching, has not been widely studied. We do examine some proxies for quality such as preservice teachers' and others' perceptions of their teacher preparation courses and program components and their general teaching abilities. However, these data, while informative, are limited as they are restricted to perceptions and aggregated across several institutions and programs. We also briefly review measures of preservice students' general aptitude and achievement, including comparisons with non–education majors. Again, while not to be dismissed, these data are nonetheless once again considerably constrained by their aggregate nature across individuals, programs, and institutions. Even when reduced to individual cases, such measures have little validity in terms of predicting eventual success as a teacher. Finally, we chose not to report follow-up studies of the quality of beginning teachers, as the host of variables that mediate teacher success over time in different school contexts render these data, at least from this perspective, less than helpful.

We cannot, of course, report what does not exist. There simply are no well conceived, large-scale studies of preservice teachers' effects on pupils they teach over time. There are no studies with multiple measures of preservice teacher performance over time into the beginning years of teaching, let alone studies of their pupils' performance or development over time.

One primary data source for describing prospective teachers generally are the ongoing Research About Teacher Education (RATE) studies sponsored by the American Association of Colleges for Teacher Education (1987, 1988, 1989, 1990). We draw on four years of RATE data: 1987 for secondary students, 1988 for foundations students, 1989 for elementary students, and 1990 for students enrolled in student teaching. The studies used a layered random sampling technique. In each of these years, five preservice students were sampled in the classrooms of up to five faculty members surveyed in each of seventy-five institutions stratified by mission. Responses over the past four years totaled 4,027 students (876 students for RATE I, 729 for RATE II, 1,141 for RATE III, and 1,281 for RATE IV).

There are few surprises in these data from the RATE studies. For example, white females continue to be overrepresented among prospective teachers, just as in the experienced teaching force. If subpopulations of teachers reflected their percentages of the U.S. population, we would expect females to be only a slight majority in the total population of preservice teachers and up to a quarter of these females to be nonwhite. Over the past several decades, gender and race composition in the experienced teacher work force have remained remarkably stable in their composition. The "typical" teacher is a white woman approaching her fortieth birthday, married and the mother of two children. She is not active politically and teaches in a suburban elementary school, staffed largely by women and administered by a male (Feistritzer, 1986). A profile of teachers in the 1980s is drawn again in the recent Darling-Hammond (1990) portrait of experienced teachers but with a slight increase in average years of experience, now over fifteen, and unfortunately with further decreases in the percentage of minority teachers.

In the RATE I, II, and IV samples, three out of four prospective teachers were female, climbing to 93 percent for RATE III when the sample was drawn from students enrolled in elementary education programs. A review of forty-four studies of teacher education students (Brookhart and Freeman, 1992) also confirms the preponderance of female teacher candidates.

These data stand in sharp contrast to the population of females enrolled in higher education generally. This percentage increased from 49.9 percent to 54.0 percent in the ten years from 1978 to 1988, as reported in 1990 by the National Center for Educational Statistics (NCES), considerably below the 75 percent of females in teaching majors.

The racial or ethnic composition of preservice students is overwhelmingly white in the RATE studies, ranging from 89 percent white in RATE I to 93 percent white in RATE III. Across the four years of data collection, there was little variability relative to African-American populations, with 5 percent reported in RATE I and IV and 4.3 percent in RATE II and 3.7 percent in RATE III. From RATE I to RATE IV, Hispanic-American students ranged from 2 to 3 percent of the samples.

The NCES (1990) examination of trends in social/ethnic enrollment in teacher education reveals that these percentages in each instance are lower than the percentage of minority groups enrolled overall in higher education. In order to determine the general participation rate in higher education, the 1990 NCES *Digest of Education* statistics compared data from the Census Bureau's current population survey with the Higher Education General Information Survey and the Integrated Postsecondary Education Data System "fall enrollment" surveys. In 1978, 31.4 percent of high school graduates indicated they were enrolled in higher education. By 1988, the percentage had risen to 37.3 percent. Thirty-one percent of white high school graduates (18 to 24 years old) were enrolled in higher education in 1978 and by 1988, 38.7 percent had enrolled. In 1978, 29.7 percent of African-American high school graduates had enrolled in higher education, but by 1988, while the total number of African-American students had increased, the percentage had dropped to 28.0 percent. Twenty-seven percent (254,000) of the

Hispanic high school graduates had enrolled in higher education in 1978 and by 1988, 30.9 percent (450,000) of the students had enrolled.

Doubtless teacher education enrollment of minorities lags behind the general student population because of the fierce competition for minorities in academic recruitment throughout higher education. Student preference is also a factor. For example, Baratz (1986) reports that about three-fourths of blacks scoring in the highest quartile on the SAT traditionally choose four majors: engineering (36 percent), health and medicine (15 percent), computer science (12 percent), and the social sciences (11 percent). Less than 1 percent of the highest quartile indicated an interest in education. Neither can we be assured that the education pipeline will deliver an increased minority teaching population, as blacks and Hispanics tend to drop out of this pipeline much faster than do Anglos (Zimpher and Yesseyan, 1987).

Location and the added costs of attending a school some distance from home are also factors. For example, most preservice teacher education students annually report that they enroll at campuses close to where they lived prior to enrolling. For example, in RATE III, three-fourths of the students were enrolled in schools a hundred miles or less from their homes. Most of the remaining sample came from less than five hundred miles away. Only 1.6 percent of these prospective teachers attended schools more than a thousand miles from their home. Astin (1992) examined all 1991 freshmen and reported that a little over 30 percent (30.7 percent) attended a college or university within fifty miles of their home; 47 percent within a hundred miles; and over 85 percent within eight hundred miles. Thus, prospective teachers represent the broader population in this regard.

Likewise, minority enrollment in different institutions is to a large degree a function of the proportions of minorities residing in that area, and in this regard, the *Almanac in Higher Education* (1991) reflects a range of minority-group enrollments from a high of 33 percent in California to a low of 2 percent in Maine.

The problem of minority enrollment is hardly limited to distance between home and university or to the degree of racial pluralism by state. In states with a higher percentage or number of minorities, other factors enter in. For example, in the RATE III study, 36 percent of the respondents were raised in small towns, 28 percent in suburban areas (compared to RATE II's response of 41 percent from suburbia), 15 percent in rural areas, 12 percent in urban areas, and only 8 percent in major metropolitan areas (over five hundred thousand). The net effect is that few teacher candidates come from urban areas of any size, where minority populations are common.

Astin also reported on the ages of all entering freshmen. About two-thirds (66.4 percent) were age eighteen and almost another quarter (23.6 percent) were age nineteen. Thus, the great majority of students still matriculate to college directly from high school. The *Almanac* (1991) reported 36 percent of those enrolled in college at ages eighteen or nineteen, 30 percent at ages twenty or twenty-one, 16 percent at twenty-two, twenty-three, or twenty-four, and the remaining 18 percent at age twenty-five and older. Based upon the RATE data, the mean age of teacher candidates would appear to exceed that portrayed for college enrollees generally. Four years ago, the average reporting age was twenty-three. For RATE II and III, the average age was closer to twenty-four and for RATE IV the average age reported was 25.7. While these teacher education candidates in the RATE studies were surveyed close to the end of their studies and typical matriculation patterns would put an eighteen-year-old freshman at age twenty-three upon completion of the program, the teacher education candidates nonetheless still appear slightly older than their counterparts in other majors. If effective teaching demands a certain level of maturity, and maturity is associated with age, these data could be construed positively. More study is needed as to what implications, if any, they suggest.

Financial Support

Given rising tuition costs and other expenses incurred in attending college, lack of finances can be a deterrent in pursuing a teaching license. The predominant source for financial support for prospective teachers comes from family resources. For RATE III, this category of support accounted for 41.4 percent of the responses (an increase of 4.3 percent from RATE II). Recall again these typically are students who proceed to college directly from high school. In rank order, sources of support beyond family resources for students in RATE III were loans, grants, employment, personal savings, scholarships and/or fellowships, and finally, work-study assistance.

In Astin's analysis (1992) of American freshmen, these students also typically draw upon multiple sources for financial aid; again, this is not surprising given the recent depressed economy and the rising costs of attending college. Over three-fourths (76.1 percent) of freshmen in 1991 received assistance from parents. Almost half of them worked (46.2 percent) and almost nine in ten reported some type of grant or scholarship (88.4 percent). Finally, almost four in ten (39.6 percent) required loan assistance. Preservice students in RATE I reported working seventeen hours a week in paid employment. In the Goodlad (1990) studies, 40 percent of the student respondents report being supported by someone else while in college and 30 percent being supported by a combination of self and others. Another two-thirds reported holding part- or full-time jobs, considerably higher than the general population.

Interest in Teaching

Prospective teachers' sense of altruism and commitment to a career have long been documented in the literature and, as Goodlad (1990) underscores, appear largely undaunted by influential others: "Most had experienced strong negative pressure regarding their career choice from parents, peers, former teachers, current professors, and even current supervisors of student teaching—sometimes from all of these" (p. 201).

While serious concerns can be raised about the apparent distance of many prospective teachers from social issues, there is little doubt that a great many of those who choose teaching do so because they genuinely care about others and wish to serve society.

Regardless of the rising costs of attending college and pressures to pursue a well-paying vocation or profession, the great majority of students in RATE III also indicate that they are "very positive" (74 percent) or "positive" (20 percent) about teaching as a career, a perception that has remained consistent over four years of RATE data collection. Ninety-three percent of the RATE III respondents intend to teach after graduation; of the remaining 7 percent, a fourth intend to go to graduate school, and another 20 percent intend to work in an education-related field.

There has been much concern about the retention of prospective candidates in teaching careers. How well do these positive feelings about teaching hold up once these preservice teachers take on a teaching assignment? Recent data suggest that they are sustained. In the Metropolitan Life survey of first-year teachers (1991b), nine in ten teachers anticipated that teaching would be a long-term career choice for them before they began their first teaching job. After this same sample's first year was completed, only a slightly lower percentage (85 percent) still held to the long-term potential of a teaching career. Another Metropolitan Life survey (1991a) sampled a thousand teachers in public schools, kindergarten through grade 12. When asked if they would leave the teaching profession to go into some different occupation, only 4 percent of teachers with less than five years of experience responded "very likely."

This is not to say that there are not serious concerns in terms of recruitment and retention. When asked if they thought a single teacher could live on today's teaching salary, only three-fourths of the respondents in RATE III thought it was adequate and almost nine in 10 (89 percent) thought that current salaries were inadequate to support a family. Similarly, Goodlad (1990) found that about half of the teacher candidates he interviewed saw teaching as being capable of supporting an individual, but only 10 percent saw this career choice as capable of providing the sole or even main support for a family.

Satisfaction with Preparation

If these prospective teachers appear satisfied generally with their choice of a profession—albeit understandably concerned about finances—it may well be related to their general satisfaction with their teacher preparation programs. The RATE III study is again typical in this regard. Slightly more than 80 percent (80.9 percent) of the students rated their preservice programs as good or excellent with only a very small percentage seeing their programs as below average.

Recall, however, these prospective teachers are by no means fully apprised of the rigors of teaching and they tend to view college in a general sense as a good time in their lives. In this regard, satisfaction levels for all college students appear generally high, particularly with regard to courses in their majors (85 percent satisfied to very satisfied), with two-thirds of those surveyed reporting satisfaction with opportunities to work with faculty, the quality of their instruction, and with campus life generally (Astin, Korn, and Green, 1987).

Teacher education students' responses are very similar in terms of affirmation of the degree of rigor in their course experiences, the extent of their investment required to succeed in education courses, and their satisfaction with education faculty instruction and faculty availability out of class. In RATE II, students were asked about teacher education faculty availability and 80 percent indicated that they were often or nearly always available to meet with them.

Student Quality

Questions raised about the quality of prospective teachers are not to be dismissed. Prospective teachers should be intellectually capable and morally responsible persons who have demonstrated consistent records of academic achievement as prerequisites for admission to a program of teacher preparation. Vance and Schlechty (1982), Lanier and Little (1986), Feistritzer (1986), and the Southern Regional Education Board (Galambos, Cornett, and Spitler, 1985) are among many who have raised legitimate concerns about test scores and other indices of the academic quality and intellectual ability of our prospective teachers. Our position is that we need nonetheless to be more thoughtful in terms of how we define and measure quality, especially in terms of intellectual abilities and personal qualities that are predictive not only of success in academic preparation but also in terms of pedagogical ability and broader teacher responsibilities. We should also note that characterizations of teacher education students derived from analyses of SAT scores raise concerns but also call for caution. These data do not represent actual teacher education students in many instances but rather those who indicated this interest. Neither are they predictive of success in teaching. Multiple, repeated measures of teacher quality or effectiveness are needed. This should begin with rigorous selection criteria and, more fundamentally, ongoing screening procedures, as we discuss later.

There have been modest efforts in this regard but only in terms of academic achievement. Fisher and Feldman (1985), for example, examined multiple measures of aptitude and achievement for teacher education students versus other majors. They examined standardized test scores, high school percentile rank, cumulative GPA and academic achievement in the major, common general studies courses and selected upper versus lower division courses. In another study conducted by the Southern Regional Education Board in 1985, an analysis of prospective teachers in a variety of arts and sciences courses was pursued. The former study suggests a more favorable portrait of prospective teachers and the latter a less flattering view. Obviously, there are differences across programs within institutions, among institutions, and likely even among regions in the country that need to be taken into account when considering such data. Nonetheless, a more positive picture does appear to be evolving in terms of the abilities of both those entering and those exiting programs of teacher preparation. Data from the RATE studies over time provides this entry profile of teacher education students:

> A parallel question asked of the faculty each year is how they would rate the quality of students in the particular teacher education program with which they are most closely affiliated. As is the situation in terms of ratings of program quality, ratings of student quality have also been consistently high and stable. These perceptual data are buttressed with other indices of quality that are also stable over time. These data indicate that these students were typically in the upper third of their high school rank and have maintained a little better than a B average in both their general studies and teacher education courses. Likewise, RATE data indicate that scores on the SAT in those institutions maintaining these data tend to fall close to 900 (898) or very close to the national average of 906. Thus, we should not be surprised that once again the majority of faculty (52.6 percent) rate the quality of their students very highly, 6 or 7 on a 7-point scale, and about another third as above average [Howey, 1993, p. 9].

Securro (1992, p. 131) also calls attention to recent exit studies:

> New evidence is accumulating which indicates that teacher education majors perform as well as or better than their non–teacher education peers when exit performance measures are the criterion. Nelli (1984) compared mean GPA differences between teacher education and non–teacher education graduates and found no significant differences. Fisher and Feldman (1985) studied several thousand graduates from Illinois State University during a 5-year period and found no significant differences in mean GPA between teacher education and non–teacher education graduates. Matczynski, Siler, McLaughlin, and Smith (1988) examined the differences in performance of secondary teacher education majors and non–teacher education majors in selected arts and science courses and found no difference in GPA.

Regardless of the evolving positive profile of preservice teachers, based upon our involvement over the past several years with the RATE studies, we also know that there is considerable variability in the quality of preservice students on standardized measures of aptitude and academic achievement.[1] This surely is in part the function of so many institutions preparing teachers (over twelve hundred).

This condition makes access to some programs available for too many who should not be admitted as a teacher candidate.

Teachers Disposed and Able to Teach All Youngsters

Even if one consistently found academically able students across all programs of preservice teacher education, a major concern still exists. The common sociodemographic profile of the preservice students in the RATE studies suggest a portrait of the future teaching pool as white and female, from a rural, small town, or suburban community. These are prospective teachers who went to a college not because of its reputation but for its proximity to home and because it was accessible and affordable. The field studies undertaken by Howey and Zimpher (1989) indicate that they tend to embrace a conservative view of schooling and have limited firsthand awareness of or engagement in many of our major social issues.

They are an essentially monolingual population. Most of them would like to stay close to their hometown to teach (79 percent). More than half (57 percent) of the RATE III sample, for example, indicated that they would like to teach in suburbia (42 percent for RATE II and 54 percent for RATE I). Another one-fourth would like to teach in rural areas. But only 15 percent reported a desire to teach in urban areas (up from 9 percent from RATE II but the same as for RATE I). This is understandable since across all schools or colleges of education, prospective teachers and their professors raise concerns about their abilities to teach in urban settings, despite their view that they are generally ready to teach. When RATE VI examined students in teacher education programs in urban settings, however, a more positive picture emerged:

> Here we have found that about a third or more of both student and faculty respondents in the past indicated that students are not adequately prepared to teach in such settings with about another third reporting but adequate or moderate preparation, and finally, only about a third reporting good or very good preparation. This year we find, by taking the top three points on the seven point scale, that almost two-thirds, or (62.8 percent) of the faculty respondents indicate that their teacher education graduates are in fact prepared to teach well in an urban setting. The student responses are even higher with over three-fourths of the students reporting that they are more than adequately prepared to teach in an urban setting. Hence we have a major deviation from prior surveys in that it appears that more faculty members and students who pursue their teacher education in institutions in urban settings believe that they are able to teach well in these settings [Howey, 1993, p. 13].

These data would appear to support the argument made earlier for recruiting more prospective teachers both from and to urban settings.

Other data from the RATE studies suggest problems. When prospective teachers are asked what types of educational settings they would seek teaching positions in and the kind of school organization and the socioeconomic and ability level of pupils they would prefer, they consistently respond that they prefer to teach in "traditional" classroom settings with middle-income children of average ability.

In summary, and of major concern, the considerable majority of prospective teachers across all institutions preparing teachers do not believe that they are very well prepared to teach in urban, multicultural settings, nor are they disposed to do so. Thus, in those schools where the needs for good teachers are often the greatest and opportunities abound, the desire to teach is least for many of our prospective teachers.

Implications

There are several implications that can be drawn from the general profile of our prospective teachers, but two seem paramount to us: (1) how can we attract more underrepresented populations into the teaching force, and (2) how can we overcome the parochial perspectives or desire to teach those with similar backgrounds, which characterize so many future teachers? In terms of the first matter, more multifaceted recruitment programs with specific responsibilities for individual faculty are in order. There is a burgeoning literature on the variety of means designed to attract minorities into teaching that suggests that longer-range strategies are needed. An example of this is the numerous teaching high schools or schools within a school where, beginning in the freshman year in high school, students with a potential interest in teaching can enroll in special programs. The emphasis is on attracting minority students. Herein they can be assigned to a teacher mentor, engage in some coursework to inform them more fully about education and teaching, participate in a future teachers club, engage in cross-age tutoring and other teaching-related activities, and come into contact with student teachers and professors from a cooperating university. Such an arrangement speaks to this longer-range view. Those who do well in these programs can be guaranteed support for college, and again, if they do well, a teaching position upon completion of their preservice preparation. We obviously need to be bolder in efforts to attract diversity as well as quality within our future teaching force.

It is also equally obvious that we need to counter some of the attitudes and values of not only preservice students but teacher education faculty. As Garcia (1991) reminds us, middle-class Americans provide standards and serve as the hub for making comparisons. He calls for viewing all cultures as coexistent, abandoning paradigms that speak of cultures as "underdeveloped," "overdeveloped," and "primitive," and discarding educational labels that describe nonwhite, nonmiddle-class students as "culturally deprived," "disadvantaged," or "culturally deficient." Transcending the narrow confines of our culture is not easy and even when accomplished it is not enough to address many of the very troubling conditions in our society. It is critical, however, that efforts to transcend our culture be undertaken in a more strenuous and structured manner in our programs of teacher education than typically done at present.

In summary, we need not only to attract greater diversity in our future teachers, but we also need to confront in a much more substantive manner existing beliefs about class and culture for all prospective teachers whatever their race or ethnicity. We will shortly address some of the naïve beliefs preservice students bring with them to their programs, perhaps none more naïve than their assumptions about class and culture.

Preservice Teacher Traits and Developmental Patterns

The RATE studies (American Association of Colleges for Teacher Education, 1990) reveal, not surprisingly, that standards for admissions for programs of teacher education have risen over the past decade. This is no surprise given the recommendations of numerous state legislators and other "blue ribbon" committees advocating largely expeditious means to the improvement of teacher education. Higher cumulative grade point averages and test scores than previously needed for admission are reported by many institutions. Certainly no one would argue with a desire to select intelligent teachers who have achieved academic success in a vocation where intelligence and discipline should be hallmark characteristics. Nevertheless, these measures should be put into perspective. Evertson, Hawley, and Zlotnik (1984), for example, concluded that various standardized measures of aptitude and common measures of performance employed during and at the end of programs of teacher education in the studies they reviewed were not consistently related to different measures of effective teacher performance. While underscoring the limitations of several of the studies reviewed, they found mixed results when different measures of aptitude and achievement were correlated with indices of teacher success, namely perceptions of effective teaching. For example, teacher on-the-job performance as assessed either by principals or by trained observers and GPA tended to show no relationship or a negative relationship as often as a small positive association. In a classic but somewhat dated example, Eash and Rasher (1977) reported that student teachers with higher grade point averages were rated more highly by their pupils than were student teachers who had lower grade point averages. Principals, on the other hand, ranked these student teachers with the higher grades superior on only two of twenty-seven items related to teaching effectiveness. In one of the few studies examining the relationship between the grades of education majors and the cognitive attainment of the pupils they taught, Denton and Smith (1984) found no statistically significant relationship. Studies of the relationship between teaching success and preservice students' performance on the present National Teacher Examination are also mixed, as would be expected since this test does not claim to have validity in predicting effective teaching however teaching effectiveness might be defined.

Beyond Admissions to Continuing Screening of Preservice Teachers

As has been noted, common criteria employed for candidate selection into programs of teacher preparation have limited predictive validity in terms of eventual teaching success. Beyond this, little further screening of candidates is conducted in any systematic manner once they are admitted to a program. Howey and Strom (1987) drew upon the literature concerned with cognitive development of adults to suggest a screening procedure. They portrayed screening as an ongoing process that is educative and embedded in the curriculum of the preservice program. It consists of a series of activities designed to assess specific qualities related to the highly moral and interpersonal role of teachers. These qualities can be feasibly measured to a reasonable degree. They are also qualities that often cannot be easily acquired in the life space of a preservice program. Feedback about these qualities is developed over time into a multidimensional profile that can be used in counseling prospective teachers and helping them better understand themselves, especially relative to the roles and functions of a teacher.

Howey and Strom assert, first, that there are human traits and psychological characteristics that are predictive of successful teaching and second, that these can be measured in multiple ways over time. They argue that good teachers, as good persons, should possess the qualities of being adaptable, questioning, critical, inventive, self-renewing, and oriented to moral principles. In teaching, such persons would evidence such qualities by considering different and conflicting perspectives in thinking and decision making; organizing and using ideas in a creative manner in problem solving; understanding and using others' perspectives in communication; seeking a beliefs-practice congruity; understanding and accommodating the needs of diverse groups; and evaluating the impact of their actions on other people. They illustrate ways that these patterns of behavior can be measured in ongoing educative activities.

Not wishing to detract from indices of academic ability and general achievement, they argue rather for a more robust consideration of what is valued in a teacher as follows:

1. When qualities such as those just mentioned . . . are made explicit, they provide a clearer and loftier vision of the type of teacher we consider desirable. These particular qualities suggest a noble and select vocation as opposed to the pedestrian, technist conception of teaching that is so prevalent in much of the literature and discussions about teachers today.
2. The vision we have of a teacher is critical for a number of reasons. Our conception of a teacher tends to be a self-fulfilling prophecy in terms of: (a) the goals toward which our teacher preparation activities are oriented, (b)

the roles assumed and behaviors modeled by teachers, and (c) the images of teaching which the public accepts and is willing to support.

3. We are largely unclear about the extent to which persons who enter teacher preparation programs possess these qualities. We believe, however, that they are important, operationally definable, and thus, to an extent measurable.

4. The assessment of selected qualities, especially across institutions over time, would allow systematic study of their relationship to measures of teaching effectiveness. The question of whether these qualities can/should be used in selection or can/should be developed within the context of teacher preparation can then be addressed [Howey and Strom, 1987, p. 9].

Support for a broader assessment or screening effort was also recently advocated by McGaghie (1991), who, in a parallel vein, stated that no professional group in the United States today is pleased, let alone sanguine, about methods used to certify or license new candidates. He identifies several reasons for this widespread satisfaction but two of these seem especially appropriate in terms of the above arguments: "1. Professional competence evaluation typically covers a narrow range of practice situations. By contrast, what professionals in many walks of life actually do is very complicated, not only involving technical skill but also requiring judgment, tact, physical endurance, and tenacity. 2. Professional competence evaluation is biased toward assessment of acquired knowledge. This is due to the established tradition of academic achievement testing (Levine, 1976), convenience, and to the sophisticated psychometric technology that underlies knowledge assessment" (McGaghie, 1991, p. 4).

We acknowledge that such procedures are fraught with methodological and ethical issues and fly in the face of powerful institutional norms and in this regard Goodlad (1990) found little evidence of such practices in his studies of programs of teacher preparation relative to procedures and criteria for initial selection and continued screening. Regardless of the apparent problems attached to screening personal qualities viewed as enabling of teaching, the authors of this chapter reassert the need for more attention to specific, desired human qualities in a teacher, which can be used to guide program development as well as screening procedures. Arnstine (1990) speaks to this concern as follows:

Once we decide that certain educational aims are worth pursuing, we have to make plans for achieving them. There are difficulties in achieving educational aims that are dispositional, however, because dispositions are not acquired in the same way one can acquire a new coat, a particular skill, or a British accent. We may point to particular behaviors as evidence of the dispositions we ascribe, but those behaviors are simply evidence, not the disposition itself. We cannot teach the behaviors that exemplify a disposition in the hopes that the disposition will follow, any more than we can teach a child how to use a ruler and then conclude that he is now disposed to measure carefully. Dispositions are cultivated rather than simply conveyed or transmitted, and a number of conditions in the learner's situation need to be attended to for their cultivation [p. 234].

Promoting Dimensions of Cognitive Development

We have suggested that aspects of mature psychological development could serve as a departure point for the counseling and screening of prospective teachers, especially given the critical human nature of teaching. What are elements of psychological development? Oja and Smulyan (1989) examined common elements in adult development constructs as put forth by such scholars as Piaget (1961), Loevinger (1966), Kohlberg (1969), Perry (1969), and Hunt (1971) with an emphasis on Loevinger's work as follows:

> The essence of development is the striving to master, to integrate, to make sense of one's experience. Development takes place in a sequence of steps along a continuum of increasing differentiation and complexity. There is a unitary nature to this scheme in describing the world and within which one perceives the world. . . . The characteristics of the successive stages of development are described in terms of one's impulse control, interpersonal style, conscious preoccupations, and cognitive style. These stages can be compared with levels of moral judgment. At the adult preconventional level are the Impulsive and Self-Protective ego stages. At the conventional levels are the Conformist, Self-Aware, and Conscientious stages. At the post-conventional levels are the Individualistic, Autonomous, and Integrated Ego stages [Oja and Smulyan, 1989, p. 127].

Common to different conceptions of human development are discernible prevailing stages or patterns of behavior that move from a more concrete, dualistic, and dogmatic processing of one's experience to more abstract, relativistic, and inquiring orientations.

Gender-related aspects of development are also being explored. Belenky, Clinchy, Goldberger, and Tarule (1986), for example, examined procedures that college-age women use in making meaning. In developing a construct of procedural knowledge, they identified two epistemological orientations, which they refer to as separate and connected knowing. They provide the following examples of these two types of knowing by comparing two women in their study: Naomi, who represents male perspectives, as identified in earlier research, and Patti, who is more representative of the women in their sample.

> Naomi, like Perry's prototypical male undergraduate at this position, asks herself, "What standards are being used to evaluate my analysis of this poem? What techniques can I use to analyze it?" As with the small boys Piaget

(1965) observed playing marbles on the sidewalks of Geneva fifty years ago, the orientation is toward impersonal rules. Borrowing a term from Gilligan (1982), we call this epistemological orientation separate knowing. Women at the same position who think more as Patti does ask instead, "What is the poet trying to say to me?" The orientation, as with the little girls Piaget observed playing hopscotch, is toward relationship. We call this epistemological orientation connected knowing [Belenky, Clinchy, Goldberger, and Tarule, 1986 p. 101].

Belenky and her colleagues suggest that this evolving construct of connected knowing while not gender specific appears gender-related. They have not observed and interviewed men in making their clinical assessments. Thus, further research is surely in order. Nonetheless, given these tentative findings and given the major gender imbalance among teachers in elementary schools, further investigation into these particular developmental patterns would be instructive, especially in terms of informing classroom interactions.

A number of recent studies have examined specific dimensions of cognitive development, focusing on prospective teachers specifically. In one study, for example, Sunal and Sunal (1985) focused on senior students majoring in early and middle childhood education and their ability to plan and teach a science unit. Their cognitive development was analyzed using the Classroom Test of Formal Reasoning (CTFR), an instrument derived from Piaget's stages of development. In their analyses of the CTFR, they found that 11 percent of these students were operating at a concrete operational level, another 56 percent at the transitional level, and only one third or 33 percent at a formal level of operations. When they looked at the relationship of these stages to a measure of teacher performance, Comparing Teacher Performance in microteaching sessions, they found a positive statistical correlation between teaching ability and the ability to function at a formal level as measured by the CTFR.

Similarly, Reyes (1987) examined the cognitive development of approximately one hundred elementary and secondary education majors using another instrument based on Piaget's stages, the Inventory of Piaget's Developmental Tasks. These students were evaluated in terms of their abilities to perform the tasks of classification, conservation, proportional reasoning, image, and relations. While the investigator did not find any differences between the two majors, he did find that fewer than half of either group demonstrated mastery of conservation, classification, and proportional reasoning.

Winitzky (1992) employed an "ordered-tree" technique wherein twenty items were grouped by fifteen elementary preservice teachers into various configurations and then in turn were analyzed. She also administered a taxonomy of reflective thinking and found a statistical relationship in a positive direction between students' ability to structure knowledge in complex ways and their ability to reflect. The major implication of the study is that once again the majority of these beginning teachers had low cognitive scores in terms of their abilities on the ordered-tree technique.

Surely further research is needed both in terms of validating distinctive qualitative patterns and dimensions of cognitive ability and conceptual development, and improving the means to assess performance against these. Nonetheless, it is clear that cognitive development is a dynamic and not a static concept with numerous independent studies suggesting a progression from more dogmatic and dualistic thinking to more abstract, relativistic, and principled thinking. These studies also suggest sharp differences among the adult population. It seems very clear that arrested cognitive development in prospective teachers would considerably constrain their more general pedagogical development.

Thus, two fundamental questions for teacher educators include, how can further insights into the cognitive developmental patterns of prospective teachers be gained and how can desired development be promoted? Among the possibilities in responding to these questions is to engage prospective teachers with various developmental constructs, adult as well as adolescent and child, early on in programs of preservice preparation. A sustaining focus on developmental patterns could be a part of the conceptual framework and the core studies guiding a program of teacher preparation. To ensure that attention to developmental patterns is manifested in a continuing way throughout the program, a profile of each preservice student could be developed with an emphasis on examining changes in these profiles over time. The screening procedure we have advocated could incorporate understandings of the cognitive development of adults as well as youngsters.

Aspects of such a strategy have been undertaken. Numerous studies, for example, have employed journals to examine prospective teachers' cognitive development and in some instances to plan activities designed to promote progression to higher stages (Packard, 1992). Sprinthall and Thies-Sprinthall (1983) experimented first with program components designed to enable cognitive development and have continued their work by guiding interactions between consulting and mentor teachers and beginning teachers, with feedback tied to developmental constructs. They draw heavily from the literature on cognitive development and incorporate formal study of this literature into their programs of study. Beyond that, they place students in situations to challenge existing perspectives and patterns of coming to know.

General Pedagogical Development

There have, of course, been other efforts to document patterns of general pedagogical development in preservice teachers and especially student teachers. The most widely cited of these is the developmental sequence identified initially by Fuller and Bown (1975). They identified a sequence of concerns that characterized preservice teachers at various stages of their preparation. Preservice or novice teachers tend understandably to focus first on themselves. Ultimately, they acquire the ability to look more fully at the teaching situation and finally are able to focus more fully on pupils and their behaviors and what contributes to these behaviors. Obviously, there are many exceptions to such a progression of patterned behavior. This developmental pattern, however, is also supported by various studies of differences between "expert teachers and novice teachers" that illustrate the qualitative differences in understanding and addressing student behavior between expert and novice teachers (Berliner, 1987).

There are other widely cited developmental constructs. Lacey (1977), for example, studied the socialization of beginning teachers over a five-year period in England and delineated a sequence of developmental stages. They begin with what he characterized as honeymoon, that is a period of almost euphoria that came from moving from student to teacher, to a period of elaborate preparation to compensate for the myriad problems novice teachers encountered in the classroom. Eventually, however, crisis or feelings of failure will occur. In most cases, teachers adopt and adapt strategies to succeed in the classroom. In this latter regard, Lacey's theoretical work identified three patterns. First, there were students who accommodated the beliefs and values of their cooperating teachers while maintaining their own beliefs and values about teaching. A second pattern was that of students who basically internalized the norms and expectations of their supervisors. A third pattern included student teachers who were able to bring about a change in their own situation as well as the beliefs and values of others.

Berliner (1988) has posited a taxonomy of skill learning based on his studies of expert and novice teachers. He identified five stages of skill development in the process of acquiring expertise in pedagogy. His five stages include novice, advanced beginner, competent teacher, proficient teacher, and expert teacher. Employing Berliner's definition of these five stages, the RATE studies (American Association of Colleges for Teacher Education, 1989) examined the perceptions of preservice students in the student teaching phase of their programs relative to these stages. The considerable majority of these preservice teachers (69 percent) assessed their developmental stage as advanced beginners or at the second level of Berliner's hierarchical construct. This particular stage has teachers moving from having learned a set of context or situation prerules to a stage where they have had experience with youngsters and are now beginning to acquire episodic or event-structured knowledge. Thus, as context begins to inform their behavior, they are able to develop strategic knowledge. Berliner notes, however, that the advanced beginner often has no real sense of discriminating among competing demands in a situation.

Buchmann's research (1987) at the National Center for Learning to Teach similarly suggests a limited pattern of general pedagogical development for many preservice or novice teachers. She argues that most college teaching, whether in general studies or in the teacher education component, does little to offset relatively naïve notions of teaching. She contends it rather extends the apprenticeship of "studenting," and the anticipatory socialization of "teaching as telling" to thirteen thousand hours. She goes on to argue that if the induction of teachers to the profession happens in most ordinary schools, it will close a circle that begins and ends with a folkways of teaching orientation. She describes the folkways of teaching as "teaching as usual," teaching that is learned in practice, in the half-conscious ways in which people go about their everyday lives, and in which they carry themselves fittingly. She argues that what demarcates teaching expertise from folkways of teaching, local mores, and private views is that teaching expertise calls for judgments of appropriateness, testing of consequences, and considerations of ends and not just means in public forums. She concludes her penetrating analysis about the development of teachers—or rather lack thereof—with the sobering conclusion that expertise is as inaccessible to the majority of American teachers as is the opportunity to become rich or to climb up the social ladder. She puts forth a provocative tadpole theory to account for most teachers' operating knowledge of teaching and she quotes Tawny (1964, cited in Buchmann, 1987) as follows to make the point graphically: "The more fortunate of the species will shed their tails, distend their mouths and stomachs, hop nimbly on to dry land, and croak addresses to their former friends on the virtues by means of which tadpoles of character and capacity can rise to be frogs" (p. 105).

She suggests that most teachers live and die as tadpoles, nothing more, and her observations are supported not only by many beginning teachers' perceived abilities of where they are but more fundamentally by the general lack of understanding of how they might get beyond this.

This brief overview of inquiries into the developmental patterns of teachers underscores three salient points: first, good teaching remains more complex than the understanding many teachers have of it; second, learning to teach is in turn more complex than many of those who would educate teachers perceive it to be; and third, there appear to be cognitive stages or developmental patterns that characterize many prospective teachers and in many instances constrain their learning to teach, let alone their ability to teach others.

Developmental Patterns: Implications for Learning to Teach on Campus

We believe that a clarion call is in order with concerted attention to the nature of conditions for enabling more complex teaching on campus as well as in elementary and secondary schools. The seeds for the disposition to continually inquire into one's instructional practice and to support that practice with principled reasoning and with decisions that are data-based and theoretically grounded need to be nurtured in pedagogical laboratories, teaching clinics, and through the utilization of instructional cases in our campus settings. Prospective teachers should, for example, critically examine teaching-learning episodes employing the lens of the linguist, the cultural anthropologist, the social-psychologist, and the sociologist as well as the perspectives of scholars of teaching and outstanding experienced teachers. They should encounter multiple ways of thinking about teaching and learning in order to move beyond a tadpole perspective of learning to teach to a highly intellectual and professional discourse about the essence of what they do.

They should view dozens of hours of video representing both principles that guide the teaching profession and the pervasive problems teachers will encounter. They should be able to do this in a context in which complex phenomena can be represented from multiple perspectives, through several media, and at a time and in a manner conducive to their learning. At present, critical examination of instructional practice is, as Buchmann (1990) suggests, neither fostered well in the lecture hall nor the teacher's workplace. It could well be that until we can send larger numbers of teachers into the workplace better disposed toward critical examination of their practice, the character and culture of teaching and schooling will not change.

In summary, what we need are pedagogical laboratories and teaching and diagnostic clinics on campuses as well as in K–12 schools.

Preservice Teacher Beliefs

Learning to teach also calls for the prospective teacher to engage in a variety of structured activities in which warrants and evidence for beliefs and decisions about teaching and learning, teachers and learners, have to pass public inspection. A fundamental principle to guide both learning and learning to teach is to begin where one is. Studies supported by the former National Center for Research on Teacher Education, and the now aptly named National Center For Research on Learning to Teach (NCRLT) sponsored by the U.S. Department of Education, Office of Educational Research and Improvement, have focused attention on the knowledge and beliefs that novice or prospective teachers bring to their programs of preservice teacher education. They begin where the beginner is.

Likewise, Calderhead's scholarly activities (1991) over the years have focused on the kinds of knowledges and beliefs that prospective teachers bring with them and a consideration of how those knowledges and beliefs interact with the teacher education curriculum. Among other conclusions that Calderhead has reached, reinforced in numerous other studies, is that student teachers' or prospective teachers' knowledge of pedagogy is not necessarily well adapted to what is actually involved in good teaching. While there are surely qualitative differences in how prospective teachers conceptualize learning to teach, they tend to embrace relatively naïve and uncomplicated beliefs. The many years of studenting have led these teachers to think of teaching as telling and showing and of learning as memorizing and as largely a passive activity. Some, for example, believe that they will be told how to teach, others believe that on-the-job experience is the best teacher. There are still others who believe that nothing special needs to be learned in order to teach, that knowledge of content is basically sufficient. Many others believe they can learn largely by observing exemplary teachers. In other instances, the belief is even more tenuous based on a rather naïve view of liking youngsters and therefore being able to help them as a teacher.

Buchmann and Schwille, researchers at the NCRLT, contend that the great majority of prospective teachers value firsthand experience more highly than intellectual discourse, especially structured intellectual discourse, which demands the kind of pedagogical reasoning that defends and supports teacher decisions in conversations with peers and/or more experienced teachers and professors. These prospective teachers, they contend, are very susceptible to the strong socializing influences of more experienced teachers and prevalent policies and practices in the schools. Buchmann and Schwille (1983) speak to why firsthand experience is so powerful for many preservice teachers: "Firsthand experience is trusted implicitly as both the means and content of education. It is 'down to earth,' personal, sensory, and practical. Ideas encountered in books are pale in contrast. Compared with life as a school of hard knocks, the school of hard books seems soft and ineffective. Immersion in the 'real world' teaches people to think and act rightly. Those who want students to know the world of work firsthand often do not challenge limits set by occupations as they presently are" (p. 31).

The importance of focusing on teacher beliefs about learning (and learning to teach) is a particularly important issue in this country, for in contrast to many other countries, the United States has no national curriculum. Even though statewide and district textbook adoptions are common, and most districts provide relatively comprehensive curriculum guides for various subjects, teachers behind the closed door of the classroom have considerable latitude and freedom to teach in the manner they deem most appropriate and efficacious.

Others, such as Britzman (1986), argue that these pedagogical beliefs really are just the tip of the iceberg, that they in fact represent a more deep-seated epistemological orientation that is often characterized by reliance on external sources of knowledge. Given findings from the studies of the cognitive and psychological development of novice teachers and college-age students briefly reviewed earlier, there surely are data that support this contention.

Whatever, teams of scholars at the NCRLT, including the research team of Wilcox, Lanier, Schram, and Lappan (1992), have initiated a program of research examining the knowledge and beliefs of prospective teachers. They instituted the Elementary Mathematics Study in the Academic Learning Teacher Preparation Strand at Michigan State University. The major purpose of their studies was to demonstrate the feasibility of developing a more conceptual level of knowledge about mathematics and the teaching and learning of mathematics in prospective elementary teachers than such teachers typically have.

The research team examined the various factors that influenced these prospective teachers' choices about what to teach and how to teach in their mathematics classes, including their view of knowledge—that is, what it means to know and how one comes to know, and their knowledge of mathematics and beliefs about what should constitute elementary mathematics curriculum and effective teaching of mathematics.

In reflecting upon their study, the research team concluded that disciplinary study is essential to develop a set of intellectual tools and a disposition to engage in mathematical inquiry by prospective teachers. They question, however, whether disciplinary study alone will be sufficient to overcome preservice teachers' deeply held beliefs about mathematics and how it should be taught. They conclude that modeling new practices and nontraditional conceptions of mathematical pedagogy, however difficult this is, might be sufficient to develop in beginning teachers the beliefs that teaching is something other than telling and more than a matter of technical competence.

In a related study at the NCRLT, another research team comprised of Bird, Anderson, Sullivan, and Swindler (1992), examined how one member of the team of teacher educators, Tom Bird, attempted to challenge prospective teachers' beliefs about teaching and learning in an introductory course specifically designed for that purpose. Among other strategies that Bird incorporated into this class was cooperative learning, an attempt to enable students' capacities collectively to connect familiar and unfamiliar ideas. The research team comments on this approach: "However, once the instructor had delegated work to small groups, the students had considerable latitude to shape the tasks according to their own conceptions and needs, and his ability to intervene was correspondingly limited. While there were many lively conversations in groups and group members did aid each other in understanding the texts, the students tended to smooth over differences of opinion and the lines of inquiry those differences might open up. They appeared to want agreement, confirmation, and closure, and in relatively short order" (p. 15).

They did not conclude that Bird failed to influence preservice students' beliefs about teaching and learning and learning to teach. Rather they underscored the difficulties involved in this endeavor. They speak to the continuing tension between establishing oneself as a knowledgeable and helpful teacher on the one hand and encouraging students to think for themselves and take risks on the other (recall again the developmental patterns of many beginning teachers); between cultivating familiar ideas and promoting unfamiliar ones; and finally, between keeping the students comfortable with and responsive to novel demands while prompting them to test their thinking and reconsider their ideas.

Ball (1989), another researcher at NCRLT, provides her prospective teachers a unique opportunity of working in two learning communities: the methods class and the public school third-grade mathematics class in which she teaches daily and in which her prospective teachers participate intermittently throughout the term.

Despite this unique experience of having a group of prospective teachers in her college classroom as well as in her elementary classroom, Ball is concerned about the time in which to learn to teach mathematics conceptually:

Ten weeks, four hours a week, is a minuscule, almost trivial, amount of time to contemplate the agenda I have set. The risk is that the tension between unsettling assumptions and generating future growth will be left unbalanced and that the continuity will be therefore interrupted. Prospective teachers may come away even less confident than they were before, more worried that they will not be able to teach mathematics so that kids can understand. They may see classrooms and children as daunting, mathematics as a vast sea of things they really do not understand. Thus unsettled, the most logical course of action would be to return to the safety of the old assumptions and habits with which they are comfortable and familiar.

At the end of the term there is evidence that the experience has had an impact on the prospective teachers' ideas, ways of seeing, and ways of acting. The extent to which this impact in fact can help to redirect the continuity of their learning to teach mathematics is an empirical question, well worth asking. But, skeptical in any case of the adequacy of a 10-week course, I think it equally worth pursuing how one might extend its duration and form in ways that would make it more likely that we could prepare teachers to learn from their own practice [Ball, 1989, pp. 12–13].

So one finds Ball and her other colleagues at NCRLT acknowledging that some progress has been made in altering obdurate beliefs about teaching and learning; however, this progress has not been made easily.

Many other scholars, not associated with the NCRLT, have also engaged in relatively intensive efforts to alter the beliefs of their prospective teachers. For example, Powell (1991) worked with sixteen career-change preservice teachers and focused on their beliefs and thinking. He reported success in moving these students from atheoretical schemata when thinking about schools and students to more theoretical schemata and eventually to an integrated schemata combining theoretical knowledge with students' practical knowledge of the school context. Based upon his study, the general age and maturity of preservice teachers and the extent to which the construct of schemata is addressed explicitly could be factors in confronting novices' beliefs about teaching and learning, and in this instance, learners.

Casey (1988) employed curriculum-based measures to test elementary-level prospective special education teachers' students' a priori hypotheses about the effectiveness of different teaching strategies. This investigator reported that teachers over time became less dogmatic in their beliefs and more accepting of the premise that many teaching strategies are working hypotheses to be tested.

Implications for Examining Teacher Beliefs

Obviously, the nature and scope of this chapter preempts reviewing in any depth the numerous studies of beginning teachers' knowledge and beliefs and their implications for learning to teach and teacher education programming. A major point we wish to underscore again, and as illustrated by the studies just referenced, is that many preservice teachers' beliefs about teaching and learning underestimate the complexity of these endeavors and, in turn, the complexity of learning to teach. Also, it appears that these beliefs are not altered easily, and this suggests that the education of teachers needs to be protracted in thoughtful ways into the early years of teaching. Two conditions are necessary from this perspective to ensure high quality continuing education for beginning teachers. First, these beginners should receive guidance from carefully selected, well qualified teachers who not only are experienced in the curriculum of local districts but are prepared as well in terms of our most contemporary understandings of teaching and learning and helping one learn to teach. Second, time is needed for sustained observation of one another and accompanying dialogue in this arrangement. We recommend one half day release time per week for both the beginning and experienced teacher.

In this regard, we have previously addressed some of the legal, structural, and economic conditions necessary to facilitate sustained and structured intellectual discourse between novice and expert teachers into the early years of teaching (Zimpher and Howey, 1992):

> The role and responsibility of those in preservice teacher education in this model is twofold. First, in a partnership arrangement, they would offer continuing, credit-bearing seminars for beginning teachers. These seminars would be congruent with major thematic goals originally addressed in preservice preparation programs. Second, and as fundamentally, those in preservice programs, along with those in K–12 schools, would offer a developmental series of courses for the experienced consulting teachers culminating in an additional certificate to a teaching license and signifying expertise as clinicians to work with the beginning teachers. While any number of titles could be employed for the veteran teachers who complete such a program, the title of consulting teacher or clinical teacher would perhaps best connote the functions performed [p. 35].

Preservice Students: Socialization and Acculturation

Increased attention to the purposeful and positive socialization of preservice teachers can be argued on several fronts. First, there is the evolving concept of learning community, which has major implications both for how teachers interact with their colleagues and how they structure learning opportunities in the classroom. This concept is increasingly advocated in various educational literatures. For example, the National Board for Professional Teaching Standards (1989) in delineating its vision of school culture speaks to a learning community.

Second, even a cursory overview of studies of teaching and learning demonstrates that the social dimension of cognitive learning is better understood today. For example, numerous studies undertaken by developers of cooperative learning arrangements such as Johnson and Johnson (1990) and Slavin (1990) point to the cognitive benefits that can be derived when groups are structured not only for individuals but for the group as a whole to succeed. In these social settings, students must share, explain, and defend their learnings with one another.

Third, while the social context promotes cognitive abilities, it is the social development of students, as well as their cognitive growth, that is a focus in these programs. Thus, the emphasis goes beyond how knowledge is best socially constructed to how the social setting or classroom society is constructed as well. This is a major point of departure in terms of how classroom instruction is viewed. The Johnsons' studies (1990), undertaken over two decades, illustrate the many positive intra- and interpersonal gains for students in various cooperative classroom arrangements, including increased respect for others, learning to work better together, and learning to resolve the conflicts that inevitably arise in social contexts.

Scholars such as Wang and Palinscar (1989) and Anderson (1989) also address the social dimensions of cognitive learnings in considerable detail in the first volume of *The Knowledge Base for the Beginning Teacher.* Cognitive and metacognitive abilities or scaffolding techniques are applicable not only for individuals in monitoring their learning but also for members of a group to monitor their collective learning and well-being as a group. A core principle in effective group functioning is that a group is responsible for its members, and principles in this regard are analogous to what the achievement/motivation literature suggests for individuals in terms of monitoring their learning.

The concept of a learning community obviously applies to teachers' development as well. There is evidence from numerous quarters, including the work of Rosenholtz (1988), Lieberman and Miller (1984), and Little (1990), that underscores the importance of various aspects of professional collegiality both at the school level and in small functioning groups. Teachers understandably work in cultures that can enable or constrain their teaching and their pupils' learning. The attributes of good or effective schools are being delineated with increasingly penetrating studies of the school setting but always there is an emphasis on the collegial functions required for success in these schools. It is clear that there has been a major transition in the view of what constitutes good continuing professional development for teachers. In recent years, the emphasis has moved from a reliance on instructional "packages" concerned with the development of specific teaching skills, later reinforced in the context of the classroom, to a concern for the creation of school cultures wherein professional development can occur in more natural, sustained, and civilized ways. This is a concept of professional development that is deeply embedded in the activities that occur naturally and daily in the schools.

Lack of Overt Attention to Socialization in Preservice Programs

Given these three conditions, one would conclude that there would be a major emphasis in the preparation of preservice teachers on the development of "learning communities" and strategies for professional collaboration. As Arnstine (1990) underscored, dispositions—such as the disposition for professional collaboration—must be thoroughly cultivated in sustained ways and one would not expect such activities to easily evolve in the absence of socialization for such collaboration in preservice preparation. Nonetheless, planned socialization and acculturation in preservice programs is uncommon.

Zeichner and Gore (1989) reviewed the teacher socialization research relative to various phases of teaching and teacher preparation. We need not speak further here to the various studies that have documented the pervasive effects of the first socialization phase, anticipatory socialization—that is, the views of teaching and learning and schooling that prospective teachers have acquired in their thousands of hours of "studenting." Since the focus in this chapter is on preservice students, neither need we dwell on studies of how teachers are socialized negatively as well as positively in their early and formative years of teaching.

Our focus is on teacher socialization in programs of preservice preparation, and when examining the effects of socialization during teacher preparation, attention needs to be paid to the broader institutional mission and milieu in which programs preparing teachers are situated. The effects of colleges and universities in general on the cognitive, moral, political, and interpersonal development of students is germane to understanding the socialization of prospective teachers. Many of these studies (Pascarella, 1985) have shown a general liberalization of values and in some instances an improved ability to reason about moral issues. Zeichner and Gore (1989) remind us, however, that this literature is also very clear that not all students change in the same way and that several factors mediate the socializing influence of the broader university or college context and culture including age, gender, race, ability, social class, and religious background.

Contextual Influence

While little attention has been paid in these studies of general college influence to *teacher* socialization, some of the variation that exists in terms of how preservice teachers are socialized can surely be attributed to differences in institutional mission and type. Such differences were clear to us in our case studies of elementary teacher education programs across three different institutional types preparing teachers: doctoral-granting research institutions, regional comprehensive universities with a priority on educating teachers, and small liberal arts institutions (Howey and Zimpher, 1989). For example, when we visited students enrolled in a program of teacher education in a Ph.D. institution with an emphasis on scholarly activity, the preservice teachers we interviewed raised questions in our initial meeting with them about the nature of our research and the nature of their involvement within it. They raised not only technical but ethical issues. This dialogue revealed a level of sophistication not encountered in meetings with prospective teachers at other campuses. For example, prospective teachers at the regional universities saw few problems in their view of teaching or the need to inquire into it. They attested rather to the value of their many experiences in schools as showing the way to being a good teacher. This student's comment was typical of those we interviewed at one of the latter institutions: "The key to effective teaching is being patient and being tolerant; realizing you're working with young children. Also, a teacher has to be well-organized and willing to be available. She has to work hard" (American Association of Colleges for Teacher Education, 1989, p. 110).

The effects of these preservice students' interaction with different faculty norms was readily apparent. However, since faculty members in preservice programs only rarely in a planful manner structure socializing activities, it should hardly be a surprise that there has been little systematic study of how prospective teachers are socialized, as important as this is, and as obvious as it is that different student norms have naturally evolved in different institutional contexts and within different programs within the same institution. In order to understand the socializing influence of teacher education program components and courses, we first need better descriptions of the purpose and character of these programs as we provided in our case studies (Howey and Zimpher, 1989), those developed by Goodlad (1990), or those undertaken at the National Center for Research on Teacher Education (NCRTE) at Michigan State.

Also, the particular beliefs and perspectives that different students bring to these experiences also needs to be delineated. Studies undertaken by Zeichner and Tabachnick (1985) are especially informative. What would be especially helpful in this regard is to move beyond descriptive studies to experimental or quasi-experimental studies wherein specific interventions or programs are designed to promote various types of socialization in preservice teachers.

There are a number of studies concerned with the socializing effects of field experiences or practicum activities on preservice students. However, those who have reviewed these literatures have characterized the socializing dimension of these experiences as ambiguous. Griffin's review (1983) of the literature also points to not well explicated aspects of many of these studies. For example, these studies often did not take into account the nature and relationship of these school-based experiences vis-à-vis the goals of the professional course sequence. Also, there are those who argue that the culture and conditions of elementary and secondary schools serve as a pervasive acculturating influence not only on preservice teachers but on experienced teachers as well (Fenstermacher, 1980). According to Zeichner and Gore (1989), however, even this premise needs more study since conditions in schools themselves in many ways are products of policy decisions, political actions, and other influences beyond the school. Also, it is clear that teachers have an impact upon the conditions in which they work and in which they are prepared just as those external conditions exert influence upon them.

Socialization and Acculturation

Better-designed studies of the socialization of preservice teachers obviously have to extend into the early years of teaching and learning to teach. Deal and Chatman (1989) speak to the problems that currently exist relative to the socialization of teachers and our understanding of that phenomenon:

> Part of the difficulty surrounding teacher socialization is rooted in the classic tension between professionals and organizations. A hospital, university, or any business that employs professionals must recognize that they are socialized by the profession first and receive secondary socialization or acculturation from the organization in which they work.

> But teaching is a semiprofession and for a variety of reasons it is not clear that the professional socialization experiences they receive are adequate. As a consequence the burden of adequately acculturating new teachers or experienced teachers taking a new position is left to the organization, that is, the local district or school. But as we have seen, the way teachers are brought into the culture of a district or school leaves much to be desired [p. 26].

Implications for Purposeful Socialization

A theme throughout this chapter is that the preservice education of teachers needs increasingly to be seen as extending in a seamless manner into the first or early years of teaching. The responsibilities for what Deal and Chatman refer to as secondary socialization or acculturation are in fact the responsibility of both those within the teacher education community who reside on campus as well as the growing number of experienced teachers who take formal responsibility for the education of novitiates in the workplace. As Tom (1991) points out:

> Thus, the professional part of teacher education is more likely to be thought of in terms of cognitive and curricular tasks than in such sociological terms as peer group, socialization, and so forth. Most teacher educators do not adequately appreciate the social nature of teaching and of professional training programs; nor do they comprehend the extent to which such programs are embedded in the politics and value structures of the contemporary university. Stated in different terms, teacher educators are too willing to accept existing intellectual and organizational structures—both in universities and in teacher education programs—as "givens" and direct their attention almost solely to what can be done within the context of those structures [p. 26].

Multiple opportunities do exist for those in programs of teacher education to attend more thoughtfully and strategically to the socialization of beginning teachers. This focus should be not only on individual teachers but as we indicated at the outset on collectives or learning communities. We have identified (Howey and Zimpher, 1989) numerous short-term cohort arrangements, designed to socialize students in specific ways while they interact with one another and with the faculty and while they engage in professional study. These short-term cohort arrangements lasting days, weeks, or even months, can contribute to (1) interpersonal development; (2) cooperative planning for instruction (almost all of the studies on teachers' planning and decision making have again focused on individual abilities and dispositions, activities that seem somewhat tangential to the idea of an effective learning community); (3) cooperative learning; (4) collaborative action research; or (5) peer- or team-teaching cadres.

Also, research and evaluation teams of students could be formed to collectively provide ongoing formative feedback about the effects of instruction in their teacher education programs. Not only is such an activity consonant with a view of teaching and learning that calls for continual monitoring and assessing the nature of how one comes to understand but it also seems the most feasible way to augment and improve the evaluation of teacher preparation.

Likewise, cohort arrangements could be put together that have a political action or critical perspective. In their review of the literature, Zeichner and Gore (1989) found little that reflected either a critical perspective of socialization or a critical inquiry into socialization. More inquiry such as that promoted by Ginsburg (1988) and Ginsburg and Clift (1989), which focus on "the influence of the 'hidden' curriculum" are surely in order.

Preservice Teachers Vis-à-Vis More Experienced and Expert Teachers

A very brief overview of some of this literature is appropriate here, for in order to understand preservice teachers it is helpful to contrast them with experienced teachers. Livingston and Borko (1989) were among the first to review research on expert-novice distinctions in teaching. They characterize teaching as a complex cognitive or intellectual skill that can be employed as a framework for understanding the differences between more expert and less expert teachers. Central to this characterization is the concept of schema, which is an abstract knowledge structure that allows one to summarize and synthesize information about many particular cases and the relationships amongst them. The cognitive schemata of experts in whatever domain typically are more elaborate, more complex, more interconnected, and more easily accessible than those of novices (Leinhardt and Greeno, 1986; Borko and Shavelson, 1990).

There are a burgeoning number of studies that provide testimony to these differences. Westerman (1991), for example, underscores differences between experts and novices while teaching in terms of their awareness of the behavioral cues from students that told them when to change their approach or to maintain the flow of the lesson. Needles (1991), when comparing novice and experienced teachers in their analysis of a teaching episode, demonstrated that experienced teachers reveal a greater understanding of the complexity of teaching and are better able to identify the interconnections of the elements of a lesson. Byra and Scherman (1991), when investigating differences in decision making between more experienced novice teachers and less experienced novice teachers, found even the more experienced novices were able to make some lesson adjustments when they perceived things were not going well while the less experienced novices continued to teach without adjustment. Sabers, Cushing, and Berliner (1988) clearly illustrated differences in expert and novice teachers in tasks characterized by simultaneity, multidimensionality, and immediacy. They report that experts were able to monitor and interpret events in much more detail and with more insight than teachers characterized as either novice or advanced.

Issues Assessing Teacher Knowledge

Better understanding of craft knowledge has obvious applications for the education of novice teachers. This presents the challenge of assessing this craft knowledge, however. Leinhardt (1990) draws attention to several of the problems and issues that are attached to assessing the practical knowledge of expert teachers or craft wisdom. The first fundamental question raised by Leinhardt is whose craft knowledge is to be explicated. Surely not all experienced teachers are expert, although some experience is a precondition for achieving expertise. In reporting on his studies of more and less experienced teachers, Berliner (1987) concluded that there were overall performance differences between the most and least experienced teachers. Nevertheless, he pointed out that many who have accumulated years of relevant kinds of experience seemed not to have profited from it. Conversely, his research team also identified many individuals who, while they did not have much experience, probably needed less of it than the investigators first imagined. There are indeed novice and postulate teachers who are motivated and reflective and are likely to excel quickly within their profession.

Leinhardt suggests that a parallel concern to that of identifying who is expert is the question of who is expert on what—that is, selecting what aspect of knowledge is to be assessed. As several scholars have revealed in expert-novice studies, teachers as individuals possess important and insightful pieces of information on what is best done under specific situations (pedagogical content knowledge). They also know about the specific subject matter that they are teaching (content knowledge). It is clear, however, that not all teachers are "expert" in all things and surely not at all times. As Leinhardt points out, at one extreme one could consider anything offered as practice-based knowledge as wisdom. However, most teachers, as she reminds us, have not had to separate their unverified opinion from probable "truth."

Leinhardt goes on to point out an even more fundamental problem in capturing the knowledge of experts:

> Up to this point there have been suggestions on how to select the source of craft knowledge, how to winnow kernels of knowledge from the chaff of superstition, how to generate examples of the wisdom, and how to use that wisdom to generate exercises. There has, however, been no discussion of totality. Totality is an issue under discussion right now. In the rush to include items that capture the wisdom of practice, it is imperative that theoretical knowledge of learning, development, and subject matter be a part of any assessment of teachers. Balance between theory and practice, and between a range from small-scale structure to larger issues of curriculum and pedagogical content, must also be dealt with. It is the next step. For now, researchers have only guides for the capturing of craft [Leinhardt, 1990, p. 23].

This latter concern appears to have major implications for thinking through how craft knowledge can best be incorporated into programming for preservice teachers, and we will return to this shortly when we discuss the notion of teaching clinics in the implication section.

Variations on Teacher Reasoning

Central to the conception of teaching as a complex cognitive skill and to explaining differences between experts and novices is the concept of pedagogical reasoning. Shulman (1987) defines pedagogical reasoning as a process of transforming subject matter knowledge "into forms that are pedagogically powerful and yet adaptive to the variations and ability and background presented by the students" (p. 15). Thus, the problem for teacher educators is not only how to capture the wisdom and reasoning of experienced teachers but to enable novice teachers in similarly acquiring those reasoning abilities themselves, to avoid a continuation of the tadpole conception of development offered by Buchmann (1987). There is a growing corpus of studies that address the structure of pedagogical reasoning (Fenstermacher, 1986; Morine-Dershimer, 1987; Rentel, 1988). Shulman (1987) identified aspects of pedagogical reasoning in a cyclic set of intellectual activities that begin with comprehension and proceed through transformation (which includes preparation, representation, selection, and adaptation and tailoring to student characteristics and assessment), followed by reflection, which leads in turn to new comprehensions.

This teacher pedagogical reasoning is not formal conditional reasoning but is rather better defined as practical reasoning. Practical reasoning is based upon abstract, pragmatic rules of inference related to particular context, relationships, and inferential goals (Rentel, 1988).

Understandably, there are distinctive qualities to teachers' pedagogical reasoning. Teachers generally think alone when they plan for their teaching or reflect on their actions, and they typically do this without the benefit of intellectual discourse about that teaching from colleagues. Rentel argues that because of the constant need for teachers to act spontaneously, combined with the complexity of the endeavor and the absence of explicit rules of practice, teachers' actions appear to be more artful than thoughtful. His research, however, suggests such is not the case, for when given an opportunity to examine pedagogical issues or problems in detail, he found that teachers' conceptual systems can be made explicit and that their actions are predicated on (1) complex practical arguments that evolve into highly reasoned principles of action, (2) simple principles that are based on such arguments, and (3) poorly understood or described professional norms. Though not all, or even most, teaching acts are solidly grounded in warranted belief, studies are beginning to reveal that there are basic forms of reasoning underlying teachers' actions.

A study undertaken by Rentel and Pinnell (1989) is a good example of this research. They studied experienced teachers who participated in a yearlong training program preparing them to be Reading Recovery teachers. As part of this training, teachers worked daily with children in thirty-minute lessons and then met in weekly seminar sessions with a group of their peers, during which extensive use was made of a one-way glass for observation of one of their colleagues teaching and subsequent discussion of that lesson. Each of the twelve teachers is engaged in the cycle of tutoring a child while being observed by the other eleven members of the group. The training sessions were designed to enable participants to justify their decisions by relating general background theory to specific claims about individual children or to support these claims by grounding them in other evidence such as research studies.

Rentel and Pinnell (1987), as well as scholars such as Morine-Dershimer (1987) and Shulman (1987), provide clues in terms of how teachers can develop justifications for teaching that are both data-based and principled in nature. The type of training activity engaged in by experienced teachers in the Reading Recovery Program lends itself to novice teachers as well as experienced teachers. It also underscores again the power of socializing students to be fully invested in learning communities, communities engaged in intellectual discourse.

An Emphasis on Moral Reasoning

As we close this brief overview of studies that can guide the design of preservice programs, we should underscore again that both novice teachers and consulting or clinic teachers need instruction in focusing on the moral and ethical dimensions of teaching and the many aspects of social justice that pervade teaching and schooling. Strike (1990) speaks to the need for formal instruction in this regard:

Teacher education programs thus should include instruction in basic ethical concepts. This should be distinguished from teaching abstract moral philosophy. Teachers must be taught how to apply ethical principles to *concrete* [emphasis ours] situations by learning to perceive a situation as involving an ethical issue and by reflecting on how principles are appropriately applied to the case. Since case studies provide a means of simulating the real world classroom, they are pedagogically useful.

The emphasis should be on teaching those ethical concepts that are central to the activities of teachers. Among the most important are intellectual liberty and intellectual honesty, respect for appropriate diversity, due process in such matters as discipline and grading, fairness in punishment, and equity in the distribution of educational resources such as the teachers' time [p. 208].

Strike's insightful and instructive comments also provide guidance in focusing the structured discourse between novice teachers who are learning to teach and those who are assisting them in this regard.

Expert-Novice Interactions: Implication for Programming

One can envision teaching clinics wherein novice teachers observe veteran teachers and the initial discourse is on the reasons advanced by veteran teachers for why they taught they way they did in particular lessons that the novices have observed. Employing videotape to examine the instruction and engaging pupils involved in the lesson as well would add even more power to this method "of learning to teach." Considerable care should be given on how to structure the discourse between veterans and novice in this regard given the examples above. Developmentally, it would seem that novices might best begin with the observation of and structured discourse with veteran teachers—acknowledging that the distance between more experienced and more expert teachers and less experienced and less expert novices may be such that the discourse is constrained by the shorthand that the experienced teachers employ. Thus, a mediating function by a teacher educator could be envisioned. If this dialogue is structured and sustained over time, it should help these veteran teachers "unpack" and make more explicit and elaborate their "theories in use."

In a second phase, novice teachers could engage more fully in videotaped self-analysis and reflection of their own teaching enabled by interaction with their peers as part of a learning community. In a third phase, there would be more engagement with a veteran teacher again but this time with an emphasis on the novice's instruction.

Such a developmental sequence appears reasonable but looks quite different from activities designed to promulgate learning to teach as manifested in most programs of preservice preparation at present. The prevalent approach (American

Association of Colleges for Teacher Education, 1990) is feedback of somewhat increasing frequency to the novice with little if any analysis first of the experienced teacher's or professor's instruction, no involvement of students in these classes in such analyses, and no opportunities for self-analytic practice before peers; then ultimately more expert feedback is inserted into a dialogue about the novice's teaching. Beyond this, there appears to be little attention in most instances to either personal theories or general principles or relationships between them.

Student Development and the Use of Portfolios

A theme throughout our review of what we know about students and their various abilities, beliefs, and stages of development is that considerable attention should be given to new or revised conditions and structures in programs of teacher preparation to both enable and evaluate learning to teach. Thus, in the final section of this chapter, we take time briefly to illustrate how preservice students might assume a central role in the assessment of their own learning and at the same time help assess the effects of these various activities and conditions designed to enable their teaching and learning.

We believe a key vehicle for accomplishing this is the use of portfolios by preservice students. These portfolios should be embedded in a conceptual framework and tied to the various dimensions of student development and learning to teach that have been articulated throughout this chapter. For example, a preservice teacher portfolio, from this perspective at least, should not be judged so much by the diversity or richness of materials contained therein but rather by how well these materials inform the student and her advisors and instructors of her progress and her development over time. At the same time, the ongoing analysis and assessment of the activities and materials reflected in the portfolios should inform the faculty in a continuing manner of the effects of their instruction and various program activities. They should also serve as a primary means of formative program evaluation. Evaluation of teacher education programs is generally lacking on several counts. Nominal resources are turned over to the endeavor, and just as is often the situation in elementary and secondary school evaluation, it is a periodic, externally driven activity, largely uncoupled from ongoing instruction. This portfolio approach is an opportunity to draw upon an obvious but major resource for evaluation of our teacher education programs.

The portfolio could be grounded in the thematic goals of the program. A coherent interrelated program of preservice preparation would have explicit conceptual bases; the adult developmental framework we alluded to earlier is but one example of a conceptual base. Constructivist principles of learning or a critical perspective on schooling in a social democracy would obviously provide guidance as well and fill out a framework to guide program design. Once such a framework is explicit, a reasonable number of principles to guide perhaps eight to ten key dispositional abilities desired in preservice students can be derived. A few examples might be these:

1. Learning builds on prior knowledge and beliefs.
2. Learning is active, and much knowledge is ultimately socially constructed.
3. Teaching is an intellectual activity focused on conceptual development.
4. Teaching is a highly interpersonal and moral activity.

The prospective student documents in a repeated manner in the portfolio how such principles are adhered to and how her abilities as a teacher are progressing in this regard. Obviously, the students' portfolios serve as a needed mirror to the faculty as well in order for them to examine what the program is doing, individually and collectively, to enable these novice teachers to achieve these essential goals.

A second possibility in defining and guiding the portfolios would be to highlight the human qualities that give definition to a vision of the good teacher that guides the program. Earlier in this chapter, we called for a revisiting of what should be involved in the selection and screening of prospective teacher candidates, especially from the vantage point of desired human qualities. Thus, dimensions of the portfolio, which would be initiated early in the program, could also include attention to whether and how such general qualities as the following are manifested:

1. Acknowledging, even soliciting, the perspectives of others
2. Inquiring about the effects of one's behavior on others
3. Assessing the correspondence of one's espoused beliefs and behavior
4. Tolerating conflict and ambiguity

Ultimately, however, we suggest that the portfolio should be anchored in what we know about prospective teachers from those literatures that we have reviewed however briefly here. Thus, we suggest that, among other possibilities, preservice students' activities be monitored over time in a portfolio to assess developmentally

1. Changes in their beliefs about schooling, teaching, learning, and coming to know, from a perception of teaching as telling and an emphasis on control and performance to conceptions of active learning that are both self- and group-monitored and developmental in nature
2. Changes in the locus of their concerns, again from a preoccupation with cosmetic appearance and performance as a "teacher" to a focus on causal relationships that might help explain student behavior
3. Changes in their reasoning about teaching, from unexamined assumptions and unsupported warrants to decisions and actions that are repeatedly subject to

public discourse and supported by multiple forms of data with full consideration of their ethical consequences

4. Changes in their efficaciousness (not just sense of efficacy); the basic source of knowledge about teaching efficacy is pupils; thus, the progression here for the novice teacher would be from relatively intermittent and uneven self-assessment to a continuing pattern of feedback from pupils: evaluation blended with, indistinguishable from, instruction

A preservice teacher portfolio, carefully constructed by the prospective teacher, is central to the view of teaching and learning just articulated in number 4 above. Its powerful byproducts should be at least twofold. First, engaging prospective teachers in such ongoing assessment activities will, one hopes, result in teachers who more fully understand measurement and evaluation and whose practices as experienced teachers eventually could put standardized measures in proper perspective. Second, it could lead to teacher educators taking more seriously than at present an examination of their own instructional practices as they receive continuing feedback.

In summarizing this section of the chapter, we have provided an illustration of how a carefully conceived prospective teacher portfolio could draw from what we presently know about preservice students and their developmental patterns. If such a practice of documenting the development of prospective teachers along several dimensions were widespread, we could speak much more fully to the quality of our prospective teachers than we have been able to here. Our hope would be to do just that in a sequel.

Note

1. The Research About Teacher Education studies were initiated in 1986, and we have been members of the research team that conducted these annual studies since their inception. Sponsored by the American Association of Colleges for Teacher Education, the analyses are undertaken at Ohio State University. Other members of the research team at present include Richard Arends, Central Connecticut University; Gary Galluzzo, Northern Colorado; and Sam Yarger, University of Miami.

References

Almanac in Higher Education (1991). Chicago: University of Chicago Press.

American Association of Colleges for Teacher Education (1987). *Teaching teachers: Facts and figures (RATE I)*. Washington, D.C.: American Association of Colleges for Teacher Education.

American Association of Colleges for Teacher Education (1988). *Teaching teachers: Facts and figures (RATE II)*. Washington, D.C.: American Association of Colleges for Teacher Education.

American Association of Colleges for Teacher Education (1989). *Teaching teachers: Facts and figures (RATE I).* Washington, D.C.: American Association of Colleges for Teacher Education.

American Association of Colleges for Teacher Education (1990). *Teaching teachers: Facts and figures (RATE II).* Washington, D.C.: American Association of Colleges for Teacher Education.

Anderson, L. M. (1989). "Learners and learning." In M. C. Reynolds (ed.), *Knowledge base for the beginning teacher.* New York: American Association of Colleges for Teacher Education.

Arnstine, B. (1990). "Rational and caring teachers: Reconstructing teacher preparation." *Teachers College Record, 92*(2), 230–247.

Astin, A. W. (1992). "Fact-file: Freshman characteristics and attitudes." *Chronicle of Higher Education, 38*(20), A30–A31.

Astin, A. W., Korn, W., and Green, K. (1987). "Retaining and satisfying students." *Educational Record, 68*(1), 36–42.

Ball, D. L. (1989). *Breaking with experience in learning to teach mathematics: The role of a preservice methods course.* East Lansing, Mich.: National Center for Research on Teacher Education.

Baratz, J. C. (1986). *Black participation in the teacher pool.* New York: Carnegie Forum on Education and the Economy.

Belenky, M. F., Clinchy, B. M., Goldberger, N. R., and Tarule, J. M. (1986). *Women's ways of knowing.* New York: Basic Books.

Berliner, D. C. (1987). "Laboratory settings and the study of teacher education." *Journal of Teacher Education, 36,* 2–8.

Berliner, D. C. (1988). "The development of expertise in pedagogy." Lecture presented at the annual meeting of the American Association of Colleges for Teacher Education, New Orleans, La.

Bird, T., Anderson, L. M., Sullivan, B. A., and Swidler, S. A. (1992). *Pedagogical Balancing Acts: A Teacher Educator Encounters Problems in an Attempt to Influence Prospective Teacher Beliefs.* East Lansing, Mich.: National Center for Research on Teacher Learning.

Borko, H., and Shavelson, R. J. (1990). "Teachers' decision making." In B. Jones and L. Idols (eds.), *Dimensions of thinking and cognitive instruction.* Hillsdale, N.J.: Erlbaum.

Britzman, D. P. (1986). "Cultural myths in the making of a teacher: Biography and social structure in teacher education." *Harvard Educational Review, 56,* 442–472.

Brookhart, S. M., and Freeman, D. J. (1992). "Characteristics of entering teacher candidates." *Review of Educational Research, 62*(1), 37–66.

Buchmann, M. (1987). *Teaching knowledge: The lights that teachers live by.* East Lansing, Mich.: National Center for Research on Teacher Education.

Buchmann, M. (1990). *Making new or making do: An inconclusive argument about teaching.* East Lansing, Mich.: National Center for Research on Teacher Education.

Buchmann, M., and Schwille, J. R. (1983). "Education: The overcoming of experience." *American Journal of Education, 91,* 30–51.

Byra, M., and Scherman, M. (1991). "Preactive and interactive decisions of experienced and inexperienced novice teachers." Roundtable presentation at the annual meeting of the American Educational Research Association, Chicago.

Calderhead, J. (1991). "The nature and growth of knowledge in student teaching." *Teaching and Teacher Education, 7,* 531–535.

Casey, K. (1988). "Teacher as author: Life history narratives of contemporary women teachers working for social change." University of Wisconsin (unpublished doctoral dissertation).

Darling-Hammond, L. (1990). "Teachers and teaching: Signs of a changing profession." In W. R. Houston (ed.), *Handbook of research on teacher education.* New York: Macmillan.

Deal, T. E., and Chatman, R. M. (1989). "Learning the ropes alone: Socializing new teachers." *Action in Teacher Education, 11*(1), 21–29.

Denton, J. J., and Smith, N. L. (1984). "Alternative teacher preparation programs: A cost-effectiveness comparison." Paper presented at the annual meeting of the American Educational Research Association, New Orleans, La.

Eash, M. J., and Rasher, S. P. (1977). "An evaluation of changed inputs on outcomes in teacher education curriculum." Paper presented at the annual meeting of the American Educational Research Association, New York.

Evertson, C. M., Hawley, W. D., and Zlotnik, M. (1984). "The characteristics of effective teacher preparation programs: A review of research." Paper prepared for the Education Analysis Center, Office of Planning, Budget and Evaluation, U.S. Department of Education, Vanderbilt University, Nashville, Tenn. Feistritzer, C. E. (1986). *Profile of teachers in the U.S.* Washington, D.C.: National Center for Education Information.

Fenstermacher, G. D. (1980). *Teacher personnel policies: A case of inappropriate means to appropriate ends.* Washington, D.C.: National Institute of Education.

Fenstermacher, G. D. (1986). "Philosophy of research on teaching: Three aspects." In M. C. Wittrock (ed.), *Handbook of research on teaching.* (3rd ed.). New York: Macmillan.

Fisher, R., and Feldman, M. (1985). "Some answers about the quality of teacher education students." *Journal of Teacher Education, 36,* 37–40.

Fuller, F., and Bown, O. H. (1975). "Becoming a teacher." In K. Ryan (ed.), *Teacher education.* (74th yearbook of the National Society for the Study of Education). Chicago: University of Chicago Press.

Galambos, E. C., Cornett, L. M., and Spitler, H. D. (eds.) (1985). *An analysis of transcripts of teachers and arts and sciences graduates.* Atlanta: Southern Regional Education Board.

Garcia, R. L. (1991). *Teaching in a pluralistic society: Concepts, models, strategies.* New York: Harper-Collins.

Gilligan, C. (1982). *In a different voice: Psychological theory and women's development.* Cambridge, Mass.: Harvard University Press.

Ginsburg, M. B. (1988). *Contradictions in teacher education and society: A critical analysis.* Washington, D.C.: Falmer Press.

Ginsburg, M. B., and Clift, R. T. (1989). "Hide and seek: Researching the hidden curriculum of preservice teacher education." In W. R. Houston (ed.), *Handbook of research on teacher education.* New York: Macmillan.

Goodlad, J. I. (1990). *Teachers for our nation's schools.* San Francisco: Jossey-Bass.

Griffin, G. A. (1983). *Clinical preservice teacher education: Final report of a descriptive study.* Austin: Research and Development Center for Teacher Education, University of Texas.

Howey, K. R., and Strom, S. M. (1987). "Teacher selection reconsidered." In M. Haberman (ed.), *Advances in teacher education.* Norwood, N.J.: Ablex.

Howey, K. R., and Zimpher, N. L. (1989). *Profiles of preservice teacher education: Inquiry into the nature of programs.* Albany: State University of New York Press.

Hunt, D. (1971). *Matching models in education.* Toronto: Ontario Institute for Studies in Education.

Johnson, D. W., and Johnson, R. T. (1990). "Social skills for successful group work." *Educational Leadership, 47*(4), 29–33.

Kohlberg, L. (1969). "Stage and sequence: The cognitive-developmental approach to socialization." In D. Goslin (ed.), *Handbook of socialization.* Skokie, Ill.: Rand McNally.

Lacey, C. (1977). *The socialization of teachers.* London: Methuen.

Lanier, J. E., and Little, J. W. (1986). "Research on teacher education." In M. C. Wittrock (ed.), *Handbook of research on teaching.* (3rd ed.). New York: Macmillan.

Leinhardt, G. (1990). "Capturing craft knowledge in teaching." *Educational Researcher, 19*(2), 18–25.

Leinhardt, G., and Greeno, J. (1986). "The cognitive skill of teaching." *Journal of Educational Psychology, 78*(2), 75–95.

Levine, M. (1976). "The academic achievement test: Its historical context and social functions." *American Psychologist, 31,* 228–238.

Lieberman, A., and Miller, L. (1984). *Teachers, their world and their work: Implications for school improvement.* Alexandria, Va.: Association for Supervision and Curriculum Development.

Little, T. W. (1990). "The persistence of privacy: Autonomy and initiative in teachers' professional relations." *Teachers College Record, 91,* 4.

Livingston, C., and Borko, H. (1989). "Expert-novice differences in teaching: A cognitive analysis and implications for teacher education." *Journal of Teacher Education, 40,* 36–42.

Loevinger, J. (1966). "The meaning and measurement of ego development." *American Psychologist, 21,* 195–206.

Matczynski, T. J., Siler, E. R., McLaughlin, M. L., and Smith, J. W. (1988). "A comparative analysis of achievement in arts and science courses by teacher education and non–teacher education graduates." *Journal of Teacher Education, 39*(3), 23–36.

McDiarmid, G. W. (1989). *What do prospective teachers learn in their liberal arts courses?* East Lansing, Mich: National Center for Research on Teacher Education.

McGaghie, W. C. (1991). "Professional competence evaluation." *Educational Researcher, 20*(1), 3–9.

Metropolitan Life (1991a). *Coming to terms: Teachers' views on current issues in education.* New York: Metropolitan Life Insurance Co.

Metropolitan Life (1991b). *The first year: New teachers' expectations and ideals.* New York: Metropolitan Life Insurance Co.

Morine-Dershimer, G. (1987). "Practical examples of the practical argument: A case in point." *Educational Theory, 37,* 395–407.

National Board for Professional Teaching Standards (1989). Hearing before the Subcommittee on Postsecondary Education of the Committee on Education and Labor. Washington, D.C.: House of Representatives.

National Center for Educational Statistics (1990). *Digest of education statistics.* Washington, D.C.: U.S. Department of Education, Office of Educational Research and Improvement.

Needles, M. (1991). "Comparison of student, first-year and experienced teachers' interpretations of a first-grade lesson." *Teaching and Teacher Education, 7*(3), 269–278.

Nelli, E. (1984). *Phi Delta Kappa grade point average study: Final report.* Lexington: University of Kentucky. (ED 242–724)

Oja, S. N., and Smulyan, L. (1989). *Collaborative action research: A developmental approach.* Washington, D.C.: Falmer Press.

Packard, M. H. (1992). "A study of the use of dialogue journals in an introductory course in preservice teacher education for the purpose of assessing and promoting cognitive development." Ohio State University (unpublished doctoral dissertation).

Pascarella, E. T. (1985). "College environmental influences on learning and cognitive development: A critical review and synthesis." In J. Smart (ed.), *Higher education: Handbook of theory and research,* Vol. 1. New York: Agathon Press.

Perry, W. G. (1969). *Forms of intellectual and ethical development during the college years.* Austin, Texas: Holt, Rinehart & Winston.

Piaget, J. (1961). "The genetic approach to the psychology of thought." *Journal of Educational Psychology, 52,* 275–281.

Piaget, J. (1965). *The moral judgment of the child.* New York: Free Press. (Originally published in 1932.)

Powell, R. (1991). "Acquisition and use of pedagogical knowledge among career-change preservice teachers." *Action in Teacher Education, 13,* 17–23.

Rentel, V. M. (1988). "Becoming a science teacher: First lessons." Paper presented at the American Association for the Advancement of Science Convention, Boston.

Rentel, V. M., and Pinnell, G. S. (1987). "A study of practical reasoning in reading recovery instruction." Paper presented at the National Reading Conference, St. Petersburg, Fla.

Rentel, V. M., and Pinnell, G. S. (1989). "Stake that claim: The content of pedagogical reasoning." Paper presented at the National Reading Conference, Austin, Texas.

Reyes, D. (1987). "Cognitive development of teacher candidates: An analysis." *Journal of Teacher Education, 38,* 18–22.

Rosenholtz, S. J. (1988). *Teachers' workplace: A social organizational analysis.* White Plains, N.Y.: Longman.

Sabers, D. S., Cushing, K. S., and Berliner, D. C. (1988). "Differences among teachers in a task characterized by simultaneity, multidimensionality, and immediacy." *American Educational Research Journal, 28*(1), 63–88.

Securro, S., Jr. (1992). "Quality of teacher education and non–teacher education graduates: Fact or artifact?" *Journal of Research and Development in Education, 25*(3), 131–135.

Shulman, L. S. (1987). "Knowledge and teaching: Foundations of the new reform." *Harvard Educational Review, 57,* 1–22.

Slavin, R. E. (1990). "Research on cooperative learning: Consensus and controversy." *Educational Leadership, 47*(4), 52–55.

Sprinthall, N. A., and Thies-Sprinthall, L. (1983). "The need for theoretical frameworks in educating teachers: A cognitive-developmental perspective." In K. R. Howey and W. E. Gardner (eds.), *The education of teachers: A look ahead.* White Plains, N.Y.: Longman.

Strike, K. A. (1990). "The legal and moral responsibility of teachers." In J. I. Goodlad, R. Soder, and K. A. Sirotnik (eds.), *The moral dimensions of teaching.* San Francisco: Jossey-Bass.

Sunal, D., and Sunal, C. (1985). "Teacher cognitive functioning as a factor in observed variety and level of classroom teaching behavior." *Journal of Research in Science Teaching, 22,* 631–648.

Tom, A. R. (1991). "Stirring the embers: Reconsidering the structure of teacher education programs." Paper prepared for the Conference on Teacher Development, Vancouver, British Columbia.

Vance, V. S., and Schlechty, P. C. (1982). "The distribution of academic ability in the teaching force: Policy implications." *Phi Delta Kappan, 64*(1), 22–27.

Wang, M. C., and Palinscar, A. S. (1989). "Teaching students to assume an active role in their learning." In M. C. Reynolds (ed.), *Knowledge base for the beginning teacher.* Elmsford, N.Y.: Pergamon Press.

Westerman, J. E. (1991). "Minimum state teacher certification standards and their relationship to effective teaching: Implications for teacher education." *Action in Teacher Education, 11*(2), 25–32.

Wilcox, S. K., Lanier, P., Schram, P., and Lappan, G. (1992). *Influencing beginning teachers' practice in mathematics education: Confronting constraints of knowledge, beliefs, and context.* East Lansing, Mich.: National Center for Research on Teacher Education.

Winitzky, N. E. (1992). "Structure and process in thinking about classroom management: An exploratory study of prospective teachers." *Teaching and Teacher Education, 8*(1), 1–14.

Zeichner, K. M., and Gore, J. M. (1989). *Teacher socialization.* East Lansing, Mich.: National Center for Research on Teacher Education.

Zeichner, K. M., and Tabachnick, B. R. (1985). "The development of teacher perspectives: Social strategies and institutional control in the socialization of beginning teachers." *Journal of Education for Teaching, 11,* 1–25.

Zimpher, N. L., and Howey, K. R. (1992). *Policy and practice toward the improvement of teacher education.* Oak Brook, Ill.: North Central Regional Educational Laboratory.

Zimpher, N. L., and Yesseyan, S. (1987). "Recruitment and selection of minority populations into teaching." *Metropolitan Education, 5,* 57–71.

Annotated Bibliography

Brookhart, S. M., and Freeman, D. J. (1992). "Characteristics of entering teacher candidates." *Review of Educational Research, 62*(1), 37–60.
These authors review forty-four studies examining characteristics of candidates upon entry to programs in teacher preparation. Their review is guided by two sets of related questions: first, what characteristics of entering teacher candidates have been studied, and what has been learned, and second, what forms of inquiry have been employed in these studies and how might these studies have been improved? Suggestions for future research are included in this synthesis of studies. Four major categories were identified as foci: (1) demographics and high school record, (2) motivation to teach and career aspirations, (3) confidence or anxiety about teaching, and (4) perceptions of the nature of teachers and teaching.

Darling-Hammond, L. (1990). "Teachers and teaching: Signs of a changing profession." In W. R. Houston (ed.), *Handbook of research on teacher education*. New York: Macmillan.
This chapter provides a brief historical analysis of teaching as an occupation and commonly accepted attributes of a profession. It examines sociodemographic data relative to the teaching force. Matriculation patterns, both in terms of preparation for teaching and throughout the teaching career, are also identified. A major contribution of the manuscript is the analysis of incentives and disincentives for entering or remaining in teaching. In this regard, licensing procedures, teacher preparation, and induction into the profession are examined as they impact the supply and distribution of teachers.

Goodlad, J. I. (1990). *Teachers for our nation's schools*. San Francisco: Jossey-Bass.
This book presents the results of a major five-year study of institutions preparing teachers in which Professor Goodlad served as principal investigator. A major focus is the quality of preservice teachers and their preparation. A central thesis of the book and the study on which it is based is that the education of teachers should be driven by a clear and thoughtful conception of expectations for our schools and correspondingly for our teachers. Further guiding the study are nineteen postulates or essential presuppositions against which extant conditions in teacher education were judged. In addition to naturistic study, survey responses were obtained from over twelve hundred teacher education faculty members in a variety of institutions including liberal arts colleges and regional and national public and private institutions engaged in the education of teachers.

Zeichner, K. M., and Gore, J. M. (1990). "Teacher socialization." In W. R. Houston (ed.), *Handbook of research on teacher education*. New York: MacMillan.
This review of the literature examines the means through which individuals become part of the society of teachers. It examines competing explanations of teaching socialization including the functionalist, interpretive, and critical perspectives of socialization and variations therein. It also examines socialization influences on predictive variables prior to teacher preparation, during this structured educative period and finally throughout the teaching career. Competing hypotheses are examined to explain the apparent limited impact of initial teacher education in terms of teacher socialization.

The Research About Teacher Education (RATE) studies are sponsored by the American Association of Colleges for Teacher Education and are conducted annually. These studies focus on the nature and quality of teacher education faculty and students and the various programs and institutions in which teacher education is conducted. Prospective teachers are examined in terms of sociodemographic data, measures of aptitude and achievement, matriculation patterns, and career development, along with several indicators of their success in these various settings.

CHAPTER TWENTY-ONE

PHILOSOPHICAL AND STRUCTURAL PERSPECTIVES IN TEACHER EDUCATION

JANICE GROW-MAIENZA

In the newest wave of calls for educational reform, many teacher education faculties are changing the structure of their programs. Some are making substantive changes as well. Those faculties who are not changing are pressured to define and justify what they have. It is important that teacher education programs be coherent courses of study tied to what teachers need to know and what teachers need to be able to do in a society that is an information technology society and that is global and diverse. Thus, there is an increasing demand today for teacher education programs to articulate their respective knowledge bases and the philosophical assumptions on which those knowledge bases are founded. Faculties best able to design and articulate their programs so that the knowledge base is clear and salient will be those who will have examined and articulated the philosophical assumptions on which their programs are based.

In an effort to help faculties place their own programs in context, the beginning of this chapter addresses the structure and substance of teacher education in relation to the philosophical perspectives that can be said to have influenced teacher education since the beginnings of colonial and American education. The end of the chapter attempts to meld the conceptual and organizational aspects of structure in teacher education by examining how specific faculties who have made recent changes in their programs looked at underlying assumptions about their own organizational structures, defined a knowledge base, and then redefined their programs. Looking at first the conceptual alternatives outlined in the first part of the chapter, and then the change processes experienced by specific faculties in doing just that, may help other faculties to look more carefully and thoughtfully at the underlying assumptions of their own programs and to then define and articulate those programs.

Philosophical Orientations

American schools grew out of the needs of an emerging industrialized nation in a democratic political structure where most students were taught the three R's and the rules of the society. The elite, in addition, were taught the Western classical traditions that have their cultural roots in the Greek philosophers and the Judeo-Christian heritage. The reforms of the nineteenth century that resulted from the rise of science and the notion of the malleability of humankind and society changed the educational system significantly. But once again, as we enter the twenty-first century, demands on the educational system have changed dramatically. Today our schools must serve an information technology, must take a more global perspective, and must meet the needs of all students from diverse cultures. To meet the requirements of education today, say the reformers, schools must change. Restructuring of schools must necessarily call for a reexamination of teacher education.

Both the structure and the substance of teacher education programs are related to the philosophical assumptions on which the various movements and countermovements in education are built. Typically in the past, each teacher education institution has determined its own best way of educating teachers with little or no attention to other institutions or to the research literature (Houston, 1990). But the roots of teacher education, as in schooling, are in the culture (Joyce, 1975; Medley, 1979; Zeichner, 1983; Schubert, 1989). This chapter argues that conceptions of what the functions of education should be have explicitly driven various movements and countermovements in education. But the implicit underlying assumptions of those movements have been historical conceptualizations of humankind and of learning.

Today we have at least four or five basic approaches to teacher education reflecting the philosophical origins and changing thought in American society. Writers have placed these approaches or models of teaching into various taxonomies with identical or similar classifications (Joyce, 1975; Zeichner, 1983; Scardamalia and Bereiter, 1989; Feiman-Nemser, 1990; Tabachnick and Zeichner, 1991). Each approach is based upon a distinctive, though not necessarily exclusive, knowledge base.

The approaches can be viewed as being influenced to a greater or lesser extent either by traditional or by so-called progressive notions of what the aims of education should be (Tanner and Tanner, 1990). These two strands can be seen in the history of education since the age of Erasmus but have been played out in uniquely American style in four major reform movements of the late nineteenth century, described later below.

Traditional and Progressive Strands in the Aims of Education

The traditionalist movement in education is essentially an economic model with a view of the function of education as one to provide workers and professionals for the society. It is a view that includes the building of good citizens as one of the goals of education, a goal that evolved in the early nineteenth century into one geared to the building of an American national identity. It is a view that selects some for leadership, others to follow. The traditional approach has as its aim the transmission of the culture. Its philosophical foundations are in Plato and Aristotle, in the dualistic notions of prescientific theocracy and faculty psychology and a belief in the permanence of Truth.

The theocentric Christian traditionalism brought from Europe to colonial America is still strong today and is reflected in the perennialist and essentialist movements of the nineteenth and twentieth centuries. As late as the late nineteenth century, textbooks in public schools still referred to God, God's will, and man's soul (Tanner and Tanner, 1990). In 1870, teachers of philosophy in the academies and colleges were still clergymen. Strands of Christian traditionalism can be seen in the influence of the fundamentalists in the schools even today. In 1985, the California State Curriculum Development Commission found that no science texts gave adequate treatment to evolution and other topics of a controversial nature (cited in Tanner and Tanner, 1990).

The term *progressive*, when applied to education, has been used by writers in various ways. Some use the term to describe the movement that saw people as creators of their culture, knowledge as emergent, the movement that dominated the progressive era of Dewey and others who were putting the pragmatist philosophy into educational terms in the early part of the twentieth century (Joyce, 1975). Others use the term to categorize the various reform movements of the late nineteenth century, which were reactions to the traditional approach to education (Tanner and Tanner, 1990). In this chapter, the term *progressive movement* is used to refer to those reforms with their foundations in the late nineteenth century that were a result of the rise of science and the child study movement, the beginnings of the study of education as a science, the constructionist approach to knowledge, and the recognition of the malleability of humans and society with the concomitant notion that one of the aims of education should be the transformation of the society (Kliebard, 1986). The reforms are viewed here from Kliebard's perspective as reactions not so much to traditionalist content but to the way content was delivered in the schools.

The progressive movement essentially created innovation models with a view of the function of education as creating a better life for all citizens and thus a better democracy for the society. The roots of the progressive movement are in the pre- and postrevolution era, and the movement survives in the work of Franklin, Jefferson, Lester Ward, Horace Mann, and John Dewey (cited in Tanner and Tanner, 1990, and in Cremin, 1962) and in the behaviorist psychology that saw people moving society. The same progressive views surface today in the work of Schön and Shulman (see, for example, Schön, 1987, and Shulman, 1987) in their notions about the reflective professional, in school-based management, in the role of teachers as curriculum builders and policy makers, and in the view of the nature of children as constructing their own knowledge. The models of teacher education in-fluenced by the progressive reform movements discussed below have as their aim not only the transmission of the culture in a set of permanent truths but also the construction of new truth and the transmission of that part of the culture that will enable the society to transform itself, to make a better society for a more and more inclusive society.

The tension that exists between the traditional and progressive movements of philosophical and political thought can be traced back beyond the beginnings of American education and have to do with the two primary notions of what should be the aim of education. One strand can be called a traditional approach to ed-ucation, the other progressive. One holds to the authority and legitimacy of the prior and valued, the other moves for social change. One calls for the transmis-sion of the culture, the other for the transformation of the society. The presence of one strand in an approach to education need not preclude the presence of the other. Every teacher education program in practice may well have some char-acteristics of many, if not all, of the models, though the emphasis is upon the char-acteristics of one or another of the models.

Traditional and Progressive Approaches

Drawing on Kliebard's analysis of the various interest groups that have vied for control of the primary and secondary school curriculum in the twentieth century, Zeichner and his colleagues have discussed teacher education in the light of four reform movements to interpret aspects of various approaches to teacher educa-tion (Zeichner and Liston, 1987; Zeichner and Tabachnick, 1991). Placing vari-ous conceptualizations in the context of the four reform movements described by Kliebard (1986) and others who have applied Kliebard's conceptualization to a taxonomy of models can be very helpful here.

In the traditional economic or industrial model of teacher education, which persists today in some programs, the beginning teacher must know the functions to be performed in the classroom, know the content of subjects to be handed down to students, and be trained in predetermined skills to teach that knowledge (Joyce, 1975; Zeichner, 1983). The aim is to transmit the culture that remains permanent and static and to prepare good citizens to meet the needs of the industrialized so-ciety. Learning occurs through the authority of the teacher and the disciplining of the mind.

The rise of science and the conceptualization of humankind and society as malleable, not predetermined, gave rise to four liberal reform movements in the late nineteenth century. The four major reform movements have been char-acterized as (1) the humanist movement with its ideal for a liberal education for all and the importance of a common curriculum, (2) the developmentalist move-ment with its emphasis on looking to the stages of development in the child to determine what should be taught, (3) the social efficiency movement, which focused on examining teaching behaviors that bring results, and (4) the social melioration movement with its ideal of using the school to reconstruct society (Kliebard, 1986).

Though the reform movements were in reaction to the industrial model, none challenged the economic view of the individual. Rather, the progressives would move toward the egalitarian in their focus on extending educational opportunity to include more members of society in education and thus in its economic benefits (Joyce, 1975). In the progressive or social innovation models, one of the aims is still the transmission of a certain part of the culture. The knowledge base would necessarily include the notion of democracy and the role of the citizen in democracy. Working with groups and the reflection necessary for problem solving will be very important in some of the progressive models. In models in which teachers are viewed as facilitators, it is important that teachers have autonomy and supportive resources to select and adapt materials to the needs of children, whereas the needs of children are not usually considered in the industrial approach to education (Dewey, 1916; James, 1939; Thelen, 1954; Cremin, 1962; Joyce, 1975; Zeichner, 1983).

Academic Approach

The academic approach to teacher education is an influence of the humanist movement that dominated the National Education Association's powerful Committee of Ten of 1892. For the humanists of the nineteenth century, the development of reasoning power was the central function of the schools, and that was best accomplished through the study of five basic liberal arts and by learning and applying the skills of accurate observation, correct recording, classification, categorization, and correct inferences (Kliebard, 1986). In the academic approach to teacher education, the child is viewed as a developing scholar and the teacher is to be trained to think like a scholar and practice the disciplines with children. The knowledge base is in the core disciplines of the liberal arts and sciences.

For some, the professional component in this approach comes from a constructionist point of view and would focus on teachers knowing the cognitive processes involved in learning and the structures of the discipline (Piaget, 1952, 1955; Ausubel, 1963; Bruner, 1963; Schwab, 1963; Goodlad, 1964; Joyce, 1975; Tanner and Tanner, 1990). In Shulman's application of the academic approach (1987), knowledge of subject matter is just one focus of teacher education, representation and translation of subject matter knowledge to promote student understanding being a very important second focus (Zeichner and Tabachnick, 1991).

Some proponents of the academic approach, such as E. D. Hirsch (1987) and others who take the perennialist perspective, see the primary task of education to be to inculcate core ideas from the Western tradition, and therefore they are not necessarily constructionist in bent. In the perennialists' view, we see a pull to the traditionalist notion of what should be taught: that which is prior and valued.

Personalistic Approach

The developmentalist or personalistic approach to teacher education grew out of the child study movement initiated by Stanley Hall and others as an outgrowth of the new status of science in the nineteenth century (cited in Kliebard, 1986). The developmentalist approach focuses on the stages of development of the child. Proponents of this model have a view of humanity influenced by Rousseau, Froebel, Horace Mann, and the notion that the natural order of development in the child is the most significant and scientifically defensible basis for deciding what should be taught (Joyce, 1975; Kliebard, 1986).

Because for the developmentalists education should facilitate the unfolding natural goodness of the child, the aims of education become individual and idiosyncratic, and thus learning outcome standardization is deemphasized. For the teacher, there are no standard competencies to be acquired. The focus is instead on coming to terms with self, acquiring knowledge of the stages of child development, and demonstrating an empathetic relationship with students more as equals than in an authoritarian role. In the personalistic approach to teacher education that developed in the twentieth century, coming to terms with oneself in the knowledge base for teachers includes clarifying one's values and discovering one's personal meaning and style in teaching (Maslow, 1954; Neill, 1960; Combs, 1965; Perls, Hefferline, and Goodman, 1971; Glasser, 1968; Rogers, 1969; Freire, 1970; Greene, 1973). For developmentalists, the teacher is viewed as a naturalist, an artist, or a researcher of child development (Zeichner and Liston, 1987).

Competency Approach

The competency or outcomes-based approaches to teacher education originated in the social efficiency movement whose advocates at the turn of the century shared the developmentalists' view that the key to successful education lay in scientific data on the child. But these approaches began to focus on the study of teaching activities and moved ultimately to notions about application of scientific management techniques successful in increasing efficiency in industry. The competency approach is an industrial model of education, with a mechanistic view of the child and of what should be taught. For proponents of the competency and outcomes-based approaches, knowledge is made up of discrete competencies that can be taught and assessed separately. The aim of the social efficiency reformers was standardization and efficiency in the curriculum. Outcomes were specified for the training of teachers, and supervision of teaching activities was considered essential.

The competency orientation to teacher education developed in the 1960s and 1970s was the culmination of the development of various interaction analysis systems (Withall and Lewis, 1963; Flanders, 1970; Medley and Mitzel, 1950; Bellack, 1966; Taba, Levine, and Ellzey, 1964) and a large body of process/product research, much of it summarized in Medley (1977), Smith (1983), and Brophy and Good (1986). Today the outcomes model of teacher education is focused on the intelligent use of generic strategies suggested by research on teaching (Zeichner and Tabachnick, 1991).

Social Reconstructionist Approach

In the social reconstructionist or reconceptualist approach to teacher education, school settings are seen as uncertain, dynamic, and problematic (Zeichner, 1983; Shulman, 1986a, 1986b, 1987; Schubert, 1989). Reconceptualization is the basis of Zeichner's view of the inquiry model of teacher education that has its roots in the progressive social melioration movement (Zeichner, 1983) and would seem to be the basis of current attempts in teacher education reform to further professionalize the work of teaching (Shulman, 1986b, 1987; Holmes Group, 1986; Carnegie Task Force, 1986).

The knowledge base for the social reconstructionists comes out of the progressive social melioration movement, a blend of the child study movement, and the writings of John Dewey and the neo-Marxists of the early twentieth century. People are viewed not as raw material for the industrial society, but as an organic unity, as intelligent and emotional, social beings, members of a society that has responsibility for intelligent action. Knowledge is viewed as constructionist—a product of thinking rather than something that is static and permanent. The aim of education is to facilitate children in their struggle to become, and to reconstruct the society that, like the individual and knowledge, is constructivist in nature, struggling to become.

The knowledge base for the teacher in the social reconstructionist approach must include awareness of political and social contexts of schooling. Teachers must be prepared to assess classroom actions for their ability to contribute to equity and social justice in school and in society. Thus, problem solving and group dynamics are very important skills, as are those activities that foster the reflective capacities of observation, analysis, critical thinking, and decision making (Zumwalt, 1987; Schön, 1987; Shulman, 1986b, 1987; Zeichner and Liston, 1987; Doyle, 1990; Holmes Group, 1986; Carnegie Task Force, 1986). As in the constructivist versions of the academic model, the knowledge to be learned is uncertain and constructed by the student interacting with the environment rather than by passive reception.

Synthesis View

The political and intellectual perspectives undergirding teacher education are not necessarily mutually exclusive, nor do teacher education programs generally reflect one orientation exclusively (Zeichner, 1983). One reconceptualist model proposed by Shulman, for instance, addresses the transformation of subject matter, as does the academic model of teacher education. Shulman also cites the process/product research that would be part of the pedagogical knowledge necessary for teachers and the cognitive development of critical thinking skills of both teachers and students—characteristics, respectively, of the competency and developmental approaches to teacher education. Thus, in Shulman's model, rather than rules and prescriptions for classroom application, knowledge and methods of inquiry useful in deliberating about teaching problems and practices are in the knowledge base (Shulman, 1986b; Doyle, 1990).

Scardamalia and Bereiter (1989) in the handbook *Knowledge Base for the Beginning Teacher* suggest that modern research has provided a strong empirical basis for each approach, but research has also made it possible to identify more clearly the core problems that arise when these conceptions are carried into action. Scardamalia and Bereiter further suggest that within given conceptions of teaching, expert teachers confront the core problems, while inexpert teachers avoid them. Since dealing with the core problems involves going outside the boundaries of a single conception of teaching, Scardamalia and Bereiter suggest that as teachers become more expert, their teaching increasingly reflects all conceptions. Tom (1991) proposes that walls separating four reform traditions be broken down and that teacher educators attempt a synthesis of the traditions. "Each tradition," writes Tom, "holds the promise of throwing light on a different domain of the riddle of teacher education: the student and the teacher-in-training (developmentalist), subject matter (academic), social context (reconstructionist), and scientific understanding of teaching-learning processes (social efficiency)" (Tom, 1991, p. 28).

The teacher education faculty that would reflect today on the four commonplaces of schooling described by Schwab (1973)—the student, the teacher, the subject matter, and the context of schooling—would necessarily be influenced by the impact of the four reform movements of the nineteenth century. The child study movement, for instance, changed the view of the child from the soul that must be saved through regimentation and strict discipline to the physical and emotional individual that would construct his or her own knowledge. The social efficiency movement saw the beginnings of the science of teaching with its focus on behavior, attitudes, and interactions of the teacher. The academic movement forced the focus on subject matter from an emphasis on rote memorization of a fixed body of knowledge to be passively received on the basis of the authority of the teacher to a focus on the transformation of knowledge to fit the cognitive stages of the learner.

Relationship of the Knowledge Base to the Structure of Teacher Education

Just as there has been tension, and often conflict, among philosophical camps in teacher education throughout the history of education, there has been tension about structural elements in teacher education between the adherents of liberal and technical education regarding the relevance of the theoretical and the practical, and between the forces for campus-based and field-based education. There is tension too between adherents of traditionally packaged teacher education and extended programs. The tension between traditional and progressive forces has also impacted the structure of teacher education.

Before the beginning of the first normal school, founded under Horace Mann, who was then Secretary of Education in Massachusetts, and the normal schools that followed, teacher education did not exist in any formal way. Girls and the sons of the common folk were taught at home or in the dame schools (school taught by women in their homes) and later in town schools. Sons of the elite were taught in private grammar schools and academies.

Just as now, candidates in the nineteenth century went into teaching from diverse educational backgrounds. Some entered the teaching profession from the colleges, some from the academies, and some from short-term teaching courses offered by the towns and counties. Some candidates had only a smattering of postelementary education before entering the schools as teachers (Herbst, 1989; Urban, 1990). Though the first normal school was established in 1837, the normal school movement occurred in response to the needs of the burgeoning common schools in the cities and rural counties in the mid-nineteenth century. Horace Mann's vision of the normal school was an attempt to professionalize the teaching career in order to recruit a more highly educated and stable work force.

Teacher educators in those earlier years were concerned mainly with the elaboration of the function of normal schools and with the establishment of instructional programs for teacher education (Su, 1986). From 1837 to 1890, normal schools were single purpose, autonomous, often private, and functioned to prepare elementary teachers for the town and rural schools. When the normal school movement was at its peak, educators in the normal schools were very much influenced by the notions of Rousseau, the method of Herbart and Pestalozzi. Thus, a blending of the child study movements and the beginnings of the study of the science of teaching was occurring.

Though even at the peak of the normal school movement at the turn of the century only 24 percent of teachers came out of the normal schools, it is the public normal school that represents the distinctive nineteenth century approach to teacher education (Feiman-Nemser, 1990). Also, the focus of the normal school, for a while, was on preparing teachers for the elementary schools. Those preparing to teach at the secondary level, on the other hand, were prepared in the disciplines at the university, where pedagogy was not seen as important. Knowledge of the content area was viewed as sufficient preparation for secondary teaching. Departments of education that were created in the major research universities at the turn of the century focused on the preparation of educational administrators and researchers, largely a male population (Feiman-Nemser, 1990; Clifford, 1985; Herbst, 1989).

Movement to upgrade normal schools and to provide general education for populations in rural areas ended in the demise of the single purpose, autonomous, professional school for the education of teachers and in the emergence of dual-purpose teachers' colleges, later contained within the comprehensive university (Smith, 1980; Su, 1986; Herbst, 1989). Today, teacher education is offered in liberal arts colleges, in university undergraduate and graduate programs, and in alternative certification programs in some states, and some districts provide their own inservice professional development (Feiman-Nemser, 1990).

But it was in the period at the turn of the twentieth century that three elements of the structure of teacher education as we know it today began to take shape. Teacher education programs began to be comprised of three components still widely held: academic studies, professional studies, and practice teaching (Su, 1986). The first reform of the teacher education curriculum began in 1889 with the appointment of James Russell as dean of Teachers College at Columbia University. There the components of teacher education were expanded to four: general culture, special scholarship, professional knowledge, and technical skill (Cremin, 1977). It was in this move that a marriage first occurred between the disciplines represented in the liberal arts and sciences and in the science of education with its focus on learning, methodology, and child development. The general culture and special scholarship components provided knowledge in the liberal arts and sciences; the professional knowledge and technical skill components provided knowledge of the nature of learning and of pedagogy. American teacher education for nearly a century has developed around those four components with little real variation in teacher education programs (Cremin, 1977; Su, 1986).

But other reforms and trends in research have impacted the structure and knowledge base of teacher education. Reports from the American Council on Education in the 1940s reflect an advancement of the knowledge base that evolved in the progressive period with a focus on the need for teacher education institutions to be sensitive to social realities and democratic ideals (Su, 1986). A 1946 report of the Commission on Teacher Education urged, also, recognition of the need for institutions to improve programs and the need for interinstitution cooperation—part of the beginnings of the move to accreditation and professionalization of teaching (Su, 1986).

Russell's reform at Teachers College did not settle the debate between liberal and technical studies representing two perspectives: the academic or liberal arts perspective that was traditionally viewed in the preparation of secondary teachers and the normal school perspective held by professional educators engaged largely in the preparation of elementary teachers (Borrowman, 1956; Su, 1986). The rationale of proponents of the liberal arts and sciences in the twentieth century was that there was so little substance to pedagogy that the basic education of teachers should be in liberal arts and sciences, followed by an apprenticeship in the trade (Bestor, 1953; Su, 1986).

There were also studies in this period, however, that spoke to the professionalization of teaching and the knowledge and skills needed by professional teachers (Lieberman, 1956; Conant, 1963). The quarrel over liberal arts and the technical side of teaching, the latter position birthing the development and application of various performance-based models of teacher education, continued into the 1970s when conscientious research into the knowledge of teaching began. This trend toward what is often called process/product research is summarized at its various stages in several studies (for example, Ryan, 1975; Gage, 1978; Smith, 1983; Brophy and Good, 1986). Many of today's reformers, recognizing both the need for strong liberal arts and sciences and the need for professional education, call for both and would place the latter in a graduate year (Holmes Group, 1986; Carnegie Task Force, 1986).

Also in the 1970s and 1980s, several models outlining what could be called a knowledge base for teacher education were put forth, some forming the foundation of a specific program or innovation in program, all calling for reform (for example, Howsam's *Educating a Profession*, published by the American Association of Colleges for Teacher Education, 1976, and Clark and Guba's 1977 study published at the National Institute for Education, which speaks to the relationship of structural and curricular reform). B. O. Smith's knowledge base of pedagogical education (1980) became a blueprint for professional schools of pedagogy and how to educate teachers in a clinical mode.

D. C. Smith (1983) summarized the process/product line of research of the previous twenty years in an attempt to reach a description of effective teaching. He categorized the essential knowledge necessary for beginning teachers into six classifications: (1) instructional planning, (2) management of instruction, (3) management of conduct, (4) context variables, (5) diagnosis and measurement, and (6) evaluation. These classifications formed the knowledge base for teacher education at the University of Florida in the 1980s.

On the other side of the academic debate, Andrew (1974) wrote a design for teacher education very different from those using competencies models derived from the process/product research. Andrew's model was published by the Association of Teacher Educators and formed the basis for the curriculum in a new five-year teacher education program at the University of New Hampshire (Andrew, 1984). In that model, philosophical foundations form a core for the curriculum in teacher education, and all courses focus on the development of critical thinking skills. Various other models have been described for specific programs (Lanier and Little, 1986; De Vitis and Sola, 1989; Zeichner and Liston, 1987; Andrew, 1986; Feiman-Nemser, 1990; Grow-Maienza, 1990, 1991).

Shulman (1986b, 1987) proposed a view of teacher education that speaks not only to the professionalization of teachers but to the knowledge base as well, dividing it into knowledge of (1) content, (2) curriculum and foundational studies, (3) pedagogy, and (4) the wisdom of practice. In response to the National Commission on Excellence in Education's *Nation at Risk* document (1983), which was highly critical of American public education, many reform reports were written speaking to the need for the increased professionalization of teachers (California Commission on the Teaching Profession, 1985; National Commission for

Excellence in Teacher Education, 1983; Holmes Group, 1986; Carnegie Task Force, 1986).

Melding Conceptual and Organizational Aspects of Teacher Education

Writers at several schools that have created both substantive and structural change and innovation in their teacher education programs in recent years have written about that process of reflection and about coming to consensus on the knowledge base for their programs. They describe the consensus process as engaging not only their faculty but various publics as well—students, teachers, and state agency representatives. A brief review of some of that literature can inform faculties who are preparing to examine their own programs (Smith, Krogh, Ross, and Kinzer, 1983; Andrew, 1984; Freeman, 1985, 1989; De Vitis and Sola, 1989; Grow-Maienza, 1990, 1991).

The analysis of data in one case study that described four such programs that had gone to extended five-year formats reveals that innovations in each case were in place only after clear explication of the respective program (Grow-Maienza, 1991). Definition and explication of each program came about only after examination and consideration of the goals and the philosophical foundations of the respective program. The programs were in widely varying institutions. One program was in the institution that served as the flagship in the state university system. Another was in a large state land grant institution. A third program was housed in a small state university with its origins in a nineteenth-century normal school. And the fourth program was in a tiny private liberal arts college. In each case, faculties came to consensus on a knowledge base for the program and in many instances articulated a unique model for its program (De Vitis and Sola, 1989; Grow-Maienza, 1991). Ways of defining programs and coming to consensus were diverse.

A new five-year program was designed twenty years ago in one flagship state university around a full-blown model for teacher education reform (see Andrew, 1974). In that program, philosophical foundations form a core for the curriculum in teacher education, and all courses focus on the development of critical thinking skills. The faculty credits the success of the innovations to the preexisting model that addressed the traditional criticisms of teacher education and kept the momentum going during initial internal discussions and to a series of planning and coordinating committees that involved graduate students, faculty, school personnel, and representatives of state agencies to define and refine details of the program (Andrew, 1984, 1986).

Documents at one large state university, one of the original land-grant institutions, describe the restructuring of one campus with a focus on the new process/product research literature on effective teaching just surfacing in the early

1980s and reflected in the later work of D. C. Smith (1983); Smith, Krogh, Ross, and Kinzer (1983); and Brophy and Good (1986). Groups of task forces comprised of faculty, graduate students, school personnel, and representatives of the state categorized their perceptions of the essential knowledge necessary for beginning teachers into six classifications (Smith, Krogh, Ross, and Kinzer, 1983; Carroll, 1989). The result was the basis for the knowledge base for a restructured program that combined knowledge from the process/product research with the program's previous humanistic focus on the importance of personal development.

The result did not come without conflict, of course. Diverse views of the faculty are still accommodated, as evidenced in later literature about that program (for example, Ross, Johnson, and Smith, 1992). Ross, Johnson, and Smith cite ongoing research and evaluation at that institution that demonstrates that the program continues to evolve, now more toward a reflective personal development focus based on a constructivist approach to learning but with a tolerance for other points of view. That programs evolve and seldom remain stable is of course a principle of formative evaluation and certainly a necessary condition for healthy programs. The literature from all the programs mentioned here elaborates on the dialogue and process of continual revision that takes place at the respective institutions.

A small state university with its mission in the liberal arts and sciences restructured its teacher education program yet another way. Evolved from a nineteenth-century normal school, it has become rather selective and recently phased out its four-year program for a five-year Master of Arts in Education program. The five-year plan, based on reform notions in the recent literature (for example, Scannell, 1983; National Commission for Excellence in Teacher Education, 1985), was approved by the state Coordinating Board for Higher Education in 1986.

When ready to define its knowledge base, the faculty instituted a series of faculty workshops at which several other models for reform and program models found in the literature were reviewed (Smith, 1980; Smith, 1983; Andrew, 1984; Schön, 1987; Smith, Krogh, Ross, and Kinzer, 1983). Faculty looked at the concepts implied in the models and programs reviewed and came to some kind of consensus on what was believed in common about what teachers needed to know and experience. A paradigm was created from the results of a faculty questionnaire requesting information about courses that addressed questions in the standards of a national professional accrediting agency. Finally, faculty came to consensus on how courses fit into the model and the extent to which the model represented delivery of the knowledge base in the curriculum (Grow-Maienza, 1990, 1991).

A small, private liberal arts college, goaded by its administration to reform, took the pulse of alumni and in the spirit of the 1960s reorganized the structure of teacher education there. Documents from the college indicate that the program changed from a behaviorally oriented program containing one common set of skills to be received by the students to a student-centered approach featuring the development of the individual in unique ways (Freeman, 1985, 1989). Again, later documents from the college reflect the well-known principle that no healthy program remains stable for long. Conceptualization of program, even after structure is in place, continues to evolve. At that college, credits have been rearranged, field experiences changed somewhat, and the work of Shulman (1987), Giroux and McLaren (1986), Short (1987), and Zeichner (see Kennedy and Zeichner, 1989) is reflected in the stated knowledge base. Today, say the documents, every course is driven by the four notions of collaboration, inquiry, reflection, and critique (Pierce and others, 1991).

Implications for Teacher Education Faculties for Defining and Articulating the Knowledge Base

Faculties will have a better sense of their own programs and a greater chance of having coherent, integrated programs if they first look at the programs and articulate the assumptions underlying them. Secondly, faculties will need then to articulate the knowledge base they will deliver to their students to meet the objectives of their programs, given their assumptions about what teachers should know and be able to do and how best they can come by that knowledge and those skills.

Placing programs in the context of a broad framework, such as one provided by Kliebard (1986) around four reform movements of the nineteenth century, may help faculties be more conscious and systematic in thinking about their own conceptualizations. Faculties and their beliefs are of course diverse. But laying out the assumptions of each reform movement, detailing the implications for what teacher education must provide for teachers, and asking faculty to identify their beliefs about the nature and purpose of education can do wondrous things for demonstrating commonalities in diverse faculties. Such an exercise can also help a faculty come to consensus on a shared knowledge base—a conception of what teachers should know and be able to do, which is generally what drives the courses and integration of courses in teacher education.

In addition to an examination of the broad conceptualizations of teacher education, to help design and come to consensus on their own program models, faculties might also investigate recently designed models for teacher education articulated in varying degrees of detail and specificity (for instance, Smith, 1980; Andrew, 1974; Tom, 1980; Shulman, 1986b, 1987; and others in De Vitis and Sola, 1989). Again, analyzing widely distributed models and coming to consensus about what is in—or what might be in—one's own program can help a faculty conceptualize its own unique model.

A practical third step might be to examine individual programs whose authors have described not only the reconceptualization and knowledge base of their programs but also how consensus and articulation of the knowledge base was accommodated.

Many examples of programs that have articulated their philosophies and knowledge bases concurrent with and following some of the reform reports of the 1980s can be found in the recent literature. Several five-year models were cited above. Disregarding the advantages or disadvantages of innovations made in those programs and the presence of substantive change or mere structural change, it may be useful for faculties of other programs to investigate how these programs examined the assumptions underlying the changes they made, the processes through which those faculties came to consensus, and how they articulated their knowledge bases on what teachers need to know, what teachers need to be able to do, and the best way to deliver that knowledge base to future teachers.

Conclusion

The purpose of this volume is to describe a common body of information and knowledge that a teacher education faculty needs to have in order to establish collectively a modern teacher education program at the college and university levels. This chapter has attempted to describe philosophical perspectives that have been influences on teacher education and its structure and to bring to the reader's attention models that have been proposed for teacher education in recent years. Finally, this chapter tries to meld conceptual aspects with the structural, with a look at four programs that have in recent years explicated their assumptions and articulated the knowledge base for their programs. It has been the intent of the chapter to encourage other faculties to place their own programs in perspective and to provide some direction for defining and articulating programs in place.

References

Andrew, M. D. (1974). *Teacher leadership: A model for change.* (Bulletin no. 37). Washington, D.C.: Association of Teacher Educators.

Andrew, M. D. (1984). *Restructuring teacher education: The University of New Hampshire's five year program.* (Report no. SP 025 588). Washington, D.C.: National Commission on Excellence in Teacher Education. (ED 250 310)

Andrew, M. D. (1986). *The University of New Hampshire's five year teacher education program: A status report after 12 years, 1974–1986.* (Report no. SP 027 289). Durham: University of New Hampshire. (ED 267 039)

Ausubel, D. P. (1963). *The psychology of meaningful verbal learning.* Philadelphia: Grune & Stratton.

Bellack, A. (1966). *The language of the classroom.* New York: Teachers College Press.

Bestor, A. (1953). *The restoration of learning.* New York: Knopf.

Borrowman, M. S. (1956). *The liberal and technical in teacher education.* New York: Teachers College Press.

Brophy, J. B., and Good, T. L. (1986). "Teacher behavior and student achievement." In M. C. Wittrock (ed.), *Handbook of research on teaching.* (3rd ed.). New York: Macmillan.

Bruner, J. (1963). *The process of education.* Cambridge, Mass.: Harvard University Press.

California Commission on the Teaching Profession (1985). *Who will teach our children?* Sacramento: California Commission on the Teaching Profession.

Carnegie Task Force on Teaching as a Profession (1986). *A nation prepared: Teachers for the twenty-first century.* New York: Carnegie Forum on Education and the Economy.

Carroll, R. G. (1989). "PROTEACH: The content and context of change in teacher education at the University of Florida." In J. L. De Vitis and P. A. Sola (eds.), *Building bridges for educational reform. New approaches to teacher education.* Ames: Iowa State University Press.

Clark, D. L., and Guba, E. G. (1977). *A study of teacher education institutions as innovators, knowledge producers and change agencies.* Washington, D.C.: National Institute of Education. (ED 139 805)

Clifford, G. J. (1985). "The formative years of schools of education in America: A five-institution analysis." *American Journal of Education, 94*(1), 427–446.

Combs, A. W. (1965). *The professional education of teachers: A humanistic approach to teacher preparation.* Needham Heights, Mass.: Allyn & Bacon.

Conant, J. B. (1963). *The education of American teachers.* New York: McGraw-Hill.

Cremin, L. A. (1962). *The transformation of the school: Progressivism in American education, 1876–1957.* New York: Knopf.

Cremin, L. A. (1977). *The education of the educating profession.* Washington, D.C.: American Association of Colleges for Teacher Education.

De Vitis, J. L., and Sola, P. A. (1989). *Building bridges for educational reform: New approaches to teacher education.* Ames: Iowa State University Press.

Dewey, J. (1916). *Democracy and education.* New York: Macmillan.

Doyle, W. (1990). "Themes in teacher education research." In W. R. Houston (ed.), *Handbook of research on teacher education.* New York: Macmillan.

Feiman-Nemser, S. (1990). "Teacher preparation: Structural and conceptual alternatives." In W. R. Houston (ed.), *Handbook of research on teacher education.* New York: Macmillan.

Flanders, N. A. (1970). *Analyzing teacher behavior.* Reading, Mass.: Addison-Wesley.

Freeman, B. (1985). *Exploring new frontiers in teacher education: The Austin teacher program.* (Report no. SP 025 173). Austin, Texas: Austin College. (ED 249 187)

Freeman, B. (1989). "Exploring new frontiers in teacher education: The Austin teacher program." In J. L. De Vitis and P. A. Sola (eds.), *Building bridges for educational reform: New approaches to teacher education.* Ames: Iowa State University Press.

Freire, P. (1970). *Pedagogy of the oppressed.* New York: Seabury Press.

Gage, N. L. (1978). *The scientific basis of the art of teaching.* New York: Teachers College Press.

Giroux, H. A., and McLaren, P. (1986). "Teacher education and the politics of engagement: The case for democratic schooling." *Harvard Educational Review, 56*(3), 213–238.

Glasser, R. (1968). *Schools without failure.* New York: HarperCollins.

Goodlad, J. I. (1964). *School curriculum reform in the United States.* New York: Fund for the Advancement of Education.

Greene, M. (1973). *Teacher as stranger.* New York: Teachers College Press.

Grow-Maienza, J. (1990). "Doing or being done to: The complexities and realities of a new MAE program." Paper presented at annual meeting of the American Association of Colleges for Teacher Education, Chicago.

Grow-Maienza, J. (1991). "Teacher education and the role of external actors: Four case studies." Paper presented at annual meeting of the American Educational Research Association, Chicago.

Herbst, J. (1989). *And sadly teach: Teacher education and professionalism in American culture.* Madison: University of Wisconsin Press.

Hirsch, E. D., Jr. (1987). *Cultural literacy: What every American needs to know.* Boston: Houghton Mifflin.

Holmes Group (1986). *Tomorrow's teachers: A report of the Holmes Group.* East Lansing, Mich.: Holmes Group.

Houston, W. R. (ed.) (1990). *Handbook of research on teacher education.* New York: Macmillan.

Howsam, R. B. (ed.) (1976). *Educating a profession.* Washington, D.C.: American Association of Colleges for Teacher Education.

James, W. (1939). *Talks to teachers on psychology.* Austin, Texas: Holt, Rinehart & Winston.

Joyce, B. R. (1975). "Conceptions of man and their implications for teacher education." In K. Ryan (ed.), *Teacher education.* (74th yearbook of the National Society for the Study of Education). Chicago: University of Chicago Press.

Kennedy, M. M., and Zeichner, K. M. (1989). "Kenneth Zeichner reflecting on reflection." *Colloquy, 2*(2), 15–21.

Kliebard, H. M. (1986). *The struggle for the American curriculum, 1893–1958.* New York: Routledge & Kegan Paul.

Lanier, J. E., and Little, J. W. (1986). "Research on teacher education." In M. C. Wittrock (ed.), *Handbook of research on teaching.* (3rd ed.). New York: Macmillan.

Lieberman, M. (1956). *Education as a profession.* Englewood Cliffs, N.J.: Prentice Hall.

Maslow, A. (1954). *Motivation and personality.* New York: HarperCollins.

Medley, D. M. (1977). *Teacher competence and teacher effectiveness: A review of process-product research.* Washington, D.C.: American Association of Colleges for Teacher Education. (ED 143 629)

Medley, D. M. (1979). "The effectiveness of teachers." In P. L. Peterson and H. Walberg (eds.), *Research on teaching: Concepts, findings, and implications.* Berkeley, Calif.: McCutchan.

Medley, D. M., and Mitzel, H. E. (1950). "A technique for measuring classroom behavior." *Journal of Educational Psychology, 49,* 86–92.

National Commission on Excellence in Education (1983). *A nation at risk: The imperative for educational reform.* Washington, D.C.: U.S. Government Printing Office.

National Commission for Excellence in Teacher Education (1985). *A call for change in teacher education.* Washington, D.C.: American Association of Colleges for Teacher Education.

Neill, A. S. (1960). *Summerhill.* New York: Hart.

Perls, F. S., Hefferline, R. F., and Goodman, P. (1971). *Gestalt therapy: Excitement and growth in the human personality.* New York: Julian Press.

Piaget, J. (1952). *The child's conception of number.* Atlantic Highlands, N.J.: Humanities Press.

Piaget, J. (1955). *The language and thought of the child.* New York: World.

Pierce, V. L., and others (1991). "Restructuring teacher education: The Austin teacher program response." Paper presented at the annual meeting of the Association of Teacher Educators, New Orleans, La.

Rogers, C. (1969). *Freedom to learn.* Columbus, Ohio: Merrill.

Ross, D. D., Johnson, M., and Smith, W. (1992). "Developing a professional teacher at the University of Florida." In L. Valli (ed.), *Reflective teacher education: Cases and critiques.* Albany: State University of New York Press.

Ryan, K. (ed.). *Teacher education.* (74th yearbook of the National Society for the Study of Education). Chicago: University of Chicago Press.

Scannell, D. (1983). *Educating a profession: Profile of a beginning teacher.* Washington, D.C.: American Association of Colleges for Teacher Education.

Scardamalia, M., and Bereiter, C. (1989). "Conceptions of teaching and approaches to core problems." In M. C. Reynolds (ed.), *Knowledge base for the beginning teacher.* Elmsford, N.Y.: Pergamon Press.

Schön, D. (1987). *Educating the reflective practitioner.* San Francisco: Jossey-Bass.

Schubert, W. H. (1989). "Reconceptualizing and the matter of paradigms." *Journal of Teacher Education, 40*(1), 27–32.

Schwab, J. J. (1963). *The biology teacher's handbook.* New York: Wiley.

Schwab, J. J. (1973). "The practical three: Translation into curriculum." *School Review, 81,* 501–522.

Short, E. C. (1987). "Curriculum decision making in teacher education: Policies, programs development, and design." *Journal of Teacher Education, 38*(4), 2–12.

Shulman, L. S. (1986a). "Paradigms and research programs in the study of teaching: A contemporary perspective." In M. C. Wittrock (ed.), *Handbook of research on teaching.* (3rd ed.). New York: Macmillan.

Shulman, L. S. (1986b). "Those who understand: Knowledge growth in teaching." *Educational Researcher, 15*(2), 4–14.

Shulman, L. S. (1987). "Knowledge and teaching: Foundations of the new reform." *Harvard Educational Review, 57*(1), 1–22.

Smith, B. O. (1980). *A design for a school of pedagogy.* Washington, D.C.: U.S. Government Printing Office.

Smith, D. C. (1983). *Essential knowledge for beginning educators.* (Report no. SP 022 600). Washington, D.C.: American Association of Colleges for Teacher Education. (ED 237 455)

Smith, D. C., Krogh, S. L., Ross, D. D., and Kinzer, S. M. (1983). *Reconceptualizing teacher education at the University of Florida.* (Report no. SP 022 796). Detroit: American Association of Colleges for Teacher Education. (ED 232 976)

Su, Z. (1986). *Teacher education reform in the United States, 1890–1986.* (Report no. EA 020 323). Seattle: Center for Educational Renewal, Washington University. (ED 298 647)

Taba, H., Levine, S., and Ellzey, F. (1964). *Thinking in elementary school.* San Francisco: San Francisco State University Press.

Tabachnick, B. R., and Zeichner, K. M. (eds.) (1991). *Issues and practices in inquiry-oriented teacher education.* Washington, D.C.: Falmer Press.

Tanner, D., and Tanner, T. (1990). *History of the school curriculum.* New York: Macmillan.

Thelen, H. A. (1954). *Dynamics of groups at work.* Chicago: University of Chicago Press.

Tom, A. R. (1980). "Teaching as a moral craft: A metaphor for teaching and teacher education." *Curriculum Inquiry, 10,* 317–323.

Tom, A. R. (1991). "Whither the professional curriculum for teachers?" *Review of Education, 14,* 21–30.

Urban, W. J. (1990). "Historical studies of teacher education." In W. R. Houston (ed.), *Handbook of research on teacher education.* New York: Macmillan.

Withall, J., and Lewis, W. W. (1963). "Social interaction in the classroom." In N. L. Gage (ed.), *Handbook of research on teaching.* Skokie, Ill.: Rand McNally.

Zeichner, K. M. (1983). "Alternative paradigms of teacher education." *Journal of Teacher Education, 34*(3), 3–9.

Zeichner, K. M., and Liston, D. P. (1987). "Teaching student teachers to reflect." *Harvard Educational Review, 57*(1), 23–48.

Zeichner, K. M., and Tabachnick, B. R. (1991). "Reflections on reflective teaching." In B. R. Tabachnick and K. M. Zeichner (eds.), *Issues and practices in inquiry-oriented teacher education.* Washington, D.C.: Falmer Press.

Zumwalt, K. K. (1987). "Tomorrow's teachers: Tomorrow's work." *Teachers College Record, 88*(3), 436–441.

Annotated Bibliography

History of teacher education:
Feiman-Nemser, S. (1990). "Teacher preparation: Structural and conceptual alternatives." In W. R. Houston (ed.), *Handbook of research on teacher education.* New York: Macmillan. The author gives a detailed historical overview of the structure of teacher education in America, chronicling various approaches used in teacher education from the early normal schools to present-day university programs and outside alternatives.

Another overview of the history of teacher education is found in Urban (1990). Revisionist approaches to the history of education are found in Herbst (1989) and Clifford (1985). Herbst suggests that the education of teachers, particularly elementary teachers, has been subject to an elitist male bias among the leaders and policy makers in teacher education. Clifford chronicles the elitist male bias in the research agenda of teacher education in her analysis of five schools of education in America.

Philosophical foundations of education:
De Vitis, J. L., and Sola, P. A. (1989). *Building bridges for educational reform: New approaches to teacher education.* Ames: Iowa State University Press.
   Authors of each chapter in this edited book describe and discuss specific programs that have made substantive and structural changes in going to an extended teacher education model. The programs are described in detail and change processes discussed.

Smith, B. O. (1980). *A design for a school of pedagogy.* Washington, D.C.: U.S. Government Printing Office.
   Examination of models designed for specific reforms or specific programs may provide direction for faculties who are engaged in articulating their own programs. In this document, the author presents a blueprint for the clinical model of teacher education that is widely used today. Examples of other documents worth examining are found in Andrew (1974), D. C. Smith (1983), Scannell (1983), and Shulman (1986b, 1987).
   Andrew (1974), in *Teacher Leadership: A Model for Change,* presents a design for teacher education in which philosophical foundations form a core for the curriculum, and all courses develop critical thinking skills. D. C. Smith (1983), in *Essential Knowledge for Beginning Educators,* summarized in detail competencies derived from the process/product research, which became the foundation for a competency-based program. *Educating a Profession: Profile of a Beginning Teacher,* by Scannell (1983), was a widely distributed model that is cited in many new programs and many reform reports today.
   In Shulman (1986b), the author advocates new methods of inquiry and reflection for teachers that circumvent the traditional bifurcation in pedagogy between subject matter and professional knowledge and that would develop both subject matter expertise and knowledge of general pedagogy for teachers. In Shulman (1987), the author's model of pedagogical reasoning focuses first on comprehension of content, then on transformation of the content so that it can be absorbed by the student, and then on reflection. The author discusses the implications of his model for the professionalization of teachers.

Tanner, D., and Tanner, T. (1990). *History of the school curriculum.* New York: Macmillan.
   Tanner and Tanner's treatise provides an excellent summary of the philosophical foundations in American education, showing the tension between the traditional and progressive spirit. The authors give excellent explanations of the traditional perennialist movement of the nineteenth century, the humanitarian and pragmatic movements at the turn of the twentieth century, and the academic movement that was a reaction to the essentialist movement in the late twentieth century.
   Other conceptualizations of the philosophical foundations of education that may help faculties place their own programs into perspective can be found in Joyce (1975), Kliebard (1986), and Zeichner and Liston (1990). Joyce's is an early work that addresses the alternative views of man in a classic conceptualization of the models of teaching. Kliebard categorizes models of schooling today as having been shaped by four forces that were to struggle for control of the American curriculum in the late nineteenth and early twentieth centuries. Zeichner and Liston discuss four traditions

of reform in twentieth-century U.S. teacher education, drawing on Kliebard's analysis of the various interest groups that have vied for control of the primary and secondary school curriculum in this century and on several recent analyses of alternative conceptual orientations in teacher education (Feiman-Nemser, 1990; Joyce, 1975; Zeichner, 1983).

CHAPTER TWENTY-TWO

PROGRAM STRUCTURES AND LEARNING TO TEACH

RICHARD ARENDS AND NANCY WINITZKY
with Arlene Ackerman Burek

An often heard argument among teacher educators (and policy makers as well) in debates about how to improve teacher education is that changing the ways programs are structured will *not* make any difference if what goes on inside the structure remains the same. Heard almost as often is the counterpoint to this argument, that simply doing more of the same old thing, *without* new structures, will not amount to much more than "straightening the chairs on the Titanic." Both of these arguments have elements of truth in them, and each can be compelling. Both, however, can also be deceiving and lead faculties and policy makers astray in their quest for improvement of teacher education.

The position taken in this chapter will be that teacher education needs to be reformed and that many of the identified weaknesses—lack of depth in liberal arts preparation, lack of depth in pedagogical knowledge, lack of integration across the various course components, and lack of articulation between college-based and field-based experiences—will require changes in the way teacher education programs are structured. We view basic program structures in teacher education as not being fundamentally different from the basic structures we create in the physical world, such as our homes or our public buildings or our highways and telephone networks. In and of themselves, these structures do not guarantee quality of family or work lives or our ability to move from one place to

We wish to thank the reviewers of the draft version of the manuscript for alerting us to the Katz and Raths (1992) analysis and for making several other suggestions that have been incorporated into the chapter.

another or communicate with friends and colleagues. Structures in every setting do, however, strongly influence the capabilities that exist and facilitate or restrict the type and quality of activities that can occur. For instance, the twentieth-century freeway structure greatly facilitated interstate commercial transportation and trade and enhanced the individual's ability to move quickly from one community or region to another. These structures have influenced the locations of our work, the composition of our communities, and countless other aspects of our family life and leisure. At the same time, our reliance on this particular transportation structure has also been restrictive. It has established economic conditions that retard the development of reliable public transportation, and it has been one of the major factors in creating adverse environmental conditions.

The way teacher education is structured cannot guarantee quality programs or world-class graduates; it can (and does), however, facilitate or restrict opportunities for particular kinds of actions and results. Based on our own experiences and the incomplete literature that exists, we take the position that program structures can make a difference in the education of teachers. We also take the position, as Katz and Raths (1992) did, that often the structure question becomes one of "optimal value."

That is, it is not a question of one structure over another but what the optimal level of a particular structure is. Take for instance the structural issues surrounding the use of cohorts, which we will describe more fully later. What is the optimal level of cohort use? Having students take classes at random with no attention to getting them into cohort groups (zero use of cohort) probably leads to lack of program coherence and fails to use the power of peer learning groups. At the same time, students could be so highly organized and controlled in cohort groups that "group think" would be encouraged and creativity by students and faculty discouraged. Exploring alternative program structures and analyzing their advantages and disadvantages with an eye toward delineating optimal structural features is the purpose of this chapter.

Three internal structures that impinge on the conduct of teacher education and on the way individuals learn to teach will be described and analyzed: time structures, degree structures, and curriculum and activity structures. Other structures such as the way childhood, middle, and secondary teacher education programs are organized or the various structural features of certification, accreditation, or the placement of schools of education within the larger university could have been considered. We limit our discussion to time, degree, and curriculum and activity structures because we think these three structures have dominated the contemporary debate about how to improve teacher education.

A brief history lesson will be used to introduce each of the three structures to show that many of the structures that exist today have histories and represent action (or omission) by teacher educators and policy makers as they strived to solve real-world problems in earlier eras. Also, we will analyze each structure through the lens of the educational reform efforts of the 1980s and the 1990s. This aspect of the discussion will describe reforms that were proposed, the stakeholders who were advocating particular changes, and the rationale behind their beliefs and actions. Each section will also include alternative structures currently being tried in the various teacher education institutions around the country. Evidence in the form of experience or research that supports continued use or discontinuation of particular structures will be included when it exists. On the latter point, we want to alert our readers that the discussions in the literature of "program structures" are currently filled much more with *prescription* than with *description*.

Time Structures

The term *time structures* refers to the amount of time devoted to particular teacher education programs and to the way time is allocated across various programmatic components. The results of most human endeavors are greatly influenced by time, a resource that always seems to be in short supply. This is true for the time we have to spend with loved ones on weekends, to use for our vacations in the summer, or to write articles and books. The Academic Learning Time research of the 1970s highlighted the strong relationship that exists between the amount of time devoted to teaching a particular subject and student performance in that subject. The position taken by many reformers over the past two decades has been that time, particularly the lack of it, has been the albatross that has hung around the neck of teacher education from the beginning.

Historical Sketch

The history of formal teacher preparation in the United States since the creation of the first normal school in 1836 has been an evolution of preparation from a few months of preparation in the period prior to the Civil War to two years and three years in the late nineteenth and early twentieth century and more recently to the contemporary four-year baccalaureate program that became the norm after World War II. The major components of teacher education programs have consisted of three parts: studies in the liberal arts education to satisfy a belief that teachers should be reasonably well-educated adults, specialization in a teaching field to support the belief that it is important to know something to teach it, and professional knowledge or command of pedagogy. These components took shape during the seventy-year period between 1840 and 1910 and consolidated during the 1920s and 1930s (Cremin, 1953, 1978; Johnson, 1989). Although not fully understood by some critics, the liberal and academic preparation of teachers has been substantial throughout most of the twentieth century. Elementary teacher candidates, for the most part, have been required to satisfy the same general education requirements as other students at colleges and universities, and secondary teacher candidates have taken the same courses in particular fields as have the non–teaching majors. This situation has left little time within a four-year (120 semester hours) college program for the professional and pedagogical component of teacher education, and unlike other fields where time for professional preparation increased significantly in the twentieth century, hours devoted to professional preparation of teachers has remained essentially the same since the 1920s, actually decreasing slightly overall and significantly in some states (for example, Texas and New Jersey). Kerr (1983) summarized credit hours devoted to professional studies between 1929 and 1979 in four career fields: teaching, law, pharmacy, and engineering. Whereas total credits required in law, pharmacy, and engineering increased from 10 to 20 percent during the fifty-year period, the total credit hours of professional studies required in secondary education decreased by 2 percent between 1929 and 1979 and by 12 percent in elementary education during this same period.

Although it may be true that extended teacher education programs will be the norm in the future, they are not yet adopted widely. For instance, the Research About Teacher Education (RATE) studies, sponsored by the American Associate of Colleges for Teacher Education (AACTE) in the late 1980s found a pattern of courses and credit hours in elementary and secondary teacher education similar to those reported by Kerr (American Associate of Colleges for Teacher Education, 1987, 1989, 1990). A recent survey of teacher education institutions by Wong and Osgathorpe (1993) shows the same situation. The pattern that still exists shows that elementary and secondary teacher candidates spend well over two-thirds of their college work on general studies and study in a teaching field and of the professional studies required, almost half consists of field experiences and student teaching.

Recent Reform Proposals

In the ten-year period between 1976 and 1986, five major proposals for reform for teacher education were published: *Educating a Profession* (Howsam, Corrigan, Denmark, and Nash, 1976), *A Design for a School of Pedagogy* (Smith, 1980), "The Phoenix Agenda" (Joyce and Clift, 1984), *Tomorrow's Teachers* (Holmes Group, 1986), and *A Nation Prepared: Teachers for the 21st Century* (Carnegie Forum on Education and the Economy, 1986). Each addressed a wide array of issues and problems associated with teacher education, but each argued that keeping teacher education within a four-year undergraduate program had severely limited the development of professional studies in teacher education, and each proposal had as its central reform the call for extending the time spent in teacher preparation.

In 1974, AACTE appointed a commission on Education for the Profession of Teaching and charged that group to study and issue a report on the "structures, processes, and governance" of teacher education to celebrate the American bicentennial. The commission was composed primarily of deans of education and prominent teacher educators of the day. After extended dialogue both within the commission and with reactor panels from across the country, they came forward with *Educating a Profession* in 1976. The report contained fifty-one recommendations, but the one that captured the most attention and generated the most controversy among AACTE's membership was the recommendation that teacher education be extended into a fifth year to afford it "adequate life space."

In 1977, a year after the bicentennial report, a study was commissioned by the National Teacher Corps and the U.S. Office of Education to review previous studies and to develop a plan for reform of teacher education. Under the leadership of B. O. Smith, a review was conducted and a series of conferences held where a wide range of issues were considered. Although Smith did not organize *A Design for a School of Pedagogy* (1980) around specific recommendations, an analysis of his overall proposal finds over twenty actions required to improve teacher education. Smith concluded that time, as it was then allocated, was insufficient for the preparation of teachers and recommended two years of graduate study leading to a master's degree in pedagogy, thus making teacher education a six-year program.

In 1984, *Educational Researcher* published a piece by Bruce Joyce and his colleague Rene Clift. The analysis found in the "Phoenix Agenda" was based on a series of studies on teacher education conducted during the late 1970s and early 1980s. Speaking as educational researchers but not necessarily for the research community, Joyce and Clift offered eighteen recommendations in the form of propositions aimed at improving teacher education. Like Smith, they recommended extending teacher education and making it into a two-year graduate program.

With considerable fanfare (prior to and following), *Tomorrow's Teachers* was published in 1986. With support of the Carnegie, Ford, Johnson, and New York Times foundations, *Tomorrow's Teachers* was written by and represented the views of a group of deans (called the Holmes Group) in colleges of education located in major research universities. *Tomorrow's Teachers* called for reform in teacher education, particularly at large, multipurpose research universities, and corresponding reform in the teaching profession itself. Specific recommendations for action number slightly over twenty but included, as did previous reports, the strong recommendation that teacher education be extended to include five years of study leading to a bachelor's degree in the arts and sciences and a master's degree in education.

A Nation Prepared: Teachers for the 21st Century also appeared in 1986. This report was a result of the work of a fourteen-member task force funded by the Carnegie Forum on Education and the Economy. Members of the task force included the presidents of both teachers' unions, the governor of New Jersey, presidents of major corporations, as well as policy-level educators working in the various states and foundations. A series of workshops and twelve commissioned papers provided the data base on which the Carnegie report rested. The report's eight major recommendations could be translated into over twenty specific proposals for improving teaching and teacher education. Prominent among them was the proposal to extend teacher education beyond four years and to conduct much of the preparation in pedagogy as part of a graduate program.

Although the five reports vary in the way they were produced and the way the data were used to support various recommendations, the arguments for extending teacher education programs can be summarized into two major points: (1) four years was viewed as insufficient time for teacher candidates to acquire a good general education, depth in a teaching field, and command of pedagogical knowledge, and (2) extending and providing graduate-level teacher preparation was believed to make better preparation possible while also enhancing the teaching profession.

Contemporary Alternatives

Currently, there are a number of teacher education programs that *extend* beyond four years. These programs can provide a glimpse of what the future may hold in terms of time structures. For the purposes of this chapter, we will describe four major reconceptualizations of time: (1) the extended, integrated five-year program leading to a bachelor's degree; (2) the extended, integrated five-year program leading to a bachelor's degree and a master's degree; (3) a fifth-year or 4 + 1 program leading to a master's degree; and (4) the six-year or 4 + 2 program leading to a master's degree.

Several extended teacher-education programs could have been chosen for illustrative purposes in the discussion that follows. We based our selection on two major criteria: (1) we knew something about the program firsthand and knew that it had been implemented pretty much as the designers had intended, and (2) some evaluation or descriptive information existed on the program.

Extended Integrated Five-Year Programs. Much of the early discussion about issues of time focused primarily on how to get more of it and the simplest way to do that was to extend the teacher preparation program from four to five years without tackling the issues associated with graduate education and advanced degrees. One of the earliest extended, integrated five-year programs was planned at the University of Kansas (KU).

Conceptualized in the late 1970s, the KU five-year program began during the 1981–82 academic year and graduated its first teachers in 1986. The program requires five years of full-time study to complete. Graduates receive a bachelor of science degree in education at the end of four years (126 hours). At the end of the fifth year, candidates receive certification for teaching in elementary, middle, or secondary schools and may have accrued fifteen hours of graduate credit, which can be applied toward a future master's degree at KU.

Teacher candidates in the KU program are required to satisfy the sixty hours of general education required of all KU students. These hours are spread across various fields (literature, social science, science, math) in a fairly typical fashion.

All secondary teaching candidates are required to complete a forty-plus-hour major in a particular teaching field. This work is similar to (and sometimes exceeds) the requirements of the major in the discipline. Elementary teaching candidates are required to complete thirty-six hours in a teaching field and to develop two twenty-hour minor fields.

Depending on the field, teacher candidates are required to complete fifty-six to sixty-two hours of professional coursework. This requirement includes courses taken during a candidate's first and second years in introduction to education, multicultural education, and human development and a traditional array of methods courses taken during years three and four. During year five, candidates take twelve to fifteen hours of graduate credit in classroom management, special education, schools, and history of education.

Field experiences are required from year one in the KU program with a great portion of the fifth year devoted to field experiences. Teacher candidates take twelve to fifteen hours of graduate-level coursework in education during the fifth year but most of it is devoted to clinical experiences. Candidates take six weeks of student teaching during the first semester and then do an unpaid "internship" for the complete second semester.

Extended Integrated Program Leading to a Bachelor's and a Master's Degree.
One of the major structural reforms called for in the previously described Holmes and Carnegie reports was to extend teacher education beyond four years and to move much of the professional preparation to the graduate level. Faculty at the University of Virginia had been studying their teacher education programs for several years when both the Holmes Group and Carnegie Forum reports were issued. Although they attribute their program design to the work of the bicentennial commission and B. O. Smith's *Design for a School of Pedagogy*, they became known as one of the first Holmes institutions to implement a graduate-level teacher preparation program where successful candidates were awarded a master's degree.

The University of Virginia (UVA) implemented its extended teacher preparation program during the 1986–87 academic year and graduated its first teachers in 1991. The program requires five years of full-time study to complete. At the end of the fifth year, two degrees are awarded simultaneously: a bachelor's degree in the arts and sciences and a master of teaching degree in education. Successful candidates can be certified to teach in elementary, secondary, or special education.

Teacher candidates complete the same general education (forty to forty-five semester hours) required of all UVA students, including coursework in the sciences, mathematics, humanities, social sciences, and history. Some general education coursework is specified for teacher candidates, such as a required course in economics for elementary teachers.

Teacher candidates complete the same requirements as other students, in particular arts and science majors. Areas in which elementary candidates can major, however, are restricted to language studies, science, mathematics, history, and social sciences. Elementary candidates are also required to complete a fifteen-semester-hour minor. The total credits for this aspect of the program consist of fifty-six to seventy-two hours, depending on the teaching field.

Overall, students complete approximately fifty-five hours in professional coursework and clinical experiences. The UVA faculty makes distinctions between generic professional studies and special professional studies. All students (elementary, secondary, and special education) complete coursework in teaching as a profession, learning and development, exceptionality, instructional planning, foundations of schools, contemporary issues, and professional ethics. These generic professional courses begin in year two and continue through year five. Specialized methods are taken by teacher candidates during years four and five.

Field and clinical experiences begin in year two and are required in each subsequent year. Clinical experiences, for the most part, are connected to the generic professional coursework. In the fall semester of the fifth year, students have a full-semester field experience called "teaching associateship." Clinical studies account for twelve to fifteen hours of the fifty-five-hour professional component.

The fall semester of the fifth year consists of the teaching associateship experience (twelve semester hours) and a seminar (three semester hours) conducted to support the teaching associateship experience. During the spring semester, candidates complete a field project in their specialty area, take a course in contemporary educational issues, and pursue six to nine hours of advanced coursework in the teaching field, after the teaching associateship provides candidates with a different and more realistic view about the content they are expected to teach.

Fifth-Year (4 + 1) Program Leading to a Master's Degree. Faculties who support the integrated programs described above have argued that introducing teacher candidates to professional studies early in their university careers and connecting liberal education with professional studies are critical for the preparation of good teachers. Others, however, have taken a different perspective. They have challenged the benefits of early career decisions and have argued that because of the way many modern universities are structured, opportunities are not afforded for integration of studies, regardless of how hard particular faculties may try. This perspective also recognizes the mobile student population found in many universities situated in urban centers. Students simply do not attend one institution of higher education for four or five years. Instead, they frequently transfer from two-year to four-year institutions and from one four-year institution to another. This situation makes planned integration and articulation across various courses and experiences, if not impossible, highly improbable. Finally, it is argued that better teachers can be prepared if we allow undergraduate students to focus on their education in the arts and sciences before making a career decision and entering a postbaccalaureate, graduate-level program as do candidates in other professional fields. A good example of this type of program is the one developed by faculty at the University of Maryland, College Park, in the mid 1980s.

Called the Maryland Master's Certification Program (MMCP), the program was implemented in 1985 and designed for students who had completed baccalaureate degrees in particular academic fields. The program consists of one calendar year of study and culminates with a master's degree and a certificate to teach in elementary or secondary schools. Teaching candidates start their studies during the first week in July and finish one year later. This schedule translates into two six-week summer school semesters and two academic year semesters.

Students are required to have a bachelor's degree from an accredited institution and a 3.0 grade point average to be admitted to the MMCP. The program accepts the general education background that candidates bring with them and makes no additional requirements. This means that the final candidate pool will bring varied and diverse general education backgrounds with them.

As with general education, the MMCP accepts, for the most part, the major as it was defined at the institution where the candidates secured their bachelor's degrees. However, transcripts are reviewed during the admission process and applicants who do not have strong academic majors that correspond to particular teaching fields are denied admission. Further, the program has space for candidates to take two or three courses in the teaching field. These courses are agreed upon between the candidate and the advisor. Most often courses are chosen that update a candidate in a particular field, particularly if the candidate has been out of school for some time, or that fill a particular gap, such as a course in U.S. history for the European history major or a course in composition for the literature major. Secondary candidates are required to have a major in the field they want to teach; various majors are accepted for elementary candidates, including such fields as business, accounting, and social work.

The MMCP features several new types of courses in pedagogy: Research on Teaching, Cognitive Psychology of Learning, Principles of Teaching, Action Research for Teachers. These courses constitute the professional core and are taken by elementary and secondary candidates as a cohort group.

Candidates in the MMCP are required to participate in a three-hour practicum during the fall semester of the program, during which they spend time in schools working with children and completing assignments attached to the various generic and special method courses. In the spring semester, students complete a twelve-week internship. Interns spend full days in the classroom but are brought to campus for two one-week workshops.

The last two weeks of the spring semester and the six-week summer semester are devoted to completing an action research project, taking comprehensive examinations, and participating in a variety of activities affording reflection and synthesis of knowledge.

Six-Year Program Leading to Master's Degree. Smith (1980), in his *Design for a School of Pedagogy,* argued, as did Joyce and Clift (1984), for a teacher education program that extends two years beyond the baccalaureate degree. To our knowledge, no institution has developed this type of program. Nonetheless, it is a serious alternative proposed by eminent educators and we will describe it here, relying mainly on Smith's conceptualization.

The six-year program outlined by Smith included (1) four years of study in the arts and sciences culminating in a bachelor's degree and (2) two years of study in pedagogy culminating in a master's degree. Unlike other reformers of that era, Smith was willing to be very prescriptive about the arts and science courses required of elementary and secondary teachers and clustered these under the following areas of knowledge: (1) the arts and symbolics of information; (2) the physical, biological, psychological, and social sciences; (3) the historical, sustaining, regulatory, and disseminative sciences; and (4) the Zetetica and integrative sciences.

Smith was also very prescriptive with his two-year (four-semester) program in pedagogy. The first semester was to be devoted to acquiring clinical knowledge and skills and would include two courses in clinical observation, clinical psychology, evaluation, evaluation laboratory, and school and community laboratory. The second semester was to focus on curriculum and instruction (both generic and content-specific), including a curriculum laboratory and a series of specialized methods courses. Semesters three and four were to be full-time work in a laboratory school where teacher candidates would teach and attend a variety of clinical seminars.

Alternative Certification Programs. We would be remiss if we did not include (albeit briefly) proposals aimed at extending teacher education beyond the traditional four-year program but that shorten the time spent in professional studies. These programs, such as the ones currently found in the states of New Jersey, Texas, and Connecticut and nationally under the auspices of "Teach for America," have several common features. Program organizers believe, as do other teacher educators, that strong liberal arts and subject-specific preparation is important. To accomplish this goal, individuals are recruited who already have bachelor's degrees in liberal arts. Candidates are given brief (four to six weeks) training in the summer prior to a school year and then are given a classroom assignment (called an internship) for which they get paid and for which, in most instances, they assume the same responsibilities as other first-year teachers. In the better alternative programs, interns are assigned a mentor and participate in special seminars. These programs normally are not associated with higher education and depend mainly on apprenticeships for completion.

Extended Programs: Evidence and Arguments Pro and Con. Most extended teacher preparation programs have not been in existence long enough for long-term studies to be conducted. At the same time, the effects of more traditional programs have likewise gone unstudied for a long time. Three sources of evidence might be considered by faculties who are thinking about redesign of teacher education and about extending the length of their programs beyond four years. These would include (1) expert judgment in regard to the efficacy and cost of extended teacher preparation programs, (2) content analysis of programs to see if the additional time has been used to address traditional weaknesses of teacher education, and (3) an emerging literature comparing graduates in four- and five-year programs. Unfortunately, studies have yet to be done that look specifically at the performance of graduates from either four-year or extended teacher preparation programs.

Expert Judgment. One very strong argument for extended programs is that every major reform report over the past two decades has recommended them. It is not that "experts can't be wrong," but when an array of different and often prestigious individuals (deans of education, educational researchers, teachers and their union leaders, as well as business executives and executives in private foundations) study a particular problem and come up with a similar solution, it carries a singular weight and validity that a sole recommendation from a particular group would not.

On the other hand, there have been some strong arguments by eminent educators against extending teacher preparation programs. These arguments fall basically into two categories: costs and efficacy. Several policy analysts, such as Hawley (1987, 1990) and Darrell (1990), have argued that without evidence showing that graduates of extended teacher education programs are better teachers or in greater demand by employing agencies, the costs of adding a fifth or sixth year of schooling cannot be justified. Others, such as Tom (1986), have argued, as we pointed out in the beginning of this chapter, that extending the time devoted to teacher preparation, without simultaneously addressing other features of programs, will make little difference.

Content Analysis. Reform of teacher education has normally aimed at two weaknesses that sufficient time would help correct: (1) insufficient subject matter knowledge and (2) insufficient integrated experiences among coursework in the arts and sciences, coursework in pedagogy, and clinical or field experiences.

An analysis of the programs we studied in preparing this chapter shows that extended teacher preparation programs have increased the number of subject matter courses taken by teacher candidates. All of the extended programs, except the University of Kansas, now require what constitutes a subject matter major for both its elementary and secondary teacher candidates. However, currently we do not have any evidence that this increased subject matter emphasis has produced a superior teacher (see McDiarmid, 1990). We can, however, observe that if programs are given more time, faculties will decide to devote some of this time to additional studies in the arts and sciences.

From an analysis of programs described in this chapter, we could find no evidence that extended programs produced more integration between coursework in the arts and sciences and coursework in pedagogy. In fact, it may be that programs such as the one at the University of Maryland or the one proposed by Smith might lead to less integration because students will pursue studies in the arts and sciences separately and before they begin their studies in pedagogy. At the same time, it would appear that designers of extended programs sought to increase the amount of clinical and field experiences and to connect these more tightly to coursework in pedagogy. Most of the extended programs we reviewed had ongoing practica or clinical experiences connected to various courses in pedagogy. All programs (with the exception of the one at the University of Maryland) also extended the amount of time devoted to field experiences and to internships.

Looking at program description and course titles makes us believe that some of the content in courses in extended programs has remained the same as that found in four-year programs. We observe courses and activities broken into the rather traditional categories of foundations courses, methods courses, and field work. A few slight departures were observed, such as the following:

- Generic coursework in teaching and learning for elementary and secondary candidates found in the University of Maryland and the University of Virginia programs
- Coursework in research and a required action research project found in the University of Maryland's program
- Work in foundations coming after the major field experience found in the University of Virginia's program

Research and Evaluation Evidence. Over the past few years, several empirical studies have been completed comparing graduates and various features of more traditional programs with extended teacher preparation programs. Although all of these studies are methodologically weak, they do provide some initial insights about the effects of extending teacher education.

In the fall of 1988, faculty at the University of Kansas conducted telephone surveys of their 1985 through 1988 graduates (see School of Education Follow-Up Studies, 1990). The 1985 respondents were graduates from the University's four-year program while the later graduates were from the five-year program. While performance data on graduates is missing, the University's evaluation group reported that graduates from the five-year program rated their degree and teacher preparation significantly higher than did graduates of the four-year program.

Headed by Michael Andrew from the University of New Hampshire, a team of researchers (see Andrew and Schwab, 1993; Oja, Barton, Smith, and Wiseman, 1993; and Kull and Bailey, 1993) surveyed graduates from eleven teacher education programs. Surveys were sent to 2,906 individuals who graduated from selected programs between 1985 and 1990. Forty-eight percent (1,394) of the graduates responded to the survey. In addition, 481 principals of these graduates responded to the survey. Researchers reported that a higher percentage of graduates from extended programs (90 percent) found jobs than did graduates of four-year programs (80 percent) and that the retention rate was higher for graduates of extended programs (87 percent) than four-year programs (78 percent). Like University of Kansas researchers, this group found that graduates from extended programs had a more positive attitude toward their teacher preparation programs than did their four-year-program counterparts. Although positive evaluations by graduates alone is certainly not a compelling reason to adopt an extended teacher education program, it is nonetheless important, particularly since graduates of teacher education programs have been among its most severe critics.

Another team of researchers from the University of Maryland (Caples and others, 1993) surveyed and interviewed forty-two graduates from Maryland's Master's Certification Program and thirty-seven graduates from four-year programs. Respondents were matched on years of experience, gender, age, and subject or grade level taught. Attitudinal scales measured teacher sense of efficacy and dispositions toward research. Performance tests measured respondents' decision-making and classroom management skills.

Respondents from the extended teacher preparation program were found not to differ from graduates of four-year programs on sense of efficacy. However, they did report a more positive disposition toward research, and they acknowledged using research in making classroom decisions more frequently than did respondents who were graduates of four-year programs. Graduates from the Master's Certification Program were also found to be more effective on a series of classroom management, problem-solving tasks than were graduates from the four-year programs.

Degree Structures

Beyond the question about how much time should be devoted to teacher education, there have been ongoing concerns about what kind of degree should be awarded to the beginning teacher.

Historical Overview

Historically, several alternatives have existed: institutions that offer a bachelor of science (B.S.) degree; institutions that provide postbaccalaureate work and award no degree; those that offer a master's in education (M.Ed.) degree; those that offer a master's of arts in teaching (M.A.T.), or a master's in teaching (M.T.) degree. Proposals have been made to create a bachelor's degree and master's degree in pedagogy.

The Bachelor's Degree. In the years following World War II, the bachelor's degree quickly became the requirement for acquiring a teaching certificate. In some institutions, the bachelor's degree for teachers is offered by colleges of arts and sciences, whereas in others it is offered by departments, schools, or colleges of education. In most institutions, the bachelor's degree is offered to teachers after they have met the general education requirements of the institutions and have completed a major (defined by the institution) and required coursework. Today, this degree requires 120 to 130 semester hours of study and can be completed in four years of full-time study. This situation has remained the norm for over a half century.

Postbaccalaureate Work Without an Additional Degree. In the 1960s, the state of California started to require all teachers to obtain a noneducation bachelor's degree and to fulfill postbaccalaureate work that leads to a teaching certificate but not to a second or advanced degree. A survey of teacher education programs by RATE researchers has shown that postbaccalaureate study not leading to a particular degree increased significantly between 1986 and 1991 (see American Association of Colleges for Teacher Education, 1989, 1990). In most instances, teacher candidates acquiring certification through postbaccalaureate work are not enrolled in special, extended teacher preparation programs, such as those described at Kansas University or the University of Maryland. Instead, candidates take a series of courses (those required for certification) already being offered by the institution as part of their regular, undergraduate teacher education program.

Recent Reform Trends

Master's Degree in Education. Several schools have extended their teacher education programs to a fifth year and offer an already existing degree (M.Ed.) to successful graduates. This is the case with the already described program at the University of Maryland and holds true for other institutions as well, such as ones at the University of Connecticut, University of Florida, University of New Hampshire, University of Massachusetts, and UCLA. Faculties at these universities have held to the belief that postbaccalaureate work should carry graduate credit, and they have strived to make the content and criteria for success in professional coursework meet the standards of graduate studies. This has been accomplished by requiring teacher candidates to read primary research and knowledge base materials rather than syntheses of this research; it also has required the completion of traditional graduate-level activities such as research papers, action research projects, and comprehensive examinations. Critics, however, argue that beginning methods courses and student teaching, regardless of what it is called, should not carry graduate level credit. They also point out that awarding the M.Ed. to the beginning teacher cheapens the degree because it is at the same level as degrees given to experienced teachers for advanced work and for certification of more highly specialized professionals, such as principals, reading specialists, or school counselors.

Master's Degree in Teaching. The criticisms described above have led some faculties to create a new degree for the beginning teacher. Among the first to take this action was the University of Virginia. The master of teaching (M.T.) degree, approved by the University of Virginia's Board of Regents, is awarded only to students who complete the University's teacher education program, thus allowing the UVA faculty to maintain their more traditional M.Ed. and M.S. degrees for experienced teachers who have completed advanced programs in particular fields such as educational leadership, curriculum and instruction, or school psychology.

Master of Arts in Teaching. Started as early as the 1930s, the master of arts in teaching (M.A.T.) degree was popularized and expanded during the 1960s at several prestigious institutions such as Harvard and Yale. Although several schools of education today are offering this degree, it originally was a new degree awarded to the beginning teacher by departments in colleges of arts and sciences. It was created to replace the regular M.A. or M.S. degree offered by arts and science departments. M.A.T. programs were originally confined to teacher candidates who had bachelor's degrees and who wanted to teach in secondary schools. Most of these yearlong programs consisted of fifteen credit hours of graduate coursework in the teaching field, two or three courses in education (methods and human development) and a semesterlong internship. In their heyday, M.A.T. programs received considerable support from the Ford Foundation, and, like several of the contemporary alternative teacher certification programs, were seen as a way to address the teacher shortage by recruiting the best and the brightest liberal arts graduates.

Evidence

There have been no comparisons that we know of among different degree structures and what effect they may have on programs and their graduates. Likely, faculties approach degree decisions as policy issues rather than as pedagogical issues. For example, discussions may center on the impact of a certification/master's degree on the institution's existing graduate programs; would it cause enrollment to diminish over time? Another consideration is the beginning teacher's marketability; some districts, in an effort to keep costs down, may not want to hire new teachers with master's degrees. Faculty also wonder if they will in effect price themselves out of the market for candidates; from the eyes of a prospective teacher, time added to training adds costs and if these costs do not result in something tangible such as an advanced degree, improved employability, or higher salary prospects, then strong disincentives exist for extended programs and advanced degrees.

Curriculum and Activity Structures

Curriculum and activity structures refer to the ways the content of teacher education is organized and presented beyond the level of individual courses. Traditionally, this content has been organized in three strands: general education, subject area major, and professional coursework, which itself in turn is broken down into foundations courses, methods courses, and field work. A persistent tension in the organization of these strands has centered on the conflicting pulls between a "liberal" orientation versus a "technical" orientation. Reformers in the liberal tradition have often critiqued the lack of intellectual rigor in teacher education, while others have maintained that teachers need to be grounded in the realities of the classroom (Bestor, 1955; Borrowman, 1956; Conant, 1963; Feiman-Nemser, 1990; Goodlad, 1990; Koerner, 1963).

Historical Overview

As we have described, the transition from normal school-based to university-based teacher education brought with it shifts from teacher educator–controlled, pragmatically oriented programs to programs held at arm's length from the schools. As teacher education became one among many functions of higher education, responsibility for teacher education programs became more diffuse. The resulting fragmentation has been much decried (Arends, 1990, 1991; Barnes, 1987; Lanier and Little, 1986). The argument is that programs of teacher education, as currently constructed, comprise too weak an intervention to challenge, much less overcome, teacher candidates' preconceptions about teaching. Many of the common goals of teacher education—for example, to induce novice teachers to replace recitation teaching with more variety in approaches, to reduce the amount of teacher talk and increase student talk, to promote more collegial workplace norms, to ground teaching in empirically, theoretically, and morally defensible practices—require more than a mere scattering of courses and field experiences. Recent proposals to reform curriculum and activity structures center around mechanisms to increase the power of teacher education through increasing program coherence and articulation.

Coherence is more often described in terms of what it is not than what it is. A coherent program would not be conceptually scattered (Barnes, 1987), responsibility for running programs would not be fragmented across the university and public school system (Goodlad, 1990), teacher educators would not advocate teaching methods that they themselves do not practice, the cultural chasm between the university and the schools would be closed (Winitzky, Stoddart, and O'Keefe, 1992). Terms like *coherence* and *course integration* seem to mean that there is some consistency across program experiences; the consistency can come from a theoretical perspective held constant across discrete courses or some other set of unifying ideas or practices.

Recent Reform Proposals

Fragmentation and the perceived disjuncture between "liberal" and "technical" were problems tackled by the Holmes Group (1986). These reformers resolved the tension between the technical and the liberal by recommending that (1) all candidates obtain a bachelor's degree in a particular content area, a nod to liberal pressures to enhance the intellectual quality of programs, and (2) universities and schools link more closely together in professional development schools (PDSs), a nod to technical pressures to enhance the pragmatic value of programs. The Carnegie Forum's recommendations (1986) were virtually identical—move teacher education to the graduate level, and develop clinical schools, analogous to teaching hospitals, that would link university and school people in teaching, teacher education, and inquiry. Ameliorating the liberal-technical tension and establishing stronger links between universities and public schools would, it was hoped, enhance program coherence and integration. Most recent program reform efforts have centered on PDSs. There are, however, three other reforms advanced to increase program coherence: cohort organization, thematic programs, and collaboration with arts and sciences faculty.

Contemporary Alternatives

In addressing these four reforms, we will provide the rationale for each, report any evidence of efficacy, and give an example from an institution that has implemented the reform.

Professional Development Schools. Without a strong link between theory and practice, between the university and the field, any hope for program coherence is futile. Many scholars have documented that once candidates enter field experiences, the influence of the cooperating teacher overwhelms and washes out the influence of university-based coursework (see Evertson, Hawley, and Zlotnik, 1985). Therefore, the recommendations of the Holmes Group and the Carnegie Forum to build school-university partnerships resonate with many university faculty.

Field experiences have always been a part of teacher education (Guyton and McIntyre, 1990). The importance of observing exemplary practice has long been recognized as a critical component in educating teachers (Watts, 1987). Student teaching has traditionally been the capstone experience, and for many candidates, student teaching represented their first exposure to the classroom setting during their professional training. A recent trend has been to begin field experiences earlier and expand the time spent in the field in order to better ground novices in classroom realities (Guyton and McIntyre, 1990; Watts, 1987; Zeichner, 1981). The downside to this has been that beginners are socialized to often nonexemplary practices even earlier, and it has also meant sacrificing other parts of the curriculum, especially foundations (Lanier and Little, 1986). This exacerbated concerns that teacher preparation was favoring the liberal too greatly over the technical (Lanier and Little, 1986).

Organizationally, for both student teaching and early field experiences, candidates' placements have often been scattered in several sites, wherever amenable cooperating teachers could be found. While this arrangement may have provided the most congenial and accomplished cooperating teachers, the side effect has been that candidates were dispersed across numerous classrooms and schools, each representing a diversity of approaches, rendering the linking of theory to practice, and the achievement of harmony and coherence between the university's teacher education curriculum and the school's almost impossible to achieve.

It was in part this perceived watering down and fragmenting of program impact that generated the PDS reform. Another in a long tradition of school-university partnership reform proposals, the PDS was designed to serve as a site of exemplary practice (see Winitzky, Stoddart, and O'Keefe, 1992). Rather than widely scattering field placements, candidates are to be clustered in PDS sites in order to maximize the impact of limited university resources. Since the university is to work closely with the schools, it is assumed that over time, philosophy and practices will converge, thus optimizing program coherence and easing the tension between technical and liberal pressures. The functions of the PDS are threefold: to serve as field placement site for teacher candidates, to promote the professional development of experienced teachers, and to advance the knowledge base on teaching and learning by supporting reflection, inquiry, and research. It is hoped that by focusing on such system-level change, meaningful reform for both schools and teacher education can take place. (For a review of university-school partnership reforms, such as lab schools and portal schools, see Stallings and Kowalski, 1990.)

Does the professional development school improve learning in teacher candidates? For example, are candidates better able to make connections between theory and practice when they pursue field experiences in PDSs rather than in traditional field settings? Are they more reflective? Are they enabled to better serve the educational needs of diverse students? As a relatively new reform, little evidence has accumulated as to PDS efficacy. However, there is some indication, albeit small, that PDSs may live up to their promise.

Stallings, Bossung, and Martin (1990) compared student teachers placed in PDSs with those placed in conventional settings. Forty-four candidates in the Houston Teaching Academy (an inner-city PDS) were compared with twenty-five control student teachers placed in middle-class, multicultural settings, both urban and suburban. A key element of this particular PDS program was a weekly seminar: student teachers met with their university supervisor for forty-five minutes and then were joined by the cooperating teachers. Multiple data sources were used to assess the effectiveness of the PDS experience: observations, questionnaires, interviews, journals. Based on the observational data, PDS candidates outperformed controls on questioning, praise and support, percent of students on task, and percent of academic statements. Follow-up studies (Stallings, 1992) revealed that many graduates of this inner-city PDS program had obtained employment in multiracial schools and were happy in these positions.

Harris (1992) assessed the utility of PDSs from an economic perspective, analyzing the costs and benefits of school-university partnerships at his institution. While he did not quantify all variables in order to determine a numeric cost-benefit ratio, he specified eight tangible and intangible variables that have a bearing on PDS effectiveness. The tangible cost variables to both university and school were increased time demands, expenses for travel and other items, and use of facilities. Additional intangible costs were increased pressures in expanding and modifying job roles, need for communication, and diminishment of control over one's own sphere. These costs, Harris argued, were offset in part by several benefits: for example, while there were more demands on facilities in one's own institution, facilities in the other institution opened up. By the same token, diminishment of control in one's own sphere paradoxically contributed to a sense of empowerment overall; formerly isolated teachers experienced increased status, for example, through university professors overtly valuing their work, even though teachers had to sacrifice some control by turning classrooms over to teacher candidates. Harris also presented preliminary evidence that the PDS was effective. For example, surveys of parents revealed highly positive attitudes about PDSs. No data were reported regarding effects on teacher candidates.

The University of Wisconsin, Milwaukee, was an early leader in PDS development. As such, their experiences in enacting PDSs can be useful. Their story is important, because from it can be gleaned a sense of what outcomes PDSs might engender and what program features and implementation practices might best produce these outcomes.

Pugach and Pasch (forthcoming) described the process of developing an "unfinished" urban elementary PDS located in a poor, inner-city neighborhood. At the outset of its partnership with University of Wisconsin, Milwaukee, the school had little special support, and turnover for students and teachers was high. The school had participated in a mandated reform effort grounded in the effective schools literature; that effort had failed to produce increases in student achievement. Because of the rigors of this environment, teachers there placed little faith in professional growth and development and exuded a sense of professional powerlessness.

Following a collaborative site selection process, initial partnership efforts focused on building trust and familiarity and on easing teacher candidates into the setting through early field experiences, not student teaching. A faculty member was assigned as a liaison to the building; the professor was brought out of one course in order to devote time to this role. The liaison visited classrooms, attended school meetings, and worked with the principal "to identify ways of supporting teacher growth" (Pugach and Pasch, forthcoming). Informal informational meetings were held with teachers to apprise them of the university's teacher education program. Further, teacher candidates made group visits to the school in conjunction with an Introduction to Teaching class.

During the ensuing years of the partnership, the primary focus was on staff development. The process of determining staff development goals became a more teacher-directed decision. Further, staff development goals evolved from short-term, technique-oriented aims to more extensive, long-term projects. The pedagogy of staff development changed from workshop plus coaching to workshop plus coaching plus action research. Student teachers began to be placed in the school, and they too became involved in the staff development process. Additional university personnel were attached to the school with the help of external funding. External funds were also used to release a teacher from classroom duties three afternoons per week to assist with coordinating PDS activities, especially supervising student teachers.

What has been learned from the Milwaukee experience? Through dedicating faculty time to the building, eased entry of student teachers, a long-term commitment to working together, collaboratively generated staff development, and the willingness of both parties to be open to influence by the other, the Milwaukee PDS was able to achieve several Holmesian goals. After four years' involvement with the university, the teachers in the Milwaukee PDS changed: they felt empowered, they became more active in influencing what happened in their building, they reached out proactively to improve their own teaching practice. Classroom practices in the school and those advocated and taught in the university moved toward congruence, thus impacting the problems of program continuity and coherence. Graduates of the Milwaukee PDS felt more comfortable and confident about working in inner-city schools.

Cohorts. Another solution to the problem of lack of articulation and coordination has been the creation of cohorts, in which students proceed through a course of study together as a group, providing opportunities for articulation and continuity among program components. The rationale for a cohort structure has centered on professional socialization. "Programs for the education of educators must be characterized by a socialization process through which candidates transcend their self-oriented student preoccupations to become more other-oriented in identifying with a culture of teaching" (Goodlad, 1990, p. 288). Goodlad suggested the use of cohort groups as one way to accomplish this needed socialization. He contrasted programs in other professions with programs of teacher education and found the cohort structure present in others but lacking in the preparation of teachers (Goodlad, 1990; Schlechty, 1985).

Lanier and Little (1986) also saw a cohort structure as a vehicle for socialization. They cited Lortie's criticism of teacher education, specifically the absence of a "shared ordeal," an important component of socialization in other professions. The shared ordeal is thought to perform several functions: "assisting occupational identity formation, encouraging collegial patterns of behavior, fostering generational trust, and enhancing self-esteem" (Lortie, cited in Lanier and Little, 1986, p. 549). Lanier and Little noted that candidates undergo the "ordeal" part during student teaching and their first year or two on the job but that the "shared" part is missing. Since the ordeal is individual rather than collective, beginning teachers are deprived of "a sense of solidarity with colleagues" (p. 549).

There is a long history of social psychological research on groups that would also suggest the utility of cohorts in teacher education programs. McGrath (1984) summarizes this research: "Proximity increases chances of interpersonal encounter, hence of communication. Communication leads to attraction, hence to subsequent communication. When a set of people communicate, and are attracted, they generate forces toward agreement on . . . those issues related to their common situation. Such forces toward agreement constitute social pressures on the individual to modify his or her attitudes and opinions . . . in accord with those of the group" (p. 240).

This attraction between members of a group is termed *cohesiveness.* Highly cohesive groups are more effective at solving problems and resolving conflicts than groups low in cohesiveness (McGrath, 1984). The assumption is that by placing teacher candidates in cohort groups—that is, by placing them in situations with greater proximity to each other—we can more effectively instill the professional attitudes we value and in so doing more effectively guide professional socialization.

Recent work in learning theory would also support the efficacy of cohorts (Black and Ammon, 1992). The role of interaction and, most important, interaction with peers has been recognized as central in the learning process. Cohort arrangements provide a mechanism within which this interaction can occur.

While the evidence on PDSs is meager, the direct evidence on the efficacy of cohorts is nonexistent. It represents a promising but as yet untested idea. Even the prevalence of cohorts is difficult to assess. Cohort structures are assumed to facilitate learning to teach through providing an emotional support system, through a more effective professional socialization process, through providing a milieu within which peers can interact and engage more deeply in the content, through building group cohesiveness, and through improving program continuity and coherence. This makes sense, but we have no direct evidence that any of this takes place; by the same token, we have no direct evidence that it does not.

The University of Utah implemented a cohort structure in the early 1980s, initially in their secondary program. It grew out of a perception of the disconnectedness of individual courses and the feeling that there was really no "program" in any sense of the word. At that time, the professional segment of the secondary program consisted of three elements: a curriculum course, an instruction course, and student teaching, all taught by different people. It was relatively simple to adjust schedules and assign one instructor to all three courses and to assign one group of students to that instructor.

A few years later, cohorts were implemented in the more complicated elementary program. Elementary faculty adapted the cohort idea by adding an ongoing seminar taught by the cohort leader, a tenure-track or clinical faculty member. Methods faculty rotated in and out of the cohort, but the cohort leader stayed with one group of students for a year. The cohort leader took responsibility for helping students integrate information across methods classes, facilitating clinical assignments, supervising candidates, and helping methods faculty coordinate their courses with each other and with cooperating teachers. Classes were scheduled as a block, and faculty coordinated their classes and field work within that block.

Both the secondary and elementary programs have expanded since first implementing cohorts, and the cohort structure has remained a strong component of each. Cohorts have become one of the most positively regarded aspects of the Utah program, highly rated on in-house surveys by teacher candidates and cooperating teachers alike. Candidates report that they appreciate the support system and collegiality that come from the cohort organization. The cohorts also created a structure within which faculty were supported in working together and in which program continuity could be supported through the cohort leader, now a feature of the secondary program as well. The structure also facilitated coordination with schools. As the cohorts developed, cohort leaders were assigned to specific schools, ensuring continuity from year to year. Meetings are held on-site at least quarterly between school and university faculty, facilitated by the cohort leader, to discuss aims, assignments, and logistics.

The cohort structure has become institutionalized at the University of Utah, but it would be misleading to leave the impression that the transition was an easy one. The change was relatively uncontroversial for the secondary faculty because most considered themselves generalists and had taught each of the individual components separately. However, there were conflicts among the elementary faculty about whether the benefits outweighed the costs. The central issue revolved around faculty autonomy. Professors had been accustomed to teaching their courses in the way they thought best without consultation with anyone. To make scheduling, curriculum, or instructional concessions to colleagues was troubling for some. More problematic though were field placements. Accompanying the shift to cohorts was a concurrent shift from scattered field placements, coordinated by individual methods professors to obtain the best classroom models in their specific subject area, to field placements concentrated in just a few sites. What was gained was the ability to build more collegiality and continuity into the experience for candidates and to increase the opportunity for coordinating with cooperating teachers. What was lost was the use of several exemplary practitioners in particular subject areas. The disagreements were resolved initially by allowing certain adamant professors to opt out of the cohort structure. Of course, this weakened the integrative aspects of the experience for candidates, but for the department, the action provided a temporary bridging maneuver between the former laissez-faire system and the current one, in which virtually all faculty buy into the cohort rationale and organization.

An additional problem area has surfaced. The cohort structure appears indeed to engender greater group cohesiveness and emotional support. But the higher levels of agreement can be for desired or undesired attitudes. Sometimes teacher candidates come to value the place of reflection, lifelong learning, and the importance of research as a source of knowledge; sometimes they become socialized earlier and more thoroughly to norms in opposition to intellectual rigor and reflection. The evidence is only anecdotal but bears more systematic research.

Thematic Programs. Some argue that tinkering with program features such as program length (four versus five years) or cohort structures by themselves is bound to be ineffectual (Feiman-Nemser, 1990). Of more value is to directly confront the conceptually scattered nature of teacher education by infusing themes into programs—that is, by organizing programs around a particular conceptual orientation. "An orientation refers to a set of ideas about the goals of teacher preparation and the means for achieving them. Ideally, a conceptual orientation includes a view of teaching and learning and a theory about learning to teach. Such ideas should give direction to the practical activities of teacher preparation" (Feiman-Nemser, 1990, p. 220). Feiman-Nemser makes a distinction between program structure and conceptual orientation, arguing that an orientation can express itself in many forms. We take the view, however, that orientation is itself a structural feature and that in turn a particular structure should emerge from a particular orientation.

Barnes (1987) supports the use of thematic programs: "Individual courses typically skim the surface of knowledge from a variety of disciplines that are thought to inform the teaching process without offering serious and in-depth study of these domains. Because field experiences typically are not articulated with the theoretical (albeit fragmented) views of teaching offered within campus-based courses, prospective teachers develop a sketchy vision of teaching, which frequently includes bits and pieces of professional knowledge but lacks coherence, stability, and grounded justification for teaching practice" (p. 14).

Barnes describes the move to thematic programs as a response to the realization that traditional programs were too weak to have any impact on prospective teachers' thinking or practice. The hope is that a "set of coherent coursework experiences" will "significantly increase the power of formal teacher preparation to overcome students' naïve conceptions about teaching and create alternative views of effective teaching practice" (p. 14).

Little research has accumulated as to the prevalence of program themes or the efficacy of these themes in helping teacher candidates learn. The most comprehensive evidence available comes from the University of California, Berkeley; developmental researchers Ammon, Black, Levin, Hutcheson, and Kroll have conducted a number of studies demonstrating the effects of Berkeley's Developmental Teacher Education (DTE) program. Relying on a teacher development framework devised by Ammon and Hutcheson (see Ammon and Hutcheson, 1989; Ammon, Hutcheson, and Black, 1985), Levin and Ammon (1991) conducted a case study on four graduates of the DTE program. They found that teachers' pedagogical conceptions progressed, albeit unevenly, over the course of the program and through their third year of teaching, moving from an initial "naïve empiricism" toward the "integrated constructivism" taught in the program.

Teacher educators at Michigan State have developed several alternative thematic programs. In the Academic Learning Program, for example, the focus is on subject matter, and the aim is to foster deep understanding of academic disciplines. Coursework emphasizes the structure of the disciplines and conceptual over algorithmic instruction. The emphases in the Heterogeneous Classrooms Program, however, are on teaching diverse students, on the use of education to promote social justice, and on the origins and organization of diversity in our society. Through comparing responses on entry, exit, and follow-up questionnaires, Barnes (1987) reported that "graduates of thematic programs are generally more satisfied with the quality of their programs than is true of alumni from the traditional program" (p. 16). Further, perceptions of program impact were higher for graduates of thematic programs than for the traditional program. Thematic programs also seemed to engender greater sensitivity to the importance of teacher expectations and to heighten expectations for all students. Finally, "those completing thematic programs also were more likely to report a preference to negotiate classroom rules and to work with low motivated students" (p. 17). (See also Howey and Zimpher, 1989, for more descriptions of thematic programs.)

The program at UC Berkeley was organized around a developmental-constructivist theory of learning. Black and Ammon (1992) describe it as grounded in Piagetian developmental theory and research: "In the Piagetian view, learning in the sense of making associations (i.e., memorizing) is subordinated to a more fundamental process of active assimilation whereby new information is interpreted in terms of existing understandings. These understandings evolve as the lack of fit between newly assimilated information and old understandings forces a reformulation. Reformulation takes time as bits and pieces of information are recombined, and higher-level understandings typically emerge after repeated (recursive) interactions with the problem at hand" (p. 324).

This developmental-constructivist theme colors program structure, curriculum, and instructional practices. The two-year program is organized around three areas of study: developmental theory and research, teaching methods, and field studies. Fifteen to twenty teacher candidates begin the program each year and progress as a cohort, sharing few if any courses with other students.

During the first year, "the series of core program seminars emphasizes developmental theory and research first and classroom applications second" (Black and Ammon, 1992, p. 326). These seminars, on cognitive and language development, social and moral development, and psychological development, help candidates to become grounded in knowledge about children, how they think and grow, and to consider the implications of children's development on the classroom. In addition, they take mathematics, reading, language arts, social studies, and science methods classes as well as multicultural education. Field experiences also figure largely during the first year. Three separate placements give candidates familiarity with classroom dynamics and the opportunity for limited practice teaching in different grade levels and in different communities; a seminar is taken in conjunction with field work.

During the second year of the program, "the core program seminars for teaching mathematics, science, and literacy are now directed at integrating theory and practice within a developmental framework. Theoretical and practical material covered separately in the first year is reintroduced at a higher level for purposes of integration" (Black and Ammon, 1992, p. 329). Additional coursework includes short classes on teachers' legal rights and responsibilities and on mainstreaming. Candidates continue to pursue diverse field experiences and take an accompanying seminar, assuming increasing responsibilities. Candidates also complete a master's project at the end of the second year involving research on developmental teaching. "In terms of academic achievement, the master's project represents a culmination of lessons learned about applying developmental theory and research to teaching. In many cases the results are incorporated into the DTE curriculum" (p. 331).

Collaboration with Arts and Sciences.

Collaboration with Arts and Sciences. All of the above reforms represent changes in how teacher education itself is structured. But what about the academic studies that precede teacher education? If teacher education programs are conceptually scattered and difficult to articulate, the problem is exacerbated when the focus is broadened to include other units in the university. Many have critiqued undergraduate education on the same grounds as teacher education, for a lack of intellectual rigor, relevance, depth, and coherence (Barzun, 1993; Boyer, 1987; Schwab, 1969), and the connections between subject matter preparation and teacher education are tenuous. The remedy has been to improve the links between education faculty and faculties in other disciplines through increased collaboration. As a very recent structural innovation, no empirical studies have yet been conducted.

The Project 30 Alliance is a consortium of thirty institutions of higher education whose aim is to produce "better educated, better prepared teachers through collaborative curriculum redesign" (Project 30 Alliance, 1991, p. iii). Education faculty and arts and sciences faculty are jointly engaged in the reform process. Each institution is developing its own strategies and programs. Of special interest is the program under development at the University of Delaware. Faculty there have tackled the problem of subject matter preparation for elementary teachers and are in the process of reworking the existing separate subject minors into an interdisciplinary major. Five approaches to such a redesign are being considered:

1. *Philosophy of subject matter.* Rather than take a variety of courses within a single field, students would study the philosophy of each subject area, the philosophy of science, history, aesthetics, and so on. It is hoped that students would come to understand the fundamentals and underlying structure of each area.

2. *Text approach.* Students would study the great books and the commonly

used school textbooks in each domain. This would provide students with under-standing about the origins of the organizing ideas in each discipline.

3. *Genetic epistemology.* Students would study the process of development of knowledge within each domain and come to understand the constraints operat-ing at each stage of development. In so doing, they would necessarily come to un-derstand the subject itself; for example, tracking children's development of a sense of number would entail exploring number theory.

4. *Cognitive psychology.* Students would explore, for example, how the mind "does" math. "Each area would be approached from the perspective of how we think about and know the content in question" (Project 30 Alliance, 1991, p. 28).

5. *Pedagogical content knowledge.* The object of study within this approach is the juncture between knowledge of teaching and knowledge of subject matter. Stu-dents would explore what constitutes a good example, analogy, question, or theme within each discipline.

Discussion

All of these reforms make sense, and there is some evidence that they are more effective than traditional programs. If that is the case, why are not more institu-tions implementing them? We suspect that collaborative programs with arts and science, PDSs, cohorts, and thematic programs are difficult to implement for similar reasons. Building coherence requires building shared understanding, which takes dialogue, time, and compromise. The diffuse nature of teacher education means these reforms require articulating across specialties, units, and institutions, and this can be laborious logistically and frustrating conceptually. There are few institutional rewards for the work of building coherence, and there are few means for estab-lishing the benefits that might accrue from coherent programs. In higher educa-tion, a long tradition of academic freedom and faculty autonomy works against collaboration. The necessary adjustments needed to produce coherence are also hampered because in the university, district, and state bureaucracies, every ac-commodation requires approval by every other unit. By the time changes are ap-proved, the parties most intimately involved in implementing the change have often changed their thinking themselves in response to new experience and new research.

Surprisingly, coherence as an aim in redesigning teacher education programs is not universally seen as a good thing. Buchmann and Floden (1992), for exam-ple, argue that too often coherence is operationalized as consistency and that con-sistency is miseducative: "A program that is too consistent fits students with blinders . . . and encourages complacency. Remember that being focused is good only if people are heading in a good direction. . . . [I]f learners are repeatedly presented with objects of thought that others have trimmed to fit patterns, they lack op-portunities for responsibly making sense" (p. 4).

Buchmann and Floden seem to have confused program coherence with a transmission model of the curriculum. Thematically driven, conceptually coherent programs, such as Berkeley's, the program under discussion at Delaware, and others, are designed precisely to give teacher candidates the experience of discovering their own patterns, for constructing their own theoretically and ethically defensible understandings about teaching and learning. Consistency is not necessarily miseducative; it depends on how it is done. For example, a program can be designed to consistently require candidates to reflect on their practice in light of child development theory, social justice concerns, the process-product research, and/or their own experiences as learners. This type of consistency would be very different from one that, for example, promulgated one and only one model of classroom management in every course and every field experience. At bottom, these issues remain empirical questions; we do not know the effects of coherence and consistency, however they are operationalized, on prospective teachers. We do know, however, that something is amiss with the fragmented nature of current programs, and we would argue that it is premature to critique coherence before it has even been tried.

Changing Structures and Reform

We have reviewed available information on time structures, degree structures, and curriculum and activity structures, such as professional development schools, cohorts, thematic programs, and collaborations with arts and sciences. The reforms we have described are promising but largely untested. The problem is quantity: we need more case studies of the type conducted by the Berkeley group that give us detailed information on how teacher knowledge progresses, and we need more comparative studies like those done at Michigan State, Houston, and Maryland, which tell us how variations in programs lead to different outcomes. Also, as with any type of innovation, studies of the process of development and implementation of PDSs, themes, extended programs, and so on, would be very helpful.

The impediments to doing such research, however, are many. As a field, we lack valid outcome measures. What outcomes are important to us, and how can we accurately measure them? Also, such research is politically dangerous, running the risk of intimating that one school or one program is good, while another, which lacks a cohort or PDS or some other innovation, is bad. How do you persuade comparison programs to participate in such studies? There are in addition all the logistical difficulties of coordinating across numerous stakeholders (teachers, candidates, professors, and so on). This coupled with the fact that teacher educators control only a portion of their professional programs means that many designs, especially experimental ones in which causal conclusions could be drawn, are not possible. Further, research is time-consuming, and all the time and energy of people interested in reform are being channeled into program development, with little left over for evaluation. Perhaps the most serious impediment is the uncertainty about the value added of any particular study. Given the multiplicity of factors that contribute to candidates' learning and the evolutionary nature of most reforms (for example, many schools are labeled PDSs that are actually still in the long process of becoming PDSs), the likelihood of detecting program effects may be very small. If you have a stake in a program, or if editors are biased in favor of studies that show positive effects, why take the risk? In addition, of course, there is little or no money to support research and evaluation in teacher education.

As we strive to improve the knowledge base on the effects of program structure on learning to teach, however, we must remember the caveat with which we opened this chapter. Structural factors provide the boundaries surrounding teacher education, but these factors are not sufficient in themselves to guarantee excellent programs. The "stuff" that goes on inside the structure must be excellent, too; by the same token, good things are much less likely to happen within a faulty structure. We need to improve program structures in teacher education, but at the same time, we need to improve everything else.

References

Andrew, M. D., and Schwab, R. (1993). "An outcome assessment of graduates of eleven teacher education programs." Paper presented at annual meeting of American Educational Research Association, Atlanta.

American Association of Colleges for Teacher Education (1987). *Teaching teachers: Facts and figures I (RATE I)*. Washington, D.C.: American Association of Colleges for Teacher Education.

American Association of Colleges for Teacher Education (1988). *Teaching teachers: Facts and figures II (RATE II)*. Washington, D.C.: American Association of Colleges for Teacher Education.

American Association of Colleges for Teacher Education (1989). *Teaching teachers: Facts and figures (RATE III)*. Washington, D.C.: American Association of Colleges for Teacher Education.

American Association of Colleges for Teacher Education (1990). *Teaching teachers: Facts and figures (RATE IV)*. Washington, D.C.: American Association of Colleges for Teacher Education.

Ammon, P., and Hutcheson, B. P. (1989). "Promoting the development of teachers' pedagogical conceptions." *Genetic Epistemologist, 17*(4), 23–29.

Ammon, P., Hutcheson, B. P., and Black, A. (1985). "Teachers' developing conceptions about children, learning, and teaching: Observations from a clinical interview." Paper presented at the annual meeting of the American Educational Research Association, Chicago.

Arends, R. I. (1990). "Connecting the university and the school." In B. R. Joyce (ed.), *Changing school culture through staff development*. (1990 yearbook of the Association of Supervision and Curriculum Development). Alexandria, Va.: Association of Supervision and Curriculum Development.

Arends, R. I. (1991). "Challenging the regularities of teaching through teacher education." In N. B. Wyner (ed.), *Current perspectives on the culture of schools*. Boston: Brookline Books.

Barnes, H. L. (1987). "The conceptual basis for thematic teacher education programs." *Journal of Teacher Education, 38*, 13–18.

Barzun, J. (1993). *The American university: How it runs, where it is going.* (2nd ed.). Chicago: University of Chicago Press.

Bestor, A. (1955). *The restoration of learning.* New York: Knopf.

Black, A., and Ammon, P. (1992). "A developmental-constructivist approach to teacher education." *Journal of Teacher Education, 43,* 323–335.

Borrowman, M. S. (1956). *The liberal and technical in teacher education: A historical survey of American thought.* New York: Teachers College Press.

Boyer, E. L. (1987). *The undergraduate experience in America.* New York: HarperCollins.

Buchmann, M., and Floden, R. E. (1992). "Coherence, the rebel angel." *Educational Researcher, 21*(9), 4–9.

Caples, M., and others (1993). "Graduate teacher evaluation project." Paper presented at annual meeting of the American Educational Research Association, Atlanta.

Carnegie Forum on Education and the Economy (1986). *A nation prepared: Teachers for the 21st century.* New York: Carnegie Foundation.

Conant, J. B. (1963). *The education of American teachers.* New York: McGraw-Hill.

Cremin, L. A. (1953). "The heritage of American teacher education" (parts 1 and 2). *Journal of Teacher Education, 3,* 163–170, 246–250.

Cremin, L. A. (1978). "The education of the educating professions." Lecture presented at the annual meeting of the American Association of Colleges for Teacher Education, Washington, D.C.

Darrell, L. R. (1990). "Estimating the economic worth of a 5th-year licensure program for teachers." *Educational Evaluation and Policy Analysis, 12,* 25–39.

Evertson, C. M., Hawley, W. D., and Zlotnik, M. (1985). "Making a difference in educational quality through teacher education." *Journal of Teacher Education, 36*(13), 2–12.

Feiman-Nemser, S. (1990). "Teacher preparation: Structural and conceptual alternatives." In R. W. Houston (ed.), *Handbook of research on teacher education.* New York: Macmillan.

Goodlad, J. I. (1990). *Teachers for our nation's schools.* San Francisco: Jossey-Bass.

Guyton, E., and McIntyre, D. J. (1990). "Student teaching and school experiences." In R. W. Houston (ed.), *Handbook of research on teacher education.* New York: Macmillan.

Harris, C. R. (1992). "Cost-benefit analysis of partner schools." Paper presented at the annual meeting of the American Educational Research Association, San Francisco.

Hawley, W. D. (1987). "The high costs and doubtful efficacy of extended teacher-preparation programs." *American Journal of Education, 95,* 275–298.

Hawley, W. D. (1990). "Systematic analysis, public policy-making, and teacher education." In W. R. Houston (ed.), *Handbook of research on teacher education.* New York: Macmillan.

Holmes Group (1986). *Tomorrow's teachers.* East Lansing, Mich.: Holmes Group.

Howey, K. R., and Zimpher, N. L. (1989). *Profiles of preservice teacher education: Inquiry into the nature of programs.* Albany: State University of New York Press.

Howsam, R. B., Corrigan, D. C., Denmark, G. W., and Nash, R. J. (1976). *Educating a profession.* Washington, D.C.: American Association of Colleges for Teacher Education.

Johnson, W. R. (1989). "Teachers and teacher training in the twentieth century." In D. Warren (ed.), *American teachers: Histories of a profession at work.* New York: Macmillan.

Joyce, B. R., and Clift, R. T. (1984). "The Phoenix agenda: Essential reform in teacher education." *Educational Researcher, 13,* 5–18.

Katz, L. G., and Raths, J. D. (1992). "Six dilemmas in teacher education." *Journal of Teacher Education, 43,* 376–385.

Kerr, D. H. (1983). "Teaching competence and teacher education in the United States." In L. S. Shulman and G. Sykes (eds.), *Handbook of teaching and policy.* White Plains, N.Y.: Longman.

Koerner, J. D. (1963). *The miseducation of American teachers.* Boston: Houghton Mifflin.

Kull, J., and Bailey, J. (1993). "Perceptions of recent graduates: Leadership and standing out." Paper presented at annual meeting of American Educational Research Association, Atlanta.

Lanier, J. E., and Little, J. W. (1986). "Research on teacher education." In M. C. Wittrock (ed.), *Handbook of research on teaching.* (3rd ed.). New York: Macmillan.

Levin, B. B., and Ammon, P. (1991). "The development of beginning teachers' pedagogical thinking: A longitudinal analysis of four case studies." Paper presented at the annual meeting of the American Educational Research Association, Chicago.

Lortie, D. C. (1975). *Schoolteacher: A sociological study.* Chicago: University of Chicago Press.

McDiarmid, G. W. (1990). "The liberal arts: Will more result in better subject matter understanding? *Theory into Practice, 29,* 21–29.

McGrath, J. E. (1984). *Groups: Interaction and performance.* Englewood Cliffs, N.J.: Prentice Hall.

Oja, S. N., Barton, R. Smith, D., and Wiseman, D. (1993). "Perceived self-efficacy and its relationship to selected items on the survey of graduates in the eleven-university survey." Paper presented at annual meeting of American Educational Research Association, Atlanta.

Project 30 Alliance (1991). *Project 30 year two report: Institutional accomplishments.* Newark: University of Delaware.

Pugach, M. C., and Pasch, S. H. (forthcoming). The challenge of creating urban professional development schools." In R. Yinger and K. N. Borman (eds.), *Restructuring education: Issues and strategies for communities, schools, and universities.* Norwood, N.J.: Ablex.

School of Education Follow-Up Studies (1990). *A longitudinal appraisal of program outcomes: Composite report.* Lawrence: University of Kansas.

Schlechty, P. C. (1985). "Teaching as a profession: What we know and what we need to know." Paper presented at the annual meeting of the American Educational Research Association, Chicago.

Schwab, J. J. (1969). *College curriculum and student protest.* Chicago: University of Chicago Press.

Smith, B. O. (1980). *A design for a school of pedagogy.* Washington, D.C.: U.S. Government Printing Office.

Stallings, J. A. (1992). "Lessons learned from a four-year case study of preparing teachers for inner-city schools." Paper presented at the annual meeting of the American Educational Research Association, San Francisco.

Stallings, J. A., Bossung, J., and Martin, A. (1990). "Houston Teaching Academy: Partnership in developing teachers." *Teaching and Teacher Education, 6,* 355–365.

Stallings, J. A., and Kowalski, T. J. (1990). "Research on professional development schools." In W. R. Houston (ed.), *Handbook of research on teacher education.* New York: Macmillan.

Watts, D. (1987). "Student teaching." In M. Haberman and J. M. Backus (eds.), *Advances in teacher education,* Vol. 3. Norwood, N.J.: Ablex.

Winitzky, N. E., Stoddart, T., and O'Keefe, P. (1992). "Great expectations: Emergent professional development schools." *Journal of Teacher Education, 43,* 3–18.

Wong, M. J., and Osgathorpe, R. T. (1993). "The continuing domination of the four-year teacher education program: A national survey." *Journal of Teacher Education, 44,* 64–70.

Zeichner, K. M. (1981). "Reflective teaching and field-based experience in teacher education." *Interchange, 12*(4), 1–22.

Annotated Bibliography

Goodlad, J. I. (1990). *Teachers for our nation's schools.* San Francisco: Jossey-Bass.
Goodlad reports the findings of his extensive study on the education of educators. Through exhaustive observations, interviews, and surveys, Goodlad paints a picture of contemporary teacher education programs. Based on these findings, he makes a series of recommendations for its reform, among them that schools of teacher education should become entities detached from the university as a whole, analogous to law schools and medical schools.

Holmes Group (1990). *Tomorrow's schools: Principles for the design of professional development schools.* East Lansing, Mich.: Holmes Group.
The Holmes Group presents the rationale, goals, and a general framework for professional development schools (PDSs). An eloquent, well-reasoned, and solidly research-based argument is presented for PDSs. This volume launched the current major reform effort in teacher education.

Howey, K. R., and Zimpher, N. L. (1989). *Profiles of preservice teacher education.* Albany: State University of New York Press.
Howey and Zimpher present case studies of six Midwest teacher education programs housed at a variety of institutions. Through careful and detailed exposition of the data (observations and interviews), they demonstrate some of the exemplary practices and some of the problems inherent in programs of teacher education. Their cross-case analysis highlights the key issues and offers suggestions for effective programs.

Howsam, R. B., Corrigan, D. C., Denmark, G. W., and Nash, R. J. (1976). *Educating a profession.* Washington, D.C.: American Association of Colleges for Teacher Education.
Although some of the ideas expressed in it are now dated, this is still an important book for teacher educator audiences interested in program structures. It provided the first full rationale and justification for extending teacher education beyond four years and influenced many of the early fifth-year and five-year programs.

Woolfolk, A. E. (ed.) (1989). *Research perspectives on the graduate education of teachers.* Englewood Cliffs, N.J.: Prentice Hall.
Woolfolk brings together a number of scholars who examine the graduate preparation of teachers from a variety of research perspectives. Individuals studying teacher preparation, classroom instruction, educational policy, the development of teaching expertise, educational philosophy, instructional psychology, student cognition, and educational administration each bring their own unique focus to analyzing extended programs.

CHAPTER TWENTY-THREE

PROGRAM PEDAGOGY

KATHY CARTER AND DEBORAH ANDERS

This chapter contains a survey of the core pedagogical approaches and strategies available today to the teacher education community. The emphasis is on conveying the nature of these approaches and strategies, the assumptions that underlie their design, the research upon which they are based, the arguments for and against their use, and the factors that must be considered in actually using them for the education of teachers.

The scope of the chapter is restricted to pedagogy for the professional sequence, those experiences that are directed primarily to the exercise of teaching responsibilities, rather than for courses in general education, foundations, or specialized subject matter preparation. Moreover, although teacher education is best thought of as a continuum that spans both preservice and inservice phases, we concentrate primarily on pedagogy for initial teacher preparation. This is a somewhat narrow stipulation since there are exciting pedagogies emerging in many of the contexts in which teacher education takes place. However, this delimitation serves two important purposes. First, it prevents overlap with other chapters in this volume that concentrate on field experiences, student teaching, and inservice activities. Second, it specifies an identifiable and manageable body of literature within the field of teacher education.

Choices of pedagogy depend of course on what one thinks the enterprise of teacher education is about and how it works. When it was thought that teacher education was largely a process of skill training, considerable emphasis was given to protocol materials, laboratory experiences, and videotaped feedback (see Cruickshank and Metcalf, 1990, for the authoritative review of this work). With the modern emphasis on cognition, reflection, and personal perspectives in teacher preparation, narrative and dialogue methods have become prominent in discussions of ways to educate teachers to think richly about teaching (see Carter, 1993; Clandinin, 1992; Shulman, 1992; Sykes and Bird, 1992). Thus, it is not easy to separate pedagogy from curriculum in teacher education or from basic assumptions about how teachers learn to teach (see Carter, 1990b). The discussion of pedagogical approaches and strategies in this chapter is framed therefore within an analysis of alternative views of what is to be accomplished in the education of teachers.

For analysis and discussion, teacher education pedagogies have been grouped into three broad categories: (1) teaching laboratories and simulations, (2) field-based pedagogies, and (3) narrative methods, including the use of cases and story. Within these categories, attention is given to pedagogical issues in professional development schools and to cooperative methods for teacher education. Although we have attempted to be comprehensive, space limitations have forced us to be selective in our treatment of many of the issues and nuances of meaning in this area. It is our hope that the present discussion, one of the few of its kind in the professional literature, will create a foundation for theory, research, and development related to teacher education pedagogy and prompt others to devote their energies to this important domain.

Pedagogy and the Enterprise of Teacher Education

The preservice preparation that teachers receive is primarily an enterprise of colleges and universities. As a result, much of what happens in teacher education is shaped by the dominant structures—credit hours, courses, class schedules, the design of classroom space—and the prevailing pedagogical forms—lectures, term papers, examinations—of these institutions. As Doyle (1990b) remarks, "the form of most professional coursework is indistinguishable from the rest of undergraduate education" (p. 6).

Professional offerings that reflect these conventional features of university teaching have been denounced over the years by critics (Conant, 1963) and graduates (Yamamoto and others, 1969) alike, who tend to place special value on the learning of teaching by apprenticeship during student teaching. Partially in response to these criticisms, teacher educators have over the years struggled to devise pedagogies that promise to increase the power and effectiveness of preservice experiences. These efforts have in turn been driven by a variety of conceptions about the purposes and functions of teacher education, conceptions that are not always consistent or even compatible. To understand the full range of teacher education pedagogies, therefore, it is necessary to review the prevailing frameworks and emerging conceptions that have shaped and are shaping development in this area.

Frameworks for Teacher Education Pedagogy

Drawing upon analyses by Doyle (1990b), Feiman-Nemser (1990), and Zeichner (1983), we can identify five major orientations to teacher education that have substantial implications for the design and/or selection of teacher education pedagogies. These include (1) a practical/craft orientation, (2) a technological orientation, (3) a personal orientation, (4) an academic orientation, and (5) a critical/social orientation. As will be seen in the following brief discussion, each of these orientations reflects a somewhat different stance toward the goals and nature of teacher preparation.

Three considerations must be kept in mind throughout the discussion. First, these orientations represent clusters of ideas rather than clearly distinguishable categories. At the edges of each orientation, there is frequently a blending with aspects of other orientations. Moreover, individuals may often find kinship with more than one orientation, depending upon the issue at hand. Second, across orientations there is a common belief that teacher education is an instrument for improving schooling. Thus, teacher education is typically set against "traditional" school practice as a force for innovation and change (see Joyce and Clift, 1984). Most agree, in other words, that teachers should be taught how to teach but not to teach in conventional ways. Finally, we are currently in the midst of a profound shift in the core conceptions of teaching and teacher education, one that is transforming basic notions in the field. This shift will be reflected in the discussion and then addressed specifically in the section, which follows this one, on the emerging conception of teachers as reflective professionals.

The Practical/Craft Orientation.

From a practical/craft perspective, emphasis in teacher education is on preparing teachers to deal effectively with the "real world" of schooling—the management of classes, the conduct of lessons, and the performance of the many other tasks a teacher faces throughout the school day and year. Of course, the teaching methods to be used or the models to be emulated may well represent the latest advances in teaching (for example, whole language, math for conceptual understanding, and so forth); however, the stress is not just on theory but rather on practical ways of carrying out these approaches. Indeed, "theory" is often a shibboleth for "irrelevance" in the education of teachers.

With respect to teacher education pedagogy, this orientation fosters an interest in demonstration lessons, exemplary models, and apprenticeships with especially competent and committed practitioners. Novice teachers are also often encouraged to collect artifacts, materials, and other practical tools used by outstanding teachers.

Practicality, craft knowledge, and apprenticeship in teacher education have often been seen as unscientific and conservative against the promise of professionalization, innovation, and reform arising from psychological research or philosophical premises (Buchmann, 1987). Recently, however, cognitive scientists have extolled the virtues of situated cognition, communities of practice, and apprenticeship modes of learning (Brown, Collins, and Duguid, 1989). Moreover, the craft perspective has been given new energy within an emerging focus on the special knowledge or "wisdom" teachers derive from the actual practice of teaching and from examining and reflecting on their own experiences (Grimmett and MacKinnon, 1992). This theme will be explored more fully shortly.

The Technological Orientation. The technological perspective in teacher education has roots in behavioral psychology and the associated procedures of task analysis and instructional design, exemplified, for instance, in programmed instruction (see McDonald, 1973). From this perspective, teaching competence is a composite of discrete skills, especially skills that have been shown to be associated with high student achievement, and teacher education is a process of skill training (see Gliessman, 1984). The most renowned version of this approach went under the name of Performance (or Competency) Based Teacher Education in the 1970s (see Gage and Winne, 1975). This orientation also shaped teacher evaluation schemes used widely in school districts and state assessment programs (see Medley, Coker, and Soar, 1984).

Pedagogies that are especially compatible with this orientation include laboratory skill training methods (for example, microteaching and minicourses), intensive observation and feedback strategies, peer coaching, and training-oriented simulations (see Cruickshank and Metcalf, 1990).

Technologists sometime have a skeptical attitude toward field experiences and apprenticeships in conventional classrooms because these experiences foster a survival mentality and often train prospective teachers in traditional practices rather than research-based skills. They occasionally argue therefore that laboratory training experiences can serve as substitutes for field observations and even student teaching (see Smith, Cohen, and Pearl, 1969).

With the emphasis on thinking, reflection, and decision making in teacher preparation, this area of teacher education pedagogy is undergoing a fundamental reappraisal (see Zumwalt, 1982).

The Personal Orientation. Perhaps the most vigorous line of work in teacher education today is that focused on teachers' personal knowledge and stories (see Carter, 1993; Elbaz, 1991; Goodson, 1992; Raymond, Butt, and Townsend, 1991; Schubert and Ayers, 1992; Witherell and Noddings, 1991). In this work, the focus often ranges beyond the immediately technical issues of curriculum and classroom lessons to encompass teachers' biographies. Thus, teaching events are framed within a context of a teacher's life history or narrative. As a result, the central themes are often moral and philosophical, having more to do with feelings, purposes, images, aspirations, and personal meanings than with teaching skills or method in isolation from personal experience or biography. For an individual teacher, theory and practice are integrated through her or his narrative unity of experience (see Connelly and Clandinin, 1990).

A personal perspective in teacher education is not new. There is a long tradition, grounded in counseling psychology and developmental theory, of personalized teacher education that focuses on coming to terms with oneself, maximizing a sense of self-efficacy, clarifying one's values, and discovering one's own personal meaning and style in teaching (see Combs, 1965). In the reemergence of this viewpoint, however, emphasis is being placed on teachers' voice (see Carter, 1993; Elbaz, 1991). At issue in the discussion of voice is the extent to which the conventional language of educational research and teaching skill undermines the authentic expression by teachers (largely women) of their experiences and concerns and serves to subordinate teachers to policy makers and administrators (typically men).

Traditionally, personalized teacher education rested on pedagogies derived from counseling, such as interviews with a caring person, support groups, journals, and the like. The modern emphasis on personal knowledge has expanded these pedagogies to include opportunities for reflection, the study and writing of stories and cases, action research, and the like (see Carr and Kemmis, 1986; Russell and Munby, 1992).

The Academic Orientation. An emphasis on solid preparation in the core academic disciplines of the university curriculum has always been strong, especially among faculty in the liberal arts and sciences (see, for example, Bestor, 1953). Proponents of this position are particularly wary of the substance and rigor of pedagogical courses offered in education departments. They prefer rather that teachers be educated through a rigorous program of academic preparation followed by an apprenticeship with a skilled and academically prepared teacher. As the table of contents of the present volume demonstrates, subject matter preparation is certainly at the heart of the teacher education agenda today. It is a central theme in the influential report of the Holmes Group (1986) on teacher education reform, and it is the focus of substantial research programs on pedagogical content knowledge (see Grossman, 1990; Gudmundsdottir, 1991; Shulman, 1987) and subject matter teaching (see Ball and McDiarmid, 1990). There is a distinct emphasis in this emerging area on the use of cases as exemplars for teacher preparation.

The Critical/Social Orientation. The political stance inherent in the recent discussions of teachers' voice receives its full elaboration among scholars who see power as the pivotal issue in teacher preparation (see Ginsburg and Clift, 1990; Smyth, 1987). Central to this work is the notion of teacher empowerment; that is, the essential role of teachers as owners of their knowledge and their destinies (see Garrison, 1988).

One prominent theme in this work is a rejection of the technical rationality of the behaviorist tradition of research on teaching effectiveness and, in some quarters, a renunciation of science as a legitimate way of gaining knowledge about teaching. In turn, there is an emphasis on teachers' personal understanding of a situation and their own purposes, values, and associations. Practitioner knowledge, it is argued, is highly tentative, situational, idiosyncratic, intuitive, and embedded in the particulars of practice. The emphasis in teacher education therefore is on processes that stimulate personal reflection, such as action research (Carr and Kemmis, 1986) or life histories (Woods, 1987), methods that start from a teacher's own understandings and construction of meaning.

Emerging Conceptions of the Reflective Professional

Implicit in this survey of orientations is a fundamental change in the conceptual underpinnings of teacher education. On several fronts, there is an emerging cognizance of the essential role of teachers' reflective capacities of observation, analysis, interpretation, and decision making in professional practice (Russell and Munby, 1992; Schön, 1983; Zeichner and Liston, 1987). The emphasis, in other words, is on teachers' ability to inquire into teaching and think critically about their work using their craft and personal knowledge as well as the knowledge derived from studies of learning, development, and society.

This array of assumptions and commitments, reflecting cognitive, personal, and constructivist ancestry, has underscored narrative, dialogue, and inquiry in the preparation of teachers. As will be seen through the present chapter, this movement has had and is continuing to have a profound impact on both the curriculum and the pedagogy of teacher preparation.

Teaching Laboratories and Simulations

Keeping in mind the preceding overview of the various goals and assumptions that compel debates about teacher education pedagogy, the discussion now turns to the clusters of program pedagogies that form the nucleus of the chapter. Attention turns first to laboratory and simulations methods as an array of pedagogies grounded in the scientific study of both teaching practice and behavior change. As noted, this cluster reflects a technological orientation that has had a profound impact on teacher education practices and on the character of teacher evaluation. This review is followed by a consideration of field-based pedagogies and then cases and case methods.

Laboratory training methods, which began to flourish in the 1960s, were hailed as the harbinger of professionalization in teaching because they placed teacher preparation on a solid scientific, technological, and practical base (see Allen and Ryan, 1969). Through these methods, scientific knowledge about effective teaching behaviors and about changing human performance could be combined with the emerging technologies of systematic classroom observation and videotape recording to produce highly skilled teachers who could actually teach effectively in the nation's schools. The principal theme of this development was that teaching is best thought of as an aggregate of discrete skills that can be observed, discussed, modeled, and learned through guided practice. Moreover, it was argued that teaching laboratories enable novices to acquire these skills in safe environments that allow for provisional efforts to try out teaching behaviors and not have damaging effects on elementary and secondary students.

This convergence of scientific and technical ideas gave rise to three somewhat distinct traditions: (1) observation and feedback strategies, (2) laboratory skill training designs, and (3) simulations (see Cruickshank and Metcalf, 1990; Gliessman, 1984). The first tradition centers on systematic observation systems (for example, Flanders, 1970) and their use for recording teacher behavior and providing feedback concerning performance. The modal form of this pedagogy consisted of a teacher education student being observed while teaching in a field setting, usually by a nonparticipant observer, and then, after teaching, taking part in a data-based discussion of the performance record with the observer. In essence, this is a field-based pedagogy that will be discussed more fully in the next section. For present purposes, it can be noted, however, that multiple versions of this form arose, involving, for example, immediate feedback during performance and self-observation and feedback using audio or video recordings (see Cruickshank and Metcalf, 1990). Moreover, some attempts were made to determine whether training in an observational category system would itself affect classroom performance in the absence of observation and feedback (see Furst, 1967). Finally, all forms of laboratory-based instruction incorporate some form of a category system to observe and analyze performance.

The second and third traditions—skills training and simulations—are more properly thought of as laboratory pedagogies and therefore will be discussed in more detail here. Given the slight differences in format and research results, these pedagogies will be discussed separately.

Laboratory Skill Training

The model form of laboratory skill training in teacher education consists of the following steps or phases (see Allen and Ryan, 1969):

1. Studying written descriptions and visual models of a specific teaching skill (often known as protocol materials)
2. Teaching under "laboratory" conditions, that is, for a short period of time with a small number of "real" or peer students with the intent of using the target skill as often as possible
3. Feedback, using a video recording of the teaching performance and/or discussion with an observer and sometimes students, on the extent to which the skill was used accurately and on appropriate occasions during the lesson
4. Repetition of the study, teaching, and feedback cycle as necessary to achieve mastery of the target skill

As with systematic observation techniques, many versions of this basic structure have appeared and considerable attention has been given to specific steps in the process (for example, Borg, Kelley, Langer, and Gall, 1970). Protocol materials for a wide variety of teaching skills have been developed; variations in the mode and sources of feedback and coaching have been examined, including visual displays and audio ("bug in the ear") prompts during performance; and schedules for moving from laboratory to more real settings have been proposed.

One interesting variation on laboratory training is the reflective teaching approach developed by Cruickshank and his associates at Ohio State University to foster deliberation about teaching processes (see Cruickshank, 1987). For this training, novices are assembled into small groups with a designated teacher who prepares and teaches a reflective-teaching lesson with preestablished goals and content. After the lesson, learners are tested with respect to the goals of the lesson and their satisfaction, and this information, together with their experience of the lesson itself, forms the basis of a discussion of specific and general issues about teaching.

Despite these variations, there is sufficient commonality in basic structure across versions to summarize with reasonable confidence the rather large body of research that has accumulated in the area. Drawing on recent reviews (such as Copeland, 1982; Cruickshank and Metcalf, 1990; Gliessman, 1984), it is possible to formulate the following general conclusions about laboratory skill training in teacher education:

1.   There is a general sense that you get what you train for. That is, novice (and sometimes experienced) teachers acquire the target skills of a training laboratory, at least within the context of the laboratory setting. Most studies also indicate that considerable improvement in performance is apparent in the second round of teaching.

2.   It is not altogether clear that the features of any one component of a laboratory are crucial. In studies in which some form of each of these components was present, it is apparent that considerable variation in protocol representation, teaching situation, and feedback mode can occur without major differences in consequences.

3.   Some evidence suggests that learning what a teaching skill actually is and how to recognize it in operation is a key ingredient of laboratory training. Wagner (1973), for instance, found that cognitive discrimination training (learning to recognize the skill in protocol materials) was as effective as microteaching in acquisition of a teaching skill. This has led to an emphasis on concept teaching and cognition in laboratory pedagogies (see Gliessman and Pugh, 1987).

4.   Transfer of teaching skills from the laboratory to the classroom is a serious problem: a skill acquired and assessed in a laboratory context is not necessarily used in actual teaching situations unless that behavior has already become part of the classroom ecology (see, especially, Copeland, 1975, 1977). This trans-

fer problem has underscored the importance of coaching and other strategies to bridge the distance between the laboratory and the classroom (see Joyce and Showers, 1981).

    5. Teaching laboratories remain a popular component of many teacher education programs (see Cruickshank and Metcalf, 1990).

Simulations

Simulations[1] are comparable to teaching laboratories in that a teacher's experience occurs in a scaled-down or modified situation that approximates but is not actually a real-world classroom. A simulation has one important feature, however: it is designed to enable an operator to perform experiments, to act in ways that change the situation. The situation used in a simulation is necessarily and intentionally a simplified model. Nonetheless, if the simulation is designed well, the model will behave in a manner that is congruent with the behavior of the real system.

Familiar examples of simulations include the driving simulator in driver's education and the flight simulator in pilot training. Recently, fairly sophisticated simulations have been developed for court trials in law and for patient management in medicine. The major advantage of a simulation is that it can efficiently provide directed experiences with the behavior of a system under conditions that maximize attention to relevant features and minimize the harmful consequences of mistakes. Thus, a flight simulator enables a pilot to know what severe turbulence feels like without having to risk life and equipment by flying into an actual storm.

One of the key features of a simulation is its interactive capacity. In a simulation, the operator must be able to act on the model system in ways that affect the course of its behavior. This interactive feature distinguishes a simulation from a good description, a film or videotape, or a case. Interaction is also the most difficult feature to design in a simulation.

A teaching simulation, then, is a model environment that behaves like a classroom while engaging a teacher in a task or tasks congruent with those encountered in a real classroom. By acting in the model environment, the operator is afforded an opportunity to experience the consequences of different courses of action as they would occur in a real classroom setting.

In the past few years, there has been considerable interest in the development of teaching simulations for use in the clinical preparation of teachers (see Doak, Hipple, and Keith, 1987). Many of the early teaching simulations were developed within a skill training framework. Brown and Gliessman (1987), for example, developed a program at Indiana University that used interactive video to train teachers to identify instances of need, achievement, sociometric status, and scholastic ability among pupils in brief videotaped classroom segments. Students viewed an episode and rated the level at which the concept seemed applicable. Knowledge of results and explanations were provided immediately for "correct" and "incorrect" responses, and a test was administered at the end of each concept unit. The emphasis in this program was largely on concept formation, labeling, and problem solving by proposing solutions to problems depicted in the videotaped scenes. The solutions were not, however, carried out within the simulation environment.

A skill training model also underlies the simulation developed by Strang and his colleagues (see Strang, Landrum, and Lynch, 1989). In this system, an IBM PC with separate monitor displays is used to train teachers in giving feedback for correct and incorrect answers and to adjust the pace of question asking during lessons. A trainee and a computer operator are in separate rooms in front of separate monitors but linked by a sound system. The trainees' task is to design instruction to teach a list of spelling words to sixteen pupils represented on a monitor. In a separate room, an operator rapidly codes trainee verbal statements, feeds this information into the computer, and instructs the computer to reply to the trainee. Interaction with the computer is mediated, in other words, by a human operator who interprets the trainee's statements and feeds codes to the computer. The computer selects from a dictionary of replies to different codes. This interaction continues until the word list is covered. The computer also records the operator's codes and delay times for the trainee's responses, and a printout of this information is available for feedback and debriefing after each teaching session.

An alternative to this emphasis on skill training has begun to emerge in teacher education and is changing the intellectual context for the development of simulations in the field. In this alternative view, teaching is seen not as skill enactment but as situated *cognition* (see Brown, Collins, and Duguid, 1989; Carter and Doyle, 1987). Teaching, in other words, is seen to involve processes of recognition, comprehension, and problem solving in a complex social environment characterized by multidimensionality, unpredictability, and immediacy. Accomplishing the tasks of achieving order and enacting curriculum in these settings requires event structured knowledge: knowledge of the rhythms, patterns, and action-situation connections that occur in classrooms.

Teaching simulations, as models of how classrooms work, would seem to be especially valuable for providing experiences that help teachers construct the event structured knowledge needed for comprehension and problem solving. One useful example is the planning simulation developed by Morine-Dershimer and Shelly at Syracuse University (see Morine-Dershimer, 1987). The core of the simulation is an extensive computer-stored data bank on fourteen elementary school children entering fifth grade. The tasks involve decisions about the preliminary grouping of pupils for instruction in reading and the allotment of time for instruction. After preliminary decisions are made, the computer often gives students additional information and asks them to reconsider their decisions, record any changes they make, and explain why. At the conclusion, the computer gives feedback concerning the merits of their decisions in the form of a discussion of limitations on the various forms of data and a probable "best placement" for each pupil based on an experienced teacher's analysis of a combination of test records, teacher comments, and grades.

Copeland (1987a, 1987b, 1989) has been especially successful in getting a computer to behave like a classroom and thus in providing students with an opportunity for "real time" clinical reasoning about classrooms. His Arithmetic Drill Game uses an Apple II microcomputer to simulate lessons. The monitor displays five pupils and the simulation begins by displaying an arithmetic problem (for example, 8 x 4). The operator selects a pupil to respond (some of the students raise their hands and some do not). By this time, the problem is no longer displayed but an answer is. The operator must now verify whether the answer is correct or not. Then a new problem is posed. If the operator called on a volunteer last time, he or she must call on a nonvolunteer this time. The task requires, in other words, both situational memory and divided attention. The lesson continues in this fashion with two additional tasks added on. First, a pupil is displayed in the upper right corner of the screen. This pupil is supposed to be working independently on an assignment. On a random schedule, the pupil raises his or her head up from the work. If the operator catches the student quickly, extra points are awarded. Second, on a random schedule, a pupil spells a word over an audio track, and again the operator must verify whether the spelling is correct or not. Initial results of testing indicated that students have positive reactions to the game and that the game evokes thought processes and emotions characteristic of managing actual classrooms. Scores on the instrument also predict supervisor ratings of management proficiency in classroom teaching (see Copeland, 1987a).

Advances in computer technology have opened up the prospect for exciting work on simulating teaching episodes in ways that enable novices to engage in realistic interactive decision making. With the use of laser discs and advances in the capacity of personal computers, it is now possible to achieve a high degree of realism for teaching simulations. At the same time, production costs are quite high, and thus few operating systems are widely available and little research has been accumulated on their cognitive or behavioral consequences in teacher education (see Doak, Hipple, and Keith, 1987).

Using Teaching Laboratories and Simulations

Teaching laboratories and simulations are extolled for their practicality, clarity, utility, scientific foundation, and technical originality. But the central issue to face in deciding to use these pedagogies is curricular: Is the technical rationality that underlies these approaches, with its emphasis on training in discrete skills, an appropriate representation of what it takes to be a professional teacher? This question has been forcefully raised in recent years by several teacher education specialists who underscore the complex intellectual, emotional, and moral foundations of teaching practice (Carter and Doyle, 1987; Schön, 1983; Smyth, 1987; Zumwalt, 1982). These discussions have prompted efforts to reformulate purposes and strategies in this area, with an emerging emphasis on deliberation, inquiry, and problem solving to replace the former concentration on skill mastery. This trend is especially apparent in the development of simulations as problem spaces for real-time reasoning about the task of teaching in classroom environments (Copeland, 1987b).

Once the decision is made to use laboratory pedagogies in teacher education, several other practical issues emerge. Of particular importance are the problems of creating the necessary space and securing adequate materials, equipment, and personnel to run such an enterprise. A fully operating teaching laboratory, for example, requires a designated space, protocol materials, "students" (whether peers or actual elementary and secondary pupils), video and sound equipment, and people to organize the schedule, run the equipment, and provide feedback. Simulations often require computers with peripheral video and/or sound equipment as well as trained personnel to manage the operation. Moreover, the range of available simulations is quite limited.

Assuming that these resource issues can be solved, two additional concerns must be confronted: namely, evaluation and transfer. How is performance in a teaching laboratory or on a simulation to be interpreted? There is little strong evidence to assume that performance in such settings predicts teaching success. Moreover, such experiences are perhaps best viewed as diagnostic rather than criterial, as occasions to instruct and counsel the student rather than judge teaching ability. Furthermore, if the emphasis is on deliberation and inquiry, what sense can one make of how an individual teaches in the laboratory? Finally, the evidence clearly shows that transfer from the laboratory to the classroom is hardly automatic. As a result, some effort needs to be invested in helping students connect their laboratory experiences to actual classroom tasks and processes.

Two helpful suggestions would seem to flow from this discussion. First, it would seem especially useful to form small cohort groups of students to work together on laboratory and simulation tasks. Such groups would provide a supportive context for exploring teaching practices and deliberating about their features, uses, and value. This group context, together with judicious feedback and questioning from the instructor, can contribute to the development of a solid foundation for clinical reasoning (Copeland, 1989). Second, if laboratory pedagogies are closely tied to experiences in school sites, then students will be able to discern connections between laboratory or simulation environments and real-world situations. This prospect is explored more fully in the next section on field-based pedagogies.

Summary

Laboratory-based pedagogies offer contexts within which teacher education candidates can direct attention to specific aspects of the performance of teaching. These methods are especially recommended for their clarity, practicality, and concentration on the details of teaching performance. They also appear to help students develop concrete understandings of how teaching is actually accomplished and perhaps to achieve "self-confidence and reduce the chances that they will reject appropriate practices" (Knowles and Holt-Reynolds, 1991, p. 109). Finally, if properly structured, they can become locales for deliberation, inquiry, and problem solving and thus supply a foundation for developing a reflective capacity among beginning teachers.

Field-Based Pedagogies

In keeping with the long tradition of apprenticeship in learning to teach, field experiences have been a central ingredient in teacher preparation for many years. Recently, however, their use has expanded in both the number of occasions offered during teacher education and the amount of time devoted to such events (see Guyton and McIntyre, 1990). This expansion reflects in part the importance of field experiences in the movement to ground teacher education in practice and to link it closer to schools so that the functions of teaching and the education of teachers intertwine. Moreover, recent advances in our understanding of classroom knowledge (Carter and Doyle, 1987), case methods (Sykes and Bird, 1992), practical arguments (Fenstermacher and Richardson, 1993), reflection (Russell and Munby, 1992), and the process of learning to teach (Carter, 1990b) have contributed to a reformulation of conceptions of the role of field experiences in becoming a teacher. As a result, considerable energy is being directed to creating and elaborating the pedagogical aspects of field experiences.

The issues surrounding the full range of field experiences in teacher education are treated elsewhere in this volume (see the chapter by Knowles and Cole). The present discussion is focused therefore more narrowly on pedagogies that promise to maximize the benefits students derive from field experiences. Special attention is given here to early field experiences operated in conjunction with general and special methods courses and thus to pedagogies that appear to help integrate field experiences more closely with the overall goals and outlook of a teacher education program. Given this focus, little attention will be directed to the broader issues of curriculum and pedagogy in student teaching.

Learning from Experience

Field experiences have traditionally reflected a practical/craft orientation to teacher preparation. By spending time in the field, candidates for teaching learn what the "real world" of teaching is all about, are able to watch models of exemplary practice, can tap the practical wisdom of experienced professionals, and in a variety of other ways begin their apprenticeship in teaching.

Consistent with this orientation, the central pedagogical issues associated with field experiences have customarily been (1) the selection of exemplary sites that provide models teacher educators would want candidates to emulate, (2) the provision of observation guides to focus students' attention on key aspects of the teaching process, and (3) the structuring of assignments to be carried out in field settings (for example, tutoring, teaching a reading lesson to a small group, grading papers, and the like) that contribute worthwhile background for entering teaching.

Recently, there has been a surge of interest in the preconceptions and personal histories that candidates for teaching bring with them into teacher education (see, for example, Armaline and Hoover, 1989; Carter, 1990b; Knowles, 1992; Weinstein, 1988; Zeichner and Gore, 1990). Novices often come to teacher education with robust notions about what teaching will be like and how they intend to teach, notions often formed early in their experience as students. In addition, many students in teacher education report employment in day care centers and nurseries, experience working with children in summer or day camps, in Sunday school classes and 4-H clubs, babysitting, tutoring, or assisting teachers in junior high and high school. An interest in these early conceptions among teacher educators has served to counterbalance the traditional focus on *what is to be learned* in field settings with a concern for *how candidates interpret* what they see and construct personal meanings from the incidents they witness or in which they participate. This new awareness is consistent with the modern emphasis on reflection, but it is also motivated by findings that suggest that novices' conceptions mediate the impact of preservice programs. All of these factors have given rise to a number of pedagogical innovations involving journals, life histories, and personal narratives, and these pedagogies are being found attractive to advocates of personal, academic, and critical/social orientations toward teacher education (see Carter, 1993; Goodson, 1992; Zeichner and Gore, 1990).

Of particular relevance to the development of field-based pedagogies are the academic histories of candidates for teaching. Students arrive in teacher education with finely polished skills, developed over their many years in schools, for navigating the traditional academic rituals of reading textbooks, writing term papers, and cramming for exams. The knowledge to be acquired in these familiar situations is characteristically predigested, and the task is to remember how others have thought about a topic or subject. For the most part, everyday personal experiences are irrelevant to academic success. Soon after their arrival, however, candidates for teaching are immersed in field settings and thus confronted with the alien task of formally learning from their own experiences. This transition from an academic to an experiential base for learning presents special challenges for field-based teaching.

Specific Pedagogies

In this section, we briefly review several types of field-based pedagogies designed to help novice teachers to either order the complexity of field contexts or to develop an awareness of their evolving conceptions of specific pedagogies for teaching. Following this survey, we turn to the research base for field-based pedagogies.

Observation Guides. Classrooms and schools are enormously complex settings. Although novice teachers have been students for many years, their looking in classrooms has been framed by the demands of the student role. As a result, it may be difficult for them to recognize the structures and rhythms by which teaching is carried out. They may benefit therefore from guidance in how to observe teaching. Typically, this guidance is provided through observation schedules or guides that students take with them to the field and complete during or immediately after their observations.

The development of observation guides received considerable technical impetus from the work on interaction analysis (Flanders, 1970) and the vast number of similar efforts to devise systematic observational tools for the study of teaching (see Evertson and Green, 1986). These category systems were extolled for their objectivity, scientific precision, and analytical rigor, and numerous studies were conducted to ascertain their impact on novice teachers' performance (see Cruickshank and Metcalf, 1990). These instruments also provided a common language for talking about teaching and thus in some situations helped to promote an analytical perspective among candidates and to tie field observations more closely to the content of preparation programs. On the other hand, learning to use these systems often required extended technical training and considerable amounts of time for data processing. Moreover, the category labels and data summaries derived from codes using these labels did not always correspond to the terminology of either the textbooks, the field practitioners, or the teacher educators. For these reasons, the use of research instruments for teacher preparation can easily become cumbersome.

An alternative means of helping novices sort through the complexities of teaching in real-world situations is to provide them with conceptual frameworks rather than a list of specific observation categories (see Carter and Doyle, 1989). From this perspective, novices begin their field observations by studying descriptive and explanatory conceptions designed to capture the dynamics of classroom order and academic task systems, for example, rather than memorizing discrete categories. The use of conceptual frameworks rather than predetermined categories is consistent with the use of qualitative or ethnographic methods for studying situations (see Florio-Ruane, 1989).

Explanatory conceptions help make aspects of the familiar settings of classrooms conspicuous and thus direct candidates' observations to essential aspects of teaching. In addition, they provide an intellectual context within which to interpret what they see in classrooms and thus assist them in learning to think like a teacher. These frameworks can also be used, then, to ground postobservation discussions.

Structured Assignments. The complexity of field experience is also reduced frequently through the use of assignments designed to enable novices to practice parts of the total array of teaching responsibilities. Thus, candidates are often asked to assist the regular teacher in distributing supplies or grading papers, to tutor individual students or teach brief lessons to small groups, and the like. Such structured experiences are recommended for their practicality in introducing teacher education students to teaching responsibilities and for providing a common basis for discussions about teaching. Their function, in other words, can be seen as akin to that of teaching laboratories. At the same time, their realism can be questioned on the grounds that they take place within the context of management and curriculum decisions made by the regular teacher rather than the candidate. It is quite difficult, that is, to pull apart the teaching role in real-world settings.

Opportunities to Write About Teaching. As noted above, substantial attention has been devoted recently to pedagogies designed to assist novices to make explicit their preconceptions about teaching, to understand how their unique biographies have shaped their preferences and understandings, and to monitor their evolving personal constructions of what teaching is. Many of these pedagogies involve having students write about teaching. In this section, we describe a sampling of such pedagogies to give the reader a sense of the developments in this area. These methodologies are discussed further in the following section on narrative methods.

Journal writing appears to be a mainstay in reports of practices that promote reflection in teacher thinking (Bolin, 1988; Knowles and Holt-Reynolds, 1991; Rovegno, 1992; Tabachnick and Zeichner, 1984; Zeichner and Liston, 1987). Rovegno (1992) reports that students wrote in "dialogue journals, reflecting on their progress toward becoming effective teachers" (p. 71). Journals also provide students with opportunities to "vent frustrations, express enthusiasm for teaching, cope with the pain of leaving students, and reflect on all the complex dimensions of preservice development" (Zulich, Bean, and Herrick, 1991, p. 19) as well as revealing "many of the catalysts and inhibitors in prospective teachers' past and contemporary experiences, and in their thinking about future practices" (Knowles and Holt-Reynolds, 1991, p. 108).

Bolin (1988) recommends that teacher educators respond to journal entries by asking questions and commenting on the content of the writing, thus providing opportunities for the teacher educators to uncover uncertainty in students' thinking or locate events that cause dissonance. Bolin also argues that journals provide "a useful tool in guiding (students) and assessing the extent to which [they] have become more deliberative teachers" (p. 53). Zeichner and Liston (1987) state that journals provide information to the supervisors about the context of the students' field experiences as well as a picture of the students' development as teachers. For the teacher education students, Tabachnick and Zeichner (1984) report that journals enabled clarification of perspectives and the adoption of a "reflective or analytic stance toward teaching practice" (p. 34).

On a practical level, Bean and Zulich (1989) relate how they used dialogue journals in a preservice, content-area reading course. Time was provided at the beginning of each class for students and the professor to write in journals. At the end of this time, the professor collected four to six student journals and had one student take the professor's journal to write responses. While Bean and Zulich recognize that reading and responding to students journals can be quite time consuming, they found that reading only a few each week and limiting their responses to the same length as the original entry served the purpose of engendering reflectiveness on the part of the preservice teachers. In addition, Bean and Zulich strongly recommended that more research be conducted around the practice of using reflective or dialogue journals in teacher education.

Carter (1994) has devised a writing task involving well-remembered events that is especially suited to helping novices learn from field experiences. A well-remembered event is an incident or episode that a student observes in a school situation and considers, for his or her own reasons, especially salient. Events are standardized to include three parts: (1) a detailed description of the event itself; (2) an analysis of the event, which may be drawn from considering a variety of sources, including recent research on teaching and learning, class discussions, and/or the practical perspectives of the writer; and (3) the teaching implications the writer uncovers as a result of experiencing and analyzing the event. In exploratory studies, Carter (1994) and Carter and Gonzalez (1993) obtained preliminary evidence that these well-remembered events provide a window to the cognitive world of teaching and to the acquisition of teachers' event knowledge of classrooms.

A variety of "life history" methods have emerged recently that consist of having teacher education students write autobiographical accounts (see Crow, 1987; Goodson, 1992; Knowles, 1992; Woods, 1987). These personal stories are grounded in the notion of narrative unity—that is, the coherence and continuity of an individual's experience. Connelly and Clandinin (1985) argue, for instance, that a teaching act is a "narrative-in-action," an "expression of biography and history . . . in a particular situation" (1985, p. 184). Thus, for an individual teacher, theory and practice are integrated through her or his narrative unity of experience. The construction of life histories typically involves a very close, long-term collaboration between teacher educators and novices. This collaboration involves observation, conversation, and mutual construction.

These writing-based pedagogies are closely related to the work on cases and case methods. Issues associated with the latter methods are discussed more fully in the section on cases in this chapter.

Seminars and Conversations. Another practice that appears prominently in writing about field experiences is dialogue. Bolin (1988) notes that journals furnish opportunities for students to talk with each other about their experiences, whether through a "roving" journal or in a seminar setting. Rovegno (1992) recommends on-campus class discussions about observations as well as individual conferences

The Teacher Educator's Handbook

with the teacher educators. Killian and McIntyre (1988) suggest placements that offer multiple opportunities for students of teaching to talk with their cooperating teachers. Applegate and Lasley (1982), Tabachnick and Zeichner (1984), and Zeichner and Liston (1987) all advocate weekly seminars that provide opportunities for students, cooperating teachers, and university faculty (in some combination) to reflect about experiences through conversations. The seminars have the potential to expose misconceptions, fears, and frustrations from all participants, as well as offer opportunities to celebrate successes (see also MacKinnon and Grunau, 1991). Pulling together students from several classrooms within a school allows for "the plurality of vision that is essential to a more comprehensive understanding" of classroom processes (Elbaz, 1988, p. 177). Both practices, journals and seminars, model for prospective teachers strategies for continued growth based on interactions with others and in practice begin to refute the traditional notion that teaching is an isolating occupation.

Supervision would seem to provide an ideal setting for conversations about teaching, but it is most often discussed in relation to student teaching rather than early field experiences (see Glickman and Bey, 1990). A major part of the reason for this neglect may be that field experiences are not customarily supervised very closely, especially by college or university personnel. Extrapolating from the literature on student teaching (see Griffin, 1986), it appears that most supervisory conferences are focused on procedural matters and dominated by the supervisor. Such conversations are unlikely to be efficacious for developing self-awareness or reflection among teaching candidates.

One innovative and theoretically grounded pedagogy developed by Fenstermacher and Richardson (1993) involves the elicitation of "practical arguments," the premises upon which teachers ground their decisions about which actions to take to achieve particular goals in particular circumstances. Practical arguments are elicited in a dialogue or interview process with an "other" who is intimately familiar with the teacher's situation and intentions (Richardson and Fenstermacher, 1992). As a result, the elicitation of practical arguments tends to be a lengthy and labor-intensive process. The existing work on practical argument interviews has been conducted with experienced teachers in staff development settings. Nevertheless, the approach would seem to hold promise for encouraging future teachers to begin to examine their beliefs about teaching and learning, especially with respect to action decisions they make in laboratory or field settings.

An emphasis on reflection and dialogue is pronounced among those within the academic orientation who espouse a constructivist view of knowledge and learning (see, for example, Duckworth, 1987; Warren and Rosebery, 1995). Here the emphasis is on having prospective and experienced teachers examine their own understandings or constructions of academic content (especially in science and mathematics) as a prerequisite for exploring and practicing constructivist pedagogy in their own classrooms. The premise, in other words, is that teachers must understand their own understandings of content if they are to interpret the meaning children make of their curricular experiences.

Working largely from a critical/social perspective, Cochran-Smith (1991; see also Cochran-Smith and Lytle, 1992) advocates that students learn to teach through systematic and self-critical inquiry within teacher research communities of novices, cooperating teachers, and university-based teacher educators. The inquiry begins with a reflective essay on one's own experiences and how they shaped ideas of schools, teaching, race, and diversity. Subsequently, students gather information in groups about the culture of the school and the community, analyze children's learning opportunities and their constructions of meaning in small-scale observation studies, and engage with their colleagues on constructing reconstructionist pedagogy. A fundamental aim of this approach is to develop teachers who regard teaching as a political activity and embrace social change as a part of their professional responsibility.

The Research Base for Field Pedagogies

Although considerable enthusiasm typically accompanies descriptions of field-based pedagogies, there is little solid evidence concerning the impact of field experiences in general or of specific intervention strategies (see Guyton and McIntyre, 1990; Zeichner, 1987). Studies indicate that training in systematic observation systems (particularly interaction analysis) influences what students see in classrooms (Cruickshank and Metcalf, 1990), but most pedagogies in this area are based on logical rather than empirical arguments. Part of the problem here is that it is quite difficult to know what impact to study (behavior? cognition? attitude?) or to single out the specific contributions of a given field experience or pedagogy within the larger context of candidates' experiences in colleges and schools (see Zeichner and Gore, 1990). Too, perhaps outcome is not the most critical issue. It may well be more pivotal to understand the pedagogical process itself, what happens as the pedagogies are being carried out, as demonstrated, for instance, in the works of Crow (1987) and Clandinin (1992).

There are, however, three findings that merit attention because of their relevance to program pedagogy:

1. Preconceptions and predispositions of candidates for teaching would appear to be quite robust and probably resistant to changes during preservice experiences (see Carter, 1990b; Zeichner and Gore, 1990).
2. Field experiences may well engender survival and craft orientations among candidates, thus reinforcing conservative predispositions and thwarting program objectives related to more general understandings and attitudes toward education and teaching (Feiman-Nemser, 1983).
3. Particularly in the area of culture and diversity, teaching candidates may readily acquire (or have reinforced) in their courses and field experiences

stereotypical notions about ethnic groups or special populations of students (see Cazden and Mehan, 1989).

These findings underscore the challenge teacher educators face in making explicit the underlying conceptions and motivations that candidates carry with them into teacher preparation and helping them come to terms with these influences on their developing notions of teaching and the issues with which teachers deal. Field experiences and field-based pedagogies, while part of a much larger set of program processes, can play a key role in this undertaking.

Issues in the Use of Field-Based Pedagogies

We conclude our consideration of field-based pedagogies with a discussion of three important issues having to do with sites for field experience, supervision and evaluation, and time. These issues impinge directly upon the use of these pedagogies in teacher education practice.

Sites. The selection of and coordination with field sites is one of the central and enduring issues to be faced in designing and organizing field experiences. Since schools exist primarily to educate students rather than prepare teachers, resolving this issue can be difficult.

In selecting a site, it is important to consider whether it offers a suitable range of approaches and models and an adequate diversity of students and teachers. Moreover, is there among the staff some common interest in and commitment to the preparation of novices for teaching? Once a site has been selected, it is necessary to build cooperation between the university and the school site personnel in setting goals, defining roles, and articulating expectations (Applegate and Lasley, 1982; Killian and McIntyre, 1988; Zeichner and Liston, 1987). Cooperating teachers can have an especially powerful influence on the students (Bunting, 1988) as well as on the content and process of teacher education. It is especially important therefore that their voices be heard in the planning of field experiences and that they be able to model the goals of the program (see Copeland, 1981; Goodman, 1988).

Finally, teaching candidates must be prepared to enter field settings in terms of what tasks they can accomplish, what they can expect to learn from their experiences, and how they should conduct themselves as professionals within these contexts (Applegate and Lasley, 1982). In particular, they need to understand how to interpret what they are seeing, how to discern what tasks are being accomplished and what problems are being addressed by a school staff, and how to talk ethically and prudently about their observations and experiences (see Erickson, 1986, on the issues of site entry and involvement). Failure to provide this preparation can have embarrassing consequences for all the participants.

The inauguration of professional development schools would seem to be especially suited to a resolution of the problems of site selection and coordination outlined here (see Stallings and Kowalski, 1990). Such sites provide an "invisible campus" where faculty from both public schools and universities convene to engage in the enterprise of educating new teachers, creating new roles of equal status for all faculty members. Although the issues of resource limitations and the lack of a shared conception are not automatically solved in these settings, they do provide an overall structure within which these issues can be addressed (see Rushcamp and Roehler, 1992; Zimpher, 1990).

Supervision and Evaluation. In general, it appears that the supervision of early field experiences is irregular at best, especially by campus-based teacher educators. This state of affairs reflects the characteristic lack of resources in teacher education programs, but it also places heavy burdens on school personnel and often results in unsystematic or unfocused experiences by teaching candidates. It also raises serious questions about how field experiences can be satisfactorily evaluated and novices' commitment to and developing competence in teaching be assessed (Applegate and Lasley, 1982).

Time. Without a doubt, field experiences and many of the pedagogies recommended for use in conjunction with them are enormously labor-intensive for both candidates and teacher educators. For example, McDiarmid (1990) described a four-week experience that explored the teaching of operations with positive and negative numbers. During the four weeks, students did observations in a third-grade math class, held class discussions, interviewed the teacher and her students, wrote about their experiences, questions, concerns, and finally taught similar content to someone else. This was a four-week exercise that covered just one topic in the third-grade math curriculum. At the end of the exercise, McDiarmid still was not sure that his students' preconceptions had changed.

Goodman (1988) argues that efforts to design field experiences "that promote serious reflection, experimentation, and responsible decision making" will require significant changes in the work of teacher educators (p. 47). Not only will additional personnel be needed but supervisors must be provided with time to engage in extensive dialogue with the teachers-to-be and with practicing teachers who serve as the mentors in field situations. This will require financial support beyond the traditional allocations of money and personnel. Moreover, as faculty are encouraged to spend more time working with novices in their field placements, this work should be rewarded rather than dismissed as less important than on-campus coursework, service, or research.

Summary

There is a rich variety of pedagogies available in teacher education that are especially useful in conjunction with field experiences. Traditionally, these pedagogies were designed principally to help reduce the complexity of practice settings by focusing students' attention on specific dimensions to observe or structuring opportunities to participate in segments of the total teaching function. The dramatic growth of interest in reflection and the potency of the preconceptions candidates for teaching bring with them into teacher education has prompted the invention of pedagogies designed to enlarge, through writing and/or dialogue, candidates' personal awareness of how their prior and current experiences have shaped and are shaping their conceptions of teaching.

At the same time, these pedagogies are very labor-intensive for candidates and for field-based and campus-based teacher educators. A full realization of their educative potential will depend upon substantial changes in role definitions, school-campus structures, and reward systems in teacher education.

Cases and Case Methods

Cases and case methods have been a customary part of clinical teaching in the professions of medicine, law, architecture, and business for most of this century (Carter and Unklesbay, 1989; Doyle, 1990a). Similarly, examples, vignettes, and cases have been used for a long time in teacher education to illustrate approaches and encourage problem solving (see, for example, Sperle, 1933). In the past few years, however, there has been a massive increase in enthusiasm for cases and case methods in the education of teachers (see Merseth, 1991; Sykes and Bird, 1992). As a result, several casebooks and collections on case methods have recently appeared and a rich array of cases, ranging from short episodes to lengthy descriptions of yearlong experiences and from general teaching dilemmas to subject-specific reasoning, are now readily available to teacher educators (see Hinely and Ford, 1994; Greenwood and Parkay, 1989; Kowalski, Weaver, and Hensen, 1990; Shulman and Colbert, 1987, 1988; Silverman, Welty, and Lyon, 1991).

This escalation of activity around cases reflects several factors impinging upon teaching: for example, a shift from quantitative to qualitative approaches in research; a growing focus on cognitive, theoretical, and reflective dimensions of teaching practice; a heightened concern for professional status and school reform; and an increased awareness of issues of gender, power, and voice in teaching. At the same time, the wide variety of approaches being taken in this field has provoked considerable discussion about what constitutes a case, what cases teach, and how cases can be used to accomplish the goals of teacher preparation (see Grossman, 1992). Sykes and Bird (1992) use the label *case idea* to signify the heterogeneity of views, purposes, and beliefs that characterize this movement.

The Uses of Cases in Teacher Preparation

In this section, we survey some of the major suggestions being made for adopting cases and case methods in teacher preparation. This survey is organized around three general purposes for using cases: (1) as illustrations or exemplars, (2) as problem situations for analysis and inquiry, and (3) as frames for eliciting or developing storied knowledge of teaching.

Illustrations and Exemplars. One quite common use of cases in teacher education is to exemplify or illustrate a general principle or a model of practice. Here the basic purpose of a case is to depict vividly such matters as the complexity of teaching environments, the way in which a method is actually carried out in a classroom (such as teaching for understanding), or the complicated ways a general proposition about learning or development manifests itself in a particular situation.

The motivations underlying this use of cases are often practical and technical. The use of real-world instances and demonstrations is in general seen as a valuable tool for moving teacher preparation from the abstractions of theory to the concrete and practical, for holding candidates' interests, or for persuading them to adopt a particular perspective or approach. In more specific ways, designers of teaching laboratories have used written or recorded models of teaching skills that trainees are to emulate in their own laboratory lessons.

The illustration of abstract ideas with concrete instances has much to recommend it as a method for helping candidates clarify their understanding of foundational and craft knowledge in teaching (see Sykes and Bird, 1992). At the same time, the use of cases as prototypes to be emulated reflects an emphasis on performance rather than reasoning in the education of teachers.

Cases as Problematic Situations. A second important use of cases in teacher education centers on analysis, inquiry, and problem solving. Here teaching is construed not simply as the following of rules or the enactment of particular skills but rather as an intricate process of interpretation and decision making, of connecting knowledge to complex situations. From this perspective, cases are not just illustrations or models to imitate. Rather, they are precedents in much the way that cases exist in other professions (see Carter and Unklesbay, 1989). As Doyle (1990a) notes, a case written for this purpose "exemplifies not only how a lesson was conducted but also what the problematics of the performance were" (p. 10).

The overall goal of using cases as precedents is twofold: (1) to help students acquire the situated knowledge of teaching they need in order to "think like a teacher" (Kleinfeld, 1992, p. 35) and (2) to engender habits of analysis, inquiry, and reflection that will empower them to continue to grow in their professional understandings and abilities. There is also some evidence to suggest that learning from cases is especially suited to the development of cognitive flexibility and the acquisition of knowledge in ill-structured domains (see Spiro and others, 1987).

Brief cases depicting problem situations in teaching have been around for a long time as textbook exercises or exam questions, and some casebooks contain expanded versions of these incidents with the intent of stimulating discussions. But the movement is toward richer and more comprehensive representations of teaching situations. In contrast to cases constructed to illustrate a point, model a skill, or start a discussion, cases as precedents are complex and incomplete and are likely to be lengthy so that a range of events, impinging factors, and relevant contexts can be portrayed. In addition, expert commentaries, often with conflicting explanations and suggestions, are sometimes supplied with the case. In dealing with such cases, students take an active role in investigating and interpreting the circumstances depicted and bringing an assortment of propositions, viewpoints, and metaphors to bear on the specific predicaments represented (see Carter, 1990a). The students' task, in other words, is not to find the right answer but to interpret the situation and understand the theoretical issues involved. As a result, days or even weeks can be devoted to presentation of and deliberation about a case.

Within this context, it is possible to begin to think of laboratory and field experiences as "cases," episodes that furnish opportunities to think about the intricacy and perplexity of teaching, rather than simply lessons for the learned. Such an extension of laboratory and field pedagogies is consistent with the emphasis on reflection in teacher education.

Cases as Storied Knowledge. Beyond the enthusiasm for cases as occasions for clinical reasoning, there is an emerging sense that cases capture the essentially storied nature of teachers' knowledge (see Carter, 1993). This view of cases as stories reflects a conviction that narrative is not only a powerful pedagogical tool for representing teaching but also a means of capturing the concerns and motivations of novice teachers and helping them acquire understandings and dispositions that reflect the fundamental way in which teachers, regardless of their experience, know and think about their work (Carter, 1993; Clandinin, 1992; Gudmundsdottir, 1991; Elbaz, 1991).

A combined emphasis on biography and story in teacher education leads to pedagogies in which novices tell their own stories—that is, write their own cases (see Clandinin, 1992; Richert, 1992). Carter's idea (1994) of well-remembered events, described earlier in conjunction with field-based pedagogies, can, for example, be viewed as "short stories" from a novice's stream of experience that reflect the interpretive structures being used to organize his or her growing knowledge of teaching.

One important implication of the view of cases as stories is their inherent ambiguity. Stories seem to resist such singular interpretations and thus teach in ambiguous ways. This feature is both the strength and the weakness of case teaching. Stories convey the multiplicity of connections between actions and situations and thus represent well the complex demands of teaching. At the same time, they can confuse and frustrate novices who lack the situated frames within which to interpret such portrayals. As Carter (1993) notes, we clearly have "a great deal to learn about the interpretive space within which story can become teacher education pedagogy" (p. 10).

The Research Base for Case Teaching

Sykes and Bird (1992) note that support for the case idea in teacher education is characterized more by enthusiasm than empiricism. But this is also true for case methods in other professions (Carter and Unklesbay, 1989). Few attempts have ever been made to examine or verify systematically the consequences of studying cases. At the same time, the case idea is consistent with a large body of literature on situated learning (see Brown, Collins, and Duguid, 1989) and reflection in action (Schön, 1983). This indirect backing for the case idea provides a foundation, at least, for further development and inquiry in this particular field of teacher education pedagogy.

Considerations for Case Teaching

In this section, we turn to the issues surrounding the actual use of cases in teacher preparation (see also Carter, 1993). The discussion is organized around the topics of finding a case literature, deciding how to represent a case, and setting the context for deliberation about a case.

A Case Curriculum. The first issue that needs to be faced in deciding to introduce cases into teacher education is selecting the cases that should be taught. Although the number of available casebooks in teaching has increased substantially in the past few years and promises to grow even larger, the grounds upon which these cases are constructed varies widely across developers and there are no clear curricular frameworks or guidelines within which to interpret the total corpus of cases.

The selection of cases is fundamentally a curriculum problem: it reflects a conception of what teaching is and what knowledge is needed to teach successfully. Decisions about case pedagogy must begin therefore with this thorny issue. A closely related issue is the interrelation achieved across cases. Given that much of teachers' knowledge is conditional and context-specific, multiple representations will be needed to help teachers develop the professional knowledge required for practical reasoning about classroom tasks. This suggests that each case should not be treated independently but rather that common themes and issues might best be represented in several cases. It might even be possible to create comprehensive cases that candidates work with across courses throughout their programs.

Cases can of course be developed locally to meet local needs and purposes. Especially within the context of professional development schools, cases can be constructed collaboratively by teacher educators, classroom teachers, and teacher education students. Such collaboration is likely to be a great benefit to all concerned, especially novices, and can become a useful context for clarifying understandings and coordinating campus and field conceptions of teaching and teacher education. At the same time, it must be recognized that case writing is a very time-consuming and not necessarily highly rewarded process.

Form of Representation. Cases of teaching come these days in a variety of forms, ranging from the traditional written text to video recordings integrated with hypermedia computer systems (see Goldman, Barron, and Witherspoon, 1991; Sykes and Bird, 1992). Indeed, simulations of the kind Copeland (1987a) has developed might well be regarded as cases that move in response to decisions by the "reader." Nontraditional representations have the advantage of vividness and realism. At the same time, such representations often require large amounts of time, equipment, and other resources for their creation and use.

Contexts for Deliberation About Cases. The achievement of particular purposes in teaching with cases is not automatic (see Grant, 1992). In many respects, the impact of a case on learning to teach depends upon how it is framed in the immediate environment in which it is introduced and taught. How a teacher educator sets the tasks to be accomplished with respect to a case, what interpretive resources (for example, expert commentaries) are supplied during deliberation, and how alternative interpretations are treated all influence what candidates make of their encounters with cases. The use of small groups for case discussions and collaborative groups of teacher educators, classroom teachers, and candidates can provide a fruitful climate for case deliberation. Regardless of the group arrangements, however, if the purpose of case teaching is to promote analysis and reflection, then it is important that the case itself represent dilemmas and problematics of teaching, that time be made available for students to become familiar with a case and work with it from a variety of perspectives, and that the discussion not be directed toward one right answer. The balance here is tricky since novices often lack the practical knowledge needed to interpret complex classroom events and experts often find it difficult to convey the nature of their reasoning about particular incidents.

Awareness of the delicate balance required in framing cases is especially important in evaluating what candidates learn from cases. One useful perspective is to focus on reasoning rather than correctness in judging responses to cases. Richardson (1992), for example, attempted to capture the effects of case methods on changes in preservice teachers' perspectives on thinking about classrooms. She was particularly interested in the shift in novices' thinking from a student frame to that of an experienced teacher. To accomplish this assessment, she focused on responses to cases in terms of such features as students' language use, the extent of negative judgments about observed behaviors, extent of negative judgments about observed behaviors, changes in orientation from teacher-centered to child-centered approaches, increases in functional rather than behavioral descriptions of teachers' actions, and the movement from simple descriptions to those that were "rich and deep" (p. 15).

Summary

Cases and case methods represent one of the most vigorous developments within the field of program pedagogy in teacher education. Cases provide rich illustrations of abstract conceptions, exemplars of particular approaches and instructional methods, portrayals of the dilemmas and problematics of teaching, and frames for representing personal and professional knowledge in teaching. The case literature is growing rapidly, as are the conceptional foundations for this approach to teacher preparation and the modes for representing cases. Case teaching is by no means inexpensive in terms of money, personnel, equipment, energy, and time, but the promise of case methods is at present strongly motivating teacher educators to pursue this domain enthusiastically.

Reflections on Program Pedagogies

In this final section, we reflect back on the previous survey of program pedagogies and attempt to draw out some general themes that appear to have emerged from this discussion. We conclude with some suggestions for future directions in this area.

Our review clearly indicates that considerable energy and excitement currently surrounds the area of program pedagogy across the various orientations to teacher education. This is a creative and invigorating time in the field, one that reflects multiple purposes and emerging sources of knowledge and motivation. It is one area of teacher education that is certainly being taken seriously by some of the best minds in education, and the promise for the future is bright.

As we look back over the pedagogies we have reviewed, four topics—discreteness, supervision, impact, and research—seem to cut across the entire domain of program pedagogy in teacher education. The issues associated with these topics would seem to represent the cutting edge of development in this area. A brief discussion of each of these topics will clarify this view.

Discreteness

Few would disagree with the view that successful teaching requires a complex and finely integrated mosaic of knowledge and skill. Yet program pedagogies typically focus on discrete aspects of teaching competence, whether it be separate teaching skills to be learned in laboratories, individual field experiences, or autonomous cases. It is often difficult to find more than passing attention to the continuum of content underlying teaching or the integration of the various components of teaching expertise. This would certainly seem to be an area that warrants attention, especially with the contemporary emphasis on narrative or biographical unity in teachers' knowledge.

Supervision

Issues of supervision, accountability, and evaluation within teacher education programs are for the most part ignored or treated only superficially. Yet supervision is an essential part of laboratory and field pedagogies, and accountability and evaluation are a necessary part of teaching regardless of one's pedagogical philosophy. Given the reputation teacher education has for ease of entry and exit, it is appropriate that teacher educators deal with these difficult issues internally rather than leave them by default to external regulatory agencies.

Impact

The question of the impact of program pedagogies, especially those practiced within university-based preservice preparation, lurks in the shadows of nearly all discussions of teacher education. The general perception seems to be that teacher education is at best a weak influence on candidates for teaching, in part because of the power of their apprenticeship of observation as longtime students and in part because very little that is explicit and useful is offered in teacher education courses. It may also be that we do not know how to ferret out the actual power of teacher education pedagogies. Moreover, the enterprise itself is very fragmented across university and field settings with multiple participants who often send quite contradictory messages about the value and relevance of teacher education experiences (see Ginsburg and Clift, 1990). Achieving a reasonable degree of consensus in this cacophony of voices is a perennial issue in teacher education programs.

Research

It is customary to call for more research at the conclusion of nearly all essays in education, and certainly research on program pedagogy is not a highly developed area. Yet we are reluctant to issue such a call, especially if it conjures up images of effectiveness studies pitting one pedagogy against another and comparing their consequences by some common standard. We have long known that the results of such "methods" studies are often inconclusive and that positive results usually reflect a match at the level of curriculum between the winning method and the test (see Walker and Schaffarzick, 1974). A large number of issues concerning learning, knowledge, curriculum, and enactment surround program pedagogies in teacher education and many of these can benefit from systematic inquiry (see Sykes and Bird, 1992). But research will contribute only to the extent that it reflects the contemporary spirit and energy of this field.

Conclusion

We are pleased with the current state of program pedagogies and optimistic about the future in this area. There is much that can be learned about teaching and about collegiate and professional education from teacher education.

Note

1.   The authors are deeply indebted to Walter Doyle for his substantial contributions to this section on simulations in teacher education.

References

Allen, D., and Ryan, K. (1969). *Microteaching.* Reading, Mass.: Addison-Wesley.

Applegate, J. H., and Lasley, T. J. (1982). "Cooperating teachers' problems with preservice field experience students." *Journal of Teacher Education, 33*(2), 15–18.

Armaline, W. D., and Hoover, R. L. (1989). "Field experience as a vehicle for transformation: Ideology, education, and reflective practice." *Journal of Teacher Education, 40*(2), 42–48.

Ball, D. L., and McDiarmid, G. W. (1990). "The subject-matter preparation of teachers." In W. R. Houston (ed.), *Handbook of research on teacher education.* New York: Macmillan.

Bean, T. W., and Zulich, J. (1989). "Using dialogue journals to foster reflective practice with preservice, content-area teachers." *Teacher Education Quarterly, 16*(1), 33–40.

Bestor, A. (1953). *The restoration of learning.* New York: Knopf.

Bolin, F. S. (1988). "Helping student teachers think about teaching." *Journal of Teacher Education, 39*(2), 48–54.

Borg, W. R., Kelley, M. L., Langer, P., and Gall, M. D. (1970). *The minicourse: A microteaching approach to teacher education.* New York: Macmillan.

Brown, J. S., Collins, A., and Duguid, P. (1989). "Situated cognition and the culture of learning." *Educational Researcher, 18*(1), 32–42.

Brown, L., and Gliessman, D. H. (1987). "The role of interactive video in the acquisition of teaching skills." In E. D. Doak, T. Hipple, and M. Keith (eds.), *Simulation and clinical knowledge in teacher education.* Knoxville: College of Education, University of Tennessee.

Buchmann, M. (1987). *Teaching knowledge: The lights that teachers live by.* (Issue Paper no. 87–1). East Lansing, Mich.: National Center for Research on Teacher Learning.

Bunting, C. (1988). "Cooperating teachers and the changing views of teacher candidates." *Journal of Teacher Education, 39*(2), 42–46.

Carr, W., and Kemmis, S. (1986). *Becoming critical: Education, knowledge, and action research.* Washington, D.C.: Falmer Press.

Carter, K. (1990a). "Meaning and metaphor: Case knowledge in teaching." *Theory into Practice, 29,* 109–115.

Carter, K. (1990b). "Teachers' knowledge and learning to teach." In W. R. Houston (ed.), *Handbook of research on teacher education.* New York: Macmillan.

Carter, K. (1993). "The place of story in research on teaching and teacher education." *Educational Researcher, 22*(1), 5–12.

Carter, K. (1994). Preservice teachers' well-remembered events and the acquisition of event-structured knowledge." *Journal of Curriculum Studies, 26,* 235–252.

Carter, K., and Doyle, W. (1987). "Teachers' knowledge structures and comprehension processes." In J. Calderhead (ed.), *Exploring teachers' thinking.* London: Cassell Educational.

Carter, K., and Doyle, W. (1989). "Classroom research as a resource for the graduate preparation of teachers." In A. E. Woolfolk (ed.), *Research perspectives on the graduate preparation of teachers.* Englewood Cliffs, N.J.: Prentice Hall.

Carter, K., and Gonzalez, L. (1993). "Beginning teachers' knowledge of classroom events." *Journal of Teacher Education, 44,* 223–232.

Carter, K., and Unklesbay, R. (1989). "Cases in teaching and law." *Journal of Curriculum Studies, 21,* 527–536.

Cazden, C. B., and Mehan, H. (1989). "Principles from sociology and anthropology: Context, code, classroom, and culture." In M. C. Reynolds (ed.), *Knowledge base for the beginning teacher.* Elmsford, N.Y.: Pergamon Press.

Clandinin, D. J. (1992). "Narrative and story in teacher education." In T. Russell and H. Munby (eds.), *Teachers and teaching: From classroom to reflection.* Washington, D.C.: Falmer Press.

Cochran-Smith, M. (1991). "Learning to teach against the grain." *Harvard Educational Review, 61,* 279–310.

Cochran-Smith, M., and Lytle, S. L. (1992). "Interrogating cultural diversity: Inquiry and action." *Journal of Teacher Education, 43*(2), 104–115.

Combs, A. W. (1965). *The professional education of teachers: A perceptual view of teacher education.* Needham Heights, Mass.: Allyn & Bacon.

Conant, J. B. (1963). *The education of American teachers.* New York: McGraw-Hill.

Connelly, F. M., and Clandinin, D. J. (1985). "Personal practical knowledge and the modes of knowing: Relevance for teaching and learning." In E. W. Eisner (ed.), *Learning and teaching the ways of knowing.* (84th yearbook of the National Society for the Study of Education, Part 2). Chicago: University of Chicago Press.

Connelly, F. M., and Clandinin, D. J. (1990). "Stories of experience and narrative inquiry." *Educational Researcher, 19*(5), 2–14.

Copeland, W. D. (1975). "The relationship between microteaching and student teacher classroom performance." *Journal of Educational Research, 68,* 289–293.

Copeland, W. D. (1977). "Some factors related to student teacher classroom performance following microteaching training." *American Educational Research Journal, 14,* 147–157.

Copeland, W. D. (1981). "Clinical experiences in the education of teachers." *Journal of Education for Teachers, 7,* 3–16.

Copeland, W. D. (1982). "Laboratory experiences in teacher education." In H. E. Mitzel (ed.), *Encyclopedia of educational research.* New York: Free Press.

Copeland, W. D. (1987a). "Classroom management and student teachers' cognitive abilities: A relationship." *American Educational Research Journal, 24,* 219–236.

Copeland, W. D. (1987b). "Teacher information processing in the management of classrooms." In E. D. Doak, T. Hipple, and M. Keith (eds.), *Simulation and clinical knowledge in teacher education.* Knoxville: College of Education, University of Tennessee.

Copeland, W. D. (1989). "Technology-mediated laboratory experiences and the development of clinical reasoning in novice teachers." *Journal of Teacher Education, 40*(1), 10–18.

Crow, N. A. (1987). "Preservice teacher's biography: A case study." Paper presented at the annual meeting of the American Educational Research Association, Washington, D.C..

Cruickshank, D. R. (1987). *Reflective teaching: The preparation of students of teaching.* Reston, Va.: Association of Teacher Educators.

Cruickshank, D. R., and Metcalf, K. K. (1990). "Training within teacher preparation." In W. R. Houston (ed.), *Handbook of research on teacher education.* New York: Macmillan.

Doak, E. D., Hipple, T., and Keith, M. (eds.) (1987). *Simulation and clinical knowledge in teacher education.* Knoxville: College of Education, University of Tennessee.

Doyle, W. (1990a). "Case methods in the education of teachers." *Teacher Education Quarterly, 17,* 7–15.

Doyle, W. (1990b). "Themes in teacher education research." In W. R. Houston (ed.), *Handbook of research on teacher education.* New York: Macmillan.

Duckworth, E. (1987). *The having of wonderful ideas.* New York: Teachers College Press.

Elbaz, F. (1988). "Critical reflection on teaching: Insights from Freire." *Journal of Education for Teaching, 14,* 171–181.

Elbaz, F. (1991). "Research on teachers' knowledge: The evolution of a discourse." *Journal of Curriculum Studies, 23,* 1–19.

Erickson, F. (1986). "Qualitative methods in research on teaching." In M. C. Wittrock (ed.), *Handbook of research on teaching.* (3rd ed.). New York: Macmillan.

Evertson, C. M., and Green, J. L. (1986). "Observation and inquiry and method." In M. C. Wittrock (ed.), *Handbook of research on teaching.* (3rd ed.). New York: Macmillan.

Feiman-Nemser, S. (1983). "Learning to teach." In L. S. Shulman and G. Sykes (eds.), *Handbook of teaching and policy.* White Plains, N.Y.: Longman.

Feiman-Nemser, S. (1990). "Teacher preparation: Structural and conceptual alternatives." In W. R. Houston (ed.), *Handbook of research on teacher education.* New York: Macmillan.

Fenstermacher, G. D., and Richardson, V. (1993). "The elicitation and reconstruction of practical arguments in teaching." *Journal of Curriculum Studies, 25,* 101–114.

Flanders, N. A. (1970). *Analyzing teaching behavior.* Reading, Mass.: Addison-Wesley.

Florio-Ruane, S. (1989). "Social organization of classes and schools." In M. C. Reynolds (ed.), *Knowledge base for the beginning teacher.* Elmsford, N.Y.: Pergamon Press.

Furst, N. (1967). "The effects of training in interaction analysis on the behavior of student teachers in secondary schools." In E. J. Amidon and J. B. Hough (eds.), *Interaction analysis: Theory, research, and application.* Reading, Mass.: Addison-Wesley.

Gage, N. L., and Winne, P. H. (1975). "Performance-based teacher education." In K. Ryan (ed.), *Teacher education.* (74th yearbook of the National Society for the Study of Education, Part 2). Chicago: University of Chicago Press.

Garrison, J. W. (1988). "Democracy, scientific knowledge, and teacher empowerment." *Teachers College Record, 89,* 487–504.

Ginsburg, M. B., and Clift, R. T. (1990). "The hidden curriculum of preservice teacher education." In W. R. Houston (ed.), *Handbook of research on teacher education.* New York: Macmillan.

Glickman, C. D., and Bey, T. M. (1990). "Supervision." In W. R. Houston (ed.), *Handbook of research on teacher education.* New York: Macmillan.

Gliessman, D. H. (1984). "Changing teacher performance." In L. G. Katz and J. D. Raths (eds.), *Advances in teacher education,* Vol. 1. Norwood, N.J.: Ablex.

Gliessman, D. H., and Pugh, R. C. (1987). "Conceptual instruction and intervention as methods of acquiring teaching skills." *International Journal of Educational Research, 11,* 149–154.

Goldman, E., Barron, L., and Witherspoon, M. L. (1991). "Hypermedia cases in teacher education: A context for understanding research on the teaching and learning of mathematics." *Action in Teacher Education, 13*(1), 28–36.

Goodman, J. (1988). "University culture and the problem of reforming field experiences in teacher education." *Journal of Teacher Education, 39*(5), 45–53.

Goodson, I. F. (ed.) (1992). *Studying teachers' lives.* New York: Teachers College Press.

Grant, G. E. (1992). "Using cases to develop teacher knowledge: A cautionary tale." In J. H. Shulman (ed.), *Case methods in teacher education.* New York: Teachers College Press.

Greenwood, G. E., and Parkay, F. W. (1989). *Case studies for teacher decision making.* New York: Random House.

Griffin, G. A. (1986). "Issues in student teaching: A review." In J. D. Raths and L. G. Katz (eds.), *Advances in teacher education,* Vol. 2. Norwood, N.J.: Ablex.

Grimmett, P. P., and MacKinnon, A. M. (1992). "Craft knowledge and the education of teachers." In G. E. Grant (ed.), *Review of research in education,* Vol. 18. Washington, D.C.: American Educational Research Association.

Grossman, P. L. (1990). *The making of a teacher: Teacher knowledge and teacher education.* New York: Teachers College Press.

Grossman, P. L. (1992). "Teaching and learning with cases: Unanswered questions." In J. H. Shulman (ed.), *Case methods in teacher education.* New York: Teachers College Press.

Gudmundsdottir, S. (1991). "Story-maker, story-teller: Narrative structures in curriculum." *Journal of Curriculum Studies, 23,* 207–218.

Guyton, E., and McIntyre, D. J. (1990). "Student teaching and school experiences." In W. R. Houston (ed.), *Handbook of research on teacher education.* New York: Macmillan.

Hinely, R., and Ford, K. (1994). *Education in Edge City: Cases for reflection and action.* New York: St. Martin's Press.

Holmes Group (1986). *Tomorrow's teachers.* East Lansing, Mich.: Holmes Group.

Joyce, B. R., and Clift, R. T. (1984). "The phoenix agenda: Essential reforms in teacher education." *Educational Researcher, 13*(4), 5–18.

Joyce, B., and Showers, B. (1981). "Transfer of training: The contribution of coaching." *Journal of Education, 163,* 163–172.

Killian, J. E., and McIntyre, D. J. (1988). "Grade level as a factor in participation during early field experiences." *Journal of Teacher Education, 39*(2), 36–41.

Kleinfeld, J. (1992). "Learning to think like a teacher: The study of cases." In J. H. Shulman (ed.), *Case methods in teacher education.* New York: Teachers College Press.

Knowles, J. G. (1992). "Models for understanding preservice and beginning teachers' biographies: Illustrations from case studies." In I. F. Goodson (ed.), *Studying teachers' lives.* New York: Teachers College Press.

Knowles, J. G., and Holt-Reynolds, D. (1991). "Shaping pedagogies through personal histories in preservice teacher education." *Teachers College Record, 93,* 87–113.

Kowalski, T. J., Weaver, R. A., and Hensen, K. T. (1990). *Case studies in teaching.* White Plains, N.Y.: Longman.

McDiarmid, G. W. (1990). "Challenging prospective teachers' beliefs during early field experience: A quixotic undertaking?" *Journal of Teacher Education, 41*(3), 12–20.

McDonald, F. J. (1973). "Behavior modification in teacher education." In C. E. Thoresen (ed.), *Behavior modification in education.* (72nd yearbook of the National Society for the Study of Education, Part 1). Chicago: University of Chicago Press.

MacKinnon, A. M., and Grunau, H. (1991). "Teacher development through reflection, community, and discourse." Paper presented at the annual meeting of the American Educational Research Association, Chicago.

Medley, D. M., Coker, H., and Soar, R. S. (1984). *Measurement-based evaluation of teacher performance: An empirical approach.* White Plains, N.Y.: Longman.

Merseth, K. K. (1991). *The case for cases in teacher education.* Washington, D.C.: American Association of Colleges for Teacher Education/American Association of Higher Education.

Morine-Dershimer, G. (1987). "Creating a recycling center for teacher thinking." In E. D. Doak, T. Hipple, and M. Keith (eds.), *Simulation and clinical knowledge in teacher education.* Knoxville: College of Education, University of Tennessee.

Raymond, D., Butt, R. F., and Townsend, D. (1991). "Contexts for teacher development: Insights from teachers' stories." In A. Hargreaves and M. G. Fullan (eds.), *Understanding teacher development.* London: Cassells Educational.

Richardson, V. (1992). "The use of videocases in teacher education." Paper presented at the annual meeting of the American Educational Research Association, San Francisco.

Richardson, V., and Fenstermacher, G. D. (1992). "The role of the 'other' in school change." Paper presented at the annual meeting of the American Educational Research Association, San Francisco.

Richert, A. E. (1992). "Writing cases: A vehicle for inquiry into the teaching process." In J. H. Shulman (ed.), *Case methods in teacher education.* New York: Teachers College Press.

Rovegno, I. (1992). "Learning to teaching in a field-based methods course: The development of pedagogical content knowledge." *Teaching and Teacher Education, 8,* 69–82.

Rushcamp, S., and Roehler, L. R. (1992). "Characteristics supporting change in a professional development school." *Journal of Teacher Education, 43*(1), 19–27.

Russell, T., and Munby, H. (eds.) (1992). *Teachers and teaching: From classroom to reflection.* Washington, D.C.: Falmer Press.

Schön, D. (1983). *The reflective practitioner: How professionals think in action.* New York: Basic Books.

Schubert, W. H., and Ayers, W. C. (eds.) (1992). *Teacher lore: Learning from our own experience.* White Plains, N.Y.: Longman.

Shulman, J. H. (ed.) (1992). *Case methods in teacher education.* New York: Teachers College Press.

Shulman, J. H., and Colbert, J. A. (eds.) (1987). *The mentor teacher casebook.* San Francisco: Far West Laboratory for Educational Research and Development.

Shulman, J. H., and Colbert, J. A. (eds.) (1988). *The intern teacher casebook: Cases and commentaries.* San Francisco: Far West Laboratory for Educational Research and Development.

Shulman, L. S. (1987). "Knowledge and teaching: Foundations of the new reform." *Harvard Educational Review, 57,* 1–22.

Silverman, R., Welty, W. M., and Lyon, S. (1991). *Case studies for teacher problem-solving.* New York: McGraw-Hill.

Smith, B. O., Cohen, S. B., and Pearl, A. (1969). *Teachers for the real world.* Washington, D.C.: American Association of Colleges of Teacher Education.

Smyth, J. (ed.) (1987). *Educating teachers: Changing the nature of pedagogical knowledge.* Washington, D.C.: Falmer Press.

Sperle, D. H. (1933). *The case method technique in professional training: A survey of the use of case studies as a method of instruction in selected fields and a study of its application in a teachers college.* (Teachers College Contributions to Education, no. 571). New York: Teachers College Press.

Spiro, R. J., and others (1987). "Knowledge acquisition for application: Cognitive flexibility and transfer in complex domains." In B. C. Britton (ed.), *Executive control processes.* Hillsdale, N.J.: Erlbaum.

Stallings, J. A., and Kowalski, T. J. (1990). "Research on professional development schools." In W. R. Houston (ed.), *Handbook of research on teacher education.* New York: Macmillan.

Strang, H. R., Landrum, M. S., and Lynch, K. A. (1989). "Talking with the computer: A simulation for training basic teaching skills." *Teaching and Teacher Education, 5,* 143–153.

Sykes, G., and Bird, T. (1992). "Teacher education and the case idea." In G. E. Grant (ed.), *Review of research in education,* Vol. 18. Washington, D.C.: American Educational Research Association.

Tabachnick, B. R., and Zeichner, K. M. (1984). "The impact of the student teaching experience on the development of teacher perspectives." *Journal of Teacher Education, 35*(6), 28–36.

Wagner, A. C. (1973). "Changing teacher behavior: A comparison of microteaching and cognitive discrimination training." *Journal of Educational Psychology, 64,* 299–305.

Walker, D. C., and Schaffarzick, J. (1974). "Comparing curricula." *Review of Educational Research, 44,* 83–111.

Warren, B., and Rosebery, A. S. (1995). "Equity in the future tense: Redefining relationships among teachers, students, and science in linguistic minority classrooms." In E. Fennema, W. G. Secada, and L. Byrd (eds.), *New directions for equity in mathematics.* Cambridge: Cambridge University Press.

Weinstein, C. S. (1988). "Preservice teachers' expectations about the first year of teaching." *Teaching and Teacher Education, 4,* 31–40.

Witherell, C., and Noddings, N. (eds.) (1991). *Stories lives tell: Narrative and dialogue in education.* New York: Teachers College Press.

Woods, P. (1987). "Life histories and teacher knowledge." In J. Smyth (ed.), *Educating teachers: Changing the nature of pedagogical knowledge.* Washington, D.C.: Falmer Press.

Yamamoto, K., and others (1969). "As they see it: Culling impressions from teachers in preparation." *Journal of Teacher Education, 20*(4), 465–475.

Zeichner, K. M. (1983). "Alternative paradigms of teacher education." *Journal of Teacher Education, 34*(3), 3–9.

Zeichner, K. M. (1987). "The ecology of field experience: Toward an understanding of the role of field experiences in teacher development." In M. Haberman and J. M. Backus (eds.), *Advances in teacher education*, Vol. 3. Norwood, N.J.: Ablex.

Zeichner, K. M., and Gore, J. M. (1990). "Teacher socialization." In W. R. Houston (ed.), *Handbook of research on teacher education*. New York: Macmillan.

Zeichner, K. M., and Liston, D. P. (1987). "Teaching student teachers to reflect." *Harvard Educational Review, 57*, 23–48.

Zimpher, N. L. (1990). "Creating professional development school sites." *Theory into Practice, 29*, 42–49.

Zulich, J., Bean, T. W., and Herrick, J. (1991). "Charting stages of preservice teacher development and reflection in a multicultural community through dialogue journal analysis." Paper presented at the annual meeting of the American Educational Research Association, Chicago.

Zumwalt, K. K. (1982). "Research on teaching: Policy implications for teacher education." In A. Lieberman and M. W. McLaughlin (eds.), *Policy making in education.* (81st yearbook of the National Society for the Study of Education, Part 1). Chicago: University of Chicago Press.

Annotated Bibliography

Cruickshank, D. R., and Metcalf, K. K. (1990). "Training within teacher preparation." In W. R. Houston (ed.), *Handbook of research on teacher education*. New York: Macmillan.
This chapter is the authoritative review of the long tradition of laboratory skill training in teacher preparation. Basic terms are defined and the major approaches and research programs are summarized.

Fosnot, C. T. (1989). *Enquiring teachers, enquiring learners: A constructivist approach for teaching.* New York: Teachers College Press.
Fosnot suggests that "a thorough overhauling of pedagogical education" is needed in order to "empower teachers to do what must be done in schools, rather than one that tells teachers what to do" (p. xi). Her book, as the title suggests, offers a constructivist approach to teacher education that will "empower teachers" by providing opportunities for inquiry. Dialogue reproduced from many of Fosnot's classes, workshops, and seminars provide the substance through which she explores criteria for constructivist teacher education programs, describes sample activities for concept construction, demonstrates teachers defining themselves as learners, and provides details for implementation of a constructivist program. The use of dialogue draws the reader into Fosnot's classroom for a glimpse of how she puts her theory into practice for both preservice and inservice teachers. Not surprisingly, then, we come to understand the power of discourse among communities of learners who are becoming reflective and action-oriented.

Goodson, I. F. (ed.) (1992). *Studying teachers' lives.* New York: Teachers College Press.
Goodson writes, "The crucial focus for life history work is to locate the teacher's own life story alongside a broader contextual analysis, to tell, in Stenhouse's words, 'a story of action, within a theory of context'" (p. 6). To this end, Goodson offers four reasons for studying teachers lives: (1) to gain a perspective on schooling reform issues; (2) to understand socializing influences such as the apprenticeship of observation; (3) to de-

scribe the experience of women's lives in teaching, the "gendered profession"; and (4) to contribute to the production of teacher-centered professional knowledge, knowledge that was previously decontextualized. The volume consists of seven "studies" of teachers' lives, which cover a range of topics from pedagogy to school improvement, while at the same time offering fresh perspectives on the issues of ethics and methods inherent in studying teacher's lives. The issues cited by Goodson include process and procedure, the nature of interpretation and of the text, the role of the teacher's voice, the relationship between the teacher and the researcher as well as the "relationship of the studies of teachers' lives to the academy" (p. 238). He recommends a "requirement of procedural clarification" as a means of addressing these dilemmas (p. 247). The authors whose works are contained in this volume are, argues Goodson, "facing squarely the dilemmas of studying people's lives" (p. 15).

Posner, G. J. (1989). *Field experience: Methods of reflective teaching.* White Plains, N.Y.: Longman.
Posner writes in his preface that "we benefit from our experiences by preparing for and reflecting on them" (p. ix). He suggests that his book can be used by novices for early field experiences as well as for student teaching and into the first years of teaching. The book has been designed to be used more than once because it presents a "cyclical" approach: preparation, engagement, and reflection. The first chapters focus on orientation to the field experience and to the school community. The middle chapters assist the student in recognizing and defining his or her perspective on teaching and learning as well as making sense of the current experience. The final chapters are intended to promote reflection on the experiences and prepare for the next experience, thus completing the cycle. Posner also includes an appendix of sample progress reports written by students in field experiences and a list of suggested readings. With the addition of close supervision, this book can provide the vehicle necessary for successful completion of the practicum experience.

Russell, T., and Munby, H. (eds.) (1992). *Teachers and teaching: From classroom to reflection.* Washington, D.C.: Falmer Press.
Russell and Munby have gathered a collection of chapters focused on reflection: in teaching, in and from cases, through narrative, and in teacher education. These chapters, the editors argue, "provide the potential of novel frames for understanding teachers and teaching" (p. 8). Several chapters present cases of individual teachers (including one autobiographical case) that address the question of what it means to be a reflective teacher. Other chapters describe research projects aimed at understanding these processes as experienced by preservice and inservice teachers, the writing of cases and the development of case literatures, and the use of cases in teacher education to develop reflection. The authors seem particularly pleased that within the chapters in the book the authors have "reframed" traditional notions of research on teaching and of teacher education from that of "telling" to a concerted effort to understand teachers and their work from the teachers' perspective.

Shulman, J. H. (ed.) (1992). *Case methods in teacher education.* New York: Teachers College Press.
In the foreword, Sykes suggests that "cases . . . are helpful in teaching about subject matter, classroom management, inquiry and reflection on teaching, and knowledge traditionally conveyed in foundations courses" (p. vii). Shulman's latest collection of cases is similarly eclectic, providing a wide variety of cases and suggestions for using them that "portray the complexity of teaching" and learning to teach. This is a book about teaching with cases. The cases provide opportunities for "prospective teachers to grapple with the ambiguities and dilemmas of schooling such as grading, plagiarism, diversity, appropriate instructions, and uncooperative students" (p. xiv). The authors of

many of the cases in this book have been writing and dialoguing about cases, case development, and their potential for use in teacher education for some time: Anna Richert, Pam Grossman, Kathy Carter, Katherine Merseth, and Judith Kleinfeld. These scholars have suggested that cases can be used to teach concepts and to develop reflective inquiry through the writing of them. Included in this volume are several research-based cases as well as a discussion of the limitations of a case approach. Finally, there is promise that the teaching and learning resulting from the use of cases will contribute heartily to the development of a knowledge base of teaching.

Sykes, G., and Bird, T. (1992). "Teacher education and the case idea." In G. E. Grant (eds.), *Review of research in education,* Vol. 18. Washington, D.C.: American Educational Research Association.

Sykes and Bird have provided a state-of-the-field review of the emerging work on case teaching in the preparation of teachers. Given the diversity of the field and the lack of clear research or theory, the authors use the phrase *case idea* to characterize the field as a whole. In addition to surveying the rapidly expanding body of case literature in the field, the authors examine issues of the relationship of cases to the curriculum of teacher education, the development of cases for teacher education, and learning to teach from cases. They conclude with suggestions for research on the case idea. This chapter is essential reading for anyone interested in case-based pedagogy in teacher education.

Witherell, C., and Noddings, N. (eds.) (1991). *Stories lives tell: Narrative and dialogue in education.* New York: Teachers College Press.

This book is about the power of narrative both in human lives and in educational practice and research. Three major themes emerge from the fourteen chapters. First, story and narrative are primary tools in the work that educators and counselors do. As the editors argue so persuasively, "those engaged in this work can penetrate cultural barriers, discover the power of self and the integrity of the other, and deepen their understanding of their respective histories and possibilities" (p. 4). Second, education means taking seriously both the quest for meaning and the call to care for persons, and third, the use of narrative and dialogue can serve as a model for teaching and learning across the boundaries of disciplines, professions, and cultures. Subsequently, narrative studies serve three purposes: (1) narrative as a way of knowing, (2) narrative as a way of understanding self and other, and (3) narrative as a way of modeling education and research. Through stories, we can both explain and learn. Through stories, we come to know and understand. Through stories, we can envision change. Through stories, we can capture the richness, the complexity, the connectedness of people's lives.

CHAPTER TWENTY-FOUR

CHANGES AND CHOICES
IN TEACHING METHODS

BARBARA SENKOWSKI STENGEL AND ALAN R. TOM

No issue in the professional education curriculum arouses stronger opinions than does the topic of "methods courses." Some see courses on methodology as the only truly useful part of a future teacher's curriculum besides student teaching. They often advocate wide-ranging methods study, including general methods as well as subject- and age-level-specific courses. For others, methodology courses take up curricular space that could be better devoted to additional subject matter study in the arts and sciences. They recommend more and broader liberal arts study as the panacea for ineffective teacher preparation. Still others view time spent studying methodology as pedagogically important in principle but in reality impractical and out of touch with the day-to-day challenges of classroom teaching. They lament that methods courses are taught by professors in university classrooms rather than by practicing elementary and secondary teachers on site. Yet another position is taken by those who support research-based methods instruction offered by university faculty but who worry that present practice does not acknowledge the complex developmental nature of the process of learning to teach. They advocate reformulating methods study to incorporate qualitative research findings and such pedagogical strategies as case study. In short, few seem neutral about the importance and utility of methods courses.

There is good reason for this. Traditional teacher education programs are typically marked by three components: foundations of schooling and learning, teaching methodology, and practice teaching. Within this framework, methods study is at the heart of the teacher education enterprise. Whereas history, philosophy, and psychology courses provide background for the act of teaching, and student teaching supplies an opportunity to practice one's skills, it is in methods courses that one presumably learns to teach.

This traditional framework is under intense scrutiny as a result of a variety of political initiatives, teacher education reform efforts, and new lines of research on teaching and learning to teach. Policy changes in Texas (stringent credit limits) and California (postbaccalaureate certification) that place external restrictions on teacher educators' options have given way to heated discussions about which components in the traditional framework can be cut or altered. Certification guidelines such as New Jersey's allow liberal arts graduates to begin teaching in public schools without formal preparation in teacher education, thus calling into question the value of methods instruction. Efforts such as the Carnegie-funded Project 30 Alliance and several Association of American Colleges' National Endowment for the Humanities–funded initiatives have gathered program review teams from various institutions to stimulate conversation and action toward integrating liberal arts and professional study in teacher education. Coalitions of institutions educating teachers, such as the Renaissance Group and the Holmes Group, have addressed the conceptual and political issues underlying such reform and offered guidelines and principles for proceeding. Research programs such as those undertaken at Michigan State's National Center for Research on Learning to Teach and Stanford's Knowledge Growth in Teaching Project have extended our understanding of teaching as a content- and context-specific endeavor. Studies inspired by Donald Schön's conception of the reflective practitioner (1983), as well as other cognitivist and constructionist views, have forced recognition that teachers are not technicians applying skills in prescribed situations but responsible decision makers interpreting ill-structured and complex situations and acting in response.

The structure of this book reflects the changes (still very much in process) in our conceptualization of teacher education programs. This chapter on methods is not grouped under the heading of "curriculum content" but located with other "program structures." What then does "methods" mean? We know what it used to mean to most of us: topically oriented study of planning for, delivery of, management of, special problems regarding, and professional concerns implicit in instruction. However, what "methods" are in those programs that have begun to struggle through the reconceptualization process is a very interesting question— and very much an open question underlying the issues we raise in this chapter.

We do not align ourselves here with any *one* of the positions concerning the value of methods coursework outlined in the opening paragraph. In fact, these four positions are not merely opinions about methods instruction but indicators of one's priorities (perhaps even what might be called one's "paradigm") regarding teacher education generally. Together, they form the boundaries of the political field on which decisions about methods are played out.

We maintain that underlying each of these paradigms is a legitimate concern regarding the education of future teachers: respectively, command of professional knowledge and skill, strong content preparation, substantial field-based coaching, and attention to the realities of the process of learning to teach, all of which can be used as criteria to judge the value of particular teacher education programs. These criteria are addressed thoroughly elsewhere in this volume and implicitly throughout this chapter.

There is, lurking beneath any discussion about methods preparation, a very basic question. Can we teach someone to teach? There is a common view (held even by some teacher educators) that one either has a knack for teaching or one does not. No amount of instruction will make a poor teacher into a good one. This is, in our estimation, a flawed view. It is surely true that some people have more talent for teaching than do others, just as some have more talent for musical composition or for playing basketball than do others. It also seems true that some (a very few) need virtually no formal instruction to develop their talent for teaching, just as Mozart and Michael Jordan needed little formal instruction in their respective fields. Nonetheless, it is reasonable to believe that persons of modest talent can be "taught" to enhance and expand their abilities, just as innumerable accomplished, though perhaps not virtuoso, composers and basketball players have been.

We begin this chapter with the assumption that persons (with a moderate level of talent for teaching) *can* be taught to teach and that methods instruction is the effort to do that. As will become clear as this chapter unfolds, we are still in the process of learning just how to do that. The answer to the "how" question is a function not only of ongoing research and theorizing about teaching and learning to teach but also and always a function of the models and assumptions that guide the thinking of the teacher education faculty (here we include all university faculty who have direct contact with future teachers and/or a voice in program construction).

Because we hold the view that teacher education faculties in particular institutions must frame local responses to the practical, theoretical, and political issues outlined in this introduction, we have constructed this chapter around assumptions to be examined and questions to be answered by any faculty in the process of making decisions about methods instruction.

In our first two sections, we focus on two sets of assumptions about methods instruction that rarely receive explicit attention. The first of these is the purpose of methods study or more accurately the alternate purposes that can be attributed to the study of teaching methodology. The second set of assumptions is the varying ways in which general methods can be seen as differing from special methods.

In the third section, we address the practical questions that teacher education faculties typically decide about the study of methodology: (1) How many methods courses should be required? (2) What balance ought there be between the study of general and special methods? (3) How should methods courses be sequenced and linked, both among themselves and among such other areas of study as subject matter and teaching practice?

Figure 24.1 represents our view of the interaction of paradigms, metaphors, and models, assumptions about purposes for and kinds of methods instruction, and issues in methods decision making. Note that local decisions about methods instruction are embedded in various levels of conceptual, professional, and programmatic assumptions and prior questions.

This discussion will be capped, in the final section, by a consideration of four examples of possible methods instruction sequences, analyzing these examples for the coherence of their assumptions and answers as well as for their adequacy in addressing the concerns of those who hold the four positions described earlier.

The Purposes for Methods Instruction

Explicit consideration of the goals and desired outcomes of methods instruction is extremely important since even the teachers of methods courses often fail to think rigorously about the purposes for their instruction (Floden, McDiarmid, and Wiemers, 1989), and the goals they do propose for their courses may not be related to the attributes these same instructors believe to be essential for becoming competent K-12 teachers (Katz and Raths, 1982).

The parameters of "methods" are partially established by teacher education faculties in choosing the metaphors and models that ground their programs and that express their conceptions of teaching. How is it then that you and your colleagues think about teaching? As a craft, a science, an art, a calling, a political endeavor? (Dawe, 1984; Freeman, 1930; Giroux and McLaren, 1986; Rubin, 1985; Tom, 1984). What assumptions and implications are bound up in your dominant metaphor? Do you think of teaching as primarily skill-based, as intrinsically moral, as creative, as intuitive, as logical, as reliant on formal/basic research, as grounded in the "wisdom of practice," as (inter)personal, as professional, as dependent on the educated judgment of the individual teacher? The assumptions you hold about the essence of teaching constitute the lens through which our discussion of purposes and variants of methods instruction can be considered, understood, and dismissed or utilized (Gideonse, 1986; Richards and Gipe, 1992). In what follows here, we discuss four plausible purposes for methods instruction. Depending on program philosophy and guiding metaphors, one or more purposes may become the foci of methods study for your program.

The four purposes are (1) intellectual command of the concepts and schemata of teaching, (2) demonstration of skillful teaching practice, (3) interpretation of the complexities of content and context, and (4) socialization into self-understanding with respect to the professional role of teacher. While we do not argue that these are the only four goals conceivable for methods courses, we believe that our categories include most of the goals typically put forward for methods instruction. While we also do not argue that these four goals can *only* be achieved through "methods instruction," we do insist that all four goals *should* be achieved in the course of a

FIGURE 24.1. CHANGES AND CHOICES IN TEACHING METHODS.

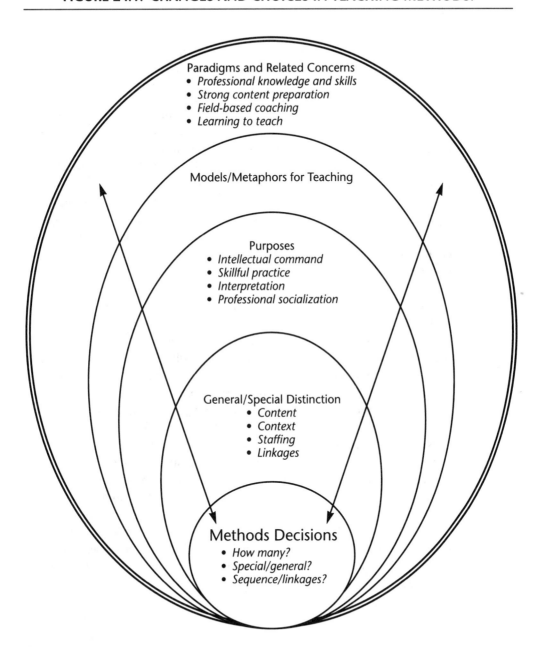

Paradigms and Related Concerns
- *Professional knowledge and skills*
- *Strong content preparation*
- *Field-based coaching*
- *Learning to teach*

Models/Metaphors for Teaching

Purposes
- *Intellectual command*
- *Skillful practice*
- *Interpretation*
- *Professional socialization*

General/Special Distinction
- *Content*
- *Context*
- *Staffing*
- *Linkages*

Methods Decisions
- *How many?*
- *Special/general?*
- *Sequence/linkages?*

well-designed teacher education program and *can* be achieved as a result of methods courses.

Intellectual Command of Concepts, Principles, and Schemata

In general, future teachers are expected to comprehend principles of, develop schemata for, and articulate models of basic approaches to teaching practice. Whether one considers methods textbooks (see, for example, Arends, 1991; Kauchak and Eggen, 1989), research compendia (Reynolds, 1989), or practitioners' handbooks (Pennsylvania State Education Association, 1993), the topical list of indispensable teaching knowledge is relatively stable: instructional processes and planning, classroom management and discipline, "special" student needs, assessment of student learning, and professionalism issues. While each of these sources (predictably) offers a different treatment of these topics—more or less practical, more or less theoretical, more or less immediate and concrete—each source provides a propositional version of what teachers should know about teaching.

Is the acquisition of this kind of propositional knowledge the primary goal of methods instruction? Should it be? There are three plausible answers. First, the traditional response is yes: intellectual command of propositional knowledge about teaching is the ground on which a future teacher builds effective practice through field experience. Second, the Deweyan revival headlined by Donald Schön (1983, 1987) says yes and no: intellectual command of propositional knowledge about teaching results *from* reflective practice as much as it leads *to* it. Therefore, theory and practice should not be separated in learning to teach. Third, the response emerging from a relatively new line of teacher thinking research is no—not because intellectual command of knowledge about teaching is unimportant but because the propositional form of knowledge is inappropriate for the practice of teaching. That is, expert teachers do not hold and access their knowledge in terms of general rules and principles (Clark and Lampert, 1986; Lampert and Clark, 1990; Leinhardt, 1990; Petrie, 1992).

The traditional yes response, while not totally discredited, is clearly under fire from researchers who have demonstrated that students may have clear command of knowledge about teaching yet not be able to teach in a way that demonstrates the practice of such understandings (Brown, Collins, and Duguid, 1989). This calls into question the value of propositional knowledge as *the* focal point for methods instruction and lends credibility to the other two responses. Questioning the value of propositional knowledge does not mean that intellectual command of the craft knowledge of teaching is unimportant; however, it does force us to reconceive the notion of the intellectual dimensions of teacher knowledge. This is in fact one result of both reflective practice studies and teacher thinking research in that intellectual command and skillful practice become flip sides of the same coin of purpose, of the same knowledge.

Demonstration of Skillful Practice

An obvious potential outcome of methods study is demonstration of teaching practice with at least a minimal level of skill. If skillful practice is a goal of methods instruction, then discussion topics, texts, and instructional activities must be designed to foster the acquisition of appropriate skills and the use of such skills in instructional settings. There are two possible avenues to pursue: laboratory applications and field-based practice.

The former includes microteaching and peer reaction, videotaping and analysis, forms of case study that emphasize decision making (Shulman, 1992), and various forms of simulation exercises (Berliner, 1985). Such activities have the strength of being controlled experiences in which students can practice specific techniques or apply theory-based strategies in simplified and/or low-pressure contexts.

The latter involves either short-term or extended experiences in public schools. These approaches have the strength of being "real" opportunities to try one's hand at teaching but involve settings not under the control of the course instructor. Neither the preservice teacher nor the university instructor determines the curriculum or the approach to classroom management. For example, a methods instructor may direct field experience students to "practice" various features of cooperative learning, but the student will not be able to do so if placed in the classroom of a teacher who never uses this strategy. Similarly, students directed to attend to children's cultural and socioeconomic differences as these factors affect learning patterns will be hard pressed to do so if assigned to classrooms in which there are relatively homogeneous students. In professional development schools or other similar collaborative arrangements (Holmes Group, 1986, 1990), however, prospective teachers should have opportunities for "real" practice while certain factors (such as the cooperating teacher's approach and the school curriculum) can be controlled or at least predicted.

Interpretation and Response

Several strands of educational thought and research in the past decade suggest that teaching is a subject-specific affair (Grossman, Wilson, and Shulman, 1989; Shulman, 1986) and that teachers can become curriculum makers, not merely content deliverers (Grumet, 1989; Ben-Peretz, 1990; Clandinin and Connelly, 1992). At what point in the teacher education program do students come to grips with this role, attaining competence in interpreting complex instructional situations and responding appropriately?

The renewed realization that content and method ought to be interrelated in a prospective teacher's preparation, a realization partly resulting from the failure by teaching effectiveness researchers to discover general principles of teaching (Shulman, 1987), points to the conclusion that consideration of complex curricular issues does fall within the realm of methods. How one conceptualizes the nature and purposes of subject matter affects the planning of particular units and lessons. Further, what understandings, skills, and attitudes one assesses as potential outcomes of curriculum materials and media also shape instructional strategy decisions by which these materials and media are employed.

Consider the decisions facing a high school social studies teacher. Is the curriculum to be organized in an interdisciplinary or disciplinary way? What themes, events, persons, and relationships demand emphasis and why? What political, cultural, and civic interests are served? What texts, video presentations, computer simulations, and discussion topics are most likely to help achieve one's goals and how is the quality of all of these decisions to be assessed? Even more basic, is the purpose of social studies education the mastery of disciplinary thinking, the deepening of historical and cultural literacy, or the development of critical citizens? The way teachers conceptualize the social studies curriculum will shape their choices about how it is to be taught. While the "how" is more commonly assumed to be the heart of methods study, the "what" is the blood to be pumped and cannot be ignored.

Note that a focus on curriculum and context issues shifts the purpose of methods study away from command of identifiable theories and demonstration of skills toward exploration of the complexity of content and contexts that require interpretation and response (Ben-Peretz, 1990). This is a more open-ended goal, less capable of specification, requiring more tolerance for ambiguity among teacher educators and students alike. Case study formats that are inquiry oriented are potentially useful pedagogical tools here (Shulman, 1992).

This interpretive turn brings the self of the teacher and the selves of students into the picture, further complicating the process of curricular deliberation. Who *you* are shapes what you want for your students—that is, your objectives. Who *they* are shapes the particular "course of study" that will enable you and them to achieve these broadly conceived objectives (see, for example, Jackson, 1990; Cuban, 1993). Curriculum is dependent both on who students are and what they already know and on how teachers understand their task as well as how they understand themselves. The theories and techniques of teaching become intelligible and meaningful within the context of curriculum study.

Professionalism and Self-Understanding

Teacher education students must acquire a sense of themselves as teachers while shedding (at least certain aspects of) the role of student. What does this mean? At minimum, teachers have a language, a loose set of legal and ethical mores, and a role-bound perspective. There are a variety of ways of conceptualizing teaching (one's metaphor for teaching, as mentioned earlier) and a range of theories as to how teaching brings about learning, as well as dispositions on the part of teachers to act upon this knowledge (Katz and Raths, 1985). Moreover, the profession of teaching has a history rooted in particular gender and class relations. Teacher education students may be prompted to think about such matters in social and psychological foundations courses and to confront them in student teaching. Still, "becoming a professional" is a potential purpose of methods instruction in that methods used in teaching embody the words, theories, and points of view that are properly professional.

We raise this purpose here so that what has been typically implicit can be made explicit and strengthened. We also raise the goal of professional self-understanding because of the growing consensus, from educators holding varied points of view, that teaching is more than a purely technical activity, that teaching inherently involves the exercise of informed ethical judgment and action (Goodlad, Soder, and Sirotnik, 1990; Sockett, 1993; Strike and Soltis, 1985; Noddings, 1992; Tom, 1984). Moreover, there is a tradition within methods instruction for raising the political awareness of prospective teachers about the ways in which political and social action can be linked to teaching (Adler and Goodman, 1986; Hesch, 1990).

Thus, our view of teacher socialization is not grounded in the belief that the purpose of methods instruction is to better organize the induction of prospective teachers into schooling as it is currently practiced but rather we see the opportunity for prospective teachers to play an active role in their own "socialization" into the role of teacher (Zeichner and Gore, 1990; Ayers, 1990). Those faculty responsible for making decisions about methods instruction need to reflect upon the way(s) both the form and content of methods instruction foster the professional self-understanding of prospective teachers.

A Matter of Relative Emphasis

Our discussion of the purposes of methods instruction is not meant to be an either/or affair, forcing choices among the purposes listed. It is not enough to assume the value of one purpose and ignore the others. All must be addressed, if not in methods courses, then in some other component of the teacher education program. The question here is the relative emphasis to be given to each of the four purposes in methods instruction per se. In planning for methods instruction, conscious deliberation by decision makers about the relative importance of each purpose is needed to ensure the quality of prospective teachers' preparation.

General and Special Methods: Prior Assumptions

Acknowledging and exploring multiple purposes for methods study suggest the possibility of multiple kinds of methods courses. In fact, methods study has traditionally been divided into "general" and "special" methods. As we rethink other aspects of teacher education, this taken-for-granted distinction is also subject to scrutiny.

Rather than discussing this conceptual distinction, we suggest uncovering assumptions by focusing on a complex operational question: what is the difference between general and special methods courses with reference to programmatic considerations, specifically (1) the substance/content of methods courses, (2) the context specificity of such study, (3) instructional staffing, and (4) linkages among teacher education program components?

Substance and Content of Methods Courses

Presumably, certain topics—planning, instructional strategies, student evaluation, and so forth—are common to both general and special methods. Is it also true that some topics are only attributable to one or the other? For example, at first review, curriculum issues and reading in the content area strategies seem to belong properly to special methods in that these are topics embedded in subject matter concerns. Still, one could make a case that there are generic curriculum models that are given particular instantiation in each subject area and that there is a general set of reading strategies that may or may not be appropriate to a particular subject area.

Similarly, one might assume that classroom management is a generic topic, more properly located in a general methods course than in a special methods course. However, surely there are management issues that are domain-specific—the organization of science labs, for instance, or the procedures for independent library research in history—and which are properly treated in a special methods course.

Shulman (1986, 1987), among others, maintains that all teaching is content- and context-bound and can only be defined, planned, and evaluated in that light. If one takes this position seriously, then all "true" methods instruction must be special methods. General methods courses would be allotted only those topics and activities common to all teachers whatever their subject domain.

One alternative to distributing different topics to the two types of methods courses is to view general methods and special methods as differing points of view on the same phenomenon. That is, general methods examines teaching practice from the point of view of the teaching profession in general, while special methods examines teaching practice from the point(s) of view of particular teachers in particular contexts. Given this understanding, the topics considered and questions asked would be quite similar in both general and special methods, but the answers constructed would be intentionally more or less specific to particular contexts.

Placing general and special methods on a continuum allows us to value and integrate the findings of both process-product and interpretive research in methods instruction as well as the kind of reflection on teaching that has been described as "teacher lore" (Schubert and Ayers, 1992). The process-product/effective teaching research that produces generalizations regarding teaching becomes the centerpiece of general methods work while qualitative/ethnographic research and the "wisdom of practice" fit better with methods courses that are subject-specific or age-level-specific.

Context Specificity of Methods Study

Future teachers are being prepared and certified to work in specific contexts. Subject matter and student developmental levels are the primary determinants of what makes special methods "special," but sociocultural setting and institutional culture are also factors that affect a teacher's instructional decision making (that is, decision making and implementation of "methods"). As suggested in the previous section, context specificity does not seem to be a mutually exclusive set of categories (general versus special) but a continuum (more or less specific to a given instructional context). Where is the line to be drawn between general and special methods?

The rationale is most often expressed in typical course titles. "Principles of Teaching" or "Classroom Processes and Instruction" clearly represent general methods courses. "Teaching Mathematics in Secondary Schools" is a special methods course, focused on a particular subject matter for a particular developmental/age group. Similarly, "Art in the Elementary School" is a special methods course.

"Problems in Secondary Education" would be special as to developmental/age group but general as to subject matter. It is difficult to imagine a course that is special as to subject matter but general as to student population, though perhaps "Reading in the Content Areas" would be a candidate.

Examining course titles leaves many questions unanswered, however. Consider "Teaching Mathematics in the Secondary School." Teaching mathematics includes teaching algebra, geometry, trigonometry, calculus, and business math to students of varying ability and ambition. One can be an effective teacher of trigonometry to college-bound students while being woefully ineffective teaching business math to the non-college-bound (Grossman, Wilson, and Shulman, 1989; Hashweh, 1987). How specific (special) can such a course actually be? The general-special distinction again appears to be one of degree.

Thorough attention to the notion of context specificity suggests that the general-special distinction is not based only on subject matter and developmental level but also on social, cultural, and economic factors. For example, many teacher education programs currently require a multicultural education course. Such courses do more than merely provide future teachers with cultural information, aiming instead to develop sensitivity to the cultural characteristics of varying student populations as well as to explore appropriate instructional strategies for particular student audiences (Erb and Keesbury, 1992; Grant, 1991; Ryan and Robinson, 1990). Other programs have urban and/or rural education courses or concentrations, which prepare future teachers to work in specific geographic and economic environments. Specifically, methodological coursework focused on gender issues has developed slowly for prospective teachers (for exceptions, see Sadker and Sadker, 1982; Streitmatter, 1994), though courses using gender as a lens to consider texts and curricula as well as classroom interaction have proliferated.

Interestingly, the very existence of specific coursework for multicultural, rural, urban, and gendered instructional environments raises the question of how general "general methods" really are. General methods courses may simply be courses specific to white, middle-class, male-dominant, suburban, and small-town environments and appropriate for curricula defined in the same ways.

Instructional Staffing

Who can and should teach general methods? Special methods? What kind of expertise is needed and who possesses that expertise? There is an outdated but still extant assumption that content is covered in liberal arts courses taught by disciplinary experts, while how to teach that content is developed in methods courses taught by education faculty. In this view, liberal arts faculty cannot have pedagogical expertise, education faculty cannot have disciplinary expertise, and expert public school teachers have no role to play in the education of teachers. Taken literally, this view assigns education faculty to the teaching of general methods courses and leaves special methods courses in limbo.

More recent discussion and research surrounding the subject-specific nature of instruction also suggests scrutiny of the staffing of special methods courses. If a teacher's organization of subject matter, bridges to students' prior knowledge, and representational repertoire are essential elements in instruction, then special methods courses should address the nature of future teachers' understanding of their subject fields and their knowledge of students' cultural backgrounds.

Mastering methods of teaching is more than acquiring useful pedagogical tactics. It involves insight into multiple perspectives on each discipline as well as knowledge of the role played by each discipline (for example, mathematics) in our society and everyday life (Ball, 1991). Such mastery requires knowledge of students from diverse cultural backgrounds, including the meaning that these students have constructed from their out-of-school experiences as well as from their encounters with subject matter inside the school (McDiarmid, 1991). How can this content best be taught and who possesses the relevant expertise?

It is doubtful that more liberal arts study can simply replace special methods coursework to achieve the goal of a pedagogical understanding of subject matter (Grossman, 1990; McDiarmid, 1992). While it seems obvious that deepening one's subject matter knowledge will make a good teacher better, it does not follow that knowing a lot results in effective teaching. As Dewey points out (1916), it is the ability to make one's understanding of the world accessible to particular learners that marks the effective teacher.

Consider the example of an earth science teacher in an urban middle school. It is as important to attend to the shape of one's knowledge of general science and to its connections with the environment of one's students as it is to require a substantial amount of academic study from the teacher. Who, then, can assist future teachers in shaping their knowledge of the sciences in pedagogically effective ways so that content, method, and learners become "seamless" in actual teaching?

The earth science professor brings subject matter depth but typically has little awareness of shaping content for diverse learners, in particular minorities and possibly females. The effective public school science teacher has substantial experience with the process of instructional decision making in complex circumstances but often has little formal subject matter preparation beyond his or her bachelor's degree. The curriculum and instruction faculty member has mastered the literature of the teaching profession in general but may not have an understanding of science beyond his or her own undergraduate general education requirements. The science educator who has integrated substantial subject matter expertise with study of curriculum and instruction seems the ideal candidate for teaching a course in the teaching of science but may be limited by functioning primarily in the university environment, somewhat removed from the everyday realities of the teaching profession and school students. The multicultural or special needs expert offers a valuable perspective on the individual character of each learner but may have no experience with middle-school students. Despite these realities, we must make staffing decisions that will ensure adequate attention to the purposes of professionalism, of content and context, of skillful practice, and of knowledge of teaching concepts and schemata.

General methods courses can integrate standard teaching strategies, ethical dimensions, and the formal research that grounds the teaching profession. In this case, the teaching of such courses seems properly the province of education generalists or perhaps a team of subject specialists (for example, Moore and Scott, 1981). Questions remain, however, concerning the staffing of special methods courses. Who has the expertise required to synthesize subject matter, methodological, and contextual variables in teaching and to enable future teachers to do so as well? Is team teaching indicated? Are joint appointments (across academic departments and between university and public school) appropriate? Are ties between various courses and field experiences appropriate in order to generate shared expertise and broad-based experience and reflection for future teachers? All of these are among the suggestions appearing in the teacher education reform literature, yet few have been thoroughly conceptualized, researched, and evaluated.

Linkages Among Program Components

Should methods courses stand alone or be linked to other courses and/or experiences? This may be the most fruitful focus for the substantive reform of teacher education (Valli, 1992).

Programs treat methods courses in a variety of ways, sometimes linking several methods courses, often incorporating some form of early field experience.

Coupling general methods and special methods courses could enable future teachers to see the connections between the subject-specific practice and the effective teaching research, but a more common approach is to join general methods and educational psychology (Duell and Yeotis, 1981). Another possibility is to "block" subject-specific methods courses for elementary education majors to facilitate the development of integrated units of instruction for elementary students, especially if joint planning and/or team teaching is employed (Lasley, 1990; Schivley, De Cicco, and Millward, 1982).

Incorporating early field experiences in methods courses or the teaching of methods courses in school settings can encourage the application of methodological techniques and tactics to practice, thus developing both instructional skill and intellectual schemata concurrently but also requiring special planning efforts by the faculty (Freeland, 1988). However, the developers of some methods courses reject or deemphasize the use of field experiences (for example, Peck and Connell, 1991) or even the concept of a special methods course (Trumbull, 1991) on the presumption that prospective teachers may well need to have their own views of subject matter reconstructed before they can productively spend time working with elementary or secondary school students.

Some programs incorporate general and/or special methods with student teaching out of the belief that schemata and related teaching techniques can best be learned by linking methods instruction with opportunities to practice these ideas (Ross, 1988), with the added possibility that the teacher education faculty in charge of methods content can also supervise the student teaching component of the professional semester (Bagheri, Kretschmer, and Sia, 1991; Cohn, Gellman, and Tom, 1987). The more common practice, however, is to require that general methods be taken prior to student teaching (often also prior to special methods work). This is done in order to develop the intellectual frameworks needed for subsequent reflection on teaching practice as well as to avoid the ways that learning from experience can actually arrest thought or mislead novices into thinking that they have understood central aspects of teaching when they have not done so (Feiman-Nemser and Buchmann, 1985).

Methods coursework can also be profitably linked with liberal arts courses, both general education and academic major requirements. By placing methods coursework alongside general education requirements for elementary education majors, for instance, students' perceptions of the conceptual power of various disciplines is enhanced (Lasley and Payne, 1993). Their learning how to teach a subject contributes to their understanding of that subject's structure.

Several suggestions have been advanced for linking special methods work with "content" or major courses for prospective secondary teachers. One development is the design of new courses specially constructed to explore disciplinary structure and syntax and to examine the discipline's modes of inquiry for their pedagogical potential. Another is linking special methods courses (for example, methods of teaching English) with particular disciplinary requirements (for example, language study and/or American literature) and related study in other disciplines (for example, American history or art history) to allow the (inter)disciplinary content to become grist for the methods mill. Yet another alternative is pedagogical seminars, associated with specific disciplinary courses so that the teaching and learning of the course content for different audiences can be considered without the formal structure of a separate methods course (see especially Project 30 Alliance, 1991, but also Johnston, Spalding, Paden, and Ziffren, 1989).

Linkages between methods courses and field experiences (both early and capstone), as well as those between special methods courses and disciplinary study, offer relatively simple ways to help students build important connections in the process of learning to teach. Such ties may provide the most promising (and least costly) path toward reform and revitalization of methods instruction in light of institutional structures characterized by departmental "turf" wars, competition over credit-hour production, and difficulty in replacing lost faculty lines.

General or Special: A Legitimate Distinction?

In trying to describe the operational import of the taken-for-granted distinction between general and special methods courses, we have suggested that (1) the distinction might express two ends of a continuum rather than mutually exclusive categories and (2) staffing issues and contextual challenges direct us to consider linking various kinds of methods courses with each other and with other teacher education program components. The end result of this is to blur the very distinction we started out assuming. This is intentional. As we reconceptualize teacher education, few assumptions can be taken for granted.

Decision Questions

The preceding discussion of the assumptions that undergird decisions about methods instruction enables us to consider the "decision questions" identified at the beginning of this chapter in quick succession.

How Much Methods?

How many methods courses and/or credits are required to develop a beginning teacher who is at least minimally proficient? The simplistic answer of course is "enough" to accomplish the goals established for the methods sequence. If the designated methods component of the teacher education program were oriented primarily toward the goal of gaining intellectual command of the general concepts, principles, and schemata of teaching, then one course (with or without a field experience) would be sufficient. However, if, as we suggest, the development of professionalism and interpretive curricular competence are desiderata of methods study, then far more time and attention are required than three credits allow. Furthermore, if skillful teaching practice is a goal as well, then field experience linked with methods coursework will require still more time. Articulation of the goals of methods instruction is therefore an integral part of judgments about whether one more course is needed, or two.

As suggested earlier, nothing in what we say requires separate courses or experiences devoted to the four distinguishable purposes of methods instruction we have identified. It is conceivable that all four of the purposes, or some combination thereof, could be integrated into whatever methods sequence is ultimately designed. The point we wish to make clear is that the adoption of multiple goals for methods study requires a commensurate investment of time in instruction. For the prospective secondary education teacher, numbers of course credit hours are not as important as is careful consideration of how to link methods instruction with other components of the future teacher's education, especially subject matter preparation. Few would question the need for some specialization with regard to age group and subject matter. Further, methods instruction needs to take account of a variety of institutional realities that confront the typical secondary teacher who daily must encounter no less than one hundred students, cope with a growing proportion of undermotivated students, make several course preparations, and face the prospect of new forms of statewide testing designed to "manage" curriculum decision making at the local level. Methods instruction also needs to address other social and political realities: an increasingly culturally diverse student population, expanded responsibility for and contact with special needs students, and the ever-present possibility that the violence of the larger society will spill over into the schoolhouse.

While the secondary teacher faces large numbers of students, the elementary teacher faces multiple subject matters. The challenges are different but equally daunting. Multiple subject matters mean multiple curricula, which in turn mean multiple lesson plans. To further complicate matters, many prospective elementary teachers are not well versed in all the subjects that they are to teach and may even have substantial subject matter misconceptions that must be overcome. Prospective elementary teachers require a range of subject-specific methods courses to enable careful consideration of curricular organization, instructional objectives, and teaching materials. It may be that integrated methods courses can be designed to allow prospective elementary teachers to acquire broad methodological competence more efficiently and effectively than is accomplished in the typical system of separate methods courses for each subject area. It may be possible to link methods study with subject matter courses to enhance understanding. However achieved, acquiring the interpretive skills that lead to curricular competence is a critical component in an elementary teacher's preparation program.

General-Special Balance?

What balance ought there be between general and special methods in a teacher education curriculum? The answer to this question is quite likely different for elementary and secondary education students.

Secondary teacher education programs typically require one course in generic methods of teaching and one course more clearly devoted to subject-specific pedagogy but may also include coursework related to special education, multicultural concerns, or reading in the content areas. Teacher preparation programs that require the teaching of multiple school subjects (elementary education and special education) or multiple age groups (K-12 certification programs) often dispense with a general methods course in favor of several special methods courses. In such programs, however, a course in educational psychology that is practice-oriented—taught under the rubric of "psychological foundations of teaching" or "principles of teaching"—may actually function as a general methods course.

The traditional two-course sequence in secondary education is acceptable as far as it goes. If both the general and special methods courses have as a goal becoming knowledgeable about teaching, then the general methods course can lean heavily toward professionalism issues while the special methods course leans heavily toward interpretation of content and context of instruction. Still, relationships between theory and practice, between content and method, between thought and action, and between the schools and the society they serve are not clearly developed in this framework. Efforts to reformulate and enhance the two-course methods sequence should take these relationships into account.

Typically, many more methods courses—often all "special" in one way or another—comprise the elementary education curriculum. These range from four or more required courses in subject matter methods to topical offerings such as creative arts, children's literature, cultural diversity, and special needs students. Subject matter methods study can be justified based on the premise that teaching is a subject-specific affair and that appropriate response requires content-rich and methodologically sound curricular competence. The value of the other methods-related courses in stand-alone form probably requires justification in light of calls for more substantive liberal arts study for future elementary teachers. This does not mean that methods work addressing each student's special needs is expendable, only that the form of this instruction should be carefully considered.

There is nothing magical about the general/special methods distinction per se. What we need to maintain is attention paid to the goals each kind of methods course is intended to achieve.

When and How to Sequence and Link?

It should be clear from the discussion regarding the differences between general and special methods instruction that the question of sequencing and integrating has been broadened to include not only the order of methods courses to be taken but the sequence of methods instruction vis-à-vis other components of the professional education curriculum (educational foundational study, field experiences, and student teaching), as well as other components of the overall undergraduate curriculum (general education and academic major).

Standard practice in professional education sequencing involves situating methods instruction before student teaching but after foundations study. Prospective teachers learn about the context of their actions (social and psychological foundations) before forming schemata for the activities (methods) that they will apply in school settings (student teaching). This is a stance that is generally supported by the effective teaching literature—that is, by the view that the teacher is a technical decision maker applying appropriate theories to particular educational situations. Little if any attention is paid to linkages with general education or academic major requirements.

Current educational reform literature suggests at least two alternatives to this fairly typical approach. First, the Holmes Group view (1986) implies the need to demonstrate mastery of general knowledge and subject matter *before* any methods instruction and to link intellectual mastery of teaching methods with substantial practica; hence, this position calls for postbaccalaureate teacher preparation programs featuring immersion in professional issues, literature, research, and practice based in professional development schools. Foundations study, methods study, and student teaching are woven together in a professional year.

Second, the present incarnation of the academic reform tradition (Feiman-Nemser, 1990; Zeichner and Liston, 1990) shifts the focus to subject matter as the "missing paradigm" in teacher thinking, suggesting subject matter as the point of departure for methodological decisions; hence, this position relies on case study analysis, pedagogical seminars, and other mechanisms that emphasize the subject-specific character of teaching. Subject matter expertise and subject-specific pedagogical expertise are developed concurrently. Student teaching is the capstone experience in that it is the quintessential opportunity to learn subject matter in its teachable form by teaching and learning with "real" students.

We do not know for certain if it matters whether students take foundations before or after methods, study theories of teaching before or during student teaching, or know biology thoroughly before thinking about teaching methods specific to biology instruction. We *do* know that prospective teachers must construct the connections between various kinds of knowledge related to teaching and actual teaching practice. Making connections explicit in the structure of teacher education programs situated in the departmental bureaucracy of universities presents particular challenges that must be met if methods instruction is to be as rich as actual teaching practice requires and if the four purposes outlined earlier are to be achieved.

Examples and Analysis

Suppose a teacher education faculty exposes assumptions and answers decision questions as we have suggested. What might those responses look like? How can they be evaluated? Each of the models below is based on a particular institution's response to practical, theoretical, and political concerns about methods instruction, but the ideas suggested are not necessarily unique to those particular teacher education programs.

Teacher as Artist

"Teacher as artist" is the guiding model for an elementary curriculum in a medium-sized urban state system campus. Within this model, several assumptions are clear. Self-awareness and conscious awareness of one's art and one's audience are critical. All of the purposes for methods study described in the first section of this chapter are important in this program, but the focus is self-understanding. Intellectual command, technical skill, and interpretive skill form a seamless whole in the service of a sense of oneself as responsible for what happens in schools.

The "teacher as artist" approach is developed programmatically through two education "studio courses" (a combination of traditional foundations and general methods courses) thematically linked to liberal arts courses and several subject-specific teaching arts courses (the programmatic analog of special methods courses) that lead naturally into a student teaching experience. Virtually every course, liberal arts or teacher education, is designed to highlight the question of self as teacher and to examine possible responses to that challenge.

This methods sequence is congruent with the model that supports it. Moreover, it demonstrates a high degree of attention to subject matter competence, professional knowledge, and practical experience. Finally, this methods sequence evidences a well-developed view of how one learns to teach (Grumet, 1989; Project 30 Alliance, 1991).

Teacher as Responsible Decision Maker

At one Eastern state teachers' college-turned-state-university, the program model calls for teachers who are responsible decision makers. That is, teachers must be capable of using the knowledge of four domains—general education, professional knowledge, specialty studies, and field experience—to formulate morally and politically worthy goals and to accomplish those goals with students.

The overall framework of the secondary teacher education program is a traditional sequence of foundations courses (psychological and social) in the sophomore year, a methods block (one special methods and one general methods) in the junior year, and a full-semester student teaching experience in the senior year. However, the program provides for a series of linkages throughout to help students make the connections among the four domains of knowledge from which the teacher as responsible decision maker draws. A first-year case study–based seminar focuses on the value of general education/liberal arts study for the teacher-to-be and begins a process of portfolio development. Field experiences of progressive length and responsibility are linked with all professional courses.

"Pedagogy seminars," one-credit seminars attached to courses in the student's academic major, provide special opportunities to consider subject-specific pedagogy and curricular issues as well as to integrate content and method. Student teaching has a four-day/one-day design: four days in a public school with substantial teaching responsibilities and one day on campus with a classroom management seminar and a kind of "grand rounds" pedagogy, in which students present their own "cases" (drawn from their actual experience) for the consideration of their peers and supervisor.

In this program, there are designated "methods" courses (in the junior year) devoted to a blend of intellectual command of teacher knowledge and skillful practice, but there is methods instruction going on in virtually every phase of the program, from academic major through wide-ranging field experiences. Strong content preparation and guided teaching practice are not sacrificed to methods study but linked with it (Stengel, 1993).

Reflective Pedagogical Thinking

A large midwestern university, with a longtime commitment to teacher education, has adopted and adapted the notion of reflective pedagogical thinking as the core concept for the program. A key component of this program, for both elementary and secondary teachers, is an eight-credit block that includes three classes—Curriculum and Methods, Social Aspects of Education, and Measurement and Evaluation—and a specially designed field experience. The block involves cross-class assignments (including journal writing, microteaching, peer evaluations, and case studies) and collaboration and interaction by all three instructors. Students enroll in this block just prior to student teaching.

This block has a methods component in two courses, Curriculum and Methods and Measurement and Evaluation, but what is most noteworthy is the *linking* of methods instruction with foundations study and clinical experience. The stated purpose of the block, to promote reflective pedagogical thinking, has roots in all four of the possible purposes of methods instruction discussed previously but is probably most closely linked to professionalism and self-understanding, learning to think—technically, morally, politically—like a teacher. We should acknowledge, however, that methods instruction alone is not expected to accomplish this goal. It is methods instruction linked with the other experiences that makes the achievement of the overall program goal possible (Sparks-Langer and others, 1990).

Craft and Reflection

At one private university, the department of education is located in the College of Arts and Sciences. This institutional as well as philosophical link between the liberal arts and teacher education contributes to an elementary education program that begins with a view of teaching as a complex intellectual activity. It is at once a craft requiring the ability to make and carry out a seemingly infinite number of on-the-spot decisions and a practice demanding from-a-distance reflection—the ability to consider the realities of classroom life thoughtfully and critically in order to generate alternative ways of acting.

Here, too, integrating professional education courses and clinical experiences seems to be the key to achieving the goal of effective and reflective practice. In one professional semester, students are enrolled in four courses—Reading Methods, Mathematics Methods, Children's Literature, and Principles of Teaching—and a modified student teaching experience. The Principles of Teaching course is a general methods course that considers lesson and unit planning, classroom management and control, questioning strategies and problem solving. Each of the other three are special methods courses that provide the subject-specific examples of the general principles. The student teaching experience (four days per week) allows students to experiment with various techniques explored in class (the fifth day each week) and to reflect on the relationship between theory and practice.

The blocking of these courses and experiences addresses the primary concern of each of the paradigmatic positions outlined at the outset of this chapter: a clear vision of how one learns to teach, plenty of coached experience, substantial professional knowledge, and even strong content preparation (by creating more space in the curriculum for liberal arts study!). Moreover, methods study, both general and special, is designed to serve the overall program emphases of craft and reflection (Johnston, Spalding, Paden, and Ziffren, 1989).

Analysis

On what basis can we assess the value of these local responses, and in turn on what basis can you evaluate your own programmatic response to the concerns and issues surrounding methods instruction?

First, as we indicated at the outset, any decision about methods instruction must acknowledge the legitimacy of calls for strong content preparation (especially content *for* teaching), substantial professional knowledge and skill, field-based coaching, *and* a vision of learning to teach. A direct and thorough discussion of each of these criteria is outside the scope of this chapter, yet they cannot be ignored because they are indicative of the preconceptions faculty members bring to the decision-making process. Each of the models outlined above addresses all four of these considerations, responds coherently, and in doing so offers reassurance that creative and integrative programs of teacher education are possible.

Second, a response should be internally coherent (Buchmann and Floden, 1992) to be likely to achieve its desired effect. The program model or metaphor should be congruent with the program structure. The stated philosophy and the concepts used to express it should be evident in student assignments and assessment, faculty interactions, and even course titles. At the same time, experience and coursework should not be so tightly controlled as to misrepresent the complex reality of teaching and learning and limit the possibility of creative response. Each of the programs discussed maintains a productive balance between unified design and real-world variability. The metaphors employed (teacher as artist, as responsible decision maker, as reflective thinker, as intellectual artisan) suggest the unique character of the teacher's response in any particular instructional situation, while the program structures each demonstrate a unity of intention and intelligibility.

Third, the purposes of methods instruction within the overall program framework should be clear. Students and instructors need to know the planned outcomes of any particular program component. Common to all of the models discussed is an effort to link content and method as well as theory and practice. The purposeful linking of various program components (in different ways!) is a very powerful pedagogical feature of these program models, but it presents a potential danger as well. Care must taken to constantly reiterate and articulate the alignment of courses and experiences with the critical *methodological* outcomes of intellectual command of concepts, demonstration of skillful practice, interpretation of context and content, and professional self-understanding.

This analysis does not address the thorny empirical question of whether better teachers are the result of implementing a particular methods sequence. A conceptually well-designed program is a necessary though not sufficient condition for educating good teachers. Also needed is ongoing assessment of student learning and program effectiveness. At present, data regarding the methods sequences we have outlined above is clearly encouraging, but it is not conclusive (see, for example, Sparks-Langer and others, 1990).

Conclusion

Curriculum decision making in teacher education today is very often a university-wide responsibility involving faculty from arts and sciences departments as well as education faculty outside the curriculum and instruction area. In addition, such decision making occurs in external political contexts that prescribe and/or set specific limits on allowable education coursework and methods instruction. While there usually are good reasons behind decisions about methods instruction, those who have not traditionally been included in the decision making (particularly arts and sciences faculty) are entitled to question past practice. We who are directly responsible for methods instruction must be able to articulate the reasons and purposes that underlie such instruction and to interrogate the assumptions of those who are critical of methods coursework. We can only do that intelligently if we are clear about our own assumptions.

Three decision questions (course? kinds? sequence and linkages?) rely on the articulated consideration of the program assumptions and goals. We urge those in the process of reconceptualizing methods instruction to consider the ways in which methodological goals can be accomplished efficiently and effectively by linkages among already extant program components and by cooperative efforts between liberal arts and teacher education faculty.

As was the case with the four sample methods sequences we described and analyzed, we maintain that methods sequences can be conceptually analyzed both internally—that is, based on program coherence—and externally—that is, based on how well the methods instruction addresses the legitimate concerns voiced at the outset of this chapter. We also maintain that this assessment must be an ongoing process on the part of teacher education faculty, supported by research on teacher education programming.

In this chapter, we have admittedly raised as many questions as we have answered. There are two reasons for this. First, there is much about effective methods instruction that we do not know. Issues of sequencing, for example, are just beginning to be studied systematically. Case studies of beginning teachers have given us mere first steps toward understanding the nature and mastery of subject-specific pedagogy. For this reason, the questions asked in this essay constitute an ongoing research agenda regarding methods instruction in teacher education. Second, there are some "prior questions"—questions of philosophy, of assumptions, of commitments that cannot be adjudicated by research or prescription, that should be asked and answered by program faculty as programmatic decisions are made. Once the assumptions underlying the decision questions have been clarified, our suspicion is that the decisions to be made become clearer as well.

The four positions regarding methods instruction outlined in the opening paragraph of this chapter are not mutually exclusive. It *is* possible to integrate strong content preparation, professional knowledge and skill, and field-based coaching within a developmental framework of learning to teach. A well-thought-out methods component within a coherent teacher education program is a (perhaps the) critical factor in making this integration possible.

References

Adler, S. A., and Goodman, J. (1986). "Critical theory as a foundation for methods courses." *Journal of Teacher Education, 37*(4), 2–8.

Arends, R. I. (1991). *Learning to teach.* (2nd ed.). New York: McGraw-Hill.

Ayers, W. C. (1990). "Rethinking the profession of teaching: A progressive option." *Action in Teacher Education, 12*(1), 1–6.

Bagheri, H., Kretschmer, D., and Sia, A. (1991). "Restructuring teacher education: Integrating science/mathematics methods course and student teaching—the Northridge experience." Paper (revised version) presented at the annual meeting of the Association of Teacher Educators, New Orleans, La. (ED 338 604).

Ball, D. L. (1991). "Teaching mathematics for understanding: What do teachers need to know about subject matter?" In M. M. Kennedy (ed.), *Teaching academic subjects to diverse learners.* New York: Teachers College Press.

Ben-Peretz, M. (1990). *The teacher-curriculum encounter: Freeing teachers from the tyranny of texts.* Albany: State University of New York Press.

Berliner, D. C. (1985). "Laboratory settings and the study of teacher education." *Journal of Teacher Education, 36*(6), 2–8.

Brown, J. S., Collins, A., and Duguid, P. (1989). "Situated cognition and the culture of learning." *Educational Researcher, 18*(1), 32–42.

Buchmann, M., and Floden, R. E. (1992). "Coherence: The rebel angel." *Educational Researcher, 21*(9), 5–9.

Clandinin, D. J., and Connelly, F. M. (1992). "Teacher as curriculum maker." In P. W. Jackson (ed.), *Handbook of research on curriculum.* New York: Macmillan.

Clark, C. M., and Lampert, M. (1986). "The study of teacher thinking: Implications for teacher education." *Journal of Teacher Education., 37*(5), 27–31.

Cohn, M. M., Gellman, V., and Tom, A. R. (1987). "The secondary professional semester." *Teaching Education, 1*(2), 31–37.

Cuban, L. (1993). "The lure of curricular reform and its pitiful history." *Phi Delta Kappan, 75,* 182–185.

Dawe, H. A. (1984). "Teaching: A performing art." *Phi Delta Kappan, 66,* 548–552.

Dewey, J. (1916). *Democracy and education.* New York: Free Press.

Duell, O. K., and Yeotis, C. (1981). "Integrating methods and educational psychology in teacher preparation." Paper presented at the annual meeting of the Association of Teacher Educators, Dallas, Texas. (ED 204 260).

Erb, D. J., and Keesbury, F. (1992). "Seeing the island from the other shore: Attempts to bring together teacher education students from predominantly white and historically black institutions." Paper presented at the annual meeting of the American Association of Colleges for Teacher Education, San Antonio, Texas. (ED 343 852).

Feiman-Nemser, S. (1990). "Teacher preparation: Structural and conceptual alternatives. In W. R. Houston (ed.), *Handbook of research on teacher education.* New York: Macmillan.

Feiman-Nemser, S., and Buchmann, M. (1985). "Pitfalls of experience in teacher preparation." *Teachers College Record, 87*(1), 53–65.

Floden, R. E., McDiarmid, G. W., and Wiemers, N. (1989). *What are they trying to do? Perspectives on teacher educators' purposes.* (Research Report no. 89–6). East Lansing, Mich.: National Center for Research on Teacher Education. (ED 320 854).

Freeland, K. (1988). "A collaborative effort in field experiences." *Teacher Educator, 24*(2), 22–28.

Freeman, F. N. (1930). "Teaching as an applied science." *Journal of Educational Methods, 9,* 448–455.

Gideonse, H. D. (1986). "Guiding images for teaching and teacher education." In T. J. Lasley (ed.), *The dynamics of change in teacher education,* Vol. 1: *Background papers from the National Commission for Excellence in Teacher Education.* Washington, D.C.: American Association of Colleges for Teacher Education. (ED 272 512).

Giroux, H. A., and McLaren, P. (1986). "Teacher education and the politics of engagement: The case for democratic schooling." *Harvard Educational Review, 56,* 213–238.

Goodlad, J. I., Soder, R., and Sirotnik, K. A. (eds.) (1990). *The moral dimensions of teaching.* San Francisco: Jossey-Bass.

Grant, C. A. (1991). "Culture and teaching: What do teachers need to know?" In M. M. Kennedy (ed.), *Teaching academic subjects to diverse learners.* New York: Teachers College Press.

Grossman, P. L. (1990). *The making of a teacher: Teacher knowledge and teacher education.* New York: Teachers College Press.

Grossman, P. L., Wilson, S. M., and Shulman, L. S. (1989). "Teachers of substance: Subject matter knowledge for teaching." In M. C. Reynolds (ed.), *Knowledge base for the beginning teacher.* Elmsford, N.Y.: Pergamon Press.

Grumet, M. R. (1989). "Generations: Reconceptualist curriculum theory and teacher education." *Journal of Teacher Education, 40*(1), 13–17.

Hashweh, M. Z. (1987). "Effects of subject matter knowledge in the teaching of biology and physics." *Teaching and Teacher Education, 3,* 109–120.

Hesch, R. (1990). "Aboriginal teachers as organic intellectuals." Paper presented at the Mokakit's biennial conference, Quebec. (ED 334 041).

Holmes Group (1986). *Tomorrow's teachers.* East Lansing, Mich.: Holmes Group.

Holmes Group (1990). *Tomorrow's schools: Principles for the design of professional development schools.* East Lansing, Mich.: Holmes Group.

Jackson, P. W. (ed.) (1990). *The handbook of research on curriculum.* New York: Macmillan.

Johnston, J. S., Jr., Spalding, J. R., Paden, R., and Ziffren, A. (1989). *Those who can: Undergraduate programs to prepare arts and sciences majors for teaching.* Washington, D.C.: Association of American Colleges.

Katz, L. G., and Raths, J. D. (1982). "The best intentions for the education of teachers." *Action in Teacher Education, 4*(1), 8–16.

Katz, L. G., and Raths, J. D. (1985). "Dispositions as goals for teacher education." *Teaching and Teacher Education, 1,* 301–307.

Kauchak, D. P., and Eggen, P. D. (1989). *Learning and teaching: Research-based methods.* Needham Heights, Mass.: Allyn & Bacon.

Lampert, M., and Clark, C. M. (1990). "Expert knowledge and expert thinking in teaching: A response to Floden and Klinzing." *Educational Researcher, 19*(5), 21–23.

Lasley, T. J. (1990). "Designing a curriculum that uses the knowledge base." Paper presented at the annual meeting of the Association of Teacher Educators, Las Vegas, Nev. (ED 318 697).

Lasley, T. J., and Payne, M. (1993). "Creating a core curriculum that integrates knowledge." Paper presented at the annual meeting of the American Educational Research Association, Atlanta.

Leinhardt, G. (1990). "Capturing craft knowledge in teaching." *Educational Researcher, 19*(2), 18–25.

McDiarmid, G. W. (1991). "What teachers need to know about cultural diversity: Restoring subject matter to the picture." In M. M. Kennedy (ed.), *Teaching academic subjects to diverse learners.* New York: Teachers College Press.

McDiarmid, G. W. (1992). *The arts and sciences as preparation for teaching.* (Issue Paper no. 92–3). East Lansing, Mich.: National Center for Research on Teacher Learning. (ED 348 358).

Moore, K. D., and Scott, C. V. (1981). "A team approach to secondary methods." *College Student Journal, 15,* 255–258.

Noddings, N. (1992). *The challenge to care in schools: An alternative approach to education.* New York: Teachers College Press.

Peck, D. M., and Connell, M. L. (1991). "Developing a pedagogically useful content knowledge in elementary mathematics." Paper presented at the annual meeting of the American Educational Research Association, Chicago. (ED 332 875).

Pennsylvania State Education Association (1993). *A guide to success for new teachers.* Harrisburg: Pennsylvania State Education Association.

Petrie, H. (1992). "Knowledge, practice, and judgment." *Educational Foundations, 6*(1), 35–48.

Project 30 Alliance (1991). *Project 30 year two report: Institutional accomplishments.* Newark: University of Delaware.

Reynolds, M. C. (ed.) (1989). *Knowledge base for the beginning teacher.* Elmsford, N.Y.: Pergamon Press.

Richards, J. C., and Gipe, J. (1992). "Beginning professionals' metaphors in an early field placement." Paper presented at the annual meeting of the American Educational Research Association, San Francisco. (ED 348 353).

Ross, E. W. (1988). "Preparing students of teaching: A professional semester for secondary social studies teachers." *Teaching Education, 2*(2), 80–83.

Rubin, L. J. (1985). *Artistry in teaching.* New York: Random House.

Ryan, P. M., and Robinson, K. S. (1990). "Enhancing preservice teachers' contextual understandings about their learners." Paper presented at the annual meeting of the American Association of Colleges for Teacher Education, Chicago. (ED 319 707).

Sadker, M. P., and Sadker, D. M. (1982). *Sex equity handbook for schools.* White Plains, N.Y.: Longman.

Schivley, W., De Cicco, E., and Millward, R. (1982). *Junior block: A field-oriented curriculum design for the blending of theory and application in elementary teacher education.* Indiana, Pa.: Indiana University of Pennsylvania. (ED 222 453).

Schön, D. A. (1983). *The reflective practitioner: How professionals think in action.* New York: Basic Books.

Schön, D. A. (1987). *Educating the reflective practitioner.* San Francisco: Jossey-Bass.

Schubert, W. H., and Ayers, W. C. (eds.) (1992). *Teacher lore: Learning from our own experience.* White Plains, N.Y.: Longman.

Shulman, J. H. (1992). *Case methods in teacher education.* New York: Teachers College Press.

Shulman, L. S. (1986). "Those who understand: Knowledge growth in teaching." *Educational Researcher, 15*(2), 4–14.

Shulman, L. S. (1987). "Knowledge and teaching: Foundations of the new reform." *Harvard Educational Review, 57,* 1–22.

Sockett, H. (1993). *The moral base for teacher professionalism.* New York: Teachers College Press.

Sparks-Langer, G. M., and others (1990). "Reflective pedagogical thinking: How can we promote it and measure it?" *Journal of Teacher Education, 41*(4), 23–32.

Stengel, B. S. (1993). "Secondary education: Self, student, school, and society." Millersville University (unpublished curriculum proposal).

Streitmatter, J. L. (1994). *Toward gender equity in the classroom: Everyday teachers' beliefs and practices.* Albany: State University of New York Press.

Strike, K. A., and Soltis, J. F. (1985). *The ethics of teaching.* New York: Teachers College Press.

Tom, A. R. (1984). *Teaching as a moral craft.* White Plains, N.Y.: Longman.

Trumbull, D. J. (1991). "Education 301: Knowing and learning in science and mathematics." *Teaching Education, 3*(2), 145–150.

Valli, L. (1992). "Beginning teacher problems: Areas for teacher education improvement." *Action for Teacher Education, 14*(1), 18–25.

Zeichner, K. M., and Gore, J. M. (1990). "Teacher socialization." In W. R. Houston (ed.), *Handbook of research on teacher education.* New York: Macmillan.

Zeichner, K. M., and Liston, D. P. (1990). "Traditions of reform in U.S. teacher education." *Journal of Teacher Education, 41*(2), 3–20.

Annotated Bibliography

Brown, J. S., Collins, A., and Duguid, P. (1989). "Situated cognition and the culture of learning." *Educational Researcher, 18*(1), 32–42.

Brown, Collins, and Duguid make a case for the situated nature of knowledge, arguing that all knowledge is in part a product of the activity, context, and culture in which it is developed and used. They discuss how such a view alters our understanding of learning as well as shapes our approaches to teaching.

Feiman-Nemser, S. (1990). "Teacher preparation: Structural and conceptual alternatives." In W. R. Houston (ed.), *Handbook of research on teacher education.* New York: Macmillan.

Feiman-Nemser examines various ways of conceiving and carrying out teacher preparation, surveying alternatives from a historical perspective (normal school, liberal arts college, and university school of education traditions), a structural perspective (undergraduate, extended, graduate, and alternative certification programs), and a conceptual perspective (academic, practical, technological, personal, and critical/social orientations). She describes the research efforts that are necessary to support choices among these traditions, program structures, and intellectual orientations.

Floden, R. E., McDiarmid, G. W., and Wiemers, N. (1989). *What are they trying to do? Perspectives on teacher educators' purposes*. (Research Report no. 89–6). East Lansing, Mich.: National Center for Research on Teacher Education. (ED 320 854).
Floden, McDiarmid, and Wiemers interviewed teacher educators about the purposes of the methods courses they taught, using a syllabus-guided interview methodology. Respondents were not at all clear about their purposes, often including class activities that went beyond stated goals, and paying little attention to subject matters as active fields of inquiry.

Gideonse, H. D. (1986). "Guiding images for teaching and teacher education." In T. J. Lasley (ed.), *The dynamics of change in teacher education*, Vol. 1: *Background papers from the National Commission for Excellence in Teacher Education*. Washington, D.C.: American Association of Colleges for Teacher Education. (ED 272 512).
Gideonse explores four images of the teachers' role: (1) teacher as artist, (2) teacher as moral craftsperson, (3) teacher as applied scientist, and (4) teacher as decision maker. He discusses how the adoption of a particular image of teacher affects other considerations, specifically, the knowledge base required, the preparation model for teaching, and the selection criteria for future teachers.

Grossman, P. L., Wilson, S. M., and Shulman, L. S. (1989). "Teachers of substance: Subject matter knowledge for teaching." In M. C. Reynolds (ed.), *Knowledge base for the beginning teacher*. Elmsford, N.Y.: Pergamon Press.
Grossman, Wilson, and Shulman explore the facets of teachers' subject matter knowledge—content knowledge, substantive knowledge, and syntactic knowledge—as well as teachers' beliefs about subject matter.

Johnston, J. S., Jr., Spalding, J. R., Paden, R., and Ziffren, A. (1989). *Those who can: Undergraduate programs to prepare arts and sciences majors for teaching*. Washington, D.C.: Association of American Colleges. (ED 316 082).
Johnston, Spalding, Paden, and Ziffren offer guidelines for approaches to teacher education that integrate liberal arts and professional education. At the book's conclusion, the authors describe eleven programs that have already undertaken the kinds of innovations proposed.

Lampert, M., and Clark, C. M. (1990). "Expert knowledge and expert thinking in teaching: A response to Floden and Klinzing." *Educational Researcher, 19*(5), 21–23.
In this article, Lampert and Clark contribute to an ongoing discussion regarding the notion of expertise in teaching and its relation to teacher thinking and knowledge use in practice. Specifically, they connect recent cognitive science research with the process of teacher education, arguing that we must know not only how experts structure their knowledge but also how they acquired it and how they use knowledge in practical contexts.

Project 30 Alliance (1991). *Project 30 year two report: Institutional accomplishments*. Newark: University of Delaware. (ED 355 179).
This document provides extended descriptions of efforts by Project 30 institutions (thirty-two colleges and universities) to improve teacher education through the integration of liberal arts and professional education. A variety of program innovations and initiatives are detailed.

CHAPTER TWENTY-FIVE

EDUCATING TEACHERS
FOR RESTRUCTURED SCHOOLS

MARSHA LEVINE

If we expect new teachers to use the knowledge contained here, we must create conditions for learning which are most conducive to subsequent implementation of that knowledge. If we expect our students to engage in cooperative learning with their students, we must provide meaningful practice, critique, and reflection around cooperative learning. If we want new teachers to understand the complexity, problems, and possibilities associated with working across a range of students, including those considered to be at risk, we must engage ourselves and our students with real-life school environments that demonstrate these characteristics. If we believe that it is important for prospective students to develop the disposition to question seriously business as usual, we must promote such questioning in our own institutions and place our students in elementary and secondary schools where nothing is taken for granted.

Last, as we work toward including in our teacher preparation programs the knowledge presented here, we must cooperate with our elementary and secondary teacher educator colleagues toward the creation and maintenance of school sites that reinforce and complement our intentions. It will do no one a service if we compound the conventional belief that higher education programs of teacher education have little or nothing in common with what goes on in the nation's lower schools. What is called for is a systematic collaborative activity whereby higher education faculty and elementary and secondary school faculty come together to learn from one another such that the various components of our prospective teachers' professional preparation are as smoothly and powerfully reinforcing as is the education we desire for our children.

GARY GRIFFIN, 1989, P. 286

The opening quotation serves as the premise and the starting point for this chapter on teacher education and school reform.

Earlier chapters in this volume describe and define the knowledge bases upon which decisions in teacher education should be made. This chapter seeks to illustrate how the lens of school reform provides a rubric for making decisions that will restructure teacher education.

There is a striking parallel in the changes we expect to take place in the education of our children and what we will need to achieve in the education of their teachers. We need to help both students and their teachers to become users of knowledge, to develop habits of mind that include a problem-solving orientation, to be able to view things from multiple perspectives, and to build the skills of collaboration and self-assessment. We expect both teacher and student to become researchers, to continuously use the skills of inquiry and examination and reflection. In short, the goal for students and teachers is learning for understanding. This parallel is not coincidental, nor is it a novel idea. John Dewey, almost a century ago (Dewey, 1974), described the role of knowledge, experience, and practice in the development of the "thinking" individual, whether student or teacher. As teacher candidates move through the process of their own education, they should experience the kind of learning that they will be expected to support in their students. Like a mirror, the restructuring of teacher education will reflect the transformation of schools.

This chapter briefly describes the vision of schooling that is embedded in the reform movement of the 1990s. The implications of that vision for teacher education will then be addressed. The chapter concludes with a discussion of the professional development school, a new institution that can play a key role in transforming learning for students and teachers.

A Changing Vision of Schools

By the year 2000, American students will leave grades four, eight, and twelve having demonstrated competency in challenging subject matter including English, mathematics, science, history, and geography, and every school in America will ensure that all students learn to use their minds well, so they may be prepared for responsible citizenship, further learning, and productive employment in our modern economy (National Education Goals Report, 1992).

Underlying this statement and the entire set of National Goals for Education is a new vision for America's public schools. It is a vision in which *all* students are helped to achieve high standards, a vision in which high standards include deep knowledge and understanding and the ability to use that knowledge and not just recall information. It has been articulated one way or another by numerous national reports and calls to action over the past decade (Carnegie Forum on Education and the Economy, 1986; Holmes Group, 1986; National Education

Goals Panel, 1992). Whether driven by a concern for the nation's economic competitiveness or by a commitment to values of equity and excellence for all students, this vision is spawning efforts to restructure learning, teaching, schooling, and whole systems of public education. New networks have been created to support school-based reform efforts (for example, the Coalition for Essential Schools, the Comer Project, the Accelerated Schools Project), large and small school districts have supported districtwide reform (Hill, Wise, and Shapiro, 1989; Elmore and McLaughlin, 1988), and whole states have committed to systemic change (Kentucky being the premier example of such a comprehensive approach). All of these developments are in pursuit of a vision of schooling that enables all children to use their minds well.

Today's schools, designed one hundred years ago, have functioned like efficient sorting machines, separating students on the basis of a narrow definition of learning, favoring abstract reasoning and information recall, and allowing uneven expectations for performance. Education reform of the last decade challenges those practices that support this sorting process (for example, tracking; heavy reliance on textbook teaching; standardized basic skills testing; and passive, isolated, often rote, learning). The challenges have been driven by arguments coming from three directions: by economic and social demands on the schools to produce more and better educated students and by developments in cognitive science that provide substantive bases for restructuring schools to support student and adult learning.

Economic Arguments for School Reform

Over the last ten years, economists, educators, and political leaders have stressed education as a basic ingredient in our economic health and in our ability to be competitive in the world economy (Kearns and Doyle, 1988; Commission on the Skills of the American Workforce, 1990; Committee for Economic Development, 1985, 1987). While the relationship between education and the economy has long been a theme of education reformers (for example, see the works of Callahan, 1962; Mann, 1965), contemporary arguments, as we shall see, have very different implications for what schools ought to be like and therefore for how teachers need to be prepared.

With much simplification, the strands of the argument include the following: we simply cannot afford to leave any child behind. The youth cohort is smaller than it has ever been, particularly in contrast with a steadily growing aging population. Tomorrow's workplace will be different from today's and will continue to change. Change in fact is the only constant. Employers are looking for people who know how to read, write, communicate, and think. Employers want people who can recognize a problem and figure out how to solve it. Employers want people who can work well with their colleagues. The public schools must provide such young men and women if the schools are to keep the support of society.

Research relating education to employability (Berryman and Bailey, 1992; Levine, 1985; Natriello, 1989) has produced a vision of schools that embraces a broader definition of how people learn, which, in turn, relies on important research on learning in work settings (Resnick, 1987; Scribner and Sachs, 1991; Scribner and Stevens, 1989). These findings have led to a set of recommendations for how to change schools (Berryman and Bailey, 1992; Kearns and Doyle, 1988; Resnick, 1987). For example, Resnick's descriptions of learning in school and out of school draw sharp contrasts and raise questions about the artificiality of school-based learning. She describes out-of-school learning as being contextualized, social, concrete, and specific, as opposed to symbolic, individual, abstract, and general, characteristics of most in-school learning. Berryman's observations on learning out of school suggest a set of recommendations for change that focus on reducing or eliminating the characteristic tension in traditional schooling between educating "head and hand" (Berryman and Bailey, 1992).

Social Concerns and the Argument for School Reform

Who are today's students? What do teachers need to know about them in order to support their success in school? The limitations of this chapter preclude an in-depth discussion of these questions but I will refer to an excellent synthesis of the literature by Pechman (1992) to highlight the ways in which today's school children differ from school populations of the past.

Student diversity challenges teachers' skills and knowledge in a number of ways. Where exclusionary practices historically have "protected" schools from having to address the needs of children with a broad range of abilities and backgrounds, today's schools are filled with children with special learning and physical needs as well as with a very broad range of learning styles and approaches to learning. The schools' success in dealing with these needs, however, is dependent on flexibility and adaptation, both organizational and instructional.

In addition to the range of student ability now present in school, cultural diversity abounds. Hodgkinson (1992) points out that the current wave of immigration is the largest in recent times. The schools have always been a fulcrum for diverse cultures. However, the sheer number of different immigrant groups represented in our schools today challenges the teachers' abilities to find effective instructional strategies to allow these children to flourish.

Similarly, changes in the role and structure of the American family have far-reaching implications for schools. Economic and social pressures on the American family have resulted in large numbers of children growing up without access to the critical social structure traditionally provided by family. In addition, community structures have been weakened. The roles of churches, community groups, neighborhood networks, and youth organizations have been eroded and no longer provide the support system to children that they have in the past. The breakdown of these important social systems has left the schools unsupported in their work with youngsters. This problem extends across economic and social classes; it is not only a problem of the poor.

Finally, poverty is perhaps the biggest challenge to today's schools. It is estimated that 25 percent of all children and 17 percent of school-aged children live in poverty. Poor health care, prenatal through adolescence, poor nutrition, and inadequate housing result in these children being extremely disadvantaged with respect to their readiness for learning and their ability to function in the social structure of the school. These are not the only children in today's schools but projections indicate that they will continue to be an increasingly large proportion of the public school's population (Hodgkinson, 1992).

The difficulty of meeting these challenges is further compounded by the long-standing inequities throughout public schools both in terms of expectations and services (Kozol, 1991). There is a growing imperative to use what we already know about how children learn and about how organizations can support learning.

How Students Learn

While arguments for school change are coming from the business community, and while the social agenda for the schools grows as society changes, there is an equally powerful impetus for the redesign of schools that comes from an increasing understanding of how children learn. Here again, Pechman's (1992) synthesis of the literature forms the basis of my discussion.

Studies of children as natural learners (Piaget, 1964, 1967; Sternberg, 1982) and studies of learning as it occurs in natural and structured environments suggest a divergence between school learning and learning as it takes place out of school (Resnick, 1987; Scribner and Sachs, 1991). One conclusion is that much of school learning depends upon a very narrow view of intellectual activity and therefore does not provide the range of opportunities that would maximize broad student success. Out-of-school learning is most often social: people learn collaboratively and through interaction with one another. In contrast, school learning is designed for individual activity. In nonschool settings, tools are an important part of the learning process. Schools typically demand that performance be abstract and not assisted with tool manipulation. The vision of schooling in which *all* children are held to high performance standards will require that teachers are able to engage students in many different ways according to their needs and their strengths.

Another stream of cognitive research, as Pechman observes, is leading to convergence on a constructivist view of learning. Drawing on the work of Piaget (1964, 1967) and Bruner (1966), today's cognitive scientists describe the processes by which knowledge is built. They elaborate on the elements of conflict, contradiction, and collaboration out of which learners make meaning of experience. Duckworth (1987) describes the engagement with phenomena and the challenge to explain it as the essential tasks in such learning.

In addition to studying how learning takes place, some cognitive psychologists have focused on how to describe and assess various forms of intelligence and achievement. Gardner (1985), for example, describes seven kinds of intelligence (musical, bodily kinesthetic, logical-mathematical, linguistic, spatial, interpersonal, and intrapersonal). Sternberg (1982) distinguishes practical intelligence from the formal thinking associated with schooling. Solving school-posed problems typically requires a particular form of academic intelligence. Such problems usually have one right answer; they are not devised by the learner but imposed by somebody else; all necessary information necessary to respond is usually provided; the problems are typically separate from real-life situations; and finally, they are symbolically represented.

Expectations for children's performance also affect how they will perform (Rosenthal, 1991). Curricula and tests that are devised with the expectation that only a few will reach the highest levels of achievement set clear limits for student performance. Problems requiring practical intelligence set no such limits. Finally, the assessment procedures of school reflect the narrow range of skills and abilities valued by the school. Performance assessments now being developed are more likely to cover a broader range of such abilities by virtue of their offering the opportunity for demonstration of otherwise difficult-to-assess abilities. For example, organizational abilities, negotiating skills, and interpersonal skills can be demonstrated in performance assessments if they are valued.

Strategies for Reform

Driven by economic and social forces, and guided by principles extracted from advances in cognitive research, the last ten years have been witness to numerous attempts to restructure America's public schools.

The Restructured School: A Bottom-Up Approach. The limits of this chapter do not permit a long discussion of restructuring schools but a working definition is necessary. The concept of a restructured school undergirding this chapter is that of a school that supports meaningful student and adult learning. The goal is a school that is organized to support teachers in their ongoing pursuit of ways to support student success. Schools that can do this are likely to bear certain general characteristics:

1. Learning

    A shared vision of learning for understanding as active, social, and contextual

    Clearly articulated and high standards for all students and teachers

    Opportunities for children to learn in a variety of ways

    Appropriate and varied ways of assessing what students actually know and are able to do

2. Community

    An organization that permits meaningful relationships to develop among teachers, among students, and between the two groups

    An organization that supports teacher inquiry, problem solving, and collegiality, and that is focused on students' collective and individual needs

3. Organization

    Management that is focused on achievement of results rather than delivery of programs

    Flexibility in the use of space, time, and resources

    Differentiated staffing patterns

    Shared decision making

Teachers and administrators, supported by their communities, are making changes in the organization, structure, and governance of their schools in a number of places. Often guided by a set of principles or understandings about how children learn, these schools illustrate various models of bottom-up restructuring. Among the most well-known efforts are the Coalition of Essential Schools (Sizer, 1986), the Comer Schools Project (Comer, 1988), the Accelerated Schools (Levin 1987, 1988, 1991), and a group of schools guided by the concept of multiple intelligences promulgated by Howard Gardner (1985).

These individual school restructuring projects, some of which have been quite successful, have not, however, resulted in major widespread school reform.

Frameworks for Restructuring: The Top-Down Approach. In order to provide an infrastructure or framework to support more widespread bottom-up school reform, some educators and policy makers have focused their attention on various policy reforms that might provide leverage (Cohen and Spillane, 1991; Elmore and McLaughlin, 1988; Fullan, 1991). Thus, for example, the potential power of curriculum standards (Smith, O'Day, and Cohen, 1990) and standards for professional practice (National Board for Professional Teaching Standards, 1991) and performance assessment strategies (Simmons and Resnick, 1993) have been explored and major projects have been undertaken to initiate them.

Curriculum Standards. The development of national curriculum standards, defining what students should know and be able to do in specific content areas, is an unprecedented activity in the United States. While there is considerable debate about the implications of such policy, it seems inevitable that some voluntary system of standards will be adopted. These standards are significant in two very important ways. First, they seek to establish standards for all students, not just the top 10 percent. Second, they are establishing expectations for deep content knowledge, understanding, and the ability to use knowledge. The implications for teachers' knowledge of content in order to be able to teach to these standards are profound. They will require teachers to have a level of understanding in subjects that is not typical of today's teacher preparation candidates—or other undergraduates, for that matter. If we are serious about preparing teachers to work with these standards, we must be serious about redesigning their liberal arts and science education to prepare them to be able to teach those subjects. Many believe that the establishment of such standards will provide direction and goals for school-based restructuring, allowing educators to develop alternative approaches to achieving the same ends.

National Assessment Strategies. The movement toward the development of a national system for assessing student performance, coupled with the emphasis on alternative assessment strategies that are more appropriate than standardized multiple choice tests for measuring what students actually know and are able to do, also have significant implications for the preparation of teachers. The use of assessment strategies embedded in the instructional process, an understanding of the distinction between assessment and accountability, and the development of teacher skills to employ performance-based assessment techniques must be incorporated into the professional education of teachers.

Professional Teaching Standards. The National Board for Professional Teaching Standards (NBPTS), created in 1987, is developing standards for excellence in teaching practice and evaluation techniques to measure teacher performance against these standards. The members of the NBPTS include both practitioners and education policy makers. The link between the NBPTS standards and school reform lies in part in the influence the board standards have in shaping teacher education programs in ways that will support the development of those standards.

Systemic reform, an approach that acknowledges the interrelatedness of various dimensions of school policy and practice, has now moved into the center of the reform arena and will make significant demands upon teacher education to adequately prepare practitioners. Teacher educators have a critical role to play in ensuring that there is not a major gap between what policy is demanding of teacher performance and student performance and the ability of practitioners to execute it.

Assumptions About Teacher Education

This vision of restructured schools and the school reform movement that surrounds it have serious implications for *what* teachers need to learn and what they need to be able to do. Similarly, the vision has implications for *how* teachers should learn and *where* that learning should take place. Before teacher educators can address these implications, however, it is useful to make explicit some of the basic assumptions that underlie their work today and the ways in which current teacher education institutions are organized.

Traditional Assumptions

The assumptions that underlie teacher education today tend to resemble the assumptions that more generally underlie teaching and learning in schools.

First, teacher education programs make assumptions about the *nature of teaching*. Such assumptions may range from a view of teaching as craft, as art, as technical work, and—more recently, and still embedded in only a few programs—the view of teaching as intellectual work. The particular orientation toward teaching shapes course design, practicum programs, internships, requirements, and prerequisites.

Second, there is an assumption about *where knowledge about teaching resides*. Traditionally, the belief is generally held that the university is the source of important knowledge related to teaching. If one looks at the lack of rigor in clinical programs as compared with courses within university-based programs, one can see an implicit hierarchy with respect to knowledge: the wisdom of practice is not on the same plane as theoretical knowledge and prototypical research. What is most important is learned at the university; it is the student's job to translate that knowledge into practice. Technical skills and "tricks of the trade" can be learned while student teaching by merely observing experienced teachers. In contrast, for example, medical schools rely heavily on clinical faculty and practitioners for the development of expert knowledge about practice to complement course teaching.

The third assumption has to do more specifically with the *relationship between the practitioner and research*. The traditionally oriented teacher education program defines the teacher as a user of research. Further, it implies a hierarchical relationship; university-based researchers do the research and then pass it *down* to the practitioner. Research agendas are usually determined by university faculty; research is done *on* schools.

A fourth, and far-reaching, assumption is about who has responsibility for educating new teachers. This responsibility falls unequivocally to the university; cooperating teachers merely do just that: cooperate. They do not determine standards for achievement; they do not determine who will be recommended into the profession.

Changing Assumptions

The view of teaching as intellectual work is at the heart of the restructured school, where practice is not prescribed and where considerable professional responsibility is placed on teachers for making professional judgments based on the best available knowledge.

With this orientation, the traditional relationship among practitioner, university faculty, research, and knowledge is changing. Educators increasingly acknowledge that wisdom about teaching resides in the practitioner community as well as in the academy (Grossman, 1990; Shulman, 1986, 1987). Greater attention is now paid to practitioner research as a source of professional knowledge (Cochran-Smith and Lytle, 1990; Levine, 1992). Further, inquiry is becoming viewed as an integral part of teaching for the "practitioner intellectual."

As a corollary of this view of teaching, the goals of teacher education are increasingly seen as learning for understanding and for performance (that is, the goal is to impart the ability to use knowledge in practice). The preparation of new teachers is increasingly being viewed as a shared responsibility of practitioners and academics. The implications of these changes for organization and structure are profound. As an example, restructured faculty roles in schools of education must support faculty to do research and teach in both the university and school settings (Lampert, 1991).

What Teachers Have to Know

This new vision of schooling has implications for the content of teacher education programs. Prospective teachers need to know about their students and need to understand the relationship between what they know about them and how schools are structured. For example, the need to establish community, to develop significant relationships with students, and to support student relationships with one another in meaningful ways becomes very important given both what we know about the social nature of learning and the needs children bring to school. As Pechman (1992) concludes, two distinct but related goals for teacher education are implied. Prospective teachers must learn to value these characteristics of school settings and understand their relevance to learning. Second, they also must learn ways to bring about desirable school settings.

How Children Learn. A second vital aspect of the new vision of schooling deals with the learning that is encouraged. Traditionally, school learning is characterized by large amounts of memorization and by the application of formulas to solve neat, limited problems. In restructured schools, student learning becomes more active, diverse, and product oriented. The goal shifts from the accumulation of knowledge to the ability to use it. What then becomes the teacher's role? The teacher can no longer be the giver of information, the source of all knowledge. She must shape an environment in which the student has both access to knowledge and the opportunities to do something with it. Students' work becomes the work of designing, building, using, defining, analyzing, comparing, contrasting, explaining, negotiating, and synthesizing; the teachers' strategies must change to support such activity. The repertoire of instructional approaches of the teacher in the restructured school includes inquiry teaching, cooperative learning, group problem solving, decision making, co-learning, collaborative planning, reciprocal teaching, project work with real consequences, and experience with diverse technologies.

One view is that the teacher's job should focus on providing helpful cognitive constructs, known as scaffolding, and gradually withdraw that scaffolding as students gain control of their own cognitive strategies. In other words, the teacher is coaching the students as their thinking skills develop (Collins, Brown, and Newman, 1989).

Many of these strategies are meant to provide contextualized or situated learning experiences; they are strategies designed to allow the conditions for practical intelligence to be developed. Further, they are associated with certain outcomes for the learners. On the way to those outcomes, however, the student is required to engage in certain practices and experiences. For example, students are asked to invent and to create, to explain and to describe, to elaborate and extend ideas, to defend their own positions and knowledge. This in turn leads the students to analyze and practice what they know through performances of various kinds, to integrate what they think, to expand what they know, and to evaluate positions and ideas. The learning outcomes associated with such strategies are engagement, ownership, and deep understanding.

Gardner (1991) describes what schools might look like if they took seriously the variations of intelligence and the developmental stages of learning for understanding. In these schools, learning environments would be constructed that are appropriate to the stage of development of the age group. Gardner breaks down the generally monolithic structure of schooling and introduces the idea that schools could and should be organized differently, in accordance with the work to be done. In other words, kindergarten through third grade would focus on exploration for the learner; grades four through six might concentrate on providing apprenticeship opportunities in which the learner can develop skills, learn to work with others, and learn to reflect and assess his or her own work; and the upper grades would be designed to support deep content learning and what Gardner terms *robust understandings*. As examples of such environments, Gardner points to several schools and networks of schools dedicated to restructuring learning and teaching (for example, the Accelerated Schools designed by Henry Levin, 1987, 1988; James Comer's schools, 1988; children's museum settings; the Key School in Indianapolis based on Gardner's own work on multiple intelligences, 1985; and the Coalition for Essential Schools initiated by Theodore Sizer, 1986).

In addition, the school restructuring and systemic reform movement have implications for the range of roles teachers will play as well as what they will need to know. The organizational requirements of redesigned schools will create a demand for teachers to develop school-based roles that they do not play in traditional settings. Teachers will be called upon to work collegially and in small groups in order to address the learning needs of the children. They will be called upon to deal with schoolwide issues such as grading policies and community relations and to do so in collaborative group settings. Decision-making skills, problem-framing and problem-solving skills, communication skills, and management skills will be an important part of the teacher's repertoire. Among those areas to be developed, teacher educators might consider the areas described below.

Education Policy. In order to be leaders and decision makers in schools, teachers need to understand the policy context in which they work. They need to be educated about accountability, assessment, equity issues, governance of public education, and finance of schools. Only then will they be able to intelligently carry out their roles as members of site-based management teams and share in the leadership of their organizations.

Study of Schools as Organizations. Teachers are typically educated to be instructional experts in the classroom. Restructured schools will require them to function as members of the school community in unfamiliar ways. They therefore need to understand the context in which they will provide leadership—the school as an organization and the roles of leadership, power, authority, and so forth.

Applications of Technology to Learning. In order to achieve the goals set for students, teachers will have to provide rich and varied learning opportunities for them. They undoubtedly will have to rely on sophisticated new technologies to help them to do this. Teachers will be able with this emerging technology to create active learning environments, individualize learning, and encourage intellectual activity not now possible in the classroom (for instance, manipulation of data bases in complex problem solving, computer modeling, and simulations). Teachers will need to become well acquainted with the potential of technology to support learning. In order to do this, prospective teachers will need important learning experiences themselves with such technologies.

How Teachers Will Learn

The design for student learning in restructured schools suggests the pedagogies for teacher learning. Teachers need deep content knowledge if they are going to support learning for understanding in *their* students. Both practitioners and students should become knowledge users. Group learning experiences may help them acquire the social skills for learning together. Just as students must be guided through progressive stages of learning—exploration, apprenticeship, and robust understandings (Gardner, 1991)—so too must prospective teachers.

Without the opportunity to develop real expertise, teachers, like students, will revert to the "gut dynamic" or the "lay dynamic" to guide their actions (Gardner, 1991). Novice teachers, as all learners, come with ideas, both right and wrong, already in place. If their assumptions and orientations are not recognized and challenged where necessary and appropriate expertise developed, those traditional models will prevail.

Elements of a Redesigned Professional Education Program

Using the framework of teaching as intellectual practice, the redesigned professional education program will become distinctive in several important ways. First, it will have a strong emphasis on utilizing knowledge, which suggests it will have a much stronger practice orientation. Second, the coursework will be more related to the site-based experience. It will be designed to promote the novice teacher's active engagement with groups of fellow students in a problem-solving mode. Cases will be employed in a systematic way to encourage both the uncovering of concepts and principles as well as to teach the use of the case method. These strategies will be described in greater detail below.

Problem-Based Learning. The problem-based learning approach can resolve some of teacher education's problems and provide a way to reinforce the kind of culture and practice that characterizes the reform movement. Currently, novice teachers enrolled in education programs are inundated with large quantities of information that they do not know how to use. They typically experience a sense of poor fit between what they know and what they have to do now and in the future. Finally, they are not expected to capitalize on what they bring to their own education, their individual experiences and characteristics; they are all taught the same things in the same way.

Problem-based learning operates on the principle that less is more; teacher candidates may "cover" less material but they will emerge knowing how to *use* what they have learned. Underlying this pedagogy is also the principle that learners need to be active. They need stimuli to recall what they have learned; they need to develop their practical intelligence and therefore need practical, as opposed to academic, problems; and they need to interact with each other. Problem-based learning also can be self-directed and open, allowing for broad, personalized, and interdisciplinary learning.

The strategies of problem-based learning are discussed in other chapters of this volume. The purpose of this discussion is to stress the coherence between this pedagogy and the orientation toward teaching embedded in school reform and in efforts to restructure schools. Problem-based learning provides opportunities for the prospective teacher to develop skills and habits of thinking that she will work to develop in her own students. These are also skills and strategies she will use as a practitioner working with colleagues.

Case Study. There is an overlap between problem-based learning and the second strategy, that of using case methods. Some cases are problems to be solved; others are stories or examples. Different kinds of cases can be used to common or complementary ends, but it is important to note that there is a choice as to what those ends might be. Case study over the years has become a staple of professional education in the United States. It was pioneered by the Harvard Business School, which teaches entirely through cases. The use of this methodology has now spread through schools of law, medicine, and public policy.

The case method is more than a way to develop a knowledge base: it can be used to develop a common set of values and strategies among potential practitioners (Kleinfeld, personal communication, 1991). Particular instructional strategies are associated with the different uses of cases (Christensen, 1987; Sykes and Bird, 1992; Merseth, 1992). Thus, law schools tend to use cases to introduce law students to the adversarial culture in which they will practice. The goal of law school case study is to find weaknesses among competing arguments rather than to seek "truth." This models the culture of the courtroom. Business schools use cases to help students develop expertise in justifying competing interests, reinforcing the culture of that world. Case teaching can help to develop a collaborative culture and to get people to work together to agree on a solution. This is the context for students in public policy or international relations.

Cases can be used in teacher education to develop a culture, as well. The question is what culture is to be developed? Currently, in schools the culture is one of acceptance: everybody's ideas are acceptable and valid (Sykes and Bird, 1992). Things are accepted in schools because they have always been done that way. If we want to develop a culture of expertise, a knowledge-based and knowledge-using culture, one that is collegial and oriented toward solving problems, then the way in which we use cases in teacher education must model that. Another possibility is to use cases to help teachers develop a problem-framing, problem-solving orientation and the skills to go along with that. Through analysis and study of cases, novice teachers can learn to examine situations from various perspectives, bring available knowledge to bear on questions, and take action in a considered, thoughtful manner. They also can learn to do this with colleagues, in team settings.

Cases can be real or fictitious, they can be problems seeking solution or resolution, or they can be stories or examples. They can be used to motivate learning or to demonstrate knowledge. They can be used in one or more of these ways. How they are used, however, should reflect what the teacher educator thinks is important for the learner at the time. That in turn will be determined by the particular orientation the teacher educator has toward teaching and his or her assessment of the learning teacher's needs (Merseth, 1992).

Applications of Technology. As with case methodology, and perhaps in combination with it, interactive multimedia technology is a technique that can be used to support the development of decision making, judgment developing, knowledge utilization, analytical skills, observation, and other skills associated with the work of the practitioner-intellectual (Merseth, 1992). It creates the opportunity for the learner to explore in a nonlinear fashion the multiple facets of the practical world of teaching. It allows for staged learning and development in a complex but controlled environment. Its power as a pedagogical tool is beginning to be explored and developed (Merseth, 1992). Research and development at Michigan State University (Lampert and Ball, 1990), Vanderbilt University (Goldman and Barron, 1990), and the American Federation of Teachers Center for Restructuring in collaboration with the Apple Multimedia Laboratory (Woolsey and others, 1990) have explored the applications of multimedia for teacher learning.

Designing and Implementing Professional Practice Schools

Professional practice schools, also called professional development schools, are new institutions being designed and developed to support teacher learning in real schools.

This section of the chapter will define what a PPS is and then address what new teachers (and inservice teachers, as well) have to learn in clinical settings. It will continue with some strategies being developed in the PPSs to help them do that. A brief discussion of the state of the art will follow with attention to some of the issues that arise in the implementation of the PPS. The section concludes with a discussion of the policy questions that must be addressed if professional practice schools are to be able to live up to their potential as an important lever for school reform.

Definition of a Professional Practice School

Professional practice schools are meant to be the educational equivalent of what the teaching hospital is in medicine. They are real schools, often in low-income, urban districts with large numbers of students who are educationally disadvantaged. These schools have joined in an institutional partnership with universities, colleges, and schools of education in order to create settings that foster a three-part mission: to support student learning for understanding, to support teacher learning in deliberate ways, and to support research and inquiry directed at the continuous improvement of practice. Professional practice schools are meant to become *the* clinical settings for all student teaching, internship, and practicum experiences. They are also intended to become models of restructured schools that support professional practice. Just as the standards for good medical practice and for hospitals are modeled in the teaching hospital, so will professional practice schools be model institutions, and, as teaching hospitals support clinical research focused on improving medical practice, professional practice schools will support practitioner research.

Certain principles that guide the process of design and implementation have been developed by various groups that have initiated work in this area, including the Holmes Group (1990), the American Federation of Teachers (Levine, 1988, 1990), the Ford Foundation Clinical Schools Project, and the American Association of Colleges of Teacher Education (Anderson, 1993). These principles tend to be organized around beliefs about learning, community, and organization, the same domains that shape the principles undergirding many restructuring schools. These principles tend to reflect the following beliefs:

- Acceptance of a constructivist view of learning spanning adults and students in schools

- A commitment to building collaborative, collegial work environments for adults and students in schools
- A commitment to inquiry as a central component of learning for teachers and students in schools
- A commitment to university/school collaboration in educating teachers and in improving student learning

These principles are not unique; what is unique is that they are applied to students and teachers at the same time. Underlying them is the belief that student and teacher learning are intimately tied together and an environment that supports one implies the support of the other (Dewey, 1974; Shaefer, 1967).

Schools that are collaboratively governed and organized around the support of student learning, teacher education, and research in practice will take on identifiable characteristics. One ought to be able to identify indicators of the implementation of these principles in certain areas of the school's activity: professional development, assessment approaches, the research agenda, the use of time, space, and resources, and the nature of discourse and interaction that characterizes the daily life of students and teachers (Houston, 1992).

Characteristic of a commitment to student learning for understanding would be the kinds of assessment approaches used and the promotion and graduation requirements for students. Performance-based assessments and the use of appropriate and varied approaches would characterize the school.

Characteristic of a commitment to community, collegiality, and inquiry would be the presence and valuing of practices that support teacher interaction, such as study groups, problem-solving clinics, research teams, and documentation groups. The incorporation of research findings into school practice would suggest a high value placed on such activity.

Characteristic of a commitment to new teacher learning would be evidence of a thoughtful curriculum for novices and structures that would support the kind of learning that needs to take place. Because this chapter is about the implications of school reform for the education of new teachers, we will concentrate on these characteristics: what there is to learn and how it may be supported in the professional practice school.

What New Teachers Need to Learn in a Professional Practice School

The curriculum of the professional practice school, or professional development school, is in its formative stages. The questions of what novice teachers have to learn and how they should learn it underlie the work.

Kinds of Expertise. There are four distinct kinds of expertise associated with practitioner knowledge (Kennedy, 1987, 1992). The first kind of expertise has to do with the development of technical skills—particular instructional strategies or questioning techniques. The conditions and requirements for this kind of learning are identified by Joyce and Showers (1980). They advocate the development of such skills in controlled environments before transferring them into real settings.

The second kind of expertise involves the application of principles and concepts in practice. Kennedy notes there is less literature available on this particular form of expertise but that conventional wisdom, as demonstrated in most professional education programs, is that the practitioner first learns the concepts and principles and then is expected to apply them in clinical settings. This is the pattern of programs preparing practitioners in medicine, engineering, business, architecture, and teaching.

The third form of expertise Kennedy describes is that of critical analysis. It is the ability to "critically analyze a situation and generate multiple interpretations of it" (Kennedy, 1992, p. 64). In order to do this, the practitioner must be knowledgeable about concepts and principles and their applicability to situations. She must be able to determine which concepts and situations may apply to each other, with the awareness that multiple matches may be made. Lawyers are skilled as critical analysts and they become so through the case analyses methods that characterize their training. They learn the content along with the process simultaneously.

The fourth form of expertise Kennedy calls deliberate action. It builds on critical analysis but goes further to culminate in an action. Deliberate action requires the practitioner to recognize that multiple goals may be possible in a situation and that professional practice involves making a choice among those goal possibilities and then selecting appropriate courses of action, drawing on relevant principles and concepts. It is the most difficult to develop and the one most often cited as absent from teacher preparation. Novice practitioners need to develop all four kinds of expertise but it is the last form that the professional practice school is uniquely designed to foster.

Teacher Knowledge. What do teachers know, that only *they* know, and how can that knowledge be made accessible to learners? Some of teacher knowledge pertains to content-specific, pedagogical knowledge (Shulman, 1986, 1987; Grossman, 1990; Grossman, Wilson, and Shulman, 1989). Examples of such pedagogical content knowledge are the best ways to teach concepts in math, science, or social studies; the most successful metaphors for ideas and relationships; the analogies, projects, problems, and approaches that work under defined circumstances. Other teacher knowledge centers on decision-making and information-processing knowledge and practical knowledge, including personal and classroom knowledge (Carter, 1990). It is this teacher knowledge base that is now being identified and codified and that is an important focus of the curriculum of the professional practice school.

Socialization into School Culture. Socialization has always been a product of student teaching (Lortie, 1975; Waller, 1932). Novice teachers quickly learn the norms of behavior in the school setting and they are reinforced through evaluation and isolation.

Professional practice schools also carry a socialization function but it is to initiate new teachers into a culture that is distinctly different from the traditional school setting. Socialization is a deliberate part of the curriculum for the learning teacher. The socialization curriculum includes learning and integrating the norms of collegiality and inquiry, norms associated with improved student performance and heightened teacher satisfaction (Little, 1982) and characterized by teachers' working together, solving problems, and doing research to find better solutions to their problems and by public practice with an eye toward schoolwide improvement.

Structures to Support Learning in Practice

In order to accomplish these curricular goals, professional practice schools have to separate themselves dramatically from past practice. They must build and maintain a culture and design deliberate structures to support learning in practice.

Structures for a New Culture. Lieberman and Miller (1992) describe several approaches that can support the growth of a new culture in schools. Through their review of the literature on school change and school culture, they identify five elements that have emerged as essential ingredients for creating a school culture that supports professional practice:

1. Norms of colleagueship, openness, and trust
2. Opportunities and time for disciplined inquiry
3. Teacher learning of content in context
4. Reconstruction of leadership roles
5. Networks, collaborations, and coalitions

In addition to the norms of practice, the novice has a great deal to learn about skills, decision making, judgments, evaluations, and the use of knowledge. Professional practice schools are developing specific structures for these purposes.

Structures to Support Acquiring Teacher Knowledge. There are many questions and some answers as to how teacher knowledge is uncovered by the experienced teacher for the novice. Research on novice/teacher interactions in professional development school settings is contributing to the knowledge base of how this learning takes place (Feiman-Nemser and Buchmann, 1986; Feiman-Nemser and Parker, 1990).

A major difficulty in helping student teachers develop the kind of expertise described above is that it is typically unobservable. It goes on inside teachers' heads. Often they do not have language to describe the process, and it goes on at times when teachers may not be available to novices as they think about their practice.

These problems suggest a set of conditions for structuring learning in professional practice schools (Kennedy, 1992, pp. 71–72):

1. Novices must have *responsibilities that require deliberate action:* responsibilities for establishing their own goals and for selecting their own actions. . . .
2. Novices must have the opportunity to deliberate. . . .
3. Supervisors or mentors must be able to *monitor* novices' deliberations. . . .
4. Supervisors or mentors must be able to *influence novices' deliberations*—by offering contrary evidence rival hypotheses, and by criticizing novices' hypotheses in light of recognized concepts, theories, and principles of teaching and learning. . . .

Other areas of research have promise for designing strategies for teacher learning in context. The cognitive apprenticeship represents one rich source of knowledge about cognitive development that may be transferred from student learning to teacher learning.

Cognitive Apprenticeship. The concept of cognitive apprenticeship adapts the features of traditional apprenticeship to the teaching and learning of cognitive skills in schools (Collins, Brown, and Holum, 1991). The same concepts of apprenticeship can be adapted to teacher learning. While the traditional form of apprenticeship may be applicable to the development of technical expertise and the application of principles and concepts, the development of critical analytic expertise and the skills of deliberate action will require a learning approach that can uncover the thinking of expert teachers and make it visible to the learning practitioner.

There are several key features to the apprenticeship (Collins, Brown, and Holum, 1991). First, it provides a "picture of the whole." The learner knows where he or she is going because of the opportunity to observe the master. Second, the apprenticeship is typically set in a social context in which the apprentice is surrounded by other expert practitioners, with access to other models of expertise and the chance to observe that there may be alternative ways to perform the task. Also, of equal importance, the apprentice can view other learners and observe different rates of learning and levels of skill among them. In this way, the learner gets a more realistic sense of his or her own learning.

The most important difference between a traditional apprenticeship and a cognitive apprenticeship is that in a cognitive apprenticeship the thinking processes of the teacher and the learner must be made visible. Cognitive research identifying cognitive and metacognitive processes is making this possible. A second difference is the need to situate cognitive tasks in contexts that make sense to students. In a traditional apprenticeship, they are already so situated.

A third requirement for cognitive apprenticeship is the need to vary the diversity of situations in which a skill is learned and to help the students generalize about them so they can transfer learning. In traditional apprenticeships, "the skills to be learned inhere in the tasks themselves" (Collins, Brown, and Holum, 1991, p. 9).

In designing strategies for learning in practice in professional practice schools, the idea of cognitive apprenticeship should be explored. The challenge is to make accessible the tacit knowledge of the expert practitioner. As research on teaching provides more information about how teachers think, make choices and decisions, plan, evaluate, and select with respect to students and curriculum, the idea of being able to make that information available in a systematic learning process modeled on the cognitive apprenticeship seems both possible and appropriate.

There are several instructional strategies that are effective in uncovering thinking processes. They include reciprocal teaching, small problem-solving groups, class demonstrations, control strategies to direct student learning tasks, and post mortem analyses. Professional practice schools are being designed to support this kind of learning. For example, clustering of student teachers within the professional practice school provides the opportunity for observation and interaction with other learners. Some professional practice schools are pairing student teachers in one classroom or with teams of teachers (Lemlech and Foliart, 1992). This encourages reciprocal teaching, one strategy in a cognitive apprenticeship. Professional practice schools, by design, encourage groups of teachers to share responsibility for student teachers. This allows the student teachers to have access to more than one role model, to see more than one way to practice, to hear more than one explanation of why something is done. Placed in a professional practice school, the student teacher is surrounded by models of good practice.

These strategies, and others, need to be explored as a part of the design of curricula and teacher learning experiences in the professional practice school.

State of the Art in Professional Practice Schools

It is estimated that over 250 professional development schools or professional practice schools have been created all over the country. Some are directly related to Holmes Group activity; others are initiatives undertaken by various organizations such as the American Federation of Teachers, the American Association of Colleges of Teacher Education, the Massachusetts Consortium for Higher Education, and the National Network for Educational Renewal, associated with John Goodlad's Center for Educational Renewal. Most of these initiatives are foundation funded and are viewed as projects. Some are closely associated with efforts to restructure schools, others are not at all. They all involve some partnership between schools and university, and some also include the teachers' organization and the school district as active partners.

A literature on implementation of professional practice schools and professional development schools is now developing (Abdal-Haqq, 1993). Case studies have begun to appear that document and detail the issues, problems, and possibilities in creating these new institutions (Darling-Hammond, 1994). Many of these cases identify a set of shared issues.

The Challenge of Collaboration

Deciding to move toward the creation of collaboratively governed professional practice schools represents a major decision for both schools and universities. Designing and implementing professional practice schools holds many challenges for both. Neufeld (1992) described the issues involved in three major areas: interinstitutional collaboration, policy contexts, and orientation toward teaching and learning.

Neufeld warned that the creation of collaborative institutions such as the PPS will make it necessary for all participants to examine their assumptions and beliefs about teaching and learning and learning to teach. The assumptions embedded in the mission and principles of such schools challenge traditional orientations. One cannot overestimate the difficulty and depth of learning that must go on for people to change the way they behave based on changes in their beliefs.

If that were not enough, enormous institutional barriers exist within both the schools and the universities that serve to further block implementation. Each will have to confront the incentive systems within their institution to determine how they may need to be changed to influence behavior in the agreed upon directions.

Some policy contexts are more conducive to these institutions' development and survival than others. Preexisting policies for teacher licensure, certification, induction, mentoring, and staff development may be supportive or problematic. The problems may be deeply ingrained in the orientation toward teaching embedded within them. All of this comes quickly to bear on implementation.

Many of the developmental issues that arise in building a new culture can be observed in the early projects. The establishment of norms of collegiality, inquiry, and a disposition toward problem solving involve teachers in roles not typically supported by school organization and bureaucracy.

Policy Issues in Developing the Potential of Professional Practice Schools

If professional practice schools are to be more than local projects involving the voluntary collaboration of a university and a school, increasing attention needs to be paid to joining these efforts to developing infrastructures in the policy arena. This can serve to strengthen professional practice schools and provide them with the leverage they need in order to successfully forge the link between a vision of school reform and a reality.

Accountability. As described, professional practice schools are not only schools where novices learn to teach, they are also schools that are intended to promote professional practice in teaching (Darling-Hammond, 1992, 1994). In this way, they have a crucial role in establishing a structure for professional accountability.

Darling-Hammond (1988) points out there are three goals along the path to professional accountability in education. The professional practice school has a role to play in each of those goals. The first is to guarantee that all entrants into the profession are adequately prepared. This implies that all candidates have successfully demonstrated a level of knowledge and competence. The placement of interns and student teachers in unstructured, undefined, clinical education settings, with no identified curriculum, standards of practice, requirements for supervision, or agreed upon outcomes results in many candidates emerging who are ill equipped to assume professional responsibility. State control on recruitment, licensure, and certification can and often does result in lowering of standards to fill shortages. The assumption of responsibility for standards of practice by the profession itself, through the institutions of professional practice schools, can shift that responsibility to ensure that high standards are safeguarded. No practitioner finds an incompetent colleague agreeable.

To date, the state of the art is such that professional development schools or professional practice schools are only beginning to recognize the need to develop these standards and are very gingerly approaching their positions of potential power. The negotiation of this power among the collaborators—schools, universities, union, district, and state—will be a difficult process, particularly for universities that have technically exercised this control, although not always very effectively.

The second goal of professional accountability is to ensure that where knowledge about good practice exists, it will be used; and where it does not, it will be individually and collectively sought. Darling-Hammond points out that this goal can only be met by altering the structure and organization of the school. In this area, professional development schools and professional practice schools have begun to make considerable progress. There is a body of literature emerging from PPS projects to document the political and developmental processes of change to school organizations and cultures (Anderson, 1993; Darling-Hammond, 1994; Trachtman, 1991, 1992). What we see emerging is the establishment of some of those structures that support teacher learning, which are identified by Lieberman and Miller (1992) and described above. The tension between the political and the developmental processes is clearly observable in many sites. There is not always agreement about where knowledge about good practice resides.

The third goal of professional accountability is to ensure that the primary commitment of the practitioner is to the welfare of the client. Here the professional practice school concept has demonstrated a distinct advantage over other restructuring efforts that have been more focused on governance changes—that is, site-based management. At the heart of the professional practice school is a focus on improving learning for all students. It is too early to determine the long-term effects on student performance as a result of the changes in school structure and practice, but changes in teacher behavior associated with improved student performance are observable (Little, 1982; Trachtman, 1991, 1992).

As Darling-Hammond (1992) has pointed out, standards for good practice cannot be legislated down to practitioners. The definition of professionalism includes the involvement of practitioners as a collective group in defining, transmitting, and enforcing professional standards of practice and ethics. The most powerful role that professional practice schools can play is through the establishment of standards for good practice and of institutional standards to support good practice. By definition, they are the vehicles for the transmission of the standards and exemplars for other schools of the institutional structures and norms that support such practice.

The National Board for Professional Teaching Standards. Few have begun to examine the relationships that might be drawn between the developing standards in professional practice schools and the standards for advanced certification being developed by the National Board for Professional Teaching Standards. NBPTS standards may be used to select clinical faculty and school faculty for professional practice schools. The curriculum for learning to teach can be made consistent with the NBPTS standards, so there is a connection between the preparation and expectations held for professional practice.

State Requirements for Internship. Similarly, little focused attention has been paid to how state policy moving in the direction of required internships, as in Minnesota, will strengthen the development of the professional practice school or to how such policies introduced in other states will create an incentive for their development.

When these connections are finally made, they can have a powerful influence on both the content and process of teacher education programs, as well as on the standards for the practicing profession.

Conclusion

Viewing decisions about teacher education through the lens of school reform focuses our attention not only on what teachers will need to know and be able to do but also on what are the best ways to help them learn those things. Restructuring teacher education to emphasize active, problem-based learning and clinical or site-based experiences will provide prospective teachers with experiences in learning that are like those they will be expected to create for their students. It also provides them with learning environments more suited to education for practice. Defining content informed by the national goals, world class curriculum standards, and standards for professional practice will further ensure that there is a bridge between policy and practice.

When schools of education, in collaboration with the practicing profession, assume their joint responsibilities for developing professional practitioners, they will also be laying the groundwork for new roles and relationships between universities and schools that can further enrich and enhance each institution, respectively.

References

Abdal-Haqq, I. (1993). *Resources on professional development schools: An annotated bibliography.* Washington, D.C.: ERIC Clearinghouse on Clinical Schools.

Anderson, C. R. (ed.) (1993). *Voices of change: A report of the clinical schools project.* Washington, D.C.: American Association of Colleges of Teacher Education.

Berryman, S. E., and Bailey, T. R. (1992). *The double helix of education and the economy.* New York: Institute on Education and the Economy, Columbia University Teachers College.

Bruner, J. (1966). *Toward a theory of instruction.* Cambridge, Mass.: Harvard University Press.

Callahan, R. E. (1962). *Education and the cult of efficiency: A study of the social forces that have shaped the administration of the public schools.* Chicago: University of Chicago Press.

Carnegie Forum on Education and the Economy (1986). *A nation prepared: Teachers for the 21st century.* Washington, D.C.: Carnegie Foundation.

Carter, K. (1990). "Teachers' knowledge and learning to teach." In W. R. Houston (ed.), *Handbook of research on teacher education.* New York: Macmillan.

Christensen, C. R. (1987). *Teaching and the case method.* Cambridge, Mass.: Harvard Business School.

Cochran-Smith, M., and Lytle, S. L. (1990). "Research on teaching and teacher research: The issues that divide." *Educational Researcher, 19*(2), 2–11.

Cohen, D. K., and Spillane, J. P. (1992). "Policy and practice: Relations between governance and instruction." In G. E. Grant (ed.), *Review of research in education,* Vol. 18. Washington, D.C.: American Educational Research Association.

Collins, R., Brown, I., and Holum, A. (1991). "Cognitive apprenticeship: Teaching the crafts of reading, writing, and mathematics." *American Educator, 15*(3), 6–11, 38–46.

Collins, R., Brown, I., and Newman, S. E. (1989). "Cognitive apprenticeship: Teaching the crafts of reading, writing, and mathematics." In L. B. Resnick (ed.), *Knowing, learning, and instruction: Essays in honor of Robert Glaser.* Hillsdale, N.J.: Erlbaum.

Comer, J. P. (1988). "Educating poor minority children." *Scientific American, 259*(5), 42–48.

Commission on Skills of the American Workforce (1990). *America's choice: High skills or low wages.* Rochester, N.Y.: National Center on Education and the Economy.

Committee for Economic Development (1985). *Investing in our children.* New York: Committee for Economic Development.

Committee for Economic Development (1987). *Children in need: Investment strategies for the educationally disadvantaged.* New York: Committee for Economic Development.

Darling-Hammond, L. (1988). *Sharing the responsibility: Preparing teachers for urban schools in Northwest Indiana.* Gary: Urban Teachers Education Program, Indiana University Northwest.

Darling-Hammond, L. (1992). "Accountability for professional practice." In M. Levine (ed.), *Professional practice schools: Linking school reform to teacher education.* New York: Teachers College Press.

Darling-Hammond, L. (ed.) (1994). *Professional development schools: Schools for developing a profession.* New York: Teachers College Press.

Dewey, J. (1974). "The relation of theory to practice in education." In R. D. Archambault (ed.), *John Dewey on education: Selected writings.* Chicago: University of Chicago Press. (Original work published in 1904.)

Duckworth, E. (1987). *The having of wonderful ideas and other essays on teaching and learning.* New York: Teachers College Press.

Elmore, R. F., and McLaughlin, M. W. (1988). *Steady work: Policy, practice and the reform of American education.* Santa Monica, Calif.: RAND.

Feiman-Nemser, S., and Buchmann, M. (1986). *When is student teaching teacher education?* (Research Series no. 178). East Lansing. Mich.: Institute for Research on Teaching.

Feiman-Nemser, S., and Parker, M. B. (1990). "Making subject matter part of the conversation in learning to teach." *Journal of Teacher Education, 41*(3), 32–43.

Fullan, M. G. (1991). *The new meaning of educational change.* New York: Teachers College Press.

Gardner, H. (1985). *Frames of mind: The theory of multiple intelligences.* New York: Basic Books.

Gardner, H. (1991). *The unschooled mind: How children think and how schools should teach.* New York: Basic Books.

Goldman, E., and Barron, L. (1990). "Using hypermedia to improve the preparation of elementary teachers." *Journal of Teacher Education, 41*(3), 21–31.

Griffin, G. (1989). "Coda." In M. C. Reynolds (ed.), *Knowledge base for the beginning teacher.* Elmsford, N.Y.: Pergamon Press.

Grossman, P. L. (1990). *The making of a teacher: Teacher knowledge and teacher education.* New York: Teachers College Press.

Grossman, P. L., Wilson, S. M., and Shulman, L. S. (1989). "Teachers of substance: Subject matter knowledge for teaching." In M. C. Reynolds (ed.), *Knowledge base for the beginning teacher.* Elmsford, N.Y.: Pergamon Press.

Hill, P. T., Wise, A. E., and Shapiro, L. (1989). *Educational progress: Cities mobilize to improve their schools.* Santa Monica, Calif.: RAND.

Hodgkinson, H. S. (1992). *A demographic look at tomorrow.* Washington, D.C.: Institute for Educational Leadership.

Holmes Group (1986). *Tomorrow's teachers: A report of the Holmes Group.* East Lansing, Mich.: Holmes Group.

Holmes Group (1990). *Tomorrow's schools: A report of the Holmes Group.* East Lansing, Mich.: Holmes Group.

Houston, H. M. (1992). "Institutional standard-setting in professional practice schools: Initial considerations." In M. Levine (ed.), *Professional practice schools: Linking teacher education and school reform.* New York: Teachers College Press.

Joyce, B. R., and Showers, B. (1980). "Improving inservice training: The message of research." *Educational Leadership, 37,* 279–385.

Kearns, D. T., and Doyle, D. P. (1988). *Winning the brain race: A bold plan to make our schools competitive.* San Francisco: ICS Press.

Kennedy, M. M. (1987). "Inexact sciences: Professional education and the development of expertise." In E. Z. Rothkopf (ed.), *Review of research in education,* Vol. 14. Washington, D.C.: American Educational Research Association.

Kennedy, M. M. (1992). "Establishing professional schools for teachers." In M. Levine (ed.), *Professional practice schools: Linking teacher education and school reform.* New York: Teachers College Press.

Kozol, J. (1991). *Savage inequalities.* New York: Crown.

Lampert, M. (1991). "Looking at restructuring from within a restructured role." *Phi Delta Kappan, 72,* 670–674.

Lampert, M., and Ball, D. L. (1990). *Using hypermedia technology to support a new pedagogy of teacher education.* (Issue Paper no. 90–5). East Lansing, Mich.: National Center for Research on Teacher Education.

Lemlech, J. K., and Foliart, H. (1992). "Restructuring to become a professional practice school: Stages of collegiality and the development of professionalism." Paper presented at annual meeting of American Educational Research Association, San Francisco.

Levin, H. M. (1987). "Accelerating elementary education for disadvantaged students." Report prepared for Stanford University.

Levin, H. M. (1988). *Accelerated schools for at-risk students.* (CPRE Research Report Series RR-010). New Brunswick, N.J.: Center for Policy Research in Education, Eagleton Institute of Politics, Rutgers University.

Levin, H. M. (1991). *Accelerating the progress of all students.* (Rockefeller Institute Special Report no. 31). Albany, N.Y.: Rockefeller Institute of Government.

Levine, M. (1985). "Survey of employer needs." Paper prepared for the Committee for Economic Development.

Levine, M. (ed.) (1988). *Professional practice schools: Building a model.* Washington, D.C.: American Federation of Teachers.

Levine, M. (ed.) (1990). *Professional practice schools: Building a model,* Vol. 2. Washington, D.C.: American Federation of Teachers.

Levine, M. (1992). "Professional practice schools: A conceptual framework." In M. Levine (ed.), *Professional practice schools: Linking teacher education and school reform.* New York: Teachers College Press.

Lieberman, A., and Miller, L. (1992). "Teacher development in professional practice schools." In M. Levine (ed.), *Professional practice schools: Linking teacher education and school reform.* New York: Teachers College Press.

Little, J. W. (1982). "Norms of collegiality and experimentation: Workplace conditions of school success." *American Educational Research Journal, 19,* 325–340.

Lortie, D. C. (1975). *Schoolteacher: A sociological study.* Chicago: University of Chicago Press.

Mann, H. (1965). *Horace Mann on the crisis in education.* Yellow Springs, Ohio: Antioch Press.

Merseth, K. K. (1992). "Weaving stronger fabric: The pedagogical promise of hypermedia and case methods in teacher education." Harvard University Graduate School of Education (unpublished paper).

National Board for Professional Teaching Standards (1991). "What teachers should know and be able to do." In *Toward high and rigorous standards for the teaching profession: Initial policies for the NBPTS.* Detroit: National Board for Professional Teaching Standards.

Natriello, G. (1989). *What do employers want in entry-level workers? An assessment of the evidence.* (Document no. OS-7). New York: Institute on Education and the Economy, Columbia University Teachers College.

Neufeld, B. (1992). "Professional practice schools in context: New mixtures of institutional authority." In M. Levine (ed.), *Professional practice schools: Linking teacher education and school reform.* New York: Teachers College Press.

Pechman, E. (1992). "Child as a meaning maker: The organizing theme for professional practice schools." In M. Levine (ed.), *Professional practice schools: Linking teacher education and school reform.* New York: Teachers College Press.

Piaget, J. (1964). "Development and learning." In R. Ripple and V. Rockcastle (eds.), *Piaget rediscovered.* Ithaca, N.Y.: Cornell University Press.

Piaget, J. (1967). *Six psychological studies.* New York: Random House.

Resnick, L. B. (1987). "Learning in school and out." *Educational Researcher, 16*(9), 13–20.

Reynolds, M. C. (ed.) (1989). *Knowledge base for the beginning teacher.* Elmsford, N.Y.: Pergamon Press.

Rosenthal, R. (1991). "Teacher expectancy effects: A brief update 25 years after the Pygmalion experiment." *Journal of Research in Education, 1*(1), 3–12.

Scribner, S., and Sachs, P. (1991). *Knowledge acquisition at work.* (Document no. T-22). New York: Institute on Education and the Economy, Columbia University Teachers College.

Scribner, S., and Stevens, J. (1989). *Experimental studies on the relationship of school math and work math.* (Document T-4). New York: Institute on Education and the Economy, Columbia University Teachers College.

Shaefer, R. J. (1967). *The school as a center of inquiry.* New York: HarperCollins.

Shulman, L. S. (1986). "Those who understand: Knowledge growth in teaching." *Educational Researcher, 15,* 4–14.

Shulman, L. S. (1987). "Knowledge and teaching: Foundations of the new reform." *Harvard Educational Review, 57*(1), 1–22.

Simmons, W., and Resnick, L. B. (1993). "Assessment as a catalyst of school reform." *Educational Leadership, 50*(5), 11–15.

Sizer, T. (1986). "Rebuilding: First steps by the coalition of essential schools." *Phi Delta Kappan, 68*(1), 38–42.

Smith, M., O'Day, J., and Cohen, D. K. (1990). "National curriculum American style." *American Educator, 14*(4), 10–17, 40–47.

Sternberg, R. J. (1982). "Reasoning, problem solving, and intelligence." In R. J. Sternberg (ed.), *Handbook of human intelligence.* New York: Cambridge University Press.

Sykes, G., and Bird, T. (1992). *Teacher education and the case idea.* East Lansing, Mich.: National Center for Research on Teacher Learning.

Trachtman, R. (1991). "Documentation of the planning year." Report prepared for the American Federation of Teachers Professional Practice School Project.

Trachtman, R. (1992). "Documentation of implementation, year 1." Report prepared for the American Federation of Teachers Professional Practice School Project.

U.S. Department of Education (1992). *The national education goals report: Building a nation of learners.* Washington, D.C.: U.S. Government Printing Office.

Waller, W. (1932). *Sociology of teaching.* New York: Wiley.

Woolsey, K. H., and others (1990). *Restructuring: An interactive multimedia prototype for educators.* San Francisco and Washington, D.C.: Apple Multimedia Laboratory/Center for Restructuring, American Federation of Teachers.

Annotated Bibliography

Berryman, S. E., and Bailey, T. R. (1992). *The double helix of education and the economy.* New York: Institute on Education and the Economy, Columbia University Teachers College.
Berryman and Bailey explore the relationship between economic activity and learning, focusing on two features: the human capital needs of a restructuring U.S. economy and the changes that this economy suggests for learning and schooling. Their discussion and recommendations for school reform are grounded in cognitive research that stresses the interactive, social, and inquiring nature of learning. The second area of research that grounds their recommendations comprises studies of learning in work and nonwork settings. They conclude with three recommendations for school reform: prepare all students for a high-skills workplace, dissolve the dualism between academic and vocational education that results in decontextualized academics and debased vocational education, and organize learning around effective practices.

Darling-Hammond, L. (1994). *Professional development schools: Schools for developing a profession.* New York: Teachers College Press.
Darling-Hammond brings together an important set of case studies of early efforts to create professional development schools, written by participants involved in implementation. She elaborates on the multiple roles of such institutions in supporting and initiating education reform as well as in teacher education. Comparisons are made with procedures used in other professions to integrate and support the preparation of practitioners.

Goodlad, J. I. (1990). *Teachers for our nation's schools.* San Francisco: Jossey-Bass.
Goodlad presents the results of a five-year study of teacher training programs. He contends teachers are as ill prepared to teach as they are to restructure schools. He identifies the conditions that determine the poor quality of many programs: low prestige, state-mandated curricula and credential requirements, and emphasis and rewards to university faculty for scholarly publications over teaching. He makes recommendations for institutional changes to create an infrastructure for strong teacher education programs.

Holmes Group (1986). *Tomorrow's teachers.* East Lansing, Mich.: Holmes Group.
This report presents the results of a fifteen-month analysis of teacher education by the Holmes Group, research universities engaged in teacher education. The group lays out five major goals for the restructuring of teacher education: to make education of teachers intellectually sound; to recognize differences in knowledge, skills, and commitment among teachers through the creation of three levels in teaching: novices, professional teachers, and career professionals; to create relevant and defensible standards of entry to the profession of teaching; to connect schools of education with schools; and to make schools better places for practicing teachers to work and learn.

Levine, M. (ed.) (1992). *Professional practice schools: Linking teacher education to school reform.* New York: Teachers College Press.
Chapter authors Marsha Levine, Mary Kennedy, Linda Darling-Hammond, Ann Lieberman and Lynne Miller, Holly Houston, Barbara Neufeld, and Ellen Pechman lay out a conceptual design for professional practice schools, the educational equivalent to teaching hospitals in medicine. The PPS is a real school, collaboratively governed with a triple mission: to support student learning for understanding, to support the education of teachers, and to support research directed at the improvement of practice. Policy issues, curricular questions, and institutional barriers are discussed as well as the pivotal role such institutions can play in making school reform a reality.

Schön, D. (1987). *Educating the reflective practitioner.* San Francisco: Jossey-Bass.
Recognizing that professional practitioners must draw on their knowledge and make decisions in the process of practice, Schön addresses the question of how best to prepare them. He proposes that the professional's education should center on "reflection in action" or learning by doing. He argues that this prepares students for the complex and unpredictable problems of actual practice. He uses examples from many disciplines and describes in detail coaching methods used by master teachers. He then proposes his recommendations for educating the reflective teacher.

Shaefer, R. J. (1967). *The school as a center of inquiry.* New York: HarperCollins.
Shaefer lays out a vision of schools where students and teachers are learners and where their inquiry and pursuit of knowledge is supported. He challenges the traditional notion of schooling as the transmission of information and maintains that only when schools support teacher learning will student success be at hand.

CHAPTER TWENTY-SIX

DEVELOPING PRACTICE THROUGH FIELD EXPERIENCES

J. GARY KNOWLES AND ARDRA L. COLE

I found the [field experience component] to be more detrimental than positive even though it is a necessary evil. . . . I tried to conform. I was lucky on my first practicum to work with a teacher with whom I identified greatly. The way she taught was the way I wanted to teach. I was very fortunate. For the other sessions, it wasn't at all like that. [The cooperating teachers] taught in ways in which I could never be successful and I started to feel inadequate. My fears overcame me. . . . In the practicum you get to feel pinned into a tight situation and you feel you have to be "that way."

FIRST-YEAR SECONDARY SCHOOL TEACHER[1]

The field experience, though commonly touted as the most meaningful part of preservice teacher preparation, is not without flaws and does not escape criticism. Those contributing to the literature on teacher education, those in faculties and schools of education, experienced teachers and administrators in schools, first-year teachers, and even preservice teachers themselves offer myriad criticisms and suggestions for improvement of the field experience component of preservice programs. Some are not at all optimistic about field experiences of the future. Yates (1981), for example, asserts that, "Student teaching problems are unchanging, persistent and universal. . . . The problems are unsolvable" (p. 44). While we are more hopeful, we do acknowledge that, in order for substantive and systemic change to take place and be sustained, a fundamental reconceptualization of preservice teacher education needs to occur.

In this chapter, we explore the general question, "How might field experiences in preservice teacher education better prepare teachers for the multiple roles and contextual complexities of life in schools and for careers as inquiring professionals?"

Orientation

Authors of contemporary literature on field experiences suggest that field experiences might be improved with an emphasis on the following:

- *An inquiry orientation* to encourage preservice teachers to variously engage in systematic reflection on and inquiry into teaching, learning, and schooling (for example, Bullough, Knowles, and Crow, 1991; Calderhead and Gates, 1993; Clandinin, Davies, Hogan, and Kennard, 1993; Cruickshank, 1987; Floden and Buchmann, 1990; Feiman-Nemser, 1990; Gitlin and Teitelbaum, 1983; Holmes Group, 1990; Zeichner and Liston, 1987; Zeichner and Teitelbaum, 1982)
- *A broader view of teaching* that more accurately depicts the complexity of teaching and life in schools and classrooms (for example, Lasley and Watras, 1991; Taylor, Borys, and La Rocque, 1992; Zeichner, 1992; Zeichner and Teitelbaum, 1982) and takes into account the social and political conditions of schools and society (for example, Zeichner, 1992; Zeichner and Liston, 1987)
- *School- as well as classroom-based field experiences* to provide opportunities for preservice teachers to gain insights into the complexity of teachers' roles (for example, Guyton and McIntyre, 1990; McNay and Cole, 1993b; Taylor, Boris, and La Rocque, 1992; Zeichner, 1987, 1990, 1992)
- *A focus on the relational elements* of working in schools (for example, Boydell, 1991; Griffin and others, 1983; Guyton and McIntyre, 1990; MacKinnon, 1989; Wood, 1991)
- *Collaborative links between schools of education and schools in the field* in order to provide a better integration of field and university components of preservice programs (for example, Clandinin, Davies, Hogan, and Kennard, 1993; Goodlad, 1990; Hathaway, 1985; Holmes Group, 1986; Sirotnik and Goodlad, 1988; Stallings and Kowalski, 1990; Watson and Fullan, 1991)
- *The importance of using research* to enhance the learning-to-teach process (for example, Borko, 1989; Buchmann, 1984; Carter and Doyle, 1989; Cruickshank, 1987; Guyton and McIntyre, 1990; Lanier and Little, 1986)

We build on these foundational concepts to facilitate a rethinking and reorganization of field experiences.

Our view of field experiences is strongly influenced by preservice and beginning teachers' perspectives and experiences. We broadly define the knowledge base informing teacher education and development to include practice and experience as seen through the eyes of preservice, beginning, and experienced teachers, and others, including school administrators and university and school faculty supervisors. We also include perspectives from formal inquiry as evidenced in relevant research and literature on learning to teach; preservice and inservice teacher education, particularly field experiences; and teacher socialization and development (for example, Feiman-Nemser and Buchmann, 1987; Guyton and McIntyre, 1990; Hoy and Woolfolk, 1989; Kagan, 1992; Knowles and Cole with Presswood, 1994; Lanier and Little, 1986; Taylor, Boris, and La Rocque, 1992; Watts, 1987; Zeichner, 1992; Zeichner and Gore, 1990; Zeichner and Liston, 1987).

We write with a developmental perspective on the processes of learning to teach and becoming a teacher and with a focus on self-directed learning, facilitation of ongoing professional development, and inquiry. Reflected in our writing is a view of teacher education as a lifelong process of continuing growth with preservice programs, including field experiences, providing the contexts for the formal beginnings of careerlong development. Our perspective is also based on the belief that people who enter teacher education programs bring with them established conceptions about teachers' roles and practices and about classrooms and schools. These preconceptions, along with more recent ones developed in the preservice preparation period, converge in the creation of images and expectations of practice that strongly influence preservice teachers' actual experiences of learning communities. Finally, we place value on the learning potential provided by experience and maintain that preservice field experiences are potentially invaluable educative opportunities that too often are perceived by some preservice teachers as mis- or noneducative, even dysfunctional.

The following general questions are infused throughout our thinking and writing as we make use of the broad knowledge base associated with the field experience component of precertification teacher education and as we articulate a particular framework for developing field experiences:

- What is the fundamental rationale for field experiences and what principles might guide their design and conduct?
- What are the goals of field experiences and how do they relate to the overall goals for teacher education? How can goals of field experience (and their actualization) be melded with broader program goals?
- How does the knowledge base for teacher education and development relate to field experience components? What research should inform the development of field experiences and their actualization?
- What roles can the various responsible and invested parties play in facilitating ongoing professional development of new teachers engaged in field experiences?
- How might institutes of preservice teacher education—university faculties and schools of education, and public and private schools—work together to facilitate preservice teachers' access to and use of the various knowledge sources of teacher education in ways that are meaningful, relevant, and conducive to their ongoing professional development and renewal?
- How can field experience components be conceptualized and structured to provide professional development opportunities for both inexperienced and experienced practitioners?

Framework for Developing Field Experiences

To facilitate a discussion and consideration of issues and questions about field experiences in teacher preparation, we use a matrix based on an inquiry framework (see Figure 26.1). This requires consideration of the curriculum elements identified along the horizontal axis of the inquiry framework in conjunction with the programmatic elements along the vertical axis.

The inquiry framework is based on the beliefs that inquiry fosters understanding and that commitment to continuing professional development is facilitated by self-directed learning. Prospective teachers can begin to take charge of their own professional development through systematic reflection and analysis of emerging practice within both the narrow confines of classrooms and the broader boundaries of schools, communities, and regions. We assume that with appropriate attention to individuals, contexts, and programmatic arrangements, field experiences can provide opportunities and contexts for preservice teachers to engage in such personal and contextual inquiry. In so doing, the potential of field experiences to more effectively facilitate teacher development can be realized.

Curricular Elements in Field Experiences

The inquiry focus we propose works in a cyclical yet spiral fashion (see Figure 26.2). Preservice teachers begin by focusing on self for the purposes of gaining insights into personal history influences on their developing conceptions of schools, teachers, learners, teaching, and learning. Inquiry then moves outward to explorations of teaching, learning, and educational and institutional contexts, then to professional relationships within those contexts and finally back to self as emerging and self-directed professionals. Through this process, preservice teachers explore questions that are fundamental to the development of inquiring, or reflexive, teachers:

1. Who am I as teacher?
2. What are schools and classrooms like? What goes on and who works in educational institutions?
3. Who are the students? How do I develop relationships with the many participants in the learning community?
4. How do I learn about and understand teaching, and how can I forge my own ongoing professional development?

Inquiry into Self in Relation to Prior Experiences

Many aspects of a teacher's life make a teacher the way she is. When I think about [that] I look to my own background. . . . A teacher's past is the most determining factor of the future.

ELEMENTARY PRESERVICE TEACHER

FIGURE 26.1. FRAMEWORK FOR DEVELOPING FIELD EXPERIENCES.

Curriculum For Field Experiences				
Programmatic Elements for Consideration	Curricular Elements for Consideration			
	1. Inquiry into Self in Relation to Prior Experiences	2. Inquiry into Contexts and Personnel Roles	3. Inquiry into Relationships	4. Inquiry into Self and Ongoing Professional Development
Structure of Field Experiences				
Administration and Governance of Field Experiences				
Contexts for Field Experiences				
Preparation for Field Experiences				
Supervision and Evaluation of Field Experiences				

> *When I think about becoming a good teacher, I think about my former teachers, my experiences, all my past. I pull from my background experiences. I say, "All right, I didn't like it when a teacher did that, so I'm going to try obviously not to do that". . . . I make my ideal teacher in my head.*
>
> SECONDARY PRESERVICE TEACHER

> *The placement of preservice teachers in their early field experiences is crucial. The first experiences back in schools again reinforces or refutes their memories of schools and classrooms. . . . Early experiences [should] be structured to challenge the preconceptions about the profession of teaching and set preservice teachers on appropriate paths of development.*
>
> UNIVERSITY SUPERVISOR

FIGURE 26.2. AN INQUIRY FRAMEWORK FOR FIELD EXPERIENCES.

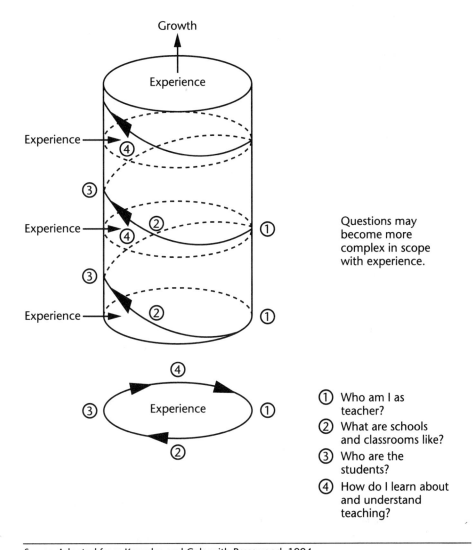

Questions may become more complex in scope with experience.

① Who am I as teacher?

② What are schools and classrooms like?

③ Who are the students?

④ How do I learn about and understand teaching?

Source: Adapted from Knowles and Cole with Presswood, 1994.

Students entering formal preservice preparation programs bring with them beliefs, attitudes, ideals, influences, and expectations developed over years of life experience and exposure to a wide variety of teaching and learning situations and contexts. Studies of preservice teachers' experiences upon reentry to schools (for example, Aitken and Mildon, 1991; Britzman, 1991; Crow, 1987a, 1987b; Knowles, 1992; McDaniel, 1991; Mcneely and Mertz, 1990; Weinstein, 1990) provide evidence of how firmly grounded in personal history are preservice teachers' expectations and understandings of schools, teachers, teaching, and students. Preservice teachers often have well-rooted images of themselves as teachers and high ideals and aspirations for teaching, and they strive to enact or play out their personal images despite contextual realities that are often at odds with them. Thus, when preconceived images are at odds with realities presented in the field, difficulties often arise (Aitken and Mildon, 1991; Bullough, 1991; Bullough and Knowles, 1990; Cole, 1990; Cole and Knowles, 1993; Kagan, 1992; Knowles, 1992; Knowles and Hoefler, 1989; Zeichner and Tabachnick, 1981).

Since Lortie (1975) proclaimed a need for attention to the role of prior experiences in the process of becoming a teacher, a field of investigation on the topic has developed. Now, it is quite widely accepted that formal teacher education has an important but secondary influence on teachers' thinking and practice, the latter being indelibly imprinted by life, school, and career experiences prior to entry to formal programs of teacher preparation.[2] Because understandings rooted in prior experiences form the foundation for developing practice and because such understandings usually are incomplete and often derive from negative experiences, it is important to help preservice teachers make explicit for examination both education-related elements of their personal histories and their preconceptions of teaching (see, also, Goodman, 1988; Gunstone and Northfield, 1987; Knowles, 1993; Knowles and Holt-Reynolds, 1991; Ross, 1987; Zeichner and Grant, 1981). The idea behind this argument is that unexamined constructs are likely to remain unchallenged, therefore static and potentially unreflected-upon elements of practice.

Because we cannot deny the power differential between the influences of experiences prior to and during preservice programs, the challenge is to find ways of *understanding* early influences on developing and emerging practices. Also, because field experiences offered in teacher preparation programs provide the first formalized opportunity for preservice teachers to verify, challenge, and modify their preconceptions, it is essential that contexts be provided for students of teaching to reflect on and make sense of their field experiences in light of their prior experiences. As Feiman-Nemser (1983) states, "The likelihood that professional study will affect what powerful early experiences have inscribed on the mind and emotions will depend on its power to cultivate images of the possible and desirable and to forge commitments to make those images a reality" (p. 154).

Most field experiences are too short, too structured, too focused on the immediacy of classroom action, and too detached from the personal; consequently, they often provide little more than superficial, "rites of passage" experiences. Field experiences that are not constructed to take into account, celebrate, and nurture human individuality and complexity run the risk of preparing teachers with more technical than introspective orientations and with intimate knowledge of nonindividualistic learning opportunities. These teachers who will essentially continue to teach as they were taught, with little understanding of either the pedagogical or the personal principles underlying such practices.

How, then, can field experiences be designed to provide preservice teachers opportunities and a basis for acknowledging and examining the history of their tacitly held beliefs and contexts for considering practical alternatives? To answer may require both a reconsideration of the existing structures and curricula of field experiences and a reorientation of the processes used to give meaning to those experiences.

Questions for Consideration

- How can preservice teachers' experiences as students—especially their understandings of teaching practices and the role of teachers—be melded with the most appropriate and current understandings of theory and practice?
- How can preservice teachers' implicit theories about teaching and the role of teachers be legitimized in the formal context of teacher education, especially the field experience component?
- How can field experiences be structured to facilitate preservice teachers' inquiry into their views of self as teacher in relation to both their prior experiences and their future work as professional educators?
- How can programs provide opportunities for substantive, extensive, critical reflection on past experiences of learning and classrooms, schools and other places of learning, in the already time-pressured demands of existing state-mandated or directed curricular requirements?
- What kinds of field experience sites—that is, teaching and learning contexts—facilitate preservice teachers to explore the place of their prior experiences and thinking in relation to their developing conceptions of themselves as teachers?

Inquiry into Contexts and Personnel Roles

I thought I knew what schools were like. Well, I just wasn't prepared for the demands of working in schools. Actually, there were two levels of unpreparedness. [The first] had to do with my preparedness to work with kids only a few years younger than I, [the second] had to do with understanding the various ways that I could act and interact in the school and classroom so as to benefit my [growth]. Really, this second [one] is much more important, and it was the one that was not done.

SECONDARY PRESERVICE TEACHER

Perhaps we need to provide a [block of time] when the [preservice teachers] literally spend all their time getting used to the school, meeting and talking to experienced teachers, floating around and observing, getting a feel for the place when there's no pressure whatsoever placed on them. Then they could go back to the faculty, kick some ideas around, and then come back to do some teaching.

                                                                 EXPERIENCED ELEMENTARY TEACHER

The early [field] experience ought to be a time for [preservice teachers] to get a sense of the lay of the land. It should help new teachers answer the question: "Do I and how do I want to be a teacher?"

                                                                 FIRST-YEAR-ELEMENTARY TEACHER

School placements [for teachers in preparation] are crucial from several perspectives. . . . But what's interesting here is that we seem to have forgotten that teachers' work is much more than classroom practice. Those "other" things are what seem to get lost in the process. Simply "shadowing" a teacher for a day, a week, or a month, does not address the great dearth in understanding about the more comprehensive practice of teachers. [Preservice teachers] need to figure out processes that will help them understand and function more like experienced teachers.

                                                                 SECONDARY SCHOOL PRINCIPAL

Past personal experiences of schools and teaching, combined with relatively simplified or stereotypical depictions of the teaching profession in the mass media, contribute to the formation of inappropriate images and inadequate expectations of teaching as a career and profession (for example, Barone, 1992; Joseph and Burnaford, 1994; Shack, 1965). As Book, Beyers, and Freeman (1983) assert, about a quarter of those entering teacher preparation programs in the United States maintain that there is little they need to learn to become successful teachers because they already have pedagogies in place in their thinking.

The relatively recent shift to a qualitative approach to research on teaching and teacher development has resulted in an increase in descriptive research that more accurately depicts the complexity of teaching and life in schools and classrooms (for example, Britzman, 1991; Bruckerhoff, 1991; Clandinin, 1986; Cohen, 1991; Freedman, 1990; Jackson, 1990; Kidder, 1989; McLaren, 1986; Polansky, 1986). Also, the work of Johnson (1990), Lieberman and Miller (1992), Little and McLaughlin (1993), Lortie (1975), Nias, Southworth, and Yeomans (1989), and Rosenholtz (1989), among others, highlights teaching and teachers' work as a complex set of interdependent concepts rather than as a discrete classroom-based enterprise. But because educational literature is not widely read by those not already in the profession, few preservice teachers enter formal preparation programs with either comprehensive or realistic understandings about teaching and the roles of teachers.[3]

Preservice programs often do little to help preservice teachers expand the relatively narrow conceptions of teachers' work that they hold on entering formal teacher preparation. Placing preservice teachers in individual classrooms and keeping their attention focused almost exclusively within the walls of that classroom and on the more technical aspects of teaching reinforces those narrow conceptions of teachers' work, fosters the perpetuation of norms of isolation, and contributes to the reality shock often experienced by beginning teachers. Also, lack of attention to the community within which the school is situated and the role of the school within the community does little to help preservice teachers understand and appreciate the contextual and cultural makeup of the students (Comer, 1988; Cummins, 1986; Zeichner, 1992).

Most preservice teacher education programs place relatively little emphasis on the contextual realities of schools or on the complexity of teaching, focusing instead on what takes place between students and teachers within the confines of classrooms. In other words, most preservice preparation programs concentrate almost entirely on teaching preservice teachers *to teach*; relatively little attention is placed on helping them *to become teachers* in the broadest sense. Consequently, preservice teachers are ill prepared for the working realities of schools and for the overall complexities associated with teaching and the roles of teachers. As Lasley and Watras (1991) observe, "The preoccupation with the knowledge base and with accountability has encouraged the adoption of simplified pedagogy and educational reductionism. . . . Teaching is emerging in the popular educational literature as a linear process, something that moves through discrete steps. . . . Preservice teachers learn the steps, and then during . . . field practica they are evaluated on those skills. The linear approach is reinforced by the reliance school districts place on . . . packaged approaches. . . . Even in teacher education programs . . . students [for the most part] go into field placements and work with teachers who possess the 'right' method. . . ." (p. 6).

Thus, they go on to argue, preservice teachers have little opportunity to understand and appreciate the complexity of teaching and schooling and to treat teaching as more than a narrow, applied field. Such a confining perspective focuses exclusively on the technical and procedural elements of teaching and forgoes developing understandings of the complex nature of the profession and its context.

Questions for Consideration

- How might field experiences be structured to promote and sustain preservice teachers' substantial inquiries into the contexts of schools, classrooms, and teaching as well as into the personnel roles within those contexts?
- How can field experiences move beyond primarily providing opportunities

for development of practice embedded in immediate classroom demands and prepare teachers for professional activities beyond classroom teaching?

- How can field experiences move beyond relatively superficial and artificial explorations of schools and the roles of teachers?

Inquiry into Relationships

I always look forward to having preservice teachers in my classroom. They come with such fresh, new perspectives and, even though they are just feeling their way in the classroom, my teaching is greatly enlightened [by their presence]. I grow as these new teachers ask me about my practice, as they seek clarification of my actions, and as they begin to interact with students and inquire into the goings-on of the school and classroom. . . . They also greatly enrich the learning of my students.

ELEMENTARY COOPERATING TEACHER

At first I perceived the job [of being a cooperating teacher] as one in which I was offering something to the student teachers. Then I realized it was a two-way street. Student teachers provide fresh blood, new faces, new ideas. They keep me up to date with current trends. It's [an opportunity for] adult contact—a team approach in a sometimes solitary profession. It also provides time for me to observe my class.

ELEMENTARY COOPERATING TEACHER

The so-called triad [of cooperating teacher, university supervisor, and preservice teacher] is important. I like to see the faculty advisor come in [to the classroom] because then I feel that it's teamwork and that I have some support. Regardless of what we talk about, it makes me feel like a part of the whole rather than an isolated element.

ELEMENTARY COOPERATING TEACHER

Realizing the identity of the "prime movers" in the school was an eye opener for me. . . . Many of the problems I faced [during my field experience] were solved by the school secretary, custodian, librarian, or media center director.

SECONDARY PRESERVICE TEACHER

By returning to the same school [for several field components] we were able to experience the school community. The children we met in our first two practicum periods would hold our hands at recess, and even students who didn't have a student teacher in their classroom recognized us and greeted us in the halls. It was a great feeling to be welcomed back by the students. And, those of us who went back to observe or teach in the classrooms we were in before could see the progression or development of the students.

SECONDARY PRESERVICE TEACHER

Field experiences provide some preservice teachers with their first realization that schools, as professional communities, are made up of numerous persons in varied roles: students, parents, administrators, professional and nonprofessional support staff, and other teachers in the school as well as members of the professional community at large. Field experiences can provide opportunities for preservice teachers to develop relationships with many of these community members and to understand how such relationships can variously influence their development. Of primary (but by no means sole) significance to most preservice teachers are the relationships they develop with other teachers in the school, particularly the experienced teachers with whom they spend most of their time, with university personnel or other persons with supervisory responsibilities, and with students. Opportunities to develop productive working relationships with members of the learning community are an important part of facilitating preservice teacher development.

Relationships with Cooperating Teachers. Morris and Morris (1980) report that the supervisory aspect of relationships with cooperating teachers is one of the main sources of stress for preservice teachers. Numerous reports of field experience studies (for example, Beynon, 1991; Campbell and Williamson, 1983; MacKinnon, 1989) indicate that the development of a positive and productive working relationship between cooperating and preservice teachers is the most significant factor in determining successful field experiences. In turn, the key to developing a significant relationship is communication (Beynon, 1991; Guyton and McIntyre, 1990). "What is said, what is meant, and how it is understood constitute the key issues in the development of relationships between the cooperating teacher and the student teacher" (Beynon, 1991, p. 17).

Issues of role definition and expectations are integral to any discussion about relationships in field experiences. There is general agreement, both in the literature and in the field, that the role of the cooperating teacher is poorly defined and that expectations related to the role are ambiguous, diverse, and often overlapping or at odds (for example, Applegate and Lasley, 1982, 1984; Cole and Sorrill, 1992; Griffin and others, 1983; Grimmett and Ratzlaff, 1986; O'Neal, 1983). Expectations for cooperating teachers' roles in facilitating preservice teachers' learning through field experiences are determined both at individual and institutional levels, and it is little wonder that so much discrepancy exists.

Griffin and others (1983) observe that university- and school-based educators rarely agree on or even articulate policies and practices to guide student teaching. What results, according to Feiman-Nemser and Buchmann (1987) and Guyton and McIntyre (1990), is a less productive and less educative field experience than is possible. Negotiating a role and developing a productive working relationship with cooperating teachers is one key to a successful and fulfilling field experience.

Relationships with University Supervisors. There is also considerable ambiguity associated with the role of the university supervisor in facilitating preservice teacher development within the context of field experiences. Examination of the literature on field experiences reveals that there is considerable uncertainty surrounding what we know about the roles, practices, and influences of university supervisors (for example, Boydell, 1991; Grimmett and Ratzlaff, 1986; Guyton and McIntyre, 1990; O'Connell Rust, 1988; Richardson-Koehler, 1988). Funk, Hoffman, Keithley, and Long (1982) and Griffin and others (1983) report a prevalence of preservice teacher dissatisfaction with the role of the university supervisor; others (Emans, 1983; Koehler, 1984; Zeichner, 1980) suggest that university supervisors have a questionable influence on preservice teachers' learning in the field. Nevertheless, university supervisors are seen as an important part of the field experience triad (preservice teacher, cooperating teacher, and university supervisor) and a complement to cooperating teachers (Alverman, 1981; Becher and Ade, 1982; Friebus, 1977; Zimpher, de Voss, and Nott, 1980).

Studies examining university supervisors' involvement in field experiences indicate the variety of roles and functions they perform: setting goals and expectations for field experiences, orienting student teachers to field placement sites, acting as a liaison between the university and the field and reinforcing university perspectives, reducing conflict in field settings and serving as mediators in cases of problems, observing and providing constructive feedback and assessment, and supporting student teachers and facilitating their development in a variety of ways not necessarily directly related to classroom practice (Alverman, 1981; Koehler, 1984; Zahorik, 1988; Zimpher, de Voss, and Nott, 1980). The nature of these roles is complex and sometimes conflicting; they are fraught with potential to confound preservice teachers' opportunities for educative field experiences. It is for this reason that we concur with the suggestion of Emans (1983) and Richardson-Koehler (1988) for a reconceptualization of the role of the university supervisor (see our discussion of this under the heading "Supervision and Evaluation of Field Experiences"). A reconceptualization of this role would involve greater attention to the preservice teacher-university supervisor relationship.

Relationships with Students. Frequently, preservice teachers have inappropriate or unrealistic expectations about the students they are to teach (Gomez and Comeaux, 1990; Kagan, 1992), perhaps a result of limited knowledge of those students (Florio-Ruane and Lensmire, 1990). For many preservice teachers, re-entry to schools through field experiences delivers a mild to severe shock when they find that their images of students, teachers, and schools are inappropriate. Some of these discrepancies rest in a commonly held perception that the students whom preservice teachers encounter will be like *they* themselves were as students (Hollingsworth, 1989; Knowles and Holt-Reynolds, 1991; Holt-Reynolds, 1994). Understanding who students are and developing relationships with them are essential for successful field experiences. Guillaume and Rudney (1991), reporting on a yearlong study of preservice teachers' changing concerns, observed that developing and maintaining positive relationships with students was a concern of preservice teachers throughout their preservice program and that strong and productive relationships in particular occupied a significant portion of student teachers' writings about their classroom experiences.

A study of university supervisors' perceptions of preservice teachers who failed student teaching points out how critical it is for preservice teachers to attend to students and their relationships with them (Knowles, Skrobola, and Coolican, 1995; see also, Sudzina and Knowles, 1993). There was a general consensus among university supervisors in these studies that most preservice teachers who fail are unable to determine and respond to students' needs and relate to students well enough to engage their interest and participation. Supervisors reported that unsuccessful preservice teachers typically become preoccupied with themselves and their ability to "survive the semester," often at the expense of students. This kind of detrimental self-absorption is explained and supported in research linking preservice teacher development with professional role identity (see Kagan, 1992).

Feiman-Nemser and Floden (1986) discuss student-teacher relationships in terms of norms governing interactions. They assert that tension between themes of authority and friendship creates a fundamental ambiguity in how teachers view their roles and relate to students. This conflict is borne out time and time again in the literature on beginning teacher development (for example, Bullough, 1989; Bullough, Knowles, and Crow, 1991; Cole, 1990; Thiessen, 1991).

Preservice and beginning teachers regularly talk of the importance of being able to respond to the diverse backgrounds, experiences, abilities, and interests of their soon-to-be students; yet few understand or are prepared for the diversity that awaits them in many classrooms. Studies of cultural sensitivity and teaching preferences of preservice teachers by Larke (1990), Larke, Wiseman, and Bradley (1990), and Ross and Smith (1992) reveal low levels of tolerance and sensitivity toward minority students. Recent emphasis in preservice preparation programs on preparing teachers for diversity (for example, Cooper, Beare, and Thorman, 1990; Grant and Secada, 1990; Larke, Wiseman, and Bradley, 1990; Liston and Zeichner, 1990; Ross and Smith, 1992; Ryan and Robinson, 1990) comes none too soon. Field experiences are prime opportunities for preservice teachers to develop an experiential understanding of the students they are likely to teach and to develop strategies for fostering appropriate relationships.

Questions for Consideration

- How might preservice teachers' inquiry into their relationships with individuals within school systems—teachers, administrators, professional and nonprofessional support staff, parents, and students—be fostered within the field experience?
- What are the implications for placement, time commitment, roles, and responsibilities if preservice teachers are to focus their energies on exploring and developing relationships within learning communities?
- How might preservice teachers be encouraged to develop strong (collegial)

relationships with university supervisors? How might the conditions under which supervisors are expected to work be changed so that quality relationships may be established with preservice teachers?

Inquiry into Self and Ongoing Professional Development

The conclusion of student teaching is the edge of a new frontier. I have learned much but there is much more to learn.

SECONDARY PRESERVICE TEACHER

The affection and trust [that students] so willingly gave me has rekindled my desire to be the best teacher I can be. It has also caused some doubts to surface. I wonder how long I will wonder if I have the "right stuff" to be a teacher. How will I know?

ELEMENTARY PRESERVICE TEACHER

Internalizing what you have learned in teachers' college takes several years. [One new teacher, for example,] was well versed at the [university] in [small group work] but it isn't as yet part of his experience. So even though a concept has been "delivered," it hasn't necessarily been internalized.

SECONDARY PRINCIPAL

[Being a cooperating teacher] makes me sit down and consider some of the things I do in the classroom, really examine some of the objectives I've set for the children and for myself. I learn a lot [working with preservice teachers]. I try to [tell] them that you don't become a teacher at the end of teachers' college or at the end of your first or second year. It's a lifelong thing. I face every year with the attitude that there is always room for improvement—[teaching] is an ongoing growth experience.

ELEMENTARY COOPERATING TEACHER

Teachers redefine their professional knowledge as they act and interact in their professional contexts. What takes place in preservice teacher preparation programs and in institutions in which teachers begin their teaching careers influences their development in important ways. Although many university teacher educators may argue that preservice teacher education programs only intend to prepare teachers to *begin* teaching, until recently there has been little systematic follow-up in the field, so in a sense new teachers *are* expected to be as fully prepared as their experienced colleagues. It is no secret that the first year of teaching is often a traumatic time for many new teachers, characterized more as a struggle for survival than as a period of continuing and sustained professional growth. Balancing responsibilities associated with both the job and work of teaching (Feiman-Nemser and Floden, 1986) is a major source of anxiety for beginning teachers as they shoulder the full impact of their new responsibilities and struggle to maintain a sense of balance in their lives (for example, Bullough, 1989; Bullough, Knowles, and Crow, 1991; Chester, 1991; Cole, 1990, 1991a, 1991b; Cole and Knowles, 1992; Kane, 1991; Kilbourne and Roberts, 1991; Knowles, 1988, 1992, 1994; Marso and Pigge, 1987; Ryan, 1970, 1986, 1992; Ryan and others, 1980; Thiessen, 1991).

As many claim, much has *not* been covered in formal preparation programs. This suggests that focus on processes that facilitate continued and ongoing learning may be the wisest strategy for preservice teacher education. If we hope to reconceptualize teacher education to reflect the developmental nature of becoming a teacher and to more fully acknowledge the complexity and individuality of teaching practice, we must begin to think about how best to facilitate the process along a continuum. Preservice programs need to be thought of as the formal starting (but not ending) point of personal and professional inquiry. They also need to be thought of as contexts for providing opportunities for alternative rates of progress and differing degrees of intensity and focus by individual prospective teachers.

Skills in, habits of, and appropriate attitudes toward reflective practice and professional development must be fostered throughout the formative years of teaching and beyond. This means going past the preservice program and practicum to the classrooms and schools that receive new teachers. Those at the university need to begin to focus attention on working with those in the field to prepare contexts that are facilitative of ongoing growth, that welcome and support new teachers and help them to engage in systematic self-assessment, and that foster attitudes of professionalism.

Through a variety of curricular and programmatic modifications, many schools of education have begun to consider ways of bridging the gap between campus and classroom (for example, Sirotnik and Goodlad, 1988; Stallings and Kowalski, 1990; Watson and Fullan, 1991). A shift towards experiential or field-based programs has placed the field experience at the center of teachers' learning. Collaboration between schools and universities has enabled closer integration of field experiences and full-time teaching positions. Incorporation into the preservice curriculum of issues pertaining to preparation for the first year of teaching and beyond helps to balance specific knowledge expected by the field with appropriate processes for continuing professional growth. Thus, the curriculum could include establishing expectations for year one, interviewing and selecting a school/position, accessing resources, assessing social and political contexts, preparing for day one and week one, establishing support networks, engaging in action research and reflective practice, and developing a professional growth plan. These and similar efforts mark new beginnings in attempts to improve teacher education and the place and value of the field experience component. In addition, they have one thing in common: they define the knowledge base for teacher education and development more broadly than it has traditionally been defined and situate that knowledge base both in the academy and in the field. In so doing, field experiences become the focal point for personal-professional and programmatic development.

Questions for Consideration

- What experiences might foster preservice teachers' personal investment in principles of ongoing professional development? What processes and experiences establish the place of professional development practices in preservice teachers' professional lives?
- How can structured field experiences move both preservice teachers and experienced teachers beyond status quo practices in classrooms and learning communities? How can field experiences and associated preparation, seminars, and support be viewed and function as professional development?
- At the conclusion of field experiences, how can preservice teachers most appropriately analyze and evaluate their learning experiences to prepare them for future work in the field?
- How can preservice teacher education programs prepare teachers for the transition to full-time teaching?
- What conditions for first-year teachers are most conducive to their ongoing professional development? How can schools and faculties of education work together to facilitate teacher development along a continuum of professional learning?
- What in particular is the role of the university in facilitating teacher development beyond the preservice program?

In Conclusion

Kagan (1992) acknowledges that "the practice of classroom teaching remains forever rooted in personality and experience and that learning to teach requires a journey into the deepest recesses of one's self-awareness, where failures, fears, and hopes are hidden" (pp. 164–165). According to Kagan, teacher development consists of at least five components: a developing awareness of initial and changing knowledge and beliefs about pupils and classrooms, a reconstruction of idealized and inaccurate images of students and a reconstruction of early images of "self as teacher," a shift in attention to students and instruction upon resolution of one's own professional identity, acquiring and becoming comfortable with standard classroom procedures, and growth in problem-solving skills. When and how development takes place depend on at least three factors: the novice teacher's biography or personal history (clarity of image of self as teacher and readiness to acknowledge and accept that some beliefs and images may be inaccurate), the configuration of the preservice teacher education program (including the amount of time spent in educational contexts), and the contexts in which student and beginning teaching occur (nature of pupils, beliefs of and relations with other teachers, availability of materials, principal's beliefs, and relationships with parents). Thus, in concert with Kagan's observations, we suggest an approach to field experiences rooted in inquiry into self, contexts, relationships, and ongoing professional development.

Tools for Facilitating Field Experience Inquiry

We propose two primary methods for exploring field experiences through inquiry: (1) gathering *internal* information through autobiographical writing and (2) gathering *external* information through extensive explorations of educational contexts and the people and their roles within those contexts, primarily through the use of ethnographic research activities. Both of these approaches provide tools for teachers' lifelong explorations of their profession and their professional development. The former includes journal writing, personal history accounts, reflective papers, and professional development summaries. The latter involves developing expertise in observing, interviewing, and collecting artifactual information and interpreting and representing such information. The latter also includes interactive peer observations and group or peer school- and classroom-based inquiry projects of various kinds.[4] These ideas are extensively represented in teacher education and development literature on "teacher as researcher" (for example, Bissex and Bullock, 1987; Brause and Smayher, 1991; Connelly and Clandinin, 1988; Cochran-Smith and Lytle, 1993; Duckworth, 1986; Goswami and Stillman, 1987; Kincheloe, 1991; Tabachnick and Zeichner, 1991).

Programmatic Elements of Field Experiences

The challenge for those responsible for the organization, design, and conduct of field experiences is to determine ways and means of providing preservice teachers opportunities to engage in ongoing examination of self as teacher within the contexts of classrooms, schools, and the broader professional community. This requires consideration of the elements identified along the vertical axis of the inquiry framework matrix in conjunction with the curriculum elements (see Figure 26.1): structure of field experiences, administration and governance, contexts for field experiences, preparation for field experiences, and evaluation and supervision of field experiences.

Structure of Field Experiences

Even when I reflected on my experience [in the teacher education program] I was not able to make sense of the organization of the various experiences that made up the whole program. I was especially dumbfounded by the inattention to the matter of theory at the university and practice in the school. I was also dismayed at the lack of attention to my development as a teacher. It seemed as though they expected us to all progress through at the same speed.

SECONDARY PRESERVICE TEACHER

There ought to be very sound reasons behind the structure of teacher training programs. In particular, field experiences should be arranged in ways that also take advantage of the cycles of school activities, the strengths of personnel, as well as the coursework at the university.

ELEMENTARY PRINCIPAL

The structure of field experiences should reflect the unique philosophical and pedagogical elements of the teacher education program while at the same time accommodate the individual and collective professional development of cohorts of preservice teachers. If structures were more flexible there would be greater chances of meeting the development needs of everyone concerned.

UNIVERSITY SUPERVISOR

The sequence, timing, and duration of field experiences—those elements constituting the structure of field experiences—have been cited as possible areas of focus for the improvement of preservice teachers' learning in the field (for example, Holmes Group, 1986; Turney, Eltis, Towler, and Wright, 1985), although, interestingly, as Guyton and McIntyre (1990) suggest, there is little research about the structural elements of field experiences. Nevertheless, while we agree that timing, sequence, duration, and other structural elements are important considerations, substantive and systemic improvement of teacher education requires that these be considered as part of a much larger and more complex discussion of field experiences as they relate to university-based components of teacher preparation.

The behavioristic, personalistic, and traditional craft orientations to field experiences identified by Zeichner (1983) are supported by most existing field experience structures. In these approaches to teacher preparation, little time is needed to engage in extensive explorations of the processes and contexts associated with learning to teach and learning to be a teacher. As Feiman-Nemser (1990) observes, "the apprenticeship model does encourage novices to learn the practices of the master, but it does not necessarily preclude consideration of underlying principles or the development of conceptual understanding" (p. 223). Similarly, Zeichner and Teitelbaum (1982) describe the traditional field experience structures as supporting a view of teaching as an enterprise "separated from its ethical, political, and moral roots" (p. 96). Given our inquiry orientation to field experiences and lifelong professional development, we set our comments on the structure of field experiences within the context of overall program goals.

In their review of research on student teaching and school experiences, Guyton and McIntyre (1990) conclude that improvements in field experiences will depend on a clear explication and mutual understanding of their goals. Even in programs in which goals are articulated, however, the nature and range of the goals and the activities designed for their achievement are still wanting. For example, Cole and McNay (1989) studied goals for field experiences articulated in several preservice programs and observed little in the way of a conceptual framework or theoretical foundation. For the most part, handbooks used to describe and guide field experiences provided only unrationalized lists of goals and activities in which preservice teachers are expected to engage. With a closer look, it became apparent that the goals articulated for field experiences, though certainly appropriate for teacher education and development, were long-term, even lifelong, goals realistically achievable neither during the period of preservice teacher preparation nor even in the first year of teaching. Cole and McNay (1993) suggested that a renewal of teacher education might be possible if the appropriate placement of goals in the teacher education process, and the timing of and contexts for activities related to the achievement of those goals, were worked out more fully.

There is a need for all elements of field experiences to be aligned and congruent with other elements of the curriculum. Field experiences must not be thought of as being either separate from or in addition to the curriculum of teacher education; the two are integrally connected and symbiotic. Our focus on the structure of field experiences therefore calls for an acknowledgment of the ways in which field experiences are related to the goals of the whole teacher preparation program, and these must be considered in light of the developmental nature of learning to teach.

Questions for Consideration

- How can the structure of field experiences promote preservice teachers' inquiry into the following: self in relation to prior experiences? contexts and personnel roles? relationships? self and ongoing professional development?
- How does the field experience component relate to other elements of the preservice teacher education program in the university and the inservice professional development program in the field? What proportion of preservice programs should be devoted to field experiences? How much time in the field is appropriate for the purposes delineated by the overall program?
- Where are field experiences situated in the preservice program calendar? What is their relationship to specific elements of the overall program? What are appropriate levels of integration between formal coursework and field experiences?
- What are some alternatives to traditional models of field experiences? Given that traditional models imply student teaching to be the cornerstone of

preservice teacher preparation, what other configurations of practice development make inherent sense?

- How can field experiences be educative for all involved: preservice teachers, cooperating teachers, university supervisors, and classroom students?
- What activities and exploration of educational concepts are most meaningful and educative in unison with field experiences and at what times during the period or periods of field experience?
- How might varieties of field experience models, which are more appropriate to individual development, be structured and implemented?

Administration and Governance of Field Experiences

It is a must to work with teachers' colleges. . . . They bring an experience and a perception of teaching that is not necessarily present in schools. . . . Teacher education is something that doesn't stop at teachers' college or with the schools. Both [parties] have to see it as an ongoing thing.

ELEMENTARY SCHOOL PRINCIPAL

There is an age-old dispute around teacher preparation about who has what power, where the requirements are fulfilled, and where the monies are allocated. What's said and done here [in the schools] is valid; what the [professors] want to do is valid. It's just that there are conflicting agendas. And ultimately, when it comes to certification [the school] doesn't count for a whole lot. . . . Both places have something important to contribute but as it is, it's really a loggerhead relationship.

ELEMENTARY COOPERATING TEACHER

School districts have a major interest [in preservice teacher education] because they are going to hire the student teachers. The colleges of education have a more thoughtful approach to education. The [government] needs to be involved because they're concerned about the whole system. It doesn't seem to be anyone's single responsibility. It has to be shared.

ELEMENTARY COOPERATING TEACHER

Although the idea that preservice programs can fully prepare teachers for a lifelong career has been pretty much abandoned, in reality that idea is still in the forefront of much talk about practice. School personnel still complain that "the university has not done its job," that new teachers are not fully prepared when they begin teaching. Similarly, first-year teachers lay claims of inadequate preparation against the university. University teacher educators retaliate with an argument for a developmental approach to teacher education, insisting that the preservice program is only the first formal step along a continuum of lifelong growth and that there was never any intention to prepare teachers "fully." Why is there such discrepancy? The noticeable absence of a mutually developed and shared understanding of the goals of preservice programs in general and field experiences in particular and little sense of shared responsibility may provide some explanation.

For the most part, preservice teachers and those in schools perceive the material taught at the university as mainly irrelevant to the "real" world of teaching and schools. The understanding is that theory and practice are distinct entities; the theory learned at the university and the practice residing and experienced in schools have little connection. The problem is systemic. From the university perspective, there is a concern that the activities taking place during field experiences are often too focused on the immediacy of classroom action, narrowly defined, and too technically oriented. Frequently, preservice teachers enter preparation programs with preconceptions that experiences in the field are all that really matter in the learning-to-teach endeavor, that the university component is to be endured but not taken seriously. These preconceived ideas all too often become reinforced in the field by those with whom they interact. Until we begin to think differently about the theory-practice relationship and view teacher education as a lifelong endeavor and shared responsibility, not much is likely to change.

As researchers on school-university partnerships point out (for example, McNay and Cole, 1993a; Sirotnik and Goodlad, 1988; Stallings and Kowalski, 1990; Watson and Fullan, 1991), though fraught with dilemmas and challenges, such collaboration is an idea well worth pursuing. A study of this body of literature would be an important first step for those interested in strengthening links and sharing responsibility for teacher education. As Hathaway (1985) suggests, "The university and the school district are each other's best resources. Between them, school districts and universities cover virtually the whole range of human learning. That we are connected is undeniable. The challenge before us is to realize and build upon the extent, the possibilities, and the necessity of our connection and dependence" (p. 4).

Questions for Consideration

- How can the administration and governance of field experiences promote preservice teachers' inquiry into the following: self in relation to prior experiences? contexts and personnel roles? relationships? self and ongoing professional development?
- What are the institutional and personnel commitments required to secure optimum learning opportunities from field experiences?
- How can schools and experienced teachers become partners in the development, administration, and governance of field experiences?

- How can professional teachers/teacher educators in the field be integrally involved with university-based teacher educators and others, in all stages of the learning-to-teach endeavor?
- How can institutes of teacher education more accurately portray their philosophical positions with regard to the practice of teaching and becoming a teacher, within the context of field experiences, so that personal and professional goals of prospective teachers may be appropriately met?
- How can models of field experience be developed that are not constrained by fiscal and bureaucratic considerations? How and to what extent can the financial costs associated with field experiences (and teacher preparation in general) be shared with the other institutes and agencies involved?
- Who is involved in the actual day-to-day facilitation of field experiences and what are their responsibilities? How are these various roles and responsibilities defined?
- In what ways do field experience sites and practices reflect institutional and hierarchical power structures? How can field experiences reflect more collaborative organizational structures?
- What is the role of preservice teachers in decision making associated with field experiences?

Contexts for Field Experiences

There are benefits to spending one's entire student teaching experience in one school. The continuity of the experience far outweighs any benefits of a variety of exposure. If student teachers could gain greater confidence from feeling part of a system, they would feel better prepared for their first year of teaching. They would know better how a system worked and could then apply their knowledge and experience to whatever situation they found themselves in the first year. No practice teaching situation can duplicate an actual teaching situation when you are in control of your own class but perhaps this idea would come close. The need for variety could perhaps be met by short visits and observations in other schools.

ELEMENTARY COOPERATING TEACHER

[By adopting a whole school approach to the practicum in our school] we have opened the doors to how adults . . . learn and grow and develop. . . . This [whole school approach] has given [the staff] one more impetus to look at themselves.

ELEMENTARY PRINCIPAL

Professional development school sites can offer teachers in preparation a crucial mix of experiences that revolves around a community bringing its energies to bear on creatively resolving the problems of the school and of students' learning. This may be schools at their very best—at least as we know them. . . . The sheer numbers of students [of teaching] in the building provides opportunities for support and learning. . . . But, while there may be support in numbers, the flip side of the coin rests on the potential for preservice teachers to get lost in the maze and hive of activity.

SECONDARY COOPERATING TEACHER AT A PROFESSIONAL DEVELOPMENT SCHOOL

Structured experiences in the field are a vital part of learning to teach. But as Dewey (1938) reminds us, "It is not enough to insist upon the necessity of experience, nor even of activity in experience. Everything depends upon the *quality* of the experience which is had. The quality of the experience has two aspects. There is an immediate agreeableness or disagreeableness, and there is its influence upon later experiences" (p. 27). A primary influence on the quality of the experience is the context in which the experience takes place.

Although most structured field experiences are situated in traditional public or private school settings, opportunities for experiences in alternative settings are also available. The process of professional development can be enhanced by attention to the possibilities afforded by different contexts of field experience: community recreation centers; tutoring and remedial learning centers; outdoor education sites; recreation sites; vacation, special interest, and sports camps; cross-cultural settings in other countries or other regions of the country (including unfamiliar urban or rural settings); churches and religion classes; child-care facilities; community volunteer or action sites; and individual and group instruction in classes for fine and performing arts. These are but some of the myriad possibilities for structured field experiences apart from and in addition to formal schools. It may be appropriate to include alternative placements as part of a program's field experience component.

As some researchers point out (for example, Feiman-Nemser and Buchmann, 1987; Guyton and McIntyre, 1990; Hoy and Woolfolk, 1989; Taylor, Boris, and La Rocque, 1992; Zeichner, 1990), in spite of the significance of field experience, little attention has been given to the contexts in which preservice teachers are placed. Classrooms and schools generally not conducive to facilitating preservice teachers' growth (Copeland, 1981, 1986; Watts, 1987) or at odds with the goals and orientations of particular preservice teacher preparation programs (Goodman, 1983; Zeichner and Liston, 1987) are for a variety of reasons not uncommon field placement sites. Zeichner (1992) identifies conceptual and structural obstacles to preservice teacher learning in the practicum: inappropriate conceptions of reflective practice; neglect of teachers' practical theories, values underlying educational practice, and the social conditions of schools; placements in individual classrooms rather than whole schools; inadequate supervisory practices; and a lack of placement in multicultural settings. Taken together, contextual factors represent a large proportion of these obstacles to educative field experiences.

In miseducative settings, preservice teachers are likely to experience confusion, disillusionment, difficulty, and even failure (for example, Knowles and Hoefler, 1989) and, in many cases, practice compliance in order to achieve a passing grade (for example, Feiman-Nemser and Buchmann, 1987). The placement of preservice teachers in field settings is a persistent problem. Decisions about placement within settings are often based more on political criteria than on criteria related to either the quality of experience for individuals involved or long-term implications related to placement issues (Cole and Sorrill, 1992; Howey, 1977). Preservice teachers who do have educative experiences often do so more by good luck than good planning. Recent attention to field experience contexts, however, is encouraging and holds promise for improving the experience. There has been attention to criteria and process of site selection and to the identification and preparation of those most directly involved in facilitating preservice teachers' learning in the field; consideration of alternative forms of placement (for example, placement of cohorts of preservice teachers in a school community or classroom rather than the more traditional one-one placement of a preservice teacher in a classroom with an experienced teacher); and attention to the curriculum of field experiences.

The professional development school concept and the "whole school approach" to field experiences, both enjoying recent popularity, hold particular promise as well. Studies of various professional development school models (for example, Clarke and La Londe, 1992; McNay and Cole, 1993b; Stallings and Kowalski, 1990; Winitzky, Stoddard, and O'Keefe, 1992) highlight opportunities for preservice teachers to develop affinity, affiliation, and professional identity; to get a better sense of the complexities of schools, teaching, and being a teacher; to "come close" to the realities of teaching; and to develop a more solid foundation for ongoing development. Schools reflecting the real complexity and diversity of modern-day classrooms and society at large hold promise as sites for teacher preparation. Not only do these contexts represent the reality of classroom and school life, they also provide contexts for preservice teachers to engage in reflection and discussion organized around critical issues in education. Thus, such contexts can help to overcome the kinds of obstacles noted by Zeichner (1992).

Questions for Consideration

- How can the contexts for field experiences promote preservice teachers' inquiry into the following: self in relation to prior experiences? contexts and personnel roles? relationships? self and ongoing professional development?
- What sites are appropriate for field experiences? What are the merits of particular kinds of sites? How might the incorporation of different kinds of field sites be facilitated?
- What criteria are appropriate for selection of placement sites?

- How can field experiences that focus on the development of practice be designed to be more collaborative and reflective of teaching contexts that represent innovative and progressive communities of learners?
- To what extent will programs and preservice teachers benefit by participation in exemplary schools/sites whose mission includes the preparation of teachers? What are the advantages and disadvantages of such sites?
- How can issues of selection be addressed so that teacher education and development, and not politics, are central to decision making?

Preparation for Field Experiences

What seems amazing is the hit-and-miss way in which [cooperating] teachers are selected [for their role]. . . . Poor student teachers! It's a wonder the system is as successful as it is.

ELEMENTARY COOPERATING TEACHER

[To prepare for my role as a cooperating teacher] I had to go completely by my own experience as a student teacher. Thank goodness it was still quite clear in my mind, and thank goodness I had some good cooperating teachers. I tried to model myself after them. There need to be some guidelines; there needs to be a focus. . . . We need more assistance to be prepared to handle many areas of concern: topics stressed at the university; writing evaluations; giving positive feedback during counseling; and staying on top of the latest research.

ELEMENTARY COOPERATING TEACHER

If we change things [for the better], the student teachers who are becoming new teachers are going to have a good attitude [toward field experiences] and will want to become cooperating teachers themselves when they have some experience. The problems [associated with field experiences] will take care of themselves in the long run. The new teachers will say, "I remember how well things worked for me when I was a student. I want to get involved myself."

ELEMENTARY COOPERATING TEACHER

The teachers who have the [preservice teachers] are often in the dark about what's expected of them. We need mechanisms to bring both groups [school and university personnel] together in planning and thinking.

ELEMENTARY SCHOOL PRINCIPAL

Whether it is a field-based teacher education model where experience in the field is the core of the overall program or a professional development school model where special attention is given to the quality of particular field experiences, neither will significantly improve the quality of field experiences unless sufficient attention is paid to preparing the context in advance both for the sites for field experiences and for the persons within those sites who will work with the preservice teachers. Preparing the context means opening the lines of communication between schools of education and elementary and secondary schools so that dialogue can take place about the purpose of field experiences and the many benefits to be derived from a collaborative approach to them, how field experiences might be designed so that they are meaningful and beneficial to all involved, and about the administrative or procedural aspects of field experiences that so often stand in the way of improvement. Many other issues need to be addressed in preparation for field experiences as well.

In almost any study of field experiences, the cooperating teacher is involved or implicated in some way. Studies of cooperating and preservice teacher relationships, preservice teachers' concerns, supervisory practices, the role of the cooperating teacher as teacher educator, influences of cooperating teachers on preservice teachers' development, and studies addressing issues related to selection, preparation, and support of cooperating teachers all point to a need for more and better attention to the role of the cooperating teacher. As Feiman-Nemser and Buchmann (1987) observe in an exploration of the question, "When is student teaching teacher education?"—"The job of cooperating teachers is to talk aloud about what they do and why, to demonstrate how to probe and extend student thinking, to alert student teachers to interpret signs of understanding and confusion in pupils, to stimulate student teachers to talk about their reasons for decisions and actions and the difficulties inherent to finding out what pupils know and what they need to learn" (p. 272).

But as they and many other researchers (including Boydell, 1991; Cole and Sorrill, 1992; Grimmett and Ratzlaff, 1986; Guyton and McIntyre, 1990; Hoy and Woolfolk, 1989) acknowledge, in order for cooperating teachers to take their role as teacher educators seriously, there has to be an emphasis on preparation and support for these individuals. Cooperating teachers typically receive little or no preparation for their role in field experiences and little or no recognition and support for their involvement; consequently, they rely heavily on their own experiences as student teachers and attempt to model themselves on what they consider to be "good" cooperating teachers (Cole and Sorrill, 1992).

Thus far, the focus has been on preparing the contexts into which preservice teachers are placed for their field experiences. Equally important is preparation of preservice teachers themselves for their reentry to schools and classrooms as developing professionals. Discussions of the philosophies that underpin programs are likely to aid preservice teachers, as are explanations of the pedagogy or curriculum for field experiences (such as we have laid out in this chapter). Attention to the processes in place to facilitate preservice teachers' development are likely to help prospective teachers in their focus and security, making for potentially more productive experiences. Given that the focus we delineate rests in an inquiry framework, attention to developing preservice teachers' expertise with the tools of inquiry and reflection *before* they enter placement sites is of utmost importance. Preservice teachers will likely greatly benefit from discussions about their expectations of and for field experiences, the ways various expectations of field experiences are realized or find resolution, some of their fantasies and fears about teaching, aspects of the "realities" of working in schools and classrooms, and the contexts into which they are about to be placed. Finally, attention to the same kinds of issues that pertain to beginning teachers entering the field (see the section "Inquiry into Self and Ongoing Professional Development") is highly appropriate.

Questions for Consideration

- How can preparation activities for field experiences promote preservice teachers' inquiry into the following: self in relation to prior experiences? contexts and personnel roles? relationships? self and ongoing professional development?
- What forms of preparation and support are required for all personnel involved in field experiences: preservice teachers, cooperating teachers, school administrators and other school personnel, university supervisors?
- What time and resource investments are required for the creation of productive field experience sites?

Supervision and Evaluation of Field Experiences

When I was practice teaching I had some wonderful cooperating teachers. I never felt I was being evaluated. [My cooperating teacher] was somebody to bounce off ideas and give feedback. I discovered things for myself by just talking about them.

FIRST-YEAR ELEMENTARY TEACHER

The system is almost too hard on student teachers because we do most of our evaluating from the back of the room near the beginning of their stint when they're most nervous, when they're feeling most ill at ease and not really comfortable with the classroom atmosphere. How can we alleviate that sort of thing? How can we get preservice teachers more involved in their evaluation?

ELEMENTARY COOPERATING TEACHER

The process that we have in place now puts too much emphasis on evaluation. Student teachers need to be evaluated but the process is too regimented and too structured. We need to consider the different rates at which these new teachers bloom and flourish. We also need to put more responsibility on the shoulders of the student teachers themselves. This is where reflective teaching has to begin.

UNIVERSITY SUPERVISOR

I liked that I had a major say in the evaluation of my progress. I think [the director of field experiences] is specifically trying to model [best] practice. But my [two] cooperating teachers didn't think that process was appropriate. They wanted to evaluate me on their criteria (which is similar to how they're evaluated . . . because the principal has all the power). They said, "[Persons] learning to be teachers cannot evaluate their own practice because they're not the experts."

SECONDARY PRESERVICE TEACHER

Supervision from the [university person] was great because it also overlapped with a regular weekly seminar [in which] we covered all the problems we experienced in the classroom. The cooperating teacher was OK, except that she kept insisting that I do things her way. There was no opportunity for me to [develop] independent practice. Except I did do things my way on occasion and she really came down hard on me in the [final] evaluation. I felt like the meat in the sandwich—between the supervisor and the cooperating teacher.

SECONDARY PRESERVICE TEACHER

The evaluation process troubled me midway through student teaching. I got annoyed when [university] supervisors came unannounced at a few routine and uninspired moments. I wanted them to see me at the times when I thought I was doing my best. The other student teachers complained too. . . . Then one of the group pointed out, "But why should they only see us when we are at our best?"

SECONDARY PRESERVICE TEACHER

The extent and quality of one's learning from field experiences depends in large part on attitudes and practices related to guidance and supervision. The way in which cooperating teachers, university supervisors, and preservice teachers work together to facilitate preservice teachers' learning during field experiences is influenced by factors such as role perceptions, goals, expectations, attitudes, and preparation for providing and accepting guidance and direction.

Guyton and McIntyre (1990) cite lack of preparation for supervision as one of the three main problems of field experiences (the other two main areas identified were lack of interpersonal and interinstitutional communication, and issues related to preservice teachers' skills, behavior, and attitudes). They summarize the research on formal supervision in this way: "[Preservice teacher-cooperating teacher] conferences are dominated by cooperating teachers and student teachers take a passive role. Conferences involve low levels of thinking: descriptions and direction-giving interactions predominate. Analysis and reflection on teaching are not common; the substantive issues of conferences tend to focus on teaching techniques, classroom management, and pupil characteristics. Craft and experiential knowledge and efficiency are rationales for most recommendations" (p. 525).

Feiman-Nemser and Buchmann (1987) add, "For student teaching to be teacher education, it must go beyond survival or extend practice in the outward forms of teaching to sort out appropriate from inappropriate lessons of experience. Well-meaning praises from cooperating teachers, coupled with a focus on management, fixes the attention of student teachers in the wrong direction" (p. 272).

It is not surprising that field experiences do not always turn out to be the learning opportunity they are intended or expected to be. Preservice teachers often experience confusion and frustration as a result of receiving inadequate or unhelpful feedback on their teaching (Feiman-Nemser and Buchmann, 1987; Griffin and others, 1983; Richardson-Koehler, 1988) or dissatisfaction with the cooperating teachers' approach to supervision (MacKinnon, 1989). Those who experience least stress and frustration and most overall satisfaction with their field experience tend to work in partnership with their cooperating teachers (MacKinnon, 1989).

Reconceptualizing the university supervisor's role (as suggested earlier) from that of formal supervision in the classroom to supervising the *process* of student teaching would be an important step toward more educative field experiences. Such a shift would reorient the university supervisor's role from supervision of actual practice to preparation of context and ongoing facilitation of professional development. It would also help to address the difficulties associated with the traditional conception of the university supervisor's role as identified by Richardson-Koehler (1988): limited amount of time in field sites; lack of time to build trust and establish rapport within the field experience context; awkwardness associated with discussing with preservice teachers anything that might seem like a criticism of the cooperating teacher's practices; and an imbalance, perceived by the cooperating and preservice teachers, in the amount of time and effort devoted to field experiences by triad members.

A reconceptualized role for university supervisors would allow closer attention to the links between field experiences and the formal aspects of the preparation program, contexts for developing emerging practice, mutual coherence of perspectives, and ways of facilitating and supporting preservice teacher development. Thus, we see university supervisors of the future placing less emphasis on evaluation and more emphasis on preparation of both the narrow and broad contexts associated with preservice teachers' learning from field experiences.

Boydell (1991) asserts that a focus on the reconceptualization of supervisory roles and preparation of university and school personnel for those roles has the potential to strengthen the traditionally weak links between school and university agenda for field experiences. We would add a role for preservice teachers and stress the importance of negotiating and developing substantial and productive working relationships focused less on the *evaluation* of practice and more on the *development* of practice.

Questions for Consideration

- How can supervision and evaluation of field experiences promote preservice teachers' inquiry into the following: self in relation to prior experiences? contexts and personnel roles? relationships? self and ongoing professional development?
- How can evaluation of field experiences and associated processes foster professional development?
- How can appropriate assistance and support systems be developed and provided to preservice teachers during field experiences? What are appropriate and optimal levels of assistance and support?
- How should field experience activities be sequenced and evaluated? How is meaning attached to these activities and concepts? To what extent (if at all) should the evaluation of field experiences be the major gatekeeper to teacher certification and the teaching profession?
- What provisions can be made to assist preservice teachers who experience failure, extreme difficulty, or other forms of marginality during field experiences?

Elements and Conditions for Experiential Learning

The experiential learning cycle is central in our conceptions of field experiences and their implementation (and to becoming a teacher). As we mentioned at the beginning of the chapter, when making known our assumptions we draw on principles of experiential learning that rest in the work of Dewey (1938) and Kolb (1984). Figure 26.3 lays out the elements of the experiential learning cycle. The basis for learning rests in the personal experience and practice of the learner. From and during that experience, information gathering and documentation occur that aid the learner in making critical reflections on the experience so that informed action or practice can eventually occur.

The value of experiential learning is predicated upon particular conditions and qualities—of the learner, the learning environment, and those facilitating the learning. Important to consider are the nature of the focus of the experience, including its self-directed nature; the preparation of the learner for the experience, as well as those in the learning environment; the focus, especially that it is appropriate for the learner and for those expected to facilitate the process; the appropriateness of the context; the level of support and feedback received by the learner, the expectation being that both are high and appropriate for the tasks at

FIGURE 26.3. EXPERIENTIAL LEARNING FROM FIELD EXPERIENCES.

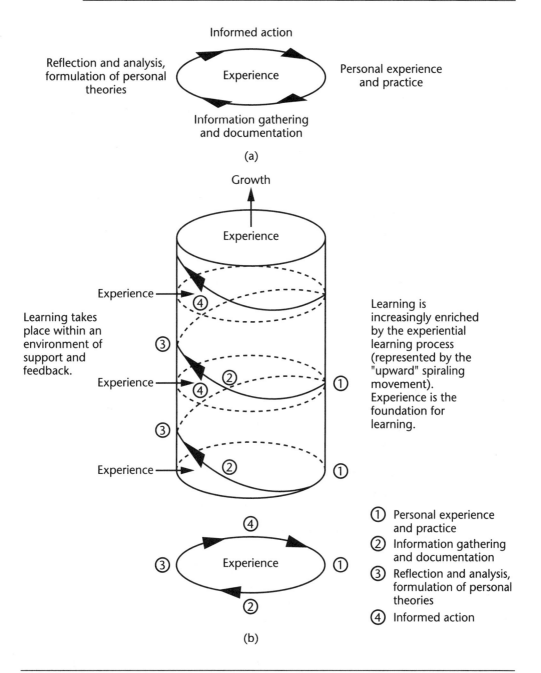

Source: Adapted from Knowles and Cole with Presswood, 1994.

hand and the nature of the experience; and the quality of experience associated with each element of the cycle.

Conclusion

In order for teacher education to be substantively and systemically improved, there must be acknowledgment of the complex nature of the knowledge informing teacher development and shared responsibility for facilitating that development. How these concepts are operationalized, however, is as individual and contextual as teaching itself. In this chapter, we did not set out to provide definitive answers, for there are none that are universally appropriate; rather, we wanted to explore curricular and programmatic elements of field experiences and raise for consideration and discussion pertinent questions and issues. It was our intention to encourage those involved in the organization, design, and conduct of field experiences to reconsider that component of teacher education in the context of the overall program and process of teacher development. If we have engendered frustration by describing what is and what could be without suggesting how to get there, then we have achieved our goal. We invite university teacher educators to consider what we, and the others whose voices are represented here, have to say about field experiences, especially in light of current practices.

> We can expect little change in the present situation [in teacher education] without a coherent, integrated, and powerful preservice program, without shared vision of the goals of both didactic learning and field experiences within that program, without carefully selected and trained university supervisors and cooperating teachers, without a curriculum (explicit and implicit) for the field experiences that gradually encourages self-direction, reflection, and analysis while developing technical competence, without a university context that rewards high-quality supervision, without a school placement that supports the goals and procedures of the preservice program, and without the constant monitoring of the entire process to determine what is really happening in the educational life of the preservice teacher [Hoy and Woolfolk, 1989, pp. 124–125].

Notes

1. The quotations from practitioners, including preservice teachers, are taken from information gathered in several research projects that are part of an ongoing program of qualitative research on learning to teach. Elements of these projects are represented in, for example, Cole (1990, 1991a, 1991b, 1992), Cole and Knowles (1992, 1993), Knowles (1988, 1992, 1994), Knowles and Cole with Presswood (1994), Knowles and Holt-Reynolds (1991), Knowles, Skrobola, and Coolican (1995), and Sudzina and Knowles (1993).

2.   For a comprehensive sense of the work conducted in this area, see literature reviews conducted by Zeichner and Gore (1990) and Kagan (1992), for example, and ongoing work by Clandinin and Connelly (for example, Clandinin, 1986; Connelly and Clandinin, 1988), Butt and Raymond (for example, Butt and Raymond, 1987; Butt, Raymond, McCue, and Yamagashi, 1992), Goodson (for example, Ball and Goodson, 1985; Goodson and Walker, 1991; Goodson, 1992; Goodson and Cole, 1994), and Knowles (1988, 1992, 1994).

3.   For a comprehensive discussion of schools as workplaces and how preservice teachers are socialized into such cultures, see Zeichner and Gore, 1990.

4.   See Knowles and Cole with Presswood (1984) for a fuller explanation of some of these tools.

References

Aitken, J. L., and Mildon, D. (1991). "The dynamic of personal knowledge and teacher education." *Curriculum Inquiry, 21,* 141–162.

Alverman, D. (1981). "The possible value of dissonance in student teaching experiences." *Journal of Teacher Education, 32*(3), 24–25.

Applegate, J. H., and Lasley, T. J. (1982). "Cooperating teachers' problems with preservice field experience students." *Journal of Teacher Education, 33*(2), 15–18.

Applegate, J. H., and Lasley, T. J. (1984). "What cooperating teachers expect from preservice field experience teachers." *Teacher Education, 24,* 70–82.

Ball, S. J., and Goodson, I. F. (eds.) (1985). *Teachers' lives and careers.* London: Falmer Press.

Barone, T. E. (1992). "A narrative of enhanced professionalism: Educational researchers and popular storybooks about school people." *Educational Researcher, 21*(8), 15–24.

Becher, R., and Ade, W. (1982). "The relationship of field placement characteristics and students' potential field performance abilities to clinical experience performance ratings." *Journal of Teacher Education, 33*(2), 24–30.

Beynon, C. (1991). "Understanding the role of the cooperating teacher." Faculty of Education, University of Western Ontario (unpublished manuscript).

Bissex, G. L., and Bullock, R. H. (1987). *Seeing for ourselves.* Portsmouth, N.H.: Heinemann Educational Books.

Book, C. L., Beyers, J., and Freeman, D. (1983). "Student expectations and teacher education traditions with which we can and cannot live." *Journal of Teacher Education, 34*(1), 9–13.

Borko, H. (1989). "Research on learning to teach: Implications for graduate teacher preparation." In A. E. Woolfolk (ed.), *Research perspectives on the graduate preparation of teachers.* Englewood Cliffs, N.J.: Prentice Hall.

Boydell, D. (1991). "Issues in teaching practice supervision research: A review of the literature." In L. G. Katz (ed.), *Advances in teacher education,* Vol. 4. Norwood, N.J.: Ablex.

Brause, R. S., and Smayher, J. S. (1991). *Search and re-search: What the inquiring teacher needs to know.* London: Falmer Press.

Britzman, D. P. (1991). *Practice makes practice: A critical study of learning to teach.* Albany: State University of New York Press.

Bruckerhoff, C. E. (1991). *Between classes: Faculty life at Truman High.* New York: Teachers College Press.

Buchmann, M. (1984). "The use of research knowledge in teacher education and teaching." *American Journal of Education, 92*(4), 421–439.

Bullough, R. V., Jr. (1989). *First-year teacher: A case study.* New York: Teachers College Press.

Bullough, R. V., Jr. (1991). "Exploring personal teaching metaphors in preservice teacher education." *Journal of Teacher Education, 42*(1), 43–51.

Bullough, R. V., Jr., and Knowles, J. G. (1990). "Becoming a teacher: Struggles of a second-career beginning teacher." *International Journal of Qualitative Studies in Education, 3*(2), 101–112.

Bullough, R. V., Jr., Knowles, J. G., and Crow, N. A. (1991). *Emerging as a teacher.* New York: Routledge & Kegan Paul.

Butt, R. F., and Raymond, D. (1987). "Arguments for using qualitative approaches in understanding teacher thinking: The case for biography." *Journal for Curriculum Theorizing, 7*(2), 62–93.

Butt, R. F., Raymond, D., McCue, G., and Yamagashi, L. (1992). "Collaborative autobiography and the teacher's voice." In I. F. Goodson (ed.), *Studying teachers' lives.* New York: Routledge & Kegan Paul.

Calderhead, J., and Gates, P. (eds.) (1993). *Conceptualizing reflection in teacher development.* London: Falmer Press.

Campbell, L. P., and Williamson, J. A. (1983). "Supervising the student teacher: What is really involved?" *National Association of Secondary School Principals Bulletin, 67*(465), 77–79.

Carter, K., and Doyle, W. (1989). "Classroom research as a resource for the graduate preparation of teachers." In A. E. Woolfolk (ed.), *Research perspectives on the graduate preparation of teachers.* Englewood Cliffs, N.J.: Prentice Hall.

Chester, M. D. (1991). "Changes in attitudes within first-year teachers in urban schools." Paper presented at the annual meeting of the American Educational Research Association, Chicago.

Clandinin, D. J. (1986). *Classroom practice: Teacher images in action.* London: Falmer Press.

Clandinin, D. J., Davies, A., Hogan, P., and Kennard, B. (1993). *Learning to teach, teaching to learn.* New York: Teachers College Press.

Clarke, R. J., and La Londe, D. E. (1992). "A case for department-based professional development sites for secondary teacher education." *Journal of Teacher Education, 43*(1), 35–41.

Cochran-Smith, M., and Lytle, S. L. (1993). *Inside/outside: Teacher research and knowledge.* New York: Teachers College Press.

Cohen, R. M. (1991). *A lifetime of teaching: Portraits of five veteran high school teachers.* New York: Teachers College Press.

Cole, A. L. (1990). "Personal theories of teaching: Development in the formative years." *Alberta Journal of Educational Research, 36*(3), 203–222.

Cole, A. L. (1991a). "Four schools, four ways of doing things: A participatory approach to the development of school-based induction programs." Paper presented at the annual conference of the Canadian Society for the Study of Education, Kingston, Ontario.

Cole, A. L. (1991b). "Relationships in the workplace: Doing what comes naturally?" *Teaching and Teacher Education, 7*(5–6), 415–426.

Cole, A. L. (1992). "Teacher development in the workplace: Rethinking the appropriation of professional relationships." *Teachers College Record, 94*(2), 375–381.

Cole, A. L., and Knowles, J. G. (1992). "Beginning teachers talk: Who listens? Who learns?" Paper presented at the annual conference of the Canadian Society for the Study of Education, Charlottetown, Prince Edward Island.

Cole, A. L., and Knowles, J. G. (1993). "Shattered images: Understanding expectations and realities in field experiences." *Teaching and Teacher Education, 9*(516), 457–471.

Cole, A. L., and McNay, M. (1989). "Induction programs in Ontario schools: Raising questions about preservice programs and practica." *Education Canada, 29*(2), 5–9, 43.

Cole, A. L., and McNay, M. (1993). "Reflections on an attempt at collaboration in a faculty/school board project." *Educational Administration and Foundations, 8*(2), 65–71.

Cole, A. L., and Sorrill, P. W. (1992). "Being an associate teacher: A feather in one's cap?" *Education Canada, 32*(3), 40–48.

Comer, J. P. (1988). "Educating poor minority children." *Scientific American, 259*(5), 42–48.

Connelly, F. M., and Clandinin, D. J. (1988). *Teachers as curriculum planners: Narratives of experience.* New York: Teachers College Press.

Cooper, A., Beare, P., and Thorman, J. (1990). "Preparing teachers for diversity: A comparison of student teaching experiences in Minnesota and South Texas." *Action in Teacher Education, 12*(3), 1–4.

Copeland, W. D. (1981). "Clinical experiences in the education of teachers." *Journal of Education for Teaching, 7*(1), 3–16.

Copeland, W. D. (1986). "The RITE framework for teacher education: Preservice applications." In J. V. Hoffman and S. A. Edwards (eds.), *Reality and reform in teacher education.* New York: Random House.

Crow, N. A. (1987a). "Preservice teachers' biography: A case study." Paper presented at the annual meeting of the Educational Research Association, Washington, D.C.

Crow, N. A. (1987b). "Socialization within a teacher education program." University of Utah (unpublished doctoral dissertation).

Cruickshank, D. R. (1987). *Reflective teaching: The preparation of students of teaching.* Reston, Va.: Association of Teacher Educators.

Cummins, J. (1986). "Empowering minority students: A framework for intervention." *Harvard Educational Review, 56*(1), 18–36.

Dewey, J. (1938). *Experience and education.* New York: Macmillan.

Duckworth, E. (1986). "Teaching as research." *Harvard Educational Review, 56*(4), 481–95.

Emans, R. (1983). "Implementing the knowledge base: Redesigning the function of cooperating teachers and college supervisors." *Journal of Teacher Education, 34*(3), 14–18.

Feiman-Nemser, S. (1983). "Learning to teach." In L. S. Shulman and G. Sykes (eds.), *Handbook of teaching and policy.* White Plains, N.Y.: Longman.

Feiman-Nemser, S. (1990). "Teacher preparation: Structural and conceptual alternatives." In W. R. Houston (ed.), *Handbook of research on teacher education.* New York: Macmillan.

Feiman-Nemser, S., and Buchmann, M. (1987). "When is student teaching teacher education?" *Teaching and Teacher Education, 3*(4), 255–273.

Feiman-Nemser, S., and Floden, R. E. (1986). "The cultures of teaching." In M. C. Wittrock (ed.), *Handbook of research on teaching.* (3rd ed.). New York: Macmillan.

Floden, R. E., and Buchmann, M. (1990). "Philosophical inquiry in teacher education." In W. R. Houston (ed.), *Handbook for research on teacher education.* New York: Macmillan.

Florio-Ruane, S., and Lensmire, T. J. (1990). "Transforming future teachers' ideas about writing instruction." *Journal of Curriculum Studies, 22,* 277–289.

Freedman, S. G. (1990). *Small victories: The real world of a teacher, her students, and their high school.* New York: HarperCollins.

Friebus, R. (1977). "Agents of socialization involved in student teaching." *Journal of Educational Research, 70,* 263–268.

Funk, E. F., Hoffman, J. L., Keithley, A. M., and Long, B. E. (1982). "Student teaching programs: Feedback from supervising teachers." *Clearing House, 55,* 319–321.

Gitlin, A., and Teitelbaum, K. (1983). "Linking theory and practice: The use of ethnographic methodology by prospective teachers." *Journal of Education for Teaching, 9*(3), 225–234.

Gomez, M. L., and Comeaux, M. A. (1990). *Start with the stone, not with the hole: Matching novices' needs with appropriate programs of induction.* East Lansing, Mich.: National Center for Research on Teacher Education. (ED 327541).

Goodlad, J. I. (1990). *Teachers for our nation's schools.* San Francisco: Jossey-Bass.

Goodman, J. (1983). "The seminar's role in the education of student teachers: A case study." *Journal of Teacher Education, 34*(3), 44–49.

Goodman, J. (1988). "Constructing a practical philosophy of teaching: A study of preservice teachers' professional perspectives." *Teaching and Teacher Education, 4*(2), 121–137.

Goodson, I. F. (ed.) (1992). *Studying teachers' lives.* New York: Routledge & Kegan Paul.

Goodson, I. F., and Cole, A. L. (1994). "Exploring the teacher's professional knowledge: Constructing identity and community." *Teacher Education Quarterly, 21*(1), 85–105.

Goodson, I. F., and Walker, R. (1991). *Biography, identity and schooling.* London: Falmer Press.

Goswami, D., and Stillman, P. R. (1987). *Reclaiming the classroom.* Portsmouth, N.H.: Boynton Cook.

Grant, C. A., and Secada, W. G. (1990). "Preparing teachers for diversity." In W. R. Houston (ed.), *Handbook of research on teacher education.* New York: Macmillan.

Griffin, G. A., and others (1983). *Clinical preservice teacher education: Final report of a descriptive study.* Austin: Research and Development Center for Teacher Education, University of Texas.

Grimmett, P. P., and Ratzlaff, H. C. (1986). "Expectations for the cooperating teacher role." *Journal of Teacher Education, 37*(6), 41–50.

Guillaume, A. M., and Rudney, G. L. (1991). "Changes in student teacher concerns: Growth toward independence." Paper presented at the annual meeting of the American Educational Research Association, Chicago.

Gunstone, R., and Northfield, J. (1987). "Constructivist views of teacher education." Paper presented at the annual conference of the South Pacific Association of Teacher Education, Ballart, Victoria.

Guyton, E., and McIntyre, D. J. (1990). "Student teaching and school experiences." In W. R. Houston (ed.), *Handbook of research on teacher education.* New York: Macmillan.

Hathaway, W. E. (1985). "Models of school-university collaboration: National and local perspectives on collaborations that work." Paper presented at the annual meeting of the American Educational Research Association, Chicago. (ED 253 973).

Hollingsworth, S. (1989). "Prior beliefs and cognitive change in learning to teach." *American Educational Research Journal, 26*(2), 160–189.

Holmes Group (1986). *Tomorrow's teachers.* East Lansing, Mich.: Holmes Group.

Holmes Group (1990). *Tomorrow's schools: Principles for the design of professional development schools.* East Lansing, Mich.: Holmes Group.

Holt-Reynolds, D. (1994). "When agreeing with the professor is bad news for preservice teacher educators: Jeanene, her personal history, and coursework." *Teacher Education Quarterly, 21*(1), 13–35.

Howey, K. R. (1977). "Preservice teacher education: Lost in the shuffle?" *Journal of Teacher Education, 28*, 26–28.

Hoy, W. K., and Woolfolk, A. E. (1989). "Supervising student teachers." In A. E. Woolfolk (ed.), *Research perspectives on the graduate preparation of teachers.* Englewood Cliffs, N.J.: Prentice Hall.

Jackson, P. W. (1990). *Life in classrooms.* (Rev. ed.). New York: Teachers College Press.

Johnson, S. M. (1990). *Teachers at work: Achieving success in our schools.* New York: Basic Books.

Joseph, P. B., and Burnaford, G. E. (eds.) (1994). *Images of schoolteachers in twentieth-century America: Paragons, polarities, complexities.* New York: St. Martin's Press.

Kagan, D. M. (1992). "Professional growth among preservice and beginning teachers." *Review of Educational Research, 62*(2), 129–169.

Kane, P. R. (ed.) (1991). *The first year of teaching: Real-world stories from America's teachers.* New York: Teachers College Press.

Kidder, T. (1989). *Among schoolchildren.* Boston: Houghton Mifflin.

Kilbourne, B., and Roberts, G. (1991). "May's first year: Conversations with a mentor." *Teachers College Record, 93*(2), 252–264.

Kincheloe, J. L. (1991). *Teachers as researchers: Qualitative inquiry as a path to empowerment.* London: Falmer Press.

Knowles, J. G. (1988). "A beginning English teacher's experience: Reflections on becoming a teacher." *Language Arts, 65*(7), 702–712.

Knowles, J. G. (1992). "Models for understanding preservice and beginning teachers' biographies: Illustrations from case studies." In I. F. Goodson (ed.), *Studying teachers' lives.* New York: Routledge & Kegan Paul.

Knowles, J. G. (1993). "Life-history accounts as mirrors: A practical avenue for the conceptualization of reflection in teacher education." In J. Calderhead and P. Gates (eds.), *Conceptualizing reflection in teacher development.* London: Falmer Press.

Knowles, J. G. (1994). "Metaphors as windows on a personal history: A beginning teacher's experience." *Teacher Education Quarterly, 21*(7), 37–66.

Knowles, J. G., and Cole, A. L., with Presswood, C. S. (1994). *Through preservice teachers' eyes: Exploring field experiences through narrative and inquiry.* New York: Macmillan.

Knowles, J. G., and Hoefler, V. B. (1989). "The student teacher who wouldn't go away: Learning from failure." *Journal of Experiential Education, 12*(2), 14–21.

Knowles, J. G., and Holt-Reynolds, D. (1991). "Shaping pedagogies through personal histories in preservice teacher education." *Teachers College Record, 93*(1), 89–113.

Knowles, J. G., Skrobola, N., and Coolican, M. (1995). "We watched them 'fail': University supervisors' perceptions of preservice teachers who 'failed' student teaching." *Journal of Qualitative Studies in Education, 8* (2).

Koehler, V. (1984). "University supervision of student teaching." Paper presented at the annual meeting of the American Educational Research Association.

Kolb, D. A. (1984). *Experiential learning.* Englewood Cliffs, N.J.: Prentice Hall.

Lanier, J. E., and Little, J. W. (1986). "Research on teacher education." In M. C. Wittrock (ed.), *Handbook of research on teaching.* New York: Macmillan.

Larke, P. J. (1990). "Cultural diversity awareness inventory: Assessing the sensitivity of preservice teachers." *Action in Teacher Education, 12*(3), 23–29.

Larke, P. J., Wiseman, D., and Bradley, C. (1990). "The minority mentorship project: Changing attitudes of preservice teachers for diverse classrooms." *Action in Teacher Education, 12*(3), 5–11.

Lasley, T. J., and Watras, J. (1991). "Teacher education at the crossroads." In L. G. Katz and J. D. Raths (eds.), *Advances in teacher education.* Norwood, N.J.: Ablex.

Lieberman, A., and Miller, L. (1992). *Teachers: Their world and their work.* New York: Teachers College Press.

Liston, D. P., and Zeichner, K. M. (1990). "Teacher education and the social context of schooling: Issues for curriculum development." *American Educational Research Journal, 27,* 610–638.

Little, J. W., and McLaughlin, M. (1993). *Teachers' work: Individuals, colleagues, and contexts.* New York: Teachers College Press.

Lortie, D. C. (1975). *Schoolteacher: A sociological study.* Chicago: University of Chicago Press.

McDaniel, J. E. (1991). "Close encounters: How do student teachers make sense of the social foundations?" Paper presented at the annual meeting of the American Educational Research Association, Chicago.

MacKinnon, J. D. (1989). "Living with conformity in student teaching." *Alberta Journal of Educational Research, 35*(1), 2–19.

McLaren, P. (1986). *Schooling as a ritual performance: Towards a political economy of educational symbols and gestures.* London: Routledge & Kegan Paul.

McNay, M., and Cole, A. L. (1993a). "Lessons from a faculty and school board attempt at collaboration in teacher education." *Educational Administration and Foundations, 8*(2), 64–71.

McNay, M., and Cole, A. L. (1993b). "A whole school approach to the practicum." *McGill Journal of Education, 28*(1), 115–131.

Mcneely, S. R., and Mertz, N. T. (1990). "Cognitive constructs of preservice teachers: Research on how student teachers think about teaching." Paper presented at the annual meeting of the American Educational Research Association, Boston.

Marso, R. N., and Pigge, F. L. (1987). "Differences between self-perceived job expectations and job realities of beginning teachers." *Journal of Teacher Education, 38*(6), 53–56.

Morris, J. E., and Morris, G. W. (1980). "Stress in student teaching." *Action in Teacher Education, 2*(4), 57–62.

Nias, J., Southworth, G., and Yeomans, R. (1989). *Staff relationships in the primary school: A study of organizational cultures.* London, England: Cassell Educational.

O'Connell Rust, F. (1988). "How supervisors think about teaching." *Journal of Teacher Education, 39*(2), 56–64.

O'Neal, S. F. (1983). *Supervision of student teachers: Feedback and evaluation.* Austin: Research and Development Center for Teacher Education, University of Texas. (ED 240 106).

Polansky, S. B. (1986). *900 shows a year.* New York: Random House.

Richardson-Koehler, V. (1988). "Barriers to the effective supervision of student teaching: A field study." *Journal of Teacher Education, 39*(2), 28–34.

Rosenholtz, S. J. (1989). *Teachers' workplace: The social organization of schools.* White Plains, N.Y.: Longman.

Ross, D. D., and Smith, W. (1992). "Understanding preservice teachers' perspectives on diversity." *Journal of Teacher Education, 43*(2), 94–103.

Ross, E. W. (1987). "Teacher perspective development: A study of preservice social studies teachers." *Theory and Research in Social Education, 15*(4), 225–243.

Ryan, K. (ed.) (1970). *Don't smile until Christmas.* Chicago: University of Chicago Press.

Ryan, K. (1986). *The induction of new teachers.* Bloomington, Ind.: Phi Delta Kappan Educational Foundation.

Ryan, K. (ed.) (1992). *The roller coaster year: Essays by and for beginning teachers.* New York: Harper-Collins.

Ryan, K., and others (1980). *Biting the apple.* White Plains, N.Y.: Longman.

Ryan, P. M., and Robinson, K. S. (1990). "Enhancing the preservice teacher's contextual understanding about their learners." Paper presented at the annual meeting of the American Association of Colleges for Teacher Education, Chicago.

Shack, S. (1965). *Armed with a primer: A Canadian teacher looks at children, schools, and parents.* Toronto, Ontario: McClelland & Stewart.

Sirotnik, K. A., and Goodlad, J. I. (eds.) (1988). *School-university partnerships in action: Concepts, cases, and concerns.* New York: Teachers College Press.

Stallings, J. A., and Kowalski, T. J. (1990). "Research on professional development schools." In W. R. Houston (ed.), *Handbook of research on teacher education.* New York: Macmillan.

Sudzina, M., and Knowles, J. G. (1993). "Personal, professional, and contextual circumstances of student teachers who 'fail': Setting a course for understanding failure in student teaching." *Journal of Teacher Education, 44*(4), 254–262.

Tabachnick, B. R., and Zeichner, K. M. (1984). "The impact of the student teaching experience on the development of teacher perspectives." *Journal of Teacher Education, 15*(6), 28–36.

Tabachnick, B. R., and Zeichner, K. M. (eds.) (1991). *Issues and practices in inquiry-oriented teacher education.* Washington, D.C.: Falmer Press.

Taylor, G., Borys, A., and La Rocque, L. (1992). "Reforming teachers' education: Toward an alternative model of practicum." *International Journal of Educational Reform, 1*(4), 376–391.

Thiessen, D. (1991). "Student-teacher relationships and the emerging professional identity of a first-year teacher." Paper presented at the annual meeting of the American Educational Research Association, Chicago.

Turney, C., Eltis, K. J., Towler, J., and Wright, R. (1985). *A new basis for teacher education: The practicum curriculum.* Sydney, Australia: Sydmac Academic Press.

Watson, N., and Fullan, M. G. (1991). Beyond school-university partnerships. In M. G. Fullan and A. Hargreaves (eds.), *Teacher development and educational change.* London: Falmer Press.

Watts, D. (1987). "Student teaching." In M. Haberman and J. M. Backus (eds.), *Advances in teacher education*, Vol. 3. Norwood, N.J.: Ablex.

Weinstein, C. S. (1990). "Prospective elementary teachers' beliefs about teaching: Implications for teacher education." *Teaching and Teacher Education, 6,* 279–290.

Winitzky, N. E., Stoddard, T., and O'Keefe, P. (1992). "Great expectations: Emergent professional development schools." *Journal of Teacher Education, 43*(1), 3–18.

Wood, P. O. (1991). "The cooperating teacher's role in nurturing reflective teaching." In B. R. Tabachnick and K. M. Zeichner (eds.), *Issues and practices in inquiry-oriented teacher education*. Washington, D.C.: Falmer Press.

Yates, J. W. (1981). "Student teaching in England: Results of a survey." *Journal of Teacher Education, 32*(5), 44–47.

Zahorik, J. A. (1988). "The observing conferencing role of university supervisors." *Journal of Teacher Education, 39*(2), 9–16.

Zeichner, K. M. (1980). "Myths and realities: Field-based experiences in preservice teacher education." *Journal of Teacher Education, 31*(6), 45–46.

Zeichner, K. M. (1983). "Alternative paradigms of teacher education." *Journal of Teacher Education, 34*(3), 3–9.

Zeichner, K. M. (1987). "The ecology of field experience: Toward understanding the role of field experiences." In M. Haberman and J. M. Backus (eds.), *Advances in teacher education*, Vol. 3. Norwood, N.J.: Ablex.

Zeichner, K. M. (1990). "Changing directions in the practicum: Looking ahead to the 1990s." *Journal of Education for Teaching, 16*(2), 105–132.

Zeichner, K. M. (1992). "Rethinking the practicum in the professional development school partnership." *Journal of Teacher Education, 43*(4), 296–307.

Zeichner, K. M., and Gore, J. M. (1990). "Teacher socialization." In W. R. Houston (ed.), *Handbook of research on teacher education*. New York: Macmillan.

Zeichner, K. M., and Grant, C. A. (1981). "Biography and social structure in the socialization of student teachers: A re-examination of the pupil control ideologies of student teachers." *Journal of Education for Teaching, 7*(3), 298–314.

Zeichner, K. M., and Liston, D. P. (1987). "Teaching student teachers to reflect." *Harvard Educational Review, 57*(1), 23–48.

Zeichner, K. M., and Tabachnick, B. R. (1981). "Are the effects of university teacher education 'washed out' by school experience?" *Journal of Teacher Education, 32*(3), 7–11.

Zeichner, K. M., and Teitelbaum, K. (1982). "Personalized and inquiry-oriented teacher education: An analysis of two approaches to the development of curriculum for field-based experiences." *Journal of Education for Teaching, 8*(2), 95–117.

Zimpher, N. L., de Voss, G., and Nott, D. (1980). "A closer look at university student teacher supervision." *Journal of Teacher Education, 31*(4), 11–15.

Annotated Bibliography

Field experiences:

Clandinin, D. J., Davies, A., Hogan, P., and Kennard, B. (1993). *Learning to teach, teaching to learn*. New York: Teachers College Press.

Learning to Teach, Teaching to Learn presents "stories of collaboration" from the perspectives of preservice teachers, cooperating teachers, and university teacher educators who joined together to explore and reimagine a teacher education experience more relevant and connected to their personal experiences.

Cochran-Smith, M., and Lytle, S. L. (1993). *Inside/outside: Teacher research and knowledge.* New York: Teachers College Press.

This book provides a framework for understanding and exploring the relationship between teacher research and university-based research. The authors challenge traditional viewpoints about the relationship between theory and practice, and about how, where, and by whom knowledge about teaching is constructed.

Knowles, J. G., and Cole, A. L., with Presswood, C. S. (1994). *Through preservice teachers' eyes: Exploring field experiences through narrative and inquiry.* New York: Macmillan.
This book presents a curriculum and pedagogy of field experiences based on and influenced by preservice teachers' perspectives and experiences. The authors write with a developmental perspective on learning to teach and learning to be a teacher and with a focus on self-directed learning, facilitation of ongoing professional development, and inquiry.

Reviews of research and literature:

Feiman-Nemser, S. (1990). "Teacher preparation: Structural and conceptual alternatives." In W. R. Houston (ed.), *Handbook of research on teacher education.* New York: Macmillan.
Feiman-Nemser provides an overview of traditional orientations and approaches to teacher preparation and offers some frameworks for considering alternative perspectives and approaches.

Kagan, D. M. (1992). "Professional growth among preservice and beginning teachers." *Review of Educational Research, 62*(2), 129–169.
Kagan offers an analysis and model of the learning-to-teach process that take into account its complex and personal nature. She highlights the role of personal history influences on learning to teach and emphasizes the importance of attending to issues associated with professional identity development, professional contexts, and relationships.

Zeichner, K. M., and Gore, J. M. (1990). "Teacher socialization." In W. R. Houston (ed.), *Handbook of research on teacher education.* New York: Macmillan.
Zeichner and Gore review the research and literature on teacher socialization conducted within various intellectual traditions, and they examine how the socialization research relates to teacher education practices.

PART FIVE

THE TEACHER EDUCATION FACULTY AND THEIR WORK

CHAPTER TWENTY-SEVEN

DEVELOPMENT OF THE TEACHER EDUCATION PROFESSORIATE

EDWARD R. DUCHARME AND MARY K. DUCHARME

In this chapter, we briefly review the history of the teacher education faculty, summarize the extant teacher education faculty literature, describe current conditions including implications of recent demographic studies of teacher education faculty, and place teacher education faculty in the context of the 1980s and 1990s reform waves.

Scholars have devoted meager attention to the serious study of education faculty as a whole, even less to that of teacher education faculty. Early writers who studied professional education in higher education often mingled teacher education faculty with education faculty in general, including faculty in educational administration, educational psychology, and other disciplines. Consequently, we will occasionally cite research or writing referring to education faculty in general and elicit the implications for teacher education faculty.

Lanier and Little (1986) contend that researchers systematically overlook teacher educators: "Research on teaching teachers stands in stark contrast to research on teaching youngsters. When teaching is studied in elementary and secondary schools, teachers are considered too important to overlook. But teachers of teachers—what they are like, what they do, what they think—are systematically overlooked in studies of teacher education. Even researchers are not exactly sure of who they are. While it is known that a teacher educator is one who teaches teachers, the composite of those who teach teachers is loosely defined and constantly changing" (p. 528).

Researchers may not have *systematically* omitted teacher educators from research, but their absence from the research literature until very recently is evident. Ducharme (1986) contends that one reason for the lack of literature about teacher educators is the lack of a clear definition: "Little is known about 'teacher educators,' the higher education faculty responsible for teacher preparation. Reasons include the lack of a definition and consequent difficulty in identifying the population, scarcity of research about teacher educators specifically, and inclusion of teacher educators in research on the education professoriate generally" (p. 1).

In the same essay, Ducharme includes only seven references to literature on the subject, several of which focus on education faculty generally, not teacher education faculty specifically, demonstrating the paucity of writing on the topic. Hazlett (1989) contends that no history of the education professoriate exists. If there is an incomplete history of the education professoriate, there is almost no history or analysis of the teacher education professoriate.

Reasons for Study

The teacher education professoriate merits serious inquiry for several reasons. First, the history of teacher education's presence in higher education is ambiguous, complex, and in need of clarification; the continuous debates about the place of teacher education in higher education affect the role and status of teacher educators. While Wisniewski and Ducharme (1989) contend that "historically, functionally, and legally, the education professoriate is secure within the academic firmament" (p. 147), others (Finn, 1991; Kramer, 1992; Judge, 1982; Clifford and Guthrie, 1988) are less sanguine. Mackay (1989), in his review of Clifford and Guthrie's *Ed School*, notes that "the ed school has been treated like Cinderella—tolerated by her academic sisters only for the work she performs" (p. 64). Conant (1963) stated his earlier extremely hostile views of education faculty when he noted that "when any issues involving benefits to the graduate school of education came before the faculty of arts and sciences, I automatically voted with contempt upon the school of education" (p. 2). Second, teacher education is influenced equally by its substantive ties to elementary and secondary schools, particularly in the use of school sites for field experiences in teacher education programs; the expectations of both those in the world of practice in elementary and secondary schools and those in higher education institutions influence the role and responsibilities of teacher educators. Third, many of the critics of teacher education (see Finn, 1991; Koerner, 1963; Conant, 1963; Kramer, 1992) base their negative images of teacher education programs and faculty on blanket condemnation and hearsay rather than a careful delineation of actual conditions and practice. Kramer is particularly virulent in her attack. Nash (1993) notes that her portrayal of teacher education faculty is "so mean-spirited and caricatured as to be virtually unrecognizable to me" (p. 71) and "Kramer's gratuitous tendency to go far beyond the evidence of her interviews in order to indict teacher education is particularly troublesome in her methodology" (p. 74). Kramer's and other superficial attacks (Koerner, 1963) cite alleged lack of consistency in programs, unclear expectations, failure to meet the needs of prospective teachers, and overreliance on theory. Scholarly inquiry and study of the teacher education professoriate are necessary to refute some of these intellectually shallow but often powerfully stated indictments. The intense education reform agenda of the 1980s and 1990s is a fourth reason for studying the teacher education professoriate. These years have been a period of close scrutiny of American public education, including substantial criticism of the education of teachers. Goodlad (1990) contends that educational reformers are finally making the connection between teacher preparation and what occurs in schools. Yet there is a lack of knowledge of who educates teachers and what they do. Informed response to the critiques necessitates accurate knowledge about teacher education and the faculty who provide it. Liston and Zeichner (1991) describe the reform history in American teacher education and suggest possible future strategies.

Historical Context

Knowledge of the historical context of teacher education is essential to understand the evolution of the role of teacher educators and the potentially contradictory perspectives inhering in their work. In the nineteenth century, teacher preparation, when it existed at all, was an apprenticeship. Some teachers left the eighth grade as students only to begin teaching others, often equipped only with an additional year of living and virtually no more preparation than the students they would teach. "Real" teacher education in America began in the 1820s and 1830s with the establishment of the first normal schools in Vermont and Massachusetts (Borrowman, 1956). Beginning in the mid 1880s, Horace Mann and other school leaders advocated the establishment of normal schools for formal teacher preparation, basing them on European models (Urban, 1990).

Borrowman (1956, 1965), Warren (1989), Clifford and Guthrie (1988), Urban (1990), Goodlad (1990), and others have written compellingly of the normal schools and the teachers' colleges of the first half of the twentieth century. Borrowman (1956, 1965) broadly describes the early history of teacher education, including its time in normal schools, relates the subsequent struggle for survival in higher education institutions once the shift occurred, and gives descriptions of some preparation programs.

In its early years, most teacher education occurred in these normal schools, institutions specifically developed for the preparation of teachers and rarely educating their students much beyond elementary school levels of instruction. With few exceptions, institutions with the sole purpose of teacher preparation no longer exist. However, a few comments on the past of teacher education are appropriate to provide a context for present-day conditions. Some knowledge of the history and reputation of normal schools and the early teachers' colleges that followed them may also explain why some noneducation faculty in colleges and universities have negative attitudes toward teacher education.

Often attached to elementary schools, the first normal schools offered little that was intellectual to their students, most of whom were uneducated. Urban (1990) describes the students and briefly comments on the curriculum: "A few students had had some high school training, whereas the great majority had attended the elementary schools for which they were preparing to teach. The single purpose of training teachers meant that the curriculum of the normal school would be mainly technical. Yet the relatively uneducated character of the normal school students meant that often the normal school would have to offer academic subjects, so that the teachers would be familiar with what they would be teaching in the schools" (p. 61).

Normal schools initially had the sole purpose of training teachers; for this purpose, they combined academic, technically oriented pedagogical study with practice in classrooms (Urban, 1990). The normal school movement spread rapidly and "By 1914, every city with a population of at least 300,000 maintained normal schools or training classes in connection with their public school systems, often integrated with the academic program of the city high schools" (Altenbaugh and Underwood, 1990, p. 149). Many city and state normal schools had short lives: "While the nation had 46 teachers' colleges and 137 state normal schools in 1920, these figures shifted profoundly in only thirteen years to 146 and 50, respectively. The number of city normal schools declined from 33 in 1920 to 16 in 1933" (p. 150). Borrowman (1956) summarizes how teacher education had both grown and changed in thirty-five years:

> The period from 1895 to 1930 had been one of fantastic expansion in every dimension of teacher education. The normal schools, besides increasing in size, had largely become teachers' colleges; the collegiate and university training of secondary teachers had mushroomed beyond all expectations; the teaching profession had not only expanded but had become highly organized; new materials for teacher education had filled thousands of volumes; and the universities, with their growing graduate schools of education, were turning up new material faster than it could be absorbed or evaluated. There was critical need for a time of stability to permit a careful resurvey of what had happened and a dispassionate analysis of existing thought and practice [p. 181].

By 1940, the term *normal school* had become obsolete (Altenbaugh and Underwood, 1990). Of those that survived, most followed a common pattern and eventually became teachers' colleges, then four-year state colleges, and finally multipurpose state colleges and universities. For example, the St. Cloud (Minnesota) State Normal School is now St. Cloud State University; the case is similar with Illinois Normal University and many state universities or colleges in New York, Massachusetts, Illinois, and California. Some of these schools, however, often do not lay claim to their own heritage of teacher preparation. Goodlad (1990) comments on the reluctance of these institutions to acknowledge their pasts: "A university we were about to visit sent us an array of documents about its history and accomplishments. Not one contained any mention of the fact that this university had recently been a normal school" (p. 73).

Critics of teacher education cite the low intellectual climate of the normal schools rather than the enormous service they provided in supplying teachers for a rapidly expanding population or the growing shift toward a more academic climate. The perception of low intellectual climate still influences the judgment of some commentators on teacher preparation, who often characterize it as anti-intellectual. Bernier and McClelland (1989) observe that "most teacher selection was determined on judgments of moral character rather than upon teaching competencies. . . . Standards of admission were minimal" (p. 19). Questions about standards of admission and other alleged indicators of quality with respect to teacher education continue to arise; having lost faith in SAT and ACT scores, some teacher educators are arguing for the validity of inherent predispositions or qualities in candidates (Jacobwitz, 1994). The debate over the relevancy of SAT and ACT scores, grade point averages, and personal characteristics as predictors of good teaching continues.

Warren (1989) includes several chapters on the history of teacher education. Herbst (1989) chronicles the move of professional education from the normal schools to the universities, showing how the move prefigured the future low status of teacher education in higher education that Judge (1982) described. Herbst observed, "As it was, by the beginning of the twentieth century, professionalism in education was to find its home in the graduate departments of educational administration and psychology, in the hierarchical establishments of state and city educational bureaucracies, and in the research-centered graduate schools of education and their programs for the continuing education of administrators and specialists. By contrast, the education of the country's largely female elementary-classroom teachers appeared to the overwhelmingly male ranks of professionals to be an unprestigious, albeit necessary and unavoidable, task not undertaken with much enthusiasm" (1989, p. 233).

Ginsburg (1988) contends that the normal schools reinforced class and gender distinctions, that the prolonged pursuit of liberal arts courses for normal schools despite an ingrained bias against them among normal school people indicated the desire of normal school leaders for status, and that all these conditions reflected societal norms of social class.

While many of the normal schools in cities and states developed because of a perceived need to serve society by preparing teachers for the nation's growing population, some scholars believe that universities were not quite as altruistic as they developed teacher preparation programs. In *Ed School,* Clifford and Guthrie (1988) provide brief histories of teacher education in the ten research institutions under their scrutiny. They indicate that universities rarely developed education departments or schools for altruistic reasons: "They launched their initially modest ventures in professional education because it directly served their *own* interests. . . .

As some elite colleges and universities found it convenient to have a theological seminary as a token to quiet critics of their 'godless materialism,' they similarly found that educating a few teachers could project an image of contributing to the public weal" (p. 123).

Schneider (1987) contends that the demise of the normal schools was inevitable, given expanding needs for teachers and the market:

> By the 1890s, it was apparent that great numbers of teachers and administrators were needed to educate America's rapidly growing school age population. . . . Given this expanding market, criticism of teacher education took a different form. Rather than dismissing teacher education as intellectually inconsequential, faculty members in universities stressed the need for teacher training programs that were academically demanding and grounded in the liberal arts tradition. . . . Once universities became intent on capturing the teacher training market, the demise of the normal school was a certain reality. Universities first attempted to increase their enrollments by lowering their admissions requirements in hopes of drawing students away from the normal schools [pp. 214–215].

Schneider's contention that the universities first lowered admissions standards in order to attract students for their teacher preparation programs, if correct, may explain some of the intellectual antipathy between arts and sciences units and teacher preparation units.

Goodlad (1990) writes of early university teacher education from a critical perspective, concluding that teacher education lost some of its identity by affiliation with or absorption by colleges and universities: "This transition was accompanied by a severe loss of identity for teacher education. . . . On none of these campuses was the education of educators (or, for that matter), the college of education, the crown jewel" (p. 73).

The move of teacher education and the study of education from normal schools and teachers' colleges to higher education or the transition from normal school to teachers' college to state college to state university was difficult. Early on, some universities, such as the University of Tennessee, attempted to add educational studies to their programs. Allison's verbal portraits (1989) of the first three professors of education at the University of Tennessee reveal the problems that have inhered in the nature of research and publication appropriate to education faculty. Palmer (1985) notes that universities have been slow to recognize and sanction teacher education and reluctant to own it, a situation relevant to Goodlad's experience mentioned above.

Judge (1982) argues that the more distant research institution faculty are from teacher education, the more status they think they have; Lanier and Little (1986) contend that regardless of the level of an institution's involvement in teacher education, arts and sciences faculty want nothing to do with it. Further: "There is an inverse relationship between professorial prestige and the intensity of involvement with the formal education of teachers" (p. 530). Clark (1987) writes of the antipathy that exists among some arts and sciences faculty members toward administrators and teachers in universities that once were teachers' colleges. He quotes one faculty member's comment about an education "colleague": "[He] is now a professor in the foundations of education, whatever the hell they do over there, and that mishmash that goes in all directions, people without disciplines, six characters in search of an author, twelve characters in search of a discipline!" He saw the educationalist old-timers as still "very much a presence here." They had "seriously hurt this college" (p. 167).

Yet despite problems of ownership, prestige, quality and quantity of scholarship, and questionable reputation, teacher education persists; over twelve hundred institutions in the nation have a school, college, or department of education that prepares teachers. Various institutions boast outstanding teacher education faculty, who are developing premier programs. A review of the programs of the recent national meetings of the American Association of Colleges for Teacher Education, the Association of Teacher Educators, and Division K of the American Education Research Association demonstrates growing scholarly activity and productivity from teacher education faculty at a rising number of institutions. Yet the picture emerging from the writers cited earlier and a few others on the subject of the early history of teacher education is that of a faculty group lacking academic identity, struggling for legitimacy in universities and colleges, and occasionally smarting under the criticisms of the faculty from the older, established disciplines. These writers relate how grudgingly and reluctantly the academy has granted teacher education the limited status it currently possesses in higher education. Status and a sense of security do not come easily.

Research and Writings About Teacher Education Faculty

In 1986, Lanier and Little described the paucity of research available about teacher educators: "The body of research leading to better understanding of those who teach teachers is modest at this time. A broad search of the literature and a weaving together of circumstantial evidence was required as part of the sense-making task called for in a review of this nature. The difficult-to-locate, easy-to-overlook, and much-maligned nature of the teacher education population lies behind the questioning perspective brought to the research studies considered in this section" (p. 535).

A considerable amount of writing about teacher education and teacher educators has appeared since Lanier and Little's 1986 observations. Some researchers have written about teacher education generally and a few have focused on teacher educators specifically. Warren (1989), Clifford and Guthrie (1988), Goodlad (1990), Wisniewski and Ducharme (1989), Popkewitz (1987), and others have either devoted lengthy sections to teacher educators or included some analysis of them in their books on the professoriate. Ginsburg (1988), in his study of teacher education, argues that teacher education reflects and reinforces the social stratification of the larger society. Howey and Zimpher (1990) wrote the chapter "Professors and Deans of Education" for the *Handbook of Research on Teacher Education,* in which they reviewed some of the studies of teacher educators; their book *Profiles of Preservice Teacher Education* (1989) focuses solely on teacher education, its students, faculty, and administrators at several institutions. Ducharme (1993) published *The Lives of Teacher Educators,* in which he reported on interviews with thirty-four teacher educators from eleven institutions. *Phi Delta Kappan,* the *Journal of Teacher Education,* and other journals have either run feature issues on teacher educators or published articles on the topic. The American Association of Colleges for Teacher Education's annual *Research About Teacher Education* (RATE) monographs have annually included a section on teacher educators. Thus, one can report considerable scholarly activity in the past seven years.

Yes, there is more material, but what does one make of it? Has the corpus of research grown both quantitatively and qualitatively? Is there now a clear image of who teacher educators are, what they do, why they do what they do? Yes and no. What exists is more detail to confirm some earlier descriptions and conceptions of teacher educators, other material to refute or call into question some of these earlier descriptions and conceptions, a deluge of information about what teacher educators do, a near glut of demographic data, and an increase in the volume of hypothetical statements about teacher educators based loosely on the emerging data.

Demographics

The results of national surveys, regional data collections, and individual studies indicate clearly the profile of campus-based teacher educators who can be described as "those who hold tenure-line positions in higher education, teach beginning and advanced students in teacher education and conduct research or engage in scholarly studies germane to teacher education" (Ducharme, 1993, p. 6).

The RATE studies (American Association of Colleges for Teacher Education, 1987–1994), the Ducharme-Agne data (1982), Ducharme's *Lives of Teacher Educators* (1993), Howey and Zimpher's *Profiles of Preservice Teacher Education* (1989), and the Howey, Yarger, and Joyce data (1978) are major sources of information about education faculty generally and teacher education faculty specifically. A faculty member, according to these and other studies, has the following characteristics: "[He] is a white male in his late forties or early fifties, tenured at either the full or associate professor level. He acquired his doctorate while studying part-time, and has been at his current place of employment for more than 15 years, during which time he has published six or seven articles in refereed publications. He taught for a minimum of three years in the lower schools prior to his employment in higher education" (Ducharme, 1994).

Most teacher education faculty taught previously in the public schools. "Nearly all teacher education faculty in the RATE study have had prior experience in the elementary and secondary schools as teachers, department chairs, and administrators, a condition reflected in other studies and writings about the education professoriate (Ducharme and Agne, 1982; Lanier and Little, 1986). Nearly 80 percent of elementary and secondary faculty had several years of prior work in elementary and secondary schools" (Ducharme and Kluender, 1990, p. 46).

Ducharme (1993) notes the reasons those teacher educators whom he interviewed gave for leaving teaching in the elementary and secondary schools: "isolation, low autonomy, poor intellectual climate, fear of becoming boring to students, and lack of personal time" (p. 52).

A number of scholars have contended that teacher educators, inasmuch as they almost always come from the ranks of teachers, reflect the social class origins of teachers. Most of Ducharme's interviewees come from working-class origins, one of whom stated, "So I actually went into teaching because it was secure and you could get a job" (p. 28). Mattingly (1975), Powell (1980), Lanier and Little (1986), and Ducharme and Agne (1989) concur that teacher educators generally come from a working-class background, and all suggest that the lower- and lower-middle social class origins affect the lives of teacher education faculty in higher education. Lanier and Little (1986) observe, "A disproportionately large number of faculty teaching teachers most directly have come from lower middle-class backgrounds. It is very likely that they obtain conformist orientations and utilitarian views of knowledge from their experiences at home, educational opportunities in school, and restrictive conditions of work as teachers before coming to higher education" (p. 535).

They also note, "Faculty in institutions of higher education are expected to value intellectual challenge, questioning, criticism, and conceptual analysis. Advancing higher learning requires that scholars enter uncharted intellectual territory, and, as they explore the not-yet-known, they must maintain a cognitive flexibility and commitment to examine alternative, sometimes competing, beliefs and assumptions. . . . Evidence suggests that the typical lineage of teacher educators has not prepared them to appreciate the traditional values of higher education" (p. 533).

We recognize that, lacking empirical data about relationships among social class origins, work habits, and professional attitudes, observations based on social class are speculative, but this condition makes them no less interesting. For example, Lanier and Little's observation that teacher educators likely have "utilitarian views of knowledge" may partially explain why some teacher educators are so quick to accept utilitarian, mechanistic movements as Competency Based Teacher Education of the 1970s, outcomes-based education, and other simplistic solutions to complex problems.

Teacher education faculty are of course much more complex than the composite cited above. The teacher education literature is replete with the work of individuals who do not admit to simple solutions to complex problems; Warren (1989), Nash (1993), Kagan (1990), and Howey and Zimpher (1989) come to mind. Further, recently hired faculty are, based on early productivity, likely to publish more in their careers than have older faculty; anticipate moving during their careers; and are somewhat more likely to be female and white (American Association of Colleges for Teacher Education, 1988, 1989). A department chair in Ducharme's study noted of new faculty, "Oh, they're better. They have richer backgrounds; they're better prepared as researchers. They're more specialists, more in-depth in certain areas. I think they do research and writing before they finish their dissertations" (1993, p. 66). McCarthy and her colleagues (1988) came to similar conclusions about professors new (six or fewer years of experience, p. 67) to educational administration faculties: "New faculty were more interested in research than were their experienced colleagues; 24 percent of the new faculty declared research to be their greatest strength, compared with 13 percent of experienced faculty. New faculty also spend considerably more time in research and scholarly activities (18 percent of the work week) than did their more experienced counterparts (12 percent of the work week)" (McCarthy, Kuh, Newell, and Iacona, p. 136).

Women in teacher education perform more field work than do men, are more likely to supervise students in early field experiences and in student teaching than males, are likely to have more advisees and spend more time in advising and in committee work. They perform these tasks even while reporting that they spend about the same number of hours per week doing their work (American Association of Colleges for Teacher Education, 1987–1994). They report spending less time than male faculty on scholarly and research activities in similar roles. Summarizing the first three years of the RATE studies, Ducharme and Kluender (1990) observed, "As indicated in the remarks on gender, men publish more frequently than women, regardless of rank, time at the institution, or type of degree. Women do more field supervision and more teaching. Therefore, women may publish less because they are often asked to assume supervisory responsibilities at a disproportionate level, and they teach more" (p. 46).

The 1988 RATE report indicated that "almost half of the females (48.3 percent) had never published compared to approximately one-third of the males (31.2 percent)" (p. 26). Because publishing plays a major role in faculty promotion, tenure, and salary, the combination of heavier teaching, advising, and supervising loads and low scholarly productivity for female faculty is untenable.

The percentage of teacher education faculty at the various professorial ranks reflect national norms. Yet women are not represented in the various ranks at the same percentage levels as they are in the professoriate generally. For example, in the 1988 RATE study, which surveyed education foundations faculty, women form 28 percent of the teacher education professoriate, yet they constitute only 12 percent of the faculty at the rank of full professor.

There is no one adequate explanation for these conditions. Later entry into professorial roles in higher education than males, interrupted career line for children, lower scholarly output than males, inappropriate assignment or acceptance of duties, prejudice and bias, lack of a female network including mentoring while in doctoral work—each is an interesting reason or cause but none suffices. None of these can be viewed singly. For example, the lower scholarly productivity may be a function of interrupted career pattern, or inappropriate assignments, or lack of mentoring, or all three.

More than 90 percent of the students in elementary teacher education programs are female while more than 50 percent of those who teach them in their professional preparation are male (RATE III). The vast majority of female graduates of these programs take positions in elementary schools with male principals. These conditions relay a clear message to females intending to be teachers: *you can teach but those who prepare you to teach and those who administer the schools in which you will teach are likely to be male.*

Some might contend that this condition merely reflects the society in general; namely, organizations headed largely by male CEOs. We contend that, even if it does, teacher education has a moral responsibility to change this pattern and demonstrate gender equity to its students, the future teachers of America.

Perhaps teacher education curricula should provide opportunities for students to study the generally prevailing conditions so as to prepare better the teachers coming to the schools. Teacher education faculty, both male and female, must provide prospective teachers with better models to confront the frequently sexist professional world and a curriculum and set of experiences enlightening and empowering them to live and teach effectively.

"The teacher education profession exists, after all, to prepare the teachers for the nation's schools; a large majority of the students are females. It ill suits the profession to have the female role models for these prospective teachers feeling unfairly treated or being unfairly treated in work load, salary, rank, and tenure" (Ducharme, 1993, p. 101).

The demographics on race are more pernicious. With the exception of the historically black colleges and universities, nearly all institutions have very small percentages of minority faculty in teacher education. In the RATE studies, regardless of the area of teacher education under study during the different years—elementary education, secondary education, educational foundations—the percentage of minority faculty (African-American, Hispanic, Native American) remains below 10 percent. The 1987 RATE report indicates only 8 percent of then-current doctoral students were minority (American Association of Colleges for Teacher Education, 1987, p. 27). Teacher education units should not take comfort in the fact that this is the general condition in higher education. Minority children currently are almost 30 percent of the student population in elementary and secondary schools (National Center for Education Statistics, 1991); predictions are that this percentage will grow. The nation must have a more diverse teaching population.

Faculty Life

Demographics and conditions of life are inextricably related; who people are, what their experiences have been, and where they come from often dramatically affect what they do. Nonetheless, there are some *unique* conditions of teacher education faculty life meriting discussion.

Use of Faculty Time

Researchers have gathered considerable data about the quality and quantity of the academic work lives of teacher education faculty, including how they actually spend their time and how they would prefer spend it (Ducharme and Agne, 1982; Gideonse, 1989; Goodlad, 1990; Ducharme and Kluender, 1990; Ducharme and Ducharme, 1991) in the traditional triad of teaching, scholarship, and service. The RATE studies from 1986 through 1991 annually asked faculty how they spent their time in those three areas, how much time they thought their institutions wanted them to spend in each area, and how much time they personally would consider ideal. The results were consistent through the five years of data collection, even though those conducting the study surveyed different subgroups each year: secondary education faculty, educational foundations faculty, elementary education faculty, student teacher supervisors. Faculty reported spending about 60 percent of their time either teaching or on activities related to teaching such as planning and reviewing student work; slightly less than 20 percent of their time on scholarship; and slightly more than 20 percent of their time on service. The faculty indicated that they thought that administrators would prefer that they spend more time on research but without stinting on either teaching or service; they themselves would also prefer to spend more time on scholarly activities.

The three broad categories may disguise other time-consuming activities demanding faculty time. Gideonse (1989), in a detailed analysis of how faculty members from three institutions (each of whom had earned "merit" salary increases) spent their time, reported they spent an average of 57 hours per week on professional work; individual faculty efforts ranged from 42.1 hours per week to 88 hours per week. He further analyzed how they spent time across five categories: teaching, scholarly activity, advising, service, and administration/governance. Advising and administration/governance accounted for an average of 4.8 and 13.7 hours per week or 15.8 hours total, about 32 percent of the reported work week, a finding consistent with data reported in the RATE studies. For example, in 1992, faculty in the RATE V study reported that they spent over 48 hours per week in professional activities, of which more than 17 hours per week, or about 36 percent time, was spent on advising, committee work, administrative tasks, or other activities (pp. 123–125).

Clear differences exist in how faculty use time, depending on the type of institution in which they work, their area of concentration within teacher education, and their own demographic characteristics. For example, foundations faculty in the RATE studies taught fewer hours, spent more time on research and produced more scholarly products, and spent far less time in the field than did their colleagues in other areas of concentration. Faculty employed in bachelor's- or master's-level institutions were more likely to spend time teaching, advising, and supervising field experiences and less likely to spend time on research (Ducharme and Kluender, 1990). As we described earlier, females were more likely than males to spend time on supervision, advising, and committee work (Ducharme and Ducharme, 1991; Ducharme and Agne, 1982; Ducharme, 1993). Clearly, inequities exist among the education disciplines and between genders and they require attention. It *may* be that faculty workload should in part be a function of the discipline taught; it *cannot* be that workload is solely a function of gender. Adjustments in philosophy and practice are requisite if the teacher education professoriate is to model appropriate roles for its students.

Research and Publication

There is lack of clarity about the degree and kind of research and publishing that teacher education faculty do. Guba and Clark (1978) argue that research productivity is lower among education faculty than among faculty in other academic units; others, including Ducharme and Agne (1982), contend that research productivity of education faculty, while uneven among institutions and individuals, is at about the level of higher education faculty generally. The 1987 and 1988 RATE studies report that approximately 50 percent of the faculty had published nothing in their professional lifetimes; 25 percent had ten publications or more, conclusions similar to those of Ducharme and Agne (1982). Teacher education faculty publish unevenly; that is, the average number of refereed publications for faculty members in a given institution might be 5.6, but individual faculty members may have as many as 26 and as few as none. The RATE studies indicate a similar conclusion with the added information that some departments or specializations within teacher education—for example, foundations faculty—publish much more than do elementary and secondary education faculty (Ducharme and Kluender, 1990, p. 46). All the demographic studies require further analysis; for example, the RATE group has never sorted publications-lifetime into the various categories of years of experience in higher education, type of institution, and nature of assignment.

The RATE data indicate that younger faculty are publishing at a pace suggesting that they will surpass their older colleagues. Schuttenberg, Patterson, and Sutton (1985) argue that younger education faculty value scholarship more highly than more mature faculty and believe their potential for scholarship to be higher as well. Some older faculty came to higher education at a time and place where pressure for publishing was minimal. Two of Ducharme's interviewees make the point clearly. The first, a veteran male faculty member, noted, "But when I came to this university, [publishing] was not emphasized, as a matter of fact, it was incidental. If you did it, it was OK, but the emphasis was on service, on work in the schools" (1993, p. 68). The second, an untenured female faculty member, commented, "The provost made it clear when we came in . . . 'Now we spent lots of money to bring you here. Like Harvard, we want you to get tenure here, the way you get tenure is to publish.'" (p. 65). Ducharme and Agne (1989) contend that recently hired faculty such as the young faculty member quoted above come to their positions with a predisposition toward becoming scholars. They also note that fewer of them have the level of experience in the elementary and secondary schools that older colleagues had prior to working on doctoral degrees.

Boyer (1990) in his 1989 national study of higher education faculty in all disciplines notes that approximately the same percentage of faculty under forty and over forty had published nothing in their careers, 27 percent and 26 percent respectively, but that 39 percent of those under forty had published one to five articles versus only 31 percent of those over forty, while 16 percent of those under forty had published six to ten articles versus 13 percent of those over forty. As would be expected with much longer time in the profession, 30 percent of those over forty had published eleven or more articles, but only 19 percent of those under forty had done so. On related matters, 53 percent of those under forty strongly agree that it is difficult to gain tenure without publishing versus 39 percent of those over forty; 38 percent of those under forty believe the number of publications is very important for tenure versus 26 percent of those over forty; and 79 percent of faculty under forty were currently engaged in scholarly work versus 63 percent of those over forty. Given the weight that the younger faculty place on publishing, it is not surprising that 34 percent of them thought that student evaluations of teaching were either fairly or very unimportant in gaining tenure versus 27 percent of older faculty; and 28 percent of younger faculty thought that teaching effectiveness should be the primary criterion for promotion of faculty versus 33 percent of older faculty. Finally, younger faculty—those under forty—clearly feel the pressure to publish and its perhaps deleterious effect on their teaching (pp. 85–126). Forty-three percent of those under forty believe that the "pressure to publish reduces the quality of teaching at my university" versus percentages between 31 and 34 for faculty between ages forty and sixty-five (p. 48).

Ducharme (1986) and Lanier and Little (1986), among others, speculate that the years that the older, in-place faculty spent in the elementary and secondary schools with their low priority for scholarship and high priority for teaching and long hours of work may contribute to some individual teacher educators' low scholarly productivity. That is, they may find it difficult to change the ingrained habits of the earlier workplace with its emphases on teaching and involvement in extracurricular activities in order to meet the loosely applied but rigidly held scholarly standards of higher education.

Work in the Field

Not only are teacher education faculty tied to the elementary and secondary schools by prior work experience but many work directly in elementary and secondary schools or indirectly through student teachers and interns. Teacher education faculty spend considerable time in the schools. For example, the elementary methods faculty reported in the 1988 RATE study that they spend an average of more than twenty-eight hours per month in the schools. The faculty in the schools likely divide their time among the following activities: observing preservice students and their early in-school observations and experiences, supervising student teaching, meeting and planning with supervisors, conducting pre- and postconferences with student teachers, occasionally teaching, or, less likely, providing in-service or workshop activities for teachers or conducting research in the schools. The faculty reported that they spend 6.8 hours per month in student teaching supervision and 1.6 hours per month in research activities.

As the faculty in teacher education programs and departments in colleges and universities determine their roles and responsibilities, they should consider the time spent in schools and how they might coordinate and utilize that time more purposefully and effectively, both to create more productive relationships with the schools as argued in the Holmes reports (1986, 1990) and to more directly affect pedagogy in the schools. They should consider that if the RATE data reflect general conditions, a teacher education faculty of five spend over 140 hours per month in schools doing one thing and another. They might reflect on several questions, including the following: Is that time well spent? Can the time and the faculty be better organized to meet student, program, and faculty needs and goals? Can faculty find ways to link the time in schools with compelling research? Can professional development relationships emerge from these hours? We ask these questions not to devalue the time that teacher education faculty spend in schools but to challenge the profession in these times of decreased resources and high need to consider how the time might yield better results. We suggest that teacher educators, teachers, and student teachers could be conducting collaborative research during some of that time.

Teacher Educators and Reform

Particularly in an era of reform, critics often depict teacher education programs and faculty as both the cause of all school problems and the source of many of its solutions. Those who view teacher education as the critical element in the sorry state of modern public education portray teacher educators as mediocre faculty doing largely unnecessary and inconsequential work with students of modest or low ability. Finn (1991) is among recent critics to charge that education schools and their faculties are purveyors of folly:

Faculties of education are the brain and central nervous system of the school establishment. They are where ideas originate and get legitimated. They are also where beliefs are held—and transmitted to teachers and principals—that fly in the face of common sense, popular preference, and the express will of democratically elected policy makers. They are where the most absurd notions are promulgated, usually with an introductory phrase such as "research shows" or "we have learned." . . . It is not, I think, coincidental that those colleges of education] are the most-despised institutions in the education universe, that alternatives to them are among the most popular reform policies being devised by governors and legislatures, and that limiting prospective educators' exposure to their teachings is one of the school renewal strategies with the greatest appeal [pp. 222–223].

Finn's remarks are in the tradition of the whipping boy school of criticism; earlier, Koerner (1963) had followed a similar strategy of undocumented assertions about quality, practice, and public opinion. Teacher education has had to struggle and must continue to do so against these frequently occurring, quasi-scholarly indictments.

Most reformers, however, see teacher education programs and faculty as potential partners in the improvement of schools. Almost all of the reform reports of the 1980s acknowledge the critical role that teachers play in student success and make a variety of recommendations to recruit, educate, and support the best teachers possible. Some, like Finn, view teacher education programs as essentially irredeemable and advocate their abolition or drastic reduction. It is both interesting and ironic that Finn and other recent critics of teacher education are themselves in or from universities, usually from the school or college of education. For most reformers, however, high-quality preparation and continued staff development are essential to the reform effort and existing teacher education programs and faculty are major contributors to that work. Commenting on the many reform documents and reports of the 1980s, Sikula (1990) observes, "From this sampling [of reports] and other analyses too numerous to elaborate upon here, it is apparent that the thrust of the major reform themes and concerns in teacher preparation centered around expanding the teacher candidate pool, regulating teacher preparation more rigorously, emphasizing the clinical nature of teacher education, mastering subject matter knowledge, and extending the formal preparation of fully certified teachers" (p. 80).

Thus, the current teacher education faculty must add another urgent need to their efforts: they must expand their focus beyond the multiple demands of teaching, research, and service and the sometimes conflicting expectations of their higher education institutions and the schools with which they work in order to come to terms with their role in the larger issues of the transformation of schools. For it is clear that teacher education's survival and meaning depend upon its ability to adapt to the changing culture and needs of the schools for which they prepare teachers and to do so in such a manner as to bring the unique perspectives of inquiry and the pursuit and application of knowledge to bear upon the practical problems of teaching and learning. Higher education's contribution to school reform must take place through the efforts of the teacher education faculty, most of whom are already hired and tenured. Ducharme (1987) notes:

> If teacher education programs are to change significantly, and they must change if they are to survive, they will do so through the efforts of existing teacher education faculty. The plethora of national reports calling for improvement in the elementary and secondary schools has led to calls for reform in teacher education programs. Advocacy for a post bachelor's program for teacher preparation is growing; demands for quality scholarship and research in education are increasing; standards for recruitment and acceptance of applicants into teacher preparation programs are rising; and resources are at their usual low ebb. These conditions must be met by a largely in-place teacher education faculty, a faculty prepared with one set of assumptions, confronted during their careers with changing emphases, and facing a future filled with change [p. 71].

Goodlad (1990) and others have reminded us that teacher educators straddle two cultures, that of higher education and that of the K–12 school system (p. 154). Kagan (1990) suggests that the same characteristics that serve as hallmarks for change in elementary schools—a common professional culture, sense of consensus about purpose and goals, an organization that promotes collaborative problem solving and growth—are the very issues that are most problematic for teacher educators. Kagan poses what she perceives as the central issue for teacher educators to make the necessary changes:

> If we are to reform teacher education, embedding it in coherent programs, education faculty may have to merge their subjective definitions of teaching and learning; collaboration rather than isolation may have to become the norm. This is a deeply troubling proposition, given the pluralistic nature of the professoriate and the importance of academic freedom. Are there any legitimate mechanisms for effecting genuine consensus among college faculty? To what degree should the dean of a college serve as an instructional leader, establishing norms of collegiality? When does the norm of collaboration become tyranny by majority rule? When does consensus within an academic unit of a university become stagnation and resistance to change? In sum, does the creation of coherent programs of teacher education require a significant loss of autonomy for individual teacher educators? [pp. 50–51].

As teacher educators work to resolve such dilemmas, the institutions in which they reside must make some concurrent commitments. Goodlad (1990) calls for significant, sustained commitment from higher education to the unique role of teacher educators to both higher education and elementary and secondary schools:

> If faculty members' time and energies are to be mobilized for renewal, they must hear an alternative drumbeat and subsequently see progress toward the promises of the drumbeat: an elevation of teacher education to a central place in institutional mission, resources allocated via a formula that recognizes the high time and energy demands of a first-rate teacher education program, and equitable share of scholarship funds and support services, additional funds for creating "teaching" schools in collaborating school districts, and faculty rewards geared to the nature of the required work. Unless it is clear that the work of planning and renewal are to be rewarded, there is little likelihood that it will begin [p. 195].

Conclusion

Teacher education faculty have a stormy and controversial history. Lauded and impugned, needed and disdained, respected and vilified, they have grown from small numbers in meager beginnings to thousands in higher education institutions of all types. The future with its desperate needs for quality and caring teachers, for humane curricula, and for schools that fulfill the needs of America's youth is filled with challenges for teacher educators. There must be a joining of the many disparate efforts of teacher educators around the nation, reaching out even beyond the nation's borders.

After decades of struggle, teacher education appears firmly placed in higher education. But it must continue to grow in its capacities to produce quality research and publication while not lessening its efforts in field-based studies and work.

The challenges of conducting needed research, of fostering pedagogy that makes a difference in the life in schools, of remaining consistent with the humane values of the profession, of building the networks with the arts and sciences faculties, of bringing new knowledge to the schools are enormous. Yet as our chapter reveals, the variety and potential within teacher education are vast. In the next decade, teacher education must show more unity, more understanding of the problems and issues of modern American society, more demonstrated effectiveness in bringing about desired outcomes in teacher education graduates, and more imagination in bridging to the world of today's youth.

The problems that inhere in the late twentieth century do not admit of easy solution. We indicated the continued low percentage of minority faculty in teacher education, a condition when coupled with the dramatic changes in the demographics of America's youth guarantees that the ranks of the teaching profession will not reflect the composition of the larger society, however hard teacher education will try to recruit minority teachers. This condition argues for dramatic changes in the education of today's majority-white teachers for tomorrow's "majority-minority" schools. Teacher education must also address the problems related to gender in the teacher education professoriate, to which we referred earlier. A profession that espouses equity cannot divide its work so that females have significantly higher teaching and advising loads, do more supervision, and have less time for scholarship. These are but two issues of high drama facing teacher education. Others include social class clashes, public impatience with educational progress, governmental interference, tight resources, and competition for candidates. Fortunately, the teacher education faculty has many individuals of high intelligence, goodwill, and strong commitment. They are the individuals, combined with the influx of newly prepared people in the next decade, who can move the profession forward. While we have described some of the starker conditions of teacher education, we must also remember that much is good. As one of Ducharme's interviewees, a senior male professor, put it, "I think the professorial life is great. It's a great life. My father *worked*" (1993, p. 112). Or as a young female assistant professor noted, "Being a professor is a good life. There is much diversity. [The] days are so exciting" (p. 102).

Teacher education will be at the center of critics' attention for some time to come. Its challenges are considerable, its resources are slim, but its will is large. The tale implicit in our chapter is one of dedication and perseverance; both are requisite for the future.

Finally, what should future teacher educators be like? Perhaps authors of a chapter titled "Development of the Teacher Education Professoriate" should not play seers, but we will. To return to the earlier description of today's composite faculty member: a faculty member with the characteristics from these and other studies is a white male in his late forties or early fifties, tenured at either the full or associate professor level; he acquired his doctorate while studying part time, has been at his current place of employment for more than fifteen years, and has published six or seven articles in refereed publications. Prior to going on for further graduate study generally concluding with either a Ph.D. or an Ed.D. and subsequent status as a faculty member in higher education, he taught for a minimum of three years in either an elementary or a secondary school.

Perhaps a faculty member composite picture in the year 2001 might look like this: she is a member of a minority, in her mid-thirties, tenured at associate professor; she acquired her doctorate while studying full time, supported by a foundation fellowship promoting educational excellence and equity; she has been at X University for seven years with one of those years spent in an exchange program in China; she has authored four articles, coauthored six articles with teachers from the schools, developed five media productions on teaching; she spends two days a month at the local middle school working with teachers and children. Prior to working on her doctorate, she taught in a rural youth center for two years and in an inner-city middle school for three years.

We depict this future faculty member in this manner to indicate that the approximate 50 percent female population in doctoral program in education (American Association of Colleges for Teacher Education, 1988, 1989) will produce a cadre of female leaders and that minority faculty must play a critical role in the evolution of the profession; that private foundations must play their role in promoting the excellence and equity they write about in brochures by supporting the development of quality teacher educators; that an international perspective will be requisite in the future; that writing and researching in collaboration with colleagues at the university and in the elementary and secondary schools of the nation will be commonplace and necessary; that teacher educators must be involved in the technological revolution; that all teacher educators will be spending time in the schools and social agencies related to schools.

References

Allison, C. (1989). "Early professors of education: Three case studies." In R. Wisniewski and E. Ducharme (eds.), *The professors of teaching: An inquiry.* Albany: State University of New York Press.

Altenbaugh, R. J., and Underwood, K. (1990). "The evolution of normal schools." In J. I. Goodlad, R. Soder, and K. A. Sirotnik, (eds.), *Places where teachers are taught.* San Francisco: Jossey-Bass.

American Association of Colleges for Teacher Education (1987). *Teaching teachers: Fact and figures. (RATE I).* Washington, D.C.: American Association of Colleges for Teacher Education.

American Association of Colleges for Teacher Education (1988). *Teaching teachers: Fact and figures. (RATE II).* Washington, D.C.: American Association of Colleges for Teacher Education.

American Association of Colleges for Teacher Education (1989). *Teaching teachers: Fact and figures. (RATE III).* Washington, D.C.: American Association of Colleges for Teacher Education.

American Association of Colleges for Teacher Education (1990). *Teaching teachers: Fact and figures. (RATE IV).* Washington, D.C.: American Association of Colleges for Teacher Education.

American Association of Colleges for Teacher Education (1991). *Teaching teachers: Fact and figures. (RATE V).* Washington, D.C.: American Association of Colleges for Teacher Education.

American Association of Colleges for Teacher Education (1992). *Teaching teachers: Fact and figures. (RATE VI).* Washington, D.C.: American Association of Colleges for Teacher Education.

American Association of Colleges for Teacher Education (1993). *Teaching teachers: Fact and figures. (RATE VII).* Washington, D.C.: American Association of Colleges for Teacher Education.

American Association of Colleges for Teacher Education (1994). *Teaching teachers: Fact and figures. (RATE VIII).* Washington, D.C.: American Association of Colleges for Teacher Education.

Bernier, N., and McClelland, A. (1989). "The social context of professional development." In M. Holly and C. McLoughlin (eds.), *Perspectives on teacher professional development.* Washington, D.C.: Falmer Press.

Borrowman, M. S. (1956). *The liberal and technical in teacher education: A historical survey of American thought.* New York: Teachers College Press.

Borrowman, M. S. (1965). *Teacher education in America: A documentary history.* New York: Teachers College Press.

Boyer, E. L. (1990). *Scholarship reconsidered: Priorities of the profession.* Princeton, N.J : Carnegie Foundation for the Advancement of Teaching.

Clark, B. R. (1987). *The academic life: Small worlds, different worlds.* Princeton, N.J : Carnegie Foundation for the Advancement of Teaching.

Clifford, G. J., and Guthrie, J. P. (1988). *Ed school.* Chicago: University of Chicago Press.

Conant, J. B. (1963). *The education of American teachers.* New York: McGraw-Hill.

Ducharme, E. R. (1986). *Teacher educators: What do we know?* Washington, D.C.: ERIC Clearinghouse on Teacher Education/American Association of Colleges for Teacher Education.

Ducharme, E. R. (1987). "Developing existing education faculty." In C. Magrath and R. Egbert (eds.), *Strengthening teacher education.* San Francisco: Jossey-Bass.

Ducharme, E. R. (1993). *The lives of teacher educators.* New York: Teachers College Press.

Ducharme, E. R. (1994). "Characteristics of teacher educators." In L. M. Anderson (ed.), *The international encyclopedia of education.* Elmsford, N.Y.: Pergamon Press.

Ducharme, E. R., and Agne, R. (1982). "The education professoriate: A research-based perspective." *Journal of Teacher Education, 33*(6), 30–36.

Ducharme, E. R., and Agne, R. (1989). "Professors of education: Uneasy residents of academe." In R. Wisniewski and E. R. Ducharme (eds.), *The professors of teaching: An inquiry.* Albany: State University of New York Press.

Ducharme, E. R., and Ducharme, M. K. (1991). "Education faculty and their perceptions of leadership in SCDEs." In American Association of Colleges for Teacher Education, *Teaching teachers: Facts and figures (RATE V).* Washington, D.C.: American Association of Colleges for Teacher Education.

Ducharme, E. R., and Kluender, M. (1990). "The RATE study: The faculty." *Journal of Teacher Education, 41*(4), 45–49.

Finn, C. (1991). *We must take charge: Our schools and our future.* New York: Free Press.

Gideonse, H. D. (1989). "The uses of time: Evocations of an ethos." In R. Wisniewski and E. R. Ducharme (eds.), *The professors of teaching: An inquiry.* Albany: State University of New York Press.

Ginsburg, M. B. (1988). *Contradictions in teacher education and society: A critical analysis.* Washington, D.C.: Falmer Press.

Goodlad, J. I. (1990). *Teachers for our nation's schools.* San Francisco: Jossey-Bass.

Guba, E. G., and Clark, D. L. (1978). "Levels of R&D productivity in schools of education." *Educational Researcher, 7*(5), 3–9.

Hazlett, S. (1989). "Education professors: The centennial of an education crisis." In R. Wisniewski and E. R. Ducharme (eds.), *The professors of teaching: An inquiry.* Albany: State University of New York Press.

Herbst, J. (1989). "Teacher preparation in the nineteenth century." In D. Warren (ed.), *American teachers: Histories of a profession at work.* New York: Macmillan.

Holmes Group (1986). *Tomorrow's teachers.* East Lansing, Mich.: Holmes Group.

Holmes Group (1990). *Tomorrow's schools: A report of the Holmes Group.* East Lansing, Mich.: Holmes Group.

Howey, K. R., Yarger, S. J., and Joyce, B. R. (1978). *Improving teacher education.* Washington, D.C.: Association of Teacher Education.

Howey, K. R., and Zimpher, N. L. (1989). *Profiles of preservice teacher education.* Albany: State University of New York Press.

Howey, K. R., and Zimpher, N. L. (1990). "Professors and deans of education." In W. R. Houston (ed.), *Handbook of research on teacher education.* New York: Macmillan.

Jacobwitz, T. (1994). "Goodlad's sixth postulate." *Journal of Teacher Education, 45*(1), 46–52.

Judge, H. (1982). *American graduate schools of education: A view from abroad.* New York: Ford
    Foundation.

Kagan, D. M. (1990). "Teachers' workplace meets the professors of teaching: A chance en-
    counter at 30,000 feet." *Journal of Teacher Education, 41*(5), 46–53.

Koerner, J. D. (1963). *The miseducation of American teachers.* Boston: Houghton Mifflin.

Kramer, R. (1992). *Ed school follies: The miseducation of American teachers.* New York: Free Press.

Lanier, J. E., and Little, J. W. (1986). "Research in teacher education." In M. C. Wittrock
    (ed.), *Handbook of research on teaching.* (3rd ed.). New York: Macmillan.

Liston, D. P., and Zeichner, K. M. (1991). *Teacher education and the social conditions of teaching.*
    New York: Routledge & Kegan Paul.

McCarthy, M., Kuh, G., Newell, L., and Iacona, C. (1988). *Under scrutiny: The educational admin-
    istration professoriate.* Tempe, Ariz.: University Council for Educational Administration.

Mackay, J. (1989). "Ed school: A brief for professional education." *Journal of Teacher Education,
    40*(4), 63–64.

Mattingly, P. H. (1975). *The classless profession.* New York: New York University Press.

Nash, R. J. (1993). "Rita Kramer's follies: The misrepresentation of America's teacher edu-
    cators." *Journal of Teacher Education, 44*(1), 71–77.

National Center for Educational Statistics (1991). *The condition of education,* Vol. 1. Washing-
    ton, D.C.: U.S. Government Printing Office.

Palmer, J. (1985). "Teacher education: A perspective from a major public university." In C.
    Case and W. Matthes (eds.), *Colleges of education: Perspectives on their future.* Berkeley, Calif.:
    McCutchan.

Popkewitz, T. S. (ed.) (1987). *Critical studies in teacher education: Its folklore, theory and practice.*
    Washington, D.C.: Falmer Press.

Powell, A. (1980). *The uncertain profession.* Cambridge, Mass.: Harvard University Press.

Schneider, B. (1987). "Tracing the provenance of teacher education." In T. S. Popkewitz
    (ed.), *Critical studies in teacher education: Its folklore, theory and practice.* Washington, D.C.:
    Falmer Press.

Schuttenberg, E., Patterson, L., and Sutton, R. (1985). *Self-perceptions of productivity of education
    faculty: Life phase and gender differences.* Washington, D.C.: American Association of Col-
    leges for Teacher Education. (ED 257 807).

Sikula, J. (1990). "National commission reports of the 1980s." In W. R. Houston (ed.), *Hand-
    book of research on teacher education.* New York: Macmillan.

Urban, W. J. (1990). "Historical studies of teacher education." In W. R. Houston, M. Haber-
    man, and J. Sikula (eds.), *Handbook of research on teacher education.* New York: Macmillan.

Warren, D. (ed.) (1989). *American teachers: Histories of a profession at work.* New York: Macmillan.

Wisniewski, R., and Ducharme, E. R. (1989). "Where we stand." In R. Wisniewski and E. R.
    Ducharme (eds.), *The professors of teaching: An inquiry.* Albany: State University of New
    York Press.

Annotated Bibliography

Borrowman, M. S. (1956). *The liberal and technical in teacher education: A historical survey of American
    thought.* New York: Teachers College Press.

    This is the classic text for learning about and understanding the history of teacher ed-
    ucation in America through the mid 1950s. It contains the description of the genesis
    of many contemporary issues such as who should control teacher education in the uni-
    versities, one of the current concerns of the National Council for the Accreditation of
    Teacher Education. He notes how one pundit asserted, "This control [of teacher edu-

cation] should include the right to designate which academic courses taught outside the college of education would be creditable and to specify those academic instructors whose offerings were acceptable" (p. 19).

Borrowman, M. S. (1965). *Teacher education in America: A documentary history.* New York: Teachers College Press.

Faculty new to the teacher education wars would do well to read this book to acquire a valuable perspective on their profession, and veterans can profit from another look at it. Much that has occurred in teacher education since Borrowman was published is the mere updating of timeless issues and problems. For example, Borrowman noted, "Many college professors of pedagogy also insisted that professional education should follow the completion of most of general education" (p. 91) and "At the beginning of the period here discussed, educational psychology was in a state of considerable confusion which amounted to a running war between varying schools of thought" (p. 213). Readers will find comments on nearly every page bearing directly on issues remaining under study and discussion in the 1990s and beyond.

Clifford, G. J., and Guthrie, J. P. (1988). *Ed school.* Chicago: University of Chicago Press.

Clifford and Guthrie's *Ed School* is a rich study in which the authors describe in some detail the ten schools of education deemed the most distinguished in the 1930s; they then follow up on the ones that are still providing such education, making substitutions where necessary (for example, for Yale, which closed its school of education). They deal with the perennial problems of the theory-practice dichotomy, questionable scholarship, uneasy relationships between practicing educators in schools and faculty in higher education, and the weak fiscal base for teacher education. Their book is a sensible follow-up to Borrowman's work. Though riddled with contradictions, such as arguing that education faculty have little to offer and then saying that the public schools and schools of education should collaborate, the book makes a major contribution by linking reform suggestions, education school analyses, and other relevant matters to research studied. Mackay (1989) noted that "*Ed School* is a timely and provocative book coming in the midst of the most sustained educational reform of the twentieth century" (p. 64). It remains so.

Ducharme, E. R. (1993). *The lives of teacher educators.* New York: Teachers College Press.

Ducharme provides insights into the professional lives of thirty-four teacher educators who range in status from first-year assistant professors to emeritus. The faculty are from ten institutions quite similar in scope to those that Howey and Zimpher studied. Divided into chapters dealing with early teaching experiences, transition to higher education, research and publication, mentoring and collaborating, and satisfactions and frustrations, the book depicts the variety inherent in the professional life. The chief strength of the book is its clear depiction of the many facets that make up the day-to-day and year-to-year work of teacher educators. The weakness is the limited sample of thirty-four individuals. Judge, in his foreword to the book, says, "We need to understand a great deal more of the lives of teacher educators, if only to avoid the pain of having to read about their collective death. This study is of importance in advancing such work" (p. ix).

Howey, K. R., and Zimpher, N. L. (1989). *Profiles of preservice teacher education.* Albany: State University of New York Press.

Howey and Zimpher provide a rich description of teacher education students, programs, and faculty in six different types of institutions, ranging from small liberal arts colleges to large state universities. The authors visited the schools and interviewed students, faculty, and administrators. On the basis of their interviews, their study of archival documents from the institutions, and their own broad understanding of teacher education, the authors present the kaleidoscope of teacher education. What emerges is a largely positive picture of the young people preparing to teach, largely dedicated faculty, and generally philosophically supportive administrators. Because Howey and Zimpher go into such detail on each institution, readers will gain many insights regarding the practice of teacher education at these various schools. Some might find the book helpful in understanding their own programs.

Judge, H. (1982). *American graduate schools of education: A view from abroad*. New York: Ford Foundation.

Judge tells the sometimes discouraging but always interesting saga of teacher education in some of the major research universities in the United States. What emerges is an uneven, generally negative picture of the importance of teacher education in these institutions. He notes the importance of faculty publishing research studies, obtaining grants, and consulting with external audiences. Some might argue that Judge's short treatise in fact provided some of the inspiration and energy resulting in the formation of the Holmes Group. A major value in Judge's book is his description of the tensions inherent among the various demands of the practical world, the academy, and the disciplines in education. This rather objective foreigner's view of American schools of education gives the reader pause as to why anything gets done in them.

CHAPTER TWENTY-EIGHT

THE CASE FOR FORMAL RESEARCH AND PRACTICAL INQUIRY IN TEACHER EDUCATION

VIRGINIA RICHARDSON

This chapter suggests that the concept of research should be broadened and deepened to include formal research as well the type of inquiry conducted by individuals or groups who are attempting to improve their teaching and their programs. The researcher-practitioners of interest in this chapter are those who prepare elementary and secondary teachers and work with them in inservice education. The styles of research to be explored are formal research that is conducted for purposes of expanding the larger community's knowledge base and practical inquiry that is conducted by teacher educators to understand their contexts, practices, and students. By conducting inquiry designed to change programs and practices, teacher educators may be able to improve their programs, model an inquiry approach to their teacher education students, and inform colleagues about useful ways of thinking about and practicing teacher education.

Thus, this chapter is directed toward teacher educators who wish to conduct research for either of two purposes. The first, *formal research,* can contribute to knowledge and understanding of teacher education for the larger community of scholars and educators; and the second, *practical inquiry,* can lead to the improvement of one's own teaching and teacher education programs. Since the two forms of research have different purposes and outcomes, an initial distinction is made between practical inquiry and more traditional, published research. The next two

I would like to acknowledge the useful guidance of the reviewers of this chapter, Gene Hall, Frank Murray, and Jerome Frieberg, and the supportive and valuable comments of my colleagues at the University of Arizona, Yetta Goodman, Gary Fenstermacher, and Kathy Short.

sections of the chapter will discuss these two approaches in some depth. However, just as formal research may lead to improvement in teaching and programs, practical inquiry may also lead to a contribution to the knowledge base and to publication. The third section will discuss the conditions under which the distinction between practical inquiry and formal research breaks down, at which point, practical inquiry is of interest to a larger community.

Formal Research

Formal research is what many of us usually think of when using the term *research*. It constitutes the content of our graduate research and methodology courses, and the products of this research are published in research journals. Formal research is designed to contribute to the more general knowledge about and understanding of teacher education processes, players, outcomes, and contexts, and the relationships between or among them. This is the type of research that is generally written about in research and research methodology chapters and is often broken down by methodological types: experimental, correlational, survey, case study, qualitative, evaluation, and so forth. I do not intend to repeat such descriptions in this chapter, in that they have been adequately addressed in numerous other publications.[1] This section will not therefore be categorized along the lines of methodological types. Rather, it will be organized along functional lines and will include brief descriptions of different methodologies as they relate to the purposes of the research and the questions being asked.

Three categories of formal research are described below. They were developed along functional lines: descriptive studies that provide information for policy makers and others involved in making decisions about programs and resource allocation, research designed to contribute to theory development, and studies that examine relationships between or among variables in teacher education or between programs and their outcomes. These are not mutually exclusive categories; descriptive studies could lead to understanding and therefore to theory development, and serendipitous findings in a relationship study could as well. However, the original purposes of studies in these three categories differ and this is the basis for their differentiation here.

Describing Teacher Education

Descriptive studies of teacher education programs and systems are extremely helpful for purposes of policy analysis, programmatic decision making, accreditation, and resource allocation. These may be large or small scale and use survey or multiple case study techniques. They are designed to provide verbal pictures of systems, the characteristics of the participants, funding sources, individual programs, the contexts in which programs find themselves, and so on.

An early descriptive study of teacher education programs around the country was developed for the U.S. Office of Education (Howey and others, 1977). This study was helpful in describing the wide variety of teacher education programs and the higher education institutions in which they take place, as well as the similarities in the basic nature of the programs. The Research About Teacher Education (RATE) project, supported by the American Association of Colleges for Teacher Education, has continued to provide yearly detailed information on various aspects of the teacher education enterprise since 1987 (American Association of Colleges for Teacher Education, 1987, 1988, 1989, 1990, 1991). Extensive surveys of a stratified random sample of ninety institutions provide detailed information on such aspects as costs of becoming a teacher, faculty salaries, the nature of secondary methods courses, and student demographics. A different emphasis is explored each year.

Descriptive studies do not always employ survey methodology. Two recent qualitative, multiple-case studies have provided important descriptive information on programs of teacher education. Howey and Zimpher's case studies (1989) of six programs of teacher education employed interview, survey, and observation data to provide descriptions of the perspectives of the various participants in university-based teacher education. The second, a large-scale, multiple-case study of teacher education, is described in Goodlad (1990) and Goodlad, Soder, and Sirotnik (1990). This study involved two teams of researchers who traveled to twenty-nine sites and used survey, interview, classroom observation, and document analysis methodologies.

It must be pointed out that both of these studies are more interpretive in their written descriptions of the studies than the survey-only studies such as RATE. Goodlad's group, for example, spent considerable time prior to the case visits developing criteria for exemplary teacher education. They organized their data collection around these criteria, but the case study design also allowed for the discovery of additional themes. For example, Goodlad found that, by and large, education deans placed their aspirations in the non-professional-preparation programs (such as comparative education and educational technology) that were least understood by their colleagues across campus (1990). The rhetorical styles selected by the authors— narrative case studies by Howey and Zimpher and cross-case theme analysis with considerable inclusion of quality judgments by Goodlad— differ considerably from the data charts and tables in RATE. But all of these studies are initially and primarily descriptive and are intended to contribute to national and local policy deliberations.

Smaller-scale descriptive studies may also be useful in policy deliberations concerning teacher education. For example, McDiarmid and Wilson (1991) examined the mathematics knowledge of fifty-five teachers who were participating in two alternate route certification programs. They concluded that these teachers, all of whom had majored in mathematics, were knowledgeable about the algorithms that are associated with the mathematics curriculum but could not explicate the concepts underlying these operations. They also found that these teachers began to learn some of the concepts from teaching them but not all of the concepts. Such descriptive information is important for policy makers who are considering alternate route programs.

Theory Development

Studies in this category are designed to contribute to an understanding of teacher education, including its organization, processes, participants, and contexts. A distinction is made between theory development and theory testing, the latter being represented in the third category below. The work here is primarily qualitative or interpretative in nature (Erickson, 1986). This means that the researchers enter the environment to be studied in a relatively open-ended manner, and the categories derived from analysis emerge from an interaction between the data and the researcher.

There are increasing numbers of such studies in education. This is due in part to the increased acceptance of qualitative methodologies and the willingness of historically quantitative journals to begin to publish qualitative articles (see Eisner and Peshin, 1990, for a history of the status of qualitative methodologies in education).

Some of the examples of theory development studies in teacher education are case studies. For example, Bolin (1988, 1990) studied two semesters of a student's student-teaching experience in a program that was intended to help students develop reflective thinking. In this study, Bolin developed a way of thinking about reflection and how a student could resist developing it: "Lou tended to describe [in his dialogue journals] what he was thinking rather than to reflect on his thoughts. . . . Lou was verbose about his teaching, but not reflective" (1990, p. 17). Bolin's work adds to our understanding of the concept of reflection and of the difficulties involved in helping students become more reflective.

The use of case study methodology has been particularly important in development and understanding of the concept of pedagogical content knowledge, defined by Shulman (1987) as an amalgam of content and pedagogical knowledge that constitutes the professional knowledge of teachers. Grossman (1990) contributed to an understanding of the concept with her case studies of six beginning English teachers who were well grounded in their content area. Three of the teachers had graduated from a fifth-year teacher education program, while three entered teaching without extensive formal pedagogical preparation. She found differences in the ways the teachers who had received pedagogical preparation both understood their content and taught their classes. For example, they considered their students' interests in planning lessons more than did those who had no pedagogical preparation, and they used more alternative procedures for motivating their students. Grossman also spent time in the subject-specific component of the teacher education program attended by the first three beginning teachers and was able to tie the content in these courses with the pedagogical content knowledge held and exercised by them.

There are also studies that use a number of subjects or sites and interpret the results in terms of categories of results and themes rather than as individual case stories. For example, Pinnegar and Carter (1990) conducted a content analysis of interviews of thirty-eight cooperating teachers to determine their theories of student learning. They then compared the teachers' theories of learning with those in three current educational psychology texts and found that they were quite different: the teachers' learning theories focused on "the relationship between teachers and students, the establishment of respect and trust, and the importance of confidence, personal interest, and enthusiasm" (p. 26).

In addition, "new" methodologies (or at least new to the field of teacher education) are being developed to deal with the complexity and interrelationships among the processes, contexts, and histories of the participants and programs. One such methodology is narrative or story, which refers both to the result or process of making sense of our lives (Witherell and Noddings, 1991) and to the methodology of capturing and writing about experience (Clandinin and Connelly, 1991; Connelly and Clandinin, 1988). Narrative inquiry, as described and conducted by Connelly and Clandinin (1988), is isomorphic to the way in which we make sense of our experience—as a story or set of stories. Narrative inquiry is a means of studying experience, one that takes into account that "a person is, at once . . . engaged in living, telling, retelling and reliving stories" (Clandinin and Connelly, 1991, p. 265). Narrative inquiry involves participant observation in which the researcher and the practitioner tell and live their own stories but in a collaborative setting. Collaboration between researcher and practitioner is clearly an important element of much of the current research in this area (see Schön, 1991). Carter (1992) recently summarized the field of narrative and story, focusing in part on the story as a way of knowing. She concludes that the analysis of story provides a way to reframe our field away from conventional research methods and to give voice to practitioners.

Narrative inquiry has been used in research on teaching but less so in teacher education. An exception is some of the work on learning to teach. For example, Russell (1988) and Munby (1986) have examined learning to teach in longitudinal studies of teachers, some from when they were preservice students. The themes that emerged from Russell's study (1988) of student and first-year teachers, for example, highlight the importance to teachers of learning by experience and the difficulties of bringing together formal theory, as learned in preservice teacher education, and teaching practice. More work on narrative inquiry in teacher education is called for; however, we must also address some of the questions asked by Tochon (1994), who points out the somewhat masked potential of narrative inquiry to manipulate and indoctrinate the practitioner because of the very strong role of the researcher in the interpretive process.

Providing Evidence of Relationships

When one thinks of traditional educational research, it is usually the methodologies in the category of providing evidence of relationships that come to mind. These include correlational studies, experiments—both "pure" and "quasi"—and program evaluations. Correlational studies are designed to test hypotheses and provide evidence of relationships among variables and between educational treatments and outcomes. It is not my purpose here to describe these methodologies since many texts have quite adequately done so (see, for example, Borg and Gall, 1989). What I wish to emphasize is that it is possible to conduct such research on one's own program and participants and/or network with others to increase sample size and by so doing produce useful additions to the knowledge base of teacher education. It is also clear in perusing many current journals that recent relationship studies in teacher education are struggling quite successfully with studies of teachers' acquisition of mental processes, including beliefs, cognitive schemata and processes, attitudes, dispositions, subject matter, and pedagogical subject matter knowledge.

Winitzky and Arends (1991), for example, reported on a set of studies designed to examine the impact of variations in teacher education classroom and field experiences on preservice students' acquisition of knowledge, skills, and abilities to reflect on teaching. The three experimental studies used a comparative treatment design, with the treatments carefully tied to theory. They used a number of different measures, including the ordered-tree technique, to assess students' schemata. These studies took place within four teacher-education institutions in Maryland.

Marso and Pigge (1989) conducted a study to determine whether there were differences in so-called levels of concerns (Fuller, 1969; Fuller and Bown, 1975; Bown 1975) as well as the attitudes of preservice teachers at three points in their education and of inservice teachers, also at three stages in their careers. They found that certain attitudes, such as the view of teaching as a career, remained stable across the different levels. However, some concerns, such as concern for instructional impact, increased over time; others, such as concern for self, decreased. They also found that the teaching field was related to changes in concern. For example, secondary teachers' concern about impact of instruction upon students decreased in the transition from student teaching to the first year of teaching, and the positive attitude of special education teachers remained the same or increased over the inservice years, but the attitudes of others decreased.

Given the interest in teachers' cognitive processes, there have been a number of studies that have tested new measures of various forms of thought and knowledge. For example, a cross-sectional comparative study of 117 first- and third-year teacher education students' views of "good teaching" conducted by Corporaal (1991) using the repertory grid technique (Kelly, 1955) included a useful discussion of the costs and benefits of a large-scale and complex measure, such as used in Corporaal's study, as compared with a more in-depth conversation process with respondents. Corporaal (1991) concluded that the "repgrid" process is suitable for eliciting prospective teachers' cognitions but, because of its labor-intensive procedures, its benefits in a large-scale application are not large enough to warrant use. Sparks-Langer and others (1990) also developed and tested a method designed to assess student teachers' development of pedagogical thinking that seems less time consuming than the repgrid process used by Corporaal (1991).

Evaluation of preservice teacher education programs is included in this category because most evaluations attempt to link program processes with outcomes (an exception being that proposed by Raths, 1987, which would compare processes and outcomes with a normative set included in his chapter). Galluzzo and Craig (1990) provide a thorough discussion of teacher education program evaluation. They suggest that purposes of such evaluations include accountability, improvement, understanding, and knowledge. Most evaluations use follow-up studies (Adams, 1987) as the primary data, in which graduates of the program complete a survey that provides demographic and work information as well as judgments of the worth of the program and its various courses in helping them in their new teaching positions. Galluzzo and Craig (1990) highlight the elementary program evaluation process at Michigan State University (Barnes, 1987; Freeman, 1986) and suggest that one reason this program is strong is because the faculty in four alternate programs are clear about the goals and processes of their individual programs and agree on them.

Program evaluations may also be qualitative in nature. Aksamit, Hall, and Ryan (1990), for example, discuss the philosophical differences between naturalistic and conventional evaluation approaches and describe the processes and results of a naturalistic evaluation of an innovative teacher education program. The evaluation, as presented in this article, focused on the processes of teacher education and the perceptions and intentions of the participants. The authors identified major process themes in the program. One, for example, related to the developmental focus of the program, another to the focus on preparing the students to be critically reflective. Such a study in combination with a follow-up study of the program's graduates would be particularly useful to a faculty engaged in teacher education.

Practical Inquiry

The term *inquiry* has been defined by Clift, Veal, Johnson, and Holland (1990) as "a deliberate attempt to collect data systematically that can offer insight into professional practice" (p. 54). This is closely associated with teacher-researcher notions, which, while often conceptually fuzzy,[2] may be helpful in our deliberations on practical inquiry for teacher educators. Burton (1991) describes teacher-researcher studies in this manner: "Simply stated, teacher-research studies are attempts to illuminate pedagogical acts by re-searching experience. The aim of the teacher-researcher is not to create educational laws (as is sometimes done in the physical science) in order to predict and explain teaching and learning. Instead, the teacher-researcher attempts to make visible the experience of teachers and children acting in the world" (p. 227). If we substitute the words *teacher educator* for *teacher* and *prospective teachers* for *children,* we will have captured the desired sense of teacher educator/researcher studies.

While practical inquiry has been advocated for elementary and secondary teachers (Cochran-Smith and Lytle, 1990; Hollingsworth and Sockett, 1994), it has only recently been explored as a process for teacher educators (see, for example, Adler, 1993). While many teacher educators are already engaging in such inquiry, colleges of education traditionally neither support nor reward such activity. What is suggested here is that practical inquiry may be improved by becoming recognized and supported as an integral element of the role of an individual teacher educator or a group of them and by becoming more systematic in its implementation.

Practical inquiry is also important for the development and use of formal research on teacher education. Because reflective inquiry is concerned with teacher education practice and learning to teach, it may help to make clear the normative foundations of practices and programs. That is, such inquiry helps individuals and groups clarify the "shoulds" of teacher education practice: conceptions of the nature of good and effective teaching, of schools as we want them to be, and of the goals of teacher education programs. Such normative clarification is essential in the conduct of practical inquiry and can be foundational to formal research that becomes useful to the improvement of practice. Normative conceptions underlie all formal research on teaching and teacher education, but they are often unexamined or tacit. Practical inquiry may provide for the articulation of normative conceptions to guide and redirect formal research in a less tacit manner. Without continual inquiry into what we want of our classes and programs, formal research may provide us only with academically interesting knowledge rather than knowledge that may help us think about, understand, and improve our programs.

There is no one research methodology that is associated with practical inquiry, although the recent acceptance of qualitative research has accompanied an increased interest in and advocacy of practical inquiry. Qualitative research allows for small sample size, in-depth, and case study research (Yin, 1984). It is interpretive and recognizes the subjective nature of all inquiry (Erickson, 1986). Thus, it allows the researcher to be a partial or full participant in the processes being studied (Spradley, 1980). However, we are not confined to qualitative research in practical inquiry, particularly in action research in which a number of teacher educators are involved. Experiments and relationship studies may also be conducted to help us understand our practices and its effects on different types of students.

The categories of practical inquiry that are described below are not meant to be mutually exclusive. They are developed in terms of both the number of people that may be involved in the inquiry as well as (or therefore) the amount and type of data that are collected and examined.

Reflective Practice

A considerable literature has developed around the concept of teacher reflection. While the notion of reflection in practice goes back some time (for example, Dewey, 1933), it has recently received prominence through the writings of scholars such as Schön (1983) and Van Manen (1977). Schön's work was important in legitimating knowledge/action processes undertaken in professional practice that are neither conscious nor linear/rational (see Clift, Houston, and Pugach, 1990, for further explication of reflective practice). Knowledge in action, Schön suggests, is inherent in the action and is based in part on the practitioner's past experiences in dealing with similar situations. For example, experience in teaching planning to a number of groups of students would suggest to a teacher educator when to slow down or try an alternative approach when she sees the look of frustration or puzzlement on the students' faces. However, the teacher may not be able to articulate such knowledge when asked: it is often tacit and emerges during the action. For Schön, knowledge in action is an essential element of the epistemology of all professional practice, including teaching.

Reflection in action, a second concept in Schön's theory, is conscious, occurs when problems appear in practice, and creates an awareness in practitioners of the thinking process that they are going through at the time of the action. Reflection on action takes place after the fact.

There are many other conceptualizations of reflection (see, for example, Cruickshank and others, 1981; and Grimmett, MacKinnon, Erickson, and Riecken, 1990). Louden (1991) has recently developed a set of categories for a broad conception of reflection that ties the different forms of reflection to cognitive interests or to the goals of reflection.[3] He includes the following forms: introspection, replay or rehearsal of professional action, systematic enquiry in action, and spontaneous action. The interests include technical, or interest in control through adherence to or development of predictive rules; personal, or an interest in making sense of an experience through relating it to biography; problematic, or dealing with a professional problem; and critical, or emancipatory interest in critiquing the social structure in which one operates. A technical interest within the classroom would be the desire to use reliable and valid diagnostic tests that would allow a teacher to place a student in a reasonably permanent ability group. A personal interest would involve tying a particular classroom incident to a similar one experienced in the past to help the teacher to remember a response that seemed to work. A problematic interest would be one in which the teacher acknowledged and worked through an instructional dilemma, such as whether to work with an individual student or the entire group of students. Finally, a critical interest would place the teacher in the position of determining whether the environment she established in the classroom marginalized certain students' voices.

In his case study of an experienced teacher, Louden (1991) found the teacher's reflection centered on personal and problematic interests more than on technical or critical. This way of tying forms of reflection with our cognitive interests in the reflective act seems particularly useful in considering how the process of reflection may be of importance to teacher educators in both their teaching and scholarship.

There are a number of ways in which reflective capacities can be enhanced. One is journal writing, in which teachers educators maintain a written record of their reflections, for example, on the results of their practices. Writing helps practitioners to understand their beliefs and goals as well as to systematically tie instruction to learning. It also enhances the process of developing and analyzing one's premises with respect to teaching and learning.

Another useful way to enhance reflection is through dialogue with others. Various forms in which this may take place are described in the next two sections. However, while the benefits of teachers talking about practice with colleagues have been examined in some depth in elementary and secondary schools (see, for example, Gitlin, 1990; Little, 1987; Rosenholtz, 1989), it has been ignored in teacher education. One can only speculate that such dialogues would be extremely useful among teacher education faculty members, both in terms of enhancing individual reflection as well as developing common languages and goals related to the teacher education program.

Clinical Analysis

The clinical inquiry processes described here involve two or sometimes more individuals in a mutually supportive activity of observation and analysis of teaching. The purpose is to help teachers understand more about their teaching and its effects on student learning and to lead to changes in practices. At the same time, the observer also learns more about teaching practices. These processes, while common in elementary/secondary schools, are unfortunately seldom seen—at least formally— in higher education (Duncan and Barnes, 1986). Team teaching, a quite common process in higher education, can provide an occasion for clinical analysis.

All forms of clinical analysis include two essential elements: observation of teaching (by someone else and/or by the teacher examining a videotape after teaching) and a dialogue around the classroom actions that were observed. Two examples from elementary/secondary education are coaching and clinical supervision. Coaching (Joyce and Showers, 1982), at least that which is not purely top-down and didactic, is a form of clinical analysis, although it is generally tied to a specific innovation. That is, if a group of teacher educators decided to implement case teaching (Merseth, 1991; Shulman, 1993), they might benefit from observation in each others' classrooms and from discussions concerning what was observed in relation to specific methods of case teaching. Clinical supervision, as described by Glickman and Bey (1990), is a "formative evaluation process involving a preconference, observation, and postconference cycle" (p. 556). It is, however, also seen as a concept that involves collegiality and inquiry (Garmen, 1986; Smyth, 1988). While there is some controversy concerning the potential for an evaluative emphasis in clinical supervision and the role of the supervisor (colleague, expert, formal supervisor/evaluator), clinical supervision can be approached as an inquiry into goals and practices in a teacher's classroom.

One promising process of clinical analysis is the practical argument (Fenstermacher and Richardson, 1993). The original notion of practical arguments is found in Aristotle's work and suggests that a practical argument consists of a set of premises that lead to an action. Green (1976) argues that the purpose of teaching is "to change the truth value of the premise of the practical argument in the mind of the child" (p. 252). Fenstermacher (1986) modifies this further to suggest that the value of research on teaching is to change or modify the premises in the minds of teachers and thus influence their actions. He provides the following example of a practical argument that was elicited from an extended conversation with a teacher:

1. It is better for children to be treated as unique individuals than as members of groups.
2. Allowing children to pace their own learning is a good way to honor their individuality.
3. If I present new material to the whole class, drill them as a group, then assign the same seatwork to all of them at the same time, I prevent them from proceeding at their own pace, and thus deny their individuality.
4. If I do these things with smaller groups of children, I come closer to honoring their individuality.
5. If I create independent work stations, with varied tasks and differing amounts of time for completion, and allow children to schedule their activities at these stations, I come as close to honoring their individuality as I possibly can.
6. There will soon be children in my class awaiting the assignment of tasks I design for them.

ACTION: (I am preparing independent learning centers, with a full range of materials at each center) [pp. 43–44].

Fenstermacher suggested that research could be introduced to teachers by encouraging them to examine their own empirical and value premises in relation to those extracted from current research.

Anders and Richardson (1991; Richardson, 1994) used the concept in a staff development process designed to help teachers examine their premises in the teaching of reading comprehension and introduce alternative premises from current research. In this form of clinical inquiry, a videotaped lesson of the teacher's classroom is used to provide a stimulus for a dialogue with the teacher about her actions. A second person, called an "other" (Richardson and Fenstermacher, 1992), views the videotape with the teacher. The other elicits beliefs that the teacher uses to explain her actions, offers alternative premises, and works with the teacher in experimenting with new practices and reconstructing the argument. The other may be another teacher, supervisor, staff developer, principal, or perhaps eventually the teacher herself (Fenstermacher and Richardson, 1993; Morgan, 1993; Vasquez-Levy, 1993). Fenstermacher and Richardson (1993) describe a practical argument process with a teacher that took place over one semester and focused on the teacher's beliefs about silent reading and reading aloud and how these beliefs affected her instruction of reading comprehension.

This process has not yet been attempted in higher education (at least not as described in the literature), and there are questions about how it would be approached. For example, initial discussions of teaching in higher education may focus more on content than on interactions with students, since so many professors use a lecture format in their teaching. Examination of a tape of teaching could explore the manner of the teacher in discussion and interactions with students. Practical arguments is a promising clinical inquiry procedure for both the improvement of practice and the building of knowledge concerning the beliefs and practices of teacher educators.

Action Research

Action research in teaching and teacher education has a long and complex history (see, for example, Noffke, 1992). Clift and colleagues (Clift, Veal, Johnson, and Holland, 1990) suggest that action research implies that changes in practices is the goal. They state, "Action research is a way of thinking that implies the use of reflection and inquiry as a way of understanding the conditions that support or inhibit change, the nature of the change (or intervention), the process of change, and the results of change" (pp. 54–55). Action research may be conducted by an individual or a group; however, most action research that is described in the literature is conducted by a group or at least involves a network of professionals who are participating in individual action research projects (Short, 1992). Currently, there are two forms of action research as described in the literature. The first is action research as defined by Clift, Veal, Johnson, and Holland (1990) as any inquiry within a classroom or school that is meant to lead to change. The second is inquiry guided by critical or neo-Marxist theory and therefore emancipatory in nature. The latter form involves questioning the underlying assumptions of the social and economic system in which the practitioner/researchers are operating.

In the first category of action research is Stenhouse's work (1975) on curriculum change in England, which was continued and extended by Elliott (1976–1977). This work helped to spawn a set of collaborative research projects in the United States, funded by the National Institute of Education (Gonzalez, 1983; Jacullo-Noto, 1984; Lieberman, 1986; Oja and Smulyan, 1989; Tikunoff, Ward, and Griffin, 1979). In these projects, researchers, teachers, and teacher educators worked together to identify and conduct research on and create solutions to problems identified by a group of teachers in a school.

The second form of action research, that which is critical or emancipatory, is advocated by Carr and Kemmis (1986), Lather (1986), and Liston and Zeichner (1991). This involves a process of reflection and inquiry that questions the underlying social and political context. The goal is to develop classroom practices that contribute to greater equity and social justice in the particular school or college as well as the society (Sirotnik and Oakes, 1990). In fact, Lather (1986, p. 263) suggests that action research that ignores these goals should not be conducted because it both contributes to the existing social status quo and lends itself to misuse by those who wish to control, through technical means, the educational system. Capper and Jamison (1993) illustrate Lather's point in their description of an incident of action research using procedures from total quality management (Demming, 1982). The teachers in a school met to focus on the problem of the large number of students who were having unproductive experiences. The solutions that were generated from this project, however, focused on what parents should do rather than on how the school should reorient itself to deal with the problem. Capper and Jamison (1993) speculate that the problem was that the teachers did not start with a common understanding of social change and the goals of the school in the change process. Further, the process did not involve students or parents.

Although action research has been described as a part of the content of teacher education and undertaken by the prospective teachers (see, for example, Clift, Veal, Johnson, and Holland, 1990; Cochran-Smith, 1991; Gore and Zeichner, 1991), it has not yet been studied as a process conducted by higher education faculties on their own program. Yet, as Kagan (1990) suggests, an action research project conducted by faculty members in a college of education could lead to cohesiveness and professional growth. In fact, she suggests that such activity on the part of teacher education faculty could "begin to resolve their collective identity crisis" (p. 53).

Bringing Practical Inquiry and Formal Research Together

Practical inquiry should be considered as an essential element of the work of individual and groups of faculty members and other teacher educators in understanding and improving their teaching and programs. This work should not necessarily be undertaken to contribute to the general knowledge base of teacher education but be valued as a part of what all educators should be doing to improve the education.

At the same time, practical inquiry may lead to its consideration as formal research and to publication. It is the purpose of this section of the chapter to address these possibilities.

Differences and Similarities

Practical inquiry and formal research have been separated in this chapter to make a distinction between inquiry conducted in one's everyday work life for purposes of improvement and research that is meant to contribute to the larger community's knowledge base. While such separation makes sense initially, some may question it, and in fact such a distinction may break down in the case of research that meets both purposes. Before examining how these two forms of research may come together, let us look at an example that highlights the differences.

Suppose a professor is employing, for the first time, case teaching in her preservice teacher education classroom. She asks the students to read the case and the relevant chapter from the text prior to class, and she structures small group discussions in which each group selects an individual to report to the rest of the groups about their deliberations. The professor listens carefully to group discussions and the reporting sessions and takes thorough notes on the quality of the concepts and analyses used by the students. She is disappointed with their reports. Following the activity, she asks the students a series of questions to which they respond in writing about what they gained from the activity and whether they enjoyed the group discussion. On the basis of the data—their written work, the reporting, and their conversations—she concludes that the students did not understand the notion of case discussion and were confused about its purposes. In the next two classes, she structures full-group case discussions, with herself as moderator, before proceeding once again with student-led small group activities.

This professor's activities represent practical inquiry. She collected and analyzed data on the activity and her students' responses to it and used it to improve her teaching. Her personal sense of validity for the inquiry was met, although she was aware that she would have to wait until the next semester to determine the effects of starting the process with full group discussions. She had little need for control groups because she had many experiences with such classes in the past. She was also aware that her "experiment" was not necessarily leading to a procedural, stable law that would guide her approach in all future classes. She saw a need for constant flexibility and experimentation within her classrooms and time for reflection on her experiences. While there are aspects of the teacher education classrooms that remain stable, she also sensed that every group of students is different, the subject matter changes and develops, and she changes as well from one year to the next.

Lindblom and Cohen (1979) suggest that this professor's knowledge gained from her inquiry is sensitive to context and is comprehensive or holistic whereas knowledge from formal research is more context-independent and selective or limited rather than comprehensive. If the lessons this professor learned were to be of interest to the larger community, she would need to take a different approach to the question and the research. She would first have to develop a question of interest to the larger community. Her initial question in practical inquiry was something like, is this activity working and if not, what can I do to make it work? For formal research, the question could become, how should case discussions be introduced in teacher education? Her notes on the discussion and the written comments from the students could begin to constitute a data source. However, it would be advantageous for the professor to introduce case discussions in several different ways in several different classrooms, perhaps working with a colleague. She would collect more systematic data on the students and their backgrounds, perhaps have them analyze a case prior to initial case discussion and toward the end of the semester to develop a sense of gain in ability to analyze.

Formal research is conducted, then, for an audience that is larger than oneself or one's immediate colleagues. There is a shared sense of validity and generalizability in the larger community that is perhaps more rigorous than one's own requirements when conducting practical inquiry. However, as one can see from the example above, practical inquiry provides a sound normative base for formal inquiry. The teacher educator came to an understanding of what it means for the activity to work, and this knowledge supplied the outcomes of value for purposes of formal research. It can help to suggest what we want students to do with cases, what we want them to learn. It also tells us what is of interest to the teacher educator and provides the beginnings of data for another study that would be of interest to many others. It may also be that, through practical inquiry, enough data has been collected to reanalyze and develop a story line that may be of interest to others. The question then becomes, how should one think about turning practical inquiry into formal research and publications?

Reconstruction for the Reader

Turning the results of practical inquiry into a publication requires two considerations, both related to the reader. The first concerns methodological and/or rhetorical standards that are understood and accepted by the community. It may be that the data and data collection procedures for the practical inquiry are not stringent enough to satisfy the potential readers. The teacher educator/researcher can then decide whether to conduct the study again using more generally acceptable procedures. The second and perhaps more important consideration concerns the story line. That is, what aspects of the practical inquiry would be of interest to the wider community, and how may these be framed? We will explore these latter two questions in some depth.[4]

Aspects of teacher educators' practical inquiry that may be of interest to others include the following: the ideas that were examined or concluded may be intriguing, the methodologies unique and creative, the particular practices useful in solving a common problem, the findings contradictory to general understanding or "myth," or the cases particularly useful for teaching purposes. Developing the story line that elucidates these interests for the wider audience may take several writing stages. The stages described below are adapted from Bos and Richardson

(1993), who outlined three purposes for writing in qualitative research:

1. *Writing to learn.* Writing helps the researcher discover, develop, and express ideas that have been germinating during the study. This type of writing should begin soon after the study begins, perhaps in journal form.

2. *Writing to record procedures.* This is particularly important in a research process that proceeds without a written research proposal. This record would include methodologies, context of the study, dates of data collection and subjects who were present, methods of storing data, and results of analyses. It is important that this record be maintained because all of the data may not be used in publication, but that which is will need to be explained thoroughly. For example, a pretest may have been given to eighteen students and a posttest to twenty, although three of the posttest students did not take the pretest. The reader will want to understand these numbers. A record of who was present and absent at each test-taking period and who added and dropped the course is critical information for later data analysis and interpretation.

3. *Writing to communicate to others.* This requires a different mind-set than the preceding two types of writing. Writing to learn focuses on ideas that the researcher is currently grappling with and ignores those that are conceptually solved. Further, the methodological records are descriptive and inclusive and will be useful only in part within a publication. For writing to communicate with others, writers must turn their attention to the reader. What issues in the field are of interest to the reader that can be addressed by the inquiry, and how can they be framed to make the publication interesting to read?

A reexamination of the research literature in the appropriate areas may help provide clues toward theory development, gaps in the knowledge base, and areas of interest that are being pursued. This literature analysis, in interaction with the inquiry itself, helps to provide the story line for the publication. It is possible, then, to frame those elements of the data and analysis that support the story line.

The writing form is also important to consider in writing for publication. Fortunately, many journals have recently been responsive to very different ways of presenting studies. New conventions are becoming more acceptable, such as the use of first person in describing decisions made by the researcher/author. Knowledge of what is acceptable may be developed by a careful reading and analysis of articles in current issues of the journals.

New Methodologies as Bridges

A number of newly accepted methodologies are making it easier for practitioners/researchers to communicate their research to others. These methodologies include qualitative case studies, research on one's own practices, narrative inquiry, collaborative research, and clinical analysis. These methodologies permit small sample sizes and allow the teacher educator to conduct research on his or her own teaching and program, either individually or in collaboration with others. In fact, collaborative inquiry with other teacher educators and with students or teachers who are being studied is an approach that is strongly advocated today. Such collaboration provides more and different perspectives on the experience and therefore leads to a richer analysis and interpretation.

There are a number of examples of teacher educator researchers who have conducted practical inquiry and formal research on their own programs. Researchers at the University of Wisconsin, for example, have been contributing to the knowledge base of teacher education for a number of years as well as being highly reflective about their program (Zeichner and Liston, 1985; Zeichner and Liston, 1987; Zeichner and Tabachnick, 1981). Cochran-Smith (1991) has produced some interesting understandings about student teachers and action research in her program at the University of Pennsylvania, and O'Loughlin (1990, 1992) has been coming to an understanding of constructivist teacher education through research on his own teaching and learning processes. These and many other examples suggest that it is possible for teacher educators to conduct research on their own teaching and programs that both helps improve their programs and contributes to the knowledge base.

Conclusion: A Need for Multiple Forms of Inquiry

While the last section of this chapter suggested that it was possible to turn practical inquiry into formal research and publication, I am not suggesting that this is necessarily a goal toward which teacher educators should be heading. These various forms of inquiry should by themselves be encouraged, supported, and rewarded.

Practical inquiry should become an integral element of teacher education programs and should not be expected necessarily to lead to publication and other formal products. Practical inquiry may provide not only the passion but the normative foundation for significant and worthwhile change in individual and programmatic teacher education. Formal research adds knowledge for the community of teacher educators and provides information that may be used in the improvement of process.

Whereas external incentives exist, however, for the production of formal research, they do not for practical inquiry. Further, the structures and norms in higher education make it difficult for teacher educators to share their practical inquiries with colleagues. It is suggested here that incentives should be developed and structures promoted that allow practical inquiry to flourish in teacher education programs. When this happens, we will perhaps see major changes and improvement in teacher education.

Notes

1. See, for example, Merwin (1989) and Galluzzo and Craig (1990) for program evalua-
    tion research, Medley (1987), Richardson-Koehler (1985), and Yarger and Smith
    (1990) for reviews and analyses of teaching and teacher education research, Erickson
    (1986) for qualitative methodology in research on teaching, and Linn (1986) for quan-
    titative methodology in research on teaching.
2. The notions range from statements that teachers are researchers in their everyday
    practice (therefore providing a definition of teaching and making the teacher-re-
    searcher designation redundant) to teachers conducting research and publishing. See
    Cochran-Smith and Lytle (1990), Elliott (1987), and Fosnot (1989) for descriptions of
    teacher-researchers.
3. Louden's formulation is developed primarily from the work of Jurgen Habermas's the-
    ory (1971) of knowledge-constitutive interests.
4. It should be pointed out that there are many difficult issues related to conducting re-
    search on one's own practice. These issues relate to the ethics of using your students as
    subjects, the different types of thinking involved in analyzing data for teaching and for
    formal research (and whether the latter detracts from the former) and the sheer ex-
    haustion in moving back and forth between practice and research. However, this topic
    warrants its own chapter.

References

Adams, R. D. (1987). "Follow-up studies of teacher education graduates." In M. Haberman
    and J. M. Backus (eds.), *Advances in teacher education*, Vol. 3. Norwood, N.J.: Ablex.

Adler, S. A. (1993). "Teacher education: Research as reflective practice." *Teaching and Teacher
    Education, 9*(2), 159–167.

Aksamit, D., Hall, S. P., and Ryan, L. (1990). "Naturalistic inquiry applied to the evaluation
    of a teacher education program." *Teaching and Teacher Education, 6*(3), 215–226.

American Association of Colleges for Teacher Education (1987). *Teaching teachers: Facts and fig-
    ures. (RATE I)*. Washington, D.C.: American Association of Colleges for Teacher
    Education.

American Association of Colleges for Teacher Education (1988). *Teaching teachers: Facts and fig-
    ures. (RATE II)*. Washington, D.C.: American Association of Colleges for Teacher
    Education.

American Association of Colleges for Teacher Education (1989). *Teaching teachers: Facts and fig-
    ures. (RATE III)*. Washington, D.C.: American Association of Colleges for Teacher
    Education.

American Association of Colleges for Teacher Education (1990). *Teaching teachers: Facts and fig-
    ures. (RATE IV)*. Washington, D.C.: American Association of Colleges for Teacher
    Education.

American Association of Colleges for Teacher Education (1991). *Teaching teachers: Facts and fig-
    ures. (RATE V)*. Washington, D.C.: American Association of Colleges for Teacher
    Education.

Anders, P., and Richardson, V. (1991). "Research directions: Staff development that empow-
    ers teachers' reflection and enhances instruction." *Language Arts, 68,* 316–321.

Barnes, H. L. (1987). "The conceptual basis for thematic teacher education programs." *Jour-
    nal of Teacher Education, 38*(4), 13–18.

Bolin, F. S. (1988). "Helping student teachers think about teaching." *Journal of Teacher Education, 39*(2), 48–55.

Bolin, F. S. (1990). "Helping student teachers think about teaching: Another look at Lou." *Journal of Teacher Education, 41*(1), 10–19.

Borg, W. R., and Gall, M. D. (1989). *Educational research: An introduction.* (5th ed.). White Plains, N.Y.: Longman.

Bos, C., and Richardson, V. (1993). "Qualitative research and learning disabilities." In S. Vaughn and C. Bos (eds.), *Learning disabilities: Theory, methodology, assessment and ethics.* New York: Springer-Verlag.

Burton, F. (1991). "Teacher-researcher projects: An elementary school teacher's perspective." In J. Flood, J. M. Jensen, D. Lapp, and J. R. Squire (eds.), *Handbook of research on teaching the English language arts.* New York: Macmillan.

Capper, C. A., and Jamison, M. T. (1993). "Let the buyer beware: Total quality management and educational research and practice." *Educational Researcher, 22*(8), 25–30.

Carr, W., and Kemmis, S. (1986). *Becoming critical: Education, knowledge and action research.* London: Falmer Press.

Carter, K. (1992). "The place of story in the study of teaching and teacher education." *Educational Researcher, 22*(1), 5–12.

Clandinin, D. J., and Connelly, F. M. (1991). "Narrative and story in practice and research." In D. A. Schön (ed.), *The reflective turn: Case studies in and on educational practice.* New York: Teachers College Press.

Clift, R. T., Houston, W. R., and Pugach, M. C. (eds.) (1990). *Encouraging reflective practice: An examination of issues and exemplars.* New York: Teachers College Press.

Clift, R. T., Veal, M. L., Johnson, M., and Holland, P. (1990). "The restructuring of teacher education through collaborative action research." *Journal of Teacher Education, 41*(2), 52–62.

Cochran-Smith, M. (1991). "Reinventing student teaching." *Journal of Teacher Education, 42*(3), 104–118.

Cochran-Smith, M., and Lytle, S. L. (1990). "Research on teaching and teacher research: The issues that divide." *Educational Researcher, 19*(2), 2–11.

Connelly, F. M., and Clandinin, D. J. (1988). *Teachers as curriculum planners.* New York: Teachers College Press.

Connelly, F. M., and Clandinin, D. J. (1991). "Stories of experience and narrative inquiry." *Educational Researcher, 19*(5), 2–14.

Corporaal, A. (1991). "Repertory grid research into cognitions of prospective primary school teachers." *Teaching and Teacher Education, 7*(4), 315–329.

Cruickshank, D. R., and others (1981). "Evaluation of reflective teaching outcomes." *Journal of Educational Research, 75*(1), 26–32.

Demming, W. E. (1982). *Quality, productivity, and competitive position.* Cambridge: Center for Advanced Engineering Study, Massachusetts Institute of Technology.

Dewey, J. (1933). *How we think.* Lexington, Mass.: Heath.

Duncan, M., and Barnes, J. (1986). "Research on teaching in higher education." In M. C. Wittrock (ed.), *Handbook of research on teaching.* (3rd ed.). New York: Macmillan.

Eisner, E. W., and Peshin, A. (1990). "Introduction." In E. W. Eisner and A. Peshin (eds.), *Qualitative inquiry in education: The continuing debate.* New York: Teachers College Press.

Elliott, J. (1976–1977). "Developing hypotheses about classrooms from teachers' practical constructs: An account of the Ford teaching project." *Interchange, 7*(2), 2–22.

Elliott, J. (1987). "Teachers as researchers." In M. Dunkin (ed.), *International encyclopedia of teaching and teacher education.* Elmsford, N.Y.: Pergamon Press.

Erickson, F. (1986). "Qualitative research on teaching." In M. C. Wittrock (ed.), *Handbook of research on teaching.* (3rd ed.). New York: Macmillan.

Fenstermacher, G. D. (1986). "Philosophy of research on teaching: Three aspects." In M. C. Wittrock (ed.), *Handbook of research on teaching.* (3rd ed.). New York: Macmillan.

Fenstermacher, G. D., and Richardson, V. (1993). "The elicitation and reconstruction of practical arguments in teaching." *Journal of Curriculum Studies, 25*(2), 101–114.

Fosnot, C. T. (1989). *Enquiring teachers, enquiring learners.* New York: Teachers College Press.

Freeman, D. J. (1986). *Overview: Program evaluation in the College of Education at Michigan State University.* (Program Evaluation Series no. 10). East Lansing: College of Education, Michigan State University. (ED 281 830).

Fuller, F. (1969). "Concerns of teachers: A developmental conceptualization." *American Educational Research Journal, 6,* 207–226.

Fuller, F., and Bown, O. H. (1975). "Becoming a teacher." In K. Ryan (ed.), *Teacher education.* (74th yearbook of the National Society for the Study of Education). Chicago: University of Chicago Press.

Galluzzo, G., and Craig, J. R. (1990). "Evaluation of preservice teacher education programs." In W. R. Houston (ed.), *Handbook of research on teacher education.* New York: Macmillan.

Garmen, N. B. (1986). "Clinical supervision: Quackery or remedy for professional development." *Journal of Curriculum and Supervision, 1*(2), 48–57.

Gitlin, A. (1990). "Understanding teaching dialogically." *Teachers College Record, 91*(4), 537–563.

Glickman, C. D., and Bey, T. M. (1990). "Supervision." In W. R. Houston (ed.), *Handbook of research on teacher education.* New York: Macmillan.

Gonzalez, R. (1983). *Collaborative research and inservice education for teachers of students with limited English proficiency.* Washington, D.C.: National Institute of Education.

Goodlad, J. I. (1990). *Teachers for our nation's schools.* San Francisco: Jossey-Bass.

Goodlad, J. I., Soder, R., and Sirotnik, K. A. (eds.) (1990). *Places where teachers are taught.* San Francisco: Jossey-Bass.

Gore, J. M., and Zeichner, K. M. (1991). "Action, research, and reflective teaching in preservice teacher education: A case study from the United States." *Teaching and Teacher Education, 7*(2), 119–136.

Green, T. (1976). "Teacher competency as practical rationality." *Educational Theory, 26,* 249–258.

Grimmett, P. P., MacKinnon, A. M., Erickson, G., and Riecken, T. (1990). "Reflective practice in teacher education." In R. T. Clift, W. R. Houston, and M. C. Pugach (eds.), *Encouraging reflective practice in education.* New York: Teachers College Press.

Grossman, P. L. (1990). *The making of a teacher.* New York: Teachers College Press.

Habermas, J. (1971). *Knowledge and human interests* (J. Shapiro, trans.). Boston: Beacon Press.

Hollingsworth, S., and Sockett, H. (eds.) (1994). *Teacher research and educational reform.* (93rd yearbook of the National Society for the Study of Education). Chicago: University of Chicago Press.

Howey, K. R., and others (1977). *Preservice teacher education.* Washington, D.C.: U.S. Office of Education. (ED 146 210).

Howey, K. R., and Zimpher, N. L. (1989). *Profiles of preservice teacher education: Inquiry into the nature of programs.* Albany: State University of New York Press.

Jacullo-Noto, J. (1984). "Interactive research and development: Partners in craft." *Teachers College Record, 86*(1), 20–22.

Joyce, B. R., and Showers, B. (1982). "The coaching of teaching." *Educational Leadership, 40*(1), 4–10.

Kagan, D. M. (1990). "Teachers' workplace meets the professors of teaching: A chance encounter at 30,000 feet." *Journal of Teacher Education, 41*(5), 46–53.

Kelly, G. A. (1955). *The psychology of personal constructs,* Vols. 1 and 2. New York: Norton.

Lather, P. (1986). "Research as praxis." *Harvard Educational Review, 56*(3), 257–277.

Lieberman, A. (1986). "Collaborative research: Working with, not working on." *Educational Leadership, 43*(5), 28–33.

Lindblom, C. E., and Cohen, D. K. (1979). *Usable knowledge.* New Haven, Conn.: Yale University Press.

Linn, R. L. (1986). "Quantitative methods in research on teaching." In M. C. Wittrock (ed.), *Handbook of research on teaching.* (3rd ed.). New York: Macmillan.

Liston, D. P., and Zeichner, K. M. (1991). *Teacher education and the social conditions of schooling.* New York: Routledge & Kegan Paul.

Little, J. W. (1987). "Teachers as colleagues." In V. Koehler (ed.), *Educators' handbook: A research perspective.* White Plains, N.Y.: Longman.

Louden, W. (1991). *Understanding teaching: Continuity and change in teachers' knowledge.* New York: Teachers College Press.

McDiarmid, G. W., and Wilson, S. M. (1991). "An exploration of the subject matter knowledge of alternate route teachers: Can we assume they know about their subject?" *Journal of Teacher Education, 42*(2), 93–103.

Marso, R. N., and Pigge, F. L. (1989). "The influence of preservice training and teaching experience upon attitude and concerns about teaching." *Teaching and Teacher Education, 5*(1), 33–41.

Medley, D. M. (1987). "Evolution of research on teaching." In M. Dunkin (ed.), *The international encyclopedia of teaching and teacher education.* Elmsford, N.Y.: Pergamon Press.

Merseth, K. K. (1991). *The case for cases in teacher education.* Washington, D.C.: American Association of Higher Education/American Association of Colleges for Teacher Education.

Merwin, J. C. (1989). "Evaluation." In M. C. Reynolds (ed.), *Knowledge base for the beginning teacher.* Elmsford, N.Y.: Pergamon Press.

Morgan, B. (1993). "Practical rationality: A self-investigation." *Journal of Curriculum Studies, 25*(2), 115–124.

Munby, H. (1986). "Metaphor in the thinking of teachers: An exploratory study." *Journal of Curriculum Studies, 18,* 197–209.

Noffke, S. E. (1992). "Action research and the work of teachers." In R. T. Clift and C. M. Evertson (eds.), *Focal points: Qualitative inquiries into teaching and teacher education.* (Teacher Education Monograph no. 12). Washington, D.C.: ERIC Clearinghouse on Teacher Education.

Oja, S. N., and Smulyan, L. (1989). *Collaborative action research: A developmental approach.* Washington, D.C.: Falmer Press.

O'Loughlin, M. (1990). "Self-reflexive pedagogy: A narrative inquiry." Paper presented at the 12th Annual Conference on Curriculum Theory and Classroom Practice, Dayton, Ohio.

O'Loughlin, M. (1992). "The discourse of pedagogy and the possibility of social change." Paper presented at the annual meeting of the American Educational Research Association, San Francisco.

Pinnegar, S., and Carter, K. (1990). "Comparing theories from textbooks and practicing teachers." *Journal of Teacher Education, 41,* 21–27.

Raths, J. D. (1987). "An alternative view of the evaluation of teacher education programs." In M. Haberman and J. M. Backus (eds.), *Advances in teacher education,* Vol. 37. Norwood, N.J.: Ablex.

Richardson, V. (ed.) (1994). *A theory of teacher change and the process of staff development: A case in reading instruction.* New York: Teachers College Press.

Richardson, V., and Fenstermacher, G. D. (1992). "The role of the 'other' in school change." Paper presented at the annual meeting of the American Education Research Association, San Francisco.

Richardson-Koehler, V. (1985). "Research on preservice teacher education." *Journal of Teacher Education, 36*(1), 23–30.

Rosenholtz, S. J. (1989). *Teachers' workplace: The social organization of schools.* White Plains, N.Y.: Longman.

Russell, T. (1988). "From preservice teacher education to first year of teaching: A study of theory and practice." In J. Calderhead (ed.), *Teachers' professional learning.* Washington, D.C.: Falmer Press.

Schön, D. A. (1983). *The reflective practitioner.* New York: Basic Books.

Schön, D. A. (1991). "Concluding comments." In D. A. Schön (ed.), *The reflective turn: Case studies in and on educational practice.* New York: Teachers College Press.

Short, K. (1992). "'Living the process': Creating a learning community among educators." *Teaching Education, 4*(2), 11–18.

Shulman, J. H. (ed.) (1993). *Case methods in education.* New York: Teachers College Press.

Shulman, L. S. (1987). "Knowledge and teaching: Foundations of a new reform." *Harvard Educational Review, 57*(1), 1–22.

Sirotnik, K. A., and Oakes, J. (1990). "Evaluation as critical inquiry: School improvement as a case in point." In K. A. Sirotnik (ed.), *Evaluation and social justice: Issues in public education.* New Directions for Program Evaluation, no. 45. San Francisco: Jossey-Bass.

Smyth, J. (1988). "A critical perspective for clinical supervision." *Journal of Curriculum and Supervision, 3*(2), 136–156.

Sparks-Langer, G. M., and others (1990). "Reflective pedagogical thinking: How can we promote it and measure it?" *Journal of Teacher Education, 41*(5), 23–32.

Spradley, J. (1980). *Participant observation.* Austin, Texas: Holt, Rinehart & Winston.

Stenhouse, L. (1975). *An introduction to curriculum research and development.* Portsmouth, N.H.: Heinemann Educational Books.

Tikunoff, W. J., Ward, B. A., and Griffin, G. A. (1979). *Interactive research and development on teaching: Final report.* San Francisco: Far West Laboratory for Educational Research and Development. (ED 186 385).

Tochon, F. V. (1994). "Presence beyond the narrative: Semiotic tools for deconstructing the personal story." *Curriculum Studies, 2*(2), 221–247.

Van Manen, M. (1977). "Linking ways of knowing with ways of being practical." *Curriculum Inquiry, 6*(2), 205–228.

Vasquez-Levy, D. (1993). "The use of practical arguments in clarifying and changing practical reasoning and classroom practices: Two cases." *Journal of Curriculum Studies, 25*(2), 125–144.

Winitzky, N. E., and Arends, R. I. (1991). "Translating research into practice: The effects of various forms of training and clinical experience on preservice students' knowledge, skill, and reflectiveness." *Journal of Teacher Education, 42*(1), 52–65.

Witherell, C., and Noddings, N. (eds.) (1991). *Stories lives tell: Narrative and dialogue in education.* New York: Teachers College Press.

Yarger, S. J., and Smith, P. L. (1990). "Issues in research on teacher education." In W. R. Houston (ed.), *Handbook of research on teacher education.* New York: Macmillan.

Yin, R. (1984). *Case study research: Design and methods.* Newbury Park, Calif.: Sage.

Zeichner, K. M., and Liston, D. P. (1985). "Varieties of discourse in supervisory conferences." *Teaching and Teacher Education, 1*(1), 155–174.

Zeichner, K. M., and Liston, D. P. (1987). "Teaching student teachers to reflect." *Harvard Educational Review, 57*(1), 1–22.

Zeichner, K. M., and Tabachnick, B. R. (1981). "Are the effects of university teacher education washed out by school experience?" *Journal of Teacher Education, 32,* 7–11.

Annotated Bibliography

Adler, S. A. (1993). "Teacher education: Research as reflective practice." *Teaching and Teacher Education, 9*(2), 159–167.

Adler proposes that the concept of research be broadened to include disciplined reflective inquiry and that teacher educators should engage in such processes. She provides examples of such inquiry in teacher education.

Bogdan, R. C., and Biklen, S. K. (1992). *Qualitative research for education: An introduction to theory and methods.* (2nd ed.). Needham Heights, Mass: Allyn & Bacon.

This book is an excellent introduction to qualitative methodology and provides useful guidelines for participant observation, interviews, and data analysis.

Carr, W., and Kemmis, S. (1986). *Becoming critical: Education, knowledge and action research.* London: Falmer Press.

Carr and Kemmis provide a framework for, and examples of, action research that is based on critical theory. They include an excellent description of the early work of Jurgen Habermas and its relationship to education.

Clift, R. T., Houston, W. R., and Pugach, M. C. (eds.) (1990). *Encouraging reflective practice in education.* New York: Teachers College Press.

The chapters in this book deal with the concept of reflective practice in teacher education and ways of improving professional practice through reflective inquiry. Examples of reflective inquiry programs are presented.

Connelly, F. M., and Clandinin, D. J. (1988). *Teachers as curriculum planners.* New York: Teachers College Press.

This book was developed to both explain the concept of narrative inquiry and to help teachers examine their own practical knowledge and narrative inquiry. It would be a useful book for teacher educators as well.

Fenstermacher, G. D. (1994). "The place of practical arguments in the education of teachers." In V. Richardson (ed.), *A theory of teacher change and the process of staff development.* New York: Teachers College Press.

This chapter is the latest explication of Aristotle's notion of practical arguments. Fenstermacher then suggests how practical arguments may be used as a process to help teachers examine their beliefs and actions.

Hollingsworth, S., and Sockett, H. (eds.) (1994). *Teacher research and educational reform.* (93rd yearbook of the National Society for the Study of Education). Chicago: University of Chicago Press.

This book contains a number of chapters that examine and provide examples of teacher research. Many are meaningful for teacher educators.

NAME INDEX

SUBJECT INDEX

A

Academic approach to teacher education, 510–511, 513
Academic Learning Time research, 528
Accreditation, 34–35
Action research, 726–727
American Association of Colleges for Teacher Education (AACTE), 48, 529
American Educational Studies Association (AESA), 382
Apprenticeship, 81–83, 638–639
Ask-the-teacher studies, 132–138; limitations of, 135–136
Assessment: of learning style, 333–334; performance-based, 50; reforms, 17, 49–51, 627; of student teacher quality, 471–473
Assisted performance, 82
Association for Supervision and Curriculum Development (ASCD), 359
Attention deficit hyperactivity disorder (ADHD), 339–340
Autobiographies, teachers', 560, 573

B

Bachelor's degrees, 22, 538–539
Binet test, 327

C

Cases and case methods, 83, 578–583, 632–633, 718; contexts for deliberations in, 582; forms of representation in, 582; in history and social studies, 299–300; as illustrations and exemplars, 579; as problematic situations, 579–580; as storied knowledge, 580; selection of cases in, 581–582
Certification and licensure: and accredited programs, 35; advanced certification, 50; alternative routes, 21, 24, 25–26, 39–43, 47–48, 535; emergency permit, 127–132; and inner-city schools, 24; lack of, 23, 24, 25–26; performance-based, 50–51; positional value of, 398; through postbaccalaureate work, 539; reforms, 49–51; and teacher skills, 127–132; tests for, 35, 36, 49–50
Classroom discipline, 136
Classroom Test of Formal Reasoning (CTFR), 479
Clinical inquiry processes, 724–726
Coaching, 724
Cognitive apprenticeship, 82, 638–639

Cognitive development: gender-related aspects, 478–479; of prospective teachers, measurement of, 478–480; social dimensions of, 488
Cognitive style, and learning style, 332
Cognitive theories, 6–7, 11, 81, 479, 549
Cohort structures, 527, 545–548
Competency approach, 511–512
Computer technology, and dialetical learning, 10
Conceptual change theory, and teacher candidates' beliefs, 81
Connected knowing, 478–479
Conservation, 430, 431, 434
Construction of meaning, 11; and gender, 478–479; reading as, 238–239
Constructivism, 248–249
Content: of learning to teach, 71–78; versus pedagogy, 166. *See also* Curriculum
Cooperating teachers, 37, 659
Cooperative grouping, 485; and cognitive benefits, 488; research on, 138
Council of Learned Societies in Education (CLSE) standards, 381, 383, 385, 411